Jimmy Dorsey

studies in jazz

Institute of Jazz Studies
Rutgers—The State University of New Jersey
General Editors: Dan Morgenstern and Edward Berger

Jimmy the fashion plate. By 1937, when this was taken on a motion-picture studio set, Jimmy had "gone Hollywood" with white jacket and dark flower in his lapel (Duncan Sheidt collection).

Jimmy Dorsey
A Study in Contrasts

Robert L. Stockdale

Studies in Jazz, No. 30

The Scarecrow Press, Inc.
Lanham, Maryland, and London
1999

Library
University of Texas
at San Antonio

SCARECROW PRESS, INC.

Published in the United States of America
by Scarecrow Press, Inc.
4720 Boston Way
Lanham, Maryland 20706

4 Pleydell Gardens, Folkestone
Kent CT20 2DN, England

British Library Cataloguing in Publication Information Available

Library of Congress Cataloging-in-Publication Data
Stockdale, Robert L. (Robert Lee), 1926-
    Jimmy Dorsey : a study in contrasts / Robert L. Stockdale.
        p.   cm.
    Includes bibliographical references and indexes.
    ISBN 0-8108-3536-3 (cloth : alk. paper)
    1. Dorsey, Jimmy, 1904-1957—Discography. I. Title.
ML156.7.D66S76   1999
016.7844'8165'092—dc21   98-36426
                                                                 CIP
                                                                 MN

⊖™ The paper used in this publication meets the minimum requirements of American National Standard for Information Sciences—Permanence of Paper for Printed Library Materials, ANSI Z39.48–1984.
Manufactured in the United States of America.

To Shirley,

who once again has set aside her own musical preferences so her husband could spend hours listening "to
all those old records." Her interest and understanding
are deeply appreciated.

Contents

Editor's Foreword

Robert L. Stockdale's justly praised *Tommy Dorsey: On the Side* (Studies in Jazz, No. 19) inevitably contained multitudinous references to the great trombonist's older brother Jimmy. The lives, private and professional, of these gifted, famous and famously combative siblings often intersected, and the period under scrutiny in *On the Side*—the twenties through the mid-thirties—culminated with their jointly led Dorsey Brothers' Orchestra.

But for a few addenda, Stockdale took leave of Tommy as his career as a big-band leader in his own right began. In Jimmy's case, however, Stockdale decided to take into his purview his subject's entire career. This proved a daunting task, but Stockdale comes through with flying colors. This work is as detailed a documentation of a musician's legacy as one could ask for, and it can be placed alongside such definitive studies as D. Russell Connor's of Benny Goodman, also in this series.

The discographic contents of this book are admirably complete, but Stockdale has also provided fascinatingly detailed records of Jimmy Dorsey's extensive work in radio and television, to which the author's wide professional experience in broadcasting brings a special perspective. With the addition of details about work in the film studios and various band itineraries, we have here a full picture of the surprising scope and diversity that a successful musician's professional life in those vintage years encompassed.

Stockdale also provides information about Jimmy's (and Tommy's) personal affairs and fortunes, adding a welcome human dimension to a career history that indeed is *A Study in Contrasts*. Anyone with a serious interest in one of the richest periods of American popular music will find this work most illuminating, and its clear organization and detailed indexes will please scholars and researchers.

We are indebted to Robert Stockdale for having done such dedicated research and bringing it to such fine fruition—without, it should be noted, the perks and supports that accrue to academics.

Dan Morgenstern
Director
Institute of Jazz Studies
Rutgers — The State University
of New Jersey

Preface and Acknowledgments

Jimmy Dorsey's early recording efforts are not as difficult to pin down as those of his brother Tommy, first because Jimmy wasn't quite as active in the studios, tending to record somewhat exclusively with the same group over lengthy periods of time, and second because his style, particularly on alto saxophone, was more certain and more identifiable than Tommy's trombone in the twenties. One reason was that Jimmy spent more time with white and black jazz musicians than Tommy did.

Nevertheless, there are times in the late twenties and especially the early thirties when Jimmy is as difficult to track as Tommy was in the author's earlier book, *Tommy Dorsey: On the Side*.

Much of the work the Dorseys did in those pioneer days was for record contractors like Ed Kirkeby, Ben Selvin and Sam Lanin. Of the three, only Kirkeby's staffing records have been available.

As a result, some of the early listings are based to some degree upon conjecture. The choice, then, was either to include those nondocumented recordings where some circumstance or sound says it is *possible* or *probable* that Jimmy took part, or to list only those where hard identification has been proven. As in his first book, the author chose the first course since listing the "possibilities" keeps the door open for discussion and further decision. Since it is becoming more and more difficult to assemble accurate information as the years go by and those with personal knowledge pass on, it is the author's hope that assembling all this material in one place will persuade those with more accurate information, many of whom, like the author, are getting on in years, to finally share it and get it into printed form before it is lost forever.

Total personnel in many of these sessions is equally difficult to pin down. Since part of the aim of this work is to provide as many examples of the early work of Jimmy Dorsey as possible, all of the known and many of the potential participants are also included.

When Jimmy's participation is certain because of printed records, definite aural identification or similar documentation, he is listed in boldface: **Jimmy Dorsey.** If it is the opinion of the author and/or others that he is *probably* present based upon reasonable aural evidence, it is shown in lightface: Jimmy Dorsey. If Jimmy's participation is *possible* based upon less certain factors, it is shown in italic: *Jimmy Dorsey.*

As more information becomes available, future editions will reflect it. For this reason the author welcomes any additions, corrections or deletions that collectors or others wish to call to his attention.

To make the discographical material a little more relevant to the times, and to help tie these sessions to the growth and development of Jimmy Dorsey's talent, some biographical and sociological references are made from time to time and especially for the later years.

As was the case with the author's prior work, reference is made to these other events to show what helped shape Jimmy's image. Unlike the prior volume, this book deals with the entire career of Jimmy Dorsey and thus includes all the recordings, films and known broadcasts and telecasts of his big bands from the thirties to the fifties, as well as many of the dates and locations of personal appearances by the Jimmy Dorsey Orchestra and the early and latter-day Dorsey Brothers' organizations.

Certain of these recordings, most particularly those Deccas of the "Green Eyes," "Amapola" and "Tangerine" era, continue to crop up almost monthly on CDs and tapes in numerous "anthologies" of the big-band era, including many unauthorized editions. It is almost impossible to list all of these because of the frequency of their release and since little is served by including them all, the author has chosen not to do so.

In assembling this discography many existing published and unpublished works were referenced and these are in the bibliography. Yet, there are some sources that have been more helpful than others.

Two excellent resources of early information have been Woody Backensto's data from the diaries and payroll books of Wallace "Ed" Kirkeby, covering the California Ramblers and other Kirkeby sessions conducted between 1925 and 1931 for Edison, Gennett, Columbia, Pathe, Plaza and American Record Corporation (ARC), and the unpublished discography of Sam Lanin, assembled in the sixties by Bert Whyatt of England.

This latter material has been updated by fellow Briton Richard Johnson and Mike Sutcliffe of Australia as a chapter in Johnson's massive revisions of Brian Rust's *American Dance Band Discography,* which I am told now exceeds 3,000 pages. Johnson and Ray Mitchell, an Eddie Lang discographer and also of England, have also been of great assistance in updating other studio sessions of the twenties and early thirties as a result of their current review of original Columbia file cards.

In addition, Red Nichols enthusiast Stan Hester, his son Steve, ARC collector Earl Young, collector Paul Burgess, Jazz Hour Records producer and archivist Ed Burke, collector Karl Pearson and *One Night Stand* researcher Harry Mackenzie have been especially supportive.

The availability of microfilm files of *Billboard, Down Beat, International Musician* and *Variety* and untold numbers of matrix number files through the Bruce Davidson International Association of Jazz Record Collectors (IAJRC) Library and the New York State Public Library have also proved extremely helpful. These publications are the main source for the travel itinerary sections, for example.

I am also deeply grateful for the "above and beyond" reference assistance of Davidson librarian and ARC researcher Bozy White, who has been especially supportive and particularly dogged in keeping this effort as accurate and nonmisleading as possible.

Frank Riordan, Jr., who grew up on the same street as the Dorseys in Lansford, Pennsylvania and was a student of the Dorseys' father, a favorite of their mother, and a longtime friend of the boys, has also been very helpful with some of the biographical details.

As was the case in my earlier volume, I believe the work of a musician of the fame and talent of Jimmy Dorsey should be collected and chronicled for future generations to look back on and for collectors to use as a benchmark before the details vanish.

List of Abbreviations

Instruments and Miscellaneous:

acc	accordion	harp	harp
accomp	accompanied	hfp	hot fountain pen
arr	arranger	ldr	leader
as	alto saxophone	mar	marimba
bar	baritone saxophone	mgr	manager
bb	brass bass (tuba or sousaphone)	mel	mellophone
bcl	bass clarinet	o	oboe
bj	banjo	org	organ
bsn	bassoon	p	piano
bsx	bass saxophone	sb	string bass
cel	violincello(cello)	ssx	soprano saxophone
celst	celeste	stg	steel guitar
cl	clarinet	tb	trombone
c-mel	C-melody saxophone	tp	trumpet
cnt	cornet	tymp	tympani
comb	tissue on comb	ts	tenor saxophone
d	drums, percussion	uke	ukulele
dir	director	vcl	vocal
fh	French horn	vcl grp	vocal group
fl	flute	vib	vibraphone
g	guitar	viola	viola
goof	goofus (Rollini)	vn	violin
harm	harmonium	vtb	valve trombone
		xyl	xylophone

Types of Releases (in sequence used in text):

78	78 rpm recording	45	45 rpm recording
CYL	Edison cylinder	EP	45 rpm extended play
ET	electrical transcription ($33^1/_3$ rpm) for radio use but also for Vitaphone Sound	LP	$33^1/_3$ rpm (long play)
		8T	8-track cartridge
		TC	4-track cassette
		CD	compact disc

Countries of Origin for Releases:

Arg	Argentina	EEC	European Economic Community
Au	Australia		
Aust	Austria	F	France
C	Canada	G	Germany
Cz	Czechoslovakia	GE	General European
E	England	GR	Greece

H	Holland	SA	South America
Hu	Hungary	Sc	Scotland
Ind	India	Sp	Spain
It	Italy	Swe	Sweden
J	Japan	Swi	Switzerland
Port	Portugal	UK	United Kingdom

Broadcasting Networks:
AFRS	Armed Forces Radio Service
ABC	American Broadcasting Company
BBC	British Broadcasting Corporation
CBS	Columbia Broadcasting System
MBS	Mutual Broadcasting System
NBC	National Broadcasting Company
NBC-Blue	Blue Network of the National Broadcasting Company (became **Blue** network, then **Blue network of the American Broadcasting Company** and eventually **ABC**)
NBC-Red	Red Network of the National Broadcasting Company (eventually known just as **NBC**)

Note: In many listings of broadcasts the network is identified (e.g., NBC-Blue) as well as the New York City flagship station for which it is listed in referenced newspapers (e.g., [WJZ]). This is done since in some cases it is not known for certain whether the broadcast was fed to all or part of the network or was carried only locally.

Time Zones:
ET or EST	Eastern (Standard) Time
CT or CST	Central (Standard) Time
PT or PST	Pacific (Standard) Time

(**_DT** rather than **_ST** denotes Daylight Time)
(**_WT** rather than **_ST** denotes War Time, which was Daylight Time observed all year during World War II)

Editorial and Format Notations

The general form followed in this discography is similar to that used by the author in *Tommy Dorsey: On the Side*. Each recording session is listed in chronological order and shows first the studio, city and date. Where these are not shown but a second group or artist name in bold-face is, it indicates that the group or artist first named for that date has changed but the band's personnel, unless noted, remains as is. If a month and year for a session are known but not the date, it is usually listed at the month's end.

Next, the name of the recording group or artist and then band personnel are listed. Where personnel are missing it is assumed they are the same as, or very similar to, the nearest preceding session for that group.

A name in *italics* means it is *possible* that that musician is present. Those interested in that musician should not accept such listings as gospel. Instruments with no known player are shown by a number if more than one, the word *unknown* and the abbreviation for that instrument or instruments. Next is a line-by-line listing of each matrix:
Matrix Number   **Title,** [lyricists; composers] Vocal and Jimmy Dorsey solo (if any)

Numbers or letters in parentheses ( ) after the matrix number indicate known *unreleased* takes; -0-in place of a matrix number indicates that the matrix number is *unknown*. Unissued takes are shown separately only if no releases were made of that matrix number or if test pressings are known to have been made and are in collectors' hands.

Lyricists and composers (if known) are listed in brackets [ ] with the lyricist(s) separated from the composer(s) by a semicolon (;). This listing is not included for unissued takes or for titles repeated within a session. The vocal indication (e.g., vIK) is based on the vocalist's name as previously listed in full in the personnel (i.e. Irving Kaufman). Releases are then listed by type. Notations such as pseudonyms are in *italics*.

Columbia, New York, N.Y. Wednesday, July 6, 1928
BEN SELVIN AND HIS ORCHESTRA
Ben Selvin (vn,ldr) Mannie Klein (tp) Tom Dorsey (tb) **Jimmy Dorsey** (cl,as) *unknown* (ts) 2 *unknown* (vn) *Eddie Lang [or] Tommy Felline* (g) *Joe Tarto* (bb) Stan King (d) Irving Kaufman (vcl)

147987-1,2   **Ain't Misbehavin'** [Andy Razaf; Thomas "Fats" Waller, Harry Brooks] vIK (as solo)
   78: Harmony 965-H, (E) 1072-H (-2), Velvet Tone 2965-G
   Harmony as MAJESTIC HOTEL DANCE ORCH.
   LP: Saville (E) SVL 165, CBS 234-2
   CD: CBS 234, HEP (Sc) 456
   (100056-1) **78:** OKeh 4567

147987 (3)   **Ain't Misbehavin'** vIK (as solo)
    78: (unissued test pressing)

In the preceding *hypothetical* example, an unknown tenor sax and two unknown violins are listed.   The guitarist could be Eddie Lang or Tommy Felline.   There is a question as to whether Joe Tarto is the one playing brass bass (tuba).   There is one lyricist (Razaf) and two composers.   For take -1,2 there are two releases on Harmony, one in the Unted States and one in England (E) and so the label is not repeated. However, the English release is known to have been made from take 2; to show this, (-2) follows the release number.

There is an LP release (SVL 165), another (CBS 234-2) is available as both an LP and CD under the same number, and the cut also appears on CD only (HEP 456).   In addition, take -1 with the number changed to 100056 was used for a release on OKeh.   If it were a *separate* matrix (a different take), it would not be in parentheses and the title, vocal, etc., would be repeated. Of the unissued take (-3) a test pressing is known to exist.

The vocalist for both the issued and unissued takes (vIK) is Irving Kaufman.   Jimmy Dorsey has an alto sax solo (as solo).   Multiple Dorsey solos on different instruments are shown in order (as,cl,as solos).

Harmony 965-H is shown released under the pseudonym *MAJESTIC HOTEL DANCE ORCH.* (the abbreviation *ORCH.* for *ORCHESTRA* is occasionally used to save space, but does not necessarily mean that it appears this way on the label. The same is true of the use of the ampersand [&] in place of the word *AND*).   The Velvet Tone and OKeh releases use Ben Selvin's name since no pseudonym appears.   CBS 234-2 is part of a two-record set but here only the single LP number is listed.

A special comment is in order regarding Brunswick releases of the thirties. File cards on these recordings, passed down through ARC and Columbia, indicate there were -A and -B takes of most selections but make no mention of which was released. In addition, neither the label or the pressing stamper carries this information.   Listings of this period that contain "-A" or "-A,-B" after the matrix number are for the most part indefinite and should not be taken as firm information.

In addition, many listings of content and references to known radio and television broadcast and movie activity of Jimmy Dorsey are included where chronologically appropriate. They are treated thusly:

> *sustaining broadcast,* Terrace Room, Mosque Theater, Newark, N.J.—CBS (WABC), 11:30-12:00 P.M.
> Tuesday, February 8, 1944

JIMMY DORSEY AND HIS ORCHESTRA

Contrasts [Jimmy Dorsey] (theme) / **Opus No. 1** [Sid Garris; Sy Oliver] / **I'm In Love With Someone** vGT / **My First Love** vPC / **Perdido** [Juan Tizol] / **When They Ask About You** [Sam H. Stept] vGT / **The Great Lie** [Cab Calloway, Andy Gibson] / **Star Eyes** [Don Raye, Gene DePaul] vPC / **King Porter Stomp** [Ferdinand "Jelly Roll" Morton] arr OH (JD cl solo)
    Entire show on **ET**: AFRS One Night Stand #137, opening theme and "Opus No. 1" on **LP**: First Heard (E) FH-19

Some special features of the broadcast and telecast listings include the location, network carrying it, the originating station in brackets [ ] and the local time of the broadcast.

In most instances the source of the information listed for broadcasts and telecasts is given. If not, the source is always transcriptions made by the networks or "off-air" by recording hobbyists and now in the hands of collectors.

In the case of motion-picture work, the listings, using a similar display style to the broadcasts, include the studio, the film title, the director (where known), major cast members and the musical content of the film. Known recorded and video releases of the sound track or film material are listed.

Purists will point out that an additional version of the film sound tracks, or at least portions of them, can be found in the coming-attractions "trailers" for each of these films. While this is true, there is little data about them so the reader may assume they exist, although they are not included in the listings.

If there are known dates and times of broadcasts (or telecasts) for which total or partial contents are *not* known they are shown in the form indicated in the example that follows.

Broadcast schedule (all Cafe Rouge): Wed., Sept. 5, NBC-Red [WEAF] 11:00-11:30 P.M. / Fri., Sept. 7, NBC-Blue [WJZ] 11:30-12:00 P.M. / Wed., Sept. 12, NBC-Red [WEAF] 10:30-11:00 P.M. / Thurs., Sept. 13, NBC-Blue [WJZ] 12:00-12:30 A.M.

In the example above the last broadcast was actually the second that evening for the band, but since it occurred after midnight, the *following* day and date are shown.

When a series of personal appearances, such as one-nighters and week long bookings, are known but not otherwise treated in the text, they are listed like this:

Travel itinerary: Thurs., June 9-Smoky Mountain Wild Flower Pageant, Knoxville, Tenn. / Fri., June 10—German Ball, Rocky Mount, N.C. / Sat., June 11—Virginia Military Institute, Lexington, Va.

Contrasts from the Start
(1904-1927)

In the first half of the twentieth century, one of the major products that northeastern Pennsylvania contributed to America was anthracite coal, mined throughout the region and shipped over the tracks of the numerous railroads that spread through the region to the homes of the greater northeast United States. Another was musicians, especially the Dorsey brothers, who were trained at home and then shipped themselves to fame and fortune in the New York City music mills.

James Francis Dorsey was the first—a leap-year baby born February 29, 1904, to Thomas Francis and Theresa (Langton) Dorsey of Mahanoy Plane, now part of Shenandoah, Pennsylvania. Jimmy's brother, Thomas Francis, Jr., was born at home twenty-one months later, the family says on November 19, 1905, though official records list the date as November 27, 1905. There were two other children: sister Mary, born two years after Tommy, and the youngest brother, Edward Francis (St. Francis was apparently the family's patron saint), who died at a very early age.

All through their lives the brothers were a study in contrasts. While both possessed strong Irish tempers, Jimmy, the calmer one, tended to be happiest as a section player and soloist, leaving the leading to others. Tommy, on the other hand, was more aggressive, at his best "out front" and handling the politics of the music business.

Their dad, Thomas Francis, Sr., was a ten-dollar-a-week coal miner by necessity and a music teacher and bandmaster by choice, who exercised a three-part theory in training his children in the fundamentals of music: practice, practice and practice.

The elder Dorsey (Mom and the kids always referred to him as "the father") started Jimmy and Tommy on slide trumpet at about age five and by seven Jimmy was playing first-chair cornet in Pop's band at the Irish Catholic Church in Shenandoah (Lee September 1940).

In 1913 at the ripe old age of nine, Jimmy told his dad he was tired of working for applause when it was money that counted. That September Jimmy made his first New York City theater appearance, working for two days with J. Carson McGee's King Trumpeters, a booking that Jimmy's father arranged for him. His father a decade later said that Jimmy played the cornet better than anyone he had ever heard play any band instrument, insisting that Jimmy's later sax playing was "maybe as good" as his cornet work at ten. Jimmy even performed as soloist in a local appearance by the famed John Phillip Sousa band (Riordan 1998).

By age ten Jimmy's father concluded that the woods were full of cornet players, even if Jimmy was superior to most. He then switched him over to C-melody saxophone in the hopes that Jimmy could rise to the top with the just-emerging saxophone. The music world was the better for it all.

Four years later, at age fourteen, Jimmy was working in the mines as

1

a messenger and general "gofer." This was short-lived, for Pennsylvania soon banned those under seventeen from mine work.

In January 1920, "the father," having received a higher paying offer from the Lansford Concert Band, moved the family twenty-five miles east to 227 E. Abbott Street in Lansford, Pennsylvania. Tommy got a job in a meat market and Jimmy lied about his age, saying he was eighteen, to get a clerical job in the mines.

A year later Jimmy and Tommy had put together the first Dorsey Brothers band, originally labeled Dorsey's Novelty Six (The Jazz Band of 'em all) and later renamed Dorsey's Wild Canaries. In addition to the Dorseys, the Canaries included "Soccer" Miller (tp), the Dorseys' cousins Jim (vn) and Kay (p) Crossan, Cliff Zug (bj) and Don Nyer (d).

In the summer of 1921 they were playing a sixteen-week booking at Carling's Amusement Park in Baltimore, Maryland, when Bill Lustig, head of the Scranton Sirens, the most prestigious of the Pennsylvania regional bands, caught them. The Canaries also became the first jazz band to broadcast on WBAL, the pioneer Baltimore radio station.

Late that year Jimmy joined the Sirens, his first big-time job. Soon, trombonist Russ Morgan left for Paul Specht's band and Jimmy cajoled Lustig into hiring "the brother." The older brother (nicknamed "Lad" by Tommy) looking out for the younger (whom Jimmy called "Mac") was to be Jimmy's quiet way for most of those early years. How ironic that in their final years the roles were reversed.

The Dorsey brothers were the first Sirens with a more than passing talent for improvising. Jimmy developed a "trademark" song, triple-tonguing "I'm Just Wild About Harry," with the band playing a stop chorus behind him, which became a big hit on the vaudeville circuit.

In 1923 Jimmy also began to hear the C-melody saxophone stylings of Rudy Wiedoeft on Cotton Pickers recordings with Phil Napoleon and Miff Mole, mannerisms that would stay with him for some time.

Jimmy's original clarinet had the "Albert System" fingering mechanism, and though he tried using the more modern Boehm system in the thirties, he could only master the left hand (or upper) section and so merged "upper Boehm" and "lower Albert" sections into what he nick-named his "Al-Boehm" clarinet (Riordan 1998).

The Sirens are generally given credit for helping to spawn the big-band style of music. They employed three-part harmony backgrounds behind the soloists, very much like what became the big-band sound.

In 1923 the Sirens were booked for the Dancing Carnival promoted by Sammy Collins, a Remick Music song plugger and promoter, at the St. Nicholas Arena on New York's West Sixty-sixth Street (Lee May 1940).

It's also believed that while the Sirens were in New York they visited the OKeh studios and cut two sides for the band's private label to be sold mostly on public appearances.

For "Three O'Clock In The Morning" Jimmy and Sid Trucker turned in a credible Hawaiian guitar imitation on their saxes.

OKeh, New York, N.Y. Late Spring 1923
SCRANTON SIRENS
Billy Lustig (vn) Fuzzy Farrar (tp) Tom Dorsey (tb) **Jimmy Dorsey**, Sid Trucker (as) Irving ["Itzy"] Riskin (p) Tommy Edwards (bj) Carey Barney (bb) Joe Settler (d) [personnel is that of the period]

SRP-S-4   **Three O'Clock In The Morning** [Dorothy Terris;
                   Julian Robledo]
   78: Sirens 1001-B
SRP-S-5   **Fate** [Cage]
   78: Sirens 1001-A

From New York it was a short trip to the Beaux Arts Cabaret in Atlantic City, New Jersey. While working the Boardwalk, Jimmy and Tommy had their first exposure to two Philadelphia area musicians, violinist Joe Venuti and guitarist Eddie Lang.

It was also in Atlantic City that Sirens' trumpeter Fred "Fuzzy" Farrar got an offer to join the Detroit-based Jean Goldkette band. Fuzzy talked up Jimmy and soon the older Dorsey, just turning twenty, "went west." As he was to do for the next half decade, Jimmy raved so much about "the brother" that soon Tommy was in Detroit as well, in time to join Jimmy on the Goldkette band's first commercial recordings.

Detroit Athletic Club, Detroit, Mich. Thursday, March 27, 1924
JEAN GOLDKETTE AND HIS ORCHESTRA
Fuzzy Farrar, Ray Lodwig, Tex Brewster (tp) Bill Rank, Tom Dorsey (tb) Doc Ryker, **Jimmy Dorsey** (cl,as) Don Murray (cl,ts) Joe Venuti (vn) Dewey Bergman (p) Howdy Quicksell (bj) Irish Henry (bb) Charlie Horvath (d)

29807-3   **In The Evening** [Walter Donaldson]
   78: Victor 19308, His Master's Voice (E) B-1865
   LP: RCA (F) FXM1-7136, The Old Masters 47
29808-2   **Where The Lazy Daisies Grow** [Cliff Friend]
   78: Victor 19308, His Master's Voice (E) B-1849, HMV (F) K-2490
   LP: RCA (F) FXM1-7136, The Old Masters 47
29809-2   **My Sweetheart** [Gus Kahn, Conley; Gene Rodemich]
   78: Victor 19313, Zonophone (E) 3782
29810-2   **It's The Blues (No. 14 Blues)**
   78: Victor 19600
   LP: RCA (F) FXM1-7136
29811-2   **Eileen** [Victor Arden] (as solo)
   78: Victor 19327

Detroit Athletic Club, Detroit, Mich. Friday, March 28, 1924
JEAN GOLDKETTE AND HIS ORCHESTRA

29812-3   **Fox Trot Classique** (medley: **From The Land Of The Sky Blue Water** [Nelle Richmond Eberhart, Charles Wakefield Cadman]; **To A Wild Rose** [Edward MacDowell]) (as solo)
   78: Victor 19345, Zonophone (E) 3793
29813-1,2,3   **Chanson Bohemienne** (unissued)
29814-4   **Cover Me Up With The Sunshine Of Virginia** [Sam Lewis; Joe Young] (as solo)
   78: Victor 19317, Zonophone (E) 3767

In less than a year, and just before Goldkette hired Leon "Bix" Beiderbecke, Jimmy returned east, spending a brief period with violinist Ray Miller's society orchestra. While Jimmy was with Miller, his father visited New York and did a sales job on Arnold Brilhart, who was then with the California Ramblers. Brilhart convinced Rambler's head Ed Kirkeby to audition the Dorseys that summer at the Alamac Hotel where the Ramblers were currently working (Healey 1996).

Tommy, who had eloped with sixteen-year-old Mildred Kraft two years before at the age of seventeen, came into New York especially for the audition, and the Ramblers were amazed at what they saw and heard. Brilhart later said the only stumbling block was convincing Jimmy to get rid of what Brilhart referred to as a "nanny-goat" vibrato (Riordan 1998).

Popular alto man Bobby Davis was leaving the group and Kirkeby persuaded Jimmy to leave Miller. Tommy held off for another six months. By the time the younger Dorsey got back to Manhattan the Ramblers were ruling the roost at their own club, Westchester County's The Ramblers Inn, in Pelham Bay Park on Long Island Sound, just north of New York City.

Columbia, New York, N.Y. Friday, November 14, 1924
THE LITTLE RAMBLERS
Ed Kirkeby (ldr) Bill Moore (tp) *Jimmy Dorsey* (cl,as) Adrian Rollini (bsx,goof) Irving Brodsky (p) Tommy Felline (bj) Stan King (d,kazoo)

140115-4,5,6   **Copenhagen** (unissued)
140116-4,5,6   **Gotta Get A Girl** (unissued)

The Kirkeby diaries say the above were remakes of sides cut on October 23 by the California Ramblers before Jimmy joined. While Jimmy is credited with being on the remakes by Kirkeby, he is not present for two other released cuts made that day. "Those Panama Mamas" (140142-4) and "Prince Of Wails" (140143-3) were made with Bobby Davis (cl,as,ssx).

Edison, New York, N.Y. Tuesday, November 18, 1924
CALIFORNIA RAMBLERS
Ed Kirkeby (ldr) Frank Cush, Bill Moore (tp) Lloyd Olsen (tb) **Jimmy Dorsey** (cl,as) Arnold Brilhart (cl,as,ssx) Fred Cusick (cl,ts) Adrian Rollini (bsx) Irving Brodsky (p) Tommy Felline (bj) Stan King (d)

9853-A,B,C   **I've Got A Garden In Sweden**
      78: Edison 51443
            as GOLDEN GATE DANCE ORCHESTRA
      LP: Riverside RLP 12-834, London (E) AL 3562
9854-A,B,C   **Southern Rose**
      78: Edison 51443
            as GOLDEN GATE DANCE ORCHESTRA

Ed Kirkeby's diaries first listed the next group as "The St. Louis Low Downs." Red Nichols later cited this as the session Nichols made before officially joining the California Ramblers, adding that it was the first time he used his hand over the trumpet bell to create a "growl" (Hester 1994).

OKeh, New York, N.Y. Tuesday, November 25, 1924
THE GOOFUS FIVE
Ed Kirkeby (ldr) Red Nichols (cnt) **Jimmy Dorsey** (cl,as) Adrian Rollini (bsx) Irving Brodsky (p) Tommy Felline (bj) Stan King (d) Billy Jones (vcl)

S-72-998-C   **Everybody Loves My Baby** [Jack Palmer; Spencer Williams] (cl solo)
    78: OKeh 40244, Odeon (G) O3162, Parlophone (E) E-5326
    LP: Retrieval (E) FJ118
S-72-999-B   **Oh! How I Love My Darling** [Leo Wood]
    78: OKeh 40244, Odeon (G) O3162, Parlophone (E) E-5326
    LP: Retrieval (E) FJ118

Plaza, New York, N.Y. c. Thursday, December 11, 1924
CALIFORNIA RAMBLERS
Personnel as November 18, 1924. Arthur Fields (vcl)

5764-1,2   **Oh! Mabel** [Gus Kahn, Ted FioRito] vAF
    78: Banner 1472, Domino 3439, Regal 9772, Ajax 17108, Apex (C) 8295, Starr (C) 8295, Imperial (E) 1418, Bell P-321
        Domino as RIALTO DANCE ORCHESTRA, Bell as BELL RECORD ORCHESTRA
    LP: Riverside RLP12-834
5765-2   **Blue-Eyed Sally** [Bernard Robinson] (as solo)
    78: Banner 1474, Bell P-319, Domino 3446, Pathe Actuelle 036199, Perfect 14380, Imperial (E) 1419, Apex (C) 8294
        Bell as GOLDEN GATE ORCH., Domino as ROY COLLINS' ORCH., Pathe Actuelle as EMPIRE DANCE ORCH., Perfect as ELITE DANCE ORCH.
5766-1,2   **Nobody Knows What A Red Head Mama Can Do** [Irving Mills, Al Dubin, Sammy Fain] (as solo)
    78: Banner 1459, 1471, Ajax 17112, Domino 3429, 3446, Oriole 504, Regal 9758, 9774, Silvertone 2606, Apex (C) 8308
        Domino 429 as HAL WHYTE'S SYNCOPATORS, 3446 as ROY COLLINS' ORCHESTRA. All Banners, Regals and Imperials from this session as GOLDEN GATE ORCHESTRA

Columbia, New York, N.Y. Saturday, December 13, 1924
CALIFORNIA RAMBLERS
Personnel as November 18, 1924. Billy Jones (vcl)

140177-1   **Oh! Mabel** [Gus Kahn, Ted FioRito] vBJ (cl solo)
    78: Columbia 268-D, (E) 3600
    LP: Jazz Supreme (It) JS101
140178-1,2,3   **Me And The Boy Friend** vBJ (unissued)

OKeh, New York, N.Y. Tuesday, December 16, 1924
THE GOOFUS FIVE
Bill Moore (tp) **Jimmy Dorsey** (cl,as) Adrian Rollini (bsx) Arthur Hand (vn) Irving Brodsky (p) Tommy Felline (bj) Stan King (d) Billy Jones (vcl) (Contd.)

THE GOOFUS FIVE (Contd.)

S-73-028-A   Oh! Mabel [Gus Kahn, Ted FioRito] vBJ (as solo)
    78: OKeh 40261
    LP: Retrieval (E) FJ118
S-73-029-C   I Ain't Got Nobody To Love [Sam Coslow, Abner
                  Silver] vBJ (as solo)
    78: OKeh 40261
    LP: Retrieval (E) FJ118

Columbia, New York, N.Y. Monday, December 22, 1924
CALIFORNIA RAMBLERS
Personnel as November 18, 1924. Billy Jones (vcl)

140178-5   Me And The Boy Friend [Sidney Clare; James V.
                  Monaco] vBJ (cl solo)
    78: Columbia 268-D, Regal (E) G-8376
        Regal as CORONA DANCE ORCHESTRA
    LP: Jazz Supreme (It) JS101

When Jimmy returned to New York City in 1924, Joe Helbock, who
would become the originator of the famed Fifty-second Street Onyx Club
in the late twenties and early thirties, was a bootlegger of some prom-
inence among show business personages. He operated a bootleg liquor
delivery system using a telephone and young bicycle messengers from a
hole-in-the-wall later occupied by Radio City.

Jimmy became acquainted with Helbock and soon they were sharing a
year's sublease in the Des Artistes Apartments on West Sixty-seventh
Street at Central Park West, near Columbus Circle (Shaw 1977).

Helbock later recalled some wild parties he and Jimmy threw there,
even after Jimmy moved out. One in late 1929 was for a young blonde
stage actress named Bette Davis who was married to a trumpet player,
and was about to leave for Hollywood for a Universal Studios screen test.
Jimmy was also best man when Helbock wed in 1928 (Shaw 1977).

Jimmy's early friendship with Helbock, ten years his senior, has been
cited by several who knew him at the time as a major reason for alcohol
becoming a lifetime companion.

"Where's My Sweetie Hiding" on Bell P-319 is credited in some
sources as being from a January 3, 1925, session by the Golden Gate
Orchestra (an Ed Kirkeby group name). It is now believed that January 3
is the date Bell assigned the release a number, not its recording date.

P-139's reverse is "Blue-Eyed Sally" from the December 11, 1924,
Plaza session and is a true Kirkeby side. However, Bell's "Where's My
Sweetie Hiding" does not match any other known take of the song by any
Ramblers group.

Bell apparently leased "Sally" from Plaza but as for "Sweetie," it is
now believed it is from Plaza matrix 5778 by Lanin's Arcadians, recorded
October 15, 1924. It does not include either Dorsey.

Columbia, New York, N.Y. Monday, January 5, 1925
CALIFORNIA RAMBLERS
Personnel as November 18, 1924.

140220-1 **Where's My Sweetie Hiding?** [Malie, Finch, Britt, Little] (as solo)
   78: Columbia 278-D
140221-1 **Why Couldn't It Be Poor Little Me?** [Gus Kahn; Isham Jones] (as solo)
   78: Columbia 278-D

OKeh, New York, N.Y. Wednesday, January 14, 1925
THE GOOFUS FIVE
Ed Kirkeby (ldr) Bill Moore (tp) **Jimmy Dorsey** (cl,as) Adrian Rollini (bsx) Irving Brodsky (p) Tommy Felline (bj) Stan King (d)

S-73-099-B **Alabamy Bound** [Buddy De Sylva, Bud Green; Ray Henderson] (as solo)
   78: OKeh 40292
   LP: Retrieval (E) FJ118
S-73-100-B **Deep Blue Sea Blues** [Clara Smith] (as solo)
   78: OKeh 40292
   LP: Retrieval (E) FJ118

Edison, New York, N.Y. Monday, January 19, 1925
CALIFORNIA RAMBLERS
Ed Kirkeby (ldr) Frank Cush, Bill Moore (tp) Lloyd Olsen (tb) **Jimmy Dorsey** (cl,as) Arnold Brilhart (cl,as,ssx) Freddy Cusick (cl,ts) Adrian Rollini (bsx) Irving Brodsky (p) Tom Felline (bj) Stan King (d,kazoo)

9947-A **Keep Smiling At Trouble** [Buddy De Sylva, Al Jolson; Lewis E. Gensler] (as solo)
   78: Edison 51491
9947-B **Keep Smiling At Trouble** (as solo)
   78: Edison 51491
   LP: Riverside RLP1008, RLP12-801, London (E) AL-3516, Biograph BLP12020, Bygone (F) AJ529089
   TC: Star Line SLC-61149
9948-A **Oh! Mabel** [Gus Kahn, Ted FioRito] (cl solo)
   78: Edison 51491
   LP: Riverside RLP12-834, London (E) AL-3562, Biograph BLP12021, Bygone (F) AJ529089
9948-C **Oh! Mabel** (cl solo)
   78: Edison 51491

Columbia, New York, N.Y. Wednesday, January 28, 1925
CALIFORNIA RAMBLERS
Ed Kirkeby (ldr) Frank Cush, Bill Moore (tp) Lloyd Olsen (tb) **Jimmy Dorsey** (cl,as) Arnold Brilhart (cl,as,ssx) Freddy Cusick (cl,ts) Adrian Rollini (bsx,xyl) Irving Brodsky (p) Tommy Felline (bj) Stan King (d,xyl)

140368-2 **Oh! Lady Be Good** [Ira Gershwin; George Gershwin]
   78: Columbia 293-D
140369-2 **Swanee Butterfly** [Billy Rose; Walter Donaldson]
   78: Columbia 293-D

Pathe, New York, N.Y. Friday, January 30, 1925
CALIFORNIA RAMBLERS
Personnel as January 19, 1925. Billy Jones (vcl)

105816   **Ain't My Baby Grand?** vBJ
    78: Pathe Actuelle 036205, 10872, Perfect 14386, Grafton (E)
    9107, Salabert (F) 149
        Grafton as WINDSOR ORCHESTRA
105817   **Cuddles And Kisses** vBJ
    78: Pathe Actuelle 036206, Perfect 14387
        as PALACE GARDEN ORCHESTRA
105818   **Where The Four-Leaf Clovers Grow**
    78: Pathe Actuelle 036207, 10961, Perfect 14388, Homochord (E)
    C-870
        Homochord as DELANEY'S ORCHESTRA

Paramount, New York, N.Y. Thursday, February 5, 1925
GOLDEN GATE ORCHESTRA
Personnel as January 19, 1925. Arthur Hall (vcl)

2006-2,3   **The One, Only One**
    78: Paramount 20380 (-2), Puritan 11380, Triangle 11462 (-3),
    Maxsa (F) 1531
2007-1   **Me And The Boy Friend** [Sidney Clare; James V.
          Monaco]
    78: Paramount 20382, Puritan 11382, Maxsa (F) 1540
2008-1   **Oh! Katharina** [L.Wolfe Gilbert; Richard Fall] vAH
    78: Paramount 20389, Puritan 11389, Maxsa (F) 1540, Kalliope
    K-997
2008-2   **Oh! Katharina** vAH
    78: Paramount 20389, Puritan 11389, Maxsa (F) 1530
    (3572) **78:** Everybody's 1035
        Everybody's as CALIFORNIA RAMBLERS

OKeh, New York, N.Y. Monday, February 9, 1925
THE GOOFUS FIVE
Personnel as January 14, 1925. Blanche Vincent, Earl Richard (vcl)

S-73-159-B   **You Better Keep The Home Fires Burning ('Cause
          Your Mamma's Getting Cold)** [Edgar Leslie, Charles
          Kinney, Percy Weinrich] vBV (as,cl solos)
    78: OKeh 40314
S-73-160-A   **Hot Tamale Molly** vER (as solo)
    78: OKeh 40314
    both sides also on **LP:** Retrieval (E) FJ118

Plaza, New York, N.Y. c. Monday, February 16, 1925
CALIFORNIA RAMBLERS
Personnel as January 19, 1925. King adds (kazoo) Vernon Dalhart [as
Charles West], Arthur Hall (vcl)

5856-1,2   **My Gal Don't Love Me Anymore** [Leon Russell;

                            Cliff Friend] vVD (2nd as solo)
        78: Banner 1502, Domino 3471, Pathe Actuelle 036227, Perfect
        14408, Regal (E) 9799, Apex (C) 8360, Leonora (Au) 10021, Starr
        (Au) 10021
                    Domino as ALAMAC HOTEL ORCHESTRA, Pathe Actuelle as
                    IMPERIAL DANCE ORCHESTRA, Perfect as ELITE DANCE
                    ORCHESTRA
5857-2   **(I Like Pie, I Like Cake) But I Like You Best Of**
                      All vAH
        78: Banner 1502, Domino 3471, Regal (E) 9799, Imperial (E)
        1432, Apex (C) 8336, Leonora (Au) 10004, Starr (Au) 10021
                    Domino as ALAMAC HOTEL ORCHESTRA
5858-   **I Ain't Got Nobody To Love**
        78: Banner 1500, Domino 3474, Regal (E) 9801, Apex (C) 8344,
        Leonora (Au) 10006, Starr (Au) 10006
                    All Banners, Leonoras and Regals as GOLDEN GATE ORCH.

By early 1925 Tommy was back and the Dorseys rented a house on
City Island on Long Island Sound. On an NBC radio salute to Red Nichols (May 31, 1952) Tommy said Red subleased a room from them there.

Cameo, New York, N.Y. Friday, February 27, 1925
VARSITY EIGHT
Ed Kirkeby (ldr) Bill Moore (tp) Tom Dorsey (tb) **Jimmy Dorsey,** Arnold
Brilhart (cl,as) Freddy Cusick (ts) Adrian Rollini (bsx,goof) Irv Brodsky
(p) Ray Kitchingman (bj) Stan King (d) 2 *unknown* (vcl)

1378 A,B,C   **(I Like Pie, I Like Cake) But I Like You Best Of**
                     All vDuet
        78: Cameo 695, Lincoln 2311, Tremont 0530 (-B,-C)
                    Tremont as MUSICAL COMRADES
1379 B   **Cheatin' On Me** [Jack Yellen; Lew Pollack]
        78: Cameo 725, Lincoln 2337, Tremont 0537
                    Lincoln and Tremont as UNIVERSITY SEXTETTE
1380 B   **No One** [Jack Yellen; Milton Ager]
        78: Cameo 694, Lincoln 2315

OKeh, New York, N.Y. Monday, March 16, 1925
THE GOOFUS FIVE
Personnel as January 14, 1925. Ernie Hare (vcl)

S-73-238-B   **I Had Someone Else Before I Had You (And I'll**
                     Have Someone After You've Gone) (as solo)
        78: OKeh 40340, Odeon (G) O3036
S-73-239-B   **(I Like Pie, I Like Cake) But I Like You Best Of**
                     All vEH (cl solo)
        78: OKeh 40340, Odeon (G) O3036
        both sides also on **LP:** Retrieval (E) FFJ118

Columbia, New York, N.Y. Monday, March 23, 1925
CALIFORNIA RAMBLERS
Ed Kirkeby (ldr) Red Nichols (cnt) Frank Cush (tp) Tom Dorsey (Contd.)

CALIFORNIA RAMBLERS (Contd.)
(tb) **Jimmy Dorsey** (cl,as,hfp) Arnold Brilhart (cl,as) Freddy Cusick (cl,ts) Adrian Rollini (bsx) Irving Brodsky (p) Tommy Felline (bj) Stan King (d)

W 140457-1   **Just A Little Drink** [Byron Gay] (cl,hfp solos)
    78: Columbia 340-D
    LP: Jazz Supreme (It) JS100, Vintage Jazz Music (E) VLP28
W 140458-3   **Dromedary** [Hagen] (as solo)
    78: Columbia 340-D
    LP: Jazz Supreme (It) JS100, Vintage Jazz Music (E) VLP28

Columbia, New York, N.Y. Monday, March 30, 1925
LITTLE RAMBLERS
Ed Kirkeby (ldr) Red Nichols (cnt) Tom Dorsey (tb) **Jimmy Dorsey** (cl,ssx,as) *Sam Ruby [or] Freddy Cusick* (ts) Adrian Rollini (bsx,goof) Irving Brodsky (p) Tommy Felline (bj) Stan King (d) Billy Jones (vcl)

W 140476-2   **Cross Words Between My Sweetie And Me** vBJ
                  [Fred Steele, Bob Schafer; Bill Heagney, Bert Reed]
                  (as solo)
    78: Columbia 346-D
    LP: Only For Collectors 48, Vintage Jazz Music (E) VLP28
    CD: Timeless (E) 1037
W 140477-1   **Don't Bring Lulu** [Billy Rose, Lew Brown; Ray Hen-
                  derson] vBJ (as solo)
    78: Columbia 346-D
    LP: Only For Collectors 48, Vintage Jazz Music (E) VLP28
    CD: Timeless (E) 1037

Paramount, New York, N.Y. Wednesday, April 1, 1925
CALIFORNIA RAMBLERS
Personnel as March 23, 1925. Arthur Hall [some as John Ryan] (vcl)

2072-2,3   **Cheatin' On Me** [Jack Yellen; Lew Pollack] vAH (as
                  solo)
    78: Paramount 20395, Puritan 11395
    LP: Bygone (F) AJ529089, The Old Masters 20
2073-1   **Ah-Ha!** [Sidney Clare; James V. Monaco] vAH (as solo)
    78: Puritan 11394
2073-2   **Ah-Ha!** vAH (as solo)
    78: Paramount 20394
2073-3   **Ah-Ha!** vAH (as solo)
    78: Everybody's 1046, Mitchell 1046, Nadsco 1285
                  *Puritan, Paramount and Everybody's as GOLDEN GATE
                  ORCHESTRA, Mitchell as A. KLEIN'S ORCHESTRA, Nadsco
                  as BIG CITY SIX*
    (2073-C) **78:** Grey Gull 1285, Rex 1285, Radiex 1285
                  *Grey Gull as BIG CITY SIX ORCHESTRA, Rex and Radiex as
                  INTERNATIONAL DANCE ORCHESTRA*
2073-4   **Ah-Ha!** vAH (as solo)
    (5883-4) **78:** Perfect 14433, Pathe Actuelle 036232, Regal 9838,

Banner 1536, Harmograph 1043, Dandy 5064, Domino 3507, Oriole 417, Apex 8355, Starr (Au) 10022, Microphone (C) 2207, Imperial (E) 1464, Domino (C) 21055, Bell 350
> *Perfect, Pathe Actuelle, Harmograph as SOUTHAMPTON SOCIETY ORCH., Oriole as BALTIMORE DANCE ORCH., Banner, Regal, Imperial as HOLLYWOOD DANCE ORCH., Domino 3507 as MISSOURI JAZZ BAND, Apex, Starr, Microphone as BEN SELVIN AND HIS ORCH., Domino (C) as THE SIX COLLEGIANS, Bell as HOTEL McALPIN ORCH.*

2074-2   **Oh Those Eyes** [Bert Kalmar, Harry Ruby, M. K. Jerome]
    78: Paramount 20394, Puritan 11394, Bell 350
    Bell as HOTEL McALPIN ORCHESTRA

Edison, New York, N.Y. Thursday, April 2, 1925
CALIFORNIA RAMBLERS
Personnel as March 23, 1925, except Rollini adds (p) (with Brodsky)

10292-A   **Charleston** [Cecil Mack (Richard McPherson), James P. Johnson] (as solo)
    78: Edison 51542
    ET: AFRS American Popular Music 49, 709
    TC: Starline 61149
10292-B   **Charleston** (as solo)
    78: Edison 51542
    LP: Bygone (F) AJ529089, Riverside RLP12-801, RLP1008, RLP 1280, Biograph BLP12020, London (E) AL3516, Monkey 40013
10292-C   **Charleston** (as solo)
    78: Edison 51542
10293-A,B,C   **On The Oregon Trail** [Edward Sedgewick, Henry Cohen] (as solo)
    78: Edison 51538
    CD: Jazz Oracle (C) BDW 8007

Cameo, New York, N.Y. Friday, April 3, 1925
VARSITY EIGHT
Ed Kirkeby (ldr) Red Nichols (tp) Tom Dorsey (tb) **Jimmy Dorsey,** Arnold Brilhart (cl,ssx,as) Freddy Cusick (ts) Adrian Rollini (bsx,goof) Irving Brodsky (p) Ray Kitchingman (bj) Stan King (d)

1399 C   **Don't Bring Lulu** [Billy Rose, Lew Brown; Ray Henderson] vBand (as solo)
    78: Cameo 714, Lincoln 2330
1400 A,C   **Nobody Knows What A Red Head Mama Can Do** [Irving Mills, Al Dubin, Sammy Fain] (as solo)
    78: Cameo 714, Lincoln 2328, Tremont 0526
1401 C   **He's The Kind Of A Man That You Like (If You Like That Kind Of Man)** [Joseph Young, Ted Snyder; Sam H. Lewis] (as solo)
    78: Cameo 711, Lincoln 2328
    Lincolns as UNIVERSITY SEXTETTE, Tremont as MUSICAL COMRADES

Pathe, New York, N.Y. Monday, April 13, 1925
CALIFORNIA RAMBLERS
Personnel as March 23, 1925. Arthur Hand (vn) added. Arthur Hall (vcl)

105963-3   **Isn't She The Sweetest Thing?** [Gus Kahn; Walter
                   Donaldson] vAH (as solo)
    78: Pathe Actuelle 036231, 10985, Perfect 14412, Grand Pree
    (Au) 18485, Salabert (F) 114, Harmograph 1032
          Grand Pree as MEYER'S DANCE ORCH.
105964   **Just A Little Drink** [Byron Gay] vAH
    78: Pathe Actuelle 036235, 10899, Apex 712, Perfect 14416,
    Microphone (C) 22503, Grand Pree (Au) 18322, Starr (Au) 23055,
    Leonora (Au) 23055
          *Grand Pree as ART LODGE AND HIS ORCH., Microphone as
          THE ARCADIANS*
105965   **Montmartre Rose** [Abe Lyman]
    78: Pathe Actuelle 036421, Perfect 14422, Leonora (Au) 23005,
    Starr (Au) 23005
          *Pathe Actuelle 036's as PALACE GARDEN ORCH., 10899 as
          MAX TERR AND HIS ORCH., Perfects and Leonoras as
          GOLDEN GATE ORCH.*

Gennett, New York, N.Y. Wednesday, April 15, 1925
BAILEY'S LUCKY SEVEN
Sam Lanin (ldr) Red Nichols (cnt) Vic D'Ippolito (tp) Sam Lewis (tb)
Jimmy Dorsey (cl,as) Chuck Muller (cl,as,ts) Lucien Smith (cl,ts) Frank
Signorelli (p) Tony Colicchio (bj) Joe Tarto (bb) Vic Berton (d)

9462   **If You Knew Susie (Like I Know Susie)** [Buddy
                   De Sylva; Joseph Meyer]
    78: Gennett 5710, 3009
    (8649) **78:** Champion 15016-A, Edison Bell Winner (E) 4353
          *Champion (labeled "Susie") as THE SEVEN CHAMPIONS,
          E.B.W. as REGENT ORCH.*
9463   **Isn't She The Sweetest Thing?**
    78: Gennett 3008
          as RAINBOW SERENADERS
9464-B   **Flag That Train (To Alabam')** [Richmond, McPhail,
                   Rothchild]
    78: Gennett 5710, 3011

Edison, New York, N.Y. Wednesday, April 22, 1925
CALIFORNIA RAMBLERS
Personnel as March 23, 1925. Arthur Hall, Vernon Dalhart (vcl)

10331 B   **Everything Is Hotsy-Totsy Now** vVD [Irving Mills;
                   Jimmy McHugh] (as solo)
    78: Edison 51551
10331 C   **Everything Is Hotsy-Totsy Now** vVD (as solo)
    78: Edison 51551
    LP: Biograph BLP 12021, Bygone (F) AJ529089, Riverside RLP
    12-801, Monkey 40013, Broadway 12021

10332 A   The Flapper Wife [Carl Rupp; Val Burton] vAH
                    (as solo)
    78: Edison 51551
    TC: Starline 61149
10332 B   The Flapper Wife vAH (as solo)
    78: Edison 51551
    LP: Riverside RLP 1008, RLP 12-801, London 3516
10332 C   The Flapper Wife vAH (as solo)
    78: Edison 51551
    LP: Monkey 40013, Bygone (F) AJ529089

Cameo, New York, N.Y. Tuesday, April 28, 1925
VARSITY EIGHT
Ed Kirkeby (ldr) Red Nichols (tp) Tom Dorsey (tb) **Jimmy Dorsey**
(cl,as) Arnold Brilhart (cl,ssx,as) Freddy Cusick (ts) Adrian Rollini
(bsx,goof) Irving Brodsky (p) Tommy Felline (bj) Stan King (d,kazoo)

1435 B   **Sweet Georgia Brown** [Maceo Pinkard, Kenneth Ca-
                    sey, Ben Bernie] (cl solo)
    78: Cameo 730, Lincoln 2340
1436 B   **Lady Of The Nile** [Gus Kahn; Isham Jones] *(as solo)*
    78: Lincoln 2339
1436 C   **Lady Of The Nile** *(as solo)*
    78: Cameo 730
1437 B   **Ah-Ha!** [Sidney Clare; James V. Monaco] (as solo)
    78: Cameo 732
1437 C   **Ah-Ha!** (as solo)
    78: Lincoln 2343
                    Lincolns as UNIVERSITY SEXTETTE

Pathe, New York, N.Y. Monday, May 4, 1925
CALIFORNIA RAMBLERS
Personnel as April 13, 1925, except no (vn)

106004   **Dustin' The Donkey** [Howdy Quicksell] (as solo)
    78: Pathe Actuelle 036260, Perfect 14441
                    Pathe Actuelle as PALACE GARDEN ORCH.
    LP: The Old Masters 20
106005   **Tiger Rag** [Harry DeCosta; Edwin Edwards, Nick La
                    Rocca, Tony Spargo, Larry Shields] (cl,as solos)
    78: Pathe Actuelle 036266, (F) P6853, Perfect 14447, Banner
    6049, Oriole 984, 1544 (some issues), Apex 8644, Domino 4011,
    21303, Rex 8380, Lucky Strike (C) 24120, Microphone (C) 22197,
    Starr (C) 10272, Salabert (F) 197
                    Perfect and both Pathes as FIVE BIRMINGHAM BABIES,
                    Banner as NEW ORLEANS JAZZ BAND, Apex as HOLLY-
                    WOOD DANCE ORCHESTRA, Domino 4011 and Rex as MIS-
                    SOURI JAZZ BAND, Domino 21303 as GOLDIE'S SYNCO-
                    PATORS, Oriole 984 as DIXIE JAZZ BAND, 1544 as TED
                    WHITE'S COLLEGIANS
    LP: Only For Collectors 38, Jazz Studies (C) JS3
    both sides also on **CD:** Village (G) VILCD 011-2

The Kirkeby pay voucher for the preceding session includes two additional titles: "Tech Triumph" and "Techland" (Hester 1994).

Edison, New York, N.Y. Monday, May 11, 1925
CALIFORNIA RAMBLERS
Ed Kirkeby (ldr) Frank Cush, Red Nichols (cnt) Tom Dorsey (tb) **Jimmy Dorsey**, Arnold Brilhart (cl,as) Freddy Cusick (cl,ts) Adrian Rollini (bsx) Irving Brodsky (p) Tommy Felline (bj) Stan King (d) Vernon Dalhart, Charles Hart (vcl)

10361 A   **Cheatin' On Me** [Jack Yellen; Lew Pollack] vVD
        78: Edison 51562
        LP: Riverside RLP1051, RLP 12-081, London (E) AL3545, Monkey 40013, Bygone (F) AJ 529089
10361 B,C   **Cheatin' On Me** vVD
        78: Edison 51562
10362 A   **When The Moon Shines On Coral Gables** [Charles Bayha] vCH (as solo)
        78: Edison 51562
        LP: Bygone (F) AJ529089, Biograph BLP 12020, Monkey 40013
10362 B,C   **When The Moon Shines On Coral Gables** vCH (as solo)
        78: Edison 51562

Cameo, New York, N.Y. Wednesday, May 13, 1925
VARSITY EIGHT
Ed Kirkeby (ldr) Red Nichols (cnt) Tom Dorsey (tb) **Jimmy Dorsey** (cl,as) Arnold Brilhart (cl,ssx,as) Freddy Cusick (ts) Adrian Rollini (bsx,goof) Irving Brodsky (p) Tommy Felline (bj) Stan King (d,kazoo)

1447 A,B   **If You Knew Susie Like I Know Susie** [Buddy De Sylva; Joseph Meyer] (as solo)
        78: Cameo 724, Lincoln 2352, Tremont 0544
            Lincoln as UNIVERSITY SEXTETTE, Tremont as MUSICAL COMRADES
1448 C   **Charleston** [Cecil Mack (Richard McPherson), James P. Johnson] (as solo)
        78: Cameo 741, Lincoln 2355
            Lincoln as UNIVERSITY SEXTETTE
        LP: Jazum 14
1449 C   **Flag That Train (To Alabam')** [Richmond, McPhail, Rothchild]
        78: Cameo 740, Lincoln 2355, Tremont 526
            Cameo as BROADWAY BROADCASTERS, Lincoln as SAM LANIN & HIS ORCH., Tremont as THE SENATORS

Columbia, New York, N.Y. Thursday, May 14, 1925
CALIFORNIA RAMBLERS
Personnel as May 11, 1925, plus Arthur Hand (vn)

W 140602-1   **Everything Is Hotsy-Totsy Now** [Irving Mills; Jimmy McHugh] (as solo)

78: Columbia 380-D
LP: Only For Collectors 48, Halcyon (E) HAL 8
TC: Halcyon (E) CHHDL 8
CD: Village (G) VILCD 011-2
W 140603-1   **Sweet Georgia Brown** [Maceo Pinkard, Kenneth Casey, Ben Bernie] arrJD (as solo)
    78: Columbia 380-D, (E) 3717
    Columbia 3717 as DENZA DANCE BAND
    LP: Only For Collectors 48, Halcyon (E) HAL 8, Saville (E) SVL 175
    TC: Saville (E) CSVL 175, Halcyon (E) CHDL 8
    CD: Village (G) VILCD 011-2

Okeh, New York, N.Y. Saturday, May 30, 1925
MELODY SHEIKS
Sam Lanin (ldr) Red Nichols (cnt) Fuzzy Farrar (tp) Miff Mole (tb) **Jimmy Dorsey,** Dick Johnson (cl,as) Bobby Davis (cl,ts) Rube Bloom (p) Tommy Felline (bj) Joe Tarto (bb) Vic Berton (d)

S-73383-A   **Ukulele Lady** [Gus Kahn; Richard Whiting]
    78: OKeh 40412, Parlophone (E) 5420, Odeon (G) 3308
S-73384-A,B   **Steppin' In Society** [Alex Garber; Harry Akst]
    78: OKeh 40387, Parlophone (E) 5400
    LP: Broadway BR-108

Columbia, New York, N.Y. Tuesday, June 2, 1925
LITTLE RAMBLERS
Red Nichols (cnt) Tom Dorsey (tb) **Jimmy Dorsey** (cl,as) Adrian Rollini (bsx,goof) Irving Brodsky (p) Tommy Felline (bj) Stan King (d)

W-140644-1,2,3   **Look Who's Here!** (unissued) *remade June 16, 1925*
W-140645-1,2,3   **Got No Time** (unissued) *remade June 16, 1925*

Columbia, New York, N.Y. Wednesday, June 3, 1925
SAM LANIN AND HIS ROSELAND ORCHESTRA
Sam Lanin (ldr) Red Nichols (cnt) Hymie Farberman (tp) Tom Dorsey (tb) **Jimmy Dorsey,** Dick Johnson (cl,as) Lucien Smith (cl,ts) Bill Krenz (p) Tony Colucci (bj) Joe Tarto (bb) Vic Berton (d)

140648-1,3   **One Smile** [Howard E. Johnson; Irving Bilbo, Bud Cooper]
    78: Columbia 396-D, (E) 3733
140649-2,3   **Who Loved You Best?** [Whipple, Wylie, Donaldson] (as solo)
    78: Columbia 396-D, (E) 3933
    Columbia (E) 3733 and 3933 as DENZA DANCE BAND

Cameo, New York, N.Y. Thursday, June 4, 1925
VARSITY EIGHT
Ed Kirkeby (ldr) Red Nichols (tp) Tom Dorsey (tb) Jimmy Dorsey, Arnold Brilhart (cl,ssx,as) Fred Cusick (ts) Adrian Rollini (bsx,goof) Irving Brodsky (p) Tommy Felline (bj) Stan King (d,kazoo)

VARSITY EIGHT (Contd.)

1488-B   **Moonlight And Roses** [Black; Moret] (as solo)
    78: Cameo 753
1489-A   **Yes, Sir! That's My Baby** [Gus Kahn; Walter Donald-
                son] vBand (as solo)
    78: Cameo 750, Lincoln 2371
    Lincoln as UNIVERSITY SEXTETTE

Pathe, New York, N.Y. Monday, June 8, 1925
SAM LANIN AND HIS ORCHESTRA
Personnel as June 3, 1925, except *unknown* (ssx). Billy Jones (vcl)

106074-   **Honey, I'm In Love With You** [William B. Fried-
                lander, Con Conrad] vBJ (as solo)
    78: Pathe Actuelle 036258, 10917, P-1897, Perfect 14439,
    Grafton (E) 9129, 9151, Homochord (E) C-829, Starck (E) 258,
    Starr (C) 10031, Domino (C) 21066, Microphone (C) 222018,
    Apex (C) 8371
            Pathe Actuelle 10917 as HOTEL BILTMORE DANCE ORCH.,
            Grafton 9129 as WINDSOR ORCH., 9151 as CALIFORNIAN
            [sic] RAMBLERS, Homochord as ELDON'S DANCE ORCH.
106075-1   **Are You Sorry?** [Benny Davis; Milton Ager] vBJ
    78: Pathe Actuelle 036259, 11031, Perfect 14440, Grafton (E)
    9186, Harmograph 1053, Salabert (F) 110
            Grafton as WINDSOR ORCHESTRA
106076-1   **No Other** [Benny Davis; Joseph Burke]
    78: Pathe Actuelle 036258, 10937, Perfect 14439, Starck (E) 258

Columbia, New York, N.Y. Tuesday, June 9, 1925
CALIFORNIA RAMBLERS
Personnel as May 14, 1925. Billy Jones (vcl)

W 140673-1   **Sonya (Yup, Alay Yup!)** [Fred Fisher, Bob Schafer]
                vBJ
    78: Columbia 419-D, (E) 3783
            3783 as DENZA DANCE BAND
W 140674-2   **I'm Gonna Charleston Back To Charleston** [Lou
                Handman, Roy Turk] (as solo)
    78: Columbia 419-D
    LP: Halcyon (E) HAL 8

Columbia, New York, N.Y. Tuesday, June 16, 1925
LITTLE RAMBLERS
Personnel as June 2, 1925.

W-140644-5   **Look Who's Here!** [Whitmer, Klages] (as solo)
    78: Columbia 403-D
    LP: Vintage Jazz Music (E) VLP28
    CD: Timeless (E) 1037
W-140645-5,6   **Got No Time** [Gus Kahn; Richard Whiting] (as solo)
    78: Columbia 403-D, (E) 3783

3783 as DENZA DANCE BAND
LP: Vintage Jazz Music (E) VLP28
CD: Timeless (E) 1037

Plaza, New York, N.Y. c. Friday, June 19, 1925
SAM LANIN'S DANCE ORCHESTRA
Sam Lanin (ldr) Red Nichols (cnt) *Hymie Farberman [or] Fuzzy Farrar* (tp) Herb Winfield (tb) **Jimmy Dorsey,** Bobby Davis (cl,as) *unknown* (ts) Rube Bloom (p) Tommy Felline (bj) Joe Tarto (bb) Vic Berton (d) Arthur Hall (vcl)

6055-1   **Marguerite** [Ben Bernie; Al Sherman] vAH (as solo)
    78: Banner 1567, Regal 9866, Domino 3538, (C) 21074, Oriole 467, Microphone (C) 22017, Beeda (Au) 108
        Microphone as CLARENCE SHERMAN'S ORCHESTRA, Oriole as BILLY JAMES' DANCE ORCHESTRA, Domino 21074 as HAL WHITE'S SYNCOPATORS
    LP: Broadway BR 108
6055-2   **Marguerite** vAH (as solo)
    78: Apex 8385, Silvertone 6067, Banner 1567, Starr (C) 10048, Leonora (Au) 10048
        Leonora as LANIN AND HIS ORCHESTRA
6056-1   **Save Your Sorrow (For Tomorrow)** [Buddy De Sylva, Al Sherman] vAH
    78: Domino (C) 21067, Apex 8370, Starr (C) 10032, Microphone (C) 22017, Olympic 1436
        Domino 3539 as MISSOURI JAZZ BAND, Olympic as DANCE ORCHESTRA, Apex as LANIN AND HIS ORCHESTRA, Microphone as CLARENCE SHERMAN'S ORCHESTRA
6056-2   **Save Your Sorrow (For Tomorrow)** vAH
    78: Banner 1564, Regal 9866, Domino 3539, Oriole 450, Imperial (E) 1490, Bell 349, Leonora (Au) 10032
        Banner as MISSOURI JAZZ BAND, Oriole as ROSELAND DANCE ORCHESTRA, Imperial as SAM LANIN'S ORCHESTRA, Bell as FRANK DAILEY'S MEADOWBROOKS, Leonora as LANIN AND HIS ORCHESTRA
6057-1   **If I Had A Girl Like You** [Billy Rose, Mort Dixon, Ray Henderson]
    78: Banner 1570, Domino 3536, Regal 9869, Oriole 469, Stradivari (G) G-5200
        Oriole as BILLY JAMES' DANCE ORCH., Stradivari as ORIGINAL AMERIKANISCHES TANZORCHESTER
6057-2   **If I Had A Girl Like You**
    78: Apex (C) 8370, Domino (C) 21076, Starr (C) 10031, Microphone (C) 22017, Vocalion (Au) 0686
        Apex as LANIN AND HIS ORCH., Microphone as CLARENCE SHERMAN'S ORCH.

Gennett, New York, N.Y. Friday, June 19, 1925
BAILEY'S LUCKY SEVEN
Sam Lanin (ldr) Red Nichols (cnt) Fuzzy Farrar (tp) Herb Winfield (tb) **Jimmy Dorsey,** Bobby Davis (cl,as) Dick Johnson (cl,as,ts) Rube Bloom

BAILEY'S LUCKY SEVEN (Contd.)
(p) *Tommy Felline* (bj) Joe Tarto (bb) Vic Berton (d) Einar Swan (arr)

9606-A   **If I Had A Girl Like You** [Billy Rose, Mort Dixon, Ray Henderson]
    78: Gennett 3093
9607-A   **Summer Nights** [Howard E. Johnson; Irving Bibo, Abe Lyman]
    78: Gennett 3094
9608-A,B   **Marguerite** [Ben Bernie; Al Sherman]
    78: Gennett 3094

Edison, New York, N.Y. Tuesday, June 23, 1925
CALIFORNIA RAMBLERS
Personnel as June 9, 1925, except no (vn).

10451-A   **Collegiate** [Moe Jaffe, Nat Bonx] vDuet (as solo)
    78: Edison 51580
    LP: Riverside RLP12-801, Biograph BLP 12020, Bygone (F) AJ528089, Monkey 40013
10451-B,C   **Collegiate** vDuet
    78: Edison 51580
    CYL: Edison Amberol 5029 (dub)
    (10451-B) **CD:** Village (G) VILCD 011-2
10452-A,B,C   **Look Who's Here!** [Ken Whitmer, Ray Klages]
    78: Edison 51591
    (10452-B) **CD:** Village (G) VILCD 011-2
    (10452-C) **CD:** Jazz Oracle (C) BDW 8007

Columbia, New York, N.Y. Thursday June 25, 1925
SAM LANIN AND HIS ROSELAND ORCHESTRA
Sam Lanin (ldr) Red Nichols (cnt) Hymie Farberman (tp) Herb Winfield (tb) **Jimmy Dorsey,** *Bobby Davis [or] Alfie Evans* (cl,as) *Dick Johnson [or] George Slater* (ts) Arthur Schutt (p) Tony Colucci (bj) Joe Tarto (bb) Vic Berton (d)

W-140720-3   **Summer Nights** [Howard E. Johnson; Irving Bibo, Abe Lyman]
    78: Columbia 414-D, (E) 3754
    3754 as DENZA DANCE BAND
W-140721-2   **If I Had A Girl Like You** [Billy Rose, Mort Dixon, Ray Henderson]
    78: Columbia 414-D, (E) 3754

Plaza, New York, N.Y. c. Thursday, July 2, 1925
CALIFORNIA RAMBLERS
Roy Johnston (tp) for Nichols. Arthur Fields [as James or Charles Potter on some labels] (vcl)

6081-1,2   **I Miss My Swiss (My Swiss Miss Misses Me)** [L. Wolfe Gilbert, Abel Baer] vAF
    78: Banner 1569, Bell 354, Domino 3535, (C) 21058, Perfect

14457, Pathe Actuelle 036276, Oriole 445, National Music Lovers 1123, Paramount 20405, Regal 9867, Kadewelt (G) 2032, Starr (C) 10074 (-1), Microphone (C) 19008 (-1), 22015, Puritan 11405 (-1), Silvertone 2544
N.M.L. as NATIONAL MUSIC LOVERS DANCE ORCH., Oriole as BALTIMORE SOCIETY ORCH., Microphone 22015 as GOTHAM DANCE ORCH., Kadewalt as ORIGINAL AMERIKANISCHES TANZORCHESTER

6082-3 **Say Arabella** [Gus Kahn; Ted FioRito] vAF
78: Banner 1568, Domino 3540, (C) 21064, Regal 9869, Apex (C) 8372, Leonora (Au) 10074, Microphone (Au) 22014, Starr (C) 10038

6083-1,2 **Oh, Say! Can I See You Tonight?** vAF (as solo)
78: Banner 1566, Bell 354, Domino 3541, Oriole 446, National Music Lovers 1124, Perfect 14457, Pathe Actuelle 036276, Regal 9864, Apex (C) 8375, Leonora (Au) 10037, Starr (C) 10037
Pathe Actuelle and Perfect as SOUTHAMPTON SOCIETY ORCHESTRA, Bell as GOLDEN GATE ORCHESTRA, National Music Lovers as MASTER MELODY PLAYERS

Cameo, New York, N.Y. Wednesday July 8, 1925
SAM LANIN AND HIS ORCHESTRA
Personnel as June 25, 1925.

1515-A **When Eyes Of Blue Are Fooling You** [Sidney Clare, James V. Monaco]
78: Cameo 755, Lincoln 2369
1516-C **Who Loved You Best?** [Whipple, Wylie, Davidson]
78: Cameo 758, Lincoln 2370
Cameos as BROADWAY BROADCASTERS, Lincolns as SAM LANIN'S DANCE ORCHESTRA

In late July, Jimmy quit the Ramblers and Sam Lanin, Tommy took some time off and the brothers visited Chicago. They also worked a session with Henry Thies at the Gennett studios in Richmond, Indiana. It has also been claimed that the brothers worked a few weeks with Thies at Castle Farms, Cincinnati, Ohio. It appears instead that they returned to New York where Tommy cut two Ramblers sessions on August 20 and 28. Some list Jimmy and Tommy on an August 31 Thies date, but the author now believes neither Dorsey was present.

Gennett, Richmond, Ind. Monday, August 17, 1925
HENRY THIES AND HIS CASTLE FARMS ORCHESTRA
Henry Thies (vn,ldr) 2 *unknown* (tp) Tom Dorsey (tb) **Jimmy Dorsey** (cl,as) *unknown* (as), (ts) Joe Reichman (p) Dan Dewey (bj) Ray Fantcher (bb) *unknown* (d)

12320,12320-A **Spanish Melody**
78: Gennett 3142, (Sa) S-20272 (-A)
12321-A **Dream Garden**
78: Gennett 3118
12322 **Just Like A Dream** (unissued)

Upon returning to New York Tommy went back to work with the California Ramblers. For a while Jimmy worked in Freddie Rich's band at the Hotel Astor, taking part in some, if not all, of the Rich recording sessions that fall.

Columbia, New York, N.Y. Tuesday, September 22, 1925
FRED RICH AND HIS HOTEL ASTOR ORCHESTRA
Fred Rich (p,ldr) *Hymie Farberman [or] Mike Mosiello [or] Leo McConville* (tp) *Lloyd Turner [or] Earl Kelly* (tb) *Jimmy Dorsey [or] Ted Klein* (cl,as) Ken "Goof" Moyer (cl,as,mel) Rudolph Adler (ts) Jimmy Johnston (bsx) Phil Oliwitz (vn) *unknown* (bj) Jack Hansen (bb) Ray Bauduc (d) Billy Jones (vcl)

141030-1   **You Told Me To Go** vBJ
    78: Harmony 37-H
141031-2   **Feelin' Kind Of Blue**
    78: Harmony 38-H
141032-2   **Miami** [Con Conrad, Buddy De Sylva, Al Jolson]
    78: Harmony 38-H

Columbia, New York, N.Y. Wednesday, October 28, 1925
FRED RICH AND HIS HOTEL ASTOR ORCHESTRA
Fred Rich (p,ldr) Red Nichols (cnt) *Lloyd Turner [or] Earl Kelly* (tb) **Jimmy Dorsey** (cl,as) Ken "Goof" Moyer (cl,as,mel) Rudolph Adler (ts) Jimmy Johnston (bsx) Phil Oliwitz (vn) *unknown* (bj) Jack Hansen (bb) Ray Bauduc (d) Franklyn Baur (vcl)

141204-1   **I'm Sitting On Top Of The World** [Sam M. Lewis,
                 Joe Young; Ray Henderson] (as solo)
    78: Harmony 64-H, Regal (E) G-8541, Silvertone 3226
141205-3   **If You Hadn't Gone Away** [Lew Brown, Billy Rose;
                 Ray Henderson]
    78: Harmony 57-H
141206-2   **When I Dream Of The Last Waltz With You** [Gus
                 Kahn; Ted FioRito] vFB (as solo)
    78: Harmony 67-H, Regal (E) G-8561, Silvertone 3224
    Regals as CORONA DANCE ORCHESTRA

In late fall 1925, anticipating an upcoming trip to New York City, Jean Goldkette contacted Jimmy and recruited him back into the Detroit-based band. For his return to the Motor City, Jimmy bought a new Chrysler, and experienced one of his first "rip-offs," not from the car dealer, but some unknown 1920's car-strippers who lifted the Chrysler's expensive bullet-shaped headlights. Jimmy later said he bought back his same headlights for twenty dollars from an auto store (Lee June 1940).

The Goldkette band was known for the antics of members like Don Murray, Howdy Quicksell and Joe Venuti. Venuti was leading the band one night. Jimmy got up to take applause for one of his by then renowned hot choruses and Venuti let loose with one of his equally famous "rasp-berries," which was heard in the back of the ballroom (Lee ibid).

Since Victor wanted to cut more sides by the band and wanted to do it in New York, Goldkette landed a two-week booking in the Roseland

Ballroom. Their tumultuous reception really pumped up the band. Former members have since likened it to the Benny Goodman success at the Palomar Ballroom in Los Angeles a decade later.

Victor, New York, N.Y. Wednesday, January 27, 1926
JEAN GOLDKETTE AND HIS ORCHESTRA
Fuzzy Farrar, Ray Lodwig (tp) Newell "Spiegel" Wilcox, Bill Rank (tb) Doc Ryker, **Jimmy Dorsey** (cl,as) Don Murray (cl,as,ts,bar) Joe Venuti (vn) Lou Longo (p) Howdy Quicksell (bj) Steve Brown (sb) Chauncey Morehouse (d) Russ Morgan (arr) Frank Bessinger (vcl)

34367-1,2,3	**(The) Roses (Brought Me You)** (unissued)
34368-1	**After I Say I'm Sorry** vFB (unissued)

Victor, New York, N.Y. Thursday, January 28, 1926
JEAN GOLDKETTE AND HIS ORCHESTRA

34368-2   **(What Can I Say) After I Say I'm Sorry** [Walter Donaldson, Abe Lyman] vFB
      78: Victor 19947, His Master's Voice (Au) EA-46, (It) R-7589
      LP: RCA (F) FXM1-7136, The Old Masters 47
34369-1   **Dinah** [Sam M. Lewis, Joseph Young; Harry Akst] (cl solo)
      78: Victor 19947, His Master's Voice (Au) EA-42, (It) R-7589
      LP: RCA (F) FXM1-7136, The Old Masters 47

Victor, New York, N.Y. Wednesday, February 3, 1926
JEAN GOLDKETTE AND HIS ORCHESTRA

34390-3   **Behind The Clouds (There's Crowds And Crowds Of Sunbeams)** vFB
      78: Victor 19965
34391-4   **Drifting Apart** vFB
      78: Victor 19975

Victor, New York, N.Y. Thursday, February 4, 1926
JEAN GOLDKETTE AND HIS ORCHESTRA

34392-2   **Sorry And Blue** vFB
      78: Victor 19962, (C) 19905, His Master's Voice (E) B-5081, Electrola (G) EG-186
34393-1,2,3,4   **Nothing Else To Do** (unissued)

Pathe, New York, N.Y. c. Thursday, February 4, 1926
THE RED HEADS
Red Nichols (cnt) **Jimmy Dorsey** (cnt,cl,as) Miff Mole (tb) Alfie Evans (cl,ts) Rube Bloom (p) Vic Berton (d) Arthur Fields (vcl)

106602   **Poor Papa (He's Got Nothin' At All)** [Billy Rose; Harry Woods] vAF (cl solo)
      78: Pathe Actuelle 36387, (E) 11134, Perfect 14568, Grafton (E) 9217, Salabert (F) 262 (Contd.)

THE RED HEADS (Contd.)

> *Pathe Actuelle 11134 as RED NICHOLS AND HIS ORCH-*
> *ESTRA, Grafton as WINDSOR ORCHESTRA*

106603   **'Tain't Cold** [Harry Barris] (as solo)
    78: Pathe Actuelle 36419, (E) 11396, Perfect 14600
106604   **Hangover** [Loring "Red" Nichols, Miff Mole] (as solo)
    78: Pathe Actuelle 36419, (E) 11396, Perfect 14600
    all sides also on **LP:** Retrieval (E) FJ-110, Ristic (E) 48, **CD:** Jazz
    Archives 15904

The last session marked the beginning of an association that was a major factor in Jimmy's rise in jazz circles. Red Nichols, Miff Mole and Jimmy Dorsey would be names followers of the white jazz scene of the twenties would avidly talk about for many years.

Alfie Evans, who plays in the last session, was a violinist who switched to sax and clarinet after receiving just three weeks of training from Jimmy (Riordan 1998).

Victor, New York, N.Y. Monday, February 8, 1926
JEAN GOLDKETTE AND HIS ORCHESTRA

34367-4 to 8   **(The) Roses (Brought Me You)** (unissued)

Pathe, New York, N.Y. c. Wednesday, April 7, 1926
THE RED HEADS
Red Nichols (cnt) **Jimmy Dorsey** (cnt,cl,as) Miff Mole (tb) Arthur Schutt (p) Vic Berton (d)

106786   **Wild And Foolish** [Edgar Smith; Don Redman] (cl,
                as solos)
    78: Pathe Actuelle 36492, (E) 11206, Perfect 14673
106787   **Hi-Diddle-Diddle** [Hal Keidel, Carlton Coon] (as,cl
                solos)
    78: Pathe Actuelle 36458, (E) 11234, Perfect 14639, Pathe (F) X-
    6900, Salabert (F) 382, Apex 752, Domino 21520, Lucky Strike (C)
    24504, Microphone (C) 22517, Starr (C) 25042
                Some issues of Apex as TEN BLACK BIRDS
106788   **Dynamite** [Fletcher Henderson, Jack Palmer] (cl solos)
    78: Pathe Actuelle 36458, (E) 11456, Perfect 14639, Pathe (F) X-
    6903, Salabert (F) 378
    all sides also on **LP:** Retrieval (E) FJ-110, Ristic (E) 48, **CD:** Jazz
    Archives 15904

Victor, Camden, N.J. Thursday, April 22, 1926
JEAN GOLDKETTE AND HIS ORCHESTRA

34796-1   **(The) Roses (Brought Me You)**
    78: Victor 20033, His Master's Voice (F) K-3564, (It) R-7561
    LP: The Old Masters 47
34797-1,2,3,4   **Jig Walk** (unissued)

Victor, Camden, N.J. Friday, April 23, 1926
JEAN GOLDKETTE AND HIS ORCHESTRA
Franklyn Baur [as Carl Mathieu], Wilfred Glenn [as James Stanley] (vcl)

34798-1   **Gimme A Little Kiss, Will Ya, Huh?** [Roy Turk,
                 Jack Smith; Maceo Pinkard] vBand (as solo)
      78: Victor 20031, His Master's Voice (E) B-5080, (Au) EA-65,
      (F) K-3564, (It) R-7561
34799-1   **Lonesome And Sorry** [Benny Davis, Con Conrad]
                 vFB, WG
      78: Victor 20031, 79866, His Master's Voice (Au) EA-76
      LP: The Old Masters 47

While in New York with Goldkette, Jimmy is said to have been tapped
by Sam Lanin to take part in a couple of recording sessions, which are
dealt with next. There is a question as to whether Lanin actually directs
the June 1 date or Jimmy is present, but the one on June 9 is certainly
Lanin's, and Jimmy's participation is equally certain.

Plaza, New York, N.Y. c. Tuesday, June 1, 1926
PLAZA STUDIO ORCHESTRA
Sam Lanin [or] Adrian Schubert (ldr) Red Nichols (cnt) *unknown* (tp) Miff
Mole (tb) Jimmy Dorsey, Dick Johnson (cl,as,bar) *unknown* (cl,ts), (vn)
Arthur Schutt (p) Tony Colucci (bj) Joe Tarto (bb) *unknown* (d) Billy
Jones (vcl)

6643-2   **Who Wouldn't?** [Gus Kahn; Walter Donaldson] vBJ
      78: Banner 1780, Regal 8085, Broadway 1029, Oriole 675,
      Domino 3750, Apex (C) 8525, Starr (C) 10186
                 *Banner and Domino as MISSOURI JAZZ BAND, Starr as
                 LANIN AND HIS ORCHESTRA, others as IMPERIAL DANCE
                 ORCHESTRA*
6644-2   **Am I Wasting My Time On You?** [Howard E. John-
                 son; Irving Bibo] vBJ *(as solo)*
      78: Banner 1779, Domino 3754, Imperial (E) 1636
      Oriole 675, Regal 8091, Bon Marche (Au) 1015
                 *Banner and Domino as HOLLYWOOD DANCE ORCH.,
                 Oriole as BALTIMORE SOCIETY ORCH., Regal, Bon Marche
                 and Imperial as IMPERIAL DANCE ORCH.*
6645-2   **Barcelona** [Gus Kahn; Tolchard Evans] vBJ
      78: Banner 1777, Broadway, 1024, Regal 8086, Maxsa 1575,
      Kalliope (G) K919, National Music Lovers 1160, Puritan 11466,
      Paramount 20466, Oriole 667, Domino 3753, (C) 21198, Apex
      8514, Leonora (Au) 10169, Bon Marche (Au) 1020, Dahlmont (Au)
      102
                 *Broadway, Puritan, Regal, Apex and Bon Marche as HOLLY-
                 WOOD DANCE ORCHESTRA, Banner, Domino as IMPERIAL
                 DANCE ORCHESTRA, Oriole as BALTIMORE SOCIETY
                 ORCHESTRA, Leonora as LANIN AND HIS ORCHESTRA,
                 NML as NATIONAL MUSIC LOVERS DANCE ORCHESTRA,
                 Canadian Domino as HAL WHYTE'S SYNCOPATORS, Dahl-
                 mont as WOODLAND DANCE ORCHESTRA*

Plaza, New York, N.Y. c. Wednesday, June 9, 1926
SAM LANIN'S TROUBADORS
Sam Lanin (ldr) Red Nichols (cnt) Harold Peppie (tp) Miff Mole (tb) **Jimmy Dorsey,** Andy Sanella (cl,as) Norm York (ts) Irving Brodsky (p) Tony Colucci (bj) *unknown* (d) Irving Kaufman (vcl)

6653-2   **Someone Is Losin' Susan** [Roy Turk; George Meyer] vIK (as solo)
78: Banner 1779, Domino 3754, Lucky Strike 24044, Microphone (C) 22128, Bon Marche (Au) 1018, Dahlmont (Au) 104, Leonora (Au) 10186, Regal 8088, Paramount 20465, Puritan 11465, Broadway 1023, Apex (C) 8526, Domino (C) 21184, Starr (C) 10186, Usiba 1011, National Music Lovers 1161
    Bell as ROSELAND DANCE ORCH., Dahlmont as WILCOX HARMONY ORCH., Broadway, Paramount and Puritan as SAM LANIN'S ORCH., Leonora as LANIN & HIS ORCH., NML as MANHATTAN MUSICIANS
6653-3   **Someone Is Losin' Susan** vIK (as solo)
78: Oriole 672
    as ORIOLE VARSITY TEN, (others listed as take 2 may be 3)
6654-1   **In A Little Garden (You Made Paradise)** [Whittemore, Lula] vIK
78: Domino 3748, Bell 436
    Bell as ROSELAND DANCE ORCH.
6654-2   **In A Little Garden (You Made Paradise)** vIK
78: Banner 1782, Domino 3748, Oriole 671, Regal 8091, Broadway 1030, Apex (C) 8524, Puritan 11472, Paramount 20472, Imperial (E) 1652, Edison Bell Winner (E) 4544, Domino (C) 21185, Lucky Strike (C) 24042, Microphone (C) 22123, Starr (C) 10183, Leonora (Au) 10183, Bon Marche (Au) 1015
    Broadway, Puritan, Paramount as SAM LANIN & HIS ORCH., Apex as LANIN ORCH., Oriole as YANKEE TEN ORCH., Imperial as SAM LANIN & HIS DANCE ORCH., EBW as DIPLOMAT NOVELTY ORCH., Leonora as LANIN & HIS ORCH.
6655-1   **For My Sweetheart** [Gus Kahn; Walter Donaldson] vIK (cl solo)
78: Domino 3748, Broadway 1032, Kalliope (G) K968, Puritan 11474, Paramount 20474, National Music Lovers 11161, Silvertone 2763
    Paramount, Puritan as SAM LANIN & HIS ORCH., NML as MANHATTAN MUSICIANS, Silvertone as RIALTO DANCE ORCH.
6655-2   **For My Sweetheart** vIK (cl solo)
78: Bell 438, Banner 1782
    Bell as CALIFORNIA MELODY MEN
6655-3   **For My Sweetheart** vIK (cl solo)
78: Banner 1782, Domino 3748, (C) 21199, Regal 8090, Apex (C) 8526, Starr (C) 10184, Lucky Strike (C) 24060, Microphone (C) 22128, Leonora (Au) 10184, Bon Marche (Au) 1016, National Music Lovers 11161, Silvertone 2763
    NML as MANHATTAN MUSICIANS, Silvertone as RIALTO

DANCE ORCHESTRA
6655-4   **For My Sweetheart** vIK
   78: Oriole 720, Paramount (test)
     as BOB GREEN'S DANCE ORCHESTRA

Finally the Goldkette band went back to Michigan, where it split into two summer units: at Hudson Lake near South Bend, Indiana, and Blue Lantern Dance Hall on Island Lake, Michigan, forty miles from Detroit.

Jimmy drew the Island Lake gig along with fellow reed man Don Murray, Ray Lodwig (tp), Bill Rank (tb), Howdy Quicksell (bj), Steve Brown (sb), Fred Bergen (p) and Chauncey Morehouse (d). The band members relied heavily on Dixieland and scaled-down Goldkette charts.

The Goldkette "summer units" attracted a lot of musicians from Chicago who came over to Island Lake and especially Hudson Lake to catch the bands they had all been hearing about.

That summer Jimmy hobnobbed with names like Dave Tough, Frank Teschemacher, Eddie Condon, Benny Goodman, Glenn Miller and Jimmy McPartland (Lee July 1940).

But when summer was over, Jimmy again got the itch for New York. Saxophonist Doc Ryker, who stayed on with Goldkette, has said that when Jimmy left the band they lost some of their spark (Lee ibid.) Goldkette's loss was the New York white jazz scene's gain, since Jimmy returned to New York to work with the Ramblers and Red Nichols.

However, all was not "jazzy," for later in the year when he went back with Sam Lanin, Jimmy became part of the "Lanin School Of Music," as Red Nichols, Miff Mole, Tommy and Jimmy, Joe Venuti, Artie Schutt, Joe Tarto and Vic Berton called themselves (Burgess 1977).

Pathe, New York, N.Y. c. Tuesday, September 14, 1926
THE RED HEADS
Red Nichols, Leo McConville (tp) Miff Mole (tb) **Jimmy Dorsey** (cl,as) *Fred Morrow* (as) *Alfie Evans* (cl,ts) Art Schutt (p) Dick McDonough (bj, g) Vic Berton (d)

107094   **Alabama Stomp** [Henry Creamer; Jimmy Johnson]
          (cl solo)
   78: Pathe Actuelle 36527, (E) 11236, Perfect 14708, Pathe (F) X-6946, Salabert (F) 471
107095-A,B   **The Hurricane** [Paul Mertz]
   78: Pathe Actuelle 36536, (E) 11331, Perfect 14717, Salabert (F) 467, Apex 26009, Domino 21580, Leonora (Au) 23093, Starr (C) 23093
     Domino as THE RED DANDIES
107096   **Brown Sugar** [Harry Barris]
   78: Pathe Actuelle 36527, (E) 11236, Perfect 14708
   all three sides also on **LP**: Retrieval (E) FJ-110, Ristic (E) 48, **CD**: Jazz Archives 15904

Edison, New York, N.Y. Wednesday, October 13, 1926
RED AND MIFF'S STOMPERS
Red Nichols (mgr,cnt) Miff Mole (tb) **Jimmy Dorsey** (cl,as) Alfie Evans (as) Arthur Schutt (p) Joe Tarto (bb) Vic Berton (d)

RED AND MIFF'S STOMPERS (Contd.)

11245-A,B   **Alabama Stomp** [Henry Creamer; Jimmy Johnson]
                 (cl solo)
        78: Edison 51854, Steiner-Davis (dubbing) 106
        LP: Historical HLP-8, Biograph BLP 12057, Riverside RLP 1048
11245-C   **Alabama Stomp** (cl solo)
        LP: Only For Collectors 36, London (E) AL-3541, Riverside SPD-
        11
11246-A,B,C   **Stampede** [Fletcher Henderson] (as solo)
        78: Edison 51854, Steiner-Davis (dubbing) 106
        LP: Historical HLP-8, Biograph BLP 12057, Only For Collectors
        36, London (E) AL-3541
        TC: Riverside SPD-11
        all six takes also on **CD:** Jazz Oracle (C) BDW 8007. 11245-A and
        11246-A also on **CD:** Biograph BCD 129

     Frank Trumbauer is listed by some sources on the next Pathe session,
but Red Nichols has said he only made one session with Trumbauer, that
being at Victor on October 26, 1927 (Hester 1997).

Pathe, New York, N.Y. October 1926
CLIFF EDWARDS and His Hot Combination
Red Nichols (cnt) Miff Mole (tb) Jimmy Dorsey (cl,as) Arthur Schutt (p)
Dick McDonough (g,bj) Cliff Edwards (uke,vcl) Vic Berton (d)

107160-A   **Sunday** [Chester Conn, Ned Miller; Jule Styne,
                 Bennie Kreuger] vCE (as solo)
        78: Perfect 11633, Pathe Actuelle 25199
        LP: Ristic (E) 39 (10"), Bateau Chinois (E) A-1 (10"), Retrieval (E)
        FV203, Columbia 77763 (in sets C3l-35, CL2229), New World 279
107160-B   **Sunday** vCE (as solo)
        78: Perfect 11633, Pathe Actuelle 25199, Starck 199
107161-A   **I Don't Mind Being All Alone (When I'm All Alone
                 With You)** [Clarence Gaskill, Jimmy McHugh, Irving
                 Mills] vCE (as solo)
        78: Pathe Actuelle 25198, Starck 198
        LP: Bateau Chinois (E) A-1 (10"), Ristic (E) 39 (10"), Retrieval (E)
        FV203
107161-B   **I Don't Mind Being All Alone (When I'm All Alone
                 With You)** vCE (as solo)
        78: Perfect 11632, Starck 199

Pathe, New York, N.Y. Early November 1926
CLIFF EDWARDS and His Hot Combination
Personnel as last but **Jimmy Dorsey** sure, *Vic Berton or Ray Bauduc* (d)

107181   **Meadow Lark (Every Evening In The Park Dear
                 When It's Dark)** [Hal Keidel; Ted FioRito] vCE
        78: Pathe Actuelle 25199, (E) 11341, Perfect 11633, Starck 199,
        Philips (E) BBL-7434
        LP: Ristic (E) 39 (10"), Bateau Chinois (E) A-1 (10"), Columbia

50275 (in sets C4L-18, CL1524)
107182-A   **I Never Knew What The Moonlight Could Do** [Sam
                Coslow; Harry R. Spier] vCE (cl solo)
        78: Pathe Actuelle 25200, (E) 11365, Perfect 11634, Starck 200
        LP: Ristic (E) 39 (10"), Bateau Chinois (E) A-1 (10")

Pathe, New York, N.Y. Early November 1926
CLIFF EDWARDS and His Hot Combination
Mole omitted, Dorsey (bar), Joe Venuti (vn) added

107194-2   **I'm Tellin' The Birds, I'm Tellin' The Bees** [Lew
                Brown; Cliff Friend] vCE
        78: Pathe Actuelle 25200, (E) 11341, Perfect 11634, Starck 200
        LP: Ristic (E) 39 (10"), Bateau Chinois (E) A-1 (10")
                "If You Can't Land Her On The Old Veranda" by Cliff
                Edwards is sometimes attributed to this session. It was made in
                September 1926 with solo uke backing by Edwards.

Edison, New York, N.Y. Wednesday, November 10, 1926
RED AND MIFF'S STOMPERS
Personnel as October 13, 1926

11291-A,B   **Hurricane** [Paul Mertz] (cl,as solos)
        78: Edison 51878, Steiner-Davis (dubbing) 105
        LP: Riverside RLP-1448 (-B)
11291-C   **Hurricane** (unissued test)
11292-B,C   **Black Bottom Stomp** [Ferdinand "Jelly Roll" Morton]
                (cl,as solos)
        78: Edison 51878, Steiner-Davis 105 (dubbing)
        all five takes of 11291 and 11292 also on **CD:** Jazz Oracle (C) BDW
        8007. 11291 and 11292 (take unknown) also on **LP:** Historical
        HLP-8, Biograph BLP 12057, Only For Collectors (Arg) 36,
        London (E) AL-3541, **CD:** Biograph BCD 129
-0-   **Five Pennies** [Loring"Red" Nichols]
        LP: Historical HLP-8

Pathe, New York, N.Y. c. Thursday, November 11, 1926
THE RED HEADS
Red Nichols, Leo McConville (tp) Miff Mole (tb) **Jimmy Dorsey** (cl,as)
Arthur Schutt (p) Dick McDonough (bj,g) Vic Berton (d)

107204-1   **That's No Bargain** [Loring "Red" Nichols] (as solo)
        78: Pathe Actuelle 36576, (E) 11331, Perfect 14757
Brad Gowans (cnt) added for next selection only:
107205-2   **Heebie Jeebies** [Boyd Atkins, Connie Boswell]
        78: Pathe Actuelle 36557, (E) 11289, Perfect 14738, Pathe (F) X-
        6963, Salabert (F) 565
107206-A-B   **Black Bottom Stomp** ["Jelly Roll" Morton] (cl solo)
        78: Pathe Actuelle 36557, (E) 11289, Perfect 14738, Pathe (F) X-
        6965, Salabert (F) 565
        All sides also on **LP:** Ristic (E) 49 (10"), Retrieval (E) FJ-110, **CD:**
        Jazz Archives 15904

Pathe, New York, N.Y. c. Friday, November 26, 1926
ORIGINAL MEMPHIS FIVE
Phil Napoleon (tp), Miff Mole (tb) **Jimmy Dorsey** (cl) Frank Signorelli (p) Jack Roth (d)

107239   **Missouri Squabble** (unissued)
107240   **The Chant**
    78: Pathe Actuelle 36565, 11295, Perfect 14746
107241   **One Sweet Letter From You** [Lew Brown, Sidney
                Clare; Harry Warren] (cl solo)
    78: Pathe Actuelle 36565, 11295, Perfect 14746
107242   **Go, Joe Go** [Phil Napoleon, Steve Kretzmer, Frank
                Signorelli] (cl solos)
    78: Pathe Actuelle 36576, Perfect 14757

In liner notes for a 1940 Decca album (A-135), Jimmy confirmed his participation in the previous session and that his is the clarinet solo heard on "One Sweet Letter From You."
It was after the next session that Vic Berton is credited with creating the band's name by suggesting to Brunswick's recording chief Jack Kapp that the group be called "Red Nichols And His Five Pennies." The suggestion, made as a joke, stuck regardless of the size of the band in later years (Hester 1995).

Brunswick, New York, N.Y. Wednesday, December 8, 1926
RED NICHOLS AND HIS FIVE PENNIES
Red Nichols (cnt) **Jimmy Dorsey** (cl,as) Arthur Schutt (p) Eddie Lang (g) Vic Berton (d,tymp)

E-20992-3   **Washboard Blues** [Hoagy Carmichael, Fred B. Cal-
                lahan, Irving Mills] (cl solo)
    78: Brunswick (Arg) 40608
    (E-4178) **78:** Vocalion 15498
    LP: Coral COPS6795, Natchez WEP-805, Classic Jazz Masters 24,
    Swaggie (Au) 836
E-20993-3   **Washboard Blues** (cl solo)
    78: Brunswick 3407, 6814, 80072, (C,E,Au) 3407, (E) O1801,
    (G) A-222
    (E-4179) **78:** Vocalion 1069
    LP: Coral (G) 6495, 97024, Ace Of Hearts (E) AH-63, Classic Jazz
    Masters 24, Brunswick BL-58009, Swaggie (Au) 836, Affinity (E)
    AFS-1038
E-20994-4   **That's No Bargain** [Loring"Red" Nichols] (as solo)
    78: Brunswick 3407, (Arg) 40608
    (E-4180) **78:** (unissued)
    LP: Natchez WEP-805, Classic Jazz Masters 24, Swaggie (Au) 836
E-20995-5   **That's No Bargain** (as solo)
    78: Brunswick 3407, 6814, 80072, (E) O1801, (G) A-222
    (E-4181) **78:** Vocalion 1069, 15498
    LP: Coral (G) 97016, MCA 1518, 2-4061, (J) 3001, Ace Of Hearts
    (E) AH-63, Classic Jazz Masters 24, Brunswick BL-58009, (E)
    LAT-8166, LAT-8307, Universal Record Club 462, Swaggie (Au)

836, Affinity (E) AFS-1038, Herwin (E) 116

Brunswick, New York, N.Y. Monday, December 20, 1926
RED NICHOLS AND HIS FIVE PENNIES
Miff Mole (tb) added. *Dick McDonough* (g) replaces Lang.

E-21594-   **Buddy's Habits** [Arnette Nelson, Charley Straight]
                  (as solo)
          78: Brunswick 3477, 6815, 80071, (C,E,Au) 3477, (E) O1802,
          (G) A-358
          (E-4263) **78:** Vocalion 1076, 15573
          LP: Brunswick BL-58009, Ace Of Hearts (E) AH-63, Classic Jazz
          Masters 24, Coral (G) 6795, 6925, 97024, Swaggie (Au) 836, ASV
          Living Era AJA 5025, Affinity (E) AFS-1038
          CD: ASV Living Era AJA 5025
E-21597-   **Boneyard Shuffle** [Hoagy Carmichael, Irving Mills]
                  (as solo)
          78: Brunswick 3477, 6815, 80071, (C,E,Au) 3477, (E) O1802,
          (G) A-358
          (E-4260) **78:** Vocalion 1076, 15573
          LP: Brunswick BL-58009, 54008, (F) LAT-8307, Ace Of Hearts
          (E) AH-63, Classic Jazz Masters 24, Coral (G) 6795, 97204,
          Swaggie (Au) 45, 836, ASV Living Era AJA 5025, Affinity (E)
          AFS-1038, Universal Record Club 462
E-21598-   **Boneyard Shuffle** (as solo)
          78: (unissued test pressing)
          LP: Classic Jazz Masters 24, Swaggie (Au) 836

Cameo, New York, N.Y. Wednesday, December 29, 1926
JOE CANDULLO AND HIS EVERGLADES ORCHESTRA
Joe Candullo (vn,ldr) Sylvester Ahola (tp) *unknown* (tb) **Jimmy Dorsey**
(cl,as) *unknown* (as) Foster Morehouse (ts) *unknown* (p),(bj),(bb),(d)
Johnny Ryan (vcl)

2263-A   **Delilah** [Horatio Nicholls] vJR
          78: Cameo 1077, Romeo 317
          Romeo as TONY GRAVELLO AND HIS ORCHESTRA.

    Reportedly only one side was cut at the last session because Jimmy
arrived late.

Pathe, New York, N.Y. December 1926
CLIFF EDWARDS and His Hot Combination
Red Nichols (cnt) **Jimmy Dorsey,** Jimmy Lytell (cl,as) Bill Haid (p) John
Cali (bj) Cliff Edwards (uke,vcl) *Joe Tarto* (bb) Ray Bauduc (d)

107281   **Lonely Eyes** [Lou Davis; Harry Akst] vCE
          78: Pathe Actuelle 25203, Perfect 11637
          LP: Ristic (E) 39 (10"), Bateau Chinois (E) A-1 (10")
107282   **Since I Found You** [Sidney Clare; Hary Woods] vCE
          78: Pathe Actuelle 25203, Perfect 11637
          LP: Ristic (E) 39 (10"), Bateau Chinois (E) A-1 (10") (Contd.)

CLIFF EDWARDS and His Hot Combination (Contd.)

107283   I Know That You Know [Anne Caldwell; Vincent
                  Youmans] vCE
       78: Pathe Actuelle 25204, Perfect 11638, Supertone 25201, Starck
       204
       LP: Ristic (E) 39 (10"), Bateau Chinois (E) A-1 (10")

Columbia, New York, N.Y. Tuesday, January 4, 1927
SAM LANIN AND HIS FAMOUS PLAYERS
Sam Lanin (ldr) *Red Nichols, Leo McConville* (tp) Tom Dorsey (tb)
Jimmy Dorsey (cl,as,bar) *Andy Sanella* (cl,as,stg) *Merle Johnston* (cl,ts)
2 *unknown* (vn) *Arthur Schutt* (p,celst) Harry Reser (g,bj) Joe Tarto (bb)
Vic Berton (d) Irving Kaufman (vcl) Einar Swan (arr)

W 80281-B   In A Little Spanish Town [Sam M. Lewis, Joseph
                  Young; Mabel Wayne] vIK
       78: OKeh 40740, Parlophone (E) R-3319, (Au) A-2147, (G)
       A-4505, Odeon (G) 04004
W 80282-C   Moonlight On The Ganges [Chester Wallace, Monta-
                  gue Ewing; Sherman Myers] vIK (cl, bar solos)
       78: OKeh 40740, Parlophone (Au) A-2147, (G) A-4505, Odeon
       (G) 04004

Einar Swan, who was Sam Lanin's primary arranger from 1924 to
1929, played trumpet and also later wrote, as E. A. Swan, "When Your
Lover Has Gone" and "A Room With a View."

Columbia, New York, N.Y. Tuesday, January 4, 1927
THE CHARLESTON CHASERS
Red Nichols (cnt) Miff Mole (tb) **Jimmy Dorsey** (cl) Arthur Schutt (p)
Dick McDonough (bj,g) Joe Tarto (bb) Vic Berton (d)

143258-(1,2,3)   Someday Sweetheart (unissued)
143259-(1,2,3)   After You've Gone (unissued)

Columbia, New York, N.Y. Tuesday, January 4, 1927
THE ARKANSAS TRAVELERS
Red Nichols (cnt) Miff Mole (tb) **Jimmy Dorsey** (cl) Fred Morrow (as)
Arthur Schutt (p) Vic Berton (d)

143260-3   Washboard Blues [Hoagy Carmichael, Fred B. Cal-
                  lahan, Irving Mills]
       78: Harmony 332-H
       LP: Columbia CL-1524, C4L-18
143261-1   That's No Bargain [Loring "Red" Nichols]
       78: Harmony 383-H
       LP: Columbia CL-1524, C4L-18
143262-3   Boneyard Shuffle [Hoagy Carmichael, Irving Mills]
       78: Harmony 332-H
       LP: Columbia CL-1524, C4L-18

Plaza, New York, N.Y. c. Wednesday, January 5, 1927
SAM LANIN AND HIS (DANCE) ORCHESTRA
Sam Lanin (ldr) Leo McConville (tp) *Tom Dorsey [or] Abe Lincoln* (tb)
Jimmy Dorsey (cl,as) *Larry Abbott, unknown* (cl,ts) Artie Schutt (p) John
Cali (bj,g) *Joe Tarto* (bb) Vic Berton (d) Billy Jones (vcl)

7036-1,2,3   **Nesting Time** [Mort Dixon; James V. Monaco] vBJ
     78: Banner 1928
          7036 was remade January 7, 1927.
7037-1,3   **I'm Looking Over A Four Leaf Clover** [Mort Dixon;
                   Harry Woods] vBJ (cl solo)
     78: Banner 1924, Regal 8241, Domino 3893, Oriole 825,
     Homestead 16432, Imperial (E) 1798, Paramount 20497, Puritan
     11497, Silvertone 3583, Challenge 563, Broadway 1055, Edison
     Bell Winner (E) 4654, Mimosa (E) P160, Jewell 5000, Bon Marche
     (Au) 221
          Oriole, Homestead as ROY COLLINS' DANCE ORCH., Par-
          amount, Puritan, Silvertone, Broadway as THE BADGERS,
          Edison Bell Winner as PAVILION PLAYERS, Challenge as
          CHALLENGE DANCE ORCH., Bon Marche as LAURIE KIN-
          LOCK'S DANCE ORCH., Jewell as LOU CONNOR'S COL-
          LEGIANS, Mimosa as MIMOSA DANCE ORCH.

OKeh, New York, N.Y. Thursday, January 6, 1927
SAM LANIN AND HIS FAMOUS PLAYERS
Sam Lanin (ldr) Red Nichols (cnt) Leo McConville (tp) Miff Mole, Tom
Dorsey (tb) **Jimmy Dorsey** (cl,as,bar) Alfie Evans (as) Merle Johnston
(cl,ts) *Artie Schutt [or] Frank Black* (p) *John Cali* (bj) Joe Tarto (bb) Vic
Berton (d) Les Reis [as Russell Douglas] (vcl) Einar Swan (arr)

W 80288-A   **It Made You Happy When You Made Me Cry** [Wal-
                   ter Donaldson] vLR (bar solo)
     78: OKeh 40738, Parlophone 2144, (E) R-3318, (Au) A-2144,
     Odeon (G) A-189005
     LP: World Records (E) WR SH424
W 80289-A   **I Gotta Get Myself Somebody To Love** vLR [Lewis,
                   Young, Handman] (cl solo)
     78: OKeh 40738, Parlophone (E) R-3318, (Au) A-2144, Odeon
     (G) A-189005
     LP: World Records (E) WR SH424

Plaza, New York, N.Y. Friday, January 7, 1927
SAM LANIN AND HIS (DANCE) ORCHESTRA
Billy Jones (vcl)

7042-2   **Nesting Time** vBJ
     78: Banner 1928, Regal 8242, Domino 3899, Oriole 848, Imperial
     (E) 1784, Bell 504, Broadway 1059, Curry (E) 299, Apex 25042
          Oriole as BOB GREEN'S DANCE ORCHESTRA, Broadway as
          NEWPORT SOCIETY ORCHESTRA, Curry as CURRY'S
          DANCE ORCHESTRA. 7042 is a remake of 7036 recorded
          January 5, 1927.

Cameo, New York, N.Y. c. Monday, January 10, 1927
SAM LANIN AND HIS ORCHESTRA
Sam Lanin (ldr) *unknown* (tp) Tom Dorsey (tb) **Jimmy Dorsey** (cl,as,bar)
Merle Johnston (ts) Arthur Schutt (p) *unknown* (bj) Joe Tarto (bb) Vic
Berton (d) *Arthur Hart* (vcl)

2290-B   **Here Or There (As Long As I'm With You)** [Lou
                    Davis; Jesse Greer] v*AH*
    78: Cameo 1088
         as BROADWAY BROADCASTERS
2291-A   **High-High-High Up In The Hills** [Sam H. Lewis, Joe
                    Young; Maurice Abrahams] v*AH* (bar solo)
    78: Cameo 1090, Romeo 335, Lincoln 2602
         Romeo as THE TROUBADORS
2292-B   **You Went Away Too Far And Stayed Away Too
                    Long** v*AH* (bar solo)
    78: Cameo 1092, Romeo 338, Lincoln 2604
         Lincoln as THE RANGERS

Brunswick, New York, N.Y. Wednesday, January 12, 1927
RED NICHOLS AND HIS FIVE PENNIES
Red Nichols (cnt) Miff Mole (tb) **Jimmy Dorsey** (cl,as) Arthur Schutt (p)
Eddie Lang (g) Vic Berton (d,tymp)

E-22981   **Alabama Stomp** [Henry Creamer; Jimmy Johnson]
                    (as solo)
    78: Brunswick 3550, 6817, (C,E,Au) 3550, (E) O1804, (G) A-
    456
    LP: Classic Jazz Masters 24, Swaggie (Au) 836, Swingfan (G)
    1004, Living Era AJA 5025
E-22982   **Alabama Stomp** (as solo)
    (E-4383) **78:** Vocalion 15566
    LP: Classic Jazz Masters 24, Jazz Studies (E) JS2, Swaggie (Au)
    836
E-22983   **Alabama Stomp** (as solo)
    78: Brunswick 3550
    LP: Classic Jazz Masters 24, Swaggie (Au) 836
E-22984   **The Hurricane** [Paul Mertz] (cl,as solo)
    78: Brunswick 3550, 6817, (C,E,Au) 3550, (G) A-456
    (E-4385) **78:** Vocalion 15566
    LP: Classic Jazz Masters 24, Swaggie (Au) 836, Swingfan (G)
    1004, Living Era AJA 5025
E-22985   **The Hurricane** (cl,as solo)
    78: Brunswick 3550, (E) O1804
    LP: Classic Jazz Masters 24
E-22986   **The Hurricane** (cl,as solo)
    78: Brunswick 3550
    LP: Classic Jazz Masters 24, Swaggie (Au) 836

Plaza, New York, N.Y. c. Thursday, January 20, 1927
SAM LANIN'S DANCE ORCHESTRA
Personnel as January 5, 1927. Billy Jones (vcl)

7060-2   **Since You Went Away** [Riddick, Smith] vBJ
      78: Homestead 16432
      as ROY COLLINS' DANCE ORCHESTRA
7061-3   **Song Of The Wanderer (Where Shall I Go?)** [Neil
      Moret] vBJ
      78: Banner 1939, Regal 8262, Edison Bell Winner (E) 4677, Dom-
      ino 3912, Oriole 849, Apex 8602, Starr (C) 10244, Broadway 1059
      Broadway as NEWPORT SOCIETY ORCH., Oriole as BOB
      GREEN'S DANCE ORCH., Apex, Starr as LANIN & HIS
      ORCH., Edison Bell Winner as PAVILION PLAYERS

OKeh, New York, N.Y. Monday, January 24, 1927
SAM LANIN AND HIS FAMOUS PLAYERS
Personnel as January 6, 1927. Vaughn deLeath (vcl)

W 80326-A   **Blue Skies** [Irving Berlin] vVdL
      78: OKeh 40754, Odeon (G) A-189009, Parlophone (E) R-3319,
      (G) A-4513, (Au) A-2157, Lindstrom (G) A-4513
W 80327-A,B   **Yankee Rose** [Sidney Holden; Abe Frankel] vVdL
      78: OKeh 40754, Odeon (G) A-189009, Parlophone (E) R-3325,
      (G) A 4513, (Au) A 2157, Lindstrom (G) A-4513

Pathe, New York, N.Y. Tuesday, January 25, 1927
SAM LANIN AND HIS ORCHESTRA
Sam Lanin (ldr) *Red Nichols [or] Leo McConville* (tp) Tom Dorsey (tb)
Jimmy Dorsey (cl,as) Bobby Davis (cl,ts) Arthur Schutt (p) *unknown* (bj)
Joe Tarto (bb) Vic Berton (d) Art Fowler (vcl)

E-2654-2   **Collette** [Gus Kahn; Abel Baer]
      78: Pathe Actuelle 36581, (E) 11425, Perfect 14762, Apex 26022,
      Domino (C) 21596, Starr (C) 23103, Grafton (E) 9279
      Apex as LANIN & HIS ORCHESTRA, Grafton as IRVING'S
      BROADWAY PLAYERS, Domino as THE ARCADIANS
E-2655-3   **He's The Last Word** [Gus Kahn; Walter Donaldson]
      vAF
      78: Pathe Actuelle 36580, (E) 11379, (F) X-6136, Perfect 14761
E-2656-1   **Don't Somebody Want Somebody To Love?** [Billy
      Rose, Ted FioRito] vAF
      78: Pathe Actuelle 36579, (E) 11425, Perfect 14760
      Pathe Actuelles as LANIN'S ARCADIANS
E-2657-2   **Forgive Me** [Jack Yellen; Milton Ager] vAF
      78: Pathe Actuelle 36579, (E) 11379, Perfect 14760, Imperial (E)
      1805, Bon Marche (Au) 1240, Maxsa 1625
      Pathe Actuelles as LANIN'S ARCADIANS, Imperial as IM-
      PERIAL DANCE ORCH., Bon Marche as LAURIE KIN-
      LOCK'S DANCE ORCH.
      (7202-2) **78:** Banner 1979, Regal 8311, Domino 3957, Broadway
      1073, Oriole 905, Apex 26037, Challenge 239, Edison Bell Winner
      (E) 4680
      Banner, Domino as IMPERIAL DANCE ORCH., Regal as
      HOLLYWOOD DANCE ORCH., Broadway as THE BADG-
      ERS, Oriole as AL LYNCH ORCH.

OKeh, New York, N.Y. Wednesday, January 26, 1927
SAM LANIN AND HIS FAMOUS PLAYERS
Sam Lanin (ldr) Red Nichols (cnt) Leo McConville (tp) Tom Dorsey (tb) **Jimmy Dorsey**, Alfie Evans (cl,as) Merle Johnston (cl,ts,ssx) 2 *unknown* (vn) Artie Schutt (p) *John Cali* (bj) Joe Tarto (bb) Vic Berton (d) Irving Kaufman (vcl)

W 80342-A,B   **Moonbeam! Kiss Her For Me** [Mort Dixon; Harry Woods] vIK
    78: OKeh 761, Parlophone (E) E-5823, Odeon (G) A189020, A193036, Ariel (E) 4229
        OKeh as OKeh MELODIANS, Ariel as ARIEL DANCE ORCH., Parlophone as PARLOPHONE MELODIANS
W 80343-B   **I'm Looking Over A Four Leaf Clover** [Mort Dixon; Harry Woods] vIK
    78: OKeh 40766, Parlophone (E) R-3325, Odeon (G) A189020

Columbia, New York, N.Y. Thursday, January 27, 1927
THE CHARLESTON CHASERS
Red Nichols (cnt) Miff Mole (tb) **Jimmy Dorsey** (cl,as) Arthur Schutt (p) Dick McDonough (bj,g) Joe Tarto (bb) Vic Berton (d)

143258-4,6   **Someday, Sweetheart** (unissued)
143258-5   **Someday, Sweetheart** [John and Benjamin Spikes] (cl solo)
    78: Columbia 861-D, 4419, 0920 (E) DB-5005, (It) CQ-1416, (G) DW-4361
    LP: Columbia 4CL18, VJM (E) VLP26
    CD: BBC (E) 664, ABC (Au) 36185
143259-4,6   **After You've Gone** (unissued)
143259-5   **After You've Gone** [Henry Creamer; Turner Layton] (as solo)
    78: Columbia 861-D, 4419, 0920 (E) FB-1108, test pressing AYG-1
        Columbia 0920 as DENZA DANCE BAND, FB-1108 as "RED" NICHOLLS [sic] AND THE CHARLESTON CHASERS
    LP: Columbia 4CL18, VJM (E) VLP26, Fontana (E) TFE17267

Cameo, New York, N.Y. Friday, January 28, 1927
SAM LANIN AND HIS ORCHESTRA

2311-B,D   **Moonbeam! Kiss Her For Me** [Mort Dixon; Harry Woods] vocal
    78: Cameo 1104, Lincoln 2608, Variety 5043, Romeo 364
        Romeo as THE TROUBADORS, Lincoln as THE RANGERS, Variety as THE SENATORS
2312-C   **There's Everything Nice About You** [Arthur Terker, Alfred Bryan; Pete Wendling] vocal
    78: Cameo 1103, Lincoln 2609, Romeo 344
        Romeo as DIXIE MUSIC MAKERS. This side was remade on February 10, 1927.

The next Trumbauer session with Bix Beiderbecke, together with the Charleston Chasers date on January 27, begin a series of recordings that many consider Jimmy's best jazz work. Not that he didn't play well later, but given his youth, coupled with the freedom of the roaring twenties and its fixation on jazz, he experimented, whereas a decade later he had to be more conservative if he wanted to meet payrolls and feed his family.

There are several stories about Jimmy and Bix and their drinking prowess but none more colorful than that recounted by Miff Mole who tells how he, Jimmy, Bix, Vic Berton and Artie Schutt showed up for a Gennett session with two quarts of bootleg gin.

After an hour and a half of drinking and a half hour of questionable playing, they were told to leave. Undaunted, the quintet boarded the open top of a double-decker Fifth Avenue bus and entertained the populace all the way back home (Shapiro, Hentoff 1955, 276). Sadly, any masters that might have been attempted during this Gennett date have never surfaced.

Columbia, New York, N.Y. Friday, February 4, 1927
FRANKIE TRUMBAUER AND HIS ORCHESTRA
Frank Trumbauer (c-mel,ldr) Bix Beiderbecke (cnt) Bill Rank (tb) **Jimmy Dorsey** (cl,as) Paul Mertz (p,arr) Eddie Lang (g) Chauncey Morehouse (d)

80391-C   **Trumbology** [Frankie Trumbauer]
          78: OKeh 40871, Columbia 36280, Parlophone (E) R-3419, R-2465, (Swi) PZ-11245, Odeon (F) 165171, (G) A-189128
          LP: Swaggie (Au) 1242, Parlophone (E) PMC7113, Joker (It) SM3560, World Records (E) SH413, Columbia CJ 45450
          TC: Columbia CT 45450
          CD: Columbia CK 45450, JSP (E) CD-316, MFP (E) 6046, Masters Of Jazz (F) CD-MJ7, IRD (It) BIX 2, Origin Jazz Library BXCD 1-3, Giants of Jazz 53017
Doc Ryker (as) added:
80392-A   **Clarinet Marmalade** [Edwin B. Edwards, Nick La-
                    Rocca, Tony Spargo, Larry Shields] (cl solo)
          78: OKeh 40772, Columbia 37804 (dubbing), Vocalion 3010, 4412, Parlophone (E) R-3323, R-2304, (Au) A-7534, Odeon (F) 165093, (Arg) 194718, A-189019, (G) A-286089
          LP: Columbia CL845, CBS 62374, CJ 45450, Swaggie (Au) 1242, Parlophone (E) PMC7064, Joker (It) SM3560, World Records (E) SH413
          TC: Columbia CT 45450
          CD: Columbia CK 45450, JSP (E) CD-316, Masters Of Jazz (F) CD-MJ7, Flapper (E) 9765, Saville (E) 201, IRD (It) BIX 2, CDS (E) CD-620, Origin Jazz Library BXCD 1-3
80393-B   **Singin' The Blues (Till My Daddy Comes Home)**
                    [Sam M. Lewis, Joe Young; Con Conrad, J. Russell
                    Robinson] (cl solo)
          78: OKeh 40772, Columbia 37804 (dubbing), Brunswick 7703, Parlophone (E) R-3323, R-1838, (Au) A-6235, (It) B-27597, TT-9073, Odeon (F) 165093, (Arg) 295124, (It) A-2409, A-189019, (G) A-286085
          LP: Columbia CL845, CBS 62374, Columbia CJ 45450 (Contd.)

FRANKIE TRUMBAUER AND HIS ORCHESTRA (Contd.)

> Swaggie (Au) 1242, Parlophone (E) PMC7064, ASV Living Era (E) AJA5080, Joker (It) SM3560, World Records (E) SH413, Odeon (G) SMS13
> TC: Columbia CT 45450, ProArte Digital PCD490
> CD: Columbia CK 45450, JSP (E) CD-316, ASV Living Era(E) CD-AJA5080, CD-AJA5117, ProArte Digital CDD490, MFP (E) 6046, Saville (E) 201, Masters Of Jazz (F) CD-MJ7, IRD (It) BIX 2, Origin Jazz Library BXCD 1-3, Drive 41065

OKeh, New York, N.Y. Saturday, February 5, 1927
SAM LANIN AND HIS FAMOUS PLAYERS
Sam Lanin (ldr) Red Nichols, Leo McConville (tp) Tom Dorsey (tb) **Jimmy Dorsey** (cl,as) Andy Sanella (cl,as,stg) Merle Johnston (cl,ts) 2 *unknown* (vn) *Art Schutt [or] Irv Brodsky* (p) *Harry Reser [or] Tony Colucci* (bj,g) Joe Tarto (bb) Vic Berton (d) Les Reis [as Russell Douglas] (vcl)

W 80382-B   **I Want To Be Miles From Everyone (And A Little Bit Closer To You)** vLR
      78: OKeh 40782, Parlophone (E) E-5823, Odeon (G) A-189021
W-80383-C   **It All Depends On You** [Buddy De Sylva, Lew Brown, Ray Henderson] vLR
      78: OKeh 40761, Parlophone (E) E-5823, Odeon (G) A-193036
      OKehs as OKeh MELODIANS, Parlophones as PARLOPHONE MELODIANS

Cameo, New York, N.Y. Thursday, February 10, 1927
SAM LANIN AND THE TROUBADORS
Sam Lanin (ldr) Red Nichols (cnt) Hymie Farberman (tp) Tom Dorsey (tb) **Jimmy Dorsey** (cl,as) Andy Sanella (cl,as,stg) *Merle Johnston* (cl,ts) *unknown* (vn) Arthur Schutt (p) *unknown* (bj,g) *Joe Tarto* (bb) Vic Berton (d) *unknown* (vcl) Einar Swan (arr)

2312-D,G   **There's Everything Nice About You** [Arthur Terker, Alfred Bryan; Pete Wendling] vocal
      78: Cameo 1103, Lincoln 2609, Romeo 344
      Romeo as DIXIE MUSIC MAKERS. These are remakes of a side first cut January 28, 1927.
2335-C   **I Wonder How I Look When I'm Asleep?** [Buddy De Sylva, Lew Brown, Ray Henderson] vocal (as solo)
      78: Cameo 1106, Lincoln 2607
2336-A   **It All Depends On You** [Buddy De Sylva, Lew Brown, Ray Henderson] vocal arr ES (as solo)
      78: Cameo 1107, Lincoln 2652, Romeo 356
      Lincolns as THE RANGERS, Romeo as THE TROUBADORS

Victor, New York, N.Y. Friday, February 11, 1927
RED AND MIFF'S STOMPERS
Red Nichols (cnt) Miff Mole (tb) **Jimmy Dorsey** (cl,as) Arthur Schutt (p) Tony Colucci (bj) Vic Berton (d)

37768-2   **Delirium** [Arthur Schutt] (cl,as solos)
     78: Victor 20778
     LP: RCA LES9, (F) PM43179, (F) NL89606, Saville (E) SVL146
37768-3   **Delirium** (cl,as solos)
     LP: Jazz Archives JA-21, RCA (F) PM43179, (F) NL89606
     TC: RCA 3136, Radio Yesteryear Stack 45
     CD: RCA 3136
37769-2   **Davenport Blues** [Leon "Bix" Beiderbecke] (cl solo)
     78: Victor 20778
     LP: RCA LES9, (F) PM43179, (F) NL89606, Saville (E) SVL146
     TC: RCA 3136
     CD: RCA 3136, BBC (E) 664, ABC (Au) (Au) 36185
37769-3   **Davenport Blues** (cl solo)
     LP: Jazz Archives JA-21, RCA (F) PM43179, Whitakers Wax
     Works 265 **TC:** Radio Yesteryear Stack 45

Columbia, New York, N.Y. Monday, February 14, 1927
THE CHARLESTON CHASERS
Red Nichols (cnt) Miff Mole (tb) **Jimmy Dorsey** (cl) Arthur Schutt (p)
Dick McDonough (bj,g) Joe Tarto (bb) Vic Berton (d) Kate Smith (vcl)

143476-3   **One Sweet Letter From You** [Lew Brown, Sidney
                  Clare; Harry Warren] vKS (cl solo)
     78: Columbia 911-D
     TC: Radio Yesteryear Stack 14
     LP: Sunbeam MFC-13
143476-3   **I'm Gonna Meet My Sweetie Now** [Benny Davis;
                  Jesse Greer] vKS (cl solo)
     78: Columbia 911-D
     TC: Radio Yesteryear Stack 14
     LP: Sunbeam MFC-13

Brunswick, New York, N.Y. Monday, February 21, 1927
VINCENT LOPEZ AND HIS HOTEL PENNSYLVANIA ORCH.
Vincent Lopez (ldr) Pete Gentile, Einar Swan (tp) Charlie Butterfield (tb)
Larry Abbott, (cl,as) George Napoleon (as) **Jimmy Dorsey** (cl,as) Xavier
Cugat, Daniel Yates (vn) Arthur Schutt (p) Frank Reino (bj,g) Joe Tarto
(bb) Willie Kessler (d) Frank Bessinger (vcl)

E-21574   **So Blue** [Buddy De Sylva, Lew Brown; Ray Hender-
                  son] (waltz) vFB
     78: Brunswick 3473
E-21576   **What Does It Matter?** [Irving Berlin] (waltz) vFB
     78: Brunswick 3473

OKeh, New York, N.Y. Wednesday, February 23, 1927
SAM LANIN AND HIS FAMOUS PLAYERS
Sam Lanin (ldr) Red Nichols, Leo McConville (tp) Tom Dorsey (tb)
Jimmy Dorsey (cl,as) Andy Sanella (cl,as,stg) Merle Johnston (cl,ts) 2
unknown (vn) Irving Brodsky (p) *Tony Colucci* (bj,g) *Joe Tarto* (bb) Vic
Berton (d) Les Reis [as Russell Douglas] (vcl)
                         (Contd.)

SAM LANIN AND HIS FAMOUS PLAYERS (Contd.)

W 80476-A   **Rio Rita** [Joseph McCarthy; Harry Tierney] vLR
    78: OKeh 40781, Parlophone (E) R529, E-4515, (Au) A2377, (G)
    B-12520, (J) E-5116, Odeon (G) A193000, 04030, A189014,
    A221098, (It) 167232, Lindstrom (G) A4515, Ariel (E) Z4610
        *Ariel as ARIEL DANCE ORCHESTRA, Odeon 167232 as SAM
        LANIN AND HIS ORCHESTRA*
W 80477-B   **The Kinkajou** [Joseph McCarthy; Harry Tierney] vLR
    78: OKeh 40781, Parlophone (E) R529, E-4515, (Au) A2377, (G)
    B-12520, (J) E-5116, Odeon (G) 04030, A189014, A221098,
    Lindstrom (G) A4515

Columbia, New York, N.Y. Friday, February 25, 1927
THE CHARLESTON CHASERS
Red Nichols (cnt) Miff Mole (tb) **Jimmy Dorsey** (cl,as) Arthur Schutt
(p,arr) Dick McDonough (bj,g) Joe Tarto (bb) Vic Berton (d)

143533-1   **Farewell Blues** [Elmer Schoebel, Paul Mares, Joseph
            Leon Rappolo] arrAS (as,cl solos)
    78: Columbia 1539-D
    ET: Columbia Special (unnumbered)
    EP: Fontana (E) 17266
    LP: Columbia C4L18, CL-1523, Vintage Jazz Music (E) VLP26,
    Fontana (E) G) J73810
143534-1   **Davenport Blues** [Leon "Bix" Beiderbecke] arrAS
            (as,cl solos)
    78: test pressing AYG-1B, Columbia (J) 218
    LP: Fontana (E) TFE17267
143534-2   **Davenport Blues** arrAS (as,cl solos)
    78: Columbia 909-D, 909-D (Blue Wax), 4453, (E) FB-1108
        *FB-1108 as "RED" NICHOLLS [sic] AND THE CHARLES-
        TON CHASERS*
    LP: Columbia C4L18, VJM (E) VLP26
143537-1   **Wabash Blues** [Dave Ringle; Fred Meinken] arrAS
            (cl solo)
    78: Columbia (J) 218
    LP: Fontana (E) TFE17267
143537-2   **Wabash Blues** (cl solo)
    78: Columbia 909-D, 909-D (Blue Wax), 4419, (J) 219,
    Parlophone (E) R-2211, (Au) A-6510, B-71143, Odeon (Norway)
    D-517
    LP: Columbia C4L18, CL1523, VJM (E) VLP26, ASV Living
    Era (E) AJA5002, Fontana (G) J73810
    CD: BBC (E) 664, ABC (Au) 36185, Jazz Roots 56071

Pathe, New York, N.Y. Friday, February 25, 1927
SAM LANIN AND HIS ORCHESTRA
Sam Lanin (ldr) Red Nichols (cnt) *unknown* (tp) Tom Dorsey (tb) *Jimmy
Dorsey,* Andy Sanella (cl,as) *unknown* (ts) *Joe Venuti* (vn) Arthur Schutt
(p) *Tony Colucci [or] Harry Reser* (bj) Joe Tarto (bb) Vic Berton (d)
Scrappy Lambert [as Ross Doolittle] (vcl)

107385   **Hello Cutie** [Cliff Friend] vSL
    78: Pathe Actuelle 36602, Perfect 14783, Apex (C) 26025,
Domino (C) 21596, Starr (C) 23105
    Domino as THE MIDNIGHT SERENADERS
107386-2   **What Does It Matter?** [Irving Berlin] vSL (waltz)
    78: Pathe Actuelle 36596, (E) 11442, Perfect 14777, Imperial
(E) 1807
    Imperial as HOLLYWOOD DANCE ORCH.
107387   **A Lane In Spain** [Al Lewis; Carmen Lombardo] vSL
    78: Pathe Actuelle 36602, (E) 11381, Perfect 14783, (E) P-300,
Apex (C) 26025
    Perfect P-300 as THE PERFECT DANCE ORCHESTRA
107388   **Swanee River Trail** [Irving Caesar, Al Jolson] vSL
    78: Pathe Actuelle 36603, (E) 11452, Perfect 14784, Grafton (E)
9285
    All Pathe Actuelles from this session as LANIN'S ARCA-
DIANS, Grafton as WINDSOR ORCHESTRA

Brunswick, New York, N.Y. Thursday, March 3, 1927
RED NICHOLS AND HIS FIVE PENNIES
Red Nichols (cnt) Miff Mole (tb) **Jimmy Dorsey** (cl,as) Joe Venuti (vn)
Arthur Schutt (p) Eddie Lang (g) Vic Berton (d,tymp)

E-21718-   **Bugle Call Rag** [Jack Pettis, Elmer Schoebel, Billy
    Meyers] (as solo)
    78: Brunswick 3490, 3510, 6816, (E) O1803, (G) A-7556, (Au)
3490
    (E-4643) **78:** Vocalion 15536
    ET: AFRS America's Popular Music 49
    45: Brunswick 980169
    LP: Brunswick LP-54008, (E) LAT307, Coral (G) 6795, (G)
97024, Classic Jazz Masters 24, Swaggie (Au) 45, 836, Affinity
(E) AFS-1038, Universal Record Club VJ462
    CD: Best Of Jazz (F) 4041
E-21719-   **Back Beats** [Frank Guarente] (as solo)
    78: Brunswick 3490, 3510, 6816, (E) O1803, (G) A-7556, (Au)
3490
    (E-4640) **78:** Vocalion 15536
    LP: Ace Of Hearts (E) AH-63, Classic Jazz Masters 24, Swaggie
(Au) 836

OKeh, New York, N.Y. Monday, March 7, 1927
MIFF MOLE'S MOLERS
Red Nichols (cnt) Miff Mole (tb) **Jimmy Dorsey** (cl,as) Arthur Schutt
(p) Dick McDonough (bj,g) Joe Tarto (bb) Ray Bauduc (d)

80501-B   **Davenport Blues** [Leon "Bix" Beiderbecke] (cl,as
    solos)
    78: OKeh 40848, Parlophone (E) R-3362, (G) A-4903, Odeon
(Arg) 193053, A-189176
    LP: Columbia CAL18CL, Parlophone (E) PMC-7, PMC-7120,
Swaggie (Au) 1295, World (E) SH-503 (Contd.)

MIFF MOLE'S MOLERS (Contd.)

CD: BBC (E) 664, ABC (Au) 36185, Jazz Roots 56071
80502-A   **The Darktown Strutters' Ball** [Shelton Brooks]
                 (cl solo)
      78: OKeh 40784, Vocalion (dubbing) 3041, Parlophone (E) R-
      3326, (Au) A-2188, A-4903, Odeon (Arg) 193008, 194865
            Vocalion dubbing omits the spoken introduction. According
            to Joe Tarto, Nichols and Mole tried to get OKeh executives
            to reject this cut because Artie Schutt had dropped a few
            measures in his solo (Hester 1996).
      LP: Columbia CAL18CL, Parlophone (E) PMC-7, PMC-7120,
      Swaggie (Au) 1295, World (E) SH-503
80503-B   **A Hot Time In The Old Town Tonight** [Joe Hayden;
                 Theodore H. Metz] (as solo)
      78: OKeh 40784, Vocalion (dubbing) 3041, Parlophone (E) R-
      3326, (Au) A-4903, Odeon (Arg) 193008
      LP: Parlophone (E) PMC-7120, Swaggie (Au) 1295, World (E)
      SH-503
      CD: BBC (E) 664, ABC (Au) 36185

Brunswick, New York, N.Y. Friday, March 18, 1927
RED NICHOLS AND HIS FIVE PENNIES

E-5143/4/5   **Alabama Stomp** (unissued)
E-5146/7/8   **Hurricane** (unissued)

Plaza, New York, N.Y. c. Wednesday, March 23, 1927
THE SIX HOTTENTOTS
Red Nichols (tp) Miff Mole (tb) **Jimmy Dorsey** (cl,as) Arthur Schutt (p)
Joe Tarto (bb) Vic Berton (d) Irving Kaufman (vcl)

7173-2,3   **I'm In Love Again** [Cole Porter] vIK
      78: Banner 1964, Broadway 1069, Domino 3935, (C) 21279,
      Oriole 880, Paramount 20511, Pathe Actuelle 36643, Perfect
      14824, (E) P-306, Regal 8289, Apex (C) 8624, Leonora (Au)
      10256, Lucky Strike (C) 24097, Imperial (E) 1803, Bon Marche
      (Au) 240, Maxsa (G) 1623
            Oriole as DIXIE JAZZ BAND, Pathe Actuelle as SOUTH-
            AMPTON SOCIETY ORCH., Perfect P-306 as RAYNER'S
            DANCE ORCH., Imperial as SAM LANIN'S TROUBADORS,
            Bon Marche as LAURIE KINLOCK'S AUSTRALIANS
      LP: Jazz Studies (E) JS2, Fountain (E) FJ-110
7174-2   **Sometimes I'm Happy** [Leo Robin, Clifford Grey;
                 Vincent Youmans] vIK
      78: Imperial (E) 1845
      TC: Neovox (E) 861
7174-3   **Sometimes I'm Happy** vIK
      78: Banner 6008, Domino 3975, 21274, Oriole 933, Regal 8333,
      National Music Lovers 1208, Pathe Actuelle 36643, 11477, Apex
      (C) 8614, 26050, Leonora (Au) 10249, Perfect 14824, (E) P-306,
      Microphone (C) 22165, Lucky Strike (C) 24091, Maxsa (G) 1623

Oriole as YANKEE TEN ORCHESTRA, Pathe Actuelle as SOUTHAMPTON SOCIETY ORCHESTRA
LP: Fountain (E) FJ-110
7175-1   **Rosy Cheeks** [Richard A. Whiting, Seymour Simons] vIK (cl solo)
78: Banner 1962, Broadway 1070, Domino 3931, (C) 21275, Oriole 883, Paramount 20512, Regal 8289, Apex (C) 8614, Leonora (Au) 10250, Maxsa (F) 1623
Oriole as DIXIE JAZZ BAND
LP: Jazz Studies (E) JS-2, Only For Collectors (Arg) 26, Fountain (E) FJ-110
TC: Neovox (E) 862
7175-3   **Rosy Cheeks** vIK (cl solo)
78: Oriole 883
LP: Jazz Studies (E) JS-3

Okeh, New York, N.Y. Friday, March 25, 1927
SAM LANIN AND HIS FAMOUS PLAYERS
Sam Lanin (ldr) Red Nichols (cnt) Leo McConville (tp) Tom Dorsey (tb) **Jimmy Dorsey**, Arnold Brilhart (cl,as) Merle Johnston (cl,ts) 2 *unknown* (vn) Irving Brodsky (p) *Tony Colucci* (bj,g) Johnny Marvin (uke,vcl) Joe Tarto (bb) Vic Berton (d,chimes) Einar Swan (arr)

W 80674-B   **It's A Happy Old World After All** [Malie, Steiger, Ash] vJM (as solo)
78: OKeh 40810, Parlophone (E) E-5854, Odeon (G) 04017, (Arg) 193009
Parlophone as PARLOPHONE MELODIANS
W 80675-B   **Side By Side** [Harry Woods] arrES vJM (as solo)
78: OKeh 40810, Parlophone (E) R-3346, Odeon (G) 04017, (Arg) 193009

Brunswick, New York, N.Y. Tuesday, March 29, 1927
VINCENT LOPEZ AND HIS CASA LOPEZ ORCH.
Vincent Lopez (ldr) Pete Gentile, Einar Swan (tp) Charlie Butterfield (tb) Larry Abbott, (cl,as) George Napoleon (as) **Jimmy Dorsey** (cl,as) Xavier Cugat, Dan Yates (vn) Arthur Schutt (p) Frank Reino (bj,g) Joe Tarto (bb) William Kessler (d) Keller Sisters and Lynch (vcl)

E-22150/3   **I'll Just Go Along** vKS&L (unissued)
E-22154/5   **A Lane In Spain** vKS&L (unissued)

Pathe, New York, N.Y. Thursday, March 31, 1927
SAM LANIN AND HIS ORCHESTRA
Sam Lanin (ldr) Red Nichols (cnt) Leo McConville (tp) *Sam Lewis* (tb) **Jimmy Dorsey** (cl,as,bar) *unknown* (cl,as) Joe Dubin (ts) Art Schutt (p) *Tony Colucci* (bj,g) *Joe Tarto* (bb) Vic Berton (d,xyl) Frank McGrath (vcl)

107454   **You're The One For Me** [Walter Donaldson; Paul Ash] vFM (bar solo)
78: Pathe Actuelle 36621, Perfect 14802 (Contd.)

SAM LANIN AND HIS ORCHESTRA (Contd.)

107455-A   **My Idea Of Heaven** [Al Sherman, Harry Tobias, Arnold Johnson] vFM (cl,as solos)
   78: Pathe Actuelle 36622, (E) 11452, Perfect 14803, (E) P-309, Domino (C) 21616, Apex (C) 26047
       Perfect P-309 as HAL READFORD'S DANCE ORCHES-TRA, Domino as THE ARCADIANS, Apex as LANIN AND HIS ORCHESTRA
107456-A   **Sunny Disposish** [Ira Gershwin; Phil Charig] vFM
   78: Pathe Actuelle 36621, (E) 11443, Perfect 14802, Apex (C) 26035
       Pathe Actuelle 11443 as LANIN'S ARCADIANS
107457-A,B   **Doll Dance** [Nacio Herb Brown] (as solo)
   78: Pathe Actuelle 36619, (E) 11426, Perfect 14800, (E) P-301, Imperial (E) 1805
       Pathe Actuelle 36619 as RAMBLING RAGADORS, Perfect P-301 as PERFECT DANCE ORCHESTRA, Imperial as IM-PERIAL DANCE ORCHESTRA
   (7192-2,4,5,6) **78:** Banner 1981, Regal 8311, Domino 3949, Broadway 1074, Jewell 5028, Edison Bell Winner (E) 4671, Maxsa (G) 1625, Curry (E) 308, Apex (C) 26037, Bell 506, Oriole 906, Silvertone 21503, Ideal-Scala 7196
       Banner, Domino as IMPERIAL DANCE ORCHESTRA, Broadway as MIAMI BELL BOYS, Regal and Jewell as HOLLYWOOD DANCE ORCHESTRA, Edison Bell Winner as DIPLOMAT NOVELTY ORCHESTRA, Bell as LANIN'S MELODY ORCHESTRA, Oriole as BILLY JAMES DANCE ORCHESTRA, Ideal-Scala as ASTORIA ORCHESTRA. It is possible 7192 takes 4,5,6 are dubs of 107457.

In the late twenties, Brunswick issued a series of about 500 different selections in its 78 rpm Mood Accompaniment Library, which had the same selection on both sides. Most appear to be identical to regular Brunswick instrumental sides of the period. E-22223 from the next session was used for one of these "mood" releases (Hester 1997).

Brunswick, New York, N.Y. Saturday, April 2, 1927
CARL FENTON AND HIS ORCHESTRA
Red Nichols, *unknown* (tp) Miff Mole (tb) **Jimmy Dorsey** (cl,as) *Fud Livingston [or] Pee Wee Russell* (cl,ts) *unknown* (vn) Art Schutt (p) Dick McDonough (bj) Joe Tarto (bb) Vic Berton (d) G. H. Hamilton (xyl)

E-22223   **Doll Dance** [Nacio Herb Brown]
   78: Brunswick 3519, (E) 3519, (G) A-406, Brunswick Mood Accompaniment Library 82L
   (E-4865) **78:** Vocalion 15555
       Vocalion as TUXEDO ORCHESTRA
E-22226   **Delirium** [Arthur Schutt] (as solo)
   78: Brunswick 3519, (E) 3519, (G) A-406
   (E-4868) **78:** Vocalion 15556

Vocalion as TUXEDO ORCHESTRA
LP: Coral 52057, (G) COPS 8869

Brunswick, New York, N.Y. Saturday, April 9, 1927
VINCENT LOPEZ AND HIS CASA LOPEZ ORCH.
Personnel as March 29, 1927.

E-22331   **A Lane In Spain** [Al Lewis, Carmen Lombardo]
                 vKS&L
     78: Brunswick 3517
E-22334   **I'll Just Go Along** [Gus Kahn; Ted Fiorito]
                 vKS&L (as solo)
     78: Brunswick 3517

Billboard (April 9, 1927) reported that J. Dorser [*sic*] of the Vincent Lopez sax section was quitting Lopez in two weeks.
By 1927 Sophia Kalish-Abuza had become better known as Sophie Tucker, "The Last of the Red Hot Mamas." Her loud and robust singing style was a hit in many vaudeville appearances and later in the Ziegfeld Follies, Earl Carroll's Vanities and London revues.

Okeh, New York, N.Y. April 11, 1927
SOPHIE TUCKER (accomp. by MIFF MOLE'S MOLERS)
Red Nichols (cnt) Miff Mole (tb) **Jimmy Dorsey** (cl,as) Ted Shapiro (p) Eddie Lang (g) Joe Tarto (bb) Vic Berton (d) Sophie Tucker (vcl)

80716-B   **After You've Gone** [Henry Creamer, Turner Layton]
                 vST
     78: OKeh 40837, Parlophone (E) R-3353, (Aus) A-2588, (G) A-4568, Odeon (F) 165138, (G) O4099
     LP: World Records (E) SH-503, Parlophone (E) PMC7006, PMC7120, (J) E-5483, Columbia CL2604, Swaggie (Au) S1295
     CD: Flapper (E) 7807
80717-C   **I Ain't Got Nobody** [Roger Graham, Dave Peyton; Spencer Williams] vST
     78: OKeh 40837, Parlophone (E) R-3353, (Aus) A-2588, (G) A-4568, (J) E-5483, Odeon (F) 165138, (G) O4099
     LP: World Records (E) SH-503, Parlophone (E) PMC7120, (J) E-5483, Columbia CL2604, Swaggie (Au) S1295

Okeh, New York, N.Y. Friday, April 15, 1927
SOPHIE TUCKER (accomp. by MIFF MOLE'S MOLERS)
Red Nichols (cnt) Miff Mole (tb) **Jimmy Dorsey** (cl,as) Ted Shapiro (p) Eddie Lang (g) Joe Tarto (bb) Vic Berton (d) Sophie Tucker (vcl)

80737-B   **One Sweet Letter From You** [Lew Brown, Sidney Clare; Harry Warren] vST
     78: OKeh 40813, Parlophone (E) R-3342, (Aus) A-2219, (G) A-4569, Odeon (F) 165137, (G) O4100
     Title on R-3342 is "One Sweet Letter From Home"
     LP: World Records (E) SH-503, Parlophone (E) PMC7120, Columbia CL2604, Swaggie (Au) S1295 (Contd.)

SOPHIE TUCKER (Contd.)

80738-A   Fifty Million Frenchmen Can't Be Wrong [Willie
                 Raskin, Billy Rose; Fred Fisher] vST (cl solo)
    78: OKeh 40813, Parlophone (E) R-3342, (Aus) A-2219, (G) A-
    4569, Odeon (F) 165137, (G) O4100
    LP: World Records (E) SH-503, Parlophone (E) PMC7120,
    Columbia CL2604, Swaggie (Au) S1295
    CD: Flapper (E) 7807

Plaza, New York, N.Y. c. Monday, May 2, 1927
SAM LANIN AND HIS ORCHESTRA
Sam Lanin (ldr) Red Nichols (cnt) Miff Mole (tb) **Jimmy Dorsey**
(cl,as,bar) Lucien Smith, *unknown* (cl,ts) Art Schutt (p) Tony Colucci
(bj,g) Joe Tarto (bb) Vic Berton (d) Irving Kaufman [as Charles Dixon
on Challenge 639] (vcl)

7239-3   **Lazy Weather** [Jo Trent; Peter DeRose] vIK
    78: Banner 1982, Domino 3954, Regal 8315, Broadway 1080
                 *Broadway as THE BADGERS, Regal as SOUTHAMPTON
                 SOCIETY ORCHESTRA*
7240-1   **Just Like A Butterfly That's Caught In The Rain**
                 [Mort Dixon, Harry Woods] vIK
    78: Banner 1983, Domino 3951, Regal 8309, Apex 8629, Starr
    (C) 10261, Edison Bell Winner (E) 4728, Broadway 1080,
    Challenge 631, Jewell 5026
                 *Edison Bell Winner as GAIETY DANCE BAND, Broadway
                 as THE BADGERS, Challenge and Jewell as TENNESSEE
                 HAPPY BOYS*
7244-1   **Hallelujah!** [Leo Robin, Clifford Grey; Vincent You-
                 mans] vIK
    78: Edison Bell Winner (E) 4659, 4749, Oriole 901, Broadway
    1077, Imperial 1818, Beltona 1303
                 *Broadway as MISSOURI JAZZ BAND, Beltona as PALM
                 BEACH PLAYERS, Edison Bell Winners as PAVILION
                 PLAYERS*
7244-2   **Hallelujah!** vIK
    78: Regal 8314
7244-3   **Hallelujah!** vIK
    78: Challenge 639, Domino 3952, Broadway 1077, Banner 1984,
    Regal 8314
                 Challenge as BILLY JAMES DANCE ORCH.
7244-5   **Hallelujah!** vIK
    78: Oriole 901
                 as BILLY JAMES DANCE ORCH.
7244-6   **Hallelujah!** vIK
    78: Banner 1984, Regal 8314
                 Banner as MISSOURI JAZZ BAND.

    There is a possibility that takes 5 and 6 of 7244 were made at a
different session at which Jimmy was not present, but this is not
confirmed.

Plaza, New York, N.Y. Monday, May 2, 1927
THE SIX HOTTENTOTS
Red Nichols (tp) Miff Mole (tb) **Jimmy Dorsey** (cl,as) Arthur Schutt (p)
Joe Tarto (bb) Vic Berton (d)

7241-2   **The Memphis Blues** [William C. Handy] (cl solo)
        78: Banner 1986, Oriole 952, Regal 8310, 8335
        LP: Fountain (E) DFJ 110, Only For Collectors (Arg) OFC26
                Oriole as DIXIE JAZZ BAND
        TC: Neovox (E) 861
7241-3   **The Memphis Blues** (cl solo)
        78: Domino 3956

Columbia, New York, N.Y. Tuesday, May 10, 1927
THE ARKANSAS TRAVELERS
Red Nichols (tp) Miff Mole (tb) **Jimmy Dorsey** (cl) Fred Morrow (as)
Arthur Schutt (p) Vic Berton (d)

144119-3   **Ja Da** [Bob Carleton]
        78: Harmony 421-H, Velvet Tone 1421-V, Diva 2421-G
144120-2   **Sensation (Stomp)** [Original Dixieland Jazz Band]
        78: Harmony 421-H, Velvet Tone 1421-V, Diva 2421-G
144121-2   **Stompin' Fool** [Ford]
        78: Harmony 459-H, Velvet Tone 1459-V, Diva 2459-G
        All three matrices also on **LP:** Columbia C4L-18, CL-1524

Pathe, New York, N.Y. Monday, May 16, 1927
THE SIX HOTTENTOTS
Personnel as May 2, 1927

7264-1   **Melancholy Charlie** [Frank Crum]
        78: Banner 6009, Domino 3975, Oriole 931
                Oriole as TED WHITE'S COLLEGIANS
        LP: Only For Collectors (Arg) OFC26
7264-3   **Melancholy Charlie**
        78: Oriole 931, Regal 8333, Mouldy Fygge 103,
        test pressing also exists
                Oriole as TED WHITE'S COLLEGIANS
        LP: Fountain (E) DFJ-110
7265-1   **Hurricane** [Paul Mertz]
        78: Banner 6009, Domino 3976, (C) 21580, Mouldy Fygge 103
                Domino 21580 as THE RED DANDIES
        LP: Only For Collectors (Arg) OFC26, Fountain (E) DFJ-110
        TC: Neovox (E) 861
7265-2   **Hurricane**
        78: Regal 8335, Oriole 931
                Oriole as TED WHITE'S COLLEGIANS

Columbia, New York, N.Y. Wednesday, May 18, 1927
THE CHARLESTON CHASERS
Red Nichols (tp) Miff Mole (tb) **Jimmy Dorsey** (cl,as) Arthur Schutt
(p,arr) Dick McDonough (bj,g) Joe Tarto (bb) Vic Berton (d) (Contd.)

THE CHARLESTON CHASERS (Contd.)

144168-2   **My Gal Sal** [Paul Dresser] (as solo) arrAS
    78: Columbia 1539-D
    EP: Fontana (E) 17266
    LP: Columbia C4L18, VJM (E) VLP26, Fontana (G) J73810
144169-3   **Delirium** [Arthur Schutt] arrAS
    78: Columbia 1076-D, 4562, (J) 300, Parlophone (E) R-2540,
    Odeon (Norway) D-517
    LP: Columbia C4L18, CL-1523 Vintage Jazz Music (E) VLP26,
    ABC (Au) REB 644
    TC: ABC (Au) 2CF644
    CD: BBC (E) 664, ABC (Au) 36185
    Both tunes also appear on a Columbia 16" test pressing.

Jimmy had earned a reputation on the alto sax by 1927, authoring a
booklet titled *100 Hot Breaks For The E-flat Alto Sax.* A major
accomplishment for a twenty-three-year-old who hadn't finished school,
it became a "must-read" for anyone wanting to play jazz alto.
    Jimmy's increased fame led Paul Whiteman to use him in the next
session and in July to add him to the band full-time. By 1928 the senior
of the Dorsey siblings was taking home $200 a week, $50 more than
singer Bing Crosby was getting. Whiteman's crew included Bix
Beiderbecke, Frankie Trumbauer, Joe Venuti and Eddie Lang and later
would include Jack and Charlie Teagarden.
    Neither of the Dorseys worked with the Whiteman band on the
Broadway show *Lucky*, which opened March 22, 1927, for seventy-one
performances.

Victor, New York, N.Y. Tuesday, May 24, 1927
PAUL WHITEMAN AND HIS ORCHESTRA
Paul Whiteman (dir) Henry Busse, Vic D'Ippolito, Red Nichols (tp)
Wilbur Hall (tb,g) Jack Fulton (tb,vcl) **Jimmy Dorsey,** Chester Hazlett,
Hal McLean (cl,as) Charles Strickfaden (as,bar) Max Farley (cl,
as,ts,arr) Kurt Dieterle, Mischa Russell (vn) Mario Perry (vn,acc)
Chester Gaylord (vn,vcl) Matt Malneck (vn,viola) Harry Perella and/or
Ferdé Grofe [or] Ray Turner (p) Mike Pingitore (bj) John Sperzel (bb)
Vic Berton (d) Austin Young, The Rhythm Boys [Bing Crosby, Al
Rinker, Harry Barris] (vcl)

38778-(1,2,3,4)   **Broken Hearted** vJF,CG&AY (unissued)
38779-1   **Magnolia (Mix The Lot—What Have You Got?)**
    [Buddy De Sylva, Lew Brown, Ray Henderson] vRB
    arrMF (as solo)
    78: Victor 20679, His Master's Voice (E) B-5317, Electrola (G)
    EG-582, Decatur 505 (dub?)
    LP: Jazum 39, Jonzo (E) JZ1, RCA (F) PM42413, Grannyphone
    (H) 03306

Okeh, New York, N.Y. Tuesday, May 24, 1927
SAM LANIN AND HIS FAMOUS PLAYERS
Sam Lanin (ldr) Red Nichols (cnt) Leo McConville (tp) Tom Dorsey (tb)

Jimmy Dorsey (cl,as) *unknown* (ts) Artie Schutt (p) *unknown* (g) Joe Tarto (bb) Vic Berton (d,chimes) Jerry Macy, Ed Smalle (vcl)

W 80934-C **She's Got "It"** [L. Wolfe Gilbert, Benny Davis; Harry Akst] vJM&ES
78: OKeh 40833, Parlophone (E) R-3348, (Au) A-2269, (G) B-12515, (Swe) 12515, Odeon (G) A-189063, (Arg) 193048
LP: Broadway BR 105
W 81099-A **Sa-Lu-Ta** vJM&ES
78: OKeh 40833, Parlophone B-12515, (E) R-3348, (Au) A-2268, (Swe) 12515, Lindstrom (G) A-4522, Odeon (Arg) 193048

Brunswick, New York, N.Y. Monday, June 20, 1927
RED NICHOLS AND HIS FIVE PENNIES
Red Nichols (cnt,ldr,arr) Miff Mole (tb) **Jimmy Dorsey** (cl,as) Adrian Rollini (bsx) Arthur Schutt (p) Eddie Lang (g) Vic Berton (d,tymp)

E-23665 **Cornfed** [Bob Effros, Phil Wall] arrRN (as solo)
78: Brunswick 3597, 6818, (E) 3597
(E-6302) **78:** Vocalion 15602
LP: Classic Jazz Masters 24, Swaggie (Au) 836, Swingfan (G) 1004
E-23666 **Cornfed** arrRN (as solo)
78: Brunswick 3597, (C,E,Au) 3597, (E) O1805, (G) A-7543
(E-6303) **78:** Vocalion 15602
LP: Classic Jazz Masters 24, Swaggie (Au) 836, Living Era (E) AJA 5025
TC: Living Era K-15888
CD: Living Era (E) AJA 5025
E-23668-A **Five Pennies** [Loring "Red" Nichols] arrRN (as solo)
78: Brunswick 3855, 6821, (E) 3819, O1851, (C) 4844, (Au) 3855, Columbia (Au) DO-1354
LP: Coral (G) 97024, Classic Jazz Masters 24, Swaggie (Au) 837
Some copies of Brunswick (C) 4844 use E-26751 (not a Red Nichols item) in error.

Brunswick, New York, N.Y. Saturday, June 25, 1927
RED NICHOLS AND HIS FIVE PENNIES

E-23752 **Mean Dog Blues** (unissued)
E-23753 **Mean Dog Blues** [Lou Jackson] (as solo)
78: Brunswick 3597, (E) O1805, (G) A-7543
(E-6300) **78:** Vocalion 15602
LP: Coral (G) 97024, Classic Jazz Masters 25, Swaggie (Au) 837, Living Era (E) AJA 5025
E-23754 **Mean Dog Blues** (unissued)
E-23755 **Mean Dog Blues** (as solo)
78: Brunswick 6818
LP: Classic Jazz Masters 25, Living Era AJA 5025
TC: Living Era AJA K-15888
CD: Living Era AJA 5025

Victor, New York, N.Y. Thursday, August 11, 1927
PAUL WHITEMAN AND HIS ORCHESTRA
Paul Whiteman (dir) Henry Busse, Vic D'Ippolito, *Charlie Margulis [or]*
Bob Mayhew (tp) Jack Fulton (tb) Wilbur Hall (tb,g) Tom Dorsey,
Boyce Cullen (tb) **Jimmy Dorsey,** Chester Hazlett (cl,as) Hal McLean
(as) Charles Strickfaden (as,bar) Max Farley (cl,ts) Kurt Dieterle,
Mischa Russell, Moses Freedman (vn) Mario Perry (vn,acc) Matt
Malneck (vn,viola) *Ferdé Grofe [or] Ray Turner* (p) Mike Pingitore (bj)
Al Armer (sb) Harold McDonald (d) Don Redman (arr)

A39559-1(2)   **Whiteman Stomp** [Thomas "Fats" Waller, Don Red-
                   man, Jo Trent] arrDR (as solos)
    LP: RCA LPV570, (F) PM42413
A39559-3   **Whiteman Stomp** arrDR (as solos)
    78: Victor 21119, His Master's Voice (E) B-5577, Electrola (G)
    EG-807
    LP: RCA RD8090, Grannyphone (H) 03306
    CD: ASV Living Era AJA 5170
A39560 (1,2,3)   **Sugar Your Tea Stomp** (unissued)
A39561-1   **Sensation Stomp** [Original Dixieland Jazz Band]
                   arrDR (cl,as solos)
    78: Victor 21119, His Master's Voice (E) B-5577, Electrola (G)
    EG-807
    LP: RCA (F) PM42413
A39561-3   **Sensation Stomp** arrDR (cl,as solos)
    LP: Grannyphone (H) 03306

Victor, Camden, N.J. Monday, August 15, 1927
PAUL WHITEMAN AND HIS ORCHESTRA
Paul Whiteman (dir) Henry Busse, *Bob Mayhew* (tp) Tom Dorsey (tb)
Jimmy Dorsey, Chester Hazlett (cl,as) Charles Strickfaden (as,bar) Nye
Mayhew (cl,ts) Matty Malneck (vn) Harry Perella (p) Mike Pingitore
(bj) Wilbur Hall (g) John Sperzel (bb) Harold McDonald (d) Austin
Young (vcl)

A39564-3   **Cheerie-Beerie-Bee** vAY
    78: Victor 20881, His Master's Voice (E) B-5376, EA-396,
    Electrola (G) EG-659

Victor, Camden, N.J. Tuesday, August 16, 1927
PAUL WHITEMAN AND HIS ORCHESTRA
Paul Whiteman (dir) Henry Busse, Vic D'Ippolito (tp) Tom Dorsey (tb)
Jimmy Dorsey, Chester Hazlett (cl,as) Charles Strickfaden (as,bar) Max
Farley (cl,ts) Matty Malneck (vn) Harry Perella (p) Mike Pingitore (bj)
Wilbur Hall (g) Al Armer (sb) Harold McDonald (d) The Rhythm Boys
[Crosby, Rinker, Barris], Austin Young (vcl)

A39569-2   **Five Step** [Buddy De Sylva, Lew Brown, Ray Hender-
                   son] vRB (as solo)
    LP: Jonzo (E) JZ2
A39569-3   **Five Step** vRB (as solo)
    78: Victor 20883, His Master's Voice (E) B-5511, Electrola (G)

EG-700
LP: Jazum 40, Jonzo (E) JZ2
unknown (tb), 3 *unknown* (vn) added:
A39570-3   **Broadway** [Buddy De Sylva, Lew Brown; Ray Hend-
                  erson] vAY
    78: Victor 20874

Victor, Camden, N.J. Wednesday, August 17, 1927
PAUL WHITEMAN AND HIS ORCHESTRA
Jack Fulton, Chester Gaylord, Austin Young (vcl)

39572-(1,2,3,4)   **Oooh! Maybe It's You** vJF,CG&AY (unissued)
39573-(1,2,3)   **Shaking The Blues Away** (unissued)

Victor, Camden, N.J. Friday, August 19, 1927
PAUL WHITEMAN AND HIS ORCHESTRA
Paul Whiteman (dir) Henry Busse (tp) Tom Dorsey, Wilbur Hall (tb,g)
Jimmy Dorsey, Chester Hazlett (cl,as) Charles Strickfaden (as,bar) Nye
Mayhew (cl,ts) Matty Malneck (vn) Harry Perella (p,celst) Mike
Pingitore (bj) Al Armer (sb) Harold McDonald (d) Bing Crosby, Jack
Fulton, Chester Gaylord, Austin Young (vcl)

A39575-2   **The Calinda** [Herman Hupfield] vBC,JF,CG&AY
    78: Victor 20882, His Master's Voice (E) B-5384, EA-476,
    Electrola (G) EG-659
    LP: Jazum 40, Jonzo (E) JZ2
A39576-4   **Just A Memory** [Buddy De Sylva, Lew Brown; Ray
                  Henderson]
    78: Victor 20881, His Master's Voice (E) B-5376, EA-231, R-
    4875, Electrola (G) EG-659

Victor, Camden, N.J. Saturday, August 20, 1927
PAUL WHITEMAN AND HIS ORCHESTRA
Paul Whiteman (dir) Henry Busse, Bob Mayhew (tp) Tom Dorsey
(cnt,tb) Boyce Cullen (tb) **Jimmy Dorsey,** Chester Hazlett (cl,as)
Charles Strickfaden (as,bar) Nye Mayhew (cl,ts) Matty Malneck (vn)
Harry Perella (p) Mike Pingitore (bj) Wilbur Hall (g) Al Armer (sb)
Harold McDonald (d) The Rhythm Boys [Crosby, Rinker, Barris] (vcl)

A39577-8   **It Won't Be Long Now** [Buddy De Sylva, Lew
                  Brown; Ray Henderson] vRB (cl solo)
    78: Victor 20883, His Master's Voice (E) B-5555, Electrola (G)
    EG-700
    LP: Jazum 40, Jonzo (E) JZ2, Grannyphone (H) 03306, Broadway
    BR112

Victor, Camden, N.J. Monday, August 22, 1927
PAUL WHITEMAN AND HIS ORCHESTRA
Personnel as Aug. 16. Jack Fulton, Chester Gaylord, Austin Young (vcl)

39572-7   **Oooh! Maybe It's You** vJF,CG&AY
    LP: Jonzo JZ2   (Contd.)

PAUL WHITEMAN AND HIS ORCHESTRA (Contd.)

39572-8   Oooh! Maybe It's You vJF, CG, AY
    78: Victor 20885, His Master's Voice (E) B-5415, X-2607
    (export), (Au) EA-313, Electrola (G) EG-662
39573-5   Shaking The Blues Away [Irving Berlin]
    78: Victor 20885, His Master's Voice (E) B-5415, X-2607
    (export), (F) K-5647, Electrola (G) EG-662
    LP: Halcyon (E) HAL21

OKeh, New York, N.Y. Thursday, August 25, 1927
IRWIN ABRAMS AND HIS HOTEL MANGER ORCHESTRA
Irwin Abrams (ldr) Julian Hess (tp) Tom Dorsey (tb) Jimmy Dorsey
(cl,as) Frankie Trumbauer (c-mel) *Joe Venuti* (vn) *Lennie Hayton [or]
Arthur Schutt* (p) Carl Kress (bj) *unknown* (bb), (d) Seger Ellis (vcl)

W 81271-C   Shaking The Blues Away [Irving Berlin] vSE
    78: OKeh 40880, Parlophone (E) R-3460, Odeon 189108
W 81272-B   It All Belongs To Me [Irving Berlin] vSE
    78: OKeh 40880, Parlophone (E) R-3460, Odeon 189108
    Parlophones as TAMPA BLUE ORCHESTRA

Jimmy is erroneously listed in some discographies as participating in
an October 7, 1927, California Ramblers session. (It is Pete Pumiglio.)
    Jimmy and Tommy were on the road with Paul Whiteman, and while
at the Indiana Theater in Indianapolis, the Dorseys went to the Gennett
recording studio in Richmond, Indiana, for a Hoagy Carmichael date.

Gennett, Richmond, Ind. Friday, October 28, 1927
HOAGY CARMICHAEL AND HIS PALS
Hoagy Carmichael (p,cnt,ldr) Andy Secrest, Bob Mayhew (cnt) Tom
Dorsey (tb) Jimmy Dorsey (cl,as) Nye Mayhew (ts) Mischa Russell (vn)
unknown (g), (bb), (d)

13183-A   One Night In Havana [Hoagy Carmichael] (as,cl solos)
    78: Gennett 6311, Champion 15420
    Champion as MALCOMB WEBB AND HIS GANG
    LP: Sentry 4011, Fountain (E) FJ109, Arcadia (C) LP1003
    CD: Giants of Jazz 53017
13184-A   One Last Kiss [Hoagy Carmichael] (waltz)
    LP: Broadway BR112

Back in Indianapolis, Whiteman overheard Hoagy "noodling" "Washboard Blues" in the room Jimmy Dorsey and arranger Bill Challis
shared. Though Red Nichols and others had recorded it nearly a year
before, the "King of Jazz," having made a "new discovery," recorded it
on their return to Chicago (Sanford 1972).
    Challis and Jimmy had been roommates for the tour until Saturday,
November 5, 1927, when Jimmy wed Jane Porter, Miss Detroit of 1927,
who remained with Jimmy for twenty-two years. Jimmy had met her in
1926 while working with Goldkette. Jimmy called his new bride "Beebe," also using the name for one of his famous solos.

Victor, Chicago, Ill. Friday, November 18, 1927
PAUL WHITEMAN AND HIS ORCHESTRA
Paul Whiteman (dir) Bix Beiderbecke (cnt) Tom Dorsey, Boyce Cullen (tb) **Jimmy Dorsey** (cl,as) Chester Hazlett (cl) Charles Strickfaden (as,bar) Kurt Dieterle, Mischa Russell (vn) Matt Malneck (viola) Hoagy Carmichael (p,vcl) Wilbur Hall (g) Steve Brown (sb) Harold McDonald (d,vib) Bill Challis (arr)

40901-1   **Washboard Blues** [Hoagy Carmichael, Irving Mills, Fred B. Callahan] arrBC vHC (cl solos)
     78: Victor 36877, 36186
     LP: RCA (F) 741093, LSA3180, (G) NL89096, Joker (It) SM3563, Divergent 301, BIX 6B, Indiana Historical Society 038, Timeless (H) 013
     TC: Radio Yesteryear Stack #82
     CD: Masters Of Jazz (F) MJ-16, Timeless (H) CBC 1-011, King Jazz 154, IRD (It) BIX 4, Smithsonian 381, RCA (F) 66540, Giants of Jazz 53017
40901-4   **Washboard Blues** arrBC vHC (cl solos)
     78: unissued test pressing
     LP. RCA (F) 741093, Joker (It) SM3563
     CD: IRD (It) BIX 4

Victor, Chicago, Ill. Tuesday, November 22, 1927
PAUL WHITEMAN AND HIS ORCHESTRA
Paul Whiteman (dir) Henry Busse, *Charlie Margulis* (tp) Tom Dorsey (tb) *Jimmy Dorsey, Chester Hazlett* (cl,as) Charles Strickfaden (as) *Nye Mayhew* (cl,ts) Kurt Dieterle, Mischa Russell, *Matt Malneck, Mario Perry* (vn) Harry Perella (p) Mike Pingitore (bj) Mike Trafficante (bb) Steve Brown (sb) Harold McDonald (d)

40934-4   **Among My Souvenirs** [Edgar Leslie; Horatio Nichols] vJF,CG&AY
     78: (12-inch) Victor 35877, His Master's Voice (E) C-1472
     LP: Sunbeam MFC-18

Victor, Chicago, Ill. Wednesday, November 23, 1927
PAUL WHITEMAN AND HIS ORCHESTRA
Paul Whiteman (dir) Henry Busse, Charlie Margulis (tp) Bix Beiderbecke (cnt) Wilbur Hall, Tom Dorsey (tb) Chester Hazlett, Hal McLean (as) **Jimmy Dorsey,** Nye Mayhew, Charles Strickfaden (as,bar) Kurt Dieterle, Mischa Russell, Matt Malneck, Mario Perry (vn) Harry Perella (p) Mike Pingitore (bj) Mike Trafficante (bb) Steve Brown (sb) Harold McDonald (d) Bing Crosby, Al Rinker, Harry Barris, Jack Fulton, Chester Gaylord, Austin Young (vcl) Bill Challis (arr)

40937-2   **Changes** [Walter Donaldson] vBC,AR,HB,JF,CG&AY (as solo)
     78: Victor 25370
     LP: RCA (It) 50004, (E) RD-27225, BIX 6B, Joker (It) SM-3563, Jonzo (E) JZ2, *Victor LPM-2323, *RCA RD-27225, BBC (E) REB-704

PAUL WHITEMAN AND HIS ORCHESTRA (Contd.)

CD: ProArte Digital CDD-490, Masters Of Jazz (F) MJ-16, IRD
(It) BIX 4, Living Era (E) AJA-5005
   *Victor extracted only the Bix Beiderbecke solo in
   preparing the LP releases of take 2.*
40937-3   Changes vBC,AR,HB,JF,CG&AY (as solo)
78: Victor 21103, His Master's Voice (E) B-5461, (E) B-8913, (It)
GW-1785, (Swi) JK-2809, (F) K-5368, (Ind) N-4475, Electrola
(G) EG-690, Biltmore 1032 (dub)
LP: Joker (It) SM-3563
CD: Masters Of Jazz (F) MJ-16, IRD (It) BIX 4, RCA (F) 66540,
ASV Living Era (E) AJA-5170

Victor, Chicago, Ill. Friday, November 25, 1927
PAUL WHITEMAN AND HIS ORCHESTRA

40945-2   Mary (What Are You Waiting For?) [Walter Don-
                 aldson] vBC (as solo)
78: Victor 21103, His Master's Voice (E) B-5461, (E) B-8913,
(Au) EA-291, (F) K-5368, Electrola (G) EG-771, Biltmore 1032
(dub)
LP: Divergent 301, RCA (F) 741093, Ariston 12015, BIX 7A,
Jonzo (E) JZ2, Joker (It) SM-3563
CD: Affinity (E)AFS 1021-2, Masters Of Jazz (F) MJ-16, IRD (It)
BIX 4
40945-4   Mary (What Are You Waiting For?) vBC (as solo)
78: Victor 26415
LP: Victor LPV-584, LSA-3094, RCA (F) 731036, "X" LVA-
3040, HMV (E) EA-2764, Jonzo (E) JZ2, BIX 7A, Joker (It) SM-
3563
CD: Masters Of Jazz (F) MJ-16, IRD (It) BIX 4

   The Whiteman company continued its road tour for most of the
remainder of 1927 and it was early 1928 before Jimmy returned to the
recording studios.

The Studio Scene
(1928)

Jimmy and Tommy were out on the road at the end of 1927. The band returned to New York for the holidays and brother Tom parted company with Paul Whiteman. Jimmy stayed on a month longer.

This marks a good point to pause and look at some of the contrasts already developing between the brothers, especially the difference in their playing styles after five years as professionals.

Tommy's early years were spent mostly with such "square" names as Goldkette, Lanin and Whiteman, while Jimmy also worked often with Nichols, Mole, Trumbauer and the like. Though he paid the bills with the studio dates, Jimmy was "looser" than Tommy, who even then dreamed of his own band while Jimmy was happy to be a section player.

However, it is doubtful that the Dorsey Brothers dates that follow would have been just "Tommy Dorsey Orchestra" sessions, due to a strong sibling tie that saw each brother quietly looking out for the other. This held true no matter what their surface troubles, including the traumatic breakup in 1935. Even while not talking to one another, each quietly worked behind the scenes to protect the other all through their lives.

There were other factors that would come into play. Network radio was becoming a major industry; on Broadway, musicals were thriving; and the magic of sound had been added to motion pictures, many of which were musical and being made on Long Island.

Cameo, New York, N.Y. Monday, January 2, 1928
ALABAMA RED PEPPERS
Bob Haring (ldr) Mike Mosiello, *unknown* (tp) Charlie Butterfield (tb) **Jimmy Dorsey** (cl,as) Andy Sanella (cl,as,stg) *unknown* (p), (bj), (bb), (d) Arthur Fields (vcl)

2788-A,C   **San** [Lindsay McPhail, Walter Michaels] vAF (cl solo)
        78: Cameo 8109, Lincoln 2763, Romeo 532, Dominion (E) A-29
        Dominion as JAY WILBUR AND HIS ORCHESTRA

Victor, New York, N.Y. Wednesday, January 4, 1928
PAUL WHITEMAN AND HIS ORCHESTRA
Paul Whiteman (dir) Henry Busse, Charlie Margulis (tp) Bix Beiderbecke (cnt) Bill Rank (tb) **Jimmy Dorsey,** Chester Hazlett (cl,as) Nye Mayhew (cl,ts) Rube Crozier (cl,ssx,as,ts,bsn) Hal McLean (cl,ssx,as,o) Charles Strickfaden (as,bar) Kurt Dieterle (vn) Harry Perella (p) Wilbur Hall (g) Mike Trafficante (bb) Steve Brown (sb) Harold McDonald (d) Bill Challis (arr) Jack Fulton, Al Rinker, Austin Young (vcl) (Contd.)

PAUL WHITEMAN AND HIS ORCHESTRA (Contd.)

41294-1   **Smile** [Donald Heywood] vAR,JF arrBC (as solo)
          LP: Broadway BR102
Add Frank Trumbauer (c-mel), Mischa Russell (vn), Matty Malneck (viola):
41295-1   **Lonely Melody** [Benny Meroff, Sam Coslow; Hal Dyson] arrBC (cl solo)
          78: Victor 21214, His Master's Voice (E) B-5516, (Aus) EA-371, Biltmore 1017 (dubbing)
          LP: Victor 2323, RCA (E) RD27225, (F) 741093, PM42413, (It) 50004, Joker (It) SM3563
          CD: Masters Of Jazz (F) MJ-16, IRD (It) BIX 4
41295-3   **Lonely Melody** arrBC (cl solo)
          78: Victor 25366
          LP: Victor 2323, RCA LPV570, "X" LVA3040, (E) RD27225, (F) 731036, Joker (It) SM3563
          CD: Masters Of Jazz (F) MJ-16, IRD (It) BIX 4
          Jimmy is not on this session's matrix 41293-2 ("Ramona").

Victor, New York, N.Y. Thursday, January 5, 1928
PAUL WHITEMAN AND HIS ORCHESTRA
Paul Whiteman (dir) *Bix Beiderbecke* (cnt) Henry Busse, *Bob Mayhew [or] Charlie Margulis* (tp) Boyce Cullen, Bill Rank, Jack Fulton, *unknown* (tb) **Jimmy Dorsey,** Chester Hazlett (cl,as) Nye Mayhew (cl,ts) Charles Strickfaden (as,bar) Frank Trumbauer (c-mel) Kurt Dieterle, Mischa Russell, Mario Perry, John Bowman (vn) Matt Malneck (vn,viola) Harry Perella (p) Mike Pingitore (bj) Wilbur Hall (g) Mike Trafficante (bb) Steve Brown (sb) Harold McDonald (d) Domenico Savino (arr)

41296-2   **O Ya Ya** arrDS
          78: Victor 21304, His Master's Voice (E) B-5488, (Au) EA-340
          Jimmy is not on matrix 41297-4 ("Dolly Dimples") also made this session.

OKeh, New York, N.Y. Monday, January 9, 1928
FRANKIE TRUMBAUER AND HIS ORCHESTRA
Frank Trumbauer (c-mel,ldr) Bix Beiderbecke (cnt) Bill Rank (tb) **Jimmy Dorsey** (cl,as) *Charlie Strickfaden* (as) Min Leibrook (bsx) Matty Malneck (vn) Tom Satterfield (p,celst) Harold McDonald (d)

400003-B   **There'll Come A Time** [Mannone, Mole] (cl,as solos)
          78: OKeh 40979, Parlophone (E) R-3526, R-2097, (Aus) A-6311, A-7692, DP-255, Odeon (F) 165330, (Arg) 193128, (It) A-2399, A-189143
          LP: Parlophone (E) PMC7100, Joker (It) SM3563, Columbia CL845, CBS 62374, World Records (E) SH415
          TC: Columbia CT 45450
          CD: Columbia CK 45450, Masters Of Jazz (F) MJ-16, JSP (E) CD317, IRD (It) BIX 4

Charlie Margulis (tp) added:
400004-C   **Jubilee** [Hoagy Carmichael] (as solo)
     78: OKeh 41044, Parlophone (E) R-161, R-2054, Odeon (F)
     165539, A-189203, (G) A-286091
     LP: Parlophone (E) PMC7100, Joker (It) SM3563, World Records
     (E) SH415
     TC: Columbia CT 45450
     CD: Columbia CK 45450, Masters Of Jazz (F) MJ-16, JSP (E)
     CD317, IRD (It) BIX 4

Victor, New York, N.Y. Wednesday, January 11, 1928
PAUL WHITEMAN AND HIS ORCHESTRA
Paul Whiteman (dir) Henry Busse, Charlie Margulis (tp) Bix Bei-
derbecke (cnt) Bill Rank, Wilbur Hall, Jack Fulton, Boyce Cullen (tb)
Chester Hazlett (cl,bcl,as) Hal McLean (cl,as) Charles Strickfaden
(cl,ts) **Jimmy Dorsey** (cl) Frankie Trumbauer (c-mel) Kurt Dieterle,
Mischa Russell, Matt Malneck, Mario Perry, John Bowman (vn) Harry
Perella (p,celst) Mike Pingitore (bj) Mike Trafficante (bb) Steve Brown
(sb) Harold McDonald, *unknown* (d) Bill Challis (arr) Bing Crosby (vcl)

27268-11   **Parade Of The Wooden Soldiers** [Leon Jessel]
     78: Victor 21304, His Master's Voice (E) B-5488, (F) K-5620
41607-2   **Ol' Man River** [Oscar Hammerstein II; Jerome Kern]
                  vBC arrBC (as solo)
     78: Victor 21218, 25249, His Master's Voice (E) B-5471, B-
     8929, BD-5066, (Ireland) IM-129, (Swi) JK-2882, (F) K-5448,
     (It) R-4697, Electrola (G) EG-838, Temple 4008, Sentry 4008
     LP: Divergent 301, RCA LPV584, Phontastic (Swe) NOST7604,
     Jonzo (E) JZ2, Joker (It) SM3563
     TC: Columbia CT 45450, ProArte Digital PCD490
     CD: Columbia CK 45450, Masters Of Jazz (F) MJ-16, ProArte
     Digital CDD490, IRD (It) BIX 4, Drive 41065

Victor, New York, N.Y. Thursday, January 12, 1928
PAUL WHITEMAN AND HIS ORCHESTRA
Bix Beiderbecke, *Tom Dorsey* (cnt) Charlie Margulis (tp) **Jimmy Dorsey**
(cnt,cl,as) Bill Rank (tb) Frankie Trumbauer (c-mel) Min Leibrook (bsx)
Matty Malneck (vn,viola) Bill Challis (p,arr) Carl Kress (g) Harold
McDonald (d,chimes)

30172-6   **San** [Lindsay McPhail, Walter Michaels] arrBC
                  (as, cl solos)
     78: Victor 24078, His Master's Voice (E) B-5581, Biltmore
     1031
     LP: Only For Collectors 34, RCA "X" LVA3040, Joker (It)
     SM3563, RCA (F) 75490, 741093, BBC (E) REB590, Living Era
     (E) AJA5080
     TC: BBC (E) TC590, ProArte Digital PCD490
     CD: ProArte Digital CDD490, BBC (E) CD590, Living Era (E)
     CD-AJA5080, Masters Of Jazz (F) MJ-16, IRD (It) BIX 4, RCA
     68777

(Contd.)

PAUL WHITEMAN AND HIS ORCHESTRA (Contd.)

30172-7   **San** arrBC (as, cl solos)
    78: Victor 25367
    LP: Victor 2323, RCA (E) RD27225, (F) 731036, (J) RA5298,
    (It) 50004, Camden CAL446, Herwin 116, Joker (It) SM3563
    CD: Masters Of Jazz (F) MJ-16, IRD (It) BIX 4

In *Billboard* (September 10, 1938, 12) Paul Whiteman claims that his January 12, 1928 recording of "San" had a three-way "trumpet" chorus played by Bix, Jimmy and Tommy Dorsey. Tommy left the payroll weeks earlier so it is more probably Margulis.
Also recorded were 30173-8 and 30174-6, remakes of the 1924 "Rhapsody In Blue" parts 1 and 2, only released on German Electrola EH-86. It is doubtful that Jimmy participated, although some claim that he played the familiar clarinet opening solo.

Victor, New York, N.Y. Saturday, January 21, 1928
PAUL WHITEMAN AND HIS ORCHESTRA
Paul Whiteman (dir) Bix Beiderbecke (cnt) Henry Busse, Charlie Margulis, Bob Mayhew (tp) Bill Rank, Wilbur Hall, Jack Fulton (tb,vcl) Boyce Cullen (tb) Chester Hazlett (cl,bcl,as) Hal McLean (cl,as) Charles Strickfaden (cl,ts) **Jimmy Dorsey** (cl,as) Frank Trumbauer (c-mel) Kurt Dieterle, Mischa Russell, Matty Malneck, Mario Perry, John Bowman (vn) Harry Perella (p) Mike Pingitore (bj) Mike Trafficante (bb) Steve Brown (sb) Harold McDonald (d)

41635-3   **Together** [Buddy De Sylva, Lew Brown; Ray Hender-
                son] vJF (12-inch)
    78: (12-inch) Victor 35883, His Master's Voice (E) C-1472
    LP: Sunbeam MFC18

Victor, New York, N.Y. Tuesday, January 24, 1928
PAUL WHITEMAN AND HIS ORCHESTRA
Personnel as January 4, 1928, except no strings are used on "Smile."
Jack Fulton, Chester Gaylord, Austin Young, Al Rinker (vcl)

41294-4   **Smile** [Donald Heywood] vJF,CG,AY&AR arrBC
                (as solo)
    LP: Victor (F) 741093, Broadway BR102, Joker (It) SM3563
    CD: Masters Of Jazz (F) MJ-16, IRD (It) BIX 4
41294-5   **Smile** vJF,CG,AY,AR arrBC (as solo)
    78: Victor 21228, His Master's Voice (E) B-5465, Biltmore
    1017 (dub)
    LP: Divergent 301, Ariston 12025, Living Era (E) AJA5002,
    Joker (It) SM3564
    CD: Masters Of Jazz (F) MJ-16, IRD (It) BIX 4
41465-3   **My Heart Stood Still** [Lorenz Hart; Richard Rodgers]
                vJF,CG,AY&AR arrBC
    78: Victor 35883 (12-inch)
            as PAUL WHITEMAN AND HIS CONCERT ORCH.
    LP: Sunbeam MFC18

Victor, New York, N.Y. Saturday, January 28, 1928
PAUL WHITEMAN AND HIS ORCHESTRA
Personnel as January 21, 1928, except Bill Challis (dir,arr) for
Whiteman, Tom Satterfield (p,arr) added and Mayhew (tp), Fulton (tb)
and Hazlett (cl,as) omitted.

41471-3   **Back In Your Own Back Yard** [Dave Dreyer, Al
                 Jolson, Billy Rose] arr BC (cl solos)
      78: Victor 21240, His Master's Voice (E) B-5564, K-5606,
      Electrola (G) EG-1161
      LP: Divergent 302, Joker (It) SM3564
41471-4   **Back In Your Own Back Yard** (cl solos)
      78: Victor 27689
      LP: RCA LPM523, "X" LVA3040, (E) RD7865, (F) 731036

Rain or Shine opened February 9, 1928 at the George M. Cohan
Theater with Joe Cook and Tom Howard. Don Voorhees' pit band
included Jimmy Dorsey, Fuzzy Farrar, Mannie Klein, Arnold Brilhart,
Charlie Butterfield, Dudley Fosdick, Max Farley, Joe Venuti, Frank
Signorelli and Chauncey Morehouse.

OKeh, New York, N.Y. Friday, February 10, 1928
SAM LANIN AND HIS FAMOUS PLAYERS
Sam Lanin (ldr) Mannie Klein (tp) Tom Dorsey (cnt,tb) Sammy Lewis
(tb) **Jimmy Dorsey** (cl,as) Andy Sanella (as,stg) Dick Johnson,
unknown (cl,ts) *Joe Venuti [or] Murray Kellner* (vn) *Rube Bloom [or]
Arthur Schutt* (p) John Cali, *unknown* (bj,g) *Joe Tarto [or] Hank Stern*
(bb) *Harry Ring [or] Vic Berton* (d) Scrappy Lambert (vcl)

W 400079-B   **Together** (waltz) [Buddy De Sylva, Lew Brown; Ray
                 Henderson] vSL
      78: OKeh 40990, 16289, Parlophone (E) R104, E-6063, (Au) A-
      2454, Odeon 193169, (G) A-221066, Ariel (E) 4301
            Ariel as ARIEL DANCE ORCHESTRA
W 400080-B   **Ramona** (waltz) [L. Wolfe Gilbert; Mabel Wayne]
                 vSL (as solo)
      78: OKeh 40990, 16289, Parlophone (E) R-158, E-6063, (Au)
      A-2454, (G) A-4545, B-12642, Odeon (G) 04072, A-189114, A-
      189150, Columbia (J) M-84
            Parlophone E-6063 as THE MERTON ORCHESTRA
W 400081-C   **There Must Be A Silver Lining (That's Shining For
                 Me)** vSL
      78: OKeh 40991, Parlophone (E) R-104, (Au) A-4539, Odeon
      (G) A221095
            OKeh as JUSTIN RING'S OKeh ORCHESTRA

Some discographies claim Jimmy played cornet on Whiteman's February 13 recording, "From Monday On". Jimmy never confirmed this.

OKeh, New York, N.Y. Tuesday, February 14, 1928
DORSEY BROTHERS AND THEIR ORCHESTRA
Tom Dorsey (cnt,tb,ldr) Leo McConville, Fuzzy Farrar (tp) (Contd.)

DORSEY BROTHERS AND THEIR ORCHESTRA (Contd.)
Jimmy Dorsey (cl,as) Arnold Brilhart (as,o) Herb Spencer (ts) Carl Kress (g) Hank Stern (bb) Chauncey Morehouse (d,chimes) Irving Kaufman [as Noel Taylor] (vcl)

W 400082-B   **Mary Ann** [Benny Davis; Abner Silver] vIK (cl,as solos)
    78: OKeh 40995, 16311, Parlophone (E) R-181, (Au) A-2469, (G) A-4534, Odeon (Arg) 193246, (F) A-221092, (F) 04055
    LP: The Old Masters 14, Broadway BR112, World Records (E) SHB67, (Au) R-09520
    TC: World Records (E) CSHB67
W 400083-C   **Persian Rug** [Gus Kahn; Neil Moret] (as solos)
    78: OKeh 40995, 16311, Parlophone (E) R-202, (Au) A-2469, Odeon (Arg) 193246
    LP: The Old Masters 14, World Records (E) SHB67, (Au) R-09520
    TC: World Records (E) CSHB67
    Both sides also on **CD:** Jazz Oracle (C) BDW 8004

OKeh, New York, N.Y. Wednesday, February 15, 1928
SAM LANIN AND HIS FAMOUS PLAYERS
Sam Lanin (ldr) Mannie Klein (tp) Sammy Lewis (tb) **Jimmy Dorsey** (cl,as) Andy Sanella (as) Dick Johnson, *unknown* (cl,ts) *Joe Venuti [or] Murray Kellner* (vn) *Rube Bloom [or] Arthur Schutt* (p) John Cali, *unknown* (bj,g) *Joe Tarto [or] Hank Stern* (bb) *Harry Ring [or] Vic Berton* (d) Irving Kaufman [as Noel Taylor], *unknown [Venuti]* (scat vcl)

400084-A   **My Miami Moon** vIK
    78: OKeh 40996, Parlophone (E) E-6024, (G) A-2606, Odeon (G) 04064
400085-B   **I'm Always Smiling** vIK
    78: OKeh 40996, Parlophone (E) E-6024, (G) A-2606, Odeon (G) 04064
    Both sides: Parlophone A-2606 as BILLY HAYS AND HIS ORCHESTRA, Odeon 04064 as OKeh MELODIANS
400086-B   **I Just Roll Along (Havin' My Ups And Downs** [Jo Trent; Peter De Rose] vIK,*scat*
    78: OKeh 41002, Parlophone (E) R-158, (G) A-2476, Odeon (G) 189135, A221095

Columbia, New York, N.Y. Wednesday, February 29, 1928
BEN SELVIN AND HIS ORCHESTRA
Ben Selvin (vn,ldr) 2 *unknown* (tp) Tom Dorsey, *unknown* (tb) **Jimmy Dorsey** (cl,as) *unknown* (ts,bsx), (p), (bj,g) Joe Tarto (bb) Stan King (d) Irving Kaufman [as Frank Harris], band (vcl)

W 145694-3   **When** [Bob Schafer, Andy Razaf; J. C. Johnson] vIK,band (cl solo)
    78: Columbia 1321-D, (E) 4911
W 145695-2   **Tell Me You're Sorry** vIK (cl,as solos)
    78: Columbia 1321-D, (E) 4911

OKeh, New York, N.Y. Wednesday, March 14, 1928
DORSEY BROTHERS AND THEIR ORCHESTRA
Tom Dorsey (cnt,tb,ldr) Mickey Bloom, Fuzzy Farrar (tp) **Jimmy Dorsey** (cl,as) Arnold Brilhart (as) Herb Spencer (ts) *Arthur Schutt* (p) Carl Kress (bj) Hank Stern (bb) Chauncey Morehouse (d) Scrappy Lambert [as Bill Dutton] (vcl)

W 400144-B   **Coquette** [Gus Kahn; Johnny Green, Carmen Lombardo] vSL (as solo)
        78: OKeh 41007, Parlophone (E) R-142, (Au) A-2475, (G) A-4543, Odeon (Arg) 193160, (G) A-189133, (F) 04072
        LP: The Old Masters 14,World Records (E)SHB67, (Au)R-09520
        TC: World Records (E) CSHB67
W 400145-C   **The Yale Blues** [Vivian Ellis, Collie Knox] vSL (as, cl solos)
        78: OKeh 41007, Parlophone (E) E-6051, (Au) A-2475, Odeon (Arg) 193160, (G) A-189133
                Parlophone E-6051 as COMPETITION ORCHESTRA
        LP: The Old Masters 14,World Records (E)SHB67, (Au)R-09520
        TC: World Records (E) CSHB67
        Both sides also on **CD:** Jazz Oracle (C) BDW 8004

The author now believes neither Dorsey is present on a March 17, 1928, Ben Selvin session for Columbia.

Columbia, New York, N.Y. Friday, March 23, 1928
BOYD SENTER AND HIS SENTERPEDES
Boyd Senter (cl,ldr) Mickey Bloom (tp) Tom Dorsey (tb) **Jimmy Dorsey** (as) Jack Russell (p) Eddie Lang (g)

W 400168-A   **I Wish I Could Shimmy Like My Sister Kate** [Armon J. Piron]
        78: OKeh 41018, Odeon 156335, (Arg) 193162, A-189174, Clarion 5194-C, Velvet Tone 7120-V, Vocalion 3015
        LP: Parlophone (E) PMC7133, Harlequin (E) HQ 2044, Swaggie (Au) S1299
        CD: Timeless (H) CBC-1032
W 400169-B   **Mobile Blues** [Rose, Short] (as solo)
        78: Parlophone R-143, Odeon (F) 165335, (Arg) 193162
        LP: Parlophone (E) PMC7133, Harlequin (E) HQ 2044, Swaggie (Au) S1299
        CD: Timeless (H) CBC-1032

Okeh, New York, N.Y. Wednesday, April 11, 1928
SEGER ELLIS (accompanied by OKeh NOVELTY ORCHESTRA)
Tom Dorsey (cnt,tb) **Jimmy Dorsey** (cnt,cl,as) Joe Venuti (vn) Rube Bloom (p) Eddie Lang (g) Seger Ellis (vcl)

W 400605-A   **If I Can't Have You (I Want To Be Lonesome, I Want To Be Blue)** [Walter Donaldson] vSE (as solo)
        78: OKeh 41047, Parlophone (E) R-165, (Au) A-2518, Odeon (G) 16370 (Contd.)

SEGER ELLIS (Contd.)

> *Parlophones as TAMPA BLUE ARTISTES AND THEIR SINGER*

W 400606-C   **Coquette** [Gus Kahn; Johnny Green, Carmen Lombardo] vSE
          78: OKeh 41024, Parlophone (Au) A-2499, Odeon (F) 165364, (Au) 193175
W 400607-A   **I Must Be Dreaming** [Al Dubin; Al Sherman] vSE (cnt duet with TD)
          78: OKeh 41024, Parlophone (E) R-281, (Au) A-2499, Odeon (G) A-193183
> *Parlophones as SEGER ELLIS & TAMPA BLUE ARTISTES*

By April 1928, both Jimmy and brother Tom were also keeping busy in Dr. Eugene Ormandy's twenty-plus member silent-movie pit band at the Capitol Theater. Ormandy also led two of the 1928 Dorsey sessions.

OKeh, New York, N.Y. Tuesday, April 24, 1928
DORSEY BROTHERS AND THEIR ORCHESTRA
Tom Dorsey (cnt,tb,ldr) Mickey Bloom, Fuzzy Farrar (tp) **Jimmy Dorsey** (cl,as) Arnold Brilhart (as) Herb Spencer (ts) Adrian Rollini (bsx) *Art Schutt* (p) Carl Kress (g) Chauncey Morehouse (d) Seger Ellis (vcl)

W 400633-B   **Indian Cradle Song** [Gus Kahn; Mabel Wayne] vSE
          78: (unissued test pressing)
          LP: Broadway BR-112
W 400633-C   **Indian Cradle Song** vSE
          78: OKeh 41032, Parlophone (E) R-202, (Au) A-2591, Odeon (Arg) 193215, (G) A-189166
          LP: Broadway BR112, The Old Masters 14, World Records (E) SHB67, (Au) R-09520
          TC: World Records (E) CSHB-67
W 400634-A   **My Melancholy Baby** [George Norton; Ernie Burnett] vSE (cl,as solos)
          78: (unissued test pressing)
          LP: Broadway BR-112
W 400633-C   **My Melancholy Baby** vSE (cl,as solos)
          78: OKeh 41032, Parlophone (E) R-181, (Au) A-2591, Odeon (Arg) 193214, (G) A-189166, (F) A-221092
          LP: Columbia C4L18, Broadway BR-112, The Old Masters 14, World Records (E) SHB-67, (Au) R-09520
          TC: World Records (E) CSHB-67, Radio Yesteryear Stack 15
          CD: Jazz Greats (E) 036
          All sides and takes also on **CD**: Jazz Oracle (C) BDW 8004

Columbia, New York, N.Y. Monday, April 30, 1928
BEN SELVIN AND HIS ORCHESTRA
Ben Selvin (ldr) *2 unknown* (tp) Tom Dorsey (tb) *Jimmy Dorsey* (cl,as) *unknown* (bsx), (ts) Charlie Magnante (acc) *unknown* (p), (bj) *Joe Tarto* (bb) Stan King (d) Jack Parker, Three Melodians [*Frank Luther, Phil Dewey, Jack Parker*] (vcl)

W 146282-3   **I'm Afraid Of You** vJP
    78: Columbia 1399-D
W 146283-3   **What's The Reason?** v3M
    78: Columbia 1398-D
        as THE KNICKERBOCKERS

Next are three sessions illustrating the further inroads Jimmy had been making on the New York City jazz scene.

Cameo, New York, N.Y. April 1928
ALABAMA RED PEPPERS
Leo McConville (tp) Tom Dorsey (tb) **Jimmy Dorsey** (cl,as) *Fud Livingston* (ts) *Arthur Schutt* (p) *Dick McDonough* (bj,g) Stan King (d)

3070-A   **River Boat Shuffle** [Hoagy Carmichael]
    78: Cameo 8204, Lincoln 2859, Romeo 634
3071-A   **Eccentric (Rag)** [J. Russell Robinson] (cl solo)
    78: Cameo 8205, Lincoln 2860, Romeo 635
    LP: Mouldie Fygge (E) 101

OKeh, New York, N.Y. Thursday, May 3, 1928
BOYD SENTER AND HIS SENTERPEDES
Boyd Senter (cl,ldr) Mickey Bloom (tp) Charlie Butterfield (tb) **Jimmy Dorsey** (as) Jack Russell (p) Eddie Lang (g)

400647-B   **Original Stack O' Lee Blues** [Traditional] (as solo)
    78: OKeh 41115, Clarion 5054-C, Parlophone (E) R-501, Vocalion 3015 (dub)
    (100382-B) Diva 6044-G, Velvet Tone 7070-V
    LP: Parlophone (E) PMC7133, Harlequin (E) HQ2044, Swaggie (Au) S1299
    CD: Timeless (H) CBC-1032
400169-C,D   **Mobile Blues** (unissued)

OKeh, New York, N.Y. Tuesday, May 8, 1928
BOYD SENTER AND HIS SENTERPEDES
Tom Dorsey (tb) replaces Butterfield. Vic Berton (d) added.

W 400653-B   **Original Chinese Blues** [Moore, Gardner]
    78: OKeh 41163, Parlophone (E) R-143, (Au) A-3342, Odeon (F) 165577, (G) 193272
    LP: Parlophone (E) PMC7133, Harlequin (E) HQ2044, Swaggie (Au) S1299
    TC: Radio Yesteryear Stack 58
W 400654-B   **Somebody's Wrong** [Raymond Egan, Henry Marshall; Richard Whiting] (as solo)
    78: OKeh 41059, Odeon (F) 165577, (Au) 193272, (E) A189162, Vocalion 3031 (dub)
    LP: Parlophone (E) PMC7133, Harlequin (E) HQ2044, Swaggie (Au) S1299
    Both sides also on **CD:** Timeless (H) CBC-1032

OKeh, New York, N.Y. Tuesday, May 22, 1928
DORSEY BROTHERS AND THEIR ORCHESTRA
Tom Dorsey (cnt,tb,ldr) Mickey Bloom, Fuzzy Farrar (tp) **Jimmy Dorsey** (cl,as) Arnold Brilhart (as) Herb Spencer (ts) *Arthur Schutt* (p) Carl Kress (g) Joe Tarto (bb) Chauncey Morehouse (d) Scrappy Lambert [as Bill Dutton] (vcl)

W 400698-A   **That's My Mammy** [Ed Nelson, Harry Pease; Abel Baer] vSL (as solo)
  78: OKeh 41050, Parlophone (E) R-215, (Au) A-2529, Ariel (E) 4311, Odeon (G) A-189165, (F) A-221085
    Ariel as ARIEL DANCE ORCHESTRA, Odeon A-221085 as ROOF GARDEN ORCHESTRA
  LP: The Old Masters 14, World Records (E) SHB67, (Au) R-09520
W 400699-C   **Dixie Dawn** [Joseph Trent; Peter De Rose] vSL (cl, as solos)
  78: OKeh 41032, Parlophone (E) R-280, (Au) A-2654, Odeon (G) A-189165
  LP: The Old Masters 14, World Records (E) SHB67, (Au) R-09520, Broadway BR112
  Both sides also on **TC:** World Records (E) CSHB67, **CD:** Jazz Oracle (C) BDW 8004

Brunswick, New York, N.Y. Tuesday, May 29, 1928
RED NICHOLS AND HIS FIVE PENNIES
Red Nichols, Leo McConville, Mannie Klein (tp) Miff Mole (tb) Fud Livingston (cl) **Jimmy Dorsey** (as) Arthur Schutt (p) Carl Kress (g) Vic Berton (d)

E-27605-   **Panama** [William N. Tyers] (as solo)
  78: Brunswick 3961, (E) O3499 (dub), (Ind) 3961 (Au) 3961, Decca (F) BM-1197 (dub), United Hot Clubs Of America 20
  LP: Classic Jazz Masters 27, Swaggie (Au) 838
E-27606-   **There'll Come A Time** [Mannone, Mole] (as solo)
  78: Brunswick 3955, 3850, 6822, (G) A-7849, A-9932, (Ind) 3961, (Au) 3961
  LP: Classic Jazz Masters 27, Ace of Hearts (E) AH-63, Coral (G) 97024, ASV Living Era AJA 5025, Swaggie (Au) 838
  TC: ASV Living Era 15888
  CD: ASV Living Era (E) AJA 5025

OKeh, New York, N.Y. Monday, June 4, 1928
DORSEY BROTHERS AND THEIR ORCHESTRA
Tom Dorsey (cnt,tb,ldr) Mickey Bloom, Fuzzy Farrar (tp) **Jimmy Dorsey** (cl,as) Arnold Brilhart (as) Herb Spencer (ts) *Arthur Schutt* (p) Carl Kress (g) Hank Stern (bb) Chauncey Morehouse (d) Scrappy Lambert (vcl)

W 400740-B   **Evening Star** [Roy Turk; Fred E. Ahlert] vSL (as, cl solos)
  78: OKeh 41065, Parlophone (E) R-215, (Au) A-2535, (G) A-4549, (Sp) B-25257, Odeon (F) 165368, 040706, (Arg) 193207, 193333,

(G) A-189157
LP: The Old Masters 14, World Records (E) SHB67, (Au) R-09520, Broadway BR112
TC: World Records (E) CSHB67
W 400740-C　　　**Evening Star** vSL (as,cl solos)
　　　78: (unissued test pressing)
　　　LP: Broadway BR112
W 400741-A　　　**Forgetting You** [Buddy De Sylva, Lew Brown; Ray Henderson] vSL (cl,as solo)
　　　78: OKeh 41065, Parlophone (Au) A-2535, (G) A-4549, (Sp) B-25257, Odeon (F) 165368, 040706, (Arg) 193207, (G) A-189157
　　　LP: The Old Masters 14, World Records (E) SHB67, (Au) R-09520, Broadway BR112
　　　TC: World Records (E) CSHB67
W 400740-C　　　**Forgetting You** vSL (cl,as solo)
　　　78: (unissued test pressing)
　　　LP: Broadway BR112
　　　All sides and takes also on **CD:** Jazz Oracle (C) BDW 8004

OKeh, New York, N.Y. Monday, June 11, 1928
SAM LANIN AND HIS FAMOUS PLAYERS
Sam Lanin (ldr) Phil Napoleon, Harold Peppie (tp) Tom Dorsey (tb) *Frank Teschemacher, Jimmy Dorsey* (cl,as) *unknown* (ts) (p) (bj) *Jimmy Mullen* (bb,sb) *unknown* (d) Three Star Singers [Frank Luther, Jack Parker, Phil Dewey] (vcl grp)

W 400775-C　　　**Sorry For Me** v3S
　　　78: OKeh 41063, Parlophone (Au) A-2534, (G) A-4548, Odeon 193205, (G) 04075, A-189158
　　　Australian Parlophone as SAM LANIN'S ORCH.
　　　LP: World Records SH-424
W 400776-A　　　**Don't Keep Me In The Dark, Bright Eyes** [Alfred Bryan; Pete Wendling] v3S
　　　78: Parlophone (E) R-214
W 400776-B　　　**Don't Keep Me In The Dark, Bright Eyes** v3S
　　　78: OKeh 41063, Parlophone (G) A4548, (Au) A-2684, Odeon 193205, (G) 04075, A189158
　　　LP: World Records SH-424

OKeh, New York, N.Y. Tuesday, June 12, 1928
EMMETT MILLER'S GEORGIA CRACKERS
Leo McConville (tp) Tom Dorsey (tb) **Jimmy Dorsey** (cl) Arthur Schutt (p) Eddie Lang (g) Stan King (d) Emmett Miller, Dan Fitch (vcl)

W 400781-A　　　**God's River Blues** [Hackett] vEM (cl solo)
　　　78: OKeh 41438, Parlophone (E) R-198
W 400782-C　　　**I Ain't Got Nobody** [Roger Graham, Dave Peyton; Spencer Williams] vEM,DF (cl solo)
　　　78: OKeh 41062, Odeon (F) 165494
　　　400781 and 400782 also on **LP:** The Old Masters 1
W 400783-B　　　**Lovesick Blues** [Irving Mills; Cliff Friend] vEM
　　　　　　　　　　　　　　　(Contd.)

EMMETT MILLER'S GEORGIA CRACKERS (Contd.)

78: OKeh 41062, Odeon (F) 165494, Parlophone (E) R-198
*Parlophone R-198 as EMMETT MILLER assisted by THE
UNIVERSITY FIVE*
LP: The Old Masters 1, Parlophone (E) PMC7006
W 400784-A　　　**The Lion Tamers** [Emmett Miller, Dan Fitch] vEM,DF
78: OKeh 41205
All sides this session also on **CD:** Columbia CK 66999

Brunswick, New York, N.Y. Wednesday, June 13, 1928
ORIGINAL MEMPHIS FIVE
Phil Napoleon (tp,ldr) Tom Dorsey (tb) **Jimmy Dorsey** (cl,as) Frank
Signorelli (p) *Stan King [or] Jack Roth* (d)

E 7367　　　　　**I'm More Than Satisfied** [Raymond W. Klages;
　　　　　　　　　Thomas "Fats" Waller] (cl solos)
78: Vocalion 15712
E 7368　　　　　**My Angeline** [Jack Palmer] (cl,as solos)
78: Vocalion 15712
E 7369　　　　　**Fireworks** [Spencer Williams] (as,cl solos)
78: Vocalion 15761
LP: Historical HLP-25
all three sides also on **CD:** Timeless (H) CBC 1-049

Victor, New York, N.Y. Thursday, June 21, 1928
RED NICHOLS AND HIS ORCHESTRA
Red Nichols (cnt) Leo McConville (tp) Miff Mole (tb) Dudley Fosdick
(mel) Fud Livingston (cl) **Jimmy Dorsey** (as) Arthur Schutt (p) Carl
Kress (g) Chauncey Morehouse (d,vib,vcl) Glenn Miller (arr)

45814-2　　　　　**Harlem Twist** [Fud Livingston, Chauncey Morehouse]
　　　　　　　　　vCM arrGM (as solo)
78: Victor 21560
LP: RCA (F) PM43179, Saville (E) SVL146, Living Era (E)
AJA5025
TC: Living Era (E) 15888
45814-3　　　　　**Harlem Twist** vCM arrGM (as solo)
78: Victor 21560
LP: RCA (F) NL89606, Living Era (E) AJA5025
45815-2　　　　　**Five Pennies** [Loring "Red" Nichols]
78: Victor 21560
LP: RCA (F) PM43179, Saville (E) SVL146
45815-3　　　　　**Five Pennies**
LP: Broadway BR110, Victor LPM 1455

OKeh, New York, N.Y. Monday, July 16, 1928
DORSEY BROTHERS AND THEIR CONCERT ORCHESTRA
Eugene Ormandy (ldr) Leo McConville, Mickey Bloom, Fuzzy Farrar,
Mannie Klein (tp) Tom Dorsey, Carl Loeffler (tb) **Jimmy Dorsey** (cl,as)
Max Farley (as,fl) Arnold Brilhart (as) Bill Green (ts) Al Duffy, Leo
Kroucrick, 2 *unknown* (vn) Arthur Schutt (p) Jack Hansen (bb) Jimmy

Mullen (sb) Charles Dondron (vib) Smith Ballew (vcl) Nye Mayhew, Hal Kemp, Saxie Dowell, Skinnay Ennis (quartet) George Crozier (arr)

W 400871-B   **Was It A Dream?** [Sam Coslow, Larry Spier] (pt. 1)
    78: OKeh 41083, Parlophone (E) R-226, (Au) A-2567, Odeon
    (F) 165382, (Arg) 193219
    LP: World Records (E) SHB-67, (Au) R-09520
    TC: World Records (E) CSHB-67
W 400872-C   **Was It A Dream?** (pt. 2) vSB&quartet (as solo)
    (same issues as part 1)
500021-C   **Was It A Dream?** vSB & quartet (as solo)
    78: (12 inch) *Harmony 6000-H,* Odeon (G) 3237
        confirmation of 6000-H's release is lacking.
    LP: World Records (E) SHB-67
    TC: World Records (E) CSHB 67, ProArte Digital PCD-519
    CD: ProArte Digital CDD-519
500021-D   **Was It A Dream?** vSB & quartet (as solo)
    78: (12-inch) (unissued test pressing)
    All sides, all takes also on **CD:** Jazz Oracle (C) BDW 8005

OKeh, New York, N.Y. Tuesday, July 24, 1928
JOE VENUTI AND HIS NEW YORKERS
Leo McConville, *Fuzzy Farrar* (tp) Charlie Butterfield (tb) Arnold Brilhart, **Jimmy Dorsey** (cl,as) Fud Livingston (ts) Joe Venuti (vn) Frank Signorelli (p,celst) Tony Colucci (bj) Eddie Lang (g) Joe Tarto (bb) Chauncey Morehouse (d) Scrappy Lambert (vcl)

400884-C   **Pickin' Cotton** [B. G. De Sylva, Lew Brown; Ray
    Henderson] vSL *(as solo)*
    78: OKeh 41087, Parlophone (E) R-309, (Aus) A-2702, Odeon
    (Arg) 193234, A-189191
    LP: The Old Masters 8, JSP (E) 1111
    TC: Radio Yesteryear Stack 22
        *Parlophone R-309 as JOE VENUTI AND HIS CONCERT
        ORCH., Parlophone A-2702 as LANG'S DANCE ORCH.*
400885-B   **I'm On The Crest Of A Wave** [B. G. De Sylva, Lew
    Brown; Ray Henderson] vSL (as solo)
    78: OKeh 41087, Parlophone (E) R-309, (Aus) A-2702, Odeon
    (Arg) 193234, A-189191, Ariel (E) 4363
        *Parlophone R-309 as JOE VENUTI AND HIS CONCERT
        ORCH., Parlophone A-2702 as LANG'S DANCE ORCH.,
        Ariel as ARIEL DANCE ORCH.*
    LP: The Old Masters 8, JSP (E) 1111
    TC: Radio Yesteryear Stack 22
    both sides also on **CD:** JSP (E) CD309

OKeh, New York, N.Y. Friday, August 3, 1928
SAM LANIN AND HIS FAMOUS PLAYERS
Sam Lanin (ldr) Phil Napoleon, Harold Peppie (tp) Tom Dorsey (cnt,tb) **Jimmy Dorsey** (cl,as) *unknown* (as), (ts) Arthur Schutt (p) Smith Ballew (g) Jimmy Mullen (bb) *Stan King* (d) Three Star Singers [Emmett Miller, Dan Fitch, Ballew] (vcl) (Contd.)

SAM LANIN AND HIS FAMOUS PLAYERS (Contd.)

W 401053-A   Ten Little Miles From Town [Gus Kahn; Elmer Sch-
                    oebel] v3S
      78: OKeh 41097, Parlophone (E) R-214, (Au) A-2604, Odeon
      (Arg) 193232
          OKeh and Odeon as BILLY HAYS & HIS ORCHESTRA
      LP: The Old Masters 28
W 401054-A   If You Don't Love Me [Jack Yellen, Milton Ager]
                    v3S (as solo)
      78: OKeh 41097, Parlophone (E) E-6114, (Au) A-2604, Odeon
      (Arg) 193232
          OKeh and Odeon as BILLY HAYS & HIS ORCHESTRA
W 401055-B   Why? (Do I Love You Like I Do) [Gold, Hills, Rock-
                    well] v3S
      78: OKeh 41091, Parlophone (E) E-6114, A-4556, Odeon (G)
      A-189178, 04088
                    *Parlophone E-6114 as SOUTHERN MELODY ARTISTS,
                    OKeh, Odeons and Parlophone A-4556 as BILLY HAYS &
                    HIS ORCHESTRA*

OKeh, New York, N.Y. Thursday, August 9, 1928
EMMETT MILLER'S GEORGIA CRACKERS
Mannie Klein (tp) Tom Dorsey (tb) **Jimmy Dorsey** (cl,as) Arthur Schutt
(p) Eddie Lang (g) Stan King (d) Emmett Miller (vcl)

W 404060-A   Any Time [Herbert "Happy" Lawson] vEM
      78: OKeh 41095, Odeon (F) 165415
W 404061-B   St. Louis Blues [William C. Handy] (cl solo)
      78: OKeh 41095, Odeon (F) 165415, Parlophone (E) R-2270
      Both sides on **LP:** The Old Masters 1, **CD:** Columbia CK 66999

Columbia, New York, N.Y. Friday, September 14, 1928
EMMETT MILLER'S GEORGIA CRACKERS
Miff Mole (tb) replaces Tom Dorsey

W 401116-C   Take Your Tomorrow (And Give Me Yesterday)
                    [Andy Razaf; J. C. Johnson] vEM
      78: OKeh 41135, Parlophone (E) R-314
W 401117-C   Dusky Stevedore [Andy Razaf; J. C. Johnson]
                    vEM (cl solo)
      78: OKeh 41095, Odeon (F) 165415, Parlophone (E) R-2270
                    *Parlophones as EMMETT MILLER, accompanied by MIFF
                    MOLE AND IIIS MOLERS*
      Both sides on **LP:** The Old Masters 1, **CD:** Columbia CK 66999

OKeh, New York, N.Y. Wednesday, September 26, 1928
SAM LANIN AND HIS FAMOUS PLAYERS
Sam Lanin (ldr) Leo McConville, Jack Purvis (tp) Tom Dorsey (tb)
Jimmy Dorsey (cl,as) Fud Livingston (as,vcl) *unknown* (cl,ts) Rube
Bloom (p) *unknown* (bj) *Hank Stern* (bb) *unknown* (d)

W 401148-C   **Roses Of Yesterday** [Irving Berlin] vFL
    78: OKeh 41121, Parlophone (E) R-297, (G) A4558, (Au) A-
    2613, Odeon (G) 04090, A-189185, Ariel (E) 4352
            Ariel as ARIEL DANCE ORCHESTRA
W 401149-A   **Jumping Jack** [Rube Bloom, Seaman, Smolev] (Rube
            Bloom piano, JD as solos)
    78: OKeh 41121, Parlophone (E) E-6138, (Au) A-2613, (G)
    A4558, Odeon (G) 04090, A-189185
            Parlophone (E) as PARLOPHONE NOVELTY ORCH.

OKeh, New York, N.Y. Thursday, September 27, 1928
JOE VENUTI'S BLUE FOUR
Joe Venuti (vn,ldr) **Jimmy Dorsey** (cl,as,bar) Rube Bloom (p,vcl) Eddie
Lang (g) Paul Graselli (d)

401159-A   **The Blue Room** [Lorenz Hart; Richard Rodgers] vRB
            (cl solo)
    78: OKeh 41144, Parlophone (E) R-1916, Odeon (F) 165535,
    (Arg) 193271, Vocalion 3011 (possible dub)
    LP: Columbia C3L35, Parlophone (E) PMC7091
    CD: JSP (E) CD309
401160-A   **Sensation (Stomp)** [Original Dixieland Jazz Band]
            vRB (bar solo)
    78: OKeh 41144, Harmony 1420-H, Clarion 5467-C, Velvet
    Tone 2527-V, Parlophone (E) R-596, Odeon (Arg) 193271, (It)
    A-2316, (G) A-286010
            *Clarion, Harmony and Velvet Tone as ALL STAR RHYTHM
            BOYS, Bloom vocal as JERRY MILLS*
    LP: Parlophone (E) PMC7091, The Old Masters 8, Odeon (G)
    SMS2
    CD: JSP (E) CD309

Cameo, New York, N.Y. Thursday, September 27, 1928
SAM LANIN AND HIS ORCHESTRA
Sam Lanin (ldr) Phil Napoleon, Harold Peppie (tp) Tom Dorsey (tb)
Jimmy Dorsey, *unknown* (cl,as) *unknown* (cl,ts) *Rube Bloom* (p,celst)
unknown (g) Jimmy Mullen (bb) *unknown* (d) Scrappy Lambert [as
William Smith] (vcl)

3370-A   **I Still Belong To You** vSL
    78: Cameo 8338, Lincoln 2986, Romeo 761, Pathe Actuelle
    36879, Perfect 15060
            Cameo, Lincoln, Romeo as BROADWAY BROADCASTERS
3371-A   **Avalon Town** [Grant Clarke; Nacio Herb Brown] vSL
    78: Cameo 8343, Lincoln 2991, Romeo 766, Dominion (E) A-
    103, Pathe Actuelle 36879, Perfect 15060
            *Cameo, Lincoln, Romeo and Dominion as SAM LANIN
            AND HIS TROUBADORS*
3372-A   **Sonny Boy** [Buddy De Sylva, Lew Brown, Al Jolson;
            Ray Henderson] vSL (as solo)
    78: Cameo 8333, Lincoln 2981, Romeo 756, Dominion (E) A-
    46, Angelus (Au)3081, Starr (Au)729, Sterling (Au)1169 (Contd.)

SAM LANIN AND HIS ORCHESTRA (Contd.)

> *Angelus as THE NEW YORKERS, Starr as THE PLAZA DANCE BAND, Sterling as ROY GREEN'S MANHATTAN ORCH., others as SAM LANIN AND HIS TROUBADORS*
> (108351-) **78:** Perfect 15039
> *as ARTHUR LANGE'S SYMPHONY ORCHESTRA*

OKeh, New York, N.Y. Saturday, September 29, 1928
DORSEY BROTHERS AND THEIR ORCHESTRA
Tom Dorsey (cnt,tb,ldr) Fuzzy Farrar, *Nat Natoli* (tp) Jack Teagarden (tb) **Jimmy Dorsey** (cl,as) Arnold Brilhart (as) Frank Teschemacher (cl,ts) Herb Spencer (ts) Frank Signorelli (p) Carl Kress (bj,g) Hank Stern (bb) Stan King (d) Smith Ballew (vcl)

W 401169-B   **'Round Evening** [Steiner; Richard A. Whiting, J. Fred Coots] vSB (as solos)
          78: OKeh 41124, Parlophone (Au) A2620, (F) 22231, Odeon (Arg) 193257, (G) A-189198
          LP: The Old Masters 14, World Records (E) SHB67, (Au) R-09520, Time-Life STL-J23
          TC: World Records (E) CSHB67
W 401170-B   **Out Of The Dawn** [Walter Donaldson] vSB (as,cl solos)
          78: OKeh 41124, Parlophone (E) R-256, (Au) A2632, (F) 22231, Odeon (Arg) 193257, (G) A-189198, Ariel (E) 4324
          Ariel as ARIEL DANCE ORCHESTRA
          LP: The Old Masters 14, World Records (E) SHB67, (Au) R-09520, Time-Life STL-J23
          TC: World Records (E) CSHB67
          Both sides also on **CD:** Village (G) VILCD 014-2, Jazz Oracle (E) BDW 8004

OKeh, New York, N.Y. Saturday, September 29, 1928
BIG ACES
Tom Dorsey (cnt) Nat Natoli (tp) Jack Teagarden (tb) **Jimmy Dorsey,** Don Redman (cl,as) Frank Teschemacher (cl,ts) George Thomas (ts,vcl) Frank Signorelli (p) Carl Kress (g) Hank Stern (bb) Stan King (d,vib)

W 401171-A   **Cherry** [Don Redman, Ray Gilbert] vGT (as solo)
          78: OKeh 41136, Parlophone (E) R-365, (E) R-2541, Odeon (F) 165125
          Parlophone as THE BIG CHOCOLATE DANDIES, Odeon as THE LITTLE ACES
          LP: Time-Life STL-J23, Parlophone PMC7038, Swaggie (Au) S1249
          CD: Village (G) VILCD 014-2
W 401171-C   **Cherry** vGT (as solo)
          78: OKeh 41136, Parlophone (E) R-365
          Parlophone as THE BIG CHOCOLATE DANDIES
          LP: IAJRC 2, Time-Life STL-J23
          CD: Village (G) VILCD 014-2

The "Big Aces" evolved when Don Redman and George Thomas showed up at the Brothers' session with the "Cherry" score. Both were members of McKinney's Cotton Pickers and knew the Dorseys from Detroit where the "Pickers" were managed by Jean Goldkette.

Brunswick, New York, N.Y. Tuesday, October 2, 1928
RED NICHOLS AND HIS FIVE PENNIES
Red Nichols (tp,ldr,arr) Mannie Klein (tp) Dudley Fosdick (mel) Fud Livingston (cl) **Jimmy Dorsey** (as) *Walter Livingston* (ts) Arthur Schutt (p) Carl Kress (g) Vic Berton (d)

E-28326-A   **A Pretty Girl Is Like A Melody** [Irving Berlin]
                   arrRN (as solo)
       78: Brunswick 4456, 6826, (E) O1854, (F) 1033, (G) A-8337,
       (Au) 4456
       LP: Sunbeam MFC-12, Class. Jazz Mast. 28, Swaggie (Au) 838
       TC: Radio Yesteryear Stack 31
E-28327-A,B   **I Must Have That Man** (unissued)

Columbia, New York, N.Y. Thursday, October 4, 1928
IPANA TROUBADORS
Sam Lanin (ldr) Phil Napoleon, Harold Peppie (tp) Tom Dorsey (tb) *Jimmy Dorsey [or] Frank Teschemacher* (cl,as) *unknown* (as), (ts) Rube Bloom (p) Smith Ballew (g,vcl) (g) Jimmy Mullen (bb) *unknown* (d)

W 147040-3   **I Can't Make Her Happy (That Old Girl Of Mine)**
                   [Sidney Clare; Lew Pollack] vSB
       78: Columbia 1586-D, Regal (Au) G-20380
       LP: Broadway BR104
W 147041-3   **Heart Broken And Lonely** [Sam Coslow, Con Con-
                   rad, Ben Bernie] vSB (as solo)
       78: Columbia 1586-D, Regal (Au) G-20380
                   Regals as STELLAR DANCE BAND

OKeh, New York, N.Y. Thursday, October 4, 1928
JOE VENUTI AND HIS NEW YORKERS
Joe Venuti (vn,ldr,*scat vcl*) Leo McConville, *Mannie Klein [or] Fuzzy Farrar* (tp) Tom Dorsey (tb) **Jimmy Dorsey** (cl,as) Arnold Brilhart (cl,as) Max Farley (cl,ts,fl) Frank Signorelli (p) Eddie Lang (g) Joe Tarto (bb) Chauncey Morehouse (d,*scat vcl*)

W 401193-B   **Doin' Things** [Joe Venuti, Eddie Lang]
       78: OKeh 41133, Odeon (F) 165679, (Arg) 193256, A-189219,
       (F) A-221110
       LP: The Old Masters 8, JSP (E) 1111
       CD: JSP (E) CD309
W 401194-B   **I Must Have That Man!** [Dorothy Fields; Jimmy
                   McHugh] vCM or JV
       78: OKeh 41133, Odeon (F) 165679, (Arg) 193256, A-189219,
       (F) A-22110, Parlophone (E) R-280
                   Parlophone as ED LANG'S WONDER ORCHESTRA
       LP: The Old Masters 8, Broadway BR108, JSP (E) 1111

Pathe, New York, N.Y. c. Thursday, October 4, 1928
SAM LANIN AND HIS ORCHESTRA
Sam Lanin (ldr) Bill Moore, *Mannie Klein* (tp) Jack Teagarden (tb) **Jimmy Dorsey**, *Arnold Brilhart* (cl,as) Jack Pettis (cl,ts) *Rube Bloom* [or] *Arthur Schutt* (p) *unknown* (bj), (bb), (d) Scrappy Lambert (vcl)

108410-2   **My Blackbirds Are Bluebirds Now** [Irving Caesar; Cliff Friend] vSL (as solo)
        78: Pathe Actuelle 36880, Perfect 15061
        (3387-A) **78:** Cameo 8349, Lincoln 2997, Romeo 772, Angelus (Au) 3082, Worth (Au) 7036, Gracelon (Au) 4026
            Angelus as THE NEW YORKERS, Worth as ART CARROLL AND HIS BAND, others as BROADWAY BROADCASTERS
108411-1   **A Happy Ending** vSL
        78: Pathe Actuelle 36893, Perfect 15074
-0-   **On Candlelight Lane** vSL
        78: Pathe Actuelle 36878, Perfect 15059
            as BROADWAY BROADCASTERS (possibly not from this session)

Columbia, New York, N.Y. Monday, October 8, 1928
THE KNICKERBOCKERS
Ben Selvin (ldr,vcl) Leo McConville, Mannie Klein (tp) Tom Dorsey (tb) **Jimmy Dorsey** (cl,as) *unknown* (ts), (bsx), (vn), (p,celst) *Tony Colucci [or] Carl Kress* (g) *unknown* (bb), (d)

W 147043-2   **Happy Days And Lonely Nights** [Billy Rose; Fred Fisher] vBS (cl solo)
        78: Columbia 1596-D
W 147044-3   **Doin' The Raccoon** [Ray Klages; J. Fred Coots] vBS
        78: Columbia 1596-D

Columbia, New York, N.Y. Wednesday, October 17, 1928
BEN SELVIN & HIS ORCHESTRA
Ben Selvin (vn,ldr) Mannie Klein, Leo McConville (tp) *Tom Dorsey [or] Chuck Campbell (tb)* **Jimmy Dorsey** (cl,as,bar) *unknown* (ss), (ts), (p) *John Cali* (bj) Joe Tarto (bb) *Joe Green* (d,xyl) Jack Parker, *Three Melodians [Frank Luther, Phil Dewey, Jack Parker]* (vcl)

W 147048-2   **I'm Sorry Sally** [Gus Kahn; Ted FioRito] vJP,3M
        78: Columbia 1617-D
147049 (1,2,3) **I'm Sorry Sally** (unissued)
W 147050-2   **There's A Rainbow 'Round My Shoulder** [Dave Dreyer, Billy Rose, Al Jolson] vJP (as solo)
        78: Columbia 1605-D, (E) 5226

Pathe, New York, N.Y. c. Thursday, October 18, 1928
BROADWAY BROADCASTERS
Sam Lanin (ldr) Leo McConville, *Mannie Klein* (tp) Tom Dorsey (tb) Jimmy Dorsey, Fud Livingston (cl,as) *unknown* (cl,ts) Rube Bloom (p) *unknown* (bj) Hank Stern (bb) *unknown* (d) Scrappy Lambert [as Chester Hale on Pathe Actuelle, Perfect] (vcl)

108426-2   **Don't Be Like That** [Maceo Pinkard, Archie Gottler,
                  Charles Tobias] vSL
   78: Pathe Actuelle 36876, Perfect 15057
   (3400-) **78:** Cameo 8348, Lincoln 2996, Romeo 771
      *Cameo as SAM LANIN AND HIS ORCHESTRA, Romeo and
      Lincoln as THE CAROLINERS*
108426-3   **Don't Be Like That** vSL
   78: Cameo 8348
108427-1   **Everybody Loves You** [Al Dubin; George Little] vSL
   78: Pathe Actuelle 36876, Perfect 15057
   (3401-C) **78:** Cameo 8351, Lincoln 2999, Romeo 774
108428-1   **Come On, Baby!** vSL
   78: Pathe Actuelle 36890, Perfect 15071
   (3402-A) **78:** Cameo 8352, Lincoln 3000, Romeo 775

Cameo, New York, N.Y. Friday, October 19, 1928
SAM LANIN AND HIS ORCHESTRA
Sam Lanin (ldr) Leo McConville, *unknown* (tp) Tom Dorsey (tb) **Jimmy
Dorsey,** *unknown* (cl,as) *unknown* (cl,ts) Rube Bloom (p) *unknown* (bj)
Hank Stern (bb) *unknown* (d) Scrappy Lambert (vcl)

3415-B   **Bring Me Your Tears** vSL
   78: Cameo 8370, Lincoln 3018, Romeo 793
3416-A   **Adorable Dora** [Sidney Clare, Maceo Pinkard;
                  Archie Gottler] vSL (cl solo)
   78: Cameo 9008, Lincoln 3037, Romeo 812
      Cameo and Romeo as BROADWAY BROADCASTERS
   (108442-1) **78:** Pathe Actuelle 36894, Perfect 15075
      as CASINO DANCE ORCHESTRA

Columbia, New York, N.Y. Friday, October 19, 1928
BEN SELVIN AND HIS ORCHESTRA
Ben Selvin (vn,ldr) 2 *unknown* (tp) Tom Dorsey (tb) **Jimmy Dorsey**
(cl,as,bar) *unknown* (ts), (vn), (p) John Cali (bj,g) *unknown* (bb) Stan
King (d) Jack Parker (vcl)

W 147140-3   **You're The Cream In My Coffee** [Buddy De Sylva,
                  Lew Brown; Ray Henderson] vJP (as solo)
   78: Columbia 1604-D, Regal (E) G-9334
      *Columbia as BROADWAY NITELITES, Regal as THE
      RHYTHMIC TROUBADORS*
W 147141-2   **Billie** (waltz) [George M. Cohan] vJP
   78: Columbia 1603-D
      as EDDIE THOMAS' COLLEGIANS

Pathe, New York, N.Y. c. Friday, October 26, 1928
SAM LANIN AND HIS ORCHESTRA
Sam Lanin (ldr) Leo McConville, *unknown* (tp) Tom Dorsey (tb) **Jimmy
Dorsey** (cl,as) *unknown* (cl,as) *unknown* (cl,ts) Rube Bloom (p) *unknown*
(bj) *Hank Stern* (bb) *unknown* (d) Scrappy Lambert [as Chester Hale or
Harold Lang on Pathe, Perfect] (vcl)

SAM LANIN AND HIS ORCHESTRA (Contd.)

108451-1   **Marie** [Irving Berlin] vSL[CH] (cl solo)
          78: Pathe Actuelle 36885, Perfect 15066
108451-3   **Marie** vSL[CH] (cl solo)
          78: Pathe Actuelle 36885, Perfect 15066
          (3448-C) **78:** Cameo 8365, Lincoln 3013, Romeo 788, Gracelon
          (Au) 4024
108452-1   **Where Is The Song Of Songs For Me?** [Irving Ber-
                    lin] vSL[HL]
          78: Pathe Actuelle 36885, Perfect 15066
          (3447-A) **78:** Cameo 8364, Lincoln 3012, Romeo 787
                    for 3447-A and 3448-C: Cameos, Lincolns and Romeos as
                    BROADWAY BROADCASTERS
108452-2   **Where Is The Song Of Songs For Me?** vSL[HL]
          78: Pathe Actuelle 36885, Perfect 15066
108453-2   **Wings** [Ballard MacDonald; J. S. Zamecnik]
                    vSL (cl,as solos)
          (3449-B) **78:** Cameo 8372, Lincoln 3020, Romeo 795
108453-3   **Wings** vSL[CH] (cl,as solos)
          78: Pathe Actuelle 36886, Perfect 15067
          as BROADWAY BROADCASTERS

Pathe, New York, N.Y. c. Wednesday, October 31, 1928
SAM LANIN AND HIS ORCHESTRA
Sam Lanin (ldr) Leo McConville, *unknown* (tp) Tom Dorsey (tb) *Jimmy
Dorsey, unknown* (cl,as) *unknown* (cl,ts), (vn) Rube Bloom (p) *unknown*
(bj) *Hank Stern* (bb) *unknown* (d) Scrappy Lambert (vcl)

108467-2   **Marion** (waltz) vSL
          78: Pathe Actuelle 36898, Perfect 15079
          (3437-A) **78:** Cameo 9010, Lincoln 3039, Romeo 814, Starr (Au)
          720
                    *Cameo, Lincoln and Romeo as SAM LANIN AND HIS
                    TROUBADORS, Starr as THE PLAZA BAND*
108468-1   **Lenora** vSL
          78: Pathe Actuelle 36898, Perfect 15079
108469-2   **Sally Of My Dreams** [William Kernell] vSL
          78: Pathe Actuelle 36893, Perfect 15074
          (3439-A) **78:** Cameo 8373, Lincoln 3021, Romeo 796, Angelus
          (Au) 3070, Melotone (Au) 10073

Cameo, New York, N.Y. c. Thursday, November 8, 1928
IRVING MILLS ORCHESTRA
Jimmy McPartland, unknown (tp) *Jack Teagarden* (tb) Jimmy Dorsey
(cl,as) *Larry Binyon* (cl,ts) unknown (p) (bj) (d) *Irving Mills* (vcl)

3454-B   **I Found My Sunshine In The Rain** vIM
          78: Cameo 9020, Lincoln 3049, Romeo 824
                    as THE LUMBERJACKS
3455-A   **Star Dust** [Mitchell Parrish; Hoagy Carmichael] (cl
                    solo)

78: Cameo 9012, Lincoln 3041, Romeo 816
as THE DETROITERS
(108499) Pathe Actuelle 36903, Perfect 15084
as GOODY'S GOOD TIMERS
LP: VJM (E) VLP7
3456- **Oh, Boy! It's A Pleasure** vIM
78: Cameo 9007, Lincoln 3036, Romeo 811
as THE LUMBERJACKS

Some believe that the next Meyer Davis sessions are Dorsey Brothers' dates using Davis' name because of the Dorseys' OKeh contract.

Brunswick, New York, N.Y. c. Monday, November 12, 1928
MEYER DAVIS AND HIS ORCHESTRA
Tex Brewster, *Eddie Wade* (tp) Tom Dorsey (tb) *Jimmy Dorsey or Pete Pumiglio* (cl,as) *Arnold Brilhart* (as) *Babe Russin* (ts) Ernest Charles (p) *unknown* (bj), (bb), (d) *Al Shayne,* Smith Ballew (vcl)

E-28629-B **There's A Rainbow 'Round My Shoulder** [Dave Dreyer, Billy Rose, Al Jolson] v*AS*
78: Duophone (E) D-4016
as MIDNIGHT BROADCASTERS
E-28630-B **Blue Grass** v*AS*
78: Duophone (E) D-4021
as DAVY'S BROADWAY SYNCOPATORS
E-28631-B **Moonlight Madness** v*AS*
78: Duophone (E) D-4040
as DAVY'S BROADWAY SYNCOPATORS
E-28750-B **Halfway To Heaven** [Al Dubin; J. Russell Robinson] vSB (as solo)
78: Duophone (E) D-4027
as DAVE MEYER'S BOSTONIANS
LP: Sunbeam SB MFC23
E-28751-B **Jo-Anne** vSB
78: Duophone (E) D-4034
as THE HOMETOWNERS
E-28752-B **Let's Do It (Let's Fall In Love)** [Cole Porter]
78: Duophone (E) D-4045
as CROSS ROADS INN ORCHESTRA
E-28753-B **Coquette** [Gus Kahn; Johnny Green, Carmen Lombardo] vSB
78: Duophone (E) D-4019
as THE HOMETOWNERS

Brunswick, New York, N.Y. Thursday, November 15, 1928
MEYER DAVIS AND HIS ORCHESTRA
Smith Ballew (vcl)

E-28645-A **Buy, Buy For Baby** [Irving Caesar; Joseph Meyer] vSB (as solo)
78: Duophone (E) D-4044
as CROSS ROADS INN ORCHESTRA (Contd.)

MEYER DAVIS AND HIS ORCHESTRA (Contd.)

    LP: Sunbeam SB MFC23
E-28646-A   **Yascha Michaelofsky's Melody**
    78: Duophone (E) D-4059
E-28647   (unknown)
E-28648-B   **She's Wonderful** vSB
    78: Duophone (E) D-4017
       Pseudonyms for D-4017 and D-4059, if any, are unknown

Pathe, New York, N.Y. Friday, November 16, 1928
GOODY AND HIS GOOD TIMERS
Jimmy McPartland (cnt) Jack Teagarden (tb) **Jimmy Dorsey,** *Benny Goodman* (cl,as) *Bud Freeman* (ts) Matty Malneck (vn) Frank Signorelli (p) Dick Morgan (bj) Harry Goodman (bb) Ben Pollack (d) Irving Mills [as Erwin Magee on Pathe Actuelle or Goody Goodwin on Perfect] (vcl)

108485-1   **'Cause I'm In Love** [Frank Signorelli, Matty Malneck, Irving Mills] vIM (cl solo)
    78: Pathe Actuelle 36924, Perfect 15105
    (3503) **78:** Cameo 9004, Lincoln 3033, Romeo 808
       Cameo, Lincoln and Romeo as DIXIE DAISIES
108486-1   **Diga Diga Doo** [Dorothy Fields; Jimmy McHugh] vIM (as,*cl* solo)
    (3502-A) **78:** Cameo 9004, Lincoln 3033, Romeo 808
       as DIXIE DAISIES
108486-2   **Diga Diga Doo** vIM (as,*cl* solo)
    78: Pathe Actuelle 36902, (F) X6279, Perfect 15083
    (3502-B) **78:** Romeo 808
       Romeo as DIXIE DAISIES
    LP: Epic LN24045, Columbia (E) 33SX1545, Vintage Jazz Music Society (E) 6, Connoisseur (F) 523

Plaza, New York, N.Y. Saturday, November 17, 1928
SAM LANIN AND HIS ORCHESTRA
Sam Lanin (ldr) Leo McConville, *unknown* (tp) Tom Dorsey (tb) **Jimmy Dorsey,** *unknown* (cl,as) *unknown* (cl,ts) Rube Bloom (p) *unknown* (bj), (bb), (d) Jack Parker [as Jack Fuller on Banner or Perry Smith on some Orioles], Alta Cohen (Kahn) [as "Cookie—The California Sunshine Girl"] (vcl)

8321-2   **Everybody Loves You** [Al Dubin; George Little] vJP (as solo)
    78: Banner 6211, Domino 4225, 31011, Regal 8667, Oriole 1397, Apex (C) 8857, Lucky Strike (C) 24363, Microphone (C) 22363, Starr (Au) 10415
       Domino 4225 as SAM LANIN'S TROUBADORS, Domino 31011 and Microphone as THE ARCADIANS, Oriole as ORIOLE DANCE ORCH.
8322-3   **I Must Have That Man** [Dorothy Fields; Jimmy McHugh] vAC (as solo)

78: Banner 6214, 6298, Domino 4225, Oriole 1399, Jewel
5446, Regal 8667
> *Domino as SAM LANIN AND HIS TROUBADORS, Jewel as*
> *JEWEL DANCE ORCH., Oriole as ORIOLE DANCE ORCH.*
> *[or] MAJESTIC DANCE ORCH.*

8323-3   **Me And The Man In The Moon** [Edgar Leslie;
              James V. Monaco] vJP [PS on Oriole]
78: Banner 6213, Domino 4228, 31040, Regal 8671, Oriole
1394, Apex (C) 8883, Lucky Strike (C) 24385, Microphone (C)
22385, Imperial (E) 2023, Kristall (G) 4019, Conquerer 7209
> *Conquerer as JOHN VINCENT'S CALIFORNIANS, Domino*
> *31040 as THE ARCADIANS, Imperial as SAM LANIN'S*
> *DANCE ORCH., Oriole as ORIOLE DANCE ORCH.*

Brunswick, New York, N.Y. c. Saturday, November 17, 1928
MEYER DAVIS AND HIS ORCHESTRA
Tex Brewster, *unknown* (tp) Tom Dorsey (tb) **Jimmy Dorsey** (cl,as)
Arnold Brilhart (as) *Babe Russin* (ts) *unknown* (p),(bj),(bb),(d) Scrappy
Lambert (vcl)

E-28656-B   **To Know You Is To Love You** [Buddy De Sylva,
              Lew Brown; Ray Henderson] *vSL*
78: Duophone (E) D-4053
E-28657-B   **Do You? That's All I Want To Know** [Jack Yellen,
              Henry Tobias, Harry Tobias; Benee Russell] vSL
              (as solo)
78: Duophone (E) D-4046
> *as THE MIDNIGHT BROADCASTERS*
LP: Sunbeam MFC23
E-28658   (unknown)
E-28659-B   **You're The Cream In My Coffee** [Buddy De Sylva,
              Lew Brown; Ray Henderson] *vSL*
78: Duophone (E) D-4053

OKeh, New York, N.Y. Wednesday, November 21, 1928
DORSEY BROTHERS AND THEIR ORCHESTRA
Tom Dorsey (tb,ldr) Leo McConville, Fuzzy Farrar, Phil Napoleon (tp)
Glenn Miller (tb,arr) **Jimmy Dorsey** (cl,as) Arnold Brilhart (cl,as,f)
Herbert Spencer (ts) 3 *unknown* (vn) Arthur Schutt (p) Tony Colucci
(bj) Eddie Lang (g) Hank Stern (bb) Stan King (d) Smith Ballew (vcl)

W 401385-B   **Sally Of My Dreams** [William Kernell] vSB&Chorus
              (as solo)
78: OKeh 41151, Parlophone (E) R-316, (Au) A-2670, (G) A-
4559, (E) E-4595, (F) 22378, Odeon (F) 165544, (F) A-221122,
(F) 04087, (Au) 933270, Ariel (E) 4360
> *Ariel as ARIEL DANCE ORCHESTRA, Parlophone E-4595*
> *as RIVER CLUB ORCHESTRA*
LP: The Old Masters 14, World Records (E) SHB67, (Au) R-
09520, Columbia Special Products P-16355
TC: World Records (E) CSHB67
CD: Jazz Oracle (C) BDW (E) 8004 (Contd.)

DORSEY BROTHERS AND THEIR ORCHESTRA (Contd.)

W 401386-A   **(I Got A Woman Crazy For Me) She's Funny That Way** [Neil Moret; Richard Whiting] vSB (as solo)
    78: OKeh 41158, Parlophone (E) R-331, (Au) A-2720, Odeon (G) 193286, (F) 165544, 165579, (Sp) 182478, 189226
    Odeon 193286 as DAVEY BROTHERS' ORCHESTRA
    LP: The Old Masters 14, World Records (E) SHB67, (Au) R-09520, Columbia Special Products P-16355
    TC: World Records (E) CSHB67
    CD: Jazz Oracle (C) BDW (E) 8004
W 401386-B   **(I Got A Woman Crazy For Me) She's Funny That Way** vSB (as solo)
    78: (unissued test pressing)
    LP: Broadway BR112
W 401387-B   **Cross Roads** [Raymond W. Klages, David Mendoza; Harry Akst] vSB (as solo)
    78: OKeh 41151, Parlophone (Au) A-2682, (G) A-4559, Odeon (Au) 193270, (G) A-189225, (F) 04089
    LP: The Old Masters 14, World Records (E) SHB67, (Au) R-09520, Columbia Special Products P-16355
    TC: World Records (E) CSHB67
    CD: Jazz Oracle (C) BDW (E) 8004

Edison, New York, N.Y. Wednesday, November 28, 1928
CALIFORNIA RAMBLERS
Ed Kirkeby (ldr) Frank Cush, Mickey Bloom (tp) Carl Loeffler (tb) **Jimmy Dorsey,** Harold Marcus (cl,as) Sam Ruby (ts) Lawrence Kosky (vn) Chauncey Gray (p) Tommy Felline (g) Ward Lay (bb) Stan King (d) Trio [Ed Kirkeby, Cyril Potts, Tom Muir] (vcl)

18907-A,B,C   **Happy Days And Lonely Nights** vTrio (unissued)
18908-A,B,C   **I Loved You Then As I Love You Now** [Ballard MacDonald; Harry Akst, David Mendoza] vTrio
    78: Edison 52515
    (N-602-A,B) (unissued)

Brunswick, New York, N.Y. c. November 28-30, 1928 (three sessions?)
MEYER DAVIS AND HIS ORCHESTRA
Tom Dorsey (tb,ldr) Leo McConville, *Tex Brewster [or] Fuzzy Farrar,* Phil Napoleon (tp) Glenn Miller (tb,arr) **Jimmy Dorsey** (cl,as) Arnold Brilhart (cl,as,f) Herbert Spencer (ts) *Joe Venuti,* 2 *unknown* (vn) Arthur Schutt (p) Tony Colucci (bj) Eddie Lang (g) Hank Stern (bb) Stan King (d) *Al Shayne,* Scrappy Lambert (vcl)

E-28673-A   **Dream House** [Earl Foxe; Victor Schertzinger] v*AS*
    78: Duophone (E) D-4023
        as TEX BREWSTER'S ORCHESTRA
E-28674   (unknown)
E-28675-B   **My Blue Heaven** [George Whiting; Walter Donaldson] v*AS* (cl solo)
    78: Duophone (E) D-4022

          as TIP TOP CLUB ORCHESTRA
   LP: Sunbeam MFC23
E-28676   (unknown)
E-28677-B   **Sunny Skies** [Jack Meskill, Raymond W. Klages; Vincent Rose] v*AS*
   78: Duophone (E) D-4049
          as TEX BREWSTER'S ORCHESTRA
   LP: Sunbeam MFC23
E-28678-A   **Down Where The Sun Goes Down** [Verne Buck; Isham Jones] vSL (as solo)
   78: Duophone (E) D-4019
          as TIP TOP CLUB ORCHESTRA
   LP: Sunbeam MFC23, Broadway BR113
E-28679-A,B   **Ho-Ho-Hogan** vSL
   78: Duophone (E) D-4041
          as DAVY'S BROADWAY SYNCOPATORS
E-28680-A   **Tiger Rag** [Harry De Costa; Edwin Edwards, Nick LaRocca,Tony Spargo,Larry Shields] (cl,as,cl solos)
   78: Duophone (E) D-4034
          as THE HOMETOWNERS
   LP: Sunbeam MFC23, The Old Masters 15
   CD: Jazz Greats (E) 036
E-28681-A,B   **I Ain't Got Nobody** [Roger Graham, Dave Peyton; Spencer Williams] vSL (as solos)
   78: Duophone (E) D-4020
          as THE MIDNIGHT BROADCASTERS
   LP: Sunbeam MFC23
E-28682-A   **Louisiana** [Bob Schafer, Andy Razaf; J. J. Johnson] (as solo)
   78: Duophone (E) D-4030
          as CROSS ROADS INN ORCHESTRA
   LP: Sunbeam MFC23, Broadway BR112
E-28683-B   **Mississippi Mud** [James Cavanaugh, Harry Barris] vSL
   78: Duophone (E) D-4020
          as THE HOMETOWNERS
   LP: Sunbeam MFC23
   E-28680 through E-28683 also on **TC:** Neovox (E) 902

Next is a session that was inadvertently omitted from the author's book on Tommy Dorsey.

Okeh, New York, N.Y. Monday, December 3, 1928
HARRY RING'S SOUTHERN MELODY ARTISTS
Tommy Gott, Phil Napoleon (tp) Tom Dorsey (tb) Arnold Brilhart, **Jimmy Dorsey** (as) Alfie Evans (ts) Sid Harris, Joe LaFaro (vn) Arthur Schutt (p) Eddie Lang (g) Hank Stern (bb) Stan King (d)

401422-A   **You Can't Take My Mem'ries From Me**
   78: OKeh 45285
401423-A   **Tennessee (I'm Coming Home)**
   78: OKeh 45285

OKeh, New York, N.Y. Wednesday, December 5, 1928
SAM LANIN AND HIS FAMOUS PLAYERS
Sam Lanin (ldr) Leo McConville, *unknown* (tp) Tom Dorsey (tb) *Jimmy Dorsey, unknown* (cl,as) *unknown* (cl,ts) Rube Bloom (p) *unknown* (bj) *Hank Stern* (bb) *unknown* (d) Irving Kaufman (vcl)

W 401246-B   **Sweethearts On Parade** [Charles Newman; Carmen Lombardo] vIK
    78: OKeh 41159, Parlophone (E) R-296, (Au) A-2763, (G) B-12734, Odeon (G) A-189211
W 401247-C   **Everybody Loves You** [Al Dubin; George Little] vIK
    78: OKeh 41159, Parlophone (Au) A-2700, (J) E-5080, Odeon (G) A-189211, (It) B-12734
W 401248-A   **Dreaming Of The Day** vIK
    78: OKeh 41162, Parlophone (Au) A-2700, Odeon (G) A189221
    OKeh and Odeon as NEW YORK SYNCOPATORS

Pathe, New York, N.Y. c. Monday, December 10, 1928
SAM LANIN AND HIS ORCHESTRA
Sam Lanin (ldr) Leo McConville, *unknown* (tp) Tom Dorsey (tb) **Jimmy Dorsey,** *unknown* (cl,as) *unknown* (cl,ts) Rube Bloom (p) *unknown* (bj) *Hank Stern* (bb) *unknown* (d) Scrappy Lambert [as Chester Hale, Frank Keyes or Harold Lang] (vcl)

108521-2   **(I've Got A Woman Crazy For Me) She's Funny That Way** [Neil Moret; Richard Whiting] vSL[CH]
    78: Pathe Actuelle 36910, Perfect 15091
3517-A   **(I've Got A Woman Crazy For Me) She's Funny That Way** vSL
    78: Cameo 9023, Lincoln 3052, Romeo 827, Dominion (E) A-122, Angelus (Au) 3095, Plaza (Au) 3095
        Dominion as SAM LANIN AND HIS TROUBADORS, Angelus and Plaza as EMIL SEIDEL AND HIS ORCHESTRA
3517-C   **(I've Got A Woman Crazy For Me) She's Funny That Way** vSL
    78: Cameo 9023, Lincoln 3052, Romeo 827
108522-2   **I'll Get By (As Long As I Have You)** [Roy Turk; Fred Ahlert] vSL[FK]
    78: Pathe Actuelle 36909, Perfect 15090
    (3518-B) **78:** Cameo 9022, Lincoln 3051, Romeo 826
108523-2   **My Mother's Eyes** [L. Wolfe Gilbert; Abel Baer] vSL[FK]
    78: Pathe Actuelle 36914, Perfect 15095
    as FRANK KEYES AND HIS ORCHESTRA
3519-A   **My Mother's Eyes** vSL[HL]
    78: Cameo 9046, Lincoln 3075, Romeo 850, Angelus (Au) 3086, Starr (Au) 941
    Angelus and Starr as EMIL SEIDEL AND HIS ORCH.
3519-C   **My Mother's Eyes** vSL[HL]
    78: Cameo 9046, Lincoln 3075, Romeo 850
    All Cameos, Lincolns and Romeos from this session as BROADWAY BROADCASTERS

Victor, New York, N.Y. Tuesday, December 11, 1928
NEW ORLEANS BLACK BIRDS
Phil Napoleon (tp) Miff Mole (tb) **Jimmy Dorsey** (cl,as) Matty Malneck
(vn) Frank Signorelli (p) Dick McDonough (g) Joe Tarto (bb) Ted
Napoleon (d)

49248-1   **Red Head** [Germain, Lilliard] (cl solo)
    78: Victor 38027
49248-2   **Red Head** (cl solo)
    78: Victor 38027, Bluebird B-6611
    LP: RCA (EC) NL-89606, Arcadia (C) 2013
49249-2   **Playing The Blues** [Matt Malneck, Frank Signarelli,
                 Irving Mills] (as solo)
    78: Victor 38027
    LP: Arcadia (C) 2013
49249-3   **Playing The Blues** (as solo)
    78: Victor 38027, Bluebird B-7881
    LP: RCA (EC) NL-89606

OKeh, New York, N.Y. Wednesday, December 12, 1928
JOE VENUTI'S BLUE FOUR
Jimmy Dorsey (cnt,bar) Joe Venuti (vn) Rube Bloom (p,vcl) Eddie
Lang (g) Paul Graselli (d)

401449-A   **My Honey's Lovin' Arms** [Herman Ruby; Joseph
                 Meyer] vRB (cnt solo)
    78: OKeh 41251, Odeon 165763, 193327
    LP: The Old Masters 8, Swaggie (Au) 817
401450-A   **Goin' Home** [William A. Fisher] vRB (bar solo)
    78: OKeh 41251, Vocalion 3043, Odeon 165763, 193327
    LP: The Old Masters 8, Swaggie (Au) 817
    Both sides also on **CD:** JSP (E) CD310

OKeh, New York, N.Y. Thursday, December 13, 1928
THE GOOFUS FIVE AND THEIR ORCHESTRA
Ed Kirkeby (ldr,vcl) Angie Rattiner, Al King (tp) Ted Raph (tb) **Jimmy
Dorsey** (cl,as) Sam Ruby (as) Harold Marcus (ts) Lawrence Kosky (vn)
Chauncey Gray (p) Tommy Felline (g) Ward Lay (sb) Stan King (d)
Trio [Cyril Potts, Tom Muir, Kirkeby] (vcl)

W 401451-A   **(I Love You) Sweetheart Of All My Dreams** [Art
                 Fitch, Bert Lowe] vTrio (as solo)
    78: OKeh 41169, Odeon A-189227, A-189252, (Arg) 193281,
    Parlophone (E) R-315, (G) A-4574, B-12749
W 401452-B   **My Troubles Are Over** [Edgar Leslie; James V.
                 Monaco] vTrio
    78: Parlophone (E) R-364
W 401453-A   **That's How I Feel About You, Sweetheart** vTrio
    78: OKeh 41169, Odeon A-189227, A-189252, (Arg) 193281,
    Parlophone (E) R-364, (G) A-4574, B-12749
                 *All Parlophones this session as ED KIRKEBY WALLACE
                 AND HIS GOOFUS ORCHESTRA*

Edison, New York, N.Y. c. Wednesday, December 19, 1928
SEVEN BLUE BABIES
Ed Kirkeby (ldr) Angie Rattiner (tp) Tom Dorsey (tb) **Jimmy Dorsey**
(cl,as) Chauncey Gray (p) Tommy Felline (bj) Stan King (d) Jack
Kaufman (vcl)

18954(A,B,C)   **I Love To Bumpity Bump On A Bumpy Road
                  With You** vJK (unissued)
N-645 (A,B)   **I Love To Bumpity Bump On A Bumpy Road
                  With You** vJK (unissued cylinder)
18955-A,B,C   **I'm Wild About Horns On Automobiles (That Go
                  "Ta-Ta-Ta-Ta")** [Clarence Gaskill] vJK
      78: Edison 52508
N-646 (A,B)   **I'm Wild About Horns On Automobiles (That Go
                  "Ta-Ta-Ta-Ta")** vJK (unissued cylinder)

Plaza, New York, N.Y. Wednesday, December 26, 1928
SAM LANIN AND HIS ORCHESTRA
Sam Lanin (ldr) *Phil Napoleon, Leo McConville* (tp) Tom Dorsey (tb)
Jimmy Dorsey, Andy Sanella (cl,as) *Merle Johnston* (cl,ts) Arthur
Schutt (p) *Tony Colucci* (bj) Jimmy Mullen (bb) *Stan King* (d) Irving
Kaufman [as George Beaver], Arthur Fields (vcl)

8421-1,2,3   **I'm Bringing A Red, Red Rose** [Gus Kahn; Walter
                  Donaldson] vAF
      78: Banner 6273, Domino 4263, 31047, Conquerer 7252, Regal
      8705, Apex (C) 8889, Broadway 1241, Starr (Au) 10435 Imperial
      (E) 2144, Edison Bell Winner (E) 4899, 4961, Embassy (Au) 8009
            *Conquerer as SAM LANIN'S DANCE ORCH., Broadway as
            HARRY'S MELODY MEN, Imperial as SAM LANIN AND
            HIS DANCE ORCH., Edison Bell Winner as MURRAY'S
            MELODY MAKERS, Embassy as CHICAGO RED HEADS*
8422-1   **Happy Days And Lonely Nights** [Billy Rose; Fred
                  Fisher] vIK (as solo)
      78: Banner 6261, Regal 8701, Domino 4256, (C) 31022,
      Broadway 1238
            *Broadway as EARL RANDOLPH'S ORCHESTRA, Domino
            31022 as THE ARCADIANS*
      LP: Jazz Studies (E) JS1
8422-2   **Happy Days And Lonely Nights** vIK (as solo)
      78: Apex (C) 8867, Starr (Au) 10420, Microphone (C) 22369
8422-3   **Happy Days And Lonely Nights** vIK (as solo)
      78: Banner 6261, Domino 4256, Oriole 1449, Regal 8701,
      Broadway 1238, Challenge 980
            *Oriole as TED WALLACE AND HIS ORCHESTRA, Regal as
            THE ROUNDERS, Broadway as EARL RANDOLPH'S OR-
            CHESTRA*
8423-1   **If You Want The Rainbow (You Must Have The
                  Rain)** [Billy Rose, Mort Dixon; Oscar Levant] vIK
      78: Banner 6262, Regal 8701, Oriole 1446, Broadway 1243
            *Broadway as THE BADGERS, Oriole as THE UNIVERSITY
            BOYS [or] BOB GREEN'S DANCE ORCHESTRA*

8423-3   **If You Want The Rainbow (You Must Have The Rain)** vIK
        78: Banner 6262, Domino 4256, (C) 31033, Broadway 1243, Regal 8701, Apex (C) 8876
        Banner as CAMPUS BOYS [or] THE BADGERS

Paving the way for the first solo, non-Victor, non-Paul Whiteman recording by Bing Crosby since Crosby joined the Whiteman organization was a contract recently signed by Whiteman switching the band from Victor to Columbia, which also permitted Whiteman's featured performers to record with other organizations.

The Whiteman switch was considered so important in the music world that a newsreel company captured a small portion of the first Whiteman Columbia recording session. Released on a videotape (Yazoo 514) it provides the only sample of Bix Beiderbecke performing in a sound film, though not as a soloist.

Columbia, New York, N.Y. Friday, December 28, 1928
IPANA TROUBADORS
Sam Lanin (ldr) Leo McConville, Mannie Klein (tp) Tom Dorsey (cnt) *Chuck Campbell* (tb) **Jimmy Dorsey**, Merle Johnston (cl,as) Arnold Brilhart (cl,ts) 2 *unknown* (vn) Arthur Schutt (p) *John Cali* (bj) Joe Tarto (bb,arr) Vic Berton (d) Bing Crosby (vcl)

W 147545-3   **I'll Get By (As Long As I Have You)** [Roy Turk; Fred Ahlert] vBC arrJT (as solo)
        78: Columbia 1694-D, (E) 5391, (Au) 01647
        LP: Epic EE22013/4, Columbia P4-13153, Jonzo (E) JZ-7
        TC: Radio Yesteryear Stack 26
        CD: Columbia Special Products A2-201
W 147546-3   **Rose Of Mandalay** [Ted Koehler; Frank Magine] vBC arrJT
        78: Columbia 1694-D, (E) 5541, 35093, Pelican 104
        LP: Sunbeam SB P502, Columbia C4X 44429, Jonzo (E) JZ-7
        TC: Memory Lane 2042

Harmony, New York, N.Y. Monday, December 31, 1928
BUDDY GOLDEN AND HIS MICHIGAN WOLVERINES
Ben Selvin (ldr) *Mannie Klein, unknown* (tp) Tom Dorsey (tb) *Jimmy Dorsey, Merle Johnston [or] Arnold Brilhart* (cl,as) *unknown* (cl,ts) *Arthur Schutt* (p) *John Cali* (bj) *Hank Stern [or] Joe Tarto* (bb) *Vic Berton* (d) Irving Kaufman (vcl)

147738-(1,2,3)   **Button Up Your Overcoat** vIK (unissued)
147739-(1,2,3)   **I Want To Be Bad** vIK (unissued)

Buildup to an Awful Letdown
(1929)

And still things got better and better. The prosperity of the country had never been higher. There appeared to be no end to the growth of the nation's economy. It seemed like every bellhop and cab driver you met was "in the market, on margin of course," and the New York music industry was along for the ride .

For Jimmy and Tommy, the phonograph records, radio broadcasts, Broadway musicals and even the fledgling sound-movie studios on Long Island were still bringing what seemed like nonstop engagements.

OKeh, New York, N.Y. Tuesday, January 8, 1929
EMMETT MILLER'S GEORGIA CRACKERS
Mannie Klein (tp) Tom Dorsey (tb) **Jimmy Dorsey** (cl,as) Arthur Schutt (p) Eddie Lang (g) Stan King (d) Emmett Miller, Charles Chiles (vcl)

W 401509-A   **I Ain't Gonna Give Nobody None of This Jelly Roll**
        [Spencer Williams; Clarence Williams] vEM
    78: OKeh 41280, Parlophone (E) R-2163, Odeon 165812
    CD: Columbia CK 66999
W 401510-B   **(I Got A Woman Crazy For Me) She's Funny That Way** [Neil Moret; Richard Whiting] vEM
    78: OKeh 41182
    LP: The Old Masters 1
    CD: Columbia CK 66999
W 401511-C   **You Lose** [Emmett Miller, Charles Chiles] vEM&CC
    78: OKeh 41205, Parlophone (E) R-1155
    CD: Columbia CK 66999

Pathe, New York, N.Y. Wednesday, January 9, 1929
SAM LANIN AND HIS ORCHESTRA
Sam Lanin (ldr) Phil Napoleon, *unknown* (tp) Tom Dorsey (tb) **Jimmy Dorsey,** Andy Sanella (cl,as) *Merle Johnston* (cl,ts) Arthur Schutt (p) *Tony Colucci* (bj) Jimmy Mullen (bb) *Stan King* (d) Scrappy Lambert [as James Denton on some] (vcl)

108581-2   **I'd Rather Be Blue Over You (Than Happy With Somebody Else)** [Billy Rose; Fred Fisher] vSL
    78: Pathe Actuelle 36926, Perfect 15107
        as LEVEE LOUNGERS
    (3574-A) **78:** Cameo 9045, Lincoln 3074, Romeo 849
        Cameo as VINCENT RICHARDS AND HIS ORCH.
108582-3   **If I Had You** [Jimmy Campbell, Reg Connelly, Ted Shapiro] vSL

78: Pathe Actuelle 36926, Perfect 15107, Angelus (Au) 3100
(3610-B) **78:** Cameo 9043, Lincoln 3072, Romeo 847, Regent
(Au) 1077, Starr (Au) 744
> *Cameo, Romeo, Lincoln as BROADWAY BROADCASTERS,*
> *Regent as REGENT DANCE ORCHESTRA, Angelus as SAM*
> *LANNIN [sic] AND HIS ORCHESTRA, Starr as VAN CARL-*
> *SON AND HIS HALF-MOON ORCHESTRA*

108583-3   **(So Far, So Good, So Good, So Far) Whatcha Gonna Do, Do Now?** vSL[JD]
    78: Pathe Actuelle 36927, Perfect 15108
(3575-A) **78:** Cameo 9043, Lincoln 3072, Romeo 847
> *Cameo and Lincoln as BROADWAY BROADCASTERS*

108584-3   **That's Her Now!** vSL[JD]
    78: Pathe Actuelle 36927, Perfect 15108
> *as DEEP RIVER ORCHESTRA*

(3806-) **78:** Cameo 9146, Lincoln 3173, Romeo 948

Brunswick, New York, N.Y. Thursday, January 10, 1929
THE WHOOPEE MAKERS
Bill Moore, Phil Hart (tp) Paul Weigan (tb) Jack Pettis (cl,as,c-mel)
Jimmy Dorsey (cl,as) Matty Malneck (vn) Al Goering (p) Clay Bryson
(bj) Merrill Kline (bb) Dillon Ober (d)

E-28948   **Rush Inn Blues**
    78: Vocalion 15769
E-28949   **Freshman Hop** [Al Goering, Jack Pettis, Irving Mills]
    78: Vocalion 15769
E-28950   **I've Never Been Loved By Anyone Like You**
    78: Vocalion 15768
    All three sides also on **LP:** Harrison LP-L

Columbia, New York, N.Y. Saturday, January 12, 1929
BUDDY GOLDEN AND HIS MICHIGAN WOLVERINES
Sam Lanin (ldr) *Leo McConville, Mannie Klein* (tp) Tom Dorsey (tb)
Jimmy Dorsey, *Merle Johnston* (cl,as) *unknown* (cl,ts), (vn) Arthur
Schutt (p) *John Cali* (bj) *Hank Stern [or] Joe Tarto* (bb) Vic Berton (d)
Irving Kaufman [as Marvin Young where shown] (vcl)

147776 3   **Button Up Your Overcoat** [Buddy De Sylva, Lew
Brown; Ray Henderson] vIK
    78: Harmony 855-H, Follow-Thru 1011-P, Velvet Tone 1855-V,
Puritone 1061
147777-3   **My Lucky Star** [Buddy De Sylva, Lew Brown; Ray
Henderson] vIK
    78: Harmony 855-H, Follow-Thru 1012-P, Velvet Tone 1854-V
> *as ARTHUR ROSS AND HIS WESTERNERS*

147778-2   **I Want To Be Bad** [Buddy De Sylva, Lew Brown;
Ray Henderson] vIK[MY]
    78: Harmony 854-H, Follow-Thru 1011-P, Velvet Tone 1855-V,
Puritone 1061
> *Follow-Thru sides were made for lobby sales at the musical*
> *comedy of the same name, which included these three songs.*

Columbia, New York, N.Y. Thursday, January 17, 1929
FRED RICH AND HIS ORCHESTRA
Fred Rich (p,ldr) Leo McConville (tp) Tom Dorsey (tb,tp) **Jimmy Dorsey,** *unknown* (cl,as) *unknown* (ts) 2 *unknown* (vn) Carl Kress (g) Joe Tarto (bb,sb) *unknown* (d) Billy Murray (vcl)

W 147785-3   **As Long As We're In Love** [Dorothy Fields; Jimmy McHugh] vBM (cl solo)
        78: Columbia 1713-D
W 147786-3   **Let's Sit And Talk About You** [Dorothy Fields; Jimmy McHugh] vBM (as solo)
        78: Columbia 1713-D

Pathe, New York, N.Y. c. Friday, January 18, 1929
SAM LANIN AND HIS ORCHESTRA
Sam Lanin (ldr) Phil Napoleon, *unknown* (tp) Tom Dorsey (tb) **Jimmy Dorsey,** Andy Sanella (cl,as) *Merle Johnston* (cl,ts) Arthur Schutt (p) *Tony Colucci* (bj) Jimmy Mullen (bb) *Stan King* (d) Irving Kaufman [as Jack Manning where shown] (vcl)

108605-1   **I'm Bringing A Red, Red Rose** [Gus Kahn; Walter Donaldson] vIK
        78: Pathe Actuelle 36938, Perfect 15119
            as DEEP RIVER ORCHESTRA
        (3595-A) **78:** Cameo 9055, Lincoln 3084, Romeo 859, Angelus (Au) 3096
            Angelus as JARDIN ROYAL ORCHESTRA
108614-2   **Dream Train** [Charles Newman; Billy Baskette] vIK[JM]
        78: Pathe Actuelle 36932, Perfect 15113
        (3596-A) **78:** Cameo 9056, Lincoln 3085, Romeo 860, Angelus (Au) 3170
            Cameo, Romeo and Lincoln as BROADWAY BROADCAST-ERS, Angelus as THE RED MILL ORCHESTRA (vcl IK)
108615-1   **The Waltz I Can't Forget** vIK
        78: Pathe Actuelle 36934, Perfect 15115
            as LOUIS SHERRY'S DANCE ORCHESTRA
        (*3597*) **78:** Cameo 9107, Lincoln 3134, Romeo 909
            as SOCIETY NIGHT CLUB ORCHESTRA (vcl JM)

OKeh, New York, N.Y. Saturday, January 19, 1929
EMMETT MILLER'S GEORGIA CRACKERS
Mannie Klein [or] Leo McConville (tp) Tom Dorsey (tb) **Jimmy Dorsey** (cl,as) Arthur Schutt (p) Eddie Lang (g) Stan King (d) Joe Tarto (sb) Emmett Miller (vcl)

W 401546-B   **Right Or Wrong** [Benny Davis, Billy Rose; Harry Akst] vEM
        78: OKeh 41280, Odeon (F) 165812
        CD: Columbia CK 66999
W 401547-C   **That's The Good Old Sunny South** [Jack Yellen; Milton Ager] vEM (cl solo)

78: OKeh 41438
LP: The Old Masters 1
CD: Columbia CK 66999
W 401548-C   You're The Cream In My Coffee [Buddy De Sylva,
                Lew Brown; Ray Henderson] vEM (cl solo)
     78: OKeh 41182
     LP: The Old Masters 1
     CD: Columbia CK 66999

Pathe, New York, N.Y. c. Monday, January 21, 1929
SAM LANIN AND HIS ORCHESTRA
Sam Lanin (ldr) Phil Napoleon, Bob Effros (tp) Miff Mole (tb) **Jimmy Dorsey,** Andy Sanella (cl,as) Merle Johnston (cl,ts) Arthur Schutt (p) Tony Colucci (bj) Jimmy Mullen (bb) *Stan King* (d) Irving Kaufman [as George Beaver on Banner, Ray Winn on Broadway] (vcl)

8479-1,2,3   **Good Little, Bad Little You** [Bud Green; Sam H.
                Stept] vIK
     78: Banner 6298, Domino 4272, (C) 31091, 181087, Oriole
     1489, Regal 8721, Apex (C) 8939, Crown (C) 81087
                Oriole as TED WHITE'S COLLEGIANS, Domino 31091 as
                THE ARCADIANS, 181087 as PIERROT SYNCOPATORS
8480-2   **If I Had You** [Jimmy Campbell, Reg Connelly, Ted
                Shapiro] vIK
     78: Broadway 1253, Domino 4271, Regal 8718, Oriole 1477,
     Jewel 5511, Conquerer 7245, Apex (C) 8891, Edison Bell
     Winner (E) 4928
                Broadway as THE BADGERS, Jewel as TED WHITE'S
                COLLEGIANS, Conquerer as JOHN VINCENT'S CALI-
                FORNIANS, Edison Bell Winner as GAIETY DANCE BAND
     (2029-2) **78:** Banner 6287
8481-1,3   **Who Wouldn't Be Jealous Of You?** [Haven Gilles-
                pie; Larry Shay] vIK
     78: Banner 6289, Domino 4270, 31048, Regal 8719, Broadway
     1250, Oriole 1475, Conquerer 7246, Apex (C) 8891, Imperial
     (E) 2064
                Broadway as THE BADGERS, Oriole as TED WHITE'S
                COLLEGIANS, Conquerer as MONTMARTE ORCH.

Victor, New York, N.Y. Tuesday, January 22, 1929
NAT SHILKRET ORCHESTRA
Nat Shilkret (ldr) Mike Mosiello, Del Staigers (tp) Tom Dorsey (tb) **Jimmy Dorsey,** Andy Sanella (cl,as) Max Farley (cl,ts,fl) Lou Raderman (vn) Milt Rettenberg (p) Carl Kress (g) *Joe Tarto* (bb) Joe Green (d) Belle Mann, Johnny Marvin (vcl)

BVE 49671-2   **You Wouldn't Fool Me, Would You?** [Buddy De
                Sylva, Lew Brown; Ray Henderson] vJM
     78: Victor 21859, His Master's Voice (Au) EA-670
BVE 49672-2   **I Want To Be Bad** [Buddy De Sylva, Lew Brown;
                Ray Henderson] vBM (cl solo)
     78: Victor 21859, His Master's Voice (Au) EA-670

Columbia, New York, N.Y. Wednesday, January 23, 1929
IPANA TROUBADORS
Sam Lanin (ldr) Leo McConville, Mannie Klein (tp) *Tom Dorsey [or] Chuck Campbell* (tb) **Jimmy Dorsey,** Merle Johnston (cl,as) Arnold Brilhart (as,ts) Arthur Schutt (p) John Cali (bj) Joe Tarto (bb) Vic Berton (d) Irving Kaufman (vcl)

W 147886-3   **(It's) A Precious Little Thing Called Love** [Lou Davis; J. Fred Coots] vIK (as solo)
        78: Columbia 1717-D, (E) 5391, (Au) 01468
W 147887-3   **Mississippi (Here I Am)** [Arthur Sizemore; Bernie Grossman] vIK
        78: Columbia 1717-D

OKeh, New York, N.Y. Friday, January 25, 1929
SAM LANIN AND HIS FAMOUS PLAYERS
Sam Lanin (ldr) Phil Napoleon, Bob Effros (tp) Tom Dorsey (tb) **Jimmy Dorsey,** Andy Sanella (cl,as) *Merle Johnston* (cl,ts) Arthur Schutt (p) *Tony Colucci* (bj) Jimmy Mullen (bb) *Stan King* (d) Bing Crosby (vcl)

W 401555-B   **I'm Crazy Over You** [Al Lewis; Al Sherman] vBC
        78: OKeh 41228, Odeon ONY 41228, (F) 193314, Parlophone (E) E6148, (Au) A2747
                Odeon ONY 41228 as EDDIE GORDON'S ORCHESTRA, Parlophone E6148 as WILL PERRY'S ORCHESTRA
        LP: World Records (E) SH424, Columbia 35093, C4X 44429, Jonzo (E) JZ-7
        CD: Affinity (E) AFS 1021-2
W 401556-B   **Susianna** [Spencer Williams] vBC (cl,as solos)
        78: OKeh 41228, Odeon ONY 41228, (G) A-221112, (It) O-10094, Parlophone (E) R339, (Au) A2790, Ariel (E) Z-4364
                Odeon ONY 41228 as EDDIE GORDON'S ORCHESTRA, Ariel as ARIEL DANCE ORCHESTRA
        LP: Epic E2E-202, World Records (E) SH424, Columbia P4 13153, Parlophone (E) PMC7006, Jonzo (E) JZ-7
        CD: Timeless (H) 004, Affinity (E) AFS 1021-2, Columbia Special Products A2-201
W 401557-C   **If I Had You** [Jimmy Campbell, Reg Connelly, Ted Shapiro] vBC (cl solo)
        78: OKeh 41188, Parlophone (E) E6148, (Au) A2737, Odeon (G) A189234
                Parlophone E6148 as WILL PERRY'S ORCHESTRA
        LP: Epic E2E-202, Parlophone (E) PMC7006, Columbia P4 13153, World Records (E) SH424, Jonzo (E) JZ-7
        TC: Radio Yesteryear Stack 26
        CD: Columbia Special Products A2-201, Affinity (E) AFS 1021-2

OKeh, New York, N.Y. Saturday, January 26, 1929
DORSEY BROTHERS AND THEIR ORCHESTRA
Tom Dorsey (tp,tb,ldr) Leo McConville, Fuzzy Farrar, Phil Napoleon (tp) Glenn Miller (tb,arr) **Jimmy Dorsey** (cl,as) Arnold Brilhart (cl,as,fl) Herbert Spencer (ts) *unknown* (vn) Arthur Schutt (p) Eddie

Lang (g) Hank Stern (bb) Stan King (d) Bing Crosby (vcl)

W 401560-B   **The Spell Of The Blues** [Harry Ruby, Dave Dryer; Arthur Johnston] vBC arrGM (cl solo)
    78: OKeh 41181, Parlophone (E) R-385, (Au) A-2738, Odeon (Arg) 193287, A-189235, (F) A-221169
    LP: Epic E2E 201, E2E 202, World Records (E) SHB67, (Au) R-09520, Columbia Special Products P5-16354, P4-13153, Parlophone (E) PMC 7006, CBS CE2 E201, (E) M66210, (Au) S2BP 234579, Jonzo (E) JZ-7
    TC: World Records (E) CSHB67, Nostalgia (E) MRT40045
    CD: Columbia Special Products A2 201, Timeless (H) 004, Affinity (E) AFS 1021-2, Jazz Oracle (C) BDW 8005
W 401561-B   **Let's Do It (Let's Fall In Love)** [Cole Porter] arrGM vBC (cl,as solos)
    78: OKeh 41181, Parlophone (E) R-331, Odeon (Arg) 193287, A-189235
    LP: Epic E2E 201, E2E 202, World Records (E) SHB67, (Au) R-09520, Columbia Special Products P5-16354, P4-13153, Parlophone (E) PMC 7006, CBS CE2E 201, (E) M66210, (Au) S2BP 234579, Jonzo (E) JZ-7, ASV Living Era (E) AJA 5004
    TC: Columbia/Legacy 3CT52862, World Records (E) CSHB67, Nostalgia (E) MRT40045, ASV Living Era (E) ZC AJA 5004, Old Bean (E) COLD 15, Radio Yesteryear Stack 26
    CD: Columbia Special Products A2 201, Columbia/Legacy 3CK52862, CK64642, Timeless (H) 004, Old Bean (E) DOLD 15, Affinity (E) AFS 1021-2, West End (E) WEC 304, Jazz Oracle (C) BDW 8005
W 401562-B   **My Kinda Love** [Jo Trent; Louis Alter] arrGM vBC (as solos)
    LP: Columbia C4X 44229
W 401562-C   **My Kinda Love** arrGM vBC (as solos)
    78: OKeh 41188, Parlophone (E) R-374, (E) R-2475, (Au) A-2858, (It) B-27044, Odeon A-189234
    LP: World Records (E) SHB67, (Au) R-09520, Epic E202, Columbia Special Products P 16355, Columbia C3L35, CBS (E) BPG 62545, (E) M66210, Jonzo (E) JZ-7, Broadway BR112, Biograph BLP C13
    TC: Columbia CT44306, World Records (E) CSHB67, Radio Yesteryear Stack 15
    CD: Columbia CK44306, Timeless (H) 004, Affinity (E) AFS 1021-2, Jazz Oracle (C) BDW 8005

The Dorsey Brothers session was the first time Bing Crosby and Eddie Lang recorded together.

Pathe, New York, N.Y. c. Monday, January 28, 1929
SAM LANIN AND HIS ORCHESTRA
Sam Lanin (ldr) 2 *unknown* (tp) Tom Dorsey (tb) **Jimmy Dorsey**, 2 *unknown* (cl,as) Merle Johnston (ts) *Arthur Schutt* (p) *unknown* (bj), (bb) *Stan King* (d) Scrappy Lambert [as William Smith, Harold Lang or Chester Hale] (vcl) (Contd.)

SAM LANIN AND HIS ORCHESTRA (Contd.)

108601   When The World Is At Rest [Benny Davis; Sammy
               Fain] vSL
     78: Pathe Actuelle 36933, Perfect 15114
          as LARRY RICH AND HIS ORCHESTRA
108604-1   (It's) A Precious Little Thing Called Love [Lou
               Davis; J. Fred Coots] vSL (as solo)
     78: Pathe Actuelle 36933, Perfect 15114
          as LARRY RICH AND HIS ORCHESTRA
     (3614-A,C) 78: Cameo 9062, Lincoln 3091, Romeo 866, Starr
     (Au) 741, Angelus (Au) 3095, Plaza (Au) 3095
          *Starr as ELMER GROSSO AND HIS ORCHESTRA, Angelus
          and Plaza as EMIL SEIDEL AND HIS ORCHESTRA*
108616-1   Mississippi (Here I Am) [Arthur Sizemore; Bernie
               Grossman] vSL[HL on Pathe, Perfect, WS on others]
     78: Pathe Actuelle 36932, Perfect 15113
     (3613-A) 78: Cameo 9064, Lincoln 3093, Romeo 868
          Cameo, Lincoln, Romeo as THE WASHINGTONIANS

     Okeh matrix 401580-B ("A Precious Little Thing") by Milt Shaw was
released in error on Parlophone (E) as the Dorsey Brothers Orchestra.

Victor, New York, N.Y. Wednesday, January 30, 1929
BOYD SENTER AND HIS SENTERPEDES
Boyd Senter (cl,ldr) Phil Napoleon (tp) Tom Dorsey (tb) Jimmy Dorsey
(as) Frank Signorelli (p) Carl Kress (g) Stan King (d) *unknown* (scat vcl)

BVE 49701-2   Wabash Blues [Dave Ringle; Fred Meinken] (as solo)
     78: Victor 21864, Bluebird B-5545, Regal Zonophone (E) MR-
     1316, His Master's Voice (Au) EA-1392, (E) R-14133
     LP: Gardenia (It) 4003
     CD: Timeless (H) CBC-1032
BVE 9702-2   Goin' Back To Tennessee [Boyd Senter] vocal (as
               solo tag)
     78: Victor 21864, Bluebird B-6203, His Master's Voice (E) R-
     14133
     LP: Gardenia (It) 4003, Sunbeam MFC-1
     CD: Timeless (H) CBC-1032

Okeh, New York, N.Y. Thursday, January 31, 1929
HARRY RING'S SOUTHERN MELODY ARTISTS
Tommy Gott, Phil Napoleon (tp) Tom Dorsey (tb) Arnold Brilhart, Jimmy Dorsey (as) Alfie Evans (ts) Sid Harris, Joe LaFaro (vn) Art Schutt
(p) Eddie Lang (g) Hank Stern (bb) Stan King (d) Smith Ballew (vcl)

401573-A,B,C   Carolina Moon vSB (waltz) (unissued)
401574-C   My Angeline [Jack Palmer] vSB (waltz)
     78: OKeh 41198, Odeon A-189251, Parlophone (E) E-6202
          Parlophone as MERTON ORCHESTRA
401575-C   Dear, When I Met You vSB (waltz)
     78: OKeh 41229, Odeon A-189253

OKeh, New York, N.Y. Saturday, February 2, 1929
JOE VENUTI AND HIS NEW YORKERS
Joe Venuti (vn,ldr) Leo McConville, Fuzzy Farrar (tp) Tom Dorsey
(tb,tp) **Jimmy Dorsey** (cl,as) Jimmy Crossan (as) Alfie Evans (ts)
Arthur Schutt (p) Eddie Lang (g) Joe Tarto (bb) Chauncey Morehouse
(d,xyl) Smith Ballew (vcl)

W 401584-C   **That's The Good Old Sunny South** [Jack Yellen;
                Milton Ager] vSB (as solos)
      78: OKeh 41192, Parlophone (E) R-340, 22305, Odeon 193295,
      A-189244, (F) A-221111
            Parlophones as JOE VENUTI'S CONCERT ORCHESTRA
      LP: The Old Masters 7, JSP (E) 1111
      CD: JSP (E) CD310
W 401585-A   **Weary River** [Grant Clark; Louis Silvers] vSB
      78: OKeh 41192, Parlophone (E)R-341, 22304, Odeon (Arg)
      193295, A-189244, Ariel (E) 4563
            *Parlophones as JOE VENUTI'S CONCERT ORCHESTRA,
            Ariel as ARIEL DANCE ORCHESTRA*
      LP: The Old Masters 7, JSP (E) 1111
      CD: JSP (E) CD310

Pathe, New York, N. Y. c. Tuesday, February 5, 1929
SAM LANIN AND HIS ORCHESTRA
Personnel as January 28, 1929. Joe Venuti (vn) Scrappy Lambert (vcl)

108628-2   **Button Up Your Overcoat** [Buddy De Sylva, Lew
                Brown; Ray Henderson] vSL
      78: Pathe Actuelle 36941, Perfect 15122
            as MAJESTIC DANCE ORCHESTRA
      (3699) **78:** Cameo 9093, Lincoln 3120, Romeo 895
            as VINCENT RICHARDS AND HIS ORCHESTRA
108629-1   **Weary River** [Grant Clark; Louis Silvers] vSL
      78: Pathe Actuelle 36943, Perfect 15124
            as FRANK KEYES AND HIS ORCHESTRA
      (3648-2) **78:** Cameo 9072, Lincoln 3101, Romeo 876, Dominion
      (E) A-134, Angelus (Au) 3104
            *Cameo, Romeo, Lincoln, Dominion as VINCENT RICHARDS
            AND HIS ORCH., Angelus as JARDIN ROYAL ORCH.*
108630-2   **I Want To Be Bad** [Buddy De Sylva, Lew Brown;
                Ray Henderson] vSL (as solo)
      78: Pathe Actuelle 36941, Perfect 15122
            as MAJESTIC DANCE ORCHESTRA
      (3685-3) **78:** Cameo 9084, Lincoln 3111, Romeo 886
            as BROADWAY BROADCASTERS

Pathe, New York, N. Y. c. Wednesday, February 6, 1929
SAM LANIN AND HIS ORCHESTRA
Scrappy Lambert [as James Denton where noted] (vcl)

108631-2   **That's The Good Old Sunny South** vSL
      78: Pathe Actuelle 36954, Perfect 15135 (Contd.)

SAM LANIN AND HIS ORCHESTRA (Contd.)

> *as SAM LANIN AND HIS TROUBADORS*
108632-2   **Deep Night** [Rudy Vallee; Charlie Henderson] vSL
> **78:** Pathe Actuelle 36940, Perfect 15121
> *as TEN FRESHMEN (vcl James Denton)*
> (3633-B) **78:** Cameo 9081, Lincoln 3108, Romeo 883, Dominion
> A-155, Angelus (Au) 3126
> *Dominion as SAM LANIN AND HIS TROUBADORS, Angelus*
> *as SAM LANNIN [sic] AND HIS ORCHESTRA*
108633-1   **I'll Never Ask For More** [Roy Turk; Fred E. Ahlert]
> vSL
> **78:** Pathe Actuelle 36939, Perfect 15120
> (3634-A,B) **78:** Cameo 9082, Lincoln 3109, Romeo 884,
> Dominion A-135
> *as VINCENT RICHARDS' ORCHESTRA*

Victor, New York, N.Y. Wednesday, February 6, 1929
BOYD SENTER AND HIS SENTERPEDES
Boyd Senter (cl) Phil Napoleon, *unknown* (tp) Charlie Butterfield (tb)
Jimmy Dorsey (as) Frank Signorelli (p) Carl Kress (g) Stan King (d)

BVE 48335-3   **Rich Man, Poor Man, Beggar Man, Thief** [Boyd
> Senter]
> **78:** Victor 22010, Electrola (G) EG-1627
> *Electrola as VICTOR ARDEN—PHIL OHMAN AND THEIR*
> *ORCHESTRA*
BVE 48336-3   **I'm In The Jailhouse Now** [Jimmy Rogers]
> **78:** Victor 22010, Bluebird B-5545, Regal Zonophone (E) MR-
> 1316, His Master's Voice (E) EA-1392
> Both sides also on **LP:** Gardenia (It) 4003, **CD:** Timeless (H)
> CBC-1032

Columbia, New York, N.Y. Friday, February 8, 1929
JACK HART (accomp. by SAM LANIN AND HIS ORCHESTRA)
Sam Lanin (ldr) *Phil Napoleon, unknown* (tp) Tom Dorsey (tb) **Jimmy
Dorsey,** *unknown* (cl,as) *Merle Johnston* (ts,fl) 2 *unknown* (vn) *Art
Schutt* (p,celst) *unknown* (bj), (bb), (d) Jack Parker [as Jack Hart] (vcl)

147947-2,3   **You Were Meant For Me** [Arthur Freed; Nacio Herb
> Brown] vJH
> **78:** Harmony 845-H, MGM 1010-P, 1035-P, Diva 2845-G,
> Velvet Tone 1845-V, Puritone 1043, Regal (Au) G-20508
> *1035-P as THE CAPITOLIANS*
147948-1,3   **Broadway Melody** [Arthur Freed; Nacio Herb Brown]
> vJP
> **78:** Harmony 845-H, MGM 1010-P, 1035-P, Diva 2845-G,
> Velvet Tone 1845-V, Puritone 1043, Regal (Au) G-20508
> *1035-P as THE CAPITOLIANS*
147949-1   **Josephita** vJP
> **78:** Harmony 905-H, Diva 2905-G, Velvet Tone 1905-V

Columbia, New York, N.Y. Tuesday, February 19, 1929
FRED RICH AND HIS ORCHESTRA
Fred Rich (ldr) Leo McConville (tp) Tom Dorsey (tb,cnt) **Jimmy Dorsey** (cl,as) *unknown* (p) Carl Kress (g) Joe Tarto (bb,sb) *unknown* (d) The Rollickers (vcl grp)

W 147969-4   **Wedding Bells (Are Breaking Up That Old Gang Of Mine)** [Irving Kahal, Willie Raskin; Sammy Fain] vR
       78: Columbia 1740-D
W 147970-3   **I'll Tell The World** vR
       78: Columbia 1751-D

Columbia, New York, N.Y. Wednesday, February 20, 1929
ANNETTE HANSHAW (accomp. by NEW ENGLAND YANKEES)
Ben Selvin (ldr) Tom Dorsey (cnt) *Tommy Gott* (tp) Charlie Butterfield (tb) **Jimmy Dorsey,** *unknown* (cl,as) *unknown* (ts) Al Duffy, *unknown* (vn) *unknown* (p), (g), (bb),(d) Annette Hanshaw (vcl)

147974-2   **(It's) A Precious Little Thing Called Love** [Lou Davis; J. Fred Coots] vAH
       78: Harmony 859-H, Diva 2859-G Velvet Tone 1859-V
147976-2   **Mean To Me** [Roy Turk; Fred E. Ahlert] vAH (as solo)
       78: Harmony 859-H, Diva 2859-G, Velvet Tone 1859-V
       Both sides also on **LP:** World Records (E) SH146

Pathe, New York, N.Y. c. Wednesday, February 20, 1929
SAM LANIN AND HIS TROUBADORS
Sam Lanin (ldr) 2 *unknown* (tp) *unknown* (tb) Jimmy Dorsey, *unknown* (cl,as) *Merle Johnston* (ts) Arthur Schutt (p) *unknown* (bj), (bb) *Stan King* (d,chimes) Scrappy Lambert [as William Robyn] (vcl)

108657-2   **Wedding Bells (Are Breaking Up That Old Gang Of Mine)** [Irving Kahal, Will Raskin; Sammy Fain] vSL
       78: Pathe Actuelle 36948, Perfect 15129
       as MAJESTIC DANCE ORCH.
       (3654-D) **78:** Cameo 9085, Lincoln 3112, Romeo 887, Angelus (Au) 3121
            Cameo, Lincoln, Romeo as VINCENT RICHARDS AND HIS ORCH., Angelus as ERNIE GOLDEN AND HIS ORCH.
108658-1   **Broadway Melody** [Arthur Freed; Nacio Brown] vSL
       78: Pathe Actuelle 36947, Perfect 15128
       (3656-A,B) **78:** Cameo 9026, Lincoln 3113, Romeo 888, Angelus (Au) 3101, Starr (Au) 745
            Cameo, Lincoln, Romeo as VINCENT RICHARDS AND HIS ORCH., Angelus as SAM LANNIN [sic] AND HIS ORCH., Starr as VAN CARLSON AND HIS HALF-MOON ORCH.
108659-1   **You Were Meant For Me** [Arthur Freed; Nacio Herb Brown] vSL
       78: Pathe Actuelle 36947, Perfect 15128
       (3655-A,C) **78:** Cameo 9101, Lincoln 3128, Romeo 903, Dominion (E) A-137

"Broadway Melody" and "You Were Meant For Me" from the preceding session were introduced by Charles King in MGM's first "all talking-all singing" musical *Broadway Melody*, which won the 1929 Academy Award for best film and opened the floodgates for movie musicals. It also produced a demand for New York musicians, including the Dorseys, to appear in one-reelers filmed on Long Island.

Columbia, New York, N.Y. Thursday, February 21, 1929
IPANA TROUBADORS
Sam Lanin (ldr) Leo McConville, Mannie Klein (tp) Tom Dorsey (tb) **Jimmy Dorsey**, *unknown* (cl,as) *unknown* (cl,ts) Arthur Schutt (p) *John Cali* (bj) *Hank Stern* (bb) Vic Berton (d) Smith Ballew (vcl)

W 147989-2   **Some Sweet Day** [Nat Shilkret, Lew Pollack] vSB
                          (as solo)
        78: Columbia 1747-D
W 147990-3   **Deep Night** [Rudy Vallee; Charlie Henderson] vSB
                          (cl solo)
        78: Columbia 1747-D, (E) 5373, (Au) 01539

Pathe, New York, N.Y. c. Wednesday, February 27, 1929
SAM LANIN AND HIS ORCHESTRA
Sam Lanin (ldr) Phil Napoleon, *unknown* (tp) Tom Dorsey (tb) **Jimmy Dorsey** (cl,as) Andy Sanella (cl,as) *Merle Johnston* (cl,ts) Art Schutt (p) *unknown* (bj) Jimmy Mullen (bb) *Stan King* (d) Scrappy Lambert [as Harold Lang or Chester Hale on Pathe and Perfect] (vcl)

108667-2   **The Wedding Of The Painted Doll** [Arthur Freed;
                          Nacio Herb Brown] vSL [HL on Pathe, Perfect]
        78: Pathe Actuelle 36949, Perfect 15130
                as LARRY RICH AND HIS FRIENDS
        (3686-A,B) **78:** Cameo 9095, Lincoln 3122, Romeo 897, Angelus
        (Au) 3100, Starr (Au) 744
                Angelus as SAM LANNIN [sic] AND HIS ORCH., Starr as
                VAN CARLSON AND HIS HALF-MOON ORCH.
108672-3   **Mean To Me** [Roy Turk; Fred E. Ahlert] vSL[CH]
                          (as solo)
        78: Pathe Actuelle 36960, Perfect 15141, Pathe (F) X-6726
                as MAJESTIC DANCE ORCHESTRA
        (3718-B) **78:** Cameo 9103, Lincoln 3130, Romeo 905
-0-   **Hello, Sunshine, Hello!** [Murray, Tobias] vSL[CH]
        78: Pathe Actuelle 36957, Perfect 15138
                as SAM LANIN AND HIS TROUBADORS

Plaza, New York, N.Y. Wednesday, March 6, 1929
SAM LANIN AND HIS ORCHESTRA
Personnel as c. February 27, 1929.   Scrappy Lambert [as Jack Blue, Rodman Lewis or Roland Lance] (vcl)

8593-3   **He, She And Me** vSL (as solo)
        78: Banner 6328, Domino 4298, Regal 8745, Challenge 960,

Jewel 5550, Apex (C) 8917, Oriole 1513, Broadway 1261, Crown
81038, Kalliope (G) K1438
> *Oriole as ORIOLE DANCE ORCH., Challenge, Jewel as*
> *MIAMI SOCIETY ORCH., Broadway, Kalliope as THE*
> *BADGERS, Crown as LLOYD HALL AND HIS ORCH.*

8594-2   **My Castle In Spain Is A Shack In The Lane** [Irving
               Caesar; Cliff Friend] vSL[RL]
78: Banner 6326, Domino 4297, Regal 8743, Conquerer 7321,
Apex (C) 8914, Crown 81025, Broadway 1263
> *Conquerer as JOHN VINCENT'S CALIFORNIANS, Crown as*
> *ERNIE NOBLE AND HIS ORCHESTRA, Broadway as THE*
> *BADGERS*

8595-1,3   **There's A Four-Leaf Clover In My Pocket (And A**
               Horseshoe Over My Door) vSL (cl,as solos)
78: Banner 6325, Domino 4296, 31081, Challenge 959, Regal
8747, Apex (C) 8922, Broadway 1272
> *Challenge as MIAMI SOCIETY ORCHESTRA, Broadway as*
> *THE BADGERS*

Pathe, New York, N.Y. Friday, March 8, 1929
MILLS' MUSICAL CLOWNS
2 *unknown* (tp) Tom Dorsey (tb) **Jimmy Dorsey,** *unknown* (cl,as)
unknown (ts), (p), (bj), (bb), (d) Irving Kaufman (vcl)

108684-1   **The Sorority Stomp** [Irving Mills] vIK
               78: Pathe Actuelle 37042, Perfect 15223
> *as WHOOPEE MAKERS*
               (3698-A) **78:** Cameo 9098, Lincoln 3125, Romeo 900, 976
> *Cameo, Lincoln and Romeo 900 as VARSITY EIGHT, Romeo*
> *976 as TEN BLACK BERRIES*

Columbia, New York, N.Y. Monday, March 11, 1929
RUTH ETTING
Tom Dorsey (cnt) Charlie Butterfield (tb) **Jimmy Dorsey** (cl) *Joe Venuti*
(vn) *Frank Signorelli* (p) Eddie Lang (g) *Joe Tarto* (sb) Ruth Etting (vcl)

W 148029-3   **Button Up Your Overcoat** [Buddy De Sylva, Lew
               Brown; Ray Henderson] vRE
               78: Columbia 1762-D, (E) 5600
               LP: Biograph C11, Columbia C3l35, P2-11919, Living Era (E)
               AJA 5008
W 148030-2   **Mean To Me** [Roy Turk; Fred E. Ahlert] vRE
               (cl solo)
               78: Columbia 1762-D, (E) 5446
               LP: Columbia ML5050, Living Era (E) AJA 5008
               Both sides also on **CD:** Living Era (E) ASV 5008

Victor, New York, N.Y. Wednesday, March 13, 1929
BOYD SENTER AND HIS SENTERPEDES
Boyd Senter (cl,ldr) Mickey Bloom (tp) Tom Dorsey (tb) **Jimmy Dorsey**
(as) Frank Signorelli (p) Eddie Lang (g) Stan King (d) Paul Small (vcl)

BOYD SENTER AND HIS SENTERPEDES (Contd.)

BVE 49780-2   Doin' You Good [Boyd Senter] vPS (as solo)
    78: Victor 21912, His Master's Voice (It) R-14160, (Swe) X-
    4493, Electrola (G) EG-1422
    LP: Gardenia (It) 4003
BVE 49781-3   Shine [Cecil Mack, Lew Brown; Ford T. Dabney]
                   vPS (as solo)
    78: Victor 21912, His Master's Voice (It) R-14160, (Swe) X-
    4493, Electrola (G) EG-1422
    LP: Gardenia (It) 4003

OKeh, New York, N.Y. Friday, March 15, 1929
DORSEY BROTHERS AND THEIR ORCHESTRA
Tom Dorsey (tb,ldr) Leo McConville, Fuzzy Farrar, Phil Napoleon (tp)
Glenn Miller (tb,arr) Jimmy Dorsey, Arnold Brilhart (cl,as) Herbert
Spencer (ts) unknown (vn) Arthur Schutt (p) Eddie Lang (g) Hank Stern
(bb) Stan King (d) Smith Ballew, chorus (vcl)

W 401715-B   Mean To Me [Roy Turk; Fred E.Ahlert] arrGM vSB,
                   chorus (cl solo)
    78: OKeh 41210, Parlophone (E) R-374, (Au) A-2781, (F)
    22413, (It) B-27044, Odeon (F) 165685, (Arg) 193307
    ET: AFRS END-390-67
    LP: The Old Masters 15, Columbia Special Products P-16355,
    World Records (E) SHB67, (Au) R-09520
    TC: World Records (E) CSHB67
    CD: Jazz Oracle (C) BDW 8005
        World Records LP liner notes claim that its release is from
        "take -C" of 401715. The author has been unable to sub-
        stantiate the existence of such a take, even in a test pressing,
        and now believes this is a typo.
W 401716-C   Button Up Your Overcoat [Buddy De Sylva, Lew
                   Brown; Ray Henderson] arrGM vSB,chorus (cl solo)
    78: OKeh 41210, Parlophone (E) R-374, (F) 22378, (It)
    B-27045, Odeon (F) 165685, (Au) 193307, (F) A-221169
    LP: The Old Masters 15, World Records (E) SHB67, (Au)
    R-09520, Columbia Special Products P16355
    TC: World Records (E) CSHB67
    CD: Jazz Oracle (C) BDW 8005
W401717-A   I'll Never Ask For More [Roy Turk; Fred E. Ahlert]
                   arrGM vSB,chorus
    78: OKeh 41220, Parlophone (E) E-6179, (Au) A-2827, Ariel
    (E) 4424, Odeon (F) A221154, (F)165765, (Arg) 193315
        Ariel as ARIEL DANCE ORCHESTRA, Parlophone (E) as
        WILL PERRY'S ORCHESTRA, Odeon A221154 as RIVER
        CLUB ORCHESTRA
    LP: The Old Masters 15, World Records (E) SHB67, (Au)
    R-09520, Columbia Special Products P16355
    TC: World Records (E) CSHB67
    CD: Jazz Oracle (C) BDW 8005

Columbia, New York, N.Y. Friday, March 22, 1929
FRED RICH AND HIS ORCHESTRA
Fred Rich (ldr) Leo McConville (tp) Tom Dorsey (tb,cnt) **Jimmy Dorsey,** *unknown* (cl,as) *unknown* (ts) Joe Venuti, *unknown* (vn) Arthur Schutt (p,celst) Carl Kress (g) Joe Tarto (bb,sb) *unknown* (d)   The Rollickers (vcl)

W 148124-2   **Yours Sincerely** [Lorenz Hart; Richard Rodgers] vR
                 (cl solo)
     78: Columbia 1778-D, (E) CB-99
W 148125-3   **I Kiss Your Hand, Madame** [Sam M. Lewis, Joe
                 Young, Fritz Rotler] vR
     78: Columbia 1778-D

Columbia, New York, N.Y. Friday, March 22, 1929
SAM LANIN AND HIS ORCHESTRA
Sam Lanin (ldr) Leo McConville, *unknown* (tp) Tom Dorsey (tb) **Jimmy Dorsey,** *Merle Johnston [or] Arnold Brilhart* (cl,as) Frank Teschemacher (cl,ts) Arthur Schutt (p,celst) *Tony Colucci* (bj) Joe Tarto (bb) Stan King (d) Willard Robison, Smith Ballew (vcl)

148126-3   **Wake Up! Chillun, Wake Up!** [Willard Robison, Jo
                 Trent] vWR (as solo)
     78: Columbia 1747-D
148127-4   **Old Fashioned Lady** [Abner Silver, Al Sherman, Al
                 Lewis] vSB (cl solo)
     78: Columbia 1747-D, (E) 5373
     148126 & 148127 as IPANA TROUBADORS
W 401734-A   **The One That I Love Loves Me** [Roy Turk; Fred
                 Ahlert] vSB (cl solo)
     78: OKeh 41264
     as SAM LANIN AND HIS FAMOUS PLAYERS
W 401734-B   **The One That I Love Loves Me** vSB (cl solo)
     78: OKeh 41264, Parlophone (E) R-401, Odeon ONY-41264,
     (Arg) 193356, (G) A-189251, Ariel (E) Z-4400
     *Parlophone as SAM LANIN AND HIS FAMOUS PLAYERS,
     OKeh and Odeon as NEW YORK SYNCOPATORS, Ariel as
     ARIEL DANCE ORCH.*
     LP: The Old Masters 28
W 401735-C   **The Wedding Of The Painted Doll** [Arthur Freed;
                 Nacio Herb Brown] (as solo)
     78: OKeh 41215, Parlophone (E) R-367, (Au) A2775, (G) A-
     4572, Odeon 193305, (G) A-189251, Ariel (E) Z-4400
W 401736-C   **The Toymaker's Dream** [John Golden] vSB
     78: OKeh 41215, Parlophone (E) R-367, (Au) A2775, (G) A-
     4572, B-12787, Odeon (G) A-189251, Ariel (E) 4399
     *For 401735 & 401736: Ariel as ARIEL DANCE ORCH., all
     others as SAM LANIN AND HIS FAMOUS PLAYERS*

Plaza, New York, N.Y. Monday, March 25, 1929
SAM LANIN AND HIS ORCHESTRA
Sam Lanin (ldr) Phil Napoleon, *unknown* (tp) Tom Dorsey (tb) **Jimmy**

SAM LANIN AND HIS ORCHESTRA (Contd.)
Dorsey, *unknown* (cl,as) Merle Johnston (ts) Arthur Schutt (p) *unknown*
(bj) Jimmy Mullen (bb) *unknown* (d) Irving Kaufman (vcl)

8635-2   **The Toymaker's Dream** [John Golden] vIK
        78: Banner 6354, Oriole 1540, Apex (C) 8937, Broadway 1267,
        Imperial (E) 2128, Crown (C) 81086, Domino (C) 181086,
        Sterling (C) 281086, Edison Bell Winner (E) 4919, Edison Bell
        Radio (E) (8-inch dub) 1224, Kristall (G) 4023, Embassy (Au)
        8060, Savoy (Au) 1060, Arcadia (Au) 2052
              Oriole as TED WHITE'S COLLEGIANS, Broadway as THE
              BADGERS, Crown as RENDEZVOUS DANCE ORCH., Do-
              mino, Sterling as BLUE ROOM CLUB ORCH., Edison Bell
              Winner as MURRAY'S MELODY MAKERS, Edison Bell Ra-
              dio as THE BLUE JAYS, Savoy as SAVOY DANCE ORCH.,
              Arcadia as ARCADIA DANCE BAND, Embassy as AMBAS-
              SADOR'S DANCE ORCH.
8636-2   **The Wedding Of The Painted Doll** [Arthur Freed;
                       Nacio Herb Brown] vIK (as solo)
        78: Banner 6350, Regal 8765, Domino 4320, 31076, (C)
        181086, Oriole 1548, Conquerer 7343, Jewel 5578, Apex (C)
        8924, Broadcast (Au) W-509, Broadway 1270, Crown (C) 81026,
        Imperial (E) 2079, Embassy (Au) 8000, Edison Bell Winner (E)
        4919, Savoy (Au) 1002
              Conquerer as JOHN VINCENT'S CALIFORNIANS, Jewel as
              BOB GREEN'S DANCE ORCH., Domino 181086 and Crown
              as RENDEZVOUS CAFE ORCH., Broadway as THE BAD-
              GERS, Edison Bell Winner as MURRAY'S MELODY
              MAKERS, Embassy as HOLLYWOOD DANCE ORCH.,
              Broadcast as LOS ANGELES AMBASSADORS, Savoy as
              NEW YORK SYNCOPATORS
8637-2   **Dance Of The Paper Dolls** [Johnny Tucker, Joe Schu-
                       ster, John Siras] vIK
        78: Banner 6358, Domino 4320, Regal 8765, Conquerer 7343,
        Oriole 1543, Apex (C) 8937, Imperial (E) 2079, Edison Bell
        Radio (E) (8-inch dub) 1224, Broadway 1267, Crown (C) 81085,
        Edison Bell Winner (Au) 511, Broadcast (Au) W-511
              Conquerer as JOHN VINCENT'S CALIFORNIANS, Oriole as
              TED WHITE'S COLLEGIANS, Broadway as THE BADG-
              ERS, Edison Bell Radio as THE BLUE JAYS, Broadcast as
              ROXY DANCE ORCHESTRA, Crown as JIMMIE POL-
              LACK'S ORCHESTRA
        (108858) **78:** Pathe 37009, Perfect 15190
              as BEN FRANKLIN HOTEL DANCE ORCHESTRA

Columbia, New York, N.Y. Tuesday, March 26, 1929
SAMMY FAIN "The Crooning Composer"
Tom Dorsey (cnt) **Jimmy Dorsey** (cl) *Rube Bloom* (p) Eddie Lang (g)
Sammy Fain (vcl)

148139-2   **What Didja Wanna Make Me Love You For?**
                       [Harry Warren, Mort Dixon] vSF (cl solo)

78: Harmony 904-H, Diva 2904-G, Velvet Tone 1904-V
148140-3   **(You Can't Take Away) The Things That Were Made For Love** [Charles Tobias, Irving Kahal; Peter De Rose] vSF (cl solo)
78: Harmony 904-H, Diva 2904-G, Velvet Tone 1904-V

Brunswick, New York, N.Y. Wednesday, March 27, 1929
COTTON PICKERS
Tom Dorsey (cnt,ldr) Glenn Miller (tb) **Jimmy Dorsey** (cl,as) Arthur Schutt (p) Perry Botkin (bj) Joe Tarto (sb) Stan King (d) Hoagy Carmichael, Marlin Hurt (vcl)

E 29523$\frac{1}{2}$-A   **Rampart Street Blues** [J. R. Robinson] (cl,as solos)
    78: Brunswick 4325, (E) 02505, (G) A-8261, (F) A-81004
    LP: Arcadia (C) 2013
E 29523$\frac{1}{2}$-B   **Rampart Street Blues** vHC&SL (cl,as solos)
    78: Brunswick 4325, (E) 05037
    LP: Arcadia (C) 2013, Halcyon (E) HLP37
E 29524-A   **St. Louis Gal** [J. R. Robinson] vHC&SL (cl solo)
    78: Brunswick 4440, (F) 1035
    LP: Arcadia (C) 2013, Halcyon (E) IILP37
E 29524-B   **St. Louis Gal** vHC&SL (cl solo)
    LP: Arcadia (C) 2013, Broadway BR115
    CD: Timeless (H) CBC 1-011
E 29525-A   **Kansas City Kitty** [Edgar Leslie; Walter Donaldson] (cl,as solos)
    78: Brunswick 4325, (E) 05037, (G) A-8261, (F) A-81004
    LP: Arcadia (C) 2013
    all sides also on **CD:** Timeless (H) CBC 1-049

A series of errors occurred with the above session: the "$\frac{1}{2}$" matrix designation came from a clerical goof using 29523 for two unrelated sessions; the same matrix number is assigned to both a vocal and non-vocal version of the same song; some issues of English Brunswick 02505 were pressed from 29525 but labeled "Rampart Street Blues."

Plaza, New York, N.Y. Friday, March 29, 1929
FRED RICH AND HIS ORCHESTRA
Fred Rich (ldr) Leo McConville (tp) Tom Dorsey (tb,cnt) **Jimmy Dorsey** (cl,as) *unknown* (as), (ts), (p) Carl Kress (g) Joe Tarto (bb) *unknown* (d) Irving Kaufman [as George Beaver, Charles Dickson, Roland Lance or Ray Winn on some] (vcl)

8646-1   **Some Sweet Day** [Nat Shilkret, Lew Pollack] vIK [GB, Broadway as RW] (as solo)
    78: Banner 6346, Broadway 1269, Challenge 998, Conquerer 7333, Domino 4313, 31086, Oriole 1535, Regal 8761, Apex 8928, Embassy (Au) 8008
        Broadway as FRANK RAYMOND'S DANCE ORCH., Challenge as Jewel DANCE ORCH., Oriole as ORIOLE DANCE ORCH., Embassy as CHICAGO REDHEADS
                (Contd.)

FRED RICH AND HIS ORCHESTRA (Contd.)

8647-3   **(You Can't Take Away) The Things That Were Made For Love** [Charles Tobias, Irving Kahal; Peter De Rose] vIK [RL on Broadway]
     78: Banner 6351, Broadway 1269, Conquerer 7340, Domino 4315, Paramount 20710, Regal 8760
          Broadway and Paramount as FRANK RAYMOND'S DANCE ORCHESTRA
8648-1,2   **I Get The Blues When It Rains** [Marcy Klauber; Harry Stoddard] vIK [RL on Broadway, CD on Oriole and Jewel] (as solo)
     78: Banner 6360, Broadway 1271, Challenge 999, Conquerer 7333, Oriole 1542, Paramount 20712, Regal 8761, Apex (C) 8944, Crown 81050, Perfect 15142, Jewel 5569
          Broadway and Paramount as FRANK RAYMOND'S DANCE ORCHESTRA, Perfect as FRANK KEYES AND HIS ORCHESTRA, Challenge and Jewel as Jewel DANCE ORCHESTRA, Oriole as ORIOLE DANCE ORCHESTRA, Crown as LLOYD HALL AND HIS ORCHESTRA

Pathe, New York, N.Y. Late March-Early April 1929
PATHE STUDIO BAND
Sam Lanin (ldr) *Phil Napoleon, unknown* (tp) Tom Dorsey (tb) **Jimmy Dorsey,** *unknown* (cl,as) Merle Johnston (ts) *unknown* (vn) Art Schutt (p) *unknown* (bj) *Jimmy Mullen* (bb) *unknown* (d) Irving Kaufman (vcl)

108706-2   **My Sugar And Me** vIK
     78: Pathe Actuelle 36967, Perfect 15148
          as HAROLD WHITE AND HIS ORCHESTRA
108707-1   **I'll Never Forget** vIK
     78: Pathe Actuelle 36966, Perfect 15147
          as DAN RITCHIE AND HIS ORCHESTRA

Pathe, New York, N.Y. Late March-Early April, 1929
PATHE STUDIO BAND
Personnel mostly as preceding. Scrappy Lambert [as Larry Rich or Chester Hale] (vcl)

108715-2   **I'm Marching Home To You** vSL[LR]
     78: Pathe Actuelle 36967, Perfect 15148
          as FRANK KEYES AND HIS ORCHESTRA
108716-1   **I Get The Blues When It Rains** [Marcy Klauber; Harry Stoddard] vSL[CH]
     78: Pathe Actuelle 36961, Perfect 15142
          as FRANK KEYES AND HIS ORCHESTRA
     (3804-) **78:** Cameo 9143, Lincoln 3170, Romeo 945
          as VARSITY EIGHT

Pathe, New York, N.Y. Late March-Early April, 1929
SAM LANIN AND HIS ORCHESTRA
Personnel mostly as Pathe Studio Band preceding. Irving Kaufman (vcl)

108735-2,3 **My Heart Is Bluer Than Your Eyes, Cherie** vIK
78: Pathe Actuelle 36968, Perfect 15149
(3777) 78: Cameo 9134, Lincoln 3161, Romeo 936
*Pathe and Perfect as HAROLD WHITE AND HIS ORCH-
ESTRA, others as THE CAROLINERS. Which Pathe matrix (if
any) matches 3777 is unknown. It is also uncertain whether
this is truly from a Lanin session.*
108746-1 **Lady Divine** [Richard Kountz, Nat Shilkret] vIK
(as solo)
78: Pathe Actuelle 36971, Pathe (F) X-6728, Perfect 15152
*as FRANK KEYES AND HIS ORCHESTRA, Pathe (F) as
PATHE ORCHESTRA*
(3771-A) 78: Cameo 9128, Lincoln 3155, Romeo 930, Dominion
(E) A-157, Angelus (Au) 3136
*Angelus as ELMER GROSSO AND HIS ORCHESTRA, others
as VINCENT RICHARDS AND HIS ORCHESTRA*

A popular radio program of the period, *The Atwater-Kent Dance
Hour,* featured an orchestra led first by Joseph Pasternack, then Don
Voorhees and later Victor Young.
The thirty-member band often included the Dorseys and was heard
Sundays, 9:00 to 10:00 P.M., on the NBC-Red network, sponsored by a
radio-set manufacturer (Sanford 1972).

OKeh, New York, N.Y. Monday, April 1, 1929
SEGER ELLIS
Justin Ring (ldr) Fuzzy Farrar (tp) Tom Dorsey (tb) **Jimmy Dorsey** (cl,
as) Murray Kellner (vn) Rube Bloom (p) Eddie Lang (g) Harry Ring (d)
Seger Ellis (vcl)

W 401764-C **(Try To Forget The Name Of) Coquette** [Irving
Berlin] vSE
78: OKeh 41221, Parlophone (E) R-396, Ariel (E) 4428, Kismet
K-708, Odeon (Arg) 193750
Ariel as NORMAN THORNE
TC: Neovox (E) 932
W 401765-C **Louise** [Leo Robin; Richard Whiting] vSE (as solo)
78: OKeh 41221, Parlophone (E) R-405, Ariel (E) 4455, Kismet
K-708, Odeon (Arg) 193750
Kismet K-708 as CHARLES HADDON
TC: Neovox (E) 932

For a period in early to mid-1929 the brothers were booked and managed by Lown-Vallee Orchestras, Inc., formed in late March 1929 by
bandleader Bert Lown and singer Rudy Vallee. They also booked Red
Nichols, Miff Mole, Stan King, Irving Brodsky, Leo McConville, Tommy Felline and others (*Orchestra World,* April 1929).
Next, the Dorseys make another try at emulating Paul Whiteman's
style with Justin Ring as leader. While these Dorsey Brothers releases in
1928 and 1929 met with fairly good sales results, the group never quite
attained the status for which OKeh was looking.

OKeh, New York, N.Y. Wednesday, April 3, 1929
DORSEY BROTHERS AND THEIR CONCERT ORCHESTRA
Justin Ring (ldr) Leo McConville, Fuzzy Farrar, Phil Napoleon (tp)
Tom Dorsey, Glenn Miller (tb) **Jimmy Dorsey** (cl,as) Ollie Boyd (cl)
Arnold Brilhart (as) Jim Crossan (ts) Irving Kohn (o) Phil Raines (bsn)
Murray Kellner, Sam Rates, Nat Brusiloff, Sam Freed (vn) Emil Stark
(cel) Arthur Schutt (p) Eddie Lang (g) Hank Stern (bb) Joe Tarto (sb)
Stan King (d) Chauncey Morehouse (d,vib) George Crozier (arr) Smith
Ballew (vcl)

W 401775-B   **Lover, Come Back To Me** (part 1) [Oscar Hammer-
                    stein II; Sigmund Romberg] vSB
          78: OKeh 41223, Parlophone (E) R-391, Ariel (E) 4418, Odeon
          (Brazil) 2541
                    Ariel as ARIEL SYMPHONY ORCHESTRA
          LP: World Records (E) SHB67, (Au) R-09520, Columbia Special
          Products P5-16354
          TC: World Records (E) CSHB67
          CD: Jazz Oracle (C) BDW 8005
W 401776-E   **Lover, Come Back To Me** (part 2)
          All issues same as 401775-B

The first two titles next are remakes of rejected takes from January 18
and February 11, 1929, sessions with Jimmy replacing Benny Goodman.

Plaza, New York, N.Y. Thursday, April 4, 1929
IRVING MILLS AND HIS ORCHESTRA
Jimmy McPartland (cnt) Tommy Thunen (tp) Jack Teagarden (tb,vcl)
Jimmy Dorsey (cl,as) Gil Rodin (as) Larry Binyon (ts) Vic Breidis (p)
Dick Morgan (bj,g) Harry Goodman (bb,sb) Ray Bauduc (d) Jack
Kaufman (vcl)

8476-3   **Tiger Rag** [Harry De Costa; Edwin Edwards, Nick
                La Rocca, Tony Spargo, Larry Shields] (cl solo)
          78: Banner 6355, 0839, Cameo 9195, 0439, Challenge 822,
          Domino 4322, Jewel 5577, 6089, Lincoln 3222, Oriole 1544,
          2089, Regal 8768, 10145, Romeo 997, 1453
                *Banner 6355 as KENTUCKY GRASSHOPPERS, Banner
                0839, Cameo 0439, Jewel 6089, Oriole 2089, Regal 10145
                & Romeo 1453 as TEN BLACKBERRIES, Cameo 9195,
                Lincoln 3222 and Romeo 997 as THE COTTON PICKERS,
                Domino 4322 and Regal 8768 as JIMMY BRACKEN'S TOE
                TICKLERS, Challenge, Jewel 5577 and Oriole 1544 as TED
                WHITE'S COLLEGIANS*
          (108864-3) Pathe Actuelle 37013, Perfect 15194
                as WHOOPEE MAKERS
8543-4   **Makin' Friends** [Jack Teagarden; Jimmy McPartland]
                vJT
          78: Banner 6360, Challenge 999, Domino 4322, Jewel 5569,
          Oriole 1537, Regal 8768, Columbia 36010, (J) M-673
                *Banner as KENTUCKY GRASSHOPPERS, Columbias as
                JACK TEAGARDEN AND THE WHOOPEE MAKERS,*

Challenge, Jewel, Oriole as DIXIE JAZZ BAND
8657-1   **Sweet Liza** vJK
    78: Banner 6358, Jewel 5575, Oriole 1540
    *Banner as KENTUCKY GRASSHOPPERS, Jewel and Oriole
    as DIXIE JAZZ BAND*

Brunswick, New York, N.Y. Friday, April 5, 1929
ORIGINAL MEMPHIS FIVE
Phil Napoleon (tp,ldr) Tom Dorsey (tb) **Jimmy Dorsey** (cl,as) Frank
Signorelli (p) Joe Tarto (sb) Stan King (d) Dick Robertson (vcl)

E 29579-1   **Memphis Blues** [George A. Norton; William C.
                 Handy] vDR (cl solos)
    78: Vocalion 15805
E 29580-1   **Beale Street Blues** [William C. Handy] vDR (cl solo)
    78: Vocalion 15805
E 29580-G   **Beale Street Blues** (cl solos)
    78: (unissued test pressing)
E 29581-1   **Kansas City Kitty** [Edgar Leslie; Walter Donald-
                 son] vDR (cl solo)
    78: Vocalion 15810
    all four sides also on **CD:** Timeless (H) CBC 1-049

Columbia, New York, N.Y. Friday, April 12, 1929
FRED RICH AND HIS ORCHESTRA
Fred Rich (p,ldr) Leo McConville, *unknown* (tp) Tom Dorsey (tb)
Jimmy Dorsey, *unknown* (cl,as) *unknown* (ts) 2 *unknown* (vn) Carl
Kress (g) Joe Tarto (bb) *unknown* (d) The Rollickers (vcl)

W 148426-3   **Why Can't You?** [Buddy De Sylva, Lew Brown; Ray
                 Henderson] vR (cl,as solos)
    78: Columbia 1878-D, (E) 5545
    LP: The Old Masters 27
    CD: The Old Masters 101
W 148427-3   **Used To You** [Buddy De Sylva, Lew Brown; Ray
                 Henderson] vR
    78: Columbia 1878-D, (E) 5545

Columbia, New York, N.Y. Monday, April 15, 1929
IPANA TROUBADORS
Sam Lanin (ldr) Leo McConville, Mannie Klein (tp) *Tom Dorsey [or]
Chuck Campbell* (tb) **Jimmy Dorsey,** *Merle Johnston [or] Arnold
Brilhart* (cl,as) *unknown* (cl,ts) Arthur Schutt (p) *John Cali* (bj) *Hank
Stern [or] Joe Tarto* (bb) Vic Berton (d) Smith Ballew (vcl)

W 148439-3   **Building A Nest For Mary** [Billy Rose, Jesse Greer]
                 vSB
    78: Columbia 1815-D, (Au) 01617
W 148440-3   **I Used To Love Her In The Moonlight (But She's
                 In The Limelight Now)** vSB (cl solos)
    78: Columbia 1815-D, (Au) 01617
    LP: Harrison LP-I

OKeh, New York, N.Y. Friday, April 19, 1929
MIFF MOLE'S MOLERS
Leo McConville, Mannie Klein (tp) Miff Mole (tb) **Jimmy Dorsey** (cl,as) Arthur Schutt (p) Eddie Lang (401815 only) (g) Stan King (d)

401815-C   **I've Got A Feeling I'm Falling** [Billy Rose; Harry Link, Thomas "Fats" Waller] (as,cl solos)
    78: OKeh 41232, Parlophone PNY-41232, (E) R-421, R-2355, (Au) A-2976, Odeon (F) 279695, (G) A-189260
       Parlophone PNY as JOE CURRAN AND HIS ORCH.
    LP: Parlophone (E) PMC7126, Swaggie (Au) 1297
401816-A   **That's A-Plenty** [Lew Pollack] (cl solo)
    78: Odeon (F) 279695, Parlophone (E) R-421, R-2336, Odeon (Arg) 286090
    LP: Swaggie (Au) 1297
401816-B   **That's A-Plenty** (cl solo)
    78: OKeh 41232, Parlophone PNY-41232, (E) R-421, R-2336, (Au) A-2964
       Parlophone PNY as JOE CURRAN AND HIS ORCH.
    LP: Parlophone (E) PMC7126, Swaggie (Au) 1297
401816-C   **That's A-Plenty** (cl solo)
    78: Odeon (G) A-189260

Pathe, New York, N.Y. c. Friday, April 26, 1929
SAM LANIN AND HIS ORCHESTRA
Sam Lanin (ldr) 2 *unknown* (tp) Miff Mole (tb) **Jimmy Dorsey** (cl,as) *Merle Johnston* (cl,ts) Arthur Schutt (p) *Tony Colucci* (bj) Jimmy Mullen (bb) *Stan King* (d) Scrappy Lambert (vcl)

8715-2,-3   **Do Something!** [Bud Green; Sam Stept] vSL (cl solo)
    78: Banner 6388(-2), Domino 4337, Regal 8783, Oriole 1574 (-2), Broadway 1274(-2), Conqueror 7354(-2), Apex (C) 8939(-3), Crown 81048(-2), Imperial 2099
8716-3   **From Sunrise To Sunset (From Sunset 'Til Dawn)** [Ben McLaughlin; Jack Miller] vSL
    78: Banner 6382, Domino 4336, Regal 8784, Oriole 1584, Broadway 1274, Conqueror 7355, Apex (C) 8965, Crown 81142
8717-3   **I'm Just A Vagabond Lover** [Leon Zimmerman, Rudy Vallee] vSL
    78: Banner 6379, Domino 4340, Regal 8786, Oriole 1573, Broadway 1278, Challenge 825, Apex (C) 8955, Crown 81094, Imperial 2222, Kristall (G) 4025
       For this session: Broadways as THE BADGERS, Orioles as MIAMI SOCIETY ORCH., Apexes as LANIN & IIIS ORCH., Crown 81048 as SOUTHERN NIGHT HAWKS, 81094 as ERNIE NOBLE & HIS ORCH., Kristall as LOU GOLD UND SEIN ORCHESTER

Columbia, New York, N.Y. Monday, April 29, 1929
ARTHUR ROSS AND HIS WESTERNERS
2 *unknown* (tp) Tom Dorsey (tb) **Jimmy Dorsey** (cl,as) *unknown* (ts) Art Schutt (p) *unknown* (bj), (bb), (d) Irving Kaufman [as Tom Frawley,

Robert Wood or Jim Andrews] (vcl)

148389-2   **Do Something!** [Bud Green; Sam H. Stept] vIK[TF]
                  (cl solo)
      78: Harmony 913-H, Diva 2913-G, Velvet Tone 1913-V
148390-2   **The One In The World** [Little; Ekersley] vIK[RW]
      78: Harmony 907-H, Diva 2907-G, Velvet Tone 1907-V
148391-2   **Jericho** [Leo Robin; Richard Myers] vIK[TF] (as
                  solo)
      78: Harmony 908-H, Diva 2908-G, Velvet Tone 1908-V
148392-2   **Alabamy Snow** vIK[JA] [Lee David, Fred Rose] (cl
                  solo)
      78: Harmony 926-H, Diva 2926-G, Velvet Tone 1926-V

Pathe, New York, N.Y. Late April 1929
SAM LANIN AND HIS ORCHESTRA
Sam Lanin (ldr) *Leo McConville, unknown* (tp) Tom Dorsey (tb) **Jimmy
Dorsey,** *unknown* (cl,as) Merle Johnston (cl,ts) *unknown* (vn) Art Schutt
(p) *unknown* (bj) Jimmy Mullen (bb) Stan King (d) *unknown* (xyl)
Scrappy Lambert [as Andrew Lawrence or "Wee" Willie Robyn] (vcl)

108760-1   **I've Got A Feeling I'm Falling** [Billy Rose; Harry
                  Link, Thomas "Fats" Waller] vSL[WR] (as solos)
      78: Pathe Actuelle 36983, Perfect 15164
      as CASINO DANCE ORCHESTRA
      (3793-A) **78:** Cameo 9165, Lincoln 3192, Romeo 967, Angelus
      (Au) 3192
      *Angelus as THE CLEVELANDERS, all others as CLIFF
      ROBERTS AND HIS ORCHESTRA*
108762-1   **Louise** [Leo Robin; Richard Whiting] vSL
      78: Pathe Actuelle 36979, Perfect 15160
      as DAN RITCHIE AND HIS ORCHESTRA
      (3795-A) **78:** Cameo 9157, Lincoln 3184, Romeo 959, Starr (Au)
      748, Dominion (E) A-164, Angelus (Au) 3103
      *Cameo, Lincoln and Romeo as BROADWAY BROAD-
      CASTERS, Angelus as EMIL SEIDEL AND HIS ORCH.,
      Starr as ELMER GROSSO AND HIS ORCH.*
108763-1   **(You Can't Take Away) The Things That Were
                  Made For Love** [Charles Tobias, Irving Kahal, Peter
                  De Rose] vSL (cl solo)
      78: Pathe Actuelle 36982, Perfect 15163
      as THE TEN FRESHMEN
      (3796-A) **78:** Cameo 9156, Lincoln 3183, Romeo 958
      as BROADWAY BROADCASTERS
108764-1   **(When I'm Walking With My Sweetness) Down
                  Among The Sugar Cane** [Charles Tobias, Sidney
                  Clare; Peter De Rose] vSL (as solo)
      78: Pathe Actuelle 36977, Perfect 15158
      (3797-A) **78:** Cameo 9140, Lincoln 3167, Romeo 942
      Cameo, Lincoln, Romeo as BROADWAY BROADCASTERS
108770-1,2   **Jericho** [Leo Robin, Richard Myers] vSL[AL] (as
                  solo)   (Contd.)

SAM LANIN AND HIS ORCHESTRA (Contd.)

> **78:** Pathe Actuelle 36979, Perfect 15160 *as FRANK KEYES & HIS ORCHESTRA*
> (3801-B) **78:** Cameo 9145, Lincoln 3172, Romeo 942, Dominion (E) A-163, Angelus (Au) 3116
>> *Dominion as DEAUVILLE DANCE ORCHESTRA, Angelus as JARDIN ROYAL ORCHESTRA, others as CLIFF ROBERTS & HIS ORCHESTRA*

108771-1   **Love Me Or Leave Me** [Gus Kahn; Walter Donaldson] vSL[AL] (cl solo)
> **78:** Pathe Actuelle 36978, Perfect 15159
>> *as MAJESTIC DANCE ORCHESTRA*
> (-0-) **78:** Cameo 9141, Lincoln 3168, Romeo 943
>> *as PAUL MILLS' MERRY-MAKERS*

3810-A   **Coquette** [Gus Kahn; Johnny Green, Carmen Lombardo] vSL
> **78:** Cameo 9151, Lincoln 3178, Romeo 953
>> *as VINCENT RICHARDS AND HIS ORCHESTRA*

Brunswick, New York, N.Y. April 1929
THE EIGHT RADIO STARS
Tommy Gott (tp) Tom Dorsey (tb) **Jimmy Dorsey** (cl) Andy Sanella (as) Rube Bloom (p) Joe Tarto (bb) George Hamilton Green (xyl) Stan King (d) Scrappy Lambert (vcl)

E-29466   **A Happy Ending** vSL (cl solo)
> **78:** Brunswick 4311, (F) A-8394
E-29467   **Always In My Heart** [Bert Kalmar; Harry Ruby] vSL
> **78:** Brunswick 4312, (E) 3996
E-29468   **Under The Stars Of Havana** [Coleman, Blue] vSL
> **78:** Brunswick 4311, (F) A-8394

OKeh, New York, N.Y. Wednesday, May 1, 1929
JOE VENUTI AND HIS NEW YORKERS
Joe Venuti (vn,ldr) Leo McConville, Fuzzy Farrar, Phil Napoleon (tp) Tom Dorsey (tb) **Jimmy Dorsey,** Jimmy Crossan (cl,as) Alfie Evans (cl,ts) Arthur Schutt (p) Eddie Lang (g) Joe Tarto (bb) Stan King (d) Smith Ballew (vcl)

W 401846-B   **I'm In Seventh Heaven** [Al Jolson, Buddy De Sylva, Lew Brown; Ray Henderson] vSB (as solo)
> **78:** OKeh 41263, Parlophone (E) R-427, (Au) A-2947, B-12802, Odeon (Γ) 165813, (Arg) 193374, A-189265
> **LP:** The Old Masters 7, JSP (E) 1111
W 401847-C   **Little Pal** [Buddy De Sylva, Lew Brown; Ray Henderson] vSB
> **78:** OKeh 41263, Parlophone (E) R-427, (Au) A-2947, B-12802, Odeon (F) 165813, (Arg) 193374, A-189265, Ariel (E) 4452
>> *Ariel as ARIEL DANCE ORCHESTRA, Parlophone R-427 as JOE VENUTI AND HIS CONCERT ORCHESTRA*
> **LP:** The Old Masters 7, JSP (E) 1111

Plaza, New York, N.Y. c. Friday, May 3, 1929
FRED RICH AND HIS ORCHESTRA
Fred Rich (ldr) Leo McConville, *unknown* (tp) Tom Dorsey (tb) **Jimmy
Dorsey,** *unknown* (cl,as) *unknown* (ts), (p) Carl Kress (g) Joe Tarto
(bb,sb) *unknown* (d) Irving Kaufman [as Ray Wynn on some] (vcl)

8729-1,3   **Jericho** [Leo Robin; Richard Myers] vIK [RW on
                  Broadway]
        78: Banner 6383, Broadway 1278, Oriole 1575, Imperial 2099,
        Paramount 20719, Apex (C) 8945, Crown 81047, Edison Bell
        Radio (E) 1261
                *Broadway as FRANK RAYMOND'S DANCE ORCHESTRA,
                Crown as JACK MARSHALL'S ORCHESTRA, Edison Bell
                Radio (an 8-inch dub from the original) as THE BLUE JAYS*
8730-2   **The One In The World** [George Little, Ekersley]
                  vIK [RW on Broadway, Paramount]
        78: Banner 6392, Broadway 1280, Domino 4336, Paramount
        20721, Regal 8784, Conqueror 7355
                Broadway as FRANK RAYMOND'S DANCE ORCHESTRA
8731   **That's Living** vIK[RW]
        78: Broadway 1280
                as FRANK RAYMOND'S DANCE ORCHESTRA

Pathe, New York, N.Y. c. Wednesday, May 8, 1929
SAM LANIN AND HIS ORCHESTRA
Sam Lanin (ldr) *Leo McConville, unknown* (tp) Tom Dorsey (tb) *Jimmy
Dorsey, unknown* (cl,as) *unknown* (cl,ts) Rube Bloom (p) *unknown* (bj),
(bb), (d) Scrappy Lambert [as Larry Rich on some] (vcl)

108785-1   **Pagan Love Song** [Arthur Freed; Nacio Herb Brown]
                  vSL[LR]
        78: Pathe Actuelle 36987, Perfect 15168
        (3825-A) **78:** Cameo 9159, Lincoln 3186, Romeo 961
                *Pathe Actuelle and Perfect as LARRY RICH AND HIS
                FRIENDS, others as VINCENT RICHARDS AND HIS ORCH.*

Pathe, New York, N.Y. c. Friday, May 10, 1929
SAM LANIN AND HIS ORCHESTRA
Sam Lanin (ldr) Phil Napoleon, *unknown* (tp) *Tom Dorsey [or] Miff
Mole* (tb) **Jimmy Dorsey,** Andy Sanella (cl,as) *Merle Johnston* (cl,ts)
Arthur Schutt (p,celst) Tony Colucci (bj) Jimmy Mullen (bb) Stan King
(d) Scrappy Lambert [as Larry Rich on some] (vcl)

108788-2   **Bless You! Sister** vSL
        78: Pathe Actuelle 36991, Perfect 15172
        (3839-A) **78:** Cameo 9161, Lincoln 3188, Romeo 963
                *Cameo, Lincoln and Romeo as VINCENT RICHARDS AND
                HIS ORCHESTRA*
108789-   **Wake Up! Chillun, Wake Up!** [J. Russell Robinson,
                  Jo Trent] vSL [LR on Pathe Actuelle, Perfect] (as
                  solo)
        78: Pathe Actuelle 36987, Perfect 15168 (Contd.)

SAM LANIN AND HIS ORCHESTRA (Contd.)

>   *as LARRY RICH AND HIS FRIENDS*
>   (3838-A) **78:** Cameo 9160, Lincoln 3187, Romeo 962, Perfect
>   15168
>   *as DIXIE DAISIES*
108790-2   **Do Something!** [Bud Green; Sam H. Stept] vSL
>   **78:** Pathe Actuelle 36990, Perfect 15171
>   *as TUXEDO DANCE ORCHESTRA*
>   (3837-A) **78:** Cameo 9158, Lincoln 3185, Romeo 960, Dominion
>   A154, Angelus (Au) 3116, Plaza (Au) 3116
>   *Angelus, Plaza as JARDIN ROYAL ORCH., Cameo, Lincoln,*
>   *Romeo, Dominion as BROADWAY BROADCASTERS*
>   **LP:** Harrison LP-H, The Old Masters 28 (labeled as "#2")

Columbia, New York, N.Y. Friday, May 10, 1929
FRED RICH AND HIS ORCHESTRA
Fred Rich (ldr) Leo McConville (tp) Tom Dorsey (tb) **Jimmy Dorsey,**
Tony Parenti, *unknown* (cl,as) *unknown* (p) Carl Kress (g) Joe Tarto
(bb,sb) *unknown* (d) The Rollickers (vcl)

W 148502-3   **Singin' In The Rain** [Arthur Freed; Nacio Herb
>   Brown] vR
>   **78:** Columbia 1838-D, (E) 5561, (Au) 01628
>   **LP:** The Old Masters 50, Saville (E) SVL 175
>   **TC:** Saville (E) CSVL 175
W 148503-3   **Nobody But You** [Joe Goodwin; Gus Edwards] vR
>   (cl solo)
>   **78:** Columbia 1838-D, (E) 5561, (Au) 01628
>   **LP:** The Old Masters 27, Vintage Jazz Music Society VLP56
>   **CD:** The Old Masters 101

   The following session has been carried for decades (including in the
author's recent book and even Columbia LP liner notes) as being made
on June 13, 1929. Both Richard Johnson, revising the Brian Rust *American Dance Band Discography* volumes and Ray Mitchell, researching an
Eddie Lang discography, found the error recently in the original
Columbia file cards.

OKeh, New York, N.Y. Monday, May 13, 1929
JAMES DORSEY (WITH ACCOMPANIMENT)
Jimmy Dorsey (cl,as) Leo McConville, Mannie Klein (tp) Tom Dorsey
(tb) Alfie Evans (as) Paul Mason (ts) Arthur Schutt (p) Eddie Lang (g)
Joe Tarto (sb) Stan King (d)

W 401877-B   **Beebe** [James Dorsey] (as solo)
>   **78:** OKeh 41245, Parlophone (It) B-27059, (E) R-449, Odeon
>   (F) 165757, (Arg) 193336, A-189279, (G) A-286001
>   **LP:** Columbia C4L18, Odeon (G) SMS1, Parlophone PMC7133,
>   Swaggie (Au) S1299
>   **TC:** Radio Yesteryear Stack 15
>   **CD:** Jazz Oracle (C) BDW 8005

W 401878-C   **Prayin' The Blues** [James Dorsey] (cl solo)
    78: OKeh 41245, Parlophone (E) R-511, (Au) A-3245, (It) B-27059, Odeon (F) 165757, (Arg) 193336, A-2320, A-189291, (G) A-286012, Columbia 36063 (in set C-51)
    LP: The Old Masters 15, Odeon (G) SMS3, Parlophone PMC-7133, Swaggie (Au) S1299
    CD: Jazz Oracle (C) BDW 8005, Jazz Greats (E) 036

Pathe, New York, N.Y. c. Monday, May 13, 1929
SAM LANIN AND HIS ORCHESTRA
Sam Lanin (ldr) *Leo McConville, unknown* (tp) Tom Dorsey (tb) **Jimmy Dorsey,** *unknown* (cl,as) *unknown* (cl,ts) Rube Bloom (p) *unknown* (bj), (bb), (d) Scrappy Lambert (vcl)

108793-2   **The Desert Song** [Oscar Hammerstein II, Otto Harbach; Sigmund Romberg] vSL
    78: Pathe Actuelle 36986, Perfect 15167
    (3861-2) **78:** Cameo 9169, Lincoln 3196, Romeo 971, Angelus (Au) 3063
108794-2   **One Alone** [Oscar Hammerstein II, Otto Harbach; Sigmund Romberg] vSL
    78: Pathe Actuelle 36986, Perfect 15167
    (3860-2) **78:** Cameo 9168, Lincoln 3195, Romeo 970, Angelus (Au) 3063
        For 108793 and 108794: Cameo, Lincoln and Romeo as BROADWAY BROADCASTERS, Angelus as LOU GOLDEN & HIS ORCH.

Victor, New York, N.Y. Tuesday, May 14, 1929
NAPOLEON'S EMPERORS
Phil Napoleon (tp) Tom Dorsey (tb) **Jimmy Dorsey** (cl,as) Joe Venuti (vn) Frank Signorelli (p) Ed Lang (g) Joe Tarto (sb) Stan King (d)

BVE 53615-3   **Mean To Me** [Roy Turk; Fred E. Ahlert] (as solos)
    78: Victor V-38057, Bluebird B-6574, B-7101
    LP: The Old Masters 13, Victor "X" LVA 3036, (J) RA5334, Jazz Archives ZET715, Bluebird AD83136
    TC: Bluebird AD83136, Stack of 78's #71
BVE 53616-2   **My Kinda Love** [Jo Trent; Louis Alter] (as,cl solos)
    78: Victor V-38057, Bluebird B-6574, B-7101
    LP: The Old Masters 13, Victor "X" LVA 3036, (J) RA5334, Jazz Archives ZET715, Bluebird AD83136
    TC: Bluebird AD83136, Stack of 78's #71
    Both sides also on **CD:** Jazz Archives ZET715, Bluebird 3136-2-RB, Timeless (H) CBC 1-049

Columbia, New York, N.Y. Tuesday, May 14, 1929
IPANA TROUBADORS
Sam Lanin (ldr) Leo McConville, Mannie Klein (tp) *Tom Dorsey [or] Chuck Campbell* (tb) **Jimmy Dorsey,** *Merle Johnston* (cl,as) *unknown* (cl,ts) Arthur Schutt (p) *John Cali* (bj) *Hank Stern [or] Joe Tarto* (bb) Vic Berton (d) Smith Ballew (vcl)

IPANA TROUBADORS (Contd.)

W 148526-2   **That's Living** vSB
   78: Columbia 1840-D
W 148527-3   **To Be In Love (Espesh'lly With You)** [Roy Turk;
                  Fred E. Ahlert] vSB
   78: Columbia 1840-D, (E) 5541, (Au) 01660

Columbia, New York, N.Y. Tuesday, May 14, 1929
ETHEL WATERS
Mannie Klein (tp) Tom Dorsey (tb) **Jimmy Dorsey** (cl) Frank Signorelli
(p) Joe Tarto (sb) Ethel Waters (vcl)

W 148531-3   **Birmingham Bertha** [Grant Clarke; Harry Akst]vEW
   78: Columbia 1837-D, (E) 5534, 01739, (Arg) A-8600
   LP: CBS CL2792
   CD: Timeless (H) CBC 1-007, Classics (F) 688
W 148532-2   **Am I Blue?** [Grant Clarke; Harry Akst] vEW (cl
                  solo)
   78: Columbia 1837-D, (E) 5534, 01739, (Arg) A-8600
   LP: Columbia Special Products P2-11919, CBS CL2792
   CD: ASV (E) AJA5031, Timeless (H) CBC1-007, Classics (F) 688
W 148532-3   **Am I Blue?** vEW (cl solo)
   LP: CBS CL2230, C3L35

Brunswick, New York, N.Y. c. Wednesday, May 15, 1929
ROGER WOLFE KAHN AND HIS ORCHESTRA
Roger Wolfe Kahn (ldr) Tony Gianelli, John Egan (tp) Charlie But-
terfield (tb) Dudley Fosdick (mel) Fred Morrow, **Jimmy Dorsey** (cl,as)
Babe Russin (ts) Joe Venuti, Henry Whiteman (vn) Jack Russin (p) Tony
Colucci (bj) Joe Tarto (bb) Chauncey Morehouse (d) Frank Munn (vcl)

E-29840   **Pretty Little Thing** vFM
   78: Brunswick 4374, 5033
E-29841   **Heigh-Ho, Everybody, Heigh-Ho** [Harry Woods]
               vFM
   78: Brunswick 4374, 5033

Brunswick, New York, N.Y. Thursday, May 16, 1929
COTTON PICKERS
Tom Dorsey (cnt,ldr) Glenn Miller (tb) **Jimmy Dorsey** (cl,as) Arthur
Schutt (p) *Carl Kress* (g) Joe Tarto (sb) Stan King (d) Dick Robertson
(vcl)

E 29847-A   **No Parking** [Napoleon, Rah, Chase] (as,cl solos)
   78: Brunswick 4440, (F) 1033
   LP: Arcadia (C) 2013, Broadway BR115
   CD: Timeless (H) CBC 1-049
E 29848-A   **Sweet Ida Joy** [Harris, Abrahms] vDR (as,cl solos)
   78: Brunswick 4404, (F) 1011
   LP: Arcadia (C) 2013
   CD: Timeless (H) CBC 1-049

OKeh, New York, N.Y. Friday, May 17, 1929
SAM LANIN AND HIS FAMOUS PLAYERS
Sam Lanin (ldr) Phil Napoleon, *unknown* (tp) Tom Dorsey (tb) **Jimmy Dorsey**, Andy Sanella (cl,as) *Merle Johnston* (cl,ts) Arthur Schutt (p) *Tony Colucci* (bj) *Jimmy Mullen* (bb) *Stan King* (d) Smith Ballew (vcl)

W 401896-A   **Now I'm In Love** vSB
        78: OKeh 41264, Parlophone (E) R-401, (Au) A-2790, A-2858,
        Odeon ONY-41264, (Arg) 193356
        Odeon ONY and OKeh as NEW YORK SYNCOPATORS
W 401897-A   **When My Dreams Come True** [Irving Berlin] vSB
        (as solo)
        78: OKeh 41257, Parlophone (E) R-418, (G) B-12841, (Au) A-2813, Odeon (G) A-189226
W 401898-A   **This Is Heaven** [Jack Yellen; Harry Akst] vSB
        same relesaes as 401898.

Pathe, New York, N.Y. c. Friday, May 17, 1929
SAM LANIN AND HIS ORCHESTRA
Sam Lanin (ldr) *Leo McConville, unknown* (tp) Tom Dorsey (tb) **Jimmy Dorsey,** *unknown* (cl,as) *unknown* (cl,ts) Rube Bloom (p) *unknown* (bj), (bb), (d) Scrappy Lambert (vcl)

3865-A   **Sleepy Valley** [Andrew Sterling, James F. Hanley]
        vSL (as solo)
        78: Cameo 9172, Lincoln 3199, Romeo 974
        as CLIFF ROBERTS & HIS ORCHESTRA
        (108820-A) **78:** Pathe Actuelle 36993, Perfect 15174
        as SAM LANIN AND HIS TROUBADORS
3866   **Blue Hawaii** vSL
        78: Cameo 9173, Lincoln 3200, Romeo 975
        (-0-) **78:** Pathe Actuelle 36988, Perfect 15169
        Pathe Actuelle and Perfect as TEN FRESHMEN

Brunswick, New York, N.Y. Monday, May 20, 1929
RED NICHOLS AND HIS FIVE PENNIES
Bob Haring (dir) Red Nichols, Leo McConville, Mannie Klein (tp) Jack Teagarden (tb,vcl) Glenn Miller (tb,arr), Herb Taylor (tb) Bill Trone (mel) **Jimmy Dorsey** (cl,as) Alfie Evans, Arnold Brilhart (cl,as,bsn,fl,o) Larry Binyon (ts,fl,o) Murray Kellner, Joe Raymond, Lou Raderman, Henry Whiteman (vn) Lucien Schmidt (cel) Arthur Schutt (p,arr) Carl Kress (g) Joe Tarto (bb) Vic Berton (d) Scrappy Lambert (vcl)

XE-29957-A   **Sally, Won't You Come Back?** [Gene Buck; Dave
        Stamper] vJT,SL (cl solo) arrGM
        78: (12-inch) Brunswick 20092, (C) 20092, (E) O101
        LP: Ace Of Hearts (E) AH-168, Sunbeam MFC-12, Affinity (E)
        AFS-1038, Swaggie (Au) 840 **TC:** Radio Yesteryear Stack 31
        CD: Tax (Swe) S-5-2
CE-29957-G   **Sally, Won't You Come Back?** arrGM
        78: (12-inch) (unissued)

Brunswick, New York, N.Y. Monday, May 20, 1929
COTTON PICKERS
Phil Napoleon (tp) Glenn Miller (tb) **Jimmy Dorsey** (cl,as) *unknown* (cl, ts) *Art Schutt* (p) Joe Tarto (sb) Vic Berton (d) Scrappy Lambert (vcl)

E-29958   **Sugar Is Back In Town** [Landay, Springer] vSL
                   (cl,as solos)
       78: Brunswick 4404, 1011
       LP: Arcadia (C) 2013
       CD: Timeless (H) CBC 1-049

Pathe, New York, N.Y. c. Tuesday, May 21, 1929
SAM LANIN AND HIS ORCHESTRA
Personnel as May 17, 1929. Scrappy Lambert [as William Smith or Chester Hale on some] (vcl)

108809-2   **What A Day!** [Harry Woods] vSL[WS]
       78: Pathe Actuelle 36998, Perfect 15179
              as HAROLD WHITE AND HIS ORCHESTRA
       LP: The Old Masters 28
       (3939-A) **78:** Cameo 9211, Romeo 1013, Lincoln 3238
108810-3   **The World Is Yours And Mine** [Bud Green, James
                   F. Hanley, Sam H. Stept] vSL[CH on Pathe, Perfect]
                   (cl solos)
       78: Pathe Actuelle 36993, Perfect 15174
              as SAM LANIN AND HIS TROUBADORS
       (3882-) **78:** Cameo 9189, Lincoln 3216, Romeo 991
              as BROADWAY BROADCASTERS
108811-1,3   **Heigh-Ho! Everybody, Heigh-Ho!** [Harry Woods]
                   vSL
       78: Pathe Actuelle 36994, Perfect 15175
              as MAJESTIC DANCE ORCHESTRA
       (3873) **78:** Cameo 9182, Lincoln 3209, Romeo 984

OKeh, New York, N.Y. Wednesday, May 22, 1929
EDDIE LANG AND HIS ORCHESTRA
Eddie Lang (g,ldr) Leo McConville (tp) Tom Dorsey (cnt,tb) **Jimmy Dorsey** (cl,as) Arthur Schutt (p) Joe Tarto (sb,bb) Stan King (d)

W 401958-C   **Bugle Call Rag** [Jack Pettis, Elmer Schoebel, Billy
                   Myers] (as,cl solos)
       78: OKeh 41410, Clarion 5461-C, Harmony 1415-H, Velvet
       Tone 2521V, Parlophone (E) R-510, Odeon (G) A286003, 028500
              Clarion, Harmony, Velvet Tone as TENNESSEE MUSIC MEN
       LP: Columbia C4L18, Odeon (G) SMS1, Parlophone (E) PMC-
       7133, Swaggie (Au) S1299
       CD: ABC CD-36200
W 401959-B   **Freeze An' Melt** [Dorothy Fields; Jimmy McHugh]
                   (cl,as solos)
       78: OKeh 8696, 41253, Parlophone (E) R-448, 22429, Odeon
       (Arg) 193397, A189327, (G) A286000, (Norway) D5034, 028500
       LP: Columbia C4L18, Odeon (G) SMS1, Parlophone (E) PMC-

7133, Swaggie (Au) S1299
W 401960-C   **Hot Heels** [Al Goering, Jack Pettis, Irving Mills]
                  (cl solos)
    78: OKeh 8696, 41253, Parlophone (E) R-596, 22429, (Au)
    A7404, Odeon (Arg) 193397, A2316, A189327, (G) A286010
    LP: Swaggie (Au) S1299
    All three sides also on **CD:** ASV Living Era AJA 5061

On "Hot Heels" (really a take off on Louis Armstrong's "King of the
Zulus") Tommy Dorsey hits several successively higher notes. Close
listening however will show that the last of these is actually played by
Jimmy on clarinet. Talk about brotherly support!

Victor, New York, N.Y. Thursday, May 23, 1929
PHIL NAPOLEON'S EMPERORS
Phil Napoleon (tp,ldr) Tom Dorsey (tb) **Jimmy Dorsey** (cl,as) Joe
Venuti (vn) Frank Signorelli (p) Eddie Lang (g) Joe Tarto (bb) Ted
Napoleon (d)

BVE 53506-2   **Gettin' Hot (Waterloo)** [Ray Stillwell] (cl solo)
    78: Victor 23039, His Master's Voice (E) B-4890
          as JOE VENUTI AND HIS ORCHESTRA
    LP: The Old Masters 13, Victor "X" LVA 3036, Jazz Archives
    ZET715, Bluebird AD83136
    TC: Bluebird 3136
    CD: RCA 3136, Jazz Archives (F) ZET715, Timeless (H) CBC 1-
    049
BVE 53507-2   **Anything (*Thunder In My Dreams)** [Phil Napol-
          eon, Frank Signorelli] (cl solo)
    78: Victor V-38069, His Master's Voice (E) B-4955, *Bluebird
    B-7039
    LP: The Old Masters 13, Broadway BR-117, Jazz Archives ZET-
    715, Bluebird AD-83136
    CD: RCA 3136, Jazz Archives (F) ZET-715, Timeless (H) CBC
    1-049
BVE 53508-1   **You Can't Cheat A Cheater** [Phil Napoleon, Tom
          Dorsey, Frank Signorelli] (cl solos)
    78: Victor V-38069, His Master's Voice (E) BD-120
    LP: The Old Masters 13, Broadway BR117, Jazz Archives ZET-
    715, Bluebird AD-83136
    TC: Bluebird 3136
    CD: RCA 3136, Jazz Archives (F) ZET-715
BVE 53508-2   **You Can't Cheat A Cheater** (cl solos)
    78: His Master's Voice (E) B-4955
    LP: Victor "X" LVA-3036
    CD: Timeless (H) CBC 1-049

Brunswick, New York, N.Y. Friday, May 24, 1929
IRVING MILLS AND HIS HOTSY TOTSY GANG
Bill Moore (cnt) Tom Dorsey (tb) **Jimmy Dorsey** (cl,as) Irving Mills
(vn,vcl) *unknown* (vn) Jack Cornell (acc) Al Goering (p) Clay Bryson
(bj) Merrill Kline (bb) Dillon Ober (d)

E 29946-A   **What A Girl! What A Night!** [Joe Sanders] vIM
    78: Brunswick 4998, (G) A-8831
    LP: The Old Masters 12, Retrieval (E) FJ122
E 29947-A   **St. Louis Blues** [William C. Handy] (cl solo)
    78: Banner 32701, Melotone M-12051, M-12632, Oriole 2654,
    Perfect 15738, Polk P-9031, Romeo 2027, Vocalion 15860
    LP: The Old Masters 12, Retrieval (E) FJ122
E 29948-A   **I Wonder What My Gal Is Doin' Now** (unissued)

Irving Mills was probably the sharpest and undoubtedly one of the
most aggressive men behind the scenes of the late twenties music world
in New York City. A songwriter and singer-of-sorts as well as a prin-
cipal in the publishing firm Mills Music, Inc., he is probably best known
as the manager who propelled Duke Ellington to stardom. But despite
his fondness for the Cotton Club and the music of Harlem he very
seldom used its musicians on record dates under his own name.

Cameo, New York, N.Y. c. Wednesday, May 29, 1929
SAM LANIN AND HIS ORCHESTRA
Sam Lanin (ldr) *Leo McConville, unknown* (tp) Tom Dorsey (tb) Jimmy
Dorsey (cl,as) *unknown* (as), (ts) *Rube Bloom* (p) *unknown* (bj), (bb), (d)
Sid Garry (vcl)

3891-B   **You Oughta Know** vSG
    78: Cameo 9201, Lincoln 3228, Romeo 1003
        as MILLS' MERRY MAKERS
3892-A   **Tell Me You're My Pretty Baby** vSG
    78: Cameo 9199, Lincoln 3227, Romeo 1001
        as VINCENT RICHARDS AND HIS ORCHESTRA
3893-A   **My Baby Is Back Again** vSG
    78: Cameo 9200, Lincoln 3226, Romeo 1002
        as REGENT CLUB ORCHESTRA

Columbia, New York, N.Y. Friday, May 31, 1929
ANNETTE HANSHAW (accomp. by THE NEW ENGLANDERS)
Ben Selvin (ldr) *Phil Napoleon* (tp) *unknown* (tb) **Jimmy Dorsey** (cl)
Hymie Wolfson (cl,ts) *unknown* (vn) Art Schutt (p) Tony Colucci (g)
Hank Stern [or] Joe Tarto (bb) Stan King (d) Annette Hanshaw (vcl)

148647-1   **Am I Blue?** [Grant Clarke; Harry Akst] vAH
    78: Harmony 940-H, Publix 1022-P, (Lobby Record) 1038-P
    CD: Take Two 408
148647-3   **Am I Blue?** vAH
    78: (test pressing)
    LP: World Records (E) SH246
148648-4   **Daddy Won't You Please Come Home?** [Sam Cos-
            low] vAH (cl solo)
    78: Harmony 940-H, Publix 1021-P
    LP: Sunbeam MFC-17, Columbia P-14302, World Records (E)
    SH246
    TC: Columbia/Legacy C2T 52943, CT52932
    CD: Columbia/Legacy C2K 52943, Take Two 408

Pathe, New York, N.Y. May 1929
LA PALINA BROADCASTERS (Fred Rich and His Orch.)
Fred Rich (ldr) Leo McConville, *unknown* (tp) Tom Dorsey (tb,cnt)
Jimmy Dorsey, Tony Parenti (cl,as) Fred Cusick (cl,as,ts) Al Duffy
(vn) *unknown* (p) Carl Kress (g) Joe Tarto (bb,sb) Stan King (d) Irving
Kaufman (vcl)

-0-   **Oh, Sweetheart, Where Are You Tonight?** vIK
    78: Pathe Actuelle 36989, Perfect 15170
108778-3   **The Rainbow Man** vIK
    78: Pathe Actuelle 36980, Perfect 15161
108779-1   **Christina (waltz)** vIK
    78: Pathe Actuelle 36980, Perfect 15161
108780   **Nobody's Fault But Your Own** vIK
    78: Pathe Actuelle 36981, Perfect 15162
108801-3   **Evangeline** [Billy Rose, Al Jolson] vIK
    78: Pathe Actuelle 36991, Perfect 15172
    (3907-3) **78:** Cameo 9199, Lincoln 3266, Romeo 1001
    Cameo and Romeo as FREDDIE RICH AND HIS ORCH.
    (8807) **78:** Banner 6436, Domino 4360, Regal 8804, Apex (C)
    8991, Crown (C) 81135, Oriole 1623, Conqueror 7374, Broadway
    1288, Embassy (Au) 8037
        *Banner as IMPERIAL DANCE ORCHESTRA, Domino, Regal
        and Apex as HOLLYWOOD DANCE ORCHESTRA, Crown
        as RENDEZVOUS CAFE ORCHESTRA, Conqueror as CALI-
        FORNIA COLLEGIANS, Broadway as EARL RANDOLPH
        AND HIS ORCHESTRA, Embassy as THE AMBASSADORS*
108802-2   **When My Dreams Come True** [Irving Berlin] vIK
                 (cl solo)
    78: Pathe Actuelle 36997, Perfect 15178
    (3858) **78:** Cameo 9166, Lincoln 3192, Romeo 968
    Cameo and Romeo as FREDDIE RICH AND HIS ORCH.

Plaza, New York, N.Y. Monday, June 3, 1929
SAM LANIN'S DANCE ORCHESTRA
Sam Lanin (ldr) Phil Napoleon, *unknown* (tp) *Tom Dorsey [or] Al
Philburn* (tb) **Jimmy Dorsey,** Larry Abbott (cl,as), *unknown* (cl,ts)
Arthur Schutt (p) *Tony Colucci* (bj) *unknown* (bb) *Stan King* (d) Scrappy
Lambert [as Rodman Lewis or Ralph Haines on some] (vcl)

8790-3   **Here We Are** [Gus Kahn; Harry Warren] vSL
    78: Banner 6426, Domino 4359, Regal 8802, Oriole 1609, Apex
    (C) 8969, Microphone (C) 22487, Broadcast (Au) W-512
        *Oriole as MIAMI SOCIETY ORCHESTRA, Microphone as
        THE ARCADIANS, Broadcast as LOS ANGELES AMBAS-
        SADORS*
8791-3   **Finding The Long Way Home** [Harry Warren] vSL
    78: Domino 4399, Regal 8844, Broadway 1289, Broadcast (Au)
    W-540
        *Broadway as THE BADGERS, Broadcast as ROXY DANCE
        ORCHESTRA*
                    (Contd.)

SAM LANIN'S DANCE ORCHESTRA (Contd.)

8792-1   **Love Me Or Leave Me** [Gus Kahn; Harry Warren]
                vSL[RH on Banner, Domino, Regal, RL on Broad-
                way]
     78: Banner 6410, Domino 4350, Regal 8805, Oriole 1604,
     Conqueror 7369, Apex (C) 8963, Imperial (E) 2144, Broadway
     1285, Jewel 5628, 5652
                Broadway as THE BADGERS, Oriole and Jewel as MIAMI
                SOCIETY ORCHESTRA, Conqueror as JOHN VINCENT'S
                CALIFORNIANS

OKeh, New York, N.Y. Tuesday, June 4, 1929
SEGER ELLIS
Louis Armstrong (tp) Tom Dorsey (tb) **Jimmy Dorsey** (cl) Harry
Hoffman (vn) Justin Ring (p,cel) Stan King (d) Seger Ellis (vcl)

W 402416-B   **S'posin'** [Andy Razaf; Paul Denniker] vSE
     78: OKeh 41255, Parlophone (E)R-475, Ariel (E) 4459, Odeon
     (Arg) 193379
                Ariel as NORMAN THORNE
     TC: Neovox (E) 932
     CD: Columbia CK 46148, Azure (E) CD 22
W 402417-C   **To Be In Love (Espesh'lly With You)** [Roy Turk;
                Fred E. Ahlert] vSE (cl solo)
     78: OKeh 41255, Parlophone (E)R-475, Ariel (E) 4460, Odeon
     (Arg) 193379
                Ariel as NORMAN THORNE
     TC: Neovox (E) 932
     CD: Columbia CK 46148, Azure (E) CD 22

Pathe, New York, N.Y. Early June 1929
FRED RICH AND HIS ORCHESTRA
Fred Rich (ldr) Leo McConville, *unknown* (tp) Tom Dorsey (tb,tp)
Jimmy Dorsey, *unknown* (cl,as) Fred Cusick (cl,as,ts) *unknown* (vn),
(p) Carl Kress (g) Joe Tarto (bb,sb) *unknown* (d) Irving Kaufman (vcl)

108830-3   **Kids Again** [Natoll, Stokes] vIK (cl solo)
     78: Pathe Actuelle 37005, Perfect 15186
                Perfect as LA PALINA BROADCASTERS
     (3895) **78:** Cameo 9194, Lincoln 3221, Romeo 996
108831-1   **A Night In May** vIK
     78: Pathe Actuelle 37035, Perfect 15216
                Perfect as DAN RITCHIE AND HIS ORCHESTRA

Pathe, New York, N.Y. c. Tuesday, June 4, 1929
SAM LANIN AND HIS ORCHESTRA
Sam Lanin (ldr) *Leo McConville, Mannie Klein* (tp) Tom Dorsey (tb)
Jimmy Dorsey (cl,as) Andy Sanella (as,stg) *unknown* (ts) Rube Bloom
(p) *unknown* (bj), (bb), (d) Scrappy Lambert [as William Smith, Roland
Lance or Chester Hale on some] (vcl)

108832-2   **Maybe—Who Knows?** [Joseph Shuster, Ruth Etting;
                Joseph Tucker] vSL[WS] (cl solo)
        78: Pathe Actuelle 37007, Perfect 15188
                as DAN RITCHIE AND HIS ORCHESTRA
        (3923-A,B) **78:** Cameo 9209, Lincoln 3236, Romeo 1011
                as BROADWAY BROADCASTERS
        (9095-2) **78:** Banner 6566, Oriole 1752, Broadway 1329, Apex
        (C) 41055
                Oriole as MIAMI SOCIETY ORCHESTRA, Broadway as THE
                BADGERS (vRL)
108833   **Or What Have You?** [Grace Henry; Morris Hamil-
                ton] vSL[CH]
        78: Pathe Actuelle 37000, Perfect 15181
108834   **I've Made A Habit Of You** vSL[CH]
        78: Pathe Actuelle 37000, Perfect 15181
                108833, 108834 as SAM LANIN'S TROUBADORS

A rarity in the next session is trombonist Jack Teagarden playing a
trumpet solo on "It's So Good." While his brother Charlie made a
musical life out of playing it, including several years in Jimmy's band,
Jack could play trumpet only passably and that because his father first
introduced him to it (sound familiar?). Two other siblings, Norma (p)
and Clois (d), were also professional musicians.
    At the time of these recordings, Teagarden had been in New York
about a year and was working with Ben Pollack's band.

Plaza, New York, N.Y. Thursday, June 6, 1929
IRVING MILLS ORCHESTRA
Jimmy McPartland (cnt) *Tommy Gott* (tp) Jack Teagarden (tp,tb,vcl)
Jimmy Dorsey, Gil Rodin (cl,as) Bud Freeman, Pee Wee Russell (cl,ts)
Vic Breidis (p) Dick Morgan (bj,vcl) Harry Goodman (bb) Ray Bauduc
(d) Jack Kaufman (vcl)

8761-5,6   **After You've Gone** [Henry Creamer; Turner Layton]
                vJK
        78: Banner 6441, Conqueror 7389, Domino 4381, Jewel 5648,
        Oriole 1624, Regal 8826
                Jewel and Oriole as DIXIE JAZZ BAND, all others as JIM-
                MY BRACKEN'S TOE TICKLERS
8762-6   **Twelfth Street Rag** [Euday L. Bowman] vDM
        78: Banner 6441, Conqueror 7382, Domino 4369, Jewel 5648,
        Oriole 1624, Regal 8813
                Jewel and Oriole as DIXIE JAZZ BAND, all others as JIM-
                MY BRACKEN'S TOE TICKLERS
        (108931-6) **78:** Pathe Actuelle 37036, Perfect 15217
                as THE WHOOPEE MAKERS
8763-5   **It's So Good** [Ben Pollack, Gil Rodin, Benny Good-
                man, Jack Teagarden] vJT
        78: Banner 6483, Conqueror 7382, Domino 4369, Jewel 5685,
        Oriole 1668, Regal 8813
                Jewel and Oriole as DIXIE JAZZ BAND, all others as JIM-
                MY BRACKEN'S TOE TICKLERS

IRVING MILLS ORCHESTRA (Contd.)

(108930-5) **78:** Pathe Actuelle 37036, Perfect 15217, United Hot
Clubs Of America (dubbing) 39
*Pathe Actuelle and Perfect as THE WHOOPEE MAKERS,
UHCA as JACK TEAGARDEN & THE WHOOPEE MAKERS*

Columbia, New York, N.Y. Friday, June 7, 1929
ETHEL WATERS
Ben Selvin (ldr) Bob Effros (tp) Tom Dorsey (tb) **Jimmy Dorsey** (cl,as)
Frank Signorelli (p) *unknown* (vn) Tony Colucci (g) Joe Tarto (sb) Stan
King (d) Ethel Waters (vcl)

W 148671-4   **True Blue Lou** [Leo Robin, Sam Coslow, Richard A.
Whiting] vEW (cl solo)
78: Columbia 1871-D, (E) 5648
LP: Columbia KG31571, P14302
CD: Timeless (H) CBC 1-007, Classic (F) 721
W 148672-1   **Do I Know What I'm Doing?** [Leo Robin, Sam Cos-
low, Richard A. Whiting] vEW (cl solos)
78: Columbia 1905-D, (E) 5690
LP: Columbia P14302
CD: Timeless (H) CBC 1-007, Classic (F) 721
W 148673-2   **Shoo Shoo Boogie Boo** [Leo Robin, Sam Coslow,
Richard A. Whiting] vEW
78: Columbia 1905-D, (E) 5690
CD: Timeless (H) CBC 1-007, Classic (F) 721

Brunswick, New York, N.Y. Friday, June 7, 1929
RED NICHOLS AND HIS FIVE PENNIES
Bob Haring (dir) Red Nichols (tp,arr) Tommy Thunen, *Mannie Klein
[or] Phil Hart* (tp) Jack Teagarden (tb,vcl) Glenn Miller, Herb Taylor
(tb,arr) **Jimmy Dorsey** (cl,as) Jimmy Crossan (cl,as) Arnold Brilhart
(cl,as,bsn,fl,o) Larry Binyon (ts,fl,o) Murray Kellner, Joe Raymond,
Henry Whiteman, Lou Raderman (vn) Lucian Schmidt (cel) Arthur
Schutt (p,arr) Carl Kress (g) Art Miller (sb) Joe Tarto (bb) Vic Berton
(d) Scrappy Lambert (vcl)

XE-29994-A   **It Had To Be You** [Gus Kahn; Isham Jones] arrAS
vSL
78: (12-inch) Brunswick 20092, (C) 20092, (E) O101
LP: Family (It) DP 693, Sunbeam MFC-12, Swaggie (Au) 840
TC: Radio Yesteryear Stack 31
CD: Tax (Swe) S-5-2
CE-29994-G   **It Had To Be You** (unissued)
XE-29995-A   **I'll See You In My Dreams** [Gus Kahn; Isham Jones]
arrGM vSL (cl solo)
78: (12-inch) Brunswick 20091, (C) 20091
LP: Family (It) DP 693, Sunbeam MFC-12, Swaggie (Au) 840
TC: Radio Yesteryear Stack 31
CD: Tax (Swe) S-5-2

CE-29995-G   **I'll See You In My Dreams** (unissued)
XE-29996-A   **Some Of These Days** [Shelton Brooks] arrRN&HT
                 vJT&SL (as solo)
    78: (12-inch) Brunswick 20091, (C) 20091
    LP: Family 693, Sunbeam MFC-12
    TC: Radio Yesteryear Stack 31
    CD: Tax (Swe) S-5-2
CE-29996-G   **Some Of These Days** (unissued)

Columbia, New York, N.Y. Monday, June 10, 1929
SAM LANIN AND HIS ORCHESTRA
Sam Lanin (ldr) Phil Napoleon, *unknown* (tp) Tom Dorsey (tb) **Jimmy
Dorsey**, Andy Sanella (cl,as) Merle Johnston (cl,ts) Art Schutt (p) *Tony
Colucci* (bj) Jimmy Mullen (bb) *Stan King* (d) Irving Kaufman [as Tom
Frawley] (vcl)

148676-1   **I Don't Want Your Kisses** [Fred Fisher; Martin
                 Broones] vIK (as solo)
    78: Harmony 1029-H, Velvet Tone 2029-V, Diva 3029-G,
    Publix 1062-P, MGM 1080-P
        1062-P as PUBLIX TEN, 1080-P as THE CAPITOLIANS
148677-2   **Campus Capers** [Greenwood; Martin Broones] vIK
    78: Harmony 1029-H, Velvet Tone 2029-V, Diva 3029-G,
    MGM 1082-P
148678-1   **Sophomore Prom** [Raymond Klages; Jesse Greer]
                 vIK (as solo)
    78: Harmony 1036-H, Velvet Tone 2036-V, Diva 3036-G,
    MGM 1082-P
        1082-P (both sides) as THE CAPITOLIANS
148679-3   **The World's Greatest Sweetheart Is You** vIK
    78: Harmony 952-H, Diva 2952-G, Velvet Tone 1952-V

Columbia, New York, N.Y. Wednesday, June 12, 1929
FRED RICH AND HIS ORCHESTRA
Fred Rich (ldr) Leo McConville, *unknown* (tp) Tom Dorsey (tb) **Jimmy
Dorsey** (cl,as) *unknown* (cl,as) Fred Cusick (cl,as,ts) *unknown* (vn), (p)
Carl Kress (g) Joe Tarto (bb) *unknown* (d) Rollickers (vcl)

W 148692-3   **Until The End** [Fisher, Brown, Broasberg] vR (as
                 solo)
    78: Columbia 1979-D
W 148693-3   **Wishing And Waiting For Love** [Grant Clarke;
                 Harry Akst] vR (as solo)
    78: Columbia 1924-D, 5622
    LP: The Old Masters 27
    CD: The Old Masters 101

Pathe, New York, N.Y. Mid-June 1929
PATHE STUDIO BAND
Sam Lanin (ldr) *Leo McConville, Mannie Klein* (tp) Tom Dorsey (tb)
Jimmy Dorsey (cl,as) Andy Sanella (as,stg) *unknown* (ts) Rube Bloom
(p) *unknown* (bj), (bb), (d) Irving Kaufman (vcl)

PATHE STUDIO BAND (Contd.)

3921-2   **Baby, Oh Where Can You Be?** [Ted Koehler; Frank
                  Magine] vIK (as solo)
    78: Pathe Actuelle 37012, Perfect 15193, Cameo 9237, Lincoln
    3264, Romeo 1039
           *Pathe Actuelle and Perfect as FRANK KEYES AND HIS OR-
           CHESTRA, others as BROADWAY BROADCASTERS*
108???   **I've Never Seen A Smile Like Yours** vIK
    78: Pathe Actuelle 36989, Perfect 15170
           as FRANK KEYES AND HIS ORCHESTRA

Columbia, New York, N.Y. Monday, June 17, 1929
IPANA TROUBADORS
Sam Lanin (ldr) Leo McConville, Mannie Klein (tp) Chuck Campbell
(tb) **Jimmy Dorsey,** *Merle Johnston [or] Arnold Brilhart* (cl,as)
unknown (cl,ts) Arthur Schutt (p) *John Cali* (bj) *Hank Stern [or] Joe
Tarto* (bb) Vic Berton (d) Smith Ballew (vcl)

W 148699-2,3   **There Was Nothing Else To Do** [Bert Kalmar, Harry
                  Ruby; Harry Warren] vSB (cl solo)
    78: Columbia 1881-D, (Au) 01703
W 148700-1,3   **Just A Little Glimpse Of Paradise** [Bert Kalmar,
                  Harry Ruby; Harry Warren] vSB
    78: Columbia 1881-D, (Au) 01699

Seemingly, whenever Jimmy organized and/or led smaller Dorsey
Brothers recording sessions, they were invariably released under the
name "The Travelers." The arrangements are much less elaborate than
on the earlier sessions, and the playing is much looser, which might also
have influenced the group name change.

OKeh, New York, N.Y. Wednesday, June 19, 1929
THE TRAVELERS (Dorsey Brothers Orchestra)
Jimmy Dorsey (cl,as,ldr) Leo McConville, Mannie Klein (tp) Tom
Dorsey (tp,tb) Alfie Evans (as) Paul Mason (ts) Arthur Schutt (p,arr)
Tony Colucci (bj) Hank Stern (bb) Stan King (d) Irving Kaufman (vcl)

W 402465-B   **Am I Blue?** [Grant Clarke; Harry Akst] vIK (as solo)
    78: OKeh 41259, Odeon ONY-41259, Parlophone (E) R-426,
    (E) R-2475, 22432, (It) B-27285, Odeon (F) 165786, 19337, A-
    189261, (E) OR-2475, Kismet K-742
    LP: The Old Masters 15, World Records (E) SHB67, (Au) R-
    09520
    TC: World Records (E) CSHB-67, Columbia/Legacy CT 52855
    CD: Columbia/Legacy CK 52855, Jazz Oracle (C) BDW 8005
           *Parlophone R-426 as SAM LANIN'S ARKANSAW [sic]
           TRAVELLERS, Kismet as CASINO ORCHESTRA*
W 402466-B   **Baby, Oh! Where Can You Be?** [Ted Koehler;
                  Frank Magine] vIK
    78: OKeh 41260, Parlophone (E) R-426, (Au) A-2837, (It) B-
    27045, Odeon (Arg) 193377

LP: The Old Masters 15, World Records (E) SHB67, (Au) R-09520
TC: World Records (E) CSHB-67
CD: Jazz Oracle (C) BDW 8005
W 402467-C   **Breakaway** [Sid Mitchell, Archie Gottler; Con Conrad] arrAS (as,cl solos)
    78: OKeh 41260, Parlophone (E) E-6197, (Au) A-2837, (It) B-27045, Odeon (F) 165766, (Arg) 193377
    LP: The Old Masters 15, World Records (E) SHB67, (Au) R-09520
    TC: World Records (E) CSHB-67
    CD: Jazz Oracle (C) BDW 8005
    Parlophone as WILL PERRY'S ORCHESTRA, all Odeons as DORSEY BROTHERS' ORCHESTRA

Pathe, New York, N.Y. Mid-June 1929
FRED RICH AND HIS ORCHESTRA
Fred Rich (ldr) Leo McConville, *unknown* (tp) Tom Dorsey (tb) **Jimmy Dorsey,** Tony Parenti (cl,as) Fred Cusick (cl,as,ts) Al Duffy (vn) *unknown* (p) Carl Kress (g) Joe Tarto (bb,sb) *unknown* (d) Irving Kaufman (vcl)

108849-3   **Now I'm In Love** vIK
    78: Pathe Actuelle 37010, Perfect 15191, Pathe (F) X-6282
    (3916) **78:** Cameo 9203
108850-1   **Lonely Little Cinderella** [Gill, Richey] vIK
    78: Pathe Actuelle 37012, Perfect 15193
108851-1   **Singin' In The Rain** [Arthur Freed; Nacio Herb Brown] vIK
    78: Pathe Actuelle 37008, Perfect 15189, Pathe (F) X-6282
    Pathe Actuelle and Perfect as LA PALINA BROADCASTERS
    (4143) **78:** Cameo 9300, Lincoln 3327, Romeo 1109
    as FREDDIE RICH AND HIS ORCHESTRA

Columbia, New York, N.Y. Friday, June 28, 1929
THE CHARLESTON CHASERS
Phil Napoleon (tp) Miff Mole (tb) **Jimmy Dorsey** (cl,as) Arthur Schutt (p,harm) Joe Tarto (sb) Dave Tough (d) Eva Taylor (vcl)

148762-2   **Ain't Misbehavin'** [Andy Razaf; Thomas "Fats" Waller, Harry Brooks] vET (as,cl solos)
    78: Columbia 1891-D, 5610
    LP: The Old Masters 6, VJM (E) VLP44
148763-3   **Moanin' Low** [Howard Dietz; Ralph Rainger] vET (as solo)
    78: Columbia 1891-D, (E) CB-207
    LP: The Old Masters 6, VJM (E) VLP44

Pathe, New York, N.Y. Late June 1929
SAM LANIN AND HIS ORCHESTRA
Sam Lanin (ldr) Phil Napoleon, *unknown* (tp) Tom Dorsey (tb) **Jimmy**

SAM LANIN AND HIS ORCHESTRA (Contd.)
Dorsey, Andy Sanella (cl,as) *unknown* (cl,ts) Art Schutt (p) *Tony Colucci* (bj) Jimmy Mullen (bb) *Stan King* (d) Scrappy Lambert (vcl)

3924-A   **I Don't Want Your Kisses (If I Can't Have Your Love)** [Fred Fisher; Martin Broones] vSL (cl solo)
          78: Cameo 9206, Lincoln 3233, Romeo 1008
          (108853-1) **78:** Pathe Actuelle 37065, Perfect 15246
          Cameo, Lincoln, Romeo as BROADWAY BROADCASTERS, others as SAM LANIN AND HIS TROUBADORS
108854-3   **Campus Capers** [Greenwood; Martin Broones] vSL
          78: Pathe Actuelle 37065, Perfect 15246
          as SAM LANIN AND HIS TROUBADORS
108855-3   **My Song Of The Nile** [Alfred Bryan; George W. Meyer] vSL
          78: Pathe Actuelle 37008, Perfect 15189
          as DAN RITCHIE AND HIS ORCHESTRA
          (3940-A) **78:** Cameo 9212, Lincoln 3239, Romeo 1014, Angelus (Au) 3151
          Angelus as SAM LANNIN [sic] AND HIS ORCHESTRA
          (8829-3) **78:** Banner 6488, Broadway 1292, Domino 4367, (C) 181130, Oriole 1626, Regal 8812, Imperial 2361
          Banner, Domino 4367, Regal as BUDDY BLUE AND HIS TEXANS, Domino 181130 as FRED COOPER'S DANCE ORCHESTRA, Broadway, Oriole as GARY DAWSON AND HIS COLLEGIANS

Pathe, New York, N.Y. Late-June 1929
FRED RICH AND HIS ORCHESTRA
Fred Rich (ldr) Leo McConville, *unknown* (tp) Tom Dorsey (tb,tp) **Jimmy Dorsey,** *unknown* (cl, as) Fred Cusick (cl,as,ts) *unknown* (vn), (p) Carl Kress (g) Joe Tarto (bb,sb) *unknown* (d) Irving Kaufman (vcl)

108879-1   **I'm Walkin' Around In A Dream** vIK
          78: Pathe Actuelle 37019, Perfect 15200
          (8938-2) **78:** Regal 8847, Banner 6501
          (3945) **78:** Cameo 9220, Lincoln 3247, Romeo 1022
108880-2   **Ain't Misbehavin'** [Andy Razaf; Thomas "Fats" Waller, Harry Brooks] vIK (cl solo)
          78: Pathe Actuelle 37016, Perfect 15197
          (4024) **78:** Cameo 9243, Lincoln 3270, Romeo 1045, Angelus (Au) 3151
          Cameo, Lincoln, Romeo as FREDDIE RICH & HIS ORCH.
108881-3   **I Want To Meander In The Meadow** vIK
          78: Pathe Actuelle 37019, Perfect 15200
          (8844) **78:** Regal 8815, Broadway 1297, Banner 6444, Oriole 1631, Embassy 8058, Broadcast (Au) W-529
          Broadway as ROYAL DANCE ORCHESTRA, Banner as HOLLYWOOD DANCE ORCHESTRA, Oriole as ORIOLE DANCE ORCHESTRA, Embassy as BROADWAY SYNCO-PATORS, Broadcast as ROXY DANCE ORCHESTRA

Columbia, New York, N.Y. Monday, July 1, 1929
FRED RICH AND HIS ORCHESTRA
Kress adds (bj) Smith Ballew (vcl)

W 148771-2   **Don't Hang Your Dreams On A Rainbow** [Irving
                  Kahal; Arnold Johnson] vSB (cl solo)
    78: Columbia 1893-D
W 195006-1   **Don't Hang Your Dreams On A Rainbow** (cl solo)
    78: Columbia (SA) 3613-X
W 148772-1   **Song Of The Moonbeams** [Harry Tobias; Vincent
                  Rose] vSB
    78: Columbia 1893-D
W 195007-1   **Song Of The Moonbeams**
    78: Columbia (SA) 3613-X

Brunswick, New York, N.Y. Tuesday, July 9, 1929
COTTON PICKERS
Tom Dorsey (tb,ldr) Phil Napoleon (tp) **Jimmy Dorsey** (cl,as) Arthur
Schutt (p) *unknown* (bj,g) Joe Tarto (bb) Stan King (d) Libby Holman,
Marlin Hurt (vcl)

E 30326   **Moanin' Low** [Howard Dietz; Ralph Rainger] vLH
                  (as,cl solos)
    78: Brunswick 4446, (F) 1038
    LP: Broadway BR115
E 30327   **Moanin' Low**
    78: Brunswick (G) (unknown if ever released)
E 30328   **He's A Good Man To Have Around** [Jack Yellen;
                  Milton Ager] vLH (cl solo)
    78: Brunswick 4447
E 30329   **He's A Good Man To Have Around** (as,cl solos)
    78: Brunswick (G) A-8406
E 30330-A   **Shoo Shoo Boogie Boo** [Leo Robin, Sam Coslow,
                  Richard A. Whiting] vMH (cl solos)
    78: Brunswick 4447
E 30331   **Shoo Shoo Boogie Boo** (cl solos)
    78: Brunswick (G) A-8406
    all released sides also on **LP:** Arcadia (C) 2013, **CD:** Timeless (H)
    CBC 1-049

Columbia, New York, N.Y. Tuesday, July 9, 1929
IPANA TROUBADORS
Sam Lanin (ldr) Leo McConville, Mannie Klein (tp) *Tom Dorsey [or]
Chuck Campbell* (tb) **Jimmy Dorsey,** Arnold Brilhart (cl,as) *unknown*
(cl,ts) 2 *unknown* (vn) Arthur Schutt (p) John Cali (bj) Hank Stern (bb)
Vic Berton (d) Smith Ballew (vcl)

W 148736-3   **Do What You Do** [Ira Gershwin, Gus Kahn; George
                  Gershwin] vSB (cl solo)
    78: Columbia 1903-D
                        (Contd.)

IPANA TROUBADORS (Contd.)

W 148737-3   **Liza (All The Clouds'll Roll Away)** [Ira Gershwin, Gus Kahn; George Gershwin] vSB
     78: Columbia 1903-D
     LP: Columbia Special Products P2-15974, Halcyon (E) HAL112

Plaza, New York, N.Y. Wednesday, July 10, 1929
SAM LANIN AND HIS ORCHESTRA
Sam Lanin (ldr) Phil Napoleon, *unknown* (tp) Tom Dorsey (tb) **Jimmy Dorsey,** Andy Sanella (cl,as) *unknown* (cl,ts) Arthur Schutt (p) *Tony Colucci* (bj) Jimmy Mullen (bb) *Stan King* (d) Scrappy Lambert [sometimes as Ralph Haines, Chester Hale, Rodman Lewis or Roland Lance, as indicated below] (vcl)

8853-1,2,3   **Wishing And Waiting For Love** [Grant Clarke; Harry Akst] vSL[RodL on Domino, RolL on Broadway] (cl solo)
     78: Banner 6445, Domino 4373, 181134, Regal 8817, Conqueror 7386, Apex (C) 8988, Crown 81134, Sterling (C) 281134, Broadway 1298, Embassy (Au) 8073
          Conqueror as JOHN VINCENT'S CALIFORNIANS, Crown, Domino 181134, Sterling as BLUE ROOM CLUB ORCHESTRA, Broadway as THE BADGERS, Embassy as EMBASSY DANCE BAND
8854-2   **Miss You** [Harry, Charles and Henry Tobias] vSL [RH on Banner, RolL on Broadway]
     78: Banner 6447, Domino 4372, Regal 8818, Apex 8997, Imperial (E) 2192, Broadway 1297, Edison Bell Winner (Au) W-530, Oriole 1635
          Broadway as THE BADGERS, Oriole as BILLY JAMES DANCE ORCHESTRA, Edison Bell Winner as ROXY DANCE ORCHESTRA
     (4061-) **78:** Cameo 9264, Lincoln 3291, Romeo 1066
          as BROADWAY BROADCASTERS
     (108916-) **78:** Pathe Actuelle 37033, Perfect 15214
          as SAM LANIN AND HIS TROUBADORS (vCH)
8855-2   **What A Day!** [Harry Woods] vSL
     78: Banner 6452, Domino 4371, Regal 8818, Conqueror 7387, Broadway 1298, Edison Bell Winner (Au) W-530
          Broadway as THE BADGERS (vRolL), Conqueror as JOHN VINCENT'S CALIFORNIANS

Columbia, New York, N.Y. Thursday, July 11, 1929
SAM LANIN AND HIS ORCHESTRA
Sam Lanin (ldr) Leo McConville, Mannie Klein (tp) *Tom Dorsey [or] Chuck Campbell* (tb) **Jimmy Dorsey,** Arnold Brilhart (cl,as) *unknown* (cl,ts) 2 *unknown* (vn) Arthur Schutt (p) John Cali (bj) Hank Stern (bb) Vic Berton (d) Irving Kaufman [as George Kay or Arthur Seelig] (vcl)

148795-2   **Here We Are** [Gus Kahn; Harry Warren] vIK[AS] (cl solo)

78: Harmony 968-H, Diva 2968-G, Velvet Tone 1968-V
148796-2,3   **At Close Of Day** [Raymond Klages, Jesse Greer,
                  Martin Broones] vIK[GK]
     78: Harmony 967-H, MGM 1030-P, Velvet Tone 1967-V
148797-2   **Don't Hang Your Dreams On A Rainbow** [Irving
                  Kahal; Arnold Johnson] vIK[AS]
     78: Harmony 968-H, Diva 2968-G, Velvet Tone 1968-V

OKeh, New York, N.Y. Friday, July 12, 1929
DORSEY BROTHERS AND THEIR ORCHESTRA
Tom Dorsey (tb,ldr) Leo McConville, Mannie Klein (tp) **Jimmy Dorsey**
(cl,as) Larry Abbott (as) Lucien Smith (ts,cel) *unknown* (vn) *unknown*
(viola) Arthur Schutt (p) Eddie Lang (g) Hank Stern (bb) Stan King (d)
Irving Kaufman (vcl)

W 402531-A   **Singin' In The Rain** [Arthur Freed; Nacio Herb
                  Brown] vIK (as solo)
     78: OKeh 41272, Parlophone (E) R-433, (Au) A-2908, (It) B-
     27284, B-222514, Odeon (Arg) 193357, A-189265, A-189267, A-
     189817, (F) A-221176, ONY-41272, Ariel (E) 4445
          Ariel as ARIEL DANCE ORCHESTRA
     LP: The Old Masters 15, World Records (E) SHB67, (Au)
     R-09520
     TC: World Records (E) CSHB67
     CD: Jazz Oracle (C) BDW 8005
W 402531-B   **Singin' In The Rain** vIK (as solo)
     78: OKeh 41272, Parlophone (E) R-433, (Au) A-2908, (It)
     B-27284, B-222514, Odeon (Arg) 193357, A-189265, A-189267,
     A-189817, (F) A-221176, ONY-41272, Ariel (E) 4445
          Ariel as ARIEL DANCE ORCHESTRA
     LP: The Old Masters 15,World Records (E) SHB67, (Au)
     R-09520, Odeon (F) 165.817, Phontastic (Swe) 7608
     TC: World Records (E) CSHB67
     CD: Phontastic (Swe) 7608, Jazz Oracle (C) BDW 8005
W 402532-A   **Your Mother And Mine** [Joe Goodwin; Gus Ed-
                  wards] vIK
     78: OKeh 41272, Parlophone (E) R-433, (Au) A-1908, B-12802,
     (It) B-27284, B-222514, Odeon ONY-41272, (Arg) 193357,
     A-189265, A-189267, A-189817, (F) A-221176, Ariel (E) 4444
          Ariel as ARIEL DANCE ORCHESTRA
     LP: The Old Masters 15, World Records (E) SHB67
     TC: World Records (E) CSHB67
     CD: Jazz Oracle (C) BDW 8005
W 402533-C   **Maybe—Who Knows?** [Joseph Shuster, Ruth Etting;
                  Joseph Tucker] vIK (cl solo)
     78: OKeh 41279, Parlophone (E) R-464, (Au) A-2867, Odeon
     ONY-41279, (Arg) 193395
     LP: The Old Masters 15, World Records (E) SHB67, (Au) R-
     09520
     TC: World Records (E) CSHB67
     CD: Jazz Oracle (C) BDW 8005

The July 12 Dorsey Brothers session marked the end of the Dorseys' series on OKeh and, along with the June 19 date, has a much different sound, with much duller arrangements, almost stock in concept.

Columbia, New York, N.Y. Wednesday, July 24, 1929
LEE MORSE AND HER BLUE GRASS BOYS
Ben Selvin (ldr) Phil Napoleon (tp) Tom Dorsey (tb) **Jimmy Dorsey** (cl) Frank Signorelli (p) *Tony Colucci* (g) *Joe Tarto* (sb) Stan King (d) Lee Morse (vcl)

W 148846-1   **Moanin' Low** [Howard Dietz; Ralph Rainger] vLM
        78: Columbia 1922-D, (E) DB-370
        LP: Take Two TT201
W 148847-1   **Sweetness** [Ned Miller, Carmen Lombardo, Chester Conn] vLM
        78: Columbia 1922-D, (E) DB-161
        LP: Harlequin (E) HQ2072

Columbia, New York, N.Y. Wednesday, July 24, 1929
GAY ELLIS (accomp. by THE NEW ENGLANDERS)
Ben Selvin (ldr) Phil Napoleon (tp) Tom Dorsey (tb) **Jimmy Dorsey** (cl) Frank Signorelli (p) *Tony Colucci* (g) *Joe Tarto* (sb) Stan King (d) Annette Hanshaw [as Gay Ellis] (vcl)

148848-2   **Here We Are** [Gus Kahn; Harry Warren] vAH
        78: Harmony 981-H, Velvet Tone 1981-V, Diva 2981-G, Publix 1040-P, Columbia 01694
        LP: World Records (E) SH246
148848-3   **Here We Are** vAH
        78: Harmony 981-H, Columbia 01694
148849-2,3   **True Blue Lou** [Leo Robin, Sam Coslow, Richard A. Whiting] vAH (cl solo)
        78: Harmony 981-H, Velvet Tone 1981-V, Diva 2981-G, MGM 1071-P, Columbia 01694
        LP: Sunbeam SB P512

Columbia, New York, N.Y Friday, July 26, 1929
FRED RICH AND HIS ORCHESTRA
Fred Rich (ldr) Leo McConville, *unknown* (tp) Tom Dorsey (tb) **Jimmy Dorsey**, *unknown* (cl,as) Fred Cusick (cl,as,ts) Al Duffy (vn) *unknown* (p) Carl Kress (g) Joe Tarto (bb,sb) *unknown* (d) The Rollickers (vcl)

W 148856-4   **Tip Toe Thru The Tulips With Me** [Al Dubin; Joe Burke] vR (cl solo)
        78: Columbia 1924-D, (E) 5622, 01781
W 148857-3   **I Don't Want Your Kisses** [Fred Fisher; Martin Broones] vR (cl solo)
        78: Columbia 1979-D, (E) 01781

Vitaphone Movie Studios, Brooklyn, N.Y. July 1929
SEGER ELLIS AND HIS CLUB EMBASSY ORCHESTRA
Fuzzy Farrar (tp) Tom Dorsey (tb) **Jimmy Dorsey** (cl,as) Art Schutt (p)

Al Duffy (vn) Eddie Lang (g) Stan King (d) Seger Ellis (vcl)

VA-823-1   **After Loving You** vSE
    ET: Vitaphone VA-823-1
VA-823-2   **Am I Blue?** [Grant Clarke; Harry Akst] (as solo)
    ET: Vitaphone VA-823-2
    LP: Broadway BR-112
VA-823-2   **I've Got A Feeling I'm Falling** [Billy Rose; Thomas
    "Fats" Waller, Harry Link] vSE
    ET: Vitaphone VA-823-2

Paramount Studios, Astoria, N.Y. July 1929
ALICE BOULDEN in High Hat, directed by Joseph Santley
Tom Dorsey (tb,ldr) *Mannie Klein [or] Phil Napoleon,* Fuzzy Farrar (tp)
Jimmy Dorsey, 2 *unknown* (cl) Al Duffy (vn) *unknown* (p), (g), (bb)
Alice Boulden (vcl)

    Nobody's Sweetheart [Elmer Schoebel, Gus Kahn, Ernie Erdman,
    Billy Meyers] (theme) / (segue to:) **Get Out And Get Under The
    Moon** [Charles Tobias, William Jerome, Larry Shay] (cl solo) / **Easy
    Come, Easy Go** [Edward Heyman; Johnny Green] vAB (cl solo) /
    The One That I Love Loves Me [Roy Turk; Fred Ahlert] vAB
    All selections in **FILM:** Paramount *High Hat,* "Nobody's Sweet-
    heart," "Get Out And Get Under The Moon" on **VIDEO:** Yazoo 514

Pathe, New York, N.Y. July 1929
SAM LANIN AND HIS ORCHESTRA
Sam Lanin (ldr) Phil Napoleon, *unknown* (tp) Tom Dorsey (tb) **Jimmy
Dorsey,** Andy Sanella (cl,as) *Merle Johnston* (cl,ts) 2 *unknown* (vn)
Arthur Schutt (p) *Tony Colucci* (bj) Jimmy Mullen (bb) *Stan King* (d)
Scrappy Lambert [as Larry Rich, Chester Hale, Ralph Haines or Larry
Holton] (vcl)

108868-2   **Yours Sincerely** [Lorenz Hart; Richard Rodgers]
    vSL[LR]
    78: Pathe Actuelle 37011, Perfect 15192
    as LARRY RICH AND HIS FRIENDS
108869-1   **With A Song In My Heart** [Lorenz Hart; Richard
    Rodgers] vSL [LR]
    78: Pathe Actuelle 37011, Perfect 15192
    as LARRY RICH AND HIS FRIENDS
    (3941-A) **78:** Cameo 9213, Lincoln 3240, Romeo 1015
    as BROADWAY BROADCASTERS
108874-3   **If I Had My Way** [Waggner, Green] vSL[CH]
    78: Pathe Actuelle 37017, Perfect 15198
    as SAM LANIN AND HIS TROUBADORS
8966-2   **If I Had My Way** vSL[RH on Banner, LH on Oriole]
    78: Banner 6502, Domino 4402, Regal 8846, Oriole 1684, Apex
    (C) 41019
    *Some Banners as HOLLYWOOD DANCE ORCHESTRA,
    other Banners, plus Domino and Regal, as SAM LANIN'S*
    (Contd.)

SAM LANIN AND HIS ORCHESTRA (Contd.)

DANCE ORCHESTRA, Oriole as CONTINENTAL DANCE ORCHESTRA, Apex as LANIN AND HIS ORCHESTRA

ARC, New York, N.Y. July 1929
FRED RICH AND HIS ORCHESTRA
Fred Rich (ldr) Leo McConville, *unknown* (tp) Tom Dorsey (tb) **Jimmy Dorsey**, *unknown* (cl,as) Fred Cusick (cl,as,ts) *unknown* (vn), (p) Carl Kress (g) Joe Tarto (bb,sb) *unknown* (d) Irving Kaufman (vcl)

3978-A   **Piccolo Pete** [Phil Baxter] vIK (cl solo)
    78: Cameo 9233, Lincoln 3260, Romeo 1035
8994-3   **Piccolo Pete** vIK (cl solo)
    78: Banner 6508, Broadway 1327, Challenge 827, Conqueror 7426, Jewel 5707 Domino 4422, Oriole 1690, Paramount 20768, Regal 8869, Apex (C) 41021, Crown 81161, Imperial (E) 2191
    LP: Jazum 14
        Broadway, Paramount as FRANK RAYMOND'S DANCE ORCHESTRA, Challenge, Jewel, Oriole as TED WHITE'S COLLEGIANS, Crown as PIERROT SYNCOPATORS, Conqueror, Domino as LA PALINA BROADCASTERS, Imperial as PETE MANDEL AND HIS RHYTHM MASTERS
108901-2,3   **Piccolo Pete** vIK (cl solo)
    78: Pathe Actuelle 37024, Perfect 15205, Embassy (Au) 8067
    LP: Kenatone (Au) K-102, Collectors Items (E) 010
        as LA PALINA BROADCASTERS
3979-A   **Serenading The Moon** vIK
    78: Cameo 9234, Lincoln 3261, Romeo 1036
108900-2   **Serenading The Moon** vIK
    78: Pathe Actuelle 37025, Perfect 15206
        as LA PALINA BROADCASTERS
8895-1 (or 2412)   **Sweetness** [Ned Miller, Carmen Lombardo, Chester Conn] vIK (cl solo)
    78: Banner 6477, Broadway 1304, Challenge 828, Domino 4388, Oriole 1664, Paramount 20745, Regal 8834, Edison Bell Winner (Au) W-541, Crown 81156, Sterling 181156
        Broadway and Paramount as FRANK RAYMOND'S DANCE ORCHESTRA, Challenge and Oriole as TED WHITE'S COLLEGIANS, Sterling as JIMMY POLLACK'S ORCHESTRA, Crown as PIERROT SYNCOPATORS
108902-3   **Sweetness** vIK (cl solo)
    78: Pathe Actuelle 37022, Perfect 15203, Domino 4388
        as LA PALINA BROADCASTERS
    (-0-) **78:** Cameo 9229, Lincoln 3256, Romeo 1031

Columbia, New York, N.Y. Monday, August 12, 1929
THE KNICKERBOCKERS
Ben Selvin (ldr) Mannie Klein (tp) Tom Dorsey (cnt,tb) **Jimmy Dorsey** (cl,as) Arnold Brilhart (cl,as,o) *unknown* (vn) Joe Dubin (ts) Arthur Schutt (p) *Charles Magnante* (acc) *unknown* (bj,g) *Joe Tarto* (bb) Stan King (d) Smith Ballew (vcl)

W 148865-2   **Song Of Siberia** vSB (cl solo)
     78: Columbia 1940-D
W 148866-3   **Song Of The Blues** [Bernie Grossman; Isham Jones]
     vSB
     78: Columbia 1940-D

Columbia, New York, N.Y. Tuesday, August 13, 1929
SAM LANIN AND HIS ORCHESTRA
Sam Lanin (ldr) Mannie Klein, *unknown* (tp) Tom Dorsey (tb) **Jimmy Dorsey,** *unknown* (cl,as) *unknown* (cl,ts) Arthur Schutt (p) Tony Colucci (bj) Hank Stern (bb) *unknown* (d) Irving Kaufman [as Tom Frawley or Robert Wood] (vcl)

148871-2   **One Sweet Kiss** [Al Jolson; Ernest Dreyer] vIK[TF]
     78: Harmony 985-H, Diva 2985-G, Velvet Tone 1985-V
148872-2   **Marianne** [Roy Turk; Fred E. Ahlert] vIK[RW]
     78: Harmony 984-H, Publix 1049-P, Paramount 1056-P, MGM
     1079-P, Diva 2984-G, Velvet Tone 1984-V
     Publix and Paramount as THE PARAMOUNTEERS, MGM as
     THE CAPITOLIANS
148873-2   **I'll Close My Eyes To The Rest Of The World**
     (And Dream Sweet Dreams Of You) [Cliff Friend]
     vIK [TF] (cl solo)
     78: Harmony 985-H, Publix 1059-P, Velvet Tone 1985-V

OKeh, New York, N.Y. Friday, August 16, 1929
JUSTIN RING AND HIS ORCHESTRA
Justin Ring (p,ldr) 2 *unknown* (tp) Tom Dorsey (tb) **Jimmy Dorsey,** *unknown* (cl,as) *unknown* (ts), (vn) Eddie Lang (g) Joe Tarto (sb) Stan King (d) Scrappy Lambert (vcl)

W 402858-A   **My Song Of The Nile** [Alfred Bryan; George W.
     Meyer] vSL
     78: OKeh 41287, Parlophone (E) R-465, Ariel (E) 4461
     Parlophone as TAMPA BLUE ORCHESTRA, Ariel as ARIEL
     DANCE ORCHESTRA
W 402859-A   **Sleepy Valley** [Andrew B. Sterling; James F. Han-
     ley] vSL
     78: OKeh 41287, Parlophone (E) F-6208, Ariel (E) 4452
     Parlophone as WILL PERRY'S ORCHESTRA, Ariel as ARI-
     EL DANCE ORCHESTRA
W 402860-A   **True Blue Lou** [Leo Robin, Sam Coslow, Richard A.
     Whiting] vSL (as,cl solo)
     78: OKeh 41295, Parlophone (E) E-463, (Au) A-2427, Ariel (E)
     4462
     Ariel as ARIEL DANCE ORCHESTRA
     LP: Parlophone (E) R-3418, Vintage Jazz Music Society VLP56

Jimmy was part of the twenty-two-member Red Nichols pit band for *John Murray Anderson's Almanac,* which opened at the Erlanger Theatre on Broadway August 14, 1929, and ran for sixty-nine performances. While its run was relatively short, being cut by the stock market crash in October, it is still remembered for "I May Be Wrong, But I Think You're Wonderful."

Brunswick, New York, N.Y. Tuesday, August 20, 1929
RED NICHOLS AND HIS FIVE PENNIES
Red Nichols, Tommy Thunen, John Egan (tp) Jack Teagarden, Glenn Miller, Herb Taylor (tb) **Jimmy Dorsey,** Pee Wee Russell (cl,as) Fud Livingston (ts,arr) Henry Whiteman, Maurice Goffin (vn) Irving Brodsky (p) Tommy Felline (bj) Jack Hansen (bb) George Beebe (d) Scrappy Lambert, Red McKenzie (vcl)

E 30502-A   **I May Be Wrong, But I Think You're Wonderful**
                   [Harry Ruskin; Henry Sullivan] vSL
    78: Brunswick 4500, 6753, (Arg), (Au), (C) 4500
    LP: Sunbeam MFC-12
    TC: Radio Yesteryear Stack 31
    CD: Tax (Swe) S-5-2
E 30502-B   **I May Be Wrong, But I Think You're Wonderful**
                   vSL
    78: Brunswick 4500, 6753, (It) 4891, (G) A-8493
E 30503-G   **I May Be Wrong, But I Think You're Wonderful**
    78: Brunswick (G) A-9520
E 30504-A   **The New Yorkers** [Cole Porter] vRM (as solo)
    78: Brunswick 4500 (Arg), (Au), (C) 4500 (G) A-8493
    LP: Sunbeam MFC-12
    TC: Radio Yesteryear Stack 31
    CD: Tax (Swe) S-5-2
E 30505-B   **The New Yorkers** (as solo)
    LP: MCA 1518
E 30505-G   **The New Yorkers** (as solo)
    78: Brunswick (G) A-9520

ARC, New York, N.Y. Tuesday, August 20, 1929
FRED RICH AND HIS ORCHESTRA
Fred Rich (ldr) Leo McConville, *unknown* (tp) Tom Dorsey (tb) **Jimmy Dorsey,** *unknown* (cl,as) Fred Cusick (cl,as,ts) *unknown* (vn), (p) Carl Kress (g) Joe Tarto (bb,sb) *unknown* (d) Irving Kaufman (vcl)

108951-2,3   **Little By Little** [Walter O'Keefe; Robert Emmet Dolan] vIK (cl solo)
    78: Pathe Actuelle 37037, Perfect 15218
        as LA PALINA BROADCASTERS
    (4067) **78:** Cameo 9265, Lincoln 3292, Romeo 1067
    (8957) **78:** Banner 6503, Broadway 1316, Paramount 20757, Regal 8849, Domino 4405, Apex 41027, Challenge 848, Conqueror 7412, Jewel 5702, Oriole 1694, Crown 81158
        Broadway, Paramount as FRANK RAYMOND'S DANCE ORCH., Challenge, Jewel, Oriole as TED WHITE'S COLLEGIANS, Conqueror, Domino as LA PALINA BROAD-CASTERS, Crown as MATTY CRAWFORD'S ORCH.

108952-2   **How Am I To Know** [Dorothy Parker; Jack King]
vIK
78: Pathe Actuelle 37037, Perfect 15218
     as LA PALINA BROADCASTERS
(-0-) **78:** Cameo 9320, Lincoln 3347, Romeo 1108
(8953) **78:** Banner 6504,   Broadway 1316, Conqueror 7413,
Domino 4404, Jewel 5701, Oriole 1688, Paramount 20757, Regal
8850, Edison Bell Winner (Au) W-523
     Broadway, Paramount as FRANK RAYMOND'S DANCE
     ORCH., Jewel, Oriole as TED WHITE'S COLLEGIANS,
     Conqueror, Domino as LA PALINA BROADCASTERS
108953-3   **Wouldn't It Be Wonderful** [Grant Clarke; Harry
Akst] vIK
78: Pathe Actuelle 37041, Perfect 15222
     as LA PALINA BROADCASTERS
(4072) **78:** Cameo 9270, Lincoln 3297, Romeo 1072
(8982) **78:** Banner 6512, Broadway 1317, Domino 4406,
Oriole 1696, Paramount 20758, Regal 8848, Imperial 2278
     Broadway, Paramount as FRANK RAYMOND'S DANCE
     ORCH., Oriole as TED WHITE'S COLLEGIANS, Domino as
     LA PALINA BROADCASTERS

Columbia, New York N.Y. Friday, August 23, 1929
SEGER ELLIS
Louis Armstrong (tp) Tom Dorsey (tb) **Jimmy Dorsey** (cl,as) Joe Venuti
(vn) Art Schutt (p) Eddie Lang (g) Stan King (d) Seger Ellis (vcl)

W 402881-B   **Ain't Misbehavin'** [Andy Razaf, Harry Brooks,
Thomas "Fats" Waller] vSE (cl solo)
78: OKeh 41291, Odeon ONY-41291, (F) 165848
LP: Columbia 3CL35, CBS 65251, Smithsonian 2012
CD: Columbia CK 46148, Azure (E) CD 22
     Columbia file cards show four attempts to remake this
     matrix August 26, 1929, minus Armstrong and probably
     both Dorseys. Most list the remake session as August 27.

Columbia, New York, N.Y. Monday, August 26, 1929
SAM LANIN AND HIS ORCHESTRA
Sam Lanin (ldr) Mannie Klein, *unknown* (tp) Tom Dorsey (tb) **Jimmy
Dorsey** (cl,as) *unknown* (cl,as), (cl,ts) Arthur Schutt (p) *unknown* (bj)
Hank Stern (bb) *unknown* (d) Irving Kaufman [as Robert Wood] (vcl)

148927-3   **Perhaps** [Andy Razaf; Paul Denniker] vIK (cl solo)
78: Harmony 998-H, Diva 2998-G, Velvet Tone 1998-V
148928-2   **Ev'ry Day Away From You** [Charles Tobias; Jay
Mills] vIK
78: Harmony 998-H, Diva 2998-G, Velvet Tone 1998-V
148929-3   **Little By Little** [Walter O'Keefe; Robert Emmet
Dolan] vIK
78: Harmony 1001-H, Publix 1054-P, Diva 3001-G, Velvet
Tone 2001-V
     Publix as THE PARAMOUNTEERS (only 75 pressings made)

Columbia, New York N.Y. Tuesday, August 27, 1929
SEGER ELLIS
Mannie Klein (tp) replaces Armstrong, Seger Ellis (vcl)

W 402882-B   **There Was Nothing Else To Do** [Bert Kalmar, Harry
          Ruby; Harry Warren] vSE
     78: OKeh 41291, Odeon ONY-41291, (F) 165848
     TC: Columbia/Legacy CT 52930
     CD: Columbia/Legacy CK 52942
W 402883-B   **True Blue Lou** [Leo Robin, Sam Coslow, Richard A.
          Whiting] vSE
     78: OKeh 41290, Parlophone (E) R-522, Odeon A-189326
W 402884-B   **My Song Of The Nile** [Alfred Bryan; George W.
          Meyer] vSE (cl,as solos)
     78: OKeh 41290, Parlophone (E) R-522, Odeon A-189326

Brunswick, New York, N.Y. Tuesday, August 27, 1929
RED NICHOLS AND HIS FIVE PENNIES
Irving Brodsky adds (celst) Scrappy Lambert (vcl) Glenn Miller (arr)

E 30712-A,B   **They Didn't Believe Me** [Michael E. Rourke; Jer-
          ome Kern] vSL (arrGM)
     78: Brunswick 4651, 6827
     LP: Gaps (H) 180
     CD: Tax (Swe) S-5-2
E 30713-G   **They Didn't Believe Me** (arrGM)
     78: Brunswick (G) A-8655
XE 30714-A   **Say It With Music** [Irving Berlin] (theme); **They
          Didn't Believe Me** vSL (arrGM)
     78: (12-inch) Brunswick Brevities #29 Program E, pt. 2
     LP: Jazz Archives JA-43, Fanfare LP20-120
     CD: IAJRC CD1011
XE 30715-A   **Say It With Music** (theme); **I May Be Wrong, But I
          Think You're Wonderful** [Harry Ruskin; Henry
          Sullivan] vSL (as solo)
     78: (12-inch) Brunswick Brevities #30 Program E, pt. 5
     LP: Jazz Archives JA-43, Fanfare LP20-120
     CD: IAJRC CD1011
XE 30716-A   **Say It With Music** (theme); **The New Yorkers** [Cole
          Porter]
     78: (12-inch) Brunswick Brevities #31 Program E, pt. 3
XE 30717-A   **Say It With Music** (theme); **On The Alamo** [Gus
          Kahn; Isham Jones] vSL
     78: (12-inch) Brunswick Brevities #32 Program E, pt. 4
     LP: Jazz Archives JA-43, Fanfare LP20-120
     CD: IAJRC CD1011
XE 30718-A   **Say It With Music** (theme); **That's A-Plenty** [Lew
          Pollack] (as solo)
     78: (12-inch) Brunswick Brevities #33 Program E, pt. 6
     LP: Jazz Archives JA-43, Fanfare LP20-120
     CD: IAJRC CD1011
          Unissued "B" takes are known to have been made for all

"Brevities" sides cut in this session for broadcast use. No test pressings of these "B" takes are known to have surfaced.

ARC, New York, N.Y. Tuesday, August 27, 1929
SAM LANIN AND HIS ORCHESTRA
Sam Lanin (ldr) Mannie Klein, *unknown* (tp) Tom Dorsey (tb) **Jimmy Dorsey**, *unknown* (cl,as) Larry Abbott (cl,ts) Art Schutt, *Oscar Levant* (p) Tony Colucci (bj) Hank Stern (bb) *unknown* (d) Irving Kaufman (vcl)

108921-1   **Used To You** [Buddy De Sylva, Lew Brown, Al Jolson; Ray Henderson] vIK
   78: Pathe Actuelle 37029, Perfect 15210
         as FRANK KEYES & HIS ORCHESTRA
   (3989) **78:** Cameo 9242, Lincoln 3269, Romeo 1044
         as CLIFF ROBERTS & HIS ORCHESTRA
   (8920-3) **78:** Domino 4389, Regal 8835, Imperial (E) 2132, Broadway 1310, Paramount 20751, Domino (C) 181173, Crown (C) 81173, Conqueror 7405
         Domino and Crown as PIERROT SYNCOPATORS, Broadway, Paramount as MIDNIGHT SERENADERS
108929 3   **Lovable And Sweet** [Sidney Clare; Oscar Levant] (2 pianos) vIK (cl solo)
   78: Pathe Actuelle 37032, Perfect 15213, Domino 4386
         as BEN FRANKLIN HOTEL DANCE ORCHESTRA
   (4068-A) **78:** Cameo 9266, Lincoln 3293, Conqueror 7404, Domino (C) 181147
         Cameo and Lincoln as BUDDY FIELDS AND HIS ORCHESTRA, Conqueror as VICTOR KING AND HIS CONQUEROR ORCHESTRA, Domino as THE ROUNDERS, Domino (C) as RENDEZVOUS CAFE ORCHESTRA
   (8921-3) **78:** Banner 6483, Regal 8831, Oriole 1668, Romeo 1068, Jewel 5685, Imperial (E) 2172, Paramount 20751
   LP: Sunbeam MFC-17
         Banner and Regal as THE CAMPUS BOYS, Oriole and Jewel as UNIVERSITY BOYS, Paramount as MIDNIGHT SERENADERS, Imperial as BUDDY BLUE AND HIS TEXANS
108945-1   **I May Be Wrong, But I Think You're Wonderful** [Harry Ruskin; Henry Sullivan] vIK
   78: Pathe Actuelle 37038, Perfect 15219
         as SAM LANIN'S TROUBADORS
   (8975-1) **78:** Banner 6540, Domino 4426, Regal 8871, Oriole 1725, Jewel 5729, Imperial (E) 2225, Broadway 1317, Crown 81206, Domino (C) 181206, Broadcast (Au) W-621
         Oriole, Jewel as MIAMI SOCIETY ORCH., Crown, Domino (C) as ERNIE NOBLE & HIS ORCH., Broadcast as MANHATTAN MELODY MAKERS, Broadway as THE BADGERS

Columbia, New York, N.Y. Thursday, August 29, 1929
ANNETTE HANSHAW
Ben Selvin (ldr) Tom Dorsey (cnt) *Mannie Klein* (tp) Charlie Butterfield (tb) **Jimmy Dorsey** (cl,as) Arthur Schutt (p) Tony Colucci (bj,g) Hank Stern (sb) Stan King (d) Annette Hanshaw (vcl)

ANNETTE HANSHAW (Contd.)

W 402887-A   **Moanin' Low** [Howard Dietz; Ralph Rainger] vAH
                  (cl solo)
    78: OKeh 41292, Parlophone (E) R-850
    LP: World Records (E) SH246
    TC: Columbia Legacy CT52932
    CD: Columbia Legacy CK52943
W 402888-D   **Lovable And Sweet** [Sidney Clare; Oscar Levant]
                  vAH
    78: OKeh 41292, Parlophone (E) R-477, (Au) A-2961
    LP: World Records (E) SH246, Living Era (E) AJA5017
    CD: Living Era (E) ASV 5017

Frances Williams was a vaudeville and musical comedy star who
appeared in *The Cocoanuts* (1925), *Artists And Models* (1925), *George
White's Scandals* (1926, 1928, 1929), *The New Yorkers* (1930) and
Everybody's Welcome (1931), the latter with the Dorsey Brothers' pit
band. The next sides were probably cut in two sessions.

Brunswick, New York, N.Y. Late August 1929
FRANCES WILLIAMS
Mannie Klein (tp) **Jimmy Dorsey** (cl,as) *unknown* (g), (sb), (d,xyl)
Frances Williams (*p,*vcl)

E-30595-   **It's Unanimous Now** [Bud Green; Sam H. Stept]
                  vFW (cl solo)
    78: Brunswick 4499
E-30597-   **Then You've Never Been Blue** [Sam M. Lewis, Joe
                  Young; Ted FioRito] vFW
    78: Brunswick 4499
E-30710-   **Bottoms Up** [George White; Cliff Friend] vFW
    78: Brunswick 4503
E-30711-   **Bigger And Better Than Ever** [Irving Caesar; Cliff
                  Friend] vFW (as solo)
    78: Brunswick 4503

ARC, New York, N.Y. Late August 1929
FRED RICH AND HIS ORCHESTRA
Fred Rich (ldr) Leo McConville, *unknown* (tp) Tom Dorsey (tb) **Jimmy
Dorsey,** *unknown* (cl,as) Fred Cusick (cl,as,ts) Al Duffy (vn) *unknown*
(p) Carl Kress (g) Joe Tarto (sb) *unknown* (d) Smith Ballew (vcl)

108971-2   **All That I'm Asking Is Sympathy** [Benny Davis;
                  Joseph A. Burke] vSB
    78: Pathe Actuelle 37047, Perfect 15228
        as LA PALINA BROADCASTERS
    (4108) **78:** Cameo 9282, Lincoln 3309, Romeo 1084
108971-3 (9008-2) **All That I'm Asking Is Sympathy** vSB
    78: Banner 6517, Broadway 1322, Challenge 844, Domino
    4409, Jewel 5711, Oriole 1701, Paramount 20773, Regal 8856,
    Imperial (E) 2239

> *Challenge, Jewel, Oriole as TED WHITE'S COLLEGIANS,*
> *Domino, Regal, Imperial as LA PALINA BROADCASTERS,*
> *Broadway, Paramount as FRANK RAYMOND'S DANCE*
> *ORCHESTRA*

108972-1(9009-1,2) **Sweetheart, We Need Each Other** [Joseph Mc-
Carthy; Harry Tierney] vSB (cl solo)
78: Banner 0508, Broadway 1321, Cameo 0108, Domino 4408,
Jewel 5761, Oriole 1760, Paramount 20762, Regal 8854, Imperial
(E) 2194, Crown (C) 81188, Apex (C) 41030

> *Broadway, Paramount as RON CHADWICK'S ORCH-*
> *ESTRA, Jewel, Oriole as TED WHITE'S COLLEGIANS,*
> *Crown as JIMMIE POLLACK & HIS ORCHESTRA, Domino,*
> *Regal, Imperial as LA PALINA BROADCASTERS*

108972-2   **Sweetheart, We Need Each Other** vSB (cl solo)
78: Pathe Actuelle 37043, Pathe (F) X-6296, Perfect 15224

> *as LA PALINA BROADCASTERS*

108973-2   **Pal Of My Sweetheart Days** [Benny Davis; J. Fred
Coots] vSB
78: Pathe Actuelle 37047, Perfect 15228

> *as LA PALINA BROADCASTERS*

(9010 2) **78:** Banner 6517, Broadway 1327, Domino 4409,
Paramount 20778, Regal 8856, Apex (C) 41031

> *Regal as LA PALINA BROADCASTERS, Broadway, Para-*
> *mount as FRANK RAYMOND'S DANCE ORCHESTRA*

OKeh, New York, N.Y. Thursday, September 5, 1929
EMMETT MILLER'S GEORGIA CRACKERS
Leo McConville (tp) Tom Dorsey (tb) **Jimmy Dorsey** (cl,as) Art Schutt
(p) Eddie Lang (g) Joe Tarto (sb) Stan King (d) Phil Pavey, Emmett
Miller (vcl)

W 402932-A   **Lovin' Sam (The Sheik Of Alabam)** [Jack Yellen;
Milton Ager] vEM (cl solo)
78: OKeh 41305, Odeon ONY-41305
LP: Parlophone (E) R2270, The Old Masters 1
W 402933-A   **Big Bad Bill Is Sweet William Now** [Jack Yellen;
Milton Ager] vEM (cl solo)
78: OKeh 41305, Odeon ONY-41305
LP: Parlophone (E) R2270, The Old Masters 1
W 402934-B   **The Ghost Of The St. Louis Blues** [Billy Curtis; J.
Russell Robinson] vEM,PP (cl solo)
78: OKeh 41342, Parlophone PNY-34013, (E) R-1138, Odeon
(F) 238013, A-286056
LP: Smithsonian 9
All sides also on **CD:** Columbia CK 66999

Columbia, New York, N.Y. Thursday, September 5, 1929
FRED RICH AND HIS ORCHESTRA
Fred Rich (ldr) Leo McConville, *unknown* (tp) Tom Dorsey (tb) **Jimmy
Dorsey**, *unknown* (cl,as) Fred Cusick (cl,as,ts) *unknown* (vn), (p) Carl
Kress (g) Joe Tarto (bb,sb) *unknown* (d) The Rollickers (vcl)

FRED RICH AND HIS ORCHESTRA (Contd.)

W 148973-2   **Revolutionary Rhythm** vR (cl solo)
          78: Columbia 1965-D, (E) 5632, (Arg) A-8824
          LP: The Old Masters 27, Stack of 78's #71
          CD: The Old Masters 101
W 148974-2   **When The Real Thing Comes Along** vR
          78: Columbia 1965-D, (E) 5632, (Arg) A-8824

Brunswick, New York, N.Y. Friday, September 6, 1929
RED NICHOLS AND HIS FIVE PENNIES
Red Nichols, Tommy Thunen, John Egan (tp) Jack Teagarden, Glenn
Miller, Herb Taylor (tb) **Jimmy Dorsey,** Pee Wee Russell (cl,as) Fud
Livingston (ts,arr) Henry Whiteman, Maurice Goffin (vn) Irving
Brodsky (p) Tommy Felline (bj) Jack Hansen (sb) George Beebe (d)
Scrappy Lambert, Dick Robertson (vcl)

E 30531-A,B   **Wait For The Happy Ending** [Jack Yellen; Milton
          Ager] vSL arrFL
          78: Brunswick 4510, (E) 1043
          LP: Gaps (It) 180, Emanon ESL1, Origin OJL-8106
          CD: Tax (Swe) S-5-2
E 30532-G   **Wait For The Happy Ending** (unissued)
E 30533-A,B   **Can't We Be Friends?** [Paul James; Kay Swift] vDR
          (as solo) arrFL
          78: Brunswick 4510, 6827, (C) 45100 (E) 1043
          LP: Gaps (It) 180
          CD: Tax (Swe) S-5-2
E 30534-G   **Can't We Be Friends?** (unissued)

Brunswick, New York, N.Y. Monday, September 9, 1929
RED NICHOLS AND HIS FIVE PENNIES
Red Nichols, Mickey Bloom, Tommy Thunen (tp) Jack Teagarden,
Glenn Miller, Bill Trone (tb) Benny Goodman (cl) **Jimmy Dorsey**
(cl,as) Rube Bloom (p) Tommy Felline (bj) Joe Tarto (bb) Dave Tough
(d) Scrappy Lambert (vcl)

E 30538-A   **Nobody Knows (And Nobody Seems To Care)** [Irv-
          ing Berlin] vSL (cl solo)
          78: Brunswick 4790, 6832, (C) 4790, (E) O2505, (F,G) 8744
          LP: Sunbeam SB-137
          CD: Tax (Swe) S-5-2
E 30539-G   **Nobody Knows (And Nobody Seems To Care)**
          (unissued)
E 30540-A   **Smiles** [J. Will Callahan, Lee G. Roberts] vSL
          78: Brunswick 4790, 6832, (C) 4790, (F,G) 8744
          LP: Sunbeam SB-137, Ace Of Hearts (E) AH168, Gaps (H) 180,
          Affinity (E) AFS-1038
          CD: Tax (Swe) S-5-2
E 30541-G   **Smiles** (unissued)
E 30542-A,B   **Say It With Music** vSL (unissued)
E 30543-G   **Say It With Music** (unissued)

Brunswick, New York, N.Y. Tuesday, September 10, 1929
LOUISIANA RHYTHM KINGS
Red Nichols (tp,ldr) Tommy Thunen (tp) Glenn Miller (tb) **Jimmy Dorsey** (cl,as) Irving Brodsky (p) Dave Tough (d)

E 30544   **Waiting At The End Of The Road** [Irving Berlin] (cl solo)
     78: Vocalion 15833
     LP: Broadway BR-110
E 30545   **Little By Little** [Walter O'Keefe; Robert Emmet Dolan] (cl solo)
     78: Vocalion 15841
     LP: Broadway BR-110
E 30546   **Marianne** [Oscar Hammerstein II; Sigmund Romberg] (as solo)
     78: Vocalion 15833
     LP: Broadway BR-110
     CD: Tax (Swe) S-5-2

Columbia, New York, N.Y. Wednesday, September 11, 1929
TEDDY JOYCE AND HIS PENN STAGE RECORDERS
Unknown (tp), (tb) **Jimmy Dorsey** (cl) Teddy Joyce (vn,vcl) *unknown* (p), (bj), (sb), (d)

148990-3   **Collegiate Sam** vTJ (cl solo)
     78: Harmony 1009-H, Velvet Tone 2009-V, Diva 3009-G, MGM 1076-P
     LP: Sunbeam MFC-17
     TC: Radio Yesteryear Stack 12
148991-3   **Gotta Feelin' For You** [Jo Trent; Louis Alter] vTJ
     78: Harmony 1009-H, Velvet Tone 2009-V, Diva 3009-G, MGM 1076-P

OKeh, New York, N.Y. Thursday, September 12, 1929
EMMETT MILLER'S GEORGIA CRACKERS
Tom Dorsey (cnt) Jack Teagarden (tb,vcl) **Jimmy Dorsey** (cl,as) Art Schutt (p) Eddie Lang (g) Joe Tarto (sb) Gene Krupa (d) Emmett Miller (vcl)

W 402948-C   **Sweet Mama** [Harold Frost, Billy Rose; George Little] vEM (cl solo)
     78: OKeh 41342, Parlophone PNY-34013, Odeon (F) 238013
     LP: Parlophone (E) PMC7006
W 402949-C   **The Pickaninnie's Paradise** [Sam Coslow; Arthur Johnston] vEM
     78: OKeh 41377
     LP: The Old Masters 1
W 402950-C   **The Blues Singer (From Alabam')** vEM&JT
     78: OKeh 41377, Parlophone (E)R-1115, Odeon (G)A-286054
     LP: The Old Masters 1, Odeon (G) SMS9
     all three sides also on **CD:** Columbia CK 66999

Columbia, New York, N.Y. Friday, September 13, 1929
IPANA TROUBADORS
Sam Lanin (ldr) Leo McConville, *unknown* (tp) Tom Dorsey (tb) *Pete Pumiglio,* **Jimmy Dorsey** (cl,as) *Babe Russin* (cl,ts) Arthur Schutt (p) *unknown* (bj) *Hank Stern* (bb) *unknown* (d) Smith Ballew (vcl)

W 149000-1   **True Blue Lou** [Leo Robin, Sam Coslow, Richard A.
        Whiting] vSB (as solo)
    78: Columbia 1982-D, Regal (Au) 20602
        Regal as MIDNIGHT REVELLERS
W 149001-3   **There's Too Many Eyes That "Wanna" Make Eyes
        At Two Pretty Eyes I Love** [Benny Davis; J. Fred
        Coots, Ed G. Nelson] vSB (as solo)
    78: Columbia 1982-D, (Au) 01761
        01761 as MIDNIGHT REVELLERS

OKeh, New York, N.Y. Tuesday, September 17, 1929
DR. EUGENE ORMANDY'S SALON ORCHESTRA
Eugene Ormandy (ldr) Leo McConville, Mannie Klein (tp) Tom Dorsey (tb) **Jimmy Dorsey** (cl,as) Arnold Brilhart (as) Jim Crossan (ts) Murray Kellner, Nat Brusiloff, Sam Freed (vn) Emil Stark (cel) Arthur Schutt (p) Eddie Lang (g) Hank Stern (bb) Joe Tarto (sb) Chauncey Morehouse (d) Scrappy Lambert (vcl)

W 402953-C   **Go To Bed** vSL
    78: OKeh 41300, Parlophone (E) R-518
W 402954-B   **Dance Away The Night** [Harlan Thompson; Dave
        Stamper] vSL
    78: OKeh 41300, Parlophone (E) R-518
W 402955-   **Like A Breath Of Springtime** vSL
    78: OKeh 41319, Parlophone (E)R-586

Brunswick, New York, N.Y. Friday, September 20, 1929
IRVING MILLS AND HIS HOTSY TOTSY GANG
Manny Klein, Leo McConville (tp) Miff Mole (tb) **Jimmy Dorsey,** Arnold Brilhart (cl,as) Pee Wee Russell (cl,ts) Hoagy Carmichael (p,celst,vcl) Joe Tarto (bb) Chauncey Morehouse (d,vib)

E 30958   **Harvey** [Hoagy Carmichael] vHC (cl solo)
    78: Brunswick 4559
    LP: The Old Masters 12, MCA 52056, Retrieval (E) FJ-123
E 30959   **Harvey** (cl solo)
    LP: Coral (G) 0052.056
E 30960   **March Of The Hoodlums** (as solo)
    78: Brunswick 4559
    LP: The Old Masters 12, Retrieval (E) FJ-123
E 30961   **Star Dust** [Mitchell Parish; Hoagy Carmichael] (as
        solo)
    78: Brunswick 4587
    LP: The Old Masters 12, Retrieval (E) FJ-123

OKeh, New York, N.Y. Tuesday, September 24, 1929
MIFF MOLE'S MOLERS
Phil Napoleon (tp) Miff Mole (tb) **Jimmy Dorsey** (cl,as) Babe Russin
(ts) Arthur Schutt (p) Dick McDonough (g) Stan King (d)

402986-B **You Made Me Love You (I Didn't Want To Do It)**
[Joseph McCarthy; James V. Monaco] (cl solos)
78: Parlophone (E)R-647, Odeon (Arg)193622, (G)A-286015
LP: The Old Masters 13
402987-C **After You've Gone** [Henry Creamer; Turner Layton]
(cl solos)
78: OKeh 41445, Parlophone (E) R-1063, (Au) A-3339, Odeon
(Arg) 193622, (F) 238185, (G) A-286049, United Hot Clubs Of
America 24
Both sides on **LP:** Parlophone (E) PMC-7126, Swaggie (Au) 1297

Columbia, New York, N.Y. Thursday, September 26, 1929
SAM LANIN AND HIS ORCHESTRA
Sam Lanin (ldr) Mannie Klein, *unknown* (tp) Tom Dorsey (tb) **Jimmy
Dorsey** (cl,as) *unknown* (cl,as), (cl,ts) Art Schutt (p) Tony Colucci (bj)
Hank Stern (bb) *unknown* (d), Irving Kaufman [as Marvin Young] (vcl)

149053-1 **Deep In The Arms Of Love** [Davis, Ingraham] vIK
(cl solo)
78: Harmony 1017-H, Diva 3017-G, Velvet Tone 2017-V
149054-1 **Melancholy** [Walter Melrose, Marty Bloom] vIK
(cl solo)
78: Harmony 1018-H, Diva 3018-G, Velvet Tone 2018-V
149055-3 **Like A Breath Of Springtime** [Al Dubin; Joe
Burke] vIK
78: Harmony 1018-H, Diva 3018-G, Velvet Tone 2018-V

Columbia, New York, N.Y. Tuesday, October 1, 1929
IRVING BRODSKY AND HIS ORCHESTRA
Red Nichols, *Tommy Thunen [or] Jack Egan* (tp) Glenn Miller (tb) **Jimmy Dorsey** (cl,as) Pee Wee Russell, Fud Livingston (cl,ts) *Henry Whiteman, Maurice Goffin* (vn) Irving Brodsky (p) Tommy Felline (bj) Jack
Hansen (bb) George Beebe (d) Irving Kaufman [Robert Wood] (vcl)

149076-1,2 **If You Believed In Me** [L.W. Gilbert; Abel Baer]
vIK (as solo)
78: Harmony 1021-H, Velvet Tone 2021-V, Diva 3021-G,
Publix 1053-P
Publix as THE PARAMOUNTEERS (only 75 pressed)
149077-2 **The End Of The Lonesome Trail** [Herman Ruby;
Ray Perkins] vIK
78: Harmony 1041-H, Velvet Tone 2041-V, Diva 3041-G
149078-2 **I May Be Wrong, But I Think You're Wonderful**
[Harry Ruskin; Henry Sullivan] vIK
78: Harmony 1021-H, Velvet Tone 2021-V, Diva 3021-G,
Publix 1063-P, Sunshine 1063-P
Publix as THE PARAMOUNTEERS

OKeh, New York, N.Y. Thursday, October 3, 1929
CHARLES W. HAMP
Ben Selvin (ldr) Leo McConville (tp) Tom Dorsey (tb) **Jimmy Dorsey**
(cl,as) *Harry Hoffman* (vn) *Frank Signorelli* (p) *Eddie Lang* (g) Stan
King (d) Charles W. Hamp (vcl)

W 403022-C   **Perhaps** [Andy Razaf; Paul Denniker] vCH (as solo)
        78: OKeh 41308
        CD: Take Two 411
W 403023-C   **Sweetheart's Holiday** [Irving Kahal, J. Russell Rob-
                inson] vCH (cl solo)
        78: OKeh 41308, Parlophone (E) R-560
                Parlophone as TAMPA BLUE ARTISTES & THEIR SINGER

Brunswick, New York, N.Y. Tuesday, October 22, 1929
RED NICHOLS AND HIS FIVE PENNIES
Red Nichols, Mickey Bloom, Tommy Thunen (tp) Glenn Miller, Herb
Taylor (tb) **Jimmy Dorsey** (cl,as) Rube Bloom (p) Tommy Felline (g,bj)
Joe Tarto (bb) Dave Tough (d) Scrappy Lambert (vcl)

E 31266-A   **Get Happy** [Ted Koehler; Harold Arlen] vSL (as solo)
        78: Brunswick 4591, (Au) 4591, (F,G) A-8615
                as THE CAPTIVATORS, DIRECTION RED NICHOLS
        LP: IAJRC 22
        CD: Tax (Swe) S-5-2
E 31266-B   **Get Happy** vSL (as solo)
        LP: IAJRC 22
E 31267-G   **Get Happy** (as solo)
        78: Brunswick (G) A-8615, (F) A-8615
                as THE CAPTIVATORS, DIRECTION RED NICHOLS
E 31268-   **Somebody To Love Me** [Ted Klages, Jesse Greer] vSL
                (cl solo)
        78: Brunswick 4591, (Au) 4591, (F,G) A-8615
                as THE CAPTIVATORS, DIRECTION RED NICHOLS
        LP: Emanon ESL-1, Origin OJL-8106
        CD: Tax (Swe) S-5-2
E 31269-G   **Somebody To Love Me** (cl solo)
        78: Brunswick (G) A-8615, (F) A-8615
                as THE CAPTIVATORS, DIRECTION RED NICHOLS
E 31270-   **Say It With Music** [Irving Berlin] vSL
        78: Brunswick 4651, (C) 4651
E 31271-G   **Say It With Music**
        78: Brunswick (G) A-8655

Plaza, New York, N.Y. Tuesday, October 29, 1929
SAM LANIN'S ORCHESTRA
Personnel as September 26, 1929, except Joe Green (d,xyl) Scrappy
Lambert [as Rodman Lewis, Roland Lance or Chester Hale] (vcl)

9104-   **Great Day** [Edward Eliscu, Billy Rose; Vincent You-
                mans] vSL
        78: Oriole 1756

9104-2   **Great Day** vSL (RolL on Broadway)
    78: Banner 0503, Broadway 1334, Clifford (Au) 5299, Cameo
    0103
        Broadway as THE BADGERS, Clifford as SAM LANNIN'S
        [sic] ORCHESTRA
9104-3   **Great Day** vSL[as RodL on Domino]
    78: Banner 0503, Domino 4444, Pathe Actuelle 37062, Perfect
    15243, Romeo 1122, Conqueror 7440, Imperial (E) 2325
        Pathe, Perfect as SAM LANIN'S TROUBADORS (vCH),
        Conqueror as JOHN VINCENT'S CALIFORNIANS, Imperial
        as SAM LANIN'S DANCE ORCHESTRA
9104-4   **Great Day** vSL[RodL]
    78: Regal 8889
9105-3   **Without A Song** [Edward Eliscu, Billy Rose; Vincent
                Youmans] vSL[as RodL on Regal]
    78: Banner 0504, Domino 4444, Cameo 0104, Pathe Actuelle
    37062, Perfect 15243, Regal 8889, Imperial (E) 2325, Broadway
    1334, Conqueror 7440, Apex (C) 41068, Crown 81281, Angelus
    (Au) 3299, Clifford (Au) 5299
        Pathe, Perfect as SAM LANIN'S TROUBADORS (vCH),
        Imperial as SAM LANIN'S DANCE ORCHESTRA, Broadway
        as THE BADGERS (vRolL), Crown as THE TROUBADORS,
        Clifford as SAM LANNIN'S [sic] ORCHESTRA
9106-   **Somebody Mighty Like You** vSL (cl solo)
    78: Savoy 1077
9106-2   **Somebody Mighty Like You** vSL (cl solo)
    78: Banner 0511, Domino 4449, Oriole 1765, Pathe Actuelle
    37063, Perfect 15244, Regal 8893, Cameo 0111, Romeo 1129,
    Imperial (E) 2223, Broadway 1333, Angelus (Au) 3183
        Perfect, Pathe as MAJESTIC DANCE ORCH., Imperial as
        SAM LANIN & HIS ORCH., Broadway as THE BADGERS,
        Angelus as LOU GOLD & HIS ORCH.
9106-3   **Somebody Mighty Like You** vSL (cl solo)
    78: Apex (C) 41076, Embassy (Au) 8079
        Embassy as SAM LANIN'S DANCE ORCHESTRA

Brunswick, New York, N.Y. Late October 1929
IRVING MILLS' HOTSY TOTSY GANG
Mannie Klein, Leo McConville (tp) Miff Mole (tb) **Jimmy Dorsey** (cl)
Babe Russin (ts) Hoagy Carmichael (p,vcl) Joe Tarto (bb) Chauncey
Morehouse (d,vib) Irving Mills (vcl)

XE-31010-A,B   **Nobody's Sweetheart** [Elmer Schoebel, Gus Kahn,
                Ernie Erdman, Billy Myers] (cl solo)
    78: (12-inch) Brunswick Brevities #58, Program H, pt. 1
XE-31011-A   **Harvey** [Hoagy Carmichael] vHC,IM
    78: (12-inch) Brunswick Brevities #59, Program H, pt. 3
    Both on **LP:** Jazz Archives JA-21, **TC:** Radio Yesteryear Stack 45
XE-31013-B   (medley) **Rockin' Chair** [Hoagy Carmichael]; **I Can't
                Give You Anything But Love** [Dorothy Fields; Jimmy
                McHugh]
    78: (12-inch) Brunswick Brevities #61, Program H, pt. 5

Brunswick, New York, N.Y. Thursday, November 7, 1929
IRVING MILLS' HOTSY TOTSY GANG
Mannie Klein, Leo McConville (tp) Tom Dorsey (tb) **Jimmy Dorsey,**
Arnold Brilhart (cl,as) Pee Wee Russell (cl,ts) *Joe Venuti [or] Harry
Hoffman* (vn) Hoagy Carmichael (p,celst) Joe Tarto (bb) Chauncey
Morehouse (d,vib)

E 31315   **Manhattan Rag** [Hoagy Carmichael]
    78: Brunswick 4641, (G) A-8645
    LP: The Old Masters 12, Retrieval (E) FJ123, Indiana Historical
    Society 1001
E 31316   **What Kind Of Man Is You?** (as solo)
    78: Brunswick 4641, (G) A-8645
    LP: The Old Masters 12, Retrieval (E) FJ123, Indiana Historical
    Society 1001
E 31317   **My Little Honey And Me** (as solo)
    78: Brunswick 4674, (G) A-8584, (Arg) 3009
    LP: The Old Masters 12, Retrieval (E) FJ123

Columbia, New York, N.Y. Friday, November 15, 1929
FRED RICH AND HIS ORCHESTRA
Fred Rich (ldr) Leo McConville, *unknown* (tp) Tom Dorsey (tb) **Jimmy
Dorsey,** *Tony Parenti* (cl,as) Fred Cusick (cl,ts) *unknown* (vn) Arthur
Schutt (p) Carl Kress (g) Joe Tarto (bb,sb) *unknown* (d) Rollickers (vcl)

W 149429-2   **He's So Unusual** [Al Lewis, Al Sherman; Abner
                   Silver] vR (as solo)
    78: Columbia 2043-D, (Arg) A-8308, Regal (E) MR-14
        Regal as RHYTHMIC TROUBADORS
    LP: The Old Masters 27, World Records (E) SH410
    TC: Columbia Legacy CT52855
    CD: Columbia Legacy CK52855, The Old Masters 101
100340-1   **He's So Unusual** (as solo)
    78: Harmony 1063-H, Diva 3063-G, Velvet Tone 2063-V
    LP: The Old Masters 27
    CD: The Old Masters 101
W 149430-3   **Dixie Jamboree** vR (as solo)
    78: Columbia 2043-D
    LP: The Old Masters 27, World Records (E) SH410
    CD: The Old Masters 101
100341-1   **Dixie Jamboree** (as solo)
    78: Harmony 1062-H, Diva 3062-G, Velvet Tone 2062-V
        as RUDY MARLOW AND HIS ORCHESTRA
    LP: The Old Masters 27
    CD: The Old Masters 101

OKeh, New York, N.Y. Monday, November 18, 1929
ARTHUR SCHUTT AND HIS ORCHESTRA
Arthur Schutt (p,ldr) Leo McConville, *unknown* (tp) Tom Dorsey (tb)
Jimmy Dorsey (cl,as) Arnold Brilhart (as) Babe Russin (ts) Eddie Lang
(g) *Joe Tarto [or] Hank Stern* (bb,sb) Stan King (d) *Elmer Feldkamp*
(vcl)

W 403275-A   **My Fate Is In Your Hands** [Andy Razaf; Thomas
                "Fats" Waller] *vEF*
    78: OKeh 41346, Parlophone (E) R-587, (Au) A-2953, B-12865
W 403275-B?   **My Fate Is In Your Hands** *vEF*
    LP: Broadway BR112
W 403276-A   **Take Everything But You** [Maurice Abrahams, El-
                mer Colby] *vEF*
    78: OKeh 41345, Parlophone (E) R-594, (Au) A-2945, B-12865
W 403277-B   **If I'm Dreaming (Don't Wake Me Too Soon)** [Al
                Dubin; Joe Burke] vEF
    78: OKeh 41346, Parlophone (E) R-594, (Au) A-2972, Ariel (E)
    4516
            Ariel as ARIEL DANCE ORCHESTRA

Columbia, New York, N.Y. Tuesday, November 26, 1929
SAM LANIN AND HIS ORCHESTRA
Sam Lanin (ldr) Mannie Klein, *unknown* (tp) Tom Dorsey (tb) *Jimmy
Dorsey, unknown* (cl,as), (ts) Arthur Schutt (p) Tony Colucci (g) Hank
Stern (bb) *unknown* (d) Irving Kaufman [as Tom Frawley ("Fawley" on
Harmony 1065)] (vcl)

149493-2   **Hoosier Hop** vIK
    78: Harmony 1065-H, Odeon (F) A-221160, (G) A-221160,
    Velvet Tone 2065-V, Diva 3065-V
    LP: World Records (E) SH424
149494-2   **Blue Butterfly** vIK
    78: Harmony 1067-H, Diva 3067-G, Velvet Tone 2067-V
149495-2   **I'm Following You** [Ballard MacDonald; Dave Drey-
                er] vIK
    78: Harmony 1065-H, MGM 1091-P, Publix 2002-P, Diva
    3065-G, Velvet Tone 2065-V
            *MGM as THE CAPITOLIANS, Publix as THE PARA-
            MOUNTEERS*

Next is what some discographers have called a Ben Selvin session, yet
Columbia files say it is Irving Brodsky. The personnel closely mirrors
most Red Nichols' groups of the period.

Columbia, New York, N.Y. Wednesday, November 27, 1929
IRVING BRODSKY AND HIS ORCHESTRA
Red Nichols, *Tommy Thunen [or] Jack Egan* (tp) Glenn Miller (tb)
Jimmy Dorsey (cl,as) Pee Wee Russell, Fud Livingston (cl,ts) Henry
Whiteman, Maurice Goffin (vn) Irving Brodsky (p,arr) Tommy Felline
(bj) Jack Hansen (bb) George Beebe (d) Annette Hanshaw (vcl)

W 149645-2   **When I'm Housekeeping For You** [Gorney, Howard]
                vAH (as solo)
    78: Publix 1070-P
    LP: World (E) SH428
            Publix as THE PARAMOUNTEERS
W 149646-1   **I Have To Have You** [Leo Robin; Richard A. Whit-
                ing] vAH (as solo)

IRVING BRODSKY AND HIS ORCHESTRA (Contd.)

> **78:** Harmony 1075-H, Velvet Tone 2075-V, Diva 3075-G, Publix 1069-P, 2008-P
> **LP:** World (E) SH428
> > *Harmony, Velvet Tone and Diva as FRANK AUBURN & HIS ORCHESTRA, Publix as THE PARAMOUNTEERS*

W-149647-3   **Ain'tcha?** [Mack Gordon, Max Rich] vAH (as solo)
> **78:** Publix 1069-P
> **LP:** World (E) SH428
> > *Publix as THE PARAMOUNTEERS*

As the Roaring Twenties came to a whimpering end, Jimmy joined the Ted Lewis stage and recording band, replacing Frank Teschemacher. A mediocre clarinet player who used his clarinet more as a stage prop, Lewis added top clarinetists like Dorsey, Teschemacher, Don Murray and Benny Goodman to his bands to provide jazz interest.

Lewis was a native of Circleville, Ohio, and made a name for himself in vaudeville and on recordings as "The Top-hatted Tragedian of Jazz." His greeting, "Is everybody happy?", was well-known at the time, as was his theme "When My Baby Smiles At Me."

While Lewis made a couple of movies in 1929 and 1930, Jimmy doesn't appear to have been in the band at the time. The possible exception is a nine-minute Vitaphone short titled "The Cave Club" in which Ted Lewis and the band have one number.

Jimmy toured with Lewis in December in the Midwest and East. The Lewis band visited Columbia's studios when they returned. Jimmy also moonlighted with Fred Rich that Christmas Eve.

Columbia, New York, N.Y. Tuesday, December 24, 1929
TED LEWIS AND HIS BAND
Ted Lewis (ldr,cl,as,vcl) Muggsy Spanier, Dave Klein (cnt) George Brunies, Harry Raderman (tb) **Jimmy Dorsey** (cl,as,bar) Sol Klein (vn) Jack Aaronson (p) Tony Gerhardi (bj,g) Harry Barth (bb) John Lucas (d)

W-149613-2   **You've Got That Thing** [Cole Porter] vTL
> **78:** Columbia 2088-D, (Arg) A-8606
> **LP:** Gaps (H) 150

Columbia, New York, N.Y. Tuesday, December 24, 1929
FRED RICH AND HIS ORCHESTRA
Fred Rich (ldr) Leo McConville, *unknown* (tp) Tom Dorsey (tb) **Jimmy Dorsey,** *unknown* (cl,as) Fred Cusick (cl,ts) *unknown* (vn) Arthur Schutt (p) Carl Kress (g) Joe Tarto (bb,sb) *unknown* (d) The Rollickers, Smith Ballew (vcl)

W 149616-1,2,3   **If Love Were All** vR (unissued)
W 149617-3   **I'll See You Again** [Noel Coward] vSB
> **78:** Columbia 2090-D
> > *149616-5 previously listed for this session was made as part of the Fred Rich session on January 8, 1930, without Jimmy.*

A New Decade Dawns
(1930)

To save money as 1929 slid warily into 1930, Jimmy and Jane Dorsey, along with Benny Goodman, rented an apartment for several months on West Fifty-eighth Street near the radio and recording studios. Despite being married for two years, Jimmy wasn't emulating brother Tommy, who was about to become a father for the second time.

On New Year's Eve, 1929, Jimmy was feeling no pain and did an imitation of Ted Lewis playing the clarinet. When the boss took offense, Jimmy hit Ted's head with his clarinet and was nearly fired.

Columbia, New York, N.Y. Friday, January 3, 1930
SAM LANIN AND HIS ORCHESTRA
Sam Lanin (ldr) Mannie Klein, *unknown* (tp) Tom Dorsey (tb) **Jimmy Dorsey,** *unknown* (cl,as) Merle Johnston (ts) Murray Kellner (vn) Arthur Schutt (p) *John Cali* (g) Hank Stern (bb) *Vic Berton* (d) Annette Hanshaw [as Gay Ellis], Irving Kaufman [as Robert Wood] (vcl)

149728-2   **If He Cared** [Clifford Grey; Herbert Stothart] vIK [RW]
     78: Harmony 1085-H, Diva 3085-G, Velvet Tone 2085-V
     Diva and Velvet Tone as ARTHUR ROSS AND HIS WESTERNERS
149729-3   **Cryin' For The Carolines** [Sam H. Lewis, Joe Young; Harry Warren] vIK (as solo)
     78: Harmony 1083-H, Publix 2008-P, Diva 3083-G, Velvet Tone 2083-V
     Publix as THE PARAMOUNTEERS
     LP: Sunbeam MFC17
149730-3   **When I'm Housekeeping For You** vAH[GE]
     78: Harmony 1084-H, Publix 2006-P, Diva 3084-G, Velvet Tone 2084-V
     Publix as THE PARAMOUNTEERS
     LP: World Records (E) SH424

Columbia, New York, N.Y. Saturday, January 4, 1930
ARTHUR SCHUTT AND HIS ORCHESTRA
Arthur Schutt (p,ldr) Leo McConville, *Mannie Klein* (tp) Tom Dorsey (tb) **Jimmy Dorsey** (cl,as) Arnold Brilhart (as) Babe Russin (ts) Eddie Lang (g) *Joe Tarto* (bb,sb) Stan King (d) Smith Ballew (vcl)

W 403583   **I'm Following You** [Ballard MacDonald; Dave Dreyer] vSB (as solo)
     78: OKeh 41360, Odeon ONY-36025, A-189317, (Contd.)

ARTHUR SCHUTT AND HIS ORCHESTRA (Contd.)

(Arg) 193500, Parlophone PNY-34020, (E) R-587
Parlophone PNY as CYRIL MERRIVALE'S ORCH.
LP: Harrison LP-U, Emanon ESL-1, Origin OJL-8106
W 490026-A   **I'm Following You** (as solo)
78: Odeon ONY-36021, Parlophone PNY-34016
W 403584-A   **Have A Little Faith In Me** [Sam M. Lewis, Joe
Young; Harry Warren] vSB
78: OKeh   41359,   Odeon   ONY-36028,   (F)   A-221235,
Parlophone PNY-34025, (E) R-619, Ariel (E) 4446
*Parlophone PNY as CYRIL MERRIVALE'S ORCH., Ariel as
ARIEL DANCE ORCHESTRA*
W 490028-A   **Cryin' For The Carolines** (unissued)
W 403585-B   **Cryin' For The Carolines** [Sam H. Lewis, Joe
Young; Harry Warren] vSB (cl solo)
78: OKeh 41359, Odeon ONY-36028, Parlophone PNY-34024,
(E) R-619
Parlophone PNY as CYRIL MERRIVALE'S ORCH.
TC: Radio Yesteryear Stack #81
LP: Columbia P5-14320

Brunswick, New York, N.Y. Monday, January 6, 1930
IRVING MILLS' HOTSY TOTSY GANG
Mannie Klein, Bill Moore (tp) Tom Dorsey (tb) **Jimmy Dorsey** (cl,as)
Babe Russin (ts) Jack Cornell [Smelser] (acc) Hoagy Carmichael
(p,cel,vcl) Dick McDonough (bj) Joe Tarto (bb,sb) Gene Krupa (d)

E 31757   **High And Dry** [Hoagy Carmichael] vHC (cl solo)
78: Brunswick 4920, 01023
LP: The Old Masters 12, Historical HLP37, Retrieval (E) FJ123
CD: Timeless (H) CBC 1-011, King Jazz 154
E 31758   **High And Dry** (cl solo)
78: Brunswick (G) A-8883, (Arg) 4920
*Argentine release as IRVING MILLS AND HIS ORCH-
ESTRA. Second pianist is unknown but could be Smelser.*
LP: Retrieval (E) FJ127
E 31759   **Barbaric** (as solo)
78: Brunswick 4920, 01023, (G) A-8883
LP: The Old Masters 12, Historical HLP37, Retrieval (E) FJ123
E 31760   **South Breeze** (unissued)

Columbia, New York, N.Y. Monday, January 6, 1930
TED LEWIS AND HIS BAND
Ted Lewis (ldr,cl,as,vcl) Muggsy Spanier, Dave Klein (cnt) George
Brunies (tb,*harmonica*) Harry Raderman (tb) **Jimmy Dorsey** (cl,as,bar)
Sol Klein (vn) Jack Aaronson (p) Tony Gerhardi (bj) Harry Barth (bb)
John Lucas (d)

W-149734-4   **Harmonica Harry** [Phil Baxter] vTL
78: Columbia 2088-D, (Arg) A-8606, (J) J-871
LP: Gaps (H) 150

Columbia, New York, N.Y. Wednesday, January 8, 1930
TED LEWIS AND HIS BAND
George Brunies doubles on kazoo.

W-149743-4   **San** [Lindsay McPhail, Walter Michaels]
     78: Columbia 2113-D, (E) CB-63, (J) J-894
     LP: Gaps (H) 020
     CD: Take Two 423, Retrieval (E) 79014

Columbia, New York, N.Y. Friday, January 10, 1930
TED LEWIS AND HIS BAND
Four Dusty Travelers (vcl grp) added.

W-149758-2   **The Lonesome Road** [Gene Austin; Nat Shilkret]
     vTL,4DT
     78: Columbia 2181-D, 56000-D (dubbing), (E) CB-63, (Arg) A-
     8821, (J) J-891
          See January 24, 1930, session for details of 56000-D.
     LP: Biograph BLP-C7, Gaps (H) 020
     CD: Retrieval (E) 79014

ARC, New York, N.Y. Monday, January 13, 1930
THE DORSEY BROTHERS' ORCHESTRA
Tom Dorsey (tb,ldr) Mannie Klein, Frank Guarente, Muggsy Spanier
(tp) Joe Yukl (tb) **Jimmy Dorsey** (cl,as) Alfie Evans (as) Herbert
Spencer (ts) 2 *unknown* (vn) Irving Brodsky (p) Carl Kress (g) Joe Tarto
(bb,sb) Ray Bauduc (d) Scrappy Lambert (vcl)

9277-2,3   **Have A Little Faith In Me** [Sam M. Lewis, Joe
                    Young; Harry Warren] vSL
     78: Banner 0571, Broadway 1352, Cameo 0171, Conqueror
     7472, Jewel 5827, Domino 4482, Oriole 1827, Perfect 15265,
     Regal 8926, Romeo 1192, Imperial 2279, Apex 41087, Clifford
     (Au) 5235, Vocalion (Au) 595
          Broadway as MANLEY BROTHERS' ORCHESTRA
9278-1,3   **Congratulations** [Maceo Pinkard, Coleman Goetz,
                    Bud Green, Sam H. Stept] vSL (cl,as solos)
     78: Banner 0566, Cameo 0166, Domino 4486, Conqueror 7476,
     Jewel 5828, Oriole 1828, Pathe Actuelle 37088, Perfect 15269,
     Regal 8931, Romeo 1186, Apex 41096, Angelus (Au) 3278,
     Crown 81265, Clifford (Au) 5278
          Crown as FRANK LLOYD'S ORCHESTRA
9279-2   **Beside An Open** Fireplace [Paul Denniker, Will
                    Osborne] vSL (as solo)
     78: Banner 0589, Broadway 1352, Cameo 0189, Conqueror
     7476, Domino 4486, Jewel 5846, Oriole 1846, Pathe Actuelle
     37088, Perfect 15269, Regal 8931, Crown 81299, Romeo 1208,
     Apex 41124, Imperial 2263
          *Crown as RENDEZVOUS CAFE ORCHESTRA, Broadway as
          MANLEY BROTHERS' ORCHESTRA*
     9277, 9278-3 and 9279 also on **CD:** Jazz Oracle (C) BDW 8005
                              (Contd.)

THE DORSEY BROTHERS' ORCHESTRA (Contd.)

9279-3   Beside An Open Fireplace vSL (as solo)
    78: Perfect 15269

The Gershwin musical *Strike Up The Band* opened January 14, 1930, in the Times Square Theater with a Red Nichols pit band. The group originally included Benny Goodman, who was, with others, trying to take over the Ben Pollack band. Benny asked Jimmy to sub for him during Philadelphia tryouts, but when the Pollack "coup" failed, Red kept Jimmy on, along with Glenn Miller, Babe Russin and Gene Krupa, for the 191-performance run of the show (Connor 1988).

Brunswick, New York, N.Y. Friday, January 17, 1930
RED NICHOLS AND HIS *STRIKE UP THE BAND* ORCHESTRA
Red Nichols (cnt,ldr) Ruby Weinstein, Charlie Teagarden (tp) Glenn Miller, *Tom Dorsey [or] Herb Taylor* (tb) **Jimmy Dorsey** (cl,as) Sid Stoneburn (as) Babe Russin, Larry Binyon (ts) 2 *unknown* (vn) Jack Russin (p) Teg Brown (g) Joe Tarto (bb) Gene Krupa (d) *unknown* (vcl)

E 31882-B   Strike Up The Band [Ira Gershwin; George Gersh-
                    win] vocal (as solo)
    78: Brunswick 4695, 6753, (C) 4695, (G) A-8659
    LP: IAJRC 22
    CD: Best Of Jazz (F) 4041
E 31883-G   Strike Up The Band (unissued)
E 31884-A   Soon [Ira Gershwin; George Gershwin] vocal (cl solo)
    78: Brunswick 4695, (C) 4695
    LP: Collectors Must (It) M8004
            *"Soon" appears twice on the Italian LP release, including a
            second purported "released" vocal take, but the author can
            not detect differences between the two "takes". Its use may
            have resulted from misinterpreting a "2" stamper number.*
E 31885-G   Soon (unissued)

ARC, New York, N.Y. Friday, January 17, 1930
SAM LANIN AND HIS ORCHESTRA
Sam Lanin (ldr) 2 *unknown* (tp) Tom Dorsey (tb) **Jimmy Dorsey** (cl,as) *unknown* (ts) 2 *unknown* (vn) Art Schutt (p) Charles Magnante (acc) *unknown* (g) *Hank Stern* (bb) *Stan King* (d) Scrappy Lambert [as Rodman Lewis or Roland Lance on some] (vcl)

9295-1,3   Mona [Con Conrad, Sidney Mitchell, Archie Gott-
                    ler] vSL [RodL on Domino 4495, Perfect] (cl solo)
    78: Perfect 15276, Cameo 0201, Domino 4495, (C) 181296,
    Romeo 1225, Imperial (E) 2237, Regal 8945, Crown (C) 81296,
    Apex (C) 41105, Banner 0601, Oriole 1855
            Crown and Domino 181296 as THE ARCADIANS
9296-1,2   I'm On A Diet Of Love vSL [RodL on Domino 4495,
                    Perfect] (cl solo)
    78: Perfect 15276, Romeo 1225, Domino 4495, Imperial (E)
    2237, Regal 8945, Crown (C) 81297, Apex (C) 41105

Crown as THE ARCADIANS
9297-1,2   **What Is This Thing Called Love?** [Cole Porter] vSL
                [RolL on Broadway]
        78: Perfect 15282, Romeo 1244, Conqueror 7511, Broadway
        1367, Cameo 0225, Oriole 1880, Banner 0625(-1), Crown (C)
        81266, Regal 8958
                Broadway as THE BADGERS, Conqueror as JOHN VIN-
                CENT'S CALIFORNIANS, Crown as JERRY WHITE'S
                ORCH., Oriole as ROY COLLINS DANCE ORCH.

Columbia, New York, N.Y. Monday, January 20, 1930
TED LEWIS AND HIS BAND
Ted Lewis (ldr,cl,as,vcl) Muggsy Spanier, Dave Klein (cnt) George
Brunies, Harry Raderman (tb) **Jimmy Dorsey** (cl,as,bar) Sol Klein (vn)
Jack Aaronson (p) Tony Gerhardi (bj,g) Harry Barth (bb) John Lucas (d)

W-149784-3   **Aunt Hagar's Blues** [William C. Handy] vTL (cl,as
                solos)
        78: Columbia 2113-D, 3169-D, 38840, (E) CB-64, (J) J-894
        LP: Biograph BLP-C7, Gaps (H) 060, Epic LN-3170
        CD: Take Two 423, Retrieval (E) 79014

Brunswick, New York, N.Y. Monday, January 20, 1930
LOUISIANA RHYTHM KINGS
Red Nichols (cnt,ldr) Tommy Thunen (tp) Glenn Miller (tb) **Jimmy
Dorsey** (cl,as) Babe Russin (ts) Adrian Rollini (bsx) Jack Russin (p) Wes
Vaughan (bj,g,vcl) Gene Krupa (d)

E 31943   **Swanee** [Irving Caesar; George Gershwin] (cl solo)
        78: Brunswick 4845, 6834, (F) A-500325
                A-500325 as RED NICHOLS AND HIS LOUISVILLE
                RHYTHM KINGS
E 31944   **Squeeze Me** [Clarence Williams; Thomas "Fats" Wal-
                ler] (as solo)
        78: Brunswick 4953, Decca (E) O3282 (dubbing)
E 31945   **Oh! Lady Be Good** [Ira Gershwin; George Gershwin]
                (as solo)
        78: Brunswick 4706, 6829, (E) O2676, O3324, (G) A-8687,
        (Ind) O.3324, Decca (E) O3282
                6829, O2676 as RED NICHOLS & HIS FIVE PENNIES
E 31946   **Sweet Sue (Just You)** [Will J. Harris; Victor Young]
        78: Brunswick 4953, (E) O3282 (dubbing)
E 31947   **The Meanest Kind Of Blues** [Jackson] (as solo)
        78: Brunswick 4845, 6834, (C) 4843, (E) O324, (G) A-8687,
        (Ind) O.3324
E 31948   **I Have To Have You** [Leo Robin; Richard A. Whit-
                ing] vWV (as solo)
        78: Brunswick 4706, 6829, (C) 4706, (E) O2676
                6829, O2676 as RED NICHOLS AND HIS FIVE PENNIES
        All sides also on **LP:** The Old Masters 35, Coral (G) 97024

In the next session, 56000-D was another of Columbia's experiments, dubbing both W-149758-2 and W-149911-4 on one side of a disk with announcements and billing it as *Ted Lewis Presents a Miniature Dance Program*. Dubbing was done June 13, 1932, as matrix 260000-3.

Columbia, New York, N.Y. Friday, January 24, 1930
TED LEWIS AND HIS BAND
Four Dusty Travelers (vcl grp) added.

W-149911-4   **Dinah** [Sam M. Lewis, Joseph Young; Harry Akst] vTL,4DT (cl solo)
  78: Columbia 2181-D, 56000-D (dubbing), (E) CB-64, (Arg) A-8821, (Au) DO-239, (J) J-936, OKeh 41585 (dubbing)
  LP: Biograph BLP-C8, Gaps (H) 060

Brunswick, New York, N.Y. Friday, January 24, 1930
RED NICHOLS AND HIS FIVE PENNIES
Red Nichols (tp,ldr) Ruby Weinstein (tp) Tom Dorsey (tb) **Jimmy Dorsey** (cl,as) Babe Russin (ts) Adrian Rollini (bsx) Jack Russin (p) Teg Brown (bj) Gene Krupa (d) *unknown* (vcl)

E 31903   **Sometimes I'm Happy** [Leo Robin, Clifford Grey; Vincent Youmans] (as solo)
  78: Brunswick 4701, 6828, (Au) 4701, (Arg) 4701, 41057, (G) A-8673
  LP: MCA 1518, IAJRC 22
  TC: Neovox (E) 762
E 31904   **Hallelujah!** [Leo Robin, Clifford Grey; Vincent Youmans] (as solo)
  78: Brunswick 4701, 6828, (Au) 4701, (Arg) 4701, 41057(G) A-8673
  ET: AFRS Phonograph Album H-62-92
  LP: IAJRC 22
  TC: Neovox (E) 762

Brunswick, New York, N.Y. Monday, January 27, 1930
LOUISIANA RHYTHM KINGS
Personnel same as Red Nichols, January 24, 1930.

E 31911-   **O'er The Billowy Sea** [Nowlin, Smith] (cl solo)
  78: Brunswick 4908, 6837, Lucky (J) 5077
        6837 as RED NICHOLS AND HIS FIVE PENNIES
  LP: The Old Masters 35
E 31912-A   **Lazy Daddy** [LaRocca, Shields, Regas] (cl solo)
  78: Brunswick 4923, 6838
        6838 as RED NICHOLS AND HIS FIVE PENNIES
  LP: The Old Masters 35
E 31913-   **Karavan** [Abe Olman, Ray Wiedoeft] (as solo)
  78: Brunswick 4908, 6837
        6837 as RED NICHOLS AND HIS FIVE PENNIES
  LP: The Old Masters 35
E 31914-   **Pretty Baby** [Gus Kahn; Tony Jackson, Egbert Van

Alstyne] (cl solo)
78: Brunswick 4938, 6840, (G) A-81260
6840 as RED NICHOLS AND HIS FIVE PENNIES
LP: The Old Masters 35
E 31915-   **Tell Me (Why Nights Are Lonely)** [Raymond B.
Egan, Walter Reisch; Robert Stolz] (cl solo)
78: Brunswick 4938, 6840, (G) A-81260, (F) A-500325
*6840 as RED NICHOLS AND HIS FIVE PENNIES, A-
500325 as RED NICHOLS AND HIS LOUISVILLE RHYTHM
KINGS*
LP: The Old Masters 35
E 31916-A   **There's Egypt In Your Dreamy Eyes** [Brown, Spen-
cer] (as solo)
78: Brunswick 4923, 6838
6838 as RED NICHOLS AND HIS FIVE PENNIES
LP: The Old Masters 35

Columbia, New York, N.Y. Tuesday, January 28, 1930
IPANA TROUBADORS
Sam Lanin (ldr) Leo McConville, Mannie Klein (tp) Tom Dorsey (tb)
Jimmy Dorsey (cl,as) Arnold Brilhart (cl,as,fl) Babe Russin (cl,ts) 2
unknown (vn) Cornell Smelser [Jack Cornell] (acc) Arthur Schutt (p)
unknown (bj) *Hank Stern* (bb) Stan King (d) Scrappy Lambert, Harriet
Lee (vcl)

W 149921-1   **Cooking Breakfast For The One I Love** [Billy Rose;
Henry Tobias] vHL (cl solo)
78: Columbia 2117-D, (E) CB-72, (Au) DO89
W 495018-1   **Cooking Breakfast For The One I Love** (cl solo)
78: Parlophone PNY-34013, Odeon ONY-6013
Odeon as EDDIE GORDON'S BAND
(W 195072-) (unissued Columbia export)
Charles Magnante (acc) added:
W 149922-2   **Kickin' A Hole In The Sky** [Billy Rose, Ballard
MacDonald; Jesse Greer] vSL (cl solo)
78: Columbia 2117-D, (E) CB-72, (Au) DO89
W 495019-1   **Kickin' A Hole In The Sky** (cl solo)
78: Parlophone PNY-34013, (E) R-661, Odeon ONY-6013
*Odeon as EDDIE GORDON'S BAND, Parlophone R-661 as
ROOF GARDEN ORCH.*
(100361-1) **78:** Harmony 1138-H, Diva 3138-G, Velvet Tone
2138-V
as FRANK AUBURN AND HIS ORCHESTRA
LP: The Old Masters 28
(W 195073-1) (unissued Columbia export)

Tommy had rejoined Fred Rich's CBS house band by this time, while
Jimmy kept busy with the Red Nichols pit band at the new Gershwin
musical. They kept looking for other work by opening up their own
booking office, located in the Hammerstein Building in Manhattan's
busy Tin Pan Alley (*Melody Maker,* February 1930: 131). As was usually the case, Jimmy was content to leave Tommy in charge.

Brunswick, New York, N.Y. Monday, February 3, 1930
RED NICHOLS AND HIS FIVE PENNIES
Red Nichols (tp,ldr) Tommy Thunen, Mannie Klein (tp) Jack Teagarden
(tb,vcl) Glenn Miller (tb,arr) **Jimmy Dorsey** (cl,as) Babe Russin (ts)
Adrian Rollini (bsx) Jack Russin (p) Wes Vaughan (g) Jack Hansen (bb)
Gene Krupa (d)

E 31923-A   **I'm Just Wild About Harry** [Noble Sissle; Eubie
                   Blake] (as solos) arrGM
     78: Brunswick 4839, 6833 (dubbing), (E) O1121, (F) A-500405,
     (Au) 4839, (G) test pressing
           The 4839 label adds "Saxophone passage by Jimmy Dorsey."
     LP: Ace Of Hearts (E) AH-63, Gaps (H) 180
     CD: Best Of Jazz (F) 4041
E 31924-A   **After You've Gone** [Henry Creamer; Turner Layton]
                   vJT (cl solo) arrGM
     78: Brunswick 4839, 6833 (dubbing), (E) O1104, (F) A-500405,
     (G) test pressing
     LP: Ace Of Hearts (E) AH-168, Gaps (H) 180, Affinity (E) AFS-
     1038

Columbia, New York, N.Y. Thursday, February 6, 1930
MIFF MOLE'S MOLERS
Phil Napoleon (tp) Miff Mole (tb) **Jimmy Dorsey** (cl,as) Babe Russin
(ts) Adrian Rollini (bsx) Lennie Hayton (p) Carl Kress (g) Stan King (d)
Scrappy Lambert (vcl)

403740-A   **Navy Blues** [Roy Turk; Fred Ahlert] vSL (cl solo)
     78: OKeh 41371, Odeon ONY-36045, (Arg) 193500, (F)
     279684, (G) A-286018, Parlophone PNY-34040, (E) R-701, (Au)
     A-2986
           Parlophone PNY- as GILBERT MARSH AND HIS ORCH.
     LP: Parlophone (E) PMC-7126, Swaggie (Au) 1297, Odeon (G)
     SMS-4
     TC: Radio Yesteryear Stack 1
490036-A   **Navy Blues** (cl,as solos)
     78: Odeon ONY-36043, Parlophone PNY-34038
           Parlophone as GILBERT MARSH AND HIS ORCH.
     LP: Swaggie (Au) 1297
490036-B   **Navy Blues** (cl,as solos)
     LP: Parlophone (E) PMC-7126, IAJRC 2, Swaggie (Au) 1297
403741-B   **Lucky Little Devil** [Leo Wood, Mort Dixon] vSL
                   (cl solo)
     78: OKeh 41371, Odeon ONY-36045, (F) 279684, Parlophone
     PNY-34041, (E) R-702, (Au) A-2986
           Parlophone PNY- as GILBERT MARSH AND HIS ORCH.
     LP: Parlophone (E) PMC-7126, Swaggie (Au) 1297
490037-A   **Lucky Little Devil** (as,cl solos)
     78: Odeon ONY-36043, Parlophone PNY-34039
           Parlophone as GILBERT MARSH AND HIS ORCH.
     LP: Swaggie (Au) 1297
490037-B   **Lucky Little Devil** (as,cl solos)

78: (unissued test pressing)
LP: Parlophone (E) PMC-7126, Swaggie (Au) 1297

Columbia, New York, N.Y. Friday, February 7, 1930
CORNELL SMELSER AND HIS ORCHESTRA
Leo McConville, Joe Lindwurm (tp) Jack Teagarden (tb) **Jimmy Dorsey** (cl,as) Fletcher Hereford (as) Adrian Rollini (bsx) Cornell Smelser (acc) Irving Brodsky (p) Dick McDonough (g) Tex Hurst (sb) Stan King (d) Artie Dunn (vcl)

403746-A   **Collegiate Love** (as,cl solos)
    78: OKeh 41386, Odeon ONY-36069, (Arg) 194380, (G) A-286023, Parlophone PNY-34065, (E) R-785
        Parlophone R-785 as CORNELL AND HIS ORCHESTRA.
        Some releases claim a vocal on this matrix. There is none.
    LP: Biograph BLP-C2, Odeon (G) SMS4, World Records (E) SH-410
403747-A   **Accordion Joe** vAD
    78: OKeh 41386, Odeon ONY-36069, (F) A-221291, Parlophone PNY-34063, (E) R-758
        Parlohone R-758 as CABARET DANCE ORCHESTRA
    LP: World Records (E) SH-410
403748-C   **I Was Made To Love You** vAD
    78: OKeh 41395, Odeon ONY-36064, (Arg) 194380, Parlophone PNY-34059
        All Parlophone PNY's as PAUL LOCH AND HIS ORCHESTRA
    LP: World Records (E) SH-410

ARC, New York, N.Y. Friday, February 14, 1930
CHICK BULLOCK
Bob Effros (tp) Tom Dorsey (tb) **Jimmy Dorsey** (cl) Joe Venuti (vn) Frank Banta (p) Eddie Lang (g) *Dick Cherwin* (sb) Stan King (d) Chick Bullock (vcl)

9365 (1,2)   **Should I?** vCB (unissued)
9367-2,3   **St. James Infirmary** [Joe Primrose] vCB (cl solo)
    78: Banner 0647, Cameo 0247, Oriole 1903, Domino 4510, Jewel 5903, Conqueror 9500, Perfect 12594, Regal 8955, Romeo 1266, Angelus (Au) 3210

Brunswick, New York, N.Y. Friday, February 14, 1930
RED NICHOLS AND HIS FIVE PENNIES
Red Nichols (tp,ldr) Tommy Thunen, Mannie Klein (tp) Jack Teagarden, Glenn Miller (tb) **Jimmy Dorsey** (cl,as) Babe Russin (ts) Adrian Rollini (bsx) Jack Russin (p) Wes Vaughan (g) Jack Hansen (bb) Gene Krupa (d)

E 32040-A   **I Want To Be Happy** [Irving Caesar; Vincent Youmans] (cl solo)
    78: Brunswick 4724, 6830, 80007, (E) O1032, (G) A-8832, (Arg) 3005, (Au) 4724 (Contd.)

RED NICHOLS AND HIS FIVE PENNIES (Contd.)

> 45: Coral (G) 94158
> LP: Brunswick BL58008, Coral (G) 97016, Family (It) SFR-DP 649, F-693

E 32041-A   **Tea For Two** [Irving Caesar; Vincent Youmans] (cl solo)
> 78: Brunswick 4724, 6830, 80007, (E) O1032, (G) A-8832, (Arg) 3005, (Au) 4724
> ET: AFRS Popular Music Library #23, series unknown
> LP: Brunswick BL58008, Family (It) SFR-DP 649, F-693

Columbia, New York, N.Y. Friday, February 14, 1930
SAM LANIN AND HIS ORCHESTRA
Sam Lanin (ldr) Mannie Klein, *Henry Busse* (tp) Tom Dorsey (tb) **Jimmy Dorsey** (cl,as) Arnold Brilhart (as,fl), (ts) Arthur Schutt (p) *unknown* (bj) *Hank Stern* (bb) *Stan King* (d) Irving Kaufman (vcl)

149985-1   **Hangin' On The Garden Gate (Sayin' Goodnight)** [Gus Kahn; Ted FioRito] vIK
> 78: Harmony 1107-H, Diva 3107-G, Velvet Tone 2107-V
149986-1   **Gone** [Andy Razaf; Harry Link, Thomas "Fats" Waller] vIK (cl solos)
> 78: Harmony 1107-H, Diva 3107-G, Velvet Tone 2107-V
149987-2   **Keepin' Myself For You** [Sidney Clare; Vincent Youmans] vIK (cl solo)
> 78: Harmony 1109-H, Diva 3109-G, Velvet Tone 2109-V

ARC, New York, N.Y. Wednesday, February 19, 1930
CHICK BULLOCK
Personnel as February 14, 1930. Chick Bullock (vcl)

9374-2,3   **Alcoholic Ward Blues** [Clarence Gaskill] vCB (cl solo)
> 78: Banner 0647, Cameo 0247, Jewel 5903, Oriole 1903, Romeo 1266
> TC: Audio Archives 1004

Columbia, New York, N.Y. Thursday, February 20, 1930
CHARLESTON CHASERS
Phil Napoleon (tp) Tom Dorsey (tb) **Jimmy Dorsey** (cl,as) Arthur Schutt (p) Joe Tarto (sb) Stan King (d) Roy Evans (vcl)

W 150009-2   **Cinderella Brown** [Dorothy Fields; Jimmy McHugh] vRE (cl,as solos)
> 78: Columbia 1989-D, (G) A-8734, (E) 5652
> LP: The Old Masters 6, Vintage Jazz Music Society VLP44
W 150010-2   **Sing, You Sinners** [Sam Coslow, W. Franke Harling] vRE
> 78: Columbia 1989-D, (E) CB-95, 5652 (G) A-8734
> LP: The Old Masters 6, Vintage Jazz Music Society VLP44
> TC: Radio Yesteryear Stack 1

Columbia, New York, N.Y. Thursday, February 27, 1930
BEN SELVIN AND HIS ORCHESTRA
Ben Selvin (ldr) Tom Dorsey (cnt) Charlie Butterfield (tb) **Jimmy Dorsey** (cl,as) Adrian Rollini (bsx) *Bruce Yantis* (vn) Frank Signorelli (p) Carl Kress (g) Stan King (d) Charles "Buddy" Rogers (vcl)

W 150027-3   **(I'd Like To Be) A Bee In Your Boudoir** [George Marion, Jr.; Richard A Whiting] vBR (cl solo)
          78: Columbia 2183-D, (E) DB-242, (Au) DO-152
          as CHARLES "BUDDY" ROGERS, America's Boy Friend
          CD: Living Era (E) ASV 5020
W 150028 (1,2,3) **My Future Just Passed** vBR (unissued)
Rogers out, Eddie Walters (uke,vcl) added:
W 150030-3   **'Leven Thirty Saturday Night** [Jess Kirkpatrick, Earl Burnett; Bill Grantham] vEW
          78: Columbia 2137-D, (E) DB-151
W 150031-3   **Me And The Girl Next Door** vEW
          78: Columbia 2137-D, (E) DB 169
          150030 & 150031 as EDDIE WALTERS
(uke) and King (d) out. Lee Morse (kazoo,vcl) added:
W 150032-3   **'Tain't No Sin** [Edgar Leslie; Walter Donaldson] vLM (cl solo)
          78: Columbia 2136-D, (E) DB-140, (Au) A-8736
          LP: Take Two TT 213
          CD: Take Two 420
W 150033-2   **I'm Following You** [Ballard MacDonald; Dave Dreyer] vLM
          78: Columbia 2136-D
          150032, 150033 as LEE MORSE & HER BLUEGRASS BOYS

Columbia, New York, N.Y. Friday, February 28, 1930
TED LEWIS AND HIS BAND
Ted Lewis (ldr,cl,as,vcl) Muggsy Spanier, Dave Klein (cnt) George Brunies, Harry Raderman (tb) **Jimmy Dorsey** (cl,as,bar) Sol Klein (vn) Jack Aaronson (p) Tony Gerhardi (bj,g) Harry Barth (bb) John Lucas (d,vib)

W 150043-2   **On The Sunny Side Of The Street** [Dorothy Fields; Jimmy McHugh] vTL
          78: Columbia 2144-D, (E) CB-74, (Arg) A-8724, (Au) DO-239, (J) J-912
          LP: Biograph BLP-C8

Columbia, New York, N.Y. Monday, March 3, 1930
TED LEWIS AND HIS BAND

W 150050-4   **Singing A Vagabond Song** [Val Burton, Harry Richman; Sam Messenheimer] vTL (cl solos)
          78: Columbia 2144-D, (E) CB-74, (Arg) A-8724, (Au) DO-87, (J) J-912
          LP: Gaps (H) 150
          CD: Retrieval (E) 79014

Columbia, New York, N.Y. Monday, March 3, 1930
BEN SELVIN AND HIS ORCHESTRA
Ben Selvin (ldr) Mannie Klein, Bob Effros (tp) Tom Dorsey (tb) **Jimmy Dorsey** (cl,as) Louis Martin (as) Joe Dubin (ts) Adrian Rollini (bsx) 2 *unknown* (vn) Rube Bloom (p) Carl Kress (g) Hank Stern (bb) Stan King (d) Smith Ballew (vcl)

W 150054(1,2,3)   **Across The Breakfast Table (Looking At You)** vSB
                  (unissued)
W 495025-1   **Across The Breakfast Table (Looking At You)** [Irving Berlin] (cl solo)
        78: Parlophone (E) R-729
            as ROOF GARDEN ORCHESTRA
        (100377-1) **78:** Harmony 1145-H, Velvet Tone 2145-V
            as LLOYD KEATING AND HIS MUSIC
        (195086-1) (unissued Columbia export)
W 150055(1,2,3)   **Let Me Sing And I'm Happy** vSB (unissued)
100378-1   **Let Me Sing And I'm Happy** [Irving Berlin] (cl,as solos)
        78: Harmony 1137-H, Diva 3137-G, Velvet Tone 2137-V
            as RUDY MARLOW AND HIS ORCHESTRA
        (W 495026-1) **78:** (unissued Odeon test pressing)
        LP: Saville (E) SVL165
        (195081-1) **78:** (unissued Columbia export)
            Matrices 150054 and 150055 remade March 13, 1930.

Columbia, New York, N.Y. Tuesday, March 4, 1930
ARTHUR SCHUTT AND HIS ORCHESTRA
Arthur Schutt (p,ldr) Leo McConville, *unknown* (tp) Tom Dorsey (tb) **Jimmy Dorsey** (cl,as) Arnold Brilhart (as) Babe Russin (ts) Eddie Lang (g) *Joe Tarto [or] Hank Stern* (bb,sb) Stan King (d) Smith Ballew (vcl)

W 403796-A   **Montana Call** [Clifford Grey; Herbert Stothart] vSB
        78: OKeh 41391, Odeon ONY-36055, Parlophone PNY-34047, (E) R-713
W 490043-A   **Montana Call**
        78: Odeon ONY-36053, Parlophone PNY-34045
            both Parlophone PNYs as CYRIL MERRIVALE'S ORCH.

Columbia, New York N.Y. Monday, March 10, 1930
ARTHUR SCHUTT AND HIS ORCHESTRA
Personnel as last except *Hymie Wolfson* (ts) *Joe Venuti* (vn) Scrappy Lambert (vcl)

W 403840-B   **The Moon Is Low** [Arthur Freed; Nacio Herb Brown] vSL
        78: OKeh 41391, Odeon ONY-36055, Parlophone PNY-34048, (E) R-713, (Au) A-3025
W 490047-A   **The Moon Is Low**
        78: Odeon ONY-36053, Parlophone PNY-34046
W 403841-B   **It Must Be You** [Roy Turk; Fred B. Ahlert] vSL
        78: OKeh 41392, Odeon ONY-36062, Parlophone PNY-34056,

(E) R-645, (Au) A-3030
W 490048-A   **It Must Be You**
        78: Odeon ONY-36060, Parlophone PNY-34053
W 403842-A   **'Leven Thirty Saturday Night** [Jess Kirkpatrick,
                Earl Burnett; Bill Grantham] vSL (cl solo)
        78: OKeh 41400, Odeon ONY-36056, Parlophone PNY-34049,
        (E) R-672, (Au) A-3022, Odeon A-189343
                All Parlophone PNYs this session as CYRIL MERRIVALE'S
                ORCHESTRA
        LP: Harrison LP-U

Columbia, New York, N.Y. Monday, March 10, 1930
COLUMBIA STUDIO ORCHESTRA
Ben Selvin [or] Ed Kirkeby (ldr) Leo McConville, *Fuzzy Farrar [or]*
Tommy Gott (tp) Tom Dorsey (tb) **Jimmy Dorsey** (cl,as) *Lou Martin*
(as) *Hymie Wolfson* (ts) 2 *unknown* (vn) Rube Bloom (p) *Tommy Felline*
(bj,g) Hank Stern (bb) Stan King (d) Smith Ballew (vcl)

W 403843-B   **I Feel You Near Me** (waltz) [Joseph McCarthy;
                James F. Hanley] vSB
        78: OKeh 41399, Odeon ONY 36057, Parlophone PNY 34051,
        (E) R-631
W 403844-A   **A Pair Of Blue Eyes** (as solo) [William Kernell] vSB
        78: OKeh 41399, Odeon ONY-36057, Parlophone PNY-34049,
        (E) R-630
W 403845-B,D   **The "Free And Easy"** [Roy Turk; Fred E. Ahlert]
                vSB (cl solo)
        78: OKeh 41392, Odeon ONY-36061, Parlophone PNY-34055,
        (E) R-645, Ariel (E) 4638
        LP: Saville (E) SVL165, World Records (E) SH428
W 490051-A   **The "Free And Easy"** (cl solo)
        78: Odeon ONY-36060, Parlophone PNY-34054
                For this session: All Parlophone PNYs as EARL MARLOW
                AND HIS ORCHESTRA, Ariel as ARIEL DANCE ORCH-
                ESTRA, all others as ED LOYD AND HIS ORCHESTRA

Columbia, New York, N.Y. Tuesday, March 11, 1930
ANNETTE HANSHAW
Charlie Spivak (tp) Tom Dorsey (tb) **Jimmy Dorsey** (bar) *unknown* (vn)
Rube Bloom (p) Tommy Felline (g) Annette Hanshaw (vcl)

W 403847-C   **The One I Love Just Can't Be Bothered With Me**
                [Gus Kahn; Seymour Simons] vAH
        78: OKeh 41397, Parlophone PNY-34060, (E) R-697
W 403848-B   **With You** [Irving Berlin] vAH
        78: OKeh 41397, Parlophone PNY-34060, (E) R-697
                Parlophone PNYs as JANET SHAW

Columbia, New York, N.Y. Thursday, March 13, 1930
BEN SELVIN AND HIS ORCHESTRA (Columbia Studio Band)
Ben Selvin (ldr) Leo McConville, Mannie Klein (tp) Tom Dorsey (tb)
Jimmy Dorsey (cl,as) Lou Martin (as) Hymie Wolfson (ts) *unknown*

BEN SELVIN AND HIS ORCHESTRA (Contd.)
(vn) Rube Bloom (p) Eddie Walters (bj,g,vcl) Hank Stern (bb) Stan King
(d) *unknown* (xyl) Smith Ballew (vcl)

W 150054-5   **Across The Breakfast Table (Looking At You)**
           [Irving Berlin] vSB
           78: Columbia 2150-D, (E) CB-105, (Au) DO-83
W 150055-6   **Let Me Sing And I'm Happy** [Irving Berlin] vSB
           (cl solos)
           78: Columbia 2150-D, (E) CB-105, (Au) DO-83
           Matrices 150054, 150055 are remakes of rejected March 3,
           1930, takes.
W 150078-3   **The "Free And Easy"** [Roy Turk; Fred E. Ahlert]
           vEW (as solo)
           78: Columbia 2149-D, (E) CB-93, (Au) A8738, DO-80, (F) DF-
322
           2149-D as COLUMBIA PHOTO PLAYERS
           First three sides on **LP:** The Old Masters 17
           This side also on **CD:** The Old Masters MB117
W 150085-2   **Reminiscing** [Edgar Leslie; Harry Warren] vSB
           (cl solos)
           78: Columbia 2159-D, (Au) DO-227
W 150086-1   **I Love You So (Waltz from *Merry Widow*)** [Adrian
           Ross; Franz Lehár] vSB
           78: Columbia 2159-D, (Au) DO-100
W 150087-3   **It Must Be You** [Roy Turk; Fred B. Ahlert] vSB
           (cl solo)
           78: Columbia 2149-D, (E) CB-93, (Au) A8738
           2149-D as COLUMBIA PHOTO PLAYERS

ARC, New York, N.Y. Friday, March 21, 1930
CHICK BULLOCK
Unknown (tp) *Tom Dorsey [or] Charlie Butterfield* (tb) **Jimmy Dorsey**
(cl) *Matty Malneck, unknown* (vn) *unknown* (p), (g), (sb), (d) Chick
Bullock (vcl)

9410-5   **Lazy Lou'siana Moon** [Walter Donaldson] vCB
           78: Banner 0671, Cameo 0271, Domino 4542, Oriole 1927,
           Imperial 2281, Angelus (Au) 3245, Vocalion (Au) 697, Clifford
           (Au) 5245, Embassy 9245
9475-2   **Eyes Of Blue** vCB
           78: Romeo 1508, Crown 81382, Vocalion (Au) 786
9476-3   **The One I Love Just Can't Be Bothered With Me**
           [Gus Kahn; Seymour Simons] vCB (cl solo)
           78: Perfect 12604, Embassy 8105, Vocalion (Au) 566

Columbia, New York, N.Y. Friday, March 21, 1930
DR. EUGENE ORMANDY'S SALON ORCHESTRA
Eugene Ormandy (ldr) Leo McConville, Mannie Klein (tp) Tom Dorsey
(tb) **Jimmy Dorsey** (cl,as) Arnold Brilhart (as) Jim Crossan (ts) Murray
Kellner, Nat Brusiloff, Sam Freed (vn) Emil Stark (cel) Arthur Schutt
(p) Eddie Lang (g) Hank Stern (bb) *[and/or]* Joe Tarto (sb) *Stan King*

[or] Chauncey Morehouse (d) Scrappy Lambert (vcl)

W 403868-B   **I Never Dreamt (You'd Fall In Love With Me)**
        [Vivian Ellis; Donovan Parsons] vSL
    78: OKeh 41401, Odeon ONY-36063, Parlophone PNY-34057,
    (E) E-6331
        English Parlophone as WILL PERRY'S ORCHESTRA
W 403869-B   **The Verdict Is Life (With You)** vSL
    78: OKeh 41408, Odeon ONY-36063, Parlophone PNY-34058,
    (E) E-6331
        English Parlophone as WILL PERRY'S ORCHESTRA
W 403870-B   **Only A Rose** [Brian Hooker; Rudolf Friml] vSL
    78: OKeh 41401, Odeon ONY-36064, Parlophone PNY-34057,
    (E) R-675

Columbia, New York, N.Y. Monday, March 24, 1930
IRVING KAUFMAN
Ben Selvin (vn,ldr) Leo McConville (tp) Tom Dorsey (tb) **Jimmy Dorsey** (cl,as) Adrian Rollini (bsx) Frank Signorelli (p) Eddie Lang (g) Stan King (d) Irving Kaufman (vcl)

W 403875-A   **Let Me Sing And I'm Happy** [Irving Berlin] vIK
    78: OKeh 41412, Parlophone (E) E-6314, (G) A-3066, Ariel (E)
    4586
        Ariel as BRIAN WATT
W 403876-B   **To My Mammy** [Irving Berlin] vIK
    78: OKeh 41412, Parlophone (E) A-3066

Columbia, New York, N.Y. Thursday, March 27, 1930
LEE MORSE AND HER BLUE GRASS BOYS
Tom Dorsey (cnt) Charlie Butterfield (tb) **Jimmy Dorsey** (cl) Adrian Rollini (bsx) Frank Signorelli (p) Carl Kress (g) Lee Morse (kazoo,vcl)

W 150138-2   **Cooking Breakfast For The One I Love** [Billy Rose;
                Henry Tobias] vLM
    78: Columbia 2165-D, (E) DB-147
    LP: Take Two TT201
W 150139-2   **Sing, You Sinners** [Sam Coslow, W. Franke Harling]
                vLM
    78: Columbia 2165-D, (E) DB-161
    LP: Take Two TT201

Columbia, New York, N.Y. Monday, April 7, 1930
BEN SELVIN AND HIS ORCHESTRA
Ben Selvin (ldr) Leo McConville, Mannie Klein (tp) Tom Dorsey (tb) **Jimmy Dorsey** (cl,as) Louis Martin (as) Hymie Wolfson (ts,fl) 2 *unknown* (vn) Rube Bloom (p) Tommy Felline (bj,g) Hank Stern (bb) *unknown* (xyl) Stan King (d) Lew Conrad (vcl)

W 150174-3   **My Future Just Passed** [George Marion, Jr.; Richard
                A. Whiting] vLC
    78: Columbia 2187-D, (E) CB-123 (Contd.)

BEN SELVIN AND HIS ORCHESTRA (Contd.)

100383-1   **My Future Just Passed**
     78: Harmony 1145-H, Diva 3145-G, Velvet Tone 2145-V,
     Lobby Record 2024-P
          Lobby Record as THE PARAMOUNTEERS or PUBLIX TEN,
          all others as LLOYD KEATING AND HIS MUSIC
     (195090-1) **78:** Columbia (SA) 4093-X
W 150175-3   **Leave It That Way** vLC
     78: Columbia 2177-D, (Au) DO-127
100397-1   **Leave It That Way**
     78: Harmony 1175-H, Diva 3175-G, Velvet Tone 2175-V
          as RUDY MARLOW AND HIS ORCHESTRA
     (195091-1) **78:** Columbia (SA) 4094-X

Columbia, New York, N.Y. Monday, April 14, 1930
TED LEWIS AND HIS BAND
Ted Lewis (ldr,cl,as,vcl) Muggsy Spanier, Dave Klein (cnt) George Bru-
nies, Harry Raderman (tb) **Jimmy Dorsey** (cl,as,bar) Sol Klein (vn)
Jack Aaronson (p) Tony Gerhardi (bj,g) Harry Barth (bb) John Lucas (d)

W 150460-3   **The World Is Waiting For The Sunrise** [Eugene
                    Lockhart; Ernest Seitz] vTL (bar,cl solos)
     78: Columbia 2246-D, 36302 (dub), (E) CB-136, (F) DF-369,
     (Au) DO-212, (J) J-1001
     LP: Gaps (H) 150

Columbia, New York, N.Y. Wednesday, April 16, 1930
TED LEWIS AND HIS BAND

W 150467-1,2,3,4   **Three O'Clock In The Morning** vTL (unissued)

Columbia, New York, N.Y. Thursday, April 17, 1930
TED LEWIS AND HIS BAND

W 150478-2   **Somebody Stole My Gal** [Leo Wood] vTL (cl solo)
     78: Columbia 2336-D, 36301, (E) CB-215, (F) DF-460, (J) J-
     1073
     LP: Gaps (H) 060
     CD: Retrieval (E) 79014
W 150479-4   **Someday, Sweetheart** [John Spikes, Benjamin
                    Spikes] vTL (cl solo)
     78: Columbia 2336-D, (E) CB-215, (F) DF-460, (J) J-1073
     LP: Gaps (H) 060
     CD: Take Two 423

Columbia, New York, N.Y. Friday, April 18, 1930
TED LEWIS AND HIS BAND

W 150482-4   **Yellow Dog Blues** [William C. Handy] (cl,as solos)
     78: Columbia 2217-D, (E) CB-189, (Au) DO-273, *(These next
     are all dubbings of 2217-D):* Banner 33413, Melotone M-13380,

Oriole 3133, Perfect 16110, Romeo 2507, Columbia 38842
LP: Biograph BLP-C7, Gaps (H) 020, Epic LN-3170
CD: Retrieval (E) 79014

Columbia, New York, N.Y. Monday, April 21, 1930
COLUMBIA PHOTO PLAYERS
Ben Selvin (ldr) Leo McConville, Mannie Klein (tp) Tom Dorsey (tb)
Jimmy Dorsey (cl,as) Louis Martin (as) Hymie Wolfson (ts,o) 2 *unknown* (vn) Rube Bloom (p) Tony Colucci (bj,g) Smith Ballew (mandolin,vcl) Hank Stern (bb) Stan King (d) *unknown* (xyl) Rondoliers (vcl)

W 150483-1,3 **Dark Night** [Clifford Grey; Herbert Stouthart, Xavier Cugat] vR (as,cl solos)
 78: Columbia 2196-D, Regal (Au) G-20770
  Regal as THE RHYTHMIC TROUBADORS
100394-1 **Dark Night** (as,cl solos)
 78: Harmony 1162-H, Diva 3162-G, Velvet Tone 2162-V
  as RUDY MARLOW AND HIS ORCHESTRA
 (195097-1) **78:** Columbia (SA) 4171-X
W 150484-4 **Dust** [Andy Rice; Fred Fisher] vR
 78: Columbia 2196-D, (E) CB-103
 LP: The Old Masters 17, Saville (E) SVL 165
W 495035-1 **Dust**
 78: Parlophone (E) R-800
 LP: Columbia P5 14320
  as ROOF GARDEN ORCHESTRA
 (100391-1) **78:** (Harmony unissued)
 (195098-1) **78:** (Columbia export unissued)
W 150485-3 **Kiss Me With Your Eyes** [Eldred, Gillespie] vSB
 78: Columbia 2197-D
100392-1 **Kiss Me With Your Eyes** (Harmony unissued)
 (195099-1) **78:** (Columbia export unissued)
W 150486-3 **You Darlin'** [Harry M. Woods] vSB
 78: Columbia 2197-D
195100-1 **You Darlin'**
 78: Columbia (SA) 4095-X
 (100390-1) (Harmony unissued)

Columbia, New York, N.Y. Thursday, April 24, 1930
TED LEWIS AND HIS BAND
Ted Lewis (ldr,cl,as) Muggsy Spanier, Dave Klein (cnt) George Brunies, Harry Raderman (tb) **Jimmy Dorsey** (cl,as,bar) Sol Klein (vn) Jack Aaronson (p) Tony Gerhardi (bj,g) Harry Barth (bb) John Lucas (d,vib,chimes)

W 150467-7 **Three O'Clock In The Morning** (waltz) [Dorothy Terris; Julian Robledo] vTL
 78: Columbia 2246-D, (E) CB-136, (Au) DO-212
W 150467-8 **Three O'Clock In The Morning** (waltz) vTL
 78: Columbia 2246-D
W 150490-1 **Sobbin' Blues** [Art Kassel] (bar,cl solos)
 78: (unissued test pressing) (Contd.)

TED LEWIS AND HIS BAND (Contd.)

   LP: IAJRC 2
   CD: Retrieval (E) 79014
W 150490-4   **Sobbin' Blues** (bar,cl solos)
   78: Columbia 2217-D, 38842 (dubbing), (E) CB-189, (Au) DO-
   273, Okeh 41585 (dubbing)
   LP: Epic LN-3170, Biograph BLP-C7, Gaps (H) 060
   CD: Take Two 423, Retrieval (E) 79014

Over the weekend of May 2-3, 1930, both Dorseys, Bud Freeman, Bix Beiderbecke and others played three spots at Princeton University: The Colonial Club, The Ivy Club and Tiger Inn. Right after, Jimmy and Jane left for Europe with Ted Lewis, where Jimmy cut several sides.

Jimmy later said that he joined Lewis knowing of the European trip and looked upon it as a honeymoon with "Beebe" and a chance to meet those who recognized his talents much more than Americans did (Riordan 1998).

Decca, London, Eng., Friday, May 23, 1930
SPIKE HUGHES AND HIS DANCE ORCHESTRA
Muggsy Spanier (cnt) Norman Payne (tp) **Jimmy Dorsey,** Max Farley (cl,as) Philip Buchel (as) Stan Andrews (vn) Eddie Carroll (p) Leslie Smith (g) Spike Hughes (sb) Bill Harty (d)

MB-1392-1,2   **Ka-lu-a** (unissued)
MB-1393-1,2   **Avalon** (unissued)
MB-1394-1   **Dinah** (unissued)
MB-1395-2   **I Like To Do Things For You** [Jack Yellen; Milton
               Ager] (as solo)
   78: (test pressing exists)
   LP: Retrieval (E) FG-411 (Vol. 3)
   CD: Kings Cross Music (E) KCM001/002

Columbia Studio, London, Eng. Monday, July 7, 1930
VAN PHILLIPS AND HIS CONCERT BAND
Van Phillips (cl,*as*,dir) Bunny Berigan, Mickey Bloom, Norman Payne (tp) Gus Mayhew, Ted Heath (tb) **Jimmy Dorsey** (cl,as) *unknown* (cl,ts,o) 2 or 3 *unknown* (vn), *Arthur Young* (p) Len Fillis (g) *unknown* (sb) *Rudy Starita* (d,xyl) Jack Plant, Robert Carr (vcl)

W AX-5646-1   **Selections from** *Song Of The Flame* [Otto Harbach,
               Oscar Hammerstein II; George Gershwin, Herbert
               Stothart]: **Song Of The Flame; Cossack Love Song**
               vJP; **When Love Calls; One Little Drink** vRC
   LP: Columbia (E) DX-83, Shoestring SS-110
W AX-5647-2   **Selections from** *The Cuckoos* [Bert Kalmar; Harry
               Ruby]: **Wherever You Are; Alma Mater; I Love
               You So Much** vJP; **Dancing The Devil Away; All
               Alone Monday** (as solo)
   LP: Columbia (E) DX-83, Shoestring SS-110

Decca, London, Eng. Tuesday, July 15, 1930
JIMMY DORSEY (with Spike Hughes & His Three Blind Mice)
Jimmy Dorsey (cl,as) Claude Ivy (p) Alan Ferguson (g) Spike Hughes
(sb) Bill Harty (d)

MB-1618-1   **I'm Just Wild About Harry** [Noble Sissle; Eubie
                    Blake] (as,cl,as solos)
      78: Decca (E) F1876, F-9003 (dub), 703, London 344
      LP: AoC ACL1176, Retrieval(E) FG409 (vol. 2), Everest FS221
MB-1619-2   **After You've Gone** [Henry Creamer; Turner Layton]
                    (cl,as solos)
      78: Decca (E) F1876, F-9003 (dub), 703, London 344
      LP: AoC (E) ACL1176, Retrieval (E) FG-409 (vol. 2)
MB-1620-1   **Tiger Rag** [Harry De Costa; Edwin Edwards, Nick La
                    Rocca, Tony Spargo, Larry Shields] (cl,as solos)
      78: Decca (E) F1878
      LP: AoC ACL1176, Retrieval(E) FG409 (vol. 2), Everest FS221
MB-1620-2   **Tiger Rag** (cl,as solos)
      78: Decca (E) F6142, 8722, (Au) X-1300, Odeon (Arg) 284378
      LP: AoC (E) ACL1176, Retrieval (E) FG-409 (vol. 2)
MB 1621-1   **St. Louis Blues** [William C. Handy] (cl solos)
      78: Decca (E) F6142, F1878, 8722, (Au) X-1300, Odeon (Arg)
      284378
      LP: AoC ACL1176, Retrieval(E) FG409 (vol. 2), Everest FS221
      All sides also on **CD:** Kings Cross Music (E) KCM001/002
      Jimmy only plays clarinet on "St. Louis Blues"

Jimmy's solo on "Tiger Rag" became the most famous and widely
imitated jazz solo of the era. For example, pianist Art Tatum copied it
on his 1933 recording of "Tiger Rag."
    When Jimmy returned to New York from Europe on the liner *Ile de
France,* Tommy went to meet him. According to Tommy a decade
later, despite having not seen each other for months they were fighting
again within five minutes (Gleason 1971).

Columbia, New York, N.Y. Friday, August 8, 1930
SAM LANIN AND HIS FAMOUS PLAYERS
Sam Lanin (ldr) Mannie Klein, Leo McConville (tp) Tom Dorsey (tb)
Jimmy Dorsey (cl,as) Andy Sanella (as,stg) *unknown* (ts) Arthur Schutt
(p) *unknown* (g), (sb), (d) Scrappy Lambert [as Jim Andrews, Robert
Woods or Wally Edwards] (vcl)

W 404282-B   **Good Evenin'** [Tot Seymour, Charles O'Flynn; Al
                    Hoffman] vSL[JA] (as solo)
      78: Odeon ONY36129, Parlophone PNY34122, (E)R798, (E)E5215
      Parlophone PNY- and E-5215 as ALBERT MASON'S ORCH.
      (100415-1)**78:** Harmony 1202-H, Diva 3202-G, Velvet Tone 2202-V
      *Harmony and Diva as FRANK AUBURN AND HIS ORCH.,
      Velvet Tone as RUDY MARLOW AND HIS ORCH.*
W 404283-A   **Tomorrow Is Another Day** [Johnny Green, Sam H.
                    Stept] vSL[RW]
      78: Odeon ONY-36130, (G) A-221305, Parlophone PNY- (Contd.)

SAM LANIN AND HIS ORCHESTRA (Contd.)

34123 (E) R-784, (E) E-5216, (Au) A3129
Parlophone PNY- and E-5216 as ALBERT MASON'S ORCH.
(100416-1) **78:** Harmony 1202-H, Diva 3202-G, Velvet Tone 2202-V
Harmony and Diva as FRANK AUBURN AND HIS ORCH.,
Velvet Tone as RUDY MARLOW AND HIS ORCH.

W 404284-B   **Why Am I So Romantic?** [Bert Kalmar; Harry Ruby]
vSL[WE] (as,cl solos)
78: Odeon ONY-36129, Parlophone PNY-34123, (E) R-798, (E) E-5216
Parlophone PNY- and E-5216 as ALBERT MASON'S ORCH.
(100417-1) **78:** Harmony 1200-H, Diva 3200-G, Velvet Tone 2200-V, Publix 2027-P
Harmony, Diva and Velvet Tone as WALLY EDWARDS AND HIS ORCH., Publix as THE PARAMOUNTEERS

ARC, New York, N.Y. Wednesday, August 13, 1930
SAM LANIN AND HIS ORCHESTRA
Sam Lanin (ldr) Mannie Klein, Leo McConville (tp) Tom Dorsey (tb) Jimmy Dorsey (cl,as) *unknown* (as), (ts), (vn) Arthur Schutt (p) Charles Magnante (acc) *unknown* (bj), (bb), (d,xyl) Scrappy Lambert (vcl)

9937-2   **My One Ambition Is You** vSL
78: Domino 4613
9937-3   **My One Ambition Is You** vSL
78: Perfect 15340, Imperial 2365, Banner 0807, Angelus (Au) 3272, Clifford (Au) 5272
Banner as BROADWAY BROADCASTERS, Angelus and Clifford as SAM LANNIN [sic] AND HIS ORCH.
9938-3   **It's Easy To Fall In Love** [Coleman Goetz; Pete Wendling] vSL
78: Perfect 15344, Romeo 1415
as SAM LANIN AND HIS TROUBADORS
9939-1   **Maybe It's Love** vSL
78: Regal 10111
as SAM LANIN AND HIS TROUBADORS
9939-3   **Maybe It's Love** vSL
78: Perfect 15345, Oriole 2057, Conqueror 7612, Imperial 2444, Jewel 6057
Perfect as SAM LANIN AND HIS TROUBADORS, Conqueror as JOHN VINCENT'S CALIFORNIANS

Columbia, New York, N.Y. Friday, August 22, 1930
BEN SELVIN AND HIS ORCHESTRA
Ben Selvin (ldr) Mannie Klein, *unknown* (tp) Tom Dorsey (tb) **Jimmy Dorsey** (cl,as) Joe Dubin (ts) *unknown* (fl) *Rube Bloom* (p) Hank Stern (bb) *Tony Colucci* (bj,g) Stan King (d,xyl) Irving Kaufman, Charles Lawman (vcl)

W 150723-3   **I'm Yours** [E. Y. Harburg; Johnny Green] vIK

78: Columbia 2287-D, (E) CB-180
W 150724-3   **Dixiana** [Anne Caldwell; Harry Tierney] vIK
   78: Columbia 2287-D, (E) CB-180, Regal (Au) G-20980
        *Regal as THE RHYTHMIC TROUBADORS. This was remade
        August 28, 1930. What issued take is on TOM 17 is uncertain.*
   LP: *The Old Masters 17*
W 150725-2   **A Big Bouquet For You** vCL
   78: Columbia 2278-D
        as CHARLES LAWMAN with Orch. accomp.

Brunswick, New York, N.Y. circa Monday, August 25, 1930
RED NICHOLS AND HIS FIVE PENNIES*
Red Nichols (cnt) *Charlie Teagarden [or] Mannie Klein* (tp) Glenn
Miller (tb) *Jimmy Dorsey [or] Jimmy Granato* (cl,as) *Sid Stoneburn* (as)
Bud Freeman (cl,ts) Adrian Rollini (bsx) Lou Raderman (vn) Joe
Sullivan (p) *Teg Brown* (g) Gene Krupa (d) Roy Evans (vcl)

XE-34058   (medley) **Ballin' The Jack** [Jim Burris; Chris Smith];
                Walkin' The Dog [Shelton Brooks]
   78: (12-inch) *Heat* Radio Program I, Part 3
   LP: Jazz Archives JA-43, Broadway 101, Old Homestead 101
   CD: IAJRC CD1011
XE-34061   (medley) **I Lost My Gal From Memphis** (vRE), **Here
                Comes Emily Brown** [Con Conrad, Jack Meskill]
   78: (12-inch) *Heat* Radio Program H, Part 2
   LP: Merritt 18
   CD: IAJRC CD1011
        **Red Nichols researcher Stan Hester believes this is an ARC
        studio band with Nichols present, not a Nichols-led session.*

Columbia, New York, N.Y. Thursday, August 28, 1930
BEN SELVIN & HIS ORCHESTRA *(to remake August 22 matrix.)*
Personnel as August 22, 1930, except Jimmy Dorsey not certain. Irving
Kaufman (vcl)

W 150724-5   **Dixiana** [Anne Caldwell; Harry Tierney] vIK
   78: Columbia 2287-D, (E) CB-180
   LP: *The Old Masters 17*

ARC, New York, N.Y. Tuesday, September 2, 1930
SAM LANIN AND HIS ORCHESTRA
Helen Rowland [some issues as Ruth Howland] (vcl)

9973-2,3   **Live And Love Today** [King, Janis, Skinner] vHR
   78: Perfect 15349, Banner 0807, Cameo 0407, Romeo 1420
        *Perfect as SAM LANIN AND HIS TROUBADORS, Cameo as
        BROADWAY BROADCASTERS*
9974-2   **It Seems To Be Spring** [George Marion, Jr.; Richard
                A. Whiting] vHR
   78: Perfect 15347, Domino 4625, Broadway 1395, Banner 0802,
   Romeo 1418, Cameo 0402, Angelus (Au) 3260, Clifford (Au)
   5260 (Contd.)

SAM LANIN AND HIS ORCHESTRA (Contd.)
> *Domino and Perfect as SAM LANIN AND HIS TROU-*
> *BADORS, Romeo, Cameo, Banner as BROADWAY BROAD-*
> *CASTERS, Broadway, Clifford and Angelus as SAM LANNIN*
> *[sic] AND HIS ORCHESTRA*

9975-2   **I'm Only Human After All** vHR
> **78:** Perfect 15348, Domino 4626, Oriole 2056, Conqueror 7615,
> Jewel 6056
> *Perfect, Jewel as SAM LANIN AND HIS TROUBADORS,*
> *Oriole, Domino as BROADWAY BROADCASTERS, Con-*
> *queror as JOHN VINCENT'S CALIFORNIANS*

9975-3   **I'm Only Human After All** vHR
> **78:** Apex (C) 41234

Columbia, New York, N.Y. Saturday, September 6, 1930
JOE VENUTI AND HIS NEW YORKERS
Joe Venuti (vn,ldr) Charlie Margulis, Mannie Klein (tp) Tom Dorsey
(tb) **Jimmy Dorsey** (cl,as) *unknown* (as,ts) *Min Leibrook* (bsx) *unknown*
(p) Eddie Lang (g) Joe Tarto (bb) Stan King (d) Scrappy Lambert (vcl)

W 404431-C   **I'm Only Human After All** vSL (as solo)
> **78:** OKeh 41451, Odeon ONY-36138, (F) 238229, Parlophone
> PNY-34130
> **LP:** The Old Masters 7, JSP Records 1111
> **TC:** Radio Yesteryear Stack 1, Stack 22

W 404432-B   **Out Of Breath (And Scared To Death Of You)**
> [Johnny Mercer; Everett Miller] vSL (as solo)
> **78:** OKeh 41451, Odeon ONY-36138, (F) 238229, Parlophone
> PNY-34130
> **LP:** The Old Masters 7, JSP Records 1111

Victor, New York, N.Y. Monday, September 8, 1930
BIX BEIDERBECKE AND HIS ORCHESTRA
Joe Venuti (vn,ldr) Ray Lodwig (tp) Bix Beiderbecke (cnt) Boyce Cullen
(tb) Benny Goodman, Pee Wee Russell, **Jimmy Dorsey** (cl,as) Bud
Freeman (ts) Min Leibrook (bsx,sb) Irving Brodsky (p) Eddie Lang (g)
Gene Krupa (d) Wes Vaughn (vcl)

BVE 63630-1   **Deep Down South** [Monty Collins, George Green]
> vWV
> **LP:** Natchez WEP804, RCA (F) 731.131, Historical 28, Joker (It)
> 3122, 3570
> **CD:** IDR (It) BIX 9, RCA (F) 66540, Masters Of Jazz (F)
> MJCD92

BVE 63630-2   **Deep Down South** vWV
> **78:** Victor 23018, 25370, His Master's Voice (E) B-8419,
> Gramaphone (F) K-6238
> **LP:** Only For Collectors 34, RCA 6845, (F) 731.036/7, Living
> Era (E) AJA 5080, Joker (It) 3570
> **CD:** RCA 6845, Flapper (E) 9765, Living Era (E) CD-AJA 5080,
> IDR (It) BIX 9, Masters Of Jazz (F) MJCD92

BVE 63631-1   **I Don't Mind Walking In The Rain (When I'm**

Walking In The Rain With You) [Al Hoffman; Max Rich] vWV
78: Victor 23008, His Master's Voice (E) B-4889
LP: Only For Collectors 34, RCA (F) 731.036/7, Joker (It) 3570
CD: IDR (It) BIX 9, Masters Of Jazz (F) MJCD92
BVE 63631-1   **I Don't Mind Walking In The Rain** (unissued)

Venuti and Lang do not return after lunch break:
BVE 63632-1   **I'll Be A Friend "With Pleasure"** vWV (unissued)
BVE 63632-2   **I'll Be A Friend "With Pleasure"** [Maceo Pinkard] vWV (cl solo)
78: Victor 23008
LP: Victor LPM2323, RCA (E) RD27225, (F) 731.036/7, Joker (It) 3570, Jazz Collector's Items (J) RA5298
CD: IDR (It) BIX 9, Masters Of Jazz (F) MJCD92, Giants of Jazz 53192
BVE 63632-3   **I'll Be A Friend "With Pleasure"** vWV (cl solo)
78: Victor 23008, His Master's Voice (E) B-8419, B-4889
LP: RCA 6845, (F) 731.036/7, Joker (It) 3570, Only For Collectors 34
CD: RCA 6845, Flapper (E) 9765, IDR (It) BIX 9, Masters Of Jazz (F) MJCD92, Avid AMSC 568

ARC, New York, N.Y. Thursday, September 11, 1930
FRED RICH AND HIS (LA PALINA*) ORCHESTRA
Fred Rich (ldr) Bill Moore, *Mannie Klein* (tp) Tom Dorsey (tb) **Jimmy Dorsey,** Tony Parenti (cl,as) *Fred Cusick* (cl,as,ts) *unknown* (p), (g), (bb), (d) Scrappy Lambert [as Chester Hale or Eddie Gale] (vcl)

10017-2   **You Darlin'** vSL
78: Conqueror 7623, Domino 4631, Jewel 6067, Oriole 2067, Perfect 15353, Regal 10121, Romeo 1429, Banner 0815, Broadway 1407
10018-2   **Until We Meet Again, Sweetheart** vSL
78: Conqueror 7622, Domino 4630, Jewel 6065, Oriole 2065, Perfect 15352, Romeo 1428, Royal 391056, Crown 91056
10019-2   **Sing Something Simple** [Herman Hupfield]vSL[CH] (cl solo)
78: Banner 0835, Cameo 0435, Oriole 2087, Perfect 15356, Regal 10140, Challenge 898, Conqueror 7626, Domino 4634, Jewel 6087, Romeo 1448, Crown (C) 81453
10019-3   **Sing Something Simple** vSL[EG] (cl solo)
Imperial (E) 2390
         *Some, but not all, issues from this session as FRED RICH AND HIS LA PALINA ORCHESTRA.

Victor, New York, N.Y. Monday, September 15, 1930
HOAGY CARMICHAEL AND HIS ORCHESTRA
Hoagy Carmichael (vcl,dir) Bix Beiderbecke (cnt) Ray Lodwig (tp) Jack Teagarden, Boyce Cullen (tb) **Jimmy Dorsey** (cl,as) Arnold Brilhart (as) Bud Freeman (ts) Min Leibrook (bsx) Joe Venuti (vn) Irving Brodsky (p) Eddie Lang (g) Gene Krupa (d) *unknown* (vib) (on second tune only)

HOAGY CARMICHAEL AND HIS ORCHESTRA (Contd.)

BVE 63653-1   **Georgia On My Mind** [Stewart Gorrell; Hoagy
               Carmichael] vHC
    78: Victor 23013, 25494, His Master's Voice (E) B-4885, B-
    6133, B-8549, K-6525, Hot Jazz Club Of America (dub) HC-100
    LP: Divergent 302, RCA LSA 3180, CPL1-3307, (E) INTS5181,
    (EC) NL 89096, Joker (It) 3570
    TC: Radio Yesteryear Stack #81, #82
    CD: IRD (It) BIX 9, Masters Of Jazz (F) MJCD92, Giants of Jazz
    53192
Cullen (tb) out:
BVE 63654-1   **One Night In Havana** [Hoagy Carmichael] vHC
    78: Victor 23013, His Master's Voice (E) B-4885, Hot Jazz Club
    Of America (dub) HC-100
    LP: Joker (It) 3570
    TC: Radio Yesteryear Stack #82
    CD: IRD (It) BIX 9, Masters Of Jazz (F) MJCD92, Giants of Jazz
    53192
BVE 63655-1   **Bessie Couldn't Help It** [Byron H. Warner, J. S.
               Richmond, Charles A. Bayha] vHC (cl solo)
    78: Victor 22864
    LP: Divergent 302, His Master's Voice (E) DLP1106, Joker (It)
    3570
    TC: Radio Yesteryear Stack #82
    CD: IRD (It) BIX 9, Masters Of Jazz (F) MJCD92
Leibrook (bsx) leaves, Venuti switches to (sb):
BVE 63655-2   **Bessie Couldn't Help It** vHC (cl solo)
    78: Victor 25371, Jazz Classics (dubbing) 532
               *All Hot Jazz Club of America and Jazz Classics as BIX BEI-
               DERBECKE WITH HOAGY CARMICHAEL AND HIS ORCHESTRA*
    LP: RCA LSA3180, (E) INTS5181 (EC) NL 89096, Joker (It)
    3570
    CD: IRD (It) BIX 9, Masters Of Jazz (F) MJCD92

Columbia, New York, N.Y. Tuesday, September 16, 1930
SEGER ELLIS
Phil Napoleon (tp) Tom Dorsey (tb) **Jimmy Dorsey** (cl,as) Seger Ellis
(p,vcl) Eddie Lang (g)

W 404443(A,B,C) **Sleepy Time Gal** vSE (unissued)
W 404452-A   **What's The Use?** [Charles Newman; Isham Jones]
               vSE
    78: OKeh 41452, Parlophone (E) R-837
W 404453-A   **If I Could Be With You One Hour Tonight** [Henry
               Creamer; James P. Johnson] vSE
    78: OKeh 41452, Parlophone (E) R-837

ARC, New York, N.Y. Monday, September 22, 1930
SAM LANIN AND HIS ORCHESTRA
Sam Lanin (ldr) Mannie Klein (tp) Tom Dorsey (tb) **Jimmy Dorsey**
(cl,as) Arthur Schutt (p) Helen Rowland (vcl) (identified personnel)

10070-2   **Oh How I Cried The Morning After (The Night Before With You)** vHR
    78: Banner 0833, Perfect 15358, Regal 10141, Cameo 0433, Romeo 1449, Domino 4646
10071-4   **What A Fool I've Been (To Believe In You)** vHR
    78: Banner 0838, Perfect 15360, Cameo 0438, Romeo 1451, Domino 4648
10072-3   **I Am Only The Words—You Are The Melody** [Buddy De Sylva, Lew Brown; Ray Henderson] vHR
    78: Banner 0838, Perfect 15362, Cameo 0438, Romeo 1469, Jewel 6106, Oriole 2106, Conqueror 7636
    Conqueror, Perfect as BROADWAY BROADCASTERS

On Sunday, September 28, Bunny Berigan, Tommy and Jimmy Dorsey, Bud Freeman, Joe Sullivan, Dick McDonough, Gene Krupa and others auditioned for a long-term booking at Janssen's Hofbrau, a famous New York German restaurant, losing out because the manager felt that the boys were weak on solos (White and Kite, 1951-1987).

Columbia, New York, N.Y. Tuesday, September 30, 1930
CHARLESTON CHASERS
Phil Napoleon (tp) Tom Dorsey (tb) **Jimmy Dorsey** (cl,as) Frank Signorelli (p) Ward Lay (sb), Stan King (d) Eva Taylor (vcl)

W 150846-2   **Loving You The Way I Do** [Blake, Scholl, Morrisey] vET (cl solo)
    78: Columbia 2309-D, (E) CB-205
    ET: (12-inch) Columbia Tele-Focal 91963 (Prog. 8)
    LP: The Old Masters 6, Vintage Jazz Music Society (E) VLP44
W 150847-2,3   **You're Lucky To Me** [Andy Razaf; Eubie Blake] vET (as solo)
    78: Columbia 2309-D, Regal (E) MR271
    Regal as THE RHYTHMIC TROUBADORS
    LP: The Old Masters 6, Vintage Jazz Music Society (E) VLP44

Victor, New York, N.Y. Tuesday, September 30, 1930
JOE VENUTI AND HIS ORCHESTRA
Joe Venuti (vn,ldr) Mannie Klein, *Charlie Margulis* (tp) Glenn Miller (tb) **Jimmy Dorsey,** *Pete Pumiglio* (cl,as) Fud Livingston (cl,ts) Rube Bloom (p) Eddie Lang (g) Joe Tarto (sb) *unknown* (d) Irene Beasley, Frank Luther (vcl)

63682-2   **Wasting My Love On You** [Edgar Leslie; Harry Warren] vFL
    78: Victor 23018, His Master's Voice (F) K-6238
    LP: RCA (F) FXM1-7016, JSP Records 1112
63683-2   **My Man From Caroline** vIB
    78: Victor 23015, His Master's Voice (E) B-4890
    LP: RCA (F) FXM1-7016, JSP Records 1112
63684-2   **I Like A Little Girl Like That** vFL
    78: Victor 23015
    LP: RCA (F) FXM1-7016, JSP Records 1112

Columbia, New York, N.Y. Friday, October 10, 1930
SAM LANIN AND HIS ORCHESTRA
Sam Lanin (ldr) Mannie Klein, *Leo McConville,* Bob Effros (tp) Tom
Dorsey (tb) **Jimmy Dorsey** (cl,as) *unknown* (as), (ts), (vn) Arthur Schutt
(p) *Eddie Lang* (bj,g) Hank Stern (bb) Vic Berton (d) Paul Small, Smith
Ballew (vcl)

W 150871-2   **Three Little Words** [Bert Kalmar; Harry Ruby] vPS
     78: Columbia 2317-D, (E) CB203, (Au) DO-265
          as IPANA TROUBADORS
100429-1   **Three Little Words**
     78: Harmony 1232-H, Clarion 5105-C, Diva 3232-G, Velvet
     Tone 2232-V
          as RUDY MARLOW AND HIS ORCHESTRA
     (W 195124-1) **78:** Columbia (GE) DC-2028
W 150872-3   **Can This Be Love?** [Paul James; Kay Swift] vPS
          (cl solo)
     78: Columbia 2317-D
          as IPANA TROUBADORS
W 404467-B   **It's A Great Life (If You Don't Weaken)** [Leo Robin;
          Richard A. Whiting, Newell Chase] vSB (cl solo)
     78: Odeon ONY-36148, (G) A221336, Parlophone PNY-34142,
     (E) R-867
          Parlophone PNY- as THE DEAUVILLE SYNCOPATORS,
          R-867 as SAM LANIN'S PHOTO PLAYERS, Odeon as NEW
          YORK SYNCOPATORS
     (100430-1) **78:** Harmony 1234-H, Diva 3234-G, Velvet Tone
     2234-V, Regal (Au) G-20896
          as FRANK AUBURN AND HIS ORCHESTRA
     LP: The Old Masters 28
W 404468-B   **When Kentucky Bids The World Good Morning**
          [Edgar Leslie; Mabel Wayne] vSB
     78: Odeon ONY-36149, Parlophone PNY-34140, (E) R-823
          Parlophone PNY- as DEAUVILLE SYNCOPATORS, R-823 as
          ED LOYD'S ORCHESTRA, Odeon as NEW YORK SYNCO-
          PATORS
     (100453-1) **78:** Harmony 1260-H, Velvet Tone 2260-V, Regal
     (Au) G-20998
          as FORD BRITTEN AND HIS BLUE COMETS
W 404469-B   **I'm Proud Of You** vSB
     78: Odeon ONY-36152, Parlophone PNY-34145, (E) R-832,
     Ariel (E) 4671
          Parlophone PNY- as DEAUVILLE SYNCOPATORS, R-832 as
          SAM LANIN & HIS FAMOUS PLAYERS, Odeon as NEW
          YORK SYNCOPATORS, Ariel as ARIEL DANCE ORCH.
W 404470-B   **Satan's Holiday** [Irving Kahal; Sammy Fain] vSB
     78: Odeon ONY-36152, Parlophone PNY-34144
          Parlophone as DEAUVILLE SYNCOPATORS, Odeon as
          NEW YORK SYNCOPATORS
     (100441-1) **78:** Harmony 1248-H, Velvet Tone 2248-V, Diva
     3248-G
          as CHESTER LEIGHTON & HIS SOPHOMORES

George Gershwin's *Girl Crazy* opened October 14, 1930, at New York's Alvin Theater with Ethel Merman, Allen Kearns and Ginger Rogers plus Red Nichols' pit band, which included Ruby Weinstein, Charlie Teagarden (tp) Glenn Miller, Jack Teagarden (tb) Benny Goodman (cl) Jimmy Dorsey (as) Roger Edens (p) and Gene Krupa (d).

On opening night Gershwin led the band and, according to Rogers, would often play piano during the show's 272-performance run (Rogers 1991). Sixty years later the show and its story line were the nucleus for the Gershwin retrospective *Crazy For You*.

Brunswick, New York, N.Y. Wednesday, October 15, 1930
GRACE JOHNSTON
Mike Mosiello (tp) Tom Dorsey (tb) **Jimmy Dorsey** (cl) Hymie Wolfson (ts) *unknown* (vn) Rube Bloom (p) Carl Kress (g) *unknown* (bb) Grace Johnston (vcl)

E 34918-   **Loving You The Way I Do** [Blake, Scholl, Morrissey] vGJ
    78: Melotone M-12010
E 34920-   **Sweet Jennie Lee!** [Walter Donaldson] vGJ
    78: Melotone M-12010, Panachord (E) 25002

ARC, New York, N.Y. Thursday, October 16, 1930
CHICK BULLOCK
Bob Effros (tp) Tom Dorsey (tb) **Jimmy Dorsey** (cl) Andy Sanella (cl,stg) 2 *unknown* (vn) *unknown* (p), (g), (bj), (sb), (d) Chick Bullock (vcl)

10146-2,3   **Here Comes The Sun** [Arthur Freed; Harry Woods] vCB (cl solo)
    78: Banner 0865, Cameo 0465, Oriole 2114, Perfect 12651, Vocalion 719
10147-3   **Sweet Jennie Lee!** [Walter Donaldson] vCB
    78: Oriole 2148, Regal 10205, Romeo 1511, Vocalion 752
10148-3   **My Baby Just Cares For Me** [Gus Kahn; Walter Donaldson] vCB
    78: Regal 10206, Imperial 2380, Angelus (E) 3263, Clifford (Au) 5263, Crown 81491, Embassy 9263, Vocalion (Au) 719

Columbia, New York, N.Y. Friday, October 24, 1930
SAM LANIN AND HIS ORCHESTRA
Sam Lanin (ldr) Mannie Klein, Leo McConville [or] Bob Effros (tp) Tom Dorsey (tb) **Jimmy Dorsey** (cl,as) *unknown* (as), (ts), (vn) Arthur Schutt (p) *Eddie Lang [or] Tony Colucci* (bj,g) Hank Stern (bb) Vic Berton (d) Scrappy Lambert (vcl)

W 404508-B   **Oh Why?** vSL
    78: Odeon ONY-36155, Parlophone PNY-34147, (E) R-844, (Au) A3117
            Parlophone PNY- as ALBERT MASON'S ORCHESTRA
                    (Contd.)

SAM LANIN AND HIS ORCHESTRA (Contd.)

W 404509-B   **My Ideal** [Leo Robin, Newell Chase, Richard A. Whiting] vSL
     78: Odeon ONY-36154, (G) A-221336, Parlophone PNY-34146, (E) R-867, Ariel (E) Z4690
        Parlophone PNY- as ALBERT MASON'S ORCHESTRA, Ariel as ARIEL DANCE ORCHESTRA
     (100438-1) **78:** Harmony 1240-H, Velvet Tone 2240-V, 2287-V, Diva 3240-G, Clarion 5178-C
        Harmony, Diva, Velvet Tone 2240-V as FRANK AUBURN & HIS ORCHESTRA, Clarion, Velvet Tone 2287-V as LLOYD KEATING & HIS MUSIC
W 404510-B   **You're Simply Delish** [Arthur Freed; Joseph Meyer] vSL [as Tom Frawley] (cl solo)
     78: Odeon ONY-36154, Parlophone PNY-34148, (E) R-832
        Parlophone PNY- as ALBERT MASON'S ORCHESTRA
     (100463-1) **78:** Harmony 1265-H, Velvet Tone 2265-V
        Harmony, Velvet Tone as LLOYD KEATING & HIS MUSIC
W 404511-B   **If I Knew You Better** vSL
     78: Odeon ONY-36155, Parlophone PNY-34146, (E) R-891
        Parlophone PNY- as ALBERT MASON'S ORCHESTRA

Columbia, New York, N.Y. Wednesday, October 29, 1930
FRED RICH AND HIS ORCHESTRA
Fred Rich (ldr) Mannie Klein, *Bill Moore* (tp) Tom Dorsey (tb) **Jimmy Dorsey** (cl,as) unknown (ts) Joe Venuti (vn) *unknown* (p) Eddie Lang (g) *Joe Tarto* (sb) Stan King (d) Smith Ballew [as Frank James, George Walker or Chester Leighton] (vcl)

W 404533-A   **I'll Be Blue Just Thinking Of You** [George Whiting; Pete Wendling] vSB[FJ]
     78: OKeh 41466, Odeon ONY-36157, Parlophone PNY-34149, (E) E-6391
        OKeh as BUD BLUE AND HIS ORCHESTRA, Odeon as NEW YORK SYNCOPATORS, Parlophone 34149 as DEAUVILLE SYNCOPATORS, 6391 as MERTON ORCHESTRA
     LP: The Old Masters 27
     CD: The Old Masters MB101
     (150907-1) **78:** Harmony 1233-H, Clarion 5103-C, Velvet Tone 2233-V
        Clarion as LLOYD KEATING AND HIS MUSIC, others as FORD BRITTEN AND HIS BLUE COMETS
     LP: The Old Masters 27
150907-2   **I'll Be Blue Just Thinking Of You** vSB[FJ]
     78: Regal (Au) G-20897
W 404534-A   **I Got Rhythm** [Ira Gershwin; George Gershwin] vSB[GW] (as solo)
     78: OKeh 41465, Odeon ONY-36158, Parlophone PNY-34149
        OKeh as HAROLD LEM & HIS ORCHESTRA, Parlophone as DEAUVILLE SYNCOPATORS, Odeon as NEW YORK SYNCOPATORS

LP: The Old Masters 27, Phontastic (Swe) NOST7618
TC: Columbia Legacy CT52855
CD: Phontastic (Swe) NOST7618, Columbia CT52855, The Old Masters MB101
150908-2   **I Got Rhythm** vSB[GW] (as solo)
    78: Harmony 1234-H, Clarion 5104-C, Velvet Tone 2234-V
       as PAUL ASH AND HIS MERRY MAD MUSICAL GANG
    LP: CBS P215974
W 404535-A   **Ukulele Moon** [Gus Kahn; Richard A. Whiting] vSB
       [CL] (cl solo)
    78: Odeon ONY-36159, Parlophone PNY-34150
       Odeon as NEW YORK SYNCOPATORS, Parlophone as GEORGE WELLS AND HIS ORCHESTRA
    CD: The Old Masters MB101
150909-2   **Ukulele Moon** vSB[CL] (cl solo)
    78: Harmony 1241-H, Velvet Tone 2241-V
       as CHESTER LEIGHTON AND HIS SOPHOMORES
W 404536-A   **(You're Always Sure Of) My Love For You** [Gus
       Kahn] vSB[CL]
    78: OKeh 41465, Odeon ONY-36159, Parlophone PNY-34151
       OKeh as HAROLD LEM AND HIS ORCHESTRA, Parlophone as GEORGE WELLS AND HIS ORCHESTRA, Odeon as NEW YORK SYNCOPATORS
    LP: The Old Masters 27
    TC: Columbia/Legacy CT 52930
    CD: Columbia/Legacy CK 52942, The Old Masters MB101
(150910-1) **78:** Harmony 1242-H, Velvet Tone 2242-V
       as CHESTER LEIGHTON AND HIS SOPHOMORES
150910-2   **(You're Always Sure Of) My Love For You**
       vSB[CL]
    78: 2242-V, Regal (Au) G-20938
       as CHESTER LEIGHTON AND HIS SOPHOMORES
W 404537-A   **A Peach Of A Pair** vSB[CL]
    78: Odeon ONY-36158, Parlophone PNY-34150
       Odeon as TOM ROCK AND HIS ORCHESTRA, Parlophone as GEORGE WELLS AND HIS ORCHESTRA
    LP: The Old Masters 27
    CD: The Old Masters MB101
150911-2   **A Peach Of A Pair** vSB[CL]
    78: Harmony 1233-H,   Clarion 5180-C, Velvet Tone 2233-V, 2286-V, Regal (Au) G-20937
       Clarion, Velvet Tone 2286 as FRANK AUBURN AND HIS ORCHESTRA, others as CHESTER LEIGHTON AND HIS SOPHOMORES
W 404538-A   **Someone Sang A Sweeter Song To Mary** [Ballard
       ard MacDonald; Terry Shand] vSB[CL] (cl solo)
    78: OKeh 41466, Odeon ONY-36157, Parlophone PNY-34151
       OKeh as BUD BLUE AND HIS ORCHESTRA, Parlophone as GEORGE WELLS AND HIS ORCHESTRA, Odeon as TOM ROCK AND HIS ORCHESTRA
    CD: The Old Masters MB101
(Contd.)

FRED RICH AND HIS ORCHESTRA (Contd.)

150912-2   **Someone Sang A Sweeter Song To Mary** vSB[CL]
                  (cl solo)
          78: Harmony 1251-H, Clarion 5177-C, Velvet Tone 2251-V
          as CHESTER LEIGHTON AND HIS SOPHOMORES

Columbia, New York, N.Y. Thursday, October 30, 1930
SEGER ELLIS
Unknown (tp) Tom Dorsey (tb) **Jimmy Dorsey** (cl,as) Seger Ellis (p,vcl)
Eddie Lang (g)

W 404516-C   **Body And Soul** [Robert Sour, Frank Eyton; Ed-
                    ward Heyman; Johnny Green] vSE (cl solo)
          78: OKeh 41467
          CD: Azure (E) CD 22
W 404517-A   **Somebody Loves Me** vSE (unissued)
W 404518-B   **Sweet Jennie Lee!** [Walter Donaldson] vSE (as solo)
          78: OKeh 41467, Parlophone R-837
          CD: Azure (E) CD 22

Columbia, New York, N.Y. Friday, October 31, 1930
COLUMBIA STUDIO BAND
Tom Dorsey (tb,tp) **Jimmy Dorsey** (cl) *Frank Signorelli* (p) Eddie Lang
(g) *unknown* (d) Lee Morse, Roy Evans (vcl)

W 150923-2   **I'm Tickled Pink With A Blue-Eyed Baby** [Charles
                    O'Flynn; Pete Wendling] vRE
          78: Columbia 2338-D
          as ROY EVANS
W 150924-1   **Wasting My Love On You** [Edgar Leslie; Harry
                    Warren] vLM
          78: Columbia 2333-D, (E) DB-370, Regal (Au) G-20971
          as LEE MORSE AND HER BLUE GRASS BOYS
W 150925-3   **Loving You The Way I Do** [Blake, Scholl, Mor-
                    risey] vLM
          78: Columbia 2333-D, (E) DB-413
          as LEE MORSE AND HER BLUE GRASS BOYS
          LP: Take Two TT 213
W 150926-2   **It's An Old Spanish Custom** vRE (cl solo)
          78: Columbia 2338-D
          as ROY EVANS

Brunswick, New York, N.Y. October 1930
FRANK MARVIN
Mannie Klein (tp) Tom Dorsey (tb) **Jimmy Dorsey** (cl,as) Dick McDon-
ough (g) Joe Tarto (sb) Frank Marvin (vcl)

E 34831   **My Baby Just Cares For Me** [Gus Kahn; Walter
                  Donaldson] vFM
          78: Brunswick 4949, (E) 01052

E 34833-1   **You're Simply Delish** [Arthur Freed; Joseph Meyer]
                   vFM
     78: Brunswick 4949, (E) 01052

Brunswick, New York, N.Y. c. Monday, November 3, 1930
BRUNSWICK STUDIO BAND
Unknown (ldr) Bob Effros, 2 *unknown* (tp) Tom Dorsey (tb) **Jimmy
Dorsey** (cl,as) *unknown* (as) *unknown* (ts) Joe Venuti (vn) *unknown* (p),
(acc), (bb), (bj), (d), (xyl) Dick Robertson (vcl) Norman Brokenshire
(announcer)

XE 35193-A   **Turn On The Heat** [Buddy De Sylva, Lew Brown;
                   Ray Henderson] (theme); **Milenberg Joys** [Leon
                   Roppolo, Paul Mares, Ferdinand "Jelly-Roll" Mor-
                   ton] (as solo)
     ET: "HEAT" Program AA-1
     LP: Meritt 18
XE 35196-A   **Bye Bye Blues** [Fred Hamm, Dave Bennett, Bert
                   Lown, Chauncey Grey]; **My Future Just Passed**
                   [George Marion, Jr.; Richard A. Whiting]; **I Love
                   You So Much** [Bert Kalmar; Harry Ruby] vDR
     ET: "HEAT" Program AA-4
XE 35197-A   **After You've Gone** [Henry Creamer; Turner Layton]
                   vDR
     ET: "HEAT" Program AA-5
     LP: Meritt 18

Columbia, New York, N.Y. Friday, November 7, 1930
THE TRAVELERS
Jimmy Dorsey (cl,as,ldr) Charlie Margulis, Bill Moore, Louis Garcia
(tp) Tom Dorsey, Glenn Miller (tb) Arnold Brilhart (as) Bud Freeman
(ts) Arthur Schutt (p) Eddie Lang (g) Joe Tarto (bb,sb) Stan King (d)
Scrappy Lambert, Wes Vaughan (vcl)

W 404543-A   **Can This Be Love?** [Paul James; Kay Swift] vSL
     78: Odeon ONY-36160, Parlophone PNY-34152, Clifford (Au)
     5235
          Parlophone as THE MUSICAL VOYAGERS
     (100434-A) **78:** Harmony 1242-H, Clarion 5117-C, Velvet Tone
     2242-V
          Harmony as JERRY MASON'S CALIFORNIANS
     LP: Columbia Special Products P16356, The Old Masters 15,
     World Records (E) SHB67, (Au) R-0950
     TC: World Records (E) CSHB67
     CD: Jazz Oracle (C) BDW8006
W 404543-B   **Can This Be Love?** vSL
     78: Odeon ONY-36160, Parlophone PNY-34152
          Parlophone as THE MUSICAL VOYAGERS
W 404544-B   **Fine And Dandy** [Paul James; Kay Swift] vSL
                   (as solo)
     78: OKeh 41471, Odeon ONY-36160, A386043, Parlophone
     PNY-34153, (E) R-993 (Contd.)

THE TRAVELERS (Contd.)

Parlophone PNY-34153 as MUSICAL VOYAGERS, R-993 as
THE DORSEY BROTHERS' NEW DYNAMIKS
(100452-A) **78:** Harmony 1260-H
as FORD BRITTEN & HIS BLUE COMETS
LP: Columbia Special Products P16356, The Old Masters 15,
World Records (E) SHB67, (Au) R-0950, Odeon (G) SMS8,
Electrola (G) IC.054-06314
TC: World Records (E) CSHB67, Radio Yesteryear Stack 1
CD: Jazz Oracle (C) BDW8006

W 404545-A   **(I Can Make Most Anything) But I Can't Make A**
        Man [Rube Bloom; Victor Young] vWV (cl solo)
        78: OKeh 41471, Odeon ONY-36161, A2311, A286033,
Parlophone PNY-34152, (E) R-882
        Parlophone PNY- as THE MUSICAL VOYAGERS, R-882 as
        THE DORSEY BROTHERS' NEW DYNAMIKS
        LP: Columbia Special Products P16356, The Old Masters 15,
World Records (E) SHB67, Odeon (G) SMS8, Electrola (G)
IC.054-06314
        TC: World Records CSHB67, Columbia/Legacy CT 52855
        CD: Columbia/Legacy CK 52855, Jazz Oracle (C) BDW8006

After this busy recording day, another Dorsey pickup band with unknown personnel took the train to a booking in an equally unknown
location at Princeton University (Sudhalter and Evans 1974).

ARC, New York, N.Y. Friday, November 7, 1930
ARC STUDIO BAND
Bob Effros, *unknown* (tp) *unknown* (tb) Jimmy Dorsey (cl,as) *unknown*
(as), (ts) Joe Venuti, *unknown* (vn) *unknown* (p) Eddie Lang (g) Joe
Tarto (sb) *unknown* (d), (vcl)

E-35345-   **The Little Things In Life** [Irving Berlin] *vcl*
        78: Melotone M-12025
E-35346-   **The Song Of The Fool** [Sam Lewis; Jesse Greer] *vcl*
        78: Melotone M-12022, Panachord (E) 25007
        35345 & 35346 as SLEEPY HALL & HIS COLLEGIANS
E-35347-   **Don't Forget Me In Your Dreams** (waltz) [Edgar
        Leslie; Con Conrad] vcl
        78: Melotone M-12025
        as MILLS' MUSIC MAKERS

Columbia, New York, N.Y. Wednesday, November 12, 1930
JOE VENUTI'S BLUE FOUR
Joe Venuti (vn,ldr) **Jimmy Dorsey** (cl,as,bar) Frank Signorelli (p) Eddie
Lang (g) Joe Tarto (sb)

404549-B   **I've Found A New Baby** (aka **I Found A New Baby)**
        [Jack Palmer, Spencer Williams] (cl,bar,as solos)
        78: Okeh 41469, Parlophone (E) R-924, Odeon (It) A-2362, (G)
A-286036, O28324

LP: Columbia C2L24, Odeon (G) SMS7

404550-C   **Sweet Sue (Just You)** [Will J. Harris; Victor Young]
                (bar solo)
        78: Okeh 41469, Parlophone (E) R-878, (Aus) A-3340, Odeon
        (It) A-2319, (G) A-286032
        LP: The Old Masters 7, Odeon (G) SMS6
        Both sides also on **CD:** JSP (E) CD310

Brunswick, New York, N.Y. Wednesday, November 12, 1930
GRACE JOHNSTON
Mike Mosiello (tp) Tom Dorsey (tb) **Jimmy Dorsey** (cl) Hymie Wolfson
(ts) *unknown* (vn) Rube Bloom (p) Carl Kress (g) *unknown* (bb) Grace
Johnston (vcl)

E 35251   **You're Driving Me Crazy** [Walter Donaldson] vGJ
                (cl solo)
        78: Melotone M-12032, Panachord (E) 25002, P-12032,
        Embassy (Au) E122
                Embassy as SHEILA BLAKE
E 35252   **Them There Eyes** [Maceo Pinkard, William Tracey,
                Doris Tauber] vGJ
        78: Melotone M-12032, Panachord (E) P-12032, Aurora (C) A-
        22011
                Aurora as GRACE HOLT

Columbia, New York, N.Y. Tuesday, November 18, 1930
ETHEL WATERS
Ben Selvin (ldr) Mannie Klein (tp) Tom Dorsey (tb) **Jimmy Dorsey** (cl)
unknown (vn), (p), (g) Ethel Waters (vcl)

W 150966-2   **I Got Rhythm** [Ira Gershwin; George Gershwin] vEW
        78: Columbia 2346-D
        LP: Columbia (G) P2.12854
        CD: Classics (F) 721
W 150967(1,2,3) **Three Little Words** vEW (unissued)

Columbia, New York, N.Y. Wednesday, November 19, 1930
FRED RICH AND HIS ORCHESTRA
Fred Rich (ldr) Mannie Klein, Tommy Gott (tp) Tom Dorsey (tb)
Jimmy Dorsey (cl,as,cnt) *Tony Parenti [or] Louis Martin* (cl,as) *Hymie
Wolfson* (cl,ts) Joe Venuti (vn) Jack Cornell [Smelser] (acc) Frank
Signorelli (p) Eddie Lang (g) *Joe Tarto* (sb) Stan King (d) George
Hamilton Green (xyl) Smith Ballew [as Ralph Wynn, Chester Leighton
or George Walker] (vcl)

W 150753-1   **Morning, Noon And Night** vSB
        (W 404554-A) **78:** Odeon ONY-36161, Parlophone PNY-34153
                *Odeon as ED LOYD AND HIS ORCHESTRA, Parlophone as
                EARL MARLOW'S ORCHESTRA*
100439-1   **Cheerful Little Earful** [Ira Gershwin, Billy Rose;
                Harry Warren] vSB (as solo)
        78: Harmony 1249-H, Clarion 5125-C, Velvet Tone (Contd.)

FRED RICH AND HIS ORCHESTRA (Contd.)

    2249-V, Regal (Au) G-20927
        Harmony, Velvet Tone as FRANK AUBURN & HIS ORCH.,
        Clarion as CHESTER LEIGHTON & HIS SOPHOMORES
    LP: Sunbeam MFC-17
    (W 404555-B) **78:** Odeon ONY-36165, (F) A-221334, Parlophone
    PNY-34157, (E) R-857
        Odeon as NEW YORK SYNCOPATORS, Parlophone as
        DEAUVILLE SYNCOPATORS
100435-1   **Baby's Birthday Party** [Ann Ronnell] vSB (cnt solo)
    78: Harmony 1239-H, Clarion 5126-C, Velvet Tone 2239-V
        Harmony, Velvet Tone as LLOYD KEATING & HIS MUSIC,
        Clarion as CHESTER LEIGHTON & HIS SOPHOMORES
    (W 404556-A) **78:** Odeon ONY-36163, (Arg) 193741, OKeh
    41472, Parlophone PNY-34158, (E) R-855, (Au) A-3111, Ariel
    (E) 4687
        Odeon and OKeh as NEW YORK SYNCOPATORS, Parlo-
        phone PNY-34158 as DEAUVILLE SYNCOPATORS, Ariel as
        ARIEL DANCE ORCHESTRA
100436-1   **The Wedding Of The Birds** vSB
    78: Harmony 1239-H, Velvet Tone 2239-V
        as LLOYD KEATING AND HIS MUSIC
    (W 404557-B) **78:** Odeon ONY-36164, (F) A-221335, OKeh
    41472, Parlophone PNY-34158, (E) R-855, (Au) A-3111
        OKeh, Parlophone R-855 as NEW YORK SYNCOPATORS,
        Parlophone PNY- as GEORGE WELLS AND HIS ORCH.
100437-1   **The Little Things In Life** [Irving Berlin] vSB
        (cl solo)
    78: Harmony 1240-H, Clarion 5186-C, Regal (Au) G-20955
        Harmony as LLOYD KEATING AND HIS MUSIC, Clarion as
        CHESTER LEIGHTON AND HIS SOPHOMORES
    (W 404558-A) **78:** Odeon ONY-36164, Parlophone PNY-34157,
    (E) R-874, Ariel (E) 4693
        Parlophone PNY- as GEORGE WELLS AND HIS ORCH-
        ESTRA, R-874 as NEW YORK SYNCOPATORS, Ariel as
        ARIEL DANCE ORCHESTRA
100440-1   **I'm Tickled Pink With A Blue-Eyed Baby** [Charles
        O'Flynn; Pete Wendling] vSB (cnt solo)
    78: Harmony 1246-H, Clarion 5179-C, Velvet Tone 2246-V,
    Regal (Au) G-20945
        Harmony, Velvet Tone, Regal as LLOYD KEATING AND
        HIS MUSIC, Clarion as FRANK AUBURN AND HIS ORCH.
    LP: Vintage Jazz Music Society (E) VLP56
    (W 404559-A) **78:** Odeon ONY-36165, Parlophone PNY-34155,
    (E) R-856
        Odeon as NEW YORK SYNCOPATORS, Parlophone PNY- as
        EARL MARLOW'S ORCHESTRA, R-856 as SAM LANIN'S
        FAMOUS PLAYERS AND SINGERS
    All 100000 series matrices from this session also on **CD:** The Old
    Masters MB101

Victor, New York, N.Y. Thursday, November 20, 1930
HOAGY CARMICHAEL AND HIS ORCHESTRA
Hoagy Carmichael (vcl,ldr) Mannie Klein, Ray Lodwig (tp) Tom Dorsey
(tb) **Jimmy Dorsey** (cl,as) Arnold Brilhart (as) Bud Freeman (ts) Joe
Venuti (vn) Irving Brodsky (p,celst) *unknown* (sb), (d)

BVE 64365-2   **Lazy River** [Sidney Arodin; Hoagy Carmichael] vHC
                   (cl solo)
         78: Victor 23034
         LP: His Master's Voice (E) B-6500, RCA (F) FPM1-7016, RCA
         (E) INTS5181, CPL1-3307, NL89096
         TC: Radio Yesteryear Stack #82
         CD: Timeless (H) CBC 1-011
BVE 64366-1   **Papa's Gone Bye-Bye Blues** vHC (as solo)
         LP: RCA LSA3180, RCA (F) FPM1-7016, RCA (E) INTS5181,
         NL89096
BVE 64367-2   **Just Forget** vHC
         78: Victor 23034

Columbia, New York, N.Y. Friday, November 28, 1930
ETHEL WATERS
Ben Selvin (ldr) Mannie Klein (tp) Tom Dorsey (tb) **Jimmy Dorsey** (cl)
unknown (vn), (p), (g) Ethel Waters (vcl)

W 150967-5   **Three Little Words** [Bert Kalmar; Harry Ruby]
                   vEW
         78: Columbia 2346-D
         LP: Columbia KG31571
         CD: Classics (F) 721

Brunswick, New York, N.Y. Monday, December 1, 1930
RED NICHOLS AND HIS FIVE PENNIES
Red Nichols, Charlie Teagarden (tp), Wingy Manone (tp,vcl) Glenn
Miller (tb) **Jimmy Dorsey** (cl,as) Babe Russin (ts) Joe Sullivan (p) Art
Miller (sb) Gene Krupa (d)

E-35618-A   **My Honey's Lovin' Arms** [Herman Ruby; Joseph
                   Meyer] (cl solo)
         78: Brunswick 6012, (C) 6012, (E) O1121, (F) A-9005
         LP: Sunbeam MFC-12
         TC: Radio Yesteryear Stack 31
         CD: Best Of Jazz (F) 4041
E-35619-A   **Rockin' Chair** [Hoagy Carmichael] vWM
         78: Brunswick 6012, (C) 6012, (E) O1852, (F) A-9005
         LP: Sunbeam MFC-12
         TC: Radio Yesteryear Stack 31, 82

Columbia, New York, N.Y. Tuesday, December 2, 1930
SMITH BALLEW AND HIS ORCHESTRA
Smith Ballew (vcl,ldr) J. D. Wade, *unknown* (tp) Tom Dorsey (tb) **Jim-
my Dorsey** (cl,as) *Lyle Bowen* (as) Babe Russin (ts) Bruce Yantis (vn)
Arthur Schutt (p) *George Van Eps* (g) Stan King (d)

SMITH BALLEW AND HIS ORCHESTRA (Contd.)

W 150991-3   **There's Something Missing In Your Eyes** vSB
                    (as,cl solos)
     78: Columbia 2350-D
     TC: Classic Recordings 131
W 150992-3   **(Five, Six, Seven, Eight) Nine Little Miles From
                    Ten-Ten Tennessee** [Al Lewis, Al Sherman] vSB
     78: Columbia 2350-D, (E) CB-246, Regal (Au) G-20993
     TC: Classic Recordings 131

Columbia, New York, N.Y. Monday, December 8, 1930
BEN SELVIN AND HIS ORCHESTRA
Ben Selvin (vn,ldr) Mannie Klein, Tommy Gott (tp) Tom Dorsey (tb)
Jimmy Dorsey (cl,as) *unknown* (ts) Arthur Schutt (p) *unknown* (g) Joe
Tarto (bb) *Stan King* (d) Jack Miller (vcl)

151161-2   **You're Driving Me Crazy! (What Did I Do?)**
                  [Walter Donaldson] vJM (cl solo)
     78: Harmony 1251-H, Velvet Tone 2251-V, Clarion 5186-C
          as LLOYD KEATING AND HIS MUSIC
     (W 404579-A) **78:** Parlophone PNY-34159, (E) 6394, Odeon
     ONY-36167, OKeh 41475, Ariel (E) 4689
          *Parlophone PNY- as SAM NASH AND HIS ORCHESTRA,
          Parlophone (E) as ROBERT HOOD BOWERS ORCHESTRA,
          Odeon and Okeh as RAY SEELEY AND HIS ORCHESTRA,
          Ariel as ARIEL DANCE ORCHESTRA*
151161-2   **Under The Spell Of Your Kiss** vJM
     78: Harmony 1252-H, Velvet Tone 2252-V, 2281-V, Clarion
     5196-C
          *Harmony, Velvet Tone 2252-V as LLOYD KEATING AND
          HIS MUSIC, Velvet Tone 2281-V and Clarion as ROY
          CARROLL AND HIS SANDS POINT ORCHESTRA*
     (W 404585-A) **78:** Parlophone PNY-34159, (E) R872, Odeon
     ONY-36168
          *Parlophone as SAM NASH AND HIS ORCHESTRA, Parlo-
          phone (E) as ROOF GARDEN ORCHESTRA, Odeon as RAY
          SEELEY AND HIS ORCHESTRA*
151163-2   **Hurt** [Solomon; Piantadosi] vJM
     78: Harmony 1253-H, Velvet Tone 2253-V, 2284-V, Clarion
     5189-C
          *Harmony and Velvet Tone as FRANK AUBURN AND HIS
          ORCH., Clarion as LLOYD KEATING AND HIS MUSIC*
     (W 404580-A) **78:** Parlophone PNY-34160, (E) 6394, Odeon
     ONY-36168, OKeh 41475
          *Parlophone as SAM NASH AND HIS ORCHESTRA,
          Parlophone (E) as WILL PERRY AND HIS ORCHESTRA,
          Odeon and Okeh as RAY SEELEY AND HIS ORCHESTRA*
151164-1   **I Hate Myself (For Falling In Love With You)**
                  [Benny Davis, Joe Young, Milton Ager] vJM
     78: Harmony 1252-H, Velvet Tone 2252-V, Clarion 5187-C

> *Harmony and Velvet Tone as LLOYD KEATING AND HIS*
> *MUSIC, Clarion as FRANK AUBURN AND HIS ORCH-*
> *ESTRA*
> (W 404586-A) **78:** Parlophone PNY-34160, Odeon ONY-36167
> *Parlophone as SAM NASH AND HIS ORCHESTRA, Odeon*
> *as RAY SEELEY AND HIS ORCHESTRA*

ARC, New York, N.Y. Tuesday, December 9, 1930
CHICK BULLOCK
Mannie Klein (tp) *Tom Dorsey* (tb) Jimmy Dorsey (cl,as) *unknown* (p)
(bb) (d) Chick Bullock (vcl)

10314-1   **Cheerful Little Earful** [Ira Gershwin, Billy Rose;
                 Harry Warren] vCB (as solo)
     78: Perfect 12675, Regal 10237, Romeo 1543
10315-   **Laughing At Life** [Nick Kenny, Charles Kenny; Bob
                 Todd, Cornell Todd] vCB
     78: Vocalion 788

ARC, New York, N.Y. Thursday, December 11, 1930
CHICK BULLOCK
Personnel as December 9, 1930, except 2 *unknown* (vn) replace (tb)

10323-   **Longing Just For You** vCB (unissued)
10324-2   **Chasing The Clouds Away** [Gold, Sumner] vCB
                 (cl solo)
     78: Perfect 12675, Regal 10237, Romeo 1543
10325-3   **The Little Things In Life** [Irving Berlin] vCB
     78: Banner 32060, Perfect 12677, Vocalion 758

ARC, New York, N.Y. Thursday, December 18, 1930
SEGER ELLIS
Muggsy Spanier (tp) Charlie Butterfield (tb) **Jimmy Dorsey** (cl) Rube
Bloom (p) Eddie Lang (g) Stan King (d) Seger Ellis (vcl)

E-35761-A   **My Love For You** [Gus Kahn] vSE (cl solo)
     78: Brunswick 6022, (E) 01084, (Au) 6050
     CD: Azure (E) CD-22
E-35773-D   **It's A Lonesome Old Town** [Harry Tobias; Charles
                 Kisco] vSE (cl solo)
     78: Brunswick 6022, (E) 01084

Columbia, New York, N.Y. Saturday, December 20, 1930
SEGER ELLIS
Mannie Klein (tp) Tom Dorsey (tb) **Jimmy Dorsey** (cl) Rube Bloom (p)
Eddie Lang (g) Seger Ellis (vcl)

W 404582-B   **Tears** [Frank Capano; Billy Uhr] vSE
     78: OKeh 41479
W 404583-B   **You're The One I Care For** [Harry Link; Bert
                 Lown, Chauncey Grey] vSE
     78: OKeh 41479

ARC, New York, N.Y. Monday, December 22, 1930
FRED RICH AND HIS ORCHESTRA
Fred Rich (ldr) Mannie Klein, Tommy Gott (tp) Tom Dorsey (tb)
Jimmy Dorsey (cl,as) *unknown* (ts), (vn), (p) Eddie Lang (g) Joe Tarto
(sb) *unknown* (d) Scrappy Lambert, Joe White (vcl)

10332-2   **Blue Again** [Dorothy Fields; Jimmy McHugh] vSL
                   (cl solo)
       78: Banner 32068, Conquerer 7683, Jewel 6190, Oriole 2190,
       Perfect 15419, Regal 10247, Romeo 1557, Apex (C) 41290
10333-1   **When Your Hair Has Turned To Silver** [Charles
                   Tobias; Peter De Rose] vJW
       78: Oriole 2196
                   *Matrix 10333 was remade January 22, 1931, and take 5 was
                   issued on Oriole 2192. While Joe White (also known as "The
                   Silver Masked Tenor") sings on the remake, it is a different
                   band.*
10334 (1,2)   **Lonesome Lover** vSL (unissued)

America, and for that matter the rest of the world, was by now deep
in the throes of an economic downslide. It is a paradox of these bad
times, which gained the label "The Great Depression," that a cadre of
top musicians in New York (and Hollywood and Chicago as well) was
never without work.

Because of the growing opportunities in the so-called "free" or
"cheap" entertainment, most notably radio and the movies, "quick-read"
musicians like the Dorseys, Benny Goodman, Mannie Klein, Eddie
Lang, Artie Schutt, Stan King, Joe Venuti and Joe Tarto were in great
demand.

During the early thirties some of the radio orchestras that included
Jimmy Dorsey at one time or another, sometimes on the same evening,
were Andre Kostelanetz, Jacques Renard, Lennie Hayton, Fred Rich,
Victor Young and Rubinoff and his Magic Violin.

This full schedule didn't mean that all musicians were doing well.
Unemployment among New York City's music makers was on a par
with most other occupations, roughly in the 30 percent range.

This disparity in opportunities between the "favorites" and the others
would be one of the factors that led to the rise in power of James C.
Petrillo as head of the musician's union nationally.

What Depression?
(1931)

Jimmy's first 1931 recording assignment is an early example of the association between Glenn Miller and the handsome Texas-born singer Smith Ballew, who later became an actor in the "singing westerns." Miller formed a band for Ballew that later supplied much of the nucleus of the "permanent" Dorsey Brothers' Orchestra in 1934.

Columbia, New York, N.Y. Tuesday, January 6, 1931
SMITH BALLEW AND HIS ORCHESTRA
Smith Ballew (ldr,vcl) Mannie Klein, Tommy Gott (tp) Glenn Miller (tb,arr) **Jimmy Dorsey,** Pete Pumiglio (cl,as) Babe Russin (ts) Bruce Yantis, Joe Venuti (vn) Bobby Van Eps (p) George Van Eps (g) Stan King (d)

151146-3   **Overnight** [Billy Rose, Charlotte Kent; Louis Alter] vSB (as solo)
      78: Columbia 2373-D, Regal (Au) G-20994
151147-3   **To Whom It May Concern** [Sidney D. Mitchell; George W. Meyer, Archie Gottler] vSB (cl solo)
      78: Columbia 2373-D, (E) CB-274, (Au) DO-325
      TC: Columbia/Legacy C2T 52942, CT52930
      CD: Columbia/Legacy C2K 52942

Columbia, New York, N.Y. Wednesday, January 7, 1931
FRED RICH AND HIS ORCHESTRA
Fred Rich (ldr) Mannie Klein, Tommy Gott (tp) Tom Dorsey (tb) Jimmy Dorsey (cl,as) Elmer Feldkamp (cl,as,vcl) *Andy Sanella* (ts,stg) *unknown* (vn), (p) Eddie Lang (g) Joe Tarto (sb) *unknown* (d)

151183-1   **I'm So Afraid Of You** [Bert Kalmar; Harry Ruby] vEF [as Robert Wood]
      78: Clarion 5211-C, Harmony 1269-H, Velvet Tone 2276-V
      as FRANK AUBURN AND HIS ORCHESTRA
      (W 404805-A) **78:** Odeon ONY-36181, Parlophone PNY-34171, (E) R-891
      Odeon and Parlophone R-891 as NEW YORK SYNCOPAT-ORS, Parlophone PNY-34171 as DEAUVILLE SYNCOPAT-ORS
151184-1   **Lonesome Lover** [Alfred Bryan; James V. Monaco] vEF [as Tom Frawley]
      78: Clarion 5209-C, Harmony 1268-H, Velvet Tone 2268-V
      as FRANK AUBURN AND HIS ORCHESTRA
                    (Contd.)

FRED RICH AND HIS ORCHESTRA (Contd.)

(W 404806-A) **78:** Odeon ONY-36178, Parlophone PNY-34169,
(E) R-892, Ariel (E) 4744
> *Odeon and Parlophone R-892 as NEW YORK SYNCO-
> PATORS, Parlophone PNY-34169 as DEAUVILLE SYNCO-
> PATORS, Ariel as ARIEL DANCE ORCH. (151185, 151186
> recorded by Seger Ellis December 15, 1930)*

151187-1   **Falling In Love Again** [Sammy Lerner; Friedrich
> Hollander] vEF [as Marvin Young]
> **78:** Clarion 5214-C, Harmony 1270-H, Velvet Tone 2270-V
> *as JERRY MASON'S CALIFORNIANS*
(W 404807) **78:** Odeon ONY-36178, Parlophone PNY-34170
> *Odeon as NEW YORK SYNCOPATORS, Parlophone as
> DEAUVILLE SYNCOPATORS*

151188-1,2   **Peanut Vendor** vEF
> **78:** Clarion 5213-C, Harmony 1270-H, Velvet Tone 2270-V
> *as EL MANISERO—Rhumba Orch.*

151189-1   **Truly (I Love You)** [Walter Hirsch; Frank Magine]
> vEF [as Tom Frawley] (cl solo)
> **78:** Clarion 5210-C, Harmony 1268-H, Velvet Tone 2277-V
> *as LLOYD KEATING & HIS MUSIC*
(W 404808-A) **78:** Odeon ONY-36179, Parlophone PNY-34171,
(E) R-910, Ariel (E) 4707
> *Odeon as TOM ROCK & HIS ORCH., Parlophone PNY-
> 34171 as GEORGE WELLS & HIS ORCH., R-910 as ROOF
> GARDEN ORCH., Ariel as ARIEL DANCE ORCH.*

151190-1   **Would You Like To Take A Walk? (Sump'n
> Good'll Come From That)** [Mort Dixon, Billy Rose;
> Harry Warren] vEF [as Robert Wood]
> **78:** Clarion 5212-C, Harmony 1269-H, Velvet Tone 2269-V
> *as FRANK AUBURN AND HIS MUSIC*
(W 404809-A) **78:** Odeon ONY-36179, Parlophone PNY-34172,
(E) R-892, Ariel (E) 4743
> *Odeon as TOM ROCK AND HIS ORCH., Parlophone PNY-
> as GEORGE WELLS AND HIS ORCH., R-892 as NEW
> YORK SYNCOPATORS, Ariel as ARIEL DANCE ORCH.*
(W 404867) **78:** OKeh 41482

Brunswick, New York, N.Y. Thursday, January 8, 1931
BRUNSWICK STUDIO ORCHESTRA
Bob Effros, *unknown* (tp) Tom Dorsey (tb) **Jimmy Dorsey** (cl,as) *un-
known* (as), (ts) *Joe Venuti, unknown* (vn) *unknown* (p) Eddie Lang (g)
Joe Tarto (sb) *unknown* (d,xyl) Chester Gaylord, Dick Robertson (vcl)

E-35902   **Cheerful Little Earful** [Ira Gershwin, Billy Rose;
> Harry Warren] vCG (cl solo)
> **78:** Brunswick 6028, 01078
> *as CHESTER GAYLORD "The Whispering Serenader"*
E-35903   **Would You Like To Take A Walk? (Sump'n
> Good'll Come From That)** [Mort Dixon, Billy Rose;
> Harry Warren] vCG (cl solo)

78: Brunswick 6028, 01078
     as CHESTER GAYLORD "The Whispering Serenader"
E-35904   **Tie A Little String Around Your Finger** [Seymour
               Simons] vDR
78: Melotone M-12082, Panachord 25032
     as DICK ROBERTSON AND HIS ORCHESTRA
E-35905   **Would You Like To Take A Walk?** vDR (unissued)

ARC, New York, N.Y. Monday, January 12, 1931
ARC STUDIO BAND
Mannie Klein (tp) Tom Dorsey (tb) **Jimmy Dorsey** (cl) *Rube Bloom* (p)
unknown (bb) Chick Bullock, William Robyn (vcl)

10358-3   **You're The One I Care For** [Harry Link; Bert
               Lown, Chauncey Grey] vCB
78: Banner 32081, Conquerer 7694, Perfect 12680
     as CHICK BULLOCK. ARC files say remade Jan. 21, 1931.
10360-1   **Something To Remember You By** vWR (cl solo)
78: Banner 32080, Oriole 2202, Perfect 12682
10361-2   **Rockin' Chair** [Hoagy Carmichael] vCB (cl solo)
78: Banner 32080, Oriole 2202, Perfect 12682
     as CHICK BULLOCK

Columbia, New York, N.Y. Friday, January 16, 1931
ANNETTE HANSHAW
Ben Selvin (ldr) Mannie Klein (tp) Tom Dorsey (tb) **Jimmy Dorsey** (cl)
Rube Bloom (p) Eddie Lang (g) Annette Hanshaw (vcl)

151223-1,2   **I'll Lock You In My Arms** vAH
78: Clarion 5217-C
151224-3   **Crying To The Moon** vAH
78: Clarion 5216-C, Velvet Tone 2274-V

Brunswick, New York, N.Y. Tuesday, January 20, 1931
DICK ROBERTSON & HIS ORCHESTRA (Brunswick Studio Band)
Bob Effros, *unknown* (tp) Tom Dorsey (tb) **Jimmy Dorsey** (cl,as)
unknown (as), (ts) *Joe Venuti, unknown* (vn) *unknown* (p) Eddie Lang
(g) *Hank Stern [or] Joe Tarto* (sb) *unknown* (d) Dick Robertson [as
Willie Robyn, Ray Raymond on some] (vcl)

E-35934   **I Bring A Love Song** [Oscar Hammerstein II; Sig-
               mund Romberg] vDR[WR]
78: Melotone M-12084
E-35935   **Something To Remember You By** [Howard Dietz;
               Arthur Schwartz] vDR[RR]
78: Melotone M-12083
E-35936   **Tears** [Frank Capano; Billy Uhr] vDR[RR]
78: Melotone M-12083
E-35937   **Would You Like To Take A Walk? (Sump'n
               Good'll Come From That)** [Mort Dixon, Billy Rose;
               Harry Warren] vDR (cl solo)
78: Melotone M-12082

Brunswick, New York, N.Y. Wednesday, January 21, 1931
BRUNSWICK STUDIO BAND
Bob Effros, *unknown* (tp) Tom Dorsey (tb) Jimmy Dorsey (cl,as,bar)
Ronald Perry (as,ts) *Joe Venuti, unknown* (vn) *unknown* (p) Eddie Lang
(g) *Hank Stern [or] Joe Tarto* (sb) *unknown* (d,xyl) Ronald Perry,
Scrappy Lambert, Dick Robertson, Charlie Lawman (vcl)

E-35942-   **Truly (I Love You)** [Walter Hirsch; Frank Mangine]
                  vRP (bar solo)
     78: Melotone M-12081
E-35943-   **It's A Lonesome Old Town (When You're Not**
                  Around) [Harry Tobias; Charles Kisco] vSL
     78: Melotone M-12081
          35942, 35943 as ART KAHN'S ORCHESTRA
E-35944-   **When You Were The Blossom Of Buttercup Lane**
                  (And I Was Your Little Boy Blue) [Al Dubin,
                  Alfred Bryan; Joseph Meyer] vDR (bar solo)
     78: Melotone M-12088, Panachord (E) 25030, Mayfair (E)
     W32007
          Mayfair as MICKEY'S NIGHT BAND, others as MILT SHAW
          AND HIS DETROITERS
E-35945-   **They'll All Be There But Me** [Irving Kahal; Sammy
                  Fain] vDR (bar solo)
     78: Melotone M-12088, Panachord (E) 25030
          as MILT SHAW AND HIS DETROITERS
E-35946-   **Say "Hello" To The Folks Back Home** [Lou Davis;
                  Carmen Lombardo] vCL
     78: Melotone M-12089
E-35947-   **I Hate Myself (For Falling In Love With You)**
                  [Dave Oppenheim, Nick Kenny; Abner Silver] vCL
     78: Melotone M-12089
          35946, 35947 as SLEEPY HALL AND HIS COLLEGIANS

Brunswick, New York, N.Y. Friday, February 6, 1931
BRUNSWICK STUDIO BAND
Mannie Klein (tp) Tom Dorsey (tb) **Jimmy Dorsey** (cl,as) *unknown*
(bcl), (as), (ts), (p) *Eddie Lang* (g) *unknown* (sb), (d) Nick Lucas, Smith
Ballew, Seger Ellis (vcl)

E 36029   **Walkin' My Baby Back Home** [Roy Turk; Fred E.
                  Ahlert] vNL
     78: Brunswick 6048, (E) 01119
E 36030   **Falling In Love Again (Can't Help It)** [Sammy Lern-
                  er; Frederick Hollander] vNL
     78: Brunswick 6048
E 36031   **Running Between The Rain Drops** [James Dyernforth;
                  Carroll Gibbons] vNL
     78: Brunswick 6049, (E) 01119
          36029 through 36031 as NICK LUCAS AND HIS CROON-
          ING TROUBADORS
E 36032   **Just A Gigolo** [Julius Brammer, Irving Caesar; Leon
                  Casucci] vSB

78: Melotone 12094
as ROSS COLBY
E 36033   **Yours And Mine** [Johnny Burke; Steve Nelson] vSB
78: Melotone 12094
as ROSS COLBY
E-36034-A   **Tie A Little String Around Your Finger** [Seymour Simons] vSE (cl solo)
78: Brunswick 6050, 01114, (Au) 6022, Supertone S-2208
Brunswicks as SEGER ELLIS, Supertone as ARTHUR STAI-GER

Columbia, New York, N.Y. Monday, February 9, 1931
FRED RICH AND HIS ORCHESTRA
Fred Rich (ldr) 2 *unknown* (tp) Tom Dorsey (tb) **Jimmy Dorsey** (cl,as)
unknown (as), (ts), (vn), (p) Cornell Smelscr (acc) Roy Smeck (g,stg)
unknown (bb), (sb), (d) Bill Coty [as Robert Wood on some] (vcl)

W 404834-A   **Love For Sale** [Cole Porter] vBC
78: Odeon ONY-36187, Parlophone PNY-34180
Odeon as TOM ROCK AND HIS ORCHESTRA, Parlophone as DEAUVILLE SYNCOPATORS
(100487-1) **78:** Harmony 1282-H, Velvet Tone 2311-V, Clarion 5246-C
as LLOYD KEATING AND HIS MUSIC
W 404835-A,B   **By The River Sainte Marie** [Edgar Leslie; Harry Warren] vBC (cl solo)
(W 480036-A) **78:** Odeon ONY-36188, Parlophone PNY-34180
Odeon as ED LOYD AND HIS ORCHESTRA, Parlophone as DEAUVILLE SYNCOPATORS. Columbia file cards show "404835-A,B rejected, replaced by 480036-A."
(100482-1) **78:** Harmony 1282-H, Velvet Tone 2311-V, Clarion 5246-C
as LLOYD KEATING AND HIS MUSIC
W 404836-B   **Please Don't Talk About Me When I'm Gone** [Sidney Clare; Sam H. Stept] vBC
78: OKeh 41484, Odeon ONY-36189, Parlophone PNY-34181, (E) R-895
Odeon as SAM LANIN AND HIS FAMOUS PLAYERS, Parlophone PNY-34181 as EARL MARLOW'S ORCHESTRA, R-895 as ROOF GARDEN ORCHESTRA
(100498-1) **78:** Harmony 1287-H, Velvet Tone 2336-V, Clarion 5330-C
as JACK WHITNEY'S NEW YORKERS
W 404837-A   **When Your Hair Has Turned To Silver** [Charles Tobias; Peter De Rose] vBC (cl solo)
78: OKeh 41481, Odeon ONY-36191, Parlophone PNY-34181, (E) E-6412
OKeh as LESTER MOELLER'S MUSIC, Odeon as RAY SEELEY'S ORCH., Parlophone PNY- as EARL MARLOW'S ORCH., E-6412 as WILL PERRY & HIS ORCH.
(100488-1) **78:** Harmony 1284-H, Velvet Tone 2312-V, Clarion 5247-C (Contd.)

FRED RICH AND HIS ORCHESTRA (Contd.)

as FRANK AUBURN & HIS ORCHESTRA (vcl RW)
W 404838-A   **I Surrender Dear** [Gordon Clifford; Harry Barris]
        vBC
    78: OKeh 41488, Odeon ONY-36190, Parlophone PNY- 34182
    Odeon as SAM LANIN'S FAMOUS PLAYERS, Parlophone as
    SAM NASH AND HIS ORCHESTRA
    (100483-1) **78:** Harmony 1284-H, Velvet Tone 2320-V, Clarion
    5254-C
    as FRANK AUBURN AND HIS ORCHESTRA (vcl RW)
W 404839-A   **I Want You For Myself** [Irving Berlin] vBC
    78: Odeon ONY-36191, Parlophone PNY-34182
    Odeon as RAY SEELEY'S ORCHESTRA, Parlophone as SAM
    NASH AND HIS ORCHESTRA
    (100484-1) **78:** Clarion 5269-C, Velvet Tone 2335-V, Harmony
    1285-H
    Clarion and Velvet Tone as LLOYD KEATING AND HIS
    MUSIC, Harmony as JACK WHITNEY'S NEW YORKERS

In his previous book the author listed a February 17, 1931, Regent
Club Orchestra session as possibly including both Dorseys. It does not.

Brunswick, New York, N.Y. Thursday, February 19, 1931
NEW ORLEANS RAMBLERS
Ben Pollack (ldr,vcl) Bob Haring (dir) Sterling Bose, Charlie Spivak (tp)
Jack Teagarden (tb,vcl) **Jimmy Dorsey** (cl,as) Gil Rodin (as) Eddie
Miller (ts) Al Beller (vn) Gil Bowers (p) Nappy Lamare (g) Harry
Goodman (sb) Ray Bauduc (d) The Cotton Pickers (vcl quartet)

E-36104-   **That's The Kind Of Man For Me** [Jack Egan, Alfred
        Harrison] vJT
    78: Melotone M-12230, Decatur 508 (dubbing)
    LP: Ace Of Hearts (E) AH168
E-36105-   **I'm One Of God's Children (Who Hasn't Got
        Wings)** [Oscar Hammerstein II, Harry Ruskin; Louis
        Alter] vJT
    78: Melotone M-12133, Decatur 508 (dubbing)
    LP: Ace Of Hearts (E) AH168
E-36106-   **No Wonder I'm Blue** vBP
    78: Melotone M-12133
E-36107-(A,B)   **There's Rhythm In The River** vJT&CP (unissued)

Brunswick, New York, N.Y. Saturday, February 21, 1931
FRED RICH AND HIS ORCHESTRA
Fred Rich (ldr) *Lloyd Williams [or] Ruby Weinstein,* Bunny Berigan (tp)
Lloyd Turner (tb) Lyle Bowen (as) **Jimmy Dorsey** (cl,as) *unknown* (ts)
Joe Venuti (vn) Sammy Prager (p) Cornell Smelser (acc) *Carl Kress*
(g,bj) *Stan Green* (bb,sb) *Howard Goulden* (d) Smith Ballew [as Ross
Colby or Dick Harmon], Helen Rowland (vcl)

E-36132   **Ev'rything That's Nice Belongs To You** [Bud Green;

Sam H. Stept] vSB (cl solo)
78: Melotone M-12124, Panachord (E) 25054, (Au) P-12124, Mayfair (E) G-2014
Melotone as MAURICE SHERMAN & HIS COLLEGE INN ORCH., Panachords as OWEN FALLON & HIS CALI-FORNIANS, Mayfair as SOUTHERN STATE RAMBLERS
LP: Sunbeam MFC-17
CD: IAJRC CD-1013

E-36133   **Love For Sale** [Cole Porter] vHR
78: Melotone M-12108

E-36134   **If You Should Ever Need Me (You'll Always Find Me Here)** [Al Dubin; Joe Burke] vSB
78: Melotone M-12124
as OWEN FALLON AND HIS CALIFORNIANS

E-36135   **Got The Bench, Got The Park (But I Haven't Got You)** [Al Lewis, Al Sherman; Fred Phillips] vSB (as,cl solos)
78: Melotone M-12108
36133 & 36135 as RALPH BENNETT & HIS SEVEN ACES

E-36136   **Honeymoon Parade** vSB
78: Melotone M-12190, Panachord (E) 25070

E-36137   **Soldier On The Shelf** [Myers, Reeves] vSB
78: Melotone M-12190, Panachord (E) 25070
36136 and 36137 as SLEEPY HALL AND HIS COLLEGIANS

Brunswick, New York, N.Y. Thursday, February 26, 1931
THE TRAVELLERS
Jimmy Dorsey (cl,as,ldr) Charlie Margulis, Bunny Berigan, *Louis Garcia* (tp) Tom Dorsey (tb) Glenn Miller (*tb*,arr) [files list only **one** trombone] Arnold Brilhart (as) Bud Freeman (ts) Arthur Schutt (p) Eddie Lang (g) Joe Tarto (bb,sb) Stan King (d) Scrappy Lambert (vcl)

E-36186-A,B   **You Said It** [Jack Yellen; Harold Arlen] vSL
78: Melotone M-12113, Panachord P-12113

E-36187-A,B   **Sweet And Hot** [Jack Yellen; Harold Arlen] vSL (cl solo)
78: Melotone M-12113, Panachord P-12113

E-36188-A,B   **I've Got A Sweet Somebody** [Ben Ryan; Lou Handman] vSL (as solo)
78: Melotone M-12148, Panachord P-12148
TC: Radio Yesteryear Stack #83

E-36189-A,B   **Dream A Little Dream Of Me** [Gus Kahn; Wilbur Schwandt, Fabian Andre] vSL (cl solo)
78: Melotone M-12148, Panachord P-12148, Embassy E-133
Embassy as THE JOY SPREADERS.
All released sides also on **LP:** Collectors Must (It) M8003, **CD:** Jazz Oracle (C) BDW8006

Brunswick New York, N.Y. Thursday, March 5, 1931
COLONIAL CLUB ORCHESTRA
Victor Young (ldr) Bob Effros, *Mannie Klein* (tp) Tom Dorsey (tb) *Jimmy Dorsey* (cl,as) *Andy Sanella* (as,stg) (as) *Larry Binyon* (cl,ts,fl) 2

COLONIAL CLUB ORCHESTRA (Contd.)
unknown (vn) *unknown* (p), (g), (bb) *Chauncey Morehouse [or] Larry Gomar* (d) Men About Town [Phil Dewey, Frank Luther, Jack Parker] (vcl)

E-36221   **Please Don't Talk About Me When I'm Gone** [Sid-
                 ney Clare; Sam H. Stept] vMAT
     78: Brunswick 6075
E-36222   **Smile, Darn Ya, Smile** [Charles O'Flynn,
                 Jack Meskill; Max Rich] vMAT
     78: Brunswick 6077
E-36223   **All On Account Of Your Kisses (I'm No Account
                 Anymore)** [Dave Oppenheim] vMAT
     78: Brunswick 6075
E-36224   **Ev'rything That's Nice Belongs To You** [Bud Green;
                 Sam H. Stept] vFL
     78: Brunswick 6077

                 Dance, Amherst College, Friday, March 13, 1931
DORSEY BROTHERS PICKUP BAND*
Bunny Berigan, Bill Moore (tp) "Bix" Beiderbecke (cnt) Tom Dorsey,
Glenn Miller (tb) Jimmy Dorsey, *unknown* (cl,as) 2 *unknown* (as,ts) Art
Schutt (p) Carl Kress (g) *unknown* (sb) Johnny Morris (d) *(Sudhalter
and Evans 1974).

ARC, New York, N.Y. Tuesday, March 17, 1931
CHICK BULLOCK/BEN ALLEY
Mannie Klein (tp) Tom Dorsey (tb) *Jimmy Dorsey* (cl) Joe Venuti (vn)
unknown (p), (bj), (sb), (d,xyl) Chick Bullock, Ben Alley (vcl)

10500   **Walkin' My Baby Back Home** [Roy Turk; Fred E.
               Ahlert] vCB
     78: Conquerer 7785, Romeo 1615
10501   **When I Take My Sugar To Tea** [Irving Kahal,
               Pierre Norman, Sammy Fain] vCB
     78: Conquerer 7785, Romeo 1615, Vocalion (Au) 830
10502   **Two Hearts In Three-Quarters Time** [Joe Young;
               Robert Stolz] vBA
     78: Perfect 12702
10503   **I Have A Sweetheart (And Mother Is Her Name)**
               vBA
     78: Perfect 12702

Jimmy and Tommy were by now active again in Freddie Rich's CBS
house band, along with Bunny Berigan, fresh from Hal Kemp's group
(White and Kite 1951-1987).

Columbia, New York, N.Y. Wednesday, March 18, 1931
FRED RICH AND HIS ORCHESTRA
Fred Rich (ldr) Bob Effros, Bunny Berigan (tp) *Charlie Butterfield* (tb)
Jimmy Dorsey (cl,as) Louis Martin (as) *Hymie Wolfson* (ts) Joe Venuti,
2 *unknown* (vn) *unknown* (p) Eddie Lang (g) *unknown* (sb), (d) Dick
Robertson [as Chester Leighton or Bobby Dixon on some] (vcl)

W 404881-A,B   **When I Take My Sugar To Tea** [Irving Kahal,
                Pierre Norman, Sammy Fain] vDR (cl solo)
    78: OKeh 41489, Odeon ONY-36204, Parlophone PNY-34197,
    (E) R-944
            *Odeon as REX KING AND HIS SOVEREIGNS, Parlophone
            as THE DEAUVILLE SYNCOPATORS*
    (100501-1) **78:** Harmony 1307-H, Velvet Tone 2343-V,
    Clarion 5277-C
            as FRANK AUBURN & HIS ORCH. (vBD)
    LP: World Records (E) SH410, Historical 33
W 404882-A,B,C **Rockin' Chair** [Hoagy Carmichael] vDR (cl solo)
    78: (unissued)
    (100502-1,4) **78:** Harmony 1306-H, Velvet Tone 2339-V, Clarion
    5273-C
            as FRANK AUBURN & HIS ORCH. (vBD)
W 404883-B   **The Waltz You Saved For Me** [Gus Kahn; Wayne
                King, Emil Flindt] (waltz) vDR (as Bobby Dix)
    78: OKeh 41487, Odeon ONY-36205, Parlophone PNY-34198,
    (E) R-975, Ariel (E) 4753
            *OKeh as ED LOYD AND HIS ORCHESTRA, Parlophone
            PNY- as FRANK AUBURN & HIS ORCHESTRA, Parlophone
            R-975 as ROOF GARDEN ORCHESTRA, Ariel as ARIEL
            DANCE ORCHESTRA*
    (100503-1) **78:** Harmony 1306-H, Velvet Tone 2341-V, Clarion
    5275-C
            as FRANK AUBURN & HIS ORCH. (vBD)
W 404884-A   **Dream A Little Dream Of Me** [Gus Kahn; Wilbur
                Schwandt, Fabian Andre] vDR
    78: OKeh 41493, Odeon ONY-36206, Parlophone PNY-34194,
    (E) R-1037
            OKeh as GOLDEN TERRACE DANCE ORCHESTRA
    (100504-1) **78:** Harmony 1307-H, Velvet Tone 2375-V, Clarion
    5309-C
            as CHESTER LEIGHTON AND HIS SOPHOMORES (vBD)
W 404885-A   **Do I Really Deserve It From You?** vDR
    78: Odeon ONY-36206, Parlophone PNY-34195
            Parlophone as THE DEAUVILLE SYNCOPATORS
    (100505-1) **78:** Harmony 1310-H, Velvet Tone 2353-V, Clarion
    5287 C
            as LLOYD KEATING'S MUSIC
W 404886-A   **Say A Little Prayer For Me** [Horatio Nicholls, Jos-
                eph Gilbert] vDR
    78: Odeon ONY-36205, Parlophone PNY-34196
            Odeon as LLOYD KEATING'S MUSIC
    (100506-1) **78:** Harmony 1309-H, Velvet Tone 2351-V, Clarion
    5285-C
            as LLOYD KEATING'S MUSIC (vBD)

Brunswick, New York, N.Y. Thursday, March 19, 1931
BOSWELL SISTERS
Jack Purvis (tp) Tom Dorsey (tb) **Jimmy Dorsey** (cl,as) *unknown* (ts),
(vn), (p) Chauncey Morehouse (d) Boswell Sisters (vcl)

BOSWELL SISTERS (Contd.)

E-36491-A   **Wha'dja Do To Me?** [Milton Ager] vBS
    78: Brunswick 6083, 80011, (C) 80011, (E) 01113, (F,G) A-
    9066, (GR) 826, Coral (C) 80011
    LP: Vocalion (E)VLP5, ASV Living Era (E) AJA5014, Ace Of
    Hearts (E) AH116
    TC: ASV Living Era (E) AJA5014, ProArte Digital PCD5
    CD: ASV Living Era (E) AJA5014, AJA5077, Collector's
    Classics COCD-21
E-36492-A   **When I Take My Sugar To Tea** [Irving Kahal,
                  Pierre Norman, Sammy Fain] vBS (cl solos)
    78: Brunswick 6083, 80011, (C) 80011, (E) 01113, (F,G) A-
    9066, (GR) 826, Coral (C) 80011, Decca 7-3
    LP: Vocalion (E) VLP5, ASV Living Era (E) AJA5014, Ace Of
    Hearts (E) AH116, Halcyon (E) HDL118
    TC: ASV Living Era (E) ZC AJA5014, Halcyon (E) HDL118,
    ProArte Digital PCD508
    CD: ASV Living Era CD AJA5014, AJA5118, AJA5190, L'Art
    Vocal (F) 13, Collector's Classics COCD-21, Flapper 7087

Columbia, New York, N.Y. Monday, April 6, 1931
TED RAPH AND HIS ORCHESTRA
Smith Ballew (vcl,dir) Mickey Bloom, *Mannie Klein* (tp) Ted Raph (tb)
Pete Pumiglio, **Jimmy Dorsey** (cl,as) Babe Russin (ts) Bruce Yantis (vn)
Bobby Van Eps (p) *Carl Kress or George Van Eps or Dick McDonough*
(g) *unknown* (bb,sb) Stan King (d)

W 151485-2   **Ev'rything That's Nice Belongs To You** [Bud Green;
                  Sam H. Stept] vSB
    78: Columbia 2450-D, Regal (Au) G-21070
W 151486-2   **Dream A Little Dream Of Me** [Gus Kahn; Wilbur
                  Schwandt, Fabian Andre] vSB
    78: Columbia 2450-D, (E) CB-326, Regal (Au) G-21070
W 151487-2   **When I Take My Sugar To Tea** [Irving Kahal,
                  Pierre Norman, Sammy Fain] vSB
    78: Columbia 2440-D, Regal (Au) G-21068
W 151488-2   **Please Don't Talk About Me When I'm Gone** [Sid-
                  ney Clare; Sam H. Stept] vSB
    78: Columbia 2440-D, (E) CB-326, Regal (Au) G-21068

Brunswick, New York, N.Y. Saturday, April 11, 1931
REGENT CLUB ORCHESTRA
Victor Young (ldr) Mickey Bloom, Mannie Klein (tp) Tom Dorsey (tb)
Jimmy Dorsey, Chester Hazlett (cl,as) "Mutt" Hayes (ts) Harry
Bluestone, Harry Hoffman, Walter Edelstein (vn) Joe Meresco (p) Perry
Botkin (g) Arthur Bernstein (sb) Larry Gomar (d) Smith Ballew (vcl)

E-36458-A,B   **Beautiful Love** (waltz) vSB (unissued)
E-36459-A   **After The Dance** (waltz) vSB
    78: Brunswick 6099

Brunswick, New York, N.Y. Monday, April 13, 1931
GRACE JOHNSTON
Jack Purvis (tp) Tom Dorsey (tb) **Jimmy Dorsey** (cl,as) Arthur Schutt
(p) Dick McDonough (g) *unknown* (sb) Stan King (d) Grace Johnston
(vcl)

E-36461-   **I'm Crazy 'Bout My Baby** [Alex Hill, Thomas "Fats"
                Waller] vGJ
        78: Melotone M-12151, Panachord (E) 25051
E-36462-   **I Wanna Be Around My Baby All The Time**
                [George W. Meyer; Joe Young] vGJ
        78: Melotone M-12151, Panachord (E) 25050

Brunswick, New York, N.Y. Wednesday, April 22, 1931
VICTOR YOUNG AND THE BRUNSWICK ORCHESTRA
Victor Young (ldr) *Frank Guarente [or] Charlie Margulis, unknown* (tp)
Tom Dorsey (tb) *Jimmy Dorsey* (cl,as) *Bennie Krueger* (as,bar) Larry
Binyon (cl,ts,fl) *Joe Venuti [or] Harry Hoffman* (vn) Arthur Schutt (p)
Eddie Lang (g) Joe Tarto (bb) *Larry Gomar* (d,vib) Dick Robertson (vcl)

E-36647-A   **The Hour Of Parting** [Gus Kahn; Mischa Spolian
                sky] vDR
        78: Brunswick 6116
E-36648-G   **The Hour Of Parting**
        78: (possible German or Argentine issue)
E-36649-A   **In The Candlelight** vDR
        78: Brunswick 6116
E-36650-G   **In The Candlelight**
        78: (possible German or Argentine issue)

Brunswick, New York, N.Y. Thursday, April 23, 1931
BOSWELL SISTERS
Victor Young (ldr) *Mannie Klein [or] Jack Purvis* (tp) Tom Dorsey (tb)
Jimmy Dorsey (cl,as) Joe Venuti (vn) Arthur Schutt (p) Eddie Lang (g)
Joe Tarto (sb) Chauncey Morehouse (d,vib) Boswell Sisters (vcl)

E-36654-A   **Roll On, Mississippi, Roll On** [Eugene West, James
                McCaffrey, Dave Ringle] vBS
        78: Brunswick 6109, 80012, (C) 80012, (E) 01136, (F,G) A-
        9081, Coral (C) 80012
        ET: AFRS America's Popular Music (series) #310, 807, 907
        LP: Ace Of Hearts (E) AH116, ASV Living Era (E) AJA5014,
        Vocalion (E) VLP5, Columbia Special Products P16493
        TC: ASV Living Era (E) ZC AJA5014, ProArte Digital PCD508
        CD: ASV Living Era (E) AJA5014, Flapper 7087, L'Art Vocal
        (F) 13, Collector's Classics COCD-21, Fremeaux (F) 9518
E-36655-A   **Shout, Sister, Shout** [Spencer Williams, Alex Hill,
                J. Tim Brymn] vBS
        78: Brunswick 6109, 6847, 80012, (C) 6847, 80012, (E) 01136,
        01416, (F) A-9390, (G) A-9081, (It) 4898, Coral (C) 80012,
        Lucky (J) 5016, 60021
        LP: Brunswick BL-58005, Ace Of Hearts (E) AH116, (Contd.)

BOSWELL SISTERS (Contd.)

> ASV Living Era (E) AJA5014, Vocalion (E) VLP5, Columbia
> Special Products P16493
> **TC:** ASV Living Era (E) ZC AJA5014, ProArte Digital PCD508,
> Radio Yesteryear Stack 7
> **CD:** ASV Living Era (E) AJA5014, L'Art Vocal (F) 13,
> Collector's Classics COCD-21, Flapper 7087

It is also possible, based on vague notations in ARC files that rejected takes of "Sing A Little Jingle" and "I Found A Million Dollar Baby" were cut by the Boswells on this date and April 27 (see May 22, 1931).

Brunswick, New York, N.Y. Wednesday, April 29, 1931
VICTOR YOUNG AND THE BRUNSWICK ORCHESTRA
Victor Young (ldr) *Frank Guarente [or] Charlie Margulis, unknown* (tp) Tom Dorsey (tb) **Jimmy Dorsey** (cl,as) Bennie Krueger (as,c-mel) Larry Binyon (ts,o) Joe Venuti, Harry Hoffman (vn) Art Schutt (p,celst) Eddie Lang (g) Hank Stern (bb) *Larry Gomar* (d) Smith Ballew (vcl)

E-36669-A	**Yours Is My Heart Alone** [Harry Smith, Ludwig Herzer, Fritz Loehrner; Franz Lehár] vSB (as solo)
	78: Brunswick 6117
E-36670-A	**Yours Is My Heart Alone** (as solo)
	78: Brunswick (SA) 41317
E-36671-A	**Have You Forgotten?** [Leo Robin; Nat Shilkret, Dana Suesse] vSB (as tag)
	78: Brunswick 6117
E-36672-A	**Beautiful Love** [Haven Gillespie; Victor Young, E. G. Van Alstyne, Wayne King] vSB
	78: Brunswick 6009
	as REGENT CLUB ORCHESTRA

Brunswick, New York, N.Y. Friday, May 1, 1931
DICK ROBERTSON AND HIS ORCHESTRA
Bob Effros, *Jack Purvis* (tp) Tom Dorsey (tb) **Jimmy Dorsey** (cl,as) *unknown* (ts) Bennie Krueger (c-mel) *Joe Venuti, unknown* (vn) *unknown* (p) Eddie Lang (g) *Hank Stern [or] Joe Tarto* (sb) *unknown* (d) Dick Robertson (vcl)

E-36678	**Ho-Hum!** [Edward Heyman; Dana Suesse] vDR (cl solo)
	78: Melotone M-12162, Panachord (E) 25056, (Au) P-12162, Mayfair (E) G-2023
	Mayfair as BOB RICHARDSON AND HIS ORCHESTRA
	TC: Audio Archives 1013
E-36679	**(There Ought To Be A) Moonlight Saving Time** [Irving Kahal, Harry Richman] vDR (cl solo)
	78: Melotone M-12162, Banner 32187, Panachord (E) 25056, Mayfair (E) G-2023
	Mayfair as BOB RICHARDSON AND HIS ORCHESTRA
	TC: Audio Archives 1013

E-36680   **I Wanna Sing About You** [Cliff Friend, Dave Drey-
                 er] vDR (as behind vocal)
    78: Melotone M-12163, Panachord (Au) P-12163

                 Dance, Princeton University, Princeton, N.J. Friday,
                 May 8, 1931
DORSEY BROTHERS PICKUP BAND*
Bunny Berigan (tp) "Bix" Beiderbecke (cnt) Tom Dorsey (tb) Jimmy
Dorsey, Artie Shaw (cl,as) Eddie Miller (ts) Min Leibrook (bsx) Terry
Shand (p) Carl Kress (g) *Ray Bauduc [or] Gene Krupa* (d) *(Sudhalter
and Evans 1974).

Columbia, New York, N.Y. Saturday, May 9, 1931
ANNETTE HANSHAW
Jimmy Dorsey (cl) Sam Prager (p) Eddie Lang (g) Annette Hanshaw (vcl)

365007-1,2   **(There Ought To Be A) Moonlight Saving Time**
                [Irving Kahal, Harry Richman] vAH (cl solo)
    78: Harmony 1324-H, Clarion 5327-C, Velvet Tone 2393-V,
    Parlophone (Au) R-967, Odeon (F) A-221261
    LP: Sunbeam P-512
365008-2,3   **Ho-Hum!** [Edward Heyman; Dana Suesse] vAH
                (cl solo)
    78: Harmony 1324-H, Clarion 5327-C, Velvet Tone 2393-V,
    Parlophone (Au) R-967, Odeon (F) A-221261
    LP: Sunbeam P-512 (-2)
    CD: Take Two 408 (-2)

ARC, New York, N.Y. Monday, May 11, 1931
ARC STUDIO BAND
Possible personnel includes Mannie Klein (tp) Tom Dorsey (tb) Jimmy
Dorsey (cl) Dick Cherwin (sb) Mildred Hunt, Ben Alley (vcl)

10617-3   **Ho-Hum!** [Edward Heyman; Dana Suesse] vMH
    78: Oriole 2267
10618-3   **Would You Like To Take A Walk? (Sumpin'
                 Good'll Come From That)** [Mort Dixon, Billy Rose;
                 Harry Warren] vMH
    78: Oriole 2267
        10617 and 10618 as MILDRED HUNT
10619-2   **The Little Church In The Valley** vBA
    78: Banner 32182
10620-2   **I Surrender Dear** [Gordon Clifford; Harry Barris]
                 vBA
    78: Banner 32182
        10619 and 10620 as BEN ALLEY

                 Dance, Beta Theta Phi, Yale University, New Haven,
                 Conn. Friday, May 15, 1931
DORSEY BROTHERS PICKUP BAND*
Personnel as May 8, 1931 except Lennie Hayton (p) Jules Bauduc (g)
Ray Bauduc (d) are replacements. *(Sudhalter and Evans 1974).

Brunswick, New York, N.Y. Saturday, May 16, 1931
VICTOR YOUNG AND THE BRUNSWICK ORCHESTRA
Victor Young (ldr) *Frank Guarente [or] Charlie Margulis, unknown* (tp)
Tom Dorsey (tb) **Jimmy Dorsey** (cl,as,bar) *unknown* (cl,as) Larry
Binyon (cl,ts,o) Joe Venuti, Harry Hoffman (vn) Arthur Schutt (p)
Eddie Lang (g) Joe Tarto (bb,sb) *Chauncey Morehouse [or] Larry
Gomar* (d,vib) Helen Rowland, Frank Munn (vcl)

E-36695-A   **You Forgot Your Gloves** (waltz) [Edward Eliscu; Ned
                   Lehack] vHR&FM
      78: Brunswick 6123, (E) O1207
E-36696-A   **Falling In Love** (waltz) [Earle T. Crocker; Henry Sul-
                   livan] vFM (bar solo)
      78: Brunswick 6123, (E) O1207

Confusion abounds about the next Boswell Sisters recordings. There
are those who say some were first cut April 23 and 27, 1931, but went
unreleased. There is also controversy over the personnel involved. As a
result, the author lists only the certain and most probable participants.

Brunswick, New York, N.Y. Friday, May 22, 1931
VICTOR YOUNG AND THE BRUNSWICK ORCHESTRA
Victor Young (ldr) 2 *unknown* (tp), Tom Dorsey (tb) **Jimmy Dorsey** (cl,
as,bar) *unknown* (cl,as) Vernon Hayes (ts) 4 *unknown* (vn) *unknown* (p),
(g), (sb) *Larry Gomar* (d,vib) Boswell Sisters (vcl)

E-36724-A,B   **Sing A Little Jingle** [Mort Dixon; Harry Warren]
                   vBS (cl,as solos)
      78: Brunswick 6128, (E) 1193
      LP: Jazum 25, Vocalion (E) VLP5
      CD: Collector's Classics COCD-21, Jazz Roots 56082
E-36725-G   **Sing A Little Jingle** vBS (scat vocal) (cl,as solos)
      78: Brunswick (G) A9076
      LP: JASS 1
      TC: JASS J-C-1
      CD: JASS J-CD-622
E-36726-A   **I Found A Million-Dollar Baby (In A Five-And-Ten-
                   Cent Store)** [Billy Rose, Mort Dixon; Harry Warren]
                   vBS
      78: Brunswick 6128, (E) 1193
      LP: Jazum 25, Vocalion (E) VLP5
      TC: Pro-Arte Digital PCD 486, Radio Yesteryear Stack 56
      CD: Pro-Arte Digital PCD 486, L'Art Vocal (F) 13, Collector's
      Classics COCD-21
E-36727-G   **I Found A Million-Dollar Baby (In A Five-And-Ten-
                   Cent Store)** (possibly a BS scat vocal)
      78: Brunswick (G) A9076

ARC, New York, N.Y. Monday, May 25, 1931
ARC STUDIO BAND
Mannie Klein (tp) Tom Dorsey (tb) **Jimmy Dorsey** (cl,as) Arthur Schutt
(p) *unknown* (g), (bb), (d) Chick Bullock, Dick Robertson (vcl)

10672-2   **(There Ought To Be A) Moonlight Saving Time**
        [Irving Kahal, Harry Richman] vCB (as solo)
      78: Perfect 12718, Oriole 2268, Banner 32184, Romeo 1636
10673-1   **I Wanna Sing About You** [Cliff Friend, Dave Drey-
        er] vCB (cl solo)
      78: Perfect 12718, Oriole 2268, Banner 32184, Romeo 1636
        10672, 10673 as CHICK BULLOCK
10674-   **Let's Get Friendly** vDR
      78: Perfect 12719, Banner 32193, Romeo 1637
10675-   **One Night Alone With You** vDR
      78: Perfect 12719, Banner 32193, Romeo 1637
        10674, 10675 as DICK ROBERTSON

Brunswick, New York, N.Y. Tuesday, May 26, 1931
RED NICHOLS AND HIS FIVE PENNIES
Red Nichols (tp,ldr) Glenn Miller (tb) **Jimmy Dorsey** (cl,as) Babe
Russin (ts) Jack Russin (p) Perry Botkin (g) Art Miller (sb) Ray
McKinley (d,vcl) Red McKenzie (vcl)

E-36830-A   **Just A Crazy Song (Hi-Hi-Hi)** [Chick Smith;
        Spencer Williams] (cl solo)
      78: Brunswick 6133, (E) O1153, (F) A-9090, (G) A-9090
      LP: Coral (G) 94269
E-36831-A   **You Rascal, You** [Sam Theard] vRedM (cl solo)
      78: Brunswick 6133, (E) O1153, (F) A-9090, (G) A-9090
      LP: Coral (G) 94269
      CD: Best Of Jazz (F) 4041
E-36832-A   **Moan, You Moaners** vRayM [Clarence Williams]
        (as solos)
      78: Brunswick 6149, (E) O1180, (F) A-9099, (G) A-9090
      LP: IAJRC 22

Brunswick, New York, N.Y. Wednesday, May 27, 1931
BILL (BOJANGLES) ROBINSON
Mannie Klein (tp) Tom Dorsey (tb) **Jimmy Dorsey** (cl) Arthur Schutt
(p) Eddie Lang (g), Joe Tarto (bb,sb) Stan King (d) Bill Robinson (vcl)

E-36833   **Just A Crazy Song (Hi-Hi-Hi)** [Chick Smith; Spen-
        cer Williams] vBR, band (cl solo)
      78: Brunswick 6134, 7705, (E) 1168, (G) A9091, Columbia
      30184
      LP: MCA 4634/35, 3519/20
      CD: ASV (E) AJA 5031
E-36834   **Keep A Song In Your Soul** [Alex Hill; Thomas
"Fats" Waller] vBR
      78: Brunswick 6134, 7705, (E) 1168, (G) A-9091, Columbia
      30183, Decca 7-2

Columbia, New York, N.Y. Wednesday, June 10, 1931
JOE VENUTI'S BLUE FOUR
Joe Venuti (vn,ldr) **Jimmy Dorsey** (cl,as,bar) Frank Signorelli (p) Eddie
Lang (g) Harold Arlen (vcl)

JOE VENUTI'S BLUE FOUR (Contd.)

404940-B   **Pardon Me, Pretty Baby (Don't I Look Familiar To You)** [Raymond W. Klages, Jack Meskill, Vincent Rose] vHA (bar,cl solo)
78: OKeh 41506, Clarion 5358-C, Harmony 1346-H, Velvet Tone 2422-V, Parlophone (E) R-993, (Aus) A-3268, (F) 85052, Odeon (G) A-286043
Clarion, Harmony, Velvet Tone as ALL-STAR RHYTHM BOYS

404941-B   **Little Girl** [Francis Henry, Madeline Hyde] vHA (bar,cl solo)
78: Parlophone (E) R-1003, (Aus) A-3588, (F) 85052, Odeon (G) A-286044, (E) OR-1003, Ariel (E) 4827
Ariel as ARIEL DANCE ORCHESTRA
(151655-1) **78:** Columbia 2488-D, (G) DW-4102
TC: Radio Yesteryear Stack 22

404942-B   **Little Buttercup** (later as "I'll Never Be The Same") [Matty Malneck, Frank Signorelli] (cl solo)
78: OKeh 41506, Clarion 5358-C, Harmony 1346-H, Velvet Tone 2422-V, Parlophone (E) R-1252, (Aus) A-3588, (F) 85076, Odeon (G) A-286063, O31750
Clarion, Harmony, Velvet Tone as ALL-STAR RHYTHM BOYS

404943-B   **Tempo di Modernage** [Joe Venuti, Eddie Lang] (cl solo)
78: Parlophone (E) R-1063, (F) 85076, Odeon (G) A-286049
English Parlophone title is "Tempo di Barrel"
(151656-1) **78:** Columbia 2488-D, (G) DW-4102
TC: Radio Yesteryear Stack 22
All sides also on **LP:** Columbia C2L24, **CD:** JSP (E) CD310

Brunswick, New York, N.Y. Thursday, June 11, 1931
RED NICHOLS AND HIS FIVE PENNIES
Red Nichols (tp,ldr) *Ruby Weinstein [and/or] Charlie Teagarden* (tp) Glenn Miller, George Stoll (tb) **Jimmy Dorsey** (cl,as,bar) Sid Stoneburn (as) Larry Binyon (ts,fl) Edward Bergman, Wladimir Selinsky (vn) Paul Mertz (p,arr) Art Miller (sb) Gene Krupa (d) Smith Ballew (vcl)

E-36855-A   **Slow But Sure** [Charles Newman, Charles Agnew, Audree Collins] vSB
78: Brunswick 6138, (Arg) 6138, (G) A-9094
6138 as LORING NICHOLS AND HIS ORCHESTRA
LP: Collector's Must (It) M-8003

E-36856-A   **Little Girl** [Francis Henry, Madeline Hyde] vSB (cl solo)
78: Brunswick 6138, (Arg) 6138, (G) A-9094
6138 as LORING NICHOLS AND HIS ORCHESTRA
LP: Collector's Must (It) M-8003

E-36857-A   **How The Time Can Fly** [Walter Donaldson] vSB (arrPM) (bar solo)

78: Brunswick 6164, (F) A-9140
LP: Collector's Must (It) M-8003

Columbia, New York, N.Y. Monday, June 15, 1931
FRED RICH AND HIS ORCHESTRA
Fred Rich (ldr) Bunny Berigan (tp,vcl) *unknown* (tp) *Tom Dorsey* (tb)
Jimmy Dorsey (cl,as) *unknown* (as), (ts) Joe Venuti (vn) *unknown* (p),
(acc) Eddie Lang (g) *unknown* (bb), (d) Scrappy Lambert (vcl)

W 151604-1,(2)   **At Your Command** [Harry Barris, Harry Tobias,
                  Bing Crosby] vBB
    78: Columbia 2484-D
    LP: Merritt 501, Nostalgia (Swe) NOST-7638
    TC: Radio Yesteryear Stack 66
W 151604-3   **At Your Command** vSL (unissued)
W 151605-2   **The Hour Of Parting** [Gus Kahn; Mischa Spolian-
                  sky] vSL
    78: Columbia 2494-D
W 151606-1   **Pardon Me, Pretty Baby (Don't I Look Familiar
                  To You)** [Raymond W. Klages, Jack Meskill,
                  Vincent Rose] vSL
    78: Columbia 2484-D, (J) 1217, Regal (E) MR-403
W 151607-2   **As Long As You're There** [Edgar Leslie; James V.
                  Monaco] vSL (cl solo)
    78: Columbia 2494-D

Whether take three of 151604 was made as "protection" in case the
Berigan vocal was later rejected by Columbia officials, or resulted from
Lambert being late, is unknown. In any event the released version is the
first known recording of a Berigan vocal.

Brunswick, New York, N.Y. Friday, June 19, 1931
SEGER ELLIS
Unknown (tp) Tom Dorsey (tb) **Jimmy Dorsey** (cl,as) *unknown* (p)
Eddie Lang (g) *unknown* (d,vib) Seger Ellis (vcl, possibly unknown
piano)

E 36872-A,B   **Nevertheless (I'm In Love With You)** [Bert Kalmar,
                  Harry Ruby] vSE (cl,as solos)
    78: Brunswick 6135, (E) 1167, Panachord (Au) P-11982
        Panachord as HERVY POWELL
E 36873-A,B   **As Long As You're There** [Edgar Leslie; James V.
                  Monaco] vSE (cl solo)
    78: Brunswick 6135, (E) 1167, Panachord (Au) P-11981
        Panachord as HERVY POWELL

Brunswick, New York, N.Y. Wednesday, June 24, 1931
RED NICHOLS AND HIS FIVE PENNIES
Red Nichols (tp,ldr) Glenn Miller (tb) **Jimmy Dorsey** (cl,as) Babe
Russin (ts) Jack Russin (p) Perry Botkin (g) Art Miller (sb) *Ray
McKinley [or] Gene Krupa* (d) Red McKenzie (vcl)

RED NICHOLS AND HIS FIVE PENNIES (Contd.)

E-36877-A   (How Long,) How Long Blues [Leroy Carr] vRM
                   (cl solo)
          78: Brunswick 6160, (E) O1213, (G) A-9117
E-36878-A   Fan It [Frankie Jaxon, Don Howell] vRM (cl solo)
          78: Brunswick 6160, (E) O1213, (G) A-9117
          CD: Best Of Jazz (F) 4041
          Both sides also on **LP:** IAJRC 22

Columbia, New York, N.Y. Tuesday, June 30, 1931
MOUND CITY BLUE BLOWERS
Red McKenzie (comb,vcl,ldr) Muggsy Spanier (cnt) **Jimmy Dorsey**
(cl,as) Coleman Hawkins (ts) Jack Russin (p) Eddie Condon (bj,*vcl*) Jack
Bland (g) Al Morgan (sb) Josh Billings (d)

404966-C   **Georgia On My Mind** [Stewart Gorrell; Hoagy Car-
                   michael] vRM (cl solo)
          78: OKeh 41515
          (35105?) **78:** Harmony 1375-H, Clarion 5389-C, Velvet Tone
          2453-V, Parlophone (E) R-1071, 85104, Odeon (G) A-286051,
          031813, Regal (Au) G-21480, United Hot Clubs of America 51
                   *Harmony, Clarion and Velvet Tone as TENNESSEE MUSIC
                   MEN, Parlophones and Odeons as RED McKENZIE AND
                   THE CELESTIAL BEINGS, UHCA as RED McKENZIE AND
                   THE MOUND CITY BLUE BLOWERS, Regal as MISSI-
                   SSIPPI JAZZ KINGS*
404967-B   **I Can't Believe That You're In Love With Me**
                   [Clarence Gaskill; Jimmy McHugh] vRM
          78: OKeh 41515
          (35105?) **78:** Harmony 1375-H, Clarion 5389-C, Velvet Tone
          2453-V, Parlophone (E) R-1003, (Au) A-3339, 85104, Odeon (G)
          A-286044, (E) OR-1003, United Hot Clubs of America 52
                   *Harmony, Clarion and Velvet Tone as TENNESSEE MUSIC
                   MEN, Parlophones and Odeons as RED McKENZIE AND
                   THE CELESTIAL BEINGS, UHCA as RED McKENZIE AND
                   THE MOUND CITY BLUE BLOWERS*
          First two sides also on **LP:** Gardenia 4008, Odeon (G) SMS8, Jass
          607, CBS 68227, **TC:** Columbia/Legacy C2T 52942, CT52930,
          CD: Columbia/Legacy C2K 52942
404994-A   **The Darktown Strutters' Ball** [Shelton Brooks]
                   vRM [as Jack King] (cl solo)
          78: OKeh 41526
          (351052-1) Columbia 5389-C, (C) C-6180, Harmony 1378-
          H, Velvet Tone 2456-V, Parlophone (E) R-1044, 85184, (Au) A-
          3282, B-71213, Odeon (Arg) A-286048, (It) B-35638, (G)
          031813, Columbia (dubbing) 36281
                   *Columbia 5389-C as MOUND CITY BLUE BLOWERS,
                   Harmony and Velvet Tone as TENNESSEE MUSIC MEN,
                   Parlophones and Odeons as RED McKENZIE AND THE
                   CELESTIAL BEINGS, Columbia 36281 as RED McKENZIE
                   AND THE MOUND CITY BLUE BLOWERS*

LP: Gardenia 4008, Odeon (G) SMS8, Jass 607, CBS 68227
404995-A   **You Rascal, You** [Sam Theard] vRM,*EC* [as King &
                  King] (cl solo)
   78: OKeh 41526
   (130482) **78:** Harmony 1378-H,Clarion 5392-C, Velvet Tone
   2456-V, Columbia (E) DB-5007, Parlophone 85184, (Au) A-3282
   LP: Gardenia 4008, Jass 607, CBS 68227
      Harmony, Clarion and Velvet Tone as TENNESSEE MUSIC
      MEN, Parlophones as RED McKENZIE AND THE CELEST-
      IAL BEINGS, Columbia as RED McKENZIE AND THE
      MOUND CITY BLUE BLOWERS

Brunswick, New York, N.Y. Wednesday, July 8, 1931
BOSWELL SISTERS
Tom Dorsey (tb,ldr) *Mannie Klein [or] Jack Purvis* (tp) **Jimmy Dorsey**
(cl,as) Joe Venuti (vn) *Martha Boswell [or] Artie Schutt* (p) Eddie Lang
(g) Joe Tarto (sb) Stan King (d) Boswell Sisters (vcl)

E 36911-A   **It's The Girl!** [Dave Oppenheim; Abel Baer] vBS
                   (cl solo)
   78: Brunswick 6151, 80014, (C) 80014, (E) 01181, (F,G) A-
   9112, (GR) 829, Coral (C) 80014
   LP: Brunswick BL-58005, Decca (E) RALD-510, Ace Of Hearts
   (E) AH116, Halcyon (E) HDL118, Vocalion (E) VLP5, Columbia
   Special Products P16493, ASV Living Era (E) AJA5014
   TC: Halcyon (E) CHDL118, ASV Living Era (E) ZC AJA5014,
   ProArte Digital PCD550
   CD: ASV Living Era CD AJA5014, L'Art Vocal (F) 13, Col-
   lector's Classics COCD-21, Jazz Roots 56082, Fremeaux (F) 9518
E 36912-A   **It's You** [Andy Razaf; Thomas "Fats" Waller] vBS
   78: Brunswick 6151, (E) 01181, (F,G) A-9112, (GR) 829
   LP: Ace Of Hearts (E) AH116, Vocalion (E) VLP5, Columbia
   Special Products P16493, ASV Living Era (E) AJA5014
   TC: ASV Living Era (E) ZC AJA5014
   CD: ASV Living Era CD AJA5014, Collector's Classics COCD-
   21, Flapper 7087, Smithsonian 048-21, Fremeaux (F) 9518

Brunswick, New York, N.Y. Friday, July 24, 1931
CONNIE BOSWELL
Victor Young (ldr) Mannie Klein (tp) Tom Dorsey (tb) **Jimmy Dorsey,**
unknown (cl,as) Harry Hoffman, *unknown* (vn), (p) Dick McDonough
(g) Joe Tarto (sb) Chauncey Morehouse (d) Connie Boswell (vcl)

E 36987-A   **I'm All Dressed Up With A Broken Heart** [Stella
                   Unger, Harold Stern; Fred Fisher] vCB (cl solo)
   78: Brunswick 6162, (E) 1198
   LP: Take Two TT209, ASV Living Era AJA5014
E 36988-A   **What Is It?** [Harry Tobias; Harry Barris] vCB
   78: Brunswick 6162, (E) 1198, (E) 1252
   LP: Take Two TT209, ASV Living Era AJA5014
   Both sides also on **TC:** ASV Living Era ZC AJA5014, **CD:** ASV
   Living Era CD AJA5014

Victor, New York, N.Y. Wednesday, July 29, 1931
NAT SHILKRET AND THE VICTOR ORCHESTRA
Nat Shilkret (dir) 2 *unknown* (tp) *unknown* (tb) **Jimmy Dorsey**, *unknown*
(cl,as) *unknown* (ts) *unknown* (bar) 2 *unknown* (vn) *unknown* (cel), (p),
(g), (bb), (d) Paul Small, Frank Luther (vcl)

70132-1   **Kiss Me Goodnight, Not Goodbye** (waltz) [James F.
                 Hanley, Jules Firthman] vPS
    78: Victor 22782, His Master's Voice (E) B-6084, (Au) EA-953
        as THE TROUBADORS
70133-1   **A Little Less Of Moonlight (A Little More Of
                 Love)** vPS
    78: Victor 22781, His Master's Voice (Au) EA-987
70134-1   **I Apologize** [Al Hoffman, Al Goodhart, Edward G.
                 Nelson] vPS
    78: Victor 22781, His Master's Voice (E) B-6084, (Au) EA-973

Once again Jimmy leads a "Travelers" session for ARC and like the
one on February 26 the files indicate that only one trombone is present,
although others continue to list Glenn Miller as a second trombone.
There is a Miller presence, but it is only as an arranger. Additionally,
Jimmy demonstrates his command of the clarinet with some excellent
solos, especially in "I Can't Get Mississippi Off My Mind" and "Parkin'
In The Moonlight," both of which begin to hint of the Dorsey Brothers'
sound to come.

Brunswick, New York, N.Y. Thursday, July 30, 1931
THE TRAVELERS (Dorsey Brothers' Orchestra)
Jimmy Dorsey (cl,as,ldr) Bunny Berigan, *Charlie Margulis [or] Bill
Moore, Louis Garcia* (tp) Tom Dorsey (tb) Elmer Feldkamp (cl,as,vcl)
Bud Freeman (ts) Arthur Schutt (p) Eddie Lang (g) *Joe Tarto [or] Art
Bernstein* (sb) Stan King (d) Paul Small (vcl) Glenn Miller (arr)

E 36946-   **I Can't Get Mississippi Off My Mind** [Joseph
                 Young; Harry Akst] vEF (cl,as solos)
    78: Melotone M-12230
    LP: Collector's Must (It) M8003, Shoestring SS115
E 36947-   **I Apologize** [Al Hoffman, Al Goodhart, Edward G.
                 Nelson] vPS (as solos)
    78: Brunswick (F) A9146, Melotone M-12227, Panachord (E)
    25167, Mayfair (E) G-2081, Embassy (Au) E147
        *Mayfair as CLIFF BRYAN AND HIS ORCHESTRA, Embassy
        as BROADWAY ORCHESTRA*
    LP: Collector's Must (It) M8003, Shoestring SS115
E 36948-   **Beggin' For Love** [Irving Berlin] vPS (as solo)
    78: Brunswick (E) 01224, Melotone M-12227, Panachord (Au)
    P-12228
        Brunswick as JIMMY DORSEY'S TRAVELLERS [sic]
    LP: Collector's Must (It) M8003, Shoestring SS115
E 36949-   **Parkin' In The Moonlight** [Charles O'Flynn, Charles
                 Tobias; Peter De Rose] vPS (as,cl solos)
    78: Brunswick 6164, (E) 01224, (F) A-9140

> *6164 as THE NEW YORKERS, 01224 as JIMMY DORSEY'S*
> *TRAVELLERS [sic], A-9140 as THE NEW YORKERS, vocal*
> *refrain by THE BOSWELL SISTERS [sic]*
> LP: Collector's Must (It) M8003, Shoestring SS115
> CD: Hep (UK) 1005
> All sides also on TC: Radio Yesteryear Stack 66, CD: Jazz Oracle
> (C) BDW8006

Brunswick, New York, N.Y. Tuesday, August 4, 1931
DICK ROBERTSON AND HIS ORCH. (Brunswick Studio Band)
Bob Effros, *Jack Purvis* (tp) Tom Dorsey (tb) **Jimmy Dorsey** (cl,as)
unknown (as), (ts) *Joe Venuti, unknown* (vn) *unknown* (p) Eddie Lang
(g) *Hank Stern [or] Joe Tarto* (sb) *unknown* (d) Dick Robertson (vcl)

E 36999-   **I'm Just A Dancing Sweetheart** [Charles Tobias;
          Peter De Rose] vDR
   78: Melotone M-12226, Panachord (E) 25081
E 37000-   **The Kiss That You've Forgotten (Is The Kiss I
          Can't Forget)** [Dorothy Dick; Harry Link] vDR
   78: Melotone M-12226
E 37001-   **A Little Less Of Moonlight (A Little More Of You)**
          [Irving Kahal; J. Russell Robinson] vDR (as behind
          vocal)
   78: Melotone M-12229
E 37002-   **What Is It?** [Harry Tobias; Harry Barris] vDR
   78: Melotone M-12229
   TC: Audio Archives 1013

The next day, Leon "Bix" Beiderbecke died at age twenty-eight after
a bout with pneumonia. The Dorseys had known Bix since the Goldkette
days but probably never noted the similarities between Bix and themselves: Tommy's playing was also technical perfection and lyric under-
statement; Jimmy also had an affinity for alcohol, albeit less serious.
Though they had booked Bix in 1930 and early 1931, by now they were
involved with that new trumpeter from the Midwest with the same
initials (and a similar drinking problem), Bunny Berigan.

Brunswick, New York, N.Y. Monday, August 17, 1931
VICTOR YOUNG AND THE BRUNSWICK ORCHESTRA
Victor Young (ldr) *Frank Guarente [or] Charlie Margulis,* Mannie
Klein, Billy Moore (tp) Tom Dorsey, *unknown* (tb) **Jimmy Dorsey**
(cl,as) 2 *unknown* (as) *Larry Binyon* (ts) Joe Venuti, 2 *unknown* (vn)
unknown (p) Eddie Lang (g) *Joe Tarto [or] Art Bernstein* (sb) Chauncey
Morehouse (d) Paul Small, Boswell Sisters (vcl)

E-37079-   **How's Your Uncle?** [Dorothy Fields; Jimmy Mc-
          Hugh] vPS
   78: Brunswick 6171
          as JESSE STAFFORD AND HIS ORCHESTRA
E-37080-A **Makin' Faces At The Man In The Moon** [Ned Wash-
          ington, Max Rich, Kate Smith; Al Hoffman] vBS (cl
          solos) (Contd.)

VICTOR YOUNG AND THE BRUNSWICK ORCHESTRA (Contd.)

>   **78:** Brunswick 6170, (E) 1221, (G) A-9141
>   *as BOSWELL SISTERS accomp. by THE NEW YORKERS*
>   **LP:** Ace Of Hearts (E) AH116, Vocalion (E) VLP5
>   **CD:** Collector's Classics COCD-21
> E-37081-A   **Beggin' For Love** [Irving Berlin] vPS
>   **78:** Brunswick 6171
>   *as JESSE STAFFORD AND HIS ORCHESTRA*
> E-37082-A   **(With You On My Mind I Find) I Can't Write The
>   Words** [Buddy Fields; Gerald Marks] vBS (cl solos)
>   **78:** Brunswick 6170, (E) 1221, (G) A-9141
>   *as BOSWELL SISTERS accomp. by THE NEW YORKERS*
>   **LP:** Ace Of Hearts (E) AH116, Vocalion (E) VLP5
>   **CD:** Collector's Classics COCD-21, Flapper 7087

Despite conflicting beliefs that the four preceding sides were made in two sessions, August 17 and 18, the author lists all four on one date because the band personnel appears to be the same. The August 17-18 conflict probably comes from a late-hour session that went past midnight to accommodate the Boswells. Bringing the same personnel back at full session rates for two "throw-away" sides the next day rather than paying overtime for the one session is a luxury Young couldn't afford in 1931.

Brunswick, New York, N.Y. Wednesday, August 19, 1931
BING CROSBY accomp. by VICTOR YOUNG AND HIS ORCH.
Victor Young (ldr) *Frank Guarente [or] Charlie Margulis, unknown* (tp) Tom Dorsey (tb) **Jimmy Dorsey** (cl,as) Bennie Krueger (as) *unknown* (ts) Harry Hoffman, 3 *unknown* (vn) *unknown* (p) Eddie Lang (g) Hank Stern (bb) Larry Gomar (d) Bing Crosby (vcl)

> E 37085   **I Apologize** [Al Hoffman, Al Goodhart, Edward G.
>   Nelson] vBC
>   **78:** Brunswick 6179, (E) 1219, (E) 05934
>   **EP:** Brunswick BL-58001, EB-71029
>   **LP:** Brunswick LA-8741, Ace Of Hearts (E) AH88, Jonzo (E)
>   JZ-11
> E 37086   **Dancing In The Dark** [Howard Dietz; Arthur
>   Schwartz] vBC
>   **78:** Brunswick 6169, 80056, (E) 1256, (E) 02315, 9-7001
>   **ET:** AFRS "America's Popular Music" 508, 564
>   **EP:** Brunswick BL-54005, BL-58001, EB-71010
>   **LP:** Brunswick LA-8741, Ace Of Hearts (E) AH88, Jonzo (E)
>   JZ-11
>   **CD:** ASV Living Era CD AJA5072
> E 37087   **Star Dust** [Mitchell Parish; Hoagy Carmichael]
>   vBC (as solo)
>   **78:** Brunswick 6169, 80056, (E) 1252, (E) 02101, (E) 02312
>   **EP:** Brunswick 9-7001, BL-58001, EB-71010
>   **LP:** Brunswick LA-8741, Jazum 30, Ace Of Hearts (E) AH48,
>   AH88, Vocalion (E) VLP1, Jonzo (E) JZ-11
>   **CD:** ASV Living Era CD AJA5072, AJA5190

ARC, New York, N.Y. Thursday, August 20, 1931
GENE AUSTIN AND HIS ORCHESTRA (ARC Studio Band)
Bob Effros, *unknown* (tp) Tom Dorsey (tb) **Jimmy Dorsey** (cl,as)
unknown (as), (ts) *Joe Venuti, unknown* (vn) *unknown* (p) Eddie Lang
(g) Hank Stern (sb) *unknown* (d) Gene Austin (vcl)

10777-3   **Who Am I?** [Gordon Clifford; Alfred Newman] vGA
     78: Oriole 2333
10778-3   **What Is It?** [Harry Tobias; Harry Barris] vGA
     78: Perfect 15513, Banner 32259, Decca (E) F-2619, Oriole
     2333, Melotone 91197
     Decca as GENE AUSTIN AND HIS DANCE ORCH.
10779-1,2   **Maybe It's The Moon** [Richard A. Whiting] vGA
     (cl solo)
     78: Perfect 15514, Banner 32256, Oriole 2335, Conqueror 7853,
     Royale 391198 (-1)
10780-2   **How's Your Uncle?** [Dorothy Fields; Jimmy Mc-
     Hugh] vGA (as solo)
     78: Perfect 15514, Banner 32256, Decca (E) F-2619, Oriole
     2335, Royale 391198
     Decca as GENE AUSTIN AND HIS DANCE ORCII.

ARC, New York, N.Y. Friday, August 21, 1931
CHICK BULLOCK
Mannie Klein (tp) Tom Dorsey (tb) **Jimmy Dorsey** (cl,as) *unknown* (ts)
Russ Morgan (p) Dick McDonough (g) Dick Cherwin (sb) Stan King (d)
Chick Bullock (vcl)

10769-2,3   **You Rascal You** [Sam Theard] vCB (cl solo)
     78: Banner 32252, Domino 51004, Ace (C) 351004 (dub),
     Romeo 1697, Oriole 2325, Perfect 15506
     TC: Audio Archives 1004
10770-2,3   **I Can't Get Mississippi Off My Mind** [Joseph
     Young; Harry Akst] vCB (cl,as solos)
     78: Banner 32252, Oriole 2325, Ace (C) 351002 (dub), Romeo
     1697, Perfect 15506
     Ace as JACK BERGER AND HIS HOTEL ASTOR ORCH.
     TC: Audio Archives 1004

Brunswick, New York, N.Y. Thursday, August 27, 1931
BOSWELL SISTERS
Tom Dorsey (tb,ldr) Mannie Klein (tp) **Jimmy Dorsey** (cl,as) *unknown*
(vn) Martha Boswell (p) Eddie Lang (g) Joe Tarto (sb) Stan King (d)
Boswell Sisters (vcl)

E 37112-A   **Shine On, Harvest Moon** [Nora Bayes, Jack Nor-
     worth] vBS (cl solo)
     78: Brunswick 6173, 80013, (C) 80013, (E) 01218, (F,G) A-
     9143, Lucky (J) 60161, Coral (C) 80013
     LP: Brunswick BL-58005, Ace Of Hearts (E) AH116, Vocalion
     (E) VLP5, ASV Living Era AJA5014
     TC: ASV Living Era ZC AJA5014 (Contd.)

BOSWELL SISTERS (Contd.)

    CD: ASV Living Era AJA5014, Collectors Classics COCD-21, Flapper 7087

E 37113-A   **Heebie Jeebies** [Boyd Atkins, Connie Boswell] vBS (cl solo)
    78: Brunswick 6173, 80013, (C) 80013, (E) 01218, (F,G) A-9143, Coral (C) 80013
    ET: AFRS America's Popular Music #404; AFRS Scrapbook #169
    LP: Brunswick BL-58005, Ace Of Hearts (E) AH116, Vocalion (E) VLP5
    TC: ProArte Digital PCD550
    CD: ProArte Digital CDD550, Collectors Classics COCD-21, Flapper 7087

ARC, New York, N.Y. Thursday, August 27, 1931
ARC STUDIO BAND
Mannie Klein (tp) Tom Dorsey (tb) **Jimmy Dorsey** (cl,as) *unknown* (vn) Arthur Schutt (p,celst) Eddie Lang (g) Joe Tarto (sb) Stan King (d) Chick Bullock, Ben Alley (vcl)

10785-1   **(With You On My Mind I Find) I Can't Write The Words** [Buddy Fields; Gerald Marks] vCB (cl solo)
    78: Perfect 12748, Banner 32247, Romeo 1695, Oriole 2331, Conquerer 7854
10786-1   **Sweet And Lovely** [Harry Tobias, Jules Lemare, Gus Arnheim] vCB
    78: Perfect 12748, Banner 32247, Romeo 1695, Oriole 2331, Imperial 2621, Conqueror 7852
10787   **Begging For Love** [Irving Berlin] vBA
    78: issues (if any) unknown
10788   **I'm Just A Dancing Sweetheart** [Charles Tobias; Peter De Rose] vBA
    78: issues (if any) unknown

Durium, New York, N.Y. August 1931
FRED RICH'S RADIO ORCHESTRA
Fred Rich (ldr) *Tommy Gott, Bunny Berigan, unknown* (tp) *Tom Dorsey [or] Lloyd Turner, Charlie Butterfield* (tb) **Jimmy Dorsey** (cl,as) Elmer Feldkamp (cl,as,vcl) 2 *unknown* (ts) Cornell Smelser (acc) Joe Venuti (vn) *unknown* (p) Eddie Lang (g) Hank Stern (bb) *unknown* (d), vcl trio

-0-   **Little Girl** [Francis Henry, Madeline Hyde] vEF&3 (cl solo)
    78: Hit-Of-The-Week J-4
    LP: Sunbeam MFC-9, World Records (E) SH410, Sandy Hook SH 2044, Ristic (E) 51
-0-   **It's The Girl!** [Dave Oppenheim; Abel Baer] vEF&3
    78: Hit-Of-The-Week K-1
    LP: Sunbeam MFC-9, World Records (E) SH410, Sandy Hook SH 2044, Ristic (E) 51

ARC, New York, N.Y. Wednesday, September 2, 1931
GENE AUSTIN AND HIS ORCHESTRA (Ed Kirkeby house band)
Ed Kirkeby (ldr) Bob Effros, *unknown* (tp) Tom Dorsey (tb) **Jimmy
Dorsey** (cl,as) *unknown* (as) Elmer Feldkamp (ts,vcl) 2 *unknown* (vn)
unknown (p) Eddie Lang (g) Hank Stern (sb) *unknown* (d) Gene Austin
(vcl)

10777-6   **Who Am I?** [Gordon Clifford; Alfred Newman] vGA
    78: Perfect 15513, Oriole 2333, Banner 32259, Decca (E) F-
    2686, Imperial (E) 2627
10793-1,2,3   **If I Didn't Have You** vGA(unissued, *remade 9/17/31*)
10794-1,2,3   **In A Dream** vGA (unissued, *remade 9/17/31*)

ARC, New York, N.Y. Thursday, September 3, 1931
EDDIE KIRKEBY AND HIS ORCHESTRA

10791-6   **I Don't Know Why (I Just Do)** [Roy Turk; Fred E.
    Ahlert] vEF
    78: Perfect 15518, Oriole 2339, Romeo 1711, Conqueror 7857
    *Perfect as JACK BERGER AND HIS HOTEL ASTOR
    ORCH., Oriole, Romeo, Conqueror as THE ARISTOCRATS*
10795-2   **There's Nothing Too Good For My Baby** [Harry
    Akst, Benny Davis, Eddie Cantor] vEF
    78: Perfect 15524, Banner 32279, Apex 41422
    as ED KIRKEBY AND HIS ORCHESTRA
10796-2   **Guilty** [Gus Kahn; Harry Akst, Richard A. Whiting]
    vGA (cl solo)
    78: Perfect 15526, Banner 32285, Oriole 2352, Romeo 1721,
    Ace (C) 351014, Domino DL-51014, Melotone 91211, Royale (C)
    391211, Sun 251014, Imperial (E) 2617
10797-1,2   **Blue Kentucky Moon** [Walter Donaldson] vGA (cl
    solo)
    78: Perfect 15526, Banner 32285, Romeo 1721, Domino DL-
    51014, Ace (C) 351014, Melotone 91211, Royale (C) 391311, Sun
    251014
    10796 and 10797 as GENE AUSTIN AND HIS ORCHESTRA

Victor, New York, N.Y. Thursday, September 3, 1931
RUSS COLUMBO
Mike Mosiello (tp) **Jimmy Dorsey** (cl) *Lou Raderman* (vn) *Milt
Rettenberg* (p) Carl Kress (g) *Dick Cherwin* (sb) Russ Columbo (vcl)

BS-70210-1   **I Don't Know Why (I Just Do)** [Roy Turk; Fred E.
    Ahlert] vRC (cl solo)
    78: Victor 22801, His Master's Voice (E) B-4042, (Au) EA-966
BS-70211-1   **Guilty** [Gus Kahn; Harry Akst, Richard A. Whiting]
    vRC (cl solo)
    78: Victor 22801, His Master's Voice (E) B-3997
BS-70212-1   **You Call It Madness (But I Call It Love)** [Con
    Conrad, Gladys Dubois, Paul Gregory] vRC
    78: Victor 22802, Bluebird B-6503, H.M.V (E) B-3984
    all sides also on **CD:** Living Era (E) AJA 5234

Brunswick, New York, N.Y. Friday, September 4, 1931
BRUNSWICK STUDIO BAND
Victor Young (ldr) *Frank Guarente [or] Charlie Margulis, unknown* (tp)
Tom Dorsey (tb) **Jimmy Dorsey** (cl,as) *Bennie Krueger* (cl,as,bar) Larry
Binyon (cl,ts,fl) Joe Venuti, Harry Hoffman, 2 *unknown* (vn) Arthur
Schutt (p) Eddie Lang (g) Joe Tarto (sb) *Larry Gomar* (d,vib) Helen
Rowland, Frank Munn, Paul Small (vcl)

E 37150-   **Tonight Or Never** [Harold Adamson; Burton Lane]
                vHR&FM
      78: Brunswick 6178, (E) 1266
E 37151-   **Have A Heart** [Harold Adamson; Burton Lane] vFM
                (as solo)
      78: Brunswick 6178, (E) 1266
                both sides as VICTOR YOUNG & THE BRUNSWICK ORCH.
E 37152-   **Now That You're Gone** [Gus Kahn; Ted FioRito]
                vPS (as solo)
      78: Brunswick 6175
                as THE NEW YORKERS

Columbia, New York, N.Y. Thursday, September 10, 1931
FRED RICH AND HIS ORCHESTRA
Fred Rich (ldr) Tommy Gott, *Bunny Berigan [or] Mannie Klein* (tp)
Tom Dorsey (tb) **Jimmy Dorsey,** Tony Parenti (cl,as) *unknown* (ts) Joe
Venuti, Lew Conrad (vn) *unknown* (p) Eddie Lang (g) Joe Tarto (bb)
Stan King (d) Smith Ballew (vcl)

W 151777-2   **If I Didn't Have You** [E. Y. Harburg, Milton Ager]
                vSB (cl solo)
      78: Columbia 2536-D, Regal (Au) G-21344
W 151778-2   **As Time Goes By** [Herman Hupfield] vSB (cl solo)
      78: Columbia 2536-D, Regal (Au) G-21344
                as THE COLUMBIANS
      151777, 151778 also on **LP:** Bunny LP1931
W 151779-2   **I'm Just A Dancing Sweetheart** [Charles Tobias;
                Peter De Rose] (waltz) vSB
      78: Columbia 2534-D, Regal (Au) G-21189
W 151780-2   **Kiss Me Goodnight, Not Good-bye** [James F. Han-
                ley, Furthman] (waltz) vSB
      78: Columbia 2534-D, Regal (Au) G-21189

Columbia, New York, N.Y. Thursday, September 10, 1931
JOE VENUTI'S RHYTHM BOYS
Joe Venuti (vn,ldr) **Jimmy Dorsey** (cl,as,bar) Lennie Hayton (p,celst)
Eddie Lang (g) Paul Graselli (d) *Harold Arlen [or] Paul Small* (vcl)

W-151790-1   **There's No Other Girl** [J. Russell Robinson, Benny
                Davis] *vHA or PS* (cl solo)
      78: Columbia 2335-D, Parlophone (E) R-1287, (Aus) A-3463
W-151791-1   **Now That I Need You, You're Gone** *vHA or PS*
                (cl solo)
      78: Columbia 2335-D, Parlophone (E) R-1287, (Aus) A-3463

W-151792-1 **The Wolf Wobble** [Joe Venuti, Eddie Lang] (as solo)
  78: Columbia 2589-D, Parlophone (E) R-1071, (Aus) A-3292, Odeon (G) A-286051
    Parlophone (E), Odeon as JOE VENUTI'S BLUE FOUR
  LP: Odeon (G) SMS9
  TC: Radio Yesteryear Stack 22
W-151793-1 **To To Blues** [Joe Venuti, Eddie Lang] (based on "Someday Sweetheart") (cl solo)
  78: Parlophone (E) R-1115, (Au) A-3292, Odeon (G) A-286054
    Parlophone (E), Odeon as JOE VENUTI'S BLUE FOUR
  LP: Odeon (G) SMS9
  All sides also on **CD:** JSP (E) CD310

Brunswick, New York, N.Y. Monday, September 14, 1931
BRUNSWICK STUDIO BAND
Bennie Krueger (ldr) 2 *unknown* (tp) Tom Dorsey (tb) **Jimmy Dorsey** (cl,as), *unknown* (as), (ts) 3 *unknown* (vn) Joe Moresco (p) Eddie Lang (g) Artie Bernstein (sb) Larry Gomar (d,vib) Paul Small, Dick Robertson, Bing Crosby (vcl)

E 37153 **There's A Time And Place For Everything** [Roy Turk; Fred E. Ahlert] vPS
  78: Melotone M-12246
    as OWEN FALLON AND HIS CALIFORNIANS
E 37154-A **Kissable Baby** vDR
  78: Melotone M-12267
    as DICK ROBERTSON AND HIS ORCHESTRA
E 37155-A **I'm Happy When You're Jealous** vDR
  78: Melotone M-12267
    as DICK ROBERTSON AND HIS ORCHESTRA
E 37156-A **Sweet And Lovely** [Harry Tobias, Jules Lemare, Gus Arnheim] vBC
  78: Brunswick 6179, 80057, (E) 1219, (E) 2314
  LP: Brunswick BL-54005, BL-58001, (E) EB-71029, LA08741, Ace Of Hearts AH-88, Longines LW-349, Jonzo (E) JZ-11
    as BING CROSBY
E 37157-A **Me!** [Irving Berlin] vDR
  78: Melotone M-12246, Panachord (E) 15112
    Melotone as OWEN FALLON AND HIS CALIFORNIANS, Panachord as THE CAPTIVATORS

Brunswick, New York, N.Y. Wednesday, September 16, 1931
RED NICHOLS AND HIS FIVE PENNIES
Red Nichols (tp) **Jimmy Dorsey** (cl,as) Joe Venuti (vn) Artie Schutt (p) Eddie Lang (g) Vic Berton (d)

E 37204-A **Oh! Peter (You're So Nice)** [Herb Wiedoeft, Gene Rose, Jesse Stafford] (cl solo)
  78: Brunswick 6198, (E) O1233, (G) A-9170
  LP: Living Era (E) ADA-5025, Swingfan (G) 1004
  TC: Living Era (E) K-15888
(Contd.)

RED NICHOLS AND HIS FIVE PENNIES (Contd.)

E 37205-A   **Honolulu Blues** [Maurice Gunsky, Goldstein]
(cl solo)
78: Brunswick 6198, (E) O1233, (G) A-9170
LP: IAJRC 22

Brunswick, New York, N.Y. Wednesday, September 16, 1931
VICTOR YOUNG AND THE BRUNSWICK ORCHESTRA
Victor Young (ldr) *Frank Guarente [or] Charlie Margulis, unknown* (tp)
Tom Dorsey (tb) **Jimmy Dorsey** (cl,as,bar) Bennie Krueger (cl,as) Larry
Binyon (cl,ts,o) Joe Venuti, Harry Hoffman, *unknown* (vn) Arthur
Schutt (p) Eddie Lang (g) Joe Tarto (bb,sb) *Chauncey Morehouse [or]
Larry Gomar* (d) Scrappy Lambert (vcl) Three Minutemen [Lambert,
Leonard Stokes, Randolph Whatt] (vcl grp)

E 37206-A   **Love Letters In The Sand** [Nick Kenny, Charles
Kenny; J. Fred Coots] vSL
78: Brunswick 6188, (E) O1243
E 37207-   **It's The Darndest Thing** [Dorothy Fields; Jimmy
McHugh] vSL
78: Melotone M-12248
as ART KAHN'S ORCHESTRA
E 37208-A   **Let's Drift Away On Dreamer's Bay** [Harold Spina,
George McConnell] v3M (as solo)
78: Brunswick 6188

ARC, New York, N.Y. Thursday, September 17, 1931
LOU GOLD AND HIS ORCHESTRA
Lou Gold (ldr) Bob Effros, Ruby Weinstein (tp) Al Philburn (tb) **Jimmy
Dorsey** (cl,as) Andy Sanella, Elmer Feldkamp (as) Hymie Wolfson (ts)
2 *unknown* (vn) *unknown* (p), (g) Hank Stern (sb) *unknown* (d) Gene
Austin, Frank Parker (vcl)

10793-7   **If I Didn't Have You** [E.Y. Harburg; Milton Ager]
vGA
78: Banner 32281, Perfect 15521, Oriole 2345, Romeo 1716,
Apex (C) 41419, Domino DL-51012, Melotone 91205, Crown (C)
91205, Sterling (C) 291205, Imperial (E) 2627
10794-6   **In A Dream** [Fred Higman, Carmen Lombardo] vGA
78: Banner 32281, Perfect 15521, Romeo 1716, Apex (C)
41419, Domino 51012, Melotone 91205, Crown (C) 91205,
Sterling (C) 291205
*Matrices 10793 and 10794, as GENE AUSTIN AND HIS
ORCH., are remakes from September 2, 1931.*
10813-3   **Sugar** [Maceo Pinkard, Sidney D. Mitchell] vFP
78: Oriole 2351, Perfect 15529, Banner 32287, Apex (C) 41429,
Crown (C) 91215
10814-3   **Was It Wrong?** vFP
78: Oriole 2351, Perfect 15529, Banner 32287, Apex (C) 41429,
Crown (C) 91215
10813 AND 10814 as FRANK PARKER

What Depression? 209

ARC, New York, N.Y. Thursday, September 24, 1931
CHICK BULLOCK AND HIS LEVEE LOUNGERS
Mannie Klein (tp) Tom Dorsey (tb) **Jimmy Dorsey** (cl,as) 2 *unknown*
(vn) Arthur Schutt (p) Eddie Lang (g) Joe Tarto (sb) Stan King (d,xyl)
Chick Bullock (vcl)

10816-1   **River, Stay 'way From My Door** [Mort Dixon;
             Harry Wood] vCB
    78: Banner 32294, Conqueror 7900, Oriole 2359, Romeo 1734
10817-1   **When It's Sleepy Time Down South** [Milton Tag-
             gert, Mary Woolsley; Robert Sauer] vCB (as solo)
    78: Banner 32294, Conqueror 7900, Oriole 2359, Romeo 1734
10818-2   **You Can't Stop Me From Lovin' You** [Mann Hol-
             iner; Alberta Nichols] vCB (as solo)
    78: Banner 32275, Conqueror 7872, Oriole 2301, Perfect 12756
10819-1   **You Call It Madness (But I Call It Love)** [Con Con-
             rad, Gladys Dubois, Russ Columbo, Paul Gregory]
             vCB
    78: Banner 32275, Conqueror 7872, Oriole 2301, Perfect 12756
    10818 and 10819 as CHICK BULLOCK

Brunswick, New York, N.Y. Friday, October 2, 1931
RED NICHOLS AND HIS ORCHESTRA
Red Nichols (tp,ldr) Don Moore (tp) Johnny "Scat" Davis (tp,vcl)
Wilbur Schwichtenberg [Will Bradley] (tb) **Jimmy Dorsey** (cl,as) Russ
Lyon, Babe Russin (ts) Fulton McGrath (p) Tony Sacco (bj,vcl) Artie
Bernstein (sb) Vic Engle (d)

E 37233-A,B   **Get Cannibal** [Ted Weems, Phil Dooley, Loring
              "Red" Nichols] vJD
    78: Brunswick 6219, 4875, (Au) 4875, (E) 1281, O1281, (G) A-
    9191, Lucky (J) 5046
    LP: Swingfan (G) 1004
E 37234-A,B   **Junk Man Blues** [Phil Dooley, Loring "Red" Nich-
              ols] vJD (cl solo)
    78: Brunswick 6219, 4875, (Au) 4875, (E) 1225, O1225, (G) A-
    9192, Lucky (J) 5046
    LP: Swingfan (G) 1004
E 37235-A,B   **This Is The Missus** [Lew Brown; Ray Henderson] vJD
    78: Melotone M-12256, Panachord (E) 25132, Mayfair (E) 1055
              *Mayfair as THE PALERMO HOUSE BAND, others as
              SLEEPY HALL AND HIS COLLEGIANS*
E 37236-A,B   **Life Is Just A Bowl Of Cherries** [Lew Brown; Ray
              Henderson] vTS
    78: Melotone M-12256, Panachord (E) 25132, Mayfair (E)
    1055, Oriole 2336
              *Mayfair as THE PALERMO HOUSE BAND, Oriole as VIC
              IRWIN AND HIS ORCH., others as SLEEPY HALL AND HIS
              COLLEGIANS*

The same day, the Red Nichols band reportedly journeyed out to
Paramount's Astoria, Long Island, studio to cut a short. It is claimed

that two of the selections appear on an LP, but one LP cut, "My Sweetie Went Away," is a dub of Brunswick 6241, made December 15, 1931. No Jimmy Dorsey solo appears on the LP's "St. Louis Blues" excerpt.

Paramount Studios, Astoria, N.Y., Friday, October 2, 1931
RED NICHOLS AND HIS FIVE PENNIES
Unknown vocal group added

> **St. Louis Blues** [William C. Handy] vJD, vcl grp / **My Sweetie Went Away** [Roy Turk; Lou Handman] (other titles, if any, unknown)
> "St. Louis Blues" (partial) on **LP:** Bandstand BS 7127

Brunswick, New York, N.Y. Thursday, October 8, 1931
VICTOR YOUNG AND HIS ORCHESTRA
Victor Young (ldr) *Frank Guarente [or] Charlie Margulis, unknown* (tp) Tom Dorsey (tb) **Jimmy Dorsey** (cl,as) Benny Krueger (as) *unknown* (ts) Harry Hoffman, 2 *unknown* (vn) *unknown* (cel) (p) Eddie Lang (g) *Artie Bernstein* (sb) *unknown* (d) Dick Robertson, Bing Crosby (vcl)

E 37284-A   **Too Late** [Sam M. Lewis; Victor Young] vBC
    78: Brunswick 6203, 80046, (E) 1270
    EP: Brunswick BL-5800, EB-71028
    LP: Brunswick LA-8740, Ace Of Hearts (E) AH-88, Jonzo (E) JZ-11
       as BING CROSBY
E 37285-A   **Goodnight Sweetheart** [Ray Noble, Jimmy Campbell, Reg Connelly, Rudy Vallee] vBC (as solo)
    78: Brunswick 6203, 80046, (E) 1240, (E) 02314, (E) 05928
    EP: Brunswick BL-54005, BL-58000, EB-71028
    LP: Brunswick LA-8740, Ace Of Hearts (E) AH40, Longines LW-349, Jonzo (E) JZ-11
       as BING CROSBY
E 37286   **Chances Are** [Al Stillman; Robert Allen] vDR
    78: Brunswick 6193
       as THE NEW YORKERS
E 37287   **Time On My Hands** [Harold Adamson, Mack Gordon; Vincent Youmans] vDR
    78: Melotone 12263
       as ART KAHN'S ORCHESTRA

The Sammy Fain musical *Everybody's Welcome,* after a tryout in Philadelphia, opened at New York's Schubert Theater on October 13, 1931, for 139 performances with the Dorsey Brothers' Orchestra as the pit band.

Included in the score was Herman Hupfeld's "As Time Goes By," which became a hit a decade later in *Casablanca* (Lissauer 1991).

Tommy angered Fred Rich when he lured Bunny Berigan away from CBS for the pit band, which also included, among others, Glenn Miller and Jack Teagarden (tb), Mickey Bloom (tp) and Chummy McGregor (p) (White and Kite 1951-1987).

ARC, New York, N.Y. Saturday, October 17, 1931
ARC STUDIO BAND
Earl Oliver (tp) *unknown* (tb) **Jimmy Dorsey,** Andy Sanella (cl,as) Max Farley (cl,ts) Lou Raderman, Harry Hoffman, Alex Blyer (vn) Chauncey Gray (p) Carl Kress (g) Dick Cherwin (sb) *unknown* (d) Gene Austin (vcl)

10896-3 **A Faded Summer Love** [Phil Baxter] vGA
   78: Banner 32291. Romeo 1729, Oriole 2355, Perfect 12760, Apex (C) 41441, Sterling (C) 91235
10897-1 **Goodnight, Sweetheart** [Ray Noble, James Campbell, Reg Connelly] vGA
   78: Banner 32291, Romeo 1729, Oriole 2355, Perfect 12760, Apex (C) 41441, Sterling (C) 91235
   All issues this session as GENE AUSTIN

Victor Young, after coming to New York from Chicago to direct Brunswick recording studio activities, also led several studio bands at the National Broadcasting Company (NBC), including the weekly *Carnation Contented Hour* sponsored by the Carnation Milk Company.
   After *Everybody's Welcome* closed, Jimmy and Tommy both took part in some of these weekly broadcasts, which were aired on Monday nights, 8:00-8:30 P.M. on NBC-Red.
   However, Young's major association with the Dorseys was as ARC/Brunswick's recording director.

Brunswick, New York, N.Y. Sunday, October 25, 1931
VICTOR YOUNG AND THE BRUNSWICK ORCHESTRA
Victor Young (ldr) *Frank Guarante /or/ Charlie Margulis,* Mannie Klein (tp) Tom Dorsey (tb) **Jimmy Dorsey,** Arnold Brilhart (cl,as) Larry Binyon (cl,ts) Harry Hoffman, 2 *unknown* (vn) Arthur Schutt (p) Eddie Lang (g) Hank Stern (bb) Larry Gomar (d) Boswell Sisters, Connie Boswell, Bing Crosby, Frank Munn, Mills Brothers (vcl)

XE 37320-A **Gems From** *George White Scandals* [Lew Brown; Ray Henderson] (pt. 1) *Titles:* **Life Is Just A Bowl Of Cherries** (partial), **This Is The Missus** vBS, **The Thrill Is Gone** vBC, **My Song** vFM
   78: (12-inch) Drunswick 20102, 85001, (E) 0105, (G) A 5107, Lucky (J) 801
   LP: Jonzo (E) JZ-12, Jazum 30, ASV Living Era (E) AJA5014*, Ace Of Hearts (E) AH40*
XE 37321-A **Gems From** *George White Scandals* (pt. 2) *Titles:* **That's Love** vBS, **That's Why Darkies Were Born** vFM, **Life Is Just A Bowl of Cherries** vMB,CB, BC,BS
   78: (12-inch) Brunswick 20102, 85001, (E) 0105, (G) A-5107, Lucky (J) 801
   LP: Jonzo (E) JZ-12, Jazum 30, ASV Living Era (E) AJA5014*, Ace Of Hearts (E) AH40*
   CD: JSP (E) 301
   *Boswell Sisters' portions only.

Brunswick, New York, N.Y. Wednesday, October 28, 1931
BRUNSWICK STUDIO BAND
Victor Young (ldr) 2 *unknown* (tp) Wilbur Schwichtenberg [Will
Bradley] (tb) **Jimmy Dorsey**, *unknown* (cl,as) *unknown* (ts) Harry
Hoffman (vn) *unknown* (vn,viola), (p) Eddie Lang (g) Joe Tarto (bb)
Chauncey Morehouse (d) Connie Boswell, Dick Robertson (vcl)

E-37333-A   **Time On My Hands** [Harold Adamson, Mack Gor-
                   don; Vincent Youmans] vCB
     78: Brunswick 6210 (E) 01443
     LP: Take Two TT 209, Jazum 21, ASV Living Era (E) AJA5014
     CD: Fremeaux (F) 9518
E-37334-A   **Concentratin' (On You)** [Andy Razaf; Thomas "Fats"
                   Waller] vCB (cl solo)
     78: Brunswick 6210 (E) 01252
     LP: Take Two TT 216, Jazum 21, ASV Living Era (E) AJA5014
          37333, 37334 as CONNIE BOSWELL
E-37335   **Hiding In The Shadows Of The Moon** vDR
     78: Melotone M-12276
          as DICK ROBERTSON AND HIS ORCHESTRA

Brunswick, New York, N.Y. Thursday, November 5, 1931
BOSWELL SISTERS
Victor Young (ldr) Bunny Berigan (tp) Tom Dorsey (tb) **Jimmy Dorsey**
(cl,as) Joe Venuti (vn) Arthur Schutt (p) Eddie Lang (g) Artie Bernstein
(sb) Stan King (d) Boswell Sisters (vcl)

E 37354-A   **River, Stay 'Way From My Door** [Mort Dixon;
                   Harry Wood] vBS
     78: Brunswick 6218, 80014, (E) 01251, (G) A-9191, Lucky (J)
     60150
     LP: Brunswick BL-58005, Vocalion (E) VLP5, Ace Of Hearts (E)
     AH116 **TC:** ProArte Digital PCD550
     CD: Collector's Classics COCD-21, Flapper 7087
E 37355-A   **An Ev'ning In Caroline** [Walter Donaldson] vBS
                   (cl solo)
     78: Brunswick 6218, (E) 01251, A-9191
     LP: Vocalion (E) VLP5, Ace Of Hearts (E) AH116
     CD: L'Art Vocal (F) 13, Collector's Classics COCD-21

Brunswick, New York, N.Y. Friday, November 20, 1931
BRUNSWICK STUDIO BAND
Tom Dorsey (tb) **Jimmy Dorsey** (cl,as) *Bennie Krueger* (as) *unknown*
(ts) 4 *unknown* (vn) *unknown* (p) Eddie Lang (g) Hank Stern (bb)
unknown (d) Les Reis, Artie Dunn, Connie Boswell (vcl)

E 37364   **You Try Somebody Else** [Buddy De Sylva, Lew
                   Brown; Ray Henderson] vLR,AD
     78: Melotone M-12295
E 37365   **An Ev'ning In Caroline** [Walter Donaldson] vLR,AD
     78: Melotone M-12295
          Both sides as LES REIS AND ARTIE DUNN

2 *unknown* (tp) added:

E 37366-A **You Try Somebody Else** vCB (cl solo)
   78: Brunswick 6223, (E) 1257
      as CONNIE BOSWELL
   LP: Take Two TT216
E 37367-A **Should I Be Sorry** [Leader, Eller, Johnson] vCB
   78: Brunswick 6223, (E) 1257
      as CONNIE BOSWELL
   LP: Take Two TT216
E 37368-A **An Ev'ning In Caroline** vLR
   78: Melotone M-12284
      as ART KAHN'S ORCHESTRA
E 37369-A **By The Sycamore Tree** [Haven Gillespie; Pete Wend-
      ling] vLR
   78: Melotone M-12284
      as ART KAHN'S ORCHESTRA

Columbia, New York, N.Y. Tuesday, November 24, 1931
ORIGINAL MEMPHIS FIVE
Phil Napoleon (tp,ldr) Tom Dorsey (tb) **Jimmy Dorsey** (cl,as) Frank
Signorelli (p) Joe Tarto (sb) Ted Napoleon (d)

151887-2 **Jazz Me Blues** [Tom Delaney] (cl solos)
   78: Columbia 2588-D, 36064, (GE) DC-143, MC-3027,
   Parlophone (E) R-1399, (Au) A-3478
      Parlophone A-3478 as T.N.T. RHYTHM BOYS
   LP: The Old Masters 13
151888-2 **St. Louis Gal** (cl solos)
   78: Columbia 2577-D
   LP: The Old Masters 13
151889-2 **Anything** [Phil Napoleon, Frank Signorelli] (cl solo)
   78: Columbia 2588-D, 36064, Parlophone (E) R-1297
   LP: The Old Masters 13
151890-2 **My Honey's Lovin' Arms** [Herman Ruby; Joseph
      Meyer] (as,cl solos)
   78: Columbia 2577-D, (E) DC-143, Regal (E) G-21480
      Regal as MISSISSIPPI JAZZ KINGS
   LP: The Old Masters 13

ARC, New York, N.Y. Friday, November 27, 1931
VIC IRWIN AND HIS ORCHESTRA (ARC Studio Band)
Bunny Berigan, Mannie Klein (tp) Tom Dorsey (tb) Jimmy Dorsey
(cl,as) unknown (as), (ts) Harry Hoffman (vn) Vic Irwin (p) Dick
McDonough (g) *Dick Cherwin* (sb) *Larry Gomar* (d) The Eton Boys
(vcl)

11025-3 **Who's Your Little Who-Zis?** [Walter Hirsch, Ben
      Bernie, Al Goering] vEB
   78: Banner 32331, Oriole 2386, Perfect 15547, Romeo 1747,
   Crown 91243
                      (Contd.)

VIC IRWIN AND HIS ORCHESTRA (Contd.)

11026-2   Potatoes Are Cheaper, Tomatoes Are Cheaper,
                 Now's The Time To Fall In Love [Al Lewis, Al
                 Sherman] vEB
       78: Banner 32327, Oriole 2387, Perfect 15550, Romeo 1760,
       Crown 91246
       LP: Sunbeam MFC-17
11027-2   I Don't Blame You [Miller, Hoelle] vEB
       78: Banner 32331, Oriole 2386, Perfect 15547, Romeo 1747,
       Crown 91243
11028-2   She's So Nice [Lou Davis; J. Fred Coots] vEB
       78: Banner 32327, Oriole 2387, Perfect 15550, Romeo 1760,
       Crown 91246
                 Perfect 15550 as ALL STAR COLLEGIANS

Brunswick, New York, N.Y. Tuesday, December 1, 1931
RED NICHOLS AND HIS FIVE PENNIES
Red Nichols (tp,ldr) Johnny "Scat" Davis (tp,vcl) Wilbur Schwich-
tenberg [Will Bradley] (tb) Jimmy Dorsey (cl,as) Babe Russin (ts) Jack
Russin (p) Tony Starr (bj) Artie Bernstein (sb) Vic Engle (d)

E 37436-A   Slow And Easy vJD [Williams, Spencer] (cl solo)
       78: Brunswick 6767, (E) O1312
       LP: IAJRC 22, ASV Living Era (E) AJA 5025
       TC: ASV Living Era (E) K-15888
E 37437-A   Waiting For The Evening Mail [Billy Baskette] vJD
       78: Brunswick 6767, 4896, (E) O1312
       LP: IAJRC 22, ASV Living Era (E) AJA 5025
       CD: ASV Living Era (E) AJA 5025

Brunswick, New York, N.Y. Wednesday, December 2, 1931
RED NICHOLS AND HIS FIVE PENNIES
Red Nichols (cnt) Jimmy Dorsey (cl,as) Joe Venuti (vn), Arthur Schutt
(p) Eddie Lang (g) Vic Berton (d)

E 37438-A   Yaaka Hula Hickey Dula [E. Ray Goetz, Joe Young,
                   Pete Wendling] (cl solo)
       78: Brunswick 6234, (E) O1262, (G) A-9199, ARC For Theater
       Use F-210
       ET: ARC For Theater Use E-654
       LP: IAJRC 22
E 37439-A   Haunting Blues [Busse, Hirsch, Lange]
       78: Brunswick 6234, (E) O1262, (G) A-9199
       ET: ARC For Theater Use E-647
       LP: Sunbeam MFC-12, Jass 623
       TC: Radio Yesteryear Stack 31
       CD: Jass J-CD 623

Brunswick, New York, N.Y. Friday, December 4, 1931
BOSWELL SISTERS
Bunny Berigan (tp) Tom Dorsey (tb) Jimmy Dorsey (cl,as) Joe Venuti

(vn) Art Schutt (p) Eddie Lang (g) Art Bernstein (sb) Stan King (d) Boswell Sisters (vcl)

E 37445-A   **Nothing Is Sweeter Than You** [Charles] vBS
     78: Brunswick 6231, (E) 01272, (G) A-9208
     LP: Vocalion (E) VLP5, Columbia Special Products P3-16493, Ace Of Hearts (E) AH116
     TC: Neovox (E) 919, Vocalion (E) VLP5
     CD: Collector's Classics COCD-21
E 37445-B   **Nothing Is Sweeter Than You** vBS
     LP: Grannyphone (H) 03318
E 37446-A   **I Thank You Mister Moon** [Dave Oppenheim] vBS
     (cl solo)
     78: Brunswick 6231, (E) 01272, (G) A-9208, Lucky (J) 60119
     LP: Vocalion (E) VLP5, Columbia Special Products P3-16493, Ace Of Hearts (E) AH116
     CD: Collector's Classics COCD-21
E 37446-B   **I Thank You Mister Moon** vBS (cl solo)
     LP: Grannyphone (H) 03318

Columbia, New York, N.Y. Wednesday, December 9, 1931
THE DORSEY BROTHERS AND THEIR ORCHESTRA
Tom Dorsey (tb,ldr) Bunny Berigan, Lou Garcia, *unknown* (tp) Glenn Miller (tb) **Jimmy Dorsey** (cl,as) *Arnold Brilhart* (as) Foster Morehouse (ts) Art Schutt (p) Tony Sacco (bj,g,vcl) Hank Stern (bb) Stan King (d)

W 152033-2   **Home** [Harry Clarkson, Geoff Clarkson, Peter Van Steeden] vTS
     LP: Columbia P514320, Broadway BR-113, NBC #1005
     While the Columbia LP credits the vocal to Wes Vaughan, Tony Sacco confirms he was the only vocalist present.
W 152034-2   **By The Sycamore Tree** [Haven Gillespie; Pete Wendling] vTS (cl solo)
     78: Columbia 2581-D, (J) J-1340, Regal (Au) G-21289
     LP: Columbia Special Products P16356, Everest 4005/5
W 152035-2   **Why Did It Have To Be Me?** [Bud Green; Carmen Lombardo, Sam H. Stept] vTS
     78: Columbia 2589-D, (E) DC-144, Parlophone (E) R-1239, Regal (Au) G-21289
     LP: Columbia Special Products P16356, Everest 4005/5
W 152036-2   **Ooh! That Kiss** [Harry Warren, Mort Dixon, Joseph Young] vTS (as solo)
     78: Columbia 2581-D, Parlophone (E) R-1287, Regal (Au) G-21535
     LP: Columbia Special Products P16356, Everest 4005/5
all sides also on **CD:** Jazz Oracle (C) BDW8006

Brunswick, New York, N.Y. Tuesday, December 15, 1931
RED NICHOLS AND HIS FIVE PENNIES
Red Nichols (tp,ldr) Johnny "Scat" Davis (tp) Wilbur Schwichtenberg [Will Bradley] (tb) **Jimmy Dorsey** (cl,as) Babe Russin (ts) Fulton McGrath (p) Artie Bernstein (sb) Vic Engle (d) Johnny Marvin (vcl)

RED NICHOLS AND HIS FIVE PENNIES (Contd.)

E 37462-A,B   **Twenty One Years** [Bob Miller] vJM (cl solo)
    78: Brunswick 6241, (E) O1293, (G) A-9203
E 37463-A   **My Sweetie Went Away** [Roy Turk; Lou Handman]
                   (cl solo)
    78: Brunswick 6241, (E) O1293 (dubbing), (G) A-9203
    LP: IAJRC 22, Bandstand 7127

Durium, New York, N.Y. December 1931
ERNO RAPEE'S ORCHESTRA
Erno Rapee (dir) Mannie Klein, Jack Mollick (tp) *unknown* (tb) Jimmy
Dorsey (cl,as) Larry Abbott (cl,as,comb) *unknown* (ts) 2 *unknown* (vn)
unknown (p) Eddie Lang (g) *unknown* (p), (sb), (d) Paul Small, Helen
Rowland (vcl)

1184-A   **This Is The Missus** [Lew Brown, Ray Henderson]
                   vPS; **The Merry Widow Waltz** [Franz Lehár]
    78: Hit Of The Week B-4-C-1
1185-C   **River, Stay 'Way From My Door** [Mort Dixon;
                   Harry Woods]; **Some Of These Days** [Shelton
                   Brooks] vHR
    78: Hit Of The Week M-5-A-1
    LP: Sunbeam MFC-9 ("Some Of These Days" only)

"Just Around the Corner . . ."
(1932)

The year 1932 was bleak indeed with better than 30 percent of the work force continuing unemployed. The current slogan, "prosperity is just around the corner," did little to ease the pain. In New York many musicians held on as best they could, but even a hotel band job was shaky (*Orchestra World*, January 1932: 23). It was also a notable year for Jimmy personally when he and wife Jane became the parents of a girl, Julie Lou, who was one of the delights in Jimmy's life.

ARC, New York, N.Y. Tuesday, January 12, 1932
ARC STUDIO BAND
Victor Young (ldr) *Frank Guarente, unknown* (tp) *unknown* (tb) **Jimmy Dorsey** (cl,as,bar) Larry Binyon (cl,ts) Joe Venuti, Harry Hoffman (vn) *unknown* (p), (g) *Joe Tarto* (bb,sb) *Larry Gomar* (d) Chick Bullock (vcl)

11107-   **Old Time Waltz Medley No. 2** introducing: **Silver Threads Among The Gold; Dear Old Girl** [Richard H. Buck; Theodore F. Morse]; **When You Were Sweet Sixteen** [James Thornton]; **Sweet Adeline** [Richard H. Gerard; Harry Armstrong]
78: Perfect 15562
11108-   **Show Boat Medley** [P. G. Wodehouse, Oscar Hammerstein II, Jerome Kern] (introducing **Why Do I Love You?; Can't Help Lovin' Dat Man; Bill; Make Believe; Ol' Man River**)
78: Perfect 15562
     11107 and 11108 as MAJESTIC DANCE ORCHESTRA
11109-1   **Was That The Human Thing To Do?** [Joe Young; Sammy Fain] vCB
78: Banner 32365, Oriole 2411, Perfect 15563, Crown (C) 91267
     as CHICK BULLOCK AND HIS LEVEE LOUNGERS
11110-1   **How Long Will It Last?** [Max Lief; Joseph Meyer] vCB (bar solo)
78: Perfect 15565, Oriole 2412, Banner 32363, Romeo 1786
     as DAN RITCHIE AND HIS ORCHESTRA

ARC, New York, N.Y. Wednesday, January 13, 1932
ARC STUDIO BAND
Smith Ballew, Charlie Crafts, Chick Bullock, Dick Robertson (vcl)

11111-1   **Starlight (Help Me Find The One I Love)** [Joe Young; Bernice Petkere] vSB (Contd.)

ARC STUDIO BAND (Contd.)

> **78:** Conqueror 7925, Perfect 15564, Banner 32634, Crown (C) 91268
> 11112-1   **Tell Tales** [Charles O'Flynn; J. Russell Robinson, Lou Vardi] vSB
> **78:** Conqueror 7925, Perfect 15564, Banner 32634, Crown (C) 91268
> *11111, 11112 as SMITH BALLEW AND HIS ORCHESTRA*
> 11113-(1,2)   **You're My Everything** vCB (unissued)
> 11114-   **Tell Tales** vCC
> **78:** Melotone M-12306
> 11115-   **Starlight (Help Me Find The One I Love)** vDR
> **78:** Melotone M-12306
> *11114, 11115 as ART KAHN'S ORCHESTRA*
> 11116-   **Kickin' The Gong Around** [Ted Koehler; Harold Arlen] vDR
> **78:** Melotone M-12305, Panachord (E) 25196, Mayfair (E) G-2133
> *Mayfair as BOB RICHARDSON AND HIS ORCH., others as DICK ROBERTSON AND HIS ORCH.*
> 11117-   **Aw, You Dawg!** vDR
> **78:** Melotone M-12305, Panachord (E) 25196, Mayfair (E) G-2133
> *Mayfair as BOB RICHARDSON AND HIS ORCH., others as DICK ROBERTSON AND HIS ORCH.*
> 11118-2   **Can't We Talk It Over?** [Ned Washington; Victor Young] vCB
> **78:** Perfect 15573, Oriole 2423
> *as VINCENT ROSE AND HIS ORCHESTRA*
> 11119-A   **Can't We Talk It Over?** vDR
> **78:** Melotone M-12304
> 11120-A   **Lies** [George E. Springer; Harry Barris] vDR
> **78:** Melotone M-12304, Panachord (E) 25194
> *11119, 11120 as DICK ROBERTSON AND HIS ORCH.*

ARC, New York, N.Y. Tuesday, January 19, 1932
RED NICHOLS AND HIS ORCHESTRA
Red Nichols (tp,ldr), *unknown* (tp) Tom Dorsey (tb) *Jimmy Dorsey* (cl,as) *unknown* (ts) Joe Venuti (vn) *Arthur Schutt* (p,celst) Tony Sacco (g) [as Tony Starr] (vcl) *unknown* (sb), (d) Smith Ballew (vcl)

> 11139-2   **Snuggled On Your Shoulder (Cuddled In Your Arms)** [Carmen Lombardo, Joe Young] vSB
> **78:** Perfect 15566, Banner 32368, Conqueror 7928, Romeo 1787, Oriole 2415
> **LP:** Columbia Special Products P14844
> 11140-2   **Dancing On The Ceiling** [Lorenz Hart; Richard Rodgers] vSB (as solo)
> **78:** Perfect 15566, Banner 32368, Conqueror 7928, Romeo 1787, Oriole 2415
> *11139, 11140 as SMITH BALLEW AND HIS ORCHESTRA*

LP: Columbia Special Products P14844
11141   **Snuggled On Your Shoulder** vTS (unissued)
B-11142-A   **Dancing On The Ceiling** vTS (as solo)
    78: Melotone M-12311
        as SLEEPY HALL AND HIS COLLEGIANS
11143-2   **Kiss By Kiss (I'm Falling In Love)** [Billy Rose,
                 Jack Meskill; Raymond Klages] vSB
    78: Perfect 15567, Banner 32367, Conqueror 7926, Oriole 2416
        as PALM ISLAND CLUB ORCHESTRA
B-11144-A   **Kiss By Kiss (I'm Falling In Love)** vTS
    78: Melotone M-12316
        as RALPH BENNETT AND HIS SEVEN ACES
11145-1   **The Wooden Soldier And The China Doll** [Charles
                 Newman; Isham Jones] vSB
    78: Perfect 15567, Conqueror 7926, Oriole 2416, Banner 32367
        as PALM ISLAND CLUB ORCHESTRA
B-11146-A   **The Wooden Soldier And The China Doll** vTS
    78: Melotone M-12311
        as SLEEPY HALL AND HIS COLLEGIANS

ARC, New York, N.Y. Friday, January 22, 1932
ARC STUDIO BAND
Victor Young (ldr) *Frank Guarente* [or] *Charlie Margulis, unknown* (tp)
Tom Dorsey (tb) **Jimmy Dorsey** (cl,as) Larry Binyon (cl,ts,fl) Joe
Venuti, Harry Hoffman (vn) Arthur Schutt (p,celst) Herman Hupfeld
(p,vcl) Eddie Lang (g) *Hank Stern* (bb,sb) *Chauncey Morehouse* [or]
Larry Gomar (d,vib) Paul Small, Charlie Crafts (vcl)

B-11165-A   **Goopy Geer** [Herman Hupfeld] vHH
    78: Brunswick 6251
        *as VICTOR YOUNG AND HIS ORCHESTRA, Novelty Piano and
        Vocal Chorus by the Composer, Herman Hupfeld*
B-11166-A   **Down The Old Back Road** [Herman Hupfeld] vHH
    78: Brunswick 6251
        *as VICTOR YOUNG AND HIS ORCHESTRA, Vocal Chorus by the
        Composer, Herman Hupfeld*
11167-1   **Two Loves** [J. P. Murray, Barry Trivers; Vincent
                 Scotto] vPS (as solo)
    78: Banner 32361, Conqueror 7931, Oriole 2407, Perfect 15568,
    Romeo 1781, Crown (C) 91273
        as VINCENT ROSE AND HIS ORCHESTRA
B-11168-A   **Two Loves** vCC (as solo)
    78: Melotone M-12310, Panachord (E) 25207
        as CHARLIE CRAFTS AND HIS ORCHESTRA
11169-1   **Auf Wiedersehen, My Dear** [Al Hoffman, Al Good-
                 hart, Ed Nelson, Milton Ager] vPS (as solo)
    78: Banner 32361, Conqueror 7931, Oriole 2407, Perfect 15568,
    Romeo 1781, Crown (C) 91273
        as VINCENT ROSE AND HIS ORCHESTRA
B-11170-A   **Auf Wiedersehen, My Dear** vCC (as solo)
    78: Melotone M-12310
        as CHARLIE CRAFTS AND HIS ORCHESTRA

Brunswick, New York, N.Y. Friday, February 5, 1932
BOSWELL SISTERS
Tom Dorsey (tb,ldr) Bunny Berigan (tp) **Jimmy Dorsey** (cl,as) Joe
Venuti (vn) Arthur Schutt (p) Eddie Lang (g) Artie Bernstein (sb) Stan
King (d) Glenn Miller (arr) Boswell Sisters (vcl)

B-11240-A   **(We've Got To) Put That Sun Back In The Sky**
                   [Joseph Meyer] vBS
          78: Brunswick (C) 6257
          LP: JASS 1
          TC: JASS J-C-1
          CD: JASS J-CD-622
B-11241-A   **Was That The Human Thing To Do?** [Joe Young;
                   Sammy Fain] vBS
          78: Brunswick (C) 6257
          LP: JASS 1
          TC: JASS J-C-1
          CD: JASS J-CD-622
                   Both matrices were rejected for U.S. release and remade
                   February 19 with new matrix numbers.

Durium, New York, N.Y. Thursday, February 11, 1932
ERNO RAPEE'S ORCHESTRA
Erno Rapee (dir) Mannie Klein, *unknown* (tp), (tb) **Jimmy Dorsey**
(cl,as) Larry Abbott (cl,as) *unknown* (ts) 2 *unknown* (vn) *unknown* (p)
Eddie Lang (g) *unknown* (p), (bb), (d) Paul Small (vcl)

1195-A   **Save The Last Dance For Me** [Walter Hirsch;
                Frank Magine, Phil Spitalny] vPS; **Ida (Sweet As
                Apple Cider)** [Eddie Munson; Eddie Leonard] (as
                solo)
          78: Hit Of The Week B-2-3
          LP: Sunbeam MFC-9 ("Ida" only)

Everybody's Welcome, featuring the Dorsey pit band, closed on February 14, 1932, after 139 performances (White and Kite 1951-1987).

Brunswick, New York, N.Y. Monday, February 15, 1932
RED NICHOLS AND HIS FIVE PENNIES
Red Nichols (tp,ldr) Johnny "Scat" Davis (tp) Wilbur Schwichtenberg
[Bradley] (tb) **Jimmy Dorsey** (cl,as) Babe Russin (ts) Larry Binyon
(ts,fl) Harry Hoffman (vn) Jack Russin (p) Dick McDonough (g) Artie
Bernstein (sb) Stan King (d) Sid Garry, Art Jarrett, Connie Boswell (vcl)
Earle Moss (arr)

BX-11282-A   **New Orleans Medley** (Part 1): **Way Down Yonder
                    In New Orleans** vAJ; **Dear Old Southland** vCB;
                    High Society (cl solo); **Rampart Street Blues** vCB,
                    arrEM (unissued)
BX-11282-B   **New Orleans Medley** (Part 1): **Way Down Yonder
                    In New Orleans** [Henry Creamer, Turner Layton]
                    vAJ; **Dear Old Southland** [Creamer, Layton] vCB;

                    High Society [Clarence Williams; Armond J. Piron]
                    (cl solo); Rampart Street Blues [Robinson] vCB
        78: (unissued test pressing)
        LP: Meritt 9
        CD: Jass J-CD-622
BX-11283-A   New Orleans Medley (Part 2): Milneburg [sic] Joys
                    [Walter Melrose Leon Rappolo, Paul Mares, Ferdin-
                    and "Jelly Roll" Morton] (cl solo); Panama [William
                    N. Tyers]; River, Stay 'Way From My Door [Mort
                    Dixon; Harry Woods] vCB&AJ arrEM
        78: (12-inch) Brunswick 20110, (E) O118
        LP: Sunbeam MFC-12
        TC: Radio Yesteryear Stack 31
BX-11283-B   New Orleans Medley (Part 2): Milenburg Joys (cl
                    solo); Panama; River, Stay 'Way From My Door
                    vCB&AJ arrEM
        78: (test pressing exists)
        CD: JASS J-CD-622

Brunswick, New York, N.Y. Wednesday, February 17, 1932
BRUNSWICK STUDIO BAND
Unknown (tp) Tom Dorsey (tb) **Jimmy Dorsey** (cl,as) *unknown* (ts), (p),
(sb), (bj), (d) Dick Robertson, Chick Bullock (vcl)

B-11311-A   Sing A New Song [Ned Weaver; Milton Ager] vDR
        78: Melotone M-12320, Mayfair (E) G-2197
                    Mayfair as TED COLLINS AND HIS ORCHESTRA,
                    Melotone as DICK ROBERTSON AND HIS ORCHESTRA
11312-A   Sing A New Song vCB
                    (possibly issued on Perfect as THE MERRYMAKERS)
B-11313-A   Stop The Sun, Stop The Moon (My Man's Gone) [H.
                    & M. Cook; Robinson] vDR (as solo)
        78: Melotone M-12320
                    as DICK ROBERTSON AND HIS ORCHESTRA
        TC: Audio Archives 1013

Brunswick, New York, N.Y. Thursday, February 18, 1932
RED NICHOLS AND HIS FIVE PENNIES
Red Nichols (tp,ldr) **Jimmy Dorsey** (cl,as) Babe Russin (ts) Fulton
McGrath (p) Dick McDonough (g) Artie Bernstein (sb) Vic Engle (d)

B-11314-A   Clarinet Marmalade [Edwin B. Edwards, Nick La
                    Rocca, Tony Spargo, Larry Shields] (cl solo)
        78: Brunswick 6266, (E) O1301, (F) A-500176, Parlophone (E)
        R-2598, (It) B-71157, (Swe) 71157, Columbia test pressing exists
        (F151) 78: ARC Theater-Use F-151
        (E585) ET: ARC Theater-Use E-585
        LP: IAJRC 22
B-11315-A   Sweet Sue, Just You [Will J. Harris; Victor Young]
                    (cl solo)
        78: Brunswick 6266, (E) O1301, (F) A-500176, Parlophone (E)
        R-2598, (It) B-71157, Columbia test pressing exists (Contd.)

RED NICHOLS AND HIS FIVE PENNIES (Contd.)

(F152) **78:** ARC Theater-Use F-152
(E586) **ET:** ARC Theater-Use E-586
LP: Sunbeam MFC-16, Swingfan (G) 1004, Living Era AJA 5025
CD: ASV Living Era AJA 5025

Brunswick, New York, N.Y. Friday, February 19, 1932
BOSWELL SISTERS (accomp. by The Dorsey Brothers)
Tom Dorsey (tb,ldr) Bunny Berigan, Mannie Klein (tp) **Jimmy Dorsey** (cl,as) *Harry Hoffman [or] Joe Venuti* (vn) *Sammy Prager [or] Martha Boswell* (p) Dick McDonough (g) Joe Tarto (sb) Stan King (d) Boswell Sisters (vcl)

B-11320-A   **Was That The Human Thing To Do?** [Joe Young;
                    Sammy Fain] vBS (cl solo)
          78: Brunswick 6257, (C) 6257, (E) 01284, Lucky (J) 60128
          LP: Biograph BLPC-3, CBS P3 16493
          TC: Radio Yesteryear Stack 47
          CD: Collectors Classics 21, Jazz Roots 56082, L'Art Vocal (F)13
B-11320-B   **Was That The Human Thing To Do?** vBS (cl solo)
          78: Brunswick 6257, (G) A-9926
          CD: JASS J-CD-622
B-11321-A   **(We've Got To) Put That Sun Back In The Sky**
                    [Joseph Meyer] vBS (cl solo)
          78: Brunswick 6257, (E) 01284, (G) A-9926, Lucky (J) 60128
          LP: Biograph BLPC-3, CBS P3 16493, Wave (J) MFPL84802
          TC: Radio Yesteryear Stack 47
          CD: Collectors Classics 21, Jazz Roots 56082

Both Dorseys have solos next on "Tired," but on 11324 Tommy solos before and Jimmy after the vocal, and on 11325 the solos are reversed.

ARC, New York, N.Y. Saturday, February 20, 1932
ARC STUDIO BAND
Victor Young (ldr) *Frank Guarente [or] Charlie Margulis*, Bunny Berigan (tp) Tom Dorsey (tb) **Jimmy Dorsey** (cl,as) Elmer Feldkamp (as, vcl) *unknown* (ts) *Joe Meresco* (p) Dick McDonough (g) *Joe Tarto* (sb) *unknown* (d) Paul Small (vcl)

11310-1   **Strangers** [Charles O'Flynn; J. Fred Coots] vPS
          78: Conqueror 7960, Romeo 1798, Crown (C) 91285, Perfect
          15576, Banner 32379
                    *Banner as MAJESTIC DANCE ORCHESTRA, others as VIC
                    IRWIN AND HIS ORCHESTRA*
11322-1   **Love, You Funny Thing!** [Roy Turk; Fred E. Ahlert]
                    vPS
          78: Perfect 15580, Crown (C) 91292
                    as MAJESTIC DANCE ORCHESTRA
B-11323-A   **Love, You Funny Thing!** vEF
          78: Melotone M-12322, Panachord (E) 25235
                    as ART KAHN'S ORCHESTRA

11324-1   Tired [Bert Lown, Kurras] vPS (cl solo)
   78: Oriole 2429, Romeo 1801, Conqueror 7923, Perfect 15579,
   Banner 32380
             as VIC IRWIN AND HIS ORCHESTRA
   TC: Audio Archives 1002
B-11325   Tired vEF (cl solo)
   78: Melotone M-12323
             as SLEEPY HALL AND HIS COLLEGIANS
11326-2   Somebody Loves You [Charles Tobias; Peter De
                     Rose] vPS
   78: Oriole 2429, Romeo 1801, Perfect 15579
             as VIC IRWIN AND HIS ORCHESTRA
B-11327-A   Somebody Loves You vEF
   78: Melotone M-12322
             as ART KAHN'S ORCHESTRA
B-11328   Strangers vEF
   78: Melotone M-12323
             as SLEEPY HALL AND HIS COLLEGIANS

Brunswick, New York, N.Y. Tuesday, February 23, 1932
BRUNSWICK STUDIO BAND
Victor Young (ldr) *Frank Guarente [or] Charlie Margulis*, Mannie Klein
(tp) Tom Dorsey (tb) **Jimmy Dorsey**, *unknown* (cl,as) *unknown* (ts)
Harry Hoffman, *unknown* (vn) Joe Meresco (p) Eddie Lang (g) *unknown*
(bb,sb) Larry Gomar (d,vib) Bing Crosby, Connie Boswell (vcl)

B-11330-A   Love, You Funny Thing! [Roy Turk; Fred E. Ahlert]
                     vBC (cl solo)
   78: Brunswick 6268, (E) 1304, Columbia (E) DB-2009
   LP: Columbia C4X 44229, Jonzo (E) JZ-13
B-11331-A   My Woman [Max Wartell, Bing Crosby; Irving Wall-
                     man] vBC
   78: Brunswick 6268, (E) 1308
             11330, 11331 as BING CROSBY
   LP: Columbia Special Products P413153, CBS 66210, Epic EE-
   222015/6, Jonzo (E) JZ-13
   CD: Columbia Special Products A2-201
B-11332-A   I Cried For You (Now It's Your Turn To Cry Over
                     Me) [Arthur Freed; Gus Arnheim, Abe Lyman]
                     vCB (cl solo)
   78: Brunswick 6267, (E) 1298
B-11333-A   I Can't Believe That It's You [L. Wolfe Gilbert,
                     Abner Silver] vCB
   78: Brunswick 6267, (E) 1298
             11332, 11333 as CONNIE BOSWELL
   TC: Audio Archives 1002

ARC, New York, N.Y. Wednesday, February 24, 1932
ARC-BRUNSWICK STUDIO BAND
Victor Young (ldr) Bunny Berigan, *unknown* (tp) Tom Dorsey (tb) Ben-
nie Krueger (as) **Jimmy Dorsey** (cl,as) *unknown* (ts) 2 *unknown* (vn) *Joe
Meresco* (p) Dick McDonough (g) Joe Tarto (sb) Larry Gomar (d,xyl)

ARC-BRUNSWICK STUDIO BAND (Contd.)
Chick Bullock, Howard Phillips, Boswell Sisters (vcl)

11348-2   **Sing A New Song** [Ned Weaver; Milton Ager] vCB
          78: Conqueror 7959, Perfect 12789, Banner 32373
                    as CHICK BULLOCK AND HIS LEVEE LOUNGERS
11349-1   **Stop The Sun, Stop The Moon (My Man's Gone)**
                    [H. and M. Cook; Robinson] vCB
          78: Conqueror 7959, Perfect 12789, Banner 32373
                    as CHICK BULLOCK AND HIS LEVEE LOUNGERS
          CD: IAJRC CD1013
11350-1   **Let's Have Another Cup Of Coffee** [Irving Berlin]
                    vCB
          78: Perfect 15581, Oriole 2431, Banner 32381
                    *Perfect, Oriole and Banner as BOB CAUSER & HIS
                    CORNELLIANS*
B-11351-A   **Let's Have Another Cup Of Coffee** vHP (bar solo)
          78: Melotone M-12328, Decca (E) F-3045
                    as RALPH BENNETT & HIS SEVEN ACES
11352-2   **Soft Lights And Sweet Music** [Irving Berlin] vCB
                    (cl solo)
          78: Melotone M-12328, Perfect 15581, Banner 32381, Decca
          (E) F-3045, Oriole 2431
                    *Melotone as RALPH BENNETT & HIS SEVEN ACES,
                    Perfect, Oriole, Banner as BOB CAUSER & HIS CORNEL-
                    LIANS, Decca as RON ALDRIDGE & HIS RENO BOYS*
unknown (as) (ts) 2 (vn) Meresco (p) out, Martha Boswell (p) added:
B-11353-A   **Stop The Sun, Stop The Moon (My Man's Gone)**
                    vBS (cl solo)
          78: (unissued test pressing)
          LP: Columbia Special Products P16493
B-11353-B   **Stop The Sun, Stop The Moon** vBS (cl solo)
          78: Brunswick 6271, (E) 01295, (F,G) A-9232
                    as THE BOSWELL SISTERS accomp. by The Dorsey Bros.
          LP: Jazum 21, Conifer (E) CHD 136
          TC: Conifer (E) MCHD 136
          CD: L'Art Vocal (F) 13, Collector's Classics 21
B-11354-A   **Everybody Loves My Baby** [Jack Palmer; Spencer
                    Williams] vBS
          78: Brunswick 6271, 6783, (It) 4898, (E) 01295, (F,G) A-9232,
          Columbia 36520, 88026, Lucky (J) 60021
                    as THE BOSWELL SISTERS accomp. by The Dorsey Bros.
          LP: Biograph BLP C-10, BLP C-16, Jazum 43, Columbia Special
          Products P15027, P16493, CBS (F) 80074, Wave (J) MKPL84801
          TC: ProArte Digital PCD550
          CD: ProArte Digital PCD550, L'Art Vocal (F) 13, Collector's
          Classics 21, Fremeaux (F) 9518

A February 29, 1932, session with Chick Bullock, Dick Robertson
plus the Mills Brothers and Bing Crosby's famous "Shine" has been
listed as an ARC studio band, including the Dorseys. The author, who
included it in his last book, now does not believe either is on the sides.

Brunswick, New York, N.Y. Tuesday, March 1, 1932
ARC-BRUNSWICK STUDIO BAND
Victor Young (ldr) Bunny Berigan, *unknown* (tp) Tom Dorsey (tb)
Bennie Krueger (c-mel) *Jimmy Dorsey* (cl,as) *unknown* (ts) (g) 2
unknown (vn) *Dick Cherwin* (bb) *Eddie Lang* (g) *unknown* (d) Andrea
Marsh, Scrappy Lambert, Smith Ballew (vcl)

11379-1   **One Hour With You** [Leo Robin; Richard A. Whit-
                 ing] vSL
    78: Perfect 15583, Banner 32404, Oriole 2440, Romeo 1812
B-11380-A   **One Hour With You** vSB
    78: Melotone M-12331
                 as SLEEPY HALL AND HIS COLLEGIANS
11381-1   **What Would You Do?** [Leo Robin; Richard A. Whit-
                 ing] vSL
    78: Perfect 15583, Banner 32404, Oriole 2440, Romeo 1812
                 11379 & 11381 as BOB CAUSER AND HIS CORNELLIANS
    TC: Audio Archives 1002
B-11382-A   **What Would You Do?** vSB
    78: Melotone M-12335, Panachord (E) 25242, Mayfair (E) G-
2174
                 Melotone, Panachord as ED LOYD AND HIS ORCH.,
                 Mayfair as EDDIE BOYD AND HIS ORCH.
    11381 and 11382 aalso on **CD:** IAJRC CD-1013
11383-1,2   **We Will Always Be Sweethearts** [Leo Robin; Oscar
                 Straus] vAM
    78: Melotone M-12331, Perfect 15587, Oriole 2443
                 Melotone as SLEEPY HALL AND HIS COLLEGIANS, Oriole
                 and Perfect as MAJESTIC DANCE ORCHESTRA

Brunswick, New York, N.Y. Tuesday, March 8, 1932
VICTOR YOUNG AND THE BRUNSWICK ORCHESTRA
Victor Young (ldr) Mannie Klein, *Bunny Berigan* (tp) Tom Dorsey,
unknown (tb) *Jimmy Dorsey* (cl,as) Fran Frey *(as,* vcl) Larry Binyon
(ts,o) 6 *unknown* (vn) *unknown* (acc) Joe Meresco (p) *unknown* (g), (bb)
Larry Gomar (d,xyl) Bing Crosby (vcl)

BX-11416-A,B   *Face The Music* **Medley** [Irving Berlin] (part l): **Soft
                 Lights And Sweet Music** vBC; **On A Roof In Man-
                 hattan**
    78: (12-inch) Brunswick 20106
                 as VICTOR YOUNG AND THE BRUNSWICK ORCHESTRA
                 WITH BING CROSBY
    (BX-11416-B) **LP:** Biograph BLP C-13, Columbia C4X 44229,
    Jazum 39, Sunbeam P-504, Jonzo (E) JZ-13
BX-11416-C   *Face The Music* **Medley** (part 1): **Soft Lights And
                 Sweet Music** vBC; **On A Roof In Manhattan**
    LP: Jonzo (E) JZ-13
B-11417-A   **Shadows On The Window** [Ned Washington; Victor
                 Young] vBC
    78: Brunswick (C) 6276
                 as BING CROSBY (Contd.)

VICTOR YOUNG AND THE BRUNSWICK ORCHESTRA (Contd.)

LP: Jonzo (E) JZ-13
B-11417-B   **Shadows On The Window** vBC
    78: Brunswick 6276, (E) 1304
        as BING CROSBY with VICTOR YOUNG'S ORCHESTRA
    LP: Columbia C4X 44429, Jonzo (E) JZ-13
    CD: Affinity (E) AFS 1021-2
BX-11418-A   *Face The Music* Medley [Irving Berlin] (part 2):**Man-**
                    hattan Madness; Let's Have Another Cup Of
                    Coffee vFF; **I Say It's Spinach** (*as solo*)
    78: Brunswick 20106
        *as VICTOR YOUNG & THE BRUNSWICK ORCH. Also
        made this day were 11419 and 11420 by Ruth Etting and a
        small group including clarinet, but it is not Jimmy.*

ARC, New York, N.Y., Wednesday, March 9, 1932
BENNIE KRUEGER AND HIS ORCHESTRA (ARC House Band)
Bennie Krueger (as,ldr) Bunny Berigan, *unknown* (tp) *unknown* (tb)
Jimmy Dorsey (cl,as) Fran Frey (as,vcl) *unknown* (ts) Justin King (p),
(g), (bb), (d) Phil Neely (vcl)

B-11423-A,B   **Lovable** vPN (unissued)
B-11424-A   **Sing A New Song** [Ned Weaver; Milton Ager] vFF
    78: Brunswick 6280, (E) O1357
B-11425-A   **Somebody Loves You** [Charles Tobias; Peter De
                    Rose] vPN
    78: Brunswick 6280, Panachord (E) 25215
B-11426-A   **I'm So In Love** [Walter Donaldson] vFF
    78: Brunswick 6287
    TC: Audio Archives 1002
    11424 and 11426 also on **CD:** IAJRC CD1013

Brunswick, New York, N.Y. Thursday, March 10, 1932
RED NICHOLS AND HIS FIVE PENNIES
Red Nichols (tp,ldr) Johnny "Scat" Davis (tp) Tom Dorsey (tb) **Jimmy
Dorsey** (cl,as) Babe Russin (ts) Larry Binyon (ts,fl) Joe Venuti (vn) Jack
Russin (p) Dick McDonough (g) Art Bernstein (sb) Stan King (d) Sid
Garry, Art Jarrett, Connie Boswell, Boswell Sisters (vcl) Earle Moss
(arr)

BX-11427-A   **New Orleans Medley** (part 1):**Way Down Yonder In
                    New Orleans** [Henry Creamer, Turner Layton] vAJ;
                    Dear Old Southland [Creamer, Layton] vCB; **High
                    Society** [Clarence Williams; Armond J. Piron] (cl
                    solo); **Rampart Street Blues** [Robinson] vCB arrEM
    78: (12-inch) Brunswick 20110, (E) 118
    LP: Sunbeam MFC-12
    TC: Radio Yesteryear Stack 31
BX-11427-B   **New Orleans Medley** (part 1):
    78: (unissued, test pressing exists)
BX-11432-A   **California Medley** (part 1): **California, Here I Come**

[Al Jolson, Buddy De Sylva; Joseph Meyer]; **Golden Gate** [Billy Rose, Dave Dreyer, Al Jolson; Joseph Meyer] vSG; **Hello, Frisco, Hello** [Gene Buck; Louis A. Hirsch] vBS; **Chinatown, My Chinatown** [William Jerome; Jean Schwartz] (cl solo); **Rose Room** [Harry Williams; Art Hickman] vAJ; **Fight For California** arrEM

78: (12-inch) Brunswick 20107, (E) 108, (F,G) A-5112
LP: Sunbeam MFC-12

A March 11, 1932, Victor Young session the author listed in his previous book as including Jimmy Dorsey does not. It is Fran Frey.

Brunswick, New York, N.Y. Tuesday, March 15, 1932
VICTOR YOUNG AND HIS ORCHESTRA
Victor Young (ldr) *Frank Guarente [or] Charlie Margulis*, Mannie Klein (tp) Tom Dorsey (tb) **Jimmy Dorsey** (cl,as) Bennie Krueger (c-mel) Arnold Brilhart (fl,as) 3 *unknown* (vn) Eddie Lang (g) *unknown* (p), (bb) Larry Gomar (d) Bing Crosby, Chick Bullock, Les Reis (vcl)

B-11480-A   **Paradise** [Nacio Herb Brown, Gordon Clifford; Nacio Herb Brown] vBC (cl solo)
    78: Brunswick 6285, (E) 1308, Harmony 1007, Columbia 5-1190, (E) DB-1971
    LP: Columbia C4X 44429, Columbia Special Products P4 13153, CBS 66210, Epic (E) EE-22015/6, Jonzo (E) JZ-13
    TC: Columbia-Legacy CT 48974, Radio Yesteryear Stack 26
    CD: Columbia Special Products A2-201, Columbia/Legacy 48974
B-11480-B   **Paradise** vBC (cl solo)
    78: Harmony 1007
    LP: Jonzo (E) JZ-13
B-11481-A   **You're Still In My Heart** [Jack Yellen; Dan Dougherty] vBC
    78: Brunswick 6285, (E) 1434, Columbia (E) DB-2123
        11480 and 11481 as BING CROSBY
    LP: Columbia C4X 44429, Jonzo (E) JZ-13
11434-1   **I Can't Believe That It's You** [L. Wolfe Gilbert, Abner Silver] vCB
    78: Perfect 15587
B-11482-   **I Can't Believe That It's You** vLR
    78: Melotone M-12344
        as ART KAHN'S ORCHESTRA
B-11483-B   **Lawd, You Made The Night Too Long** [Sam M. Lewis; Isham Jones] vLR
    78: Melotone M-12345, Panachord (E) 25234
        as LES PEABODY AND HIS MEMPHIS RAMBLERS
11484-1   **Lawd, You Made The Night Too Long** vCB
    78: Perfect 15590, Melotone 91310
        11434 and 11484 as MAJESTIC DANCE ORCHESTRA

Numerically the following matrix falls in the middle of fourteen Theater-Use sides dubbed March 19, 1932, from Brunswick releases.

ARC, New York, N.Y. March 1932
IMPERIAL DANCE ORCHESTRA
Bunny Berigan, *unknown* (tp) *Tom Dorsey* (tb) **Jimmy Dorsey** (cl,as) *unknown* (as), (ts), (g) *Joe Meresco* (p) *Art Bernstein* (sb) Stan King (d)

E601-1   **Stop The Sun, Stop The Moon (My Man's Gone)** [H. and M. Cook; Robinson] (as solo)
        78: ARC Theater-Use E-601
        ET: ARC Theater-Use F-167
        LP: Sunbeam MFC-16
        CD: IAJRC CD1013

Brunswick, New York, N.Y. Monday, March 21, 1932
BOSWELL SISTERS
Victor Young (ldr) Mannie Klein (tp) Tom Dorsey (tb) **Jimmy Dorsey** (cl,as) Babe Russin (ts) Martha Boswell (p) Eddie Lang (g) Artie Bernstein (sb) Stan King (d) Boswell Sisters (vcl)

B-11543-A   **There'll Be Some Changes Made** [William Higgins; W. Benton Overstreet] vBS (cl solo)
        78: Brunswick 6291, (E) 01306, (G) A-9244, Columbia 36521
        LP: Biograph BLP C-3, Epic SN6059, Columbia Special Products P16493, P12965, Columbia (E) SX6152, Conifer (E) CHD 136
        TC: Conifer (E) MCHD 136, ProArte Digital PCD550
        CD: ProArte Digital PCD550, Collector's Classics 21, Flapper 7087, Sony Special Products 10266
B-11544-A   **Between The Devil And The Deep Blue Sea** [Ted Koehler; Harold Arlen] vBS
        78: Brunswick 6291, (E) 01306, (G) A-9244
        LP: Jazum 30, Columbia Special Products P16493
        TC: ProArte Digital PCD550, Columbia CT 66977
        CD: L'Art Vocal (F) 13, Collector's Classics 21, Columbia CK 66977

Brunswick, New York, N.Y. Tuesday, March 22, 1932
ARC-BRUNSWICK STUDIO BAND
Victor Young (ldr) Mannie Klein (tp) Tom Dorsey (tb) **Jimmy Dorsey** (cl,as) Bennie Krueger (c-mel,as) *Babe Russin* (ts) *Harry Hoffman* (vn) *Joe Meresco* (p) Dick McDonough (g) *Dick Cherwin* (sb) Larry Gomar (d) George Beuchler, Paul Small (vcl)

11547-   **Shadows On The Window** [Ned Washington; Victor Young] vGB
        78: Perfect 15591, Oriole 2449
B-11548-   **Ma And Pa (Send Their Sweetest Love)** vPS
        78: Melotone M-12344, Panachord (E) 25231
        as ART KAHN'S ORCHESTRA
11549-   **Ma And Pa (Send Their Sweetest Love)** vGB
        78: Perfect 15585
11550-   **My Lips Want Kisses (My Heart Wants Love)** [Dave Oppenheim, Fred Fisher; Abel Baer] vPS
        78: Perfect 15591, Oriole 2449

11547 and 11550 as VIC IRWIN AND HIS ORCHESTRA
B-11551-A   **My Lips Want Kisses (My Heart Wants Love)** vGB
    78: Melotone M-12346, Mayfair (E) G-2178, Panachord (E)
    25249
        Mayfair as JACK LOCKE AND HIS ORCHESTRA, others as
        LES PEABODY AND HIS MEMPHIS RAMBLERS
B-11552-A   **Everything Must Have An Ending** vPS
    78: Melotone M-12346
        as LES PEABODY AND HIS MEMPHIS RAMBLERS
11553-   **Everything Must Have An Ending** vGB
    78: Perfect 15585

Brunswick, New York, N.Y. Friday, March 25, 1932
RED NICHOLS AND HIS FIVE PENNIES
Red Nichols (tp,ldr) Johnny Davis (tp) Tom Dorsey (tb) **Jimmy Dorsey**
(cl,as) Babe Russin (ts) Larry Binyon (ts,fl) Joe Venuti (vn) Jack Russin
(p) Dick McDonough (g) Artie Bernstein (sb) Stan King (d) Sid Garry,
Chick Bullock, Boswell Sisters (vcl) Earle Moss (arr)

BX-11569-A   **California Medley** (part 2): **Hail, Stanford, Hail;**
                  Avalon [Buddy De Sylva, Al Jolson; Vincent Rose]
                  vBS; **Avalon Town** [Grant Clarke; Nacio Herb
                  Brown] **Whispering** [Richard Coburn, Vincent Rose,
                  J. Schonberger] **I Cried For You** [Arthur Freed; Gus
                  Arnheim, Abe Lyman] vCB; **California, Here I**
                  Come [Al Jolson, Buddy De Sylva; Joseph Meyer]
                  vSG&BS, arrEM
    78: (12-inch) Brunswick 20107, (E) 108, (F,G) A-5112
    LP: Sunbeam MFC-12
BX-11569-B   **California Medley** (part 2):
    78: (12-inch) Brunswick 20107 (second issue)
BX-11569-C   **California Medley** (part 2) (test pressing exists)

                  Davis Musical Moments, Columbia Studios, New
                  York, N.Y. March-April 1932
BEN SELVIN AND HIS ORCHESTRA
Ben Selvin (ldr) Mannie Klein (tp) Tom Dorsey (tb) **Jimmy Dorsey**
(cl,as) *unknown* (ts) Joe Venuti (vn) *Rube Bloom* (p) *unknown* (g), (sb),
(d), Paul Small, Three Nitecaps (vcl)

    Introduction (theme) / **This Is The Missus** [Lew Brown; Ray
    Henderson] vPS / **Too Many Tears** [Al Dubin; Harry Warren] vPS /
    Cheer Up (Good Times Are Comin') [Raymond Klages; Jesse
    Greer] v3NC / **Somebody Loves You** [Charles Tobias; Peter De
    Rose] / **Closing** (theme)
    Entire show on **LP:** Fanfare 105, **TC:** Old Time Radio MT-1308

Brunswick, New York, N.Y. Friday, April 8, 1932
ARC STUDIO BAND
Victor Young (ldr) *Frank Guarente,* Bunny Berigan (tp) Bennie Krueger
(c-mel,as) **Jimmy Dorsey** (cl,as) *unknown* (ts) 3 *unknown*(vn) *unknown*
(p) *Eddie Lang* (g) *unknown* (sb), (bb) (d) Les Reis (vcl)

ARC STUDIO BAND (Contd.)

11670-   **Just Play Me An Old Fashioned Waltz (Like In The Long Ago]** [waltz] vLR
   78: Perfect 15625
      as LOU GOLD AND HIS ORCHESTRA
11671-1   **Mississippi Moon** [waltz] vLR
   78: Melotone M-12379, Perfect 15619
      Melotone as OWEN FALLON AND HIS CALIFORNIANS, Perfect as LOU GOLD AND HIS ORCHESTRA
11672-1   **My Yesterdays With You** [Plant, Squires] vLR (cl solo)
   78: Melotone M-12362, Perfect 15611
      Melotone as RALPH BENNETT & HIS SEVEN ACES, Perfect as DAN RITCHIE AND HIS ORCHESTRA
11673-1   **If I Had My Way 'Bout My Sweetie** vLR (cl solo)
   78: Melotone M-12363, Perfect 15608, Banner 32454, Romeo 1849
      Melotone, Romeo as OWEN FALLON AND HIS CALIFORNIANS, Perfect and Banner as VIC IRWIN AND HIS ORCH.
   CD: Vintage Jazz Classics VJC-1009, IAJRC CD-1013
E607 (F173-1)   **Dream Sweetheart** [Bud Green]
   78: ARC Theater-Use F-173
   ET: ARC Theater-Use E-607
      as IMPERIAL DANCE ORCHESTRA
E608 (F174)   **Lovable** [Gus Kahn; Harry Woods]
   78: ARC Theater-Use F-174
   ET: ARC Theater-Use E-608
      as VIC IRWIN AND HIS ORCHESTRA
      E-609 from this date (ARC Theater-Use E-591-2) is a dub of F-159, made March 1, 1932, and includes neither Dorsey.
E610 (F175)   **When The Lights Are Soft And Low**
   78: ARC Theater-Use F-175
   ET: ARC Theater-Use E-610
E611 (F176)   **One Hour With You** [Leo Robin; Richard A.Whiting]
   78: ARC Theater-Use F-176
   ET: ARC Theater-Use E-611
E612 (F177)   **Night** [E. Y. Harburg; Milton Ager]
   78: ARC Theater-Use F-177
   ET: ARC Theater-Use E-612
E613 (F178)   **Soft Lights And Sweet Music** [Irving Berlin]
   78: ARC Theater-Use F-178
   ET: ARC Theater-Use E-613
E614 (F179-1)   **We Will Always Be Sweethearts** [Leo Robin; Oscar Straus]
   78: ARC Theater-Use F-179
   ET: ARC Theater-Use E-614
      as SOCIETY NIGHT CLUB ORCHESTRA
E615 (F180)   **Lawd, You Made The Night Too Long** [Sam M. Lewis; Isham Jones]
   78: ARC Theater-Use F-180
   ET: ARC Theater-Use E-615

On Theater-Use masters, "E" sides are 33^1/$_3$ rpm, cut inside-out for Vitaphone turntables; "F" sides, 78 rpm, are cut outside-in. It is unknown for certain if they were made concurrently using two turntables or if one is a dub of the other, but most information points to the 78 rpm as being the original. At the time, the cost of wasting two masters in the event of a mishap probably outweighed quality considerations.

Theater-Use masters were almost always instrumental and ran the range from organ solos to dance bands.

With rare exceptions they were cut exclusively for this series as part of another ARC session but are not instrumental versions of vocal arrangements, as some have suggested. They were arranged especially for theater use and to be marketable required a "different sound" than that available "over the counter" at the nearby record store.

Theater-Use releases were also pressed on better quality material than commercial issues.

Brunswick, New York, N.Y. Saturday, April 9, 1932
BRUNSWICK STUDIO BAND
Victor Young (ldr) Bunny Berigan (tp) Tom Dorsey (tb) **Jimmy Dorsey** (cl) *Joe Venuti, 2 unknown* (vn) Martha Boswell (p) Eddie Lang (g) Art Bernstein (sb) Stan King (d) Connie Boswell, Boswell Sisters (vcl)

B-11682-A   **Lullaby Of The Leaves** [Joe Young; Bernice Petkere] vCB
    78: Brunswick 6297, (E) 01315
       as CONNIE BOSWELL
    LP: Jazum 21, Columbia Special Products P14544
    TC: Columbia/Legacy CT 52932
    CD: Columbia/Legacy CK 52943
B-11683-A   **My Lips Want Kisses (My Heart Wants Love)** [Dave Oppenheim, Fred Fisher; Abel Baer] vCB (cl solos)
    78: Brunswick 6297, (E) 01315
       as CONNIE BOSWELL
    LP: Jazum 21, Take Two TT216
    TC: Audio Archives 1002
Berigan (tp), three (vn) out:
B-11684-A   **If It Ain't Love** [Andy Razaf; Don Redman, Thomas "Fats" Waller] vCB&BS (cl solo)
    78: Brunswick 6302, (E) O1330, (F,G) A-9262
       as THE BOSWELL SISTERS, accomp. by THE DORSEY BROTHERS
    LP: Biograph BLPC3, Columbia Special Products P16495, Conifer (E) CHD 136
    TC: Conifer (E) MCHD 136, Radio Yesteryear Stack 47
    CD: Collector's Classics 21, Flapper 7087
B-11685-A   **Got The South In My Soul** [Ned Washington, Lee Wiley; Victor Young] vBS (cl solo)
    78: Brunswick 6302, (E) 01330, (F,G) A-9262
       as THE BOSWELL SISTERS, accomp. by THE DORSEY BROTHERS
    LP: Jazum 21, Columbia Special Products P16495
    CD: Collector's Classics 21

Brunswick, New York, N.Y. Thursday, April 14, 1932
VICTOR YOUNG AND THE BRUNSWICK ORCHESTRA
Victor Young (ldr) *Frank Guarente [or] Charlie Margulis*, Mannie Klein
(tp) Tom Dorsey (tb) **Jimmy Dorsey** (cl,as,bar) Bennie Krueger (cl,as)
Larry Binyon (cl,ts,fl) Joe Venuti, Jacques Renard (vn) Arthur Schutt
(p) Eddie Lang (g) Joe Tarto (sb) Larry Gomar (d,vib) Frank Munn,
Mills Brothers, Fran Frey, Connie Boswell, Boswell Sisters (vcl)

BX-11704-A   **Okay, America! Medley** (part 2): **My Romance** [Ned
                    Washington; Victor Young] vFM; **The Old Man Of
                    The Mountain** [Billy Hill; Victor Young] vMB,CB,
                    FF&BS
          78: Brunswick 20112, (G) A5114, Lucky (J) 60199 ("Old Man"
          portion only)
          LP: JASS 1
          TC: JASS J-C-1
          CD: JASS J-CD-622, JSP (E) 301, Jazz Roots 56082

Brunswick, New York, N.Y. Tuesday, April 19, 1932
ARC-BRUNSWICK STUDIO BAND
Personnel as April 14, 1932, except Cornell Smelser (acc) added, *Dick
McDonough possibly replaces Lang* (g) Tarto adds (bb). Fran Frey,
Chick Bullock, Boswell Sisters, Carmen Lombardo (vcl)

BX-11720-A   **Okay, America! Medley** (part 1): **She Was Just A
                    Tartar's Daughter** [Joe Alger] vFF (cl solo); **Love
                    Me Tonight** [Bing Crosby, Ned Washington; Victor
                    Young] vCL; **Strange As It Seems** [Andy Razaf;
                    Thomas "Fats" Waller] vBS
          78: Brunswick 20112, (F,G) A5114
          LP: JASS 1
          TC: JASS J-C-1
          CD: JASS J-CD-622
                    *as VICTOR YOUNG AND THE BRUNSWICK ORCHESTRA.
                    Matrices 11721 and 11722 were assigned for dubbings of
                    Brunswick English masters by Jack Hylton's Orchestra.*
11723-1   **Crazy People** [Edgar Leslie; James V. Monaco] vFF
                    (as solo)
          78: Perfect 15602, Oriole 2462, Romeo 1838, Imperial (E)
          2742, Banner 32442, Melotone 91339, Crown 91339
                    *Perfect and Crown as ED KIRKEBY AND HIS ORCHESTRA,
                    Imperial as HOLLYWOOD DANCE ORCHESTRA, others as
                    RALPH KIRBERRY ORCHESTRA*
B-11724-1   **Crazy People** vCB (as solo)
          78: Melotone M-12363, Decca (E) F-3059
                    *Melotone as OWEN FALLON AND HIS CALIFORNIANS,
                    Decca as RON ALDRIDGE AND HIS RENO BOYS*

Brunswick, New York, N.Y. Tuesday, May 10, 1932
ARC-BRUNSWICK STUDIO BAND
Victor Young (ldr) Mannie Klein (tp) Tom Dorsey (tb) **Jimmy Dorsey**
(cl,as) *unknown* (as) Joe Venuti (vn) *unknown* (p), (g), (bb), (d,celst)

George Beuchler, Dick Robertson (vcl)

11795-1   **Am I Wasting My Time?** [Jack Manus; Sanford
                 Green] vGB (cl solo)
   78: Perfect 15613, Banner 32458, Oriole 2482
      as HAROLD WHITE AND HIS ORCHESTRA
B-11796-A   **Am I Wasting My Time?** vDR (cl solo)
   78: Melotone M-12374
      as DICK ROBERTSON AND HIS ORCHESTRA
11797-2   **While We Danced At The Mardi Gras** [Johnny Mer-
                 cer; Alfred Opler] vDR (as solo)
   78: Perfect 15612, Conqueror 7995, Banner 32453
      as MAJESTIC DANCE ORCHESTRA
B-11798-A   **While We Danced At The Mardi Gras** vGB (as solo)
   78: Melotone M-12380, Panachord (E) 25306, Decca (E) F-
   3177, Mayfair (E) G-2206
      *Decca as HARRY WOODS AND HIS ORCH., Mayfair as
      EDDIE RUSSELL & HIS ORCH., others as SLEEPY HALL
      AND HIS COLLEGIANS*
11799-1   **Good-bye Blues** [Dorothy Fields, Arnold Johnson;
                 Jimmy McHugh] vGB (cl solo)
   78: Perfect 15611, Banner 32456
      as DAN RITCHIE AND HIS ORCHESTRA
B-11800-A   **Good-bye Blues** vDR (cl solo)
   78: Melotone M-12374
      as DICK ROBERTSON AND HIS ORCHESTRA
11801-1   **Masquerade** [Paul F. Webster; John J. Loeb] vDR
   78: Melotone M-12380, Conqueror 7985, Perfect 15612,
   Panachord (E) 25261, Banner 32453, Oriole 2475
      *Oriole, Melotone, Panachord as SLEEPY HALL AND HIS
      COLLEGIANS, Banner, Perfect and Conqueror as MAJES-
      TIC DANCE ORCHESTRA*

Brunswick, New York, N.Y. Wednesday, May 11, 1932
VICTOR YOUNG AND THE BRUNSWICK ORCHESTRA
Victor Young (ldr) *Frank Guarente [or] Charlie Margulis*, (tp) Tom
Dorsey (tb) Jimmy Dorsey (cl,as) Bennie Krueger (as) *unknown* (ts) 2
unknown (vn) *unknown* (p), (g) Joe Tarto (sb,bb) *Larry Gomar* (d,
chimes) Frank Munn, band (vcl)

B-11814-A,B   **Why Can't This Night Go On Forever?** vFM
                 (unissued)
B-11815-A   **Tell Me Why You Smile, Mona Lisa** [Raymond B.
                 Egan; Walter Reisch; Robert Stoltz] vFM
   78: Brunswick 6309, (E) O1431
B-11816-A   **The Voice In The Old Village Choir** [Gus Kahn;
                 Harry Woods] (waltz) vFM,band
   78: Brunswick 6309

   The organ effect on the last selection was created by employing a
tight scoring of low-register reeds, with violins and string bass.

Columbia, New York, N.Y. Thursday, May 12, 1932
BEN SELVIN AND HIS ORCHESTRA
Ben Selvin (ldr) Mannie Klein (tp) *unknown* (tb) **Jimmy Dorsey** (cl,as)
unknown (ts) Joe Venuti (vn) *unknown* (p), (g), (sb), (d) Milt Coleman
(vcl) *The Three Nitecaps* (vcl grp)

152193-3   **Crazy People** [Edgar Leslie; James V. Monaco] v*3NC*
          (cl solo)
     78: Columbia 2661-D, Regal (Au) G-21443
     LP: The Old Masters 16
152194-   **Is I In Love? I Is** [Mercer Cook; J. Russell Robinson]
          v*3NC* (cl solo)
     78: Columbia 2661-D, Regal (Au) G-21443
     LP: The Old Masters 16
152195-2   **Lullaby Of The Leaves** [Joe Young; Bernice Petkere]
          vMC&*3NC*
     78: Columbia 2654-D
152196-2   **Whistle And Blow Your Blues Away** vMC&3NC
     78: Columbia 2654-D
170621-1,2   **Headin' For Better Times** [Charles Tobias; Murray
          Mencher] *vMC&3NC*
     78: Columbia Special Record for Dairymens' League

Brunswick, New York, N.Y. Thursday, May 19, 1932
RED NICHOLS AND HIS FIVE PENNIES
Red Nichols (tp,ldr) **Jimmy Dorsey** (cl,as) Babe Russin (ts) Jack Russin
(p) Dick McDonough (g) Artie Bernstein (sb) Vic Engle (d) Dick Robertson (vcl)

E-11868-A   **Goin' To Town** [Hughie Prince, Harold Mooney]
          (cl solo)
     78: Brunswick 6213, (G) A-9269, Columbia test pressing exists
     LP: Swingfan (G) 1004
     TC: Neovox (E) 861
E-11869-A   **Goofus** [Gus Kahn; Wayne King, William Harold]
          vDR
     78: Brunswick 6213, (G) A-9269
     LP: Columbia P5-14320, Stash ST-116
E-11870-A   **Our Home Town Mountain Band** [Arthur Fields,
          Wendell Hall] (part 1) vDR (as solo)
     78: Brunswick 6348, (E) O1343, (G) A-9269
E-11871-A   **Our Home Town Mountain Band** (part 2) vDR
          (cl solo)
     78: Brunswick 6348, (E) O1343, (G) A-9269

Jimmy's name is included in the lyrics on part 2 of the last selection.

Columbia, New York, N.Y. Tuesday, June 7, 1932
COLUMBIA STUDIO BAND
Ben Selvin (ldr) Mannie Klein (tp) Tom Dorsey (tb) **Jimmy Dorsey**
(cl,as) *Harry Hoffman [and/or] Joe Venuti* (vn) Fulton McGrath (p) Dick
McDonough (g) Joe Tarto (sb) Harlan Lattimore, Art Jarrett (vcl)

W 152205-1   **I'm Still Without A Sweetheart With Summer Coming On** vHL (cl solo)
    78: Columbia 2671-D
      as HARLAN LATTIMORE AND ORCHESTRA
W 152206-1   **Good-bye Blues** [Dorothy Fields, Arnold Johnson; Jimmy McHugh] vAJ
    78: Columbia 2672-D, Parlophone (E) R-1409
W 152207-2   **This Time It's Love** [Sam M. Lewis; J. Fred Coots] vAJ
    78: Columbia 2672-D, Parlophone (E) R-1409
      152206 and 152207 as ART JARRETT
W 152208-1   **Strange As It Seems** [Andy Razaf; Thomas "Fats" Waller] vHL (as,cl solos)
    78: Columbia 2671-D
      as HARLAN LATTIMORE AND ORCHESTRA

ARC, New York, N.Y. Tuesday, June 14, 1932
ARC STUDIO BAND
Victor Young (ldr) Mannie Klein, *unknown* (tp) *Tom Dorsey [or] Charlie Butterfield* (tb) **Jimmy Dorsey** (cl,as) *Sid Stoneburn* (as) Larry Binyon (cl,ts,fl) 2 unknown (vn) Joe Meresco (p,celst) *Carl Kress* (g) *Dick Cherwin* (sb) *Larry Gomar* (d,vib) Paul Small, Dick Robertson, Smith Ballew (vcl)

11932-1   **Come On And Sit Beside The Sea** vPS
    78: Melotone M-12409, Banner 32489, Perfect 15627
      Melotone as OWEN FALLON AND HIS CALIFORNIANS, Banner as PAUL SMALL, Perfect as PAUL SMALL AND HIS ORCHESTRA
11933-1   **You've Got Me In The Palm Of Your Hands** [Cliff Friend, Edgar Leslie; James V.Monaco] vPS (cl solo)
    78: Melotone M-12410, Perfect 15627, Conqueror 8034, Banner 32489
      Melotone as ART KAHN'S ORCH., Banner as PAUL SMALL, Perfect as PAUL SMALL & HIS ORCH.
11934-1   **If You Were Only Mine** [Charles Newman; Isham Jones] vSB (as solo)
    78: Melotone M-12410, Perfect 15626, Conqueror 8034, Banner 32486, Romeo 1871, Decca (E) F-3083
      Melotone as ART KAHN'S ORCH., Decca as RON AL-DRIDGE & HIS RENO BOYS, others as SMITH BALLEW AND HIS ORCHESTRA
11935-2   **Sleep (Come On And Take Me)** [Joe Young, Boyd Bunch] vSB (cl solo)
    78: Melotone M-12409, Perfect 15626, Banner 32486, Romeo 1871
    LP: Harrison C
      Melotone as OWEN FALLON AND HIS CALIFORNIANS, others as SMITH BALLEW AND HIS ORCHESTRA
One trumpet leaves:
11936-1   **Holding My Honey's Hand** [Walter Hirsch; Ben Bernie] vDR (Contd.)

ARC STUDIO BAND (Contd.)

> **78:** Melotone M-12408, Romeo 1865, Banner 32479, Oriole 2493

11937-1   **There's Oceans Of Love By The Beautiful Sea** [J. Fred Coots, Little Jack Little] vDR (cl solo)
> **78:** Melotone M-12408, Romeo 1865, Banner 32479, Oriole 2493
>
> *11936 and 11937 as DICK ROBERTSON*
> Last two sides also on **TC:** Audio Archives 1013

Brunswick, New York, N.Y. Tuesday, June 14, 1932
CONNIE BOSWELL
Bunny Berigan (tp) Tom Dorsey (tb) **Jimmy Dorsey** (cl,as) *unknown* (as), (ts) Joe Venuti, *unknown* (vn) Martha Boswell (p) Dick McDonough (g) Art Bernstein (sb) Stan King (d) Connie Boswell (vcl)

B-11942-A   **The Night When Love Was Born** [David Oppenheim; Abel Baer, Victor Young] vCB
> **78:** Brunswick 6332, (E) 01328
> **LP:** Jazum 21, Take Two TT209

B-11943-A   **(I've Got The Words—I've Got The Tune) Hummin' To Myself** [Herb Magidson, Monty Seigel; Sammy Fain] vCB (cl solo)
> **78:** Brunswick 6332, (E) 01328
> **LP:** Jazum 21, Take Two TT209

Brunswick, New York, N.Y. Friday, June 17, 1932
BOSWELL SISTERS (accomp. by The Dorsey Brothers Orch.)
Bunny Berigan (tp) Tom Dorsey (tb) **Jimmy Dorsey** (cl) Joe Venuti (vn) Martha Boswell (p) Dick McDonough (g) Art Bernstein (sb) Stan King (d) Boswell Sisters (vcl)

B-11948-A   **Doggone, I've Done It!** [Franklin] vBS
> **78:** Brunswick 6335, (E) 01362, 01893, (F,G) A-9285, Columbia (Au) DO-1111
> **LP:** Columbia Special Products P16493, Jazum 30, Conifer (E) CHD 136
> **TC:** Conifer (E) MCHD 136, Columbia Legacy CT52932
> **CD:** Columbia Legacy CK52943

B-11949, "Hand Me Down My Walking Cane," was also cut. No reeds are heard and it is assumed Jimmy Dorsey had left.

Brunswick, New York, N.Y. Saturday, June 18, 1932
BENNIE KRUEGER AND HIS ORCHESTRA
Bennie Krueger (as,ldr) Mannie Klein, *unknown* (tp) *unknown* (tb) **Jimmy Dorsey** (cl,as) Fran Frey (as,vcl) 2 *unknown* (vn) *unknown* (p), (g), (bb), (d) Scrappy Lambert, Paul Small (vcl)

B-11950-   **Is I In Love? I Is** [Mercer Cook; J. Russel Robinson] vFF

78: Brunswick 6331, (E) O1333
B-11951-   **Come On And Sit Beside The Sea** vFF
   78: Brunswick 6334
B-11952-   **(I've Got The Words—I've Got The Tune) Hummin' To Myself** [Herb Magidson, Monty Seigel; Sammy Fain] vSL
   78: Brunswick 6331, (E) O1333
B-11953-   **You've Got Me In The Palm Of Your Hands** [Cliff Friend, Edgar Leslie; James V.Monaco] vPS (cl solo)
   78: Brunswick 6334, (E) O1357

ARC, New York, N.Y. Saturday, June 25, 1932
CHICK BULLOCK AND HIS LEVEE LOUNGERS
Mannie Klein (tp) **Jimmy Dorsey** (cl,as,vcl) Matty Malneck (vn) Joe Meresco (p) *Carl Kress* (g) *Artie Bernstein [or] Dick Cherwin* (sb) *Stan King [or] Larry Gomar (d)* Chick Bullock (vcl)

11972-1   **Shine** [Cecil Mack, Lew Brown; Ford T. Dabney] vCB (cl,as solos)
   78: Oriole 2506, Perfect 15633
11973-1   **I Heard** [Don Redman] vCB&JD (cl,as solos)
   78: Oriole 2506, Perfect 15633
   First two sides also on **TC:** Audio Archives 1004
11974-1   **The Night When Love Was Born** [David Oppenheim; Abel Baer, Victor Young] vCB
   78: Conqueror 8043, Perfect 12825, Romeo 1866, Broadcast 3259
11975-1   **If You Were Only Mine** [Charles Newman; Isham Jones] vCB
   78: Conqueror 8043, Perfect 12825, Romeo 1866, Broadcast 3259
   11974 and 11975 as CHICK BULLOCK

ARC, New York, N.Y. Tuesday, July 12, 1932
ARC STUDIO BAND
Mannie Klein, *unknown* (tp) Tom Dorsey (tb) **Jimmy Dorsey** (cl,as) *Al Duffy* (vn) *unknown* (p) Dick McDonough (g) *unknown* (sb), (d) Chick Bullock, Scrappy Lambert (vcl)

12050-2   **Lonesome Me** [Andy Razaf; Thomas "Fats" Waller, Con Conrad] vCB
   78: Banner 32507, Perfect 15637
   as DAN RITCHIE AND HIS ORCHESTRA
B-12051-A   **Lonesome Me** vSL
   78: Melotone M-12437, Panachord (E) 25439
   as OWEN FALLON AND HIS CALIFORNIANS
12052-   **Who's To Blame?** vSL
   78: Perfect 15636, Banner 32505, Oriole 2516
   as SMITH BALLEW AND HIS ORCHESTRA
B-12053-A   **Now You've Got Me Worryin' For You** vSL (cl solo)
   78: Melotone M-12437
   as OWEN FALLON AND HIS CALIFORNIANS (Contd.)

ARC STUDIO BAND (Contd.)

12054-1   **Now You've Got Me Worryin' For You** vCB (cl
                   solo)
       78: Perfect 15646, Banner 32512
       LP: Harrison Y
                   as DAN RITCHIE AND HIS ORCHESTRA
12055-1   **Syncopate Your Sins Away** vCB (cl solo)
       78: Perfect 15641, Melotone 91390, Banner 32509
                   as CHICK BULLOCK & HIS LEVEE LOUNGERS
12056-   **Rhythm On The River** vCB (cl solo)
       78: Perfect 15641, Melotone 91390, Banner 32509
                   as CHICK BULLOCK & HIS LEVEE LOUNGERS

Brunswick, New York, N.Y. Thursday, July 14, 1932
JIMMY DORSEY (with the Dorsey Brothers' Orchestra)
Tom Dorsey (tb,ldr) Leo McConville (tp) **Jimmy Dorsey** (as) Fulton
McGrath (p) Carl Kress (g) Artie Bernstein (sb) Stan King (d)

B-12071-A   **Beebe** [Jimmy Dorsey] (as solo)
       78: Brunswick 6352, (E) 1390, (G) A-9293
       LP: Bandstand BS 7127
B-12071-B   **Beebe** (as solo)
       78: Brunswick 6352
       LP: Meritt 11
B-12072-A   **Three Moods** (Tom Dorsey trombone solo)
       78: unissued test pressing (remade August 6, 1932)
B-12073-A   **Oodles Of Noodles** [Jimmy Dorsey] (as solo)
       78: Brunswick 6352, (E)1361, (G) A-9293, (F)
       A-50024
       TC: ProArte Digital PCD508
       CD: ProArte Digital CDD508, Jazz Greats (E) 036
B-12073-B   **Oodles Of Noodles** [Jimmy Dorsey] (as solo)
       78: Columbia 36063 (dub) (in Set C 51)
       all takes are also on **CD:** Jazz Oracle (C) BDW8006

ARC, New York, N.Y. Monday, August 1, 1932
CHICK BULLOCK & HIS LEVEE LOUNGERS (ARC Studio Band)
Bunny Berigan, Mannie Klein (tp) Tom Dorsey (tb) **Jimmy Dorsey,**
unknown (cl,as) Larry Binyon (cl,ts) 3 *unknown* (vn) Joe Meresco (p)
Dick McDonough (g) *Artie Bernstein [or] Dick Cherwin* (sb) *Larry
Gomar [or] Stan King* (d) Chick Bullock (vcl)

12117-1   **We Just Couldn't Say Good-bye** [Harry Woods]
                   vCB (as solo)
       78: Banner 32510, Conqueror 7996, Melotone M-12451, 91397,
       Oriole 2523, Perfect 15643, Panachord (E) 25261, Mayfair (E) G-
       2200
                   *Melotone 12451 and Panachord as RALPH BENNETT & HIS
                   SEVEN ACES (ALL ELEVEN OF 'EM), Banner and Mel-
                   otone 91397 as CHICK BULLOCK & HIS LAZY LEVEE
                   LOUNGERS, Mayfair as AL GREEN AND HIS ORCH.*

TC: Audio Archives 1004
12118-3   **My Heart's At Ease** [Joe Young; Thomas "Fats"
                 Waller] vCB (cl,as solos)
   78: Conqueror 7996, Oriole 2523, Melotone M-12452, Perfect
   15643, Banner 32510
         *Melotone as ART KAHN'S ORCHESTRA, Banner as CHICK
         BULLOCK AND HIS LAZY LEVEE LOUNGERS*
   TC: Audio Archives 1004
12136-1   **We Were Only Walking In The Moonlight** [Johnny
                 Burke, Harold Spina; Johnny Green] vCB
   78: Conqueror 8026, Perfect 15657, Banner 32538, Melotone
   M-12453
         *Banner as CHICK BULLOCK, Melotone as ART KAHN'S
         ORCHESTRA*
12137-1   **Sheltered By The Stars (Cradled By The Moon)**
                 [Thomas "Fats" Waller; Victor Young] vCB (cl solo)
   78: Conqueror 8026, Oriole 2542, Melotone M-12454, Banner
   32538, Perfect 15657
         *Banner as CHICK BULLOCK, Melotone as SLEEPY HALL
         AND HIS COLLEGIANS*

Brunswick, New York, N.Y. Friday, August 5, 1932
ADELAIDE HALL
Mannie Klein (tp) **Jimmy Dorsey** (cl,as) Art Tatum, Francis J. Carter
(p) Dick McDonough (g) *unknown* (sb) Adelaide Hall (vcl)

B-12148-A   **Strange As It Seems** [Andy Razaf; Thomas "Fats"
                   Waller] vAH (cl solo)
   78: Brunswick 6376, (E) 1348
   LP: Collector's Items (E) 011
B-12148-B   **Strange As It Seems** vAH
   LP: Meritt 24
B-12149-A   **I'll Never Be The Same** [Gus Kahn; Matty Malneck,
                   Frank Signorelli] vAH
   78: Brunswick 6362, (E) 1348
   LP: Collector's Items (E) 011
B-12149-B   **I'll Never Be The Same** vAH
   LP: Meritt 24

Brunswick, New York, N.Y. Saturday, August 6, 1932
TOM DORSEY (Trombone Solo with The Dorsey Brothers' Orch.)
Mannie Klein (tp) Tom Dorsey (tb) **Jimmy Dorsey** (cl,as) Larry Binyon
(cl) Fulton McGrath (p) Carl Kress (g) Art Bernstein (sb) Stan King (d)

B-12150-A   **Three Moods** [Tommy Dorsey] (cl solos)
   78: Brunswick (E) O1367, (G) A-9293, (F) A-500204
   LP: Broadway BR113, Emporium 039
   TC: Neovox (E) 804
   CD: Le Jazz (ECC) 8106, Classics (F) 833, Best Of Jazz (F)
   4029, Jazz Oracle (C) BDW8006
B-12150-B   **Three Moods** (cl solo)
   CD: Jazz Oracle (C) BDW8006

BOSWELL SISTERS (accomp. by The Dorsey Bros. Orch.)
Personnel as last (same session). Boswell Sisters (vcl) Glenn Miller (arr)

B-12151-A   **We Just Couldn't Say Good-bye** [Harry Woods] vBS
     78: Brunswick 6360, (E) 01347, (G) A-9299
     LP: Biograph BLP C-3, Columbia Special Products P16493
     CD: Jazz Roots 56082
B-12151-B   **We Just Couldn't Say Good-bye** vBS
     LP: JASS 1
     TC: JASS J-C-1
     CD: JASS J-CD-622
B-12152-A   **Sleep (Come On And Take Me)** [Joe Young, Boyd
                    Bunch] vBS (as solo)
     LP: Columbia Special Products P16493
     TC: Columbia CT 66977
     CD: Jazz Roots 56082, Columbia CK 66977
B-12152-B   **Sleep (Come On And Take Me)** vBS (as solo)
     LP: JASS 1
     TC: JASS J-C-1
     CD: JASS J-CD-622, Retrieval (E) RTR 79009
B-12153-A   **Down Among The Sheltering Palms** [James Brock-
                    man; Abe Olman] vBS (cl solo)
     78: Brunswick 6418, (E) 01347, (G) A-9299, Columbia 36522
     LP: Columbia Special Products P16493, Jazum 30
     CD: Jazz Roots 56082
B-12153-B   **Down Among The Sheltering Palms** vBS (cl solo)
     78: Brunswick 6418
     LP: Biograph BLP C-3, JASS 1
     TC: JASS J-C-1
     CD: JASS J-CD-622

Brunswick, New York, N.Y. Monday, August 8, 1932
VICTOR YOUNG AND HIS ORCHESTRA
Victor Young (ldr) *Frank Guarente [or] Charlie Margulis, Bob Effros*
(tp) Tom Dorsey (tb) **Jimmy Dorsey** (cl,as,bar) Bennie Krueger (cl,as)
Larry Binyon (cl,ts) Joe Venuti, Harry Hoffman (vn) Arthur Schutt (p)
Eddie Lang (g) Joe Tarto (bb,sb) Larry Gomar (d,vib) Frank Luther,
Zora Layman (Mrs. Frank Luther) (vcl)

B-12154-A   **Moonlight On The River** [Bud Green] vZL&FL
     78: Brunswick 6361, (E) 1358
B-12155-A   **While We Danced At The Mardi Gras** [Johnny Mer-
                    cer; Alfred Opler] vZL&FL (as solo)
     78: Brunswick 6361, (E) 1358, Lucky (J) 60169
B-12156-G   **Carnaval (While We Danced At The Mardi Gras)**
                    (as solo)
     78: Brunswick (Arg) (# unknown), ARC Theater-Use F-236 (dub)
               Brunswick as LOS GRANADIANS
     ET: ARC Theater-Use E-681 (dub)
12157-1   **I'm Yours For Tonight** [Edgar Leslie; James V.
                    Monaco] vFL
     78: Melotone M-12455, Conqueror 7996, Perfect 15656, Banner

32537, Oriole 2541
12158-1   **Here's Hoping** [Harold Adamson; J.Fred Coots] vFL
   78: Melotone M-12456, Conqueror 8027, Perfect 15656, Oriole
2541, Banner 32537, Panachord (E) 25405
     *For 12157 and 12158: Melotones, Panachord as OWEN
FALLON & HIS CALIFORNIANS, others as BOB CAUSER
& HIS CORNELLIANS.*

ARC, New York, N.Y. Thursday, August 11, 1932
ARC STUDIO BAND
Mannie Klein, Frank Guarente (tp) Tom Dorsey (tb) **Jimmy Dorsey,**
Bennie Krueger (cl,as) *Larry Binyon* (ts) *Walter Edelstein, Harry
Hoffman, unknown* (vn) Emil Seidel (p,celst) Dick McDonough (g) Dick
Cherwin (sb) *Larry Gomar* (d,vib) Smith Ballew (vcl)

12171-1   **Don't Tell A Soul (We're In Love)** [Harry S. Pep-
          per] vSB
   78: Melotone M-12455, Perfect 15654, Banner 32554
     *Banner as SMITH BALLEW AND HIS ORCHESTRA, others
as RALPH BENNETT AND HIS SEVEN ACES*
12172-1   **I'm Forgetting Myself For You** vSB (as solo)
   78: Melotone M-12456, Panachord (E) 25334, Perfect 15654,
Banner 32554
     *Banner as SMITH BALLEW AND HIS ORCHESTRA, others
as OWEN FALLON AND HIS CALIFORNIANS*
12173-1   **Goodnight, Vienna** [Marvell, George Posford] vSB
          (as solo)
   78: Melotone M-12466, Oriole 2550, Perfect 15664
     *Melotone, Perfect as SLEEPY HALL AND HIS COL-
LEGIANS, Oriole as BUDDY BLUE AND HIS TEXANS*
12174-1   **Living In Clover** [Marvell, George Posford] vSB
   78: Melotone M-12466, Oriole 2550, Perfect 15664
     *Melotone, Perfect as SLEEPY HALL AND HIS COL-
LEGIANS, Oriole as BUDDY BLUE AND HIS TEXANS*

Brunswick, New York, N.Y. Tuesday, August 16, 1932
ARC STUDIO BAND
Mannie Klein (tp) Tom Dorsey (tb) **Jimmy Dorsey** (cl,as) *unknown* (as),
(ts) *Harry Hoffman, unknown* (vn) Fulton McGrath (p) *Carl Kress [or]
Dick McDonough* (g) Artie Bernstein (sb) Chauncey Morehouse (d,vib)
Chick Bullock, Annette Hanshaw (vcl)

12192-2   **Love Me Tonight** [Bing Crosby, Ned Washington;
          Victor Young] vCB
   78: Oriole 2547
     as MAJESTIC DANCE ORCHESTRA
12193-1   **You're Blasé** [Bruce Sievier; Hamilton J. Ord] vCB
          (cl solo)
   78: Melotone M-12465, Perfect 15660, Banner 32542, Oriole
2547
     *Melotone as RALPH BENNETT AND HIS SEVEN ACES,
Perfect and Banner as MAJESTIC DANCE ORCH.* (Contd.)

ARC STUDIO BAND (Contd.)

Unknown (as) (ts) (vn) out:
12198-A   **It Was So Beautiful** [Arthur Freed; Harry Barris]
                 vAH
    LP: Sunbeam P-512, Halcyon (E) HDL-119
    TC: Halcyon (E) CHDL-119, CTP5
12199-A   **We Just Couldn't Say "Goodbye"** [Harry Woods]
                 vAH (cl solos)
    78: Banner 32541, Conqueror 8046, Melotone M-12471, Oriole
    2546, Perfect 12835, Panachord (E) 25270, Broadway (E) 4018
        Broadway as MARGARET STONE, others as ANNETTE
        HANSHAW
    LP: Sunbeam P-512, Halcyon (E) HDL-119
    TC: Halcyon (E) CHDL-119, CTP5, ASV Living Era AJA 5210

ARC, New York, N.Y. Thursday, August 18, 1932
ARC STUDIO BAND
Mannie Klein, *unknown* (tp) *Russ Morgan* (tb) **Jimmy Dorsey** (cl,as)
Benny Kreuger (as) Matty Malneck, Harry Hoffman (vn) Fulton
McGrath (p) *Carl Kress [or] Dick McDonough* (g) Artie Bernstein (sb)
Chauncey Morehouse (d,vib) Will Osborne, Annette Hanshaw (vcl)

12205-1   **I Guess I'll Have To Change My Plans (Blue Pa-**
                 jama Song) [Howard Dietz; Arthur Schwartz] vWO
    78: Melotone M-12462, Panachord (E) 25334, Banner 32549,
    Conqueror 8035, Perfect 15665
        Melotone, Panachord as OWEN FALLON AND HIS CALI-
        FORNIANS, others as HAROLD WHITE AND HIS ORCH.
12206-1   **Three's A Crowd** [Al Dubin, Irving Kahal; Harry
                 Warren] vWO
    78: Melotone M-12463, Panachord (E) 25294, Conqueror 8025,
    Perfect 15663, Imperial (E) 2782
        Melotone and Panachord as ART KAHN'S ORCHESTRA,
        others as WILL OSBORNE AND HIS ORCHESTRA
12207-1   **Sweethearts Forever** [Irving Caesar; Cliff Friend]
                 vWO
    78: Melotone M-12463, Panachord (E) 25294, Conqueror 8025,
    Perfect 15663, Imperial (E) 2782
        Melotone and Panachord as ART KAHN'S ORCHESTRA,
        others as WILL OSBORNE AND HIS ORCHESTRA
12208-1   **Strange Interlude** [Ben Bernie, Walter Hirsch; Phil
                 Baker] vWO
    78: Melotone M-12462, Panachord (E) 25316, Banner 32549,
    Conqueror 8035, Perfect 15665
        Melotone, Panachord as OWEN FALLON AND HIS CALI-
        FORNIANS, others as HAROLD WHITE AND HIS ORCH.
12209-1   **Love Me Tonight** [Bing Crosby, Ned Washington;
                 Victor Young] vAH
    78: Banner 32541, Conqueror 8046, Melotone M-12471, Oriole
    2546, Perfect 12835, Panachord (E) 25270, Broadway (E) 4018
        Broadway as MARGARET STONE, others as ANNETTE

HANSHAW
LP: Sunbeam P-512, Halcyon (E) HDL-119
TC: Halcyon (E) CHDL-119, CTP5

Brunswick, New York, N.Y. Thursday, September 8, 1932
ARC STUDIO BAND
Mannie Klein (tp) *unknown* (tb) **Jimmy Dorsey,** Bennie Krueger (cl,as) *unknown* (ts) *unknown* (vn) Fulton McGrath (p) *Carl Kress [or] Dick McDonough* (g) *unknown* (sb), (d) Chick Bullock (vcl)

12258-1   **Something In The Night** vCB
       78: Melotone M-12477, Panachord 25379, Perfect 15673
              Perfect as DAN RITCHIE AND HIS ORCHESTRA, others as ART KAHN'S ORCHESTRA
12259-1   **Me Minus You** vCB
       78: Melotone M-12493, Perfect 15671, Oriole 2564
              Melotone as OWEN FALLON AND HIS ORCHESTRA, Perfect and Oriole as BOB CAUSER AND HIS CORNEL-LIANS
12260-1   **Everyone Says "I Love You"** [Bert Kalmar; Harry Ruby] vCD
       78: Melotone M-12477, Panachord 25406, Oriole 2564, Mayfair (E) G-2255, Broadcast (E) B-110
              Oriole and Broadcast as BOB CAUSER AND HIS COR-NELLIANS, Mayfair as JACK REYNOLDS AND HIS OR-CHESTRA, others as ART KAHN'S ORCHESTRA
12261-(1,2)   **Always In My Heart (Forever In My Mind)** vCB
              (unissued) *(recut September 18, 1932, without Jimmy)*

Brunswick, New York, N.Y. Friday, September 9, 1932
VICTOR YOUNG AND HIS ORCHESTRA
Victor Young (ldr) *Frank Guarente [or] Charlie Margulis, unknown* (tp) Tom Dorsey (tb) **Jimmy Dorsey** (cl,as,bar) Bennie Krueger (cl,as) Larry Binyon (cl,ts) Harry Hoffman, *unknown* (vn) *unknown* (viola) Arthur Schutt (p) *unknown* (g,stg) Joe Tarto (bb,sb) Larry Gomar (d,xyl) Frank Munn (vcl)

BX-12267   **Sylvia** [Clinton Scollard; Oley Speaks] vFM
       78: (12 inch) Brunswick 20118, (E) 0115
              as VICTOR YOUNG & BRUNSWICK CONCERT ORCH.
B-12268-A   **Whisper Waltz** vFM
       78: Brunswick 6421, (E) 01412, Lucky (J) 60089

Theater-Use E-673/F-224 ("Love Me Tonight") credited to September 9, 1932, is a dub of a side cut August 30, 1932, by other personnel.

Brunswick, New York, N.Y. Saturday, September 10, 1932
CONNIE BOSWELL
Victor Young (ldr) Mannie Klein (tp) Tom Dorsey (tb) **Jimmy Dorsey** (cl,as) Larry Binyon (ts) 2 *unknown* (vn) Fulton McGrath (p) Dick McDonough (g) Art Bernstein (sb) Stan King (d) Connie Boswell (vcl)

B-12278-A   **Say It Isn't So** [Irving Berlin] vCB (cl solo)
          78: Brunswick 6393, (E) 01373, Columbia Special Edition SE-
          5002-S (1948 dub)
          LP: Jazum 21, Take Two TT209
B-12279-A   **Where? (I Wonder Where)** [Milton Drake, Walter
                    Kent, Terry Shand] vCB (cl solo)
          78: Brunswick 6393, (E) 01373
          LP: Jazum 21, Take Two TT209

Brunswick, New York, N.Y. Tuesday, September 13, 1932
BOSWELL SISTERS (accomp. by THE DORSEY BROTHERS)
Jimmy Dorsey (cl,ldr) Mannie Klein (tp) Tom Dorsey (tb) Larry Binyon
(ts,fl) Martha Boswell (p) Dick McDonough (g) Art Bernstein (sb) Stan
King (d) Boswell Sisters (vcl)

B-12290-A   **Down On The Delta** vBS
          78: Brunswick 6395, (E) 01403, (G) A-9329
          LP: Columbia Special Products P16493, CBS 80074
B-12290-B   **Down On The Delta** vBS
          78: Brunswick 6395
          LP: Jazum 21
B-12291-A   **Charlie Two-Step** vBS
          78: Brunswick 6418, (E) 01403, (G) A-9317, (It) 4803, Lucky
          (J) 60023
          LP: Jazum 30, Columbia Special Products P16493
          CD: Smithsonian 381, Fremaux 2741
B-12291-A   **Sentimental Gentleman From Georgia** [Mitchell
                    Parish; Frank Perkins] vBS
          78: Brunswick 6395, (E) 01379, (G) A-9329, (It) 4879,
          Columbia 36522 (dub), Rex 8910
          LP: Biograph BLP C-3, Columbia Special Products P16493,
          Conifer (E) CHD 136
          TC: Conifer (E) MCHD 136, ProArte Digital PCD550, Columbia
          CT 66977, Radio Yesteryear Stack 47
          CD: ProArte Digital CCD550, Columbia CK66977, Flapper 7087

ARC, New York, N.Y. Wednesday, September 14, 1932
ANNETTE HANSHAW
Mannie Klein (tp) **Jimmy Dorsey** (cl) Fulton McGrath (p,celst) *unknown
(vn) Carl Kress [or] Dick McDonough* (g) Artie Bernstein (sb) Chauncey
Morehouse (d,vib) Annette Hanshaw (vcl)

12283-2   **Say It Isn't So** [Irving Berlin] vAH (cl solo)
          78: Banner 32565, Broadway 4022, Melotone M-12486, Oriole
          2561, Perfect 12842, Romeo 1935, Panachord (E) 25324
          LP: Sunbeam P-512, Halcyon (E) HDL-119
          TC: Halcyon (E) CHDL-119, CTP5
          CD: Take Two 408
12284-1   **You'll Always Be The Same Sweetheart To Me**
                    [Charles Tobias, Peter De Rose, Joe Burke] vAH (cl
                    solo)
          78: Banner 32565, Broadway 4022, Melotone M-12486, Oriole

2561, Perfect 12842, Romeo 1935, Conqueror 8044, Panachord
(E) 25324
LP: Sunbeam P-512, Halcyon (E) HDL-119
TC: Halcyon (E) CHDL-119, CTP5

Only two other sides were cut that day by ARC, 12281 and 12282 by
Singin' Sam (Harry Frankel). One of these, "For Old Times Sake," as
Singin' Sam and Orchestra, could include some of the above musicians.

Brunswick, New York, N.Y. Thursday, September 15, 1932
VICTOR YOUNG AND HIS BRUNSWICK ORCHESTRA
Victor Young (ldr) *Frank Guarente [or] Charlie Margulis*, *Mannie Klein*
(tp) Tom Dorsey (tb) **Jimmy Dorsey,** *unknown* (cl,as) *Larry Binyon* (ts)
unknown (vn), (p), (g) *Art Bernstein* (sb) Stan King (d) Frank Munn,
Len Stokes (vcl)

B-12289-A   **We're Dancing Together Again** vFM
    78: Brunswick 6384
B-12295-A   **Rock-A-Bye Moon** [Johnson, Steele, Lang] vFM&LS
    78: Brunswick 6398, (E) 1396
B-12296-A   **When Mother Played The Organ (And Daddy Sang
                 A Hymn)** [Dick Sanford; George McConnell] vFM&
                 LS (cl solo)
    78: Brunswick 6398, (E) 1412
B-12297-   **You'll Always Be The Same Sweetheart To Me**
                 [Charles Tobias, Peter De Rose, Joe Burke] vFM
    78: Brunswick 6384, (E) 1412

Brunswick, New York, N.Y. Saturday, September 17, 1932
VICTOR YOUNG AND THE BRUNSWICK ORCHESTRA
Victor Young (ldr) *Frank Guarente [or] Charlie Margulis*, Bunny Beri-
gan (tp) Tom Dorsey (tb) Bennie Krueger (c-mel,as) **Jimmy Dorsey**
(cl,as) 2 *unknown* (ts), (vn) *Fulton McGrath* (p) *Dick McDonough* (g)
Artie Bernstein (sb) *unknown* (harp), *Larry Gomar* (d) Harlan Lattimore,
Dick Robertson, Frank Munn (vcl)

B-12310-A   **How Do You Do It?** [E. Y. Harburg; Lewis E. Gen-
                 sler] vHL
    78: Brunswick 6380
    TC: Audio Archives 1002, Columbia/Legacy CT 52930
    CD: Columbia/Legacy CK 52942, IAJRC CD-1013
B-12311-A   **Riddle Me This** [E. Y. Harburg; Jay Gorney] vDR
                 (cl solo)
    78: Brunswick 6380
            12310 & 12311 as ABE LYMAN & HIS CALIFORNIA ORCH.
B-12312-   **A Shine On Your Shoes** [Howard Dietz; Arthur
                 Schwartz] vDR (cl solo)
    78: Brunswick 6382
B-12313-   **Alone Together** [Howard Dietz; Arthur Schwartz]
                 vFM
    78: Brunswick 6382
    LP: CBS P514320

Brunswick, New York, N.Y. Thursday, September 22, 1932
THE SONG FELLOWS
Jimmy Dorsey (cl) *unknown* (p) *Dick McDonough* (g) *unknown* (d) The
Song Fellows (3 males) (vcl grp)

12352-   **Me Minus You** vSF
    78: Melotone M-12504
12353-   **So Ashamed** vSF
    78: Melotone M-12504
12354-   **It Don't Mean A Thing (If It Ain't Got That Swing)**
              [Irving Mills; Edward K. "Duke" Ellington] vSF
    78: Melotone M-12508
12355-   **Sentimental Gentleman From Georgia** [Mitchell
              Parish; Frank Perkins] vSF
    78: Melotone M-12508

Brunswick, New York, N.Y. Saturday, September 24, 1932
THE DORSEY BROTHERS' ORCHESTRA
Tom Dorsey (tb,ldr) Bunny Berigan (tp) **Jimmy Dorsey** (cl,as) Larry
Binyon (ts) Fulton McGrath (p) Dick McDonough (g) Artie Bernstein
(sb) Stan King (d) Jean Bowes (vcl)

B-12362-A   **Someone Stole Gabriel's Horn** [Ned Washington,
              Edgar Hayes, Irving Mills] vJB (cl solo)
    78: Brunswick (E) 01386, (G) A9332
    TC: Columbia/Legacy CT 48908, (H) 37169-4
    CD: Columbia/Legacy CK 48908, (H)37169-2, Hep (UK) 1005
B-12363-A   **I'm Gettin' Sentimental Over You** [Ned Washing-
              ton; George Bassman] vJB (as solo)
    78: Brunswick 6409, (E) 01386, (G) A9332, (F) A81743
    LP: Epic L2N6022, Columbia P12858, P13929, CBS 88026,
    Columbia Special Products P15028
    TC: Columbia Special Products P13929, Columbia/Legacy CT
    48908, (H) 37169-4
    CD: Columbia/Legacy CK 48908, (H) 37169-2
B-12363-B   **I'm Gettin' Sentimental Over You** vJB (as solo)
    78: Columbia 36065
    EP: Columbia C-51 (36065)
    all sides also on **LP:** HEP (Sc) 1005, **CD:** Hep (UK) 1005

ARC, New York, N.Y. Monday, September 26, 1932
CHICK BULLOCK & HIS LEVEE LOUNGERS (ARC Studio Band)
Victor Young (ldr) Bunny Berigan (tp) **Jimmy Dorsey** (cl,as) *Harry
Hoffman* (vn) Fulton McGrath (p), Dick McDonough (g) Art Bernstein
(sb) Stan King (d) Chick Bullock (vcl)

12364-1   **Underneath The Harlem Moon** [Mack Gordon,
              Harry Revell] vCB
    78: Conqueror 8015, Melotone M-12502, Oriole 2575, Perfect
    15678, Romeo 1941
12365-1   **Mighty River** [Billy Baskette] vCB (cl solo)
    78: Conqueror 8015, Melotone M-12502, Oriole 2575, Perfect

15678, Romeo 1941
Both Bullock sides also on **TC:** Audio Archives 1002, **CD:** IAJRC
CD1013
Unknown (tp) Tom Dorsey (tb) *unknown* (as) Larry Binyon (ts) 2
unknown (vn) added:
E682 (F233)   **Here's Hoping** [Harold Adamson; J. Fred Coots]
    78: ARC Theater-Use F-233
    ET: ARC Theater-Use E-682
E683 (F228)   **You're Telling Me** [Gus Kahn; Walter Donaldson]
    78: ARC Theater-Use F-228
    ET: ARC Theater-Use E-683
E684 (F229)   **Say It Isn't So** [Irving Berlin]
    78: ARC Theater-Use F-229
    ET: ARC Theater-Use E-684
E685 (F230)   **All-American Girl** [Al Lewis] (cl solo)
    78: ARC Theater-Use F-230
    ET: ARC Theater-Use E-685
      as ALL-STAR COLLEGIANS
    LP: Sunbeam MFC-16
    CD: IAJRC CD-1013
E686 (F231-1)   **Please** [Leo Robin; Ralph Rainger]
    78: ARC Theater-Use F-231
    ET: ARC Theater-Use E-686
E687 (F232)   **Underneath The Harlem Moon** [Mack Gordon, Harry
      Revel] (cl solos)
    78: ARC Theater-Use F-232
    ET: ARC Theater-Use E-687

Brunswick, New York, N.Y. Tuesday, September 27, 1932
THE DORSEY BROTHERS' ORCHESTRA
Tom Dorsey (tb,ldr) Bunny Berigan (tp) **Jimmy Dorsey** (cl,as) Larry
Binyon (ts) Harry Hoffman, *unknown* (vn on first tune only) Helvetica
Boswell (cel) Fulton McGrath (p) Dick McDonough (g) Artie Bernstein
(sb) Stan King (d) Connie Boswell, Jean Bowes (vcl)

B-12378-A   **I'll Never Have To Dream Again** [Charles Newman;
      Isham Jones] vCB
    78: Brunswick 6405, (E) 01382, Columbia 5002-S (dub)
    LP: Jazum 21, Take Two TT209
B-12379-A   **Me Minus You** [Paul Webster; John Jacob Loeb]
      vCB (cl solo)
    78: Brunswick 6405, (E) 01382
      12378, 12379 as CONNIE BOSWELL with Dorsey Bros. Orch.
    LP: Jazum 30, Take Two TT 209, ASV Living Era (E) AJA5060
    TC: ASV Living Era (E) ZC AJA5060
    CD: ASV Living Era (E) CD AJA5060
B-12380-A   **Sing (It's Good For You)** [Harold Mooney, Prince]
      vJB (cl,as solos)
    78: Brunswick 6409, (E) 1413
    LP: Biograph BLP C-10, HEP (Sc) 1005
    TC: Columbia/Legacy CT 48908, (H) 37169-4
    CD: Columbia/Legacy CK 48908, (H) 37169-2, Hep (UK) 1005

Brunswick, New York, N.Y. Friday, October 14, 1932
BING CROSBY
Victor Young (ldr) *Mannie Klein* (tp) Tom Dorsey (tb) **Jimmy Dorsey** (cl) *Bennie Krueger* (as) *unknown* (ts) 4 *unknown* (vn) Lennie Hayton (p) *Eddie Lang* (g) *unknown* (sb), (d) Bing Crosby (vcl)

B-12472-A   **How Deep Is The Ocean?** [Irving Berlin] vBC (cl solo)
    78: Brunswick 6406, (E) 1421, Columbia (E) 4301-M, (E) 4417-M, (E) DB-1985
    ET: AFRS America's Popular Music #55, AFRS The Swinging Years #245,137
    EP: Columbia 33S-11313, SEG-7522, Fontana (E) TFR-6012
    LP: Columbia CL-6027, (J) Z-1051, Harmony HL-7094, HS-11313, Realm 52069, Hallmark HM520, Philco LP-435, Fontana (E) TFE-17179, Z-4027, Book-Of-The-Month Club 60-5256
    8T: Book-Of-The-Month Club 10-5637
    TC: Book-Of-Month Club 90-5636, Columbia-Legacy CT48974
    CD: Columbia-Legacy CD48974, ASV Living Era (E) 5072, Affinity (E) AFS 1021-2
B-12473-A   **Here Lies Love** [Leo Robin, Ralph Rainger] vBC
    78: Brunswick 6406, (E) 1380, Columbia (E) DB-1990
    LP: Columbia C2L43, CL-2749, Columbia Special Products P4 13153, CBS 66206
    CD: Charly (E) QBCD 29, Living Era (E) AJA 5043
B-12474-A   **(I Don't Stand) A Ghost Of A Chance With You** [Bing Crosby, Ned Washington; Victor Young] vBC (cl solos)
    78: Brunswick 6454, (E) 1423, Columbia (E) DB-2030
    TC: Columbia-Legacy CT 48974
    CD: Columbia-Legacy CD 48974
B-12474-B   **(I Don't Stand) A Ghost Of A Chance With You** vBC (cl solos)
    78: Columbia (E) 4533-M, 5-1167, Harmony 1003
    EP: Fontana (E) TFE-17186 TFR-6012
    LP: Columbia CL-6027, CL-6105, (J) Z-1051, Harmony HL-7094, HS-11313, Hallmark HM520, Realm 52069

ARC, New York, N.Y. Thursday, October 20, 1932
ARC STUDIO BAND
Mannie Klein, unknown (tp) Tom Dorsey (tb) **Jimmy Dorsey** (cl,as) *unknown* (ts) 2 *unknown* (vn) Fulton McGrath (p) Dick McDonough (g) Art Bernstein (sb) Stan King (d) Harlan Lattimore, Ella Logan (vcl)

12488-1,2   **Take Me In Your Arms** [Mitchell Parish; Fritz Rutler, Alred Markush] vHL
    78: Banner 32601, Conqueror 8080, Melotone M-12512, Oriole 2591, Perfect 15691, Romeo 1963, Panachord (E) 25407
12489-1   **Someday We'll Meet Again** [Al Hoffman, Al Goodhart, Milton Ager] vHL
    78: Banner 32603, Oriole 2594, Melotone M-12511, Conqueror 8079, Perfect 15690, Romeo 1958, Panachord (E) 25340

TO 1215   **Someday We'll Meet Again**
    78: (unissued test pressing)
12490-1   **A Little Street Where Old Friends Meet** [Gus Kahn;
                   Harry Woods] vHL
    78: Banner 32601, Conqueror 8080, Melotone M-12512, Oriole
    2591, Perfect 15691, Romeo 1963, Panachord (E) 25404
            12488, 12490 as OWEN FALLON AND HIS CALIFORNIANS
12491-2   **Just A Little Home For The Old Folks (A Token
                   From Me)** [Edgar Leslie; Fred E. Ahlert] vHL
    78: Banner 32603, Oriole 2594, Melotone M-12511, Conqueror
    8079, Romeo 1958, Perfect 15690, Panachord (E) 25340
            12489, 12491 as ED LOYD AND HIS ORCHESTRA
Unknown (tp), (ts) 2 *unknown* (vn), Tom Dorsey (tb) out:
TO 1216-1   **Dinah** [Sam M. Lewis, Joseph Young; Harry Akst]
                   vEL (cl solo)
    78: Test Only 1216
    LP: Meritt 11
    CD: Hep (UK) 1005

ARC, New York, N.Y. Wednesday, October 26, 1932
GENE AUSTIN
Tom Dorsey (tb) **Jimmy Dorsey** (cl,as) Larry Binyon (ts,fl) Joe Venuti,
2 *unknown* (vn) *Joe Meresco [or] Fulton McGrath* (p) Dick McDonough
(g) *Art Bernstein* (sb) Gene Austin (vcl)

12511-2   **(I Don't Stand) A Ghost Of A Chance With You**
                   [Bing Crosby, Ned Washington; Victor Young] vGA
                   (cl solo)
    78: Banner 32729, Melotone M-12658, Oriole 2673, Perfect
    12901, Romeo 2046, Decca (E) F-3332
    CD: Living Era (E) AJA5217
12512-1   **Just A Little Home For The Old Folks (A Token
                   From Me)** [Edgar Leslie; Fred E. Ahlert] vGA
    78: Banner 32614, Conqueror 8081, Melotone M-12529, Oriole
    2595, Perfect 12862, Decca (E) F-3332
12513-2   **A Little Street Where Old Friends Meet** [Gus Kahn;
                   Harry Woods] vGA
    78: Banner 32614, Conqueror 8081, Melotone M-12529, Oriole
    2595, Perfect 12862, Decca (E) F-3392

Matrix 12514 also cut by Austin this session has no brass or reeds.

ARC, New York, N.Y. Thursday, October 27, 1932
ARC STUDIO BAND
Victor Young (ldr) *Frank Guarente [or] Charlie Margulis*, Mannie Klein
(tp) *Tom Dorsey [or] Charlie Butterfield* (tb) **Jimmy Dorsey** (cl,as) Sid
Stoneburn (as) Larry Binyon (cl,ts,fl) Joe Venuti, Harry Hoffman
[*and/or*] Al Duffy (vn) Joe Meresco (p) Carl Kress (g) Dick Cherwin
(sb) *Larry Gomar* (d,vib) Dick Robertson (vcl)

12508-1   **More Beautiful Than Ever** vDR
    78: Banner 32602, Oriole 2589, Perfect 15692, Romeo (Contd.)

ARC STUDIO BAND (Contd.)

1964, Melotone M-12532, Panachord (E) 25438
12509-1   **You'll Get By (With The Twinkle In Your Eye)**
[Roy Turk; J. Fred Coots] vDR
78: Banner 32602, Oriole 2589, Perfect 15692, Romeo 1964,
Melotone M-12532
For 12508 and 12509: Panachord as ED LOYD AND HIS
ORCH., others as BOB CAUSER AND HIS CORNELLIANS
12516 (1,2)   **Lonely Street** vDR (unissued)
12517-2   **It's A Funny World** vDR
78: Banner 32743, Melotone M-12678, Oriole 2683, Perfect
15758, Romeo 2056
as ART KAHN'S ORCHESTRA

ARC, New York, N.Y. Friday, October 28, 1932
BRUNSWICK STUDIO BAND
Lennie Hayton (p,ldr) Mannie Klein (tp) Tom Dorsey (tb) **Jimmy**
Dorsey (cl,as), (as) 2 *unknown* (vn) *unknown* (viola) Eddie Lang (g)
unknown (sb), (d) Bing Crosby (vcl)

B-12510-A   **Let's Put Out The Lights (And Go To Sleep)** [Her-
man Hupfeld] vBC
78: Brunswick 6414, (E) 1404, Columbia 4530-M, 5-1166, (E)
DB-2208
EP: Fontana (E) TFR-6000
LP: Columbia CL6105, C4X44429, Fontana (E) TFE 17179,
Z4027
TC: Columbia-Legacy CT 48974, Memory Lane 2042
CD: Columbia-Legacy CD 48974
B-12519-A   **I'll Follow You** [Roy Turk; Fred Ahlert] vBC (cl solo)
78: Brunswick 6427, (E) 1421, Columbia (E) DB-2019
12510 and 12519 as BING CROSBY
LP: Columbia C4X 44429
CD: Charly (E) QBCD 29
E688-   **Louisiana Hayride** [Howard Dietz; Arthur Schwartz]
78: ARC Theater-Use F237
ET: ARC Theater-Use E883
as ED LOYD AND HIS ORCHESTRA
E689-   **Let's Put Out The Lights And Go To Sleep**
78: ARC Theater-Use F238
ET: ARC Theater-Use E689
E690-   **A Shine On Your Shoes** [Howard Dietz; Arthur
Schwartz]
78: ARC Theater-Use F239
ET: ARC Theater-Use E690
E691-   **A Million Dreams** [Gus Kahn; J. C. Lewis]
78: ARC Theater-Use F240
ET: ARC Theater-Use E691
E692-   **You'll Get By With The Twinkle In Your Eye** [Roy
Turk; J. Fred Coots]
78: ARC Theater-Use F241

ET: ARC Theater-Use E692
E693-   **I'll Follow You**
    78: ARC Theater-Use F242
    ET: ARC Theater-Use E693
E694-   **I'll Never Have To Dream Again** [Charles Newman;
                        Isham Jones]
    78: ARC Theater-Use F243
    ET: ARC Theater-Use E694
E695-   **How Deep Is The Ocean?** [Irving Berlin]
    78: ARC Theater-Use F244
    ET: ARC Theater-Use E695
E696-   **Someday We'll Meet Again** [Al Hoffman, Al Good-
                        Goodhart, Milt Ager]
    78: ARC Theater-Use F245
    ET: ARC Theater Use E696

ARC, New York, N.Y. Monday, November 7, 1932
VICTOR YOUNG AND HIS ORCHESTRA
Victor Young (ldr) Mannie Klein, Tommy Gott, Hymie Farberman (tp)
Tom Dorsey, Eph Hannaford (tb) **Jimmy Dorsey** (cl,as) Arnold Brilhart
(as,fl) Morris Pierce (ts) Bert Hirsch, Irv Praeger (vn) Herbert Bodkin
(viola) Charles Magnante (acc) Joe Meresco (p) *unknown* (harp) John
Cali (bj) Al Moss (bb) James Melton, Dick Robertson (vcl)

B-12540-A   **Deep In Your Eyes** [LeBaron; Jacobi] vJM
    78: Brunswick 6428, (E) 01418
B-12541-A   **I May Never Pass Your Way Again** [Irving Kahal;
                    Harry Warren] vJM
    78: Brunswick 6428, (E) 01418
    12540, 12541 as JAMES MELTON, WITH ORCHESTRA
B-12542-A   **Play, Fiddle Play** [Jack Lawrence; Emery Deutsch;
                    Arthur Altman] (waltz) vDR
    78: Brunswick 6421

ARC, New York, N.Y. Wednesday, November 9, 1932
ARC STUDIO BAND
Victor Young (ldr) *Frank Guarente [or] Charlie Margulis, unknown* (tp)
Tom Dorsey (tb) **Jimmy Dorsey** (cl,as) *unknown* (as), (ts) 2 *unknown*
(vn) *unknown* (p,cclst), (g), (sb), (d) Will Osborne, Chick Bullock (vcl)

12545-1   **I'm Sure Of Everything But You** [Charles O'Flynn;
                    Pete Wendling] vWO
    78: Banner 32619, Melotone M-12530, Oriole 2600, Perfect
    15699, Romeo 1975, Panachord (E) 25417, Mayfair (E) G-266
    Mayfair as BILLY COOMBE AND HIS ORCHESTRA
12546-1   **Out Of The Darkness (You Have Come To Me)**
                    [Roy Turk; Victor Young, V. Lawnhurst] vWO
    78: Banner 32619, Melotone M-12530, Oriole 2600, Perfect
    15699, Romeo 1975, Panachord (E) 25437
12547-1   **I Found My Romance For Ten Cents A Dance** vWO
    78: Banner 32626, Melotone M-12555, Oriole 2610, Perfect
    15708, Romeo 1981 (Contd.)

ARC STUDIO BAND (Contd.)

12548-1   **(I Only Know I Love You) That's All That Matters
                 To Me** vWO
    78: Banner 32626, Melotone M-12555, Oriole 2610, Perfect
    15708, Romeo 1981, Panachord (E) 25512
        *except as noted, 12545 through 12548 as WILL OSBORNE &
        HIS ORCHESTRA*
12549-2   **We Better Get Together Again** [Cliff Friend; Con
                 Conrad] vCB (cl solos)
    78: Banner 32617, Melotone M-12531, Oriole 2605, Perfect
    15695, Romeo 1973, Panachord (E) 25439
        as CHICK BULLOCK AND HIS LEVEE LOUNGERS

ARC, New York, N.Y. Thursday, November 10, 1932
ARC STUDIO BAND
Personnel as November 9, 1932, except Mannie Klein (tp) present and
no celeste used. Chick Bullock, Paul Small, Greta Keller (vcl)

12551-1   **My Wishing Song** [Irving Kahal; Johnny Burke] vPS
    78: Banner 32620, Conqueror 8110, Melotone M-12552, Oriole
    2602, Perfect 15700, Romeo 1976
12552-1   **Play, Fiddle Play** [Jack Lawrence; Emery Deutsch,
                 Arthur Altman] vPS
    78: Banner 32620, Conqueror 8110, Melotone M-12552, Oriole
    2602, Perfect 15700, Romeo 1976, Panachord (E) 25407
        12551, 12552 as OWEN FALLON & HIS CALIFORNIANS
12553-1   **Brother, Can You Spare A Dime?** [E. Y. Harburg;
                 Jay Gorney] vCB
    78: Banner 32617, Melotone M-12531, Oriole 2605, Perfect
    15695, Romeo 1973, Broadcast (E) 3290
        *Broadcast as CHICK BULLOCK—Vocal with Orchestra,
        others as CHICK BULLOCK & HIS LEVEE LOUNGERS*
    LP: Sunbeam MFC-17
B-12554-A   **(I Don't Stand) A Ghost Of A Chance With You)**
                 [Bing Crosby, Ned Washington; Victor Young] vGK
    78: Decca (E) F-3295
B-12555-A   **Say It Isn't So** [Irving Berlin] vGK
    78: Decca (E) F-3295
        12554 and 12555 as GRETA KELLER

ARC, New York, N.Y. Tuesday, November 22, 1932
BOSWELL SISTERS
Victor Young (ldr) Bunny Berigan, Mannie Klein (tp) Tom Dorsey (tb)
Jimmy Dorsey (cl) Larry Binyon (ts) Harry Hoffman (vn) Martha Bos-
well(p) Carl Kress (g) Art Bernstein (sb) Stan King (d) Boswell Sisters
(vcl)

B-12639-A   **It Don't Mean A Thing (If It Ain't Got That Swing)**
                 [Irving Mills; "Duke" Ellington] vBS (cl solo)
    78: Brunswick 6442, (E) 01436, (G) A-9350, (It) 4819,
    Vocalion 4546, Rex (E) 8873, Columbia (E) DB-1994, Lucky (J)

60184, 60453
LP: Biograph BLP C-16, Conifer (E) CHD 136, Columbia Special Products P16496, Jazum 43, Wave (J) MFPL84802
TC: Conifer (E) MCHD 136
CD: Hep (UK) 1005
B-12640-A   **Louisiana Hayride** [Howard Dietz; Arthur Schwartz] vBS
78: Brunswick 6470, (E) 01625, (G) A-9378, (G) A-9507, (It) 4803, Lucky (J) 60025, 60453
LP: Jazum 30, Conifer (E) CHD 136, Columbia Special Products P16496, Wave (J) MFPL84802
TC: Conifer (E) MCHD 136, Columbia CT 66977
CD: Columbia CK 66977, Hep (UK) 1005
B-12641-A   **Minnie The Moocher's Wedding Day** [Ted Koehler; Harold Arlen] vBS
78: Brunswick 6442, (E) 01436, (G) A-9350, (It) 4879, Vocalion 4546, Lucky (J) 60285
LP: Biograph BLP C-3, Conifer (E) CHD136, Columbia Special Products P16496
TC: Conifer (E) MCHD136, Columbia CT 57111, CT 66977, Radio Yesteryear Stack 47
CD: Columbia CK 57111, CK 66977, Flapper (E) 7087

ARC, New York, N.Y. Friday, December 2, 1932
BRUNSWICK STUDIO BAND
Mannie Klein (tp) **Jimmy Dorsey** (cl) Harry Hoffman, Matty Malneck (vn) Fulton McGrath (p,celst) *Carl Kress [or] Dick McDonough* (g) Art Bernstein (sb) Chauncey Morehouse (d,vib) Annette Hanshaw (vcl)

12670-1   **I'm Sure Of Everything But You** [Charles O'Flynn; Pete Wendling] vAH (cl solo)
78: Banner 32616, Conqueror 8125, Melotone M-12551, Oriole 2598, Perfect 12866, Romeo 1972, Panachord (E) 25413, Mayfair (E) G-265
     Mayfair as MARION LEE, others as ANNETTE HANSHAW
LP: Sunbeam P-511, Halcyon (E) HDL-119
TC: Halcyon (E) CHDL-119, CTP5
12671-1   **Fit As A Fiddle** [Arthur Freed, Al Hoffman, Al Goodhart] vAH (cl solos)
78: Banner 32616, Conqueror 8125, Melotone M-12551, Oriole 2598, Perfect 12866, Romeo 1972, Panachord (E) 25413, Mayfair (E) G-265
     Mayfair as MARION LEE, others as ANNETTE HANSHAW
LP: Sunbeam P-511, Halcyon (E) HDL-119
TC: Halcyon (E) CHDL-119, CTP5
CD: ASV Living Era AJA 5220
B-12676-B   **Rise 'N Shine** [Buddy De Sylva; Vincent Youmans] vPS
78: Brunswick 6444
B-12677-A   **Turn Out The Light**
78: Brunswick 6444
     12676, 12677 as ABE LYMAN AND HIS CALIFORNIANS

ARC, New York, N.Y. Friday, December 9, 1932
BRUNSWICK STUDIO BAND
Mannie Klein (tp) Tom Dorsey (tb) **Jimmy Dorsey** (cl,as) Joe Meresco
(p) Dick McDonough (g) *Dick Cherwin* (sb) *Stan King [or] Larry Gomar*
(d) Chick Bullock, Bing Crosby (vcl)

12704-1   **The Way I Feel Tonight** vCB
        78: Melotone M-12584, Oriole 2627, Perfect 15716, Banner
        32648, Romeo 1998
12705-1   **(When It's) Darkness On The Delta** [Marty Symes,
                Al Neiberg; Jerry Livingston] vCB
        78: Melotone M-12584, Oriole 2627, Perfect 15716, Banner
        32648, Conqueror 8106, Vocalion 15874, Romeo 1998
        12704, 12705 as CHICK BULLOCK AND HIS LEVEE
        LOUNGERS
4 *unknown* (vn) added for:
B-12706-A   **Street Of Dreams** [Sam M. Lewis; Victor Young]
                vBC
        78: Brunswick 6464, (E) 1466, Columbia (E) DB-1085
        LP: Biograph BLP C-13
B-12707-A   **It's Within Your Power** [Mack Gordon; Harry Re-
                vel] vBC (cl solo)
        78: Brunswick 6464, (E) 1466
        12706 and 12707 as BING CROSBY

ARC, New York, N.Y. Friday, December 16, 1932
VICTOR YOUNG AND HIS ORCHESTRA
Victor Young (ldr) 2 *unknown* (tp) Tom Dorsey (tb) **Jimmy Dorsey,**
unknown (cl,as) Larry Binyon (cl,ts,fl) Joe Venuti, Harry Hoffman (vn)
Arthur Schutt (p) Eddie Lang (g) Joe Tarto (bb,sb) Larry Gomar (d,vib)
Paul Small, Ethel Merman, *Take A Chance* Octet (vcl)

B-12733-A(B)   **Hush-A-Bye, My Baby (Missouri Waltz)** [J. R.
                Shannon; Frederick Knight Logan] vPS
        78: Columbia (E) FB-2115
B-12734-A   **That Naughty Waltz (Take Me In Your Arms
                Again And Waltz, And Waltz, And Waltz)** [Edwin
                Stanley; Sol P. Levy] vPS
        78: Columbia (E) FB-2115
B-12735-B   **Eadie Was A Lady** [Buddy De Sylva; Richard Whit-
                ing; Nacio Herb Brown]—Part 1 vEM&TCO
        78: Brunswick 6456
        LP: Columbia CL-2751
        CD: Movie Stars 015, Razor & Tie 2144
B-12736-B   **Eadie Was A Lady**—Part 2 vEM&TCO
        Same issues as part 1.

The Brothers Build a Band
(1933)

The year 1933 was an important benchmark for the Dorsey brothers. While they had recorded and worked some college dates in the past under the Dorsey Brothers' name, these had not been permanent bands.

By 1933 Jimmy, and to a greater degree Tommy, had formed some ideas about a more cohesive unit. Several things were working in their favor, the most important being the economic conditions that made musicians more willing to stick with one band if it offered any sense of security. So as the year unfolded, the Dorsey Brothers' Orchestra began to take on a more solid form.

ARC, New York, N.Y. Wednesday, January 4, 1933
CHICK BULLOCK (AND HIS LEVEE LOUNGERS)
Unknown (tp) Tom Dorsey (tb) **Jimmy Dorsey** (cl,as) *unknown* (as), (ts) Joe Venuti (vn) *Joe Meresco* (p) Eddie Lang (g) *Artie Bernstein* (sb) Larry Gomar (d,xyl) Chick Bullock (vcl)

B-12798-1   **It's Winter Again** [Arthur Freed, Al Goodhart; Al Hoffman] vCB
    78: Melotone M-12579, Oriole 2622, Banner 32644, Broadcast (E) 3290
B-12799-1   **Just An Echo In The Valley** [Harry Woods, Jimmy Campbell, Reg Connelly] vCB (cl solo)
    78: Conqueror 8120, Melotone M-12579, Oriole 2622, Banner 32644

ARC, New York, N.Y. Wednesday, January 4, 1933
VICTOR YOUNG AND HIS ORCHESTRA
Victor Young (ldr) *Frank Guerente [or] Charlie Margulis,* Bunny Berigan (tp) Tom Dorsey (tb) **Jimmy Dorsey** (cl,as,bar) *unknown* (cl,as) Larry Binyon (cl,ts,fl) Joe Venuti *[and/or]* Harry Hoffman (vn) Arthur Schutt (p) Eddie Lang (g) Joe Tarto (bb,sb) *Chauncey Morehouse [or] Larry Gomar* (d,vib) Paul Small, Dick Robertson (vcl)

B-12733-C   **(Hush-A-Bye, My Baby) Missouri Waltz** [J. R. Shannon; Frederick Knight Logan] vPS
    78: Brunswick 6468
B-12734-C   **That Naughty Waltz (Take Me In Your Arms Again And Waltz, And Waltz And Waltz)** [Edwin Stanley; Sol P. Levy] vPS (cl solo)
    78: Brunswick 6468
B-12821-A   **My Wishing Song** [Johnny Burke; Irving Kahal] vDR
    78: Brunswick 6465   (Contd.)

255

VICTOR YOUNG AND HIS ORCHESTRA (Contd.)

B-12822-A   You're Charming [Roy Turk; Joseph Meyer] vDR
                   (cl solo)
          78: Brunswick 6465

ARC, New York, N.Y. Monday, January 9, 1933
BRUNSWICK STUDIO BAND
Victor Young (ldr) Mannie Klein (tp) Tom Dorsey (tb) Jimmy Dorsey
(cl,as) Bennie Krueger (c-mel,as) Harry Bluestone, *unknown* (vn), (p)
Eddie Lang (g) Artie Bernstein (sb) *Stan King [or] Chauncey Morehouse*
(d) Bing Crosby, Connie Boswell, Boswell Sisters (vcl)

B-12856-A   I'm Playing With Fire [Irving Berlin] vBC
          78: Brunswick 6480, (E) 01444, Columbia (E) DB-1990
                   as BING CROSBY
          LP: CBS Embassy (E) 31751, Columbia C4X 44229, Sunbeam P-
          504
          CD: Columbia CK 44305
B-12857-A   Try A Little Tenderness [Harry Woods, Jimmy Camp-
                   bell, Reg Connelly] vBC
          78: Brunswick 6480, (E) 01444, Columbia (E) DB-1985, SEG-
          7522, Biltmore 1013
                   as BING CROSBY
          LP: CBS Embassy (E) 31751, Columbia 35094, C4X 44229
          CD: Columbia CK 44305, Charly (E) QBCD 29
Martha Boswell (p) definite next, possible on Crosby sides:
B-12858-A   It's All My Fault [Joseph Meyer, Charles O'Flynn;
                   Pete Wendling] vCB
          78: Brunswick 6483, (E) 01443, Columbia 38298 (dub)
                   as CONNIE BOSWELL
          LP: Take Two TT-216
B-12859-A   Underneath The Arches [Joe McCarthy, Bud Flan-
                   agan; Reg Connelly] vCB (cl solo)
          78: Brunswick 6483, Columbia 38298 (dub)
                   as CONNIE BOSWELL
          LP: Jazum 31, Take Two TT-209
B-12860-A   Mood Indigo [Edward K. "Duke" Ellington, Barney
                   Bigard, Irving Mills] vBS (cl solo)
          78: Brunswick 6470, (E) 01543, (G) A9378, (F) A500230,
          Columbia (E) DB1960, 36251 (dub), Rex (E) 8910, Lucky (J)
          5070, 60025
                   as BOSWELL SISTERS
          LP: Jazum 31, Columbia Special Products P16494, Conifer (E)
          CHD 136, Wave (J) MFPL84801
          TC: Conifer (E) MCHD 136, ProArte Digital PCD 550
          CD: ProArte Digital CDD 550, Flapper 7087, Fremaux 2741
B-12860-B   Mood Indigo vBS (cl solo)
          LP: Biograph BLP C-3
          TC: Columbia CT52932
          CD: Columbia CK52943

ARC, New York, N.Y. Tuesday, January 10, 1933
ARC-BRUNSWICK STUDIO BAND
Victor Young (ldr) *Frank Guerente [or] Charlie Margulis,* Mannie Klein
(tp) Tom Dorsey (tb) **Jimmy Dorsey** (cl) *unknown* (cl,as) *Bennie
Krueger* (ts) 3 *unknown* (vn) *Joe Meresco* (p) *unknown* (g), (sb) *Larry
Gomar* (d,vib) Chick Bullock, Paul Small, Perla Violetta Amado, An-
drea Marsh (vcl)

12862-1   **Now We're On Our Second Honeymoon** vCB (cl
       solo)
    78: Banner 32661, Melotone M-12590, Oriole 2633, Perfect
    15722, Romeo 2006
12863-2   **I'm Playing With Fire** [Irving Berlin] vCB
    78: Banner 32661, Melotone M-12590, Oriole 2633,   Perfect
    15722, Romeo 2006
        12862, 12863 as BOB CAUSER AND HIS CORNELLIANS
B-12864-   **Jugando Con Fuego (I'm Playing With Fire)** vPVA
    78: (Latin-American release)
       as PERLA VIOLETA AMADO con la Orquesta de Victor Young
12865-1,2   **Moon Song (That Wasn't Meant For Me)** [Sam Cos-
       low, Arthur Johnston] vPS
    78: Banner 32662, Melotone M-12591, Oriole 2634, Perfect
    15723, Romeo 2007, Imperial (E) 2847
       as HAROLD WHITE AND HIS ORCHESTRA
B-12866-   **Cantando A La Luna (Moon Song)** vPVA
    78: (Latin-American release)
       as PERLA VIOLETA AMADO con la Orquesta de Victor Young
12867-1   **Moon Song (That Wasn't Meant For Me)** vCB
    78: Panachord (E) 25493
       as HARRY WOODS AND HIS NEW JERSEY ORCHESTRA
12868-1   **Twenty Million People** [Sam Coslow; Arthur Johns-
       ton] vPS (cl solo)
    78: Banner 32662, Melotone M-12591, Oriole 2634, Perfect
    15723, Romeo 2007
       as HAROLD WHITE AND HIS ORCHESTRA
B-12869-   **Viente Mil Personas (Twenty Million People)** vPVA
       (cl solo)
    78: (Latin-American release)
       as PERLA VIOLETA AMADO con la Orquesta de Victor Young
12870-   **Twenty Million People** vCB (cl solo)
    78: Panachord (E) 25493
       as HARRY WOODS AND HIS NEW JERSEY ORCHESTRA
12871-1   **You Are Too Beautiful** [Lorenz Hart; Richard Rodg-
       ers] vPS
    78: Panachord (E) 25524
       as RALPH BENNETT AND HIS SEVEN ACES
B-12872-   **Que Soy Muy Bella (You Are Too Beautiful)** vPVA
    78: (Latin-American release)
       as PERLA VIOLETA AMADO con la Orquesta de Victor Young
12873-1   **You Are Too Beautiful** vCB
    78: Banner 32677, Melotone M-12603, Oriole 2644, Perfect
    15731, Romeo 2019   (Contd.)

ARC-BRUNSWICK STUDIO BAND (Contd.)

as DAN RITCHIE AND HIS ORCHESTRA

TO-1248   **Till Tomorrow/Rock-A-Bye Moon** [Howard E. Johnson] vAM
    78: ARC test pressing TO-1248

ARC, New York, N.Y. Tuesday, January 24, 1933
ARC-BRUNSWICK STUDIO BAND
Victor Young (ldr) Charlie Margulis, Mannie Klein (tp) Tom Dorsey (tb) **Jimmy Dorsey,** *unknown* (cl,as) Joe Venuti, 2 *unknown* (vn) Joe Meresco (p) Carl Kress (g) Joe Tarto (sb) *unknown* (d) Will Osborne, Chick Bullock, Greta Keller (vcl)

12972-1   **Hey! Young Fella (Close Your Old Umbrella)** [Dorothy Fields; Jimmy McHugh] vWO
    78: Banner 32674, Conqueror 8113, Melotone M-12607, Oriole 2641, Perfect 15728, Romeo 2014, Panachord (E) 25462
                as WILL OSBORNE AND HIS ORCHESTRA
12973-1   **I Wake Up Smiling** [Edgar Leslie; Fred E. Ahlert] (waltz) vWO
    78: Banner 32674, Conqueror 8087, Melotone M-12607, Oriole 2641, Perfect 15728, Romeo 2014, Panachord (E) 25462
                as WILL OSBORNE AND HIS ORCHESTRA
12974-   **Linger A Little Longer In The Twilight** [Harry Woods, James Campbell, Reginald Connelly] vWO
    78: Banner 32697, Conqueror 8114, Melotone M-12624, Oriole 2650, Perfect 15734, Romeo 2023
                as WILL OSBORNE AND HIS ORCHESTRA
TO-1253   **The Onyx Club Review** vWO (cl solo)
    78: ARC TO-1253 (test pressing), Lucky (J) 7000A
                TO-1253 as THE NEW YORKERS, Lucky as JOE VENUTI AND FRIENDS
    LP: Broadway BR-108
12975-   **Spring Is In My Heart Again** [Johnny Mercer; William Woodin] vWO
    78: Banner 32697, Melotone M-12624, Oriole 2650, Perfect 15734, Romeo 2023
                as WILL OSBORNE AND HIS ORCHESTRA
12976-   **Hallelujah! I'm A Bum** [Lorenz Hart; Richard Rodgers] vCB
    78: Banner 32677, Melotone M-12613, Oriole 2644, Perfect 15731, Romeo 2019
                as DAN RITCHIE AND HIS ORCHESTRA
B-12977-A   **I'll Never Have To Dream Again** [Charles Newman; Isham Jones] vGK
    78: Brunswick 6506, Decca (E) F-3470
B-12978-A   **Willow, Weep For Me** [Ann Ronell] vGK
    78: Brunswick 6506, Decca (E) F-3483
B-12979-A   **I'm Playing With Fire** [Irving Berlin] vGK
    78: Decca (E) F-3483

B-12980-A   **I'm Sure Of Everything But You** [Charles O'Flynn;
                   Pete Wendling] vGK
    78: Decca (E) F-3470
    12977 to 12980 as GRETA KELLER

"Onyx Club Review" from the previous session was one of the most
colorful "underground" records of the thirties. According to Mannie
Klein, the takeoff resulted from a series of aborted attempts to cut a
"corny" waltz. It is a spoof on Johnny Mercer's "Spring Is In My Heart
Again," which follows in the session.
    Klein said that Victor Young, who is heard introducing the song, sug-
gested the "Review" as a way to get the fluffs out of the way. It was
probably roughed out during a lunch break. In addition, the "lyrics" that
Will Osborne "sings" include the first names "Joe, Mannie, Tom and
Jim," helping to further pin down the participants.
    The Onyx Club, which was located in the rear of a brownstone at 35
West Fifty-second Street, was opened by Joe Helbock as a "speakeasy"
in 1927 and by 1933 had become *the* meeting place for New York musicians, replacing Plunkett's on West Fifty-third (Shaw 1977).

ARC, New York, N.Y. Wednesday, January 25, 1933
ARC STUDIO BAND
Mannie Klein (tp) **Jimmy Dorsey** (cl) Harry Hoffman, Matty Malneck
(vn) Fulton McGrath (p) Eddie Lang (g) Artie Bernstein (sb) Chauncey
Morehouse (d,vib) Johnny Marvin, Annette Hanshaw (vcl)

B-12981-   **Rock-A-Bye-Moon** [Howard E. Johnson] vJM
    78: Melotone M-12610, Panachord (E) 25471
        as JOHNNY MARVIN
B-12982-1   **I'm Playing With Fire** [Irving Berlin] vJM
    78: Melotone M-12610, Panachord (E) 25471
        as JOHNNY MARVIN
12983-1   **Moon Song (That Wasn't Meant For Me** [Sam Cos-
                   low; Arthur Johnston] vAH
    78: Banner 32671, Conqueror 8124, Melotone M-12604, Oriole
    2638, Perfect 12882, Romeo 2011, Panachord (E) 25469, Key (E)
    K-604, Mayfair (E) G-318
        *Key as ETHEL BINGHAM, Mayfair as MARION LEE, others
        as ANNETTE HANSHAW*
    LP: Sunbeam P-511, Halcyon (E) HDL-119
    TC: Halcyon (E) CHDL-119, CTP5
    CD: ASV Living Era AJA 5220
12984-1   **Twenty Million People** [Sam Coslow; Arthur Johns-
                   ton] vAH (cl solo)
    78: Banner 32671, Conqueror 8124, Melotone M-12604, Oriole
    2638, Perfect 12882, Romeo 2011, Panachord (E) 25469, Key (E)
    K-611, Mayfair (E) G-318
        *Key as ETHEL BINGHAM, Mayfair as MARION LEE, others
        as ANNETTE HANSHAW*
    LP: Sunbeam P-511, Halcyon (E) HDL-119
    TC: Halcyon (E) CHDL-119, CTP5

ARC, New York, N.Y. Tuesday, February 7, 1933
MAE WEST, COMEDIENNE
Victor Young (ldr) Mannie Klein (tp) Tom Dorsey (tb) **Jimmy Dorsey** (cl,as) *Joe Venuti [or] Harry Hoffman* (vn) *Joe Meresco* (p) *Dick Mc-Donough* (g) *Art Bernstein* (sb) *Larry Gomar* (d) Mae West (vcl)

B-13037-A   **I Like A Guy What Takes His Time** [Ralph Rainger] vMW
    78: Brunswick 6495, (E) 1491, (F) A-500240, Columbia (Au) DO-1096
    CD: Hep (Sc) 1006, ABC (Au) 838216
B-13037-B   **I Like A Guy What Takes His Time** vMW
    78: (unissued, test pressing exists)
    LP: CBS CL-2751
    TC: Columbia Legacy CT5711
    CD: Columbia Legacy CK5711
B-13038-A   **I Wonder Where My Easy Rider's Gone** [Shelton Brooks] vMW
    78: Brunswick 6495, (E) 1491, (F) A-500240, Columbia (Au) DO-1096, Temple 545
    LP: Epic SN-6059, Columbia Special Products (Nostalgia Book Club) P4-12964
    TC: Rosetta TC-1315
    CD: Rosetta CD-1315, Hep (Sc) 1006, ABC (Au) 838216
B-13038-B   **I Wonder Where My Easy Rider's Gone** vMW
    78: (unissued, test pressing exists)

ARC, New York, N.Y. Thursday, February 9, 1933
ARC/BRUNSWICK STUDIO BAND
Victor Young (ldr) Mannie Klein (tp) Tom Dorsey (tb) **Jimmy Dorsey,** *Bennie Krueger* (cl,as) Larry Binyon (ts) Joe Venuti, 3 *unknown* (vn) Joe Meresco (p) Eddie Lang (g) Artie Bernstein (sb) Stan King (d) Chick Bullock, Bing Crosby, Kate Smith (vcl)

13041-1   **Any Time, Any Day, Anywhere** [Ned Washington; Victor Young] vCB (cl solo)
    78: Melotone M-12626, Perfect 15733, Vocalion 15874, Banner 32696
        as CHICK BULLOCK & HIS LEVEE LOUNGERS
    TC: Columbia/Legacy CT 52931
    CD: Columbia/Legacy CK 52942
13042-1   **I've Got The World On A String** [Ted Kohler, Harold Arlen] vCB (cl solo)
    78: Melotone M-12626, Perfect 15733, Banner 32696
        as CHICK BULLOCK & HIS LEVEE LOUNGERS
B-13043-A   **What Do I Care, It's Home** vBC
    78: Brunswick 6515, (E) 01503
        as BING CROSBY
    LP: Columbia C4X 44429
B-13044-A   **You've Got Me Crying Again** [Charles Newman; Isham Jones] vBC (cl solo)

78: Brunswick 6515, (E) 01503, Columbia (E) DB-1901, (Au) DB-3178, (GE) DC-497
  as BING CROSBY
LP: Columbia C4X 44429
CD: Living Era (E) ASV AJA 5043

After lunch most of the musicians (Jimmy included) returned, added a banjo to back Kate Smith on four tunes from her movie *Hello Everybody* and then cut three Theater-Use sides.

B-13045-A   **Pickaninny's Heaven** [Sam Coslow; Arthur Johnston] vKS
  78: Brunswick 6497, (E) 01479
B-13046-A   **Twenty Million People** [Sam Coslow; Arthur Johnston] vKS
  78: Brunswick 6496, (E) 01481, Lucky (J) 5069
  CD: Intersound 3553
B-13047-A   **My Queen Of Lullaby Land** [Sam Coslow; Arthur Johnston] vKS
  78: Brunswick 6496, (E) 01481
B-13048-A   **Moon Song (That Wasn't Meant For Me)** [Sam Coslow; Arthur Johnston] vKS
  78: Brunswick 6497, (E) 01479, Lucky (J) 60032
  13045 through 13048 as KATE SMITH
  LP: Epic SN-6059, Columbia Special Products (Nostalgia Book Club) P4-12964
E717 (F258)   **Night And Day** [Cole Porter]
  78: ARC Theater-Use F-258
  ET: ARC Theater-Use E-717
E718 (F259)   **I Wake Up Smiling** [Edgar Leslie; Fred E. Ahlert]
  78: ARC Theater-Use F-259
  ET: ARC Theater-Use E-718
    as SOCIETY NIGHT CLUB ORCHESTRA
E719 (F260)   **Hey! Young Fella (Close Your Old Umbrella)** [Dorothy Fields; Jimmy McHugh]
  78: ARC Theater-Use F-260
  ET: ARC Theater-Use E-719

ARC, New York, N.Y. Tuesday, February 14, 1933
ADRIAN ROLLINI AND HIS ORCHESTRA
Adrian Rollini (bsx,goof,xyl,vib,ldr) Mannie Klein (tp) Tom Dorsey (tb) **Jimmy Dorsey** (cl,as) Arthur Rollini (ts) Joe Venuti (vn) Charlie Magnante (acc) Fulton McGrath (p) Eddie Lang (g) Arthur Miller (sb) Dick Robertson (vcl)

13049-1   **Have You Ever Been Lonely? (Have You Ever Been Blue?)** [George Brown (Billy Hill); Peter De Rose] vDR (cl solo)
  78: Banner 32698, Conqueror 8153, Melotone M-12629, Oriole 2651, Perfect 15735, Romeo 2024, Vocalion 15886
    Melotone, Banner and Perfect as OWEN FALLON AND HIS
                        (Contd.)

ADRIAN ROLLINI AND HIS ORCHESTRA (Contd.)

> *CALIFORNIANS, Vocalion as ROY CARROLL AND HIS*
> *SANDS POINT ORCHESTRA*

13050-1   **You've Got Me Crying Again** [Charles Newman; Isham Jones] vDR

78: Banner 32699, Melotone M-12630, Oriole 2652, Perfect 15736, Romeo 2025, Decca (E) F-3518, Key S-610, Edison Bell Winner 5555, Peacock (E) P-105

> *Edison Bell Winner as RADIO DANCE BAND, Key as THE*
> *RHYTHM ACES, Peacock as NEW JERSEY ISLANDERS*

13051-1   **Hustlin' And Bustlin' For Baby** [Harry Woods] vDR

78: Banner 32699, Melotone M-12630, Oriole 2652, Perfect 15736, Romeo 2025, Decca (E) F-3518, Imperial 2846

> *Imperial as THE BELL BOYS OF BROADWAY*

13052-1   **You Must Believe Me** [Harry Tobias; Johnny Burke] vDR

78: Banner 32698, Conqueror 8108, Melotone M-12629, 91514, Oriole 2651, Panachord (E) 25495, Perfect 15735, Romeo 2024

> *Melotone, Perfect, Banner and Panachord as OWEN FAL-*
> *LON AND HIS CALIFORNIANS*

Frances Langford, who had recently been discovered in New Orleans by Rudy Vallee and given a spot on his radio show, was backed next by the Dorseys for the first time. Jimmy's band did the same on several occasions in the mid thirties.

Columbia, New York, N.Y. Thursday, February 16, 1933
FRANCES LANGFORD
Lennie Hayton (ldr) *unknown* (tp) Tom Dorsey (tb) **Jimmy Dorsey** (cl,bar) Phil Wall (p) Eddie Lang (g) Art Bernstein (sb) *unknown* (d) Frances Langford (vcl)

265053-1   **Stormy Weather (Keeps Rainin' All The Time)** [Ted Kohler; Harold Arlen] vFL (cl solo)

78: OKeh 41565 (possibly never released)
(405196-1) Columbia (E) DB-1124

265054-1   **You're Hi-De-Hi-Ing Me** [Jimmy Van Heusen; Harold Arlen] vFL

78: OKeh 41565 (possibly never released)
(405197-1) Columbia (E) DB-1124
Both sides also on **TC:** Columbia Legacy CT52951, **CD:** Columbia Legacy CK52943, Happy Days (E) 204

Columbia, New York, N.Y. Tuesday, February 28, 1933
JOE VENUTI-EDDIE LANG BLUE FIVE
Joe Venuti (vn,ldr) **Jimmy Dorsey** (tp,cl,as) Adrian Rollini (bsx,goof, p,vib) Phil Wall (p) Eddie Lang (g)

W-265066-2   **Raggin' The Scale** [Edward B. Claypoole] (as solo)

78: Columbia 2765-D,(E) CB-612,(F) DF-1263, (Au) DO-1036
LP: Columbia C2L24, Regal (E) REG1076, World Records (E)

SHB39, Disques Swing SW8457/8, Music For Pleasure (EC) 1161
TC: Radio Yesteryear Stack 22
W-265067-2   **Hey! Young Fella (Close Your Old Umbrella)** [Dorothy Fields; Jimmy McHugh] (cl,as,tp,cl,as solos)
    78: Columbia (E) CB-601, (F) DF-1229, (Au) DO-966, (It) DQ-1323
    LP: Columbia C2L24, Regal (E) REG1076, World Records (E) SHB39, Disques Swing SW8457/8, Music For Pleasure (EC) 1161
    CD: Jazz Greats (E) 036
W-265068-2   **Jig Saw Puzzle Blues** [Adrian Rollini] (tp,cl,as solos)
    78: Columbia 2782-D, (E) CB-612, (F) DF-1263, (Au) DO-937
    LP: Regal (E) REG1076, World Records (E) SHB39, Disques Swing SW8457/8, Music For Pleasure (EC) 1161
W-265069-2   **Pink Elephants** [Mort Dixon; Harry Woods] (as,cl, as,tp solos)
    78: Columbia (E) CB-601, (F) DF-1229, (Au) DO-966, (It) DQ-1323
    LP: Regal (E) REG1076, World Records (E) SHB39, Disques Swing SW8457/8, Music For Pleasure (EC) 1161, Capitol W2139

ARC, New York, N.Y. Tuesday, March 7, 1933
ARC-BRUNSWICK STUDIO BAND
Victor Young (ldr) Bunny Berigan (tp) Tom Dorsey (tb) **Jimmy Dorsey** (cl) Larry Binyon (ts,bsn) Joe Venuti, 2 *unknown* (vn) Fulton McGrath (p) Eddie Lang (g) Arthur Bernstein (sb) Stan King (d) Chick Bullock, Lee Wiley (vcl)

13120-1   **Going! Going!! Gone!!!** [Phil Baxter] vCB
    78: Banner 32716, Conqueror 8111, Melotone M-12645, Oriole 2665, Perfect 15743, Romeo 2038, Vocalion 15882
    LP: Meritt 501
13121-1   **Low Down Upon The Harlem River** vCB
    78: Banner 32716, Conqueror 8111, Melotone M-12645, Oriole 2665, Perfect 15743, Romeo 2038
        13120, 13121 as CHICK BULLOCK AND HIS LEVEE LOUNGERS
    LP: Meritt 501
B-13122-1   **You've Got Me Crying Again** [Charles Newman; Isham Jones] vLW (cl solo)
    78: Brunswick (test pressing)
    LP: Epic BSN159, SN6059, Philomel 1000, JASS 19
    TC: JASS J19C, Columbia Legacy CT52951
    CD: JASS CD-J-15, Vintage Jazz Classics (E) VJC1023, Hep (E) CD 1006, Columbia Legacy CK52943, L'Art Vocal (F) #15, Jazz Classics 6013
B-13122-2   **You've Got Me Crying Again** vLW (cl solo)
    78: Brunswick (test pressing)
    LP: Meritt 501
    CD: Vintage Jazz Classics (E) VJC 1023, Hep (E) CD 1006
B-13123-1   **I Gotta Right To Sing The Blues** [Ted Kohler; Harold Arlen] vLW
    78: Brunswick (test pressing)   (Contd.)

ARC-BRUNSWICK STUDIO BAND (Contd.)

> **LP:** Epic LN24442, Columbia Special Products P12856, Philomel 1000, JASS 19
> **CD:** JASS CD-J-15, Vintage Jazz Classics (E) VJC1023, Jazz Classics 6013

B-13123-2   **I Gotta Right To Sing The Blues** vLW
> **78:** Brunswick (test pressing)
> **TC:** Columbia Legacy CT52951
> **CD:** Vintage Jazz Classics (E) VJC 1023, Columbia Legacy CK52943, CK57711

ARC, New York, N.Y. Tuesday, March 14, 1933
THE DORSEY BROTHERS' ORCHESTRA
Tom Dorsey (tb,ldr) Bunny Berigan (tp) **Jimmy Dorsey** (cl,as) Larry Binyon (ts) Fulton McGrath (p) Dick McDonough (g) Artie Bernstein (sb) Stan King (d) Bing Crosby (vcl)

B-13148-A   **Mood Hollywood** [Lennie Hayton, Jimmy Dorsey] (as,cl,as solos)
> **78:** Brunswick 6537, (E) 01505, (F) A-500237, (G) A-9333
> **LP:** Franklin Mint J046, Hep (Sc) 1005
> **TC:** Jazz Tape 46, Columbia/Legacy CT 48908, (H) 37169-4
> **CD:** Columbia/Legacy CK 48908, (H)37169-2, Hep (UK) 1005
B-13148-B   **Mood Hollywood** (as,cl,as solos)
> **78:** Columbia 36066, S-10007
> **LP:** Columbia (J) PL-5020, (J) PMS53, Hep (Sc) 1005
> **CD:** Hep (UK) 1005
B-13149-A   **Someone Stole Gabriel's Horn** [Ned Washington; Edgar Hayes, Irving Mills] vBC (cl solo)
> **78:** Brunswick 6533, (E) 01498, (F) A-500238, Banner 33203, Melotone M-13170, Oriole 2998, Romeo 2372, Perfect 13055, Vocalion 2879, 4522, OKeh 2879, 4522, Columbia (E) DB1894, (Au) DO 1432, V-Disc (unissued)
> > *as BING CROSBY with The Dorsey Brothers' Orchestra*
> **LP:** Biograph BLP C-13, Historia (G) H-622, Hep (Sc) 1006, Columbia (J) HR-128-JK, C4X 44429, Joker (It), SM 3053
> **TC:** Joker (It) MC 3053, Ditto (E) 10312, Columbia/Legacy CT 48908, (H)37169-4
> **CD:** CBS CK 44229, CK 48908, (H) 37169-2, Hep (E) CD 1006, Conifer (E) CDMD 123, Affinity (E) AFS1021-2, Charly (E) QBCD29, Hep (UK) 1005, Jazz Greats (E) 036
B-13150-A   **Stay On The Right Side Of The Road** [Ted Koehler; Rube Bloom] vBC (as,cl solos)
> **78:** Brunswick 6533, (E) 01498, (F) A-500238, Banner 33202, Melotone M-13169, Conqueror 9557, Vocalion 4522, OKeh 4522, Perfect 13054, Harmony 1008, Oriole 2997, Romeo 2371, Columbia (E) DB 1964
> > *as BING CROSBY with The Dorsey Brothers' Orchestra*
> **LP:** Biograph BLP C-13, Historia (G) H-622, Hep (Sc) 1006, Joker (It) SM 3053, Columbia C4X 44429, (J) HR-128-JK

TC: Joker (It) MC 3053, Ditto 10312
CD: CBS CK 44229, Conifer (E) CHDH 123, Hep (Sc) CD 1006
B-13150-B   **Stay On The Right Side Of The Road** vBC (as
                 solo)
78: (test pressing exists)
LP: IAJRC-2, Columbia KG-31564, CBS 67273, Hep (Sc) 1006,
Fanfare LP-40-140
CD: Affinity (E) AFS 1021-2, Hep (Sc) 1006
B-13151-A   **Here Is My Heart** [Leo Robin; Ralph Rainger] vBC
78: (test pressing exists)
LP: Harmony HL-7147, Hep (Sc) 1006, CBS Embassy (E) 31751,
Columbia C4X 44429
CD: CBS CK 44229, Hep (Sc) 1006
B-13152-A   **Shim Sham Shimmy** [Jimmy Dorsey, Fulton Mc-
                 Grath] (cl solos)
78: Brunswick 6537, (E) 01505, (F) A-500237, (G) A-9333,
(Norway) S-10007, Columbia 36066 (dub labeled "-B")
LP: Hep (Sc) 1005
TC: ProArte Digital PCD508, Columbia CT 48908, (H) 37169-4
CD: ProArte Digital CDD508, Columbia CK 48908, (H) 37169-2
D-13152-D   **Shim Sham Shimmy** (cl solos)
78: (unissued test pressing)
LP: Hep (Sc) 1005
Both takes of 13152 also on CD: Hep (UK) 1005

Brunswick, New York, N.Y. Wednesday, March 22, 1933
GRETA KELLER
Bunny Berigan (tp) **Jimmy Dorsey** (cl) *unknown* (as) 3 or 4 *unknown*
(vn) Lennie Hayton (p) Art Bernstein, Spike Hughes (sb) *unknown* (d)
Greta Keller (vcl)

B-13168-A   **Maybe I Love You Too Much** vGK
78: Brunswick 6544, Decca (E) F-3562
B-13169-A   **I Wake Up Smiling** [Edgar Leslie; Fred B. Ahlert]
                 vGK
78: Decca (E) F-3586

A third tune, "Lover," made on B-13170, does not include brass or
reeds. Spike Hughes, visiting from England, and subbing for Bernstein
on one side, says the personnel listed was on hand (White 1988-1997).

ARC, New York, N.Y. Friday, March 31, 1933
VICTOR YOUNG AND HIS SERENADERS
Victor Young (ldr) Frank Guerente, Mannie Klein (tp) Tom Dorsey (tb)
Jimmy Dorsey (cl,as) *unknown* (as) Larry Binyon (ts) Joe Venuti, 2
unknown (vn) *unknown* (p) Dick McDonough (g) Joe Tarto (sb) Larry
Gomar (d,xyl) Chick Bullock (vcl)

B-13187-A   **Juanita** [Frank Guerente, Victor Young]
                 (as solo)
78: Brunswick 6539
13190-1   **Two Tickets To Georgia** [Joe Young, Charles (Contd.)

VICTOR YOUNG AND HIS SERENADERS (Contd.)

Tobias, J. Fred Coots] vCB (cl solo)
78: Banner 32731, Melotone M-12660, Oriole 2675, Romeo 2048, Perfect 15751, Vocalion 15882
> *Melotone, Banner and Perfect as ART KAHN'S ORCH., Vocalion as CHICK BULLOCK & HIS LEVEE LOUNGERS*

LP: Everybody's SWE1001, Lyric 3302

13191-1   **You'll Never Get Up To Heaven That Way** [Sammy Lerner; Abel Baer] vCB (cl solo)
78: Banner 32732, Melotone M-12661, Oriole 2676, Perfect 15752, Romeo 2049, Vocalion 15882
> *Melotone, Banner and Perfect as PHIL ROMANO AND HIS DE WITT CLINTON HOTEL ORCH., Vocalion as CHICK BULLOCK AND HIS LEVEE LOUNGERS*

LP: Everybody's SWE1001

13192-1   **Hold Me** [Little Jack Little, Dave Oppenheim, Ira Schuster] vCB
78: Banner 32732, Melotone M-12661, Oriole 2676, Perfect 15752, Romeo 2049, Vocalion 15886, Imperial 2888, Kristall (Swe) K-3504
> *Melotone, Banner and Perfect as PHIL ROMANO AND HIS DE WITT CLINTON HOTEL ORCHESTRA, Imperial, Kristall as ED LOYD AND HIS ORCHESTRA*

LP: Everybody's SWE1001

13193-1   **The Grass Is Getting Greener All The Time** [Johnny Burke, Charles Newman; Harold Spina] vCB
78: Banner 32731, Melotone M-12660, Oriole 2675, Perfect 15751, Romeo 2048, Rex (E) 8003
> *Melotone, Banner and Perfect as ART KAHN'S ORCHESTRA, Rex as BELL BOYS OF BROADWAY*

LP: Everybody's SWE1001

B-13194-A   **Tony's Wife** [Harold Adamson; Burton Lane] vCB (as solo)
78: Brunswick 6539

Unknown studio, New York, N.Y. March 1933
THE DORSEY BROTHERS' ORCHESTRA
Tom Dorsey (tb,ldr) *Mannie Klein* (tp) **Jimmy Dorsey** (cl,as) Larry Binyon (ts) Fulton McGrath (p) Dick McDonough (g) Artie Bernstein (sb) Stan King (d)

-0-   **By Heck** [L.Wolfe Gilbert; S.R.Henry] (as,cl solos)
LP: Fanfare LP-5-105

ARC, New York, N.Y. Saturday, April 8, 1933
RED NORVO (Xylophone and Marimba Solos)
Red Norvo (xyl,mar) **Jimmy Dorsey** (cl) Fulton McGrath (p) *Dick McDonough or Carl Kress* (g) Artie Bernstein (sb)

B-13205-A   **Knockin' On Wood** [Red Norvo] (cl solo)
78: Brunswick 6562, (E) O1568, (G) A-9419, Regal Zonophone

(Au) G-22242
CD: Giants Of Jazz 53283
B-13206-A   **Hole In The Wall** [Red Norvo] (cl solo)
  78: Brunswick 6562, (E) O1568, (G) A-9419, Regal Zonophone
  (Au) G-22242
  both sides also on **LP:** Columbia JEE22009, Philips (H) BBL7077,
  CD: Hep (Sc) 1044

ARC, New York, N.Y. Saturday, April 8, 1933
DORSEY BROTHERS' ORCHESTRA
Tom Dorsey (tb,ldr) Bunny Berigan (tp) **Jimmy Dorsey** (cl,as) *unknown*
(ts) Fulton McGrath (p) Carl Kress (g) Artie Bernstein (sb) Stan King (d)
Mildred Bailey (vcl) Glenn Miller, Herb Spencer (arr)

B-13207-A,B   **Maybe** [Ira Gershwin; George Gershwin]
  78: (unissued, test pressings exist)
  CD: Jazz Oracle (C) BDW 8006 (both takes)
B-13208-A   **Is That Religion?** [Mitchell Parish; Maceo Pinkard]
                   vMB (cl solo)
  78: Brunswick 6558, (E) 01544, (F) A-500269
  LP: CBS C3L-32, BPG-62098, Hep (Sc) 1006
  CD: Hep (E) CD 1006, The Old Masters MB104
B-13209-A   **Harlem Lullaby** [Millham; Robison] vMB (cl solo)
  78: Brunswick 6558 (E) 01544, (F) A-500269
  LP: CBS C3L-32, BPG-62098, Hep (Sc) 1006, ASV Living Era
  (E) AJA 5065
  TC: ASV Living Era (E) ZC AJA 5065
  CD: ASV Living Era (E) CD AJA 5065, Hep (E) CD 1006, The
  Old Masters MB104, Lifetimes 9076
          *13208, 13209 as MILDRED BAILEY (accomp. by Dorsey
          Brothers' Orch.)*
Mannie Klein (tp), Joe Venuti (vn) added, Joe Tarto (sb) for Bernstein:
TO-1287   (unknown dialogue, probably by Carl Kress)
  78: TO-1287
TO-1289   **Just An Echo In The Valley** [Harry Woods, Jimmy
                   Campbell, Reg Connelly]
  78: TO-1289
          as TOMMY DORSEY ORCHESTRA

In the spring of 1933, Jimmy took part in an Al Goodman radio
audition for Lucky Strikes, playing with Benny Goodman and Artie
Shaw on reeds, Bunny Berigan (tp), Tommy Dorsey (tb), Artie Bernstein
(sb) and Helen Ward.   The audition failed when American Tobacco
tycoon George Washington Hill fell asleep (Firestone 1993: 95).

ARC, New York, N.Y. Monday, April 10, 1933
VICTOR YOUNG AND HIS ORCHESTRA
Victor Young (ldr) *Frank Guerente [or] Charlie Margulis,* Mannie Klein
(tp) Charlie Butterfield (tb) **Jimmy Dorsey,** *Lyle Bowen* (cl,as) *unknown*
(as) *Hymie Wolfson* (cl,ts) Joe Venuti, 2 *unknown* (vn) Joe Meresco (p)
Dick McDonough [or] Carl Kress (g) Artie Bernstein (sb) Larry Gomar
(d,vib) Smith Ballew, Chick Bullock (vcl)

VICTOR YOUNG AND HIS ORCHESTRA (Contd.)

B-13210-A   **Down A Carolina Lane** [Mitchell Parish; Frank Perkins] vSB (cl solo)
          78: Brunswick 6549
13211-1   **Down A Carolina Lane** vCB (cl solo)
          78: Banner 32470, Melotone M-12669, Oriole 2680, Perfect 15755, Romeo 2053
          as CHICK BULLOCK AND HIS LEVEE LOUNGERS
B-13212-A   **Remember Me** vSB
          78: Brunswick 6549
13213-1   **Tony's Wife** [Harold Adamson; Burton Lane] vCB
          78: Banner 32743, Melotone M-12678, Oriole 2683, Perfect 15758, Romeo 2056, Vocalion 15884, Broadcast 3331
          Vocalion as BUNNY BERIGAN AND HIS ORCHESTRA, all others as HAVANA NOVELTY ORCHESTRA
13214-1   **Anything Your Little Heart Desires** [Little Jack Little, David Oppenheim; Ira Schuster] vCB
          78: Banner 32740, Melotone M-12669, Oriole 2680, Perfect 15755, Romeo 2053
          as CHICK BULLOCK AND HIS LEVEE LOUNGERS

The presence of Larry Gomar in the ARC studios for the next sides suggests that he stayed for the Boswell session that followed and/or that others from the Boswell date are also on the Gomar sides.

ARC, New York, N.Y. Tuesday, April 11, 1933
LARRY GOMAR, vibraphone solos
Mannie Weinstock [or] Mannie Klein (tp) Jimmy Dorsey (cl) *unknown* (p), *Dick McDonough* (g), *Artie Bernstein* (sb) Larry Gomar (vib)

B-13220   **Try A Little Tenderness** [Harry Woods, Jimmy Connelly]
          78: Brunswick 6565
B-13221   **Rhythmic Dream** [Larry Gomar]
          78: Brunswick 6565

ARC, New York, N.Y. Tuesday, April 11, 1933
THE BOSWELL SISTERS
Mannie Klein (tp) Tom Dorsey (tb) **Jimmy Dorsey** (cl) *Martha Boswell* (p) Dick McDonough (g) Artie Bernstein (sb) *Larry Gomar [or] Stan King* (d) Boswell Sisters (vcl)

B-13222-A   **Forty-Second Street** [Al Dubin; Harry Warren] vBS (cl solo)
          78: Brunswick 6545, (E) 01516, (G) A-9416, (It) 4825, (F) 500241, Lucky (J) 60020
          LP: Biograph BLP C-16, Columbia Special Products P16496, P12855, Epic LN24441, Wave (J) MFPL84801
          TC: ProArte Digital PCD 550, Columbia CT 66977
          CD: Jazz Roots 56082, Columbia CK 66977, Fremeaux (F) 9518

B-13222-B   **Forty-Second Street** vBS (cl solo)
    CD: JASS J-CD-622
B-13223-A   **Shuffle Off To Buffalo** [Al Dubin; Harry Warren]
                   vBS
    78: Brunswick 6545, (E) 01516, (G) A-9416, (It) 4825, (F)
    500241, Lucky (J) 60020
    LP: Biograph BLP C-16, Columbia Special Products P16496,
    P12855, Epic LN24441, Wave (J) MFPL84801
    TC: ProArte Digital PCD 550, Columbia CT 66977
    CD: ProArte Digital CDD 550, Living Era (E) ASV AJA-5139,
    Columbia CK 66977

ARC, New York, N.Y. Wednesday, April 12, 1933
CONNIE BOSWELL (ARC Studio Band)
Mannie Klein (tp) Tom Dorsey (tb) **Jimmy Dorsey** (cl) 3 *unknown* (vn)
Martha Boswell (p) Dick McDonough (g) Artie Bernstein (sb) *Larry
Gomar [or] Stan King* (d) Connie Boswell, Dick Robertson (vcl)

B-13230-A   **You'll Never Get Up To Heaven That Way** [Sammy
                   Lerner; Abel Baer] vCB
    78: Brunswick 6552, (E) 01528
    LP: Jazum 30
    TC: Audio Archives 1002
B-13231-A   **In A Little Second Hand Store** [Please, Driver, Nel-
                   son] vCB (cl solo)
    78: Brunswick 6552, (E) 01528
    LP: Jazum 30

ARC, New York, N.Y. Saturday, April 15, 1933
VICTOR YOUNG AND HIS ORCHESTRA
Victor Young (ldr) *Frank Guerente [or] Charlie Margulis,* Mannie Klein
(tp) Tom Dorsey (tb) **Jimmy Dorsey** (cl,as) *unknown* (as) Larry Binyon
(ts) Joe Venuti, Harry Hoffman, 2 *unknown* (vn) Fulton McGrath (p)
Dick McDonough (g) Artie Bernstein (sb) Larry Gomar (d,vib) Elmer
Feldkamp, Dick Robertson, Lee Wiley (vcl)

B-13248-A   **Home-Made Heaven** vEF
    78: Melotone M-12685, Panachord (E) 25530
                   *Melotone as OWEN FALLON AND HIS CALIFORNIANS,
                   Panachord as ART KAHN AND HIS ORCHESTRA*
13249-1   **Home-Made Heaven** vDR
    78: Banner 32756, Oriole 2692, Perfect 15764, Romeo 2065,
    Broadcast (E) 3323, Kristall (Swe) K-3503
                   *Banner as OWEN FALLON AND HIS CALIFORNIANS,
                   Broadcast as ED LOYD AND HIS ORCHESTRA, Kristall as
                   ED LLOYD UND HANS ORKESTER*
B-13250-A   **In The Park In Paree** [Leo Robin; Ralph Rainger]
                   vEF (cl solo)
    78: Panachord (E) 25530
                   Panachord 25530 as ART KAHN AND HIS ORCHESTRA
13251-1   **In The Park In Paree** vDR (cl solo)
    78: Banner 32750, Oriole 2686, Perfect 15761, Romeo (Contd.)

VICTOR YOUNG AND HIS ORCHESTRA (Contd.)

2059, Melotone M-12679, Broadcast (E) 3323, Vocalion 15883, Kristall (Swe) K-3503
> *Vocalion as EDDIE STONE AND HIS ORCHESTRA, Kristall as ED LLOYD UND HANS ORKESTER, others as ED LOYD AND HIS ORCHESTRA*

B-13252-A   **Look What I've Got** [Leo Robin; Ralph Rainger] vEF (cl,as solos)
> **78:** Panachord (E) 25524
> *as RALPH BENNETT AND HIS SEVEN ACES*

13253-1   **Look What I've Got** vDR (cl,as solos)
> **78:** Banner 32750, Oriole 2686, Perfect 15761, Romeo 2059, Melotone M-12679, Vocalion 15883
> **LP:** Harrison Y
> *Vocalion as EDDIE STONE AND HIS ORCHESTRA, others as ED LOYD AND HIS ORCHESTRA*

B-13254-A   **Let's Call It A Day** [Lew Brown; Ray Henderson] vLW (cl solo)
> **LP:** JASS 19
> **CD:** JASS CD-J-19, Vintage Jazz Classics VJC 1023, Jazz Classics 6013

B-13254-B   **Let's Call It A Day** vLW (cl solo)
> **TC:** Columbia Legacy CT52951
> **CD:** Vintage Jazz Classics VJC 1023, Columbia CK52943

ARC, New York, N.Y. Wednesday, April 19, 1933
ARC STUDIO BAND
Victor Young (ldr) *Frank Guerente [or] Charlie Margulis, unknown* (tp) Tom Dorsey (tb) **Jimmy Dorsey** (cl,as) *Larry Binyon* (ts) *unknown* (vn) Joe Meresco (p) Charlie Magnante (acc) Dick McDonough (g) *Joe Tarto* (bb,sb) Chauncey Morehouse (d,vib) Chick Bullock (vcl)

13263-1   **Have You Ever Been Lonely? (Have You Ever Been Blue?)** [George Brown (Billy Hill); Peter De Rose] vCB
> **78:** Banner 32751, Conqueror 8120, Melotone M-12680, Oriole 2687, Perfect 12908, Romeo 2080
> *Melotone and Perfect as CHICK BULLOCK, others as CHICK BULLOCK AND HIS LEVEE LOUNGERS*

13264-1   **Stormy Weather (Keeps Rainin' All The Time)** [Ted Kohler; Harold Arlen] vCB (cl solo)
> **78:** Banner 32751, Conqueror 8182, Melotone M-12680, Oriole 2687, Perfect 12908, Romeo 1080, Rex (E) 8008
> *Melotone and Perfect as CHICK BULLOCK, Rex as CHICK BULLOCK, The Great American Radio Singer, others as CHICK BULLOCK AND HIS LEVEE LOUNGERS*

13265-1   **In A Little Second Hand Store** [Please, Driver, Nichols] vCB
> **78:** Banner 32754, Melotone M-12683, Oriole 2690, Romeo 2063, Perfect 15762, Rex (E) 8008
> *Banner as CHICK BULLOCK, others as CHICK BULLOCK*

AND HIS LEVEE LOUNGERS
TC: Audio Archives 1004
13266-1   It's Time To Sing "Sweet Adeline" Again [Benny
                 Davis; Sammy Fain] vCB (cl solo)
       78: Banner 32754, Melotone M-12683, Oriole 2690, Romeo
       2063, Perfect 15762
                 Banner as CHICK BULLOCK, others as CHICK BULLOCK
                 AND HIS LEVEE LOUNGERS
       TC: Audio Archives 1004

What is undoubtedly the best known of the ARC "Test Only" series
was probably put together on this date. ARC files list "Just An Echo"
by "Tommy Dorsey Orchestra" (TO-1289) and "unknown dialogue"
(TO-1287), both on Saturday, April 8 (Allen and Brooks 1972), so it is
probable this is the music and dialogue dubbed together by engineers on
April 19 (the date shown in the same source for TO-1293).
     The author believes that the "unknown dialogue" (TO-1287) is the
Carl Kress "commercial" cut separately and that TO-1289 includes the
musical "bed" heard behind Kress.
     Most of the suggested musicians on this Joe Venuti-inspired farce
were at ARC earlier that Saturday (April 8) for regular sessions, and
Saturday would make it easier for the other suspected conspirators to
come to the studio "after hours." April 19 is ruled out for any original
recording because Bunny Berigan, who is definitely present, was on tour
with Paul Whiteman after April 14 (White and Kite 1951-1987).

ARC, New York, N.Y. Recorded April 8, edited April 19, 1933
ARC STUDIO BAND
Bunny Berigan, *Mannie Klein* (tp) Tom Dorsey (tb) **Jimmy Dorsey**
(cl,as) Joe Venuti (vn,vcl) Carl Kress (*g*,narrator) Joe Tarto (sb) Stan
King (d)

TO-1293   **The Joe Venuti Radio Program**, including **Just An
                 Echo In The Valley** vJV (cl solo)
       78: ARC TO-1293, Lucky (J) 7000-B
                 Lucky as JOE VENUTI AND FRIENDS
       LP: Arcadia (C) 2015, Broadway BR-108

ARC, New York, N.Y. Thursday, April 20, 1933
VICTOR YOUNG AND HIS ORCHESTRA
Victor Young (ldr) *Frank Guerente [or] Charlie Margulis,* Mannie Klein
(tp) Tom Dorsey (tb) *Jimmy Dorsey* (cl,as) *Larry Binyon* (ts) Harry
Hoffman, *Walter Edelstein* (vn) Charles Magnante (acc) *Fulton McGrath*
(p) *Dick McDonough [or] Carl Kress* (g) *Artie Bernstein* (sb) Larry
Gomar (d,xyl) Dick Robertson, Donald Novis, Arthur Tracy (vcl)

B-13261-A   **Two Tickets To Georgia** [Joe Young, Charles To-
                 bias, J. Fred Coots] vDR
       78: Brunswick 6554, (E) 01534
B-13262-A   **It's Time To Sing "Sweet Adeline" Again** [Benny
                 Davis; Sammy Fain] vDR
       78: Brunswick 6554, (E) 01534 (Contd.)

VICTOR YOUNG AND HIS ORCHESTRA (Contd.)

B-13267   (Special Record for Exhibitor's Screen Service, pos-
                       sibly a dubbing of a "Test Only" release)
B-13268-   **When The Sun Bids The Moon Goodnight** [Edgar
                       Leslie; Mabel Wayne] vDN
    78: Brunswick 6557
        as DONALD NOVIS with Victor Young and His Orch.
B-13269-A   **Gypsy Fiddles** [Allie Wrubel] vAT
    78: Brunswick 6561, Decca (E) F-3577
        as ARTHUR TRACY with Victor Young and His Orch.
B-13270-A   **In Old Vienna** vAT
    78: Brunswick 6561, Decca (E) F-3577
        ARTHUR TRACY with Victor Young and His Orch.
B-13271-   **I Lay Me Down To Sleep** [Allie Wrubel] vDN
    78: Brunswick 6557
        as DONALD NOVIS with Victor Young and His Orch.

ARC, New York, N.Y. Saturday, April 22, 1933
ARC STUDIO BAND
Unknown (tp) Tom Dorsey (tb) **Jimmy Dorsey** (cl,as) Joe Meresco (p),
Dick McDonough (g) Artie Bernstein (sb) Larry Gomar (d,vib) Dick
Robertson, Baby Rose Marie (vcl)

13272-A   **My Bluebird's Singing The Blues** [Leo Robin; Ralph
                       Rainger] vBRM
    78: Brunswick 6570, (E) 01546, Banner 32909, Perfect 12960,
    Melotone M-12852
        as BABY ROSE MARIE
13272-B   **My Bluebird's Singing The Blues** vBRM
    78: (unissued, test pressing exists)
13273-A   **Come Out, Come Out Wherever You Are** [Sammy
                       Cahn; Jule Styne] vBRM (cl solo)
    78: Brunswick 6570, (E) 01546, Banner 32909, Perfect 12960,
    Melotone M-12852
        as BABY ROSE MARIE
    LP: Personalities On Parade PP-3
2 *unknown* (vn) added:
F267   **Keep Looking Forward** vDR
    78: ARC Theater-Use F-267
        as ART KAHN AND HIS ORCHESTRA.

    ARC file cards show this was a **second** remake of F-267, first dubbed
from B-13232-A, made April 13, 1933, by Freddy Martin and released
on Banner 32756, then remade April 16, 1933, by an unknown group.

E720 (F268)   **Hold Me** [Little Jack Little, Dave Oppenheim, Ira
                       Schuster] (as solo)
    78: ARC Theater-Use F-268
    ET: ARC Theater-Use E-720
        as IMPERIAL CLUB ORCHESTRA
E721 (F269-1)   **Shuffle Off To Buffalo** [Al Dubin; Harry Warren]

78: ARC Theater-Use F-269
ET: ARC Theater-Use E-721
        as ED LOYD AND HIS ORCHESTRA
E722 (F270)   **Young And Healthy** [Al Dubin; Harry Warren]
        78: ARC Theater-Use F-270
        ET: ARC Theater-Use E-722
E723 (F271-1)   **Two Tickets To Georgia** [Joe Young, Charles To-
                    bias, J. Fred Coots]
        78: ARC Theater-Use F-271
        ET: ARC Theater-Use E-723
        as ED LOYD AND HIS ORCHESTRA
E724 (F272)   **Have You Ever Been Lonely? (Have You Ever Been
                    Blue?)** [George Brown; Peter De Rose]
        78: ARC Theater-Use F-272
        ET: ARC Theater-Use E-724
E725 (F273)   **You'll Never Get Up To Heaven That Way** [Sammy
                    Lerner; Abel Baer]
        78: ARC Theater-Use F-273
        ET: ARC Theater-Use E-725

ARC, New York, N.Y. Wednesday, May 3, 1933
BRUNSWICK STUDIO BAND
Victor Young (ldr) *Frank Guerente [or] Charlie Margulis, unknown* (tp)
Tom Dorsey (tb) **Jimmy Dorsey** (cl,as) Larry Binyon (cl,ts) Joe Venuti,
Harry Hoffman, Walter Edelstein, Lou Kosloff (vn) Fulton McGrath (p)
Dick McDonough (g) Artie Bernstein (sb) *unknown* (d) Ethel Waters,
Lee Wiley (vcl)

B-13292-A   **Stormy Weather (Keeps Rainin' All The Time)**
                    [Ted Kohler; Harold Arlen] vEW
        78: Brunswick 6564, (E) 01524, (F) A-500266, (It) 4842,
        Columbia 36329
        LP: Columbia CL2792, Hep (Sc) 1006
        CD: Timeless (H) CBC 1-007, Disky (H) DCO 5335-1, Classics
        (F) 735, Pearl Imports 7095
B-13293-A   **Love Is The Thing** [Ned Washington; Victor Young]
                    vEW (cl solo)
        78: Brunswick 6564, (E) 01524, (F) A-500266, Columbia 36329
        LP: Columbia KG31571, Hep (Sc) 1006
        CD: Classics (F) 735
        13292 and 13293 as ETHEL WATERS
B-13254-C   **Let's Call It A Day** [Lew Brown; Ray Henderson]
                    vLW (cl solo)
        CD: Vintage Jazz Classics VJC 1023
B-13254-D   **Let's Call It A Day** vLW (cl solo)
        LP: JASS 19
        CD: JASS CD-J-19, Vintage Jazz Classics VJC 1023, Jazz
        Classics 6013

Eddie Lang's name is missing from the next Joe Venuti session.
Lang (Salvatore Massaro) died at thirty-one in March 1933 from
anesthetic complications during a tonsillectomy.

His death was a great shock to all, including Bing Crosby, who had made Lang his "official" guitarist on both coasts.

Columbia, New York, N.Y. Monday, May 8, 1933
JOE VENUTI AND HIS BLUE FIVE
Joe Venuti (vn,sb,ldr) **Jimmy Dorsey** (tp,cl,as) Adrian Rollini (bsx, kazoo,p,vib) Phil Wall (p) Dick McDonough (g) Howard Phillips (vcl)

W-265116-1   **Hiawatha's Lullaby** [Walter Donaldson] vHP (cl,as cl solos)
   LP: World Records (E) SM327
W-265116-2   **Hiawatha's Lullaby** vHP (cl,as,cl solos)
   78: Columbia (E) CB-637, (Au) DO-979
      Columbia (E) as JOE VENUTI & HIS ORCH.
   LP: Regal (E) REG1076, Disques Swing SW 8457/8, Music For Pleasure (EC) 1161, World Records (E) SHB39
W-265117-2   **Vibraphonia** [Adrian Rollini] (as,tp,cl solos)
   78: Columbia 2782-D, (Au) DO-937, Parlophone (E) R-2083
   LP: Regal (E) REG1076, Disques Swing SW 8457/8, Music For Pleasure (EC) 1161, Columbia C2L24

2 *unknown* (tp) *unknown* (tb) 2 *unknown* (as) *unknown* (ts) added:
W-265118-2   **Isn't It Heavenly?** [E. Y. Harburg; Joseph Meyer] vHP
   78: Columbia 2783-D, (Au) DO-959
W-265119-2   **My Gypsy Rhapsody**
   78: Columbia (E) CB-637, (Au) DO-979
      Columbia (E) as JOE VENUTI & HIS ORCH. All Columbia (Au) as JOE VENUTI & EDDIE LANG'S BLUE FIVE

ARC, New York, N.Y. Thursday, May 11, 1933
ARC-BRUNSWICK STUDIO BAND
Mannie Klein (tp) Tom Dorsey (tb) **Jimmy Dorsey** (cl,as) Harry Hoffman, *Walter Edelstein, unknown* (vn) *Fulton McGrath* (p) *Dick McDonough [or] Carl Kress* (g) *Artie Bernstein* (sb) Larry Gomar (d) Les Reis, Helen Rowland, Greta Keller (vcl)

B-13315-   **Stormy Weather** vLR (unissued)
B-13316-   **I've Got To Sing A Torch Song** [Al Dubin; Harry Warren] vLR
   78: Panachord (E) 25548
13317-1   **I've Got To Sing A Torch Song** vHR
   78: Banner 32767, Melotone M-12696, Oriole 2700, Perfect 15771, Romeo 2073
      as ED LOYD AND HIS ORCHESTRA
B-13318-   **Remember My Forgotten Man** [Al Dubin; Harry Warren] vLR (as solos)
   78: Panachord (E) 25548
      13316 and 13318 as ALLEN BURNS AND HIS ORCHESTRA
13319-1   **Remember My Forgotten Man** vHR (as solos)
   78: Banner 32767, Melotone M-12696, Oriole 2700, Perfect 15771, Romeo 2073, Vocalion 15891

*Vocalion as BUNNY BERIGAN [sic] AND HIS ORCH.,
others as ED LOYD AND HIS ORCH.*

B-13324-A   **Stormy Weather (Keeps Rainin' All The Time)**
              [Ted Kohler; Harold Arlen] vGK
    78: Decca (E) F-3562
B-13325-A   **I Can't Remember** [Irving Berlin] vGK
    78: Decca (E) F-3586
B-13326-A   **Hold Me** [Jack Little, Dave Oppenheim] vGK
    78: Decca (E) F-3601
              13324 to 13326 as GRETA KELLER
F274   **Stormy Weather (Keeps Rainin' All The Time)**
    78: ARC Theater-Use F274
    ET: ARC-Theater-Use E728 *(dubbed May 25, 1933, from F-274)*

ARC, New York, N.Y. Thursday, May 25, 1933
ARC STUDIO BAND
Victor Young (ldr) Mannie Klein (tp) Tom Dorsey (tb) **Jimmy Dorsey**
(cl,as) Larry Binyon (ts) 2 *unknown* (vn) Joe Meresco (p) Dick
McDonough (g) Artie Bernstein (sb) Stan King (d,chimes) Dick Powell,
Chick Bullock (vcl)

13386-1   **The Gold Digger's Song (We're In The Money)** [Al
              Dubin; Harry Warren] vDP (as solo)
    78: Conqueror 8184, Romeo 2084, Perfect 12919, Broadcast
    3339
    LP: Columbia C2L-44, New World Record NW-270
    TC: ProArte Digital PCD 486, Columbia CT66978, Radio
    Yesteryear Stack 19
    CD: ProArte Digital CDD 486
13387-1   **Pettin' In The Park** [Al Dubin; Harry Warren] vDP
              (cl solo)
    78: Conqueror 8183, Perfect 12920, Broadcast 3340
    LP: Columbia C2L-44
    TC: Columbia CT66978
    CD: Timeless (E) 1020
13388-1   **Shadow Waltz** [Al Dubin; Harry Warren] vDP (cl
              solo)
    78: Conqueror 8183, Perfect 12920, Broadcast 3340
    LP: Columbia C2L-44
    TC: Columbia CT66978, Radio Yesteryear Stack 19
13389-1   **I've Got To Sing A Torch Song** [Al Dubin; Harry
              Warren] vDP
    78: Conqueror 8184, Romeo 2084, Perfect 12919, Broadcast
    3339
              13386 to 13389 as DICK POWELL
    LP: Columbia C2L-44
    TC: Columbia CT66978, Radio Yesteryear Stack 19
    13396 to 13389 also on **CD:** Columbia CK66978
13390-1   **Blue Prelude** [Joe Bishop; Gordon Jenkins] vCB
    78: Banner 32777, Conqueror 8188, Melotone M-12712, Oriole
    2705, Perfect 15775
    LP: Lyric 3302   (Contd.)

ARC STUDIO BAND (Contd.)

13391-1   There's A Cabin In The Pines [Billy Hill] vCB
                 (cl,as solos)
     78: Banner 32777, Melotone M-12712, Oriole 2705, Perfect
     15775
                 *13390, 13391 as CHICK BULLOCK AND HIS LEVEE
                 LOUNGERS*

ARC, New York, N.Y. Monday, May 29, 1933
MORTON DOWNEY
Victor Young (ldr) Mannie Klein (tp) Jimmy Dorsey (cl,as) others
unknown. Morton Downey (vcl)

13403   Sweetheart Darlin'[Gus Kahn; Herbert Stothart] vMD
     78: Melotone M-12710
13404-1   Isn't It Heavenly? [E. Y. Harburg; Joseph Meyer]
                 vMD
     78: Melotone M-12710, Broadcast (C) 3341
13409   Hold Your Man [Arthur Freed; Nacio Herb Brown]
                 vMD (cl solo)
     78: Melotone M-12734; Conqueror 8182
13410-1   Love Is The Thing [Ned Washington; Victor Young]
                 vMD (cl solo)
     78: Melotone M-12734; Broadcast (C) 3352, Rex (C) 8839

ARC, New York, N.Y. Saturday, June 3, 1933
VICTOR YOUNG AND HIS ORCHESTRA
Victor Young (ldr) *Frank Guerente,* Mannie Klein (tp) Tom Dorsey (tb)
Jimmy Dorsey (cl,as) *Larry Binyon* (ts) Harry Hoffman, Matty Malneck
(vn) Fulton McGrath (p) Dick McDonough (g) Art Bernstein (sb)
Chauncey Morehouse (d) Paul Small, Annette Hanshaw (vcl)

B 13419-A   Isn't It Heavenly? [E. Y. Harburg; Joseph Meyers]
                   vPS
     78: Brunswick 6589, (E) 01558
B 13420-A   A Fool In Love [George McQueen; Sid Lippman]
                   vPS (cl solo)
     78: Brunswick 6586, (E) 01558
B 13421-A   I've Got To Pass Your House (To Get To My
                   House) [Lew Brown] vPS
     78: Brunswick 6589, (E) 01582
Guarente, Tom Dorsey, *Binyon,* Small out.
13422-1   I Cover The Waterfront [Edward Heyman; Johnny
                 Green] vAH
     78: Banner 32788, Conqueror 8185, Melotone M-12721, Oriole
     2713, Perfect 12921, Romeo 2083, Panachord (E) 25551
     LP: Sunbeam P-511, Halcyon (E) HDL-119
     TC: Halcyon (E) CHDL-119, CTP5
13423-1   Sweetheart Darlin' [Gus Kahn; Herbert Stothart] vAH
     78: Banner 32788, Conqueror 8185, Melotone M-12721, Oriole
     2713, Perfect 12921, Romeo 2083, Panachord (E) 25551

LP: Sunbeam P-511, Halcyon (E) HDL-119
TC: Halcyon (E) CHDL-119, CTP5
13422, 13423 as ANNETTE HANSHAW

ARC, New York, N.Y. Tuesday, June 6, 1933
THE DORSEY BROTHERS' ORCHESTRA
Tom Dorsey (tb,ldr) *Mannie Klein* (tp) **Jimmy Dorsey** (cl,as) Larry
Binyon (ts) Fulton McGrath (p) Dick McDonough (g) Artie Bernstein
(sb) Stan King (d) Mildred Bailey (vcl)

B-13426-A   **Old Man Harlem** [Hoagy Carmichael, Rudy Vallee]
                   (as,cl solo)
    78: Brunswick 6624, (E) 01575, (F) A-81579, A-500304,
    Columbia (Au) DO-1235
    LP: Hep (Sc) 1005
    CD: ABC 36216, Hep (UK) 1005
B-13427-A   **There's A Cabin In The Pines** [Billy Hill] vMB
                   (cl solo)
    78: Brunswick 6587, (E) 01564, (F) A-500305
    as MILDRED BAILEY with DORSEY BROTHERS' ORCH.
    LP: Columbia C3L22, Hep (Sc) 1006, CBS BPG-62098
    CD: Hep (E) CD 1006, The Old Masters MB104
B-13428-A   **Lazy Bones** [Johnny Mercer; Hoagy Carmichael]
                   vMB
    78: Brunswick 6587, (E) 01564, (F) A-500305
    as MILDRED BAILEY with DORSEY BROTHERS' ORCH.
    LP: Columbia Special Products P14543, Hep (Sc) 1006
    CD: Hep (E) CD 1006, The Old Masters MB104, Flapper (E)
    CD7094

ARC, New York, N.Y. Saturday, June 10, 1933
CONNIE BOSWELL
Tom Dorsey (tb,ldr) *Mannie Klein* (tp) **Jimmy Dorsey** (cl,as) Larry
Binyon (ts) 2 *unknown* (vn) Fulton McGrath (p) Dick McDonough (g)
Artie Bernstein (sb) Stan King (d) Connie Boswell (vcl)

B-13445-A   **I Cover The Waterfront** [Edward Heyman; Johnny
                   Green] vCB
    78: Brunswick 6592, (E) 01555, (F) 500298
    TC: Columbia/Legacy CT52932
    CD: Columbia/Legacy CK52943, ASV Living Era (E) 5221
B-13446-A   **I Couldn't Tell Them What To Do** [Roy Turk; Vee
                   Lawnhurst] vCB (cl solo)
    78: Brunswick 6592, (E) 01547
B-13447-A   **Under A Blanket Of Blue** [Marty Symes, Al J. Nei-
                   berg; Jerry Livingston] vCB (cl solo)
    78: Brunswick 6603, 01555, (F) 500298, Lucky (J) 60200
    LP: Jazum 31
    TC: Columbia/Legacy CT52932
    CD: Columbia/Legacy CK52943, ASV Living Era (E) 5221

Columbia, New York, N.Y. Monday, June 12, 1933
ADRIAN ROLLINI AND HIS ORCHESTRA
Adrian Rollini (bsx,goof,xyl,vib,ldr) Mannie Klein (tp) Tom Dorsey (tb)
Jimmy Dorsey (cl) Arthur Rollini (ts) Fulton McGrath (p) Dick
McDonough (g) Herb Weil (d) Irene Beasley, Howard Phillips (vcl)

265131-2   **Blue Prelude** [Joe Bishop; Gordon Jenkins] vHP
                  (cl solo)
     78: Columbia 2785-D, Parlophone (E) R-2515, Regal 1076
265132-2   **Mississippi Basin** [Andy Razaf; Reginald Forsythe]
                  vIB (cl solo)
     78: Parlophone (E) R-2515, Regal 1076
265133-2   **Charlie's Home** [Harry Tobias; J. Fred Coots] vHP
                  (cl solo)
     LP: World Records (E) SH391
265134-2   **Happy As The Day Is Long** [Ted Kohler; Harold
                  Arlen] vHP (cl solo)
     78: Columbia 2785-D
All sides also on **LP:** Disques Swing SW8457/8

ARC, New York, N.Y. Tuesday, June 13, 1933
THE DORSEY BROTHERS' ORCHESTRA
Tom Dorsey (tb,ldr) Mannie Klein (tp) **Jimmy Dorsey** (cl,as) Larry
Binyon (ts) Harry Hoffman (vn) Fulton McGrath (p) Dick McDonough
(g) Art Bernstein (sb) Stan King (d,chimes) Boswell Sisters (vcl)

B-13449-A   **By Heck** [L. Wolfe Gilbert; S. R. Henry] (as,cl,as
                   solos)
     78: Brunswick 6624, (G) A81579, (E) 01575, (F) A-500304,
     Columbia (Au) DO-1235
     LP: Hep (Sc) 1005
     TC: ProArte Digital PCD 508, Columbia CT 48908, (H) 37169-4
     CD: ProArte Digital CDD 508, Columbia CK 48908, (H) 37169-
     2, Hep (UK) 1005, Jazz Greats (E) 036
B-13449-B   **By Heck** (as,cl,as solos)
     78: Columbia 36065
     LP: Hep (Sc) 1005
     CD: Hep (UK) 1005
B-13450-A   **The Gold Digger's Song (We're In The Money)** [Al
                   Dubin; Harry Warren] vBS
     78: Brunswick 6596, (E) 01556, (G) A-9443, (F) A-500217, (It)
     4830
     LP: CBS (F) 80074, Jazum 43, Biograph BLP C-16
     TC: ProArte Digital PCD 508
     CD: ProArte Digital CDD 508
B-13451-A   **It's Sunday Down In Caroline** [Marty Symes, Al J.
                   Neiberg; Jerry Livingston] vBS
     78: Brunswick 6596, (E) 01556, (G) A-9443, (It) 4830, (F) A-
     500217, 500314
          13450 and 13451 as BOSWELL SISTERS
     LP: CBS (F) 80074, Jazum 43

ARC, New York, N.Y. Thursday, June 15, 1933
THE DORSEY BROTHERS' ORCHESTRA
Personnel as June 13, 1933. Connie Boswell, Boswell Sisters (vcl)

B-13466-A   **(Stop That) Puttin' It On** vBS
    78: Brunswick 6625, (E) O1576, (G) A-9440, (It) 4849,
    Columbia (Au) DO-1228, Lucky (J) 60093
    LP: Jazum 31, Wave (J) MFPL84801
B-13467-A   **Swanee Mammy** (Boswell Sisters version of "Swanee
                Woman") vBS
    78: Brunswick 6625, (E) O1576, (G) A-9440 (It) 4849,
    Columbia (Au) DO-1228
        13466 and 13467 as BOSWELL SISTERS
    LP: Jazum 31, Wave (J) MFPL 84801
B-13468-A   **The River's Takin' Care Of Me** [Stanley Adams;
                Jesse Greer] vCB
    78: Brunswick 6603, (E) 01547
        as CONNIE BOSWELL
    LP: Jazum 31, Take Two TT209, Columbia 40847
    TC: Columbia CT40847
    CD: Columbia CK40847, Bellaphon (It) 625-50-003

ARC, New York, N.Y. Wednesday, July 12, 1933
ARC STUDIO BAND (possibly Dorsey Brothers)
Mannie Klein, *unknown* (tp) Tom Dorsey (tb) **Jimmy Dorsey** (cl,as)
Larry Binyon (ts) *unknown* (cl,ts), (vn) Joe Meresco (p) Dick McDon-
ough (g) Art Bernstein (sb) Stan King (d) Chick Bullock, Irene Taylor
(vcl)

13532-1   **Lazy Bones** [Johnny Mercer; Hoagy Carmichael] vCB
    78: Banner 32811, Conqueror 8190, Perfect 12927, Rex (E)
    8020
        Rex as CHICK BULLOCK, The Great American Radio Star
13533-1   **Mississippi Basin** [Andy Razaf; Reginald Forsythe]
                vCB (cl solo)
    78: Banner 32811, Conqueror 8190, Perfect 12927
        except for Rex, 13532 and 13533 as CHICK BULLOCK
13534-   **Shadows On The Swanee** [Johnny Burke, Joe Young;
                Harold Spina] vIT
    78: Vocalion 25003
13535-   **Don't Blame Me** [Dorothy Fields; Jimmy McHugh]
                vIT
    78: Vocalion 25003
        13534 and 13535 as IRENE TAYLOR

ARC, New York, N.Y. Tuesday, July 18, 1933
VICTOR YOUNG AND HIS ORCHESTRA
Victor Young (ldr) *Frank Guerente [or] Charlie Margulis, Mannie Klein*
(tp) Tom Dorsey (tb) **Jimmy Dorsey,** Larry Binyon (cl,as) Harry
Hoffman, Walter Edelstein, Lou Kosloff (vn) *Joe Meresco [or] Fulton
McGrath* (p) Dick McDonough (g) Artie Bernstein (sb) *Stan King [or]
Chauncey Morehouse* (d) Paul Small, Ethel Waters (vcl)

B-13558-A   **Hold Your Man** [Arthur Freed; Nacio Herb Brown]
                   vPS (cl solo)
       78: Brunswick 6612, (C) 6612
B-13559-A   **Isn't This(It*) A Night For Love?**[Val Burton; Will
                   Jason] vPS
       78: Brunswick 6612, *(C) 6612
Klein and unknown (tp), both Dorseys, Venuti, (p) and (d) return.
B-13565-A   **Don't Blame Me** [Dorothy Fields; Jimmy McHugh]
                   vEW (cl solo)
       78: Brunswick 6617, (E) 01579, (It) 4842
       LP: Columbia KG31517, Hep (Sc) 1006
B-13566-A   **Shadows On The Swanee** [Joe Young, Johnny Burke;
                   Harold Spina] vEW (cl solo)
       78: Brunswick 6617, (E) 01579
       13565 and 13566 as ETHEL WATERS
       LP: Hep (Sc) 1006
       TC: Columbia/Legacy CT 52932
       CD: Columbia/Legacy CK 52943
       both Waters sides on **CD:** Hep (E) CD 1006, Classics (F) 735

World, New York, N.Y. July-October 1933
DORSEY BROTHERS ORCHESTRA
Tom Dorsey (tb,ldr) Mannie Klein, *unknown* (tp) *unknown* (tb) **Jimmy
Dorsey** (cl,as) Larry Binyon (ts,fl) Harry Hoffman, *unknown* (vn)
unknown (p) Dick McDonough (g) Artie Bernstein (sb) Stan King (d)
unknown (vib) Betty Fredericks, Frank Luther (vcl)

-0-   **Forty Second Street** [Al Dubin; Harry Warren]
                   (cl solo)
       LP: Jazum 1
-0-   **Love Is The Sweetest Thing** [Ray Noble] vBF
-0-   **Learn To Croon** [Sam Coslow; Arthur Johnston] vFL
-0-   **This Is Romance** [Edward Heyman; Vernon Duke]
                   vBF&FL
       All on: **ET:** World demonstration record, **LP:** Fanfare LP-5-105

ARC, New York, N.Y. Saturday, August 5, 1933
CHICK BULLOCK
Mannie Klein, *unknown* (tp), (tb) **Jimmy Dorsey** (cl,as) Larry Binyon
(ts) *unknown* (cl,ts) *Harry Hoffman* (vn) Joe Meresco (p) Dick Mc-
Donough (g) Artie Bernstein (sb) Stan King (d) Chick Bullock (vcl)

13665-1   **Learn To Croon** [Sam Coslow; Arthur Johnston]
                   vCB (cl solo)
       78: Banner 32823, Conqueror 8254, Oriole 2733, Rex (E) 8020
13666-1   **Isn't This A Night For Love?** [Val Burton; Will
                   Jason] vCB (cl solo)
       78: Banner 32823, Conqueror 8254, Oriole 2733, Rex (E) 8057
                   Rex as CHICK BULLOCK, The Great American Radio Star
13735-1   **Shadows On The Swanee** [Johnny Burke, Joe Young;
                   Harold Spina] vCB (cl solo)
       78: Banner 32834, Conqueror 8222, Oriole 2740, Perfect 12933

13735-2   **Shadows On The Swanee** vCB (cl solo)
13736-1   **Lou'siana Lullaby** [Charles Newman, Johnny Burke;
                   Harold Spina] vCB (as solo)
   78: Banner 32834, Conqueror 8222, Oriole 2740, Perfect 12933
   13735-2 and 13736 also on **TC:** Audio Archives 1004

ARC, New York, N.Y. Monday, August 14, 1933
VICTOR YOUNG AND HIS ORCHESTRA
Victor Young (ldr) *Mannie Weinstock* (tp) Tom Dorsey (tb) **Jimmy Dorsey** (cl,as) *unknown* (as) *Larry Binyon* (ts) *Harry Hoffman,* 3 *unknown* (vn) *unknown* (p) Dick McDonough (g) *Artie Bernstein* (sb) *Larry Gomar* (d) Paul Small, Connie Boswell, Jack Fulton (vcl)

B-13784-A   **When Autumn Comes Around** vPS
   78: Brunswick 6630, (E) 01610
B-13785-A   **My Moonlight Madonna** [Paul Francis Webster;
                   William Scotti] (waltz) vPS
   78: Brunswick 6630, (E) 01586
B-13786-A   **It's The Talk Of The Town** [Marty Symes, Al J.
                   Neiberg; Jerry Livingston] vCB
   78: Brunswick 6632, (E) O1594
   LP: Jazum 31, Decca (E) RAL-505
B-13787-A   **This Time It's Love** [Sam M.Lewis; J. Fred Coots]
                   vCB
   78: Brunswick 6632, (E) O1594
            13786, 13787 as CONNIE BOSWELL AND ORCHESTRA
   LP: Jazum 31, Decca (E) RAL-505
13788-   **My Moonlight Madonna** [Paul Francis Webster;
                   William Scotti] vJF
   78: Vocalion 2522
13789-   **It Isn't Fair** [Richard Himber] vJF
   78: Vocalion 2522
            13788, 13789 as JACK FULTON AND ORCHESTRA

ARC, New York, N.Y. Tuesday, August 29, 1933
VICTOR YOUNG AND HIS ORCHESTRA
Victor Young (ldr) *Frank Guerente [or] Charlie Margulis, unknown* (tp) Tom Dorsey (tb) **Jimmy Dorsey** (cl,as) *Larry Binyon* (ts) *Harry Hoffman* (vn) *Joe Meresco* (p) Dick McDonough (g) Artie Bernstein (sb) *Larry Gomar* (d) Connie Boswell (vcl)

B-13891-A   **Dinner At Eight** [Dorothy Fields; Jimmy McHugh]
                   vCB (cl solo)
   78: Brunswick 6640, (E) 01595
B-13892-A   **Emperor Jones** [Allie Wrubel] vCB
   78: Brunswick 6640, (E) 01595
            13891 and 13892 as CONNIE BOSWELL
   Both sides on **LP:** Jazum 31
13893-   **The Last Round-up** (unissued)
13894-1   **Home On The Range** [Brewster Higley; Dan Kelley]
   78: Melotone M-12776
            as WILL OSBORNE AND HIS ORCHESTRA

ARC, New York, N.Y. Friday, September 1, 1933
VICTOR YOUNG AND HIS ORCHESTRA (ARC Studio Band)
Victor Young (ldr) *Mannie Klein* (tp) **Jimmy Dorsey** (cl) Harry Hoffman, Matty Malneck (vn) Fulton McGrath (p) Dick McDonough (g) Art Bernstein (sb) Stan King (d) Annette Hanshaw, Red McKenzie (vcl)

13905-1   **Don't Blame Me** [Dorothy Fields; Jimmy McHugh]
                 vAH (cl solo)
     78: Banner 32846, Conqueror 8256, Melotone M-12775, Oriole
     2747, Perfect 12937, Romeo 2120, Edison Bell Winner (E) W-20
     LP: Sunbeam P-511, Halcyon HDL-119
     TC: Halcyon (E) CHDL-119, CTP5
Tom Dorsey (tb) added:
13906-1   **It's The Talk Of The Town** [Marty Symes, Al J.
                 Neiberg; Jerry Livingston] vAH
     78: Banner 32846, Conqueror 8256, Melotone M-12775, Oriole
     2747, Perfect 12937, Romeo 2120, E.B.W. (E) W-20
          13905, 13906 as ANNETTE HANSHAW
     LP: Sunbeam P-511, Halcyon HDL-119
     TC: Halcyon (E) CHDL 119, CTP5
13933-1   **It's The Talk Of The Town** vRM (cl solo)
     78: Vocalion 2534, Panachord (E) 25599
13934-1   **This Time It's Love** [Sam M. Lewis; J. Fred Coots]
                 vRM (cl solo)
     78: Vocalion 2534, Panachord (E) 25599
          13933 and 13934 as RED McKENZIE
TO1329   **Blue River** [Ned Washington; Victor Young] vRM
     78: (unissued test pressing)
     All Red McKenzie sides also on **CD:** Hep (UK) CD 1005

ARC, New York, N.Y. Tuesday, September 5, 1933
MILDRED BAILEY (accomp. by Dorsey Brothers' Orchestra)
Tom Dorsey (tb,ldr) Bunny Berigan (tp) **Jimmy Dorsey** (cl,as) Larry Binyon (ts) Fulton McGrath (p) Dick McDonough (g) Artie Bernstein (sb) Stan King (d) Mildred Bailey (vcl)

B-13955-A   **Shoutin' In The Amen Corner** [Andy Razaf, Danny
                   Smalls] vMB (cl solo)
     78: Brunswick 6655, (E) 01593, (F) A-500335
     LP: Columbia C3L22, CBS BPG-62098, Hep (Sc) 1006
     CD: Hep (E) CD 1006, The Old Masters MB104
B-13956-A   **Snowball** [Hoagy Carmichael] vMB
     78: Brunswick 6655, (E) 01593
     LP: Hep (Sc) 1006
     CD: Hep (E) CD 1006, The Old Masters MB104

Metronome (September, October 1933) reported Jimmy playing sax in the Nat Shilkret and B. A. Rolfe NBC bands (White 1988-1997).

ARC, New York, N.Y. Monday, September 25, 1933
JOE VENUTI AND HIS ORCHESTRA
Joe Venuti (vn,ldr) Max Kaminsky, 2 *unknown* (tp) Red Bone (tb) Wal-

lace Blumberry, **Jimmy Dorsey** (cl,as) *unknown* (ts), (p) Dick McDonough (g) *unknown* (sb), (d) Don Elton (vcl)

14076-1   **You're My Past, Present And Future** [Mack Gordon; Harry Revel] vDE
          78: Banner 32874, Conqueror 8250, Domino 154, Melotone M-12816, Oriole 2776, Perfect 15832, Romeo 2149, Decca (E) F-3797
14077-1   **I Want To Ring Bells** [Maurice Sigler; J.Fred Coots] vDE (cl solo)
          78: Banner 32872, Domino 152, Melotone M-12807, 91635, Oriole 2771, Perfect 15830, Romeo 2144, Decca (E) F-3803
14078-1   **Doin' The Uptown Lowdown** [Mack Gordon; Harry Revel] vDE
          78: Banner 32874, Conqueror 8250, Domino 154, Oriole 2776, Romeo 2149, Melotone M-12816, Perfect 15832, Decca (E)F-3797
14079-1   **Gather Lip-Rouge While You May** [Buddy De Sylva, Leo Robin; Richard Whiting] vDE
          78: Banner 32872, Domino 152, Melotone M-12807, 91635, Oriole 2771, Perfect 15830, Romeo 2144, Decca (E) F-3860
          14076 through 14079 also on **LP:** JSP Records (E) 112
14080-1   **Moonglow** [Will Hudson, Eddie DeLange, Irving Mills]
          78: Banner 32883, 33113, Melotone M-12831, M-13081, 91675, Oriole 2787, 2935, Perfect 15842, 15965, Romeo 2160, 2309, Decca (E) F-5177
          LP: JSP Records (E) 112, Swingfan (G) 1017
14081-1   **Cheese And Crackers**
          78: Banner 32883, Melotone M-12831, 91675, Oriole 2787, 2935, Perfect 15842, Romeo 2160, Decca (E) F-5177
          LP: JSP Records (E) 112, Swingfan (G) 1017

ARC, New York, N.Y. Friday, October 13, 1933
CLIFF EDWARDS
Unknown (tp) **Jimmy Dorsey** (cl) *unknown* (vn) Dick McDonough (g) Cliff Edwards (uke,vcl) *unknown* (d)

D-14143-(1,2)   **It's Only A Paper Moon** vCE (unissued)
B-14144-   **Come Up And See Me Sometime** [Arthur Swanstrom; Louis Alter] vCE
          LP: Harmony 13430
B-14145-(1,2)   **You're My Past, Present And Future** vCE (unissued)
B-14146-(1,2)   **Night Owl** vCE (unissued)

When remade later none of these Cliff Edwards sides used clarinet.

ARC, New York, N.Y. Tuesday, October 17, 1933
THE DORSEY BROTHERS' ORCHESTRA
Tom Dorsey (tb,ldr) Mannie Klein, Frank Guarente, Charlie Margulis (tp) *Lloyd Turner [or] Chuck Campbell* (tb) **Jimmy Dorsey** (cl,as) Lyle

THE DORSEY BROTHERS' ORCHESTRA (Contd.)
Bowen (as) Jimmy Crossan, Larry Binyon (ts) Joe Venuti, Harry Bluestone, Serge Kostelarsky (vn) Harry Weller (vl) Fulton McGrath
(p,celst) Dick McDonough (g) Artie Bernstein (sb) Stan King (d) Jerry
Cooper, Mildred Bailey, Johnny Mercer (vcl) Bill Challis (arr)

B-14154-A   **Blue Room** [Lorenz Hart; Richard Rodgers] arrBC
                   (cl solo)
     78: Brunswick 6722, (E) 01713, (G) A-9504
     LP: Franklin Mint Jazz 33
     TC: Columbia/Legacy CT 48908, (H) 47169-4
     CD: Columbia/Legacy CK 48908, (H) 47169-2
B-14155-A   **Fidgety** [Frank Guerente]
     78: Brunswick 6722, (E) 01713, (G) A-9504
Bunny Berigan (tp) added next. All strings but Venuti out.
B-14156-A   **(I've Got A Woman Crazy For Me) She's Funny
                   That Way** [Neil Moret; Richard Whiting] vJC
                   (as solo)
     78: Brunswick 7542, (E) 01617, (G) A-9499, A-500360, 5045
     TC: Columbia/Legacy CT 48908, (H) 47169-4
     CD: Columbia/Legacy CK 48908, (H) 47169-2
Venuti (vn) out next.
B-14157-A   **(I Can Make Most Anything) But I Can't Make
                   A Man** [Rube Bloom; Victor Young] vMB (as,cl
                   solos)
     78: Brunswick 7542, (E) 01617
     TC: ProArte Digital PCD 508, Columbia/Legacy CT 48908, (H)
     47169-4
     CD: Columbia/Legacy CK 48908, (H) 47169-2, ProArte Digital
     CDD 508, The Old Masters MB104
Klein or Guarente, Margulis (tp) out, Berigan and one other remain.
B-14158-A   **Dr. Heckle And Mr. Jibe** [Dick McDonough] vJM
                   (cl, as solos)
     78: Brunswick (E) O1834
     LP: CBS H567273, Columbia KG 31564, Hep (Sc) 1005
     TC: Columbia/Legacy CT 48908, (H) 47169-4
     CD: Columbia/Legacy CK 48908, (H) 47169-2
     13154 through 14158 also on **LP:** Hep (Sc) 1005, **CD:** Hep (UK)
     1005
Second trombone out next.
B-14159-A   **Give Me Liberty Or Give Me Love** [Leo Robin;
                   Ralph Rainger] vMB
     78: Brunswick 6680, (E) 01631, (G) A-9500
     LP: Columbia C3L22, Hep (Sc) 1006, CBS BPG-62098
B-14160-A   **Doin' The Uptown Lowdown** [Mack Gordon; Harry
                   Revel] vMB (cl solo)
     78: Brunswick 6680, (E) 01631, (G) A-9500
                   *14159, 14160 as MILDRED BAILEY accompanied by
                   DORSEY BROS. ORCHESTRA*
     LP: Hep (Sc) 1006, Columbia Special Products P2-12854
     14159, 14150 also on **CD:** The Old Masters MB104

One of the Dorseys' big breaks came in October 1933 with a half-hour radio show, *American Review,* sponsored by American Oil Company (AMOCO). The Duke Ellington Orchestra was originally booked until Ellington extended a European tour. The show also featured singer Ethel Waters, comedian George Beatty and announcer Harry von Zell.

American Review—CBS Studios, New York, N.Y.
Sunday, October 22, 1933—7:00-7:30 P.M.
THE DORSEY BROTHERS' ORCHESTRA
Tom Dorsey (tb,ldr) Charlie Margulis, Mannie Klein (tp) *Jack Jenney [and/or] Lloyd Turner* (tb) **Jimmy Dorsey** (cl,as) *Lyle Bowen [and/or] Rudy Adler* (as) Larry Binyon (ts) Joe Venuti, Harry Bluestone (vn) *Artie Schutt [or] Fulton McGrath* (p) Art Bernstein (sb) Dick McDonough (g) *Chauncey Morehouse [or] Stan King* (d) Ethel Waters (vcl)

Theme / **Stay On The Right Side Of The Road** [Ted Koehler; Rube Bloom] / **Stormy Weather (Keeps Rainin' All The Time)** [Ted Kohler; Harold Arlen] (partial, intro to Ethel Waters) / **To Be Or Not To Be** vEW / **This Is Romance** [Edward Heyman; Vernon Duke] / **Dinah** [Sam M. Lewis, Joseph Young; Harry Akst] vEW / **Sweet Madness** [Ned Washington; Victor Young] / **Swingy Little Thingy** [Bud Green; Sam H. Stept] / **Stormy Weather (Keeps Rainin' All The Time)** vEW—Theme

American Review—CBS Studios, New York, N.Y.
Sunday, October 29, 1933—7:00 -7:30 P.M.
THE DORSEY BROTHERS' ORCHESTRA

Theme / **Doin' The Uptown Lowdown** [Mack Gordon; Harry Revel] / **Stormy Weather (Keeps Rainin'All The Time)** [Ted Kohler; Harold Arlen] (partial, intro to Ethel Waters) / **Harlem On My Mind** [Irving Berlin] vEW / (comedy routine: "Springfield" by George Beatty) / **This Is Romance** [Edward Heyman; Vernon Duke] / **(I Can Make Most Anything) But I Can't Make A Man** [Rube Bloom; Victor Young] (violin solo, Joe Venuti) / **(I Can Make Most Anything) But I Can't Make A Man** vEW / **It's The Talk Of The Town** [Marty Symes, Al J. Neiberg; Jerry Livingston] / **By Heck** [L. Wolfe Gilbert; S. R. Henry] / **Raisin' The Rent** [Ted Koehler; Harold Arlen] vEW / **Stormy Weather (Keeps Rainin' All The Time)** vEW — Theme

American Review—CBS Studios, New York, N.Y.
Sunday, November 5, 1933—7:00-7:30 P.M.
THE DORSEY BROTHERS' ORCHESTRA

Theme / **I Guess I'll Have To Change My Plan** [Howard Dietz; Arthur Schwartz] / (unknown selection) vEW / **Thanks** [Sam Coslow; Arthur Johnston] / **Doin' Things** [Joe Venuti, Eddie Lang] (violin solo by Joe Venuti) / (unknown selection) vEW / **Dinner At Eight** [Dorothy Fields; Jimmy McHugh] / **The Blue Room** [Lorenz Hart; Richard Rodgers] / **Give All Your Love To Me** vEW / **Stormy Weather (Keeps Rainin' All The Time)** vEW—Theme

ARC, New York, N.Y. Tuesday, November 7, 1933
VICTOR YOUNG AND HIS ORCHESTRA
Victor Young (ldr) Frank Guarente, *unknown* (tp) *unknown* (tb) Chester Hazlett, **Jimmy Dorsey** (cl,as) *unknown* (cl,ts) Joe Venuti, Walter Edelstein, *unknown* (vn) *Joe Meresco* (p) Perry Botkin (g) Artie Bernstein (sb) *Chauncey Morehouse* (d) Red McKenzie, Will Osborne (vcl)

B-14264-A   **Just A Year Ago Tonight** [Billy Rose; Lee David] vRM (cl solo)
          78: Brunswick 6692, (E) 01641
B-14265-A   **Goodnight, Little Girl Of My Dreams** [Johnny Burke, Harry Tobias] vRM (cl solo)
          78: Brunswick 6692, (E) 01641
14276-1   **What More Can I Ask?** [A. E. Wilkins; Ray Noble] vWO
          78: Banner 32894, Melotone M-12837, Oriole 2790, Perfect 15844, Romeo 2163
14277-2   **Don't You Remember Me?** vWO
          78: Banner 32894, Melotone M-12837, Oriole 2790, Perfect 15844, Romeo 2163

ARC, New York, N.Y. Saturday, November 11, 1933
JACK TEAGARDEN
Victor Young (ldr) Frank Guarente, Sterling Bose (tp) Jack Teagarden (tb,vcl) Chester Hazlett, **Jimmy Dorsey** (cl,as) Mutt Hayes (cl,ts) Walter Edelstein (vn) Joe Meresco (p) Perry Botkin (g) Artie Bernstein (sb) Larry Gomar (d)

B-14294-A   **Love Me** [Ned Washington, Victor Young] vJT (cl solo)
          78: Brunswick 6741, (E) O1703, (F) A-500398
          TC: Columbia/Legacy C2T 52942, CT52931
          CD: Columbia/Legacy C2K 52942
B-14295-A   **Blue River** [Ned Washington; Victor Young] vJT (as solo)
          78: Brunswick 6741, (E) O1703, (F) A-500398
          TC: Columbia/Legacy C2T 52942, CT52931
          CD: Columbia/Legacy C2K 52942
B-14296-A   **A Hundred Years From Today** [Ned Washington, Joe Young; Victor Young] vJT (cl solo)
          78: Brunswick 6716
B-14296-B   **A Hundred Years From Today** vJT (cl solo)
          78: Brunswick 6716, (E) O1683, (F) A-500392, Columbia (Au) DO-1172
          LP: Epic SN6044, Time-Life P3-15006
          TC: Columbia/Legacy C2T 52942, CT52931
          CD: Columbia/Legacy C2K 52942
B-14297-A   **I Just Couldn't Take It, Baby** [Mann Holiner, Alberta Nichols] vJT
          78: Brunswick 6716, (E) O1683, (F) A-500392, Parlophone (E) R-2599, Odeon (F) A-272291
          LP: Epic SN6044

American Review—CBS Studios, New York, N.Y.
Sunday, November 12, 1933—7:00-7:30 P.M.
THE DORSEY BROTHERS' ORCHESTRA

Theme / (unknown selection)/**Stormy Weather (Keeps Rainin' All The Time)** [Ted Kohler; Harold Arlen] (partial, intro to Ethel Waters) / **What's Keeping My Prince Charming?** vEW / (comedy routine: "Everybody Has A Hobby" by George Beatty) / **Love Is The Sweetest Thing** [Ray Noble]/ **Green Pastures** vEW (cl solo) / **By A Waterfall** [Irving Kahal; Sammy Fain]/ **I'll See You Again** [Noel Coward] / **Am I Blue?** [Grant Clarke; Harry Akst] vEW / **Stormy Weather (Keeps Rainin' All The Time)** vEW—Theme
"Green Pastures" on LP: Totem LP-1041

Earlier discographies, notably the Brian Rust "American Dance Band Discography" (Arlington House 1975), have listed a November 14, 1933, ARC session as Earl Harlan and His Orchestra involving regular ARC sidemen, including Jimmy Dorsey. In research nearly three decades ago, Bozy White found this to be Don Redman and His Orchestra and this is corrected in Rust's "Jazz Records" (Arlington House 1978).

ARC, New York, N.Y. Tuesday, November 14, 1933
BOSWELL SISTERS (accomp. by The Dorsey Brothers' Orch.)
Tom Dorsey (tb,ldr) Mannie Klein (tp) **Jimmy Dorsey** (cl) Larry Binyon (ts,fl) *Fulton McGrath [or] Martha Boswell* (p,celst) Dick McDonough (g) Artie Bernstein (sb) Stan King (d) Boswell Sisters (vcl)

B-14319-A   **Song Of Surrender** [Al Dubin; Harry Warren] vBS
    78: Brunswick 6733, (E) 01711, (G) A-9512, (It) 4888, Columbia (Au) DO-1526, Lucky (J) 60285
    LP: Halcyon (E) HDL 118
B-14320-B   **Coffee In The Morning (Kisses In The Night)** vBS
    78: Brunswick 6733, (E) 01711, (G) A-9512, (It) 4888, Columbia (Au) DO-1526, Lucky (J) 60184
    LP: Halcyon HDL 118, Wave (J) MFPL 84801
    Both sides also on **TC:** Halcyon CHDL 118, Columbia CT 66977, **CD:** Columbia CK 66977

American Review—CBS Studios, New York, N.Y.
Sunday, November 19, 1933 - 7:00-7:30 P.M.
THE DORSEY BROTHERS' ORCHESTRA
Personnel as October 22, 1933

Theme / **That's How Rhythm Was Born** [George Whitling, Nat Burton; J. C. Johnson] / **Stormy Weather (Keeps Rainin' All The Time)** [Ted Kohler; Harold Arlen] (partial, intro to Ethel Waters) / **Not For All The Rice In China** [Irving Berlin] vEW / **Mine** [Ira Gershwin; George Gershwin] / **Little Black Boy** vEW / **This Is Romance** [Edward Heyman; Vernon Duke] / **Underneath The Harlem Moon** [Mack Gordon; Harry Revel] vEW / **Stormy Weather (Keeps Rainin' All The Time)** vEW—Theme

Despite kind words from the critics, the Dorsey brothers left *American Review* after five weeks, reportedly because of brother Tommy's "shoot from the hip" response to the sponsor's suggestion that the band play more like George Olsen. "If you like George Olsen, why don't you get him?" Tommy reportedly said (Lee October 1940: 21).

It was an Olsen "sound-alike," Jack Denny And His Orchestra, that took over November 26, providing an important lesson for Tommy in dealing with sponsors. The incongruity of a society band leader like Denny, who was a mainstay at the time at the Waldorf-Astoria Hotel, backing a singer like Ethel Waters was typical of the decisions made by sponsors and networks in the heyday of American network radio.

Jimmy probably took part in some of the *Taystee Breadwinners* programs, but exact dates are unknown. Since details are listed in the author's book on Tommy Dorsey and other sources, we have chosen to only list the composite personnel. It is the author's opinion, however, that Jimmy's participation was limited to February or March 1934.

BEN SELVIN & HIS ORCHESTRA November 1933 to March 1934
Ben Selvin (vn,ldr) *Mannie Klein, [and/or] Ruby Weinstein [and/or] Sterling Bose* (2tps), *Tom Dorsey, Miff Mole [or] Charlie Butterfield* (1tb) *Benny Goodman, Artie Shaw [or] Jimmy Dorsey* (1cl,as) *Art Karle, Arthur Rollini [or] Hank Ross* (1ts) Harry De Costa (p) *Perry Botkin, Carl Kress or George Van Eps* (1g,bj) *unknown* (d) Billy Jones, Ernie Hare (vcl)

ARC, New York, N.Y. Tuesday, December 12, 1933
VICTOR YOUNG AND HIS ORCHESTRA
Victor Young (ldr) Frank Guarente, *Sterling Bose* (tp) Tom Dorsey (tb) **Jimmy Dorsey** (cl,as) Chester Hazlett (as) Vernon Hayes (ts) Joe Venuti (vn,vcl) Walter Edelstein, *unknown* (vn) Joe Meresco (p) Perry Botkin (g) Artie Bernstein (sb) *Chauncey Morehouse [or] Stan King* (d) Scrappy Lambert, Chick Bullock (vcl)

B-14439-A   **Masquerading In The Name Of Love** [Hoffman, Goodhart, Waggner] vSL (as solo)
    78: Brunswick 6725, (E) O1718
B-14440-A   **The Old Spinning Wheel** [Billy Hill] vSL
    78: Brunswick 6725, (E) O1702, (G) A9534
B-14441-A,B   **Venuti's Spinning Wheel** vJV (unissued)
B-14442-A   **Someday (Sometime, Somewhere)** (waltz) [Stark; Hanley] vSL (as solo)
    78: Brunswick 6731
B-14443-A   **Springtime In Old Granada** [Stark; Hanley] vSL
    78: Brunswick 6731
B-14444-A,B   **Venuti's Pagliacci #2** vJV (unissued)
Bose (tp) Edelstein (vn) Hazlett (as) out:
B-14445-A,B   **Onyx Club Review #2**
    78: Lucky (J) 7001-A
    LP: Arcadia 2015
    Lucky as JOE VENUTI AND FRIENDS
Venuti (vn) out, Edelstein (vn) Hazlett (as) return.
14446-1   **I Just Couldn't Take It Baby** [Mann Holiner;

Alberta Nichols] vCB (cl solo)
78: Banner 32922, Conqueror 8278, Melotone M-12865
as CHICK BULLOCK AND HIS LEVEE LOUNGERS
14447-1,2   **(When Your Heart's On Fire) Smoke Gets In
Your Eyes** [Otto Harbach; Jerome Kern] vCB
(cl,as solo)
78: Banner 32922, Conqueror 8278, Melotone M-12865
as CHICK BULLOCK AND HIS LEVEE LOUNGERS

ARC, New York, N.Y. Tuesday, December 19, 1933
THE DORSEY BROTHERS' ORCHESTRA
Tom Dorsey (tb,ldr) Charlie Margulis, Frank Guarente, *Sterling Bose*
(tp) *Chuck Campbell [or] Lloyd Turner* (tb) **Jimmy Dorsey** (cl,as)
Chester Hazlett (as) Larry Binyon (ts) Joe Venuti (vn) Fulton McGrath
(p) Dick McDonough (g) Artie Bernstein (sb) Stan King (d) Chick
Bullock (vcl)

14476-1   **Dixie Lee** [Alex Hill] vCB
78: Banner 32936, Melotone M-12879, Oriole 2817, Perfect
15866, Romeo 2190
as CHICK BULLOCK AND HIS LEVEE LOUNGERS
TC: Audio Archives 1004
14477-2   **Delta Bound** [Alex Hill] vCB (as solos)
78: Banner 32936, Melotone M-12879, Oriole 2817, Perfect
15866, Romeo 2190
as CHICK BULLOCK AND HIS LEVEE LOUNGERS
TC: Audio Archives 1004
14478-1   **Our Big Love Scene** [Arthur Freed; Nacio Herb
Brown] vCB
78: Banner 32947, Melotone M-12890, Oriole 2826, Perfect
12971, Romeo 2199, Rex (E) 8109
14479-1   **We'll Make Hay While The Sun Shines** [Arthur
Freed; Nacio Herb Brown] vCB
78: Banner 32947, Melotone M-12890, Oriole 2826, Perfect
12971, Romeo 2199, Rex (E) 8109, Conqueror 8263
14478, 14479 as CHICK BULLOCK
B-14480(A,B)   **Dawn Patrol** (unissued)

ARC, New York, N.Y. Friday, December 22, 1933
GENE AUSTIN
Jimmy Dorsey (cl) Joe Venuti (vn) Arthur Schutt (p) Coco Heimel (g)
Candy Candido (sb) Gene Austin (vcl)

14486-1   **Easter Parade** [Irving Berlin] vGA
78: Banner 32935, Melotone M-12878, Oriole 2816, Perfect
12968, Romeo 2189
LP: Epic LN-24441, Columbia P2-12854
14487-1   **Everything I Have Is Yours** [Harold Adamson;
Burton Lane] vGA (cl solo)
78: Banner 32935, Conqueror 8263, Melotone M-12878, Oriole
2816, Perfect 12968, Romeo 2189, Rex (E) 8110
LP: Epic LN-24301 (Contd.)

TC: Columbia/Legacy C2T 52942, CT52930
CD: Columbia/Legacy C2K 52942

ARC files also show matrices 14483 and 14484 cut December 22 as a "Personal recording for Mr. Waller," parts 1 and 2 with the artists being "Joe Venuti and His Orchestra." The nature of these sides is unknown, but given the history of Joe Venuti's antics they could be more "underground" sides. Is Mr. Waller "Fats" Waller or some ARC executive? Given the proximity of the matrix numbers, is Jimmy Dorsey present? We may never know.

The year 1934 would prove a heady one for the Dorseys. Their band would become a full-time unit as the clubs and ballrooms began to prosper once again. The musical tastes of America and the world were being influenced more and more by the sounds created by black arrangers and performers like Fletcher Henderson, Louis Armstrong, Chick Webb and Duke Ellington. The inroads being made by the popular white band Casa Loma were also not lost on the Dorseys, who were coming up with arrangements designed to compete with the Casa Loma sound.

Truly, things were clicking. But nothing was forever with the brothers, as the next eighteen months would show.

The Band Takes Off
(1934)

Brunswick, New York, N.Y. Thursday, January 4, 1934
VICTOR YOUNG AND HIS ORCHESTRA
Victor Young (ldr) *Bunny Berigan* (tp) *Tom Dorsey* (tb) **Jimmy Dorsey** (cl) Harry Hoffman, *unknown* (vn) Martha Boswell (p) Dick McDonough (g) Artie Bernstein (sb) Stan King (d) Connie Boswell, Dick Robertson (vcl)

B-14527-A   **I Had To Change The Words** vCB (cl solo)
     78: Brunswick 6640, (E) O1699
     LP: Jazum 43
Mannie Klein (tp) replaces *Berigan; Fulton McGrath* (celst) Larry Binyon (ts,fl) added:
B-14528-A   **In Other Words We're Through** vCB (cl solo)
     78: Brunswick 6640, (E) O1699
         14527, 14528 as CONNIE BOSWELL
     LP: Jazum 31
B-14529-   **Alice In Wonderland** [Murray Mencher, Charles Tobias, Jack Scholl] vDR
     78: Brunswick 6740, (E) O1718
B-14530-   **Arlene** vDR
     78: Brunswick 6740, (E) O1749

ARC, New York, N.Y. Saturday, January 13, 1934
VICTOR YOUNG AND HIS ORCHESTRA
Victor Young (ldr) Frank Guarente, Sterling Bose (tp) Jack Teagarden (tb) Chester Hazlett, **Jimmy Dorsey** (cl,as) Mutt Hayes (ts) Joe Venuti, Walt Edelstein, Lou Kosloff (vn) Joe Meresco (p) Perry Botkin (g) Art Bernstein (sb) Larry Gomar (d) Harlan Lattimore, Jane Vance (vcl)

B-14589-A   **A Day Without You** vHL
     78: Brunswick 6747, 01749, Columbia (E) DO-1173
B-14590-A   **Beloved** [Gus Kahn; Joe Sanders] vHL
     78: Brunswick 6748, 01830
B-14591-A   **This Little Piggie Went To Market** [Sam Coslow; Harold Lewis] vJV
     78: Brunswick 6747, Decca (E) F-3897
         Decca as HARRY WOODS & HIS NEW JERSEY ORCH.
B-14592-A   **Little Women (Like You)** vHL
     78: Brunswick 6748

Despite the vocal substitution on the next recording, a remake of the January 13 session, the label credits Jane Vance.

ARC, New York, N.Y. Tuesday, January 23, 1934
VICTOR YOUNG AND HIS ORCHESTRA
Personnel as January 13, 1934. Peg LaCentra (vcl) replaces Vance

B-14591-C   **This Little Piggie Went To Market** [Sam Coslow; Harold Lewis] vPLaC
    78: Brunswick 6747

A few of the personnel remained for two sides cut by Ruth Etting, but Jimmy was not one of them.

Joe Helbock's Onyx Club converted from speakeasy to night club, and opened legally on February 17, so Jimmy went with Joe to Har-lem to successfully persuade Art Tatum to be resident Onyx pianist. Thus Fifty-second Street began to desegregate as well as swing.

ARC, New York, N.Y. Monday, February 26, 1934
ADRIAN ROLLINI AND HIS ORCHESTRA
Pat Circirello (tp) **Jimmy Dorsey** (cl) Charlie Barnet (ts) Adrian Rollini (bsx) Fulton McGrath (p) *Charlie Magnante* (acc) Carl Kress (g) Gene Krupa (d) Chick Bullock (vcl)

14857-1   **Keep On Doin' What You're Doin'** [Bert Kalmar; Harry Ruby] vCB (cl solo)
    78: Brunswick 6786, (E) O1750
14858-1   **Get Goin'** [Con Conrad, Ben Oakland] vCB (cl solo)
    78: Brunswick 6786, (E) O1750
      14857, 14858 as ADRIAN'S RAMBLERS
14859-1   **A Hundred Years From Today** [Ned Washington, Joe Young; Victor Young] vCB
    78: Vocalion 2675
      as THE SPORT CLUB BOYS

ARC, New York, N.Y. Friday, March 2, 1934
VICTOR YOUNG AND HIS ORCHESTRA
Victor Young (ldr) Frank Guarente, Sterling Bose (tp) Jack Teagarden (tb,vcl) Chester Hazlett, **Jimmy Dorsey** (cl,as) Mutt Hayes (cl,ts) Joe Venuti, Lou Kosloff, Walter Edelstein (vn) Joe Meresco (p) Frank Worrell (g) Artie Bernstein (sb) Larry Gomar (d) Nappy Lamare, Vera Van (vcl)

B-14875-A   **I Like The Likes Of You** [E. Y. Harburg; Vernon Duke] vVV
    78: Brunswick 6779
B-14876-A   **Should I Be Sweet?** [Buddy De Sylva; Vincent Youmans] vVV
    78: Brunswick 6779
B-14877-A   **Fare-Thee-Well To Harlem** [Johnny Mercer; Bernard Hanighen] vJT&NL
    78: Brunswick 6780 (E) O1746, (G) A-9571, (F) A-500512
B-14878-A   **Ol' Pappy** [Al J. Neiberg, Marty Symes; Jerry Livingston] vJT&NL

78: Brunswick 6780 (E) O1746, (G) A-9571, (F) A-500512
14877, 14878 as JACK TEAGARDEN assisted by HILTON LAMARE

Victor, New York, N.Y. Friday, March 9, 1934
HOAGY CARMICHAEL AND HIS ORCHESTRA
Hoagy Carmichael (p,vcl,ldr) **Jimmy Dorsey** (cnt,cl) Tom Dorsey (tb)
Mischa Russell [or] Joe Venuti (vn) Red Norvo (*p*,xyl) Carl Kress (g)
Artie Bernstein (sb) *unknown* (d)

81909-1   **Judy** [Sammy Lerner; Hoagy Carmichael] vHC (cl
                 solo)
       78: Victor 24627
       LP: RCA CPL1-3307, RCA (E) INTS5181, NL89096
       TC: Radio Yesteryear Stack #82
       CD: Timeless (H) CBC 1-011
81910-1   **Moon Country** [Johnny Mercer; Hoagy Carmichael]
                 vHC (cl solo, cnt)
       78: Victor 24627
       LP: RCA CPL1-3307, RCA (E) INTS5181, NL89096, Book-Of-
       The-Month Club 3-LP set "Hoagy" *#unknown*
       TC: Book-Of-The-Month Club set "Hoagy" *#unknown*
       CD: Timeless (H) CBC 1-011

ARC, New York, N.Y. Wednesday, March 14, 1934
THE DORSEY BROTHERS' ORCHESTRA
Tom Dorsey (tb,tp,ldr) Bunny Berigan (tp) *Glenn Miller [or] Lloyd Turner* (tb) **Jimmy Dorsey** (cl,as) Lyle Bowen (as) Jimmy Crossan, Larry Binyon (ts) Fulton McGrath (p) Dick McDonough (g) Artie Bernstein (sb) Stan King (d) George Beuchler, Don Matteson, Kay Weber (vcl) Glenn Miller (arr)

14926-1   **Goodnight, Lovely Little Lady** [Mack Gordon;
                 Harry Revel] vGB (as solo)
       78: Vocalion 2662, Edison Bell Winner (E) W-113
              as PAUL HAMILTON AND HIS ORCHESTRA
14927-1   **(She Walks Like You, She Talks Like You) She
                 Reminds Me Of You** [Mack Gordon; Harry Revel]
                 vDM (cl,as solos)
       78: Vocalion 2662, Decca (E) F-5085, Decatur 512
              *Vocalion as PAUL HAMILTON AND HIS ORCH., Decca as
              HARRY WOODS AND HIS NEW JERSEY ORCH., Decatur
              as BUNNY BERIGAN WITH ALL STAR GROUP*
       LP: ASV Living Era (E) AJA 5060, Time-Life P15958
       TC: ASV Living Era (E) ZC AJA 5060, Columbia/Legacy CT
       48908, (H) 47169-4
       CD: ASV Living Era (E) CD AJA 5060, Columbia/Legacy CK
       48908, (H) 47169-2
14928   **Hold My Hand** [Jack Yellen, Irving Caesar; Ray Hen-
                 derson] vGB
       78: Vocalion 2660, Decca (E) F-5011, Edison Bell Winner (E)
       W-140 (Contd.)

THE DORSEY BROTHERS' ORCHESTRA (Contd.)

    Vocalion, Decca as BOB SNYDER AND HIS ORCH., Edison
    Bell Winner as HARRY WILSON AND HIS ORCH.
14929   **Sweet And Simple** vGB
  78: Vocalion 2661, Decca (E) F-5011
    Vocalion, Decca as BOB SNYDER AND HIS ORCH.
14930-1   **(Oh You) Nasty Man** [Jack Yellen, Irving Caesar;
    Ray Henderson] vKW (cl solo)
  78: Vocalion 2661, Decca (E) F-5010, Edison Bell Winner (E)
  W-118, Polydor (Cz) 1829
    Vocalion, Decca as BOB SNYDER AND HIS ORCH., Edison
    Bell Winner as HARRY WILSON AND HIS ORCH.
  TC: Columbia/Legacy CT 48908
  CD: Columbia/Legacy CK 48908
14931-1   **My Dog Loves Your Dog** vKW
  78: Vocalion 2660, Decca (E) F-5010, Polydor (Cz) 1829,
  Edison Bell Winner (E) W-118
    Vocalion, Decca as BOB SNYDER AND HIS ORCH., Edison
    Bell Winner as HARRY WILSON AND HIS ORCH.
  TC: Columbia/Legacy CT 48908, (H) 47169-4
  CD: Columbia/Legacy CK 48908, (H) 47169-2

ARC, New York, N.Y. Friday, March 16, 1934
ARC STUDIO BAND
Victor Young (ldr) *Frank Guerente, Charlie Margulis* (tp) Tom Dorsey
(tb) **Jimmy Dorsey** (cl,as) 2 *unknown* (as,ts) Harry Hoffman, 2 *unknown*
(vn) *Fulton McGrath [or] Joe Meresco* (p) Dick McDonough (g) Art
Bernstein (sb) Larry Gomar (d) Paul Small, Ethel Waters (vcl)

14953-1   **A Thousand Goodnights** [Walter Donaldson] vPS
  78: Banner 33012, Conqueror 8219, Melotone M-12971, Oriole
  2869, Perfect 15909, Romeo 2243, Edison Bell Winner (E) W-
  125, Rex (E) 8195
    Edison Bell Winner as SLEEPY HALL AND HIS COL-
    LEGIANS, Rex as HOLLYWOOD DANCE ORCHESTRA,
    others as PAUL SMALL AND HIS ORCHESTRA
  LP: Columbia Special Products P5-1484
14954   **Somebody Cares For You** vPS
  78: Banner 33025, Melotone M-12984, Oriole 2876, Perfect
  15916, Romeo 2250
    as ART KAHN'S ORCHESTRA
14955-1   **Waitin' At The Gate For Katy** [Gus Kahn; Richard
    A. Whiting] vPS (cl solo)
  78: Banner 33012, Melotone M-12971, Oriole 2869, Romeo
  2243, Perfect 15909, Edison Bell Winner (E) W-125
    Edison Bell Winner as SLEEPY HALL AND HIS COL-
    LEGIANS, others as PAUL SMALL AND HIS ORCHESTRA
  LP: Columbia Special Products. P5-1484
B-14956(A,B) **Come Up And See Me Sometime** vEW (unissued)
B-14957(A,B) **You've Seen Harlem At Its Best** vEW (unissued)
Both unissued sides remade March 30, 1934.

Sometime in early 1934, Jimmy Dorsey and Bunny Berigan were called in by Freddie Rich to the Vitaphone studios in Brooklyn for a nine-minute short he was filming. Jimmy solos on one featured song.

Vitaphone Studios, Brooklyn, N.Y. Early 1934
MIRRORS, featuring THE FREDDIE RICH ORCHESTRA
Fred Rich (ldr) Bunny Berigan (tp) **Jimmy Dorsey** (cl,as) Hank Ross (ts) others *unknown*

                             China Boy [Dick Winfree, Phil Boutelje] (cl solo)
      FILM: Vitaphone: *Mirrors*
      LP: Extreme Rarities 1008
      VIDEO: Swingtime 105, Charley (E) JAM5

Also sometime in early 1934, the Dorseys took part in thirty nine transcribed quarter-hour shows for Chrysler, one of which has survived.

                Chrysler Motors Program, unknown studio, New York, N.Y. Mid-March-May 1934
DORSEY BROTHERS' ORCHESTRA
Tom Dorsey (tb,ldr) Mannie Klein, Charlie Margulis (tp) *Glenn Miller* [or] *Don Matteson* (tb) **Jimmy Dorsey** (cl,as) Lyle Bowen (as) Larry Binyon (ts) Joe Meresco (p) Dick McDonough (g) Art Bernstein (sb) Stan King (d) Frank Luther, Betty Fredericks (vcl) Men About Town (vcl grp)

      Introduction (theme) / **It Don't Mean A Thing (If It Ain't Got That Swing)** [Irving Mills; Edward K. "Duke" Ellington] vMAT (cl solo) / *Medley:* **I Hate Myself (For Being So Mean To You)** [Benny Davis, Joe Young; Milton Ager] vBF (cl solo); **Diga Diga Doo** [Dorothy Fields; Jimmy McHugh] vFL&MAT (as solo); **Tiger Rag** [Harry De Costa; Edwin Edwards, Nick La Rocca, Tony Spargo, Larry Shields] (as solo) / **Wagon Wheels** [Billy Hill, Peter De Rose] / (What, No Mickey Mouse? vMAT piano only) / **Farewell Blues** [Elmer Schoebel, Paul Mares, Joseph L. Rappolo] (cl solo)
      The entire program is on **LP:** Fanfare LP 5-105

ARC, New York, N.Y. Thursday, March 22, 1934
CHICK BULLOCK
Sterling Bose (tp) Tom Dorsey (tb) **Jimmy Dorsey** (cl) *unknown* (as) Joe Venuti (vn) Joe Meresco (p) Perry Botkin (g) Artie Bernstein (sb) Larry Gomar (d) Chick Bullock (vcl)

14981-1   **You Oughta Be In Pictures (My Star Of Stars)** [Edward Heyman; Dana Suesse] vCB (cl solo)
      78: Banner 33010, Conqueror 8300, Melotone M-12969, Oriole 2867, Perfect 12989, Romeo 2241, Rex (E) 8173
14982-1   **Little Dutch Mill** [Ralph Freed; Harry Barris] vCB (cl solo)
      78: Banner 33010, Conqueror 8300, Melotone M-12969, Oriole 2867, Perfect 12989, Romeo 2241

ARC, New York, N.Y. Thursday, March 22, 1934
FRANCES LANGFORD
Sterling Bose, *Charlie Teagarden* (tp) Tom Dorsey (tb) **Jimmy Dorsey**
(cl,as) Larry Binyon (ts) Joe Venuti, 2 *unknown* (vn) Joe Meresco (p) Perry Botkin (g) Art Bernstein (sb) Larry Gomar (d) Frances Langford (vcl)

14983-1   **Hold My Hand** [Jack Yellen, Irving Caesar; Ray Henderson] vFL
            78: Banner 33027, Melotone M-12986, Oriole 2872, Perfect 12994, Romeo 2252, Rex (E) 8231

Teagarden (tp) Binyon (ts) 2 *unknown* (vn) leave:
14984-1   **(Oh You) Nasty Man** [Jack Yellen, Irving Caesar; Ray Henderson] vFL (cl solo)
            78: Banner 33027, Melotone M-12986, Oriole 2872, Perfect 12994, Romeo 2252, Rex (E) 8231
            TC: Columbia/Legacy CT 52951
            CD: Columbia/Legacy CK 52943

Skeets Herfurt, Roc Hillman and Don Matteson probably joined the Dorseys about this time, although Matteson does sing on the March 14, 1934 date. In Tommy's short-lived *Bandstand* magazine (January 1939) it's stated that they worked almost weekly Boswell Sisters' sessions until going on a tour of one-night stands.
Soon, rehearsals at the Rockwell-O'Keefe offices included the Dorseys, Bunny Berigan, Glenn Miller, Matteson, Herfurt, Jack Stacey, Bobby Van Eps, Delmar Kaplan, Hillman and Ray McKinley.

ARC, New York, N.Y. Friday, March 23, 1934
BOSWELL SISTERS
Victor Young (ldr) Bunny Berigan (tp) Tom Dorsey, Chuck Campbell (tb) **Jimmy Dorsey** (cl,as) Larry Binyon (cl,ts) Martha Boswell (p) Dick McDonough (g) Artie Bernstein (sb) Ray McKinley (d) Boswell Sisters (vcl)

B-14993-A   **You Oughta Be In Pictures (My Star Of Stars)** Edward Heyman; Dana Suesse] vBS
            78: Brunswick 6798, (E) 01751, (G) A-9575, (It) 4915, Columbia (Au) DO-1221
            LP: Jazum 31, Conifer (E) CHD 136
            TC: Conifer (E) MCHD 136
B-14994-A   **I Hate Myself (For Being So Mean To You)** [Benny Davis, Joe Young; Milton Ager] vBS
            78: Brunswick 6798, (E) 01751, (G) A-9575, (It) 4915, Columbia (Au) DO-1221
            LP: Jazum 31, Conifer (E) CHD 136
            TC: Conifer (E) MCHD 136, Columbia/Legacy CT 52932
            CD: Columbia/Legacy CK 52943

ARC, New York, N.Y. Wednesday, March 28, 1934
THE DORSEY BROTHERS' ORCHESTRA
Tom Dorsey (tb,ldr) Bunny Berigan, *unknown* (tp) Don Matteson (tb)

Jimmy Dorsey (cl,as) Skeets Herfurt (cl,ts,fl) Jimmy Crossan, Larry Binyon (ts) Joe Venuti (vn) Fulton McGrath (p) Roc Hillman (g) Art Bernstein (sb) Ray McKinley (d) Connie Boswell, Kay Weber (vcl)

B-15013-A   **Butterfingers** [Irving Berlin] vCB
     78: Brunswick 6862, (E) O1745
         as CONNIE BOSWELL with THE DORSEY BROTHERS' ORECHESTRA
15014-1   **Dancing In The Moonlight** [Gus Kahn; Walter Donaldson] vKW (as solo)
     78: Banner 33025, Rex (E) 8195, Oriole 2876, Conqueror 8346, Melotone M-12984, Perfect 15916, Romeo 2250
     LP: Broadway BR113
         Regal as HOLLYWOOD DANCE ORCHESTRA, all others as ART KAHN'S ORCHESTRA

ARC, New York, N.Y. Friday, March 30, 1934
ARC-BRUNSWICK STUDIO BAND
Victor Young (ldr) *Frank Guerente [or] Charlie Margulis,* Bunny Berigan (tp) Tom Dorsey (tb) **Jimmy Dorsey** (cl,as) 2 *unknown* (as,ts) *Joe Venuti [or] Harry Hoffman* (vn) *Fulton McGrath [or] Joe Meresco* (p) Dick McDonough (g) Art Bernstein (sb) Stan King (d) Ethel Waters, Frank Luther Trio [Luther, Zora Layman, Leonard Stokes], Connie Boswell (vcl)

B-14956-C   **Come Up And See Me Sometime** [Arthur Swanstrom; Louis Alter] vEW (cl solo)
     78: Brunswick 6885, (E) O1736
         as ETHEL WATERS
     LP: Columbia KG31571
     CD: Timeless (H) CBC 1-007, Classics (F) 735
B-14957-C   **You've Seen Harlem At Its Best** [Dorothy Fields; Jimmy McHugh] vEW
     78: Brunswick 6885, (E) O1736
         as ETHEL WATERS
     LP: Columbia KG31571
     CD: Classics (F) 735
15022-1   **She's Way Up Thar (I'm Way Down Yar) Introducing Broadway's Gone Hillbilly** [Lew Brown; Jay Gorney] vFLT
     78: Banner 33030, Melotone M-12989, Oriole 2881, Perfect 15920, Romeo 2255
         as FRANK LUTHER AND HIS ORCHESTRA
15023-1   **I'm Laughin'** [Lew Brown; Jay Gorney] vFLT
     78: Banner 33030, Melotone M-12989, Oriole 2881, Perfect 15920, Romeo 2255
         as FRANK LUTHER AND HIS ORCHESTRA
B-15024-A   **I Knew You When** [Herb Magidson; J. Fred Coots] vCB
     78: Brunswick 6862, 01745
         as CONNIE BOSWELL

By now the Dorseys were scurrying to find jobs for the new band and as Kay Weber later recalled, they auditioned, as did Benny Goodman's band, for a job at Billy Rose's about-to-open Music Hall (White and Kite 1951-1987). The job went to Benny, but only after weeks of waiting and a second audition by Goodman (Connor 1988).

ARC, New York, N.Y. Monday, April 23, 1934
THE DORSEY BROTHERS' ORCHESTRA
Tom Dorsey (tb,ldr) Bunny Berigan, Mannie Klein (tp) Glenn Miller (tb,arr) Don Matteson (tb,vcl) **Jimmy Dorsey** (cl,as) Skeets Herfurt (cl,ts,fl,vcl) Jimmy Crossan, Larry Binyon (ts) Joe Venuti (vn) Fulton McGrath (p) Roc Hillman (g,vcl) Art Bernstein (sb) Ray McKinley (d) Chick Bullock, Kay Weber, Trio [Matteson, Herfurt, Hillman] (vcl)

15090-1   **How Do I Know It's Sunday?** [Irving Kahal; Sammy Fain] vTrio (cl solo)
     78: Vocalion 2708
          as PAUL HAMILTON AND HIS ORCHESTRA
B-15091-A   **Judy** [Hoagy Carmichael, Sammy Lerner] (cl solo)
     78: Brunswick 6938, (E) O2006, (G) A-9738, (F) A500449, Columbia (Au) DO-1271
     LP: Emporium 003
     TC: ProArte Digital PCD508, Columbia/Legacy CT 48908, (H) 47169-4
     CD: ProArte Digital PCD508, Columbia/Legacy CK 48908, (H) 47169-2
15092-   **May I?** [Mack Gordon; Harry Revel] vCB (as solo)
     78: Vocalion 2707, Edison Bell Winner (E) W-117
          Vocalion as BOB SNYDER AND HIS ORCHESTRA, Edison Bell Winner as PAUL HAMILTON AND HIS ORCHESTRA
15093-1   **Love Thy Neighbor** [Mack Gordon; Harry Revel] vCB (cl solo)
     78: Vocalion 2707, Edison Bell Winner (E) W117, Decca (E) F-5085
          Vocalion as BOB SNYDER AND HIS ORCHESTRA, Edison Bell Winner as PAUL HAMILTON AND HIS ORCHESTRA, Decca as HARRY WOODS AND HIS NEW JERSEY ORCHESTRA
15094-1   **I've Had My Moments** [Gus Kahn; Walter Donaldson] vKW
     78: Vocalion 2708, Edison Bell Winner (E) W138
          as PAUL HAMILTON & HIS ORCHESTRA
     all sides also on **LP:** Columbia Special Products P16356

ARC, New York, N.Y. Friday, May 11, 1934
ARC STUDIO BAND
Victor Young (ldr) Frank Guarente, Mickey Bloom (tp) Jack Teagarden (tb) Chester Hazlett, **Jimmy Dorsey** (cl,as) Mutt Hayes (cl,ts) Joe Venuti, Walter Edelstein, Lou Kosloff (vn) Joe Meresco (p) Perry Botkin (g) Artie Bernstein (sb) Larry Gomar (d) Smith Ballew, Kay Weber (vcl)

15192-1   **I'm Dancing With The Girl Of My Dreams** [Benny
                   Davis; Al Sherman] vSB
       78: Banner 33060, Melotone M-13025, Oriole 2899, Perfect
       15934, Romeo 2273
15193-1   **I've Got You On The Top Of My List** vSB
       78: Banner 33078, Melotone M-13042, Oriole 2912, Perfect
       15945, Romeo 2286, Lucky (J) 1007
15194-1   **Forbidden Lips** vSB
       78: Banner 33065, Melotone M-13029, 91783 (dubbing) 91783,
       Oriole 2904, Perfect 15937, Romeo 2278, Lucky (J) 1009, 60071
       LP: Jazum 15
15195-1   **Foolin' With The Other Woman's Man** vKW
       78: Banner 33065, Melotone M-13029, 91783 (dubbing) 91783,
       Oriole 2904, Perfect 15937, Romeo 2278, Lucky (J) 1009
       LP: Columbia P5-14320
       All 78's this session as SMITH BALLEW AND HIS ORCH.

ARC, New York, N.Y. Monday, May 21, 1934
THE DORSEY BROTHERS' ORCHESTRA
Tom Dorsey (tb,ldr,vcl) Bunny Berigan, *unknown* (tp) Glenn Miller
(tb,arr,vcl) Don Matteson (tb) **Jimmy Dorsey** (cl,as) Skeets Herfurt
(cl,ts,fl) Jimmy Crossan (ts) Fulton McGrath (p) Roc Hillman (g) Art
Bernstein (sb) Ray McKinley (d) Chick Bullock (vcl)

15246-1   **On Accounta I Love You** [Bud Green; Sam H. Stept]
                   vCB (as,cl solos)
       78: Banner 33078, Melotone M-13042, Oriole 2912, Perfect
       15945, Romeo 2286
       as SMITH BALLEW AND HIS ORCHESTRA
       CD: IAJRC CD1013
15247-1   **So Help Me** [Irving Berlin] vCB
       78: Vocalion 2721, Edison Bell Winner (E) W-124
15248-   **Easy Come, Easy Go** [Edward Heyman; Johnny
                   Green] vCB (cl solo)
       78: Vocalion 2721, Edison Bell Winner (E) W-138
       15247, 15248 as PAUL HAMILTON AND HIS ORCHESTRA
       all sides also on **LP:** Columbia Special Products P16356
15249-1,2   **Annie's Cousin Fanny** v,TD,GM&band (unissued)

ARC, New York, N.Y. Wednesday, May 23, 1934
BOSWELL SISTERS
Tom Dorsey (tb,ldr) Bunny Berigan (tp) Glenn Miller, *Don Matteson*
(tb) **Jimmy Dorsey** (cl,as) Skeets Herfurt (cl,ts,fl) Jimmy Crossan, Lar-
ry Binyon (ts) Joe Venuti (vn) Fulton McGrath (p) Roc Hillman (g) Art
Bernstein (sb) Ray McKinley (d) Boswell Sisters (vcl) Vet Boswell (arr)

B-15254-A   **Alexander's Ragtime Band** [Irving Berlin] vBS (cl
                   solo)
       78: Brunswick 7412, (E) 01893, (G) A-9688, (F) A-500528,
       Vocalion 4239, Parlophone (E) R-2562, Columbia (Au) DO-1255
       LP: Jazum 44, CBS 88026, (F) 80074, Biograph BLP C16, Wave
                   (Contd.)

BOSWELL SISTERS (Contd.)

(J) MFPL84801, Book-Of-The-Month-Record-Club   60-5256,
Con-ifer (F) CHD 136
TC: Conifer (F) MCHD 136
CD: Columbia Legacy CK 57711, Fremeaux (F) 9518
B-15255-A   **The Darktown Strutter's Ball** [Shelton Brooks] vBS
78: Columbia (Au) DO-1265
LP: JASS 1
TC: JASS J-C-1, Columbia CT 66977
CD: JASS J-CD-622, Columbia CK 66977, Fremeaux (F) 9518,
Retrieval (E) RTR 79009

A series of one-nighters throughout the Northeast during the late
spring of 1934 kept the new band busy. For example, they are known to
have played at the Danceland Ballroom at Ocean Beach in New London,
Connecticut, on Sunday afternoon, May 27.

Author George Simon in his book *The Big Bands* (1974) recalled
seeing the band at Nuttings-on-the-Charles in Waltham, Massachusetts.
Simon recalls amazement at the big sound coming from just eleven men.

On a stop at the Amherst (Massachusetts) College campus the crowd
was made up mostly of the overflow from the main dance that night
featuring the Casa Loma Orchestra.

Kay Weber was called on to dance with some of the stags in those
early days. They'd inquire, "Whose band is this?" "The Dorsey
Brothers'. Isn't it wonderful?" she'd respond. The usual answer: "Never heard of them" (Lee, November 1940: 20).

ARC, New York, N.Y. Saturday, June 2, 1934
VICTOR YOUNG AND HIS ORCHESTRA
Victor Young (ldr) Frank Guarente, Sterling Bose (tp) *unknown* (tb)
Chester Hazlett, **Jimmy Dorsey** (cl,as) Mutt Hayes (ts) *Joe Venuti, Walt
Edelstein, Lou Kosloff* (vn) Joe Meresco (p) *Frank Worrell* (g) Art
Bernstein (sb) Larry Gomar (d) Frank Luther, Greta Keller (vcl)

B-15278-A   **Anchors Aweigh** [Alfred H. Miles, Royal Levell;
                   Charles Zimmerman]
78: Brunswick 6904
B-15279-A   **The Marines' Hymn** [*Henry C. Davis*]
78: Brunswick 6904
15280-   **Spellbound** vFL
78: Banner 33086, Melotone M-13050, Oriole 2916, Perfect
15949, Romeo 2290, Rex 8266
           as FRANK LUTHER AND HIS ORCHESTRA
15281-   **Don't Let It Happen Again** vFL
78: Banner 33086, Melotone M-13050, Oriole 2916, Perfect
15949, Romeo 2290
           as FRANK LUTHER AND HIS ORCHESTRA
B-15282-A   **Don't Let It Happen Again** vGK
78: Decca (E) F-5078
           as GRETA KELLER
LP: Eclipse (E) ECM-2049

B-15283-A   **Give Me A Heart To Sing To** [Ned Washington;
                   Victor Young] vGK
     78: Decca (E) F-5281
B-15284-A   **Easy Come, Easy Go** [Edward Heyman; Johnny
                   Green] vGK
     78: Decca (E) F-5078
B-15285-A   **With My Eyes Wide Open, I'm Dreaming** [Mack
                   Gordon; Harry Revel] vGK
     78: Decca (E) F-5203
     15283 through 15285 as GRETA KELLER

Greta Keller was an Austrian-born dancer-vocalist who first appeared
in America with Fred Astaire in the early thirties.
Two days later the brothers recut rejected masters from the May 21
session. In "Annie's Cousin Fanny" Glenn Miller uses an "insiders
joke," having Tommy name Annie's boyfriend "Harvey." "Harv" was a
handle used by Tommy when he couldn't recall a name. A decade later
Jimmy used it to rile Tommy during a fight at the Hotel Astor Roof.

ARC, New York, N.Y. Monday, June 4, 1934
THE DORSEY BROTHERS' ORCHESTRA
Tom Dorsey (tb,vcl,ldr) Bunny Berigan, Mannie Klein (tp) Glenn Miller
(tb,vcl,arr) Don Matteson (tb) **Jimmy Dorsey** (cl,as) Skeets Herfurt
(cl,ts,fl) Jimmy Crossan, Larry Binyon (ts) Joe Venuti (vn) Fulton
McGrath (p) Roc Hillman (g) Art Bernstein (sb) Ray McKinley (d) Kay
Weber (vcl)

15249-C   **Annie's Cousin Fanny** [Alton Glenn Miller] vTD,
                   KW,GM&Band
     78: Brunswick 6938, (E) O1834, (F) A-50049, A-9738,
     Columbia (Au) DO-1271
     LP: Columbia Special Products P16356, Bandstand BS 7106,
     Emporium 003
     TC: ProArte Digital PCD508, Columbia/Legacy CT 48908, (H)
     37169-4, Radio Yesteryear Stack 33
     CD: ProArte Digital CDD508, Columbia/Legacy CK 48908, (H)
     37169-2

Travel itinerary: Thurs., June 14—Lakewood Park, Mahanoy City, Pa.

ARC, New York, N.Y. Thursday, June 21, 1934
BOSWELL SISTERS
Victor Young (ldr) Bunny Berigan, Mannie Klein (tp) Tom Dorsey (tb)
Jimmy Dorsey (cl,as) Larry Binyon (cl,ts,fl) *Fulton McGrath [or]
Martha Boswell* (p) Dick McDonough (g) Art Bernstein (sb) Stan King
(d) Boswell Sisters (vcl)

B-15357-A   **Don't Let Your Love Go Wrong** [George Whiting,
                   Nat Schwartz; J. C. Johnson] vBS
     78: Brunswick 6929, (E) 01832, (G) A-9616, (It) 4928,
     Parlophone (E) R-2631, Columbia (Au) DO-1269, (Swe) DS-
     1462, Odeon (F) A-272287   (Contd.)

BOSWELL SISTERS (Contd.)

    LP: Halcyon (E) HDL118, CBS (F) 80074
    TC: Halcyon (E) CHDL118
    CD: Fremeaux (F) 9518
B-15358-A   **Why Don't You Practice What You Preach?** [Morris Sigler, Al Goodhart, Al Hoffman] vBS
    78: Brunswick 6929, (E) 01832, (G) A-9616, (It) 4928, Columbia (Au) DO-1269
    LP: Halcyon (E) HDL118, CBS (F) 80074
    TC: Halcyon (E) CHDL118

The Dorseys wrapped up their road touring when they played the General Motors Auto Show in Brooklyn, with Jean Goldkette fronting because the promoters insisted that the Dorsey Brothers' name didn't mean anything (Lee November 1940: 20). After this final reality check, the broth-ers went to work on sharpening the band some more.

There was added incentive for this in a recording deal with a brand new label, Decca. Jack Kapp, Decca's head, had left Brunswick under not the best of terms, taking with him the Casa Loma Orchestra, Bing Crosby, Victor Young, Guy Lombardo and the Dorsey Brothers, among others. Following their switch to the Decca label, the Dorseys made nearly sixty sides in 1934.

In most appearances the band shared billing with Bob Crosby, which didn't sit well with Tommy, who still resented their booking agency (Rockwell-O'Keefe) telling them to hire Bing's brother. According to Kay Weber, Tommy made things hot for young Bob, who was somewhat insecure working in his brother's shadow anyway.

Also in late summer, the Dorseys added four new band members. Replacing Bunny Berigan, whose drinking was proving too great a problem, was George Thow from the Isham Jones group, who says he joined while the band was playing the Brooklyn Auto Show (White and Kite 1951-1987). Tenor saxophonist Jack Stacey had also recently come on board from Will Osborne's band. To add flash to their Sands Point shows as well as to flesh out the brass, Jimmy and Stacey occasionally played trumpet parts.

Bobby Van Eps, recent pianist for Red Nichols' and crooner Russ Columbo's orchestras, was added to work with Glenn Miller as an arranger in addition to handling the keyboard chores. Other Dorsey arrangers eventually included Bernie Mayer, Joe Glover and Herb Spencer. Delmar Kaplan carted his string bass over from the Roger Wolfe Kahn and B. A. Rolfe bands (*Orchestra World* 1935).

Almost all of these changes were initiated by Tommy, who had for all intents and purposes taken over as the leader of the group. Jimmy's nature was one of follower, not leader, and he was more than content to let "the brother" run things. Though he would occasionally come out front to kick off a jump tune, it was usually Tommy who set the pace.

Sands Point Bath Club was private, situated on Long Island Sound's Manhasset Neck, across from the Pelham Bay home of the California Ramblers a decade before. In June 1934 it had reluctantly become infamous when Louisiana Governor Huey Long was punched by a member who didn't agree with the "Kingfish's" Share-Our-Wealth social ideas.

When the band opened, they became a hit with the Long Island society set, prompting NBC to ask the club's Board of Governors to let the band air three nights a week. Probably due to the club's recent exposure to the public press, approval didn't come until early September.

Decca, New York, N.Y. Tuesday, August 14, 1934
THE DORSEY BROTHERS' ORCHESTRA
Tom Dorsey (tb,ldr) Mannie Klein, George Thow (tp) Glenn Miller, Don Matteson (tb) **Jimmy Dorsey** (cl,as) Jack Stacey, Skeets Herfurt (ts) Bobby Van Eps (p) Roc Hillman (g) Delmar Kaplan (sb) Ray McKinley (d)

38301-A   **Heat Wave** [Irving Berlin] (cl solos)
   78: Decca 208, Brunswick (E) O1867, Polydor (J) 12025
   LP: MCA-Coral (G) 6.28315, (J) 3142, Franklin Mint 5058
   TC: Franklin Mint 58, Movie Play (Port) 5008, (GE) SER 5008, Ajazz C-1117
38302-A   **By Heck** [L. Wolfe Gilbert; S.R. Henry] (as,cl solos)
   78: Decca 118, 11034
   45: Decca 9-11034
   (SSL-4017-2) **ET:** AFRS Basic Music Library P-1997
   LP: Decca DL 6016, DL 8631, DLP20, 11034, 91530, MCA-Coral (G) 6.28315, (J) 3142, Coral (E) CP 27, (E) CRLM 1027, Brunswick (E) LA 8524, (E) LAT8256, Durium/King Of Jazz (It) KLJ-2009, Sunbeam HB301
   TC: Movie Play (Port) 5008, (GE) SER 5008, Radio Yesteryear Stack 15, Ajazz C-1117

Decca, New York, N.Y. Wednesday, August 15, 1934
THE DORSEY BROTHERS' ORCHESTRA
As August 14, 1934 except *Bobby Van Eps [or] Fulton McGrath* (p). Tom Dorsey, Glenn Miller, Kay Weber, Bob Crosby, Trio [Matteson, Herfurt, Hillman] (vcl)

38303-A   **Stop, Look And Listen** [George Van Eps; John Van Eps] (cl solo)
   78: Decca 208, A-254
   LP: Decca DL 8631, MCA-Coral 1505, (G) 6.28315, (J) 3142, Coral (E) CP 27, Brunswick (E) LAT 8256, Durium/King Of Jazz KLJ-20009
   TC: MCA MCAC1505, Fanfare PCD485, ProArte Digital PCD 508, Ajazz C-1117
   CD: Fanfare CDD 485, ProArte Digital CDD 508
38304-A   **I'm Gettin' Sentimental Over You** [Ned Washington; George Bassman] vBC (cl,as solo)
   78: Decca 115, 3942, BM-1107, Melotone M-30115, Brunswick (E) O2573, (F) A-81473
   ET: AFRS END-390-163
   LP: Sunbeam HB301, MCA-Coral (G) 6.28315, (J) 1342, Big Band Era (H) 20176, TQ (E) 153
   TC: Big Band Era (H) 40176, ProArte Digital PCD 508, Ajazz C-1117, Radio Yesteryear Stack 15 (Contd.)

THE DORSEY BROTHERS' ORCHESTRA (Contd.)

    CD: ProArte Digital CDD 508
38307-A   **Long May We Love** vKW (cl solo)
    78: Decca 115, Brunswick (E) O1899
    LP: Sunbeam HB301
    TC: Ajazz C-1117, Radio Yesteryear Stack 15
38308-A   **Annie's Cousin Fanny** [Alton Glenn Miller] vTrio,
                    TD,GM&KW
    78: Decca 117
    ET: AFRS END-390-602
    LP: Braba (It) BB-03
38309-A   **Dr. Heckle And Mr. Jibe** [Dick McDonough] vTrio
                    (cl,as solos)
    78: Decca 117
    LP: Braba (It) BB-03

Often considered a Dorsey Brothers' date, the next only includes them.

Decca, New York, N.Y. Monday, August 20, 1934
ETHEL WATERS (with Victor Young and His Orchestra)
Victor Young (ldr) *Mannie Klein, unknown* (tp) Tom Dorsey, *unknown* (tb) **Jimmy Dorsey** (cl,as) *unknown* (as), (ts), (vn) *Fulton McGrath* (p) *unknown* (g), (sb), (d) Ethel Waters (vcl)

38349-A   **Miss Otis Regrets (She's Unable To Lunch Today)**
                    [Cole Porter] vEW
    78: Decca 140
    LP: Jass 632, Swingtime (E) SW1031
    TC: ProArte Digital PCD 548, Radio Yesteryear Stack 62
    CD: Jass J-CD-632, ProArte Digital CCD 548, Koch 7136
38349-C   **Miss Otis Regrets (She's Unable To Lunch Today)**
                    vEW
    78: Brunswick (E) O1848
    CD: Classics (F) 735
38350-C   **Dinah** [Sam M. Lewis, Joseph Young; Harry Akst]
                    vEW
    78: Decca 234, Brunswick (E) O1975, Polydor (F) 15392, (G) 15392
    LP: Swingtime (E) SW 1031
    CD: Classics (F) 735
38350-D   **Dinah** vEW
    78: Decca 234 (in set A-348)
38351-C   **When It's Sleepy Time Down South** [Leon René,
                    Otis René; Clarence Muse] vEW
    78: Decca 4410, Brunswick (E) O1975
    LP: Swingtime (E) SW1031
    CD: Classics (F) 735
38352-A   **Moonglow** [Will Hudson, Eddie DeLange, Irving
                    Mills] vEW (cl behind vocal)
    78: Decca 140
    LP: Swingtime (E) SW 1031

38352-C   **Moonglow** vEW (cl behind vocal)
   78: Brunswick (E) O1848, (E) 03026
   CD: Classics (F) 735

On August 23, 1934, the Dorsey Brothers' Orchestra with Charlie
Spivak added made what were probably its best recordings: "Milenberg
Joys," "Honeysuckle Rose," "St. Louis Blues" and "Basin Street Blues."
Here was Jimmy's chance to shine at what he liked best.

Decca, New York, N.Y. Thursday, August 23, 1934
THE DORSEY BROTHERS' ORCHESTRA
Tom Dorsey (tb,ldr,vcl) Charlie Spivak, George Thow (tp) Glenn Miller
(tb,arr,vcl) Don Matteson (tb,vcl) **Jimmy Dorsey** (cl,as) Jack Stacey (ts)
Skeets Herfurt (ts,fl,vcl) Bobby Van Eps (p) Roc Hillman (g,vcl)
Delmar Kaplan (sb) Ray McKinley (d) Kay Weber, Bob Crosby (vcl)

38308-C   **Annie's Cousin Fanny** [Alton Glenn Miller]
                     vDM,SH,TD,KW&GM
   78: Decca 117
   TC: Ajazz C-1717
38309-C   **Dr. Heckle And Mr. Jibe** [Dick McDonough]
                     vDM&SH (cl,as,cl solos)
   78: Decca 117
   LP: Decca DL-8631, Coral (G) 6.28315
   TC: Ajazz C-1717
38407-A   **Millenberg Joys** [Walter Melrose, Leon Rappolo,
                     Paul Mares, "Jelly Roll" Morton] (as, cl solos)
   78: Decca 119, 11032, Brunswick (E) O2023, A-9732
   45: Decca 9-11032
   LP: Decca BM 1111, DL 6016, DL 8631, Coral (E) CRLM 1027,
   (E) CP 27, MCA 1505, (J) 1342, MCA-Coral (G) 6.28315,
   Brunswick (E) LAT 8256, Sunbeam HB301, Durium/King Of
   Jazz KJL-20009, Vanguard (Au) UJ 556
   TC: MCA MCAC 1505, ProArte Digital PCD 508, Ajazz C-1717
   CD: ProArte Digital CDD 508
   (SSL-4017-6) **ET:** AFRS Basic Music Library P-1997
38408-A   **St. Louis Blues** [William C. Handy] (cl,as solos)
   78: Decca 119, 3254, 11032, Brunswick (E) O1892
   (SSL-4017-5) **ET:** AFRS Basic Music Library P-1997
   45: Decca 9-11033
   LP: Decca DL 6016, DL 8631, Brunswick (E) LA 8254, (E) LAT
   8167, LAT 8256, Coral (E) CRLM 1027, (E) CP 27, MCA 1505,
   Coral (J) 1342, Sunbeam HB301, Odeon 284324, Durium/King Of
   Jazz KJL-2009, ASV Living Era (E) ZC AJA 5008, Vanguard
   (Au) UJ 556
   TC: MCA MCAC 1505, Movieplay (Port) 5008, (GE) SER 5008,
   ASV Living Era (E) ZC AJA 5008, ProArte Digital PCD 508,
   Decca 629, Ajazz C-1717, Radio Yesteryear Stack 15
   CD: ASV Living Era (E) AJA 5008, ProArte Digital CDD 508,
   Decca 629
38408-B   **St. Louis Blues** (cl,as solos)
   78: Decca 119, 3254

THE DORSEY BROTHERS' ORCHESTRA (Contd.)

> **LP:** Franklin Mint 8058, Braba (It) BB-03, Coral (G) 6.28315
> **TC:** Franklin Mint 58

38409-A   **Honeysuckle Rose** [Andy Razaf; Thomas "Fats"
                   Waller] (part 1) vDM,SH&RH
> **78:** Decca 296, 11033, Brunswick (E) O1890
> **45:** Decca 9-11033
> **EP:** Decca 91529
> **LP:** Decca DL 6016, Brunswick LA8254, (E) LAT 8256, Coral
> (E) CRLM 1027, (E) CP 27, MCA-Coral (G) 6.28315, 1505, (J)
> 1342, Sunbeam HB301, Vanguard(Au)UJ-556, Franklin Mint8058
> **TC:** MCA MCAC 1505, Start (It) LPS 40237, Franklin Mint Tape
> 58, Ajazz C-1717, ProArte Digital PCD 508
> **CD:** ProArte Digital CDD 508

38410-A   **Honeysuckle Rose** (part 2) (cl,as,cl solos)
Same releases as (part 1) (all versions)

38411-A   **Sandman** (theme) [Ralph Freed, Bonnie Lake] vKW
> **78:** Brunswick (E) RL-257

38412-A   **Basin Street Blues** [Alton Glenn Miller; Spencer
                   Williams] vBC&Chorus (cl solo)
> **78:** Decca 118, Brunswick (E) O1892, (F) A505012
> **LP:** Decca DL 8631, Coral (E) CRLM 1027, (E) CP 27, MCA-
> Coral (G) 6.28315, MCA 1505, (J) 1342, Sunbeam HB 301,
> Brunswick (E) LAT 8256, Durium/King Of Jazz KLJ-20009,
> Vanguard (Au) UJ-556, Deja Vu (It) DVLP 2063
> **TC:** MCA MCAC1505, Deja Vu (It) DVMC 2063, Movie Play
> (Port) 5008, Movie Play (GE) 5008, Ajazz C-1717, Radio
> Yesteryear Stack 15
> **CD:** MCA MCD1505, Deja Vu (It) DV 2063

38412-B   **Basin Street Blues** vBC&Chorus (cl solo)
> **78:** Decca 118
> **TC:** ProArte Digital PCD 508
> **CD:** ProArte Digital CDD 508

Decca, New York, N.Y. Thursday, August 30, 1934
THE DORSEY BROTHERS' ORCHESTRA
Personnel as August 23, 1934, with Spivak (tp) out. Bob Crosby (vcl)

38484-A   **Mama, Yo Quiero Un Novio (Mama, I Long For A
                   Sweetheart)** [Collazo, Raven]
> **78:** Decca (SA) 445, Brunswick (E) RL-257
> **TC:** Ajazz C-1717

38485-A   **I Ain't Gonna Sin No More** [Herb Magidson; Con
                   Conrad] vBC&Band (cl solo)
> **78:** Decca 116, Brunswick (E) RL-243
> **TC:** Ajazz C-1733

38486-A   **I Can't Dance (I Got Ants In My Pants)** [Clarence
                   Williams; Charlie Gaines] vBC&Band (as,cl,as solos)
> **78:** Decca 116, Brunswick (E) O1867
> **TC:** Ajazz C-1733

38487-   **Gracias (Thanks)** [Mayers, Rake]
      78: Decca (SA) 445
      TC: Ajazz C-1733
      All sides this session also on **LP:** Braba (It) BB-03

According to *New York Times* radio listings, there were two weeks of Wednesday and Friday night remotes from Sands Point. If there was a third weekly remote as mentioned in *Orchestra World,* it was aired later than midnight and thus not in the listings, which also showed confusion in the minds of the paper's radio editors who call it the "D'Orsey Orchestra," a name similar to "D'Orsay," a society band at the time.

Broadcast schedule (all Sands Point): Wed., Sept. 5, NBC-Red [WEAF], 11:00-11:30 P.M.; Fri., Sept. 7, NBC-Blue [WJZ], 11:30-12:00 P.M.; Wed., Sept. 12, NBC-Red [WEAF], 11:00-11:30 P.M.; Fri., Sept. 14, NBC-Blue [WJZ], 11:30-12:00 P.M.

The designation -Blue or -Red used in the text for the NBC networks originally derived from the colors used by AT&T telephone technicians to differentiate the patching jacks they used for making network connections across the country (CBS was green and MBS was orange).

NBC picked up the "colorful" tags to keep its own two divisions separate while still retaining the National Broadcasting Company name.

On the strength of those Sands Point airings the band is alleged to have made three NBC studio broadcasts, the dates and times of which do not appear in any radio listings, in the period between closing at Sands Point and opening September 19 at Ben Marden's Riviera.

It is possible this confusion resulted from subsequent misreading of the *Orchestra World* article cited above and from pictures showing the Dorsey band in the NBC studios which are actually from rehearsals arranged by Rockwell-O'Keefe, who had offices in the same building.

In a September 19 *New York Times* advertisement for the Riviera opening, the billing headlined comedian Harry Richman and as an added attraction "the Dorsey Brothers and Their Orchestra with Bob Crosby, Bing's Glorious Voiced Young Brother."

Broadcast schedule (all Riviera): Wed., Sept. 19, NBC-Blue [WJZ], 11:30-12:00 P.M.; Thursdays, Sept. 20, 27, Oct. 4, 11, 18, 25, NBC-Red [WEAF], 11:30-12:00 P.M. Of the seven broadcasts only the next aircheck survives.

                    sustaining broadcast—Riviera Club, Fort Lee,
                    N.J.—WEAF (NBC-Red), 11:30-12:00 P.M. Thurs-
                    day, September 20, 1934
THE DORSEY BROTHERS' ORCHESTRA

  Sandman [Ralph Freed, Bonnie Lake] (theme) / **Is That Religion?**
  [Mitchell Parish; Maceo Pinkard] vBC (cl solo)
     Both selections on **LP:** Fanfare LP-5-105. An acetate of the entire broadcast shows Bing Crosby and the Boswell Sisters also present.

Decca, New York, N.Y. Friday, September 21, 1934
THE DORSEY BROTHERS' ORCHESTRA
Kay Weber, Bob Crosby (vcl) (Contd.)

THE DORSEY BROTHERS' ORCHESTRA (Contd.)

38705-A   **Lost In A Fog** [Dorothy Fields; Jimmy McHugh]
                 vBC (as solo)
      78: Decca 195, Brunswick (E) O1900
38706-A   **I Couldn't Be Mean To You** [Stanley Adams; Jesse
                 Greer] vBC (cl solo)
      78: Decca 195, Brunswick (E) RL-215
38707-A   **How Can You Face Me?** [Andy Razaf; Thomas
                 "Fats" Waller] vBC
      78: Decca 196, Brunswick (E) O1963
      All issued sides this session also on **LP:** Braba (It) BB-03, **TC:**
      Ajazz C-1733
38708-A,B   **The Moon Was Yellow** vKW (unissued)

Decca, New York, N.Y. Monday, September 24, 1934
THE DORSEY BROTHERS' ORCHESTRA
Don Matteson, Skeets Herfurt, Kay Weber, Bob Crosby (vcl)

38719-A   **Don't Let It Bother You** [Mack Gordon; Harry
                 Revel] vDM&SH (as,cl solo)
      78: Decca 207, Brunswick (E) RL-205
      LP: Coral (G) 6.28315
38720-A   **The Breeze (That's Bringing My Honey Back To
                 Me)** [Tony Sacco, Richard B. Smith, Al Lewis] vKW
      78: Decca 207
      LP: Braba (It) BB-03
38721-A   **Out In The Cold Again** [Ted Kohler; Rube Bloom]
                 vBC (cl solo)
      78: Decca 206, X-1157, Brunswick (E) O1899
      LP: Braba (It) BB-03
38722-A   **Day Dreams** [Grant Clarke] vBC (bar solo)
      78: Decca 206, X-1157
      LP: Braba (It) BB-03
      All sides this session also on **TC:** Ajazz C-1733

Decca, New York, N.Y. Friday, September 28, 1934
THE DORSEY BROTHERS' ORCHESTRA

38708-D   **The Moon Was Yellow** [Edgar Leslie; Fred E.
                 Ahlert] vKW
      78: Decca 196, Brunswick (E) O1900
      LP: Braba (It) BB-03
      TC: Ajazz C-1733
38754-   **Okay, Toots** [Gus Kahn; Walter Donaldson]
                 vDM&SH (cl,as solos)
      78: Decca 259, Brunswick (E) O1954
      LP: Sunbeam HB 301
      TC: Radio Yesteryear Stack 15, Ajazz C-1733
38755-A   **An Earful Of Music** [Gus Kahn; Walter Donaldson]
                 vKW (cl solo)
      78: Decca 258, Brunswick (E) O1954

LP: Braba (It) BB-03
TC: Ajazz C-1733
38756-A   **When My Ship Comes In** [Gus Kahn; Walter Don-
aldson] vBC (as solo)
   78: Decca 259, Brunswick (E) O1955
   LP: Sunbeam HB 301
   TC: Radio Yesteryear Stack 15, Ajazz C-1733
38757-A   **Your Head On My Shoulder** [Harold Adamson;
Burton Lane] vKW (as,cl solos)
   78: Decca 258, Brunswick (E) O1955
38758-A   **Missouri Misery** [E. Y. Harburg; Dana Suesse] vBC
   78: Decca 297
   38757 and 38758 also on **LP:** Braba (It) BB-03, **TC:** Ajazz C-1743

Decca, New York, N.Y. Wednesday, October 24, 1934
THE DORSEY BROTHERS' ORCHESTRA

38883-A   **Fun To Be Fooled** [Ira Gershwin, E. Y. Harburg;
Harold Arlen] vBC
   78: Decca 260
38884-A   **Let's Take A Walk Around The Block** [Ira Gershwin, E. Y. Harburg; Harold Arlen] vKW
   78: Decca 260
   Both sides also on **LP:** Braba (It) BB-03,
   TC: Ajazz C-1743

Ben Marden was quick to capitalize on the budding popularity of the
Dorsey Brothers' band. He moved the band from the Riviera New
Jersey roadhouse to his Palais Royale night club at Broadway and West
Forty-eighth Street in the Times Square district of New York City, a
mecca for tourists and visiting businessmen. Marden was also an early
advocate of radio broadcasts for promoting his club to the hinterlands.
   An opening day ad in *The New York Times* (Sunday, October 28,
1934) promoted the Dorseys along with tenor Morton Downey, Dan and
Nancy Healy (comedians), The Tick Tock Girls, Mildred and Maurice
(dance team) and Vince Brayle's Orchestra. Charlie Spivak was added
on trumpet during the Riviera stay.
   The next day the band cut a couple of sides for Decca that had only
modest success. Originally a Mexican favorite, "What A Diff'rence" is
known under two versions using either "Made" or "Makes" as the last
word in the title. Dinah Washington's 1959 recording and a 1975 version
by Little Esther Phillips hit the top of the charts as "Makes." In 1934 it
was another story. Perhaps "what a diff'rence a *word* makes."

Decca, New York, N.Y. Monday, October 29, 1934
THE DORSEY BROTHERS' ORCHESTRA

38914-A   **What A Diff'rence A Day Made** [Stanley Adams,
Maria Grever; Maria Grever] vBC
   78: Decca 283, Brunswick (E) O1956
   LP: Coral (G) 6.28315
   TC: Movie Play (GE) 5008 (Contd.)

THE DORSEY BROTHERS' ORCHESTRA (Contd.)

38919-A   **Dream Man (Make Me Dream Some More)** vBC
        78: Decca 291, Brunswick (E) O1964
38920-A   **What Can I Say In A Love Song?** [Ira Gershwin,
                E. Y. Harburg; Harold Arlen] vKW (as solo)
        78: Decca 283
        All sides also on **TC:** Ajazz C-1743

Broadcast schedule (all Palais Royale): Tues., Oct. 30, NBC-Blue [WJZ], 11:30-12:00
P.M.; Sat., Nov. 3, NBC-Blue [WJZ], 7:15-7:30 P.M.; Tues., Nov. 6, NBC-Blue
[WJZ], 11:30-12:00 P.M.

Decca, New York, N.Y. Wednesday, November 7, 1934
THE DORSEY BROTHERS' ORCHESTRA

38883-C   **Fun To Be Fooled** [Ira Gershwin, E. Y. Harburg;
                Harold Arlen] vBC
        78: Decca 260
38963-A   **Hands Across The Table** [Mitchell Parish; Jean Del-
                ettre] vKW
        78: Decca 291, Brunswick (E) O1963
38964-A   **Love Is Just Around The Corner** [Leo Robin; Lewis
                E. Gensler] vBC (cl solo)
        78: Decca 311, Brunswick (E) O1950
        Also on **LP, CD:** Phontastic (Swe) NOST 7653
38965-A,B   **Here Is My Heart** [Leo Robin; Ralph Rainger] vBC
        78: Decca 311, Brunswick (E) O1950 (-A only)
        All sides also on **TC:** Ajazz C-1743

Broadcast schedule (Palais Royale): Tues., Nov. 13, NBC-Blue [WJZ], 11:30-12:00
P.M.

Decca, New York, N.Y. Thursday, November 15, 1934
THE DORSEY BROTHERS' ORCHESTRA

38411-C   **Sandman** (theme) [Ralph Freed, Bonnie Lake] vKW
        78: Decca 297
39020-A   **Apache** vKW
        78: Decca 314, Brunswick (E) RL-269
39021-A   **It's Dark On Observatory Hill** [Johnny Burke;
                Harold Spina] vBC
        78: Decca 314, Brunswick (E) 01956
        LP: Coral (G) 6.28315
39022-   **Blame It On My Youth** [Edward Heyman; Oscar Le-
                vant] vBC
        78: Decca 320
        All sides also on **TC:** Ajazz C-1743

Broadcast schedule (all Palais Royale): Tues., Nov. 20, NBC-Blue [WJZ], 11:30-
12:00 P.M.; Wed., Nov. 21, NBC-Blue [WJZ], 11:00-11:30 P.M.; Sat. Nov. 24, NBC-
Blue [WJZ], 11:00-11:30 P.M.

Decca, New York, N.Y. Tuesday, November 27, 1934
THE DORSEY BROTHERS' ORCHESTRA
Don Matteson, Skeets Herfurt, Kay Weber (vcl)

39102-B   **Anything Goes** [Cole Porter] vDM&SH (cl,as solo)
     78: Decca 318, Brunswick (E) RL-249
     LP: Sunbeam HB 301, Coral (G) 6.28315, Jass 632
     CD: Jass J-CD-632, Disky (H) DCO 5335-1
39103-A   **All Through The Night** [Cole Porter] vKW
     78: Decca 318, Brunswick (E) RL-249
     LP: Sunbeam HB 301
     39102, 39103 also on **TC:** Radio Yesteryear Stack 15
39104-A   **You're The Top** [Cole Porter] vDM
     78: Decca 319, Brunswick (E) RL-248
     All sides also on **TC:** Ajazz C-1753

Decca, New York, N.Y. Friday, November 30, 1934
THE DORSEY BROTHERS' ORCHESTRA
Skeets Herfurt, Kay Weber, Bob Crosby (vcl)

39116-A   **Down 't Uncle Bill's** [Johnny Mercer; Hoagy Car-
                 michael] vSH
     78: Brunswick (E) O1964
39117-A   **I'd Like To Dunk You In My Coffee** vBC
     78: Decca 321
39118-A   **I Get A Kick Out Of You** [Cole Porter] vKW
     78: Decca 319, Brunswick (E) RL-248
     LP: Coral (G) 6.28315
     CD: Jass J-CD-632
39119-A,B   **You Didn't Know Me From Adam** [Robert Burk;
                 John Jacob Loeb] vKW
     78: Decca 320
39120-A   **If It's Love** vBC
     78: Decca 321
     Except for 39116, all sides also on **TC:** Ajazz C-1753

Broadcast schedule (all Palais Royale): Sat., Dec. 1, NBC-Blue [WJZ], 11:00-11:30
P.M.; Sat., Dec. 8, NBC-Blue [WJZ], 11:00-11:30 P.M.; Sat., Dec. 15, NBC-Blue
[WJZ], 11:00-11:30 P.M.; Sat., Dec. 22, NBC-Blue [WJZ], 11:00-11:30 P.M.

Decca, New York, N.Y. Friday, December 21, 1934
THE DORSEY BROTHERS' ORCHESTRA
Bob Crosby. Kay Weber (vcl)

39181-A,B   **I Believe In Miracles** [Sam M. Lewis; George W.
                 Meyer, Pete Wendling] vBC
     78: Decca 335, Brunswick (E) RL-225, (F) A-9764
39182-A   **Dancing With My Shadow** [Harry Woods] vKW
     78: Decca 335, Brunswick (E) RL-205
39183-A,B   **Home Ties** vBC
     78: Decca 340

THE DORSEY BROTHERS' ORCHESTRA (Contd.)

39184-A   The Church Bells Told vKW
    78: Decca 340, Brunswick (E) RL-225, (F) A-9764
    All sides also on TC: Ajazz C-1753

Decca, New York, N.Y. Friday, December 28, 1934
THE DORSEY BROTHERS' ORCHESTRA
Kay Weber, Bob Crosby, Don Matteson, Skeets Herfurt (vcl)

39209-A   Rhythm Of The Rain [Jack Meskill; Jack Stern] vKW
    78: Decca 358, Brunswick (E) RL-224
39210-A   Au Revoir L'Amour vBC
    78: Decca 357, Brunswick (E) RL-223
    39209 & 39210 also on TC: Ajazz C-1753
39211-A   Singing A Happy Song [Jack Meskill; Jack Stern]
                 vDM,SH (cl solo)
    78: Decca 357, Brunswick (E) RL-223
39212-A   I Was Lucky [Jack Meskill, A. Horenz; Jack Stern]
                 vBC
    78: Decca 358, Brunswick (E) RL-224
    39211 & 39212 also on TC: Ajazz C-1763

Because the Palais Royale was primarily a night club designed to attract tourists and visiting salesmen, it included in its shows "The Tick Toc Girls," a line of chorus girls dancing with little covering behind large balloon "bubbles."

This led to something of a minor embarrassment, recounted by author George Simon. It seems Ray McKinley, who was encouraged by the Dorseys to use his natural showmanship abilities, carried his talents a bit too far. Using rubber bands as sling shots, Ray fired pins at the girls' bubbles, bursting them (Simon 1971).

Since the bubbles were intended to imply that the girls had nothing on, the revelation that they were really covered to the minimum required by law didn't sit well with the management (nor apparently with the audience).

And the Band Plays On
(1935)

As 1935 dawned, the Dorsey Brothers' Orchestra began what no one suspected at the time would be the last months of its existence. One warning sign of the symptoms that would lead to its demise came when Glenn Miller tired of acting as arbitrator in the brothers' fights, jumping at the chance to organize an American band for British bandleader Ray Noble at the brand-new Rainbow Room atop Radio City. Joe Yukl moved over from Joe Haymes' band to replace Miller on trombone.

Decca, New York, N.Y. Friday, January 4, 1935
THE DORSEY BROTHERS' ORCHESTRA
Tom Dorsey (tb,ldr) George Thow (tp) Joe Yukl, Don Matteson (tb) **Jimmy Dorsey** (cl,as) Jack Stacey (ts) Skeets Herfurt (ts,vcl) Bobby Van Eps (p) Roc Hillman (g) Delmar Kaplan (sb) Ray McKinley (d) Kay Weber, Bob Crosby (vcl)

39223-A,B	**I Thrill When They Mention Your Name** vKW (unissued)
39224-A	**Night Wind** [Bob Rothberg; Dave Pollack] vBC (cl solo)
	78: Decca 376
39225-	**I'm Just A Little Boy Blue** vKW
	78: Decca 348
39226-	**(I've Got A) New Deal In Love** [J.Russell Robinson; Bill Livingston] vBC
	78: Decca 348

All sides also on **TC:** Ajazz C-1763

Broadcast schedule (Palais Royale): Sat., Jan. 5, NBC-Blue [WJZ], 11:00-11:30 P.M.

Decca, New York, N.Y. Friday, January 11, 1935
THE DORSEY BROTHERS' ORCHESTRA
Charlie Spivak (tp) added for recording only

39241-A	**Dinah** [Sam M. Lewis; Joseph Young; Harry Akst] vBC (cl,as solos)
	78: Decca 376, BM-1107, M-30115, Brunswick (E) O2573, (F) A-81473
	LP: Coral (G) 6.28315, Coral 57224, CJE-100
	TC: Movie Play (Port) 5008, (GE) SER 5008, Ajazz C-1763
39242-(A,B)	**You Ain't Been Livin' Right** vBC (unissued)
39243-	**Solitude** [Irving Mills, Eddie DeLange; Edward K. "Duke" Ellington] vKW (cl,as solo) (Contd.)

THE DORSEY BROTHERS' ORCHESTRA (Contd.)

> **78:** (12-inch) Decca 15013, 29238, K-867, Brunswick (E) O135, A-600, A-131
> **LP:** Decca DL8045, Brunswick (E) LAT 8037, Coral (G) 6.28315
> **TC:** ProArte Digital PCD 508, Ajazz C-1763
> **CD:** ProArte Digital CDD 508

Broadcast schedule (Palais Royale): Sat., Jan. 12, NBC-Blue [WJZ], 11:00-11:30 P.M.

The next week the band closed and so did Palais Royale for the installation of a new rollaway stage designed to provide more space for a dance floor.

One of the major suppliers of 33$^{1/3}$ rpm electrical transcription services to radio stations was Associated Transcriptions, Inc., which recorded the band at two sessions in early 1935 at the studios of Electrical Research Products in the Bronx.

World Transcriptions later secured rights to some of the disks. For their releases the numbers which follow "World" denote "type" (hyphen) "cut (track) number" on an ET with four "cuts" to a side. The "200" series denoted instrumentals, while "300" was for vocals.

Following this system through, "913" is the first track on side one of an instrumental ET designated as 200-913/920. The last track on side one is "916," the last track on side two is "920."

Electrical Research Prods., Bronx, N.Y. Thursday, January 17, 1935
DALY BROTHERS' ORCHESTRA (Dorsey Brothers' Orchestra)
Bob Crosby [as Bert Castle] (vcl)

AA-133/SS-8194   **Eccentric (Rag)** [J. Russell Robinson] (cl solo)
  ET: Associated 50-000A, World 200-913 (913/920)
  LP: Design DLP-20, Circle CLP-20
  CD: Circle CCD-20
AA-133/SS-8194   **Rhythm Of The Rain** [Jack Meskill; Jack Stern]
  ET: Associated 50-000A, World 200-914 (913/920)
  LP: Design DLP-20, DLP-147, DLP-258, Gala Int'l (E) GLP-307, Pickwick PR 108, Circle CLP-20, Int'l Award AK/AKS 203
  TC: Nostalgia (E) MRT 40053
  CD: Circle CCD-20
AA-133/SS-8194   **Night Wind** [Bob Rotheberg; Dave Pollack] vBC
         (cl solo)
  ET: Associated 50-000A, World 300-915 (913/920)
  LP: Design DLP-20, DLP-147, Gala Int'l (E) GLP-307, Pickwick PR 108, Circle CLP-20, Int'l Award AK/AKS 203
  TC: Nostalgia (E) MRT 40053
  CD: Circle CCD-20
AA-133/SS-8194   **Dipper Mouth Blues (Sugarfoot Stomp)** [Joe "King" Oliver, Louis Armstrong] (cl solo)
  ET: Associated 50-000A, World 200-916 (913/920)
  LP: Design DLP-20, DLP-147, Gala Int'l (E) GLP-307, Pickwick PR 108, Circle CLP-20, Int'l Award AK/AKS 203
  TC: Nostalgia (E) MRT 40053

CD: Circle CCD-20
A-135/SS-8194   **Solitude** [Irving Mills, Eddie DeLange; Edward K. "Duke" Ellington] (cl,as solos)
    ET: Associated 10003A, RA1006A, World 200-917 (913/920)
    LP: Design DLP-20, DLP-147, Gala Int'l (E) GLP-307, Pickwick PR 108, Circle CLP-20, Int'l Award AK/AKS 203
    TC: Nostalgia (E) MRT 40053
    CD: Circle CCD-20
A-135/SS-8194   **By Heck** [L. Wolfe Gilbert; S. R. Henry] (as solos)
    ET: Associated 10003A, RA1006A, World 200-918 (913/920)
    LP: Design DLP-20, DLP-147, Gala Int'l (E) GLP-307, Pickwick PR 108, Circle CLP-20, Int'l Award AK/AKS 203
    TC: Nostalgia (E) MRT 40053
    CD: Circle CCD-20
A-135/SS-8194   **I Was Lucky** [Jack Meskill, A. Horenz; Jack Stern] vBC (as solo)
    ET: Associated 10003A, RA1006A, World 300-919 (913/920)
    LP: Design DLP-20, DLP-147, Gala Int'l (E) GLP-307, Pickwick PR 108, Circle CLP-20, Int'l Award AK/AKS 203
    TC: Nostalgia (E) MRT 40053
    CD: Circle CCD-20
A-135/SS-8194   **Dese, Dem And Dose** [Alton Glenn Miller] (cl solo)
    ET: Associated 10003A, RA1006A, World 200-920 (913/920)
    LP: Design DLP-20, Circle CLP-20
    TC: Nostalgia (E) MRT 40053
    CD: Circle CCD-20
A-136/SS-8373   **Don't Let It Bother You** [Mack Gordon; Harry Revel] (as solo)
    ET: Associated 10003B, World 200-949 (945/952)
    LP: Design DLP-20, DLP-147, Gala Int'l (E) GLP-307, Pickwick PR 108, Circle CLP-20, Int'l Award AK/AKS 203
    CD: Circle CCD-20
A-136/SS-8373   **I Believe In Miracles** [Sam H. Lewis; George W. Meyer, Pete Wendling] vBC
    ET: Associated 10003B, World 200-950 (945/952)
    LP: Design DLP-20, DLP-147, Gala Int'l (E) GLP-307, Pickwick PR 108, Circle CLP-20, Int'l Award AK/AKS 203
    TC: Nostalgia (E) MRT 40053
    CD: Circle CCD-20
A-136/SS-8373   **(I've Got A) New Deal In Love** [J. Russell Robinson; Bill Livingston]
    ET: Associated 10003B, World 200-951 (945/952)
    LP: Design DLP-20, DLP-147, Gala Int'l (E) GLP-307, Pickwick PR 108, Circle CLP-20, Int'l Award AK/AKS 203
    TC: Nostalgia (E) MRT 40053
    CD: Circle CCD-20
A-136/SS-8373   **When You Climb Those Golden Stairs** [Gordon Jenkins] vBC
    ET: Associated 10003B, World 300-952 (945/952)
    LP: Circle CLP-20
    CD: Circle CCD-20

Decca, New York, N.Y. Friday, January 18, 1935
THE DORSEY BROTHERS' ORCHESTRA
Tom Dorsey (tb,ldr) George Thow (tp) Joe Yukl, Don Matteson (tb,vcl)
Jimmy Dorsey (cl,as) Jack Stacey (ts) Skeets Herfurt (ts,vcl) Bobby Van
Eps (p) Roc Hillman (g,vcl) Delmar Kaplan (sb) Ray McKinley (d) Kay
Weber, Bob Crosby (vcl)

39264-A	**Tiny Little Fingerprints** [Charles Newman, Sam H. Stept, Charles Tobias] vKW
	78: Decca 367, Brunswick (E) RL-215
39265-A,B	**I'm Facing The Music** vBC (as solo)
	78: Decca 367
39266-A	**I Threw A Bean Bag At The Moon** [Stanley Adams; Milton Ager] vBC
	78: Decca 368, Brunswick (E) RL-246, (F) A-9782
39267-B	**The Farmer Takes A Wife** vKW,DM,SH&RH
	78: Decca 368
	All sides also on **TC:** Ajazz C-1763

Decca, New York, N.Y. Friday, January 25, 1935
THE DORSEY BROTHERS' ORCHESTRA
Kay Weber, Bob Crosby (vcl)

39278-A	**Don't Be Afraid To Tell Your Mother** [Pinky Tomlin, Coy Poe, Jimmie Greer] vBC (cl,as solo)
	78: Decca 371, Brunswick (E) RL-243
	TC: Ajazz C-1763

Decca, New York, N.Y. Saturday, January 26, 1935
THE DORSEY BROTHERS' ORCHESTRA

39280-A	**Lullaby Of Broadway** [Al Dubin; Harry Warren] vBC&band (cl solo)
	78: Decca 370, Brunswick (E) RL-245
	LP: Coral (G) 6.28315
	TC: Movie Play (Port) 5008, Movie Play (GE) SER 5008
	CD: Jass J-CD-641, Reader's Digest RC7-007-1
39281-A,B	**The Words Are In My Heart** [Al Dubin; Harry Warren] vKW (as solo)
	78: Decca 370, Brunswick (E) RL-245
39282-A	**I'm Goin' Shoppin' With You** [Al Dubin; Harry Warren] vBC (cl solo)
	78: Decca 371, Brunswick (E) RL-246
	All sides also on **TC:** Ajazz C-1773

A short note in *Variety* (January 29, 1935), that said Glen Gray and
the Casa Lomans wouldn't be returning to Glen Island Casino the
coming summer, set the stage for a big break for the Dorsey brothers.
Other stories at about this same time revealed that the Dorseys had been
booked into an undisclosed Baltimore location for later that month, and
that the Dorsey Brothers were Decca's fourth best-selling artists.
    A few days later the band returned to 2826 Decatur Avenue, up in the

Bronx, the location of the studios of Electrical Research Products, to cut some more tunes for Associated Transcriptions. Though not subsequently leased to World, some of these eventually made it to the Muzak wired background music circuit.

Electrical Research Prods., Bronx, N.Y. Friday, February 1, 1935
DALY BROTHERS' ORCHESTRA (Dorsey Brothers' Orchestra)
Tom Dorsey (tb,ldr) George Thow (tp) Joe Yukl, Don Matteson (tb) **Jimmy Dorsey** (cl,as) Jack Stacey, Skeets Herfurt (ts) Bobby Van Eps (p) Roc Hillman (g) Delmar Kaplan (sb) Ray McKinley (d) Bob Crosby [as Bob Tompkins] (vcl)

A-143   **Weary Blues** [Artie Matthews] (cl solo)
    ET: (unissued)
    CD: Circle CCD-20
A-144   **Weary Blues** (cl solo)
    ET: Associated 208A, Muzak 174
    EP: Bravo (E) BR 340
    LP: Design DLP-20, DLP-147, Gala Int'l (E) GLP-307, Pickwick
    PR 108, Int'l Award AK/AKS 203
    TC: Nostalgia (E) MRT 40053
A-143   **Dinah** (unissued)
A-144   **Dinah** [Sam M. Lewis; Joseph Young; Harry Akst]
    ET: Associated 208A, Muzak 174
A-145   **Wild Honey** [George Hamilton]
    ET: Associated 157B
A-145   **With Every Breath I Take** [Leo Robin; Ralph Rainger]
    ET: Associated 157B
A-146   **Tailspin** [Frank Trumbauer, Jimmy Dorsey]
    ET: Associated 271A, Muzak 498
A-146   **I've Got Your Number** [Bonnie Lake]
    ET: Associated 271A, Muzak 498
A-147   (Medley:) **Whispering** [Richard Coburn, Vincent
                    Rose, J. Schonberger]; **Do You Ever Think Of Me?**
                    [Earl Burtnett]; **Margie** [Con Conrad, J. Russell
                    Robinson]; **Avalon** [Vincent Rose]; **Japanese Sand-
                    man** [Richard Whiting]
    ET: Associated 353B
A-147   **Alexander's Ragtime Band** [Irving Berlin]
    ET: Associated 353B
A-148   (Medley:) **I'm Gettin' Sentimental Over You** [Ned
                    Washington; George Bassman]; **Tiger Rag** [Edwin
                    Edwards, Nick LaRocca, Tony Spargo, Larry
                    Shields]; **I'm A Ding Dong Daddy (From Dumas)**
                    [Phil Baxter]
    ET: Associated 160B, R-37A, R-12014
A-149   **St. Louis Blues** (unissued)
A-150   **St. Louis Blues** (unissued)
A-149   **Annie's Cousin Fanny** vBC&band (unissued)
A-150   **Annie's Cousin Fanny** vBC&band (unissued)

Decca, New York, N.Y. Wednesday, February 6, 1935
THE DORSEY BROTHERS' ORCHESTRA
Jimmy Dorsey adds (cnt). Glenn Miller (arr)

39337-A   **Harlem Chapel Chimes** [Spencer]
    78: Brunswick (E) O2149, Decca (E) BM 02149
39338-A   **I've Got Your Number** [Connie Lake] (cl solo)
    78: Decca 515
39339-A   **You're Okay** [Mitchell Parish; Mickey Bloom] arrGM
          (as solo)
    78: Decca 1304
39340-A   **Weary Blues** [Artie Matthews] (cl solo)
    78: Decca 469, 11035, Brunswick (E) O2149
    (SSL-4017-3) **ET:** AFRS Basic Music Library P-1997, AFRS H-
    62-90
    45: Decca 9-11035
    EP: Decca 91530
    LP: Decca DL 6016, DL 8631, Coral (E) CRLM 1027, (E) CP
    27, MCA 1505, (J) 1342, Coral (G) 6.28315, Brunswick (E) LA
    5254, (E) LAT 8256, Durium/King Of Jazz KJL-20009, Vanguard
    (Au) UJ 556
    TC: MCA MCAC 1505
39341-A   **Weary Blues** (12-inch version) (cl,as solos)
    78: Decca 15013, Brunswick (E) O135, A-131
    LP: Decca DL 8045, MCA (J) 1342, Coral (G) 6.28315,
    Brunswick (E) LAT 8037
    TC: ProArte Digital PCD 508
    CD: ProArte Digital CDD 508
39342-A   **Tailspin** [Frank Trumbauer, Jimmy Dorsey] (as solo)
    78: Decca 560, 4202, BM-1111, Brunswick 87097
    LP: Decca DL 8045, DL 8631, Coral (E) CRLM 1027, (E) CP
    27, MCA 1505, (J) 1342, Coral (G) 6.28315, Brunswick (E) LAT
    8256, Durium/King Of Jazz KJL-20009, Vanguard (Au) UJ 556
    TC: MCA MCAC 1505, ProArte Digital PCD 508
    CD: ProArte Digital CDD 508
39343-C   **Eccentric (Rag)** [J. Russell Robinson] (cnt solo)
    78: Decca 1304, Brunswick (E) 03191
    LP: Decca DL 8631, Coral (E) CRLM 1027, (E) CP 27, MCA
    1505, (J) 1342, Coral (G) 6.28315, Brunswick (E) LAT 8256,
    Durium/King Of Jazz KJL-20009, Vanguard (Au) UJ 556
    TC: MCA MCAC 1505
39344-A   **Dese, Dem, Dose** [Alton Glenn Miller] (cl solo)
    78: Decca 469, 11035
    45: Decca 9-11034
    (SSL-4017-4) **ET:** AFRS Basic Music Library P-1997
    LP: Decca DL 6016, DL 8631, Coral (E) CRLM 1027, (E) CP
    27, MCA 1505, (J) 1342, Coral (G) 6.28315, Brunswick (E) LA
    5254, LAT 8256, Durium/King Of Jazz KJL-20009, Vanguard
    (Au) UJ 556
    TC: MCA MCAC 1505, Deja Vu (It) DVLC 2063
39345-A   **Dipper Mouth (Blues) (Sugar Foot Stomp)** ["King"
          Oliver, Louis Armstrong] (cl solo)

78: Decca 561, 11035, Brunswick (E) O3191
(SSL-4017-1) ET: AFRS Basic Music Library P-1997
EP: Decca 91530
LP: Decca DL 6016, DL8631, Brunswick (E) LA 5254, (E) LAT 8256, Coral (E) CRLM 1027, (E) CP 27, (G) 6.28315, MCA 1505, (J) 3142, Durium/King Of Jazz KLJ 20009, Vanguard (Au) UJ-556
TC: MCA MCAC 2505, ProArte Digital PCD 508
39346-A   **Tomorrow's Another Day** [Alton Glenn Miller] vKW
                 (cl solo)
78: Decca 515
LP: Coral (G) 6.28315
Except for 39337, all sides this session also on **TC:** Ajazz C-1773

Jimmy and a group of other musicians, including Glenn Miller, Jack Jenney, Art Bernstein, Harry Bluestone, Mannie Klein and Jerry Colonna, plus arranger Gordon Jenkins, contributed $100 each to help pianist-conductor Lennie Hayton and his manager, Jack Colt, open The Famous Door, a night spot at 35 West Fifty-second Street (Shaw 1977).

Billboard (April 20, 1935) revealed that all the Dorseys' summer contracts, including a six-week tour of Balaban and Katz movie houses, would have to be canceled because of their booking at Glen Island Casino. Kay Weber saved a routing sheet that shows over twenty one-nighters in thirty days, plus two "transcription sessions" in New York City (April 18-19) that either never developed or were really balance checks of the band for the Dorseys to check out before Glen Island.

Travel itinerary: Thurs., Apr. 4—Purdue University, W. Lafayette, Ind. / Fri., Apr. 5 to Thurs., Apr. 11—Fox Theater, Detroit, Mich. / Fri., Apr. 12—Silver Slipper, Toronto, Ont. / Sat., Apr. 13—Erie, Pa. / Sun., Apr. 14—The Trianon Ballroom, Cleveland, Ohio. / Sat., Apr. 20—Pottstown, Pa. / Sun., Apr. 21—New London, Conn. / Mon., Apr. 22—Nuttings-on-the-Charles, Waltham, Mass. / Sun., Apr. 28—Lake Compounce, Bristol, Conn.

While the Dorseys worked a policeman's ball on Monday, April 29, in Troy, New York, Bob Eberle, a local boy from nearby Hoosick Falls, made himself (and his guitar) known to the Dorseys.

Since Bob Crosby was leaving soon, the brothers asked Eberle to join them at the next night's engagement, Tuesday, April 30, at The Gables in Deerfield, Massachusetts. Eberle did just that and hung around for ten years, becoming one of Jimmy's best friends and a mainstay of the band's popularity. And so, while tensions continued to develop between the brothers, the tour ground on:

Travel itinerary: Wed., May 1-Scranton, Pa. / Thurs., May 2—Lakewood Park, Mahanoy City, Pa. (two stops where they were caught by a proud Mom and Pop Dorsey) / Fri., May 3—Union College, Schenectady, N.Y. / Sat., May 4—Dartmouth College, Hanover, N.H. / Sun., May 5—Kantor's Hall, Passaic, N.J. / Mon., May 6—Madrid Club, Harrisburg, Pa. / Tues., May 7—Pittsfield, Mass. / Wed., May 8—Hamilton Park, Waterbury, Conn. / Thurs.,, May 9—Rhode Island State College, Providence, R.I. / Fri., May 10—Loyola College, Baltimore, Md. / Sat., May 11—Mealy's Ballroom, Allentown, Pa.

The road tour ended when the band settled in Thursday, May 16, at Glen Island Casino, "on Long Island Sound, just off the Shore Road in New Rochelle, New York," as the radio announcers used to say.

Decca, New York, N.Y. Monday, May 27, 1935
THE DORSEY BROTHERS' ORCHESTRA
Tom Dorsey (tb,ldr) George Thow (tp) Joe Yukl (tb) Don Matteson (tb,vcl) **Jimmy Dorsey** (cl,as) Jack Stacey (ts) Skeets Herfurt (ts,vcl) Bobby Van Eps (p) Roc Hillman (g,vcl) Slim Taft (sb) Ray McKinley (d) Kay Weber, Bob Eberle (vcl)

39539-A   **Footloose And Fancy Free** [Gus Kahn; Carmen Lombardo] vDM,SH&RH (cl solo)
   78: Decca 482, Brunswick (E) RL-269
   LP: Coral (G) 6.28315
   TC: Movie Play (Port) 5008, Movie Play (GE) SER 5008
39540-A   **Every Little Moment** [Dorothy Fields; Jimmy McHugh] vKW (cl solo)
   78: Decca 480, Brunswick (E) RL-256
   LP: Sunbeam HB 301
   TC: Radio Yesteryear Stack 15
39540-B   **Every Little Moment** vKW (cl solo)
   78: Decca 480
39541-A   **You're All I Need** [Gus Kahn; Bronislaw Kaper, Walter Jurmann] vBE (as solo)
   78: Decca 482
   39539 through 39541 also on **TC:** Ajazz C-1773
39542-A   **I'll Never Say "Never Again" Again** [Harry Woods] vDM&SH (cl solo)
   78: Decca 480, Brunswick RL-269
   LP: Sunbeam HB301, Coral (G) 6.28315, Reader's Digest RBA-136-5
   TC: Reader's Digest KRB-136/A/3, Radio Yesteryear Stack 15
   CD: Reader's Digest RC7-007-1
39543-A   **Chasing Shadows** [Benny Davis; Abner Silver] vBE
   78: Decca 476, Brunswick (E) RL-255
   CD: Reader's Digest RC7-007-1
39544-A   **Every Single Little Tingle Of My Heart** [Simon; Lowman, Roberts] vKW (cl solo)
   78: Decca 476, Brunswick (E) RL-255
   39542 through 39544 also on **TC:** Ajazz C-1783

In some perverse way Jimmy took pleasure in needling his brother while Tommy was leading, referring to him as "the big star." And according to Ray McKinley, when Glen Island owner Mike DeZutter took Jimmy as a drinking buddy it only added to Tommy's resentment, for it was Tommy who was driving the band as leader, setting up the dance numbers and radio programs, pushing the bookers for more jobs.

Two weeks into the Glen Island stand on Thursday, May 30, Tommy counted off a tempo for "I'll Never Say 'Never Again' Again" that wasn't to Jimmy's liking. Jimmy, some say "a bit in his cups," said as much and Tommy stalked off the stand, out of the casino and back to his home in New Jersey. The day, which happened to be Memorial (or Decoration) Day, became known as the brothers' "Separation Day."

It fell to Jimmy to keep the band going, with his biggest problem being a replacement for Tommy's trombone. Pals like Jack Jenney and Jerry Colonna sat in briefly, but none wanted the job full-time nor could they handle Tommy's tough solos.

Jimmy solved the problem by bringing in Bobby Byrne, a sixteen-year-old trombonist he had caught during a Detroit booking. Byrne arrived at Glen Island with three trombones, a harp and a huge ego, amazing those expecting a neophyte by proving himself an able replacement.

Despite its troubles the band was renewed at Glen Island until October 1 (*Billboard,* July 20, 1935, 12), while Corky O'Keefe and his partner Tommy Rockwell worked hard at getting the boys back together. Bobby Byrne confirmed (1991) that Tommy returned in late August 1935, fronting the band at Glen Island until August 30 (Seavor 1997).

Then he began appearing only one hour nightly until September 21. Byrne confirms that Tommy also took part in the August 1 and August 14 sessions at Decca Records (Seavor ibid.).

Decca, New York, N.Y. Thursday, August 1, 1935
THE DORSEY BROTHERS' ORCHESTRA
Tom Dorsey (ldr) George Thow (tp) Joe Yukl, Bobby Byrne (tb) Don Matteson (tb,vcl) **Jimmy Dorsey** (cl,as) Jack Stacey (ts) Skeets Herfurt (ts,vcl) Bobby Van Eps (p) Roc Hillman (g,vcl) Slim Taft (sb) Ray McKinley (d) Kay Weber, Bob Eberle (vcl)

39797-A   **My Very Good Friend The Milkman** [Johnny Burke; Harold Spina] vKW,BE,DM,SH&RH (cl solo)
    78: Decca 519
    LP: Coral (G) 6.28315
39798-A   **You're So Darn Charming** [Johnny Burke; Harold Spina] vDM
    78: Decca 520, Brunswick (E) RL-299
39799-A   **No Strings** [Irving Berlin] vDM,RH&SH (as solo)
    78: Decca 516, Brunswick (E) RL-307
    LP: Sunbeam HB-301, MCA (G)6.28315, Old Bean (E) OLD 14
    TC: Old Bean (E) COLD 14, Radio Yesteryear Stack 15
    CD: Old Bean (E) DOLD 14
39800-A   **Top Hat, White Tie And Tails** [Irving Berlin] vDM, RH&SH (cl solo)
    78: Decca 516, Brunswick (E) RL-307
    LP: Sunbeam HB-301, MCA (G) 6.28315, Old Bean (E) OLD 14, ASV Living Era (E) AJA 5068
    TC: Old Bean (E) COLD 14, ASV Living Era (E) ZC AJA 5068, Radio Yesteryear Stack 15
    CD: Old Bean (E) DOLD 14, ASV Living Era (E) CD AJA 5068
39801-A   **You Saved My Life** vKW (cl solo)
    78: Decca 520, Brunswick (E) RL-299
39802-A   **I Couldn't Believe My Eyes** [Walter G. Samuels, Leonard Whitcup, Teddy Powell] vKW (cl solo)
    78: Decca 519, Brunswick (E) RL-302, (F) A-9833
    All sides also on **TC:** Ajazz C-1783

Decca, New York, N.Y. Wednesday, August 14, 1935
BING CROSBY (accomp. by Dorsey Brothers' Orchestra)
Tom Dorsey (tb,ldr) George Thow (tp) Joe Yukl, Bobby Byrne, Don
Matteson (tb) **Jimmy Dorsey** (cl,as) Jack Stacey, Skeets Herfurt (ts)
Bobby Van Eps (p) Roc Hillman (g) Slim Taft (sb) Ray McKinley (d)
Bing Crosby (vcl)

39852-A   **From The Top Of Your Head** [Mack Gordon; Harry
                  Revel] vBC (as solo)
    78: Decca 547, 11005, Y-5028, Brunswick (E) 02082, (G) A-
    9855
    LP: Decca DL-4250, DL-6009, Brunswick (E) BING-1, (E) LA
    8723
    CD: ASV Living Era AJA 5185
39853-A   **I Wish I Were Aladdin** [Mack Gordon; Harry Revel]
                  vBC
    78: Decca 547, 11005, Y-5028, Brunswick (E) 02082, (G) A-
    9831
    LP: Decca DL-4250, DL-6009, Brunswick (E) BING-1, (E) LA
    8723
39854-A   **Takes Two To Make A Bargain** [Mack Gordon;
                  Harry Revel] vBC (cl,as solos)
    78: Decca 548, 11004, Y-5013, Brunswick (E) 02070, (G) A-
    9856
    LP: Decca DL-4250, DL-6009, Brunswick (E) BING-1, (E) LA
    8723
39855-A   **Two For Tonight** [Mack Gordon; Harry Revel] vBC
    78: Decca 543, 11006, Y-5029, Brunswick 02083, (G) A-9856
    LP: Decca DL-4250, DL-6009, Brunswick (E) BING-1, (E) LA
    8723, MCA (G) 6.28315 Dance Band Days (G) DBD 14
39856-A   **Without A Word Of Warning** [Mack Gordon; Harry
                  Revel] vBC
    78: Decca 548, 11004, Y-5013, Brunswick (E) 02083, (G) A-
    9856
    LP: Decca DL-4250, DL-6009, Brunswick (E) BING-1, (E) LA
    8723
    CD: Pearl-Flapper (E) PAST CD 9784, Radio Years (It) 32,
    Reader's Digest RC7-007-1
    All sides also on **TC:** Ajazz C-1783

After finishing "Without A Word Of Warning," Bing and Decca
owner-producer Jack Kapp got into a heated exchange, which was
recorded and has been passed down for years in bootleg copies:
-0-   Dialogue between Bing Crosby and Jack Kapp
    LP: For Collectors Only (no #), Curtain Calls 100/2
    TC: Listeners Digest 67
39857-A   **I Wished On The Moon** [Dorothy Parker; Ralph
                  Rainger] vBC
    78: Decca 543, 11001, Y-5013, Brunswick (E) 02070, (G) A-
    9831
    LP: Decca DL-4250, DL-6009, Brunswick (E) BING-1, (E) LA
    8723, MCA (G) 6.28315, World Records (E) SM 293

TC: ProArte Digital PCD 508
CD: ProArte Digital CDD 508, Radio Years (It) 32, Reader's
Digest RC7-007-1

The August 14 Decca session was partly why Bing Crosby had come
to New York City at this time, another reason being an appearance the
next evening (August 15) with the Dorsey brothers (without the band) on
the *Kraft Music Hall*. It was to be a sort of reunion harking back to the
1927 days with Paul Whiteman. Bing hadn't yet taken over "the Hall"
but when he did Jimmy would back him with his band for eighteen
months. Whiteman, along with his orchestra, was Kraft's host at the
time, and the hour show aired Thursday nights on NBC, just as it would
with Bing at the helm.
    The band made one more Decca session under the Dorsey Brothers'
name, but without brother Tommy, who by then had signed with Victor.

Decca, New York, N.Y. Wednesday, September 11, 1935
THE DORSEY BROTHERS' ORCHESTRA
Jimmy Dorsey (cl,as,ldr) George Thow (tp) Joe Yukl, Bobby Byrne,
Don Matteson (tb) Jack Stacey, Skeets Herfurt (ts) Bobby Van Eps (p)
Roc Hillman (g) Slim Taft (sb) Ray McKinley (d) Kay Weber, Bob
Eberle (vcl)

39962-A   **The Gentleman Obviously Doesn't Believe (In Love)**
                 [Michael Carr, Edward Pola] vKW
      78: Decca 561
39963-A   **I've Got A Feelin' You're Foolin'** [Arthur Freed;
                 Nacio Herb Brown] vBE (as solo)
      78: Decca 560, Brunswick (E) RL-301
39964-A   **On A Sunday Afternoon** [Arthur Freed; Nacio Herb
                 Brown] vKW
      78: Decca 559, Brunswick (E) RL-301
39965-A   **You Are My Lucky Star** [Arthur Freed; Nacio Herb
                 Brown] vBE
      78: Decca 559, Brunswick (E) RL-302

Now Jimmy was truly on his own. At thirty-one, "Lad" was the
reluctant leader of his own band. How he must have yearned to be back
as a sideman, with "Mac" taking charge. Fortunately, he would soon
locate several top arrangers, including Fud Livingston, Larry Clinton,
and Joe Lippman, and, even more important retain such top musicians
as Skeets Herfurt, Ray McKinley, Roc Hillman, Don Matteson and Bobby Van Eps to carry him through the early days on his own.
    But the most important binding force was probably his new trom-
bonist, Bobby Byrne, who helped forge Jimmy's brass section into one
of the best in the nation. Byrne's style became the bridge between Tommy's pioneer efforts and the later work of trombonists like Urbie Green
and Kai Winding.
    Jimmy had also added Salvatore ("Toots") Camarata to the trumpet
section. Far more important, Camarata developed the distinctive Jimmy
Dorsey sound as an arranger over the next decade. Later he became
"Tutti" Camarata and then just "Camarata."

324   JIMMY DORSEY: A Study in Contrasts

By the time of the next Decca session, the band had fully assumed Jimmy's name. This first session for Jimmy was made up of some Cole Porter songs from *Jubilee*. It took three years for rival clarinetist Artie Shaw to make a hit of still another *Jubilee* song, "Begin The Beguine."

Decca, New York, N.Y. Thursday, September 19, 1935
JIMMY DORSEY AND HIS ORCHESTRA
Jimmy Dorsey (cl,as,ldr) George Thow (tp) Toots Camarata (tp,arr) Bobby Byrne, Don Matteson, Joe Yukl (tb) Fud Livingston (as,ts,arr) Jack Stacey (as) Skeets Herfurt (ts) Bobby Van Eps (p) Roc Hillman (g) Slim Taft (sb) Ray McKinley (d) Kay Weber, Bob Eberle (vcl)

39983-A   **When Love Comes Your Way** [Cole Porter] vKW
        78: Decca 570
        LP: Ajax LP 103
39984-A   **A Picture Of Me Without You** [Cole Porter] vKW,
                BE (cl solo)
        78: Decca 571
        LP: Ajax LP103, Joyce LP6038
39985-A   **Me And Marie** [Cole Porter] vBE (as solo)
        78: Decca 570
        LP: Ajax LP103, Joyce LP6038
39986-A   **Why Shouldn't I?** [Cole Porter] vKW
        78: Decca 571
        LP: Ajax LP103
        All four sides also on **TC:** Radio Yesteryear Stack 59

The first two Dorsey Brothers' sessions for Associated Transcriptions had been so well received that the band was scheduled for another, but by the time the date arrived it was Jimmy at the helm. And as had been the case with the Dorsey Brothers, Associated changed the band's name on its releases. They cut thirty-one tunes in this marathon session.

Electrical Research Prods., Bronx, N.Y. Monday, September 23, 1935
JIMMY DORSEY AND HIS ORCHESTRA as JIMMY DALTON AND HIS ORCHESTRA
Roc Hillman, Don Matteson, Skeets Herfurt (as Trio and singly), Kay Weber, Bob Eberle (vcl)

A 700   **I've Got A Feelin' You're Foolin'** [Arthur Freed;
                Nacio Herb Brown] vBE (as solos)
        ET: Associated 201A-1, Muzak 85
A 700   **You Are My Lucky Star** [Arthur Freed; Nacio Herb
                Brown] vBE
        ET: Associated 201A-2, Muzak 85
        LP: London (E) 180032, HMG5022, Rumbleseat RS102
A 701   **On A Sunday Afternoon** [Arthur Freed; Nacio Herb
                Brown] vKW
        ET: Associated 200A-1, Muzak 84
A 701   **Dorsey Stomp (Dusk In Upper Sandusky)** [Larry
                Clinton, Jimmy Dorsey] (as solos)
        ET: Associated 200A-2, Muzak 84

LP: London (E) 180032, HMG5022, 180032, Rumbleseat RS102, Queen Disc 028
TC: Demand Performance DPC-822
A 702   East Of The Sun (And West Of The Moon) [Brooks Bowman] vBE (cl, as solos)
ET: Associated 201B-1, Muzak 85
LP: London (E) 180032, HMG5022, Rumbleseat RS102
TC: Demand Performance DPC-822
A 702   Double Trouble [Leo Robin; Ralph Rainger, Richard Whiting] vTrio (as solo)
ET: Associated 201B-2, Muzak 85
All A 700, A 701 and A 702 cuts also on TC: Ajazz 1549
A 703   My Very Good Friend The Milkman [Johnny Burke; Harold Spina] vKW&BE
ET: Associated 203A-1
A 703   From The Top Of Your Head [Mack Gordon; Harry Revel] vBE
ET: Associated 203A-2
A 704   I Wished On The Moon [Mack Gordon; Harry Revel] vBE
ET: Associated 200B-1, Muzak 84
TC: Ajazz 1551
A 704   I've Got A Note [Edward Pola] vSH&KW (as solo)
ET: Associated 200B-2, Muzak 84
TC: Ajazz 1551
A 705   A Picture Of Me Without You [Cole Porter] vKW&BE
ET: Associated 203B-1
A 705   Why Shouldn't I? [Cole Porter] vKW
ET: Associated 203B-2
A 706   The Gentleman Obviously Doesn't Believe [Michael Carr, Edward Pola] vKW
ET: Associated 202A-1, Muzak 175
TC: Ajazz 1551
A 706   Top Hat, White Tie And Tails [Irving Berlin] vTrio (cl solo)
ET: Associated 202A-2, Muzak 175
LP: London (E) 180032, HMG5022, Rumbleseat RS102, Queen Disc 028
TC: Demand Performance DPC 822, Ajazz 1551
A 709   No Strings [Irving Berlin] vTrio (as solo)
ET: Associated 206B-1
LP: London (E) 180032, HMG5022, Rumbleseat RS102
TC: Ajazz 1549
A 709   Cheek To Cheek [Irving Berlin] vKW
ET: Associated 206B-2
LP: London (E) 180032, HMG5022, Rumbleseat RS102
TC: Demand Performance DPC-822, Ajazz 1549
A 710   Tap Dancer's Nightmare [Larry Clinton] (cl solo)
ET: Associated 202B-1, Muzak 175
LP: London (E) 180032, HMG5022, Rumbleseat RS102, Queen Disc 028
TC: Ajazz 1551   (Contd.)

JIMMY DALTON AND HIS ORCHESTRA (Contd.)

A 710   **Me And Marie** [Cole Porter] vBE
    ET: Associated 202B-2, Muzak 175
    TC: Ajazz 1551
A 711   **You're What The Doctor Ordered** vTrio (as solo)
    ET: Associated 204A-1, Muzak 86
    TC: Ajazz 1551
A 711   **I'm On A See-Saw** [Desmond Carter; Vivian Ellis]
                 vBE&KW
    ET: Associated 204A-2, Muzak 86
    TC: Ajazz 1551
A 712   **I'm Painting The Town Red** [Charles Tobias; Charles
                 Newman] vDM
    ET: Associated 206A-1
    TC: Ajazz 1549
A 712   **Beebe** [Jimmy Dorsey] (as solo)
    ET: Associated 206A-2
    LP: London (E) 180032, HMG5022, Rumbleseat RS102, Queen
    Disc 028
    TC: Demand Performance DPC-822, Ajazz 1549
A 712   **Sandman** (theme) [Ralph Freed, Bonnie Lake]
    ET: Associated 206A-3
    LP: Queen Disc 028
    TC: Ajazz 1549
A 713   **Simply Grand** vBE (cl solo)
    ET: Associated 204B-1, Muzak 86
    TC: Ajazz 1551
A 713   **The Peanut Vendor** [Marion Sunshine, L. Wolfe Gil-
                 bert; Moises R. Simons] (cl solo)
    ET: Associated 204B-2, Muzak 86
    LP: London (E) 180032, HMG5022, Rumbleseat RS102, Queen
    Disc 028
    TC: Ajazz 1551
A 714   **Three Little Words** [Bert Kalmar; Harry Ruby] (cl,as,
                 cl solos)
    ET: Associated 205A-1, Muzak 320
    LP: London (E) 180032, HMG5022, Rumbleseat RS102
    TC: Demand Performance DPC-822
A 714   **It Never Dawned On Me** vKW
    ET: Associated 205A-2, Muzak 320
    LP: London (E) 180032, HMG5022, Rumbleseat RS102
    TC: Demand Performance DPC-822
A 715   **I Wish I Were Aladdin** [Mack Gordon; Harry Revel]
                 vBE
    ET: Associated 205B-1, Muzak 320
A 715   **Someone Stole Gabriel's Horn** [Ned Washington; Ed-
                 gar Hayes, Irving Mills] vKW
    ET: Associated 205B-2, Muzak 320
A 716   **Wolverine Blues** [Ferdinand "Jelly Roll" Morton, Ben-
                 jamin F. Spikes, John C. Spikes] (cl solo)
    ET: Associated 207A-1, Muzak 319

LP: London (E) 180032, HMG5022, Rumbleseat RS102, Queen
Disc 028
TC: Demand Performance DPC-822, Ajazz 1549
A 716   **Stuff Is Here And It's Mellow** vTrio (cl solo)
ET: Associated 207A-2, Muzak 319
LP: Queen Disc 028
TC: Ajazz 1549
The "B" Side of ET 207 is by accordionist Charles Magnante.

Decca, New York, N.Y. Thursday, October 10, 1935
JIMMY DORSEY AND HIS ORCHESTRA

60032-A   **Washington Grays**
78: Decca 655, (Au) X-1120, Brunswick (E) O2172
LP: Ajax LP103
60033-   **Tap Dancer's Nightmare** [Larry Clinton] (as,bar,
cl solos)
78: Decca 655, (Au) X-1120, Brunswick (E) O2172
LP: Ajax LP103, Swingfan (G) 1007, Bandstand BS7120
CD: Aero Space AS7120
60034-A   **Dorsey Stomp (Dusk In Upper Sandusky)** [Larry
Clinton, Jimmy Dorsey] (as solos)
78: Decca 607
LP: Ajax LP103, Coral COPS7449, (G) 6.28219, Time-Life STB-
B10, Bandstand BS7104
TC: Time-Life 4TL-0006
CD: Time-Life 4TL-0006
60035-A   **Stop, Look And Listen** [George Van Eps, John Van
Eps] (cl solo)
78: Decca 208, Brunswick (E) O2172
LP: Coral COPS7449, (G) 6.28219
Decca 208 was originally issued from matrix 38303-A, recorded
August 15, 1934, on the Decca sundial label. The Jimmy Dorsey
version appears on blue-label Deccas.
60036-A   **Where Am I?** [Al Dubin; Harry Warren] vKW
78: Decca 602, Brunswick (E) O2224
LP: Ajax LP103
60037-A   **You Let Me Down** [Al Dubin; Harry Warren] vBE
(cl solo)
78: Decca 602, Brunswick (E) O2224
LP: Ajax LP103, Joyce LP6038
60038-A   **Broadway Cinderella** vKW
78: Brunswick (E) O2225
60039-A   **I'm A Gambler** vBE
78: Decca 607
LP: Ajax LP103, Joyce LP6038
All sides except 60035 and 60038 also on **TC:** Radio Yesteryear
Stack 59

Variety (December 25, 1935, 40) cited Bing Crosby's move to
Hollywood and reported that Jimmy's band would have twenty-four
pieces but this expansion never took place.   Jimmy moved everybody to

California including Kay Weber and Bob Eberle. While Eberle didn't appear on the Kraft show, he was needed for other work (Sanford 1972).

The trek to the West Coast began in mid-October by automobile and included a six-week stint at "The Grove," a nitery in Houston, Texas. It was here that Jimmy acquired an insatiable taste for spareribs, Texas style, which he retained for the rest of his life.

The entire crew arrived in Hollywood in late November. While Bing Crosby became host of the Kraft Music Hall on January 2, 1936, for four weeks prior to that he was heard in inserts from Hollywood with backing by Jimmy's band, while retiring host Paul Whiteman broadcast from New York City.

Broadcast schedule (Kraft Music Hall): Thurs., Dec. 5, 12, 19, 26, NBC-Red 7:00-8:00 P.M. (PST) (backing Bing Crosby on inserts in Paul Whiteman program).

Although the band did play the Palomar on New Year's Eve it was a one-nighter only. Hollywood Local 42 of the musicians' union had a residency requirement that needed to be met before the band could do any regular work except the broadcasts for Bing.

After playing the Palomar on New Year's Eve, there was a costume party, with Jimmy bedecked as one of the Three Musketeers, Ray McKinley as Groucho Marx, Skeets Herfurt as Mickey Mouse, and a large number of others in drag, including Roc Hillman, Bobby Byrne, Bob Eberle and George Thow. Kay Weber, by contrast, came in black face as Topsy.

Bing, Booze and Cheese
(1936-1937)

Burbank, north of Hollywood in the San Fernando Valley, was where Jimmy and his wife Jane rented a Spanish-style house (what else in the thirties in southern California?) and settled in for what was to become a year-and-a-half stay under the sun.

Bob Eberle lived here as well, and it was Jimmy's hospitality, despite Bob's status as excess baggage, that helped make Eberle such a loyal employee, spurning numerous offers in the early forties to go out on his own in the style of Frank Sinatra.

The holiday period was no time for Jimmy to have time on his hands. He had joined The Lakeside, Bing's country club, and did some of his best playing at the nineteenth hole. He did fairly well on the course as well, usually hitting in the eighties, playing frequently with movie names like Bette Davis, Cass Daley and Oliver Hardy.

This partying and reliance on booze were beginning to cause tensions in Jimmy's relationship with his wife Jane. His radio boss, Bing Crosby, had faced a similar problem earlier, but his wife, actress Dixie Lee, had succeeded in controlling it.

January 2, 1936, marked the beginning of the Jimmy Dorsey band's full participation in the Kraft broadcasts. Known as *The Kraft Music Hall with Bing Crosby,* the program originated in the NBC studios in Hollywood, California, and was aired Thursdays on NBC's Red network from 7:00-8:00 P.M. Pacific Time (10:00-11:00 P.M. Eastern Time). The only other regulars were announcer Don Wilson and comedian Bob Burns, "the Arkansas Traveler," who stayed with Bing for five years.

Contents of the early Kraft shows are sketchy; however, the published guest list for each broadcast will be shown chronologically as the following. The listings assume that Bing Crosby vocalizes and is host and that Bob Burns is the regular comedian, unless otherwise indicated.

Kraft Music Hall, Thurs., Jan. 2. Guests: Eleanor Whitney (tap dancer) Cecil B. DeMille (director) Ruggero Ricci (vn) Kay Weber, Four Blackbirds Quartet (vcl) Paddy Patterson (bj)

The reviews of that first show in the trade press were anything but complimentary. The main criticism seemed to center around the format and pacing of the show, as well as the show's boring patter. As a result, the producers quickly brought in writer Carrol Carrol and the script improved. The *Variety* reviewer (January 8, 1936, 34) also bemoaned that Jimmy's band wasn't given sufficient time on the show. On the other hand, *Billboard* (January 11, 1936, 8) was a little kinder to the revised "Hall," noting that the main problem with the first outing was that there were too many acts on the show. The reviewer also sagely observed that

329

Jimmy Dorsey's Orchestra played in the style of the Dorsey Brothers.

On Wednesday, January 8, 1936, the band succeeded Joe Venuti's group and began a full-blown stay at the Palomar Ballroom, at Vermont and Second Avenues in Los Angeles, where Benny Goodman had made swing music history four months earlier.

Jimmy would remain at the Palomar until April 14, thanks in part to the club's management failing to complete a deal with Ted FioRito's band (*Billboard,* March 28, 1936, 13).

This work for Jimmy was worlds apart from the experiences of Tommy, who a decade later called the winter of 1935-1936 a long five months of freezing in a bus, playing one-nighters and hearing the Crosby program, with Jimmy out in California soaking up the sunshine.

On January 9, Jimmy's old pal Joe Venuti visited the Kraft show. Surviving recorded parts show how stilted Bing was in those early days.

Kraft Music Hall, NBC Studios, Hollywood, Cal.—
NBC-Red, 7:00-8:00 P.M. PST, Thursday, January 9,
1936
JIMMY DORSEY AND HIS ORCHESTRA
Bing Crosby (host,vcl) Bob Burns (comedian) Guests: Mischa Levitski (p) Joe Venuti (vn) author Rupert Hughes, The Clark Sisters (vcl grp) Radio Rogues (comedy imitations)

> **Where The Blue of The Night Meets The Gold Of The Day** [Roy Turk, Bing Crosby, Fred E. Ahlert] (theme) / **Pardon Me, Pretty Baby (Don't I Look Familiar To You)** [Raymond W. Klages, Jack Meskill, Vincent Rose] (JV,vn) / (background music, intro to Rupert Hughes) / **Some Of These Days** [Shelton Brooks] vBC (cl solo) / **Ida, Sweet As Apple Cider** [Eddie Leonard] (Bob Burns, "Bazooka") / **Rock and Roll** [Sidney Claire; Richard A. Whiting] vCS (rhythm section only) / **When I Grow Up** [Edward Heyman; Ray Henderson] vCS / unknown piano solo (ML,p) / **Dorsey Dervish (Waddlin' At The Waldorf)** [Larry Clinton] (as solo) / (unknown background music for Radio Rogues) / **With All My Heart** [Gus Kahn; Jimmy McHugh] vBC / **Where The Blue Of The Night** (theme)
> "Some Of These Days," "With All My Heart" on **LP:** Spokane 14

Beginning January 16, Jimmy's female vocalist, Kay Weber, became a regular participant on Bing's program. For obvious reasons, Bob Eberle got no exposure on the show. The few male guest singers during the next two seasons were usually of the concert or operatic variety.

Kraft Music Hall, Thurs., Jan. 16. Guests: John Barrymore (actor) Nina Koshetz (soprano) Radio Rogues (comedy) Park Sisters, Kay Weber, Roberts Brothers (vcl) Raphael (concertina)
Kraft Music Hall, Thurs., Jan. 23. Guests: Joe E. Brown (comedian) Park Sisters, Kay Weber (vcl) Percy Grainger
Kraft Music Hall, Thurs., Jan. 30. Guests: Nina Koshetz (soprano) Park Sisters, Kay Weber, Dixie Dunbar (vcl) Leopold Stokowski (conductor)
Kraft Music Hall, Thurs., Feb. 6. Guests: Josef Lhevinne (p) Marina Shubert (soprano) Kay Weber, Cleo Brown (vcl) Walter Huston (actor)

Kraft Music Hall, Thurs., Feb. 13. Guests: Alice Faye, Vi Bradley, Kay Weber (vcl) Andres Segovia (g) Spencer Tracy (actor)
Kraft Music Hall, Thurs., Feb. 20. Guests: Charles Ruggles (comedian) Leonard Pennario (p) Kay Weber (vcl) Dorothy Wade (vn)
Kraft Music Hall, Thurs., Feb. 27. Guests: Lotte Lehman (soprano) Ann Sothern, Kay Weber (vcl)

Kay Weber's name does not appear on the Kraft show during March. Whether this indicates her absence, perhaps on vacation, or merely a failure on the part of the show's publicists to include her name is unknown.

Kraft Music Hall, Thurs., Mar. 5. Guests: Jack Oakie (comedian) Alexander Brailowsky (p) Marina Schubert (soprano) Wini Shaw (vcl)
Kraft Music Hall, Thurs., Mar. 12. Guests: Patsy Kelly (comedienne) Owen Davis, (playwright)
Kraft Music Hall, Thurs., Mar. 19. Guests: Lyda Roberti (comedienne) Fred, Dorothy, Paula Stone (actor, actresses) Emanuel Fuerhman (cello)
Kraft Music Hall, Thurs., Mar. 26. Guests: Grete Stueckgold (soprano) Virginia Bruce(actress) Jean Hersholt (actor)

Decca, Los Angeles, Cal. Saturday, March 28, 1936
JIMMY DORSEY AND HIS ORCHESTRA
Jimmy Dorsey (cl,as,ldr) George Thow (tp) Toots Camarata (tp,arr) Bobby Byrne, Don Matteson, Joe Yukl (tb) Dave Matthews (as,ts) Fud Livingston (cl,as,arr) Skeets Herfurt (ts,vcl) Jack Stacey (ts) Bobby Van Eps (p) Roc Hillman (g,vcl) Slim Taft (sb) Ray McKinley (d) Kay Weber, Bob Eberle, Trio (Camarata, Byrne, Hillman) (vcl) Larry Clinton, Pat McCarthy (arr)

DLA-312-A   **'Tain't No Use** [Herb Magidson; Burton Lane] vTrio
      78: Decca 808, Brunswick (E) O2128
      LP: Ajax LP103
DLA-313-A   **Welcome Stranger** vKW (cl solo)
      78: Decca 768, Brunswick (E) O2237
      LP: Ajax LP103
DLA-314-A   **Serenade To Nobody In Particular** [Pat McCarthy, Jimmy Dorsey] (arrPM) (as solos)
      78: Decca 1040, Brunswick (E) O2373
      LP: Ajax LP103, Bandstand BS7104, Living Era (E) ASV 5052
      CD: Living Era (E) ASV 5052
DLA-315-A   **Robins and Roses** [Edgar Leslie; Joe Burke] vKW (as solo)
      78: Decca 776, Brunswick (E) O2226, (F) A-81038, (South Africa) SA-1087
      LP: Ajax LP103
DLA-316-A   **Sing, Sing, Sing** [Louis Prima] vTC,BB,RH&band (as solo)
      78: Decca 776, Brunswick (E) O2274
      LP: Ajax LP114, Coral (G) COPS7449, 6.28219
      All five sides also on **TC:** Radio Yesteryear Stack 59

Decca, Los Angeles, Cal. Sunday, March 29, 1936
JIMMY DORSEY AND HIS ORCHESTRA

DLA-317-A   **You Never Looked So Beautiful** vBE (as solo)
    78: Decca 764, (Au) X-1151, Brunswick (E) O2240
    LP: Ajax LP114, Joyce LP6038
DLA-318-A   **Wah-Hoo!** [Cliff Friend] vTC,BB&RH (as,cl solos)
    78: Decca 762, Brunswick (E) O2188
    LP: Ajax LP114
DLA-319-A   **Is It True What They Say About Dixie?** [Irving
                   Caesar, Sammy Lerner; Gerald Marks] vBE (cl solo)
    78: Decca 768, Brunswick (E) O2188, (F) A-81038
    LP: Ajax LP114, Joyce LP6038
    DLA-317 to DLA-319 also on **TC:** Radio Yesteryear Stack 59
DLA-320-A   **I'll Stand By** [Benny Davis; J. Fred Coots] vKW
    78: Brunswick (E) O2225
DLA-321-A   **What's The Reason (I'm Not Pleasin' You?)** [Coy
                   Poe, Jimmie Greer, Truman "Pinky" Tomlin, Earl
                   Hatch] (cl solos)
    78: Decca 764, 32108, Brunswick (E) O2274
    LP: Ajax LP114
    TC: Radio Yesteryear Stack 33, 59
    CD: Kaz (E) 309

   "What's The Reason" was a cornball take-off on what was in itself a
corny tune. Jimmy's "solos" include imitations of laughter and tricky
obbligatos hiding in the guise of amateurism. It's an example of the fun
things that Jimmy sometimes used to ease the tensions in the band.

Kraft Music Hall, Thurs., Apr. 2. Guests: Albert Spalding (vn) Binnie Barnes (actress)

Decca, Los Angeles, Cal. Friday, April 3, 1936
JIMMY DORSEY AND HIS ORCHESTRA
Bill Thorpe (g) for Hillman. Bob Eberle, Seger Ellis, Ginger Rogers
(vcl)

DLA-332-B   **You** [Harold Adamson; Walter Donaldson] vBE (cl
                   solo)
    78: Decca 764, (Au) X-1151, Brunswick (E) 02240
    LP: Ajax LP114, TQ (E) 153
DLA-333-A,B   **I Want To Be Discovered (By You)** vSE (unissued)
DLA-334-A   **It's No Fun** [Milton Ager, Murray Mencher, Charles
                   Newman] vSE (as solo)
    78: Decca 782, (Au) X-1158, Brunswick (E) O2237
        as JIMMY DORSEY AND HIS SEGER ELLIS [sic]
DLA-335-A   **I'm Putting All My Eggs In One Basket** [Irving
                   Berlin] vGR
    78: Decca (E) F-5963, (Au) X-1126
        *as GINGER ROGERS accompanied by Jimmy Dorsey and
        His Orchestra*
DLA-336-A   **Let Yourself Go** [Irving Berlin] vGR
    78: Decca (E) F-5963, (Au) X-1126

(top) Don Murray and Jimmy Dorsey clown for the camera during a 1926 photo session with the Jean Goldkette band at the Victor Studios in New York City. **(bottom)** The Dorsey Brothers arranging team is shown at NBC in mid-September 1934 while between jobs at Sands Point Beach Club and Ben Marden's Riviera Club. Standing are Bernie Mayer, Joe Glover and Herb Spencer. Bobby Van Eps is at the piano, Glenn Miller leans at right (both photos-Duncan Sheidt collection).

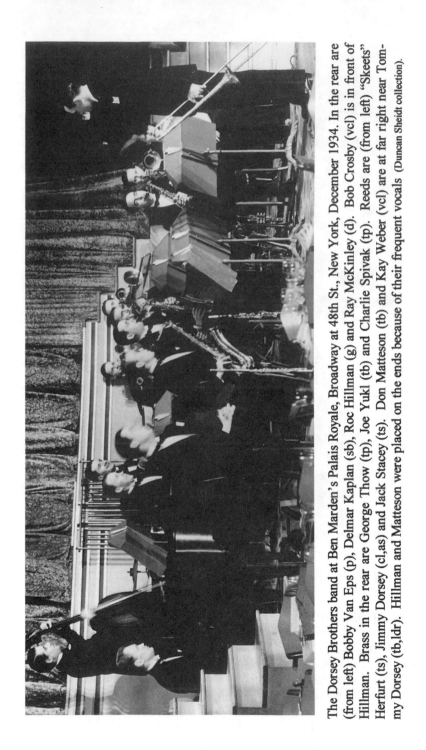

The Dorsey Brothers band at Ben Marden's Palais Royale, Broadway at 48th St., New York, December 1934. In the rear are (from left) Bobby Van Eps (p), Delmar Kaplan (sb), Roc Hillman (g) and Ray McKinley (d). Bob Crosby (vcl) is in front of Hillman. Brass in the rear are George Thow (tp), Joe Yukl (tb) and Charlie Spivak (tp). Reeds are (from left) "Skeets" Herfurt (ts), Jimmy Dorsey (cl,as) and Jack Stacey (ts). Don Matteson (tb) and Kay Weber (vcl) are at far right near Tommy Dorsey (tb,ldr). Hillman and Matteson were placed on the ends because of their frequent vocals (Duncan Sheidt collection).

Shown is the Jimmy Dorsey Orchestra, which worked the Bing Crosby *Kraft Music Hall* Show in Hollywood, January 1936 to July 1937. In the rear row from left are (seated) Bobby Byrne, Joe Yulk, Don Matteson (tb) and George Thow (tp); (standing) Roc Hillman (g), Ray McKinley (d), Slim Taft (sb) and Bobby Van Eps (p). Reeds seated at front, right, are Fud Livingston (cl,as), Jack Stacey and "Skeets" Herfurt (ts). Standing at center are Bob Eberly (vcl) (who never appeared on the show), comedian Bob "Bazooka" Burns, Kay Weber (vcl) and Jimmy Dorsey (Duncan Sheidt collection).

(top) Louis Armstrong and Jimmy Dorsey pose a gag shot, swapping instruments during the August 1936 filming of Bing Crosby's *Pennies From Heaven* (Duncan Sheidt collection). **(bottom)** Helen O'Connell, dressed "college style," sings the sensuous lyrics to "Green Eyes" at the University of North Carolina, Chapel Hill, June 6 or 7, 1941, and Jimmy keeps an eye on the boys in the crowd (Walter Scott collection).

(top) Jimmy smiles admiringly at the tenor sax solo that Herbie Haymer is belting out at the Strand Theater in New York during a three-week stand in June 1940 (photo by Walter Scott, used by permission). **(middle)** The Queen and King of any stage in the early forties. Jimmy proudly introduces his two vocal stars, Helen O'Connell and Bob Eberly (Duncan Sheidt collection). **(bottom)** Shown is the Original Dorseyland Jazz Band c. 1950. From left are Cutty Cutshall (tb), Frank Maynes (ts) Jimmy Dorsey (cl) and Charlie (Little "T") Teagarden (tp) (rear) Bill Lolatte (sb), Ray Bauduc (d) (Duncan Sheidt collection).

In the top photo, caught by Duncan Sheidt in May 1953 at the Indiana Roof Ballroom, Indianapolis, Ind., Jimmy has just rejoined Tommy. From left: Lee Castle (tp), Tommy Dorsey (tb), Buzzy Brauner (ts), Bob Carter (p), Billy Cronk (sb) and Jimmy Dorsey (cl) (photo © Duncan Sheidt. Used by permission). **(bottom)** The Tommy Dorsey Orchestra Featuring Jimmy Dorsey is pictured "north of the border up Canada way." The exact location is unknown, but personnel shown place the photo as the summer of 1953 (Duncan Sheidt collection).

It's late September 1953 at the Hotel Syracuse, Syracuse, N.Y., where to meet a dead line, the Dorseys taped voice and musical tracks for a 1954 March of Dimes radio program. **(top)** Tommy and Jimmy duet on Jackie Gleason's Emmy Award-winning "Melancholy Serenade." **(below)** Jimmy directs the band while Lynn Roberts interprets "Green Eyes" (both photos from author's collection).

(top) Pat Dorsey Hooker, Tommy's daughter by his first marriage, visits her dad and uncle backstage at the Mosque Theater, Richmond, Va., on March 31, 1954.

(center) Jimmy and Tommy Dorsey flank pal Jackie Gleason backstage at CBS-TV Studio 50 in New York during a 1954 *Stage Show.*

(left) New York's Hotel Statler was the location for the fifty-first birthday celebration for Tommy on November 19, 1956. Helping are Mom Dorsey and Jimmy, neither of whom suspected this would be Tommy's last birthday (all from Walter Scott collection).

> *as GINGER ROGERS accompanied by Jimmy Dorsey and*
> *His Orchestra*
> LP: Ace Of Hearts (E) AH-67

The last two songs in the previous session were from the Ginger Rogers-Fred Astaire RKO movie *Follow The Fleet*.

Recording sessions and the nightly work at the Palomar were all that kept Bob Eberle busy during early 1936. For Kay Weber there were also the spots on *Kraft Music Hall*, but otherwise little else. With so much time to kill, Bob and Kay did some dating, but a romance between the two never seemed to blossom.

It was nevertheless a time of wonder for Eberle because most of the band's arrangements were being done with Bing Crosby in mind, and Bing was Bob's lifelong idol. He admitted he got a great thrill from singing the Crosby charts at the Palomar and the band's other dance dates. Five years later, Crosby would call Eberle the best male vocalist around.

Though he wasn't on *Kraft Music Hall* Eberle attended all the rehearsals and was often something of a tension-breaker with his quick wit. Eberle later revealed that several of his ad-lib remarks were used by Bob Burns on the show (Simon 1974.)

Decca, Los Angeles, Cal. Saturday, April 4, 1936
JIMMY DORSEY AND HIS ORCHESTRA
Don Matteson, Seger Ellis (vcl)

DLA-341-A   **I Love To Sing-A** [E. Y. Harburg; Harold Arlen]
                       vDM (as solo)
   78: Decca 808, Brunswick (E) O2292
   LP: Ajax LP114, Living Era (E) ASV 5052
   CD: Living Era (E) ASV 5052
DLA-342-A   **Moonrise On The Lowlands** [Al J. Neiberg; Jerry
                       Livingston] vSE
   78: Decca 782, (Au) X-1158
      as JIMMY DORSEY & HIS ORCH. with SEGER ELLIS

Kraft Music Hall, Thurs., Apr. 9. Guests: Rudolph Ganz (p) Ernestine Schumann-Heink (soprano) Joan Crawford (actress)

Jimmy and the band closed their three-and-a-half-month stay at the Palomar Ballroom on Tuesday, April 14, and were replaced by Dick Jurgens' Orchestra.

Kraft Music Hall, Thurs., Apr. 16. Guests: Zazu Pitts (comedienne) Ephrem Zimbalist (vn) Maxine Lewis, Paul Taylor Choristers (vcl)
Kraft Music Hall, Thurs., Apr. 23. Guests: Grete Stueckgold (soprano) Fred Keating (comedian) Fritz Leiber (actor)

Kay Weber tired of the "easy life" about this time and returned to the East Coast for a job with her former coworker Bob Crosby and The Bob-Cats. She soon married Crosby's (later Tommy's) trombonist Ward Silloway (Sanford 1972).

Kraft Music Hall, Thurs., May 7. Guests: Toscha Seidel (vn) George Raft (actor) Una
Merkel (actress)
Kraft Music Hall, Thurs., May 14. Guests: program scheduled but guests unknown
Kraft Music Hall, Thurs., May 21. Guests: Mischa Levitsky (p) Avalon Boys (vcl)
Frank Morgan (actor)
Kraft Music Hall, Thurs., May 28. Guests: Rose Braynton (contralto) Dr. John Ersk-
ine (p) Bette Davis (actress)

Billboard (May 30, 1936, 13) said that the Dorsey band was playing
one-nighters along the West Coast, but it included no details.

Since Bing's show only required two days a week from the band, it
was able to pick up a heavy schedule of one-nighters, which became the
start of Bob Eberle's grooming as a romantic baritone able to attract the
female teenagers to the road appearances.

Meanwhile, *Variety* (June 3, 1936, 36) reported that the Kraft-Phenix
cheese people had picked up the band's option until the end of 1936.

Kraft Music Hall, Thurs., June 4. Guests: Feodor Chaliapin (basso) Norma Talmadge,
George Jessell in sketch from *June Bride,* Edith Fellows (child actresses), Jackie Searle
(child actor)
Kraft Music Hall, Thurs., June 11. Guests: Ernest Hutchinson (p) Bert Wheeler (comedian) Virginia Bruce (vcl)

In its June 24, 1936, issue (page 36) *Variety* observed that Jack Kapp,
the president of Decca Records, was in Chicago and would soon drive
west to Hollywood for recording sessions with Bing Crosby, Victor
Young, Jimmy Dorsey and others, again demonstrating Kapp's "hands-
on" managerial style.

Kraft Music Hall, Thurs., June 25. Guests: Toscha Seidel (vn) Bert Wheeler (come-
dian) Jean Arthur (actress)
Kraft Music Hall, Thurs., July 2. Guests: Toscha Seidel (vn) Frank Morgan (actor)
Martha Raye (comedienne) Frances Farmer (actress)

Seeing the need for a new theme to replace "Sandman," carried over
from the Dorsey Brothers' days, Jimmy had "Toots" Camarata write
"Hollywood Pastime" featuring himself on clarinet, as the new signature
piece. The band recorded two rejected takes at the next session.
However, Jimmy soon dropped exclusive use of "Hollywood Pastime"
and developed a medley of "Beebe," "Sandman" and "Pastime" for his
personal and non-Kraft air appearances.

At the time, Jimmy was attempting to establish himself as a clarinet-
playing leader, but later, in the face of stiff Benny Goodman-Artie Shaw
competition, he wisely changed his emphasis to the alto.

At the same session, under the watchful eye of Decca head Jack
Kapp, Jimmy cut one of his most successful band instrumentals, "Parade
Of The Milk Bottle Caps."

Decca, Los Angeles, Cal. Tuesday, July 7, 1936
JIMMY DORSEY AND HIS ORCHESTRA
Roc Hillman (g) replaces Thorpe. Pat McCarthy (arr) added to staff.
Trio (Toots Camarata, Bobby Byrne, Hillman) (vcl)

DLA-419-A   **Ah-Woo!, Ah-Woo! To You** vTrio (as solo)
     78: Decca 873, Brunswick (E) O2282
     LP: Ajax LP114
DLA-420-A,B   **Hollywood Pastime** (theme) (unissued)
DLA-421-A   **There's No Substitute For You** vTrio (as solo)
     78: Decca 873, Brunswick (E) O2282
     LP: Ajax LP114, Coral (G) COPS7449, 6.28219
DLA-422-A   **Funiculi, Funicula** [traditional Italian folk song] (as
                   solo)
     78: Decca 1086, Brunswick (E) O2364
     LP: Ajax LP114
DLA-423-A   **Parade Of The Milk Bottle Caps** [Pat McCarthy;
                   Jimmy Dorsey] (arrPM) (as solo)
     78: Decca 941, 3334 (in set A-135), Coral 60063, 56008,
     Brunswick (E) O2322
     (SSL-3933-1) **ET:** AFRS Basic Music Library P-1945
     LP: Decca DL(7)4853, Coral (G) COPS7449, 6.28219, Brunswick
     (G) 87095, MCA 2-4073, Time-Life STB-B10, Ajax LP114
     TC: Time-Life 4TL-0006
     CD: Time-Life 4TL-0006, GRP-Decca GRD-626, Kaz (E) 309

Kraft Music Hall, Thurs., July 9. Guests: Bert Wheeler (comedian) Jean Arthur (actress) Henri Deering (p)
Kraft Music Hall, Thurs., July 16. Guests: Rose Brampton (contralto) Robert Taylor (actor) Marjorie Gateson (actress)

Decca, Los Angeles, Cal. Friday, July 17, 1936
BING CROSBY with JIMMY DORSEY AND HIS ORCHESTRA
Bing Crosby, quartet (Camarata, Byrne, Hillman, Livingston) (vcl)

DLA-440-A   **I Can't Escape From You** [Leo Robin; Richard A.
                   Whiting] vBC (cl solo)
     78: Decca 871, 11009, (Au) Y-5108, Brunswick (E) 02285,
     02926
     LP: Decca DL(7)-4251, DL-6010, Brunswick BING-2, LA-8726
DLA-441-A   **The House Jack Built For Jill** vBC (as solo)
     78: Decca 905, (Au) Y-5126, Brunswick (E) 02285
DLA-441-B   **The House Jack Built For Jill** vBC (as solo)
     78: Decca 11009
     LP: Decca DL(7)-4251, DL-6010, Brunswick BING-2, LA-8726,
     Columbia B-1521, CL-2502, Fontana (E) TFR-6000, Z-4027,
     662009-TR, 687127-YZL
DLA-442-A   **I'm An Old Cow Hand (From The Rio Grande)**
                   [Johnny Mercer] vBC, quartet (cl solo)
     78: Decca 871, 2679, 11008, 25001, (Au) Y-5108, Coral 60093,
     91119, Brunswick (E) O2270, O2925, (F) A-81056
     LP: Decca BM-1151, DL-4006, DL(7)-4251, DL-5107, DL-6010,
     DL-8210, DL-34002, DXB-7184, Brunswick BING-2, LA-8726,
     LAT-8152, LAT-8368
     CD: Living Era (E) ASV 5160, ASV 5175, Pearl 9739, Radio
     Years (It) 32, Flapper (E) CD 7094, 9739

Appearing on Bing Crosby's show served as an entree to movie work, much of it "off-screen." Jimmy and parts of the band are heard on the soundtrack of 1937's *That Girl From Paris* but get no screen credit.

RKO Studios, Hollywood, Cal. Summer 1936
THAT GIRL FROM PARIS: Leigh Jason, director
JIMMY DORSEY AND HIS ORCHESTRA (in various combinations)
Jack Oakie, Lily Pons, Gene Raymond, Frank Jenks (vcl) "Fud" Livingston (arr)

Auld Lang Syne [traditional] (cl solo)/ **Love and Learn** [Edward Heyman; Arthur Schwartz] vJO (cl solo) / **Moonface** [Heyman; Schwartz] vJO (as solo) / **Blue Danube** [Johann Strauss] arrFL, vLP (cl solos) / **Our Nephew From Nice** [Heyman; Schwartz] vGR, FJ,JO&Band
All selections in **FILM:** RKO *That Girl From Paris*

The July 23 *Kraft Music Hall* was preempted for a speech by Kansas Governor Alfred M. Landon accepting the Republican presidential nomination. This gave the band a chance to go into the Decca studios for some sides. Bob Eberle, however, was back in the East on vacation.

Decca, Los Angeles, Cal. Thursday, July 23, 1936
JIMMY DORSEY AND HIS ORCHESTRA
Toots Camarata (arr) Trio (Byrne, Matteson, Hillman) (vcl)

DLA-454-A   **Don't Look Now** vTrio (as solo)
    78: Decca 941, Brunswick (E) O2322
    LP: Ajax LP114
DLA-455-A   **It Ain't Right** vDM (as solo)
    78: Decca 901, Brunswick (E) O2334
    LP: Ajax LP114
DLA-456-A   **The Boston Tea Party** vDM&Trio (as solo)
    78: Decca 901, Brunswick (E) O2334
    LP: Ajax LP114, Coral (G) COPS7449, 6.28219
DLA-457-A   **Mutiny In The Brass Section** [Toots Camarata]
        arrTC (as solo)
    78: Decca 1256
    LP: Ajax LP117, Swingfan (G) 1007, Bandstand BS7104
DLA-458-A   **Hollywood Pastime** [Toots Camarata] (theme) arrTC
        (cl solo)
    78: Decca 1200
    LP: Ajax LP117, Swingfan (G) 1007, Bandstand BS7104

For an excellent example of the contribution Bobby Byrne's trombone was making to Jimmy's band, listen to "In A Sentimental Mood," recorded next. As an extra, Jimmy records two now fairly scarce sides with Bing's wife Dixie Lee.

Decca, Los Angeles, Cal. Monday, July 27, 1936
JIMMY DORSEY AND HIS ORCHESTRA
Dixie Lee Crosby (vcl)

DLA-467-A   **When A Lady Meets A Gentleman Down South**
                   [Michael Cleary, Jacques Krakeur, David Oppen-
                   heim] vDLC
   78: Decca 892
       as DIXIE LEE CROSBY ACCOMPANIED BY JIMMY
       DORSEY AND HIS ORCHESTRA
DLA-468-A   **(It Will Have To Do) Until The Real Thing Comes**
                   Along [Mann Holiner, Alberta Nichols, Sammy
                   Cahn, Saul Chaplin, L. E. Freeman] vDLC
   78: Decca 892
       as DIXIE LEE CROSBY ACCOMPANIED BY JIMMY
       DORSEY AND HIS ORCHESTRA
DLA-469-A   **In A Sentimental Mood** [Manny Kurtz, Irving Mills;
                   Edward K. "Duke" Ellington] (as solo)
   78: Decca 882, Brunswick (E) O2354, (F) A-81162
   LP: Bandstand BS7120, Coral (G) COPS7449, 6.28219, Ajax
   LP117, Living Era (E) ASV 5052
   CD: Living Era (E) ASV 5052, GRP-Decca CD-GRP-626, Aero
   Space AS7120, Kaz (E) 309
DLA-470-A   **Stompin' At The Savoy** [Andy Razaf; Benny Good-
                   man, Chick Webb, Edgar Sampson] (as solo)
   78: Decca 882, BM-1073, Brunswick (E) O2354, Polydor (It) A-
   61090
   LP: Bandstand BS7120, Coral (G) COPS7449, 6.28219, Swingfan
   (G) 1007, Ajax LP117, Living Era (E) ASV 5052
   CD: Living Era (E) ASV 5052, GRP-Decca CD-GRP-626, Aero
   Space AS7120
DLA-471-A,B   **Chicken Reel** (unissued)

Kraft Music Hall, Thurs., July 30. Guests: Albert Spalding (vn) Dolores Costello Barrymore (actress) Vera Van, Paul Taylor Chorus (vcl)

A "sports" note made the "Bands and Orchestras" section of *Billboard*
(August 1, 1936, 20), revealing for all to see that Jimmy had shot a
hole-in-one at golf that week.
    Though not mentioned in the story, in all probability the feat was
performed at Jimmy's club, the Lakeside.

Decca, Los Angeles, Cal. Monday, August 3, 1936
JIMMY DORSEY AND HIS ORCHESTRA
Frances Langford, Bob Eberle (vcl)

DLA-508-A   **Easy To Love** [Cole Porter] vFL (as solo)
   78: Decca 940, (Au) X-1215, Brunswick (E) O2359, (F) A-
   81118
       as FRANCES LANGFORD with Jimmy Dorsey and His
       Orchestra
   CD: Happy Days (E) 204, ASV Living Era (E) 5219
DLA-509-A   **Rap-Tap On Wood** [Cole Porter] vFL (cl solo)
   78: Decca 939, (Au) X-1213, Brunswick (E) O2358 (F) A-81117
   LP: Living Era (E) ASV 5052, 5219
                             (Contd.)

JIMMY DORSEY AND HIS ORCHESTRA (Contd.)

>   *as FRANCES LANGFORD with Jimmy Dorsey and His*
>   *Orchestra*
>   **TC:** ProArte Digital PCD485
>   **CD:** ProArte Digital CDD485, Living Era (E) ASV 5052
> DLA-510-A   **So Do I** [Johnny Burke; Arthur Johnston] vBE
>   (as solo)
>   **78:** Decca 950, (Au) X-1217, Brunswick (E) O2319
>   **LP:** Ajax LP117, Joyce LP6038
>   **CD:** Empress (E) 817
> DLA-511-A   **One, Two, Button Your Shoe** [Johnny Burke; Ar-
>   thur Johnston] vBE (as solo)
>   **78:** Decca 951, Brunswick (E) O2319
>   **LP:** Ajax LP117, Joyce LP6038

Many jazz and swing fans are quick to criticize Jimmy for the abundance of "Mickey Mouse" recordings in his Decca files. These can be attributed to Jimmy's longtime respect for Decca President Jack Kapp, coupled with Jimmy's tendency to go along with other's ideas as long as it didn't "hurt the band." One of Kapp's tenets was to cater to the masses (much as today's television executives) and he often insisted on brassy, novel arrangements that would do well on juke boxes.

Decca, Los Angeles, Cal. Tuesday, August 4, 1936
JIMMY DORSEY AND HIS ORCHESTRA
Bob Eberle, Bing Crosby (vcl) Larry Clinton (arr)

DLA-518-A   **Chicken Reel** [traditional] (cl solo)
          78: Decca 1086, Brunswick (E) O2364
          LP: Coral (G) COPS7449, 6.28219, Ajax LP117
DLA-519-A   **Pennies From Heaven** [Johnny Burke; Arthur Johns-
                    ton] vBE (cl solo)
          78: Decca 951, Brunswick (E) O2318
          LP: Ajax LP117, Joyce LP6038, Living Era (E) ASV 5052
          CD: Living Era (E) ASV 5052
DLA-520-A   **Dorsey Dervish** (aka **Waddlin' At The Waldorf**)
                    [Larry Clinton] (arrLC) (as solo)
          78: Decca 1040, Brunswick (E) O2373
          LP: Coral (G) COPS7449, 6.28219, Bandstand BS7104, Swingfan
          (G) 1007, Ajax LP117, Living Era (E) ASV 5052
          CD: Living Era (E) ASV 5052
DLA-521-A   **Shoe Shine Boy** [Sammy Cahn; Saul Chaplin]
                    vBC (as solo)
          78: Decca 905, 3601, Brunswick (E) O2272, O3080
                    as BING CROSBY accomp. by Jimmy Dorsey & His Orch.
          LP: Decca BM30766, Y-5124
DLA-521-B   **Shoe Shine Boy** vBC (as solo)
          78: Decca 91612
                    as BING CROSBY accomp. by Jimmy Dorsey & His Orch.
          LP: Decca DL-8142, Ace Of Hearts (E) AH1, Festival (EC) FGL-
          12-967/3, Columbia B-1521, CL-2502, Fontana (It) TFR-6000, Z-

4027, 662009-TR, 687127-YZL

Kraft Music Hall, Thurs., Aug. 6. Guests: Ernest Hutcheson (p) Robert Taylor (actor)
Ann Sothern (actress)

Decca, Los Angeles, Cal. Friday, August 7, 1936
JIMMY DORSEY AND HIS ORCHESTRA
Frances Langford, Bob Eberle (vcl)

DLA-537-A   **I've Got You Under My Skin** [Cole Porter] vFL
    78: Decca 939, (Au) X-1213, Brunswick (E) O2358
        as FRANCES LANGFORD with Jimmy Dorsey and His Orch.
    TC: ProArte Digital PCD548, Radio Yesteryear Stack 62
    CD: ProArte Digital CDD548
DLA-538-A   **Let's Call A Heart A Heart** [Johnny Burke; Ar-
                thur Johnston] vBE (cl,as solos)
    78: Decca 950, (Au) X-1217, Brunswick (E) O2318
    LP: Ajax LP117, Joyce LP6038, Living Era (E) ASV 5052
    CD: Living Era (E) ASV 5052

Decca, Los Angeles, Cal. Friday, August 7, 1936
LOUIS ARMSTRONG with Jimmy Dorsey and His Orchestra
Jimmy Dorsey (cl,as,ldr) Louis Armstrong (tp,vcl) George Thow, Toots
Camarata (tp) Bobby Byrne, Joe Yukl (tb) Jack Stacey (cl,as) Fud
Livingston, Skeets Herfurt (cl,ts) Bobby Van Eps (p), Roc Hillman (g)
Slim Taft (sb) Ray McKinley (d)

DLA-539-A   **The Skeleton In The Closet (The Skeleton In The
                Cupboard*)** [Johnny Burke; Arthur Johnston] vLA
    78: Decca 949, (E) F-6145*, Brunswick (G) A-81135*, (F) A-
    505073, Fonit 1605, Polydor (It) A-61082
    LP: Decca DL9225, (F) 6145, Swaggie (Au) JCS33784, 702,
    Coral (G) COPS7239
DLA-540-A   **When Ruben Swings The Cuban** vLA (as solo)
    78: Decca 1049, (E) F-6324
    LP: Swaggie (Au) JCS33784, 702, MCA 1322, Coral (G)
    COPS7239
DLA-541-A   **Hurdy-Gurdy Man** [Sammy Cahn, Sam Chaplin] vLA
                (cl solo)
    78: Decca 949, (E) F-6145, Brunswick (G) A-81135, (F) A-
    505073, Fonit 1605, Polydor (It) A-61082
    LP: Swaggie (Au) JCS33784, 702, MCA 1322
DLA-542-A   **Dipper Mouth Blues (**aka **Sugarfoot Stomp)** [Joseph
                "King" Oliver, Louis Armstrong] (cl solo)
    78: Decca 906, 3796, 25155, (E) F-6202, Brunswick (E)
    OE9190, (G) A-81095, A-82503, Fonit 1606, Polydor (It) A-
    61083
    LP: Decca DL 5225, DL8284, Swaggie (Au) 702, MCA 1322,
    Coral (G) COPS7239, COPS1006
    CD: ABC CD-36200
    all sides also on **CD:** Kaz (E) 309
        as JIMMY DORSEY AND HIS ORCHESTRA (Contd.)

JIMMY DORSEY AND HIS ORCHESTRA (Contd.)

DLA-543-A   **Swing That Music** [Horace Gerlach; Louis Arm-
          strong] vLA
    78: Decca 866, 3105
    LP: Swaggie (Au) JCS33784, 702, MCA 1322
    CD: Kaz (E) 309

The explanation for the change in title on the English Decca and German Brunswick releases of "Skeleton In The Closet" was to avoid confusion. In parts of Europe "cupboard" equals a small room for clothes while "closet" is short for "water closet" (or "w.c."), which is equivalent to "toilet" in the United States.

Louis Armstrong was in Hollywood at the time primarily to be in Columbia's Bing Crosby film *Pennies From Heaven,* in which Jimmy and the band also appeared, along with Madge Evans, ten-year-old Edith Fellows and the aptly named Donald Meek.

Paramount Pictures had loaned the crooner to Columbia Pictures for the movie, which was a little more on the sentimental "family" side than were many of Bing's previous movie efforts. This one showed Bing's more serious nature, which would earn him later Oscar nominations.

Bing had another incentive for making *Pennies From Heaven* successful. It was his first venture into motion-picture production.

Columbia Pictures Studio, Hollywood Cal., August 1936
PENNIES FROM HEAVEN: Norman McLeod, director
JIMMY DORSEY AND HIS ORCHESTRA
Perry Botkin (g) Bing Crosby, Madge Evans, Louis Armstrong (vcl)

    One, Two, Button Your Shoe [Burke; Johnston] vBC
    in **FILM:** Columbia *Pennies From Heaven*

There are other songs on the soundtrack, including the title tune and "Skeleton In The Closet" which features Louis and a black band including Lionel Hampton, but Jimmy does not participate in them.

Decca, Los Angeles, Cal. Wednesday, August 12, 1936
JIMMY DORSEY AND HIS ORCHESTRA
Frances Langford, Bob Eberle (vcl)

DLA-556-A   **Swingin' The Jinx Away** [Cole Porter] vFL
    78: Decca 940, (Au) X-1215, Brunswick (E) O2359, (F) A-
    81118
          *as FRANCES LANGFORD with Jimmy Dorsey and His
          Orchestra*
    LP: Living Era (E) ASV 5052
    CD: Living Era (E) ASV 5052, 5219, Happy Days (E) 204
DLA-557-A   **Pick Yourself Up** [Dorothy Fields; Jimmy McHugh]
          vBE (as solo)
    78: Brunswick (E) 02292
    LP: Living Era (E) ASV 5052
    CD: Living Era (E) ASV 5052

Kraft Music Hall, Thurs., Aug. 13. Guests: Louis Armstrong (tp,vcl) Anita Louise, Alison Skipworth (actresses) Josephine Tumminia (soprano)

In addition to visiting Bing and Jimmy on *Kraft Music Hall,* Louis Armstrong also joined them in the Decca studios four days later.

Decca, Los Angeles, Cal. Monday, August 17, 1936
BING CROSBY, LOUIS ARMSTRONG, FRANCES LANGFORD
with Jimmy Dorsey and His Orchestra
Louis Armstrong (vcl) Bing Crosby, Frances Langford (vcl)

DLA-579-A   **Pennies From Heaven Medley** (part 1) Introducing:
              Let's Call A Heart A Heart vFL; **So Do I**
              vFL&BC; **The Skeleton In The Closet** vLA (bar
              solo) [all by Johnny Burke; Arthur Johnston]
       78: (12-inch) Decca 15027, 29226, Brunswick (E) O134
       LP: Decca DL-4251, 1-737, Coral COPS7239
       CD: ProArte Digital CDD432, GRP-Decca GRP-603, Avid (E)
       AMSC 568, ASV-Living Era (E) 5255
DLA-580-A   **Pennies From Heaven** [Johnny Burke; Arthur Johns-
              ton] (part 2) vFL,BC&LA (as solo)
       78: (12-inch) Decca 15027, 29226, Brunswick (E) O134
       LP: Decca DL-4251, 1-737, Ace Of Hearts (E) AH-139, Coral
       COPS7239, Avid (E) AMSC 568

Kraft Music Hall, Thurs., Aug. 20. Guests: Harold Bauer (p) Dorothy Lamour (vcl) Joan Bennett (actress)

After the August 20 broadcast Bing Crosby took a seven-week vaca-tion in Hawaii, leaving sidekick Bob Burns to handle the emcee chores at the "Hall," with some assistance from Jimmy.

Kraft Music Hall, Thurs., Aug. 27. Bob Burns (comedian, host). Guests: Mary Mc-Cormick, Ella Logan (vcl) Radio Rogues (comedy) Merle Oberon (actress) Pat O'Brien (actor)

On Tuesday, September 1, Jimmy opened a one-month's booking at Sebastian's Cotton Club in Culver City, California. In the heart of the movie production area of Los Angeles, Sebastian's was a favorite hang-out for movie folk. The band played for dancing as well as backing the floor show.

Kraft Music Hall, Thurs., Sept. 3. Bob Burns (comedian, host). Guests: José Iturbi (p) Alice Faye (vcl) Joel McCrea (actor) Olivia De Haviland (actress)
Kraft Music Hall, Thurs., Sept. 10. Bob Burns (comedian, host). Guests: Jack Oakie (actor) Glenda Farrell (actress) Susanne Fisher, Deane Janis (vcl)
Kraft Music Hall, Thurs., Sept. 17. Bob Burns (comedian, host). Guests: Jackie Cooper, Betty Grable (vcl) Mischa Levitsky (p) Guy Kibbee, Hoot Gibson (actors)
Kraft Music Hall, Thurs., Sept. 24. Bob Burns (comedian, host). Guests: Mario Chumlee (tenor) Jack Oakie (comedian) Vera Van (vcl) Anna Sten (actress)
Kraft Music Hall, Thurs., Oct. 1. Bob Burns (comedian, host). Guests: Rudolph Ganz (p) John Barrymore (actor) Billie Burke, Beverly Roberts (actresses)

Kraft Music Hall, Thurs., Oct. 8. Bob Burns (comedian, host). Guests: Carlos Salzedo (harp) Patricia Ellis (vcl) Jean Hersholt (actor) Madeline Carroll (actress)

Bing Crosby returned from his seven-week Hawaiian visit in time for the October 15 show. Bing's vacation had been timed a bit later than the contractual summer vacation periods typical for stars of radio network variety shows at the time. It is believed that this was because the filming for *Pennies From Heaven* ran into late August.

> *Kraft Music Hall,* NBC Studios, Hollywood, Cal.— NBC-Red, 7:00-8:00 P.M. PST, Thursday, October 15, 1936

JIMMY DORSEY AND HIS ORCHESTRA
Bing Crosby (host,vcl) Bob Burns (comedian) Guests: Elizabeth Rethberg (soprano) Ruth Chatterton (actress) Slip Madigan (coach)

One, Two Button Your Shoe [Johnny Burke; Arthur Johnston] vBC (as solo) / **So Do I** [Burke; Johnston] vBC / **Let's Call A Heart A Heart** [Burke; Johnston] vBC (cl solo) (partial contents)
All three selections on **LP:** Spokane 14

Variety (October 21, 1936, 54) in its Disc Reviews column by editor Abel Green called attention to the way in which Decca had gone all out to cover Bing Crosby's *Pennies From Heaven* movie score.

Besides Bing's own release of the title tune and three others backed by George Stoll, Green cited the several releases made by Jimmy Dorsey's band: Decca 950, 951 and the 12-inch 15027 with Bing, Jimmy, Frances Langford and Louis Armstrong.

Calling the releases "a consistently ultra job," Green also pointed out that Decca appeared to be bending over to do right by Crosby, who had a financial interest in the film and was very important to Decca.

Kraft Music Hall, Thurs., Oct. 22. Guests: Josephine Antoine (soprano) Adolphe Menjou (actor) Ann Shirley (actress)
Kraft Music Hall, Thurs., Oct. 29. Guests: Cary Grant (actor) Elissa Landi (actress) Emanuel Feuermann (cello)

In its November 4, 1936, issue *Variety* carried an ad that showed brother Tommy was now also doing well on radio row. The pitch by Raleigh and Kool cigarettes plugged the new Jack Pearl Show "with Cliff Hall and Tommy Dorsey's famous swing orchestra," which would premiere the following Monday on NBC-Blue. Also at this time, Tommy organized Tom-Dor Enterprises with offices in New York to handle his business interests. Joe Herbst was in charge of the office.

Kraft Music Hall, Thurs., Nov. 5. Guests: Bruna Castagna (contralto) Gladys George (actress) Warren Williams (actor)
Kraft Music Hall, Thurs., Nov. 12. Guests: Edmund Lowe (actor) Helen Vinson (actress) Grete Stueckgold (soprano)
Kraft Music Hall, Thurs., Nov. 19. program scheduled but guests unknown
Kraft Music Hall, Thurs., Nov. 26. Guests: Lotte Lehmann (soprano) Rochelle Hudson (actress) Ricardo Cortez (actor)

Bing was absent from the program on December 3 for an unrevealed reason. As in the late summer, Bob Burns took over as host.

Kraft Music Hall Thurs., Dec. 3. Bob Burns (comedian, host). Guests: Gene Raymond (actor) Alice Faye (vcl) Gregor Piatigorsky (cello)
Kraft Music Hall, Thurs., Dec. 10. Guests: Suzanne Fisher (soprano) Bruce Cabot (actor) Anita Louise (actress)

An article in *Variety* (December 16, 1936, 40) reported on its survey of advertising agency talent buyers for network radio programs. The study showed that higher priced big-name dance bands were faced with coming up with new programming ideas to justify using them or risk replacement by lower priced studio orchestras.

The show business weekly listed twenty-two bands, including Jimmy and Tommy Dorsey's groups, among those considered potential program choices that were no longer able to pull listeners on their name strength alone. The piece also noted that the average price paid a name band per week for an air slot was $1,200.

Kraft Music Hall, Thurs., Dec. 17. Guests: Jack Oakie (comedian) Mary Astor (actress) Nadine Connor (vcl)
Kraft Music Hall, Thurs., Dec. 24. Guests: José Iturbi (p) June Travis (actress) Jimmy Gleason (actor)
Kraft Music Hall, Thurs., Dec. 31. Guests: Pat O'Brien (actor) Art Tatum (p) Foursome (vcl grp)
Kraft Music Hall, Thurs., Jan. 7, 1937. Guests: Grete Stueckgold (soprano) Lawson Little (golfer)
Kraft Music Hall, Thurs., Jan. 14. Guests: Patricia Ellis (actress) Edward Everett Horton (comedian) Guiomar Novaes (p)
Kraft Music Hall, Thurs., Jan. 21. Guests: Rose Brampton (contralto) Lee Tracy (actor)

Variety (January 27, 1937, 45) dropped some "inside stuff" that quoted composer Arthur Schwartz as saying that the swing version of the "Blue Danube Waltz," which Lily Pons sang in RKO's *That Girl From Paris,* was arranged by Jimmy Dorsey. Actually the arranger was Fud Livingston.

Kraft Music Hall, Thurs., Jan. 28. Guests. Josephine Tumminia (soprano) Victor McLaglen (actor) Rosalind Marquis (actress)
Kraft Music Hall, Thurs., Feb. 4. Guests: Marion Claire (soprano) Basil Rathbone, William Frawley (actors)
Kraft Music Hall, Thurs., Feb. 11. Guests: Dorothy McNulty (soprano) Edward Everett Horton (comedian) Tascha Seidel (vn)
Kraft Music Hall, Thurs., Feb. 18. Guests: Marion Claire (soprano) Sophie Tucker (vcl)
Kraft Music Hall, Thurs., Feb. 25. Guests: James Cagney (actor) Sidney Skolsky (columnist) Mary Gardner (soprano)

Decca, Los Angeles, Cal. Friday, February 26, 1937
JIMMY DORSEY AND HIS ORCHESTRA
Jimmy Dorsey (cl,as,ldr) Joe Meyer (tp) Toots Camarata (tp,arr) Bobby

JIMMY DORSEY AND HIS ORCHESTRA (Contd.)
Byrne, Don Matteson, Bruce Squires (tb) Len Whitney (as) Fud
Livingston (as,ts,arr) Charles Frazier (ts) Freddy Slack (p) Roc Hillman
(g) Jack Ryan (sb) Ray McKinley (d) Vickie Joyce, Bob Eberle, Bing
Crosby (vcl)

DLA-728-A   **All God's Chillun Got Rhythm** [Bronislaw Kaper,
                Walter Jurmann, Gus Kahn] vVJ (cl solo)
    78: Decca 1256, (Au) Y-5174, Brunswick (E) O2423
    LP: Bandstand BS7104, Ajax LP117
DLA 729-A   **In A Little Hula Heaven** [Leo Robin; Ralph Rainger]
                vBC (cl solo)
    78: Decca 1210, (Au) Y-5153, Brunswick (E) 02443
        as BING CROSBY accomp. by Jimmy Dorsey and His Orch.
    LP: Decca (SA) FM5004
DLA 729-B   **In A Little Hula Heaven** vBC (cl solo)
    78: Decca 11013
        as BING CROSBY accomp. by Jimmy Dorsey and His Orch.
    LP: Decca DL-4253, DL6011, Brunswick BING3, LA8727,
    Columbia (E) B-1521, CL-2502, Fontana (E) TFR-6000, Z-4027,
    662009-TR, 687127-YZL
DLA 730-A   **Never In A Million Years** [Mack Gordon; Harry
                Revel] vBC (as solo)
    78: Decca 1210, Brunswick (E) 02453
        as BING CROSBY accomp. by Jimmy Dorsey and His Orch.

One of the most unusual recordings ever produced by Jimmy was a
twelve-inch Decca with attractive twenty-four-year-old Josephine Tumminia, first soprano of the San Francisco Opera company, who had twice
been a guest on the *Kraft Music Hall.*

Decca, Los Angeles, Cal. Sunday, February 28, 1937
JIMMY DORSEY AND HIS ORCHESTRA
Jimmy Dorsey (cl,as,ldr) Joe Meyer (tp) Bobby Byrne (tb) Fud
Livingston (as,arr) Charles Frazier (ts) Freddy Slack (p) Roc Hillman
(g) Jack Ryan (sb) Ray McKinley (d,vcl) Josephine Tumminia, Vicki
Joyce (vcl) Nat Shilkret (arr)

DLA-731-B   **La Capinera (The Wren)** vJT arrNS (cl solo of
                normally flute obligatto)
    78: (12-inch) Decca 29009, (Au) Z-750, Brunswick (E) O137
    CD: Kaz (E) 309

Bruce Squires, Don Matteson (tb) Len Whitney (as) added:
DLA-732-A   **Listen To The Mocking-Bird** [Norman Berens, Jack
                Brooks] (cl solo)
    78: Decca 1187, Brunswick (E) O2409
    LP: Bandstand BS7104, Coral (G) COPS7449, 6.28219, Swingfan
    (G) 1007, Ajax LP117, Living Era (E) ASV 5052
    CD: Living Era (E) ASV 5052
DLA-733-A   **Just Lately** vVJ (cl solo)
    78: Decca 1301

LP: Ajax LP117
DLA-734-A   **The Love Bug Will Bite You (If You Don't Watch Out)** vRM (unissued)

Decca, Los Angeles, Cal. Wednesday, March 3, 1937
JIMMY DORSEY AND HIS ORCHESTRA
Ray McKinley, Bob Eberle, Bing Crosby (vcl) Toots Camarata (arr)

DLA-735-B   **The Love Bug Will Bite You (If You Don't Watch Out)** [Pinky Tomlin] vRM (as solo)
   78: Decca 1187, Brunswick (E) O2409
   LP: Bandstand BS7104, Time-Life STB-B10, Ajax LP118, Living Era (E) ASV 5052
   TC: Time-Life 4TL-0006
   CD: Time-Life 4TL-0006, Living Era (E) ASV 5052
DLA-736-A   **Jamboree** [Harold Adamson; Jimmy McHugh] vBE (cl solo)
   78: Decca 1200, Brunswick (E) O2423
   LP: Ajax LP118, Joyce LP6038
DLA-737-A   **What Will I Tell My Heart?** [Jack Lawrence, Peter Tinturin, Irving Gordon] vBC
   78: Decca 1185, Brunswick (E) O2402
      as BING CROSBY (accompanied by JIMMY DORSEY AND HIS ORCHESTRA)
DLA-738-A   **Too Marvelous For Words** [Johnny Mercer; Richard A. Whiting] vBC
   78: Decca 1185, 25139, 60164, (Au) Y-5163, Brunswick (E) 02452 (some copies)
      as JIMMY DORSEY AND HIS ORCHESTRA (Vocal Chorus by Bing Crosby)
   LP: Decca DL-5343, Brunswick LA-8624
   CD: Flapper (E) CD 7094, Pearl (E) 7802
DLA-738-B   **Too Marvelous For Words** vBC
   78: Brunswick (E) 02452 (some copies)
      as JIMMY DORSEY AND HIS ORCHESTRA (Vocal Chorus by Bing Crosby)
   LP: Coral CPS-79, Decca BM-30518, Columbia (E) B-1521, CL-2502, Fontana (E) TFR-6000, Z-4027, 662009-TR, 687127-YZL
DLA-739-A   **Peckin'** [Ben Pollack, Harry James] vBC (cl solo)
   78: Decca 1301, Brunswick (E) O2481
      as JIMMY DORSEY AND HIS ORCHESTRA (Vocal Chorus by Bing Crosby)
   LP: Bandstand BS7104
DLA-740-A   **I Got Rhythm** [Ira Gershwin; George Gershwin] arrTC (cl,as solos)
   78: Decca 1508, 3861, (E) M-30085, Brunswick (E) 02481, (F) A-81302
   LP: Coral CRL-56033, Ajax LP118, Ace Of Hearts (E) AH114
   CD: GRP-Decca CD-GRD-626, Kaz (E) 309

"I Got Rhythm" proved to be another of Jimmy's top instrumentals. Charlie Frazier gets his only known recorded tenor solo.

Kraft Music Hall, Thurs., Mar. 4. Guests: Mischa Auer (comedian) Douglas Fairbanks, Jr. (actor)

Kraft Music Hall, Thurs., Mar. 11. Guests: Mary Brian (actress) Lee Tracy (actor) Andres Segovia (g)

Decca, Los Angeles, Cal. Wednesday, March 17, 1937
JIMMY DORSEY AND HIS ORCHESTRA
Josephine Tumminia, Bob Eberle, Don Matteson (vcl) Fud Livingston (arr)

DLA-757-A   **The Blue Danube Waltz** [Johann Straus] arrFL vJT
    78: (12-inch) Decca 29009, (Au) Z-750, Brunswick (E) O137
DLA-758-A   **Slap That Bass** [Ira Gershwin; George Gershwin]
               vBE,band (cl solo)
    78: Decca 1203, (Au) X-1352, Brunswick (E) O2433
    LP: Coral CRL-56033, (G) COPS7449, 6.28219, Bandstand
    BS7120, Ajax LP118, Joyce LP6038, Living Era (E) ASV 5052
    CD: Living Era (E) ASV 5052, Aero Space AS7120
DLA-759-A   **They All Laughed** [Ira Gershwin; George Gershwin]
               vDM (cl solo)
    78: Decca 1204, (Au) X-1352, Brunswick (E) O2434
    LP: Coral CRL-56033, Ajax LP118
DLA-760-A   **They Can't Take That Away From Me** [Ira Gershwin; George Gershwin] vBE (cl solo)
    78: Decca 1203, Brunswick (E) O2433
    LP: Coral CRL-56033, Bandstand BS7120, Ajax LP118, Joyce
    LP6038, Living Era (E) ASV 5052
    CD: Living Era (E) ASV 5052
DLA-759-A   **Let's Call The Whole Thing Off** [Ira Gershwin; George Gershwin] vDM (as solo)
    78: Decca 1204, Brunswick (E) O2434
    LP: Coral CRL-56033, Bandstand BS7120, Ajax LP118
    CD: Aero Space AS7120

With the exception of "Blue Danube," all the above are from *Shall We Dance?* Nat Shilkret, musical director of the film, hired Jimmy and the band as the nucleus of a fifty-piece studio orchestra including strings. Again, Jimmy receives no screen credit though he is heard in solo work.

RKO Studios, Hollywood, Cal. April-May, 1937
SHALL WE DANCE?: Mark Sandrich, director
Jimmy Dorsey and His Orchestra augmenting RKO studio musicians.
Fred Astaire, Ginger Rogers (vcl) Fud Livingston (arr)

    (I've Got) Beginner's Luck / **Slap That Bass** vFA (cl solo) / **Walkin' The Dog** (aka **Promenade**) (cl solo) / **(I've Got) Beginner's Luck** vFA / **They All Laughed** vGR (cl solo) / **Let's Call The Whole Thing Off** vFA,GR / **They Can't Take That Away From Me** vFA / **Shall We Dance?** vFA [entire score: Ira Gershwin; George Gershwin]
    All selections in **FILM:** RKO *Shall We Dance?;* **LP:** EMI (E) MTC102; **VIDEO:** TCM 6394V. All except part of "Walkin' The

Dog" on **CD:** Chansons Cinema (F) CIN007, Rhino 72957
Recorded but not used in film: **Hi-Ho / Wake Up Brother, And Dance** [both by Ira Gershwin; George Gershwin]

"Shall We Dance?", "They Can't Take That Away From Me" and "Slap That Bass" finally made it to Broadway, in *Crazy For You,* the nineties' highly successful Gershwin retrospective musical.

Kraft Music Hall, Thurs., Mar. 18. Guests: Basil Rathbone (actor) Rudolph Ganz (p) Vronsky and Badin (two pianos) Harriet Hilliard (vcl)
Kraft Music Hall, Thurs., Mar. 25. Guests: Betty Jaynes (soprano) Gail Sondergaard, Walter Brennan (Oscar winners)

Travel itinerary: Sat., Mar. 27—Mission Beach Ballroom, San Diego, Cal.

Kraft Music Hall, Thurs., Apr. 1. Guests: Ernest Schelling (p) Amelia Earhart (aviatrix) George Palmer Putnam, John Barrymore (actors) June Travis (actress) Charlie Grimm (Chicago Cubs manager)
Kraft Music Hall, Thurs., Apr. 8. Guests: Katherine Meisle (contralto) Victor Mc-Laglen (actor) Florence Lake (actress)
Kraft Music Hall, Thurs., Apr. 15. Guests: Percy Grainger (p) Harry Barrls (vcl) Frances Farmer (actress) Lionel Stander (actor)
Kraft Music Hall, Thurs., Apr. 22. Guests: Rose Brampton (soprano) Ernest Schelling (p) Foursome Quartet (vcl) Walter Connolly (actor)

Variety (April 28, 1937, 46) reported that Bing Crosby had signed a two-season contract, renewing the *Kraft Music Hall* through all of 1938, with a new deal giving him $3,500 a broadcast, $500 more than before. Jimmy and the band, however, were not included in the new agreement.
   In the same issue (page 54) the weekly newspaper called attention to the 12-inch Decca (29009) that Jimmy had made with Josephine Tumminia. Particularly noted in the review were the "swinging arrangements by Fud Livingston." The trade paper also notes that Tumminia's score for "Blue Danube" (actually the only Livingston-arranged side), is the same as used for Lily Pons in RKO's *That Girl From Paris.*

Kraft Music Hall, Thurs., Apr. 29. Guests: Grete Stueckgold (soprano) Mischa Auer (comedian) Madelene Carroll (actress) Paul Taylor Choristers
Kraft Music Hall, Thurs., May 6. Guests: Connie Boswell, Janie Porter (vcl) Basil Rathbone (actor) Mary Gardner (soprano)
Kraft Music Hall, Thurs., May 13. Guests: Elissa Landi (actress) Josephine Tumminia (soprano) John McCormack (tenor) Lionel Stander (actor)
Kraft Music Hall, Thurs., May 20. Guests: Connie Boswell (vcl) Lionel Stander, Lee Tracy, William Gargan (actors)

Jimmy's and Les Hite's bands began a four-week stay on Friday, May 21, playing continuous evening dance music at the Pan-Pacific Auditorium in Hollywood (*Variety,* May 19, 1937, 49).
   Sunday, May 23, Hollywood's first ever Swing Concert took place at the Pan-Pacific. Produced by the Crosby brothers (Bing, Everett and Larry) as a tribute to the ailing pianist Joe Sullivan, it included the bands of Jimmy Dorsey, Jimmy Grier, Earl Hines, Ray Noble, Louis Prima

and Victor Young along with Seger Ellis and his Choir of Brass, Candy Candido's Jazz Band, Joe Yukl's Jazz Band and pianist Art Tatum.

Singers included Connie Boswell, Bing Crosby, Dorothy Lamour, Ella Logan, Johnny Mercer and Martha Raye (Brown 1996).

> *Kraft Music Hall,* NBC Studios, Hollywood, Cal.— NBC-Red, 7:00-8:00 P.M. PST, Thursday, May 27, 1937

JIMMY DORSEY AND HIS ORCHESTRA
Jimmy Dorsey (cl,as,ldr) Joe Meyer, Toots Camarata (tp) Bobby Byrne, Don Matteson, Bruce Squires (tb) Len Whitney (as) Fud Livingston (as,ts) Charles Frazier (ts) Freddy Slack (p) Roc Hillman (g) Jack Ryan (sb) Ray McKinley (d) Bing Crosby (host,vcl) Bob Burns (comedian, "bazooka" [iron pipe and funnel, blown through]) Guests: Rudolph Ganz (p) Zasu Pitts (comedian) Gail Patrick (actress) Paul Taylor Chorus (vcl)

> **How Could You?** [Al Dubin; Harry Warren] vBC (cl solo) / **My Melancholy Baby** [George Norton; Ernie Burnett] (partial) (vZP,BC) / **You're Here, You're There** vBC / **From The Land Of The Sky Blue Waters** [Nelle Eberhart, Charles Cadman] (Bob Burns, bazooka) / **Time On My Hands** [Harold Adamson, Mack Gordon; Vincent Youmans] vBC&Chorus / **My Little Buckaroo** [Jack Scholl; M. K. Jerome] vBC / *Forgotten Waltz (RG,p) / *Puerta D'el Gato (RG,p) / *Lullaby For Bazooka (BB"bazooka,"RG,p) / **Flight Of The Bumble Bee** [Rimsky-Korsakov] (as solo) / **Where Are You?** [Harold Adamson; Jimmy McHugh] vBC,Chorus (* does not include Jimmy or the band)
>
> Entire broadcast on **LP:** Spokane 7. **TC:** Best of Old Time Radio 10090

Kraft Music Hall, Thurs., June 3. Guests: Charlie Ruggles (comedian) Natalie Bodanya (soprano) McClelland Barclay (illustrator)
Kraft Music Hall, Thurs., June 10. Guests: Harriet Hilliard (vcl) Douglas Fairbanks, Jr., William Frawley (actors)

At about this time vocalist Vickie Joyce left and was briefly replaced by Martha Tilton, a member of the Meyer Alexander Chorus, who made no recordings with Jimmy's band. A month later she was hired by Benny Goodman, on whose radio show she had worked with Alexander.

Kraft Music Hall, Thurs., June 17. Guests: José Iturbi (p) Pat O'Brien (actor) Katherine DeMille (actress) Paul Taylor Chorus

Decca, Los Angeles, Cal. Wednesday, June 23, 1937
JIMMY DORSEY AND HIS ORCHESTRA
Shorty Sherock replaces Meyer (tp). Toots Camarata (vcl,arr) Bobby Byrne, Roc Hillman, Bob Eberle, Don Matteson (vcl)

DLA-819-A,B   **(I Want It) Sweet Like You** vTC,BB&RH (unissued)
DLA-820-A   **Flight Of The Bumble-Bee** [Nikolai Rimsky-Korsakov] arrTC (as solo)
    78: Decca 1508, 3333 (in set A-135)

(SSL-3934) **ET:** AFRS Basic Music Library 1946
LP: Bandstand BS7120, Coral (G) CRL-56004, Ajax LP118
CD: Aero Space AS7120
DLA-821-A   **The Moon Got In My Eyes** [Johnny Burke; Arthur Johnston] vBE (cl solo)
    78: Decca 1377, (E) M-30089, Brunswick (E) O2527, (F) A-81375
    LP: Ajax LP118, Living Era (E) ASV 5052
    CD: Living Era (E) ASV 5052
DLA-822-A   **After You** [Sam Coslow, Al Siegal] vDM (as solo)
    78: Decca 1378, (Au) X-1429, Brunswick (E) O2527, (F) A-81375, A-81518
    LP: Ajax LP118, Living Era (E) ASV 5052
    CD: Living Era (E) ASV 5052
DLA-823-A   **All You Want To Do Is Dance** [Johnny Burke; Arthur Johnston] vBE (cl solo)
    78: Decca 1377, (E) M-30089, Brunswick (E) O2528, (F) A-81376
    LP: Ajax LP118, Living Era (E) ASV 5052
    CD: Living Era (E) ASV 5052
DLA-824-A   **It's The Natural Thing To Do** [Johnny Burke; Arthur Johnston] vDM (as solo)
    78: Decca 1378, (Au) X-1429, Brunswick (E) O2528, (F) A-81518
    LP: Ajax LP118, Living Era (E) ASV 5052
    CD: Living Era (E) ASV 5052

"Flight Of The Bumble Bee," from the previous session, was to earn Jimmy a spot in Bob Ripley's *Believe It or Not* newspaper feature in 1938 on the basis of his performing it in two breaths, at the rate of ten notes per second, sixteen notes to the bar. Then, on the CBS *Saturday Night Swing Club* March 12, 1938, he did it all in one breath.

Kraft Music Hall, Thurs., June 24. Guests: Florence George (soprano) Constance Bennett (actress) Reginald Denny (actor) Paul Taylor Choristers
Kraft Music Hall, Thurs., July 1. Guests: Mischa Levitski (p) Toby Wing, Roland Young (actors) Paul Taylor Choristers

> *Kraft Music Hall,* NBC Studios, Hollywood, Cal.—NBC-Red, 7:00-8:00 P.M. PST, Thursday, January-July, 1937

JIMMY DORSEY AND HIS ORCHESTRA
Bing Crosby (vcl)

Peckin' [Ben Pollack, Harry James] vBC,Band (cl solo)
    LP: Bandstand BS7104

Thus did Jimmy's eighteen-month California sojourn come to an end. It had been good work, it paid well, but it also cost Jimmy dearly in momentum during the phenomenal birth of the Big-Band era. The headquarters for popular music growth those days was in New York City, not Hollywood and it would take Jimmy two years to catch up.

Back to the Big Apple
(1937-1939)

The July 1, 1937, broadcast marked the end of the Jimmy Dorsey association with *Kraft Music Hall*. Bing Crosby then started his summer vacation and Bob Burns took over again as host with a new studio band led by John Scott Trotter, a former Hal Kemp pianist. Trotter's partnership with Bing would last for more than a decade.

Jimmy and the band headed back toward the East Coast. On the way there was a three-month string of one-week theater dates plus a lot of one-nighters, the details of many of them unknown.

In its July 28, 1937, issue (page 46) *Variety* said that Jimmy and the band grossed around $1,000 at the Surf Ballroom in Clear Lake, Iowa, on July 22 cutting into the gate for Frankie Masters the week before.

After the departure of Kay Weber, Jimmy had filled the female vocal chair for a short time with Vicki Joyce and Martha Tilton. Then he took what was at the time a risky move and added June Richmond. While June was bubblingly exuberant, she was also overweight, but even more daring, she was black.

Thus her debut with a big-name white band actually preceded by almost nine months that of Billie Holiday, who didn't join Artie Shaw until early 1938, making Jimmy and June apparently the pioneers in breaking the color barrier for female vocalists with prominent white bands. June took part in several of Jimmy's 1938 recording sessions and was a sensation in public appearances, bringing down the house more than once. She later went with Andy Kirk's band. Jimmy added to his integration efforts about this same time by signing Don Redman to his arranging stable.

The band played a week's engagement at the Stanley Theater, Pittsburgh, Pennsylvania, opening August 6, 1937. The week starting August 13 they spent at the Capitol in Washington, D.C. Jimmy and the band were then supposed to open at the Hotel New Yorker August 19 for an indefinite stay. This did not pan out, however, and the band was booked instead for a week starting August 20 at the Earle Theater, Philadelphia, Pennsylvania.

Variety (August 25, 1937, 46) advised that Jimmy would open at the Congress Hotel in Chicago early in October after concluding his theater tour in Philadelphia, Pennsylvania; Cleveland, Youngstown and Akron, Ohio and other locations. The paper added that Jimmy would get fourteen weekly broadcasts, four of them network, while at the Congress.

By the beginning of September Jimmy and crew were reportedly back in New York City playing a short engagement at Loew's State Theater.

However, if they participated in the theater's stage show it was a well-kept secret, for all Loew's State New York City area newspaper ads from August 27 to September 10, 1937, spotlight only The Ed Sullivan

350

Dawn Patrol Review, a swing harmonica group and the Daily News Harvest Moon Dance winners.

Probably most significant as far as the Dorsey brothers were concerned was the reunion party staged for them by Joe Helbock at the Onyx Club (Sanford 1972). By that time Tommy's band had its own commercial radio show for Raleigh cigarettes and was riding high on the strength of such record hits as "Song Of India" and "Marie." Jimmy on the other hand had been the radio studio band for Bing Crosby and had yet to have a big-selling record.

The Onyx affair was an attempt on the part of the brothers' many friends to get them back together but it would be 1942 and their father's funeral before they would again begin working together and socializing to any degree. It was also to be one of Joe Helbock's last hurrahs, as the Onyx soon went into bankruptcy.

Heading toward their Congress Hotel booking, Jimmy and the band played a week in mid-September at Eastwood Gardens, Detroit Michigan, followed by a week at the Palace Theater, Cleveland, Ohio, and a one-nighter at Valley Dale, Columbus, Ohio, on Sunday, October 3. They next played a private party on Tuesday, October 5, for Chevrolet car dealers at the brand-new Netherland Plaza Hotel in Cincinnati, Ohio, and opened the fall season for the hotel's swank new Pavillion Caprice on Wednesday, October 6.

While at the Cincinnati hotel, the band experienced a most unusual local broadcast "blackout" when WLW and WSAI were forbidden by the stations' conservative managements to carry any locally originated "swing music" programs. As a result, while Jimmy's band was fed by WLW engineers to NBC-Blue on opening night from 10:30-11:00 P.M. (CST) it was not aired on WLW, although brother Tommy's band, carried by NBC from New York, *was* heard by WLW listeners.

Finishing the Cincinnati sojourn on Tuesday, October 19, the band finally made it to that oft-trumpeted engagement at the Casino Room in Chicago's Congress Hotel, opening Thursday, October 21.

Billboard (October 23, 1937, 21) reported that the band played that fall for a debutante "coming-out" party in Pittsburgh, Pennsylvania, but gave no date. The only possible ones would be Monday, October 4, before Cincinnati, or Wednesday, October 20, after Cincinnati and before opening in Chicago, where they stayed for the rest of 1937.

Broadcast schedule (all Congress Hotel, all times Central): Tues., Oct. 26, NBC-Blue, 10:30-11:00 P.M. / Tues., Nov. 2, NBC-Blue, 10:30-11:00 P.M. / Fri., Nov. 5, NBC-Blue, 9:45-10:00 P.M. / Tues., Nov. 9, NBC-Blue, 10:30-11:00 P.M. / Tues., Nov. 16, NBC-Blue, 10:30-11:00 P.M. / Tues., Nov. 23, NBC-Blue, 10:30-11:00 P.M. / Thurs., Nov. 25, NBC-Red, 10:30-11:00 P.M. / Tues., Nov. 30, NBC-Blue, 10:30-11:00 P.M. / Tues., Dec. 7, NBC-Blue, 10:30-11:00 P.M. / Tues., Dec. 14, NBC-Blue, 10:30-11:00 P.M. / Wed., Dec. 15, NBC-Red 10:30-11:00 P.M.

In his "Airing the Bands" column, *Billboard* writer Maurice Zolotow was enthusiastic after monitoring one of the Congress NBC air slots:

Jimmy Ain't Sentimental

At the risk of starting the Jimmy-Tommy feud all over again, we venture the opinion that Jimmy Dorsey [WJZ] from the Congress Casino, Chicago is dishing out as healthy a brand of swing these days as his more refined brother Thomas. It all goes to show that hot Chicago style still has some meaning today. (*Billboard,* November 13, 1937, 12)

The band played a swing concert on Sunday, December 19, an off-day at the Congress Hotel, which pitted Jimmy's band against a quintet featuring trumpeter Roy Eldridge. An overcapacity crowd of more than 750 jammed the Congress at $1.50 a head.

Jimmy started the three-hour shindig with a session well received by the crowd, at least 70 percent of whom were Chicago area musicians.

After Eldridge filled the next sixty minutes, Jimmy came back for an hour more of swing and a finale that ended with the Eldridge quintet joining in and bringing the house down.

Broadcast schedule (all Congress Hotel, all times Central): Tues., Dec. 21, NBC-Blue, 10:30-10:45 P.M. / Tues., Dec. 28, NBC-Blue, 10:30-11:00 P.M. / Sun., Jan. 2, 1938, NBC-Red, 10:00-10:30 P.M. / Tues., Jan. 4, NBC-Blue, 10:30-11:00 P.M.

Closing at the Congress on Wednesday, January 5, 1938, the band moved up to Minneapolis, Minnesota, for a three-week engagement at the Nicollet Hotel, where Jimmy brought in several local groups and his own band on Sunday, January 16, to help a school for crippled children.

According to *Billboard* (February 5, 1938, 16) Jack Kapp, Decca's president, was in Minneapolis for some Decca sessions with Jimmy, probably at one of the city's major radio stations.

Unknown studio, Minneapolis, Minn. Tuesday, January 25, 1938
JIMMY DORSEY AND HIS ORCHESTRA
Jimmy Dorsey (cl,as,ldr) W. C. Clark, Shorty Sherock (tp) Toots Camarata (tp,arr) Bobby Byrne, Don Matteson (tb,vcl) Bruce Squires (tb) Noni Bernardi (as) Dave Matthews (as,ts,arr) Charles Frazier (ts,fl) Leonard Whitney (ts) Freddy Slack (p,arr) Roc Hillman (g,vcl) Jack Ryan (sb) Ray McKinley (d) Bob Eberle (vcl)

63201-A   **Doctor Rhythm** vDM,RH&BE (as,cl solos)
          78: Decca 1651
          LP: Bandstand BS7104, Coral (G) COPS7449, 6.28219, Swingfan (G) 1007, Ajax LP118
63202-A   **On The Sentimental Side** [Johnny Burke; James V. Monaco] vBE (cl,as solos)
          78: Decca 1651
          LP: Bandstand BS7120, Ajax LP118
          CD: Aero Space AS7120
63203-A   **How'dja Like To Love Me?** [Frank Loesser; Burton Lane] vDM (as,cl solos)
          78: Decca 1671, (E) F-6740, Brunswick (F) A-81672, Polydor (It) A-61175
          LP: Ajax LP124
63204-A   **I Fall In Love With You Every Day** [Sam H. Stept] vBE (cl solos)
          78: Decca 1671, (E) F-6740, Brunswick (F) A-81672, Polydor

(It) A-61175
LP: Ajax LP124
63205-A   **Love Is Here To Stay** [Ira Gershwin; George Gershwin] vBE (cl solos)
78: Decca 1660, (E) F-6712, Brunswick (F) A-81606
LP: Coral CRL-56033, Bandstand BS-7120, Ajax LP124
CD: Aero Space AS7120

Unknown studio, Minneapolis, Minn. Friday, January 28, 1938
JIMMY DORSEY AND HIS ORCHESTRA

63206-A   **Smoke From A Chimney** vBE (as solo)
78: Decca 1652
LP: Ajax LP124
63207-A,B   **It's The Dreamer In Me** vBE (unissued)
63208-A   **I Was Doing All Right** [Ira Gershwin; George Gershwin] vBE (as solo)
78: Decca 1660
LP: Coral CRL-56033, Ajax LP124, Bandstand BS7210
63209-A   **My First Impression Of You** [Charles Tobias; Sam H. Stept] vDM (as,cl solos)
78: Decca 1652
LP: Ajax LP124

After closing at the Nicollet there were some one-nighters to keep the band from getting rusty until they could return to the Hotel New Yorker. One of these was Sunday, January 30, at the Cleveland, Ohio, Trianon Ballroom, run by Charlie Horvath, from the Detroit days. The band received $750 plus 50 percent of the gross (*Variety,* January 12, 1938, 47).

Travel itinerary: Sun., Feb. 20—Ritz Ballroom, Bridgeport, Conn. / Tues., Feb. 22—Foot National Guard Armory, Hartford, Conn.

By Tuesday, March 1, when the band opened at the Ice Terrace Room of Hotel New Yorker, the personnel shaped up like this:

JIMMY DORSEY AND HIS ORCHESTRA
Jimmy Dorsey (cl,as,ldr) Ralph Muzillo, Shorty Sherock (tp) Bobby Byrne, Don Matteson (tb,vcl) Bruce Squires (tb) Milt Yaner, Leonard Whitney (as) Charles Frazier (ts,fl) Herbie Haymer (ts) Freddy Slack (p,arr) Roc Hillman (g) Jack Ryan (sb) Ray McKinley (d) Bob Eberle, June Richmond (vcl)

Hotel magnate Ralph Hitz hosted an opening night party attended by most of the music publishers. Brother Tommy turned up later in the week, surprising those who thought the brothers were still battling.

Broadcast schedule (all New Yorker unless noted): Tues., Mar. 1, MBS [WOR], 11:30-midnight / Wed., Mar. 2, MBS [WOR], 11:30-midnight / Mon., Mar. 7, CBS [WABC], 11:00-11:30 P.M. / Tues., Mar. 8, MBS [WOR], 11:30-midnight / Wed., Mar. 9, MBS [WOR], 11:30-midnight / Fri., Mar. 11, CBS [WABC], 11:00-11:30 P.M. / Mon., Mar. 14, CBS [WABC], 11:30-midnight.

Saturday, March 12, the CBS *Saturday Night Swing Club* had Jimmy as a guest soloist, doing his "Flight Of The Bumble Bee" in one breath.

Variety (March 16), in revealing this, also reported Jimmy had been a recent guest on the WNEW *Sunday Morning Swing Concert*.

This highly popular local broadcast was aired from the stage of the Criterion Theatre on Times Square and featured a WNEW house band led by Merle Pitt.

Decca, New York, N.Y. Tuesday, March 15, 1938
JIMMY DORSEY AND HIS ORCHESTRA

63429-A   **Two Bouquets** [Jimmy Kennedy; Michael Carr] vBE
               (as solo)
  78: Decca 1723, (E) F-6692, (Au) X-1589
  LP: Ajax LP124
      X-1589 as THE RHYTHM KINGS
63430-A   **I Can't Face The Music (Without Singin' The
               Blues)** [Ted Kohler; Rube Bloom] vJR (as,cl solos)
  78: Decca 1746
  LP: Time-Life STB-B10, Ajax LP124
  TC: Time-Life 4TL-0006
  CD: Time-Life 4TL-0006, GRP-Decca CD-GRD-626
63431-A   **Joseph! Joseph!** [Sammy Cahn, Saul Chaplin; Nellie
               Casman, Samuel Steinberg] vJR (as solo)
  78: Decca 1723, (E) M-30195, Brunswick (E) O2698, (F) A-
  1589
  LP: Ajax LP124
63432-A   **At A Perfume Counter** [Edgar Leslie; Joe Burke]
               vBE (cl solo)
  78: Decca 1724, (E) F-6799, Brunswick (F) A-81775, Polydor
  (It) A-61200
  LP: Ajax LP124

Broadcast schedule (New Yorker): Tues., Mar. 15, MBS [WOR], 11:30-midnight.

Decca, New York, N.Y. Wednesday, March 16, 1938
JIMMY DORSEY AND HIS ORCHESTRA
Sonny Lee (tb) Don Redman (arr)

63433-A   **It's The Dreamer In Me** [Jimmy Van Heusen; Jim-
               my Dorsey] vBE (cl solo)
  78: Decca 1733
  LP: Ajax LP124
63434-A   **Don't Be That Way** [Mitchell Parish; Edgar Samp-
               son, Benny Goodman] arrDR (as,cl solos)
  78: Decca 1733
  (SSL-3819) **ET:** AFRS Basic Music Library 1903
  LP: Ajax LP124, Bandstand BS7120, Coral CRL-56008, (G)
  COPS7449, 6.28219
  CD: GRP-Decca CD-GRD-626, Aero Space AS7120, Kaz (E) 309
63435-A   **Love Walked In** [Ira Gershwin; George Gershwin]

vBE (cl solo)
78: Decca 1724, (E) F-6712, Brunswick (F) A-81606
LP: Coral CRL-56033, Ajax LP124
63436-A   **The Week-End Of A Private Secretary** [Johnny
                 Mercer; Bernard Hanighen] vJR (cl solo)
                 78: Decca 1745, (Au) X-1630
                 LP: Ajax LP124

Broadcast schedule (all New Yorker): Wed., Mar. 16, MBS [WOR], 11:30-midnight /
Fri., Mar. 18, CBS [WABC], 11:00-11:30 P.M. / Mon., Mar. 21, CBS [WABC],
11:00-11:30 P.M. / Tues., Mar. 22, MBS [WOR], 11:00-11:30 P.M. / Wed., Mar. 23,
MBS [WOR], 11:30-midnight / Fri., Mar. 25, CBS [WABC], 11:00-11:30 P.M. /
Mon., Mar. 28 CBS, [WABC], 11:00-11:30 P.M.

Decca, New York, N.Y. Tuesday, March 29, 1938
JIMMY DORSEY AND HIS ORCHESTRA
Bobby Byrne, Don Matteson, Roc Hillman, Bob Eberle (vcl)

63496-A   **Lost And Found** [Pinky Tomlin, Harry Tobias] vBE
                 (cl solo)
                 78: Decca 1746
                 LP: Ajax LP128
63497-A   **Stop! And Reconsider** vBB,DM&RH (cl solo)
                 78: Decca 1745, (Au) X-1649
                 LP: Ajax LP128, Coral (G) COPS7449, 6.28219, Bandstand
                 BS7104
63498-A   **I Cried For You (Now It's Your Turn To Cry Over
                 Me)** [Arthur Freed; Gus Arnheim, Abe Lyman] (cl
                 solos)
                 78: (12-inch) Decca 15041, 29240, (Au) Z-781
                 LP: Decca DL-8045, Brunswick (E) LAT-8037, Ajax LP128, Ace
                 Of Hearts (E) AH-114
                 CD: GRP-Decca CD-GRD-626, Kaz (E) 309

Broadcast schedule (all New Yorker): Tues., Mar. 29, MBS [WOR], 11:30-midnight /
Wed., Mar. 30, MBS [WOR], 11:30-midnight / Fri., Apr. 1, CBS [WABC], 11:00-
11:30 P.M. / Sat., Apr. 2, MBS [WOR], 10:00-10:30 P.M. / Mon., Apr. 4, CBS
[WABC], 11:00-11:30 P.M. / Tues., Apr. 5, MBS [WOR], 11:30-midnight / Fri., Apr.
8, CBS [WABC], 11:00-11:30 P.M. / Mon., Apr. 11, CBS [WABC], 11:00-11:30 P.M.
/ Fri., Apr. 15, CBS [WABC], 11:00-11:30 P.M. / Mon., Apr. 18, CBS [WABC],
11:00-11:30 P.M. / Wed., Apr. 20, MBS [WOR], 11:30-midnight.

It wasn't long after the band's return to the East Coast that it became
apparent Jimmy's personal life was becoming strained. More and more
his wife Jane and their daughter Julie were living separately from him.
This was a way of life that continued off and on for fourteen more years.
     About a week before the next session, trombonist Sonny Lee left
Bunny Berigan, where he had been playing lead and jazz solo, and
joined the Jimmy Dorsey band. Higher pay offered by Jimmy was the
incentive. It is not certain if he moonlighted on the March 16 Decca
session (Bozy White 1988-1997).

Decca, New York, N.Y. Friday, April 22, 1938
JIMMY DORSEY AND HIS ORCHESTRA
Sonny Lee (tb) added. Ray McKinley, Bob Eberle, Don Matteson (vcl)

63655-A   **Popcorn Man** [Will Hudson, Lou Klein, Bill Living-
                 ston] vRM (cl solo)
     78: Decca 1799
     LP: Ajax LP128, Swingfan (G) 1007
63656-A   **I Love You In Technicolor** vBE (cl,as solos)
     78: Decca 1921
     LP: Ajax LP128
63657-A   **At Your Beck And Call** [Eddie DeLange; Buck Ram]
                 vBE (cl,as solos)
     78: Decca 1784, (E) F-6798, (Au) X-1523, Brunswick (F) A-
     81753, Polydor (It) A-61175
     LP: Ajax LP128
63658-A   **Cowboy From Brooklyn** [Johnny Mercer; Harry War-
                 ren] vRM (as solo)
     78: Decca 1799
     LP: Ajax LP128, Bandstand BS7140
63659-A   **Who Do You Think I Saw Last Night?** vDM
                 (cl,as solos)
     78: Decca 1784, (Au) X-1581
         X-1581 as THE RHYTHM KINGS
     LP: Ajax LP128

Jimmy and Tommy attended a jam session at the Paradise Cafe on
Times Square on Sunday, April 24, an off-day for both Dorseys.

Broadcast schedule (all New Yorker): Mon., Apr. 25, CBS [WABC], 11:00-11:30 P.M.
/ Wed., Apr. 27, MBS [WOR], 10:30-11:00 P.M. / Fri., Apr. 29, MBS [WOR], 10:00-
10:30 P.M.; CBS [WABC], 11:00-11:30 P.M.

"John Silver," recorded next, was the only hit ever written by Ray
Krise, who later migrated to Syracuse, New York, working for more
than two decades on radio and TV as newsman Ray Owens.
    The arrangements in this session show the varied jazz directions the
band was taking, sometimes two-beat dixie, other times the four-beat
rhythms of swing.

Decca, New York, N.Y. Friday, April 29, 1938
JIMMY DORSEY AND HIS ORCHESTRA
Ray Krise, Larry Clinton (arr) June Richmond (vcl)

63689-A   **John Silver** [Ray Krise, Jimmy Dorsey] arrRK
     78: Decca 1860, 3334 (in set A-135), (E) M-30211, Brunswick
     (E) O2719, (F) A-81990, Polydor (It) A-61175
     (SSL-3933-2) **ET:** AFRS Basic Music Library P-1945
     LP: Bandstand BS7120, Coral CRL-56008, (G) COPS7449,
     6.28219, Decca DL-74853, MCA 2-4073, Time-Life STB-B10,
     Ajax LP128
     TC: Time-Life 4TL-0006

CD: Time-Life 4TL-0006, Aero Space AS7120, GRP-Decca CD-GRD-626, Kaz (E) 309

63689-B **John Silver** arrRK
78: Coral 60396
LP: Decca DL-4006, DL-4853, Brunswick (G) 87098, MCA 2-4073

63690-A **Song Of The Volga Boatman** [Russian folk song] (as solo)
78: (12-inch) Decca 15041, (E) BM-30824, (Au) Z-781
LP: Decca DL8045, Coral (G) COPS7449, 6.28219, Brunswick (E) LAT-8037, Ajax LP128, Bandstand BS7120
CD: Aero Space AS7120

63691-A **The Darktown Strutters' Ball** [Shelton Brooks] vJR (cl solo)
78: Decca 1939, (E) BM-1076, M-30201, (Au) X-1650, Coral 60000, Brunswick (E) O2706, (F) A-81998
LP: Ajax LP128
CD: GRP-Decca CD-GRD-626, Kaz (E) 309

63692-A **Dusk In Upper Sandusky** [Larry Clinton, Jimmy Dorsey] arrLC (as solos)
78: Decca 1939, (E) M-30201, (Au) X-1650, Coral 60000, Brunswick (E) O2706, (F) A-81998
LP: Decca DL-74853, MCA 2-4073, Time-Life STB-B10
TC: Time-Life 4TL-0006
CD: Time-Life 4TL-0006, Kaz (E) 309

63692-B **Dusk In Upper Sandusky** arrLC (as solos)
78: Decca 1939, 3333 (in set A-135), Coral 60000, Brunswick (E) O2706
LP: Ajax LP128, Swingfan (G) 1007
CD: GRP-Decca CD-GRD-626

Broadcast schedule (all New Yorker): Mon., May 2, CBS [WABC], 11:05-11:30 P.M. / Tues., May 3, MBS [WOR], 10:30-11:00 P.M.

Decca, New York, N.Y. Friday, May 6, 1938
JIMMY DORSEY AND HIS ORCHESTRA
June Richmond, Bob Eberle (vcl)

63718 A **If You Were In My Place** vJR (unissued)
63719-A **I Let A Song Go Out Of My Heart** vJR (unissued)
63720-A **I Hadn't Anyone Till You** [Ray Noble] vBE (cl solos)
78: Decca 1834, (E) F-6798, Brunswick (F) A-81753, Polydor (It) A-61218
LP: Ajax LP128

Broadcast schedule (all New Yorker): Fri., May 6, CBS [WABC], 11:05-11:30 P.M. / Sat., May 7, MBS [WOR], 11:05-11:30 P.M. / Mon., May 9, CBS [WABC], 11:05-11:30 P.M. / Tues., May 10, MBS [WOR], 10:30-11:00 P.M. / Thurs., May 12, NBC-Red [WEAF], 1:00-1:30 A.M. / Fri., May 13, CBS [WABC], 11:05-11:30 P.M. / Sat. May 14, MBS [WOR], 11:05-11:30 P.M. (see Addenda)

June Richmond left the band for a while during the Hotel New Yorker stay, prompting charges in some black publications that she was a victim of racial prejudice by hotel management.

Though denied in the trade press by hotel executives, the charges were reinforced when Jimmy and the band ended their New Yorker stay on Sunday, May 15, and June rejoined the group in time for Monday's session with Jack Kapp. The band then took two weeks off, and followed with a month of one-nighters.

Decca, New York, N.Y. Monday, May 16, 1938
JIMMY DORSEY AND HIS ORCHESTRA
June Richmond, Vi Mele, Bob Eberle, Don Matteson (vcl)

63787-A   **There's A Far Away Look In Your Eyes** [Irving Taylor; Vic Mizzy] vBE (as solo)
          78: Decca 1834, (Au) X-1697
          LP: Ajax LP128
63788-A   **Any Old Time At All** vVM (as solos)
          78: Decca 1921
          LP: Ajax LP134
63789-A   **I Let A Song Go Out Of My Heart** [Henry Nemo, John Redmond, Irving Mills; Edward K. "Duke" Ellington] vJR (as solo)
          78: Decca 1809, (E) F-6767, (Au) X-1589
          X-1589 as THE RHYTHM KINGS
          LP: Ajax LP134
63790-A   **That Feeling Is Gone** [Babe Wallace; Walter Hirsch] vDM (as solo)
          78: Decca 1860
          LP: Ajax LP134
63791-A   **If You Were In My Place** [Henry Nemo, John Redmond, Irving Mills; Edward K. "Duke" Ellington] vVM (as solo)
          78: Decca 1809, (E) F-6767
          LP: Ajax LP134
63792-A   **Arkansas Traveler** [David Stevens] (cl solo)
          78: Decca 2363, 32108
          LP: Ajax LP134, Bandstand BS7120
          CD: Aero Space AS7120

An indication that Jimmy was climbing in recognition on college campuses came in the annual poll of Syracuse University seniors. The upstate New York students put Tommy Dorsey first, Benny Goodman second, Hal Kemp third and Jimmy's band fourth.

Memorial Day weekend kicked off Jimmy's next road tour:

Travel itinerary: Sat., May 28—Hampton Beach Casino, N.H., where he outdrew Artie Shaw's band with 1,800 admissions / Sun., May 29—Ocean Pier, Wildwood, N.J. / Mon., May 30—Hamid's Steel Pier, Atlantic City, N.J.

The June 8, 1938, issue of *Variety* (page 34) carried a quarter-page promotional ad for Rockwell-O'Keefe, Inc., with the general theme that

Jimmy and company had in three years become a major attraction in radio, theaters, ballrooms, motion pictures and records.

Travel itinerary: Thurs., June 9—Smoky Mountain Wild Flower Pageant, Knoxville, Tenn. / Fri., June 10—German Ball, Rocky Mount, N.C. / Sat., June 11—Virginia Military Institute, Lexington, Va. / Sat., June 18—Long Island Beach Point Club, Mamaroneck, N.Y. / Fri., June 24 to Thurs., June 30—Stanley Theater, Pittsburgh, Pa. / Fri., July 1 to Thurs., July 7—Hamid's Steel Pier, Atlantic City, N.J.

On Wednesday, July 13, the band opened for the first time at the prestigious Paramount Theater in New York for a two-week booking. Sharing the bill were the Andrews Sisters and country comedian Rufe Davis. The two-week stay grossed $71,000, the largest Paramount box-office of the summer.

Patti, Maxene and LaVerne Andrews were a sister act from Minneapolis, Minnesota, who were spotted by Jack Kapp while they were singing with Leon Belasco's Orchestra at the Hotel Edison in New York in 1937. By mid-1938 they had risen to stardom through such hits as "Bei Mir Bist Du Schoen," "Joseph, Joseph" and "Ti-Pi-Tin."

Partly on the strength of seeing them together at the Paramount, Kapp called on Jimmy to cut some sides with the Sisters twice in 1938. The first session is listed below, while the second on November 21 included one of the Sisters' top hits, "Hold Tight."

Billy Burton, ice-show promoter and producer for two years with Rockwell-O'Keefe, quit there on July 15 and came to work for Jimmy as his personal manager. Burton had other ties to the music world as the brother of lyricist Nat Burton ("White Cliffs of Dover," "When The Roses Bloom Again"). *Variety* (July 20, 1938, 40) reported that the band would continue to be booked by the Rockwell-O'Keefe office.

Decca, New York, N.Y. Wednesday, July 27, 1938
JIMMY DORSEY AND HIS ORCHESTRA
Sam Rubin (Rubinowitch) (as) replaces Whitney, Vi Mele (vcl) out. Andrews Sisters, Ray McKinley (vcl)

64350-A   **Tu-Li-Tulip Time** vAS
    78: Decca 1974, (E) M-30170, (Au) X-1576, Brunswick (E) O2654, (F) A-505181
    as ANDREWS SISTERS with Jimmy Dorsey & His Orchestra
    LP: Coral (G) 6.28219, Ajax LP134
    TC: Ajazz C-1657
64351-A   **I Haven't Changed A Thing** vJR (as solos)
    78: Decca 1961, (E) X-1649
    LP: Ajax LP134
64352-A   **Sha-Sha** vAS&band (cl solo)
    78: Decca 1974, (E) M-30170, (Au) X-1576, Brunswick (E) O2665
    as ANDREWS SISTERS with Jimmy Dorsey & His Orchestra
    LP: Ajax LP134, Joker (It) 3240
    TC: Ajazz C-1657
    CD: Flapper (E) 9766
64353-A   **Killy-Ka-Lee (Indian Love Talk)** (Contd.)

JIMMY DORSEY AND HIS ORCHESTRA (Contd.)

[Irving Taylor; Vic Mizzy] vRM (as solo)
78: Decca 1961, (E) X-1630, M-30211, Brunswick O2719, A-81990, Polydor (It) A-61218
LP: Ajax LP134

Because of the Jimmy Dorsey—Andrews Sisters pairing above, some claim that the Jimmy Dorsey Orchestra, but without Jimmy, backed the trio's August 6, 1938, New York Decca session. The band opened in Chicago August 5, ruling out this theory.

Decca, New York, N.Y. Friday, July 29, 1938
JIMMY DORSEY AND HIS ORCHESTRA
Bob Eberle, Bobby Byrne, Don Matteson, Roc Hillman (vcl)

64365-A   **Change Partners** [Irving Berlin] vBE (as solo)
      78: Decca 2002, (E) M-30195, (Au) X-1567, Brunswick (E) O2698, (F) A-81930
      LP: Ajax LP134
      Also on **TC & CD:** Good Music MSC-37083
64366-A   **Love Is Where You Find It** [Earl K. Brent; Nacio Herb Brown] vBE (as solo)
      78: Decca 1970
      LP: Ajax LP134
64367-A   **The Yam** [Irving Berlin] vBB,DM&RH (as,cl,as solos)
      78: Decca 2002, (Au) X-1567
      LP: Ajax LP134, Bandstand BS7120
      CD: Aero Space AS7120
64368-A   **Garden Of The Moon** [Al Dubin; Johnny Mercer; Harry Warren] vBE (cl solo)
      78: Decca 1970, (Au) X-1569
      LP: Ajax LP134
            X-1569 as THE RHYTHM KINGS

Starting August 5, 1938, the band began a long summer booking at the exclusive Bon Air Country Club in the northwestern Chicago suburb of Wheeling, Illinois. As a replacement for June Richmond, who left the band to return to New York, Jimmy added a Chicago-area radio singer named Lee Leighton. It was rumored that Richmond had been replaced because of the exclusive Bon Air Country Club booking.
The initial four-week stay, soon extended until September 15, meant fifteen weekly air-shots over Mutual (MBS) for Jimmy and the band. It also meant an opportunity for Jimmy to spend some extended time on the golf course. To beef up the sound during the Bon Air engagement, Jimmy added trumpeters Yank Lawson and Charlie Spivak. Lawson joined the band full-time in January 1939.
There were additional broadcasts to those listed next but they were not carried in New York City, or were limited to the Midwest Mutual Network segment, and information about them is lacking.

Broadcast schedule (Bon Air): Mon., Aug. 15, MBS, 10:15-10:30 P.M. CDT

American Rhythm Masters, NBC Studios [WGN], Chicago, Ill.—NBC-Red, Monday, August 22, 1938
JIMMY DORSEY AND HIS ORCHESTRA

Beebe [Jimmy Dorsey] (as solo); **Sandman** [Ralph Freed, Bonnie Lake] (theme) / **Hollywood Pastime** [Toots Camarata] arrTC (cl solo) / **It's The Dreamer In Me** [Jimmy Van Heusen; Jimmy Dorsey] vBE (cl solo) / **Parade Of The Milk Bottle Caps** [Pat McCarthy, Jimmy Dorsey] (as solo) / **Flight Of The Bumble Bee** [Rimsky-Korsakov] (arrTC) (as solo) / **Beebe** [Jimmy Dorsey] (as solo); **Sandman** [Ralph Freed, Bonnie Lake] (theme)
Entire program on **CD:** Jazz Hour JH-1053

Broadcast schedule (all Bon Air, all times Central): Mon., Aug. 29, MBS, 10:30-11:00 P.M. / Fri., Sept. 2, MBS, 11:30-12:00 P.M. / Fri., Sept. 9, MBS, 11:30-12:00 P.M. / Mon., Sept. 12, MBS, 10:30-11:00 P.M. / Fri., Sept. 16, MBS, 12:00-12:15 A.M.

While in Chicago Jimmy ran into pianist Squirrel Ashcraft, an old friend from the Sirens-Ramblers days. Ashcraft and another friend, attorney Jim O'Keefe (no relation to Corky), advised Jimmy to look more carefully at what his band was costing him. A little pruning here and there could turn it into a real money machine, they counseled. Jimmy angrily rejected breaking up the band he loved (Sanford 1972).

After ending his six-week engagement at the Bon Air, Jimmy and the band struck out on a series of one-nighters throughout the Midwest. An exception to the one-night bookings was a week at the Corn Palace in Mitchell, South Dakota, from September 26 to October 1.

The Dorsey band and four Kansas and Missouri University bands played one night (Thursday, September 22) of a multi-evening dance-a-thon called Jubilesta at the Municipal Auditorium in Kansas City, Missouri. The 8,600 who turned out far exceeded the other evenings which featured Jimmy Grier, Rudy Vallee and the Hoosier Hot Shots.

By contrast, the promoter just broke even when the band did one night at King's Ballroom, Lincoln, Nebraska, on Saturday, October 15.

On Tuesday, October 18, while on the way to another one-nighter in Nebraska, Jimmy was injured near Omaha when he drove his car into a ditch to avoid a truck. Apparently not hurt too seriously, he continued to Norfolk, Nebraska, for a scheduled dance. On Friday, October 21, the band began a week at the Orpheum Theater, Minneapolis, Minnesota.

Another of Jimmy's bookings Friday and Saturday, November 4 and 5, 1938, was a set of weekend appearances at Duke University, Durham, North Carolina. This was part of a ten-day string of southern one-nighters that began November 1 and included one at the National Theater, Greensboro, North Carolina on Tuesday, November 8.

One of the band's prime bookings that November was the Earle Theater in Philadelphia for a week, opening Friday, November 11. Sharing billing with the band were the Andrews Sisters.

Decca, New York, N.Y. Monday, November 21, 1938
JIMMY DORSEY AND HIS ORCHESTRA
Andrews Sisters, Ray McKinley, Bob Eberle, Lee Leighton (vcl) Vic Schoen (arr)

JIMMY DORSEY AND HIS ORCHESTRA (Contd.)

64757-A   **Hold Tight—Hold Tight (Want Some Sea Food, Mama)** [Leonard Kent, Edward Robinson, Leonard Ware, Jerry Brandow, Willie Spotswood] vAS arrVS (cl solos)
          78: Decca 2214, 23606, (E) M-30208, (Au) X-1662, Brunswick (E) O2717, (F) A-81977
          LP: Decca DL-4919, DL-5120, DL-8360, Ajax LP134, Coral (G) COPS7449, 6.28219, Ace Of Hearts (E) AH-21, Plaza House SL-6716, Lotus 14101
          TC: Ajazz C-1657
          CD: CEMA CDL-57395, Living Era (E) CD AJA5096, Flapper (E) 9766, L'Art Vocal (F) #17, MCA 11727
64758-A   **Billy Boy** [traditional] vAS&RM (cl solo)
          78: Decca 2214, 23606, (E) M-30208, (Au) X-1662, Brunswick (E) O2717, (F) A-81977
          TC: Ajazz C-1657
64759-A   **A Room With A View** [Al Stillman; Einar Swan] vBE (as solo)
          78: Decca 2213
64760-A   **Kinda Lonesome** [Leo Robin, Sam Coslow; Hoagy Carmichael] vLL (as solo)
          78: Decca 2213, (Au) X-1633, Brunswick (E) O2747, (F) A-82093
          X-1633 as THE RHYTHM KINGS
          64758 through 64760 also on **LP:** Ajax LP141

Travel itinerary: Fri., Sat., Nov. 25, 26—University of Georgia, Athens, Ga. / Sun., Nov. 27 to Sat., Dec. 3—Orpheum Theater, Memphis, Tenn. / Wed., Dec. 7—Orpheum Theater, Springfield, Ill. / Thurs., Dec. 8—Palace Theater, Peoria, Ill.

The band also played Chicago for a Christmas benefit sponsored by the Hearst newspapers at the Chicago Stadium on Wednesday, December 14. Others on that show included Buddy Rogers and Fletcher Henderson.

In mid-December 1938 Jimmy and the band went over to Brooklyn to make a nine-minute featurette for Vitaphone and to Astoria for a one-song short for Paramount. The female vocalist on the Vitaphone is identified as Evelyn Oakes, but is really Helen O'Connell.

Jimmy's secretary, Nita Moore, is credited with discovering Helen at the Village Barn in the Greenwich Village section of New York, where she was singing with Larry Funk's band. If Nita didn't get a bonus for that, she certainly deserved one, for Helen became the spark needed to propel the band to the top. While Helen didn't join the band until mid-February 1939, she "moonlighted" with Jimmy for the movie and a February record date.

Vitaphone Studio, Brooklyn, N.Y. Mid-December 1938
JIMMY DORSEY AND HIS ORCHESTRA: Lloyd French, director
JIMMY DORSEY AND HIS ORCHESTRA
Jimmy Dorsey (cl,as,ldr) Ralph Muzillo, Shorty Sherock (tp) Bobby Byrne, Don Matteson, Sonny Lee (tb) Milt Yaner, Sam Rubin (as)

Charles Frazier, Herbie Haymer (ts) Freddy Slack (p) Roc Hillman (g)
Jack Ryan (sb) Ray McKinley (d) Bob Eberle, Helen O'Connell [as
Evelyn Oakes] (vcl)

> **Beebe** (theme) [Jimmy Dorsey] (as solo) / **Parade Of The Milk
> Bottle Caps** [Pat McCarthy, Jimmy Dorsey] (as solo) / **It's The
> Dreamer In Me** [Jimmy Van Heusen, Jimmy Dorsey] vBE (cl solo) /
> **I Love You In Technicolor** vBE&HO'C (cl,as solos) / **Dusk In
> Upper Sandusky** [Larry Clinton, Jimmy Dorsey] (as solos)
>   All on **FILM:** Vitaphone: *Jimmy Dorsey and His Orchestra*

Paramount Studio, Astoria, Long Island, N.Y.—1938
SCREEN SONG: You Leave Me Breathless: Dave Fleischer, director
JIMMY DORSEY AND HIS ORCHESTRA
Bob Eberle (vcl)

> **You Leave Me Breathless** [Ralph Freed; Frederick Hollander] vBE
> **FILM:** Paramount Screen Song: *You Leave Me Breathless*

Originally set for Christmas week at the State Theater in Hartford,
Connecticut, Jimmy and the band instead played two weeks at the Adol-
phus Hotel, Dallas, Texas, starting December 21. The band proved so
popular it was held for a third week, closing Saturday, January 7, 1939.
    While in Texas, Jimmy caught Ella Mae Morse singing at a Dallas
jam session and signed her to replace Vi Mele. Ella only lasted a month
once Jimmy returned to New York and realized she wasn't yet experienced and disciplined enough to handle the job.   However, Jimmy's
then pianist Freddy Slack successfully used her three years later on his
first Capitol hit, "Cow Cow Boogie."
    Heading back to New York after their Texas holiday booking, Jimmy
and the band returned to the Hotel New Yorker on January 10, 1939. In
doing so they followed brother Tommy's band for a multi week engagement in the Ice Terrace Room, which promoted the deal with large ads
that trumpeted "One Good Dorsey Deserves Another."
    In his book, "Tommy & Jimmy: The Dorsey Years," Herb Sanford
relates how Tommy closed at midnight playing "Auld Lang Syne," and
segued to "Sandman," the old Dorsey Brothers' theme. Then Jimmy and
his band struck up the first performance of their new theme "Contrasts," a Freddy Slack reworking of Jimmy's "Oodles Of Noodles."

Broadcast schedule (New Yorker): Fri., Jan. 13, CBS [WABC], 11:30-12:00 P.M.

> *sustaining broadcast,* Hotel New Yorker, New
> York, N.Y.—MBS [WOR], 11:05-11:30 P.M.
> Saturday, January 14, 1939
JIMMY DORSEY AND HIS ORCHESTRA

> **A Room With A View** [Al Stillman; Einar Swan] vBE (as solo) / **I
> Cried For You** [Arthur Freed; Gus Arnheim, Abe Lyman] (cl solos)
> / **Liza** [Ira Gershwin; George Gershwin] / **At Long Last Love** [Cole
> Porter] vBE / **Bugle Call Rag** [Jack Pettis, Elmer Schoebel, Billy
> Meyers]

Sundays were days off for Jimmy at the New Yorker, which brought in Russ Morgan January 15 and 22 due to a recent musicians' local ruling barring any hotel band from working seven nights straight.

Broadcast schedule (New Yorker): Mon., Jan. 16, MBS [WOR], 11:05-11:30 P.M.

The reunion at the New Yorker worked so well it was repeated on Tommy's Raleigh-Kool show on NBC the following Wednesday.

> *Raleigh-Kool Program,* NBC Studio 8G, New York, N.Y.—NBC-Red, 8:30-9:00 P.M. Wednesday, January 18, 1939

TOMMY DORSEY AND HIS ORCHESTRA
Tommy Dorsey (tb,ldr) Andy Ferretti, Lee Castle, Yank Lawson (tp) Dave Jacobs, Ward Silloway, Elmer Smithers (tb) Johnny Mince (cl,as) Skeets Herfurt, Fred Stulce, Deane Kincaide (as) Babe Russin (ts) Howard Smith (p) Carmen Mastren (g) Gene Trexler (sb) Dave Tough (d) Jack Leonard, The Pied Pipers (vcl)

I'm Gettin' Sentimental Over You [Ned Washington; George Bassman] (theme) / **Marie** [Irving Berlin] vJL&band / **Dixieland Band** [Johnny Mercer; Bernard Hanighen] vPP

JIMMY DORSEY AND HIS ORCHESTRA
Jimmy Dorsey (cl,as,ldr) Shorty Sherock, Toots Camarata (tp) Bobby Byrne, Don Matteson, Sonny Lee (tb) Len Whitney (as) Dave Matthews (as,ts) Charles Frazier (ts) Freddy Slack (p) Roc Hillman (g) Jack Ryan (sb) Ray McKinley (d)

Contrasts [Jimmy Dorsey] (theme) (as solo) / **Pagan Love Song** [Arthur Freed; Nacio Herb Brown]

Skit: The Early Years, Lansford, Pa. Child actors play brothers taking lessons from Dad. Tommy and Jimmy play trumpets.

COMBINED BANDS:

Honeysuckle Rose [Andy Razaf; Thomas "Fats" Waller]

The show concluded with Tommy's band playing their theme song. One proposed feature involving Tommy, Jimmy and Bunny Berigan in New York, Gene Krupa on the West Coast, and Bobby Haggart from Chicago in a five-man long-distance jam session was ruled out when the Raleigh show's producers found it would involve $2,500 in broadcast wire charges (*Variety,* January 25, 1939, 44).

Broadcast schedule (all New Yorker): Thurs., Jan. 19, MBS [WOR], 11:05-11:30 P.M. / Sat., Jan. 21, MBS [WOR], 11:05-11:30 P.M. / Mon., Jan. 23, MBS [WOR], 11:05-11:30 P.M. / Thurs., Jan. 26, CBS [WABC], 11:05-11:30 P.M. / Sat., Jan. 28, MBS [WOR], 11:05-11:30 P.M. / Wed., Feb. 1, CBS [WABC], 11:30-12:00 P.M. / Fri., Feb. 3, CBS [WABC], 11:30-12:00 P.M. / Sat., Feb. 4, MBS [WOR], 11:05-11:30 P.M., 11:35-12:00 P.M. / Mon., Feb. 6, MBS [WOR], 11:05-11:30 P.M.

Beginning with the next session, the author begins using Bob Eberle's new last name spelling, a change Bob has said was made to avoid confusion with brother Ray (Glenn Miller's male vocalist). Why Bob, who got there first, felt he should be the one to make the change is a mystery.

Decca, New York, N.Y. Friday, February 10, 1939
JIMMY DORSEY AND HIS ORCHESTRA
Bob Eberly, Helen O'Connell (vcl) Don Redman (arr)

65001-A   **Let's Stop The Clock** [Haven Gillespie; J. Fred Coots] vBE (cl solo)
   78: Decca 2293, (Au) X-1736, Brunswick (E) O2736, (F) A-82046
65002-A   **(I'm Afraid) The Masquerade Is Over** [Herb Magidson; Allie Wrubel] vBE (cl solo)
   78: Decca 2293, Brunswick (E) O2747, (F) A-82093, Polydor (It) A-6121
   TC: Good Music MSC-37083
   CD: Good Music MSC-37083
65003-A   **Good For Nothin' (But Love)** [Eddie DeLange; Jimmy Van Heusen] vBE (cl solo)
   78: Decca 2294, (Au) Y-5425, Brunswick (E) O2797, (F) A-822210, Polydor (It) A-61261
65004-A   **Deep Purple** [Mitchell Parish; Peter De Rose] vBE arrDR (cl solo)
   78: Decca 2295, (Au) X-1708, Brunswick (E) O2736, (F) A-82046
   TC: Good Music MSC-37083
   CD: Good Music MSC-37083
65005-A   **Romance Runs In The Family** [Al Goodhart, Al Hoffman, Manny Kurtz] vHO'C (as solo)
   78: Decca 2294, (Au) Y-5395
   LP: Ajazz LP505
65006-A   **(It Was) Fate (When I First Met You)** vBE (cl solo)
   78: Decca 2295
   All sides this session also on **LP:** Ajax LP141

Broadcast schedule (all New Yorker): Fri., Feb. 10, CBS [WABC], 11:30-12:00 P.M. / Sat., Feb. 11, MBS [WOR], 11:05-11:30 P.M.

The Sunday, February 12, replacement at the New Yorker was Jack Teagarden's band, advertised as "presented by Jimmy Dorsey." Red Nichols was the substitute band, Sunday, February 26.

Broadcast schedule (all New Yorker): Mon., Feb. 13, MBS [WOR], 11:30-12:00 P.M. / Thurs., Feb. 16, CBS [WABC], 11:05-11:30 P.M. / Fri., Feb. 17, CBS [WABC], 11:30-12:00 P.M. / Sat., Feb. 18, MBS [WOR], 11:05-11:30 P.M. / Mon., Feb. 20, MBS [WOR], 11:45-12:00 P.M.

Decca, New York, N.Y. Tuesday, February 21, 1939
JIMMY DORSEY AND HIS ORCHESTRA
Bob Eberly, Helen O'Connell (vcl)

JIMMY DORSEY AND HIS ORCHESTRA (Contd.)

65051-A   **I Get Along Without You Very Well** [Hoagy Carmichael] vBE (cl solo)
    78: Decca 2322, (Au) Y-5395, Brunswick (E) O2728
    LP: Ajax LP141
    TC: Good Music MSC-37083
    CD: Good Music MSC-37083
65052-A   **It's Anybody's Moon** vBE (as solo)
    78: Decca 2322
    LP: Ajax LP141
65053-A   **It's All Yours** [Dorothy Fields; Arthur Schwartz] vHO'C (as solo)
    78: Decca 2332, (Au) Y-5554
    LP: Ajax LP141, Ajazz LP505
65054-A   **This Is It** [Dorothy Fields; Arthur Schwartz] vBE (as solo)
    78: Decca 2332
    LP: Ajax LP141
65054-B   **This Is It** vBE (as solo)
    78: Decca (Au) Y-5659

Broadcast schedule (all New Yorker): Thurs., Feb. 23, CBS [WABC], 11:05-11:30 P.M. / Fri., Feb. 24, CBS [WABC], 11:30-12:00 P.M. / Sat., Feb. 25, MBS [WOR], 11:05-11:30 P.M. / Thurs., Mar. 2, CBS [WABC], 11:05-11:30 P.M. / Fri., Mar. 3, MBS [WOR], 8:30-9:00 P.M. and CBS [WABC], 11:30-12:00 P.M. / Sat., Mar. 4, MBS [WOR], 11:15-11:45 P.M.

Decca, New York, N.Y. Friday, March 3, 1939
JIMMY DORSEY AND HIS ORCHESTRA

65098-A   **Our Love** [Larry Clinton, Buddy Bernier, Bob Emmerich] vBE (cl solo)
    78: Decca 2352, Brunswick (E) O2778
    LP: Ajax LP141
65099-A   **All Of Me** [Seymour B. Simons, Gerald Marks] vHO'C (as solo)
    78: Decca 2352, 25069
    LP: MCA 2-4073, Ajax LP148, Joyce LP6038, Time-Life STB-B10, Music Of Your Life 17003
    TC: Time-Life 4TL-0006, Good Music MSC-2-35489
    CD: Time-Life 4TL-0006, GRP-Decca CD-GRD-626, Kaz (E) 309, Good Music 35489
65200-A   **You're So Desirable** [Ray Noble] vBE (cl solo)
    78: Decca 2363, (Au) Y-5417
    LP: Ajax LP148

"All Of Me" on the last session is quite often cited as one of Helen O'Connell's best and the type of song she preferred to sing.

Broadcast schedule (all New Yorker): Mon., Mar. 6, MBS [WOR], 10:00-10:30 P.M. and CBS [WABC], 11:30-12:00 P.M.

The next night marked the end of their stay at the hotel. Replaced by Henry Busse and his band, they were once more "on the road":

Travel itinerary: Wed., Mar. 8 to Tues., Mar. 14—State Theater, Hartford, Conn. / Thurs., Mar. 16—Penn Athletic Club Ballroom, Philadelphia, Pa. / Fri., Mar. 17 to Thurs., Mar. 23—Paramount Theater, Newark, N.J.

The Hartford date was Helen O'Connell's first stage show experience. Jimmy also backed vocalist Connie Boswell, who shared billing.

On Friday, March 24, 1939, the band opened at the Strand Theater, Broadway and West 47th Street in New York City, whose ads plugged Bob Eberly, Helen O'Connell and Ray McKinley in addition to Jimmy and the band. In between the four-a-day shows, and an extra one Saturday and Sunday nights, Strand customers saw Humphrey Bogart in "You Can't Get Away With Murder."

The band also squeezed in a half-hour Mutual Network *Show Of The Week* on Sunday, March 26. The program, with Ernest Chappell as announcer-emcee, has partially survived on the reverse side of a disk found among the Red Nichols transcription collection at the University of Kansas by Nichols researcher Steve Hester.

Show Of The Week, Mutual Studios, New York, N.Y.—MBS [WOR], 6:30-7:00 P.M. Sunday, March 26, 1939
JIMMY DORSEY AND HIS ORCHESTRA

Honolulu [Gus Kahn; Harry Warren] (cl solo)/ **It's Anybody's Moon** vBE (as solo) / **Undecided** [Sid Robin; Charlie Shavers] (as solo) / **All Of Me** [Seymour B. Simons, Gerald Marks] vHO'C (as solo) / **This Can't Be Love** [Lorenz Hart; Richard Rodgers] (cl solo) / (drum solo by Ray McKinley) / **Deep Purple** [Mitchell Parish; Peter De Rose] vBE (other selections unknown)

Just after finishing the air show, Jimmy was told that his father, who had suffered a serious stroke while Jimmy was in Hollywood, experienced a second one that afternoon at Tommy's Bernardsville, New Jersey, home. Band leader-singer Will Osborne stepped in as leader at the Strand for two Sunday night shows and the first show Monday morning. After being convinced his father was recovering, Jimmy returned to New York in time for the second Monday show.

On closing day at the Strand (Wednesday, April 5) Jimmy competed with Tommy's opening at the Paramount. Friday, April 7, the band began a week at the Flatbush Theater, Brooklyn, New York, and then hit the road as Bob Eberly returned to his hometown.

Travel itinerary: Fri., Apr. 14—PBA Ball, N.Y. State Armory, Troy, N.Y. / Sat., Apr. 15—Sunnybrook Ballroom, Pottstown, Pa. / Sun., Apr. 16—Ritz Ballroom, Bridgeport, Conn. where 1,700 dancers turned out for a gross of $1,496 / Tues., Apr. 18—Glen Park Casino, Williamsville (Buffalo), N.Y. / Fri., Apr. 21 to Thurs., Apr. 27—Palace Theater, Cleveland, Ohio / Fri., Apr. 28 to Wed., May 3—Circle Theater, Indianapolis, Ind. / Thurs., May 4 to Sun., May 7—Palace Theater, Akron, Ohio / Mon., May 8 to Thurs. May 11—Palace Theater Youngstown, Ohio / Fri., May 12 to

Thurs., May 18—Rivoli Theater, Toledo, Ohio / Fri., May 19—Rutgers University, New Brunswick, N.J.

In announcing its 1939 poll of music preferences at colleges, *Billboard* (April 15, 1939, 3) revealed that the Jimmy Dorsey band finished in tenth place out of thirty behind (one to nine) Artie Shaw, Kay Kyser, Tommy Dorsey, Benny Goodman, Larry Clinton, Hal Kemp, Guy Lombardo, Horace Heidt and Glen Gray.

Jimmy signed a two-year renewal with Decca Records, effective May 1. This followed several months of negotiations during which trade-press gossips had Jimmy switching to Brunswick-Vocalion. At the same time, brother Tommy was rumored to be leaving Victor for a new label that former Victor A&R man Eli Oberstein was setting up.

The next major stop that year was Frank Dailey's Meadowbrook in New Jersey, opening Saturday, May 20. Dailey had booked the band partly because of Jimmy's exposure at The New Yorker and partly as a result of urging from Jimmy's manager, Billy Burton. The result was a bonanza for Dailey and the band. Young fans who had heard Jimmy on the radio from the New Yorker, but couldn't afford the hotel's cover charge, flocked to Cedar Grove "on the Newark-Pompton Turnpike," to again quote the remote announcers.

Jimmy's band broke every record there, including those set by brother Tommy, Glenn Miller and Woody Herman. One night alone 1,600 showed up (the capacity was 1,200). New Jersey police reportedly were turning cars back two miles away, because the Meadowbrook was full.

> *sustaining broadcast,* Meadowbrook Ballroom, Cedar Grove, N.J.—NBC-Blue [WJZ], 8:00-8:30 P.M. Saturday, May 20, 1939

JIMMY DORSEY AND HIS ORCHESTRA

Deep Purple [Mitchell Parish; Peter DeRose] vBE / **Pagan Love Song** [Arthur Freed; Nacio Herb Brown] / **Liza** [Ira Gershwin, George Gershwin]

Broadcast schedule (all Meadowbrook): Wed., May 24 MBS [WOR], 8:00-8:15 P.M. / Sat., May 27 NBC-Blue [WJZ], 8:00 to 8:30 P.M. and MBS [WOR], 10:00-10:30 P.M.

Decca, New York, N.Y. Friday, May 26, 1939
JIMMY DORSEY AND HIS ORCHESTRA
Jimmy Dorsey (cl,as,ldr) Ralph Muzzillo, Seymour "Sy" Baker, Shorty Sherock (tp) Bobby Byrne, Don Matteson (tb,vcl) Sonny Lee (tb) Milt Yaner, Sam Rubin (as) Charles Frazier, Herbie Haymer (ts) Freddy Slack (p) Roc Hillman (g) Jack Ryan (sb) Ray McKinley (d,vcl) Bob Eberly, Helen O'Connell, (vcl)

65659-A   **Romance** [Edgar Leslie; Walter Donaldson] (cl solo)
     78: Decca 2536, 4202, 25290, (F) Y-5602
     LP: Ajax LP148
65660-A   **A Home In The Clouds** [Kay Parker; Bob Henderson,
                 Benny Carter, Benny Goodman] vHO'C (as solo)
     78: Decca 2522

LP: Ajax LP148, Ajazz LP505
65661-A   **My Love For You** [Edward Heyman; Harry Jacobson]
                 vBE (cl solo)
    78: Decca 2522, Brunswick (E) O2798, (F) A-82210
    LP: Ajax LP148
65662-A   **Shoot The Meatballs To Me, Dominick Boy!** [Toots
                 Camarata, Jimmy Dorsey] vRM (as solo)
    78: Decca 2612, (E) BM-1163, (Au) Y-5437, Brunswick (E)
    O2905
    LP: Ajax LP148, Bandstand BS7104, Swingfan (G) 1007
65663-A   **All I Remember Is You** [Eddie DeLange; Jimmy Van
                 Heusen] vHO'C (as solo)
    78: Decca 2523, (Au) Y-5468
    LP: Ajax LP148, Ajazz LP505
65664-A   **Show Your Linen Miss Richardson** [Johnny Mercer;
                 Bernie Hanighan] vRM (as solo)
    78: Decca 2523
    LP: Ajax LP148

Broadcast schedule (Meadowbrook): Fri., June 2, NBC-Red [WEAF], 11:00-11:30 P.M.

            sustaining broadcast, Meadowbrook Ballroom, Cedar
            Grove, N.J.—NBC-Blue [WJZ], 8:00-8:30 P.M. Sat-
            urday, June 3, 1939
JIMMY DORSEY AND HIS ORCHESTRA

In The Middle Of A Dream [Al Stillman; Einar Swan] vHO'C (cl
solo) / **'Tain't What You Do (It's The Way What'cha Do It)** [Sy
Oliver; James "Trummy" Young] vRM / **Carolina In The Morning**
[Gus Kahn; Walter Donaldson] (cl solo) / **If I Didn't Care** [Jack
Lawrence] vBE / **All I Remember Is You** [Eddie DeLange; Jimmy
Van Heusen] vHO'C / **Parade Of The Milk Bottle Caps** [Pat
McCarthy, Jimmy Dorsey] (as solo)

Decca, New York, N.Y. Tuesday, June 6, 1939
JIMMY DORSEY AND HIS ORCHESTRA
Bob Eberly, Helen O'Connell (vcl) Toots Camarata (arr)

65739-A   **This Is No Dream** [Benny Davis; Ted Shapiro, Tom-
                 my Dorsey] vBE (as solo)
    78: Decca 2536, (Au) Y-5528
    LP: Ajax LP148
65740-A   **I Poured My Heart Into A Song** [Irving Berlin]
                 vBE (as solo)
    78: Decca 2553, (E) F-7193
    LP: Ajax LP148
65741-A   **Especially For You** [Orrin Tucker, Phil Grogan]
                 vHO'C (as solo)
    78: Decca 2554, (E) F-7176 (Au) Y-5417
    LP: Ajax LP148, Ajazz LP505
65742-A   **An Old Fashioned Tune Always Is New** [Irving
                 Berlin] vDM (as solo)   (Contd.)

JIMMY DORSEY AND HIS ORCHESTRA (Contd.)

> **78:** Decca 2553, (E) F-7193
> **LP:** Ajax LP148
> 65743-A   **All Or Nothing At All** [Jack Lawrence; Arthur Alt-
>   man] vBE (cl solos)
> **78:** Decca 2580, (Au) Y-5554, Y-5823, Brunswick (E) O3422
> **LP:** Decca DL (7) 4853, MCA 2-4073, Ajax LP148

Broadcast schedule (all Meadowbrook): Wed., June 7, NBC-Blue [WJZ], 5:00-5:30
P.M. (see Addenda) / Fri., June 9, NBC-Red [WEAF], 11:00-11:30 P.M. / Sat. June 10,
NBC-Blue [WJZ], 8:00-8:30 P.M. / Sun. June 11, NBC-Blue [WJZ], 5:00-5:30 P.M. /
Tues., June 13, NBC-Blue [WJZ], 5:00-5:30 P.M. (see Addenda) and MBS [WOR],
7:30-8:00 P.M. / Wed., June 14, NBC-Blue [WJZ], 5:00-5:30 P.M. / Thurs., June 15,
NBC-Blue [WJZ], 5:00-5:30 P.M.

The Dorsey brother's feud was fodder for a segment on *The Story Of
Swing,* on New York's WMCA on Sunday, June 11. On the broadcast
the brothers staged a fight and the Boswell Sisters also appeared.

Decca, New York, N.Y. Friday, June 16, 1939
JIMMY DORSEY AND HIS ORCHESTRA

> 65835-A   **Whisper While We Dance** vBE (cl,as solos)
> **78:** Decca 2567, Brunswick (E) O3473
> **LP:** Ajax LP148
> 65836-A   **Back To Back** [Irving Berlin] vHO'C (as solo)
> **78:** Decca 2554, (E) F-7274
> **LP:** Ajax LP156, Ajazz LP505
> 65837-A   **Stairway To The Stars** [Mitchell Parish; Matty Mal-
>   neck, Frank Signorelli] vBE (as solo)
> **78:** Decca 2567, (E) F-7176, BM-1137
> **LP:** Ajax LP156
> also on **TC:** and **CD:** Good Music MSC-37083
> 65838-A   **The Lamp Is Low** [Mitchell Parish; Peter De Rose,
>   Bert Schefter] vBE
> **78:** Decca 2579, (E) F-7274
> **LP:** Ajax LP156

The trade press revealed that Bobby Byrne would soon be leaving the
band to start his own group, with financial help from Jimmy.
On Friday, June 16 Jimmy guested on the *Raymond Paige Hour* on
CBS, 9:00-10:00 P.M. playing "Tiger Rag" and "Rhapsody In Blue."

*Broadcast schedule (**Meadowbrook**):* Fri., June 16, NBC-Red [WEAF], 11:00-11:30
P.M. / Sat., June 17, NBC-Red [WEAF], 8:00-8:30 P.M. and MBS [WOR], 10:00-10:30
P.M.

The Dorsey band's increased airings were a direct result of the
phenomenal crowds they were drawing to the Meadowbrook.   The
owner, Frank Dailey, himself a musician and bandleader, also fully
understood the value of radio time in attracting teenage dancers.

Broadcast schedule (all Meadowbrook): Wed., June 21, NBC-Blue [WJZ], 5:00-5:30 P.M. (The last quarter hour is reported to also have been carried on NBC-Red) and MBS [WOR], 8:15-8:30 P.M. / Thurs., June 22, NBC-Blue [WJZ], 5:00-5:30 P.M.

Decca, New York, N.Y. Friday, June 23, 1939
JIMMY DORSEY AND HIS ORCHESTRA

65876-A   **In The Middle Of A Dream** [Al Stillman; Einar Swan] vHO'C arrTC (cl solo)
   78: Decca 2580, (E) F-7189, BM-1137, (Au) Y-5402
   LP: Ajax LP156, Ajazz LP505
65877-A   **Begone** vHO'C arrTC (as solo)
   78: Decca 2579, (E) F-7288
   LP: Ajax LP156, Ajazz LP505
   CD: Empress (E) 852
65878-A   **Rendezvous Time In Paree** [Al Dubin; Jimmy Mc-Hugh] vBE arrTC (as solo)
   78: Decca 2577, (Au) Y-5575
   LP: Ajax LP156
65879-A   **Is It Possible?** [Al Dubin; Jimmy McHugh] vHO'C arrTC (as,cl solos)
   78: Decca 2577, (Au) Y-5560
   LP: Ajax LP156
65880-A   **Body And Soul** [Robert Sour, Edward Heyman, Frank Eyton; Johnny Green] vBE (as solo)
   78: Decca 2735, 25069, (E) BM-1163, Brunswick (E) O2905
   LP: Decca DL-8609, Ajax LP156

Broadcast schedule (all Meadowbrook): Fri., June 23, NBC-Blue [WJZ], 11:00-11:30 P.M. / Sat., June 24, NBC-Blue [WJZ], 8:00-8:30 P.M. / Sun., June 25, NBC-Blue [WJZ], 5:15-5:30 P.M. / Tues., June 27, MBS [WOR], 7:30-7:45 P.M. / Wed., June 28, NBC-Red [WEAF], 12:00-12:30 A.M. and 5:15-5:30 P.M. and MBS [WOR], 9:30-10:00 P.M. / Thurs., June 29, NBC-Blue [WJZ], 5:00-5:30 P.M. and MBS [WOR], 11:30-12:00 P.M. (opposite brother Tommy from the Hotel Pennsylvania Roof on NBC-Blue) / Fri., June 30, NBC-Red [WEAF], 11:00-11:30 P.M. / Sat., July 1, MBS [WOR], 1:30-2:00 A.M. and NBC-Blue [WJZ], 8:00-8:30 P.M.

Ray McKinley, kingpin of the Dorsey rhythm section since the early thirties, left Jimmy in early July 1939 to join Will Bradley in a band that would soon have as many tensions as the Dorsey Brothers'. Despite hits like "Beat Me Daddy, Eight To the Bar," "Down The Road Apiece" and "Celery Stalks At Midnight," the band lasted only about three years. Dave Tough temporarily, and more permanently Buddy Schutz, replaced Ray at drums. With McKinley's departure the driving beat that he had brought to the band seemed to disappear.

Broadcast schedule (all Meadowbrook): Sun., July 2, NBC-Blue [WJZ], 5:30-5:45 P.M. and MBS [WOR], 7:30-8:00 P.M.

On Tuesday, July 4, the Meadowbrook was closed and Jimmy took the band to Hershey Park Ballroom in Hershey, Pennsylvania. In the town that chocolate built, the band drew 2,200 dancers, earning the senior Dorsey $1,311 in holiday income (*Billboard,* July 15, 1939, 10).

On Thursday, July 6, the Meadowbrook unveiled an outdoor summer garden adjacent to its 1,200-seat ballroom.

Broadcast schedule (all Meadowbrook): Thurs., July 6, NBC-Blue [WJZ], 5:00-5:30 P.M. and MBS [WOR] 11:30-12:00 P.M. (again opposite Tommy) / Fri., July 7, NBC-Red [WEAF], 11:00-11:30 P.M. / Sat., July 8, MBS [WOR], 1:30-2:00 A.M. and NBC-Blue [WJZ], 8:00-8:30 P.M. / Sun., July 9, NBC-Blue [WJZ], 5:15-5:45 P.M. / Thurs., July 13, NBC-Blue [WJZ], 5:00-5:30 P.M. / Fri., July 14, NBC-Red [WEAF], 11-11:30 P.M. / Sat., July 15, MBS [WOR], 1:30-2:00 A.M. and NBC-Blue [WJZ], 8:00-8:30 P.M.

Decca, New York, N.Y. Friday, July 14, 1939
JIMMY DORSEY AND HIS ORCHESTRA

65966-A   **A Man And His Dream** [Johnny Burke; James V. Monaco] vBE (cl,as solos)
   78: Decca 2650, (E) F-7271
   LP: Ajax LP156, Big Band Archives LP-1203
65967-A   **The Jumpin' Jive (Jim Jam Jump)** [Cab Calloway, Frank Froeba, Jack Palmer] vHO'C (as solo)
   78: Decca 2612, (E) BM-1159, Brunswick (E) O2908
   LP: Ajax LP156, Ajazz LP505, Coral (G) COPS7449, 6.28219
65968-A   **Dixieland Detour** [Toots Camarata, Jimmy Dorsey] arrTC (as solo)
   78: Decca 2735, (E) BM-1159, (Au) Y-5437, Brunswick (E) O2908
   (SSL-3819) **ET:** AFRS Basic Music Library 1903
   45: Coral 9-60349
   LP: Ajax LP156, Coral CRL-56008, (G) COPS7449, 6.28219
   CD: Empress (E) 852
65969-A   **Go Fly A Kite** [Johnny Burke; James V. Monaco] vHO'C (as solo)
   78: Decca 2650, (E) F-7271
   LP: Ajax LP156, Ajazz LP505

In the 1939 *Make Believe Ballroom* popularity poll on WNEW, New York, Jimmy's band moved from seventeenth place in 1938 to seventh, a good showing but still behind Benny Goodman, Artie Shaw, Tommy Dorsey, Glenn Miller, Sammy Kaye and Gene Krupa.

On Sunday, July 16, Jimmy staged a benefit concert, attended by over 2,000, for Charles Levine, a waiter at the Meadowbrook who was hospitalized after a State Police car struck him in front of the ballroom.

Broadcast schedule (all Meadowbrook): Sun., July 16, NBC-Blue [WJZ], 5:15-5:30 P.M. / Thurs., July 20, NBC-Blue [WJZ], 5:00-5:30 P.M. / Fri., July 21, NBC-Blue [WJZ], 11:00-11:30 P.M. / Sat., July 22, MBS [WOR], 1:30-2:00 A.M. and NBC-Blue [WJZ], 8:00-8:30 P.M. / Sun., July 23, NBC-Blue [WJZ], 5:15-5:45 P.M. / Tues., July 25, NBC-Blue [WJZ], 7:30-8:00 P.M. and NBC-Red [WEAF], 11:30-12:00 P.M. / Wed., July 26, MBS [WOR], 10:00-10:15 P.M.

The next evening Jimmy was replaced by Charlie Barnet.

Travel itinerary: Fri., July 28—Willows Ballroom, Pittsburgh, Pa. / Wed., Aug. 2 to Sat., Aug. 5—unknown locations in New England / Sun., Aug. 6—Pleasure Beach Ballroom, Bridgeport, Conn., where 1,539 paid $1,354 (*Billboard*, Aug. 19, 1939, 9) / Tues., Aug. 8—Thousand Island Casino, Clayton, N.Y. / Wed., Aug. 9—Russell's Danceland, Sylvan Beach, between Syracuse and Utica, N.Y. / Thurs., Aug. 10—Lakewood Park, Mahanoy City, Pa. / Fri., Aug. 11 to Sun., Aug. 13—three unknown locations in New England.

Jimmy's song "So Many Times" in the next session also got "cover" recordings by Tommy, Jack Teagarden and Tommy Tucker. The Bob Eberly vocal seemed to be the most popular, but despite all the releases the song never went far.

Decca, New York, N.Y. Monday, August 14, 1939
JIMMY DORSEY AND HIS ORCHESTRA

66082-A   **One Sweet Letter From You** [Lew Brown, Sidney Clare; Harry Warren] vHO'C (cl solo)
    78: Decca 2702, Brunswick (E) O3015
    LP: Ajax LP156, Ajazz LP505, Bandstand BS7120
    TC: Good Music 35489
    CD: Aero Space AS7120, Good Music 35489
66083-A   **So Many Times** [Don DeVito; Jimmy Dorsey] vBE (cl solo)
    78: Decca 2727
    LP: Ajax LP156
66084-A   **It's Funny To Everyone But Me** [Dave Franklin, Isham Jones] vBE (as solo)
    78: Decca 2702, (Au) Y-5468, Brunswick (E) O3249
    LP: Ajax LP164
66085-A   **Take A Tip From The Whippoorwill** vHO'C (as solo)
    78: Decca 2727
    LP: Ajax LP164, Ajazz LP505

The band spent the hot days of mid-August at the Surf Beach Club, Virginia Beach, Virginia, where it worked the week beginning Saturday, August 19.

In a feature article in *Billboard* (August 26, 1939, 22), titled "Contrasting Music—Swing and Sweet," Jimmy laid out his philosophy as a bandleader, and showed he was slowly becoming dollar oriented: "I would go nuts after about two sessions with a Mickey Mouse band." He added that featuring swing was fine, but it pleased only the musicians who "always come in on passes anyway" and the jitterbugs who "keep their checks in two figures—on the right side of the decimal point."

Conversely, Jimmy said that sweet music was fine, but limited a band to hotels they couldn't afford to play twelve months of the year. The answer was to provide a balance of both styles, which he said he did in his contrasting style. This way, he concluded, a band could carry the teens into their thirties, by which time "the boys in your band will start calling you Pops."

Jimmy and the band recorded twelve tracks sometime between August 15 and 25 for the RCA Thesaurus transcription service.

Victor, New York, N.Y. Mid-August 1939
JIMMY DORSEY AND HIS ORCHESTRA

MS-037951-1   **Shine On, Harvest Moon** [Nora Bayes, Jack Norworth] (as solo)
  ET: RCA Thesaurus 711
  LP: Decca (G) 6.23550, Hindsight HSR-101
  TC: Hindsight HSC-101, MCH 415TC
  CD: Hindsight HCD-101, HCD-325, HCD-415, Pilz 2049
MS-037951-1   **So Many Times** [Don DeVito; Jimmy Dorsey] vBE (cl solo)
  ET: RCA Thesaurus 711
MS-037951-1   **Major And Minor Stomp** [Joe Lippman, Jimmy Dorsey] (as solo)
  ET: RCA Thesaurus 711
  LP: Big Band Archives LP-1203
MS-037951-1   **Just For A Thrill** [Lillian Hardin Armstrong, Don Raye] vHO'C (as solo)
  ET: RCA Thesaurus 711
  LP: Decca (G) 6.23550, Hindsight HSR-101
  TC: Hindsight HSC-101, MCH 415TC
  CD: Hindsight HCD-101, HCD-333, HCD-415
MS-037952-1   **A Man And His Drum** [Toots Camarata] (as solo)
  ET: RCA Thesaurus 710
  78: Big Band Archives LP-1203
MS-037952-1   **After All** [Bud Green; Guy Wood] vBE
  ET: RCA Thesaurus 710
MS-037952-1   **At Least You Could Say Hello** [Sammy Mysels, Dick Robertson, Charles McCarthy] vHO'C
  ET: RCA Thesaurus 710
  LP: Decca (G) 6.23550, Hindsight HSR-101
  TC: Hindsight HSC-101
  CD: Hindsight HCD-101
MS-037952-1   **Carolina In The Morning** [Gus Kahn; Walter Donaldson] (cl solo)
  ET: RCA Thesaurus 710
  LP: Decca (G) 6.23550, Hindsight HSR-101
  TC: Hindsight HSC-101, MCH 415TC
  CD: Hindsight HCD-101, HCD-325, HCD-415, Pilz 2049
MS-037953-1   **Lilacs In The Rain** [Mitchell Parish; Peter De Rose] vBE
  ET: RCA Thesaurus 711
MS-037953-1   **Dixieland Detour** [Toots Camarata, Jimmy Dorsey] (as solo)
  ET: RCA Thesaurus 711
MS-037953-1   **Melancholy Lullaby** [Edward Heyman; Benny Carter] vHO'C
  ET: RCA Thesaurus 711

MS-037953-1   **Shoot The Meat Balls To Me, Dominick Boy!**
                  [Toots Camarata, Jimmy Dorsey] (as solo)
      ET: RCA Thesaurus 711
      LP: Decca (G) 6.23550, Hindsight HSR-101
      TC: Hindsight HSR-101
      CD: Hindsight HCD-101

Travel itinerary: Sun., Aug. 27 to Tues., Aug. 29— Hamid's Million Dollar Pier, Atlantic City, N.J. / Wed., Aug. 30—New York Daily News Harvest Moon Ball, Madison Square Garden, New York, N.Y. / Sat., Sept. 2—Philmont Country Club, Philadelphia, Pa. / Sun., Sept. 3—Hunt's Ocean Pier, Wildwood, N.J.

The piano change in the next session is the result of the Will Bradley/Ray McKinley organization taking another of Jimmy's better players. Pianist-arranger Freddy Slack jumped ship in late summer to become Will and Ray's boogie-woogie expert.

Decca, New York, N.Y. Tuesday, September 5, 1939
JIMMY DORSEY AND HIS ORCHESTRA
Joe Lippman (p,arr) replaces Slack

66265-A   **Let's Make Memories Tonight** [Lew Brown, Charles Tobias; Sam H. Stept] vBE (as solo)
      78: Decca 2745, Brunswick (E) O2895
      LP: Ajax LP164
66266-A   **Are You Havin' Any Fun?** [Jack Yellen; Sammy Fain] vHO'C (cl solo)
      78: Decca 2761
      LP: Ajax LP164, Ajazz LP505
66267-A   **If I Had You** [Jimmy Campbell, Reg Connelly, Ted Shapiro] vBE (as solo)
      78: Decca 2814, Brunswick (E) O3015
      LP: Ajax LP164
66268-A   **Melancholy Lullaby** [Edward Heyman; Benny Carter] vHO'C (as solos)
      78: Decca 2761
      LP: Ajax LP164, Ajazz 510
66269-A   **Comes Love** [Lew Brown, Charles Tobias; Sam H. Stept] vHO'C (as solo)
      78: Decca 2745, (E) BM-1147, Brunswick (E) O2895
      LP: Ajax LP164, Ajazz 510
      CD: Living Era (E) ASV5087

After the last session the band took a two-week vacation made possible when Jimmy canceled a private party in Chicago that had been booked by the Dictaphone-Mimeograph mogul A. B. Dick and a one-nighter at the Lake Forest, Illinois, Pavilion in mid-September. Helen O'Connell used the time off for a tonsil operation.

Travel itinerary: Thurs., Sept. 21 to Wed., Sept. 27—Brandt's Audubon Theater, Queens, N.Y. / Thurs., Sept. 28 to Wed., Oct. 4—Carlton Theater, Jamaica, Long Island, N.Y.

The resounding success of that summer 1939 booking of Jimmy and the band brought them back for a fall date at The Meadowbrook, opening Thursday, October 5, and closing November 16. Opening night there was a Mutual pickup that has been preserved and includes the rarely heard lyrics to Glenn Miller's theme.

> *sustaining broadcast,* Meadowbrook Ballroom, Cedar Grove, N.J.—MBS [WOR], 7:30-8:00 P.M. Thursday, October 5, 1939

JIMMY DORSEY AND HIS ORCHESTRA

Contrasts [Jimmy Dorsey] (theme) (as solo) / **Shine On, Harvest Moon** [Nora Bayes, Jack Norworth] (as solo) / **Moonlight Serenade** [Mitchell Parish, Alton Glenn Miller] vBE / **Comes Love** [Lew Brown, Charles Tobias; Sam H. Stept] vHO'C (as solo) / **So Many Times** [Don DeVito; Jimmy Dorsey] vBE (cl solo) / **Dixieland Detour** [Toots Camarata, Jimmy Dorsey] (as solo) / **It's Funny To Everyone But Me** [Dave Franklin, Isham Jones] vBE (as solo) / **Go Fly A Kite** [Johnny Burke; James V. Monaco] vHO'C (as solo) / **Pagan Love Song** [Arthur Freed; Nacio Herb Brown] / **Contrasts** (theme)
    Entire broadcast on **LP:** Fanfare LP8-108

Broadcast schedule (Meadowbrook): Fri., Oct. 13, MBS [WOR], 10:45-11:00 P.M.

Decca, New York, N.Y. Friday, October 20, 1939
JIMMY DORSEY AND HIS ORCHESTRA
Jimmy Dorsey (cl,as,ldr) Ralph Muzzillo, Shorty Sherock, Sy Baker (tp) Bobby Byrne, Sonny Lee (tb) Don Matteson (tb,vcl) Milt Yaner, Sam Rubin (as) Herbie Haymer (ts) Charlie Frazier (ts,fl) Joe Lippman (p,arr) Roc Hillman (g) Jack Ryan (sb) Buddy Schutz (d) Bob Eberly, Helen O'Connell (vcl) Toots Camarata, Harold Mooney (arr)

66785-A   **Love Never Went To College** [Lorenz Hart; Richard Rodgers] vHO'C (as solo)
    78: Decca 2813
    LP: Ajax LP164, Ajazz 510
66786-A   **I Didn't Know What Time It Was** [Lorenz Hart; Richard Rodgers] vBE (as solo)
    78: Decca 2813
    LP: Ajax LP164
66787-A   **My Prayer** [George Boulanger, Jimmy Kennedy] vBE
    78: Decca 2810, Brunswick (E) O2934
    LP: Decca DL8609, DL(7)4248, MCA 2-4073, Ace Of Hearts (E) AH-114, Ajax LP164, Time-Life STB-B10
    TC: Time-Life 4TL-0006
    CD: Time-Life 4TL-0006
66788-A   **You're The Greatest Discovery (Since 1942)** vHO'C (as solo)
    78: Decca 2810
    LP: Ajax LP164, Ajazz 510
66789-A   **A Table In The Corner** [Sam Coslow; Dana Suesse]

vBE (as solo)
78: Decca 2814
LP: Ajax LP164
66790-A   **A Man And His Drum** [Toots Camarata] (as solo)
78: Decca 2961, set A-135, (Au) Y-5567, Brunswick (E) O2950,
60195
(SSL-3933-4) **ET:** AFRS Basic Music Library P-1945
LP: Ajax LP164, Coral CRL56004

As predicted, Bobby Byrne left the band after the Decca session to
form his own crew, with Jimmy's personal and some say financial
blessings. Jerry Rosa from the Van Alexander band replaced him.

Broadcast schedule (Meadowbrook): Fri., Oct. 20, MBS [WOR], 10:45-11:00 P.M.

sustaining broadcast, Meadowbrook Ballroom, Cedar
Grove, N.J.—MBS [WOR], 10:45-11:00 P.M. Fri-
day, October 27, 1939
JIMMY DORSEY AND HIS ORCHESTRA

Contrasts [Jimmy Dorsey] (theme) / **South Of The Border (Down
Mexico Way)** [Jimmy Kennedy, Michael Carr] / **My Silent Mood**
vBE (as solo) / **A Table In The Corner** [Sam Coslow; Dana Suesse]
vBE (as solo) / **Major And Minor Stomp** [Joe Lippman, Jimmy
Dorsey] (as solo) / **Contrasts** (theme)

Broadcast schedule (Meadowbrook): Sat., Oct. 28, NBC-Red [WEAF], 8:00-8:30 P.M.

The next afternoon, Sunday, October 29, the band staged another of
its popular swing concerts at the Meadowbrook. The band's stay with
Frank Dailey was extended two more weeks, closing November 15 and
canceling a November 3 date in Springfield, Massachusetts.

Decca, New York, N.Y. Friday, November 3, 1939
JIMMY DORSEY AND HIS ORCHESTRA
Johnny Mendell (tp) replaces Sherock, Jerry Rosa (tb) replaces Byrne

66825-A   **On A Little Street In Singapore** [Peter De Rose,
Billy Hill] vBE (as solo)
78: Decca 2838, Brunswick (E) O2934
LP: Ajax LP164
66826-A   **My Silent Mood** vBE (as solo)
78: Decca 2838
LP: Ajax LP172
66827-A   **You're A Lucky Guy** [Sammy Cahn; Saul Chaplin]
vHO'C (as solo)
78: Decca 2837
LP: Ajax LP172, Ajazz 510
66828-A   **Tomorrow Night** [Sam Coslow; Will Grosz] vBE (cl,
as solos)
78: Decca 2837
LP: Ajax LP172 (Contd.)

JIMMY DORSEY AND HIS ORCHESTRA (Contd.)

66829-A   **Major And Minor Stomp** [Joe Lippman, Jimmy
                 Dorsey] (as solo)
   78: Decca 2980, set A-135, (Au) Y-5700, Brunswick (E) O2950
   (SSL-3819) **ET:** AFRS Basic Music Library 1903
   LP: Coral CRL-56008, Ajax LP172, Swingfan (G) 1007

Broadcast schedule (all Meadowbrook): Fri., Nov. 3, MBS [WOR], 10:45-11:00 P.M.
/ Sat., Nov. 4, NBC-Red [WEAF], 8:00-8:30 P.M. (see Addenda) / Sun., Nov. 5, MBS
[WOR], 9:45-10:00 P.M. / Wed., Nov. 8, MBS [WOR], 9:15-9:30 P.M. / Thurs., Nov.
9, MBS [WOR], 9:15-9:30 P.M. / Fri., Nov. 10, MBS [WOR], 10:45-11:00 P.M. /
Sat., Nov. 11, NBC-Red [WEAF], 8:00-8:30 P.M. / Sun., Nov. 12, MBS [WOR],
9:45-10:00 P.M. / Wed., Nov. 15, MBS [WOR], 8:00-8:30 P.M.

                    sustaining broadcasts, Meadowbrook Ballroom, Cedar
                    Grove, N.J.—NBC October 5-November 15, 1939
JIMMY DORSEY AND HIS ORCHESTRA

   Contrasts [Jimmy Dorsey] (theme) / **Shine On, Harvest Moon**
   [Nora Bayes, Jack Norworth] (as solo) / **South Of The Border
   (Down Mexico Way)** [Jimmy Kennedy, Michael Carr] / **Pagan Love
   Song** [Arthur Freed; Nacio Herb Brown] (as solo) / **Bugle Call Rag**
   [Eubie Blake, Carey Morgan] (cl solo) / **You're A Lucky Guy**
   [Sammy Cahn; Saul Chaplin] vHO'C (as solo) / **My Prayer** [George
   Boulanger, Jimmy Kennedy] vBE
   All selections on **CD:** Jazz Hour JH-1053

   The band closed at the Meadowbrook on November 15 and was
replaced by the Glenn Miller band.

Travel itinerary: Fri., Nov. 17—Hill School, Pottstown, Pa. / Sat., Nov. 18—Arena,
New Haven, Conn. / Sun., Nov. 19—Savoy Ballroom, New York, N.Y. / Wed., Nov.
22—George F Pavilion, Johnson City, N.Y. / Sun., Nov. 26—Ritz Ballroom, Bridgeport, Conn. (1,938 patrons for a gate of $1,750).

Decca, New York, N.Y. Monday, November 27, 1939
JIMMY DORSEY AND HIS ORCHESTRA

66910-A   **Now You Know** vBE (as solo)
   78: Decca 2925
   LP: Ajax LP172
66911-A   **Do It Again** [Kay Werner, Sue Werner] vBE&HO'C
   78: Decca 2925, 25301
   LP: Ajax LP172, Ajazz 510
66912-A   **Rigamarole** [Harold Mooney] (cl,as solos)
   78: Decca 2918, set A-135, Coral 60194, Brunswick (E) O3050
   (SSL-3933-6) **ET:** AFRS Basic Music Library P-1945
   LP: Coral CRL56004, Big Band Archives LP1203, Ajax LP172
66913-A   **Swamp Fire** [Harold Mooney] (as,cl solos)
   78: Decca 2918, set A-135, (Au) Y-5786, Coral 60194,
   Brunswick (E) O3050

(SSL-3819) **ET:** AFRS Basic Music Library 1903
LP: Coral CRL56004, Big Band Archives LP1203, Swingfan (G)
1007, Ajax LP172
66914-A   **Cherokee** [Ray Noble] (cl,as solo)
78: Decca 2961, set A-135, (Au) Y-5567, Coral 60195
(SSL-3819) **ET:** AFRS Basic Music Library 1903
LP: Coral CRL56004, Ajax LP172
CD: Empress (E) 852

Travel itinerary: Thurs., Nov. 30—Roseland Ballroom, New York, N.Y. / Fri., Dec.
1—IFC Hall, Troy, N.Y. / Sat., Dec. 2—Debutante's Ball, Ritz Carlton Hotel, New
York, N.Y. / Sun., Dec. 3—Roseland Ballroom, Brooklyn, N.Y.

World, New York, N.Y. Monday, December 4, 1939
JIMMY DORSEY AND HIS ORCHESTRA

3473   **Major And Minor Stomp** [Joe Lippman, Jimmy
                Dorsey] (as solo)
        ET: World 3473/3476, B11, B21211
        LP: Circle 30, Big Band Archives LP-1203
        CD: Circle CCD30
3474   **Do It Again** [Kay Werner, Sue Werner] vBE&HO'C
                (as solo)
        ET: World 3473/3476, B11, B21211
        LP: Circle 30
        CD: Circle CCD30
3475   **Dixieland Detour** [Toots Camarata, Jimmy Dorsey]
        ET: World 3473/3476, B11, B21211
        LP: Circle 46
        CD: Circle CCD30
3476   **One Sweet Letter From You** [Lew Brown, Sidney
                Clare; Harry Warren] vHO'C (cl solo)
        ET: World 3473/3476, B11, B21211
        LP: Circle 30
        CD: Circle CCD30
3477   **Cherokee** [Ray Noble] (cl,as solos)
        ET: World 3477/3480, B11, B21211
        LP: Circle 30
        CD: Circle CCD30
3478   **Last Night** [Nick and Charles Kenny, Austen Croom-
                Johnson] vBE (as solo)
        ET: World 3477/3480, B11, B21211
        LP: Circle 30
        CD: Circle CCD30
3479   **You're A Lucky Guy** [Sammy Cahn; Saul Chaplin]
                vHO'C (as solo)
        ET: World 3477/3480, B11, B21211
        LP: Circle 30
        CD: Circle CCD30
3480   **Now You Know** [Henri Woode, Charles Carpenter,
                Larry Spier] vBE (as solo)
        ET: World 3477/3480, B11, B21211 (Contd.)

3481   **Tomorrow Night** [Sam Coslow; Will Grosz] vBE
        ET: World 3481/3484
        3480 and 3481 also on **CD:** Circle CCD30
3482   **You're The Greatest Discovery (Since 1492)** vHO'C
            (as solo)
        ET: World 3481/3484
3483   **On A Little Street In Singapore** [Peter De Rose,
            Billy Hill] vBE (as solo)
        ET: World 3481/3484
        LP: Circle 30
        CD: Circle CCD30
3484   **At Least You Could Say Hello** [Sammy Mysels,
            Dick Robertson, Charles McCarthy] vHO'C (as solo)
        ET: World 3481/3484
        LP: Hindsight HSR-101
        TC: Hindsight HSC-101
        CD: Circle CCD30, Hindsight HCD-101

Decca, New York, N.Y. Tuesday, December 5, 1939
JIMMY DORSEY AND HIS ORCHESTRA

66927-A   **Keep A-Knockin' (But You Can't Come In)** [Mays,
            Bradford] vHO'C&band arrTC (as solos)
        78: Decca 2980, set A-135, (Au) Y-5700, Brunswick (E) O3106
        LP: Coral (G) COPS7449, 6.28219, Folkways FP59, Ajax
        LP172, Ajazz LP510
        CD: Empress (E) 852
66928-A   **On The Trail** (unissued)

Travel itinerary: Thurs., Dec. 7—Roseland Ballroom, New York, N.Y. / Fri., Dec. 8
to Thurs., Dec. 14—Stanley Theater, Pittsburgh, Pa. / Fri., Dec. 15—Biltmore Hotel,
Providence, R.I. / Sat., Dec. 16—Manhattan Center, New York, N.Y. / Sun., Dec.
17—Westchester County Civic Center, White Plains, N.Y.

Eastern Service studio, Astoria, Long Island, Winter 1939
JIMMY DORSEY AND HIS ORCHESTRA: Leslie Roush, director
JIMMY DORSEY AND HIS ORCHESTRA

    Contrasts [Jimmy Dorsey] (theme) / **Beebe** [Jimmy Dorsey] (as solo)
    / **My Wubba Dolly** [Kay Werner, Sue Werner] vHO'C&band / **Only
    A Rose** [Brian Hooker; Rudolf Friml] vBE (as solo) / **John Silver**
    [Ray Krise, Jimmy Dorsey] (as solo)
        All selections on **FILM:** Paramount *Jimmy Dorsey And His
    Orchestra*, **VIDEO:** Swingtime 105

Travel itinerary: Wed., Dec. 20—Louisville, Ky. / Fri., Dec. 22—Czar Club, Cleveland, Ohio / Sat., Dec. 23—Castle Farm, Cincinnati, Ohio / Sun., Dec. 24—
Greystone Ballroom, Detroit, Mich. / Mon., Dec. 25—Grand Rapids, Mich.

    The band opened at Chicago's Hotel Sherman on Wednesday,
December 27, and began four NBC network and eight local radio feeds
weekly.

The View from On High
(1940-1941)

By 1940 the contrasts between Jimmy and his younger brother were vividly evident. To understand them one must realize that in the late thirties and early forties the top big bands were box-office royalty, so much so that when they visited anywhere out of New York City it was like the king and his court had come to town. Tommy recognized this intuitively and exuded the warmth, strong personality and stage experience that reached crowds immediately. Jimmy, on the other hand, was ill-at-ease "out front" and had little "crowd savvy," often beating off tough tempos for his own satisfaction, not that of the audience.

As a result, Tommy was rated high in the popularity polls and had a regular weekly commercial broadcast on which the band was featured and he appeared as a personality. Jimmy was not as fortunate in the polls and his commercial air exposure so far had been limited to being the house band for Bing Crosby, which ended thirty months before.

But even more a factor than differences in personality were the contrasts that existed in their business drive and ability. Tommy was by far the stronger of the two, easily making the tough decisions that affected his business future. Jimmy, on the other hand, was content to let his manager, Billy Burton, take over the finances.

Brother Tommy was always investing in other enterprises to make his money earn more. He bought a music publishing company about this time, renaming it Sun Music Company, and for a while put out his own music magazine, *Bandstand*.

By comparison, Jimmy's major successes were those that came from the actions of someone else. The big years for the band were the early forties, thanks to the popularity of Bob Eberly and Helen O'Connell. Jimmy's many movies were the result of his business manager's efforts. The one thing he was sure of was his musical talent, and that he would continue to utilize until the end.

There are those who say that Jimmy's continued acceptance by the public was in part due to the greater popularity of his brother. Tommy's success carried Jimmy along, the argument goes. Those who accept that ignore the talent that Jimmy possessed as a musician. There are an equal number of Jimmy's supporters who say he had a greater technical mastery of his instruments than did his brother. But as has all too frequently been proven by many a gifted musician, artistic talent is not necessarily bankable.

As the forties began under the clouds of war in Europe, the Jimmy Dorsey Orchestra started to take on the shape and sound that would propel it to a top spot within the year. Jimmy began the decade at the Panther Room of Chicago's famed Hotel Sherman, playing over the holidays and closing in early February.

While in Chicago the band was featured on the *Fitch Bandwagon,* sponsored by the makers of a hair shampoo for men, on Sunday, January 21, 1940, 6:30-7:00 P.M. CST over the NBC-Red network.

On Monday, February 5, they played for a dance at the University of Illinois in Champaign-Urbana. Jimmy ended the Sherman stay February 8, but not before setting new attendance highs for the Panther Room. They began a road-tour of the Midwest when Woody Herman moved in:

Travel itinerary: Sat., Feb. 10—Pla-Mor Ballroom, Kansas City, Mo. / Sun., Feb. 11—Meads Acres, Topeka, Kans. / Wed., Feb. 14—Madrid Ballroom, Louisville, Ky. / Sat., Feb. 17—Northwestern Univ. Junior Prom, Palmer House, Chicago, Ill. / Fri., Feb. 23—Masonic Temple, Lansing, Mich. / Sat., Feb. 24—dance at Hotel Cleveland, Cleveland, Ohio.

Jimmy marked his "ninth" birthday on February 29 with a party thrown by Chicago pals Squirrel Ashcraft and Jimmy O'Keefe at the Sherman. Four weeks earlier, Bob Eberly had married Florine Callahan, a Broadway dancer, thus, a double celebration (Sanford 1972).

Travel itinerary: Fri., Mar. 1, to Thurs. Mar. 7—State-Lake Theater, Chicago, Ill. / Fri., Mar. 8—Union Building, Iowa City, Iowa / Tues., Wed., Mar. 12 and 13—Univ. of Alabama, Tuscaloosa, Ala. / Thurs., Mar. 14, to Wed., Mar. 27—Blue Room, Hotel Roosevelt, New Orleans, La.

Jimmy brought the band into the Cafe Rouge of Hotel Pennsylvania on April 2, 1940, for what would turn out to be a three-month stay.

Broadcast schedule (Cafe Rouge): Sun., Apr. 7, NBC-Red [WEAF], 12:00-12:30 A.M.

Decca, New York, N.Y. Tuesday, April 9, 1940
JIMMY DORSEY AND HIS ORCHESTRA
Jimmy Dorsey (cl,as,ldr) Johnny Napton, Shorty Solomson, Nat Kazebier (tp) Jerry Rosa, Sonny Lee, Don Matteson (tb) Milt Yaner (as) Sam Rubin (as,bar) Herbie Haymer (ts) Charlie Frazier (ts,fl) Joe Lippman (p,arr) Roc Hillman (g) Jack Ryan (sb) Buddy Schutz (d) Bob Eberly, Helen O'Connell (vcl)

67505   **Julia** vBE (unissued)
67506-A   **I Bought A Wooden Whistle** [Roc Hillman, Jimmy
                   Dorsey] vHO'C (cl solo)
    78: Decca 3280, (Au) Y-5602, Brunswick (E) O3052
    LP: Ajazz LP510
67507-A   **Only A Rose** [Brian Hooker; Rudolf Friml] vBE (as
                   solo)
    78: Decca 18545
67508-A   **Six Lessons From Madame LaZonga** [Charles New-
                   man; James V. Monaco] vHO'C (as solo)
    78: Decca 3152, (Au) Y-5560, Brunswick (E) O3037
    EP: Decca ED614
    LP: Decca DL8153, (C) DL4248, Ajax LP172, Ajazz LP510,
    Time-Life STB-B10, Music Of Your Life 17003

TC: Time-Life 4TL-0006, Good Music MSC-2-35489
CD: Time-Life 4TL-0006, Good Music MSC-2-35489, Empress (E) 817
67509-A   **Boog-It** [Cab Calloway, Buck Ram, Jack Palmer] vHO'C (as solo)
78: Decca 3152, (Au) Y-5560, Brunswick (E) O3037
LP: Ajazz LP510
67506 through 67509 also on LP: Ajaz LP172
CD: Empress (E) 817
67510-A   **Let Me Dream** vBE (as solo)
78: Decca 3311
LP: Ajaz LP205

Broadcast schedule (all Cafe Rouge): Thurs., Apr. 11, NBC-Red [WEAF], 11:30-12:00 P.M. / Sun., Apr. 14, NBC-Red [WEAF], 12:00-12:30 A.M.

Decca, New York, N.Y. Thursday, April 18, 1940
JIMMY DORSEY AND HIS ORCHESTRA

67583-A   **Little Curly Hair In A High Chair** [Charles Tobias; Nat Simon] vHO'C (as solo)
78: Decca 3150, Brunswick (E) O3027 (dubbed)
LP: Ajazz LP510
TC: and CD: Good Music 35489
67584-A   **The Breeze And I** [Al Stillman, Ernesto Lecuona] vBE (cl solo)
78: Decca 3150, 18805, 25119, (Au) Y-5528, Brunswick (E) O3027 (not dubbed)
45: Decca 25119, MCA 60020
EP: Decca ED614
LP: Decca DL5091, DL8153, DL74248, (C) DL4248, MCA 2-4073, Ace Of Hearts (E) AH114, Time-Life STB-B10
TC: Time-Life 4TL-0006, Good Music MSC-37083
CD: Time-Life 4TL-0006, Good Music MSC-37083
67585-A   **Poor Ballerina** vBE (as solo)
78: Decca 3166
67586-A   **Let There Be Love** [Ian Grant; Lionel Rand] vBE (as solo)
78: Decca 3166, Brunswick (E) O3170
All sides this session also on LP: Ajaz LP205

World, New York, N.Y. Mid-April 1940
JIMMY DORSEY AND HIS ORCHESTRA
Toots Camarata, Fletcher Henderson, Ray Krise (arr)

3681   **Imagination** [Johnny Burke; Jimmy Van Heusen] vBE (as solos)
ET: World 3681/3684, Standard B72
LP: Hindsight HSR-101, Decca (GE) 6.23550
TC: Hindsight HSC 101, MCH 415TC
CD: Hindsight HCD-101, HCD-333, HCD-415, Circle CCD-46, Pilz 2049 (Contd.)

JIMMY DORSEY AND HIS ORCHESTRA (Contd.)

3682   **Let There Be Love** [Ian Grant; Lionel Rand] vBE
            (as solo)
    ET: World 3681/3684, Standard B72
    LP: Circle CLP-46
    CD: Circle CCD-46
3683   **You, You Darlin'** [Jack Scholl; M.K. Jerome] vHO'C
            (as,cl solos)
    ET: World 3681/3684, Standard B72
    (VP 602) **78:** V-Disc 217
    LP: Hindsight HSR-101, Decca (GE) 6.23550
    TC: Hindsight HSC 101, MCH 415TC, V-Disc JD#1
    CD: Hindsight HCD-101, HCD-333, HCD-415, Circle CCD-46,
    V-Disc JD#1
3684   **Boog-It** [Cab Calloway, Buck Ram, Jack Palmer]
            vHO'C arrFH (as solo)
    ET: World 3681/3684, Standard B72
    LP: Circle CLP-30
    CD: Circle CCD-30
3685   **Poor Ballerina** [Egan, Coots] vBE (as solo)
    ET: World 3685/3688, Standard B72
    CD: Circle CCD-30
3686   **The Breeze And I** [Al Stillman, Ernesto Lecuona]
            vBE arrTC (cl solo)
    ET: World 3685/3688, Standard B72
    (VP 602) **78:** V-Disc 217
    LP: Circle CLP-30
    TC: V-Disc JD#1
    CD: Circle CCD-30, V-Disc JD#1
3687   **Fools Rush In (Where Angels Fear To Tread)**
            [Johnny Mercer; Rube Bloom] vBE (cl,as solos)
    ET: World 3685/3688, Standard B72
    LP: Hindsight HSR-101, Decca (G) 6.23550
    TC: Hindsight HSC-101, MCH-415TC
    CD: Hindsight HCD-101, HCD-333, HCD-415, Pilz 2049, Circle
    CCD-46
3688   **I Bought A Wooden Whistle** [Roc Hillman, Jimmy
            Dorsey] vHO'C (cl solo)
    ET: World 3685/3688, Standard B72
    LP: Circle CLP-46
    CD: Circle CCD-46
3723   **King Porter Stomp** [Ferdinand "Jelly Roll" Morton]
            (cl solo)
    ET: World 3721/3724, 8239/8243, Standard B75
3724   **Sak House Stomp** [Harold Mooney] (as solo)
    ET: World 3721/3724, 8239/8243, Standard B75
3725   **John Silver** [Ray Krise, Jimmy Dorsey] (cl,as solos)
    ET: World 3725/3728, 8244/8248, Standard B75
    (VP279) **78:** V-Disc 117
    LP: Circle CLP-30
    TC: V-Disc JD#1

CD: Circle CCD-30, V-Disc JD#1
3726   **Contrasts** [Jimmy Dorsey] (theme) (as solos)
ET: World 3725/3728, 8244/8248, Standard B75
(VP 278) **78:** V-Disc 117
LP: Hindsight HSR-101
TC: Hindsight HSC-101, MCH-415TC
CD: Hindsight HCD-101, HCD-415, Circle CCD-46
3727   **Blue Lou** [Edgar Simpson, Irving Mills] (as solo)
ET: World 3725/3728, 8244/8248, Standard B75
LP: Hindsight HSR-101, Decca (G) 6.23550
TC: Hindsight HSC-101, MCH 415TC
CD: Hindsight HCD-101, HCD-325, HCD-415, Circle CCD-46
3728   **Romance** [Edgar Leslie; Walter Donaldson] (as solo)
ET: World 3725/3728, 8244/8248, Standard B75
CD: Circle CCD-30

Broadcast schedule (all Cafe Rouge): Sun., Apr. 21, NBC-Red [WEAF], 12:00-12:30
A.M. / Sun., Apr. 28, NBC-Red [WEAF], 12:00-12:30 A.M.

World Broadcasting System, New York, N.Y. Late April 1940
JIMMY DORSEY AND HIS ORCHESTRA
Guy Smith (g) replaces Hillman

3781   **Only A Rose** [Brian Hooker; Rudolf Friml] vBE (as
                       solo)
ET: World 3781/3784, Standard B77
LP: Circle CLP-46
CD: Circle CCD-46
3782   **Let Me Dream** [Charles; Dawes] vBE (as solo)
ET: World 3781/3784, Standard B77
CD: Circle CCD-30
3783   **Julia** [Mallory, Davis, Moran] (cl solo)
ET: World 3781/3784, Standard B77
(VP 278) **78:** V-Disc 117
LP: Hindsight HSR-101, Decca (G) 6.23550
TC: Hindsight HSC-101, MCH-415TC, V-Disc JD#1
CD: Hindsight HCD-101, HCD-415, Circle CCD-46, V-Disc
JD#1
3784   **Six Lessons From Madame LaZonga** [Charles New
                       man; James V. Monaco] vHO'C (as solo)
ET: World 3781/3784, Standard B77
LP: Circle CLP-46
CD: Circle CCD-46

Jimmy had begun to admire Johnny Hodges' work, and he and
Hodges had come in first and second in the 1940 *Metronome* All-Star
Band balloting. Since both were in Chicago, third-place winner Benny
Carter made the Victor session in New York (Simon 1971, 456).

Decca, New York, N.Y. Tuesday, April 30, 1940
JIMMY DORSEY AND HIS ORCHESTRA
Jimmy Dorsey (cl,as,ldr) Nate Kazebier, Jimmy Campbell, Shorty Sol-

JIMMY DORSEY AND HIS ORCHESTRA (Contd.)
omson (tp) Nat Lobovsky, Don Matteson (tb) Sonny Lee (tb) Milt
Yaner, Sam Rubin (as) Charles Frazier, Herbie Haymer (ts) Joe
Lippman (p,arr) Guy Smith (g) Jack Ryan (sb) Buddy Schutz (d) Bob
Eberly, Helen O'Connell (vcl) Freddy Slack (arr)

67638-A   **Latins Know How** [Irving Berlin] (as solo)
         78: Decca 3176
         EP: Decca ED614
         LP: Decca DL8153, Ajaz LP205
67639-A   **Fools Fall In Love** [Irving Berlin] vBE (as solo)
         78: Decca 3176
         LP: Ajaz LP205
67640-A   **Hear My Song, Violetta** [Buddy Bernier, Bob Emer-
                 ich; Rudolph Luckesch, Othmar Klose] vBE (cl solos)
         78: Decca 3255, (Au) Y-5536, Brunswick (E) O3133
         LP: Ajaz LP205
67641-A   **Devil May Care** [Johnny Burke; Harry Warren] vBE
                 (cl solos)
         78: Decca 3255, (Au) Y-5536, Brunswick (E) O3052
         LP: Ajaz LP205
67642-A   **Contrasts** [Jimmy Dorsey] (theme) arrFS (as solo)
         78: Decca 3198, set A-135, 11064, 25294, Brunswick (E)
         O3074
         45: Decca 1-711, DU1511
         EP: Decca ED614
         LP: Decca DL-7020, DL-8067, DL-8609, DL-74853, Coral (G)
         COPS7449, 6.28219, Ace Of Hearts (E) AH-114, Ajaz LP205,
         MCA 2-4073, Time-Life STB-B10
         TC: Time-Life 4TL-0006, ProArte Digital PCD1013
         CD: Time-Life 4TL-0006, ProArte Digital CDD1013, GRP-Decca
         CD-GRD-626, Kaz (E) 309, Empress (E) 817
67643-A   **Blue (And Broken Hearted)** [Grant Clarke, Edgar
                 Leslie; Lou Handman] vBE&HO'C (cl solos)
         78: Decca 3280, Brunswick (E) O3136
         LP: Ajaz LP205, Ajazz LP510
         Also on **TC, CD:** Good Music 35489

Broadcast schedule (all Cafe Rouge): Fri., May 3, NBC-Blue [WJZ], 7:30-8:00 P.M. /
Sun., May 5, NBC-Red [WEAF], 12:00-12:30 A.M. / Thurs., May 9, NBC-Red
[WEAF], 11:30-12:00 P.M.

Decca, New York, N.Y. Friday, May 10, 1940
JIMMY DORSEY AND HIS ORCHESTRA

67707-A   **I Can't Resist You** [Ned Weaver; Will Donaldson]
                 vBE (cl solo)
         78: Decca 3215, Brunswick (E) O3153
         LP: Ajaz LP205
         CD: Empress (E) 817
67708-A   **How Can I Ever Be Alone?** [Oscar Hammerstein II;
                 Arthur Schwartz] vBE (as solo)

78: Decca 3197
LP: Ajaz LP205
67709-A   I Love To Watch The Moonlight vHO'C (as solo)
78: Decca 3215
LP: Ajaz LP205, Ajazz LP510
67710-A   Tennessee Fish-Fry [Oscar Hammerstein II; Arthur
                 Schwartz] vHO'C (as solo)
78: Decca 3197
LP: Ajaz LP213, Ajazz LP510
67711-A   Tonight (Perfidia) [Milton Leeds; Alberto Domin-
                 guez] (cl solo)
78: Decca 3198, set A-135, (Au) Y-5575, Brunswick (E) O3133
LP: Coral (G) COPS7449, 6.28219, Ajaz LP213

Sometime that spring at the Cafe Rouge Jimmy gathered together a
group of "alumni" from the old Jean Goldkette band at the urging of
Metronome magazine. They included Newell "Spiegle" Willcox, Sonny
Lee and Lloyd Turner (tb) Fuzzy Farrar (tp) Chauncey Morehouse and
Dee Orr (d) Itzey Riskin (p) Doc Ryker (as) and Goldkette.

Broadcast schedule (all Cafe Rouge): Fri., May 10, NBC-Blue [WJZ], 7.30-8.00 P.M.
(the early Sun. NBC-Red feed was bumped by a variety show from the Worlds Fair that
reopened that weekend) / Thurs., May 16, NBC-Red [WEAF], 11:30-12:00 P.M.

World, New York, N.Y. Friday, May 17, 1940
JIMMY DORSEY AND HIS ORCHESTRA
Jimmy Dorsey (cl,as,ldr) Johnny Napton, Nate Kazebier, Shorty
Solomson (tp) Jerry Rosa, Sonny Lee (tb) Don Matteson (tb,vcl) Milt
Yaner, Sam Rubin (as) Herbie Haymer (ts) Charles Frazier (ts,fl) Joe
Lippman (p,arr) Guy Smith (g) Jack Ryan (sb) Buddy Schutz (d) Bob
Eberly, Helen O'Connell (vcl) Toots Camarata (arr)

3825   I'll Never Smile Again [Ruth Lowe] vBE (as solo)
ET: World 3825/3828, Standard B81
LP: Circle CLP-46
CD: Circle CCD-46
3826   Devil May Care [Johnny Burke; Harry Warren] vBE
                 (cl solo)
ET: World 3825/3828, Standard B81
LP: Circle CLP-46
CD: Circle CCD-46
3827   The Nearness Of You [Ned Washington; Hoagy Car-
                 michael] vBE (cl solo)
ET: World 3825/3828, Standard B81
LP: Hindsight HSR-101, Decca (G) 6.23550
TC: Hindsight HSC-101, MCH 415TC
CD: Hindsight HCD-101, HCD-333, HCD-415, Circle CCD-46,
Pilz 2049
3828   I'm Stepping Out With A Memory Tonight [Herb
                 Magidson; Allie Wrubel] vHO'C (cl solo)
ET: World 3825/3828, Standard B81
LP: Hindsight HSR-101, Decca (G) 6.23550 (Contd.)

JIMMY DORSEY AND HIS ORCHESTRA (Contd.)

  TC: Hindsight HSC-101, MCH 415TC
  CD: Hindsight HCD-101, HCD-333, HCD-415, Circle CCD-46,
  Pilz 2049
3829   **Blueberry Hill** [Al Lewis, Larry Stock, Vincent
                     Rose] vBE (as,cl solos)
  ET: World 3829/3832, Standard B81
  LP: Hindsight HSR-101, Decca (G) 6.23550
  TC: Hindsight HSC-101, MCH 415TC
  CD: Hindsight HCD-101, HCD-333, HCD-415, Circle CCD-46
3830   **All This And Heaven Too** [Eddie DeLange; Jimmy
                     Van Heusen] vBE (cl solo)
  ET: World 3829/3832, Standard B81
  LP: Circle CLP-46
  CD: Circle CCD-46
3831   **Once In A Lovetime** vBE
  ET: World 3829/3832, Standard B81
3832   **I Can't Resist You** [Ned Weaver; Will Donaldson]
                     vBE (cl solo)
  ET: World 3829/3832, Standard B81
  LP: Circle CLP-30
  CD: Circle CCD-30

                     sustaining broadcast, Cafe Rouge Hotel Pennsyl-
                     vania, New York, N.Y.—NBC-Blue [WJZ], 7:45-
                     8:00 P.M., Friday, May 17, 1940
JIMMY DORSEY AND HIS ORCHESTRA

  Contrasts [Jimmy Dorsey] (theme) (as solo) / **Mirage** / **Where Do I
  Go From You?** [Walter Bullock; Allie Wrubel] vHO'C / **Hear My
  Song, Violetta** [Buddy Bernier, Bob Emmerich; Rudolph Luckesch,
  Othmar Klose] vBE (cl solos) / (unknown instrumental) / **Contrasts**
  (theme)

Broadcast schedule (all Cafe Rouge): Sun., May 19, NBC-Red [WEAF], 12:00-12:30
A.M. / Thurs., May 23, NBC-Red [WEAF], 11:30-12:00 P.M. (see Addenda) / Fri.,
May 24, NBC-Blue [WJZ], 7:45-8:00 P.M. / Sun., May 26, NBC-Red [WEAF], 12:05
to 12:30 A.M. / Thurs., May 30, NBC-Blue [WJZ], 11:15-11:30 P.M., NBC-Red
[WEAF], 11:30-12:00 P.M. / Fri., May 31, NBC-Blue [WJZ], 7:30-8:00 P.M.

Decca, New York, N.Y. Monday, June 3, 1940
JIMMY DORSEY AND HIS ORCHESTRA

67854-A   **If I Forget You** [Irving Caesar] vBE (cl solo)
  78: Decca 3259
  LP: Ajaz LP213
67855-A   **Where Do You Keep Your Heart?** vBE (as solo)
  78: Decca 3270
  LP: Ajaz LP213
67856-A   **All This And Heaven Too** [Eddie DeLange; Jimmy
                     Van Heusen] vBE (cl solo)

78: Decca 3259
LP: Ajaz LP213
67857-A   **Shades Of Twilight** vBE (cl solo)
78: Decca 3270
LP: Ajaz LP213

On June 6, 1940, Hotel Pennsylvania ran large ads promoting Jimmy and the band, possibly anticipating confusion from the concurrent stage shows the band was starting the next day (June 7) at the Strand.

For three weeks the band doubled between the Pennsylvania, that was at East Thirty-second Street and Fifth Avenue, and the Strand Theater at Broadway and West Forty-seventh Street.

The four-a-day schedule at the theater (with an extra late show Saturday nights) included boxer-actor Slapsie Maxie Rosenbloom and The Berry Brothers dance team. On screen was *Brother Orchid* with Edward G. Robinson and Humphrey Bogart. The Strand box-office did $92,000 for the three week-stand (*Billboard*, July 6, 1940, 20).

> *sustaining broadcast,* Cafe Rouge Hotel Pennsylvania, New York, N.Y.—NBC-Blue [WJZ], 7:30-8:00 P.M. Friday, June 7, 1940

JIMMY DORSEY AND HIS ORCHESTRA

Where Do I Go From You? [Walter Bullock; Allie Wrubel] vHO'C
LP: Fanfare LP 8-108

> *sustaining broadcast,* Cafe Rouge Hotel Pennsylvania, New York, N.Y.—NBC-Red [WEAF], 11:30-12:00 P.M. Thursday, June 13, 1940

JIMMY DORSEY AND HIS ORCHESTRA

Shades Of Twilight vBE (cl solo)

Broadcast schedule (Cafe Rouge): Wed., June 19, NBC-Red [WEAF], 11:30-midnight.

While the band continued at the Pennsylvania through July, there were no broadcasts for two weeks because of a ruling by James C. Petrillo and the musicians' union against both NBC and CBS, that pulled union musicians off all hotel and ballroom remote network broadcasts in a dispute involving several other musicians' locals around the country.

In late June both Jimmy and Tommy filled in for Martin Block (on separate days) as daytime "deejays" on WNEW's *Make Believe Ballroom* while the host vacationed in California.

Jimmy had landed a contract to work a new summer radio show for Twenty Grand cigarettes. It sounded great, but as the show developed, more audience-participation prize gimmicks were pushed into it by the producers until the band's actual airtime became under four minutes. The show was short-lived, folding after three weeks.

Broadcast schedule (all Cafe Rouge unless noted): Twenty Grand Radio Show, Thurs., July 11, NBC-Blue [WJZ], 9:30-10:00 P.M. / Fri., July 12, NBC-Blue [WJZ], 7:30-7:45 P.M. / Mon., July 15, NBC-Blue [WJZ], 11:30-12:00 P.M.

That same week, the Jimmy Dorsey and Tommy Dorsey bands met in Central Park for a softball game, which Tommy's crew won 12-10 by scoring three come-from-behind runs in the ninth inning. Both leaders played, according to *Variety* (July 17, 1940, 35).

Decca, New York, N.Y. Wednesday, July 17, 1940
JIMMY DORSEY AND HIS ORCHESTRA
Nat Lobovsky (tb) returns, replacing Rosa.

67932-A   **Once In A Lovetime** vBE arrTC (as solo)
     78: Decca 3322, Brunswick (E) O3247
67933-A   **And So Do I** [Eddie DeLange; Paul Mann, Stephen Weiss] vBE arrTC (cl,as solos)
     78: Decca 3311, Brunswick (E) O3093
67934-A   **Hep-Tee-Hootie (Juke Box Jive)** [Fud Livingston, Jack Palmer] vHO'C arr TC (as solo)
     78: Decca 3312, Brunswick (E) O3136
     LP: Coral (G) COPS7449, 6.22183
67935-A   **Dolemite** [Buddy Feyne; William Johnson] arrTC (cl solo)
     78: Decca 3312, (Au) Y-5786, Brunswick (E) O3074
     (SSL-3934) **ET:** AFRS Basic Music Library 1946
     45: Coral 9-60349
     LP: CRL56008, Bandstand BS7104, Swingfan (G) 1007
     CD: GRP-Decca CD-GRD-626, Kaz (E) 309
67936-A   **While The Music Plays On** [Lupin Fein, Irving Mills; Emery Heim] vHO'C arrTC (cl solo)
     78: Decca 3322, Brunswick (E) O3247
     All sides also on **LP:** Ajaz LP213

Broadcast schedule (all Cafe Rouge unless noted): Wed., July 17, NBC-Blue [WJZ], 11:30-12:00 P.M. / *Twenty Grand Radio Show,* Thurs., July 18, NBC-Blue [WJZ], 9:30-10:00 P.M. / Fri., July 19, NBC-Blue [WJZ], 7:30-7:45 P.M.

To fulfill a special booking for a wedding in Houston, Texas, that had been firmed up before the Pennsylvania extended the band's stay, Jimmy and company were given Monday, July 22, off in addition to their normal Sunday rest day. The details of the round trip appeared in *Billboard* (August 3, 1940, 13, 27).

The unnamed host, who postponed the wedding until Monday to be sure to get the band, paid $5,800 for Jimmy and crew. They left New York Sunday at 11:00 A.M. aboard a chartered American airliner.

In addition to $2,300 for the air charter, the obviously oil-connected host paid for air-conditioned buses to bring the band to and from the Houston airport, individual rooms for all band members at the Rice Hotel (a real on-the-road luxury), chauffeured limousines for lunch at Houston's Hollywood Dinner Club, and a cocktail party where the band members were nonplaying, nonpaying guests.

The affluent host also provided a specially designed bandstand at the Houston Country Club, made certain there were two sound systems in case one broke down and provided a brand-new grand piano.

The band played from 8:30 P.M. to 12:30 A.M., was treated to a late supper and then bussed back to the airport, where they took off Tuesday morning at 3:00 A.M. for New York and the real world once again.

Broadcast schedule: Twenty Grand Radio Show, Thurs., July 25, NBC-Blue [WJZ], 9:30-10:00 P.M.

sustaining broadcast, Cafe Rouge Hotel Pennsylvania, New York, N.Y.—NBC-Blue [WJZ], 7:30-7:45 P.M.; Friday, July 26, 1940

JIMMY DORSEY AND HIS ORCHESTRA

Contrasts [Jimmy Dorsey] (theme) (as solo) / **Hear My Song, Violetta** [Buddy Bernier, Bob Emmerich; Rudolph Luckesch, Othmar Klose] vBE (cl solos) / **Dolemite** [Buddy Feyne; William Johnson] arrTC (as solo) / **Six Lessons From Madame LaZonga** [Charles Newman; James V. Monaco] vHO'C (as solo) / **Major And Minor Stomp** [Joe Lippman, Jimmy Dorsey] / **I Can't Resist You** [Ned Weaver; Will Donaldson] vBE (cl solo) / **Contrasts** (theme)

By the time the band finished its sixteen weeks at the Pennsylvania it had brought in 25,825 customers (*Variety,* July 31, 1940, 131).

One of their most successful summer bookings was a date at The Steel Pier in Atlantic City, New Jersey, Saturday and Sunday, August 3-4, with the Andrews Sisters. It was the largest weekend draw to that date for the Steel Pier and was followed by a month on the road:

Travel itinerary: Fri., Aug. 9, to Thurs., Aug. 15—Cedar Point Ballroom, Sandusky, Ohio / Fri., Aug. 16, to Thurs., Aug. 22—Michigan Theater, Detroit, Mich. / Fri., Aug. 23—Sandy Beach, Russells Point, Ohio / Sat., Aug. 24—Summit Beach Park Ballroom, Akron, Ohio (where the dance hall had its biggest crowd of the year, 3,768) / Sun., Aug. 25—Yankee Lake Ballroom, Brookfield (Youngstown), Ohio (3,600) / Mon. Aug. 26 to Wed., Aug. 28—Canadian National Exposition, Toronto, Ont., Canada / Sat., Aug. 31—Hershey Park, Hershey, Pa. (2,700 very wet dancers) / Sun., Sept. 1—Hunt's Ocean Pier, Wildwood, N.J. (Despite the fact that no busses, trains and few automobiles were able to get to the seashore, 4,400 showed up. The band made it through flood waters just in time, arriving at 8:00 P.M.) / Labor Day, Mon., Sept. 2—Lakewood Park, Mahanoy City, Pa.

Decca, New York, N.Y. Tuesday, September 3, 1940
JIMMY DORSEY AND HIS ORCHESTRA

68027-A   **Yesterthoughts** [Stanley Adams; Victor Herbert] vBE (cl solo)
    78: Decca 3395, Brunswick (E) O3241
    LP: Ajaz LP213
68028-A   **On The Trail** [Ferde Grofé] (cl solo)
    78: Decca 3395, Brunswick (E) O3241
    LP: Coral (G) COPS7449, 6.22183, Big Band Archives LP-1203, Ajaz LP213
68029-A   **Whispering Grass (Don't Tell The Trees)** [Fred Fisher; Doris Fisher] vBE (as solo) (Contd.)

JIMMY DORSEY AND HIS ORCHESTRA (Contd.)

    78: Decca 3391, Brunswick (E) O3153
    LP: Ajaz LP213
    CD: Empress (E) 817
68030-A   **Talkin' To My Heart** [Jimmy Dorsey, Anthony J.
        Franchini] vBE (as solo)
    78: Decca 3391, (Au) Y-5666
    LP: Ajaz LP221

Down Beat (September 1, 1940) named Jimmy as one of its forty-three "Immortals of Jazz," a feature of the magazine in 1939, 1940 and 1941. Tommy joined the ranks May 13, 1941.

Also in early September 1940, the band was back in the World ET studios for another session. The large number of films in the late thirties were important in keeping the band together and so were these World dates. This was the last transcription date until after World War II.

A side benefit for collectors in later years is that LP, cassette and CD releases of the World material have given them a chance to better hear the quality of the band's sound in this period as compared to the somewhat flat, sometimes noisy sound of the Decca 78s.

World, New York, N.Y. Early September 1940
JIMMY DORSEY AND HIS ORCHESTRA

3833   **On The Trail** [Ferde Grofé] arrTC (cl solo)
    ET: World 3833/3836, Standard B82
    LP: Circle CLP-30, Big Band Archives LP-1203
3834   **Shades Of Twilight** [Buddy Kaye; Jimmy Dorsey]
        vBE (cl solo)
    ET: World 3833/3836, Standard B82
    3833 and 3834 also on **CD:** Circle CCD-30
3835   **Hep-Tee Hootie (Juke Box Jive)** [Fud Livingston,
        Jack Palmer] vHO'C (as solo)
    ET: World 3833/3836, Standard B82
    LP: Circle CLP-46
    CD: Circle CCD-46
3836   **Dolemite** [Buddy Feyne; William Johnson] arrTC
        (as solo)
    ET: World 3833/3836, Standard B82
    LP: Circle CLP-46
    CD: Circle CCD-46, Empress (E) 817
3837   **Flight Of The Jitterbug** [Don Redman] arrDR (as
        solo)
    ET: World 3837/3840, Standard B82
    LP: Hindsight HSR-101, Decca (G) 6.23550
    TC: Hindsight HSC-101
    CD: Hindsight HCD-101, Circle CCD-46
3838   **While The Music Plays On** [Lupin Fein, Irving
        Mills; Emery Heim] vHO'C (cl solo)
    ET: World 3837/3840, Standard B82
    LP: Circle CLP-46

CD: Circle CCD-46
3839   **Moonlight On The River** [Bud Green] (cl,as solos)
    ET: World 3837/3840, Standard B82
    LP: Hindsight HSR-101, Decca (G) 6.23550
    TC: Hindsight HSC-101
    CD: Hindsight HCD-101, Pilz 2049, Circle CCD-46
3840   **And So Do I** [Eddie DeLange; Paul Mann, Stephen
                      Weiss] vBE (cl,as solos)
    ET: World 3837/3840, Standard B82
    LP: Circle CLP-46
    CD: Circle CCD-46

Travel itinerary: Fri., Sept. 6, to Thurs., Sept. 12—Shea's Buffalo theater, Buffalo,
N.Y. / Sat., Sept. 7—Buffalo Country Club (doubling at a debutante dance, making this
and the Shea's date in a fleet of cabs) / Sat., Sept. 14—private party for the DuPont
family, Wilmington Country Club, Wilmington, Del. / Sun., Sept. 15—Ritz Ballroom,
Bridgeport, Conn. (crowd 2,750) / Mon. and Tues., Sept. 16, 17—two locations in
New England / Thurs., Sept. 19, to Wed., Sept. 25—Flatbush Theater, Brooklyn, N.Y.
/ Thurs., Sept. 26, to Wed., Oct. 2—Windsor Theater, Bronx, N.Y.

Decca, New York, N.Y. Tuesday, October 1, 1940
JIMMY DORSEY AND HIS ORCHESTRA

68173-A   **You've Got Me This Way (Whatta Ya Gonna Do
                 About It?)** [Johnny Mercer; Jimmy McHugh]
                 vHO'C (as solo)
    78: Decca 3435, Brunswick (E) 03140
    LP: Ajaz LP221
68174-A   **A Handful of Stars** [Jack Lawrence, Ted Shapiro]
                 vBE (as solo)
    78: Decca 3446
    LP: Ajaz LP221
68175-A   **Falling Leaves** [Mack David; Frankie Carle] vBE
                 (cl solo)
    78: Decca 3446
    LP: Ajaz LP221
    TC: Good Music MSC-37083
    CD: Good Music MSC-37083
68176-A   **The Bad Humor Man** [Johnny Mercer, Jimmy Mc-
                 Hugh] vHO'C&band (cl solo)
    78: Decca 3435, Brunswick (E) 03140
    LP: Ajaz LP221, Bandstand BS7104, BS7120
    CD: Aero Space AS7120

Travel itinerary: Fri., Oct. 4, to Thurs., Oct. 10—Palace Theater, Cleveland, Ohio /
Fri., Oct. 11, to Thurs., Oct. 17—Chicago Theater, Chicago, Ill. / Fri., Oct. 18, to
Thurs., Oct. 24—Earle Theater, Philadelphia, Pa. (the jump from Chicago needed a
special American Airlines flight to make connections for the first show) / Fri., Oct. 25,
to Thurs. Oct. 31—Earle Theater, Washington, D.C. / Fri., Nov. 1, to Thurs., Nov.
7—Hippodrome Theater, Baltimore, Md. / Fri., Nov. 8, to Tues. Nov. 12—State
Theater, Hartford, Conn.

The next night (Wednesday, November 13) the Jimmy Dorsey band returned for the third time in 1940 to the Meadowbrook in New Jersey.

Broadcast schedule (all Meadowbrook): Wed., Nov. 13, MBS [WOR], 8:45-9:00 P.M. / Thurs., Nov. 14, MBS [WOR], 7:15-7:30 P.M. / Sat., Nov. 16, NBC-Blue [WJZ], 7:30-8:00 P.M.

It was a bang-up first five days for Jimmy at the Meadowbrook. The band drew 6,350 patrons in the four evenings and Sunday afternoon. Friday night's 1,900 was the best single night in Meadowbrook history.

Broadcast schedule (Meadowbrook): Tues., Nov. 19, MBS [WOR], 11:45-12:00 P.M.

sustaining broadcast, Meadowbrook Ballroom, Cedar Grove, N.J.—NBC-Blue   [WJZ],   7:30-8:00   P.M. Thursday, November 21, 1940
JIMMY DORSEY AND HIS ORCHESTRA

Contrasts [Jimmy Dorsey] (theme) (as solo) / **Let's Start With A Kiss** / **Frenesi** [Ray Charles, Bob Russell; Alberto Dominguez] / **Falling Leaves** [Mack David; Frankie Carle] vBE (as solo) / **A Million Dreams Ago** [Lew Quadling, Eddie Howard, Dick Jurgens] vBE / **You've Got Me This Way (Whatta Ya Gonna Do About It?)** [Johnny Mercer; Jimmy McHugh] vHO'C (as solo) / **The Right Mood** / **I Want To Be Happy** [Irving Caesar; Vincent Youmans]

sustaining broadcast, Meadowbrook Ballroom, Cedar Grove, N.J.—MBS [WOR], 11:45-12:00 P.M.; Tuesday, November 26, 1940
JIMMY DORSEY AND HIS ORCHESTRA

Mirage / **I Ain't Tellin'**

Broadcast schedule (all Meadowbrook): Wed., Nov. 27 MBS [WOR], 8:45-9:00 P.M. (see Addenda) / Sat., Nov. 30, NBC-Blue [WJZ], 7:30-8:00 P.M.

sustaining broadcast, Meadowbrook Ballroom, Cedar Grove, N.J.—November 1940
JIMMY DORSEY AND HIS ORCHESTRA

I Got Rhythm [Ira Gershwin; George Gershwin] (cl solo)
   TC: Hindsight MCH-415TC
   CD: Hindsight HCD-415

On November 26, 1940, Jimmy Dorsey and Decca records tore up their agreement, replacing it with a three-year deal for double the per-side guarantee offered before, plus a royalty on each record sold.
   The pact called for forty-eight sides a year. Part of the agreement guaranteed that twelve of the sides would be Dorsey originals and special arrangements (*Variety*, December 4, 1940, 47).
   The same issue reported that the band had set a new two-week attendance record for the Meadowbrook. Over 18,000 had shown up so

far, with a percentage and base contract payoff of about $3,000 a week.

Broadcast schedule (all Meadowbrook): Tues., Dec. 3, MBS [WOR], 11:45-12:00 P.M. / Wed., Dec. 4 MBS [WOR], 8:45-9:00 P.M. There was no Sat. 7:30-8:00 P.M. broadcast since NBC-Blue was carrying the Notre Dame-Southern California football game from the West Coast.

Decca, New York, N.Y. Monday, December 9, 1940
JIMMY DORSEY AND HIS ORCHESTRA
Joe Lippman (arr)

68461-A   **I Hear A Rhapsody** [George Fragos, Jack Baker, Dick Gasparre] vBE
          78: Decca 3570, (Au) Y-5659, Brunswick (E) O3192 (dubbing)
          LP: MCA 2-4073, Ajaz LP221
          also on **TC:**, **CD:** Good Music MSC-37083
68461-B   **I Hear A Rhapsody** vBE
          78: Coral 60673
68462-A   **I Understand** [Kim Gannon; Mabel Wayne] vBE (cl solo)
          78: Decca 3585, 25290, Brunswick (E) O3189
          LP: Decca DL-8609, DL74853, (C) DL4248, MCA 2-4073, Ajaz LP221
68463-A   **Turn Left** [Joe Lippman] (as solo)
          78: Decca 3647, Brunswick (E) O3175
          LP: Ajaz LP221
          CD: GRP-Decca CD-GRD-626, Kaz (E) 309
68464-A   **High On A Windy Hill** [Joan Whitney, Alex Kramer] vBE
          78: Decca 3585, Brunswick (E) O3192
          LP: Decca DL-8609, Ajaz LP221
          also on **TC**, **CD:** Good Music MSC-37083

Decca, New York, N.Y. Tuesday, December 10, 1940
JIMMY DORSEY AND HIS ORCHESTRA

68471-A   **The Mem'ry Of A Rose** vBE (cl solo)
          78: Decca 3570
          LP: Ajaz LP221

Broadcast schedule (all Meadowbrook): Wed., Dec. 11, MBS [WOR], 8:45-9:00 P.M. / Sat., Dec. 14, NBC-Red (WEAF) 10:30-11:00 P.M. / Mon., Dec. 16, NBC-Red (WEAF) (see Addenda)

When Jimmy and the band closed at the Meadowbrook in mid-December, they were replaced by Bobby Byrne, with brother Tommy's band due to come in January.

Travel itinerary: Wed., Dec. 25—Sigma Kappa Holiday dance, Penn Athletic Club, Philadelphia, Pa. (crowd of 2,612 surpassed Glenn Miller's a year before) / Sun., Dec. 29—Lyric Theater, Bridgeport, Conn. / Tues., Dec. 31—New Year's party, Mechanic's Hall, Boston, Mass.

Starting January 3, 1941, Jimmy replaced Vincent Lopez as the "house band" for another network show. Back in November, Twenty Grand Cigarettes had come up with a new NBC-Blue program, *Your Happy Birthday*, Friday nights, 9:35-10:00 P.M. where celebrities who were observing their birthdays that week were invited to appear.

The format of the show again restricted the amount of time the band received, that proved to be a blessing in disguise because Toots Camarata, Jimmy's very creative arranger, came up with the idea of featuring both Bob Eberly and Helen O'Connell on the same song in contrasting tempos, with a middle chorus that spotlighted Jimmy. The result was one of the hottest big-band formulas of the forties.

Broadcast schedule: Your Happy Birthday, Fri., Jan. 3, 1941, NBC-Blue [WJZ], 9:35-10:00 P.M.

Travel itinerary: Mon., Jan. 6—Butterfly Ballroom, Springfield, Mass. (lack of predate publicity brought out only 291)

Broadcast schedule: Your Happy Birthday, Fri., Jan. 10, 1941, NBC-Blue [WJZ], 9:35-10:00 P.M.

Travel itinerary: Sat. and Sun., Jan. 11, 12—Adams Theater, Newark, N.J. (capacity crowds totaling 15,743; Mobs trying to get in smashed lobby windows).

Broadcast schedule: Your Happy Birthday, Fri., Jan. 17, NBC-Blue [WJZ], 9:35-10:00 P.M. (Guest: Rear Admiral Richard E. Byrd)

In its year-end review *Variety* (January 8, 1941, 34) noted that the Jimmy Dorsey and Woody Herman bands had made the most significant strides forward in big-band popularity in 1940.

Following the Friday, January 17, Twenty Grand network show Jimmy and company hopped a train for Philadelphia's Town Hall to play a 12:30 to 3:30 A.M. dance for the Catholic High School Alumni.

On Sunday, January 19, 2,062 jammed the Ritz Ballroom in Bridgeport, Connecticut, to see the band. Then Monday, January 20, they opened at the Cafe Rouge in Hotel Pennsylvania, the largest hotel dancing venue in New York City. Jimmy had to provide a standby band at Cafe Rouge Friday nights while at the NBC studios.

Broadcast schedule (all Cafe Rouge unless noted): Tues., Jan. 21, NBC-Blue [WJZ], 7:40-8:00 P.M. / *Your Happy Birthday,* Fri., Jan. 24, NBC-Blue [WJZ], 9:35-10:00 P.M. (Guests: Ona Munsen, actor, and Franklin D. Roosevelt, Jr. apparently for his famous father) / Tues., Jan. 28, NBC-Blue [WJZ], 7:40-8:00 P.M. / *Your Happy Birthday,* Fri., Jan. 31, NBC-Blue [WJZ], 9:35-10:00 P.M. (Guest: Charlotte Greenwood, comedienne.)

The band drew 2,150 patrons the first week at Cafe Rouge, a third more than Woody Herman at the New Yorker and twice what Guy Lombardo drew at the Roosevelt. The next week was even better, with a total of 2,575. By the time their twelve weeks were up that April, they had attracted 31,400 *(Variety* April 30, 1941, 36).

The next recording date produced the golden egg that would propel the band to the top. Utilizing "Toots" Camarata's new formula, "Amapola" sold well, though not as well as "Green Eyes" still to come.

Decca, New York, N.Y. Monday, February 3, 1941
JIMMY DORSEY AND HIS ORCHESTRA
Jimmy Dorsey (cl,as,ldr) Nate Kazebier, Jimmy Campbell, Shorty Solomson (tp) Don Matteson, Nat Lobovsky, Sonny Lee (tb) Milt Yaner, Sam Rubinowich (as) Charles Frazier, Herbie Haymer (ts) Joe Lippman (p) Guy Smith (g) Jack Ryan (sb) Buddy Schutz (d) Helen O'Connell, Bob Eberly (vcl) Toots Camarata (arr)

68650-A   **Donna Maria** vBE
    78: Decca 3629, Brunswick (E,F) O3439
68651-A   **When The Sun Comes Out** [Ted Koehler; Harold
               Arlen] vHO'C (as solo)
    78: Decca 3657, Brunswick (E) O3189
    TC: Good Music 35489
    CD: GRP-Decca CD-GRD-626, Good Music MSC-2-35489
68652-A   **Amapola (Pretty Little Poppy)** [Albert Gamse; Jo-
               seph M. Lacalle] vBE&HO'C arrTC (cl solo)
    78: Decca 3629, 18806, 25120, (E) BM-30677, (Au) Y-5660,
    (C) 10325, Brunswick (E) O3170 (dubbing)
    45: MCA 60021
    EP: Decca ED614
    LP: Decca DL-5091, DL-8153, DL-4001, DL74248, (C) DL4248,
    MCA 2-4023, Ace Of Hearts (E) AH-114, Time-Life STB-B10,
    Music Of Your Life 17003
    TC: Time-Life 4TL-0006, Good Music MSC-37083, 35489
    CD: Time-Life 4TL-0006, Good Music MSC-37083, 35489,
    Empress (E) 852
68653-A   **Yours (Quieremé Mucho)** [Jack Sherr, Augustin Rod-
               riguez; Gonzalo Roig] vBE&HO'C arrTC (as solo)
    78: Decca 3657, 18807, 25121, 28487, (E) BM-30620, (C)
    10325, Brunswick (E) O3234
    45: Decca 25121
    EP: Decca ED614
    LP: Decca DL-5091, DL-5443, DL-8153, DL74248, DL74853,
    (C) DL-4248, MCA 2-4023, Ace Of Hearts (E) AH-114, Time-
    Life STB-B10, Music Of Your Life 17003
    TC: Time-Life 4TL-0006, Good Music MSC-37083, 35489
    CD: Time-Life 4TL-0006, Good Music MSC-37083, 35489,
    Empress (E) 852
68654-A   **Turn Right** [Joe Lippman] (as solo)
    78: Decca 3547, Brunswick (E) O3175
    ET: AFRS G. I. Jive 515
    CD: GRP-Decca CD-GRD-626, Kaz (E) 309
    all sides also on **LP:** Ajaz LP229

Broadcast schedule (all Cafe Rouge unless noted): Tues., Feb. 4, NBC-Blue [WJZ], 7:40-8:00 P.M. / *Your Happy Birthday,* Fri., Feb. 7, NBC-Blue [WJZ], 9:35-10:00 P.M. / Tues., Feb. 11, NBC-Blue [WJZ], 7:40-8:00 P.M. / *Your Happy Birthday,* Fri., Feb. 14, NBC-Blue [WJZ], 9:35-10:00 P.M.

In February, Tommy Dorsey and his band were at the Meadowbrook in New Jersey. One Saturday afternoon Jimmy paid a visit to his no longer "estranged" brother and took part in a broadcast trumpet contest that harked back to their early years in Pennsylvania. The comedic results of the visit have recently become available on compact disc.

> *Matinee At The Meadowbrook,* Meadowbrook Ballroom, Cedar Grove, N.J.—CBS [WABC], Saturday, February 15, 1941

TOMMY AND JIMMY DORSEY TRUMPET CONTEST
Tommy Dorsey, **Jimmy Dorsey** (tp)

(Trumpet scales are badly executed by both Dorseys and the contest ends in a draw.)
  CD: Jazz Hour JH-1035

Broadcast schedule (all Cafe Rouge unless noted): Tues., Feb. 18, NBC-Blue [WJZ], 7:40-8:00 P.M. / *Your Happy Birthday,* Fri., Feb. 21, NBC-Blue [WJZ], 9:35-10:00 P.M. / Tues., Feb. 25, NBC-Blue [WJZ], 7:40-8:00 P.M. / *Your Happy Birthday,* Fri., Feb. 28, NBC-Blue [WJZ], 9:35-10:00 P.M. (Guest: Babe Ruth)

Sometime in the spring of 1941, Jimmy and his band began making "Soundies." These were a comparatively short-lived craze offering three-minute, sixteen-millimeter soundfilms that were viewed in bars and similar venues on a sort of film jukebox. Called the "Panoram" it required ten cents a play, double the cost of a recorded jukebox tune.

Fox-Movietone Studios, Long Island, N.Y. March/April 1941
JIMMY DORSEY AND HIS ORCHESTRA

> **Oh! Look** vHO'C&BE (7/26/43)
> **FILM:** RCM Soundie 12701-M, 25604
>   **Bar Babble** [Pat McCarthy] (8/23/43)
> **FILM:** RCM Soundie 13001-F
>   **Man That's Groovy** vHO'C (9/13/43)
> **FILM:** RCM Soundie 13304-M
>   **La Rosita** [Allan Stuart; Paul Dupont] (10/4/43)
> **FILM:** RCM Soundie 13606-F
> **LP:** Kaydee 8
>   **Au Reet (Au Rote, Au Root)** [Fud Livingston, Arthur Russell, Bob Mosely] vHO'C (10/11/43)
> **FILM:** RCM Soundie 13701-M
>   **A Whole Bunch Of Something** vHO'C,BE&Band (11/8/43)
> **FILM:** RCM Soundie 14105-M
>   **I'm Tired Of Waiting For You** vHO'C&BE (11/22/43)
> **FILM:** RCM Soundie 14201-M
>   **My Sister And I** [Hy Zaret, Joan Whitney, Alex Kramer] vBE (12/6/43)
> **FILM:** RCM Soundie 14406, 26208
> **VIDEO:** Jazz Classics "Symphony Of Swing" JCVC 104

Produced by James Roosevelt (one of FDR's sons), composer Sam Coslow and Gordon Mills, a leading jukebox maker and head of Mills Novelty Company, the Soundies were copyrighted on the dates shown after each title. Why there is a two-year gap between filming and copyright is uncertain but contract ramifications are suspected.

Several factors ruled against a resounding success for the Soundies. First, though offered on the jukebox principle, eight of the filmed productions were on a continuous 800-foot reel of film, that meant if patrons wanted to view selection number five, for example, they might have to feed as many as seven or eight dimes into the machine before their favorite would appear (Terenzio et al. 1991).

Also, of course, jukeboxes were listened or danced to without attention from the patron. The Panoram required viewing to appreciate, much like the difference between radio and television.

As a promotion for the stage play *Life With Father,* a series of transcribed programs called *Famous Fathers* was distributed in 1941 to a number of stations in the Northeast.

Jimmy was picked for one program and, according to *Variety* (February 26, 1941, 43), related how he had to overcome the initial prejudice and objections of his mother-in-law-to-be toward a "no-account orchestra player."

There is no record of the mother-in-law's reaction a decade later when Jimmy and Jane divorced, but one can certainly imagine.

Decca, New York, N.Y. Monday, March 3, 1941
JIMMY DORSEY AND HIS ORCHESTRA
Toots Camarata (arr)

68761-A   **A Rose And A Prayer** [Remus Harris, Dan Woodward, Chester Conn] vBE (cl solo)
    78: Decca 3812, Brunswick (E) O3209 (dubbing)
    LP: Ajaz LP229
68762-A   **Au Reet (Au Rote, Au Root)** [Fud Livingston, Arthur Russell, Bob Mosely] vHO'C&band (as solo)
    78: Decca 3721
    LP: Ajaz LP229
68763-A   **Man, That's Groovy** vHO'C&band (cl solo)
    78: Decca 3721
    LP: Ajaz LP229
68764-A   **Once And For All** vBE (as solo)
    78: Decca 3737, Brunswick (E) O3199 (dubbing)
    LP: Ajaz LP229
68765-A   **La Rosita** [Allan Stuart; Paul Dupont] arrTC (cl,as solos)
    78: Decca 3711, Brunswick (E) O3200
    LP: Coral (G) 6.22183, Ajaz LP229

Broadcast schedule (all Cafe Rouge unless noted): Tues., Mar. 4, NBC-Blue [WJZ], 7:40-8:00 P.M. / *Your Happy Birthday,* Fri., Mar. 7, NBC-Blue [WJZ], 9:35-10:00 P.M. / Tues., Mar. 11, NBC-Blue [WJZ], 7:40-8:00 P.M. / *Your Happy Birthday,* Fri., Mar. 14, NBC-Blue [WJZ], 9:35-10:00 P.M. / Tues., Mar. 18, NBC-Blue [WJZ], 7:40-8:00 P.M.

Decca, New York, N.Y. Wednesday, March 19, 1941
JIMMY DORSEY AND HIS ORCHESTRA
Frank Langone (as) replaces Rubin, Don Hammond (ts) replaces Haymer. Toots Camarata (arr)

68832-A   The Things I Love [Lew Harris; Harold Barlow]
               vBE (as solo)
    78: Decca 3737, Brunswick (E) O3199 (dubbing)
68833-A   My Sister And I [Hy Zaret, Joan Whitney, Alex Kramer] vBE
    78: Decca 3710, Brunswick (E) O3210
68834-A   Maria Elena [S. K. (Bob) Russell; Lorenzo Barcelata] vBE arrTC (cl solo)
    78: Decca 3698, 18806, 25120, (C) 10325, (E) BM-30677,
    Brunswick (E) O3210
    (SSL-3934) ET: AFRS Basic Music Library 3934
    45: MCA 60021
    EP: Decca ED614
    LP: Decca DL-5091, DL8153, DL74248, DL74853, Time-Life
    STB-B10, MCA 2-4073
    TC: Time-Life 4TL-0006, Good Music MSC-37083
    CD: Time-Life 4TL-0006, Good Music MSC-37083, Empress (E)
    852
68835-A   Minnie From Trinidad [Roger Edens] vHO'C
    78: Decca 3711
68836-A   In The Hush Of The Night [Sammy Lerner; Al
               Hoffman] vBE&HO'C (as solo)
    78: Decca 3710
    TC: and CD: Good Music 35489
68840-A   Green Eyes (Aquellos Ojos Verdes) [N. Menendez,
               E. Rivera, Eddie Woods, A. Utera] vBE&HO'C
               arrTC (as solo)
    78: Decca 3698, 11064, 18805, 25119, (C) 10324, (E) BM-
    30621, BM-30646, Brunswick (E) O3200 (dubbing)
    45: Decca 1-711, MCA 60020
    EP: Decca ED614
    LP: Decca DL-5091, DL-7020, DL-8153, DL-8067, DL-1511,
    DL74853, DL74248, (C) DL-4248, MCA 2-4073, Brunswick (E)
    LAT-8695, Ace Of Hearts (E) AH-114, Longines 266, Time-Life
    STC-B10, Music Of Your Life 17003
    TC: Columbia/Legacy 3CT52862, Time-Life 4TL-0006, Good
    Music MSC-37083
    CD: Time-Life 4TL-0006, Columbia/Legacy 3CK52862, Good
    Music MSC-37083, Empress (E) 852
    all sides this session also on LP: Ajaz LP229

The January 1, 1941, broadcast ban of its music by The American Society of Composers, Authors and Publishers (ASCAP) also helped Jimmy immeasurably. To fill the gap, broadcasters organized Broadcast Music, Inc. (BMI), whose immediate sources of music included many non-ASCAP Latin-American composers and lyricists.
    Thus, much of the music played on radio in early 1941 was Latin in

origin, and Jimmy's recordings of the BMI tunes fit right in.

As part of the contract Jimmy had signed with the Strand Theater, the band was set for four weeks beginning April 11, with an option by the theater for two additional weeks. The $8,500 a week pact called for a first-week notice as to whether the Bette Davis film that shared billing with the band would play for four or six weeks. If the decision was for only four, the band was to get a week's booking at the Strand's sister theater, the Earle, in Philadelphia (*Variety,* March 19, 1941, 40).

Broadcast schedule (all Cafe Rouge): Fri., Mar. 21, NBC-Blue [WJZ], 9:35-10:00 P.M. / Tues., Mar. 25, NBC-Blue [WJZ], 7:40-8:00 P.M.

sustaining broadcast, Cafe Rouge, Hotel Pennsylvania, New York, N.Y.—NBC-Blue [WJZ], 12:05-12:30 A.M. Friday, March 28, 1941

JIMMY DORSEY AND HIS ORCHESTRA

Oh Look At Me Now [John De Vries; Joe Bushkin] vBE&HO'C / **Turn Right** [Joe Lippman] (as solo) / **In The Hush Of The Night** [Sammy Lerner; Al Hoffman] vBE&HO'C (cl solo) / **Blue Lou** [Edgar Simpson, Irving Mills] (as solo)

Broadcast schedule: Your Happy Birthday, Fri., Mar. 28, NBC-Blue [WJZ], 9:35-10:00 P.M. / Tues., Apr. 1, NBC-Blue [WJZ], 7:30-8:00 P.M. / *Your Happy Birthday,* Fri., Apr. 4, NBC-Blue [WJZ], 9:35-10:00 P.M. (Guest: Bette Davis) / *Fitch Band Wagon,* Sun., Apr. 6, NBC-Red [WEAF], 7:30-8:00 P.M. (Jimmy and daughter Julie are also interviewed)

On Good Friday, April 11, the band again opened at the Strand and at the same time played their final week at the Pennsylvania Hotel. As part of the deal to open at the Strand, the theater's ads included "courtesy Hotel Pennsylvania." The nearby Paramount Theater countered the booking with the Benny Goodman band and a Bing Crosby movie.

For the hectic stage, hotel and broadcast schedule, Jimmy again had to provide a standby band at the Pennsylvania for any early evening hours when he would be on stage at the Strand or at the broadcast studios.

Broadcast schedule: Your Happy Birthday, Fri., Apr. 11, NBC-Blue [WJZ], 9:35-10:00 P.M. / Wed., Thurs. Apr. 16, 17 NBC-Blue [WJZ], 7:30-8:00 P.M. (see Addenda) / *Your Happy Birthday,* Fri., Apr. 18, 25 NBC-Blue [WJZ], 9:35-10:00 P.M.

Decca, New York, N.Y. Tuesday, April 29, 1941
JIMMY DORSEY AND HIS ORCHESTRA
Phil Washburne (tb,vcl) replaces Matteson

69091-A   **Blue Champagne** [Jimmy Eaton, Grady Watts, Frank Ryerson] vBE (as solo)
78: Decca 3775, 25301, (Au) Y-5755, Brunswick (E) O3249
LP: Ajaz LP229, Time-Life STB-B10
Also on **TC, CD:** Time-Life 4TL-0006, Good Music MSC-37083
(Contd.)

JIMMY DORSEY AND HIS ORCHESTRA (Contd.)

69092-A   **Aurora** [Harold Adamson; Mario Lago, Roberto Roberti] vHO'C (cl solo)
          78: Decca 3772, Brunswick (E) O3209
          LP: Ajaz LP229
          CD: Empress (E) 817
69093-A   **Bar Babble** [Pat McCarthy] (as solo)
          78: Decca 3772, Brunswick (E) O3234
          LP: Bandstand BS-7104, Coral (G) COPS7449, 6.22183, Ajaz LP237
69094-A   **All Alone And Lonely** vBE (as solo)
          78: Decca 3775
          LP: Ajaz LP237

Because of the poor business generated by the Bette Davis film *The Great Lie,* the band only played four weeks, closing at the Strand May 1, with a total box office of $131,000.

On Sunday, May 4, they participated in the Seventh Annual American Federation of Musicians' Relief Fund Gala at Manhattan Center along with the bands of Guy Lombardo, Vincent Lopez, Harry James, Gene Krupa, Blue Barron, Frankie Masters, Fletcher Henderson and the Latin group Chiquito. Jimmy and the band got top billing in the event's ads.

In the *Billboard* poll of college campuses (April 26, 1941, 11), Jimmy's band jumped from tenth place in 1940 to sixth in 1941.

Coincidental with the band moving to the Earle Theater in Philadelphia, Jimmy left the Twenty Grand commercial show, that then began using different bands each Friday.

The Earle stand also proved popular with the fans, drawing a reported $25,300. Philadelphia police were called in to control the waiting lines.

On Saturday, May 17, the band played Sunnybrook Ballroom, Pottstown, Pennsylvania, coming within 100 attendees of breaking brother Tommy's record at the location (4,573 dancers crowding the hall). The next day 2,680 turned out for Jimmy's third appearance of the year at the Ritz Ballroom, Bridgeport, Connecticut.

Decca, New York, N.Y. Monday, May 19, 1941
JIMMY DORSEY AND HIS ORCHESTRA
Toots Camarata (arr)

69211-A   **Isle Of Pines** vBE
          78: Decca 3859
          LP: Ajaz LP237
69212-A   **Time Was** [S. K. (Bob) Russell; Miguel Prado] vBE &HO'C (as solo)
          78: Decca 3859, Brunswick (E) O3274
          LP: Decca DL-8609, Ajaz LP237, Music Of Your Life 17003
          TC: Good Music 35489
          CD: Good Music 35489, Empress (E) 852
69213-A   **Be Fair** vBE
          78: Decca 3812
          LP: Ajaz LP237

69214-A   **Embraceable You** [Ira Gershwin; George Gershwin]
vHO'C (as solo)
78: Decca 3928, 25294
LP: Decca DL-8609, MCA 2-4073, Ace Of Hearts (E) AH-114,
Ajaz LP237, Music Of Your Life 17003
TC: Good Music 35489
CD: Good Music 35489
69215-A   **Fingerbustin'** [Jimmy Dorsey] arrTC (as,cl solos)
78: Decca 3928
(SSL-3933-3) **ET:** AFRS Basic Music Library P-1945
LP: Bandstand BS-7104, Coral CRL-56008, Ajaz LP237

"Fingerbustin'" was developed by Toots Camarata as a showcase for
Jimmy's reed skills and is sometimes mislabled "Beebe" on reissues.

Travel itinerary: Tues. and Wed., May 20, 21—Totem Pole Ballroom, Auburndale,
Mass. (4,450 for two nights) / Fri. to Sun., May 23-25—Metropolitan Theater,
Providence, R.I. / Wed., May 28—Amalgamated Meat Cutters' Union dance, Town
Hall, Philadelphia, Pa. / Sat., May 31—Frank Gravatt's Steel Pier, Atlantic City, N.J.
/ Mon., June 2—Casa Loma, Charleston, W.Va. / Tues., June 3—Hampton-Sidney
College, Farmville, Va. / Wed. and Thurs. June 4, 5—Washington and Lee College,
Lexington, Va. / Fri. and Sat., June 6, 7—University of North Carolina, Chapel Hill,
N.C. / Mon. June 9—University of Virginia, Charlottesville, Va. / Tues., June 10—
University of Richmond, Richmond, Va. / Wed., June 11—Farmer's Warehouse,
Petersburg, Va. / Thurs., June 12, to Wed., June 18—Capitol Theater, Washington,
D.C. / Thurs., June 19—Lakewood Park, Mahanoy City, Pa.

Bob Eberly, his wife and Jimmy's band boy were injured slightly
when their car, returning from the Mahanoy City date, was hit by an-
other driven by two youths near Somerville, New Jersey.
   Though their injuries were slight, the accident was enough to cancel a
Decca recording date scheduled for the afternoon of June 20 in New
York. That evening, however, the band was able to resume its schedule:

Travel itinerary: Fri., June 20—Fraternal Order of Police dance, Convention Hall,
Philadelphia, Pa. (crowd 5,200) / Sat., June 21—Hershey Park, Hershey, Pa. (crowd
3,601) / Sun., June 22—Pier Ballroom, Geneva-on-the-Lake, Ohio / Mon., June
23—Idora Park, Youngstown, Ohio / Tues., June 24—Indian Lake, Russell's Point,
Ohio / Wed., June 25—Summit Beach, Akron, Ohio (crowd 2,011)

On Friday, June 27, the band settled down for four weeks at the
Panther Room of the Sherman Hotel in Chicago. After the breakneck
schedule in May and June, the July stay along Lake Michigan was a
much needed breather. Also, the Sherman engagement meant almost
nightly exposure on NBC (dates and times unknown, see Addenda). In
their first two weeks, Jimmy and the band drew 9,500 to the hotel.

Travel itinerary: Fri., July 25—Lakeside Park, Dayton, Ohio / Sat., July 26—Lake
Breeze Pier, Buckeye Lake, Ohio / Sun., July 27—Moonlight Gardens, Myers Lake
Park, Canton, Ohio, for a gate of $1,848 / Mon., July 28—Arena, London, Ont.,
Canada / Tues., July 29—Mutual Arena, Toronto, Ont., Canada (here the band set the
record for the Arena at 4,852, rating front-page stories in Toronto dailies [*Variety,*

Aug. 6, 1941, 37]) / Thurs., July 31—Russell's Danceland, Sylvan Beach, N.Y.

Decca, New York, N.Y. Friday, August 1, 1941
JIMMY DORSEY AND HIS ORCHESTRA

69594-A   **Jim** [Nelson Shawn; Caesar Petrillo, Edward Ross]
                vBE&HO'C
    78: Decca 3963, Brunswick (E) O3266
    LP: Ajaz LP237, Time-Life STB-B10, Music Of Your Life 71003
    TC: Time-Life 4TL-0006, Good Music MSC-2-35489
    CD: Time-Life 4TL-0006, Good Music MSC-2-35489
69595-A   **A New Shade Of Blue** vBE (cl solo)
    78: Decca 3963, Brunswick (E) O3266
    LP: Ajaz LP237
69596-A   **Charleston Alley** [Leroy Kirkland, Robert B. Wright,
                Horace Henderson] (as solos)
    78: Decca 4075
    (SSL-3933-5) **ET:** AFRS Basic Music Library P-1945
    LP: Swingfan (G)1007, Coral PCO7839, CRL56008, (G)6.22183,
    Bandstand BS-7104, Ajaz LP237
    CD: GRP-Decca CD-GRD-626, Kaz (E) 309
69597-A   **Moonlight Masquerade** [Jack Lawrence; Toots Cam-
                arata, Isaac Albeniz] vBE (cl solo)
    78: Decca 3991
    LP: Ajaz LP237
69598-A   **The Spirit's Got Me** [Joe Lippman] vBE,band (as,cl
                solos)
    78: Decca 4075
    LP: Big Band Archives LP-1203, Ajaz LP237
69599-A   **Wasn't It You?** [Ben Raleigh; Bernie Wayne] vBE
                (cl solo)
    78: Decca 3991
    LP: Ajaz LP237

After the one-day record session in New York, the band went to Atlantic City for a weekend at the Steel Pier on Saturday and Sunday August 2 and 3. They then took a day off and next worked The Cavalier Club at Virginia Beach, Virginia,on Tuesday, August 5, through Monday, August 18. After this somewhat relaxing two weeks in the sun and surf, the grueling but better-paying one-nighters resumed:

Travel itinerary: Sat., Aug. 30—Convention Hall, Asbury Park, N.J. (drawing 7,700 for Policemen's Benevolent Assoc. Ball) / Sun., Aug. 31—Fernbrook Park, Dallas, Pa. (3,837 dancers broke Ted Lewis' sixteen-year-old record) / Mon., Sept. 1—Steel Pier, Atlantic City, N.J.

Decca, New York, N.Y. Tuesday, September 2, 1941
JIMMY DORSEY AND HIS ORCHESTRA

69688-A   **If You Only Knew (Perfume D'Amor)** vBE
    78: Decca 18709
    LP: Ajaz LP237

69689-A   **What Makes Sammy Run?** [Toots Camarata] arrTC
                     (as solo)
    78: Decca 4356
    LP: Big Band Archives LP-1203, Ajaz LP245
69690-A   **It Happened In Hawaii** [Al Dubin; Mabel Wayne]
                     vBE&HO'C
    78: Decca 4034, 25255, (E) BM-30636, Brunswick (F) A-82532
    LP: Ajaz LP245
69691-A   **Tropical Magic** [Mack Gordon; Harry Warren] vBE
    78: Decca 4034, (Au) Y-5764, Brunswick (E) O3274
    LP: Decca DL8153, Ajaz LP245
    CD: Empress (E) 852

Travel itinerary: Wed., Sept. 3—Rosemont (formerly Roseland) Ballroom, Brooklyn, N.Y. (twenty police were called to handle the record crowd) / Fri., Sept. 5, to Thurs., Sept. 11—Buffalo Theater, Buffalo, N.Y.

While at the Buffalo Theater, Jimmy got a hurry-up call from Paramount Studios, pushing up the dates for his next movie. This unexpected turn forced him to cancel one-week bookings at the Stanley Theater in Pittsburgh, Pennsylvania; Orpheum Theater, Minneapolis, Minnesota; Palace Theater, Cleveland, Ohio, and Paramount Theater, Toledo, Ohio, as well as a two-week booking at the Chicago Theater, Chicago, Illinois.

Hurrying to the West Coast, Jimmy and the band began recording and filming for the Paramount movie *The Fleet's In,* that starred William Holden, Dorothy Lamour, Cass Daley, Eddie Bracken and Betty Hutton.

It was also the film that introduced "Tangerine" and the Bob Eberly-Helen O'Connell team to the movie-going public. Suddenly, thousands of big-band fans were able to see as well as hear this magnetic vocal com-bination of handsome boy and beautiful girl. More than anything else, this film solidified the top-rung hold Jimmy would claim at this juncture in his career.

Down Beat magazine (March 1, 1941, 15) had earlier reported that Jimmy would be paid $10,000 a week, with four weeks guaranteed, for the cinematic work. *Billboard* (November 8, 1941, 9) said that Jimmy's take for the film was the highest paid to any band for film work that year that had seen a glut of fourteen big-band movies.

However, *Billboard* later set Jimmy's figure at $75,000, that could possibly indicate more than four week's shooting time or a renegotiated contract because of the canceled theater dates.

Paramount studios, Hollywood, Cal. September 14-October 13, 1941
THE FLEET'S IN: Victor Schertzinger, director
JIMMY DORSEY AND HIS ORCHESTRA
Jimmy Dorsey (cl,as,ldr) Charlie Teagarden, John Napton, Shorty Solomson, Ray Linn, Billy Oblak (tp) Sonny Lee, Phil Washburne, Billy Pritchard, Al Jordan (tb) Milt Yaner, Frank Langone (as) Babe Russin, Charles Frazier (ts) Chuck Gentry (bar) Johnny Guarnieri (p) Tommy Kaye (g) Jack Ryan (sb) Buddy Schutz (d) Dorothy Lamour, Betty Hutton, Cass Daley, Bob Eberly, Helen O'Connell (vcl)

THE FLEETS IN (Contd.)

> **Contrasts** [Jimmy Dorsey] (theme) (as solo) / **Tangerine** [Johnny Mercer; Victor Schertzinger] vBE&HO'C (as solo) / **When You Hear The Time Signal** [Mercer; Schertzinger] vDL / **If You Build A Better Mousetrap** [Mercer; Schertzinger] vBE, HO'C / **Arthur Murray Taught Me Dancing In A Hurry** [Mercer; Schertzinger] vBH / **I Remember You** [Mercer; Schertzinger] vDL,HO'C&BE (cl solo) / **Tomorrow You'll Belong To Uncle Sam** [Mercer; Schertzinger] vCD
> All selections in **FILM**: Paramount: *The Fleet's In*. All except "When You Hear The Time Signal" in **LP**: Hollywood Soundstage SS405; "Tangerine" also in **LP**: Joyce LP-3005, Giants Of Jazz GOJ1023; "When You Hear The Time Signal" in **LP**: Legends 1000/4; "If You Build A Better Mousetrap" and "Arthur Murray Taught Me Dancing In A Hurry" in **LP**: Joyce LP-3005; "I Remember You" in **LP**: Joyce LP-3005, **CD**: Koch CD-100
> Recorded but not used in film: **Conga From Honga, When You Hear The Time Signal** (instrumental version), **Arthur Murray Taught Me Dancing In A Hurry** vBH (edited version used for radio promotion on: **ET**: Paramount *The Fleets In* Radio Promotion Program; **LP**: Radiola 1718)

Jimmy as well as brother Tommy are also represented in short film clips in the 1941 Paramount release *Birth Of The Blues*.

Decca, Los Angeles, Cal. Thursday, October 9, 1941
JIMMY DORSEY AND HIS ORCHESTRA

DLA-2791-A	**Any Bonds Today?** [Irving Berlin] vBE&HO'C (as solo)
	78: Decca 4044
	LP: Ajaz LP245
DLA-2792-A	**The Magic Of Magnolias** vBE (cl solo)
	78: Decca 4047
	LP: Ajaz LP245
DLA-2793-A	**Day Dream** [John Latouche; Edward K. "Duke" Ellington, Billy Strayhorn] vBE (as solo)
	78: Decca 4047
	LP: Ajaz LP245, Big Band Archives LP1203

Helen O'Connell was away from the band for a while in the fall of 1941 and Maureen O'Connor filled in for her at the Hollywood Palladium where Jimmy and crew opened Tuesday, October 14.

That Saturday, October 18, Jimmy set a new all-time attendance record for the Palladium, with 6,200 dancers crowding in and then set a new Sunday mark of 4,250 the next day.

> *sustaining broadcast,* Hollywood Palladium, Hollywood Cal.—(NBC), Monday, October 20, 1941
JIMMY DORSEY AND HIS ORCHESTRA
Bob Eberly, Maureen O'Connor (vcl)

Jug Music (as solo) / In The Hush Of The Night [Sammy Lerner; Al Hoffman] vBE&MO'C (cl solo) / Wasn't It You? [Ben Raleigh; Bernie Wayne] vBE (cl solo) / A Zoot Suit (For My Sunday Girl) [Ray Gilbert, Bob O'Brien] (cl solos) / I Don't Want To Set The World On Fire [Eddie Seiler, Sol Marcus, Bennie Benjamin, Eddie Durham] vBE / Easy Street [Alan Rankin Jones] vMO'C (as solo) / I Ain't Tellin' (cl solo)

 entire broadcast on LP: Fanfare LP8-108

They finished at the Palladium Monday, October 27, after being seen by about 30,000 fans, and then returned to Minneapolis, Minnesota, for a week at the Orpheum Theater, opening Friday, October 31. There they set a $20,000 box-office record for the house. Then it was back for a week at the 4,000-seat Balaban and Katz Chicago Theater, beginning Friday, November 7, where the gate was a brisk $40,000. Next Pittsburgh, Pennsylvania, Friday, November 14, for a $25,000 week at the Stanley.

On Friday, November 21, they opened a three-week stand at the Meadowbrook in New Jersey; 1,792 were there opening night.

That night the band also had its first appearance on *Coca Cola Spotlight Bands,* that featured bands from coast to coast and had premiered Monday, November 3, on Mutual from 10:15-10:30 P.M.

The next evening, Saturday, November 22, Jimmy cracked the all-time Meadowbrook Saturday record with 1,984, while Sunday another 1,800 turned out for the matinee and evening sessions. The three days drew better than the two weeks at the Meadowbrook two years before.

> *sustaining broadcast,* Meadowbrook Ballroom, Cedar Grove, N.J.—MBS [WOR], 9:15-9:30 P.M. Tuesday, December 2, 1941

JIMMY DORSEY AND HIS ORCHESTRA

(There'll Be Bluebirds Over) The White Cliffs Of Dover [Nat Burton; Walter Kent] vBE arrTC / The Spirit's Got Me [Joe Lippman] (as,cl solos)

Decca, New York, N.Y. Wednesday, December 3, 1941
JIMMY DORSEY AND HIS ORCHESTRA
Toots Camarata, Joe Lippman (arr)

69992-A	This Is No Laughing Matter [Buddy Kaye; Al Frisch] vBE arrTC (cl solo)
	78: Decca 4102
	LP: Ajaz LP245
69993-A	(There'll Be Bluebirds Over) The White Cliffs Of Dover [Nat Burton; Walter Kent] vBE arrTC
	78: Decca 4103
	LP: Ajaz LP245
69994-A	I Got It Bad (And That Ain't Good) [Paul Francis Webster; Edward K."Duke" Ellington] vHO'C (as solo)
	78: Decca 4103

(Contd.)

JIMMY DORSEY AND HIS ORCHESTRA (Contd.)

    LP: Ajaz LP245
    Also on **TC, CD:** Good Music MSC35489
69995-A   **I Said No** [Frank Loesser; Jule Styne] vBE&HO'C
    78: Decca 4102, Brunswick (E) O3317
    LP: Decca DL74248, (C) DL4248, Ajaz LP245
    Also on **TC, CD:** Good Music MSC35489
69996-A   **Drop Me A Line** vHO'C (as solos)
    78: Decca 4165
    LP: Ajaz LP245

WNEW, an independent music station in New York, premiered an hour-long dance pickup from the Meadowbrook on Sunday, December 7, 4:30-5:30 P.M. A scripted show, it was continuously interrupted by late-breaking Pearl Harbor news developments, that fateful Sunday.

Broadcast schedule (Meadowbrook): Tues., Dec. 9, MBS [WOR], 9:15-9:30 P.M.

Decca, New York, N.Y. Wednesday, December 10, 1941
JIMMY DORSEY AND HIS ORCHESTRA
Toots Camarata (arr)

70024-A   **I Remember You** [Johnny Mercer; Victor Schertz-
               inger] vBE
    78: Decca 4132, (Au) Y-5754, Brunswick (E) O3328
    LP: Ajaz LP245
    CD: Smithsonian RD-100-1, Empress (E) 852
70025-A   **Not Mine** [Johnny Mercer; Victor Schertzinger] vBE&
               HO'C arrTC
    78: Decca 4122, (Au) Y-5753, Brunswick (E) O3369
    LP: Ajaz LP245
    CD: Empress (E) 817
70026-A   **Arthur Murray Taught Me Dancing In A Hurry**
               [Johnny Mercer; Victor Schertzinger] vHO'C arrTC
    78: Decca 4122, (Au) Y-5753, Brunswick (E) O3369
    LP: Decca DL74248, (C) DL4248, MCA 2-4073, Ajaz LP245,
    Time-Life STB-B10, Music Of Your Life 17003
    TC: Time-Life 4TL-0006, Good Music MSC-2-35489
    CD: Time-Life 4TL-0006, Good Music MSC-2-35489, Empress
    (E) 817
70027-A   **If You Build A Better Mousetrap** [Johnny Mercer;
               Victor Schertzinger] vBE&HO'C (as solo)
    78: Decca 4132, (Au) Y-5754, Brunswick (E) O3349
    LP: Ajaz LP253
    CD: Empress (E) 817
70028-A   **Tangerine** [Johnny Mercer; Victor Schertzinger] vBE,
               HO'C arrTC (as solo)
    78: Decca 4123, 25255, (Au) Y-5755, Brunswick (E) O3328,
    (F) A-82532
    EP: Decca ED614
    LP: Decca DL8153, DL742248, (C) DL-4248, Ace Of Hearts (E)

AH-114, Longines 261, Time-Life STB-B10, MCA 2-4073, Music
Of Your Life 17003, Ajaz LP253
TC: Time-Life 4TL-0006, Good Music MSC-37083
CD: Time-Life 4TL-0006, GRP-Decca CD-GRD-626, CDS CD-
611, Flapper (E) CD 7094, ASV Living Era (E) 5230, Good
Music MSC-37083, Empress (E) 852

Jimmy's stay at the Meadowbrook concluded that evening, December
10, and the band headed into wartime New England and a week's
engagement at the RKO Boston Theater, which included another *Spot-light Bands* broadcast, Tuesday, December 16.   After grossing $23,000
at the Boston, the band stopped off at the Metropolitan Theater, Prov-idence, Rhode Island, Friday through Sunday, December 19-21.

Decca, New York, N.Y. Monday, December 22, 1941
JIMMY DORSEY AND HIS ORCHESTRA
Joe Lippman (arr)

70086-A   Ev'rything I Love [Cole Porter] vBE (cl solo)
    78: Decca 4123, Brunswick (E) O3356
    LP: Ajaz LP253
70087-A   **Absent Minded Moon** [Johnny Burke; Jimmy Van
                    Heusen] vBE (cl solo)
    78: Decca 4263, Brunswick (E) O3317
    LP: Ajaz LP253
70088-A   **I'm Glad There Is You** [Paul Madeira; Jimmy Dor-
                    sey] vBE (cl solo)
    78: Decca 4197
    LP: Decca DL8609, Ajaz LP253
70089-A   **Murderistic** [Joe Lippman] (as solo)
    78: Decca 4356
    LP: Ajaz LP253, Bandstand BS7104
    CD: Decca GRP-629
70090-A   **Hoboken Rock** [Joe Lippman]
    78: (unissued test pressing)
    LP: Coral (G) 6.22183

Jimmy and the band spent Christmas week (December 25 through 31)
at the Palace Theater in Albany, New York.
As 1941 came to a close, several major events had occured, not the
least of which was the Japanese attack on Pearl Harbor that plunged
America into World War II.
An incongruity of those days, when manpower was at a premium and
musicians were being inducted into the service, is the way many of the
top bands would grow in size during the next year.
Tommy would soon add a string section worthy of a small symphony
orchestra, and Jimmy's band, with a beefed-up brass section, already
numbered eighteen.   Other expanding bands included Harry James
(strings), Glenn Miller, Artie Shaw and Benny Goodman.
In 1942 the impact that World War II was to have on the band bus-iness would become even more apparent.   The armed forces were pull-ing away not only the band members but also the customers.

Gasoline shortages and the commandeering of interurban buses by the military would make many of the resorts, ballrooms and similar spots unreachable by both bands and fans.

This left a large number of big bands competing for a small number of hotel bookings across the country. Part of that competition began to dwindle, however, as the leaders themselves entered the services. Glenn Miller, Artie Shaw, Claude Thornhill and Sam Donahue were among the hundreds of former civilian musicians who would soon be leading service bands.

Unlike brother Tommy, Jimmy didn't take on a dozen or so new band members, although he did beef up the brass. Also unlike Tommy, he didn't fight back at the big changes that were taking place. As had been his way throughout his life, he rolled with the punches, pulled in his belt and rode out the storm.

The War Changes Things
(1942-1943)

New Year's Day 1942 was the band's opening day at the Strand Theater in New York City for a three-week booking. Jimmy had spotted the jitterbug dance team of Neallie Bohen and Bud Robinson at Virginia Beach and brought them to New York to work the stage show. Coupled with the film *The Man Who Came To Dinner,* the first week's gate was $55,000, the second, $48,000 and the closing week, $40,000.

Decca, New York, N.Y. Monday, January 12, 1942
JIMMY DORSEY AND HIS ORCHESTRA
Jimmy Dorsey (cl,as,ldr) Nate Kazebier, Jimmy Campbell, Shorty Solomson (tp) Phil Washburne, Sonny Lee, Al Jordan (tb) Milt Yaner, Frank Langone (as) Babe Russin (ts) Charlie Frazier (ts,fl) Chuck Gentry (bar) Joe Lippman (p) Guy Smith (g) Jack Ryan (sb) Buddy Schutz (d) Helen O'Connell, Bob Eberly (vcl)

70151-A   **A Sinner Kissed An Angel** [Mack David; Larry Shayne] vBE (as solo)
    78: Decca 4142
    LP: Ajaz LP253
70152-A   **You Made Me Love You (I Didn't Want To Do It)** Joseph McCarthy; James V. Monaco] vHO'C (as solo)
    78: Decca 4142, Brunswick (E) O3422
    LP: Ajaz LP253
    CD: Empress (E) 852
    Also on **TC, CD:** Good Music MSC35489
70153-A   **Tomorrow's Sunrise** vBE
    78: Decca 4197, Brunswick (E) O3310
    LP: Ajaz LP253
70154-A   **When The Roses Bloom Again** [Nat Burton; Walter Kent] vBE (cl solo)
    78: Decca 4165
    LP: Ajaz LP253
70155-A   **(At The) President's Birthday Ball** [Irving Berlin] vBE (as solo)
    78: Decca 4170
    LP: Ajaz LP253

Citing creative differences with Jimmy, arranger Toots Camarata left the band in early January (*Down Beat,* January 15, 1942, 5). After World War II Camarata began using the name "Tutti" and became a big favorite in England. Also in early 1942, Jimmy was garnering accolades from most of the trade press for his big popularity gains in 1941.

411

J. DORSEY NEW PHONO KING

NEW YORK, Jan. 10--The 1941 king of the coin phonographs is Jimmy Dorsey, who waxed more music box hits during the year than any other maestro, and wound up two hit disks to the good over Glenn Miller, 1940 champ.

Dorsey, who had cut only one hit platter during 1940, came thru with nine "Going Strong" items during the year just ended. *Maria Elena . . . Green Eyes . . . Amapola, I Hear A Rhapsody, Jim, My Sister and I, Blue Champagne, Yours* and *High On a Windy Hill* were Dorsey's . . . smash needlings of the year. (*Billboard*, January 17, 1942, 9)

The trade papers also carried reports early in 1942 that Jimmy and Tommy Dorsey's bands would make joint appearances in various key cities beginning in May to raise $100,000 for USO, Navy Relief and other wartime causes. For whatever reasons, the tour never materialized.

During the last week at the Strand, Jimmy announced he was adding three new band members. Trumpeter Charlie (Little "T") Teagarden, who had just folded his own group, baritone sax player Chuck Gentry, recently of the Benny Goodman band, and trombonist Andy Russo came on board as new chairs.

Two more theater dates were sandwiched in before the Cafe Rouge, the first at the Cleveland, Ohio, Palace January 23-27, the other at the Michigan in Detroit January 28-February 5. *Billboard* (February 21, 1942, 23) reported that souvenir-seeking teens made off with several of the band's arrangements from the Michigan pit during the film showing, but returned them after newspaper publicity broke.

Travel itinerary: Fri. and Sat. Feb. 6, 7—Valley Dale, Columbus, Ohio.

The band moved into the Cafe Rouge of Hotel Pennsylvania on February 9, 1942, and began a three-month stay. Jimmy's wife Jane, his mother Tess and sister Mary Lisella attended the opening night festivities and were pictured in *Down Beat* (March 1, 1942, 1).

Broadcast schedule (all Cafe Rouge): Fri., Feb. 13, NBC-Blue [WJZ], 7:45-8:00 P.M. / Sat., Feb. 21, NBC-Blue [WJZ], 5:30-6:00 P.M.

Billboard (February 28, 1942, 31) stated that Jimmy's band would do a guest shot on the *Lucky Strike Hit Parade* program over CBS "next month" from the Pennsylvania bandstand, because Jimmy had secured permission from AFM Local 802 to broadcast three numbers in different spots of the 45-minute commercial broadcast by remote from the hotel. A check of the published *Hit Parade* guest lists for February, March and April 1942 fails to show the Dorsey band.

Decca, New York, N.Y. Tuesday, February 24, 1942
JIMMY DORSEY AND HIS ORCHESTRA
Jimmy Dorsey (cl,as,ldr) Nate Kazebier, Jimmy Campbell, Shorty Solomson, Ray Anthony (tp) Phil Washburne (tb,vcl) Al Jordan, Sonny Lee, Andy Russo (tb) Milt Yaner, Frank Langone (as) Don Hammond (ts) Charlie Frazier (ts,fl) Chuck Gentry (bar) Johnny Guarnieri (p) Guy Smith (g) Jack Ryan (sb) Buddy Schutz (d) Helen O'Connell, Bob Eberly (vcl)

70389-A   **Rain, Rain, Rain** vHO'C&band (unissued)
70390-A   **'Tain't No Good (Like A Nickel Made Of Wood)**
                 —part 1 vPW (as solo)
    78: Decca 4262
    LP: Ajaz LP253
70391-A   **'Tain't No Good (Like A Nickel Made Of Wood)**
                 —part 2 vPW&HO'C (cl solo)
    same issues as part 1
70392-A   **Me And My Melinda** [Irving Berlin] vPW
    78: Decca 4263, Brunswick (E) O3345 (dubbing)
    LP: Ajaz LP253
70393-A   **If You Are But A Dream** [Moe Jaffee, Jack Fulton,
                 Nat Bonx] vBE
    78: Decca 4312, Brunswick (E) O3591
    LP: Ajaz LP261

Broadcast schedule (Cafe Rouge): Fri., Feb. 27, NBC-Blue [WJZ], 7:30-8:00 P.M.

Tommy Dorsey, who was in Hollywood at the time, began negotiations with MGM to film the story of the brothers' rise to fame. However Jimmy and his manager Billy Burton balked at the amount of money
MGM would pay for six weeks of shooting time.
    Press reports indicated that MGM was offering $125,000 for both
brothers' bands, which would mean $62,500 apiece. Burton pointed out
that Jimmy's band itself, without either Bob Eberly or Helen O'Connell, had received $50,000 for four weeks on *The Fleet's In.*
    Burton told reporters that he made a proposal, accepted by MGM, for
the entire Jimmy Dorsey package at $90,000, with the same for Tommy,
who said no despite Burton saying he wouldn't charge any commission.
    The last remark certainly didn't help improve relations between Bur-
ton and Tommy. The MGM picture never jelled and the multi-city tour
by both bands doing benefits for the Navy or Army also fell through.

Decca, New York, N.Y. Wednesday, March 4, 1942
JIMMY DORSEY AND HIS ORCHESTRA

70436-A   **Last Night I Said A Prayer** vBE
    78: Decca 4277
    LP: Ajaz LP261
70437-A   **My Little Cousin** [Happy Lewis, Sam Braverman,
                 Cy Cohen] vHO'C (as solo)
    78: Decca 4288
    LP: Ajaz LP261
70438-A   **(You Are) Always In My Heart** [Kim Gannon; Ern-
                 esto Lecuona] vBE (cl solo)
    78: Decca 4277, 18807, 25121, 28457, (E) BM-30620,
    Brunswick (E) O3356 (dubbing)
    45: Decca 25121
    EP: Decca ED614
    LP: Decca DL5091, DL8153, Ajaz LP261
    TC: Good Music MSC37083
    CD: Empress (E) 852, Good Music MSC37083

Broadcast schedule (all Cafe Rouge): Fri., Mar. 6, NBC-Blue [WJZ], 7:45-8:00 P.M. /
Sat., Mar. 7, NBC-Blue [WJZ], 5:30-6:00 P.M.

Jimmy's rhythm section got a boost when Billy Burton was able to
lure guitarist Allen Reuss away from Ted Weems by offering him more
pay than Weems could (*Down Beat,* March 15, 1942, 1).

Decca, New York, N.Y. Thursday, March 12, 1942
JIMMY DORSEY AND HIS ORCHESTRA
Paul McCoy (tp) replaces Campbell; Allen Reuss (g) replaces Smith.
Harold Mooney (arr)

70480-A   **Heavenly Hideaway** [Jules Loman; Louis Ricca]
                 vBE (as solo)
       78: Decca 4207
       LP: Ajaz LP261
70481-A   **Full Moon (Noche de Luna)** [Bob Russell; Gonzalo
                 Curiel, Marcelene Odette] vBE
       78: Decca 4312
       LP: Ajaz LP261
70482-A   **An Overture To Love** vBE (cl solo)
       78: Decca 4207
       LP: Ajaz LP261
70483-A   **Jersey Bounce** [Bobby Plater, Tiny Bradshaw, Ed-
                 ward Johnson, Robert B. Wright] (as solo)
       78: Decca 4288, Brunswick (E) O3348 (dubbing)
       LP: Ajaz LP261
70484-A   **Blue Skies** [Irving Berlin] arrHM (as solo)
       78: Decca 18385, Brunswick (E) O3529
       LP: Decca DL8654, Ajaz LP261, Festival (Au) FL7036
70485   **Mood In Da Groove** (unissued)

Decca, New York, N.Y. Tuesday, March 17, 1942
JIMMY DORSEY AND HIS ORCHESTRA

70525-A   **Sleepy Lagoon** [Jack Lawrence; Eric Coates] vBE
                 (cl solo)
       78: Decca 4304
       LP: Ajaz LP261
70526-A   **Someday, Sweetheart** [John and Benjamin Spikes]
                 vHO'C (as solo)
       78: Decca 18385, (C) 10029, Brunswick (E) O3529
       LP: Ajaz LP261
70527-A   **I Threw A Kiss In The Ocean** [Irving Berlin] vHO'C
       78: Decca 4304, Brunswick (E) O3349 (dubbing)
       LP: Ajaz LP261
       Also on **TC, CD:** Good Music MSC37083

                 sustaining broadcast, Cafe Rouge, Hotel Pennsyl-
                 vania, New York. N.Y.—NBC-Blue [WJZ], 7:45-
                 8:00 P.M. Friday, March 20, 1942
JIMMY DORSEY AND HIS ORCHESTRA

Sowing Wild Notes [Charlie Frazier] (as,cl solos)
  on **LP:** Hindsight HSR-153, **TC:** Hindsight HSC-153

Broadcast schedule (all Cafe Rouge): Sat., Mar. 21, NBC-Blue [WJZ], 5:00-5:30 P.M.
/ Fri., Mar. 27, NBC-Blue [WJZ], 7:45-8:00 P.M. / Sat., Mar. 28, NBC-Blue [WJZ],
5:00-5:30 P.M. / Fri., Apr. 3, NBC-Blue [WJZ], 7:45-8:00 P.M. / Sat., Apr. 4, NBC-
Blue [WJZ], 5:00-5:30 P.M. / Fri., Apr. 10, NBC-Blue [WJZ], 7:45-8:00 P.M. / Sat.,
Apr. 11, NBC-Blue [WJZ], 5:00-5:30 P.M. / Fri., Apr. 17, NBC-Blue [WJZ], 7:45-
8:00 P.M.

sustaining broadcast, Cafe Rouge, Hotel Pennsylvania, New York, N.Y.—NBC-Blue [WJZ], 5:00-
5:30 P.M. Saturday, April 18, 1942
JIMMY DORSEY AND HIS ORCHESTRA

Mood In Da Groove
  LP: Fanfare LP8-108

Broadcast schedule (all Cafe Rouge): Fri., Apr. 24, NBC-Blue [WJZ], 7:45-8:00 P.M.
/ Sat., Apr. 25, NBC-Blue [WJZ], 5:00-5:30 P.M. / Fri., May 1, NBC-Blue [WJZ],
7:45-8:00 P.M.

Decca, New York, N.Y. Friday, May 1, 1942
JIMMY DORSEY AND HIS ORCHESTRA
Jimmy Dorsey (cl,as,ldr) Nate Kazebier, Paul McCoy, Shorty
Solomson, Billy Oblak (tp) Phil Washburne (tb,vcl) Al Jordan, Sonny
Lee, Andy Russo (tb) Milt Yaner, Frank Langone (as) Babe Russin (ts)
Charlie Frazier (ts,fl) Chuck Gentry (bar) Johnny Guarnieri (p) Allen
Reuss (g) Jack Ryan (sb) Buddy Schutz (d) Helen O'Connell, Bob
Eberly (vcl)

70704-A   **On Echo Hill** vBE (cl solo)
     78: Decca 18362
     LP: Ajaz LP261
70705-A   **Take Me** [Mack David; Rube Bloom] vHO'C (cl solo)
     78: Decca 18376
     LP: Ajaz LP261
70706-A   **This Is Worth Fighting For** [Eddie DeLange; Sam H.
           Stept] vBE (as solo)
     78: Decca 18376
     LP: Ajaz LP267
70707-A   **Wonder When My Baby's Coming Home?** [Kermit
           Goell; Arthur Kent] vHO'C (as solo)
     78: Decca 18362
     LP: Ajaz LP267
     TC: Good Music 35489
     CD: Good Music 35489

Two new members of the band are listed above, former TD tenor
Babe Russin for Don Hammond and Billy Oblak for Ray Anthony.

Broadcast schedule (Cafe Rouge): Sat., May 2, NBC-Blue [WJZ], 5:00-5:30 P.M.

The band closed at the Pennsylvania on Saturday, May 2, and immediately left to fulfill a few one-nighters for promoter Billy Evans in New England and Pennsylvania.

Travel Jitinerary: Sun., May 3—Arena, New Haven, Conn. / Mon., May 4—Auditorium, Worcester, Mass. / Tues., May 5—Arena, Hartford, Conn. (crowd at 3,700) / Wed., May 6—Temple University, Philadelphia, Pa.

Helen O'Connell topped the list of favorite band vocalists (both male and female) in *Billboard's* 1942 survey (May 2, 1942, 19) of 158 college newspapers, ahead of Ray Eberle (2), Frank Sinatra (3), Bob Eberly (4) and Marion Hutton (5).

Jimmy returned the band to New York City for his second appearance of the year at the Strand Theater opening on Friday, May 8, and closing on Thursday, June 4. The four-week booking followed some very spirited bidding between Warner Brothers' Strand and the Paramount.

The reported four-week guarantee was $42,000 (*Billboard,* April 4, 1942, 24). On stage with Jimmy, Bob and Helen were impressionist Billy DeWolfe, and the Condos Brothers dance team.

For the first two weeks the Paramount countered with Claude Thornhill's band and then it was Woody Herman for the final two weeks, delighting General Amusement Corporation, which handled both bands.

Decca, New York, N.Y. Tuesday, June 2, 1942
JIMMY DORSEY AND HIS ORCHESTRA
Billy Pritchard (tb) replaces Jordan

70808-A   **Serenade In Blue** [Mack Gordon; Harry Warren] vBE (cl solo)
   78: Decca 18433, Brunswick (E) O3412, Coral 60673
   LP: Ajaz LP267
70809-A   **My Devotion** [Roc Hillman, Johnny Napton] vBE
   78: Decca 18372, Brunswick (E) O3419 (dubbing)
   LP: Decca DL-8609, Ajaz LP267
70810-A   **I've Got A Gal In Kalamazoo** [Mack Gordon; Harry Warren] vPW (as solo)
   78: Decca 18433, Brunswick (E) O3412
   LP: Coral (G) PCO7839, 6.22183, Ajaz LP267
70811-A   **Sorghum Switch** [Jesse Stone] (as solo)
   78: Decca 18372, Coral 60063, Brunswick (E) O3403 (dubbing)
   LP: Coral CRL56008, Ajaz LP267, Time-Life STB-B10
   TC: Time-Life 4TL-0006
   CD: Time-Life 4TL-0006, GRP-Decca CD-GRD-626, Kaz (E) 309
    All Coral releases of "Sorghum Switch" as "Cole Slaw."

June 2, 1942, was the day Jimmy and Tommy lost another longtime associate. Like Bix Beiderbecke before him, Bunny Berigan died but a pale shadow of his once great self at New York's Polyclinic Hospital.

A similar situation to the Strand "coup" cropped up for Jimmy's next booking, a week at the Century Theater in Buffalo, opening Friday, June 5, through Thursday, June 11. General Amusement Corporation was reported to favor the Century over Paramount's Shea's Buffalo. However, the Century suddenly canceled all stage shows for the summer. Jimmy signed instead with the Shea's Buffalo for the week starting August 28.

And so the band worked A. J. Perry's Empire Ballroom, Allentown, Pennsylvania, on Friday, June 5, attracting a record 4,200 dancers for a $5,000 gate. The following two days (June 6 and 7) the band played the Palomar Ballroom in Norfolk, Virginia, for a two-day crowd of 4,000.

On Friday, June 12, through Tuesday, June 18, Jimmy broke records again at Philadelphia's Earle Theater, grossing $37,500 and smashing Glenn Miller's 1941 top mark of $34,000 there. Jimmy celebrated by passing out bonuses to the theater staff in War Stamps.

After the Philadelphia engagement, the band took a vacation while Jimmy and Billy Burton headed for Hollywood. There they negotiated publicly with Paramount Pictures (*Down Beat*, July 15, 1942, 4), and privately with Metro Goldwyn Mayer, resulting in *I Dood It,* a Red Skelton feature, confirmed by *Down Beat* on August 1, 1942.

Jimmy and Tommy's father, 70-year-old Thomas F. Dorsey, Sr., died in Philadelphia shortly after Jimmy's return from the coast. "The father" passed away July 12 in Friends' Hospital, where he was brought from Lansford, Pennsylvania. He had retired in 1937 after nineteen years of teaching music to Lansford area youngsters.

After morning funeral services on July 14 in Lansford and burial in a cemetery in Shenandoah, Pennsylvania, where he would later also be interred, Jimmy rushed back to New York for a scheduled record date.

All record companies were pushing to get as many sides as possible "on wax" because American Federation of Musicians (AFM) President James C. Petrillo had ordered that no musicians make recordings after July 31 without an AFM contract, which he was refusing to approve.

Decca, New York, N.Y. Tuesday, July 14, 1942
JIMMY DORSEY AND HIS ORCHESTRA

71054-A   **I'm Getting Tired So I Can Sleep** [Irving Berlin]
               vBE
    78: Decca 18462, Brunswick (E) O3473
    LP: Ajaz LP267
71055-A   **Brazil** (Aquarela do Brasil) [S. K. [Bob] Russell; Ary
               Baroso] vBE&HO'C (as solo)
    78: Decca 18460, 18808, 25122, (E) BM-30646, Brunswick (E)
    O3403
    (SSL-3934) **ET:** AFRS Basic Music Library 3934
    EP: Decca ED614
    LP: Decca DL5091, DL8153, DL74258, DL4853, (C) DL4828,
    MCA 2-4073, Ajaz LP267, Time-Life STB-B10
    TC: Time-Life 4TL-0006, Good Music MSC-37083, 35489
    CD: Time-Life 4TL-0006, Good Music MSC-37083, 35489,
    Empress (E) 852
71056-A   **(At The) Crossroads (aka Malaguena)** [Bob Russell;
               Ernesto Lecuona] vBE
    78: Decca 18467, 18808, 25122, (E) BM-30842, Brunswick (E)
    O3439
    EP: Decca ED614   (Contd.)

JIMMY DORSEY AND HIS ORCHESTRA (Contd.)

    LP: Decca DL5091, DL8153, Ajaz LP267
    CD: Empress (E) 852
71057-A   **Murder! He Says!** [Frank Loesser; Jimmy McHugh]
          vHO'C (cl solo)
    78: Decca 18532, Brunswick (E) O3443
    LP: Ajaz LP267
    CD: Empress (E) 829
71058-A   **I'll Find You** vBE (as solo)
    78: Decca 18545
    LP: Ajaz LP267
71059-A   **Daybreak** [Harold Adamson; Ferde Grofé] vBE (as
          solo)
    78: Decca 18460, Brunswick (E) O3435
    LP: Ajaz LP267
71060-A   **Let's Get Lost** [Frank Loesser; Jimmy McHugh] vBE
          (cl solo)
    78: Decca 18532, Brunswick (E) O3443
    LP: Ajaz LP267
71061-A   **Manhattan Serenade** [Harold Adamson; Louis Alter]
          vBE (as solo)
    78: Decca 18467, Brunswick (E) O3435
    LP: Ajaz LP267
71062-A   **Ev'ry Night About This Time** [Ted Koehler; James
          V. Monaco] vBE (as solo)
    78: Decca 18462, Brunswick (E) O3419
    LP: Ajaz LP267
71063-A   **You Didn't Ask Me** vHO'C (as solo)
    78: Decca 18709
    LP: Ajaz LP757

General Amusement Corporation, in announcing that Jimmy Dorsey would do the Red Skelton movie for MGM (*Billboard,* July 18, 1942, 19), said that Jimmy's deal and an identical one for Glenn Miller's third film at 20th Century-Fox were the highest fees ever paid any bands for movie work, and boasted that Jimmy's price was nearly 70 percent higher than what brother Tommy got from MGM for *Ship Ahoy.* The Miller-Fox deal died when Glenn joined the Army a few weeks later.

Travel itinerary: Fri., July 17 to Thurs., July 23—Capitol Theater, Washington, D.C. / Fri., July 24, to Mon., July 27—Loew's Akron, Akron, Ohio / Fri., July 31, to Mon., Aug. 3—Paramount Theater, Toledo, Ohio / Tues., Aug. 4—Val-Air Park, Des Moines, Iowa (gate of $3,150) / Thurs., Aug. 6—Prom Ballroom, St. Paul, Minn. / Fri., Aug. 7, to Thurs., Aug. 13—Riverside Theater, Milwaukee, Wisc. (broke house record with a $23,000 gross)

While at the Riverside, Jimmy broadcast the first of a Saturday afternoon one-hour series, *The Navy Bulletin Board*, a recruiting program for the U.S. Navy, which aired 5:00 to 6:00 P.M. EWT on Mutual. In an unusual move for Jimmy, he emceed, playing little music himself and paid all the costs. His press agent Dave Dexter, Jr., wrote the scripts.

Travel itinerary: Fri., Aug. 14, to Thurs., Aug. 20—Chicago Theater, Chicago Ill. (six shows daily, seven on Sat. and Thurs., grossed $58,200 and broke house record; Jimmy netted $17,107 on a percentage deal) / Fri., Aug. 21, to Thurs., Aug. 27—Eastwood Gardens, Detroit, Mich. / Fri., Aug. 28, to Thurs., Sept. 3—Shea's Buffalo Theater, Buffalo, N.Y. ($31,700 gross, breaking Glenn Miller record set in July)

Broadcast schedule: Navy Bulletin Board, Sat., Aug. 15, MBS, 4:00-5:00 P.M. CWT / *Navy Bulletin Board,* Sat., Aug. 22, MBS, 5:00-6:00 P.M. / *Navy Bulletin Board,* Sat., Aug. 29, MBS, 5:00-6:00 P.M.

One evening at Shea's Buffalo, a six-year-old boy sneaked up behind Jimmy on stage and announced that he wanted to sing. Remembering the tot from before, but not wanting to alienate the audience, Jimmy let him sing two numbers. Subsequently, the kid and his mother, a typical "stage mom," were ejected from the theater. It wasn't the first time the woman had tried to impress Jimmy (*Variety,* September 16, 1942, 39).

Dorsey Brothers Music, Inc., a music publishing company headed by George Marlo and financed by Jimmy and Tommy, debuted in September amid the usual trade press puffery about all the composers who were anxious to get on board.

Billboard (September 5, 1942, 19) said that Marlo had to send lyrics and lead sheets on all new material to both brothers for rejection or acceptance, with approvals by both needed.

Despite all the advance buildup it took nearly a month for the firm's first tune to be published, which, given the need for joint agreement by the brothers, was not surprising.

The tune was called "I Don't Care What You Think of Me" and was written by Ruth Lowe (whose only other work was the hit "I'll Never Smile Again") along with Stephen Weiss, Paul Mann and Fred Jay.

Jimmy was reported to be set to cut it for an October 3 release and Tommy was expected to follow suit shortly thereafter. Neither band ever recorded the tune, of course, because of James C. Petrillo's August 1 ban on recordings, which was still in effect.

Jimmy brought the band into the "Midwest Home of Swing," the Panther Room of Hotel Sherman in Chicago on Friday, September 11, for what would turn out to be a very successful two-week stand. The first week the band did $17,800, the second, $15,000. *Billboard* (October 3, 1942, 11) reported that Jimmy was due 30 percent of the gross.

Broadcast schedule (all Hotel Sherman, all times CWT): Fri., Sept. 11, Blue, 10:15-10:30 P.M. / Sat., Sept. 12, *Navy Bulletin Board,* MBS, 4:00-5:00 P.M. / Sun., Sept. 13, Blue, 10:15-10:30 P.M. / Thurs., Sept. 17, Blue, 10:15-10:30 P.M.

> *sustaining broadcast,* Hotel Sherman, Chicago, Ill.—
> Blue, 10:15-10:30 P.M. CWT, Friday, September 18,
> 1942

JIMMY DORSEY AND HIS ORCHESTRA

Jimmy Dorsey (cl,as,ldr) Steve Lipkins, Nate Kazebier, Billy Oblak, Shorty Solomson (tp) Andy Russo, Billy Pritchard, Sonny Lee, Phil Washburne, (tb) Milt Yaner, Frank Langone (as) Babe Russin (ts) Charlie Frazier (ts,fl) Chuck Gentry (bar) Johnny Guarnieri (p) Tommy Kaye (g) Jack Ryan (sb) Buddy Schutz (d) Bob Eberly, Helen O'Connell (vcl)

JIMMY DORSEY AND HIS ORCHESTRA (Contd.)

Contrasts [Jimmy Dorsey] (theme) (as solo) / (At The) Crossroads [Bob Russell; Ernesto Lecuona] vBE / Sak House Stomp [Harold Mooney] (as solo) / Brazil (Aquarela do Brasil) [S. K. (Bob) Russell; Ary Baroso] vBE&HO'C (as solo)

Broadcast schedule (all Hotel Sherman, all times CWT): Sat., Sept. 19, *Navy Bulletin Board,* MBS, 4:00-5:00 P.M. / Sun., Sept. 20, Blue, 10:15-10:30 P.M. / Thurs., Sept. 24, Blue, 10:15-10:30 P.M.

After closing at the Sherman Thursday, September 24, the band played a one-nighter at the Municipal Auditorium in Kansas City, Missouri, on Friday, September 25. They then traveled to Hollywood, beginning a long stay at the Palladium on Tuesday, September 29.

Because of the wartime usage of Pullman and coach cars by the military, the twenty-six-person entourage had to book two compartment cars at a cost of $5,700 to make the trip to California.

Tommy Dorsey, who was an almost permanent resident of the West Coast by then, was on hand for Jimmy's opening, along with sister Mary, their mother and Jimmy's wife Jane. Mickey Rooney, who fancied himself something of a drummer, sat in briefly with Tommy and Jimmy for a jam session that opening night when more than 4,500 turned out. Others in the impromptu session were Ziggy Elman (tp), Bob Zurke (p) and Buddy Rich (d). Milton Berle was the master of ceremonies.

In his first two weeks of a six-week engagement at the two-year-old ballroom, Jimmy brought in 64,000, setting a Palladium record. Over the run the band drew close to 140,000 to the dance palace, many of these war workers from the nearby Lockheed plant.

Broadcast schedule (all except Navy Bulletin Board from Palladium, all times PWT) Wed., Sept. 30, CBS, 9:30-10:00 P.M. / Sat., Oct. 3, *Navy Bulletin Board,* MBS, 2:00-3:00 P.M. / Sun., Oct. 4, CBS, 8:30-9:00 P.M. / Mon., Oct. 5, CBS, 9:30-10:00 P.M. / Wed., Oct. 7, CBS, 9:30-10:00 P.M. / Sat., Oct. 10, *Navy Bulletin Board,* MBS, 2:00-3:00 P.M. / Sun., Oct. 11, CBS, 8:30-9:00 P.M. / Mon., Oct. 12, CBS, 9:30-10:00 P.M. / Wed., Oct. 14, CBS, 9:30-10:00 P.M. / Sat., Oct. 17, *Navy Bulletin Board,* MBS, 2:00-3:00 P.M. / Sun., Oct. 18, CBS, 8:30-9:00 P.M. / Mon., Oct. 19, CBS, 9:30-10:00 P.M. / Wed., Oct. 21, CBS, 9:30-10:00 P.M. (see Addenda) / Sun., Oct. 25, CBS, 8:30-9:00 P.M. / Mon., Oct. 26, CBS, 9:30-10:00 P.M. / Wed., Oct. 28, CBS, 9:30-10:00 P.M. / Sat., Oct. 31, *Navy Bulletin Board,* MBS, 2:00-3:00 P.M. / Sun., Nov. 1, CBS, 8:30-9:00 P.M. (see Addenda) / Mon., Nov. 2, CBS, 9:30-10:00 P.M. / Wed., Nov. 4, CBS, 9:30-10:00 P.M. / Sat., Nov. 7, *Navy Bulletin Board,* MBS, 2:00-3:00 P.M. / Sun., Nov. 8, CBS, 8:30-9:00 P.M. / Mon., Nov. 9, CBS, 9:30-10:00 P.M.

The *Navy Bulletin Board* programs originated in the KHJ Don Lee-Mutual studios, not at the Palladium, and attracted many Hollywood stars, musicians and servicemen from the area each week.

The band closed at the Palladium on Monday, November 9, and began work on *I Dood It* the next day at MGM. The film starred Red Skelton and Eleanor Powell with specialty acts by Lena Horne, pianist Hazel Scott and clarinetist Barney Bigard. At the same time, on another MGM set, brother Tommy's band was working on *Girl Crazy.*

Bob Eberly and Helen O'Connell had a duet and Bob got a major solo in the film, but Helen's solo was cut. A few instrumental bars of a separately recorded version are used behind a cameo appearance by Tommy with Red Skelton outside a night club where Jimmy's band is supposedly playing.

Skelton, who doesn't recognize Tommy, effusively compliments Jimmy's band, saying Tommy's band has too many strings. Tommy replies that his favorite is Bob Hope.

MGM Studios, Culver City, Cal. Tuesday, November 10—Tuesday, November 24, 1942
I DOOD IT (aka *By Hook Or By Crook*): Vincente Minnelli, director
JIMMY DORSEY AND HIS ORCHESTRA
Jimmy Dorsey (cl,as,ldr) Nate Kazebier, Shorty Solomson, Steve Lipkins, Billy Oblak (tp) Sonny Lee, Billy Pritchard (tb) Phil Washburne (tb,vcl) Milt Yaner, Frank Langone (as) Babe Russin (ts) Charlie Frazier (ts,fl) Chuck Gentry (bar) Johnny Guarnieri (p) Tommy Kaye (g) Jack Ryan (sb) Buddy Schutz (d) Helen O'Connell, Bob Eberly, Buck and Bubbles (vcl) Harold Mooney, Leo Arnaud (arr)

> **One O'Clock Jump** [William "Count" Basie] arrIIM (as,cl solos) (made 11/16/42) / **Contrasts** [Jimmy Dorsey] (as solo) / **So Long, Sarah Jane** [Lew Brown, Ralph Freed; Sammy Fain] arrHM vBE / **Lord And Lady Gate** [Don Raye, Gene DePaul] arrHM (instrumental break recorded 11/16/42 for Red Skelton-Tommy Dorsey cameo) / **Star Eyes** [Don Raye, Gene DePaul] arrHM (recorded 11/24/42 for Red Skelton-Eleanor Powell comedy dance) / **Star Eyes** arrHM (extended version made 11/24/42) vBE&HO'C (as solo) / **So Long, Sarah Jane** (reprise) / **Star Eyes** (reprise)
>
> All selections in **FILM**: *I Dood It*; "One O'Clock Jump" in **LP**: Joyce 3005, Giants Of Jazz GOJ-1023, **CD**: Rhino R272721, R75283; "Star Eyes" (extended version) in **CD**: Rhino R272721, R72908, R75283
> **Lord And Lady Gate** (arrHM) vHO'C (cl solo) (recorded 11/16/42 but not used in film)
> In **LP**: Hindsight HSR-153, **TC**: Hindsight HSC-153, **CD**: Rhino R272721
> **Shorter Than Me** [Don Raye, Gene DePaul] arrLA vB&B (recorded 11/14/42 for dance by Buck and Bubbles but not used in film)
> In **CD**: Rhino R272721

Rhino's CD releases erroneously attribute Hal Mooney's arrangements to Art Mooney. "Swingin' The Jinx Away", the movie's finale, was lifted intact from MGM's *Born To Dance* (1936) and does not include Jimmy.

The thirteen-day shooting and recording schedule ran from 8:00 A.M. to late afternoon, leaving time for visits to nearby Army and Navy bases and other one-nighters at spots like Long Beach Memorial Auditorium.

Broadcast schedule (all times PWT): Sat., Nov. 14, *Navy Bulletin Board,* MBS, 2:00-3:00 P.M. / Sun., Nov. 15, *Fitch Bandwagon,* NBC, 3:30-4:00 P.M. / Sat., Nov. 21, *Navy Bulletin Board,* MBS, 2:00-3:00 P.M.

Navy Bulletin Board, KHJ Studios, Hollywood, Cal.—2:00-3:00 P.M. Saturday, November 28, 1942
JIMMY DORSEY AND HIS ORCHESTRA

Three Little Words [Bert Kalmar; Harry Ruby] arrHM (as,cl solos) / **I Got Rhythm** [Ira Gershwin; George Gershwin] (cl solo) / **Someday Sweetheart** [John Spikes, Benjamin Spikes] vHO'C (as solo)
All selections in **LP:** Hindsight HSR-153, **TC:** Hindsight HSC-153, **CD:** Pilz (G) 2049

Broadcast schedule: (all times PWT) Sat., Dec. 5, *Navy Bulletin Board,* MBS, 2:00-3:00 P.M. / Sat., Dec. 12, *Navy Bulletin Board,* MBS, 2:00-3:00 P.M. / Sat., Dec. 19, *Navy Bulletin Board,* MBS, 2:00-3:00 P.M.

AFRS Command Performance, unknown location, Hollywood, Cal. December 1942
JIMMY DORSEY AND HIS ORCHESTRA
Francis Langford, Bob Eberly, Helen O'Connell (vcl)

Over There [George M. Cohan] (theme) (as solo) / **At Last** [Mack Gordon; Harry Warren] vFL / **Tangerine** [Johnny Mercer; Victor Schertzinger] vBE&HO'C (as solo) / **Arkansas Traveler** [traditional] (intro to Bob Burns) / **You Made Me Love You (I Didn't Want To Do It)** [Joseph McCarthy; James V. Monaco] vFL (as solo) / **One O'Clock Jump** [William "Count" Basie] (as,cl solos)
Entire program on **ET:** AFRS Command Performance 37; "Tangerine" and "One O'Clock Jump" on **LP:** Giants Of Jazz GOJ-1023, **TC:** Nostalgia CO-5373; "One O'Clock Jump" also on **LP:** Fanfare LP8-108

On Sunday, December 20, the band again boarded two costly railroad compartment cars for the trek back to New York City. The three-day rail trip took special booking to get through Chicago and cost over $6,500.
Variety (December 23, 1942, 39) included an "insiders" report that Jimmy was carrying one spare trumpet player, and Tommy two, in case the draft grabbed one of their key men on short notice.
On Christmas Day 1942 the band opened for a month's stand at the Strand Theater in mid-Manhattan, which ended January 20, 1943. The band shared billing with another Jimmy—Cagney—whose *Yankee Doodle Dandy* was playing a regular price engagement on the Strand screen.
While Jimmy was at the Strand, Tommy opened at the Roof Garden of Hotel Astor. With both brothers in town, and the rivalry between them heating up as a result of Jimmy's recent hits, it isn't surprising a real battle erupted at Tommy's Astor Roof opening. Jimmy, his manager Billy Burton and publishers Rocco Vocco and Jack Bregman were seated at a table when, near closing time, the younger Dorsey finally approached and asked Jimmy what he was doing there.
Tommy also made some critical comments about Burton. He was disturbed about Burton's presence, believing Billy was not giving Jimmy's finances proper care, to put it mildly. Tommy was suspicious of the way Burton spent money and supposedly felt it couldn't be all Billy's (Woods 1994, 41). He then reportedly suggested that Jimmy and Burton

stay away from the Astor or the next time he'd punch his brother's nose.

Jimmy came back with the suggestion that there was no time like the present, "Harv," pointedly using Tommy's nickname for anyone whose name he couldn't recall. Press accounts reported that chairs flew and fists landed for several minutes, resuming when the two reached the elevators. Both Tommy and Jimmy later admitted that the "Cain and Abel" publicity "humanized" them to their fans (Woods ibid.).

After the Strand contract, Helen O'Connell left the band to marry Clifford Smith, heir to a wealthy Maine family. Helen said that leaving Jimmy was hard, for she thought the world of him and the band, but didn't think marriage and road trips would mix (*Down Beat,* January 15, 1943, 1). She soon found that married life wasn't that great.

Helen went into radio work centered around New York City. Her first booking was the Blue Network's *Chamber Music Society of Lower Basin Street* on Monday nights beginning January 25. Jimmy hired Jack Teagarden's vocalist, twenty-one-year-old Kitty Kallen, to replace her.

The band was booked to go into Frank Dailey's Meadowbrook for a short stay on January 22 and then move to Hotel Pennsylvania. But Dailey suddenly closed the New Jersey ballroom, citing poor business due to gas rationing, and left Glen Gray, Woody Herman and Jimmy without winter bookings (*Billboard,* January 16, 1943, 21).

To fill the gap, Jimmy took a week off and then landed a week at the RKO Boston Theater from Thursday, January 28, to Wednesday, February 3, doing a brisk $33,000 box office.

They then got a conciliatory three-day stand, opening Dailey's new Terrace Room in the Mosque Theater building on Broad Street in Newark, New Jersey, Friday to Sunday, February 5 to 7. Situated in the basement of the vacant theater, the newly refinished Terrace Room attracted capacity crowds of 1,600 each of the three evenings.

Dailey had reportedly lined up airtime on WPAT in Patterson and WAAT in Jersey City, New Jersey, WNEW in New York City, the Atlantic Coast network, CBS and Mutual. Only the times and dates of the CBS airings are confirmed.

Broadcast schedule (both Terrace Room): Fri., Feb. 5, CBS [WABC], 11:30-12 P.M. / Sat., Feb. 6, CBS [WABC], 11:15-11:30 P.M.

The opening night activities at the Cafe Rouge were caught by the Blue Network (née NBC-Blue).

sustaining broadcast, Cafe Rouge, Hotel Pennsylvania, New York, N.Y.—Blue [WJZ], 12:30-1:00 A.M. Monday, February 8, 1943

JIMMY DORSEY AND HIS ORCHESTRA
Jimmy Dorsey (cl,as,ldr) Steve Lipkins, Nate Kazebier, Mario Serritello, Slim Davis, Shorty Solomson (tp) Billy Pritchard, Sonny Lee, Nick DiMaio (tb) Milt Yaner, Frank Langone (as) Babe Russin (ts) Charlie Frazier (ts,fl) Chuck Gentry (bar) Johnny Guarnieri (p) Tommy Kaye (g) Jack Ryan (sb) Buddy Schutz (d) Bob Eberly, Kitty Kallen (vcl) Sonny Burke, Harold Mooney, Otto Helbig (arr)

Contrasts [Jimmy Dorsey] (as solo) / **Just You, Just Me** (Contd.)

JIMMY DORSEY AND HIS ORCHESTRA (Contd.)

[Raymond Klages; Jesse Greer] (as solo) / **Moonlight On The Ganges** [Chester Wallace, Montague Ewing; Sherman Myers] (as solo)
All selections on LP: Hindsight HSR-153, TC: Hindsight HSC-153; "Just You, Just Me" also on CD: Pilz (G) 2049

Broadcast schedule (all Cafe Rouge): Sat., Feb. 13, MBS [WOR], 12:35-1:00 A.M. / Sun., Feb. 14, Blue [WJZ], 12:30-1:00 A.M. / Tues., Feb. 16, Blue [WJZ], 12:00-12:30 A.M. / Thurs., Feb. 18, Blue [WJZ], 12:00-12:30 A.M.

Hollywood columnist Hedda Hopper printed a rumor in early 1943 that Jimmy's band was disbanding. Many of the big bands were calling it quits, but Jimmy, on the crest of a wave of success and booked solid for months ahead, was not one of them.

Jimmy's manager Billy Burton was quoted by *Billboard* (February 20, 1943, 20) as offering a $1,000 reward for information about the rumor monger.

Sonny Burke jumped from Charlie Spivak to Jimmy's band as an arranger about this time (*Variety,* February 29, 1943, 32).

Broadcast schedule (all Cafe Rouge): Tues., Feb. 23, Blue [WJZ], 12:00-12:30 A.M. / Thurs., Feb. 25, Blue [WJZ], 12:00-12:30 A.M. / Sat., Feb. 27, MBS [WOR], 12:35-1:00 A.M. / Sun., Feb. 28, Blue [WJZ], 12:30-1:00 A.M. / Tues., Mar. 2, Blue [WJZ], 12:00-12:30 A.M. / Thurs., Mar. 4, Blue [WJZ], 12:00-12:30 A.M. / Fri., Mar. 5, CBS [WABC], 12:05-12:30 A.M. / Sat., Mar. 6, MBS [WOR], 12:35-1:00 A.M. / Sun., Mar. 7, Blue [WJZ], 12:30-1:00 A.M. / Tues., Mar. 9, Blue [WJZ], 12:00-12:30 A.M. / Wed., Mar. 10, Blue [WJZ], 12:00-12:30 A.M. / Thurs., Mar. 11, Blue [WJZ], 12:00-12:30 A.M. / Fri., Mar. 12, CBS [WABC], 12:05-12:30 A.M. / Sat., Mar. 13, Blue [WJZ], 12:30-1:00 A.M. / Sun., Mar. 14, Blue [WJZ], 12:30-1:00 A.M. / Tues., Mar. 16, Blue [WJZ], 12:00-12:30 A.M. / Wed., Mar. 17, Blue [WJZ], 12:00-12:30 A.M. / Thurs., Mar. 18, Blue [WJZ], 12:00-12:30 A.M. / Fri.,Mar. 19, CBS [WABC], 12:05-12:30 A.M.

Jimmy and the band did two forty-minute shows for 4,000 enlistees Saturday afternoon, March 20, at the dedication of a record lounge for WAVES and SPARS (female branches of the Navy and Coast Guard) at the U.S. Naval Training School, Hunter College, New York City.

sustaining broadcast, Cafe Rouge, Hotel Pennsylvania, New York, N.Y.—CBS [WABC], 12:30-1:00 A.M. Saturday, March 20, 1943
JIMMY DORSEY AND HIS ORCHESTRA

Contrasts [Jimmy Dorsey] (theme) (as solo) / **There's A Harbor of Dreamboats** vBE (as solo) / **Sak House Stomp** [Harold Mooney] (as solo) / **(I Would Do) Anything For You** [Alex Hill, Bob Williams, Claude Hopkins] (as solo) / **Don't Get Around Much Anymore** [Bob Russell; Edward K. "Duke" Ellington] vKK (as solo) / **As Time Goes By** [Herman Hupfield] vBE (cl solo) / **Jumpin' Jiminy** [Zane Van Auken] (as solo) / **Contrasts** (closing theme)

"I Would Do Anything For You" on **78:** V-Disc 195, **LP:** Fanfare
LP8-108, Golden Era GE-15011, Hindsight HSR-153, Joyce
LP2009, Sandy Hook CSH-2046, **TC:** Hindsight HSC-153,
LaserLight 79-759, Sandy Hook CSH-2046, V-Disc JD#2, **CD:**
LaserLight 15-759; "As Time Goes By" on **LP:** Fanfare LP8-108,
V-Disc JD#2; "Jumpin' Jiminy" on **LP:** Fanfare LP8-108, Golden
Era GE-15011, **TC:** LaserLight 79-759, **CD:** LaserLight 15-759;
closing theme on **LP:** Fanfare LP8-108

Broadcast schedule (all Cafe Rouge): Sun., Mar. 21, Blue [WJZ], 12:30-1:00 A.M. /
Mon., Mar. 22, CBS [WABC], 11:30-12:00 P.M. / Wed., Mar. 24, Blue [WJZ],
12:00-12:30 A.M. / Thurs., Mar. 25, Blue [WJZ], 12:00-12:30 A.M. / Fri., Mar. 26,
CBS [WABC], 12:05-12:30 A.M. / Sat., Mar. 27, Blue [WJZ], 12:30-1:00 A.M. / Sun.,
Mar. 28, Blue [WJZ], 12:30-1:00 A.M. / Mon., Mar. 29, CBS [WABC], 11:30-12:00
P.M. / Wed., Mar. 31, Blue [WJZ], 12:00-12:30 A.M. / Thurs., Apr. 1 Blue [WJZ],
12:00-12:30 A.M. / Fri., Apr. 2, CBS [WABC], 12:05-12:30 A.M. *and* 11:30-12:00
P.M. / Sat., Apr. 3, Blue [WJZ], 12:30-1:00 A.M. / Sun., Apr. 4, Blue [WJZ], 12:30-
1:00 A.M. / Mon., Apr. 5, CBS [WABC], 11:30-12:00 P.M. / Wed., Apr. 7, Blue
[WJZ], 12:00-12:30 A.M. / Thurs., Apr. 8, Blue [WJZ], 12:00-12:30 A.M.

Jimmy was ill with strep throat over the April 9 weekend, causing
cancellation of scheduled broadcasts on Friday, Saturday and Monday.
Bob Eberly fronted the band at the Cafe Rouge during Jimmy's absence.

Broadcast schedule (all Cafe Rouge): Wed., Apr. 14, Blue [WJZ], 12:00-12:30 A.M. /
Thurs., Apr. 15, Blue [WJZ], 12:00-12:30 A.M. / Fri., Apr. 16, CBS [WABC], 12:05-
12:30 A.M. and 11:30-12:00 P.M. / Sat., Apr. 17, Blue [WJZ], 12:30-1:00 A.M. / Sun.,
Apr. 18, Blue [WJZ], 12:30-1:00 A.M. / Mon., Apr. 19, CBS [WABC], 11:30-12:00
P.M. / Wed., Apr. 21, Blue [WJZ], 12:00-12:30 A.M.

The April 21 broadcast marked the last night of a thirteen-week stand
at Cafe Rouge. As they were closing at the Pennsylvania, Jimmy was
faced with replacing Johnny Guarnieri because the pianist wanted to
remain in New York to work with Raymond Scott.
     He conditionally hired Bill Rowland from the Les Brown band, but
Down Beat (April 15, 1943, 1) reported that pianist Joe Rann, recently
released from the army and looking for a job, happened to approach
Jimmy at the Cafe Rouge. Jimmy auditioned him on the spot and Rann
got the permanent slot.
     On Saturday, April 24, the band played at Town Hall, Philadelphia,
Pennsylvania, and at the New Haven, Connecticut, Arena on Sunday,
April 25, netting Jimmy $6,500 for the weekend.
     Also during April 1943, Billy Burton negotiated a new three-year
contract with Decca Records, similar to one Jack Kapp had signed with
Bing Crosby. The pact was said to ensure a minimum gross yearly.
     The amount of the guarantee was not revealed, but *Variety* (April 28,
1943, 46) said that Jimmy supposedly had earned approximately $80,000
annually from Decca over the preceding two years.
     Sometime in April, possibly between closing at the Pennsylvania and
opening at the Roxy, the band, along with the Woody Herman and Duke
Ellington crews, took part in a broadcast recorded for the BBC Home
Service and emceed by BBC staffer Alastair Cook, whose conversations

with the bandleaders were aimed at firming up relationships between the American and British allies. Jimmy's offerings included "I Got Rhythm," "Jazz Me Blues" and "Turn Left."

The band began a four-week stand on Wednesday, April 28 at New York's Roxy Theater, Seventh Avenue and West Fiftieth Street, a week earlier than planned. Trade reports indicated that they were getting $12,500 a week for five shows daily and six on Friday and Saturday.

Because Harry James was appearing at the nearby Paramount, both theaters splurged on full-page ads in the tabloids, a tactic that paid off for both—teenagers clogged Times Square. Originally the Paramount was scheduled to have Tommy Dorsey which would have made the whole thing even more interesting, but Tommy was tied up in Hollywood on a picture.

A review of Jimmy's Roxy show in *Orchestra World* (June 1943, 10) called it extremely well-staged. Reviewer Roger Kay said the band was extensively featured, was well rehearsed and had good ensemble quality. The film at the Roxy (*Crash Dive,* with Tyrone Power) added to the box-office draw which topped $252,000 for the first three weeks.

On Friday evening, May 7, the New York City area had a practice wartime "blackout" and two of Jimmy's trumpet players (not identified) were caught away from the theater when the sirens sounded.

Both key men, they got a freeze from Jimmy when they climbed on the bandstand halfway through the show (*Variety,* May 12, 1943, 42).

When the month's booking ended Tuesday, May 25, large newspaper ads were trumpeting the next day's opening at the nearby Paramount Theater by Frank Sinatra, who had just left Tommy and was striking out on his own. It was an appearance that proved to be history-making.

As the band got set to hit the road again, Billy Burton hired Dick Gabbe, the one-night booker for General Amusement Corporation as the band's road manager, freeing Burton to stay in New York. Gabbe started at the end of May with Jimmy's stay at the Earle in Philadelphia.

The bands that stayed together during the war, including Jimmy's and Tommy's, made a major contribution to the war effort both here at home through USO camp and hospital shows and overseas through Armed Forces Radio Service (AFRS) shows such as *One Night Stand, Command Performance* and *Mail Call* and recording services like V-Discs and the Basic Music Library for armed forces radio stations.

These AFRS efforts, V-Discs and some other airchecks have become the only recorded evidence of the changes that occurred in many big bands from mid-1942 until 1944, thanks to the AFM recording ban.

There are many who also say this absence from the recording studios helped set the stage for the end of the Big-Band era. With no recording exposure, the young fans, by now predominantly female, soon switched from the bands to the romance and glamour of the singers.

The result was the meteoric rise in popularity of vocal personalities like Sinatra, Crosby, Como, Haymes, Stafford, Shore and others, who could make their records without musicians, employing backup by vocal choral groups. Eventually, however, AFM head James Petrillo got most of the leading vocalists to abandon that practice as well.

Another school blames the war itself. The popularity of the big bands, so goes this theory, rested in the boys who wanted to see their favorites, with the girls going along to please them. The war took the boys from the girls, who turned to the more "romantic" singers.

Whichever cause was paramount, and perhaps both were, by the time the record ban and the war were over, the big-band business was entering its last few years of healthy life.

Among the many programs produced by AFRS during World War II was a popular music series called *Downbeat*. Jimmy's band was featured on one of the earliest broadcasts of this series, which was made up of studio introductions by Jimmy and the AFRS announcer to previously transcribed on-location band tracks.

Downbeat, Manhattan Beach Naval Base, New York, N.Y.—May 26 or 27, 1943

JIMMY DORSEY AND HIS ORCHESTRA

Jimmy Dorsey (cl,as,ldr) Bob Alexy, Nate Kazebier, Mario Serritello, Slim Davis, Shorty Solomson (tp) Billy Pritchard (tb,vcl) Sonny Lee, Nick DiMaio, Andy Russo (tb) Bill Covey, Frank Langone (as) Babe Russin (ts) Charlie Frazier (ts,fl) Bob Lawson (bar) Joe Rann (p) Tommy Kaye (g) Jack Ryan (sb) Buddy Schutz (d) Bob Eberly, Kitty Kallen (vcl)

Contrasts [Jimmy Dorsey] (theme) (as solo) / **It's Only A Paper Moon** [E. Y. Harburg, Billy Rose; Harold Arlen] (cl solo) / **As Time Goes By** [Herman Hupfeld] vBE (as solo) / **You Can't Get Stuff In Your Cuff** vBP (cl solo) / **Harbor Of Dreamboats** vBE (as solo) / **Taking A Chance On Love** [John Latouche, Ted Fetter; Vernon Duke] vKK (as solo) / **Turn Right** [Joe Lippman] (as solo) / **You'd Be So Nice To Come Home To** [Cole Porter] vBE&KK (as solo) / **Moonlight On The Ganges** [Chester Wallace, Montague Ewing; Sherman Myers] (as solo)/ **Contrasts** (theme)
Entire broadcast on ET: AFRS Downbeat #8 [H-7-27]

Closing at the Roxy on Monday, May 25, the band next stopped at the Earle Theater in Philadelphia, opening Friday, May 28, and ending on Thursday, June 3, after doing the best business of the season for the Earle, despite a heat wave. The band had Sunday off, due to the Pennsylvania "blue laws," which closed the theater, and Jimmy's refusal to play Sunday at a nearby Camden, New Jersey, theater.

Another attraction for the Earle customers on Wednesday, June 2, was watching Jimmy and the band substitute for Tommy on the half-hour NBC Raleigh/Kool show from 8:30 to 9:00 P.M. while Tommy was on vacation. The following week the band did the same thing from Jimmy's next booking in Cleveland, Ohio.

The band traveled to Cleveland for a week at the Palace Theater (Friday, June 4, to Thursday, June 10) followed by a similar week at the Michigan in Detroit (Friday, June 11, to Thursday, June 17), which had the added advantage of being the first week of school vacation. They then moved into the huge Balaban and Katz Chicago Theater for two weeks, opening Friday, June 18, and finishing Thursday, July 1.

At the Chicago the first week's box office was $50,500, with the band getting a $10,000 guarantee and a split over $42,000 each week. They played six shows a day with an extra show Saturday and Sunday.

An indication of what part wartime travel restrictions played in big-band bookings is found in *Billboard's* report (June 26, 1943, 24) that Jimmy had turned down a $3,000 guarantee per night for a string of one-nighters in the Midwest. The paper said that the Midwest ballrooms were hard to get to because of restricted bus travel, plus Jimmy was tired from his schedule of the past six months.

In mid-July Decca Records purchased World Broadcasting Corporation, thus putting Jack Kapp on a par with RCA-Victor and Columbia, which also had transcription services.

Jimmy and the band vacationed for two weeks and then began an extended booking at the Hollywood Palladium, opening Tuesday, July 20. In returning to the West Coast, Jimmy added an old pal from the twenties, trumpeter Phil Napoleon, to replace Mario Serritello.

Billboard (August 7, 1943, 12) noted that Jimmy's band used the Decca Hollywood studios on Melrose Avenue to rehearse a dozen new tunes in preparation for their eight-week stay at the Palladium.

Broadcast schedule (Palladium): Sundays, July 25-Sept. 5, CBS, 9:05-9:30 P.M. PWT.

sustaining broadcast, Hollywood Palladium, Hollywood, Cal.—Friday, August 13, 1943

JIMMY DORSEY AND HIS ORCHESTRA
Jimmy Dorsey (cl,as,ldr) Phil Napoleon, Ray Linn, Bob Alexy, Shorty Solomson, Marky Markowitz (tp) Sonny Lee, Billy Pritchard, Nick Di-Maio, Andy Russo (tb) Bill Covey, Frank Langone (as) Babe Russin, Charlie Frazier (ts,fl) Bob Lawson (bar) Dave Mann (p) Tommy Kaye (g) Bill Miller (sb) Buddy Schutz (d) Bob Eberly, Kitty Kallen (vcl)

Contrasts [Jimmy Dorsey] (theme) (as solo) / **Poinciana (Song Of The Tree)** [Buddy Bernier; Nat Simon] vBE (as solo) / **The Right Kind Of Love** [Kermit Goell; Mabel Wayne] vKK / **Nevada** [Mort Greene; Walter Donaldson] vBE / **Begin The Beguine** [Cole Porter] (as solo) / **The Very Thought Of You** [Ray Noble] / **Take Me In Your Arms** [Mitchell Parish; Fred Markush] vBE&KK (as solo) / **My First Love** vBE (as solo) / **Sak House Stomp** [Harold Mooney] (as solo) / **Contrasts** (theme)

Paul Whiteman Presents, NBC Studios, Hollywood, Cal.—NBC, 7:00-7:30 P.M. PWT, Sunday, August 29, 1943

PAUL WHITEMAN ORCHESTRA
Jimmy Dorsey (as) guest

Beebe [Jimmy Dorsey] (as solo)

sustaining broadcast, Hollywood Palladium, Hollywood, Cal.—CBS, 9:05-9:30 P.M. PWT, Sunday, September 5, 1943

JIMMY DORSEY AND HIS ORCHESTRA

Hit The Note (as solo)
LP: Hindsight HSR-153, **TC:** Hindsight HSC-153

Jimmy and wife Jane made it to the courts in Los Angeles in September when a former landlady sued them for $4,070 in alleged damages to the house she rented them in 1942. The charges claimed the Dorseys, their musician friends and dogs had damaged the property.

Jane Dorsey responded to the charge concerning the dogs by calling it libelous, and extolling the good manners of their canines (*Down Beat,* September 1, 1943, 3). No mention is made in the story of any similar defense by Jane of the musician friends (or Jimmy for that matter). The case was finally settled for $450 (*Down Beat,* September 15, 1943, 5).

unknown studio, Hollywood Cal. September, 1943
JIMMY DORSEY AND HIS ORCHESTRA

SSL-74   **Besame Mucho (Kiss Me Much)** [Sunny Skylar; Consuclo Vclaqucz] vBE,KK
     (SSL74) **ET:** AFRS Basic Music Library P-64-1
SSL-74   **That Wonderful, Worrisome Feeling** vKK (as solo)
     (SSL74) **78:** AFRS Basic Music Library P-64-2
SSL-74   **Sak House Stomp** [Harold Mooney] (as solo)
     (SSL74) **78:** AFRS Basic Music Library P-64-3

Travel itinerary: Wed., Sept. 8, to Tues., Sept. 14—Orpheum Theater, Los Angeles, Cal. / Thurs., Sept. 16, to Wed., Sept. 22—Golden Gate Theater, San Francisco, Cal. / Thurs., Sept. 23, to Wed., Sept. 29—T & D Theater, Oakland, Cal. / Sun., Oct. 3—Sweet's Ballroom, Oakland, Cal. / Mon., Oct. 4—Auditorium, Fresno, Cal. / Wed., Oct. 6—Auditorium, San Bernardino, Cal.

When Decca became the first major record label to settle with the Musicians' Union, Jimmy jumped out with a big hit, "Besame Mucho."

World, Hollywood, Cal. Thursday, October 7, 1943
JIMMY DORSEY AND HIS ORCHESTRA
Otto Helbig (arr)

L 3212-A   **My First Love** vBE (as solo)
     78: Decca 18582, (C) 10360, Brunswick (E) 03498
     (5969) **ET:** World 5969/5973
     LP: Ajaz LP275
L 3213-A   **That Wonderful, Worrisome Feeling** vKK
     (as solo)
     78: Decca 18900, Brunswick (E) 03613
     (VP 397) **78:** V-Disc 157
     (5970) **ET:** World 5969/5973
     LP: Joyce LP2009, Ajaz LP275, Sandy Hook SH-2046, Big Band Archives LP1203
     TC: Sandy Hook CSH-2046, V-Disc JD#1
     CD: V-Disc JD#2
L 3214-A   **Besame Mucho (*Kiss Me Much)** [Sunny Skylar; Consuelo Velaquez] vBE&KK
     78: Decca 18574, *Brunswick (E) 03495
     (5971) **ET:** World 5969/5973
     LP: Decca DL-8609, MCA 2-4073, Ace Of Hearts (E) (Contd.)

JIMMY DORSEY AND HIS ORCHESTRA (Contd.)

    AH-114, Ajaz LP275
    TC: Good Music 37083
    CD: Living Era (E) ASV AJA-5141, ASV AJA-5154, Good Music
    37083, Empress (E) 852
L 3215-A   **King Porter Stomp** [Ferdinand "Jelly Roll" Morton]
                arrOH (cl solo)
    78: Coral 60259, Brunswick (E) 03521
    (5994) **ET:** World 5994/5998
    (SSL-3934) **ET:** AFRS Basic Music Library 1946
    LP: Coral CRL56004, (G) PCO7839, 6.22183, Ajaz LP275
    CD: GRP-Decca CD-GRD-626, Kaz (E) 309
L 3216-A   **Star Eyes** [Don Raye, Gene DePaul] vBE&KK (as solo)
    78: Decca 18571, (C) 10146, Brunswick (E) 03498
    (VP 398) **78:** V-Disc 174
    (5972) **ET:** World 5969/5973
    LP: Decca DL-8609, Ace Of Hearts (E) AH-114, Ajaz LP275
    TC: V-Disc JD#2
    CD: Recording Arts (SWI) JZCD334, V-Disc JD#2
L 3217-A   **They're Either Too Young Or Too Old** [Frank Loes-
                ser; Arthur Schwartz] vKK (as solo)
    78: Decca 18571, (C) 10146, Brunswick (E) 03495
    (5976) **ET:** World 5974/5978
    LP: MCA 2-4073, Ajaz LP275
    CD: Lifetimes 9127, Empress (E) 852

Travel Itinerary: Fri., Oct. 8, to Sun., Oct. 10—Pacific Square Ballroom, San Diego, Cal.

20th-Century Fox Studios, Hollywood, Cal., Monday, October 11-Sunday, November 21, 1943
FOUR JILLS IN A JEEP: William Seiler, director
JIMMY DORSEY AND HIS ORCHESTRA
various strings added for some scenes.   Betty Grable, Martha Raye, Carole Landis, Dick Haymes, Kay Francis, Mitzi Mayfair, chorus (vcl)

Unidentified song fragment / **Over There** [George M.   Cohan] (segue to:) **Cuddle Up A Little Closer, Lovey Mine** [Otto Harbach; Karl Hoschna] vBG / **Over There** vCL,MR,KF&MM / **The Champ** [Sonny Burke] (cl solo) / **You'll Have To Swing It** (aka **Mr.   Paganini**) [Sam Coslow] vMR&chorus / **How Blue The Night** [Harold Adamson; Jimmy McHugh] vDH&chorus / unknown instrumental (cl solo) / unknown uptempo inst. (cl solo) / **You Send Me** [Adamson; McHugh] vDH& chorus / **How Many Times Do I Have To Tell You** [Adamson; McHugh] vDH / untitled boogie-woogie / **Crazy Me** [Adamson; Mc-Hugh] vCL
    All selections in **FILM:** TCF: *Four Jills In A Jeep*, **LP:** Hollywood Sound Stage 407, **CD:** Great Movie Themes 60029; "The Champ" on **78:** V-Disc 195, **LP:** Joyce LP2009, Sandy Hook CSH-2046, **TC:** Sandy Hook CSH-2046, V-Disc JD#2, **CD:** V-Disc JD#2

World, Hollywood, Cal. Wednesday, October 27, 1943
JIMMY DORSEY AND HIS ORCHESTRA

DLA 3246-A   **Do You Know?** vBE
(5977) **ET:** World 5974/5978
DLA 3247-A   **My Ideal** [Leo Robin, Newell Chase, Richard A.
Whiting] vBE (cl solo)
78: Decca 18574, (C) 10160, Brunswick (E) 03514
(5975) **ET:** World 5974/5978
LP: Ajaz LP275
CD: Empress (E) 852
DLA 3248-A   **Sak House Stomp** [Harold Mooney] (as solo)
78: Brunswick (E) 03521
(5995) **ET:** World 5994/5998
LP: Decca DL8654, Coral (G) PCO7839, 6.22183, Ajaz LP275,
Festival (Au) FL7036
DLA 3249-A)   **When They Ask About You** [Sam H. Stept] vKK
78: Decca 18582, Brunswick (E) 03544
(5978) **ET:** World 5974/5978
LP: Ajaz LP275

> *Downbeat,* unknown studio, Hollywood, Cal.—October 1943

JIMMY DORSEY AND HIS ORCHESTRA

That Wonderful Worrisome Feeling vKK (as solo)
ET: AFRS Down Beat 84

The *Fitch Bandwagon* was another of the network radio commercial shows spotlighting big bands in those World War II days. Aired between *Jack Benny* and the *Charlie McCarthy Show* Sunday nights at 7:30 Eastern time, it was one of the prize exposures for bands of the day.

> *Fitch Bandwagon,* NBC Studios, Burbank, Cal.—
> 4:30-5:00 P.M. PWT, Sunday, November 14, 1943

JIMMY DORSEY AND HIS ORCHESTRA
Bob Eberly, Kitty Kallen (vcl)

Smile For Me (Fitch Bandwagon theme) and **Contrasts** [Jimmy Dorsey] (theme) (as solo) / **King Porter Stomp** [Ferdinand "Jelly Roll" Martin] (cl solo) / **Star Eyes** [Don Raye, Gene DePaul] vBE (as solo) / **My First Love** vBE (as solo)/ **They're Either Too Young Or Too Old** [Frank Loesser; Arthur Schwartz] vKK (as solo) / **The Champ** [Sonny Burke] (cl solo) / themes

In mid-November, Bob Eberly entered the U.S. Army, thus completing the loss of the vocal team that had ensured success for Jimmy for four years. To replace Bob he hired movie actor Paul Carley.

Travel itinerary: Thurs., Nov. 25, to Thurs., Dec. 2—Orpheum Theater, Omaha, Neb. / Fri., Dec. 3, to Thurs., Dec. 9—Orpheum Theater, Minneapolis, Minn. / Fri., Dec. 10, to Thurs., Dec. 16—Chicago Theater, Chicago, Ill.

The following selections, released on two LPs, and purported to be from Cafe Rouge or Palladium broadcasts in December 1943 and January 1944, are mislabled, since the band did not play either location at that time. It is possible they are from earlier Palladium broadcasts or later airings from the Sherman.

sustaining broadcast(s), unknown locations—1943, 1944

JIMMY DORSEY AND HIS ORCHESTRA
Jimmy Middleton (sb) replaces Miller

Contrasts [Jimmy Dorsey] (theme) (as solo) / **Opus One** [Sid Garris; Sy Oliver] (as,cl solos) / **Perdido** [Juan Tizol] / **I Got Rhythm** [Ira Gershwin; George Gershwin] (cl solo) / **One O'Clock Jump** [William "Count" Basie] (as,cl solos)
     Theme and "Opus One" on **LP:** First Heard (E) FH-19; last three titles on **LP:** First Heard (E) FH-4

On Wednesday, December 22, 1943, the Jimmy Dorsey band opened for another four-week run at the Roxy Theater, Seventh Avenue and West Fiftieth Street. It was here that Kitty Kallen worked her last engagement with Jimmy and the boys. On stage with Jimmy at the Roxy was dancer Bill "Bojangles" Robinson, while on the screen was *The Gang's All Here,* Benny Goodman's latest film.

It was a battle of the Dorseys on Times Square for those four weeks ending January 18, 1944. At the Paramount Theater down the street brother Tommy, who had just added drummer Gene Krupa, also opened on December 22. It must have pleased Jimmy that he out-grossed Tommy $113,000 to $80,000 that first week. Both played to capacity; however, the Roxy had about 2,200 more seats than the Paramount.

A story in *Variety* (December 29, 1943, 29) announced that Jimmy and the band would go overseas for USO Camp Shows if plans worked out. The time frame for the overseas tour would follow Jimmy's 1944 date at the Sherman in Chicago. The project, however, never materialized.

Don't Get Around Much Anymore
(1944-1945)

The constraints of wartime travel continued to seriously affect the big-band business. The days of long strings of one-nighters had disappeared three years before. Missing were the visits to the ballrooms where the teenagers could afford to see them in person. Jimmy was relying more and more on long bookings at hotels to keep the band intact.

Faced with the loss of his major commercial appeal in O'Connell and Eberly, Jimmy forged on with typical Dorsey tenacity. Unlike Tommy, who has been pictured by some bandmembers as "cruel, ruthless and demanding," Jimmy is remembered as being gentle, kind and generous, often tolerating drunkenness and missed rehearsals that would have resulted in instant dismissal by Tommy. But the strain began to tell.

Though he was noted for his Irish temper, Jimmy's gentler traits often took over and he bottled up his frustrations. This sometimes led to trouble when he finally exploded. More often than not the target was his wife Jane. Soon his life began to be marked with traumatic events often triggered by the frustrations of being compared to his brother. Tommy was increasingly becoming a "West Coast cat," by then in a turbulent marriage to actress Pat Dane, and headed for his second divorce.

World, New York, N.Y. Wednesday, January 19, 1944
JIMMY DORSEY AND HIS ORCHESTRA
Jimmy Dorsey (cl,as,ldr) Phil Napoleon, Ray Linn, Bob Alexy, Shorty Solomson, Marky Markowitz (tp) Sonny Lee, Billy Pritchard, Nick Di-Maio, Andy Russo (tb) Bill Covey, Frank Langone (as) Babe Russin, Charlie Frazier (ts,fl) Bob Lawson (bar) Dave Mann (p) Tommy Kaye (g) Bill Miller (sb) Buddy Schutz (d) Paul Carley, Gladys Tell (vcl) Sonny Burke (arr)

71693-A   **I'm In Love With Someone** vGT (cl solo)
    78: Decca 18611, Brunswick (E) 03544
    LP: Ajaz LP275
71694-A   **Holiday For Strings** [David Rose] arrSB (as solo)
    78: Decca 18593, Brunswick (E) 03514
    LP: Decca DL-8609, Ajaz LP275
    CD: Empress (E) 852
71695-A   **Two Again** vPC (as solo)
    78: Decca 18616
    LP: Ajaz LP275
71696   **Star Dust** [Mitchell Parish; Hoagy Carmichael] (as solo)
    (6699) **ET:** World 6699/6703
71697   **It's A Cryin' Shame** vGT (unissued)

The previous Decca session introduced two new vocalists. While Paul Carley had been on hand since Bob Eberly left, Gladys Tell joined from Johnny Messner's band the same day as the session.

The next stop for the band was the Adams Theater, Newark, New Jersey, from Thursday, January 20, to Wednesday, January 26.

Closing night at the Adams saw Tommy sitting in Jimmy's trombone section for one number after announcing to the crowd that Jimmy had broken the Adams house record with a gross of $26,400. A week later Jimmy would be back at another spot in Newark.

Travel itinerary: Thurs. Jan. 27, to Wed., Feb. 2—RKO Theater, Boston, Mass. / Thurs., Feb. 3, to Thurs., Feb. 17—Frank Dailey's Terrace Room, Mosque Theater, Newark, N.J.

> *sustaining broadcast,* Terrace Room, Mosque Theater, Newark, N.J.—CBS [WABC], 11:30-12:00 P.M.
> Tuesday, February 8, 1944

JIMMY DORSEY AND HIS ORCHESTRA
Otto Helbig (arr)

I'm In Love With Someone vGT (cl solo) / **My First Love** vPC (as solo) / **Perdido** [Juan Tizol] (cl solo) / **When They Ask About You** [Sam H. Stept] vGT (as solo) / **The Great Lie** [Cab Calloway, Andy Gibson] (cl solo) / **Star Eyes** [Don Raye, Gene DePaul] vPC (as solo) / **King Porter Stomp** [Ferdinand "Jelly Roll" Morton] arrOH (cl solo)
Entire show on **ET**: AFRS One Night Stand #137

> *sustaining broadcast,* Terrace Room, Mosque Theater, Newark, N.J.—CBS [WABC], 11:30-12:00 P.M.
> Tuesday, February 15, 1944

JIMMY DORSEY AND HIS ORCHESTRA

King Porter Stomp [Ferdinand "Jelly Roll" Morton] arrOH (cl solo) / **I Couldn't Sleep A Wink Last Night** [Harold Adamson; Jimmy McHugh] vGT / **My First Love** vPC (as solo)/ **Holiday For Strings** [David Rose] (as solo) / **I'm In Love With Someone** vGT (cl solo) / **When They Ask About You** [Sam H. Stept] vGT (as solo) / **My Ideal** [Leo Robin, Newell Chase; Richard Whiting] vPC
Entire show on **ET**: AFRS One Night Stand #155

World, New York, N.Y. Wednesday, February 16, 1944
JIMMY DORSEY AND HIS ORCHESTRA

71773-A   **Ohio** [Betty Comden, Adolph Green; Leonard Bernstein] vGT (as solo)
    78: Decca 18593
    LP: Ajaz LP275
71774-A   **The Champ** [Sonny Burke] (cl solo)
    78: Coral 60259
    (SSL-3934) **ET:** AFRS Basic Music Library 3934
    LP: Coral CRL56004, Ajaz LP282

Travel itinerary: Fri., Feb. 18, to Thurs., Feb. 24—Shea's Buffalo Theater, Buffalo, N.Y. / Fri., Feb. 25, to Thurs, Mar. 23—Panther Room, Hotel Sherman, Chicago, Ill.

Monday, February 28 was a night off for the band at the Sherman, and Jimmy made a quick run to Indianapolis, Indiana, to visit Tommy at the Circle Theater. Along with Gene Krupa and Jan Savitt, they celebrated Jimmy's "tenth" birthday, the first time the brothers had observed Jimmy's natal day together in twelve years. The next night, leap year day, the band did the same for Jimmy at the Sherman.

sustaining broadcast, Hotel Sherman, Chicago, Ill.
March 1944
JIMMY DORSEY AND HIS ORCHESTRA

Perdido [Juan Tizol] (cl,as solos) / **Sunset Strip** [Sonny Burke, Jimmy Dorsey] (cl,as solos) / **Speak Low** [Ogden Nash; Kurt Weill] vPC / **I'm In Love With Someone** vGT (cl solo) / **My Silent Love** [Edward Heyman; Dana Suesse] / **Sak House Stomp** [Harold Mooney] (as solo) / **No Love, No Nothin'** [Leo Robin; Harry James] vGT / **King Porter Stomp** [Ferdinand "Jelly Roll" Morton] arrOH (cl solo)
    Entire broadcast on ET: AFRS One Night Stand 173; "Sunset Strip" on LP: Joyce LP1142, "Sak House Stomp" on LP: First Heard (E) FHR-4

sustaining broadcast(s), Hotel Sherman, Chicago, Ill.
March 1944
JIMMY DORSEY AND HIS ORCHESTRA

Oh, What A Beautiful Mornin' [Oscar Hammerstein II; Richard Rodgers] arrSB (cl solo) / **Sunset Strip** [Sonny Burke, Jimmy Dorsey] (cl,as solos) / **Speak Low** [Ogden Nash; Kurt Weill] vPC / **I'm In Love With Someone** vGT (cl solo) / **When They Ask About You** [Sam H. Stept] vGT (as solo) / **Poinciana** [Buddy Bernier; Nat Simon] vPC (as solo) / **Perdido** [Juan Tizol] (cl,as solos) / **Sak House Stomp** (partial) [Harold Mooney] (as solo)
    Entire contents (possibly from more than one broadcast) on ET: AFRS One Night Stand 182

Jimmy found himself and two other band members on the sick list in March during their Hotel Sherman stay. Along with Charlie Frazier and Dave Mann, Jimmy missed several days of work. Sonny Burke filled in at piano for Mann but the *Down Beat* coverage (April 1, 1944, 4) fails to tell who led the band, if any reeds were added or what the illness was.

Jimmy and Billy Burton, his manager for almost a decade, "split the blanket" during the Chicago stay and Dick Gabbe, who had left General Amusement Corporation to become Jimmy's road manager, took over.

There were several rumors in trade circles that the split was over some financial irregularities but these reports were never confirmed. It was announced that Burton would continue as a "consultant" from Hollywood (*Variety*, March 15, 1944, 53).

The band ended its stay at the Sherman Thursday, March 23, and immediately entrained for Cincinnati, Ohio, where they played a week

(Friday, March 24, to Thursday, March 30) at the Shubert Theater.

Two personnel changes occurred at the end of the Sherman engagement. Trombonist Bill Pritchard returned to New York radio work and was replaced by Si Zentner, and Tony Piccioto joined the expanded trumpet section from Boston (*Down Beat*, April 1, 1944, 4).

The band then went by train to Knoxville, Tennessee, for a one-nighter Friday, March 31, at the University of Tennessee, which paid a $2,500 guarantee against a percentage. The next night's booking at the Municipal Auditorium in Birmingham, Alabama, paid $3,500 certain against 60 percent of the gross (*Variety*, February 16, 1944, 37).

The band ended up in Miami, Florida, for three weeks at the Frolics Club. The booking paid $9,000 a week, an unprecedented amount for the times, but $1,000 less than Tommy had refused for the booking.

Jimmy got the added advantage of quite a few air shots from the Frolics on three different networks. By this time the Blue Network had become, in further transition to its permanent name, "The Blue Network of the American Broadcasting Company."

Broadcast schedule (Frolics Club): Wed., Apr. 5, Blue, 12:05-12:30 A.M.

sustaining broadcast, Frolics Club, Miami, Fla.—
Blue, 12:05-12:30 A.M. Wednesday, April 12, 1944
JIMMY DORSEY AND HIS ORCHESTRA

Contrasts [Jimmy Dorsey] (theme) (as solo) / **Sak House Stomp** [Harold Mooney] (as solo) / **Sunset Strip** [Sonny Burke, Jimmy Dorsey] (cl,as solos) / **Speak Low** [Ogden Nash; Kurt Weill] vPC / **King Porter Stomp** [Ferdinand "Jelly Roll" Morton] (cl solo) / **I'm In Love With Someone** vGT (cl solo) / **My First Love** vPC (as solo) / **No Love, No Nothin'**[Leo Robin; Harry James] vGT / **Holiday For Strings** [David Rose] (as solo) / **Oh, What A Beautiful Mornin'** [Oscar Hammerstein II; Richard Rodgers] (cl solo)
Entire show on **ET:** AFRS One Night Stand 202, "Sunset Strip" on **LP:** First Heard (E) FHR-19

Broadcast schedule (all Frolics Club): Sat., Apr. 15, MBS, 5:15-5:45 P.M. / Sun., Apr. 16, CBS, 12:30-1:00 A.M. / Wed., Apr. 19, Blue, 12:05-12:30 A.M. / Thurs., Apr. 20, CBS 12:30-1:00 A.M. / Sat., Apr. 22, MBS, 5:15-5:45 P.M. / Sun., Apr. 23, CBS, 12:30-1:00 A.M.

Mildred Bailey Revue, CBS Studios, New York, N.Y.—Spring 1944
TEDDY WILSON AND HIS ORCHESTRA
Teddy Wilson (p,ldr) Roy Eldridge (tp) Red Norvo (vib) Remo Palmieri (g) Al Hall (sb) "Specs" Powell (d) with Tyree Glenn (tb), **Jimmy Dorsey** (cl) added for:

I Got Rhythm [Ira Gershwin; George Gershwin] (cl solo)
    LP: Jazz Archives JA-36
    CD: Giants Of Jazz 53283

The year 1944 was a big movie year for Jimmy and the band. For the first of these, they worked during April and May on MGM's Abbott and Costello farce *Lost in a Harem* with John Conte and Marilyn Maxwell. In this one Jimmy and the boys, appearing as a band stranded in the Middle East, were decked out in Arab costumes from MGM's *Kismet*.

MGM Studios, Hollywood, Cal. April, May 1944
LOST IN A HAREM: Charles Reisner, director
JIMMY DORSEY AND HIS ORCHESTRA
Paul Carley, *Marilyn Maxwell* (vcl) Sonny Burke (arr)

> **Thunder And Blazes** (based on **Entry Of The Gladiators** [Julius Fucik]) (cl solo) arrSB / **Long John Silver** [Ray Krise, Jimmy Dorsey] (as,cl solos) (both cut 4/19)
> Both selections in **FILM:** MGM: *Lost In A Harem*, **LP:** Joyce LP3005, **CD:** Rhino 75283
> Recorded but not used in film: **Noche De Ronda** [Maria Teresa Lara] vPC (cl solo) (cut 4/21) / **I Know It's Wrong** [Don Raye; Gene de Paul] v*MM* (unknown ghost singer for Maxwell) (cut 5/5 and 5/26)
> Both selections on **CD:** Rhino 75283

Travel Itinerary: Fri., June 2—Auditorium, San Bernardino, Cal. / Sat., June 3—Auditorium, Ventura, Cal.

World, Hollywood, Cal. Wednesday, June 7, 1944
JIMMY DORSEY AND HIS ORCHESTRA
Jimmy Dorsey (cl,as,ldr) *Ray Linn [or] Red Rodney*, Claude Bowen, Bob Alexy, Tony Picciotto, Shorty Solomson (tp) Sonny Lee, Si Zentner, Nick DiMaio, Andy Russo (tb) Jack Aiken, Frank Langone (as) Bobby Dukoff, Charlie Frazier (ts) Bob Lawson (bar) Marvin Wright (p) Teddy Walters (g) Jimmy Middleton (sb) Buddy Schutz (d) Paul Carley, Gladys Tell (vcl)

L 3413-A   **It's A Crying Shame** vGT (as solo)
     78: Decca 18611
     (6454) **ET:** World 6454/6458
     LP: Ajaz LP282
L 3414   **This I Love Above All** vPC (as solo)
     (6455) **ET:** World 6454/6458
L 3415-A   **An Hour Never Passes** [Jimmy Kennedy] vGT (cl solo)
     78: Decca 18616
     (6456) **ET:** World 6454/6458
     LP: Ajaz LP282
L 3416   **Noche De Ronda** [Maria Teresa Lara]
     (6457) **ET:** World 6454/6458

The Decca/World session above was delayed several weeks because Jimmy was disturbed that Decca still hadn't released many of the disks he had made before leaving New York for the coast. Decca blamed a lack of production facilities plus wartime shortages of shellac but trade sources said that Decca was using its very limited production resources to fill the demands for its exclusive *Oklahoma!* original-cast four-record album, sales of which had already exceeded a million and a half copies (six million records).

Travel itinerary: Thurs., June 8—Auditorium, Bakersfield, Cal. / Fri., June 9— Auditorium, Fresno, Cal. / Sat., June 10—Fairgrounds Ballroom, Merced, Cal.

On June 13, 1944, Jimmy and the band opened at the Palladium in Hollywood for a six-week stay. Most of the cast of *Lost In A Harem,* as well as brother Tommy, were on hand opening night (Sanford 1972).

During the broadcast Tommy is referred to as "Homer Rodeheaver" and plays on "Grand Central Getaway." That part of opening night was aired regionally (network unknown) and by AFRS.

> *sustaining broadcast,* Hollywood Palladium, Holly-
> wood, Cal.—Tuesday, June 13, 1944

JIMMY DORSEY AND HIS ORCHESTRA
Paul Carley, Gladys Tell (vcl)

The Champ [Sonny Burke] (cl,as solos) / **All The Things You Ain't** [Sonny Burke, Jimmy Dorsey] (cl,as solos) / **Straighten Up And Fly Right** [Nat "King" Cole; Irving Mills] vGT (cl solo) / **This I Love Above All** vPC (as solo) / **King Porter Stomp** [Ferdinand "Jelly Roll" Morton] arrOH (cl solo) / **How Blue The Night** [Harold Adamson; Jimmy McHugh] vPC (as solo) / **Grand Central Getaway** [John Birks "Dizzy" Gillespie; Jimmy Dorsey] (as solo) / **It's A Crying Shame** vGT (as solo) / **Sak House Stomp** [Harold Mooney] (as solo)

> All the above on **ET:** AFRS One Night Stand Fill 23, "King Porter Stomp" on **LP:** First Heard (E) FHR-4

Tommy's opening night appearance was a little hypocritical since he and Jimmy, along with bandleader Phil Harris, were negotiating at the time with ballroom operator Bernie Cohen to buy Casino Gardens, a six to eight thousand capacity dance hall eight miles north of the Palladium at Mission Beach, in Santa Monica.

The move was rumored to be motivated by a desire to have a West Coast place of their own and thus circumvent the Palladium's low-salary structure, which most bandleaders considered robbery in view of the ballroom's large wartime earnings.

Jimmy's booking there for $5,500 a week had brought some earlier condemnation from other bandleaders, including Tommy, who felt the management was shortchanging big bands. The Palladium brass, meanwhile, insisted that playing there at a lower fee was a convenience for the bands while they worked on well-paying film commitments.

A week later *Variety* (June 28, 1944, 43) reported that the deal for Casino Gardens had been completed, with the brothers purportedly buying the lease on the Gardens for $50,000.

Variety (June 21, 1944, 1) gave a hint that the money wouldn't be too hard for at least Tommy to come up with, in a story indicating that he would gross over a million dollars in 1944, making him the highest paid bandleader ever, exceeding Kay Kyser, Glenn Miller and Harry James. After expenses and taxes, the trade paper estimated that Tommy would personally clear $75,000 to $100,000.

Jimmy's six-week stay at the Palladium would see near-capacity weekly crowds of 35,000, many of them coming from nearby military aircraft factories. This influx of war workers was a bonanza that was to pay off well for the Palladium owners, if not for the bands.

> *sustaining broadcast,* Hollywood Palladium, Holly-
> wood, Cal.—Friday, June 16, 1944

JIMMY DORSEY AND HIS ORCHESTRA

Contrasts [Jimmy Dorsey] (theme) (as solo) / **Take It Easy** [Albert DeBrue; Irving Taylor] vGT (cl solo) / **Noche De Ronda** [Maria Teresa Lara] vPC / **An Hour Never Passes** [Jimmy Kennedy] vGT (cl solo) / **Body And Soul** [Robert Sour, Edward Heyman, Frank Eyton; Johnny Green]

"Body And Soul" on **LP**: Hindsight HSR-153, **TC**: Hindsight HSC-153

> *sustaining broadcast,* Hollywood Palladium, Holly-
> wood, Cal.—Tuesday, June 20, 1944

JIMMY DORSEY AND HIS ORCHESTRA

Take It Easy [Albert DeBrue; Irving Taylor] (cl solo) / **I Dream Of You** [Marjorie Goetschius; Edna Osser] vGT (as solo) / **Grand Central Getaway** [John Birks "Dizzy" Gillespie; Jimmy Dorsey] (as solo)/ **How Blue The Night** [Harold Adamson; Jimmy McHugh] / **This I Love Above All** vPC (as solo) / **Perdido** [Juan Tizol] (cl,as solos) / **King Porter Stomp** ["Jelly Roll" Morton] arrOH (cl solo)

Entire broadcast on **ET**: AFRS One Night Stand #304

On *One Night Stand* #304, AFRS announces the location as "Sweet's Ballroom, Oakland, California." The commercial network announcer is Harry Mitchell, who was working at a Los Angeles radio station in 1944, which negates the AFRS designation.

> *sustaining broadcast,* Hollywood Palladium, Holly-
> wood, Cal.—Wednesday, June 21, 1944

JIMMY DORSEY AND HIS ORCHESTRA
Tommy Dorsey (tb) guest on three titles.

Contrasts [Jimmy Dorsey] (theme) (as solo) / **Together** [Buddy De Sylva, Lew Brown; Ray Henderson] arrSB (as solo) / **I'm In Love With Someone** vGT (cl solo) / **Sak House Stomp** [Harold Mooney] (as solo) / **Sunset Strip** [Sonny Burke, Jimmy Dorsey] (cl,as solos) / **Poinciana** [Buddy Bernier; Nat Simon] vPC (as solo) / **One O'Clock Jump** [William "Count" Basis] (as,cl solos) / **Do Nothin' Till You Hear From Me** [Bob Russell; Edward K. "Duke" Ellington] vGT (as solo) / **Oh, What A Beautiful Mornin'** [Oscar Hammerstein II; Richard Rodgers] arrSB (cl solo)

Entire broadcast on **ET**: AFRS One Night Stand 286; opening theme and "Together" on **LP**: Hindsight HSR-153, **TC**: Hindsight HSC-153

sustaining broadcast, Hollywood Palladium, Hollywood, Cal.—June1944
JIMMY DORSEY AND HIS ORCHESTRA

Perdido [Juan Tizol] (cl,as solos) / **Noche De Ronda** [Maria Teresa
Lara] vPC / **Sunset Strip** [Sonny Burke, Jimmy Dorsey] (cl,as solos)
/ **Holiday For Strings** [David Rose] (as solo) / **Do Nothin' Till You
Hear From Me** [Bob Russell; Edward K. "Duke" Ellington] vGT (as
solo) / **Long John Silver** [Ray Krise, Jimmy Dorsey] (as,cl solos) /
Star Eyes [Don Raye, Gene DePaul] vGT&PC (as solo) / **All The
Things You Ain't** [Sonny Burke, Jimmy Dorsey] (cl,as solos)
    Entire show on **ET:** AFRS One Night Stand 270

Among the more successful 1944 World War II propaganda film
efforts was *Hollywood Canteen,* involving a Who's Who of filmdom in a
story about the Hollywood USO club, the brainchild of Bette Davis.

Warner Brothers, Hollywood, Cal. June and July 1944 (two film
sessions)
HOLLYWOOD CANTEEN: Delmer Daves, director
JIMMY DORSEY AND HIS ORCHESTRA
Jack Carson, Jane Wyman, Joan Leslie, Dennis Morgan, Joe E. Brown,
Quartet (vcl)

King Porter Stomp [Ferdinand "Jelly Roll" Morton] arrOH (cl solo)
/ **What Are You Doing The Rest Of Your Life?** [Ted Koehler;
Burton Lane] vJC&JW / **You Can Always Tell A Yank** vDM&JEB
[E. Y. Harburg; Burton Lane] / **Sunset Strip** [Sonny Burke, Jimmy
Dorsey] (cl,as solos) / **Don't Fence Me In** [Cole Porter] / **Sweet
Dreams, Sweetheart** [Ted Koehler; M. K. Jerome] vJL&Qte
    All above selections in **FILM:** *Hollywood Canteen;* "King Porter
    Stomp" **78:** V-Disc 514 (Army), 274 (Navy), **LP:** Curtain Calls
    100-12, Joyce LP2009, Sandy Hook SH-2046, Dan (J) VC5026,
    TC: Sandy Hook CSH-2046, LaserLight 79-759, V-Disc JD1,
    CD: Recording Arts JZCD334, LaserLight 15-759, V-Disc JD2,
    Great Movie Themes 60024 (mislabeled "One O'Clock Jump");
    "What Are You Doing..." on **LP:** Curtain Calls 100-12, **CD:**
    Great Movie Themes 60024; "Sweet Dreams, Sweetheart" on **LP:**
    Curtain Calls 100-12, **CD:** Great Movie Themes 60024; "You Can
    Always Tell A Yank" on **CD:** Great Movie Themes 60024
What Are You Doing The Rest Of Your Life? (no vocal) (unused)

After finishing work in June on *Hollywood Canteen* and closing at the
Palladium, the band started a tour of the Southwest with a holiday week
at the popular Pacific Square Ballroom at Pacific Avenue and Ash Street
in San Diego, and then embarked on a series of one-nighters.

sustaining broadcast, Pacific Square Ballroom, San
Diego, Cal. (Blue)—Tuesday, July 4, 1944
JIMMY DORSEY AND HIS ORCHESTRA

Straighten Up And Fly Right [Nat "King" Cole; Irving Mills] vGT /

Long Ago And Far Away [Ira Gershwin; Jerome Kern] vPC (as solo) / Sunset Strip [Sonny Burke, Jimmy Dorsey] (cl,as solos) / All The Things You Ain't [Sonny Burke, Jimmy Dorsey] (cl,as solos) / I Dream Of You [Marjorie Goetschius; Edna Osser] vGT (as solo) / Poinciana [Buddy Bernier; Nat Simon] vPC (as solo) / One O'Clock Jump [William "Count" Basie] (as,cl solos) / Perdido (partial) [Juan Tizol] (cl,as solos)

Entire broadcast on ET: AFRS One Night Stand 331; "All The Things You Ain't" on ET: AFRS One Night Stand 416, LP: First Heard (E) FHR19, Hindsight HSR-153, Big Band Archives 1203, TC: Hindsight HSC-153; "One O'Clock Jump" on AFRS Yank Swing Session 121; "Perdido" on AFRS Yank Swing Session 108

sustaining broadcast, Pacific Square Ballroom, San Diego, Cal. (Blue)—Wednesday, July 5, 1944
JIMMY DORSEY AND HIS ORCHESTRA
Sonny Burke, Dizzy Gillespie, Andy Gibson (arr)

Swingin' On A Star [Johnny Burke; Jimmy Van Heusen] / This I Love Above All vPC (as solo) / Oh, What A Beautiful Mornin' [Oscar Hammerstein II; Richard Rodgers] arrSB (cl solo) / I Dream Of You [Marjorie Goetschius; Edna Osser] vGT (as solo) / Grand Central Getaway [John Birks "Dizzy" Gillespie; Jimmy Dorsey] (as solo) / How Blue The Night [Harold Adamson; Jimmy McHugh] vPC / The Great Lie [Cab Calloway, Andy Gibson] arrAG (cl solo)

Entire broadcast on ET: AFRS One Night Stand #353. (AFRS credits the location as the Palladium Ballroom, Hollywood.)

On July 6, 1944, Bing Crosby's *Kraft Music Hall* hosted both Tommy and Jimmy Dorsey with some memories of the mid-thirties.

Kraft Music Hall, NBC Studios, Burbank, Cal.—NBC, Thursday, July 6, 1944
JOHN SCOTT TROTTER ORCHESTRA
Bing Crosby (vcl,host) **Jimmy Dorsey** (as) Tommy Dorsey (tb)

Sandman [Ralph Freed, Bonnie Lake] / (comedy sketch with Bing, Jimmy and Tommy Dorsey, Marilyn Maxwell, Ken Carpenter) / Exactly Like You [Dorothy Fields; Jimmy McHugh] vBC (as solo), (TD tb solo) (BC cymbals)

sustaining broadcast, Pacific Square Ballroom, San Diego, Cal.—MBS, Tuesday, July 11, 1944
JIMMY DORSEY AND HIS ORCHESTRA

Sunset Strip [Sonny Burke, Jimmy Dorsey] (cl,as solos) / It's A Crying Shame vGT (as solo) / Together [Buddy De Sylva, Lew Brown; Ray Henderson] (as solo) / Oh, What A Beautiful Mornin' [Oscar Hammerstein II; Richard Rodgers] (cl solo) / I Dream Of You [Marjorie Goetschius; Edna Osser] vGT (as solo) / Perdido [Juan Tizol] (cl,as solos) arrJL / Take It Easy [Albert DeBrue;
(Contd.)

JIMMY DORSEY AND HIS ORCHESTRA (Contd.)

Irving Taylor] vGT (cl solo)
"Perdido" was dubbed from AFRS PMR-10 (July 20, 1944); entire broadcast on **ET**: AFRS One Night Stand 376; all instrumentals on **LP**: Queen Disc (I) 028; "Oh, What A Beautiful Morning" on **LP**: First Heard (E) FHR-19

Jimmy signed on Teddy Walters, who was a Frank Sinatra sound-alike, about this time. Walters had sung for Tommy's band, Gene Krupa and Ray Noble, played guitar for Jimmy's June 4 session and lately had been standby on *The Hit Parade* in case Sinatra developed throat problems or was drafted.

NBC Studios, Hollywood Cal. Wednesday, July 12, 1944
JIMMY DORSEY AND HIS ORCHESTRA
Teddy Walters (vcl) replaces Carley

VP 796   **The Great Lie** [Cab Calloway, Andy Gibson] (cl solo)
          78: V-Disc 283 (Army), 63 (Navy)
          (SSL 285) **ET**: AFRS Basic Music Library P-171-1
          LP: Joyce LP2009, Sandy Hook SH-2046, Dan (J) VC5009
          TC: Sandy Hook CSH-2046, V-Disc JD2
          CD: V-Disc JD2
VP 797   **Sunset Strip** [Sonny Burke, J. Dorsey] (cl,as solos)
          78: V-Disc 326 (Army), 106 (Navy)
          (SSL-377) **ET**: AFRS Basic Music Library P-209-1
          LP: Joyce LP2009, Big Band Archives 1203, Hindsight HSR-153, Sandy Hook SH-2046
          TC: Sandy Hook CSH2046, Hindsight HSC153, V-Disc JD1
          CD: Hep (E) CD-41, V-Disc JD1
VP 840   **Contrasts** [Jimmy Dorsey] (theme) arrFS (as solo)
          78: V-Disc 314 (Army), 94 (Navy)
          (SSL-203) **ET**: AFRS Basic Music Library P-133-1
          also on **TC** and **CD**: V-Disc JD2
VP 840   **Oh, What A Beautiful Mornin'** [Oscar Hammerstein II; Richard Rodgers] arrSB (cl solo)
          78: V-Disc 314 (Army), 94 (Navy)
          (SSL-285) **ET**: AFRS Basic Music Library P-171-2
          TC: V-Disc JD1
          CD: Pickwick (E) 54030, V-Disc JD1
SSL-285   **My First Love** vTW (as solo)
          ET: AFRS Basic Music Library P-171-3
VP 920   **Grand Central Getaway** [John Birks "Dizzy" Gillespie; Jimmy Dorsey] (as solo)
          78: V-Disc 391 (Army), 171 (Navy)
          (SSL-377) **ET**: AFRS Basic Music Library P-209-3
          LP: Joyce LP2009, Hindsight HSR-153, Sandy Hook SH-2046
          TC: Sandy Hook CSH-2046, Hindsight HSC-153, V-Disc JD1
          CD: Hep (E) CD-41, V-Disc JD1
VP 920   **All The Things You Ain't** [Sonny Burke, Jimmy Dorsey] (cl,as solos)

    78: V-Disc 391 (Army), 171 (Navy)
    (SSL-377) **ET:** AFRS Basic Music Library P-209-2, P-2463
    LP: Joyce LP2009, Big Band Archives 1203, Hindsight HSR-153,
    Sandy Hook SH-2046
    TC: Sandy Hook CSH-2046, Hindsight HSC-153, V-Disc JD1
    CD: Hep (E) CD-41, V-Disc JD1
VP 1088   **Long John Silver** [Ray Krise, Jimmy Dorsey]
                   (as,cl solos)
    78: V-Disc 409 (Army), 189 (Navy)
    LP: Joyce LP2009, Sandy Hook SH-2046
    TC: Sandy Hook CSH-2046, V-Disc JD1
    CD: V-Disc JD1
VP 1268   **Jumpin' Jehosephat** [Joe Lippman, Jimmy Dorsey] (as,
                   cl solos)
    78: V-Disc 470 (Army), 250 (Navy)
    (SSL-203) **ET:** AFRS Basic Music Library P-133-3
    LP: Coral PCO-7839, Joyce LP2009, Sandy Hook SH-2046
    TC: Sandy Hook CSH-2046, V-Disc JD2
    CD: V-Disc JD2
VP 1418   **Together** [Buddy De Sylva, Lew Brown; Ray Hender-
                   son] (as solo)
    78: V-Disc 514 (Army), 274 (Navy),
    (SSL203) **ET:** AFRS Basic Music Library P-133-2
    LP: Joyce LP2009, Sandy Hook SH-2046
    TC: Sandy Hook CSH-2046, V-Disc JD2
    CD: Hep (E) CD-41, V-Disc JD2

                      sustaining broadcast, Jerry Jones' Rainbow Randevu
                      Ballroom, Salt Lake City, Utah—Thursday, July 13,
                      1944
JIMMY DORSEY AND HIS ORCHESTRA
Teddy Walters, Gladys Tell (vcl) Otto Helbig (arr)

    Contrasts [Jimmy Dorsey] (theme) (as solo) / **Sak House Stomp**
[Harold Mooney] (as solo) / **Star Dust** [Mitchell Parish; Hoagy
Carmichael] arrSB (as solo) / **Grand Central Getaway** [John Birks
"Dizzy" Gillespie; Jimmy Dorsey] (as solo) / **No Love, No Nothin'**
[Leo Robin; Harry James] vGT (as solo) / **Do Nothin' Till You Hear
From Me** [Bob Russell; Edward K. "Duke" Ellington] vGT (as solo)
/ **King Porter Stomp** [Ferdinand "Jelly Roll" Morton] arrOH (cl
solo) / **When They Ask About You** [Sam H. Stept] vGT (as solo) /
What A Difference A Day Made [Stanley Adams, Maria Grever]
vTW (as solo) / **Contrasts** (theme)
    All the above on **ET:** AFRS One Night Stand 401; "Grand Central
Getaway" on **LP:** First Heard (E) FH-4, Big Band Archives 2204,
TC: Hindsight MCH-415TC, **CD:** Hindsight HCD-415

    The Rainbow Randevu Ballroom was at 47 East Fifth Avenue South
in Salt Lake City, Utah. Before and after that engagement, Jimmy and
the band continued a tour of one-nighters in the Rocky Mountain area
and the West Coast, which was cut short when Jimmy was called back

to Warners to shoot additional scenes for "Hollywood Canteen."

Jimmy and the band lucked out on their unexpected return to "Tinseltown." Due to a cancellation, there was an opening at the Palladium, so the band went back there while working days on the set at Warner Brothers. This, of course, also gave them additional air exposure from the popular ballroom.

sustaining broadcast, Hollywood Palladium, Hollywood, Cal.—Tuesday, July 18, 1944
JIMMY DORSEY AND HIS ORCHESTRA

The Great Lie [Cab Calloway, Andy Gibson] (cl solo) / **I'm In Love With Someone** vGT (cl solo) / **Together** [Buddy De Sylva, Lew Brown; Ray Henderson] (as solo) / **This I Love Above All** vPC (as solo) / **All The Things You Ain't** [Sonny Burke, Jimmy Dorsey] (dubbed from ONS 331, July 4, 1944) (cl,as solos) / **Take It Easy** [Albert DeBrue; Irving Taylor] vGT (cl solo) / **I Dream Of You** [Marjorie Goetschius; Edna Osser] vGT (as solo) / **Sunset Strip** [Sonny Burke, Jimmy Dorsey] (cl,as solos)

All the above on **ET:** AFRS One Night Stand 416 (AFRS announcer erroneously announces location as Frolics Club, Miami, Florida), **TC:** Radio Days CA-5-1001, **CD:** Radio Days CA-5-1001; "The Great Lie" on **LP:** First Heard (E) FHR-19, First Time FTR 1513, Onward To Yesterday OTY1513, Cicala (It) BJL-8016; "Together" on **LP:** Solid Sender SOL-505; "All The Things You Ain't" on **LP:** First Heard (E) FHR-19, Big Band Archives LP-1203; "Take It Easy" on **LP:** First Heard (E) FHR4

The same night AFRS recorded some music from the Palladium that later became a *Downbeat* half hour.

Downbeat, Hollywood Palladium, Hollywood, Cal.—Tuesday, July 18, 1944
JIMMY DORSEY AND HIS ORCHESTRA

Grand Central Getaway [John Birks "Dizzy" Gillespie; Jimmy Dorsey] (as solo) / **My First Love** vTW (as solo) / **All The Things You Ain't** [Sonny Burke, Jimmy Dorsey] (cl,as solos) / **Sunset Strip** [Sonny Burke, Jimmy Dorsey] (cl,as solos) / **I Dream Of You** [Marjorie Goetschius; Edna Osser] vGT (as solo) / **Together** [Buddy De Sylva, Lew Brown; Ray Henderson] (as solo) / **The Great Lie** [Cab Calloway, Andy Gibson] arrAG (cl solo)

Entire broadcast on **ET:** AFRS Downbeat 100 and 139; "Grand Central Getaway" on **LP:** Golden Era GE-15011; **TC:** LaserLight 759; **CD:** LaserLight 759; "My First Love" on **ET:** AFRS Basic Music Library P-171; "All The Things You Ain't" and "Sunset Strip" on **LP:** First Heard (E) FHR-19; "Together" on **LP:** Joyce LP1217, Radiola 2MR1314, Solid Sender SOL505; "The Great Lie" on **ET:** AFRS Basic Music Library P-171, **LP:** Golden Era GE-15011, Joyce LP1217, **TC:** Joyce JRC-1401, LaserLight 79-759, **CD:** LaserLight 15-759

World, Hollywood, Cal. Thursday, July 20, 1944
JIMMY DORSEY AND HIS ORCHESTRA
Sonny Burke, Andy Gibson, Dizzy Gillespie, Joe Lippman (arr)

L-3465   **Star Dust** [Mitchell Parish; Hoagy Carmichael]
                  arrSB (as solo)
       (8254) **ET:** World 8254/8258
       LP: Decca DL 8654, Ajaz LP282, Festival (Au) FL7036
L-3466   **Jumpin' Jehosephat** [Joe Lippman, Jimmy Dorsey]
                  (as,cl solos)
       (8255) **ET:** World 8254/8258
       LP: Coral (G) PCO7839, 6.22183, Ajaz LP282
L-3467   **Begin The Beguine** [Cole Porter] arrSB (as solo)
       (8256) **ET:** World 8254/8258
       LP: Coral (G) PCO7839, 6.22183
L 3468   **This I Love Above All** (as solo)
       (6455) **ET:** World 6454/6458
L 3469   **Oh, What A Beautiful Mornin'** [Oscar Hammerstein
                  II; Richard Rodgers] arrSB (cl solo)
       78: Decca 18664, 25487
       (8257) **ET:** World 8254/8258
       LP: Ajaz LP282
L 3470   **Noche De Ronda** [Maria Teresa Lara]
       (6457) **ET:** World 6454/6458

Note that L-3468 and L-3470 duplicate takes that were first made
June 7, 1944. It is not known for certain if this was because the original
takes became defective or were judged defective and were thus remade.

                  sustaining broadcast, Palladium, Hollywood, Cal.—
                  Thursday, July 20, 1944
JIMMY DORSEY AND HIS ORCHESTRA

       Contrasts [Jimmy Dorsey] (theme) (as solo) / **Together** [Buddy De
       Sylva, Lew Brown; Ray Henderson] (as solo) / **Do Nothin' Till You
       Hear From Me** [Bob Russell; Edward K. "Duke" Ellington] vGT (as
       solo) / **Open Up That Door** [Stanley Adams; Samuel H. Stept] vTW
       (as solo) / **Oh, What A Beautiful Mornin'** [Oscar Hammerstein II;
       Richard Rodgers] arrSB (cl solo) / **When They Ask About You**
       [Sam H. Stept] vGT (as solo) / **You Can Depend On Me** [Earl
       "Fatha" Hines, Charles Carpenter, Luis Dunlap] (as solo) / **What A
       Difference A Day Made** [Stanley Adams, Maria Grever] vTW (as
       solo) / **King Porter Stomp** [Ferdinand "Jelly Roll" Morton] arrOH
       (cl solo) / **Perdido** [Juan Tizol] (cl,as solos) arrJL (partial)
       All selections on **ET:** AFRS One Night Stand Popular Music
       Replacement 10, **LP:** Joyce LP1142; "Together," "Open Up That
       Door" and "You Can Depend On Me" on **LP:** Golden Era GE-
       55001, **TC:** LaserLight 79-759, **CD:** LaserLight 15-759; "Oh,
       What A Beautiful Mornin'" and "King Porter Stomp" on **TC:**
       LaserLight 15-768, **CD:** LaserLight 15-768; "Perdido" on **LP:**
       Queen Disc (I) Q-028, **ET:** AFRS One Night Stand 376

sustaining broadcast, Palladium, Hollywood, Cal.
—July 1944
JIMMY DORSEY AND HIS ORCHESTRA

I Dream Of You [Marjorie Goetschius; Edna Osser] vGT (as solo) /
Sunset Strip [Sonny Burke, Jimmy Dorsey] (cl,as solos) / **The Bells
Of Normandy** vTW / **One O'Clock Jump** ["Count" Basie] (as,cl
solos)
"Sunset Strip" on **LP:** First Heard (E) FH-4

sustaining broadcast, Palladium, Hollywood, Cal.
—Friday, July 21, or Saturday, July 22, 1944
JIMMY DORSEY AND HIS ORCHESTRA
Anita Boyer (vcl) replaces Tell.

Grand Central Getaway ["Dizzy" Gillespie; Jimmy Dorsey] (as
solo) / **Take It Easy** [Albert DeBrue; Irving Taylor] vAB (cl solo)
"Grand Central Getaway" on **LP:** First Heard (E) FH-4

The previous two selections are often credited with being from the
stage show at the Orpheum Theater on July 30, but the stage show tunes
in a review in *Billboard* as listed below do not include them.

Pocket tape recorders were unknown then and the musicians' union
regulations were strict about stage show recordings, so for the claimed
venue to be correct they would have to be "pirated" recordings, made
offstage, without Jimmy's knowledge or approval.

Jimmy and the band closed at the Palladium on Saturday, July 22.
From Tuesday, July 25, to Monday, July 31, the band worked several
stage shows daily at the Orpheum in Los Angeles.

A review of the show (*Billboard,* August 12, 1944, 20) lists these
instrumentals performed: "Contrasts," "One O'Clock Jump," "John
Silver," "Oh, What A Beautiful Morning," "Stardust," "Holiday for
Strings" and "King Porter Stomp." Anita Boyer's set included "A Hot
Time In The Town of Berlin," "It Could Happen To You" and
"Swingin' On A Star." Teddy Walters' songs were "How Blue The
Night," "I'll Be Seeing You," "It Had To Be You" and "Amor."

This lineup rules out the two songs often cited as being recordings
from the Orpheum performance.

There are unconfirmed reports that Jimmy recorded the titles listed
next for Decca (or possibly World) in Hollywood during this period, but
if this is the case, they have never been released.

**The Great Lie / Sunset Strip / Town Hall Tonight / I Can't
Believe That You're In Love With Me / Opus One / Grand
Central Getaway / Hip Hop / Am I Blue? / Perdido**

Negotiations continued for the purchase of Casino Gardens, with the
early August speculation (*Down Beat,* August 1, 1944, 6) being that
Wayne Daillard, who owned San Diego's Pacific Square Ballroom, and
bandleader Harry James were involved with the Dorseys.

Nothing came of this early speculation regarding Daillard, but he did
become involved in the Casino Gardens operation for a while later.

Travel itinerary: Wed. Aug. 2, to Tues. Aug. 8—Golden Gate Theater, San Francisco, Cal. / Wed., Aug. 9—Dream Bowl, Vallejo, Cal. / Thurs., Aug. 10—Auditorium, San Jose, Cal. / Sat., Aug. 12—Auditorium, Sacramento, Cal. / Sun., Aug. 13—Sweet's Ballroom, Oakland, Cal. / Fri., Aug. 18, to Sun., Aug. 20, and Fri., Aug. 25, to Sun., Aug. 27—Pacific Square Ballroom, San Diego, Cal.

Jimmy's differences with Decca continued. He was said to be upset with the August release of "I'm In Love With Someone," which Jimmy had cut in January, a tune that wasn't even being plugged by the publisher anymore (*Variety*, August 9, 1944, 31).

It was also rumored that the Dorseys, Harry James and Gene Krupa were looking into buying a New York City area ballroom. Among the spots being considered was Ben Marden's Riviera in New Jersey where the brothers worked a decade before in October 1934 (*Variety*, September 20, 1944, 45).

To kick off their Casino Gardens operation Tommy and Jimmy fought on a more friendly basis on Friday, September 1, when they staged a "Battle of the Bands." Jimmy also played there Saturday night, September 2.

> *Spotlight Bands #616,* Camp Cook, Santa Ana, Cal.—Blue, 6:30-6:45 P.M. PWT, Thursday, September 7, 1944

JIMMY DORSEY AND HIS ORCHESTRA
Teddy Walters, Anita Boyer (vcl)

> Coca Cola theme / **Contrasts** [Jimmy Dorsey] (theme) (as solo) / **King Porter Stomp** [Ferdinand "Jelly Roll" Morton] arrOH (cl solo) / **The Day After Forever** [Johnny Burke; Jimmy Van Heusen] vTW (cl solo) / **I Dream Of You** [Marjorie Goetschius; Edna Osser] vAB (as solo) / **Holiday For Strings** [David Rose] arrSB (as solo) / **Contrasts** / Coca Cola theme
> All above on **ET**: AFRS Spotlight Bands #461

On Friday and Saturday, September 8 and 9, Jimmy and the band again played Casino Gardens and then more service bases the following week, including another *Spotlight Bands.* Then they trained to Chicago.

> *Spotlight Bands #619,* U.S. Naval Air Station, Santa Ana, Cal.—Blue, 6:30-6:45 P.M. PWT, Monday, September 11, 1944

JIMMY DORSEY AND HIS ORCHESTRA

> Coca Cola theme / **Contrasts** [Jimmy Dorsey] (theme) (as solo) / **Java Junction** (cl,as solos) / **It's A Crying Shame** vAB (as solo) / **Together** [Buddy De Sylva, Lew Brown; Ray Henderson] (as solo) / **The Bells Of Normandy** vTW / **Contrasts** / Coca Cola theme
> All above on **ET**: AFRS Spotlight Bands #464

By mid-September, Jimmy had signed on Patti Palmer from the Ted FioRito band. She was the ex-wife of singer-leader Jimmy Palmer. While with Jimmy Dorsey's band, she married comedian Jerry Lewis.

Travel itinerary: Fri., Sept. 15, to Thurs., Sept. 21—Oriental Theater, Chicago, Ill. / Fri., Sept. 22, to Thurs., Sept. 28—Riverside Theater, Milwaukee, Wisc. / Fri., Sept. 29—College Auditorium, Lansing, Mich. / Sat., Sept. 30—International Machinists Assn., Flint, Mich. / Sun., Oct. 1—Trianon Ballroom, Toledo, Ohio. / Tues., Oct. 3, to Thurs., Oct. 5—Palace Theater, Columbus, Ohio / Fri., Oct. 6, to Thurs., Oct. 12—Michigan Theater, Detroit, Mich. / Fri., Oct. 13, to Thurs., Oct. 19—Palace Theater, Cleveland, Ohio

The following session has been carried in most discographies as being made in New York City on October 2, 1944. A recently published Decca discography lists the date as September 25. As can be seen above, the band was in Milwaukee, Wisconsin on September 25, as confirmed by *Billboard, Downbeat* and *Variety.* Also, an October 2 session in New York would have meant a fast wartime train trip from Toledo, Ohio, to New York City, and back to Columbus, Ohio.

The band's whereabouts from Friday, October 20, to Thursday, October 26, is unaccounted for in published itineraries, so the author suggests that the September 25 date is really October 25, and that the band returned from Cleveland, Ohio to New York City for some time off, and the Decca session, before going to Pittsburgh, Pennsylvania.

Decca, New York, N.Y. Wednesday, October 25, 1944
JIMMY DORSEY AND HIS ORCHESTRA
Chuck Travis (ts) replaces Dukoff. Teddy Walters (vcl)

72394-AA   **Moon On My Pillow** vTW
    78: Decca 18627, (C) 10198, Brunswick (E) 03560
72395-AA   **Sweet Dreams, Sweetheart** [Ted Koehler; M. K. Jerome] vTW (as solo)
    78: Decca 18627, (C) 10198, Brunswick (E) 03560
    Both sides also on **LP:** Ajaz LP282

Travel itinerary: Fri., Oct. 27, to Thurs., Nov. 2—Stanley Theater, Pittsburgh, Pa. / Fri., Nov. 3, to Thurs., Nov. 9—Earle Theater, Philadelphia, Pa.

For another example of Jimmy's caring ways, *Billboard* (October 28, 1944, 17) reported that he turned down a guarantee of $15,000 for five one-nighters between the Earle Theater date and New York to keep a promise made to his sidemen for some additional time off.

The Capitol Theater at Broadway and West Fifty-first Street in Manhattan was home for Jimmy and the band for five weeks beginning Thursday, November 16, with four performances a day and five on Saturday. The move to the MGM-owned Capitol from Warners' Strand was part of Jimmy's film contract with MGM *(Down Beat,* September 15, 1944, 1). Sharing the Capitol stage were comedian Henny Youngman and dancer "Peg-Leg" Bates.

In another trade report Jimmy was said to be asking the Hotel Pennsylvania, where he was set to begin for eight weeks on February 12, to keep an additional eight weeks open. *Billboard* (November 4, 1944, 14) implied that the request was tied to negotiations then under way for a radio show, and the sixteen continuous weeks would provide a steady location for the program. No details on the show were given.

World, New York, N.Y. Tuesday, November 21, 1944
JIMMY DORSEY AND HIS ORCHESTRA
Jimmy Dorsey (cl,as,ldr) Claude Bowen, Bob Alexy, Bill Robins, Tony Picciotto, Shorty Solomson (tp) Sonny Lee, Si Zentner, Nick DiMaio, Andy Russo (tb) Jack Aiken, Frank Langone (as) Bobby Dukoff, Buddy Williams (ts) Bob Lawson (bar) Marvin Wright (p) Phil Farney (g) Jimmy Middleton (sb) Buddy Schutz (d) Teddy Walters, Patti Palmer (vcl)

W72574-A   **More And More** [E. Y. Harburg; Jerome Kern] vTW
    78: Decca 18647
    (6729) **ET:** World 6729/6733
    LP: Ajaz LP282
W72575-A   **I Dream Of You** [Marjorie Goetschius; Edna Osser]
    vPP (as solo)
    78: Decca 18637, (C) 10206
    (SSL203) **ET:** AFRS Basic Music Library P-133-4
    (6731) **ET:** World 6729/6733
    LP: Ajaz LP282
W72576-A   **Magic Is The Moonlight** [Charles Pasquale; Maria Grever] vTW&PP (as solo)
    78: Decca 18637, (C) 10206
    (6732) **ET:** World 6729/6733
    LP: Ajaz LP282
W72577-A   **Don't You Know I Care? (Or Don't You Care To Know?)** [Mack David; Edward K. "Duke" Ellington] vPP (as solo)
    78: Decca 18647
    (6733) **ET:** World 6729/6733
    LP: Ajaz LP282

The Jimmy Dorsey-Decca Records feud over tardy releases continued in the trade press with a story that Jimmy had offered Decca $25,000 for a release from his contract, which still had eighteen months to go (*Variety*, November 22, 1944, 33).

When Jimmy and the band concluded their five-week booking at the Capitol on December 20, 1944, Jimmy gave the band another week's vacation over the Christmas holiday.

During the holiday period Jimmy lost his jazz tenor man when Bob Dukoff moved with his wife Anita Boyer to the West Coast because of Anita's radio and transcription duties (*Down Beat*, January 1, 1945, 1).

Travel itinerary: Thurs., Dec. 28, to Wed., Jan. 3, 1945—Adams Theater, Newark, N.J. / Thurs., Jan. 4, to Wed., Jan. 10—RKO Boston Theater, Boston, Mass.

Jimmy's record of "Besame Mucho" landed in sixth place on *Billboard* magazine's Top 10 Disks for 1944 (January 6, 1945, 14), with the only other big-band disk on the list being the Columbia reissue of Harry James' "I'll Get By," which traded on Dick Haymes' vocal.

Recordings by vocal headliners made up the remainder of the *Billboard* list, vividly demonstrating the trends that were already spelling bad news for the big bands.

World, New York, N.Y. Thursday, January 11, 1945
JIMMY DORSEY AND HIS ORCHESTRA
Irving Goodman (tp) replaces Bowen, Tino Isgro (ts) replaces Dukoff.
Teddy Walters, Patti Palmer (vcl)

W71685-AA   **Twilight Time** [Buck Ram, Morty Nevins, Artie
                 Dunn] vTW (cl solo)
    78: Decca 18656, (C) 10223
    LP: Ajaz LP282
W71686-AA   **El Rancho Vegas** vTW&PP (as solo) &
    78: Decca 18664, (C) 10230
    LP: Ajaz LP290
W71687-AA   **I Should Care** [Sammy Cahn, Axel Stordahl, Paul
                 Weston] vTW (as solo)
    78: Decca 18656, (C) 10223, Coral 60329, Brunswick (E) 03591
    LP: Ajaz LP290
W71688-AA   **If You Are But A Dream** [Moe Jaffee, Jack Fulton,
                 Nat Bonx] vTW
    78: Brunswick (E) O3591

Jimmy and crew spent another three weeks at the Frolics Club in
Miami, Florida, from Tuesday, January 16, to Monday, February 5.

Broadcast schedule (Frolics Club): Sun., Feb. 4, CBS, 12:30-1:00 A.M.

While Jimmy and the band were in Miami, at least ten Army air bases
offered to fly them to their fields and return them in time for the evening
show but wouldn't be responsible for accidents. The band declined.
   After Miami they played one-nighters at the Armory, Jacksonville,
Florida, at a tobacco warehouse in Columbia, South Carolina, and an
unknown location in Washington, D.C. *(Down Beat,* March 1, 1945, 2),
where they broadcast twice.

                 "Band Of The Week," Spotlight Bands #750, un-
                 known location, Washington, D.C.—Blue, 9:30-
                 10:00 P.M. Saturday, February 10, 1945
JIMMY DORSEY AND HIS ORCHESTRA
Chuck Travis (ts) replaces Isgro, Herb Ellis (g) replaces Farney, Jimmy
Stutz (sb) replaces Middleton

   Coca Cola theme / **Contrasts** [Jimmy Dorsey] (theme) (as solo) /
   King Porter Stomp [Ferdinand "Jelly Roll" Morton] arrOH (cl solo)
   / **Twilight Time** [Buck Ram, Morty Nevins, Artie Dunn] vTW (cl,as
   solos) / **Saturday Night (Is The Loneliest Night In The Week)**
   [Sammy Cahn; Jule Styne] vPP (cl,as solos) / **I Should Care**
   [Sammy Cahn, Axel Stordahl, Paul Weston] vTW arrSB (as solo) /
   Jumpin' Jehosephat [Joe Lippman, Jimmy Dorsey] arrJL (as,cl
   solos)
      All the above on **ET:** AFRS Spotlight Bands #595 and **LP:** Giants
   Of Jazz GOJ-1023

Broadcast schedule (unknown location): Sun., Feb. 11, CBS [WABC], 12:30-1:00 A.M.

On Monday, February 12, the band began a nine-week stay at the Cafe Rouge. Due to a booking mix-up that had the hotel expecting Jimmy on February 5, the Pennsylvania had to extend Les Brown's stay for one week. Fortunately, Brown was open that week.

sustaining broadcast, Cafe Rouge, Hotel Pennsylvania, New York, N.Y.—Blue, [WJZ], 12:00-12:30 A.M. Tuesday, February 13, 1945
JIMMY DORSEY AND HIS ORCHESTRA

King Porter Stomp [Ferdinand "Jelly Roll" Morton] arrOH (cl solo) / **I Dream Of You** [Marjorie Goetschius; Edna Osser] vPP (as solo) / **Lover** [Lorenz Hart; Richard Rodgers] arrSB (as solo) / **Twilight Time** [Buck Ram, Morty Nevins, Artie Dunn] vTW (cl solo) / **Magic Is The Moonlight** [Charles Pasquale; Maria Grever] vPP&TW / **Together** [Buddy De Sylva, Lew Brown; Ray Henderson] (as solo) / **Jumpin' Jehosephat** [Joe Lippman, Jimmy Dorsey] (as,cl solos) / **I Should Care** [Sammy Cahn, Axel Stordahl, Paul Weston] vTW arrSB (as solo) / **The Champ** (part) [Sonny Burke] (cl solo)
   Entire broadcast on ET: AFRS One Night Stand 635, "King Porter Stomp" on ET: AFRS One Night Stand #683; **LP:** First Heard (E) FHR-19, Magic (E) AWE27; "Jumpin' Jehosephat" on **LP:** First Heard (E) FHR-19

Broadcast schedule (all Cafe Rouge): Wed., Feb. 14, Blue, [WJZ], 11:30-12:00 P.M. / Sat., Feb. 17, Blue,[WJZ], and 12:00-12:30 A.M., CBS [WABC], 11:30-12:00 P.M. / Wed.,Feb. 21, Blue, [WJZ], 12:30-1:00 A.M. / Thurs., Feb. 22, Blue, [WJZ], 12:30-1:00 A.M. / Fri., Feb.23, 11:30-11:45 P.M. / Sat., Feb.24, CBS [WABC], 11:30-12:00 P.M.

The War Manpower Commission had recently ordered a curfew closing theaters, nightclubs, bars and the like at midnight, ostensibly to keep war workers "healthier." This had a chilling effect on bands in hotels with postmidnight broadcasts until it was agreed that they could air from the room without an audience present if they included a plug for war bonds (*Billboard,* March 10, 1945, 13).
   Guitarist Eddie Condon hosted a series of Saturday afternoon jazz concerts in 1944 and early 1945, first at Town Hall and later at the Ritz Theater. Jimmy took part in only one of these. Matrix numbers shown are for the AFRS release.

Eddie Condon, Ritz Theater, New York, N.Y. —Blue, 1:00-1:30 P.M., Saturday, February 24, 1945
EDDIE CONDON TOWN HALL JAZZ CONCERT #40 (AFRS #39)
Billy Butterfield (tp) Tommy Dorsey (tb) **Jimmy Dorsey** (cl) Ernie Caceres (bar) Jess Stacy (p) Sid Weiss (sb) George Wettling (d)

SSR-3-3-1   **Honeysuckle Rose** [Andy Razaf; Thomas "Fats" Waller] (cl solo)
   ET: AFRS "Eddie Condon" 47 (portion only)
SSR-3-3-1   **Baby, Won't You Please Come Home** [Charles Warfield, Clarence Williams] (cl solo) (Contd.)

EDDIE CONDON TOWN HALL JAZZ CONCERT #40 (Contd.)

Sidney Bechet (ssx) with backing by Stacy, Weiss and Wetling only, plays "China Boy" (introduced by Jimmy Dorsey).
Max Kaminsky (tp) replaces Butterfield in full ensemble:
SSR-3-3-2   **I Can't Believe That You're In Love With Me** [Clarence Gaskill; Jimmy McHugh] (cl solo)
    LP: Jazum 63
Billy Butterfield (tp) replaces Kaminsky:
SSR-3-3-2   **Royal Garden Blues** [Clarence and Spencer Williams] (cl solo)
    ET: AFRS "Eddie Condon" 48
    LP: Jazum 63
Entire group is featured:
-0-   **Impromptu Ensemble** (cl solo)
    ET: AFRS "Eddie Condon" 48 (portion, fades out during JD solo)
    LP: Jazum 63
    In addition the *entire* show appears on: **ET:** AFRS "Eddie Condon" #39; **LP:** Rarities (Denmark) 44; **CD:** Jazzology 1019

Broadcast schedule (all Cafe Rouge): Sat., Mar. 3, Blue, [WJZ], 12:30-1:00 A.M., and CBS [WABC], 11:30-12:00 P.M. / Fri., Mar. 9, CBS [WABC], 11:30-11:45 P.M. / Sat., Mar. 10, Blue, [WJZ], 12:30-1:00 A.M., and CBS [WABC], 11:30-12:00 P.M.

Perhaps one of the most unique V-Discs made in 1945 was put together at the acoustically perfect Leiderkranz Hall in New York City with thirty-eight musicians joining forces for two memorable sides. It was also originally announced that trumpeter Louis Armstrong would join the brothers for the session.

In introducing "More Than You Know," Tommy and Jimmy, along with announcer Bill Goodwin, joked and commented about Goodwin's association with Tommy's former vocalist, Frank Sinatra.

The massed musicians were conducted by Sy Oliver. Musician and writer Sgt. George Simon of V-Discs was in charge of the date. "Brotherly Jump" is highlighted by solos by many of both brothers' top musicians and a drum battle between two "Buddys," Schutz and Rich.

Leiderkranz Hall, New York, N.Y. Thursday, March 15, 1945
JIMMY DORSEY AND HIS ORCHESTRA
Jimmy Dorsey (cl,as,ldr) Irving Goodman, Ray Linn, Bob Alexy, Shorty Solomson, Tony Picciotto (tp) Nick DiMaio, Sonny Lee, Mickey Iannone, Andy Russo (tb) Jack Aiken, Frank Langone (as) Tino Isgro, Buddy Williams (ts) Bob Lawson (bar) Marvin Wright (p) Herb Ellis (g) Jimmy Stutz (sb) Buddy Schutz (d)
combined with:
TOMMY DORSEY AND HIS ORCHESTRA
Tommy Dorsey (tb,ldr) Gerry Goff, Bobby Guyer, Sal LaPertche, George Seaberg, Charlie Shavers (tp) Karl DeKarske, Dick Bellerose, Tex Satterwhite (tb) Gus Bivona (cl,as) Sid Cooper (as) Babe Fresk, Al Klink (ts) Bruce Branson (bar) Jess Stacy (p) Bob Bain (g) Joseph Park (bb) Sid Block (sb) Buddy Rich (d) Sy Oliver, Lt. Otto Helbig (arr)

VP 1242   **Brotherly Jump** (as solo) arrSO
          78: V-Disc 451 (Army) 231 (Navy)
          LP: Joyce LP2009, Sandy Hook SH-2046
          TC: Sandy Hook CSH-2046
VP 1243   **More Than You Know** [Edward Eliscu, Billy Rose;
          Vincent Youmans] (as,cl solos) arrOH
          78: V-Disc 451-A (Army) 231-A (Navy)
          LP: Joyce LP2009, Sandy Hook SH-2046
          TC: Sandy Hook CSH-2046
          both sides also on **TC** and **CD:** V-Disc #JD2

Broadcast schedule (all Cafe Rouge): Fri., Mar. 16, CBS [WABC], 11:30-11:45 P.M. /
Fri. Mar. 23, CBS [WABC], 11:30-11:45 P.M.

During the Hotel Pennsylvania stay, Patti Palmer (Mrs. Jerry Lewis)
quit to become a mother. Jean Cromwell, a Memphis, Tennessee, girl,
replaced Palmer, and Nita Rosa was added to sing Spanish tunes.

Jimmy and Tommy formed Embassy Corporation in early 1945 with
early "talkies" star Charles "Buddy" Rogers to produce a two million
dollar film based on their lives. It was originally titled *My Brother Leads
A Band.* The brothers put up no money, but were due to receive half the
picture's profits *(Billboard,* March 24, 1945, 14).

World, New York, N.Y. Wednesday, March 28, 1945
JIMMY DORSEY AND HIS ORCHESTRA
Sonny Burke, Howard Giebling (arr) Teddy Walters (vcl)

72801-A   **Dream** [Johnny Mercer] vTW
          78: Decca 18670, (C) 10234, Brunswick (E) 03586
          LP: Ajaz LP290
72802   **There, I've Said It Again** vTW (unissued)
72803-A   **J.D.'s Boogie Woogie** [Marvin Wright, Jimmy Dor-
          sey] (cl solo)
          78: Decca 18777, (C) 10295
          LP: Decca DL8654, Coral (G) PCO6997, PCO7839, 6.22183,
          Ajaz LP290, Festival (Au) FL7036

          sustaining broadcast, Cafe Rouge, Hotel Pennsyl-
          vania, New York, N.Y.—Blue [WJZ], 12:30-1:00
          A.M. Friday, March 30, 1945
JIMMY DORSEY AND HIS ORCHESTRA

Saturday Night (Is The Loneliest Night in The Week) [Sammy
Cahn; Jule Styne] / **I Should Care** [Sammy Cahn, Axel Stordahl,
Paul Weston] vTW arrSB (as solo) / **Any Old Time** vTW arrSB /
Perdido [Juan Tizol] (cl,as solos) / **Twilight Time** [Buck Ram, Mor-
ty Nevins, Artie Dunn] vTW (cl solo) / **Lover** [Lorenz Hart; Richard
Rogers] (as solo) / **This Heart Of Mine** [Arthur Freed; Harry
Warren] vTW / **King Porter Stomp** ["Jelly Roll" Morton] (cl solo) /
Jumpin' Jehosephat [Joe Lippman, Jimmy Dorsey] (as,cl solos)
Entire broadcast on **ET:** AFRS One Night Stand 621

Fitch Bandwagon, New York, N.Y.—NBC, 7:30-
8:00 P.M. (repeat 10:30-11:00 P.M.)—March 1945
JIMMY DORSEY AND HIS ORCHESTRA
Dick Powell (guest host) Teddy Walters, Jean Cromwell (vcl)

Smile For Me (Fitch theme) / **Contrasts** [Jimmy Dorsey] (theme) (as
solo)/ **King Porter Stomp** [Ferdinand "Jelly Roll" Morton] arrOH (cl
solo) / **I Should Care** [Sammy Cahn, Axel Stordahl, Paul Weston]
vTW arrSB (as solo) / **Lover** [Lorenz Hart; Richard Rodgers] arrSB
(as solo) / **Don't You Know I Care? (Or Don't You Care To
Know?)** [Mack David; Edward K. "Duke" Ellington] vJC (as solo) /
closing themes
     Entire broadcast also on **ET**: AFRS Bandwagon 143

sustaining broadcast, Cafe Rouge, Hotel Pennsylvania, New York, N.Y.—Saturday, March 31, 1945
JIMMY DORSEY AND HIS ORCHESTRA

Java Junction (cl,as solos) / **I Should Care** [Sammy Cahn, Axel
Stordahl, Paul Weston] vTW arrSB (as solo) / **I Dream Of You**
[Marjorie Goetschius; Edna Osser] vJC (as solo) / **Lover** [Lorenz
Hart; Richard Rodgers] arrSB (as solo) / **The Day After Forever**
[Johnny Burke; Jimmy Van Heusen] vJC / **Jumpin' Jehosephat** [Joe
Lippman, Jimmy Dorsey] (as,cl solos) / **Any Old Time** vTW arrSB /
Perdido [Juan Tizol] (cl,as solos) arrJL
     Entire broadcast on **ET**: AFRS One Night Stand 586; "Java
Junction" and "Any Old Time" on **LP**: First Heard (E) FHR-19

     Just before the Cafe Rouge stand ended, Jimmy lost his drummer of
seven years standing. Buddy Schutz quit, reportedly under stern doctor's orders to take a rest (*Variety*, March 28, 1945, 37). Cliff Leeman
replaced him for a while.
     The same issue of *Variety* (page 41) said that Jimmy would play his
first "concert" at the Mosque Theater, Richmond, Virginia, on an
upcoming one-nighter route. This may have never materialized.
     The Steel Pier in Atlantic City, New Jersey, had its traditional
"official opening" on Sunday, April 1, with Jimmy and the band
handling the honors on a day off at the Pennsylvania.

World, New York, N.Y. Wednesday, April 4, 1945
JIMMY DORSEY AND HIS ORCHESTRA
Cliff Leeman (d) for Schutz. Jean Cromwell (vcl) Sonny Burke (arr)

72808-A   **Can't You Read Between The Lines?** [Sammy
                 Cahn; Jule Styne] vJC (cl solo)
     78: Decca 18676, (C) 10239
     (7009) **ET:** World 7009/7013
     LP: Ajaz LP290
72809-A   **Lover** [Lorenz Hart; Richard Rodgers] arrSB (as
                 solo)
     78: Decca 18677 (C) 10295
     (7010) **ET:** World 7009/7013

LP: Decca DL8654, Ajaz LP290, Festival (Au) FL7036
72810-A   **Negra Consentida (My Pet Brunette)** [Marjorie
                 Harper; Joaquin Pardave] vTW&JC (cl solos)
     78: Decca 18676, Brunswick (E) 03764
     (7012) **ET:** World 7009/7013
     LP: Ajaz LP290
72811-AA   **There! I've Said It Again** [Redd Evans, Dave Mann]
                 vTW (as solo)
     78: Decca 18670, (C) 10234, Brunswick (E) 03586
     LP: Ajaz LP290

Broadcast schedule (Cafe Rouge): Fri., Apr. 6, CBS [WABC], 11:30-11:45 P.M.

The band closed at the Cafe Rouge the next evening, Saturday, April 7, and was replaced by Leo Reisman's Orchestra. Over the nine weeks, some 40,675 patrons came to see and dance to Jimmy and the band.

Billboard (April 14, 1945, 13) said that Jimmy replaced Mickey Iannone with trombonist Muni "Buddy" Morrow after leaving Cafe Rouge as part of General Amusement's plan to build Morrow up as a future bandleader.

Travel itinerary: Thurs., Apr. 12, to Wed., Apr. 18—Capitol Theater, Washington, D.C.

Jimmy and the band did not perform on Thursday night, or all day Friday or Saturday at the Capitol Theater. Like all entertainment spots nationwide, the Capitol was closed due to the sudden death of President Franklin D. Roosevelt on April 12 at Warm Springs, Georgia.

Travel itinerary: Fri., May 4, to Thurs., May 10—Circle Theater, Indianapolis, Ind.

When Jimmy and the band moved back to the Hotel Sherman in Chicago for a four-week engagement, opening Friday, May 11, 1945, there were some additional personnel changes. Joe Weidman (tp) replaced Ray Linn for a while, and Nita Rosa (vcl) was dropped.

Vocalist Teddy Walters was also a good jazz guitarist, and occasionally played for Jimmy, especially on theater dates. Herb Ellis, however, was also coming along, and there was less and less call for Walters to break out his guitar pick.

In addition, tenor saxist Stan Getz is reported to have been in the band briefly, this during Jimmy's absence from the band for a hernia operation in Good Samaritan Hospital, Los Angeles, on May 28. Buddy Morrow directed for the week that Jimmy was hospitalized. Jimmy returned June 4 to help close out the Sherman date, and on June 9 the band took a month's vacation, partly so Jimmy could further recuperate.

When the band opened for two weeks at Mission Beach Ballroom, San Diego, California, on Tuesday, July 3 there was a new drummer, seventeen-year-old Karl Kiffe, who would stay for quite a while, and a new male vocalist named Dick Culver.

Next it was up the coast to Ocean Park on Tuesday, July 17, for an extended stay at Casino Gardens replacing Tommy's band. The Dorseys had a new partner as well. Mission Beach owner Larry Finley had bought a third interest in the brothers' lease of the ballroom and the spot was now open six nights a week.

sustaining broadcast(s), Casino Gardens, Ocean Park, Cal.—July 1945
JIMMY DORSEY AND HIS ORCHESTRA
Karl Kiffe (d) replaces Leeman. Dick Culver, Jean Cromwell (vcl)

Oh! What A Beautiful Mornin' [Oscar Hammerstein II; Richard Rodgers] (cl solo) / **Open Up That Door** [Stanley Adams; Samuel H. Stept] (as solo) / **Together** [Buddy De Sylva, Lew Brown; Ray Henderson] (as solo) / **You Can Depend On Me** [Earl "Fatha" Hines, Charles Carpenter, Luis Dunlap] (as solo) / **El Rancho Vegas** vDC&JC (as solo) / **King Porter Stomp** [Ferdinand "Jelly Roll" Morton] arrOH (cl solo)
All on **LP:** Golden Era LP55001/3

sustaining broadcast, Casino Gardens, Ocean Park, Cal.—Sunday, July 29, 1945
JIMMY DORSEY AND HIS ORCHESTRA

Java Junction (cl,as solos) / **Star Dust** [Mitchell Parish; Hoagy Carmichael] arrSB (as solo) / **Negra Consentida** [Marjorie Harper; Joaquin Pardave] vDC&JC (cl solos) / **Saturday Night (Is The Loneliest Night In The Week)** [Sammy Cahn; Jule Styne] vJC (as solo) / **It's Only A Paper Moon** [E. Y. Harburg, Billy Rose; Harold Arlen] (cl solo) / **Twilight Time** [Buck Ram, Morty Nevins, Artie Dunn] vDC (cl solo) / ***King Porter Stomp** [Ferdinand "Jelly Roll" Morton] arrOH (cl solo) / **I Was Here When You Left Me** vJC (cl solo) / **The Champ** [Sonny Burke] (cl solo)
*"King Porter Stomp" dubbed from AFRS One Night Stand #635; all selections on **ET:** AFRS One Night Stand 683, **LP:** Magic (E) AWE27; "Java Junction" and "It's Only A Paper Moon" also used on **ET:** AFRS One Night Stand 835

sustaining broadcast(s), possibly Casino Gardens, Ocean Park, Cal.—July or August 1945
JIMMY DORSEY AND HIS ORCHESTRA

Opus One [Sid Garris; Sy Oliver] (as,cl solos) / **I Should Care** [Sammy Cahn, Axel Stordahl, Paul Weston] vDC (as solo)/ **I Was Here When You Left Me** vJC
All on **ET:** AFRS Magic Carpet 40

This Can't Be Love [Lorenz Hart; Richard Rodgers] vDC / **I'm Gonna Love That Guy** [Frances Ash] vJC / **Oh, What A Beautiful Mornin'** [Oscar Hammerstein II; Richard Rodgers] arrSB (cl solo)
All on **ET:** AFRS Magic Carpet 102

sustaining broadcast(s), Casino Gardens, Ocean Park, Cal.— August 1945

JIMMY DORSEY AND HIS ORCHESTRA

Contrasts [Jimmy Dorsey] (theme) (as solo) / **I Can't Believe That You're In Love With Me** [L. Wolfe Gilbert, Abner Silver] (cl solo) / **Perdido** [Juan Tizol] (cl,as solos) / **I Got Rhythm** [Ira Gershwin; George Gershwin] (cl,as solos)
    Above four titles on **ET:** AFRS Downbeat 154 and 188, **LP:** Joyce LP1217; "I Can't Believe That You're In Love With Me" also on **LP:** Golden Era LP55011/3, **TC:** Joyce JRC-1401, Laserlight 79-759, **CD:** Laserlight 15-759; "I Got Rhythm" also on **CD:** Recording Arts JZCD355

Contrasts [Jimmy Dorsey] (theme) (as solo) / **Opus One**[Sid Garris; Sy Oliver] (as,cl solos) / **If I Loved You** [Oscar Hammerstein II; Richard Rodgers] vDC / **One O'Clock Jump** [William "Count" Basic] (as,cl solos)
    All four titles on **ET:** AFRS Downbeat 155 and 189; last three on **LP:** Joyce LP1217

On August 14, 1945, the Emperor of Japan accepted the Allied terms of surrender and World War II was ended. But so, too, was the war-time economy that had buttressed the big-band business, especially on the U.S. coasts.

    sustaining broadcasts, Casino Gardens, Ocean Park, Cal.—Sunday, August 12 and Thursday, August 16, 1945

JIMMY DORSEY AND HIS ORCHESTRA

Contrasts [Jimmy Dorsey] (theme) (as solo) / **I Can't Believe That You're In Love With Me** [L. Wolfe Gilbert, Abner Silver] (cl solo) / **I Should Care** [Sammy Cahn, Axel Stordahl, Paul Weston] vDC (as solo) / **El Rancho Vegas** vDC&JC (as solo) / **Hip Hop** [Herb Ellis, Jimmy Dorsey] (as solo) / **Gotta Be This Or That** [Sunny Skylar] vJC (cl solos) / **Oh, What A Beautiful Mornin'** [Oscar Hammerstein II; Richard Rodgers] arrSB (cl solo) / **The More I See You** [Mack Gordon; Harry Warren] vDC (as solo) / **King Porter Stomp** ["Jelly Roll" Morton] arrOH (cl solo) / **Contrasts** (theme)
    All on **ET:** AFRS One Night Stand 713 (Side 1, August 12, Side 2, August 16); Except for "I Should Care" and "The More I See You" all selections on **LP:** Sunbeam SB-223; "I Can't Believe That You're In Love With Me" also on **LP:** Queen Disc (I) O28, Joyce LP1142, **TC:** LaserLight 79-759; **CD:** LaserLight 15-759; "El Rancho Vegas" also on **LP:** Golden Era LP55001/3, **TC:** LaserLight 79-759, **CD:** LaserLight 15-759; "Hip Hop" also on **LP:** Queen Disc (I) 028, Big Band Archives LP1203, Joyce LP1142, **TC:** LaserLight 79-768, **CD:** LaserLight 15-768; "King Porter Stomp" also on **LP:** Queen Disc (I) 028, Golden Era LP55001/3; closing theme also on **LP:** Queen Disc (I) O28

Their six-week stay at Casino Gardens ended Tuesday, August 28, and Jimmy headed back to the recording studios. Nine years after Jimmy and Bing Crosby had worked jointly on *Kraft Music Hall* and Decca sessions, they were back together, if only briefly.

Jimmy now had electric guitarist Herb Ellis in his lineup, and his unique talent would be featured increasingly in the band's arrangements.

World, Hollywood, Cal. Wednesday, August 29, 1945
BING CROSBY with JIMMY DORSEY AND HIS ORCHESTRA
Jimmy Dorsey (cl,as,ldr) Irv Goodman, Bob Alexy, Jack Dougherty, Shorty Solomson, Tony Picciotto (tp) Buddy Morrow, Dick Bellerose, Sonny Lee, Hi Kessler (tb) Jack Aiken, Frank Langone (as) Chuck Travis, Gil Koerner (ts) Bob Lawson (bar) Marvin Wright (p) Herb Ellis (g) Norman Bates (sb) Karl Kiffe (d) Bing Crosby (vcl)

L3937-B   **Give Me The Simple Life** [Harry Ruby; Rube Bloom] vBC (as solo)
    78: Decca 23469
    LP: Ajaz LP290
L3938-A,D   **It's The Talk of The Town** [Marty Symes, Al J. Neiberg; Jerry Livingston] vBC (as solo)
    78: Decca 23469
    EP: Decca ED1800
    LP: Decca DL8142, DXB152, Ace Of Hearts (E) AH-17, Ajaz LP290

World, Hollywood, Cal. Thursday, September 6, 1945
JIMMY DORSEY AND HIS ORCHESTRA
Sunny Burke, Rupert Biggadike (arr) Inez James, Dick Culver, Bing Crosby (vcl)

L3951-A   **Come To Baby, Do** [Inez James, Sidney Miller] vIJ arrSB (as solo)
    78: Decca 18716, Brunswick (E) 03724, V-Disc (unissued)
    (7245) **ET:** World 7244/7248, 8251/8258
    LP: Ajaz LP290
L3952-AA   **Autumn Serenade** [Sammy Gallop; Peter De Rose] arrRB vDC (as solo)
    78: Decca 18716, (C) 10266
    (8252) **ET:** World 8251/8258
    LP: Ajaz LP290
L3953-A   **Sweet Lorraine** [Mitchell Parish; Cliff Burwell] vBC (cl solo)
    78: Decca 23655
        as BING CROSBY WITH JIMMY DORSEY AND HIS ORCHESTRA
    EP: Decca ED1800
    LP: Decca DL8144, DXB152, Ace Of Hearts (E) AH-24, Ajaz LP290
L3954-   **A Door Will Open** [Don George; John Benson Brooks] vBC
    78: (unissued test pressing)
    LP: Crosbyana LP023
L3955-A   **Outer Drive** [Sonny Burke] (cl solo)

78: V-Disc (unissued)
(7244) **ET:** World 7244/7248, 8251/8258
LP: Ajaz LP290

Inez James, who sings the lyrics on "Come To Baby, Do" and was a joint composer of the song, was under contract to Universal Pictures. She became vocalist for the song after Jimmy made her part of his agreement to wax the tune (*Variety,* October 10, 1945, 45).

In the summer of 1945, Jimmy and the band appeared in a nine-minute short called *Headline Bands.* The details on this are not known.

In anticipation of Jimmy's return to the East Coast, four of his reed men decided to stay in sunny California. Five-year veteran alto Frank Langone opened teaching studios in Los Angeles. Jack Aiken, lead alto; Tino Isgro, tenor sax; and Bob Lawson, baritone sax, also quit.

Travel itinerary: Thurs. and Fri., Sept. 13, 14—Municipal Auditorium, Kansas City, Mo. / Thurs., Sept. 27, to Wed., Oct. 3—Riverside Theater, Milwaukee, Wis. / Thurs., Oct. 4, to Wed., Oct. 24—Oriental Theater, Chicago, Ill. / Fri., Oct. 26, to Thurs., Nov. 1—Michigan Theater, Detroit, Mich. / Sun., Nov. 11—Ritz Ballroom, Bridgeport, Conn.

As part of the hype for their upcoming film, Tommy and Jimmy were to be profiled in an issue of the *Saturday Evening Post.* Richard English, who was doing the script for the film, also wrote the story. The article finally appeared in the February 2, 1946, issue of the *Post* under the title "The Battling Brothers Dorsey." In it English claims that the brothers had grossed $6,201,000 the preceding five years. While there was no breakdown, the larger share of this was probably Tommy's.

Jimmy returned his band for a week's stay at the Terrace Room in Newark, New Jersey, beginning Tuesday, November 13, before opening at the Capitol Theater in New York City.

According to *Variety* (October 31, 1945, 48), the Terrace Room's new owners, the Rosenhaus brothers, who also were manufacturers of Serutan ("Natures spelled backwards") and Nutrex food supplements, were offering Jimmy and Benny Goodman $6,000 against 30 percent of the take per week as an inducement to play there.

The Rosenhauses were waging a price war with their former tenant Frank Dailey and were pressuring the networks on which they heavily advertised their products to open up remote time for them, according to the weekly. They were able to get four programs a week, two on Mutual, one on ABC (née the Blue Network) and one on CBS.

Jimmy added a new girl singer, Del Parker, who changed her first name to Dee to avoid confusion with another singer of the same name. Dee was the wife of Phil Brestoff, musical director of WXYZ, Detroit, Michigan, and had come to Jimmy's attention while he was performing at the Michigan Theater.

Variety (October 31, 1945, 52) claimed that Jimmy also had added a vocal group, the Stardusters, to compete with brother Tommy's Sentimentalists, changing their name to the Contrasters. If they ever were with the band, they do not show up on any recordings or airchecks from the period. Jimmy did add two new arrangers, Danny Hurd and Lou Carter, at about this time.

sustaining broadcast, Terrace Room, Mosque Theater
Building, Newark, N.J.—ABC [WJZ], 11:30-12:00
P.M. Tuesday, November 13, 1945
JIMMY DORSEY AND HIS ORCHESTRA
Jimmy Dorsey (cl,as,ldr) Irv Goodman, Bob Alexy, Jack Dougherty,
Shorty Solomson, Tony Picciotto (tp) Buddy Morrow, Dick Bellerose,
Sonny Lee, Bill Granzow (tb) Bill Covey, Cliff Jackson (as) Chuck
Travis, Gil Koerner (ts) Lou Carter (p) Herb Ellis (g) Norman Bates
(sb) Karl Kiffe (d) Dee Parker, Dick Culver (vcl)

Contrasts [Jimmy Dorsey] (theme) (as solo) / **Jumpin' Jehosephat**
[Joe Lippman, Jimmy Dorsey] (as,cl solos) / **A Door Will Open**
[Don George; John Brooks] vDP (as solo) / **Outer Drive** [Sonny
Burke] (cl solo) / **It's Only A Paper Moon** [E. Y. Harburg, Billy
Rose; Harold Arlen] (cl solo) / **How Deep Is The Ocean?** [Irving
Berlin] vDP / **Love Letters** [Edward Heyman; Victor Young] vDC
(as solo) / **The Moment I Met You** vDP (as solo) / ***Java Junction**
(cl,as solos)
    Entire broadcast on **ET:** AFRS One Night Stand 835. *The last
tune was dubbed from AFRS One Night Stand 683.

Singer Johnny Desmond had just been mustered out of the service
after an overseas assignment with Glenn Miller's AEF band and
appeared with Jimmy on a new NBC teenage-oriented program on a
Saturday morning in mid-November.

Teen Timers, NBC studios, New York, N.Y.—NBC
[WEAF], 11:00-11:30 A.M. Saturday, November 17,
1945
JIMMY DORSEY AND HIS ORCHESTRA
Johnny Desmond (vcl)

Somebody Loves Me [Ira Gershwin; George Gershwin] vJD / **Outer
Drive** [Sonny Burke] (cl solo) / **My Love** vJD / **As If I Didn't Have
Enough On My Mind** [Charles Henderson; Harry James, Lionel
Newman] vJD
    Entire show on **ET:** AFRS Teen Timers 2

Broadcast schedule (Terrace Room): Tues., Nov. 20, ABC [WJZ], 11:30-12:00 P.M.

Closing at the Terrace Room on Wednesday, November 21, Jimmy
and the band opened the next day at the Capitol Theater in Manhattan
for a month's stay, four shows a day, plus a late show on Saturdays.
    The band then moved downtown three blocks and east two, to the 400
Restaurant at Fifth Avenue and East Forty-third, opening on December
25. There were two shows a night, 7:30 and midnight. As a rule,
broadcasts from the club were aired just ahead of the last show. The
band was heard opening night 11:30 to midnight on NBC [WEAF].

sustaining broadcast, 400 Restaurant, New York,
N.Y.—MBS [WOR], 11:30-12:00 P.M. Wednesday,
December 26, 1945

JIMMY DORSEY AND HIS ORCHESTRA
Louis Mucci (tp) replaces Picciotto, Paul Chapman (vcl) replaces Culver

Opus One [Sid Garris; Sy Oliver] (as,cl solos) / **Don't You Remember Me?** vPC / **Come To Baby, Do** [Inez James, Sidney Miller] vDP arrSB / **Oh, What A Beautiful Mornin'** [Oscar Hammerstein II; Richard Rodgers] arrSB (cl solo) / **Outer Drive** [Sonny Burke] (cl solo) / **Everybody Knew But Me** [Irving Berlin] vPC / **Begin The Beguine** [Cole Porter] / **A Door Will Open** [Don George; John Benson Brooks] vDP
    Entire broadcast on ET: AFRS One Night Stand 850; "Opus One" on LP: Big Band Archives LP1203

It is believed that AFRS, known for creative editing, changed the order of the selections played and produced a second ET: AFRS One Night Stand 912. The sequence follows:

Everybody Knew But Me vPC / **Outer Drive** / **Don't You Remember Me?** vPC / **A Door Will Open** vDP / **Begin The Beguine** / **Opus One** / **Come To Baby, Do** vDP / **Oh, What A Beautiful Mornin'**
    Entire broadcast on ET: AFRS One Night Stand 912

Broadcast schedule (400 Restaurant): Sat., Dec. 29, CBS [WABC], 11:30-12:00 P.M.

    sustaining broadcast, 400 Restaurant, New York, N.Y.—NBC [WEAF], 11:30-12:00 P.M. Monday, December 31, 1945

JIMMY DORSEY AND HIS ORCHESTRA

Contrasts [Jimmy Dorsey] (theme) (as solo) / **I Can't Believe That You're In Love With Me** [L. Wolfe Gilbert, Abner Silver] (cl solo) / **The Last Time I Saw You** [Edna Osser, Marjorie Goetschius] vDP / **Ain't Misbehavin'** [Irving Razaf; Thomas "Fats" Waller]

There is extant an elaborate New Year's Eve Dancing Party put together by AFRS to mark the end of World War II and purportedly aired by AFRS stations around the world. The groups picked up included eighteen of the nation's top bands, ending with the traditional "Auld Lang Syne" from Guy Lombardo, but, significantly, not the traditional Times Square dropping of the ball.
    Jimmy's band is heard playing "I Got Rhythm" from the 400 Club. Though promoted on LP and CD reissues as having been transmitted by shortwave around the world on New Year's Eve, it's believed that all the "cut-ins" were from previous airchecks or specially recorded inserts made in advance, assembled, pressed and shipped to key AFRS stations for airing.
    The cost of so many live switches to produce such a spectacular "live" event, with the war over and AFRS budgets already being cut back would rule against the show being "live."
    Its AFRS Series data is ET: H-9, Program 124, and also appears on Radiola LP: MR-1031, TC: CMR-1031, CD: CDMR-1031.

After the Brawl Is Over
(1946-1949)

The year 1946 was a watershed one for the big bands. The war was over. Young couples, the backbone of their consumer base, were busy making babies at home instead of memories at dance pavilions. By year's end, the bands of Benny Goodman, Woody Herman, Harry James, even Tommy Dorsey, would fold, their places being taken by newer, more "hip" band leaders like Stan Kenton, Ray Anthony, the Elgarts, and, of course, Dizzy Gillespie and the whole bebop movement.

Broadcast schedule (all 400 Restaurant): Tues., Jan. 1, NBC-Red [WEAF], 11:30-12:00 P.M. / Wed., Jan. 2, MBS [WOR], 11:30-12:00 P.M. / Thurs., Jan. 3, ABC [WJZ], 11:30-12:00 P.M. / Sat., Jan. 5, CBS [WABC], 11:30-12:00 P.M.

> *sustaining broadcast,* 400 Restaurant, New York, N.Y.—MBS [WOR], 11:30-12:00 P.M. Wednesday, January 9, 1946

JIMMY DORSEY AND HIS ORCHESTRA
Jimmy Dorsey (cl,as,ldr) Bob Alexy, Sy Baker, Irving Goodman, Louis Mucci, Shorty Solomson (tp) Bob Alexander, Sonny Lee, Fred Mancusi, Don Matteson (tb) Bill Covey, Cliff Jackson (as) Chuck Travis, Gil Koerner (ts) John Dee (bar) Lou Carter (p,arr) Herb Ellis (g) Norman Bates (sb) Karl Kiffe (d) Dee Parker, Paul Chapman (vcl) Sonny Burke (arr)

> Contrasts [Jimmy Dorsey] (theme) (as solo) / **You Gotta See Baby Tonight** vDP (as solo) / **The Man With A Horn** [Eddie DeLange; Bonnie Lake, Jack Jenney] (as solo) / **Last Night I Saw You** vPC / **Outer Drive** (cl solo) / **It's The Talk Of The Town** vPC [Marty Symes, Al J. Neiberg; Jerry Livingston] arrSB (as solo) / **The Champ** (cl solo) / **Contrasts** (theme)
> Closing theme and "Man With A Horn" on **CD**: Hep (E) CD41

> *sustaining broadcast,* 400 Restaurant, New York, N.Y.—ABC [WJZ], 11:35-12:00 P.M. Thursday, January 10, 1946

JIMMY DORSEY AND HIS ORCHESTRA

> **Opus One** [Sid Garris; Sy Oliver] arrSB (as,cl solos) / **Here I Go Again** vDP (as solo) / **The Champ** (cl solo) / **Outer Drive** [Sonny Burke] (cl solo) / **I've Got A Crush On You** [Ira Gershwin; George Gershwin] arrSB vDP / **This Can't Be Love** [Lorenz Hart; Richard Rodgers] arrSB
> All except "The Champ" on **CD**: Hep (E) CD41

462

sustaining broadcast, 400 Restaurant, New York,
N.Y.—CBS [WABC], 11:35-12:00 P.M. Saturday,
January 12, 1946
JIMMY DORSEY AND HIS ORCHESTRA

Town Hall Tonight [Sonny Burke] / **Come To Baby, Do** [Inez
James, Sidney Miller] arrSB vDP / **Are These Really Mine?** vPC /
Lover [Lorenz Hart; Richard Rodgers] arrSB (as solo) / **It's The
Talk Of The Town** [Marty Symes, Al J. Neiberg; Jerry Livingston]
arrSB vDP / **The Champ** (cl solo) / **Lover Man (Oh, Where Can
You Be)** [Jimmy Davis, Roger "Ram" Ramirez, Jimmy Sherman]
vDP / **King Porter Stomp** ["Jelly Roll" Morton] arrOH (cl solo)
All except "Are These Really Mine" on **CD**: Hep (E) CD41

Broadcast schedule (400 Restaurant): Wed., Jan. 16, MBS [WOR], 11:30 12:00 P.M.

sustaining broadcast, 400 Restaurant, New York,
N.Y.—ABC [WJZ], 11:30-12:00 P.M. Thursday,
January 17, 1946
JIMMY DORSEY AND HIS ORCHESTRA

The Moment I Met You vDP / **Everybody Knew But Me** vPC / **I
Can't Believe That You're In Love With Me** [Clarence Gaskill;
Jimmy McHugh] arrSB (cl solo) / **Here I Go Again** vDP (as solo)
The Champ (cl solo) / **And Then I Looked At You** / **This Can't Be
Love** [Lorenz Hart; Richard Rodgers] arrSB
"I Can't Believe..." on **CD**: Hep (E) CD41

The arrival in Hollywood of Jimmy's attorney, John Manning, to
meet with General Artists (formerly Amusement) Corporation led to
speculation that Jimmy was looking to end his ten years with the bookers
(*Variety,* January 16, 1946, 51).

Broadcast schedule (all 400 Restaurant): Sat., Jan. 19, CBS [WABC], 11:30-12:00
P.M. / Tues., Jan. 22, NBC [WEAF], 11:30-12:00 P.M.

sustaining broadcast, 400 Restaurant, New York,
N.Y.—MBS [WOR], 11:30-12:00 P.M. Wednesday,
January 23, 1946
JIMMY DORSEY AND HIS ORCHESTRA
Buddy Hughes (vcl) replaces Chapman

Let It Snow! Let It Snow! Let It Snow! [Sammy Cahn; Vaughn
Monroe] / **This Is My Beloved** [Arnold B. Hewitt; Harry Revel]
vBH / **Super Chief** [William "Count" Basie, Jimmy Mundy] (cl solo)
/ **Everybody Knew But Me** [Irving Berlin] vPC / **I'm In The Mood
For Love** [Dorothy Fields; Jimmy McHugh] / **No Can Do** [Charles
Tobias; Nat Simon] / **Outer Drive** [Sonny Burke] (cl solo) / **Are
These Really Mine?** [Sunny Skyler, David Saxon, Robert Cook] /
Opus One [Sid Garris; Sy Oliver] (partial)
Entire broadcast on **ET**: AFRS One Night Stand 870

464   JIMMY DORSEY: A Study in Contrasts

Broadcast schedule (all 400 Restaurant): Thurs., Jan. 24, ABC [WJZ], 11:35-12:00
P.M. / Sat., Jan. 26, CBS [WABC], 11:30-12:00 P.M. / Tues., Jan. 29, NBC-Red
[WEAF], 11:30-12:00 P.M. / Thurs., Jan. 31, ABC [WJZ], 11:35-12:00 P.M. / Fri.,
Feb. 1, ABC [WJZ], 11:35-12:00 P.M. / Sat., Feb. 2, CBS [WABC], 11:30-12:00 P.M.

The Dorsey brothers bought out Larry Finley's Casino Gardens interest in early January, installing Jimmy's band manager Dick Gabbe as the
Gardens' manager, leading to rumors that Art Michaud, Tommy's personal manager, would take over Jimmy's management as well (*Billboard,* February 2, 1946, 22). This never came to pass. To replace
Gabbe, Jimmy hired Howard Christensen, a recently released service-
man, as his personal manager, and named Ted Alabaster road manager.
The next broadcast marked the band's last night at the 400 Club.

sustaining broadcast, 400 Restaurant, New York,
N.Y.—NBC [WEAF], 11:30-12:00 P.M. Tuesday,
February 5, 1946
JIMMY DORSEY AND HIS ORCHESTRA

In A Little Spanish Town [Sam M. Lewis, Joseph Young; Mabel
Wayne] (cl solo) / **Perdido** [Juan Tizol] (cl solo) / **Carolina In The
Morning** [Gus Kahn; Walter Donaldson] / **Opus One** [Sid Garris; Sy
Oliver] (as,cl solos) / **Hip Hop** [Jimmy Dorsey, Herb Ellis] / **Sunset
Strip** [Sonny Burke, Jimmy Dorsey] (cl,as solos) / **That Wonderful,
Worrisome Feeling** vDP (as solo) / **All The Things You Ain't**
[Sonny Burke, Jimmy Dorsey] (cl,as solos)
    Entire broadcast on **LP:** Big Band Archives LP-1203

World, New York, N.Y. Wednesday, February 6, 1946
JIMMY DORSEY AND HIS ORCHESTRA
Buddy Hughes, Dee Parker (vcl) Joe Lippman (arr)

W73346-A   **Ain't Misbehavin'** [Andy Razaf; Thomas "Fats"
                  Waller, Harry Brooks] vDP
    78: Decca 18799, Brunswick (E) 03705
    LP: Coral (G) CPO7839, 6.22183, Ajaz LP296
W73347-A   **I'll Always Be In Love With You** [Bud Green,
                  Herman Ruby; Sam H. Stept] vDP (cl solo)
    78: Decca 24363
    (SSL1936) **78:** AFRS Basic Music Library P-1054
    LP: Ajaz LP296
W73348-A   **I'm Glad There Is You** [Paul Madeira; Jimmy Dor-
                  sey] vDP (as solo)
    78: Decca 18799
    LP: Decca DL-8609, Ajaz LP296
W73349-A   **Perdido** [Juan Tizol] (arrJL) (cl solo)
    78: Decca 18812, (C) 10313, (Cz) 03745, Brunswick (E) 03745
    LP: Decca DL8654, Coral (G) CPO7839, 6.22183, Ajaz LP296

JIMMY DORSEY AND HIS JAMMERS
Jimmy Dorsey (as) Lou Carter (p,arr) Herb Ellis (g) Norman Bates (sb)
Karl Kiffe (d)

W73350-A   **J.D.'s Jump** [Jimmy Dorsey] (as solos)
    78: Decca 18812, (C) 10313, (Cz) 03745, Brunswick (E) 03745
    LP: Coral (G) PCO7839, 6.22183, Ajaz LP296

Travel itinerary: Mon., Feb. 11, to Wed., Feb. 13—Plymouth Theater, Worcester, Mass. / Thurs., Feb. 14, to Sun., Feb. 17—Metropolitan Theater, Providence, R.I. / Mon., Feb. 18, to Wed., Mar. 13—tour of one-nighters through the South (locations unknown) / Thurs., Mar. 14, to Wed., Mar. 20—Adams Theater, Newark, N.J. / Thurs., Mar. 21, to Wed., Mar. 27—Tunetown Ballroom, St. Louis, Mo. / Thurs., Mar. 28, to Wed., Apr. 3—RKO Boston Theater, Boston, Mass. / Thurs., Apr. 4, to Wed., Apr. 24—Terrace Room, Mosque Theater, Newark, N.J.

Broadcast schedule (Terrace Room): Sat., Apr. 6, NBC-Red [WEAF], 11:30-12:00 P.M.

> *sustaining broadcast,* Terrace Room, Newark, N.J.—
> MBS [WOR], 11:35-12:00 P.M. Wednesday, April
> 10, 1946

JIMMY DORSEY AND HIS ORCHESTRA
Jimmy Dorsey (cl,as,ldr) Tony Faso [Fasulo], Irv Goodman, Shorty Solomson, Sy Baker (tp) Don Matteson, Bob Alexander, Fred Mancusi, Chauncey Welsch (tb) Cliff Jackson, Serge Chaloff, Norm Stern (as) Gil Koerner, Vinnie Francis [Francescone] (ts) Lou Carter (p) Herb Ellis (g) Johnny Frigo (sb,vn) Karl Kiffe (d) *Buddy Hughes* [or] *Bob Carroll,* Dee Parker (vcl)

    Titles unknown
    Entire broadcast on **ET:** AFRS One Night Stand 971

Jimmy replaced Buddy Hughes with ex-Charlie Barnet vocalist Bob Carroll during the Terrace Room stay. Before going in the service and after leaving Barnet, Carroll did some transcription and radio work with NBC as a single. The trade press looked upon the Carroll signing as an attempt by Jimmy to regain some of the Bob Eberly charm.

> *sustaining broadcast,* Terrace   Room,   Newark,
> N.J.—MBS [WOR], Sunday, April 14, 1946

JIMMY DORSEY AND HIS ORCHESTRA
Bob Carroll, Dee Parker (vcl)

    Super Chief [William "Count" Basie, Jimmy Mundy] (cl solo) / **I Can't Begin To Tell You** [Mack Gordon; James V. Monaco] vBC (as solo) / **Outer Drive** [Sonny Burke] (cl solo) / **Coax Me A Little Bit** [Charles Tobias; Nat Simon] vDP (as solo)
       All selections on **LP:** Magic (E) AWE-27, **TC:** Magic (E) CWE-27; "Super Chief" and "Outer Drive" on **LP:** Golden Era GE-15011; "Super Chief" also on **TC:** LaserLight 79-759, **CD:** LaserLight 15-759

Some miscellaneous undated airchecks from the 1946 Terrace Room engagement are listed next. It is certain these are not all from one broadcast, but whether one or both networks are involved is uncertain.

sustaining broadcasts, Terrace Room, Newark,
N.J.—CBS and/or MBS, April 1946
JIMMY DORSEY AND HIS ORCHESTRA

King Porter Stomp [Ferdinand "Jelly Roll" Morton] arrOH (cl solo)/
This Can't Be Love [Lorenz Hart; Richard Rodgers] / **Perdido** [Juan
Tizol] arrJL (cl solo) / **Tea For Two** [Irving Caesar; Vincent
Youmans] / **Be-Baba-Luba** [Helen Humes] vDP&BC / **I May Be
Wrong But I Think You're Wonderful** [Harry Ruskin; Henry
Sullivan] vDP / **Royal Garden Blues** [Clarence and Spencer Wil-
liams] (cl solo) / **Just One Of Those Things** [Cole Porter] (as solo)
"Royal Garden Blues" on **LP:** Golden Era GE-15082; "Just One
Of Those Things" on **LP:** Project 3 PR-2-6036

World, New York, N.Y. Monday, April 15, 1946
JIMMY DORSEY AND HIS ORCHESTRA
Serge Chaloff switches to (bar), Bob Carroll, Dee Parker (vcl)

W73504-A   **Doin' What Comes Natur'lly** [Irving Berlin] vDP&
                  band
     78: Decca 18872, 25847
     LP: Ajaz LP296
W73505-A   **All That Glitters Is Not Gold** [Leo Kuhn; Alice Cor-
                  nett; Eddie Asherman] vDP&band (as solo)
     78: Decca 18872
     LP: Ajaz LP296
W73506-A   **(It's Gonna Depend On) The Way That The Wind
                  Blows** vBC (as solo)
     78: Decca 18900, (C) 10360, Brunswick (E) 03764
     (7939) **ET:** World 7939/7943
     LP: Ajaz LP296
W73507   **A Rose Was A Rose** vBC (as solo)
     (7941) **ET:** World 7939/7943
W73508-A   **Apache Serenade** [Jimmy Dorsey, Buddy Kaye, Joe
                  Lippman] vDP (as solo)
     78: Decca 18917
     (7942) **ET:** World 7939/7943
     LP: Coral (G) PCO7839, 6.22183, Ajaz LP296
W73509-A   **The Same Little Chapel** vBC
     78: Decca 24363
     (SSL1936) **78:** AFRS Basic Music Library P-1054
     (7943) **ET:** World 7939/7943
     LP: Ajaz LP296

Broadcast schedule (all Terrace Room): Wed., Apr. 17, MBS [WOR], 11:30-12:00
P.M. / Sat., Apr. 20, NBC-Red [WEAF], 11:30-12:00 P.M. / Wed., Apr. 24, MBS
[WOR], 11:30-12:00 P.M.

While in New York, Jimmy turned down buying an old mansion in
Forest Hills, Long Island which was proposed to be converted to a
summer band location (*Billboard,* April 27, 1946, 41).

Travel itinerary: Thurs., Apr. 25, to Sun., Apr. 28—Palace Theater, Akron, Ohio /
Mon., Apr. 29, to Wed., May 1—Palace Theater, Columbus, Ohio / Fri., May 3, to
Thurs., May 9—Castle Farms ballroom, Cincinnati, Ohio / Fri., May 10, to Thurs.,
May 16—Club Madrid, Louisville, Ky. / Fri., May 17, to Thurs., May 30—Chase
Hotel, St. Louis, Mo.

For their two-week stay at the Chase, Jimmy and the band were
reportedly paid $8,000 a week, double the hotel's normal band budget
(*Billboard,* March 30, 1946, 22).

Travel itinerary: Fri., May 31, to Thurs., June 6—Rainbo Ballroom, Chicago, Ill. /
Fri., June 7, to Mon., June 10—one-nighters in the Midwest; Tues., June
11—Oklahoma Fairgrounds Pavilion, Tulsa, Okla. / Wed., June 12, to Tues., June
18—New Plantation (a nightclub), Dallas, Tex. / Thurs., June 20, to Sat., June
29—400 Restaurant, New York City.

sustaining broadcast(s), 400 Restaurant, New York,
N.Y.—MBS [WOR], June 20-29, 1946
JIMMY DORSEY AND HIS ORCHESTRA

**Mo-Mo / Blues For Me / So, What's New? / Sweet Thing / Lul-
laby In Rhythm** [Walter Hirsch; Benny Goodman, Edgar Sampson,
Clarence Profit] / **Flyin' Home** [Sid Robin; Lionel Hampton, Benny
Goodman]
    Entire grouping on **LP:** Golden Era GE-15016

The trade press was reporting about this time that Jimmy had told
General Artists Corporation to turn down extended booking at the 400
Restaurant, preferring to take less money for a stand at the more prestigious Hotel Pennsylvania (*Down Beat,* July 1, 1946, 2). In addition,
the publication reported that Jimmy turned down an October date at the
Hotel New Yorker, requesting instead an October engagement at the
Meadowbrook.
    Jimmy returned in the summer of 1946 to Toluca Lake, California,
where Jane and Julie Lou (by then a 14-year-old heartbreaker) lived in a
twelve-room Tudor mansion in an exclusive area of North Hollywood.
    The home, adjacent to the third tee of Lakeside Country Club, had
originally been built for Dick Powell and Joan Blondell in the thirties,
and had Bob Hope and Bing Crosby as nearby neighbors (which, with a
golf course next door, was not surprising).
    Some of the home's features were secret passageways installed by
Powell, two tennis courts, a large swimming pool and a game room with
a movie projector and screen.
    For Jimmy, the home was just a convenient place to stay when he was
on the West Coast. For several years he and wife Jane had been living
separately. When they did socialize together, they drank extensively,
and often fought.
    Jimmy and the band worked their first West Coast engagement of
1946 at the "grand reopening" of a ballroom on the Pacific Coast south
of San Francisco from Wednesday, July 3, to Saturday, July 6.
Adjacent to Playland-at-the-Beach amusement park, the Edgewater had
been shuttered during the war for coastal security reasons.

sustaining broadcast, Edgewater Ballroom, San Francisco, Cal.—Friday, July 5, 1946
JIMMY DORSEY AND HIS ORCHESTRA

Unknown titles
Entire broadcast on **ET:** AFRS One Night Stand 1179

Another Dorsey sibling squabble bubbled up in early July when Jimmy balked at following Woody Herman into Casino Gardens starting August 18. Filming of the Dorsey film biography was to begin when Jimmy returned from his one-nighter tour in California, which would mean Jimmy would have to double between movie lot and ballroom.

The film, very loosely drawn about the lives of the brothers, started shooting on Monday, July 15, and concluded just after Labor Day. Cameo roles in the movie were offered to a wide array of names including Bing Crosby, Paul Whiteman, Henry Busse, Charlie Barnet, Woody Herman, Gene Krupa, Stan Kenton, Art Tatum, Duke Ellington, Lionel Hampton and banjoist Mike Pingatore, many of whom accepted.

United Artists Studios, Hollywood, Cal. c. July 15-September 15, 1946
THE FABULOUS DORSEYS: Alfred E. Green, director
"DORSEY'S WILD CANARIES"
Unknown (tp) Tommy Dorsey (tb) **Jimmy Dorsey** (cl) *unknown* (as), (ts), (p), (bj), (bb), (d)

Runnin' Wild [Joe Gray, Leo Wood; A. H. Gibbs] (cl solo)

"PAUL WHITEMAN ORCHESTRA"
Large group, including: Paul Whiteman (ldr) Henry Busse (tp) Tommy Dorsey (tb) Jimmy Dorsey (as) Mike Pingitore (bj)

At Sundown [Walter Donaldson] (as solo)

"DORSEY BROTHERS ORCHESTRA"

I'll Never Say "Never Again" Again [Harry Woods] / **Sandman** [Ralph Freed, Bonnie Lake] / **The Object of My Affection** [Pinky Tomlin, Coy Poe, Jimmie Greer] vJanet Blair

"ONYX CLUB JAM SESSION BAND"
Ziggy Elman (tp) Tommy Dorsey (tb) **Jimmy Dorsey** (cl) Charlie Barnet (ts) Art Tatum (p) *unknown* (g), (sb) Ray Bauduc (d)

Art's Blues [Art Tatum]
   LP: Collector's Items (E) 011, Extreme Rarities LP 1002

JIMMY DORSEY AND HIS ORCHESTRA
Personnel of the period. Bob Eberly, Helen O'Connell (vcl)

Green Eyes [N. Menendez, E. Rivera, Eddie Woods, A. Utera] vBE&HO'C (as solo) / **Contrasts** [Jimmy Dorsey] (theme) (as solo)
   Both selections on **CD:** Avid AVC528

UNITED ARTISTS STUDIO ORCHESTRA
Unknown personnel, plus Tommy Dorsey (tb) **Jimmy Dorsey** (as)

Double Concerto for Trombone and Sax [Leo Shuken] (as solos)
All selections on **FILM:** United Artists *The Fabulous Dorseys,*
VIDEO: Crown Music Classics 883546

Jimmy, like many of his fellow bandleaders, had become dissatisfied
with his agency, blaming them for a drop in bookings actually caused by
social changes the bookers were not able to control. In Jimmy's case, it
was General Artists Corporation, and he had been reportedly talking
with both Music Corporation of America (MCA) and William Morris
Agency (*Billboard* July 20, 1946, 18).

World, Los Angeles, Cal. Thursday, July 25, 1946
JIMMY DORSEY AND HIS ORCHESTRA
Bob Carroll, Dee Parker (vcl)

L4249-A   **The Whole World Is Singing My Song** [Mann Curtis; Vic Mizzy] vBC (cl solo)
78: Decca 18917, Brunswick (E) 03705
LP: Ajaz LP296
L4250-A   **One More Kiss** vDP (as solo)
78: Decca 18905, Brunswick (E) 03698
LP: Ajaz LP296

It took until mid-July 1946 for Jimmy and Harry James to extricate
themselves from the Casino Gardens venture. With the end of the war,
ballroom business all across the country took a nosedive and Tommy
Dorsey wound up being the sole proprietor of the Gardens.
Tommy even brought publicist Jack Egan to Hollywood from New
York to try some publicity gimmicks to boost business. They were only
modestly successful. Despite his earlier objections, Jimmy returned to
the Gardens in mid-August 1946, but not as a partner; another early sign
Tommy was taking a more active role in controlling Jimmy's destiny.
On August 18 Jimmy guested on Tommy's NBC commercial show
for the premiere of Leo Shuken's recently composed showcase for the
brothers, which was also the finale for their film, and was subtitled "The
Dorsey Concerto."

Tommy Dorsey Playshop (Tenderleaf Tea Show),
NBC Studios, Hollywood, Cal.—5:30-6:00 P.M. PDT,
Sunday, August 18, 1946
TOMMY DORSEY AND HIS ORCHESTRA
Tommy Dorsey (tb,ldr) George Seaberg, Johnny Dougherty, Mickey
Mangano, Ziggy Elman (tp) Johnny Youngman, Tex Satterwaite,
Charlie LaRue (tb) Abe Most (cl,as) Sid Cooper (as) Babe Fresk,
Boomie Richman (ts) Bruce Branson (bar) John Potaker (p) Sam Herman
(g) Sid Block (sb) Alvin Stoller (d) **Jimmy Dorsey** (as) guest

Double Concerto for Trombone and Sax [Leo Shuken] (as solos)
Entire show on **ET:** AFRS Tommy Dorsey Show 56

World, New York, N.Y. Wednesday, August 21, 1946
JIMMY DORSEY AND HIS ORCHESTRA
Dee Parker, Bob Carroll, Bing Crosby (vcl)

WL4254-A   **Make Me Know It** vDP (cl solo)
    78: Decca 18923
    (SSL1379) **78:** AFRS Basic Music Library P-697
    LP: Ajaz LP296
WL4255-A   **The Language Of Love** vBobC (as solo)
    78: Decca 18923
    (SSL1379) **78:** AFRS Basic Music Library P-697
    LP: Ajaz LP296
WL4256-A   **If I'm Lucky** [Eddie DeLange; Josef Myrow] vBobC
    (as solo)
    78: Decca 18905, Brunswick (E) 03698
    LP: Ajaz LP305
WL4257-A   **The Things We Did Last Summer** [Sammy Cahn;
    Jule Styne] vBing (as solo)
    78: Decca 23655, Brunswick (E) 03665
    as BING CROSBY WITH JIMMY DORSEY AND HIS ORCH.
    LP: Ajaz LP305

This session was Jimmy's last with Jack Kapp's Decca Records. The
end of their twelve-year association was one more manifestation of the
vast changes taking place in the pop music business. Besides the vocal
headliners, there was the new bebop influence among younger musicians
that was also taking the spotlight away from the big bands.

It is another coincidence that the last tune cut by Jimmy on Decca is
with Bing Crosby, who sang on the last true Dorsey Brothers Decca session in 1935 and had helped launch Jimmy's band on *Kraft Music Hall.*

The night before, Jimmy had opened at Casino Gardens, having apparently settled his differences with Tommy over doubling between the
ballroom and the movie studios.

               sustaining broadcast, Casino Gardens, Ocean Park,
               Cal.—Wednesday, August 21, 1946
JIMMY DORSEY AND HIS ORCHESTRA

    South America, Take It Away [Harold Rome] /**The Language Of
    Love** vBC (as solo) / **Perdido** [Juan Tizol] arrJL (cl solo) / (other
    titles unknown)
        Entire broadcast on AFRS One Night Stand 1157; "South
        America, Take It Away" and "Perdido" on **LP:** Joyce LP1101;
        "Language Of Love" and "Perdido" on **LP:** Sunbeam SB-210;
        "Perdido" on **LP:** First Heard (E) FH-19

               sustaining broadcast, Casino Gardens, Ocean Park,
               Cal.—Thursday, August 22, 1946
JIMMY DORSEY AND HIS ORCHESTRA

    Titles unknown
    Entire show on **ET:** AFRS One Night Stand 1164

sustaining broadcast, Casino Gardens, Ocean Park,
Cal.—Friday, August 23, 1946
JIMMY DORSEY AND HIS ORCHESTRA

Titles unknown
Entire show on **ET**: AFRS One Night Stand 1171

Teen Timers, NBC Studios, Los Angeles, Cal.—8:00
-8:30 A.M. PWT, Saturday, August 24, 1946
JIMMY DORSEY AND HIS ORCHESTRA

Ain't Misbehavin' [Andy Razaf; Thomas "Fats" Waller, Harry
Brooks] vDP / (other details unknown)
Entire show on **ET**: AFRS Teen Timers 30

It is also reported but unconfirmed that "Apache Serenade" with a
Dee Parker vocal appears on this program either along with or instead of
"Ain't Misbehavin'."

Teen Timers, NBC Studios, Los Angeles, Cal.—
8:00-8.30 A.M. Saturday, August 31, 1946
JIMMY DORSEY AND HIS ORCHESTRA

Perdido [Juan Tizol] arrJL (cl solo) / (other details unknown)
ET: AFRS Teen Timers 33

The documentary film series *The March Of Time* issued an edition in
August 1946 (volume 12, issue 8) that dealt with New York City
nightclub life, and Jimmy's band was shown as filmed in the spring of
1946 at the 400 Restaurant.   The series, inspired by Time Magazine,
was best known for the closing phrase "Time Marches On," always
delivered solemnly by narrator Westbrook Van Voorhees.
   Tommy's NBC commercial broadcast sponsored by Tenderleaf Tea
was aired from the United Artists set on September 15, 1946. Included
were interviews with Jimmy and Tommy, Stuart Foster and Charlie
Shavers as well as William Lundigan and Janet Blair from the *Fabulous
Dorseys* film cast.   AFRS also carried the program as Tommy Dorsey
Show #60. Jimmy did not perform musically.
   In another demonstration that the battling brothers had reconciled,
their two bands appeared jointly for two weeks at Casino Gardens
beginning Friday, September 13, and ending Thursday, September 26.
What might have been considered a publicity ploy of the Dorseys' film,
was more likely an attempt to bring crowds back to the Casino Gardens.
   Opening night featured a ceremonial "hatchet burying" episode in
which Jimmy and Tommy exchanged handshakes with a six-inch axe
under a dangling pair of giant boxing gloves overhead.
   Tommy's former vocalist, Frank Sinatra, was on hand opening night
singing "I Don't Know Why" on a broadcast from the Gardens. He also
sang songs first with Tommy's and then with Jimmy's bands during the
evening on an expanded bandstand built to accommodate both groups.
   The two bands performed together nightly on the tune "Brotherly
Jump." The Jimmy Dorsey portions of two broadcasts are shown next.

sustaining broadcast, Casino Gardens, Ocean Park,
Cal.—ABC, Thursday, September 19, 1946
JIMMY DORSEY AND HIS ORCHESTRA

Ain't Misbehavin' [Andy Razaf; Thomas "Fats" Waller, Harry
Brooks] vDP / **Oh, What A Beautiful Mornin'** [Oscar Hammerstein
II; Richard Rodgers] (cl solo) / **If I'm Lucky** [Eddie DeLange; Josef
Myrow] vBC (as solo)

JIMMY DORSEY AND HIS ORCHESTRA combined with:
TOMMY DORSEY AND HIS ORCHESTRA

Brotherly Jump (as solo)
All tunes on **ET:** AFRS One Night Stand 1150, **LP:** Joyce 1101;
"Ain't Misbehavin'" and "Oh, What A Beautiful Morning" on **LP:**
Sunbeam SB-210

sustaining broadcast, Casino Gardens, Ocean Park,
Cal.—Wednesday, September 25, 1946
JIMMY DORSEY AND HIS ORCHESTRA

Perdido [Juan Tizol] (cl solo) / **The Language Of Love** vBC (as
solo)
Both tunes on **ET:** AFRS One Night Stand 1150; **LP:** Sunbeam
SB-210; "Perdido" on **LP:** First Heard (E) FH-19

JIMMY DORSEY AND HIS ORCHESTRA combined with:
TOMMY DORSEY AND HIS ORCHESTRA

Brotherly Jump (as solo)
LP: Sunbeam SB-223

Travel itinerary: Fri., Sept. 27, to Thurs., Oct. 3—The Plantation, Dallas, Tex.

The next day, Friday, October 4 Jimmy was back in Los Angeles
helping to open Casino Gardens for the fall season while Tommy was in
Dallas for a two-week run at the famed Texas State Fair at a reported
$20,000 a week.

It was during that Texas fair date that Tommy was revealed to be
scrapping his band in a move that trade papers speculated was an attempt
to break his long-standing contract with Music Corporation of America
(MCA) (*Variety,* October 9, 1946, 1).

Travel itinerary: Thurs., Oct. 10, to Sat., Oct. 19—The Plantation, Houston, Tex. /
Fri., Oct. 25, to Thurs., Nov. 7—Chase Hotel, St. Louis, Mo. (see Addenda) / Tues.,
Nov. 19, to Mon., Dec. 9—Meadowbrook Ballroom, Cedar Grove, N.J.

There was some trade press speculation that Jimmy and Tommy
would work together for a month at the plush Denver, Colorado, resort,
Troutdale-in-the-Pines, which was owned by Jim O'Keefe, a Chicago
attorney and longtime friend. It proved to be just that, speculation.

The soaring postwar cost-of-living that followed the lifting of wartime price ceilings, coupled with a falling employment picture, was beginning to have an effect on the entertainment business and big bands in particular, as J. Q. Public cut back on discretionary spending.

Paradoxically, as business fell the American Federation of Musicians (AFM) pushed for and got scale raises of 25 to 38 percent for its musicians, which resulted in counterproductive higher fees for many of the locations booking bands. Added to this was the rapidly increasing number of new and old bands vying for a share of the declining business.

To save money, many hotels and ballrooms were taking out their remote lines or cutting back on their air shots, which in turn made them less desirable for the bands that had worked for less at these spots to get the prestige and publicity of the air exposure.

As 1946 drew to a close, a steady parade of big bands called it quits including Benny Goodman, Les Brown, Harry James, Benny Carter, Jack Teagarden, Woody Herman and Jerry Wald. Just after Thanksgiving Tommy Dorsey disbanded his orchestra despite a pending date at New York's Capitol Theater. Among Tommy's musicians who were let go was trumpeter Ziggy Elman, who immediately organized his own band including some of Tommy's crew.

The general opinion expressed in the trade press was that the superlarge orchestras, often twice to three times the size of prewar groups, coupled with the increased AFM pay scales, were causing the leaders to scrap their bands and regroup with reduced-personnel outfits later.

Jimmy Dorsey was one of the leaders cutting costs, but he was doing it by reducing over-scale salaries, slicing his weekly musicians payroll by one-third from $3,600 to $2,400 (*Variety,* November 27, 1946, 47).

Jimmy was also still casting about for a new record deal, dissatisfied with his treatment at Decca. Amid rumors that Capitol, Mercury, Signature and MGM were interested, Jimmy got release papers from Decca's remaining year-and-a-half contract in early December. Other Decca artists released that fall included Johnny Long, Glen Gray, Andy Kirk and Helen Forrest.

After Christmas, on Thursday, December 26, the band opened a six-week stay at Cafe Rouge of Hotel Pennsylvania in New York.

On the second day of the new year Jimmy switched recording companies to the brand-new MGM label and cut his first sides January 8. The first two tunes he cut were also the first matrices to be assigned a release number by MGM.

Harry Smith Studio, Steinway Hall, New York, N.Y. Wednesday, January 8, 1947
JIMMY DORSEY AND HIS ORCHESTRA
Jimmy Dorsey (cl,as,ldr) Tony Faso, Joe Graves, Irving Goodman, Shorty Solomson (tp) Bob Alexander, Don Matteson, Chauncey Welsch, Fred Mancusi (tb) Norman Stern, Cliff Jackson (as) Vinnie Francis, Gilbert Koerner (ts) Danny Bank (bar) Lou Carter (p) Herb Ellis (g) Johnny Frigo (sb) Karl Kiffe (d) Bob Carroll, Dee Parker (vcl)

47S42   **Heartaches** [John Klenner; Al Hoffman] vBC&DP
               (as solo)
    78: MGM 10001 (Contd.)

JIMMY DORSEY AND HIS ORCHESTRA (Contd.)

      LP: Lion L70063, Ajaz LP305
47S43   **There Is No Greater Love** [Marty Symes; Isham Jones] vBC (as solo)
      78: MGM 10001
      LP: Ajaz LP305
(smaller group from band for next side only:)
47S44   **Pots And Pans** vDP
      78: MGM 10023, (E) 105
      LP: Lion L70063, Ajaz LP305
47S45   **A Sunday Kind Of Love** [Barbara Belle, Anita Leonard, Stan Rhodes] vDP (as solo)
      78: MGM 10023, (E) 105
      LP: Lion L70063, Ajaz LP305

Broadcast schedule: Thursdays, Jan. 9, 16, 23, CBS [WCBS], 12:30-1:00 A.M.

The attendance figures for Jimmy's stay at the Pennsylvania were being watched closely to see if the hotel would drop its name band policy. The drawing power of the big bands had been falling steadily since the war ended, and other New York hotels were already cutting back. But Jimmy did well for the hotel, as did Frankie Carle who followed.

Also during the Pennsylvania engagement, Jimmy and Tommy recorded another example of their closer relationship. The Dorsey Concerto, written by Leo Shuken and used in *The Fabulous Dorseys,* would soon also be performed in concert in Indianapolis, Indiana. Apparently, Jimmy's contract with MGM allowed the Victor recording.

Victor, New York, N.Y. Wednesday, January 29, 1947
VICTOR STUDIO ORCHESTRA
Louis Forbes (ldr) Tommy Dorsey (tb) **Jimmy Dorsey** (cl,as) other personnel unknown, although some sources say it includes members of both Dorsey orchestras

D7VC 6902   **The Dorsey Concerto** [Leo Shuken] (part 1)(as solos)
      78: Victor 46-0009, test pressing also exists
D7VC 6903   **The Dorsey Concerto** (part two) (cl solos)
      78: Victor 46-0009, test pressing also exists

Broadcast schedule (Cafe Rouge): Thursday, Jan. 30, CBS [WCBS] 12:30-1:00 A.M. / Thursday, Feb. 6, CBS [WCBS] 12:30-1:00 A.M.

Travel itinerary: Sun., Feb. 9—Ritz Ballroom, Bridgeport, Conn.

Taking a belated cue from brother Tommy, Jimmy began casting about for other related sources of revenue. He reactivated his ASCAP publishing firm, Harmony Music, which included "¿Quien Sabe?", "Apache Serenade" and "Language of Love" in its roster.

During the sojourn at the Pennsylvania Hotel, Jimmy was away from the bandstand for several days under a doctor's care for exhaustion. The doctor ordered a three-week vacation for Jimmy before he went into the

RKO Boston theater (*Down Beat*, February 12, 1947, 3).

Part of that "vacation" involved a visit to Harrisburg, Pennsylvania, the state capital, where he and Tommy took part in the official premiere of *The Fabulous Dorseys* at Loew's Regent Theater, Wednesday, February 26. The next seven days across Pennsylvania had been designated "Dorsey week" in the film's honor.

As another part of the promotion for the film, the Dorseys' former boss Paul Whiteman featured a two-way remote pickup from the Harrisburg stage as part of his weekly Wednesday radio show on ABC.

Travel itinerary: Fri., Mar. 7, to Thurs., Mar. 13—RKO Boston Theater, Boston, Mass. / Fri., Mar. 14, to Sun., Mar. 16—State Theater, Hartford, Conn.

Jimmy and the band opened a four-week stand at the New York Paramount Wednesday, March 26, with fellow sax player Louis Jordan.

Harry Smith Studio, Steinway Hall, New York, N.Y. April 1947
JIMMY DORSEY AND HIS ORCHESTRA
Kenny Dehlin (as) replaces Stern, Jimmy Giuffre (ts) replaces Francis, Danny Bank (bar) adds (fl), Al Haig (p) replaces Carter, Steve Jordan (g) replaces Ellis, Barney Spieler (sb) replaces Frigo

47S58   **Angela Mia (My Angel)** [Lew Pollack; Erno Rapee] vBC (as solo)
     78: MGM 10316
     45: MGM K11739
     LP: Lion L70063, Ajaz LP305
47S59   **At Sundown** [Walter Donaldson] vDP (as solo)
     78: MGM 10316
     LP: Lion L70063, Ajaz LP313
47S60   **¿Quien Sabe? (Who Knows?)** [Jimmy O'Keefe, Jack Fulton, Dick Conliffe] vBC&DP
     78: MGM 10010
     ET: AFRS Basic Music Library 2392
     45: MGM K11230
     LP: Lion L70063, Ajaz LP305
47S61   **Time After Time** [Sammy Cahn; Jule Styne] vBC (as solo)
     78: MGM 10010
     LP: Ajaz LP305

When the Paramount Theater booking ended April 29, the band played the following weekend at the Terrace Room in Newark, New Jersey, and then Jimmy put the band on a five-week layoff. This led to trade press assertions that Jimmy was following the trend of other bands to further cut high payroll costs during May and June, coming back with a lower pay scale in summer when bands were still in big demand.

Harry Smith Studio, Steinway Hall, New York, N.Y. Early June 1947
JIMMY DORSEY AND HIS ORCHESTRA
Bill Lawrence, Dee Parker, Bob Carroll (vcl)

JIMMY DORSEY AND HIS ORCHESTRA (Contd.)

47S127   **Easy To Love** [Cole Porter] vBL (as solo)
    LP: Lion L70063, Ajaz LP313
47S128   **(Love's Got Me In A) Lazy Mood** [Johnny Mercer;
    Eddie Miller] vDP (as solo)
    78: MGM 10035, (E) 134
    LP: Ajaz LP305
47S129   **Ballerina** [Rob Russell, Carl Sigman] vBC (as solo)
    78: MGM 10035, (E) 134
    45: MGM K11739
    LP: Lion L70063, Ajaz LP305
47S130   **I Laughed At Love** (unissued)

Travel itinerary: Fri., June 13—unknown, Richmond, Va. / Sat., June 14, to Fri., June 20—Surf Club, Virginia Beach, Va. / Sun., June 22—Pleasure Beach Ballroom, Bridgeport, Conn. / Sat., June 28, to Sun., July 6—Steel Pier, Atlantic City, N.J.

                sustaining broadcast, Steel Pier, Atlantic City, N.J.—June 28, 29 or 30, 1947
JIMMY DORSEY AND HIS ORCHESTRA
Skylarks (George Becker, Harry Gedicke, Gilda Meaken, Jimmy Raffody, Harry Schuman) (vcl grp) added

    Contrasts [Jimmy Dorsey] (theme) (as solo) / **Green Eyes** [N. Menendez, E. Rivera, Eddie Woods, A. Utera] vDP&BC (as solo) / **Peg O' My Heart** [Alfred Bryan; Fred Fisher] vS / **At Sundown** [Walter Donaldson] vDP (as solo) / **¿Quien Sabe? (Who Knows?)** [Jimmy O'Keefe, Jack Fulton, Dick Conliffe] vDP&BC / **Parade Of The Milk Bottle Caps** [Pat McCarthy, Jimmy Dorsey] (as solo) / **A Sunday Kind Of Love** [Barbara Belle, Anita Leonard, Stan Rhodes] vDP (as solo) / **Linda** [Jack Lawrence] vBC / **Heartaches** [John Klenner; Al Hoffman] vDP&BC (as solo) / **Walkin' My Baby Back Home** [Roy Turk; Fred Ahlert] / **Contrasts** (theme)
    Entire broadcast on **ET:** AFRS One Night Stand 1430; "Parade Of The Milk Bottle Caps" on **LP:** First Heard (E) FH-4, FH-19

    The Skylarks vocal group was renamed from The Blue Moods, Woody Herman's former vocal quintet that switched to Jimmy after Woody folded his band.   AFRS also used a portion of the previous broadcast for a quarter-hour *Magic Carpet* program:

    Green Eyes [N. Menendez, E. Rivera, Eddie Woods, A. Utera] vDP&BC (as solo) / **Peg O'My Heart** [Alfred Bryan; Fred Fisher] vS / **At Sundown** [Walter Donaldson] vDP (as solo) / **¿Quien Sabe? (Who Knows?)** [Jimmy O'Keefe, Jack Fulton, Dick Conliffe] vDP&BC
    Entire broadcast on **ET:** AFRS Magic Carpet 837; "At Sundown" on **LP:** First Heard (E) FH-19

                sustaining broadcast, Steel Pier, Atlantic City, N.J.—June 28, 29 or 30, 1947

JIMMY DORSEY AND HIS ORCHESTRA

It's A Happy Mood (cl solo) / Ain't Misbehavin' [Andy Razaf; Thomas "Fats" Waller, Harry Brooks] vDP / The Whole World Is Singing My Song vBC / Parade Of The Milk Bottle Caps [Pat McCarthy, Jimmy Dorsey] (as solo)
Entire broadcast on ET: AFRS Magic Carpet 842; "It's A Happy Mood" on LP: First Heard (E) FH-19

Travel itinerary: Tues., July 8, to Tues., July 15—Convention Hall, Asbury Park, N.J. / Fri., July 25, to Thurs., July 31—Cedar Point Ballroom, Sandusky, Ohio / Fri., Aug. 22, to Thurs., Aug. 28—Lakeside Ballroom, Denver, Col. / Sun., Aug. 31—Jerry Jones' Rainbow Randevu, Salt Lake City, Utah.

Jimmy parted from General Artists Corporation on September 29, and asked the Mus-Art agency to set up a string of West Coast one-nighters to follow the Palladium stand, which ran from Friday, September 12, to Sunday, October 12 (*Billboard,* September 6, 1947, 34). Jimmy's contract at the Palladium called for $4,500 a week, and half of all gate receipts over $13,500 (*Variety*, September 29, 1947, 39).

sustaining broadcast, Hollywood Palladium, Hollywood, Cal.—Friday, September 19, 1947
JIMMY DORSEY AND HIS ORCHESTRA
John Martel (tp) added, Harry Nemo (vcl) added to The Skylarks (vcl grp)

Contrasts [Jimmy Dorsey] (as solo) / What Is This Thing Called Love? [Cole Porter] vHN&S/ As Long As I'm Dreaming [Johnny Burke; Jimmy Van Heusen] vBL / Old Devil Moon [E. Y. Harburg; Burton Lane] vDP / Easy To Love [Cole Porter] vBL (as solo) / Parade Of The Milk Bottle Caps [Pat McCarthy, Jimmy Dorsey] (as solo) / Man With A Horn [Eddie DeLange; Bonnie Lake, Jack Jenney] / Night And Day [Cole Porter] vHN&S / Green Eyes [N. Menendez, E. Rivera, Eddie Woods, A. Utera] vBL&DP (as solo)
Entire broadcast on ET: AFRS One Night Stand 1515

sustaining broadcast, Hollywood Palladium, Hollywood, Cal.—Saturday, September 20, 1947
JIMMY DORSEY AND HIS ORCHESTRA

At Sundown [Walter Donaldson] vDP (as solo) / East Of The Sun (And West Of The Moon) [Brooks Bowman] vHN&S / Perfidia [Milton Leeds; Alberto Domingo] (as solo) / Easy To Love [Cole Porter] vBL (as solo) / What Is This Thing Called Love? [Cole Porter] vHN&S / Sunset Strip [Sonny Burke, Jimmy Dorsey] (cl,as solos) / Green Eyes [N. Menendez, E. Rivera, Eddie Woods, A. Utera] vBL&DP (as solo) / Man With A Horn [Eddie DeLange; Bonnie Lake, Jack Jenney]
Entire broadcast on ET: AFRS One Night Stand 1497; "Perfidia" on LP: First Heard (E) FH-19, TC: Hindsight MCH415TC, CD: Hindsight HCD415

sustaining broadcast, Hollywood Palladium, Hollywood, Cal.—September 1947
JIMMY DORSEY AND HIS ORCHESTRA

Contrasts [Jimmy Dorsey] (theme) (as solo) / **My Heart Is A Hobo** [Johnny Burke; Jimmy Van Heusen] vDP / **(Love's Got Me In A) Lazy Mood** [Johnny Mercer; Eddie Miller] vDP (as solo) / **Easy To Love** [Cole Porter] vBL (as solo) / **Parade Of The Milk Bottle Caps** [Pat McCarthy, Jimmy Dorsey] (as solo) / **At Sundown** [Walter Donaldson] vDP (as solo) / **Green Eyes** [N. Menendez, E. Rivera, Eddie Woods, A. Utera] vBL&DP (as solo) / **Pots And Pans** vDP / **To Me** [Don George; Allie Wrubel] vBL
   Entire broadcast on ET: AFRS One Night Stand 1503; "My Heart Is A Hobo," "Lazy Mood," "Easy To Love" and "Parade Of The Milk Bottle Caps" on LP: Joyce LP1048

sustaining broadcast, Hollywood Palladium, Hollywood, Cal.—September 1947
JIMMY DORSEY AND HIS ORCHESTRA

Contrasts [Jimmy Dorsey] (as solo) / **New York, New Haven And Hartford** vS / **Maria Elena** [S. K. (Bob) Russell; Lorenzo Barcelata] vBL (as solo) / **Old Devil Moon** [E. Y. Harburg; Burton Lane] vDP / **Peg O' My Heart** [Alfred Bryan; Fred Fisher] vS / **Perfidia** [Milton Leeds; Alberto Domingo] (as solo) / **Lover** [Lorenz Hart; Richard Rodgers] arrSB (as solo) / **(Love's Got Me In A) Lazy Mood** [Johnny Mercer; Eddie Miller] vDP (as solo) / **Blue Champagne** [Jimmy Eaton, Grady Watts, Frank Ryerson] vBL (as solo)
   Entire broadcast on ET: AFRS One Night Stand 1509

MGM, Hollywood, Cal. late September/early October 1947
JIMMY DORSEY AND HIS ORCHESTRA
Cliff Jackson (as) replaces Dehling, Al Pelligrini (ts) for Giuffre, Barrett Deems (d) for Kiffe. Dee Parker, Bill Lawrence, Skylarks (vcl)

47S3167   **On Green Dolphin Street** [Ned Washington; Bronislaw Kaper] vBL (as solo)
   78: MGM 10098
   LP: Lion L70063, Ajaz LP305
47S3168   **Moon Over Miami** [Edgar Leslie; Joe Burke] vBL&S (as solo)
   78: MGM 11230
   ET: AFRS Basic Music Library 2392
   LP: Lion L70063, Ajaz LP313
47S3169   **Three O'Clock In The Morning** [Dorothy Terris; Julian Robledo] vDP,BL,HN&S
   78: MGM 10143, (E) C990
   LP: MGM SE4219, Lion L70063, Ajaz LP313
47S3170   **I Still Get Jealous** [Sammy Kahn; Jule Styne] vBL&DP (as solo)
   78: MGM 10098
   LP: Ajaz LP305

On Sunday, November 9, Jimmy and Tommy, who had reformed his band into a smaller unit, were appearing at the same time in Indianapolis, Indiana. Tommy was ending a week at the Circle Theater and Jimmy was doing a one-nighter at the Indiana Roof Ballroom (Sanford 1972, 218).

While there they signed to appear with the Indianapolis Symphony in January 1948 for a benefit performance of "The Dorsey Concerto."

Travel itinerary: Tues., Nov. 11—Tune Town Ballroom, St. Louis, Mo. / Thurs., Nov. 27, to Wed., Dec. 3—National Theater, Louisville, Ky.

The large number of sides recorded next is caused by the December 31 deadline for the second strike of the forties by the American Federation of Musicians against radio networks and recording and transcription services.

Harry Smith Studio, Steinway Hall, New York, N.Y.   Wednesday, December 10, 1947
JIMMY DORSEY AND HIS ORCHESTRA
Carol Scott (vcl) replaces Parker

47S631   **You Turned The Tables On Me** [Sidney D. Mitchell; Louis Alter] vCS (as solo)
    78: MGM 10162
47S632   **My Guitar** vBL (as solo)
    78: MGM 10162
47S633   **Azusa, Cucamonga and Anaheim** vS (as solo)
    78: MGM 10245
47S634   **Lilette** [Jack Gold] vBL&S (as solo)
    78: MGM 10245
47S635   **Confess** [Bennie Benjamin, George David Weiss] vBL, CS&S (as solo)
    78: MGM 10194
47S636   **If I Were You** vBL&S (as solo)
    78: MGM 10194
    LP: Lion70063
47S637   **I Don't Have To Tell Nobody** (unissued)
47S638   **If I Only Had A Match** [Lee Morris, Arthur Johnston, George W. Meyer] vBL (cl solo)
    78: MGM 10143
    All issued sides also on **LP:** Ajaz LP313
47S639   **The Frog** (unissued)

Travel itinerary: Mon., Dec. 15, to Wed., Dec. 17—Palace Theater, Columbus, Ohio / Fri., Dec. 19—University of Akron, Akron, Ohio / Sat., Dec. 20—Inter-Fraternity Ball, University of Pittsburgh, Pittsburgh, Pa.

The Pittsburgh college date became a legal issue for Jimmy in January 1948 when the college held back $1,250 of the $2,500 payment on the grounds that the band was not attired in tuxedos and played too much uptempo music for the ball.

Pending settlement of the argument the musicians' union placed the college on its "unfair list," blocking it from future bookings of union bands.

While this dispute was going on, Jimmy disbanded for the second time in less than a year and returned to his Toluca Lake, California, home. *Down Beat* (December 31, 1947, 6) implied that Jimmy was exhausted from a cross-country tour and wanted to spend time with his family over the Christmas holidays. The paper quoted sources as saying he would spend at least eight weeks resting.

In all probability part of Jimmy's time off was planned to attempt some "fence mending" with his wife Jane. By 1947 their marriage was in serious trouble and both reportedly had drinking problems.

Billboard (December 13, 1947, 19) also revealed Jimmy was giving up nine weeks of bookings worth about $85,000, including a two-week stay at the Ansley Hotel in Atlanta, Georgia, and a series of theater dates in Reading, Pennsylvania; Holyoke, Massachusetts; Providence, Rhode Island; Hartford, Connecticut; and Baltimore, Maryland, as a result.

During his "vacation," Jimmy returned to Indianapolis, along with brother Tommy and Tommy's band, for the benefit performance for the Symphony Pension Fund. The brothers along with Tommy's band joined the Indianapolis Symphony under the baton of Fabian Sevitsky at the Murat Theater in the Indiana city on Monday, January 26.

Selections performed included the "Dorsey Concerto" by Leo Shuken and a new composition, "The Quest," by Roy Harris, who was by then a noted classical composer. Harris had played with Tommy and Jimmy as teenagers at the Flagstaff near Mauch Chunk, Pennsylvania.

The audience of 1,800 was also treated to Tommy's playing of "Sleepy Lagoon" with the symphony combined with his own band, Jimmy's trademark performance of "Fingerbustin'" on alto and clarinet, and the two brothers "sitting in" with the symphony on the "1812 Overture," "Stars And Stripes Forever" and "Tales From The Vienna Woods."

Returning to Hollywood, Jimmy eventually assembled another band, mostly for movie work, plus a few West Coast one-nighters, and tried to get back up on the "bandwagon." But by now the big-band business was, at best, slim pickings.

During the reorganization period, Jimmy was urged by several close associates to revamp his style completely, emphasizing entertainment and comedy. Jimmy was resisting the advice, according to several trade reports. It was also uncertain what new booking agency arrangements he would make.

Also, by this time both Jimmy and wife Jane were increasingly using alcohol as a way to tolerate each other. In his book, Gene Bockey relates how, while he was a house guest, Jimmy's teenage daughter Julie would plead with him not to sneak drinks to her mother while Jimmy was at the movie studios (Bockemuehl 1996).

Jimmy's reorganized band opened Friday, April 9, at Casino Gardens for eight Friday-Saturday weekends, which fit in with the nature of Jimmy's group at the time. He was using Hollywood studio musicians or men who were otherwise tied to southern California and had other jobs as well.

The band included, among others, Charlie Teagarden and Conrad Gozzo (tp), Brad Gowans (tb) and Ray Bauduc (d).

It was also reported that Jimmy was trying to buy up Decca's surplus stock of his old instrumental recordings to distribute free to disk jockeys to promote his reorganized band.

The then current recording ban by the musicians' union was giving Jimmy no promotional tools, so he was trying to use his old sides to fill the gap, even considering asking Decca to press some new disks from the old masters (*Variety*, April 18, 1948, 48).

Also, as it later developed, Jimmy was not on good terms with MGM Records over some royalty advances he had received, which may also account for his reluctance to approach MGM.

In the early spring of 1948, Paramount Pictures turned out a seventeen-minute Technicolor featurette titled *Catalina Interlude* with a not-so-original story line about a missing girl singer (Virginia Maxey) who's found singing with Jimmy Dorsey's band on Catalina Island.

Paramount Studios, Hollywood, Cal. Early 1948
CATALINA INTERLUDE (in color): Alvin Ganzer, director
JIMMY DORSEY AND HIS ORCHESTRA
Jimmy Dorsey (cl,as,ldr) Charlie Teagarden, Conrad Gozzo, Everett McDonald (tp) Brad Gowans (vtb) Lloyd Elliot, John Halliburton (tb) Doc Clifford, Al Pelligrini (as) Bill Elliot, Art Lyons (ts) Bob Lawson (bar) Arnold Ross (p) Nappy Lamare (g) Joe Mondragon (sb) Ray Bauduc (d) Virginia Maxey, Male Quartet (vcl)

> **Muskrat Ramble** [Ray Gilbert; Edward "Kid" Ory] *(small group)* (cl solo) / **Hit The Road To Dreamland** [Johnny Mercer; Harold Arlen] vVM *(small group)* / **Perfidia** [Milton Leeds; Alberto Domingo] (cl,as,cl solos) / **Catalina** [Jay Livingston; Ray Evans] vVM&MQ (cl solo) / **My Ideal** [Leo Robin, Newell Chase, Richard A. Whiting] vVM
>
> All titles appear in **FILM:** Paramount *Catalina Interlude*, on **LP:** Joyce LP3005, **VIDEO:** CTV (C) 101094

The year 1948 was also when Jimmy and the band appeared in an equally forgettable sixty-six-minute second-feature, or "B" movie, called *Music Man* (not by any stretch of the imagination to be confused with the Meredith Willson hit that adds "The" to its title).

This one was a musical romance about a successful songwriting team of brothers (Freddie Stewart and Phil Brito) who can't get along with each other (sound familiar?) and who feud over a girl (June Preisser).

It was but another faltering step in the parade of so-so musical features Hollywood seemed to love to make. Because the story line didn't call for much creativity, they could be produced in a week or so of studio time, and the musical numbers meant a nice diversion while the crowd from the main feature cleared the theater.

In its "On The Beat in Hollywood" column, *Down Beat* (June 2, 1948, 8) revealed that, except for solos, part of the big-band soundtrack recording was not done by the Dorsey band members pictured in the film, but rather by studio contract musicians who were behind in the number of hours guaranteed them under their yearly contract.

Monogram Studios, Hollywood, Cal. Late Spring 1948
MUSIC MAN (originally "Manhattan Folk Song"): Will Jason, director
JIMMY DORSEY AND HIS ORCHESTRA
Ernie Felice (acc) added, Freddie Stewart, Phil Brito (vcl)

> (Unknown instrumental) / **The Frog** (as,cl solos) / **Shy Ann (From Old Cheyenne)** vFS / **Hello, Goodbye, Forget It** (cl solo) / Comm'e Bell'a Stagione vPB / **Little Man, You've Had A Busy Day** [Maurice Sigler, Al Hoffman; Mabel Wayne] vFS
> All titles appear in **FILM**: Monogram *Music Man*; first four titles on **VIDEO**: CTV (C) 101094.

While Jimmy and the band appear on screen for "Comm'e Bell'a Stagione" it is the studio band playing, with unseen strings and harp!

Universal Studios, Hollywood Cal. Summer 1948
JIMMY DORSEY AND HIS ORCHESTRA: Will Cowan, director
JIMMY DORSEY AND HIS ORCHESTRA
Dottie O'Brien, Bill Lawrence, The Mello-Larks (vcl)

> **Contrasts** [Jimmy Dorsey] (theme) (as solo) / **Am I Blue?** [Grant Clarke; Harry Akst] vDO / **They Never Sing About This (We Hate Cowboy Songs)** vML / **¿Quien Sabe? (Who Knows?)** [Jimmy O'Keefe, Jack Fulton, Dick Conliffe] vDO&BL (as solo) / **Jamboree Jones** [Johnny Mercer] vML / **Lover** [Lorenz Hart; Richard Rodgers] (as solo)
> All titles in **FILM**: Universal *Jimmy Dorsey And His Orchestra* and **LP**: Joyce LP3005; opening theme, "Am I Blue?", "¿Quien Sabe?" and "Lover" on **VIDEO**: CTV (C) 101094; "Am I Blue?", "They Never Sing About This" and "Lover" on **VIDEO**: MCA: Swing 80668 (Vol. 4)

Jimmy ended his eight-weekend stand at Casino Gardens on Saturday, May 29, and in early June signed again with Tommy Rockwell's General Artists Corporation, this time for a five-year management contract (*Billboard,* June 19, 1948, 17).
    In the next week's issue two items about Jimmy implied that he was all set to take a band out on the road. One noted that he was part of a schedule of bands booked for the summer at the Edgewater Beach resort in San Francisco and the other indicated that he would leave the coast in August for a cross-country tour (*Billboard*, June 26, 1948, 36).

Travel itinerary: Wed., July 14—Trianon Ballroom, Southgate, Cal.

In a 1948 Columbia "B" feature titled *"Make Believe Ballroom,"* released in early 1949, the Jimmy Dorsey band made an appearance and Jimmy was also seen as a featured sideman in a jam session. Among others in the film were Phil Napoleon, Frankie Carle and Gene Krupa.

Columbia Studio, Hollywood, Cal. September 1948
MAKE BELIEVE BALLROOM: director unknown
JIMMY DORSEY AND HIS ORCHESTRA

Hello, Goodbye, Forget It (cl solo)
FILM: *Make Believe Ballroom*, **VIDEO:** CTV (C) 101094

Jimmy Dorsey (cl) Jan Garber (vn) Pee Wee Hunt (tb) Charlie Teagarden (tp) Charlie Barnet (as) Ray Bauduc (d) join for:
Jam Session (including **Joshua Fit The Battle Of Jericho**)
FILM: *Make Believe Ballroom*, **VIDEO:** CTV (C) 101094

Unknown source, Hollywood, Cal., Fall 1948
JIMMY DORSEY AND HIS ORCHESTRA

Prayin' The Blues [Jimmy Dorsey] (cl solo) / **Ooodles Of Noodles** [Jimmy Dorsey] (as solo)
LP: Ajaz LP313

In October Jimmy returned to the New York City area to organize a new band for an extensive nine-month tour of mostly one-nighters in the Northeast, South and Midwest, which had been set up by Tommy Rockwell of General Artists Corporation, with whom Jimmy had reconciled.

Jimmy sent some of the California men by plane to New York, including Charlie Teagarden, Art Lyons, Ray Bauduc, singer Larry Noble and arranger Howard Gibeling.

Others, including road manager Gil Koerner, valve trombonist Brad Gowans and newly hired alto saxist Gene Bockey, drove Jimmy's Buick Roadmaster coast-to-coast (Bockemuehl 1996). The rest of the new band were New York Local 802 members.

JIMMY DORSEY ORCHESTRA (rehearsal, early October 1948)
Gil Koerner (ldr) Charlie Teagarden (tp,vcl) Dick Hoffman, Joe Graves, Max Gussack (tp) George Masso, Herb Winfield, Jr., Al Lorraine (tb) Brad Gowans (vtb) James "Doc" Clifford, Gene Bockey (as) Art Lyons (ts) Phil Cenicola (cl,ts,fl) Mimi LaRocca (bar,cl,bcl) Alvin Waslohn (p,arr) Nappy Lamare (g) Bill Lolatte (sb) Ray Bauduc (d) Larry Noble, Helen Lee (vcl) Howard Gibeling (arr)

After a week of eight-hour-a-day rehearsals under manager Gil Koerner at the Nola Studios on Times Square, Jimmy flew in and ran the band through its paces.

His only dissatisfaction was with the fourth trumpet, and soon a nineteen-year-old from Canada was hired as a replacement for Gussack. His name: Maynard Ferguson.

Jimmy and the band had been scheduled for a week at the Kovakas Club, Washington, D.C., beginning Sunday, October 10, but the date had to be canceled because they weren't ready. The band made its first public appearance at the Arcadia Ballroom on Broadway as part of that venue's twenty-fifth anniversary, Thursday, October 14. Jimmy had played the Arcadia with Ray Miller's band shortly after the ballroom opened.

Also on hand was brother Tommy, who "jammed" so long with his brother he almost missed a broadcast by his band at the Pennsylvania Hotel, twenty blocks away. The next day Jimmy and the band were off on the road trip to end all road trips.

Travel itinerary: Fri., Oct. 15—North Adams, Mass. Armory / Sat., Oct. 16—Lewiston, Maine Arena / Sun., Oct. 17—Valley Arena, Holyoke, Mass. / Mon., Oct. 18—Danceland, Montreal, Que., Canada / Thurs., Oct. 21—Mahanoy City, Pa. / Fri., Oct. 22—University of Pennsylvania, Philadelphia, Pa. / Sat., Oct. 23—Uline Arena, Washington, D.C. (the attendance was about 6,000) / Sun., Oct. 24—Ritz Ballroom, Bridgeport, Conn. / Mon., Oct. 25—Danbury, Conn., Armory.

The band ended October with a five-day stay (Tuesday, October 26 to Saturday, October 30) at the King Phillip Ballroom, Wrentham, Massachusetts.

A week's stay followed (Monday, November 1, through Sunday, November 7) at Club 86 in Geneva, New York, which by 1948 was the only location booking big bands in central New York state.

Then the band crossed through southern Ontario, Canada, for a series of one-night stands:

Travel itinerary: Tues., Nov. 9—Palace Pier, Peterborough, Ont. / Wed., Nov. 10—Toronto, Ont., Arena / Thurs., Nov. 11—Niagara Falls, Ont., Arena / Fri., Nov. 12— London, Ont., Arena.

Finally they came back to the United States on Saturday, November 13, for a booking at the Detroit, Michigan, Armory. Then it was on to the venerable Castle Farms, Cincinnati, Ohio, on Sunday, November 14.

Travel itinerary: Tues., Nov. 16—Murray College Auditorium, Murray, Ky. / Wed., Nov. 17—The Vendome Hotel, Evansville, Ind.

Jimmy and the band were scheduled for two nights at the Armory in Louisville, Kentucky, Thursday and Friday, November 18 and 19. When they arrived, however, they found the Armory locked up, with several hundred patrons standing out front.

The manager insisted that there was no contract, and that the ads that had appeared had been "feelers" to sound out the appeal of the band with Louisville area fans.

While there was no signed contract, Jimmy's business manager, Gil Koerner, said there was a telegram from the manager confirming the concert arrangements.

Louisville musicians' union officers insisted that their local members would refuse to play the Armory until it fulfilled the $1,250 contract. The band did not perform and it is unknown whether or not they were paid.

Billboard (October 30, 1948, 18) revealed that the brothers were looking for a buyer for their Dorsey Brothers Music Corporation, which published under ASCAP. The asking price was $150,000 and the trade paper said the reason for the sale was that Tommy was looking for a capital gains deal.

The schedule being followed by the band vividly pinpoints the change in popularity of not only Jimmy's band but all big bands by 1948. Note the number of one-nighters, covered by bus, that occurred in the "blizzard country" of Minnesota, Wisconsin, Iowa, Nebraska and the Dakotas during the next two months. In the heyday of the early forties Jimmy would have opted for Virginia or the Carolinas instead.

Note also the dearth of "easy-money" bookings. Gone are the long stays at the Pennsylvania or New Yorker. Missing are the five-a-days at the Paramount Theater on percentage. The whole music picture was changing, and not for the better.

As proof, the band had been scheduled (*Billboard,* September 25, 1948, 15) for four weeks in the Panther Room of the Sherman Hotel, after their swing through the East and Ontario. This deal fell through.

Travel itinerary: Sat., Nov. 20—return to Castle Farms, Cincinnati, Ohio / Sun., Nov. 21—Newark Theater, Newark, Ohio / Mon., Nov. 22, to Sat., Nov. 27—Vogue Terrace, Alpine Hotel, McKeesport, Pa. (across the Monongahela River from Pittsburgh) / Mon., Nov. 29—Appleton, Wisc. / Tues., Nov. 30—Nightingale Ballroom, Kaukana, Wisc. / Wed., Dec. 1—Rochester, Minn., Auditorium / Thurs., Dec. 2—Armor Ballroom, Marion, Iowa / Fri., Dec. 3—University of Nebraska, Lincoln, Neb. / Sat., Dec. 4—Frog Hop Ballroom, St. Josephs, Mo. / Sun., Dec. 5—Tomba Ballroom, Sioux City, Iowa (the band was stalled for two hours in a blizzard on the way to this engagement) / Tues., Dec. 7—The Arkota Ballroom, Sioux Falls, S.D. / Thurs., Dec. 9—Tower Ballroom, Pittsburg, Kans. / Fri., Dec. 10—University of Arkansas, Fayetteville, Ark. / Sat., Dec. 11—Pla-Mor Ballroom, Kansas City, Mo. / Sun., Dec. 12—Peony Park, Omaha, Neb. / Tues., Dec. 14—Gladys Ballroom, Montevideo, Minn. / Wed., Dec. 15—Mankato, Minn. / Thurs., Dec. 16—Crystal Ballroom, Fargo, N.D. / Fri., Dec. 17—Prom Ballroom, St. Paul, Minn. / Sat., Dec. 18—Electric Park, Waterloo, Iowa / Sun., Dec. 19—Surf Ballroom, Clear Lake, Iowa / Tues. to Thurs., Dec. 21-23,—Orpheum Theater, Madison, Wisc. / Fri. to Sun., Dec. 24-26—Indiana Roof of the Lincoln Hotel, Indianapolis, Ind. / Mon., Dec. 27— Warehouse, Dyersburg, Tenn. / Tues. to Thurs., Dec. 28-30—Croyden Hotel, Chicago, Ill. / New Year's Eve, Fri., Dec. 31—Rockford, Ill., Armory

On Saturday January 1, 1949, the band played an unknown location in Milwaukee, Wisconsin, then traveled to Columbus, Ohio, where they settled in for a month's stay at the Ionian Room of the Deshler-Wallick Hotel (January 3-29).

Jimmy and the band kicked off a new name-band policy for the hotel and made numerous broadcasts during their Columbus stay. CBS aired them from 12:05-12:30 A.M. Monday through Friday, MBS picked them up Tuesdays at 11:30 P.M. and Saturdays at 6:00 P.M., and WVKO, Columbus, fed the band to the regional Standard network nightly 7:30 to 8:00 P.M. as well as an hour on Saturday afternoons (*Columbus Citizen,* January 7, 1949).

After the closing at the Deshler-Wallick, singer Helen Lee left and the band went to Canton, Ohio, for a Sunday, January 30, date at Myer's Lake Pavilion. Here they took on a new vocalist, Claire Hogan, recently divorced from bandleader Johnny Bothwell, who would become an important part of Jimmy's band for the next two years, soon acquiring the nickname "Shanty."

Another hotel booking was announced and never came to pass. This one was for several weeks at the Peabody Hotel in Memphis, Tennessee, sometime in the spring (*Billboard,* January 15, 1949, 38).

Travel itinerary: Mon., Jan. 31—Mansfield Theater, Mansfield, Ohio / Wed., Feb. 2—unknown location, Hopkinsville, Ky. / Thurs., Feb. 3, to Wed., Feb. 9—The St. Louis Theater, St. Louis, Mo. (stage show included Mel Torme and comedian Jack E.

Leonard) / Thurs., Feb. 10—Armory, Jackson, Tenn. / Fri. and Sat., Feb. 11, 12—Mississippi State University, Starkville, Miss. / Mon., Feb. 14—Harding Gym, Louisiana State University, Baton Rouge, La. / Tues., Feb. 15—Mobile Auditorium, Mobile, Ala. / Wed., Feb. 16—Mustin Beach Club, Pensacola, Fla. / Thurs., Feb. 17—Armory, Selma, Ala. / Fri. and Sat., Feb. 18, 19—Pensacola Naval Air Base, Pensacola, Fla. / Sun., Feb. 20—Mustin Beach Club, Pensacola, Fla. / (the following dates are without Jimmy:) Mon., Feb. 21—Southern Club, Montgomery, Ala. / Tues., Feb. 22—Club Royale, Macon, Ga. / Wed., Feb. 23—Savanah Auditorium, Savanah, Ga. / Thurs., Feb. 24—Columbia Theater, Columbia, S.C. / Fri. and Sat., Feb. 25, 26—University of North Carolina, Raleigh, N.C.

The band performed without Jimmy from February 21 to 26 when he hurriedly flew to Hollywood after a $131,000 February 21 blaze destroyed the Dorseys' Toluca Lake home and severely burned Jimmy's wife Jane about the face, chest and arms.

Jane was rescued from her burning bed by Ben Murphy and his wife Victoria. Murphy, an ex-vaudevillian, had worked as butler for the Dorseys for several years. Jimmy's collection of 19,000 records dating back three decades and valued at $35,000 also melted down in the blaze. Saved from the flames, but suffering smoke damage, was Jimmy's extensive library of manuscripts.

After the southern tour, the band returned to New York for a four-day rest, which gave Jimmy eight days on the coast with Jane. On his return, Jimmy and the band went into the studios before resuming their road tour. The large number of "standards" recorded reflects changing needs of radio stations, which were beginning to use transcriptions more for "fill," relying on the new 45s and LP releases for the "current hits."

Atlas Studios, New York, N.Y. Thursday, March 3, 1949
JIMMY DORSEY AND HIS ORCHESTRA
Jimmy Dorsey (cl,as,ldr) Charlie Teagarden (tp,vcl) Dick Hoffman, Dick Murphy, Joe Graves, Maynard Ferguson (tp) George Masso, Herb Winfield, Jr., Al Lorraine, Chuck Maxon (tb) James "Doc" Clifford, Gene Bockey (as) Frank Maynes (ts) Phil Cenicola (ts,fl) Mimi LaRocca (bar) Al Waslohn (p) Nappy Lamare (g) Bill Lolatte (sb) Ray Bauduc (d) Larry Noble, Claire Hogan (vcl) Neal Hefti, Howard Gibeling, Dizzy Gillespie (arr)

SRR 1790-1   **Stop, Look And Listen** [George and John Van Eps]
          (cl solo)
    ET: Standard X-278
    LP: Hindsight HSR-165
    TC: Ajazz 1551
SRR 1790-1   **Tangerine** [Johnny Mercer; Victor Schertzinger] vCH&
          LN (as solo)
    ET: Standard X-278
    TC: Ajazz 1551
SRR 1790-1   **All Of Me** [Seymour B. Simons, Gerald Marks] vCH
          (as solo)
    ET: Standard X-278
    LP: Hindsight HSR-165
    TC: Ajazz 1554

SRR 1790-1   **On The Alamo** [Gus Kahn; Isham Jones] (as solo)
   ET: Standard X-278
   LP: Hindsight HSR-165
   TC: Hindsight MCH 415TC, Ajazz 1554
   CD: Hindsight HCD-415
SRR 1791-1   **In A Little Spanish Town** [Sam M. Lewis, Joseph
                  Young; Mabel Wayne] arrHG (as solo)
   ET: Standard X-278
   LP: Hindsight HSR-165, Big Band Archives 1203
   TC: Hindsight MCH 415TC, Ajazz 1554
   CD: Hindsight HCD-415
SRR 1791-1   **Out Of Nowhere** [Edward Heyman; Johnny Green]
                  (as solo)
   ET: Standard X-278
   LP: Hindsight HSR-165
   TC: Hindsight MCH 415TC, Ajazz 1554
   CD: Hindsight HCD-415
SRR 1791-1   **Green Eyes** [N. Menendez, E. Rivera, Eddie Woods,
                  A. Utera] vCH&LN(as solo)
   ET: Standard X-278
   TC: Ajazz 1554
SRR 1791-1   **Don't Blame Me** [Dorothy Fields; Jimmy McHugh]
                  vCH&LN
   ET: Standard X-278
   TC: Ajazz 1554

The next day, Friday, March 4, they played the lower of two ball-rooms in the same building at Yale University, New Haven, Connecticut, while the Hal McIntyre band was simultaneously working in an upstairs room (Bockemuehl, 1996).

Travel itinerary: Sat., Mar. 5—Sunnybrook Ballroom, Pottstown, Pa. / Sun., Mar. 6—Baltimore, Md., Armory / Mon., Mar. 7, to Fri., Mar. 11—Click Club, Philadelphia, Pa. / Sat., Mar. 12—Rocky Glen Park, Moosick, Pa. / Tues., Mar. 15—Arcadia Ballroom, Providence, R.I. / Wed., Mar. 16—Boston Theater, Boston, Mass. / Thurs., Mar. 17—unknown location, Kingston, N.Y. / Fri., Mar. 18— Alfred University, Alfred, N.Y. / Sat., Mar. 19—Armory, Jersey City, N.J. / Sun., Mar. 20—Valley Arena, Holyoke, Mass.

During the course of the March tour, Jimmy had his mother for company. *Variety* (April 6, 1949, 47) told its readers that the senior Mrs. Dorsey, now living in a home the brothers had bought her in California, would often get bored, call the sons, hop a plane and join one or the other for a while on their one-nighters.

Next came a welcome four-week booking at the popular Statler (née Pennsylvania) Hotel in New York City, opening Monday, March 21, and replacing Frankie Carle. Jimmy reportedly went on a drinking spree during the Statler stay, drying out for four days in his hotel room (Bockemuehl 1996, 91). Charlie Teagarden conducted and Bobby Hackett filled Teagarden's chair. The affair was glossed over in the trade press as a "hospitalization" stemming from the Toluca Lake fire.

The increasing frequency of these bouts with the bottle was another sign of Jimmy's frustrations with the band business in the postwar era coupled with his knowledge that his marriage was on the rocks.

Also during the New York City stay, Jimmy lost a longtime associate when Jack Kapp, 47, the president of Decca Records, died suddenly from a cerebral hemorrhage on March 25.

sustaining broadcast, Cafe Rouge, Hotel Statler, New York, N.Y.—Monday, March 28, 1949
JIMMY DORSEY AND HIS ORCHESTRA

This Can't Be Love [Lorenz Hart; Richard Rodgers] / **Here I'll Stay** [Alan Jay Lerner; Kurt Weill] vLN / **See Saw** [Neal Hefti] / **Green Eyes** [N. Menendez, E. Rivera, Eddie Woods, A. Utera] vLN&CH (as solo) / **Sing A Song Of Sixpence** (cl solo) / **I Can't Get Started** [Ira Gershwin; Vernon Duke] vCT / **A Little Bird Told Me** [Harvey O. Brooks] vCH / **Body And Soul** [Robert Sour, Edward Heyman, Frank Eyton; Johnny Green] / **Diz Duz Everything** [John Birks (Dizzy) Gillespie]
  Entire broadcast on **ET:** AFRS One Night Stand 1976, **LP:** Joyce LP1048; "This Can't Be Love," "See Saw," "A Little Bird Told Me" and "Body And Soul" on **LP:** Big Band Archives 1216, Jazz Anthology JA-5221, Musicdisc (F) 30JA5221

"Diz Duz Everything" was one of a half-dozen bop-influenced arrangements that Jimmy used at this time, including "Aces Up" and "Seesaw" by Neal Hefti and Howard Gibeling, and Dizzy Gillespie's "Grand Central Getaway." Jimmy wisely turned over the bop alto solos to a much younger Gene Bockey (Bockemuehl, 1996).

sustaining broadcast, Cafe Rouge, Hotel Statler, New York, N.Y.—Thursday, April 7, 1949
JIMMY DORSEY AND HIS ORCHESTRA

Melange / **All Of Me** [Seymour B. Simons, Gerald Marks] vCH (as solo) / **Big Butter And Egg Man** [Percy Venable; Louis Armstrong] vCH&CT (cl solo) / **Here I'll Stay** vLN / **Diz Duz Everything** [John Birks (Dizzy) Gillespie] / **Don't Worry 'Bout Me** [Ted Koehler; Rube Bloom] vCH / **Sing A Song Of Sixpence**
  Entire broadcast on **ET:** AFRS One Night Stand 1952, **LP:** Musicdisc (F) 30JA5221; "Melange," "Big Butter And Egg Man," "Diz Duz Everything" and "Sing A Song Of Sixpence" on **LP:** Big Band Archives 1216, Jazz Anthology JA-5221

A new television program to be called *One Night Stand* was announced about this time (*Billboard,* March 26, 1949, 1). For the proposed half-hour program the producers had already lined up Jimmy Dorsey, Gene Krupa, Count Basie, Charlie Spivak and Woody Herman. Like many another television proposal at the time this one never jelled.

sustaining broadcast, Cafe Rouge, Hotel Statler, New York, N.Y.—Early April 1949

JIMMY DORSEY AND HIS ORCHESTRA

Contrasts [Jimmy Dorsey] (theme) (as solo) / **On The Alamo** [Gus Kahn; Isham Jones] (as solo) / **Stop, Look And Listen** [George and John Van Eps] (cl solo) / **Out Of Nowhere** [Edward Heyman; Johnny Green] (as solo) / **Everywhere You Go** [Larry Shay, Joe Goodwin, Mark Fisher] / **All Of Me** [Seymour B. Simons, Gerald Marks] vCH (as solo) / **In A Little Spanish Town** [Sam M. Lewis, Joseph Young; Mabel Wayne] (as solo)
   All selections on **LP:** Hindsight HSR-165; "On The Alamo," "Out Of Nowhere" and "In A Little Spanish Town" on **TC:** Hindsight MCH-415TC, **CD:** Hindsight HCD-415

On Sunday, April 17, the day after closing at the Statler, Jimmy and company crossed the Hudson to Cedar Grove, New Jersey, for a two-week run at Frank Dailey's bistro, which ran until Sunday, May 1. The band did two network shots each night, three on Saturday and a *Matinee at the Meadowbrook* show on Saturday afternoons as well (Bockemuehl 1996, 81). The times, dates and networks are unknown.

sustaining broadcast, Meadowbrook Ballroom, Cedar Grove, N.J.—Thursday, April 28, 1949
JIMMY DORSEY AND HIS ORCHESTRA
Larry Noble, Claire Hogan, Charlie Teagarden (vcl)

Let's Fall In Love [Ted Koehler; Harold Arlen] / **Always True To You In My Fashion** [Cole Porter] vCH / **Have A Little Sympathy** vLN / **I Can't Get Started** [Ira Gershwin; Vernon Duke] vCT / **Dixie** [Daniel Emmett] / **If I Could Be With You One Hour Tonight** [Henry Creamer; James P. Johnson] vCH / **Here I'll Stay** vLN / **Green Eyes** [N. Menendez, E. Rivera, Eddie Woods, A. Utera] vCH&LN (as solo) / **This Can't Be Love** [Lorenz Hart; Richard Rodgers]
   Entire broadcast on **ET:** AFRS One Night Stand 1996; "Let's Fall In Love" and "I Can't Get Started" on **LP:** Big Band Archives 1216, Jazz Anthology JA-5221, Musicdisc (F) 30JA5221

Atlas Studio, New York, N.Y. Tuesday, May 3, 1949
JIMMY DORSEY AND HIS ORCHESTRA

SRR 1835-1   **Some Enchanted Evening** [Oscar Hammerstein II; Richard Rodgers] vLN
   ET: Standard X-281
SRR 1835-1   **Always True To You In My Fashion** [Cole Porter] vCH
   ET: Standard X-281
SRR 1835-1   **Once And For Always** [Johnny Burke; Jimmy Van Heusen] vLN
   ET: Standard X-281
SRR 1835-1   **Similau** [Harry Coleman, Arden Clar] vCH
   ET: Standard X-281
   All four cuts also on **TC:** Ajazz 1554

In his book (Bockemuehl 1996) Gene Bockey lists a May 4 recording date for Columbia Records, with whom Jimmy had just signed a reported five-year contract. This has to be a tentative date set up in case the musicians' union's commercial recording ban would end, which it didn't. After the May 3 session, it was back on the road:

Travel itinerary: Thurs., May 5—Allentown, Pa. / Fri., May 6—Lehigh University, Bethlehem, Pa. / Sat., May 7—Hershey Park, Hershey, Pa. / Mon., May 9—Danceland Ballroom, Montreal, Que., Canada / Tues., May 10—Latour Arena, Quebec City, Que. / Wed., May 11—Danceland Ballroom, Montreal, Que. / Thurs., May 12—Arena, Lewiston, Me. / Fri. and Sat., May 13, 14—Canobie Lake, Salem, N.H. / Sun. to Sat., May 15-21—King Phillip Ballroom, Wrentham, Mass.

James C. Petrillo's second recording ban ended in late May and Jimmy began his new association with Columbia. The vocal group shown next as well as guitarist Carl Kress were used only in studio work.

Columbia, New York, N.Y. Tuesday, May 24, 1949
JIMMY DORSEY AND HIS ORCHESTRA
Jimmy Dorsey (cl,as,ldr) Charlie Teagarden (tp,vcl) Dick Hoffman, Dick Murphy, Joe Graves, Maynard Ferguson (tp) Herb Winfield, Jr., Al Lorraine, Dick Bellerose (tb) James "Doc" Clifford, Gene Bockey (as) Frank Maynes, Phil Cenicola (ts) Mimi LaRocca (bar) Al Waslohn (p) Carl Kress (g) Bill Lolatte (b) Ray Bauduc (d) Larry Noble, Claire Hogan, Helen Carroll and The Swantones (vcl) Howard Gibeling (arr)

CO40803-1B   **And It Still Goes** [Charles Tobias; Sam H. Stept] vLN,HC&S (cl solo)
    78: Columbia 38523
    45: Columbia I-273
    LP: Ajaz LP313
CO40804-1D   **Fiddle Dee Dee** [Sammy Cahn; Jule Styne] vCH, band (as solo)
    78: Columbia 38523
    45: Columbia I-273
    LP: Ajaz LP313
    TC: Sony BT 28377
    CD: Sony BC 28377

Atlas Studio, New York, N.Y. Wednesday, May 25, 1949
JIMMY DORSEY AND HIS ORCHESTRA

SRR-1836-1   **Contrasts** [Jimmy Dorsey] (theme) (as solo)
    ET: Standard X-281
    LP: Hindsight HSR-165
SRR 1836-1   **"A," You're Adorable (The Alphabet Song)** [Buddy Kaye, Fred Wise] vCH
    ET: Standard X-281
    TC: Ajazz 1554
SRR 1836-1   **Everywhere You Go** [Larry Shay, Joe Goodwin, Mark Fisher] (cl solo)
    ET: Standard X-281

LP: Hindsight HSR-165
TC: Hindsight MCH 415TC, Ajazz 1554
CD: Hindsight HCD-415
SRR 1836-1   **Careless Hands** [Bob Hilliard; Carl Sigman] vCH
ET: Standard X-281
SRR 1836-1   **Bali Ha'i** [Oscar Hammerstein II; Richard Rodgers]
                  vCH (as solo)
ET: Standard X-281

For Memorial Day weekend the band went to The Surf Club, Virginia Beach, Virginia, working Friday, May 27, to Thursday, June 2.

Travel itinerary: Fri. and Sat., June 3, 4—Charlotte Hotel, Charlotte, N.C. / Sun., June 5—Carolina Theater, Durham, N.C. / Tues., June 7—Willon's Warehouse, Fayetteville, N.C. / Wed., June 8—Folly Beach Pier, Charleston, S.C. / Thurs., June 9—Hickory Hotel, Hickory, N.C. / Fri., June 10—New Hicks Hotel, Rocky Mount, N.C. / Sat., June 11—Cape Fear Hotel, Wilmington, N.C. / Mon., June 13—University of Virginia, Charlottesville, Va. / Tues., June 14—Auditorium, Roanoke, Va. / Wed., June 15—Harrisburger Hotel, Harrisburg, Pa. / Thurs., June 16—Lakewood Park, Mahanoy City, Pa. / Fri., June 17—unknown location, Cumberland, Md. / Sat., June 18—Sunnybrook Ballroom, Pottstown, Pa. /Sun., June 19—Rocky Glen Park, Moosick, Pa.

Jimmy's wife Jane wasn't the only Mrs. Dorsey to be involved in a life-threatening event in 1949. Brother Tommy and his third wife, also named Jane, were shaken up, but uninjured, when their land cruiser was rammed by a car near Wahoo, Iowa, on June 15 while they were on their way to a one-nighter. Mrs. TD was hospitalized for a checkup since she was about four months pregnant (*Variety*, June 22, 1949, 39).

At about this same time Leonard Vannerson became Jimmy's personal manager, handling liaison work between Jimmy and General Artists Corporation. An unusual aspect of this appointment was the fact that Vannerson was also Tommy Dorsey's representative on the East Coast. This doubling up, however, was to last only about half a year.

Tuesday night, June 21, the band played at a black nightclub, Regula's Corner, Riverhead, Long Island, New York. Here Jimmy pulled out all the band's jazz charts. He chartered a DC-3 airliner the next day, Wednesday, June 22, to get from Long Island in time for a booking in Saranac Lake, deep in the Adirondack Mountains of upstate New York (Bockemuehl 1996, 41).

Then it was back on the bus and into New England.

Travel itinerary: Thurs., June 23—unknown location, Clairmont, N.H. / Fri., June 24—Carousel Ballroom, Manchester, N.H. / Sat., June 25—The Pier, Old Orchard Beach, Mass. / Sun., June 26—Lake Compounce, Bristol, Conn. / Tues., June 28—Crystal Beach (an Ontario, Canada, amusement park across the Niagara River from Buffalo, N.Y.) / Wed., June 29—Uniontown, Pa. / Fri., July 1—Clarksburg, W.Va. / Sat., July 2—Chesapeake, Md. / Sun., July 3—Ephrata, Pa. / Mon., July 4—Russell's Danceland, Sylvan Beach, N.Y.

After a week's vacation, Jimmy and the band went into the Tower Theater in Philadelphia, Pennsylvania, on Tuesday, July 12, as a one-day tune-up for their debut the next day at New York's Paramount Theater.

The stay at the Paramount was for three weeks (Wednesday, July 13, to Tuesday, August 2) with six shows a day except Mondays, and a late show Saturdays. Also on the bill were Peggy Lee, the Dave Barbour Trio, comedian Georgie Kaye and the dance team, Tip, Tap and Toe.

Following the Paramount engagement, altoist Gene Bockey left to return to college and was replaced by Nino Palotti (Bockemuehl 1996).

Travel Itinerary: Sun., Aug. 21, to Sat., Aug. 27—Fair Grounds, Sioux Falls, Iowa.

Charging mental cruelty (part of the filing included the claim that Jimmy would wake her in the middle of the night to hear his latest recordings), Jimmy's wife Jane successfully ended their twenty-one-year marriage with a settlement giving her the fire-damaged Toluca Lake home, $850 a month, and a quarter of Jimmy's annual earnings over $20,000 (*Down Beat,* September 9, 1949, 8).

On Tuesday, September 13, the band settled in again for several weeks at the Hotel Statler's Cafe Rouge. Just before this, trumpeter Joe Graves and singer Larry Noble left. Graves had an unknown replacement for a while and then Jimmy brought Shorty Sherock back to the band. No male vocalist was added. Their first week at the Statler drew 1,928 patrons, impressive given the status of big bands by 1949.

Several band members have said that Jimmy used the Statler stay and his divorce to reinforce his drinking and that he failed to show up at all on the final night. Charlie Teagarden fronted the band for most of the broadcasts (Bockemuehl, 1996). The stay ended Saturday, October 1.

Also in early October, Leonard Vannerson, who had been representing both Dorsey brothers, was dropped by Tommy.

Travel itinerary: Mon., Oct. 10, to Sun., Oct. 16—Vogue Terrace Ballroom, McKeesport, Pa. / Fri., Oct. 21, to Sun., Oct. 23—State Theater, Hartford, Conn.

In late October Jimmy lost another pair of his key men when lead alto "Doc" Clifford and pianist Al Waslohn turned in their notices. In November Clifford joined the Copacabana show band in New York. Waslohn returned to the band for a brief period in early 1950.

Columbia, New York, N.Y. Tuesday, November 1, 1949
JIMMY DORSEY & HIS ORIGINAL DORSEYLAND JAZZ BAND
Jimmy Dorsey (clldr) Charlie Teagarden (tp,vcl) Cutty Cutshall (tb) Frank Maynes (ts) Dick Carey (p) Carl Kress (g) Bill Lolatte (sb) Ray Bauduc (d) Claire Hogan (vcl)

CO41829-1D   **Johnson Rag** [Guy H. Hall, Henry Kleinhauf] vCH& band (cl solos)
    78: Columbia 38649, (E) DB2671, (C) 1418
    (SSL-2776) **ET:** AFRS Basic Music Library 1482
    45: Columbia I-426, Coronet (Au) KEP054
    LP: Columbia CL-6114, Ajazz LP418
    TC: Sony BT 28377
    CD: Sony BC 28377
CO41830-1A   **Levee Blues** [Alman, Roth] vCT (cl solos)

EP: Columbia B-1950
LP: Columbia CL-608, Ajazz LP418
CO41831-1A   **When You're Smiling (The Whole World Smiles With You)** [Mark Fisher, Joe Goodwin, Larry Shay] (cl solo)
EP: Columbia B-1950
LP: Columbia CL-608, CL-6114, Ajazz LP418
CO41832-1A   **Struttin' With Some Barbecue** [Louis Armstrong, Lillian Hardin Armstrong] (cl solo)
78: Columbia 38655
(SSL-2775) **ET:** AFRS Basic Music Library 1481
EP: Columbia B-196, B-2601
LP: Columbia CL-608, CL-6095, (G) DW5042, Phillips (E) BBL7207 (Eu) B07226, Ajazz LP418

Columbia, New York, N.Y. Saturday, November 12, 1949
JIMMY DORSEY & HIS ORIGINAL DORSEYLAND JAZZ BAND
Dick Carey adds celeste. Charlie Teagarden, Claire Hogan (vcl)

CO41843-1A   **Charley, My Boy** [Gus Kahn; Ted FioRito] vCH,CT& band (as solo)
78: Columbia 38649, (E) DB2671, (C) 1418
(SSL-2776) **ET:** AFRS Basic Music Library 1481
EP: Columbia I-426
LP: Columbia CL-6114, Ajazz LP418
CO41844-1A   **Chimes Blues** [Joseph "King" Oliver] (cl solo)
78: Columbia 38655, (C) 6520
(SSL-2775) **ET:** AFRS Basic Music Library 1481
EP: Columbia B-196
LP: Columbia CL-6095, CL-608, Ajazz LP418
CO41845-1A   **South Rampart Street Parade** [Steve Allen; Ray Bauduc, Bob Haggart] (cl solos)
78: Columbia 38657, (E) DB2671, (C) 6522
(SSL-2776) **ET:** AFRS Basic Music Library 1481
EP: Columbia B-196, B-1950, B-2601, Coronet (Au) KEP054
LP: Columbia CL-608, CL-6095, (E) 33S1026, DB2671, Ajazz LP418
CO41846-1A   **Tin Roof Blues** [Paul Mares, Walter Melrose, Ben Pollack, Mel Stitzel, George Brunies, Leon Roppolo] (cl solo)
78: Columbia 38657, (C) 6522
(SSL-2775) **ET:** AFRS Basic Music Library 1481
EP: Columbia B-196
LP: Columbia CL-608, CL-6095, (E) 33S1026, Ajazz LP418
CO41847   Unknown title (unissued)
CO41848-1A   **The Jazz Me Blues** [Tom Delaney] (cl solo)
78: Columbia 38654, (C) 6519
(SSL-2775) **ET:** AFRS Basic Music Library 1481
EP: Columbia B-196, B-1747
LP: Columbia CL-608, CL-6095, (E) 33S1026, (G) DE5042, Ajazz LP418
All issued sides also in **78:** Columbia Album C-196

Columbia, New York, N.Y. Sunday, November 13, 1949
JIMMY DORSEY & HIS ORIGINAL DORSEYLAND JAZZ BAND

CO41852-1A   **Muskrat Ramble** [Ray Gilbert; Edward "Kid" Ory]
                (cl solo)
    78: Columbia 38656, (E) DB2693, (C) 6521, (Au) DO3645
    (SSL-2776) **ET:** AFRS Basic Music Library 1481
    EP: Columbia B196, B1950, B2601, Coronet (Au) KEP054
    LP: Columbia CL-608, CL-6095, (E) 33S1026, DB2693, Ajazz
    LP418
CO41853-1A   **Panama** [William N. Tyers]
    78: Columbia 38654, (C) 6519
    (SSL-2775) **ET:** AFRS Basic Music Library 1481
    EP: Columbia B196
    LP: Columbia CL-608, CL-6095, (E) 33S1026, Ajazz LP418

Frank Maynes (cl) joins Dorsey (cl), Carl Kress (chimes) added:
CO41854-1B   **High Society** [Clarence Williams; Armond Piron]
                (cl solo)
    78: Columbia 38656, (C) 6521
    (SSL-2775) **ET:** AFRS Basic Music Library 1481
    EP: Columbia B-196, B-2601
    LP: Columbia CL-608, CL-6095, (E) 33S1026, Ajazz LP418
    All sides above also in **78:** Columbia Album C-196
CO41854-2A   **High Society** (cl solo)
    78: Columbia (J) M-513

Columbia, New York, N.Y. Monday, November 14, 1949
JIMMY DORSEY AND HIS ORCHESTRA
Jimmy Dorsey (cl,as,ldr) Charlie Teagarden, Shorty Sherock, Dick
Hoffman, Dick Murphy (tp) Herb Winfield, Jr., Chuck Maxon, Dick
Bellerose (tb) Eddie Caine, Nino Palotti (as) Frank Maynes, Phil
Cenicola (ts) Mimi LaRocca (bar) Dick Carey (p) Carl Kress (g) Bill
Lolatte (b) Ray Bauduc (d) Claire Hogan, Kenny Martin (vcl)

CO41855-1A   **Lost In A Dream** [Edgar Leslie; Rube Bloom] vKM
                (cl solo)
    78: Columbia 38670
    45: Columbia I-449
    LP: Ajazz LP418
    TC: Sony BT 28377
    CD: Sony BC 28377
CO41856-1A   **I'll Hold You (In My Arms Once More)** vCH&KM
    78: Columbia 38670
    45: Columbia I-449
    LP: Ajazz LP418

Variety (November 23, 1949, 46) said that Jimmy had a string of one-
nighters in December in the Chicago area. No other details are known.

The Last Dorsey Decade
(1950-1953)

It is often said that all things change and so it is with popular music. The fifties began with a strange mix of pop vocalists and something called rock 'n roll. The abstract bop jazz style had a few years of prime glory but was beginning to lose its novelty, even though it continues to be a part of jazz today. And the new force in music was the disk jockey.

Top band names no longer included Goodman, James, Herman or Shaw. Instead it was Ralph Flanagan, Ray Anthony, Tex Beneke, Ray McKinley or Stan Kenton. However, the name Dorsey was still there, by whatever means Tommy and Jimmy could muster. Still, the brothers could not have dreamed that this was to be the last Dorsey decade.

By now Jimmy had acquired a new business manager, Janet Tremaine. The band played a return two-week engagement at the Deshler-Wallick Hotel in Columbus, Ohio, from Monday, January 2, to Sunday, January 15, 1950, then returned to New York for a Columbia record date and another stand at Hotel Statler.

Columbia, New York, N.Y. Tuesday, January 17, 1950
JIMMY DORSEY & HIS ORIGINAL DORSEYLAND JAZZ BAND
Jimmy Dorsey (cl,as,ldr) Charlie Teagarden (tp) Cutty Cutshall (tb) Frank Maynes (ts) Dick Carey (p) Carl Kress (g) Bill Lolatte (sb) Ray Bauduc (d) Kenny Martin, Claire Hogan (vcl)

CO42650-1D   **Rag Mop** [Johnnie Lee Wells, Deacon Anderson] vCH&band (cl solo)
    78: Columbia 38710, (E) DB2668, (C) 1472
    (SSL-2776) **ET:** AFRS Basic Music Library 1482
    EP: Columbia I-499
    LP: Columbia CL-6114, Ajazz LP427
    TC: Sony BT 28377
    CD: Sony BC 28377
CO42651-1C   **That's A-Plenty** [Lew Pollack] (cl solo)
    78: Columbia 38710, (E) DB2693, (Au) DO3645, (C) 1472
    (SSL-2776) **ET:** AFRS Basic Music Library 1482
    EP: Columbia I-499, (Au) KEP054
    LP: Columbia CL-608, CL-6114, Coronet (Au) KEP054, Ajazz LP427
CO42652-1A   **When You Wore A Tulip (And I Wore A Big Red Rose)** [Jack Mahoney; Percy Wenrich] vKM&band (cl solo)
    78: Columbia 38731
    EP: Columbia I-554
    LP: Columbia CL-6114, Ajazz LP427 (Contd.)

JIMMY DORSEY ORIG. DORSEYLAND JAZZ BAND (Contd.)

CO42653-1A   **Clap Hands! Here Comes Charley!** [Billy Rose,
                    Ballard MacDonald; Joseph Meyer] vCH (cl solo)
     78: Columbia 38731
     EP: Columbia I-554
     LP: Columbia CL-6114, Ajazz LP427

It should be pointed out that Cutty Cutshall and Carl Kress only
worked the Jazz Band recording sessions.
Billboard (December 24, 1949, 20) had reported that the band would
start a four-week stay at the Hotel Statler on Monday, January 23,
replacing Frankie Carle; then (January 28, 1950, 16) reset the opening
to Saturday, February 4. *Down Beat* (January 27, 1950, 8) and *Variety*
(December 14, 1949, 46) set the opening as Monday, February 6. The
last date is the more probable, based on the hotel's normal cycle.
     Pianist Al Waslohn sat in with the band in early February, as
confirmed by Jimmy on the next broadcast. Pianist Joe Rotundi was
Dick Carey's temporary full-band replacement.

                    sustaining broadcast, Hotel Statler (Pennsylvania),
                    New York, N.Y.—11:30-12:00 P.M. Tuesday, Feb-
                    ruary 7, 1950
JIMMY DORSEY AND HIS ORCHESTRA
Jimmy Dorsey (cl,as,ldr) Charlie Teagarden (tp,vcl) Dick Hoffman,
Dick Murphy, Shorty Sherock (tp) Dick Bellerose, Bob Hackman, Frank
Re-hak (tb) Eddie Caine, Nino Palotti (as) Frank Maynes, Phil Cenicola
(ts) Mimi LaRocca (bar) Joe Rotundi (p) Bill Lolatte (sb) Ray Bauduc
(d) Claire Hogan, Kenny Martin (vcl) Howard Gibeling (arr)
***Jimmy Dorsey and His Original Dorseyland Jazz Band**
Dorsey, Teagarden, Hackman, Maynes, Lolatte, Bauduc, Al Waslohn (p)

     Contrasts [Jimmy Dorsey] (theme) (as solo) / **The Moon Of
     Monakoora** [Frank Loesser; Alfred Newman] (as solo) / **Did I
     Remember?** [Harold Adamson; Walter Donaldson] (cl solo) / ***John-
     son Rag** [Guy H. Hall, Henry Kleinhauf] (cl solo) / **I Don't Know
     Why** [Roy Turk; Fred E. Ahlert] vCH&KM (as solo) / ***Muskrat
     Ramble** [Ray Gilbert; Edward "Kid" Ory] (cl solo) / **I'll Hold You
     (In My Arms Once More)** vKM&CH (as solo) / **McGee's Closet** (cl
     solo)
          entire show on **ET:** AFRS One Night Stand 2180; "The Moon Of
          Monakoora" and "I Don't Know Why" on **LP:** Golden Era GE-
          15011; "I Don't Know Why" on **TC:** LaserLight 79-759, **CD:**
          LaserLight 15-759; "Muskrat Ramble" on **LP:** Swing House (E)
          SWH-22; "McGee's Closet" on **LP:** Big Band Archives 1216, Jazz
          Anthology (F) 5221, Joyce 1127

     That same night, the *Billboard* reviewer was on hand and cited "Dixie
By Dorsey" as paving the way for Jimmy to reclaim his right to be at the
top among bands. The review also praised the well-balanced book of
arrangements used by the band. Another more extended review by John
Wilson (*Down Beat,* March 24, 1950, 3) had even more compliments,

saying Jimmy had returned to the ranks of the top bands, on the strength not only of his Dixieland features but also the band's great improvement in all departments. Wilson commented that Jimmy's own playing was more relaxed than it had been since the Dorsey Brothers days.

In February, Jimmy landed a weekly half-hour show on CBS-Radio, Saturdays from 5:00-5:30 P.M. Titled *The Jimmy Dorsey Show*, it was a sustainer with public service spots for the U.S. Treasury Department. The format highlighted Jimmy's Dixieland arrangements, with songs by Charlie Teagarden, Claire Hogan and Kenny Martin.

Broadcast schedule (all Cafe Rouge except Bill Stern Show): Tues., Feb. 14, CBS [WCBS], 12:30-1:00 A.M. / *The Jimmy Dorsey Show* Sat., Feb. 18, CBS [WCBS], 5:00-5:30 P.M. / Tues., Feb. 21, CBS [WCBS], 12:30-1:00 A.M. / Fri., Feb. 24 (with Jimmy only), *Bill Stern Show,* NBC-Radio [WNBC], 10:30-10:45 P.M. / *The Jimmy Dorsey Show,* Sat., Feb. 25, CBS [WCBS], 5:00-5:30 A.M. / Tues., Feb. 28, CBS [WCBS], 12:30-1:00 A.M.

A note in *Variety* (February 22, 1950, 45) indicated that the original four weeks at the Statler was possibly being extended through April 29.

sustaining broadcast(s), Hotel Statler (Pennsylvania), New York, N.Y.—February 1950
JIMMY DORSEY AND HIS ORCHESTRA

Tangerine [Johnny Mercer; Victor Schertzinger] vKM&CH (as solo) / **Green Eyes** [N. Menendez, E. Rivera, Eddie Woods, A. Utera] vKM&CH (as solo)
Both tunes on **TC:** Hindsight HSC-415, **CD:** Hindsight HCD-415

Columbia, New York, N.Y. Tuesday, March 7, 1950
JIMMY DORSEY & HIS ORIGINAL DORSEYLAND JAZZ BAND
Jimmy Dorsey (cl,as,ldr) Charlie Teagarden (tp,vcl) Cutty Cutshall (tb) Frank Maynes (ts) Dick Carey (p) Carl Kress (g) Bill Lolatte (sb) Ray Bauduc (d) Claire Hogan (vcl)

CO42952-1A   **It's A Long Way To Tipperary** [Jack Judge, Harry H. Williams] vCH (as,cl solos)
   78: Columbia 38879
   (SSL-3175) **ET:** AFRS Basic Music Library 1665
   EP: Columbia I-698
   LP: Columbia CL-608, Ajazz LP427
CO42953-1A   **Let A Smile Be Your Umbrella (On A Rainy Day)** [Irving Kahal, Frances Wheeler; Sammy Fain] vCH (as,cl solos)
   78: Columbia 38968
   (SSL-3175) **ET:** AFRS Basic Music Library 1665
   EP: Columbia I-793
   LP: Columbia CL-6114, Ajazz LP427
CO42954-1   **When You're Smiling (The Whole World Smiles With You)** [Mark Fisher, Joe Goodwin, Larry Shay]
   78: Columbia (Arg) 20230
CO42955   **Levee Blues** vCT (unissued)

Broadcast schedule (Cafe Rouge): The Jimmy Dorsey Show, Sat., Mar. 4, 11, 18, CBS
[WCBS], 5:00-5:30 P.M.

Jimmy also made headlines in March and April with some legal
problems. A suit, which had been brought by William G. Toney, a
Richmond, Virginia, milkman alleging that Jimmy struck him, was
dismissed. *Down Beat* (March 10, 1950, 1) reported that the milkman
claimed Jimmy struck him in the head with his clarinet after he asked
him if he was Tommy Dorsey's brother.

In other legal developments *Billboard* (April 1, 1950, 13) reported
that Loew's, Inc., and MGM Records had sought to attach Jimmy's pay-
ments from the Statler as part of a disagreement over $15,000 in royalty
advances allegedly made in 1946 and 1947. In seeking the attachment,
MGM said that Jimmy was a resident of California and the lien would
secure funds. Jimmy contended that he had not been a resident of
California since his June 1949 divorce and an attachment would leave
him unable to pay his band. New York State Supreme Court Justice
Morris Eder granted Jimmy's motion and set aside the attachment.

Travel itinerary: Sat., Apr. 8, and Sun., Apr. 9—Steel Pier, Atlantic City, N.J.

Claire "Shanty" Hogan left the band in April to go out on her own.
Despite her newly signed contract for singles with London Records,
Claire did make one more recording for Jimmy. Pat O'Connor was
signed by Jimmy for club dates, hotel and other band jobs but didn't
immediately make the recording sessions.

At the same time John Hall, Sammy Kaye's road manager, left Kaye
and joined Jimmy in the same capacity.

Columbia, New York, N.Y. Wednesday, May 17, 1950
JIMMY DORSEY AND HIS ORCHESTRA
Jimmy Dorsey (cl,as,ldr) Charlie Teagarden, Shorty Sherock, Dick
Hoffman, Dick Murphy (tp) Frank Rehak, Bob Hackman, Dick
Bellerose (tb) Ben Fussell, Nino Palotti (as) Frank Maynes, Phil
Cenicola (ts) Mimi LaRocca (bar) Dick Carey (p) Carl Kress (g) Bill
Lolatte (sb) Ray Bauduc (d) Claire Hogan, Terry Shand (vcl) Howard
Gibeling (arr)

CO42999-1A   **Kiss Me** [Redd Evans, Bob Trendler] vCH
     78: Columbia 38774, (C) C1523
     (SSL-3175) **ET:** AFRS Basic Music Library 1665
     EP: Columbia I-594
     LP: Ajazz LP427
CO43000-1A   **You Don't Have To Be A Baby To Cry** [Terry
                    Shand, Bob Merrill] vTS
     78: Columbia 38879
     (SSL-3175) **ET:** AFRS Basic Music Library 1665
     EP: Columbia I-698
     LP: Ajazz LP427
CO43001-1A   **Sweet Georgia Brown** [Maceo Pinkard, Kenneth Ca-
                    sey, Ben Bernie] arrHG (as solo)
     78: Columbia 38774, (C) C1523

(SSL-3175) **ET:** AFRS Basic Music Library 1665
EP: Columbia I-594
LP: Ajazz LP427
TC: Sony BT 28377
CD: Sony BC 28377
CO43002-1A   **In A Little Spanish Town** [Sam M. Lewis, Joseph
                 Young; Mabel Wayne] arrHG (as,cl solos)
78: Columbia 38968
(SSL-3175) **ET:** AFRS Basic Music Library 1665
EP: Columbia I-793
LP: Ajazz LP427

Travel itinerary: Fri., May 26, to Thurs., June 8—Lakeside Park, Denver, Colo. /
Fri., June 23, to Friday, June 30—various air bases in San Antonio, Tex., area / Sun.,
July 2, to Tues., July 4—Monte Carlo Casino, Reynosa, Tamaulipas, Mexico.

Jimmy and the band moved to the outdoor Beach Walk of the
Edgewater Beach Hotel in Chicago, Illinois, on Friday, August 18, for a
month stand, closing Thursday, September 14. After Labor Day the
band moved indoors to the Marine Ballroom.

> *sustaining broadcast,* Beach Walk, Edgewater Beach
> Hotel, Chicago, Ill.—NBC, Sunday, August 20, 1950

JIMMY DORSEY AND HIS ORCHESTRA
Kenny Martin, Pat O'Connor, Charlie Teagarden (vcl)

Contrasts [Jimmy Dorsey] (as solo) / **Sweet Sue (Just You)** [Will J.
Harris; Victor Young] (cl solo) / **You Don't Have To Be A Baby To
Cry** [Terry Shand, Bob Merrill] vKM (as solo) / **Charley My Boy**
[Gus Kahn, Ted FioRito] (cl solo) vPO'C&CT / **Green Eyes** [N.
Menendez, E. Rivera, Eddie Woods, A. Utera] vPO'C&KM (as solo)

> *Saturday Night Dance Date,* Beach Walk, Edgewater
> Beach Hotel, Chicago, Ill.—NBC, Saturday, August
> 26, 1950

JIMMY DORSEY AND HIS ORCHESTRA

Contrasts [Jimmy Dorsey] (as solo) / **Sweet Sue (Just You)** [Will J.
Harris; Victor Young] (cl solo) / **I've Forgotten You** vKM / **The
Answer She Is "Yes," No?** vPO'C (as solo) / **I Don't Know Why**
[Roy Turk; Fred E. Ahlert] vKM&PO'C (as solo) / **Third Man
Theme** [Anton Karas] (cl solo) / **Count Every Star** [Sammy Gallop;
Bruno Coquatrix] vKM (as solo) / **Jazz Me Blues** [Tom Delaney] (cl
solo) **Contrasts**

Columbia, Chicago, Ill. Wednesday, September 6, 1950
JIMMY DORSEY AND HIS ORCHESTRA
Jimmy Dorsey (cl,as,ldr) Charlie Teagarden, Shorty Sherock, Dick
Murphy, Dick Hoffman (tp) Frank Rehak, Ray Diehl, Dick Bellerose
(tb) Ben Fussell, Nino Palotti (as) Art Lyons, Phil Cenicola (ts) Mimi
LaRocca (bar) Bob Carter (p) Earl Backus (g) Bill Lolatte (sb) Karl
Kiffe (d) Pat O'Connor, Kenny Martin (vcl) Howard Gibeling (arr)

JIMMY DORSEY AND HIS ORCHESTRA (Contd.)

CCO 5186-1A   It's The Dreamer In Me [Jimmy Van Heusen, Jimmy
               Dorsey] vKM (cl solo)
    78: Columbia 39035
    (SSL-4070) ET: AFRS Basic Music Library 2018
CCO 5187   Sirrocco vKM arrHG (unissued)

JIMMY DORSEY & HIS ORIGINAL DORSEYLAND JAZZ BAND
Dorsey, Teagarden, Diehl, Carter, Backus, Lolatte, Kiffe

CCO 5188-1A   The Dixieland Band From Santa Claus Land vPO'C
    78: Columbia 39035
    (SSL-4070) ET: AFRS Basic Music Library 2018
    both issued sides also on EP: Columbia I-866, LP: Ajazz LP427

                    sustaining broadcast, Marine Ballroom, Edgewater
                    Beach Hotel, Chicago, Ill.—NBC, 11:30-11:55 P.M.
                    Saturday, September 9, 1950
JIMMY DORSEY AND HIS ORCHESTRA

    Partial contents: I Don't Know Why [Roy Turk; Fred E. Ahlert]
    vKM&PO'C (as solo) / Count Every Star [Sammy Gallop; Bruno
    Coquatrix] vKM (as solo) / Jazz Me Blues [Tom Delaney] (cl solo)

    After their booking at the Edgewater Beach ended, Jimmy and the
    band went on a four-week tour of one-nighters at Midwest ballrooms and
    theaters arranged by General Artists, then returned east for more one-
    nighters including the Ritz Ballroom, Bridgeport, Connecticut, on
    Sunday, October 8, where only 700 customers turned out (*Billboard,*
    October 21, 1950, 18).
    On Monday, October 16, Jimmy and crew returned to the Hotel
    Statler's Cafe Rouge in New York City for a two-month booking.
    That night several bandleaders, including Tommy, made the
    traditional "opening night" visit, and the last set of the night featured
    Jimmy, Tommy, Woody Herman, Bobby Sherwood and the Dixieland
    group swinging out "Muskrat Ramble" and "Honeysuckle Rose."

                    sustaining broadcast, Cafe Rouge, Hotel Statler, New
                    York, N.Y.—Saturday, November 4, 1950
JIMMY DORSEY AND HIS ORCHESTRA

    Goofus [Gus Kahn; Wayne King, William Harold] (as solo) / Where
    Do I Go From You? [Walter Bullock; Allie Wrubel] vPO'C / It's
    The Dreamer In Me [Jimmy Van Heusen, Jimmy Dorsey] vKM (cl
    solo) / I'll Never Be Free [Bennie Benjamin; George David Weiss]
    vPO'C / Baby-O, Baby-O vKM&PO'C (as solo) / Sirrocco vKM
    arrHG / Just Say I Love Her [Martin Kalmanoff, Sam Ward, Jack
    Val, Jimmy Dale] vKM
    ET: AFRS One Night Stand 2332

    Seven unattributed tracks appear on a Hindsight LP. Some say these are from Voice of America ETs but they seem to come from remotes that include on-site announcer introductions.

Wang Wang Blues [George Mueller, Buster Johnson, Henry Busse] (cl solo) / **Manhattan** [Lorenz Hart; Richard Rodgers] (cl solo) / **Busy Signal** (cl solo) / **Sweet Sue (Just You)** [Will J. Harris; Victor Young] (cl solo) / **Perfidia** [Milton Leeds; Alberto Dominguez] (cl solo) / **It's A Wonderful World** [Harold Adamson; Leo Watson, Jan Savitt] (cl solo) / **Undecided** [Sid Robin; Charlie Shavers] (cl solo)
All tunes on **LP:** Hindsight HSR-165

> *sustaining broadcast,* Cafe Rouge, Hotel Statler, New York, N.Y.—Tuesday, November 14, 1950

JIMMY DORSEY AND HIS ORCHESTRA
Mimi LaRocca (vcl) Marvin Wright (arr)

Contrasts [Jimmy Dorsey] (theme) (as solo) / **Nevertheless (I'm In Love With You)** [Bert Kalmar, Harry Ruby] (as solo) / **All My Love** vKM / **Alto-Tude** (arrMW) (as solo) / **It's The Dreamer In Me** [Jimmy Van Heusen, Jimmy Dorsey] vKM (cl solo) / **Can Anyone Explain? (No! No! No!)** [Bennie Benjamin, George David Weiss] vCH (cl solo) / **Everyone Wants To Go To Heaven** vML / **South Rampart Street Parade** [Steve Allen; Ray Bauduc, Bob Haggart] (cl solo) / **Sweet Sue (Just You)** [Will J. Harris; Victor Young] (cl solo)
Entire broadcast on **ET:** AFRS One Night Stand 2372; "Nevertheless" and "Alto-Tude" on **LP:** Big Band Archives 1216, Jazz Anthology (F) 5221, Project 3 PR-2-6036; "Can Anyone Explain" and "Sweet Sue" on **LP:** Golden Era GE-15011, **TC:** LaserLight 79-759, **CD:** LaserLight 15-759

Jimmy's Dixieland popularity prompted the U.S. Marine Corps to "recruit" him for twenty-six transcribed radio programs. Each show opened and closed with the "Marine Hymn" and part of "Contrasts." Jazz Oracle CD 3035, recently released, purports to be from Statler airchecks. The source is actually the following Marine Shows.

> *The U.S. Marine Corps presents The Jimmy Dorsey Show,* unknown studio, New York, N.Y.—November, December 1950

JIMMY DORSEY & HIS ORIGINAL DORSEYLAND JAZZ BAND
Jimmy Dorsey (cl,as,ldr) Charlie Teagarden (tp,vcl) Shorty Sherock (tp) Frank Rehak (tb) Artie Lyons (ts) Bob Carter (p) Bill Lolatte (sb) Karl Kiffe (d) Kenny Martin, Pat O'Connor (vcl)

On Wisconsin [W. T. Purdy] (as solo) / **It's Only A Paper Moon** [E. Y. Harburg, Billy Rose; Harold Arlen] (as solo) / **Charley My Boy** [Gus Kahn, Ted FioRito] vPO'C (cl solo) / **Struttin' With Some Barbecue** [Louis Armstrong, Lillian Hardin Armstrong] (cl,as solos)
All tunes on **ET:** Marine Transcription Program 5; "Charlie My Boy" on **LP:** Swing House (E) SH-22, Hindsight HSR-203, (E) HUK203, **TC:** Hindsight HSC-203

The U.S. Marine Corps presents The Jimmy Dorsey Show, unknown studio, New York, N.Y.—November, December 1950

JIMMY DORSEY & HIS ORIGINAL DORSEYLAND JAZZ BAND
Way Down Yonder In New Orleans [Henry Creamer, Turner Layton] (cl solo) / **Memphis Blues** [William C. Handy] (cl solo) / **Muskrat Ramble** [Ray Gilbert; Edward "Kid" Ory] (cl solo)
   All tunes on **ET:** Marine Transcription Program 6; "Way Down Yonder In New Orleans" on **LP:** Hindsight HSR-203, (E) HUK203, **TC:** Hindsight HSC-203; last two tunes on **LP:** Swing House (E) SH-22

JIMMY DORSEY AND HIS ORCHESTRA
Let's Fall In Love [Ted Koehler; Harold Arlen] (cl solo) / **Green Eyes** [N. Menendez, E. Rivera, Eddie Woods, A. Utera] vKM& PO'C (as solo) / **Third Man Theme** [Anton Karas] (cl solo)
   All tunes on **ET:** Marine Transcription Program 7; "Let's Fall In Love" and "Third Man Theme" on **LP:** Hindsight HSR-178, **TC:** Hindsight HSC-178

JIMMY DORSEY & HIS ORIGINAL DORSEYLAND JAZZ BAND
Stars Fell On Alabama [Mitchell Parish; Frank Perkins] (as solo) / **All My Life** [Sidney Mitchell; Sam H. Stept] vKM / **When You Wore A Tulip (And I Wore A Big Red Rose)** [Jack Mahoney; Percy Wenrich] vKM (cl solo) / **High Society** [Clarence Williams; Armand J. Piron] (cl solo)
   All tunes on **ET:** Marine Transcription Program 8; "Stars Fell On Alabama" on **LP:** Hindsight HSR-203, (E) HUK203, **TC:** Hindsight HSC-203

Down By The Oh-Hi-O [Jack Yellen; Abe Olman] (cl solo) / **Sweet Lorraine** [Mitchell Parish; Cliff Burwell] (as solos) / **Johnson Rag** [Guy H. Hall, Henry Kleinhauf] vPO'C (cl solo) / **Panama** [William N. Tyers] (cl solo)
   All tunes on **ET:** Marine Transcription Program 9; "Sweet Lorraine" on **LP:** Golden Era GE-15082, Swing House(E) SH-22, Hindsight HSR-178, **TC:** Hindsight HSC-178, "Johnson Rag" and "Panama" on **LP:** Swing House (E) SH-22

Carolina Moon [Benny David; Joe Burke] (as,cl solos) / **Embraceable You** [Ira Gershwin; George Gershwin] / **Levee Blues** [Alman, Roth] (cl solo) / **Jazz Me Blues** [Tom Delaney] (cl solo)
   All tunes on **ET:** Marine Transcription Program 10; "Levee Blues" on **LP:** Hindsight HSR-203, (E) HUK203, **TC:** Hindsight HSC-203, "Jazz Me Blues" on **LP:** Swing House (E) SH-22

JIMMY DORSEY AND HIS ORCHESTRA
King Porter Stomp [Ferdinand "Jelly Roll" Morton] (cl solo) / **It's The Dreamer In Me** [Jimmy Van Heusen, Jimmy Dorsey] vKM (cl solo) / **Hello And Good-bye** [Robert Lissauer] (cl solo)
   All tunes on **ET:** Marine Transcription Program 11 and **LP:** Hindsight HSR-178

JIMMY DORSEY & HIS ORIGINAL DORSEYLAND JAZZ BAND

The Sidewalks Of New York [James W. Blake, Charles B. Lawlor] (cl solo) / **It Had To Be You** [Gus Kahn; Isham Jones] (as solo) / **Beale Street Blues** [William C. Handy] (cl solo) / **That's A-Plenty** [Lew Pollack] (cl solo)

All tunes on **ET**: Marine Transcription Program 12; "Beale Street Blues" on **LP**: Swing House (E) SH-22, Hindsight HSR-203, (E) HUK203, **TC**: Hindsight HSC-203; "That's A Plenty" on **LP**: Swing House (E) SH-22

Carry Me Back To Old Virginny [James A. Bland] (cl solo) / **I Didn't Know What Time It Was** [Lorenz Hart; Richard Rodgers] vKM / **Tin Roof Blues** [Paul Mares, Walter Melrose, Ben Pollack, Mel Stitzel, George Brunies, Leon Rappolo] (cl solo) / **That's A-Plenty** [Lew Pollack] (cl solo)

All tunes on **ET**: Marine Transcription Program 13; "I Didn't Know What Time It Was" on **LP**: Hindsight HSR-178; **TC**: Hindsight HSC-178; "That's A Plenty" on **LP**: Hindsight HSR-203, (E) HUK203, **TC**: Hindsight HSC-203

(Back Home Again In) Indiana [Ballard MacDonald; James F. Hanley] (as,cl solos) / **Chimes Blues** [Joseph "King" Oliver] (cl solo) / **South Rampart Street Parade** [Steve Allen; Ray Bauduc, Bob Haggart] (cl solos)

All tunes on **ET**: Marine Transcription Program 14; "Indiana" on **LP**: Hindsight HSR-203, (E) HUK203, **TC**: Hindsight HSC-203

California, Here I Come [Al Jolson, Buddy De Sylva; Joseph Meyer] / **Chimes Blues** [Joseph "King" Oliver] (cl solo) / **Muskrat Ramble** [Ray Gilbert; Edward "Kid" Ory] (cl solo)

All tunes on **ET**: Marine Transcription Program 17; "Muskrat Ramble" on **LP**: Swing House (E) SH-22

Oklahoma! [Oscar Hammerstein II; Richard Rodgers] / **In A Sentimental Mood** [Manny Kurtz, Irving Mills; Duke Ellington] / **Let A Smile Be Your Umbrella** [Irving Kahal, Frances Wheeler; Sammy Fain] vPO'C (as,cl solos) / **Weary Blues** [Artie Mathews]

All tunes on **ET**: Marine Transcription Program 18

Missouri Waltz [J. R. Shannon; Frederick Knight Logan] (as solo) / **I Surrender Dear** [Gordon Clifford; Harry Barris] / **Sugar** [Maceo Pinkard, Sidney D. Mitchell] (as solo) / **High Society** [Clarence Williams; Armand J. Piron] (cl solo)

All tunes on **ET**:Marine Transcription Program 19
Programs 18 and 19 also on **TC**: Ajazz 1520

Jersey Bounce [Bobby Plater, Tiny Bradshaw, Robert B. Wright, Edward Johnson] / **It Had To Be You** [Gus Kahn; Isham Jones] (as solo) / **When You're Smiling (The Whole World Smiles With You)** [Mark Fisher, Joe Goodwin, Larry Shay] (cl solo) / **Struttin' With Some Barbecue** [Louis and Lillian Hardin Armstrong] (cl,as solos)

All tunes on **ET**: Marine Transcription Program 20

The U.S. Marine Corps presents The Jimmy Dorsey Show, unknown studio, New York, N.Y.—November, December 1950

JIMMY DORSEY AND HIS ORCHESTRA
Sweet Sue (Just You) [Will J. Harris; Victor Young] (cl solo) / **Sirrocco** vKM arr HG (cl solo) / **In A Little Spanish Town** [Sam M. Lewis, Joseph Young; Mabel Wayne] (as,cl solos)
All tunes on **ET:** Marine Transcription Program 21

JIMMY DORSEY & HIS ORIGINAL DORSEYLAND JAZZ BAND
My Old Kentucky Home (Old Folks At Home) [Stephen Foster] (as solo) / **Beale Street Blues** [William C. Handy] (cl solo) /**South Rampart Street Parade** [Steve Allen; Ray Bauduc, Bob Haggart] (cl solo)
All tunes on **ET:** Marine Transcription Program 22

Georgia On My Mind (Stewart Gorrell; Hoagy Carmichael] (cl solo) / **Rosetta** [Earl Hines, Henri Woode] (as solo) / **It's A Long Way To Tipperary** [Jack Judge, Harry Williams] vPO'C (as,cl solos) / **Deep In The Heart Of Texas** [June Hershey; Don Swander] (cl solo)
All tunes on **ET:** Marine Transcription Program 23; "Rosetta" on **LP:** Hindsight HSR-203, (E) HUK203, **TC:** Hindsight HSC-203

Mississippi Mud [James Cavanaugh, Harry Barris] (cl solo) / **Who's Sorry Now?** [Bert Kalmar, Harry Ruby; Ted Snyder] (as solo) / **Basin Street Blues** [Alton Glenn Miller; Spencer Williams] / **On Wisconsin** [W. T. Purdy] (as solo)
All tunes on **ET:** Marine Transcription Program 24; "Basin Street Blues" on **LP:** Hindsight HSR-203, (E) HUK203, **TC:** Hindsight HSC-203

JIMMY DORSEY AND HIS ORCHESTRA
This Can't Be Love [Lorenz Hart; Richard Rodgers] (as,cl solos) / **Them There Eyes** [Maceo Pinkard, William Tracey, Dorothy Tauber] vPO'C (as solo) / **Big Butter And Egg Man** [Percy Venable, Louis Armstrong] vPO'C&CT (cl solo)
All tunes on **ET:** Marine Transcription Program 25, **LP:** Hindsight HSR-178, **TC:** Hindsight HSC-178

JIMMY DORSEY & HIS ORIGINAL DORSEYLAND JAZZ BAND
Wolverine Blues [Ferdinand "Jelly Roll" Morton, Benjamin and John Spikes] (cl solo) / **Ain't Misbehavin'** [Irving Razaf; Thomas "Fats" Waller] vPO'C / **Johnson Rag** [Guy H. Hall, Henry Kleinhauf] vPO'C (cl solo) / **Muskrat Ramble** [Ray Gilbert; Edward "Kid" Ory] (cl solo)
All tunes on **ET:** Marine Transcription Program 26, **LP:** Swing House (E) SH-22

The next cuts are probably from programs 1,2,3,4,15 or 16:
Royal Garden Blues [Clarence and Spencer Williams] / **Farewell Blues** [Elmer Schoebel, Paul Mares, Joseph Leon Roppolo] / **Chicago** [Fred Fisher] **Fingerbustin'** [Jimmy Dorsey] / **Lover** [Lorenz Hart; Richard Rodgers] (as solo)

First three tunes on **LP**: Hindsight HSR-203, (E) HUK203, **TC**: Hindsight HSC-203; "Royal Garden Blues" on **LP**: Swing House (E) SH-22; "Fingerbustin'" and "Lover" on **LP**: Hindsight HSR-178, **TC**: Hindsight HSC-178

Jimmy also recorded for the U.S. State Department's *Voice Of America* broadcasts, taping only the music tracks.

> *Department Of State, Voice Of America Popular Dance Series,* unknown studio, New York, N.Y. —November-December 1950

JIMMY DORSEY AND HIS ORCHESTRA
Riley Norris (vcl)

Sweet Sue (Just You) [Will J. Harris; Victor Young] (cl solo) / **Lazy Lady Blues** vRN / **Nevertheless (I'm In Love With You)** [Bert Kalmar, Harry Ruby] (as solo) / **Muskrat Ramble** [Ray Gilbert; Edward "Kid" Ory] (cl solo)
   All tunes on **ET**: Voice Of America Program 13

Baby-O, Baby-O vKM&PO'C (as solo) / **Harbor Lights** [Jimmy Kennedy; Hugh Williams] vPO'C (as solo) / **I've Never Been In Love Before** [Frank Loesser] vKM (as solo) / **By Heck** [L. Wolfe Gilbert; S. R. Henry] (as solo)
   All tunes on **ET**: Voice Of America Program 18

Moonlight On The River [Bud Green] / **Cherokee** [Ray Noble] / **Romance** [Otto Harbach, Oscar Hammerstein II; Sigmund Romberg] / **Julida** (polka) (cl solo)
   All tunes on **ET**: Voice Of America Program 25

Just One Of Those Things [Cole Porter] (as solo) / **Wang Wang Blues** [George Mueller, Buster Johnson, Henry Busse] (cl solo) / **Pretty Eyed Baby** [Mary Lou Williams, William Johnson, Leo Mosley] vRN (cl solo) / **Sweet Georgia Brown** [Maceo Pinkard, Kenneth Casey, Ben Bernie] (as solo)
   All tunes on **ET**: Voice Of America Program 57

Manhattan [Lorenz Hart; Richard Rodgers] (cl solo) / **I'm Glad There Is You** [Paul Madeira; Jimmy Dorsey] vPO'C (as solo) / **Muskrat Ramble** [Ray Gilbert; Edward "Kid" Ory] (cl solo) / **Busy Signal** (cl solo)
   All tunes on **ET**: Voice Of America Program 93; "Manhattan," "Muskrat Ramble" and "Busy Signal" on **LP**: Joyce LP1127, V-Disc (It) VDL1007, **CD**: Suisa Recording Arts JZCD334; "Manhattan" and "Busy Signal" on **LP**: V-Disc (It) VDL1007 "I'm Glad There Is You" on **CD**: Suisa Recording Arts JZCD334

The preceding Suisa CD attributes false V-Disc catalogue numbers to the above cuts, copying similar data from the Italian LP release.
(Contd.)

Voice Of America Popular Dance Series (Contd.)

It's A Wonderful World [Harold Adamson; Leo Watson, Jan Savitt] (cl solo) / **Undecided** [Sid Robin; Charlie Shavers] (cl solo) / **And So To Sleep Again** [Joe Marsala, Sunny Skylar] vSE (as solo) / **Sweet Sue (Just You)** [Will J. Harris; Victor Young] (cl solo)
      All tunes on **ET:** Voice Of America Program 99

Sweet Sue (Just You) [Will J. Harris; Victor Young] (cl solo) / **Did I Remember?** [Harold Adamson, Walter Donaldson] vSE (cl solo) / **I Don't Know Why** [Roy Turk; Fred E. Ahlert] (as solo) / **Struttin' With Some Barbecue** [Louis Armstrong, Lillian Hardin Armstrong] (cl,as solos)
      All tunes on **ET:** Voice Of America Program 148

Wednesday, November 29, kicked off a three-week stand that ended Tuesday, December 19, at Times Square's Paramount Theater where the band did four shows daily (five on Saturday). The headliner was Nat King Cole. Also in the stage show were comedian Mickey Deems and the Tong Brothers dance team. On screen was an exceptionally long feature, *Let's Dance,* with Betty Hutton and Fred Astaire, which necessitated a much shorter than normal stage show.
      The rationale behind the recording of the following unissued side by Jimmy is lacking, but given the title it is certainly intriguing.

Columbia, New York, N.Y. Thursday, December 7, 1950
JIMMY DORSEY AND HIS ORCHESTRA

-0-   **March Of The Slide Trombones** (unissued)

Columbia, New York, N.Y. Monday, December 11, 1950
JIMMY DORSEY AND HIS ORCHESTRA
Jimmy Dorsey (cl,as,ldr) Shorty Sherock, Dick Hoffman, Dick Murphy, Riley Norris (tp) Frank Rehak, Ray Diehl, Dick Bellerose (tb) Doc Clifford, Nino Palotti (as) Art Lyons, Phil Cenicola (ts) Mimi LaRocca (bar) Bob Carter (p) Hy White (g) Bill Lolatte (sb) Karl Kiffe (d) Pat O'Connor, Kenny Martin (vcl) Howard Gibeling (arr)

CO44711-1A   **Just For Tonight** [John Latouche; Bronislaw Kaper] vKM&PO'C
      78: Columbia 39258
      (SSL-4070) **ET:** AFRS Basic Music Library 2018
      LP: Ajazz LP427
CO44712-1A   **Lily Of The Valley** vPO'C
      78: Columbia 39138
      78: Ajazz LP427
CO44713-1A   **By Heck** [L. Wolfe Gilbert; S. R. Henry] arrHG
              (as solo)
      78: Columbia 39138

The next three sessions further indicate the decline in the fortunes of big bands. Jimmy and Columbia's recording chief Mitch Miller, casting about for another gimmick like the Dixieland approach, came up with the idea of tapping the "polka" market.

Columbia, New York, N.Y. Tuesday, December 12, 1950
JIMMY DORSEY AND HIS ORCHESTRA
Jimmy Abato, Jimmy Carroll, Al Gallodoro (cl) Terry Snyder (percussion) added

CO44716-1A   **We're Gonna Have Some Fun Tonight** [Gale; Jimmy Dorsey] (polka) vKM&PO'C (cl solo)
    78: Columbia 39164
CO44717-1A   **Acapulco Polka** vKM&PO'C
    78: Columbia 39162
CO44718-1A   **Clarinet Polka** [traditional] arrJD
    78: Columbia 39162, (E) BF425
    All sides also on **ET:** AFRS Basic Music Library 2391, **EP:** Columbia B-229, **LP:** Columbia CL-6165

Columbia, New York, N.Y. Thursday, December 14, 1950
JIMMY DORSEY AND HIS ORCHESTRA
Abato, Carroll, Gallodoro and White not used. Carter adds (celst)

CO44740-1A   **Baby-O, Baby-O** vKM&PO'C (as solo)
    78: Columbia 39258
CO44741-1A   **Licorice Stick Polka** [traditional]
    78: Columbia 39163
CO44742-1A   **Barbara Polka** [traditional] arrJD (cl solo)
    78: Columbia 39164
    ET: AFRS Basic Music Library 2391
    44741 and 44742 also on **ET:** AFRS Basic Music Library 2391, **EP:** Columbia B-229, **LP:** Columbia CL-6165

Columbia, New York, N.Y. Monday, December 18, 1950
JIMMY DORSEY AND HIS ORCHESTRA
Jimmy Dorsey (cl,ldr) Bobby Hackett, Shorty Sherock (tp) Frank Rehak (tb) Jimmy Abato, Al Gallodoro, Paul Ricci (cl) Art Lyons (ts) Bob Carter (p) Hy White (g) Bill Lolatte (sb) Terry Snyder (d)

CO44744-1A   **Laugh Polka**
    78: Columbia 39162
    ET: AFRS Basic Music Library 2392
CO44745-1A   **Helena Polka**
    78: Columbia 39163
    ET: AFRS Basic Music Library 2391
CO44746-1A   **Julida Polka** [traditional] arrJD
    78: Columbia 39164, (E) BF425
    ET: AFRS Basic Music Library 2392
    All sides also on **EP:** Columbia B-229, **LP:** Columbia CL-6165

The first big booking for 1951 was a return to Chicago's Edgewater Beach Hotel Marine Ballroom, opening on Friday, January 26, and closing on Thursday, February 22, replacing Xavier Cugat.

Another known block of bookings was a late March and early April run of mostly one-nighters throughout the Midwest. A week at The Trocadero, in Henderson, Kentucky, from Thursday, March 16, to Wednesday, March 22, and a week at the Casa Loma Ballroom, in St. Louis, Tuesday, March 27, to Monday, April 2, were the exceptions.

Band management, which for a year or so had been in the hands of Janet Tremaine, shifted to John Hall in late April and the band gradually worked west, playing a month in the Venetian Room of the Fairmont Hotel, San Francisco, from Tuesday, May 8, to Monday, June 4.

Then came a four-week booking at Hollywood's Palladium where, on opening night, Helen O'Connell helped celebrate the band's sixteenth anniversary along with Shorty Sherock, Joanne Dru and John Ireland.

sustaining broadcast, Hollywood Palladium, Hollywood, Cal.—Tuesday, June 12, 1951

JIMMY DORSEY AND HIS ORCHESTRA

Jimmy Dorsey (cl,as,ldr) Shorty Sherock, Riley Norris, Billy Mullens, Guy Kee (tp) Frank Rehak, Dick Bellerose (tb) Rusty Nichols (tb,vcl) Doc Clifford, Nino Palotti (as) Art Lyons, Phil Cenicola (ts) Mimi LaRocca (bar,vcl) Bob Carter (p) Hy White (g) Bill Lolatte (sb) Karl Kiffe (d) Helen O'Connell, Pat O'Connor, Sandy Evans (vcl)

By Heck [L. Wolfe Gilbert; S. R. Henry] (as solo) / **Be My Love** [Sammy Cahn; Nicholas Brodsky] vSE / **Would I Love You (Love You, Love You)** [Bob Russell; Harold Spina] vPO'C / **Green Eyes** [N. Menendez, E. Rivera, Eddie Woods, A. Utera] vSE&HO'C (as solo) / **Sweet Georgia Brown** [Maceo Pinkard, Kenneth Casey, Ben Bernie] (as solo) / **Pretty-Eyed Baby** [Mary Lou Williams, William Johnson, Leo Mosely] vRN / **If** [Robert Hargreaves, Stanley Damerell; Tolchard Evans] vSE / **Muskrat Ramble** [Ray Gilbert; "Kid" Ory] (cl solo)
      Entire broadcast on ET: AFRS One Night Stand 2576

sustaining broadcast, Hollywood Palladium, Hollywood, Cal.—June 1951

JIMMY DORSEY AND HIS ORCHESTRA

Contrasts [Jimmy Dorsey] (theme) (as solo) / **Lover** [Lorenz Hart; Richard Rodgers] (arrSB) (as solo) / **Lonesome Gal** vPO'C / **Yours (Quieremé Mucho)** [Jack Sherr, Augustin Rodriguez; Gonzalo Roig] vPO'C&SE / **Sweet Sue (Just You)** [Will J. Harris; Victor Young] (cl solo) / **Sweet Georgia Brown** [Maceo Pinkard, Kenneth Casey, Ben Bernie] (cl solo) / **Unless** [Stanley J. Damerell, Tolchard Evans, Robert Hargreaves, Henry Tilsley] vSE / **Pretty Eyed Baby** [Mary Lou Williams, William Johnson, Leo Mosley] vRN (cl solo) / **Jazz Me Blues** [Tom Delaney] *(Original Dorseyland Jazz Band)*
      Entire broadcast on ET: AFRS One Night Stand 2582, **TC:** Joyce Record Club C-1516

About this time Jimmy named his third new manager in a year, selecting his road manager Danny Francis to do double duty, another sign of the economic changes Jimmy made as income plummeted.

sustaining broadcast, Hollywood Palladium, Hollywood, Cal.—Friday, July 6, 1951
JIMMY DORSEY AND HIS ORCHESTRA

Contrasts [Jimmy Dorsey] (theme) (as solo) / **One O'Clock Jump** [William "Count" Basie] / **All of Me** [Seymour B. Simons, Gerald Marks] vPO'C (as solo) / **Unless** [Stanley J. Damerell, Tolchard Evans, Robert Hargreaves, Henry Tilsley] vSE / **The Answer, She Is "Yes", No?** vPO'C (as solo) / **Pretty Eyed Baby** [Mary Lou Williams, William Johnson, Leo Mosley] vRN (cl solo) / **Too Young** [Sylvia Dee; Sidney Lipman] vSE,PO'C / **Muskrat Ramble** [Ray Gilbert; Edward "Kid" Ory] (cl solo) entire broadcast on **ET:** AFRS One Night Stand 2784; "One O'Clock Jump", "All Of Me", "Too Young" and "Muskrat Ramble" on **LP:** Project 3 PR-2-6036

Closing at the Palladium Monday, July 9, the band then went to Catalina's Casino Ballroom from Tuesday, July 10 to Sunday, July 15.

Columbia, Los Angeles, Cal. Monday, July 16, 1951
JIMMY DORSEY AND HIS ORCHESTRA
Jimmy Dorsey (cl,as,ldr) Shorty Sherock, Riley Norris, Billy Mullens, Guy Kee (tp) Frank Rehak, Don Burke, Dick Bellerose (tb) Doc Clifford, Nino Palotti (as) Steve White, Phil Cenicola (ts) Mimi LaRocca (bar,vcl) Bob Carter (p) Bob Bain (g) Bill Lolatte (sb) Karl Kiffe (d) Pat O'Connor, Sandy Evans (vcl) Howard Gibeling (arr)

RHCO4503-1A   **Mine And Mine Alone** vSE
      78: Columbia 39477
RHCO4504-1A   **Cherry Pink And Apple Blossom White** [Mack David; Louiguy] vSE&PO'C (as solo)
      78: Columbia 39526
      (SSL-4070) **ET:** AFRS Basic Music Library 2018
      LP: Harmony HL7238
RHCO4505-1B   **The World Is Your Balloon** [E. Y. Harburg, Sammy Fain] vSE (as solo)
      78: Columbia 39477
      TC: Sony BT 28377
      CD: Sony BC 28377
RHCO4506-1A   **A Kiss To Build A Dream On** [Bert Kalmar, Oscar Hammerstein II; Harry Ruby] vSE&PO'C (as solo)
      78: Columbia 39526
      (SSL-4070) **ET:** AFRS Basic Music Library 2018
      TC: Sony BT 28377
      CD: Sony BC 28377

Travel itinerary: Mon., July 16, to Sun., July 29—Tops' Restaurant, San Diego, Cal.

Columbia, Los Angeles, Cal. Monday, July 30, 1951
JIMMY DORSEY AND HIS ORCHESTRA
Glenn Woodmansee (tb) replaces Sam Levine, who temporarily replaced Don Burke; Ted Nash (ts) replaces White; Sol Schlinger (bar) replaces LaRocca. Howard Gibeling (arr)

JIMMY DORSEY AND HIS ORCHESTRA (Contd.)

RHCO4542-1N   **Manhattan** [Lorenz Hart; Richard Rodgers] arrHG
          (cl solo)
     78: Columbia 39578
     (SSL-4606) **ET:** AFRS Basic Music Library 2288
     45: Columbia 4-39578
     LP: Harmony HL-7238, HL-7277

Travel itinerary: Mon., July 30—Memorial Auditorium, San Luis Obispo, Cal. /
Tues., July 31—Rainbow Gardens Ballroom, Fresno, Cal. / Thurs., Aug. 2, to Wed.,
Aug. 15 —Thunderbird Hotel, Las Vegas, Nev.

Columbia, Los Angeles, Cal. Tuesday, August 7, 1951
JIMMY DORSEY AND HIS ORCHESTRA
Sam Levine (tb) replaces Woodmansee, Art Lyons (ts) replaces Nash.
Norman Luboff Choir (vcl grp) added

RHCO4569-1N   **Step By Step** [Haven Gillespie, Charles Rosoff]
          vSE&NLC
     78: Columbia 39558
     (SSL-4606) **ET:** AFRS Basic Music Library 2288
RHCO4570-1N   **Just One Of Those Things** [Cole Porter] arrHG
          (as solo)
     LP: Columbia CL-599
RHCO4571   Unknown title (unissued)
RHCO4572-1N   **Young Folks Should Get Married** [Dorothy Fields;
          Harry Warren] vSE (as solo)
     78: Columbia 39558
     ET: AFRS Basic Music Library 2392
RHCO4573-1N   **Jiminy Christmas** [Haven Gillespie, Irving Bilbo]
          vSE&PO'C (as solo)
     78: Columbia 39578
     45: Columbia 4-39578

Stars For Defense, possibly Radio Recorders Studio,
Los Angeles, Calif. Summer 1951
DIXIELAND BIG BAND ALL STARS
Red Nichols (cnt) Ziggy Elman, Charlie Teagarden, Mannie Klein, An-
dy Secrest, Zeke Zarchy, George Seaberg (tp) Jack Teagarden, Ted Ves-
ely, King Jackson, Moe Schneider, Si Zentner (tb) **Jimmy Dorsey** (cl)
Eddie Miller (ts) Matty Matlock, Skeets Herfurt, Babe Russin, Chuck
Gentry, Joe Rushton (cl,as,ts,bar) Jess Stacy, Marvin Ash (p) George
Van Eps (g) Ed Skrivanek (bj) Haig Stephens (sb) Country Washburne
(bb) Ben Pollack, Nick Fatool, Ray Bauduc (d) Johnny Mercer (vcl)

     High Society [Clarence Williams; Armand J. Piron] / **The Dixie-
     land Band** [Johnny Mercer; Bernard Hanighen] vJM / **Pagan Love
     Song** [Arthur Freed; Nacio Herb Brown]
          All selections on: **ET:** Office of Price Stabilization, Stars For
          Defense 20, **LP:** Bandstand BS-7128, Fanfare LP2-102, Black
          Jack (G) 3009, Jasmine (E) JASM2510

After the thirteen-week stint on the West Coast, there was another string of forty-nine mostly one-nighters in the Midwest.

Travel itinerary: Tues., Aug. 21, to Sun. Aug. 26—Peony Park Ballroom, Omaha, Neb. / Fri., Sept. 7—Coliseum, Indianapolis, Ind. / Thurs., Sept. 20, to Wed., Oct. 31—Roosevelt Hotel, New Orleans, La.

More September changes included replacing Guy Key (tp) with Ray Triscari and cutting one trombone when Rusty Nichols left. The band opened at the Cafe Rouge on Monday, November 5, for six weeks.

sustaining broadcast, Hotel Statler (Pennsylvania), New York, N.Y.—Monday, November 5, 1951
JIMMY DORSEY AND HIS ORCHESTRA
Jimmy Dorsey (cl,as,ldr) Shorty Sherock, Riley Norris, Charlie Frankhouser, Bobby Styles (tp) Frank Rehak, Jimmy Henderson, Glenn Woodmansee (tb) Doc Clifford, Nino Palotti (as) Art Lyons, Glenn Steiner (ts) Sol Schlinger (bar) Bob Carter (p) Art Ryerson (g) Bill Lolatte (sb) Karl Kiffe (d) Terry Snyder (percussion) Sandy Evans, Pat O'Connor (vcl)

Contrasts [Jimmy Dorsey] (theme) (as solo) / **Heat Wave** [Irving Berlin] (as solo) / **Young Folks Should Get Married** [Dorothy Fields; Harry Warren] vSE (as solo) / **I'm In Love Again** [Cole Porter] vPO'C (cl solo) / **A Kiss To Build A Dream On** [Bert Kalmar, Oscar Hammerstein II; Harry Ruby] vSE&PO'C / **Manhattan** [Lorenz Hart; Richard Rodgers] (cl solo) / **Tenderly** [Jack Lawrence; Walter Gross] (as solo) / **Tin Roof Blues** [Paul Mares, Walter Melrose, Ben Pollack, Mel Stitzel, George Brunies, Leon Roppolo] *(Original Dorseyland Jazz Band)* / **Cherry Pink And Apple Blossom White** [Mack David; Louiguy] vSE&PO'C / **Just One Of Those Things** [Cole Porter] (as solo)
Entire broadcast on ET: AFRS One Night Stand 2727; "Heat Wave", "I'm In Love Again," "Manhattan" and "Just One Of Those Things" on LP: Golden Era GE-15011; "A Kiss To Build A Dream On," "Tin Roof Blues" and "Cherry Pink" on LP: Project 3 PR-2-6036; "Manhattan" on TC: LaserLight 79-759, CD: LaserLight 15-759

sustaining broadcast, Hotel Statler, New York, N.Y.—NBC, Wednesday, November 7, 1951
JIMMY DORSEY AND HIS ORCHESTRA

Contrasts [Jimmy Dorsey] (theme) (as solo) / **Just One Of Those Things** [Cole Porter] (as solo) / **I'm In Love Again** [Cole Porter] vPO'C / **Young Folks Should Get Married** [Dorothy Fields; Harry Warren] vSE (as solo) / **Too Young** [Sylvia Dee; Sidney Lippman] vSE&PO'C / **Heat Wave** [Irving Berlin] (as solo) / **Vanity** [Jack Manus, Bernard Bierman; Guy Wood] / **That's A-Plenty** [Lew Pollack] (cl solo) *(Original Dorseyland Jazz Band)* / **It's A Wonderful World** [Harold Adamson; Leo Watson, Jan Savitt] (cl solo)
"That's A Plenty" on LP: Project 3 PR-2-6036

sustaining broadcast, Hotel Statler New York,
N.Y.—NBC, Wednesday, November 14, 1951
JIMMY DORSEY AND HIS ORCHESTRA

Contrasts [Jimmy Dorsey] (theme) (as solo) / **Undecided** [Sid Robin;
Charlie Shavers] (cl solo) / **I'm Glad There Is You** [Paul Madeira;
Jimmy Dorsey] vPO'C (as solo) / **Young Folks Should Get Married**
[Dorothy Fields; Harry Warren] vSE (as solo) / **It's A Wonderful
World** [Harold Adamson; Leo Watson, Jan Savitt] (cl solo) / **Yours
(Quieremé Mucho)** [Jack Sherr, Augustin Rodriguez; Gonzalo Roig]
vPO'C&SE (as solo) / **Little White Lies** [Walter Donaldson] vSE (as
solo) / **Jazz Me Blues** [Tom Delaney] (cl solo)
All except theme and "Undecided" on **LP:** Joyce LP1127

sustaining broadcast, Hotel Statler New York,
N.Y.—NBC, Wednesday, November 21, 1951
JIMMY DORSEY AND HIS ORCHESTRA

Contrasts [Jimmy Dorsey] (theme) (as solo) / **Just One Of Those
Things** [Cole Porter] arrHG (as solo) / **(It's No) Sin** [Chester R.
Schull; George Hoven] vSE (as solo) / **Love Me** [Sammy Cahn; Jule
Styne] vPO'C (as solo) / **Manhattan** [Lorenz Hart; Richard Rodgers]
arrHG (cl solo) / **And So To Sleep Again** [Joe Marsala, Sunny
Skylar] vSE (as solo) / **A Kiss To Build A Dream On** [Bert Kalmar,
Oscar Hammerstein II; Harry Ruby] vSE&PO'C / **Tin Roof Blues**
[Paul Mares, Walter Melrose, Ben Pollack, Mel Stitzel, George
Brunies, Leon Roppolo] (cl solo) / **Sweet Sue (Just You)** [Will J.
Harris; Victor Young] (cl solo)

While the implication was always that the bands that took part in so-
called public service programs did so gratis, they were always paid at
least scale from the American Federation of Musicians (AFM)
Recording Trust Fund, which was set up as part of the settlement of the
recording strikes in the forties.

As for the AFM, it was vital that it spend the monies, which had
grown so large the Justice Department was sniffing about, considering
antitrust charges. By the fifties, this income was almost essential to the
survival of bands like Jimmy's.

*Department Of State, Voice Of America Popular
Dance Series,* unknown studio, New York, N.Y.
—November-December 1951
JIMMY DORSEY AND HIS ORCHESTRA

When You Wore A Tulip (And I Wore A Big Red Rose) [Jack
Mahoney; Percy Wenrich] (cl solo) / **Kiss Me** [Redd Evans, Bob
Trendler] / **Them There Eyes** [Maceo Pinkard, William Tracey,
Doris Trauber]
All on **ET:** Voice Of America Program 189

Moon Of Monakoora [Frank Loesser; Alfred Newman] (as solo) /
Somebody Mentioned Your Name / **Muskrat Ramble** [Ray Gilbert;

Edward "Kid" Ory]
   All on ET: Voice Of America Program 233

Hello And Good-bye [Robert Lissauer] (cl solo) / **Dream A Little Dream Of Me** [Gus Kahn; Wilbur Schwandt, Fabian Andre] / **On The Alamo** [Gus Kahn, Isham Jones]
   All on ET: Voice Of America Program 241

I'll Never Be Free [Bennie Benjamin; George David Weiss] vPO'C / **Let's Fall In Love** [Ted Koehler; Harold Arlen] (cl solo)
   Both on ET: Voice Of America Program 257

Third Man Theme [Anton Karas] (cl solo) / **Johnson Rag** [Guy H. Hall, Henry Kleinhauf] vPO'C (cl solo)
   Both on ET: Voice Of America Program 274

> *Let's Go To Town, National Guard recruitment series,* unknown studio, New York, N.Y.—November, December 1951

JIMMY DORSEY AND HIS ORCHESTRA
Patti Page (vcl)

Manhattan [Lorenz Hart; Richard Rodgers] arrHG (cl solo) / **That's A-Plenty** [Lew Pollack] (cl solo) / **This Is My Song** [Dick Charles] vPP / **Let's Fall In Love** [Ted Koehler; Harold Arlen] (cl solo)
   All on ET: National Guard Program 5

(What Can I Say) After I Say I'm Sorry? [Walter Donaldson, Abe Lyman] / **Wimoweh** ["Paul Campbell" (Pete Seger, Fred Hellerman, Lee Hays, Ronnie Gilbert)] / **I Went To Your Wedding** [Jesse Mae Robinson] vPP / **South Rampart Street Parade** [Steve Allen; Ray Bauduc, Bob Haggart]
   All on ET: National Guard Program 6

The First Annual *Billboard* Band Buyers Survey of ballroom and hotel operators (November 11, 1951, 15) showed the 1951 favorite swing bands with the dancers to be Les Brown (1), followed by Ralph Flanagan (2), Harry James (3), Ray Anthony (4), Stan Kenton (5), Tommy Dorsey (6), Jimmy Dorsey (7) and Duke Ellington (8).
   It is another sign of the times that the only names listed who had successful bands in the thirties were the Dorseys and the Duke.
   It must have been somewhat like a reversal of the situation with Tommy in the winter of 1935-1936 when Jimmy read in *Billboard* (December 1, 1951, 59) that his brother and band would be spending eight weeks in early 1952 in summer-like Brazil, playing concerts and clubs and appearing on the premiere of Brazil's new TV network. The deal reportedly involved $200,000.

Columbia, New York, N.Y. Monday, December 10, 1951
JIMMY DORSEY AND HIS ORCHESTRA
Betty Cox (vcl) replaces O'Connor

514   JIMMY DORSEY: A Study in Contrasts

JIMMY DORSEY AND HIS ORCHESTRA (Contd.)

CO47264-1   The Night Is Filled With Echoes [Bernie Wayne, Richard Carle] vSE&BC
    78: Columbia 39728
    ET: AFRS Basic Music Library 2392
    TC: Sony BT 28377
    CD: Sony BC 28377
CO47265-1B   (I Stood And Threw) Confetti [Michael Carr] vSE (as solo)
    78: Columbia 39691
    (SSL-4606) ET: AFRS Basic Music Library 2288
CO47266-1A   I'll Always Be Following You [Bernie Wayne; Lee Morris] vSE
    78: Columbia 39691
    (SSL-4606) ET: AFRS Basic Music Library 2288

By the end of December, Pat O'Connor had returned and by New Years Eve at the Statler Jimmy had made some other personnel changes: **Jimmy Dorsey** (cl,as,ldr) Shorty Sherock, Riley Norris, Charlie Frankhouser, Bobby Styles (tp) Frank Rehak, Jimmy Henderson, Glenn Woodmansee (tb) Moe Koffman, Carmen Carlo (as) Buz Brauner, Glenn Steiner (ts) Al Layton (bar) Bob Carter (p) Hy White (g) Bill Lolatte (sb) Karl Kiffe (d) Sandy Evans, Pat O'Connor (vcl)
In late January the band played a week at the Seville Theater, Montreal, Quebec, exact dates unknown. Vince Ferrara (bar) replaced Al Layton for the booking. A review (*Down Beat,* February 22, 1952, 2) comments that Tommy had earlier urged the writer to "catch my brother's band as soon as you can. I hear he's going great guns."

Columbia, New York, N.Y. Monday, February 4, 1952
JIMMY DORSEY AND HIS ORCHESTRA
Jimmy Dorsey (cl,as,ldr) Shorty Sherock, Riley Norris, Billy Patterson, Roy Raye, Jimmy Blane (tp) Frank Rehak, Jimmy Henderson, Bill Ver-Planck (tb) Ben Fussell, Carmen Carlo (as) Buzzy Brauner, Glenn Steiner (ts) Al Layton (bar) Bob Carter (p) Art Ryerson (g) Bill Lolatte (sb) Karl Kiffe (d) Terry Snyder (percussion) Sandy Evans, Pat O'Connor, Chorus (vcl)

CO47315-1A,1B   **Wimoweh (Wee-Mo-Way)** ["Paul Campbell" (Pete Seger, Fred Hellerman, Lee Hays, Ronnie Gilbert)] vCh (as solo)
    78: Columbia 39651
    (SSL-4606) ET: AFRS Basic Music Library 2288
CO47316-1B   **No Other Love But Yours** [Leo Payne, Sunny Skylar] vSE&Ch (cl solo)
    78: Columbia 39691
    (SSL-4606) ET: AFRS Basic Music Library 2288
CO47317-1   **Tell Me True** vSE,PO'C&Ch
    78: Columbia 39728
    ET: AFRS Basic Music Library 2392

Another significant development in the rapidly declining big-band business was detailed in *Billboard* (February 9, 1952, 22) with a story that WNBC had announced the station would no longer carry late-hour dance band remotes, thus joining WJZ and WOR. It was implied that WCBS would soon follow suit. In all cases the New York City stations were installing all-night disk jockey shows. In one more way the charismatic disk spinner with his stack of 45 rpm rock bands and pop vocalists was replacing the live band, this time as a late evening broadcast staple.

Jimmy played a return engagement at the Casa Loma Ballroom, St. Louis, Missouri, from Tuesday, February 5, to Monday, February 11. The band then continued a series of one-night stands and weeklong theater dates in the Midwest, details of which are missing.

A story in *Variety* (April 9, 1952, 55) stated the Palladium was considering a policy which would switch it from only big bands to one adding single acts, especially singers. This actually took place October 28, 1952 (*Variety*, September 17, 1952, 49).

Tuesday, April 15, 1952, a slowly shrinking Jimmy Dorsey Orchestra began its last engagement at the famed Hollywood ballroom.

sustaining broadcast, Palladium, Hollywood, Cal.—
April 1952
JIMMY DORSEY AND HIS ORCHESTRA
Blane (tp) out (no replacement), Vince Ferraro (bar) replaces Layton, White (g) out (no replacement), Eleanor Russell (vcl) replaces O'Connor

Details unknown
ET: AFRS One Night Stand 2855

sustaining broadcast, Palladium, Hollywood, Cal.—
Thursday, April 17, 1952
JIMMY DORSEY AND HIS ORCHESTRA

Manhattan [Lorenz Hart; Richard Rodgers] arrHG (cl solo) / **Please, Mr. Sun** [Sid Frank; Ray Getzov] vSE / **Warm Hearted Woman** vER / **Sweet Georgia Brown** [Maceo Pinkard, Kenneth Casey, Ben Bernie] (cl solo) / **It's The Dreamer In Me** [Jimmy Van Heusen, Jimmy Dorsey] vER (cl solo) / **That's A-Plenty** [Lew Pollack] (cl solo) *(Original Dorseyland Jazz Band)* / **Tell Me True** / **All Of Me** [Seymour B. Simons, Gerald Marks] vER (as solo)
Entire broadcast on ET: AFRS One Night Stand 2881

Another sign of the times came in the weekly reports of record sales that showed Jimmy Dorsey with three listings, two of them nostalgic reissues: "I Hear A Rhapsody," from the original Decca side rereleased on Coral, and "Moon Over Miami," first issued by MGM in 1947. The third tune was his current "Wimoweh" (*Variety*, April 23, 1952, 33).

sustaining broadcast, Palladium, Hollywood, Cal.—
Thursday, April 24, 1952
JIMMY DORSEY AND HIS ORCHESTRA

Contrasts [Jimmy Dorsey] (theme) (as solo) / **(What Can** (Contd.)

JIMMY DORSEY AND HIS ORCHESTRA (Contd.)

I Say, Dear) After I Say I'm Sorry? [Walter Donaldson, Abe Lyman] / **Blacksmith Blues** [Jack Holmes] vER / **(I Stood And Threw) Confetti** [Michael Carr] vSE / **Wimoweh** ["Paul Campbell" (Pete Seger, Fred Hellerman, Lee Hays, Ronnie Gilbert)] vBand / **Manhattan** [Lorenz Hart; Richard Rodgers] arrHG (cl solo) / **Don't Take Your Love From Me** [Harry Nemo] vER / **Blue (And Broken Hearted)** [Grant Clarke, Edgar Leslie; Lou Handman] vSE / **Warm Hearted Woman** vER / **Sweet Georgia Brown** [Maceo Pinkard, Kenneth Casey, Ben Bernie] (cl solo) *(Original Dorseyland Jazz Band)*
Entire broadcast on **ET**: AFRS One Night Stand 2888

sustaining broadcast, Palladium, Hollywood, Cal.—
April 1952
JIMMY DORSEY AND HIS ORCHESTRA

Details unknown
ET: AFRS One Night Stand 2909

Jubilee #367, unknown studios, Los Angeles, Cal.—
AFRS, April 1952
JUBILEE ORCHESTRA
Personnel unknown. Jimmy Dorsey (cl,as) Joe "Fingers" Carr (p) Margaret Whiting (vcl) guests

Alto-Tude [Jimmy Dorsey, Marvin Wright] (as solo) / **Sweet Georgia Brown** [Maceo Pinkard, Kenneth Casey, Ben Bernie] (cl solo) / **Down Yonder** [L. Wolfe Gilbert] vMW&JFC (p)
All selections on AFRS Jubilee #367

sustaining broadcast, Palladium, Hollywood, Cal.—
Saturday, May 10, 1952
JIMMY DORSEY AND HIS ORCHESTRA

Manhattan [Lorenz Hart; Richard Rodgers] arrHG (cl solo) / **The Night Is Filled With Echoes** vSE&ER / **Warm Hearted Woman** vER / **Wimoweh** ["Paul Campbell" (Pete Seger, Fred Hellerman, Lee Hays, Ronnie Gilbert)] vBand / **Blue Tango** [Leroy Anderson] / **A Kiss To Build A Dream On** [Bert Kalmar, Oscar Hammerstein II; Harry Ruby] vSE&ER / **Perfidia** [Milton Leeds; Alberto Dominguez] (cl solo) / **Blacksmith Blues** [Jack Holmes] vER / **(I Stood And Threw) Confetti** [Michael Carr] vSE
Entire broadcast on **ET**: AFRS One Night Stand 2915

The next evening, Sunday, May 11, the band closed its stand at the Palladium and was replaced by brother Tommy's entourage for that band's first appearance at the Palladium in more than ten years. Earlier that month *Billboard* (May 10, 1952, 18) had announced that Tommy had sold the lease and equipment at Casino Gardens to a Beverly Hills auctioneer. Casino Gardens had been closed for seven months and for the previous few years had only been open in the summer.

Near the end of May the band played a one-nighter at Linn's Ball-room in Oakland, California, where they attracted over 1,000 dancers, which for the times was a large crowd (*Down Beat,* July 2, 1952, 6).

On May 31, 1952, NBC-Radio aired *Silver Plus Five,* a special tribute to Red Nichols' thirty years in show business. Both Jimmy and Tommy were speaking guests on the show. Tommy revealed how he and Jimmy had been landlords to Red in 1925 (Evans, Hester *et al,* 1997).

In early June the band did a swing through the Pacific Northwest, returned to the San Francisco-Oakland area for a couple of one-nighters and then went to Las Vegas for a two-week stand at the Thunderbird Hotel from Thursday, June 19, to Wednesday, July 2. Another two-week booking followed from Thursday, July 3, to Wednesday, July 16 at the Lakeside Gardens, Denver, Colorado.

As a thirteen-week summer replacement for its highly successful *Your Show of Shows* with Sid Caesar, NBC-TV created the *Saturday Night Dance Party,* a sixty-minute big-band, small combo show, rather poorly hosted by comedian Jerry Lester. Jimmy and his band, along with his two former vocal stars, Helen O'Connell and Bob Eberly, were featured Saturday, August 23, 9:00-10:00 P.M.

The Ritz Ballroom in Bridgeport, Connecticut, opened for the fall season on Monday, September 8, and Jimmy's band was the opening night attraction. The band went back to the Hotel Statler in New York City the next night, Tuesday, September 9.

The Second Annual *Billboard* Band Buyer's Survey (October 4, 1952, 22) showed how drastically the big-band business had changed. Among the favorite swing bands, Jimmy again placed eighth, behind Ralph Flan-agan (1), Ray Anthony (2), Billy May (3), Les Brown (4), Stan Kenton (5), Harry James (6), and Woody Herman (7). Tommy's band didn't show on either the sweet or swing lists.

Columbia, New York, N.Y. Friday, October 17, 1952
JIMMY DORSEY AND HIS ORCHESTRA
Jimmy Dorsey (cl,as,ldr) Bobby Styles, Riley Norris, Billy Patterson, Roy Raye (tp) Frank Rehak, Jimmy Henderson, Bill VerPlanck (tb) Ben Fussell, Nino Palotti (as) Buzzy Brauner, Glenn Steiner (ts) Vince Ferraro (bar) Bob Carter (p) Hy White (g) Bill Lolatte (sb) Karl Kiffe (d) Sandy Evans, Claire Hogan (vcl) The Satisfiers (vcl grp)

CO48416-1A   **Jump Back Honey** [Hadda Brooks] vCH&S (as solo)
    78: Columbia 39896
    TC: Sony BT 28377
    CD: Sony BC 28377
CO48417-1A   **Love Came Out Of The Night** [Edward G. Nelson;
              Fred Rose] vSE&S
    78: Columbia 39896
CO48418   **Serves You Right** vSE&S (unissued)
CO48419   **When They Ask About You** [Sam Stept] vCH&S
              (as solo)
    TC: Sony BT 28377
    CD: Sony BC 28377

Hotel Statler, New York, N.Y. November 1952
JIMMY DORSEY AND HIS ORCHESTRA
Nick Travis (tp) replaces Norris, Carmen Carlo (as) replaces Palotti, Johnny Hayes (ts) replaces Steiner, Hy White (g) out (no replacement), Frances Carroll (vcl) replaces Hogan

During 1952 the band made another visit to the Long Island film studios, filming a quarter-hour featurette as part of the Universal *Name Band* series, with old friend Will Cowan.

Universal studios, Long Island, N.Y. 1952
JIMMY DORSEY'S VARIETIES: Will Cowan, director
JIMMY DORSEY AND HIS ORCHESTRA

Sweet Georgia Brown [Maceo Pinkard, Kenneth Casey, Ben Bernie] (as solo) / (unknown song for tap dance routine) / **The Circus** [Bob Russell, Louis Alter] v*Female and vocal group* / **Wimoweh** ["Paul Campbell" (Pete Seger, Fred Hellerman, Lee Hays, Ronnie Gilbert)] vBand (as solo) / **Temptation** [Arthur Freed; Nacio Herb Brown] / **In The Bayou** v*Male* / **South Rampart Street Parade** [Steve Allen; Ray Bauduc, Bob Haggart] (cl solo)
> All selections in **FILM:** Universal: *Jimmy Dorsey's Varieties*; "Sweet Georgia Brown" and "South Rampart Street Parade" on **VIDEO:** MCA: Swing 80667 (Vol. 3)

Early 1953
JIMMY DORSEY AND HIS ORCHESTRA
Al Porcino (tp) replaces Travis, Phil Urso (ts) replaces Hayes, Bill Anthony (sb) replaces Lolatte, Andy Roberts (vcl) replaces Evans

The band made a fairly successful swing through Texas at the beginning of 1953 and spent two weeks at the Claridge Hotel in Memphis, Tennessee, opening Friday, January 23, and closing Thursday, February 5. This was followed by a string of one-nighters over the next three months, mostly in the East, although details are lacking. One of their last dates was at the spring dance for the University of Tennessee in Knoxville, Monday, April 21 (*Variety*, April 22, 1953, 41).

By late 1952 it had become evident that the big-band business was on its last legs. Jimmy, by now bankrupt, gave up the ghost in late April 1953. A major booking at the Hotel Statler, scheduled to begin May 4 was part of the casualties from Jimmy's decision, along with about three months of one-nighters.

Trombonist Jimmy Henderson and tenor saxophonist Buzzy Brauner went to work almost immediately for Tommy Dorsey.

Billboard (January 17, 1953, 28) had carried a story reporting that Tommy and his band would begin a six-week tour of Europe with stops both in England and on the mainland, this to follow a two-week stand at the Hotel Statler beginning March 9.

The tour as outlined never took place, and Jimmy, his brother and their managers met. *Billboard* (March 28, 1953, 20) contained a major story stating that after many weeks of on-again, off-again meetings, it was believed in the trade that the brothers would be joining forces for the first time in eighteen years.

Not yet settled, said the story, was whether the band would be called The Dorsey Brothers' Orchestra or Tommy Dorsey and His Orchestra, featuring Jimmy Dorsey.

In the same week's *Down Beat* (March 25, 1953, 1, 2) a similar general thread ran through the front-page story, with *Down Beat* also running a sidebar on page two in which Jimmy reminisced about the days of the mid-thirties Dorsey Brothers band.

Just below the Dorsey Brothers story was a short note showing that the younger Dorsey was really settling down. Titled "A Boy for TD," it reported that Tommy and Jane Dorsey had their second child, Tommy's fourth, in February. It was an eight-pound boy named Steven.

It took almost two months before all the booking agency and record commitments could be straightened out and the two brothers could be together again. Jimmy did make some appearances unofficially with Tommy's band beginning April 17, including an Easter weekend date at the University of Virginia in Charlotesville. The two brothers also dropped in at Duke University, in Durham, North Carolina, while "down South" to catch Ray Anthony's band and sat in for a few numbers. During April Tommy's band was much like the personnel shown for the upcoming May 23 *Jackie Gleason Show*. Doug Mettome was replaced by Lee Castle in June.

It was mid-May before the band was officially cleared for appearances by both brothers. Vince Carbone of Tom-Dor Enterprises did the bookings, and the trade press speculated that Mercury and Decca were interested in record deals.

The name finally chosen for the band was "Tommy Dorsey and His Orchestra, featuring Jimmy Dorsey." In reality Jimmy was just a sideman, being paid $1,000 a week by Tommy. Billing in all advertising was also to include the phrase "Those Fabulous Dorseys" to capitalize on their now six-year-old film. This billing was carried out in a big way in a two-page ad announcing the new band in *Variety* (May 6, 1953, 36, 37), which trumpeted solid bookings into the fall.

By this time the contrasts between the brothers were really evident. Tommy was strong-willed and all through life had been driven by the need to succeed. As a result he had become a music business icon and a very successful businessman. Except for rare social occasions, Tommy drank little alcohol and had given up smoking many years ago.

He was a strong disciplinarian, who ran his bands and other enterprises from a lofty perch, purposely maintaining a hands-off stance with his employees. As a result he had few real friends among those who worked for him.

Jimmy, by comparison, had given up his band, was weakened financially by divorce and personal mismanagement on the part of certain of his managers as well as himself, and was drinking and smoking more than ever.

Much of this had happened because of his inner need to be "one of the guys." As a result he was well liked by his employees and business associates, but not really respected or feared. He was trusting to a fault, often ignoring disloyalty.

This need for companionship thrust him all through his career into almost nightly social contacts with his sidemen, many of whom were typical of musicians of the time, buttressing themselves with booze, pot and other stimulants.   To be one of the "bunch" he did much of what they did, although there is no evidence he ever did more than flirt with hard drugs.

This kind of close relationship, while inwardly satisfying, was disastrous from the standpoint of maintaining the discipline necessary to build a musical empire.   By the fifties these contrasts between the brothers were most painfully evident.

Travel itinerary: Mon., May 11—Juniata College, Juniata, Pa. / Tues., May 12—Huntington, Pa. / Wed., May 13—Chippewa Lake, Ohio (drawing 1,800) / Fri., May 15—Buckeye Lake, Ohio (record crowd of 1,600) / Sat., May 16—Castle Farms, Cincinnati, Ohio (crowd, 2,100) / Sun., May 17—Keymen's Ballroom, Chicago, Ill. (record crowd of 1,400) / Mon., May 18—Indiana Roof Ballroom, Indianapolis, Ind.

In its review of the Keymen's (Chicago) appearance *Variety* (May 20, 1953, 40) noted that the brothers were appealing strongly to nostalgia, but still attracting the 18- to 25-year-old crowd.

The band then went in for a two-night stand at the Rustic Cabin, Englewood, New Jersey, Friday, May 22, to Sunday, May 24. They drew 2,600 for the two nights and caused traffic jams both nights, which police needed to clear (*Variety*, May 27, 1953, 55).

The band also had its television premiere that weekend on pal Jackie Gleason's highly popular CBS-TV show. Gleason fashioned a "Honeymooners" routine in which Ralph Cramden (Gleason) books Tommy Dorsey's band to play the bus drivers' benefit ball, and wife Alice (Audrey Meadows) books Jimmy's band.

Both brothers show up, wind up mending their long-standing feud and playing together, with the whole "reunion" revealed to a national television audience.

> *The Jackie Gleason Show,* CBS-TV Studios, New York, N.Y.—CBS-TV, 8:00-9:00 P.M. Saturday, May 23, 1953

TOMMY DORSEY & HIS ORCH. FEATURING JIMMY DORSEY Tommy Dorsey (tb,ldr) Doug Mettome, Billy Marshall, Daryl Campbell, George Cherub (tp) Johnny Amoroso (tp,vcl) Jimmy Henderson, Sam Hyster, Tak Takvorian (tb) **Jimmy Dorsey,** Marv Koral (cl,as) Allen Fields (as) Buzzy Brauner, George Cipriano (ts) Teddy Lee (bar) Doug Talbert (p) Sam Herman (g) Billy Cronk (sb) Jackie Mills (d)

> **Dry Bones / Ruby** [Mitchell Parish; Heinz Roemheld] vJA (as solo) / **South Rampart Street Parade** [Steve Allen; Ray Bauduc, Bob Haggart] (cl solo)

In addition to the personnel shown, the band at the time also included vocalists Gordon Polk and Lynn Roberts.

After the Rustic Cabin, there were a few more one-nighters including a very successful one on Sunday, May 31, at Youngstown Ohio's Idora Park that attracted 3,200 dancers. Then there was an eight-day booking at the Claridge Hotel in Memphis, Tennessee, from Saturday, June 6, to

Saturday, June 13. During the Memphis stay, better than 8,000 made their way to the hotel.

The week at the Claridge was the first opportunity the band had to rehearse about fifteen arrangements that had been prepared featuring both brothers. Up until then they played existing arrangements from either Tommy's or Jimmy's book.

There followed a string of one-nighters in Texas, Louisiana and Oklahoma including one Wednesday, June 17, at the Longhorn Ranch, Dallas, Texas (*Variety*, June 10, 1953, 66), then another string in the corn-belt of Iowa, Nebraska and Kansas including one Monday, June 22, in York, Nebraska (*Variety,* June 17, 1953, 51). The road tour ended at Lakeside Park, Denver, Colorado, where they played from Wednesday, July 1, to Tuesday, July 14.

Variety (July 22, 1953, 48) reported that the brothers were negotiating with Music Corporation of America, Tommy' bookers until 1950. However, a week later (July 29, 1953, 108) the paper revealed that the Dorseys had signed with Colonades, Inc., in Hollywood and that Vince Carbone would now run Colonades' New York office.

There was another string of one-nighters, a two-night booking at White City Ballroom, Ogden, Utah, and then two weeks at the Last Frontier, in Las Vegas, Nevada, from Saturday, August 1, to Thursday, August 13. They then played one-nighters at Pasadena Civic Auditorium, Friday, August 14; San Luis Obispo, Saturday, August 15; and Fresno, Sunday, August 16. These three dates for promoter Van Tonkins netted $6,000 (*Variety,* August 12, 1953, 46, and August 19, 1953, 46).

Billboard (August 15, 1953, 15) reported that the famous Palladium in London, England, had made a deal for the Dorsey band to play there in September as the first American band to be able to perform in England with all their sidemen. The pact called for $15,000 to the Dorseys and it was conjectured that the Ted Heath band would come to the United States in exchange. The tour, however, never took place.

The band recorded some singles for Decca on August 14 in Hollywood, but without Jimmy, who still had to get out of his Columbia contract. However, during their stay in Hollywood Tommy personally taped a collection of dance adaptations of eight semiclassical works, subsequently leasing them to Decca, which released them in an album titled "Invitation to the Dance."

After Tommy's death in 1956, his widow leased these sides to a number of other companies, further showing that Decca didn't control them and raising the possibility that Jimmy could have "moonlighted" on these sides (Seavor, 1997).

Unknown studio, Hollywood Cal. August 1953
TOMMY DORSEY & HIS ORCHESTRA
Tommy Dorsey (tb,ldr) Lee Castle, Daryl Campbell, Paul Cohen, John McCormick (tp) Johnny Amoroso (tp,vcl) Jimmy Henderson, Tak Takvorian, Sam Hyster (tb) *Jimmy Dorsey* (cl,as) Skip Galluccio, Kenny Delange (as) Buzzy Brauner, Joe Pamelia (ts) Teddy Lee (bar) Bob Carter (p) Sam Herman (g) Billy Cronk (b) Jackie Mills (d)

-0-   **Fruit Cocktail (Dance Of The Sugar Plum Fairies)**
     EP: Decca ED528 (Contd.)

TOMMY DORSEY AND HIS ORCHESTRA (Contd.)

LP: Decca DL5452, Premier PM/PS2007, Coronet CSX 234, Ajazz LP432
-0-   **Grieg's Grotto (Anitra's Dance)**
EP: Decca ED528
LP: Decca DL5452, Vocalion VL3613, Spin-O-Rama M150, Premier PM/PS2007, Coronet CSX186, CSX234, Musicdisc (F) CV1202, Ajazz LP432
-0-   **Hour Glass Special (Dance Of The Hours)**
EP: Decca ED528
LP: Decca DL5452, Spin-O-Rama M150, Premier PM/PS2007, Coronet CSX234, Musicdisc (F) CV1202, Ajazz LP432
-0-   **Juba Dance (Mexican Hat Dance)**
EP: Decca ED528
LP: Decca DL5452, Spin-O-Rama M150, Premier PM/PS2007, Coronet CSX234, Ajazz LP432
-0-   **Not So Spanish Please (Spanish Dance)**
EP: Decca ED528
LP: Decca DL5452, Spin-O-Rama M150, Premier PM/PS2007, Coronet CSX234, Ajazz LP432
-0-   **Ritual Fire Dance**
EP: Decca ED528
LP: Decca DL5452, Vocalion VL3613, MCA 2-4074, Spin-O-Rama M150, Premier PM/PS2007, Coronet CSX234, Musicdisc (F) CV1202, Ajazz LP432
-0-   **Turbans On Parade (Arab Dance)**
EP: Decca ED528
LP: Decca DL5452, Spin-O-Rama M150, Premier PM/PS2007, Coronet CSX234, Ajazz LP432

Jimmy also participated in a short Universal film, parts of which are available on videotape.

Universal Studios, Hollywood Cal. Late August 1953
THE DORSEY BROTHERS ENCORE: Will Cowan, director
TOMMY DORSEY & HIS ORCH., featuring Jimmy Dorsey
Tommy Dorsey (tb,ldr) Lee Castle, Daryl Campbell, Paul Cohen, John McCormick (tp) Johnny Amoroso (tp,vcl) Jimmy Henderson, Tak Takvorian, Sam Hyster (tb) **Jimmy Dorsey** (cl,as) Skip Galluccio, Kenny Delange (as) Buzzy Brauner, Joe Pamelia (ts) Teddy Lee (bar) Bob Carter (p) Sam Herman (g) Billy Cronk (b) Jackie Mills (d) Gordon Polk, Lynn Roberts (vcl)

Well Git It! [Sy Oliver] (cl solo) / **Ain't She Sweet** [Jack Yellen; Milton Ager] vGP / **Muskrat Ramble** [Ray Gilbert; Edward "Kid" Ory] *(Dixieland group)* (cl solo) / **Yes, Indeed!** [Sy Oliver] (cl solo) / Theme from "Street Scene" [Alfred Newman] (as solo)
All selections in **FILM:** Universal-International *Dorsey Brothers Encore*; "Well Git It!" and "Yes, Indeed!" on **VIDEO:** MCA: Swing 80666 (Vol. 2)

Variety (May 20, 1953, 40) reported a hotel booking set for September at the Ambassador Hotel, Los Angeles, but did not give any details.

The same magazine (July 8, 1953, 54) listed the band for the Terrytown Arena, Scottsbluff, Nebraska, on Monday, September 14, and its August 19, 1953, issue (page 47) noted that the band would play a short engagement at the Longhorn Ranch, Dallas, Texas, in October. Without giving any details, *Billboard* (October 31, 1953, 15) said that the band was booked from October until February 1954 with only one open date.

The music tracks and some Dorsey brothers' remarks for the *1954 March Of Dimes Program* were taped by WSYR, Syracuse, New York, while the band was at the Persian Terrace of the Hotel Syracuse in late September or early October. The tracks were later edited in New York with announcer Ray Morgan's voice tracks into a quarter-hour program.

To date the author has not been able to determine the exact dates of the band's Syracuse appearance, however, the time frame is confirmed by retired WSYR engineer Paul Abert, who originally taped the tracks.

1954 March Of Dimes Program, Hotel Syracuse, Syracuse, N.Y.—Late September, early October 1953
TOMMY DORSEY & HIS ORCH., featuring Jimmy Dorsey
Bob Varney (d) replaces Mills. Johnny Amoroso, Lynn Roberts, Gordon Polk (vcl) Ernie Wilkins (arr)

I'm Gettin' Sentimental Over You [Ned Washington; George Bassman] (theme) / **Melancholy Serenade** [Jackie Gleason] (as solo) / **Green Eyes** [N. Menendez, E. Rivera, Eddie Woods, A. Utera] vJA&LR (as solo) / **Kicking The Blues Around** [Ernie Wilkins] (cl solo) / **I'm Gettin' Sentimental Over You**
All selections used on ET: 1954 March Of Dimes Program
Walk It Off vGP (recorded but not used)

Also in late October *Variety* (October 28, 1953, 41) carried a story that hinted that Tommy and Jimmy were considering forming their own independent record label in partnership with Jack Comer, a Knoxville, Tennessee, small label owner.

Travel itinerary: Mon., Nov. 16, 1953—banquet-dance for Pontiac Division, General Motors Corp., Detroit, Mich.

On Friday, December 4, the Tommy Dorsey band now featuring Jimmy Dorsey was back at the Statler Hotel in New York, where Jimmy had taken up residence following his 1949 divorce from Jane.

On opening night the Cafe Rouge was packed with all side rooms also opened, this despite a weeklong newspaper strike. By now radio and television promotion was more important than newspapers to the success of such an affair. The flashy opening was reminiscent of similar events in the prewar days.

Just as there had been a Glenn Miller to act as go-between for the brothers in the thirties, so there was Lee Castle, who had to do the same in the fifties. Lee would be out front leading the band for dinner music from 7:00 to 8:00, then Jimmy led for an hour or so, and "the boss," Tommy, took over at 9:00 while Jimmy went back to being a sideman.

Jimmy would sometimes return out front about an hour before closing and the brothers would let down their hair. In many ways it was a bitter pill for Jimmy to swallow, but given all the other experiences he had survived the past few years, it was something of a relief as well.

Broadcast schedule (all Cafe Rouge): Sun., Dec 6, NBC [WNBC], 12:05-12:30 A.M. / Wed., Dec 9, NBC [WNBC], 11:30-12:00 P.M.

> *sustaining broadcast,* Cafe Rouge, Hotel Statler, New York, N.Y.—NBC [WNBC], 12:05-12:30 A.M. Sunday, December 13, 1953

TOMMY DORSEY & HIS ORCH., featuring Jimmy Dorsey
Bill Finnegan (arr)

Rain [Billy Hill; Peter De Rose] (as solo) / **Many Times** vJA / **Ebb Tide** [Carl Sigman; Robert Maxwell] / **I Haven't Got A Worry In The World** [Oscar Hammerstein II; Richard Rodgers] vLR / **(Back Home Again In) Indiana** [Ballard MacDonald; James F. Hanley] (small group) / **Island Queen** vGP / **Non Drastic** [Charlie Shavers]

> *sustaining broadcast,* Cafe Rouge, Hotel Statler, New York, N.Y.—NBC [WNBC], 11:30-12:00 P.M. Wednesday, December 16, 1953

TOMMY DORSEY & HIS ORCH., featuring Jimmy Dorsey
Neal Hefti (arr)

The Most Beautiful Girl In The World [Lorenz Hart; Richard Rodgers] arrNH / **Green Eyes** [N. Menendez, E. Rivera, Eddie Woods, A. Utera] vJA&LR (as solo) / **Walk It Off** vGP / **Jazz Me Blues** [Tom Delaney] (small group)

Broadcast schedule (all Cafe Rouge): Sun., Dec. 20, NBC [WNBC], 12:05-12:30 A.M. / Wed., Dec. 23, NBC [WNBC], 11:30-12:00 P.M.

Just before year's end, Jackie Gleason again wrote the Dorsey band into the script for a "Honeymooners" New Year's Eve segment on his successful television show.

> *The Jackie Gleason Show,* CBS-TV Studios, New York, N.Y.—8:00-9:00 P.M. Saturday, December 26, 1953

TOMMY DORSEY & HIS ORCH., featuring Jimmy Dorsey

I'm Gettin' Sentimental Over You [Ned Washington; George Bassman] (theme) / **Marie** [Irving Berlin] vJA (as solo) / **Puddle Wump** [Charlie Shavers] / **Auld Lang Syne** [Robert Burns; traditional]

Broadcast schedule (all Cafe Rouge): Sun., Dec. 27, NBC [WNBC], 12:05-12:30 A.M. / Wed., Dec. 30, NBC [WNBC], 11:30-12:00 P.M.

The Beginning of the End
(1954-1956)

The last Dorsey decade was now entering year four, and the brothers Dorsey were hanging on to each other because all the rest of their world was disappearing, or so it seemed.

Television, which was taking over the American home, didn't consume hours of dance band remotes like radio had in the forties, and it was keeping the public at home and out of the ballrooms, theaters and hotels, which were the bands' bread and butter.

Musically, rock 'n roll was serpentinely wooing away teenagers, the big-band customer base. A swivel-hipped singer from Tupelo, Mississippi, named Elvis Presley was about to solidify the rock movement and in another ironic twist, the brothers would soon give him his first national TV exposure.

> *All-Star Parade of Bands,* Cafe Rouge, Hotel Statler,
> New York, N.Y.—NBC, 12:05-12:30 A.M. Friday,
> January 1, 1954

TOMMY DORSEY & HIS ORCH., featuring Jimmy Dorsey
Charlie Shavers (tp) replaces Amoroso (tp only), Bob Varney (d) replaces Mills. Lynn Roberts, Gordon Polk, Johnny Amoroso (vcl) Bill Finnegan, Sy Oliver, Ernie Wilkins, Howard Gibeling, Dick Jones (arr)

> Medley: **The Old Gray Mare** [Frank Panella] (as solo), **Baby Face** [Benny Davis; Harry Akst], **Happy Days Are Here Again** [Jack Yellen; Milton Ager] (as solo) / **Peace Pipe** [Ernie Wilkins] (as solo) / **Marie** [Irving Berlin] vGP&band (as solo) / **When The Saints Go Marching In** [traditional] (cl solo) *(Dorseyland Jazz Band)* / **Dance With Me Willie** vLR (cl solo) / **Walk It Off** vGP / **Kicking The Blues Around** [Ernie Wilkins] (cl solo)

The NBC *Monitor All-Star Parade of Bands* was one of the few major outlets for big bands as the mid-fifties approached. NBC was trying hard to keep the concept of entertainment radio networks alive in the face of the television onslaught. *Monitor* would be one of NBC's last major radio ventures. The CBS programs listed for Saturdays were transcribed then, but their actual airing dates and times are unknown.

> *transcribed broadcast #1,* Cafe Rouge, Hotel Statler,
> New York, N.Y.—CBS, Saturday, January 2, 1954

TOMMY DORSEY & HIS ORCH., featuring Jimmy Dorsey

> **I'm Gettin' Sentimental Over You** [Ned Washington; George Bassman] (theme) / **Blue Love** [Jackie Gleason] (as solo) / **Ruby**

525

[Mitchell Parish; Heinz Roemheld] vJA arrHG (as solo) / **When The Saints Go Marching In** (traditional) (cl solo) *(Dorseyland Jazz Band)* / **Yes Indeed!** [Sy Oliver] vLR / **Rain** [Billy Hill; Peter De Rose] arrDJ (as solo) / **Island Queen** vGP / **Kicking The Blues Around** [Ernie Wilkins] (as solo)

transcribed broadcast #2, Cafe Rouge, Hotel Statler, New York, N.Y.—CBS, Saturday, January 2, 1954
TOMMY DORSEY & HIS ORCH., featuring Jimmy Dorsey

I'm Gettin' Sentimental Over You [Ned Washington; George Bassman] (theme) / **Melancholy Serenade** [Jackie Gleason] (as solo) / **Marilyn** vJA / **Jazz Me Blues** [Tom Delaney] *(Dorseyland Jazz Band)* (cl solo) / **Sentimental Baby** [Jack Palmer] vLR / **Blue Love** [Jackie Gleason] (as solo) / **Ain't She Sweet** [Jack Yellen; Milton Ager] vGP arrSO / **Non Drastic** [Charlie Shavers] (as solo)

sustaining broadcast, Cafe Rouge, Hotel Statler, New York, N.Y.—CBS, Sunday, January 3, 1954
TOMMY DORSEY & HIS ORCH., featuring Jimmy Dorsey

I'm Gettin' Sentimental Over You [Ned Washington; George Bassman] (theme) / **Stranger In Paradise** [Robert Wright, George Forrest] (cl solo) / **So Many Times** [Don DeVito; Jimmy Dorsey] vJA / **Jazz Me Blues** [Tom Delaney] *(Dorseyland Jazz Band)* (cl solo) / **Can't Help Lovin' Dat Man** [Oscar Hammerstein II; Jerome Kern] vLR arrSO / **Ebb Tide** [Carl Sigman; Robert Maxwell] (as solo) / **Ain't She Sweet** [Jack Yellen; Milton Ager] vGP arrSO / **Peace Pipe** [Ernie Wilkins] (as solo)

Broadcast schedule (all Cafe Rouge): Sun., Jan. 3, NBC, 12:05-12:30 A.M. / Wed., Jan. 6, NBC, 11:30-12:00 P.M. / Fri., Jan. 8, NBC, 11:30-12:00 P.M.

transcribed broadcast #1, Cafe Rouge, Hotel Statler, New York, N.Y.—CBS, Saturday, January 9, 1954
TOMMY DORSEY & HIS ORCH., featuring Jimmy Dorsey

I'm Gettin' Sentimental Over You [Ned Washington; George Bassman] (theme) / **Yesterdays** [Otto Harbach; Jerome Kern] arrDJ (as solo) / **Green Eyes** [N. Menendez, E. Rivera, Eddie Woods, A. Utera] vJA&LR (as solo) / **Ain't She Sweet?** [Jack Yellen; Milton Ager] vGP / **(Back Home Again In) Indiana** [Ballard MacDonald; James F. Hanley] *(Dorseyland Jazz Band)* (cl solo)
Entire broadcast on **TC**: Cassettes Only 0548

transcribed broadcast #2, Cafe Rouge, Hotel Statler, New York, N.Y.—CBS, Saturday, January 9, 1954
TOMMY DORSEY & HIS ORCH., featuring Jimmy Dorsey

I'm Gettin' Sentimental Over You [Ned Washington; George Bassman] (theme) / **Stranger In Paradise** [Robert Wright, George Forrest] (cl solo) / **Tangerine** [Johnny Mercer; Victor Schertzinger]

vJA&LR (as solo) / **Lovely Weather For Ducks** vGP / **That's A-Plenty** [Lew Pollack] *(Dorseyland Jazz Band)* (cl solo)
     Entire broadcast on **TC:** Cassettes Only 0548

In early January the Dorseys were reported in the final stages of a contract with Bell Records, a subsidiary of Pocket Books, Inc.   Under the agreement the Dorseys would produce their own masters and lease them to Bell, which sold 45 rpm as well as seven- and ten-inch 78 rpm singles through newsstands at thirty-five cents.   Artie Shaw was also reportedly dickering with Bell (*Billboard*, January 16, 1954, 14).

Broadcast schedule (all Cafe Rouge): Sun., Jan. 10, NBC, 12:05-12:30 A.M. / Wed., Jan. 13, NBC, 11:30-12:00 P.M. / Fri., Jan. 15, NBC, 11:30-12:00 P.M.

> *sustaining broadcast,* Cafe Rouge, Hotel Statler, New York, N.Y.—NBC, 12:05-12:30 A.M. Sunday, January 17, 1954

TOMMY DORSEY & HIS ORCH., featuring **Jimmy Dorsey**

I'm Gettin' Sentimental Over You [Ned Washington; George Bassman] (theme) / **Rain** [Billy Hill; Peter De Rose] arrDJ (as solo) / **With These Hands** [Benny Davis; Abner Silver] vJA / **When The Saints Go Marching In** (traditional) (cl solo) *(Dorseyland Jazz Band)* / **Sentimental And Melancholy** [Johnny Mercer; Richard A. Whiting] vLR / **Blue Love** [Jackie Gleason] (as solo) / **Walk It Off** vGP / **Peace Pipe** [Ernie Wilkins] (as solo)
     Entire broadcast on **TC:** Cassettes Only 0548

Broadcast schedule (Cafe Rouge): Wed., Jan. 20, NBC, 11:30-12:00 P.M.

> *The Martin Block Show,* ABC Studios, New York, N.Y.—ABC, c. Thursday, January 21, 1954

DORSEYLAND JAZZ BAND
Lee Castle (tp) Tommy Dorsey (tb) **Jimmy Dorsey** (cl) Buzzy Brauner (ts) Bob Carter (p) Billy Cronk (sb) Bob Varney (d)

I'm Gettin' Sentimental Over You [Ned Washington; George Bassman] (theme) / **Contrasts** [Jimmy Dorsey] (theme) (cl solo) / **Jazz Mc Blues** [Tom Delaney] (cl solo) / Bell recording: **You're My Everything** / **Tiger Rag** [Harry De Costa; Edwin Edwards, Nick La Rocca, Tony Spargo, Larry Shields] / **Muskrat Ramble** [Ray Gilbert; Edward "Kid" Ory] / **Does Your Heart Beat For Me?** [Mitchell Parish; Russ Morgan, Arnold Johnson] (Tommy's corny solo tribute to Russ Morgan) / Bell recording: **Granada** / **I'm Gettin' Sentimental Over You** (theme)

During the Martin Block program the brothers make reference to scheduled appearances in Buffalo, New York; Tampa, Florida; and Pittsburgh, Pennsylvania, during late February. The regular broadcast schedule from the Statler indicates that if these took place they were Sunday bookings covered by plane, but there is no confirmation of this.

Broadcast schedule (all Cafe Rouge): Fri., Jan. 22, NBC, 11:30-12:00 P.M. / Sun., Jan. 24, NBC, 12:05-12:30 A.M. / Wed., Jan. 27, NBC, 11:30-12:00 P.M. / Fri., Jan. 29, NBC, 11:30-12:00 P.M.

sustaining broadcast, Cafe Rouge, Hotel Statler, New York, N.Y.—NBC, 12:05-12:30 A.M. Sunday, January 31, 1954
TOMMY DORSEY & HIS ORCH., featuring Jimmy Dorsey

I'm Gettin' Sentimental Over You [Ned Washington; George Bassman] (theme) / Rain [Billy Hill; Peter De Rose] arrDJ (as solo) / How Do You Speak To An Angel? [Bob Hilliard; Jule Styne] vJA / Jazz Me Blues [Tom Delaney] *(Dorseyland Jazz Band)* (cl solo) / Sentimental Me [Lorenz Hart; Richard Rodgers] vLR / Falling In Love With Love [Lorenz Hart; Richard Rodgers] (as solo) / Tangerine [Johnny Mercer; Victor Schertzinger] vJA&LR (as solo) / Puddle Wump [Charlie Shavers]
Entire broadcast is on CD: Magic (E) DAWE44

The following are probably from among those dates listed above.

sustaining broadcast, Cafe Rouge, Hotel Statler, New York, N.Y.—January 1954
TOMMY DORSEY & HIS ORCH., featuring Jimmy Dorsey

I'm Gettin' Sentimental Over You [Ned Washington; George Bassman] (theme) / Autumn In New York [Vernon Duke] (cl,as solos)/ Melancholy Serenade [Jackie Gleason] (as solo) / Jazz Me Blues [Tom Delaney] *(Dorseyland Jazz Band)* (cl solo) / Sentimental Baby [Jack Palmer] vLR / Blue Love [Jackie Gleason] (as solo)/ Walk It Off vGP / Non Drastic [Charlie Shavers]
Entire broadcast on ET: AFRS One Night Stand 3517

sustaining broadcast, Cafe Rouge, Hotel Statler, New York, N.Y.—January 1954
TOMMY DORSEY & HIS ORCH., featuring Jimmy Dorsey

I'm Gettin' Sentimental Over You [Ned Washington; George Bassman] (theme) / Peace Pipe [Ernie Wilkins] (as solo)/ On The Sunny Side Of The Street [Dorothy Fields; Jimmy McHugh] arrSO / (Back Home Again In) Indiana [Ballard MacDonald; James F. Hanley] *(Dorseyland Jazz Band)* (cl solo) / Melancholy Serenade [Jackie Gleason] (as solo) / Don't Worry 'Bout Me [Ted Koehler; Rube Bloom] vLR (cl solo) / Moonlight In Vermont [John Blackburn; Karl Suessdorf] arrNH (as solo) / Lovely Weather For Ducks / Kicking The Blues Around [Ernie Wilkins] (as solo)
Entire broadcast on ET: AFRS One Night Stand 3526

sustaining broadcast, Cafe Rouge, Hotel Statler, New York, N.Y.—January 1954
TOMMY DORSEY & HIS ORCH., featuring Jimmy Dorsey

I'm Gettin' Sentimental Over You [Ned Washington; George Bassman] (theme) / **Peace Pipe** [Ernie Wilkins] (as solo) / **Ruby** [Mitchell Parish; Heinz Roemheld] arrHG vJA (as solo) / **That's A-Plenty** [Lew Pollack] (cl solo) *(Dorseyland Jazz Band)* / **Melancholy Serenade** [Jackie Gleason] (as solo) / **Dance With Me, Willie** vLR / **Mississippi Mud** [James Cavanaugh, Harry Barris] vGP / **Non Drastic** [Charlie Shavers]
Entire broadcast on **ET:** AFRS One Night Stand 3535

sustaining broadcast, Cafe Rouge, Hotel Statler, New York, N.Y.—January 1954
TOMMY DORSEY & HIS ORCH., featuring Jimmy Dorsey

I'm Gettin' Sentimental Over You [Ned Washington; George Bassman] (theme) / **Peace Pipe** [Ernie Wilkins] (as solo) / **With These Hands** [Benny Davis; Abner Silver] / **(Back Home Again In) Indiana** [Ballard MacDonald; James F. Hanley] *(Dorseyland Jazz Band)* (cl solo) / **Sentimental And Melancholy** [Johnny Mercer; Richard A. Whiting] / **One Kiss** [Oscar Hammerstein II; Sigmund Romberg] / **Yours (Quieremé Mucho)** [Jack Sherr, Augustin Rodríguez; Gonzalo Roig] / **Puddle Wump** [Charlie Shavers]
Entire broadcast on **ET:** AFRS One Night Stand 3563

Down Beat (January 27, 1954, 4) featured a review of the band at the Statler that began with this optimistic quote from Tommy: "I'm happy to report that my brother and I have been associated since last May and we haven't had one fight."
    Of all the female vocalists who had tackled "Green Eyes" for Jimmy since Helen O'Connell, Lynn Roberts came closest to Helen's style. The recording date of at least the first two tunes shown next would have to precede January 21 (see *Martin Block Show,* page 527).

Columbia, New York, N.Y. Early January 1954
TOMMY DORSEY & HIS ORCH., featuring Jimmy Dorsey
Gordon Polk, Johnny Amoroso, Lynn Roberts (vcl)

-0-   **Granada** [Dorothy Dodd; Augustina Lara] (as solo)
    78: Bell 1024
    45: Bell 1024
    ET: AFRS Basic Music Library P-3365
    LP: Colpix CP/CSP401, CP/SCP 498, 498, Ajazz LP441, Accord SJA7917, Festival (Au) CFR10-298
    CD: Blue Moon (Sp) BMCD 3055
-0-   **You're My Everything** [Mort Dixon, Joe Young; Harry Warren]
    78: Bell 1024
    45: Bell 1024
    ET: AFRS Basic Music Library P-3365
    LP: Colpix CP/SCP401, CP/CSP498, Ajazz LP441, Accord SJA7917, Festival (Au) CFR10-298
    CD: Blue Moon (Sp) BMCD 3055
                        (Contd.)

530 JIMMY DORSEY: A Study in Contrasts

TOMMY DORSEY & HIS ORCH., feat. Jimmy Dorsey (Contd.)

5001 **Marie** [Irving Berlin] vGP&Band (as solo)
78: Bell 1028
45: Bell 1028
ET: AFRS Basic Music Library P-3365
LP: Colpix CP/SCP401, CP/SCP498, Ajazz LP441, Premier PM/PMS2007, Accord (F)SJA7917, Festival (Au) FM326, CFR10-298, Musicdisc (F) CV1202
5002 **Green Eyes** [N. Menendez, E. Rivera; Eddie Woods, A. Utrera] vJA&LR (as solo)
78: Bell 1028
45: Bell 1028
ET: AFRS Basic Music Library P-3365
LP: Colpix CP/SCP 436, Festival (Au) CFR10-298, Marble Arch (E) MAL655, Pye (E) GGL0353, Ajazz LP441
5003 **Make Love To Me (Tin Roof Blues)** [Bill Norvas, Allan Copeland; Mares, Roppolo, Pollack, Brunies, Stitzel, Melrose] vGP
78: Bell 1029
45: Bell 1029
LP: Colpix CP/SCP 436, Marble Arch (E) MAL655, Pye (E) GGL0353, Ajazz LP441
5001 through 5004 also on **CD:** Blue Moon (Sp) BMCD 3055
5004 **My Friend The Ghost** [Floyd Huddelston, Bob Colby] vGP
78: Bell 1029
45: Bell 1029
LP: Colpix CP/SCP 401, Ajazz LP441, Premier PM/PMS2007, Coronet CSX234, Festival (Au) FM326, Musicdisc (F) CV1202

Broadcast schedule: Wed., Feb. 3, NBC, 11:30-12:00 P.M. / Sun., Feb. 7, NBC, 12:05-12:30 A.M. / Wed., Feb. 10, NBC, 11:30-12:00 P.M. / Sun., Feb. 14, NBC, 12:05-12:30 A.M. / Wed., Feb. 17, NBC, 11:30-12:00 P.M.

Jimmy was reportedly hospitalized in mid-February for treatment of stomach problems (*Billboard,* February 27, 1954, 21).

Broadcast schedule: Sun., Feb. 21, NBC, 12:05-12:30 A.M. / Wed., Feb. 24, NBC, 11:30-12:00 P.M. / Sun., Feb. 28, NBC, 12:05-12:30 A.M. / Wed., Mar. 3, NBC, 11:30-12:00 P.M. / Sun., Mar. 7, NBC, 12:05-12:30 A.M. / Wed., Mar. 10, NBC, 11:30-12:00 P.M.

During early 1954, Tommy and Jimmy did a series of fifteen-minute transcribed programs for the Army National Guard featuring Mindy Carson and then Patti Page. Four shows were recorded at each session.

Let's Go To Town, unknown studio, New York, N.Y.
—Early March 1954
TOMMY DORSEY & HIS ORCH., featuring Jimmy Dorsey
Mindy Carson (vcl)

Granada [Dorothy Dodd; Augustina Lara] (as solo) / **I Cried For You (Now It's Your Turn To Cry Over Me)** [Arthur Freed; Gus Arnheim, Abe Lyman] vMC / **Candy And Cake** [Bob Merrill] vMC / **Jazz Me Blues** [Tom Delaney] *(Dorseyland Jazz Band)* (cl solo)
    All on ET: National Guard Program #61

Down By The Riverside [Paul Barnes] vMC / **Moonlight In Vermont** [John Blackburn; Karl Suessdorf] arrNH (as solo) / **Vaya Con Dios** [Larry Russell, Inez James, Buddy Pepper] vMC / **Kicking The Blues Around** (cl solo)
    All on ET: National Guard Program #62

Lullaby Of Broadway [Al Dubin; Harry Warren] vMC / **Autumn In New York** [Vernon Duke] arrHG (cl,as solos) / **No Other Love** [Oscar Hammerstein II; Richard Rodgers] vMC / **Peace Pipe** [Ernie Wilkins] (as solo)
    All on ET: National Guard Program #63

Out Of Nowhere [Edward Heyman; Johnny Green] (as solo) / **But Not For Me** [Ira Gershwin; George Gershwin] vMC / **Peanuts, Popcorn** vMC / **(Back Home Again In) Indiana** [Ballard MacDonald; James F. Hanley] (cl solo) *(Dorseyland Jazz Band)*
    All on ET: National Guard Program #64

In 1954 NBC-Radio's Saturday night schedule continued to include the *All Star Parade Of Bands* as part of *Monitor,* its omnibus weekend feature. Unlike the many commercial shows enjoyed by the Dorseys in the forties, this was sustaining.

The glory days were now past for both network radio and the big bands. Television was claiming the home audiences in dimensions that were never dreamed of by radio.

The older medium's answer was the young personality disk jockey, who was aired twenty-four hours a day, playing the music he (there were few if any female deejays then) felt appealed to the teenagers of the day, which of course didn't usually embrace much big-band music.

        All Star Parade Of Bands, Cafe Rouge, Hotel Statler, New York, N.Y.—NBC, Friday, March 12, 1954
TOMMY DORSEY & HIS ORCH., featuring Jimmy Dorsey

I'm Gettin' Sentimental Over You [Ned Washington; George Bassman] (theme) / **Rain** [Billy Hill; Peter De Rose] (as solo) / **How Do You Speak To An Angel?** [Bob Hilliard; Jule Styne] vJA/ **Jazz Me Blues** [Tom Delaney] *(Dorseyland Jazz Band)* (cl solo) / **Sentimental Me** [Lorenz Hart; Richard Rodgers] vLR / **Falling In Love With Love** [Lorenz Hart; Richard Rodgers] (as solo) / **Tangerine** [Johnny Mercer; Victor Schertzinger] vJA&LR (as solo) / **Puddle Wump** [Charlie Shavers]

Broadcast schedule (all Cafe Rouge): Wed., Mar. 17, NBC, 12:05-12:30 A.M. / Sat., Mar. 20, NBC, 11:30-12:00 P.M. / Wed., Mar. 24, NBC, 12:05-12:30 A.M. / Sat., Mar. 27, NBC, 11:30-12:00 P.M. / Wed., Mar. 31, NBC, 12:05-12:30 A.M.

532 JIMMY DORSEY: A Study in Contrasts

Travel itinerary: Wed., Mar. 31—Mosque Theater, Richmond, Va.

Let's Go To Town, unknown studio, New York,
N.Y.—March 1954
TOMMY DORSEY & HIS ORCH., featuring Jimmy Dorsey
Patti Page (vcl)

Song Of India [Nicholas Rimsky-Korsakoff] / **This Is My Song**
[Dick Charles] vPP / **The Whole World Is Singing My Song** [Mann
Curtis; Vic Mizzy] vPP / **Jazz Me Blues** [Tom Delaney] *(Dorseyland
Jazz Band)* (cl solo)
All on **ET:** National Guard Program #69; Patti Page vocals on
CD: Jasmine 315

Oh, What A Dream [Chuck Willis] vPP / **Ebb Tide** [Carl Sigman;
Robert Maxwell] (as solo) / **Don't Get Around Much Anymore**
[Bob Russell; Edward K. "Duke" Ellington] vPP / **Boogie Woogie**
[Clarence "Pinetop" Smith]
All on **ET:** National Guard Program #70; Patti Page vocals on
CD: Jasmine 315

Cross Over The Bridge [Bennie Benjamin, George David Weiss]
vPP / **Hernando's Hideaway** [Richard Adler, Jerry Ross] / **Steam
Heat** [Richard Adler, Jerry Ross] vPP / **Kicking The Blues Around**
[Ernie Wilkins] (as solo)
All on **ET:** National Guard Program #71; Patti Page vocals on
CD: Jasmine 315

It's A Wonderful World [Harold Adamson; Leo Watson, Jan Savitt]
vPP / **The High And The Mighty** [Ned Washington; Dimitri
Tiomkin] (as solo) / **I Cried** [Michael Elias, Billy Duke] vPP /
That's A-Plenty [Lew Pollack] (cl solo) *(Dorseyland Jazz Band)*
All on **ET:** National Guard Program #72; Patti Page vocals on
CD: Jasmine 315

The Dorsey brothers and their crew played another string of one-
nighters in the Midwest and Southwest in April and May, including one
Tuesday, April 13, at the Plantation (formerly the Longhorn Ranch) in
Dallas, Texas *(Variety,* December 2, 1953, 65).
The band was also booked for a few weeks in May 1954, at the grand
old Hotel Claridge in Memphis where NBC picked them up on two
successive Saturday nights for *Monitor.*

All Star Parade Of Bands, Hotel Claridge, Memphis,
Tenn.—NBC, Saturday, May 1, 1954
TOMMY DORSEY & HIS ORCH., featuring Jimmy Dorsey

I'm Gettin' Sentimental Over You [Ned Washington; George
Bassman] (theme) / **Fruit Cocktail** / **Sentimental And Melancholy**
[Johnny Mercer; Richard A. Whiting] vLR / **Tenderly** [Jack
Lawrence; Walter Gross] (as solo) / **There Are Such Things** [Stanley
Adams, Abel Baer, George W. Meyer] vJA / **In A Sentimental**

Mood [Manny Kurtz, Irving Mills; Edward K. "Duke" Ellington] / **Mississippi Mud** [James Cavanaugh, Harry Barris] vGP / **(Back Home Again In) Indiana** [Ballard MacDonald; James F. Hanley] (as solo) *(Dorseyland Jazz Band)*

All Star Parade Of Bands, Hotel Claridge, Memphis, Tenn.—NBC, Saturday, May 8, 1954
TOMMY DORSEY & HIS ORCH., featuring **Jimmy Dorsey**

I'm Gettin' Sentimental Over You [Ned Washington; George Bassman] (theme) / **Hour Glass Special** [adapted from Amilcare Ponchielli] / **Haven't Got A Worry To My Name** vLR / **Deep Purple** [Mitchell Parish; Peter De Rose] (as solos) / **You're The Cause Of It All** [Sammy Cahn; Jule Style] vJA / **Ebb Tide** [Carl Sigman; Robert Maxwell] (as solo) / **Ain't She Sweet?** [Jack Yellen; Milton Ager] vGP / **That's A-Plenty** [Lew Pollack] (cl solo) *(Dorseyland Jazz Band)*

That same day the brothers' prerecorded voice tracks were used as part of an audition at CBS-Radio studios in Hollywood for a proposed one-hour show featuring Judy Canova and the Charles Dant Orchestra.

Also used was the Bell recording of "Marie." The show never aired but a tape of the audition exists.

Before returning to New York, the band worked a few dates on the West Coast and cut some sides for Bell. Several of these reflect an arrangement technique, playing on the "togetherness" of the brothers, with subtle trombone and alto duets that give a good idea of what the big-band era might have been like had there been no breakup in 1935.

Columbia, Hollywood, Cal. Late May 1954
TOMMY DORSEY & HIS ORCH., featuring **Jimmy Dorsey**
Bill Raymond (vcl) added

5031   **Wanted** [Jack Fulton, Lois Steele] vLR (as solo)
    78: Bell 1041
    45: Bell 1041
    ET: AFRS Basic Music Library P-3507
    LP: Colpix CP/SCP 436, CP/SCP498, Marble Arch (E) MAL655, Pye (E) GGL0353, Ajazz LP441
5032   **I Speak To The Stars** [Paul Francis Webster; Sammy Fain] vBR (as solo)
    78: Bell 1041
    45: Bell 1041
    ET: AFRS Basic Music Library P-3507
    LP: Colpix CP/SCP 401, Ajazz LP441
5033   **Ritual Fire Dance** [Manuel De Falla]
    78: Bell 1047
    45: Bell 1097
5034   **Lost In Loveliness** [Leo Robin; Sigmund Romberg] vBR (as solo)
    78: Bell 1043
    45: Bell 1043 (Contd.)

TOMMY DORSEY & HIS ORCH., feat. **Jimmy Dorsey** (Contd.)

      LP: Colpix CP/SCP401, Ajazz LP441
      CD: Blue Moon (Sp) BMCD 3055
5035   **It Happens To Be Me** [Sammy Gallop] vLR (as solo)
      78: Bell 1043
      45: Bell 1043
      LP: Ajazz LP441
5036   **Three Coins In The Fountain** [Sammy Cahn; Jule
      Styne] vBR (as solo)
      78: Bell 1044
      45: Bell 1044
      ET: AFRS Basic Music Library P-3507, P-3821
      LP: Colpix CP/SCP 436, CP/SCP498, Marble Arch (E) MAL655,
      Pye (E) GGL0353, Ajazz LP441
5037   **Little Girl** [Madeline Hyde, Francis Henry] vGP&LR
      78: Bell 1044
      45: Bell 1044
      ET: AFRS Basic Music Library P-3507, P-3821
      LP: Colpix CP/SCP 401, CP/SCP498, Ajazz LP441, Accord
      SJA7917
      5035 through 5037 also on **CD:** Blue Moon (Sp) BMCD 3055

    In the summer of 1954, and the winter of 1955-1956, Jackie Gleason hired the Dorsey brothers for *Stage Show*, premiering July 3, 1954, initially as the summer replacement for his CBS-TV series.
    Touted at first as a major breakthrough and well-needed infusion for the band business, the show instead became a symbolic farewell to the big-band era. Each program opened with the camera entering CBS-TV Studio 50 at Broadway and West Fiftieth (where the David Letterman Show later originated), taking the home viewers down the aisle to their "seat." The show closing was the reverse of the opening.
    Jackie Gleason, who supervised the production, was a longtime pal of the Dorseys, harking back to the mid-thirties. In addition to his comedic and acting talents, Gleason was a sometime composer and arranger whose work appeared on a best-selling series of Capitol LPs, which he directed.

           Stage Show, CBS-TV Studio 50, New York,
           N.Y.—8:00-9:00 P.M. Saturday, July 3, 1954
TOMMY DORSEY & HIS ORCH., featuring **Jimmy Dorsey**
Tommy Dorsey (tb,ldr) Billy Marshall, Doug Mettome, Lee Castle, Paul Cohen, John McCormick (tp) Jimmy Henderson, Tak Takvorian, Sam Hyster (tb) **Jimmy Dorsey** (cl,as) Skip Galluccio, Kenny Delange (as) Buzzy Brauner, Joe Pamelia (ts) Teddy Lee (bar) Doug Talbert (p) Sam Herman (g) Billy Cronk (b) Bob Varney (d) Kitty Kallen, Bill Raymond (vcl)

    Marie [Irving Berlin] vBR&band / **Granada** [Dorothy Dodd; Augustina Lara] (as solo) / **In The Chapel In The Moonlight** [Billy Hill] vKK / **Little Things Mean A Lot** [Edith Lindeman, Carl Stutz] vKK / **Dixieland Mambo** / **Puddle Wump** [Charlie Shavers]

"Marie" and both Kitty Kallen vocals on **CD**: Magic (E) DAWE44

Stage Show, CBS-TV Studio 50, New York, N.Y.
—8:00-9:00 P.M. Saturday, July 10, 1954
TOMMY DORSEY & HIS ORCH., featuring Jimmy Dorsey
Four Aces, Mindy Carson (vcl)

Song Of India [Nicholas Rimsky-Korsakoff] / **There Are Such Things** [Stanley Adams, Abel Baer, George W. Meyer] / **Maria Elena** [S. K. (Bob) Russell; Lorenzo Barcelata] / **On The Sunny Side Of The Street** [Dorothy Fields; Jimmy McHugh] / **Holiday For Strings** [David Rose] / **Sin** [Chester R. Schull; George Hoven] vFA / **Wedding Bells Are Breaking Up (That Old Gang Of Mine)** [Irving Kahal, Willie Raskin; Sammy Fain] vFA / **Three Coins In The Fountain** [Sammy Cahn; Jule Styne] vFA / **Steam Heat** vMC / **I've Got A Crush On You** [Ira Gershwin; George Gershwin] vMC / **South Rampart Street Parade** [Steve Allen; Ray Bauduc, Bob Haggart] *(Dorseyland Jazz Band)*

Stage Show, CBS-TV Studio 50, New York, N.Y.
—8:00-9:00 P.M. Saturday, July 17, 1954
TOMMY DORSEY & HIS ORCH., featuring Jimmy Dorsey
Tony Bennett, The DeMarco Sisters (vcl)

Well, Git It! [Sy Oliver] / **Summertime** [DuBose Heyward; George Gershwin] / **The Hucklebuck** [Roy Alfred; Andy Gibson] vDMS / **Hernando's Hideaway** [Richard Adler, Jerry Ross] vDMS / **Because Of You** [Arthur Hammerstein; Dudley Wilkinson] vTB / **Cold, Cold Heart** [Hank Williams] vTB / **Rags To Riches** [Richard Adler, Jerry Ross] vTB / **Stranger In Paradise** [Robert Wright, George Forrest] vTB (cl solo) / **There'll Be No Tear Drops Tonight** [Hank Williams, Nelson King] vTB / **Cinnamon Sinner** [Lincoln Chase] vTB / *Medley:* **I'll Never Smile Again** [Ruth Lowe]; **Yours (Quieremé Mucho)** [Jack Sherr, Augustin Rodriguez; Gonzalo Roig]; **Yes, Indeed!** [Sy Oliver] vLR arrSO

Stage Show, CBS-TV Studio 50, New York, N.Y.
—8:00-9:00 P.M. Saturday, July 24, 1954
TOMMY DORSEY & HIS ORCH., featuring Jimmy Dorsey
The McGuire Sisters, Bill Raymond (vcl)

Dippermouth Blues [King Oliver, Louis Armstrong] arrHG / **No Other Love** [Oscar Hammerstein II; Richard Rodgers] vBR / **Melancholy Serenade** [Jackie Gleason] (as solo) / **Jilted** [Robert Colby, Dick Manning] vMGS / **Goodnight, Well It's Time To Go** [Calvin Carter, James Hudson] vMGS
"Melancholy Serenade" on **CD**: Magic (E) DAWE44

Stage Show, CBS-TV Studio 50, New York, N.Y.
—8:00-9:00 P.M.—Saturday, July 31, 1954
TOMMY DORSEY & HIS ORCH., featuring Jimmy Dorsey
Marguerite Piazza (vcl)

Stage Show (Contd.)

Opus One [Sid Garris; Sy Oliver] / Blue Champagne [Jimmy Eaton, Grady Watts, Frank Ryerson] / This Love Of Mine [Frank Sinatra; Sol Parker, Henry Senicola] / Dry Bones [traditional] / You're Breaking My Heart [Pat Genaro, Sunny Skylar] vMP / Three Coins In The Fountain [Sammy Cahn; Jule Styne] vMP / medley of operatic arias vMP / One O'Clock Jump [William "Count" Basie]

Columbia, New York, N.Y. July 1954
TOMMY DORSEY & HIS ORCH., featuring Jimmy Dorsey
Tommy Dorsey (tb,vcl,ldr) Billy Marshall, Doug Mettome, Lee Castle, Paul Cohen, John McCormick (tp) Jimmy Henderson, Tak Takvorian, Sam Hyster (tb) Jimmy Dorsey (cl,as,vcl) Skip Galluccio, Kenny Delange (as) Buzzy Brauner, Joe Pamelia (ts) Teddy Lee (bar) Doug Talbert (p) Sam Herman (g) Billy Cronk (b) Bob Varney (d) Lynn Roberts, Bill Raymond, Gordon Polk (vcl)

5060   The Man That Got Away [Ira Gershwin; Harold
               Arlen] vLR (as solo)
        45: Bell 1054
        LP: Colpix CP/SCP 436, Marble Arch (E) MAL655, Pye (E)
        GGL0353, Ajazz LP448
5061   The High And The Mighty [Ned Washington; Dim-
               itri Tiomkin] (as solo)
        45: Bell 1054
        LP: Colpix CP/SCP 401, 498, Ajazz LP448, Accord SJA7917
5062   Tangerine [Johnny Mercer; Victor Schertzinger] vBR,
               LR (as solo)
        45: Bell 1061
        LP: Colpix CP/SCP 436, Marble Arch (E) MAL655, Pye (E)
        GGL0353, Ajazz LP448
5063   Who? [Otto Harbach, Oscar Hammerstein II; Jerome
               Kern] vBR&Band
        45: Bell 1061
        LP: Colpix CP/SCP 401, 498, Ajazz LP448, Accord SJA7917
        5060-5063 also on CD: Blue Moon (Sp) BMCD 3055
5087   Papa Loves Mambo [Al Hoffman, Dick Manning,
               Bixby Reichner] vLR&Band (as solo)
        45: Bell 1064
        ET: AFRS Basic Music Library P-3507, 3821
        LP: Colpix CP/SCP 436, Marble Arch (E) MAL655, Pye (E)
        GGL0353, Ajazz LP448
        CD: Blue Moon (Sp) BMCD 3055
5088   Not As A Stranger [Buddy Kaye; Jimmy Van Heusen]
               vBR (as solo)
        45: Bell 1064
        ET: AFRS Basic Music Library P-3507, 3821
        LP: Colpix CP/SCP 401, Ajazz LP448
        CD: Blue Moon (Sp) BMCD 3055
5114   Brothers (adapted from "Sisters") [Irving Berlin]
               vTD,JD,LR,BR&GP

45: Bell 1073
LP: Colpix CP/SCP 436, Pye (E) GGL0353, Ajazz LP448
CD: Blue Moon (Sp) BMCD 3055

5115   **It's A Woman's World** [Sammy Cahn] vLR
45: Bell 1072
LP: Colpix CP/SCP 436, Pye (E) GGL0353, Ajazz LP448

5116   **Love, You Didn't Do Right By Me** [Irving Berlin]
                 vBR (as solo)
45: Bell 1073
LP: Colpix CP/SCP 436, 498, Marble Arch (E) MAL655, Pye (E)
GGL0353, Ajazz LP448
CD: Blue Moon (Sp) BMCD 3055

5120   **In A Little Spanish Town** [Sam M. Lewis, Joseph
                 Young; Mabel Wayne] (cl solo)
45: Bell 1072
LP: Colpix CP/SCP 436, 498, Marble Arch (E) MAL655, Pye (E)
GGL0353, Ajazz LP448, Accord SJA7917
CD: Blue Moon (Sp) BMCD 3055

5151   **Silk Stockings** [Cole Porter] (as solo)
45: Bell 1084
LP: Colpix CP/SCP 401, 498, Ajazz LP448, Accord SJA7917
CD: Blue Moon (Sp) BMCD 3055

5152   **One Man** vLR
45: Bell 1084

5159   **You Too Can Be A Dreamer (If You Try)** [Mitchell
                 Parish; Jerry Livingston] vLR (cl solo)
45: Bell 1087
LP: Colpix CP/SCP 436, 498, Marble Arch (E) MAL655, Pye (E)
GGL0353, Ajazz LP448
CD: Blue Moon (Sp) BMCD 3055

5160   **Mister Rainbow** vBR (as solo)
45: Bell 1087
LP: Colpix CP/SCP 401, Ajazz LP448

Stage Show, CBS-TV Studio 50, New York,
N.Y.—8:00-9:00 P.M. Saturday, August 7, 1954
TOMMY DORSEY & HIS ORCH., featuring Jimmy Dorsey
Seymour "Red" Press (cl,as,fl,piccolo) joins. Henry "Red" Allen (tp)
Helen O'Connell, Bill Raymond (vcl) Cozy Cole Band, guests

I'm Gettin' Sentimental Over You [Ned Washington; George
Bassman] (theme) / **Who?** [Otto Harbach, Oscar Hammerstein II;
Jerome Kern] vBR&band / *South Pacific* medley: **Bali Ha'i; This
Nearly Was Mine** (as solo); **Some Enchanted Evening** [Oscar Ham-
merstein II; Richard Rodgers] (as solo) / **In The Still Of The Night**
[Cole Porter] vHO'C (as behind vocal) / **All Of Me** [Seymour B.
Simons, Gerald Marks] vHO'C / **Green Eyes** [N. Menendez, E.
Rivera, Eddie Woods, A. Utera] vHO'C / **Tangerine** [Johnny Mer-
cer; Victor Schertzinger] vHO'C / **When The Saints Go Marching
In** [traditional] vRA (cl solos) *(Dorseyland Jazz Band)* plus Cozy
Cole Band and Red Allen

538   JIMMY DORSEY: A Study in Contrasts

Stage Show, CBS-TV Studio 50, New York, N.Y.
—8:00-9:00 P.M. Saturday, August 14, 1954
TOMMY DORSEY & HIS ORCH., featuring Jimmy Dorsey
Lynn Roberts, Lillian Roth (vcl)

Just One Of Those Things [Cole Porter] / (unknown music for Peg Leg Bates dance) / **The High And The Mighty** [Ned Washington; Dimitri Tiomkin] (as solo) / **The Man That Got Away** [Ira Gershwin; Harold Arlen] vLR / **Ain't She Sweet?** [Jack Yellen; Milton Ager] vLilR / **I'm In Love With Honey** vLRo / **Goody Goody** [Johnny Mercer; Matty Malneck] vLilR / **I'll Cry Tomorrow** [Dave Dreyer, Gerald Marks, Lillian Roth] vLilR / **King Porter Stomp** [Ferdinand "Jelly Roll" Morton]

Stage Show, CBS-TV Studio 50, New York, N.Y.
—8:00-9:00 P.M. Saturday, August 21, 1954
TOMMY DORSEY & HIS ORCH., featuring Jimmy Dorsey
Louis Armstrong (tp) Monica Lewis (vcl)

I'm Gettin' Sentimental Over You [Ned Washington; George Bassman] (theme) / **Sweet Georgia Brown** [Maceo Pinkard, Kenneth Casey, Ben Bernie] (as solo) / **Looking For A Boy** [Ira Gershwin; George Gershwin] vML / **If I Give My Heart To You** [Jimmie Crane, Al Jacobs, Jimmy Brewster] vML / **Dixieland One Step** / **Rhapsody In Blue** [George Gershwin] / **Mood Indigo** [Edward K. "Duke" Ellington, Barney Bigard, Irving Mills] / **That's A-Plenty** [Lew Pollack] / *Theme Song Medley:* **Auld Lang Syne** *(Guy Lombardo),* **Got A Date With An Angel** *(Hal Kemp),* **Let's Dance** *(Benny Goodman),* **Moonlight Serenade** *(Glenn Miller),* **Ciribiribin** *(Harry James);* **When It's Sleepy Time Down South** *(Louis Armstrong)* (v,tpLA) / **South Rampart Street Parade** [Steve Allen; Ray Bauduc, Bob Haggart] (cl solo) (tpLA)

Stage Show, CBS-TV Studio 50, New York, N.Y.
—8:00-9:00 P.M. Saturday, August 28, 1954
TOMMY DORSEY & HIS ORCH., featuring Jimmy Dorsey
Dolores Hawkins, Vaughn Monroe (vcl)

Manhattan [Lorenz Hart; Richard Rodgers] / **Hey There** [Richard Adler, Jerry Ross] vDH / **Sing, You Sinners** [Sam Coslow, W. Franke Harling] vDH / **The Breeze And I** [Al Stillman; Ernesto Lecuona] / **Fools Rush In** [Johnny Mercer; Rube Bloom] / **Rain** [Billy Hill; Peter De Rose] (as solo) / **Doin' The Mambo** vVM / **Blue Moon** [Lorenz Hart; Richard Rodgers] vVM / **Racing With The Moon** [Vaughn Monroe, Pauline Pope; Johnny Watson] vVM / **Kicking The Blues Around** [Ernie Wilkins] (as solo)

Stage Show, CBS-TV Studio 50, New York, N.Y.
—8:00-9:00 P.M. Saturday, September 4, 1954
TOMMY DORSEY & HIS ORCH., featuring Jimmy Dorsey
Bill Raymond, Lynn Roberts, Toni Arden (vcl)

Non Drastic [Charlie Shavers] / **Amapola** [Albert Gamse; Joseph M. Lacalle] vBR&LR / **Boogie Woogie** [Clarence "Pinetop" Smith] /**It All Depends On You** [Buddy De Sylva, Lew Brown; Ray Henderson] vTA / **I Can Dream, Can't I?** [Irving Kahal; Sammy Fain] vTA / **Perdido** [Juan Tizol]
First three selections and "Perdido" on LP: Magic (E) AWE-30

On Friday, September 10, the boys returned to the bandstand at the Hotel Statler's Cafe Rouge for a month's run that ended Thursday, October 7. A standby band filled in at the Statler Saturday evenings while Jimmy, Tommy and the Dorsey band were at the TV studios.

Stage Show, CBS-TV Studio 50, New York, N.Y.
—8:00-9:00 P.M. Saturday, September 11, 1954
TOMMY DORSEY & HIS ORCH., featuring Jimmy Dorsey
Roy Hamilton (vcl)

Lover [Lorenz Hart; Richard Rodgers] (as solo) / **Street Of Dreams** [Sam M. Lewis; Victor Young] (as solo) / **Brazil** (Aquarela do Brasil) [S. K. (Bob) Russell; Ary Baroso] (as solo) / **Daybreak** [Harold Adamson; Ferde Grofé] / **Oh, What A Beautiful Morning** [Oscar Hammerstein II; Richard Rodgers] / **Ebb Tide** [Carl Sigman; Robert Maxwell] vRH / **You'll Never Walk Alone** [Oscar Hammerstein II; Richard Rodgers] vRH / **Deep River** [Henry Thacker Burleigh]

Stage Show, CBS-TV Studio 50, New York, N.Y.
—8:00-9:00 P.M. Saturday, September 18, 1954
TOMMY DORSEY & HIS ORCH., featuring Jimmy Dorsey
Lionel Hampton (vib) Mills Brothers (vcl)

Heaven Help Us [Deane Kincaide] / **I'm Gettin' Sentimental Over You** [Ned Washington; George Bassman] / **Contrasts** [Jimmy Dorsey] / **Melancholy Serenade** [Jackie Gleason] (as solo) / **How Blue** vMB / **Lazy River** [Sidney Arondin; Hoagy Carmichael] vMB / **The Glow-Worm** [Johnny Mercer; Paul Lincke] vMB / **Say "Si Si"** [Al Stillman; Ernesto Lecuona] vMB / **How High The Moon** [Nancy Hamilton, Morgan Lewis] (vib,LH) / **Flyin' Home** [Lionel Hampton, Benny Goodman] (vib,LH)

The September 18 telecast marked the end of the summer series. However, Jackie Gleason was so delighted with *Stage Show* that he had it return several times during the regular season.

Stars In Action (National Guard Show), unknown location, New York, N.Y.—Friday, September 24, 1954
TOMMY DORSEY & HIS ORCH., featuring Jimmy Dorsey
Georgia Gibbs (vcl)

I'm Gettin' Sentimental Over You [Ned Washington; George Bassman] (theme) / **(Back Home Again In) Indiana** [Ballard Mac-

Stars In Action (Contd.)

Donald; James F.   Hanley] (cl solo) *(Dorseyland Jazz Band)* / **Granada** [Dorothy Dodd; Augustina Lara] (as solo) / **My Blue Heaven** [George Whiting; Walter Donaldson] vGG / **No Other Love** [Oscar Hammerstein II; Richard Rodgers] vGG / **Autumn In New York** [Vernon Duke] vGG (cl,as solos) / **Moonlight In Vermont** [John Blackburn; Karl Suessdorf] arrNH (as solo) / **He's Funny That Way** [Neil Moret; Richard A.   Whiting] vGG / **Out Of Nowhere** [Edward Heyman; Johnny Green] (as solo) / **Somebody Loves Me** [Ira Gershwin; George Gershwin] vGG / **Muskrat Ramble** [Ray Gilbert; Edward "Kid" Ory] (cl solo) *(Dorseyland Jazz Band)*

>   *Let's Go To Town,* unknown studio, New York, N.Y.
>   —Early autumn 1954
TOMMY DORSEY & HIS ORCH., featuring **Jimmy Dorsey**
Mindy Carson (vcl)

Manhattan [Lorenz Hart; Richard Rodgers] / **I've Got A Crush On You** [Ira Gershwin; George Gershwin] vMC / **I Can't Get Him Off My Mind** vMC / **There Are Such Things** [Stanley Adams, Abel Baer, George W.   Meyer] arrDJ
    All on **ET**: National Guard Program #141

September Song [Maxwell Anderson; Kurt Weill] / **Mister Wonderful** [Jerry Block, Larry Holofcener, George David Weiss] vMC / **Hold Me Tight** [Johnny Nash] vMC / **Opus One** [Sid Garris; Sy Oliver]
    All on **ET**: National Guard Program #142

I Dream Of You (More Than You Dream I Do) [Marjorie Goetschius, Edna Osser] (as solo) / **I'm Nobody's Baby** [Benny Davis, Milton Ager, Lester Santly] vMC / **I'll Always Love You** [Jay Livingston, Ray Evans] vMC / **In A Little Spanish Town** [Sam M. Lewis, Joseph Young; Mabel Wayne] (cl solo)
    All on **ET**: National Guard Program #143

Once In A While [Bud Green; Michael Edwards] / **Everybody Loves My Baby** [Jack Palmer; Spencer Williams] vMC / **Wake The Town And Tell The People** [Sammy Gallop; Jerry Livingston] vMC / **Flagler Drive** [Ernie Wilkins] (as solo)
    All on **ET**: National Guard Program #144

In the year between September 1954 and August 1955, Tommy continued taping arrangements on speculation.   The recording dates are unknown but can be roughly established by the sounds of drummers Cliff Leeman, Buddy Rich and Louis Bellson. These tapes were eventually sold by Tommy's widow to Columbia Records, which assigned master numbers and released them on three LPs.

Columbia, New York, N.Y. September 1954
TOMMY DORSEY & HIS ORCH., featuring **Jimmy Dorsey**

Tommy Dorsey (tb,ldr) Lee Castle, Charlie Shavers, Billy Marshall [or] John Frosk, Paul Cohen [or] Dick Perry, John McCormick [or] Art Tancredi (tp) Tak Takvorian, Jimmy Henderson [or] Vince Forrest, Sam Hyster [or] Sonny Russo (tb) **Jimmy Dorsey** (cl,as) Skip Galluccio (as) Red Press (as,fl,piccolo) Buzzy Brauner, Joe Pamelia [or] Gale Curtis (ts) Teddy Lee (bar) Doug Talbert (p) Sam Herman (g) Billy Cronk (b) Cliff Leeman (d)

CO60082   **Wagon Wheels** [Billy Hill; Peter De Rose]
    LP: Columbia CL1150 (part of C2L-8), Harmony HL7334, Ajazz
    LP448

Dropping plans to organize a new band of his own, drummer Buddy Rich joined the Dorseys around November 15, replacing Cliff Leeman. Rich came on board during a period of one-nighters in the South (*Down Beat,* December 1, 1954, 1).

The brothers returned Friday, December 17, to the Hotel Statler for a five-week stay. Also in December they celebrated their twentieth anniversary as bandleaders. *Down Beat* (January 12, 1955, 1) announced that the Dorseys would replace Jackie Gleason again January 1 and 8, and that a survey of 1,000 New Yorkers listed *Stage Show* number three among TV programs "most desired that are now off the screens."

Tommy and Jimmy were reportedly forming their own record label in late 1954 (*Variety,* December 15, 1954, 49) and were scheduled to premiere the new label in early 1955. The move was not seen as a violation of their contract with the bargain-priced Bell Records, which allowed them to also record for a regular-priced label. The sessions that follow were part of that plan. However, the label never came into being and the tapes are among those posthumously acquired by Columbia.

Columbia, New York, N.Y. Late December 1954 to early 1955
TOMMY DORSEY & HIS ORCH., featuring **Jimmy Dorsey**
Buddy Rich (d) replaces Leeman. Deane Kincaide, Ernie Wilkins (arr)

CO60074   **Where Is That Rock?** [Deane Kincaide] (cl solo)
    LP: Columbia CL1151 (part of C2L-8)
CO60075   **Heaven Help Us** [Deane Kincaide] (cl solo)
    LP: Columbia CL1151 (part of C2L-8)
CO60083   **We've Crossed The Widest River** [Deane Kincaide]
                 (as,cl solos)
    LP: Columbia CL1150 (part of C2L-8)
CO60084   **Peace Pipe** [Ernie Wilkins] (as solo)
    LP: Columbia CL1150 (part of C2L-8)
CO60085   **How Far Is It To Jordan?** [Deane Kincaide] (cl solo)
    LP: Columbia CL1150 (part of C2L-8)
CO60087   **Judgement Is Coming** [Deane Kincaide] (as solo)
    LP: Columbia CL1150 (part of C2L-8)

              sustaining broadcast, Cafe Rouge, Hotel Statler, New
              York, N.Y.—NBC   [WNBC],   11:45-11:55   P.M.
              Friday, December 31, 1954

TOMMY DORSEY & HIS ORCH., featuring Jimmy Dorsey
Lynn Roberts, Bill Raymond (vcl)

I'm Gettin' Sentimental Over You [Ned Washington; George Bassman] (theme) / **Lover** [Lorenz Hart; Richard Rodgers] (as solo) / **It's A Woman's World** [Sammy Cahn] vLR / **Do It Yourself** [Ernie Wilkins]

At this point announcer Fred Collins switched NBC to Times Square for the traditional midnight countdown. The network then picked up Duke Ellington until 12:30, when they returned to the Cafe Rouge.

> *sustaining broadcast,* Cafe Rouge, Hotel Statler, New York, N.Y.—NBC, [WNBC], 12:30-1:00 A.M. Saturday, January 1, 1955

TOMMY DORSEY & HIS ORCH., featuring Jimmy Dorsey

Medley: **A Hot Time In The Old Town Tonight** [Joe Hayden; Theodore Metz]; **Happy Days Are Here Again** [Jack Yellen; Milton Ager] (as solo) / **Well, Git It!** [Sy Oliver] / **Perdido** [Juan Tizol] (as solo) / **In A Little Spanish Town** [Sam M. Lewis, Joseph Young; Mabel Wayne] (cl solo) / **Mister Rainbow** vBR (as solo) / **It Happens To Be Me** [Sammy Gallop] vLR (as solo) / **Stompin' Down Broadway** [Ernie Wilkins] (as solo)

> *sustaining broadcast,* Cafe Rouge, Hotel Statler, New York, N.Y.—December 1954-January 1955

TOMMY DORSEY & HIS ORCH., featuring Jimmy Dorsey

I'm Gettin' Sentimental Over You [Ned Washington; George Bassman] (theme) / **Stereophonic** [Ernie Wilkins] / **It Worries Me** / **I Should Care** [Sammy Cahn, Axel Stordahl, Paul Weston] (as solo) / **It's A Woman's World** [Sammy Cahn] vLR / **Jazz Me Blues** [Tom Delaney] *(Dorseyland Jazz Band)* (cl solo) / **Tangerine** [Johnny Mercer; Victor Schertzinger] vBR&LR (as solo) / **Silk Stockings** [Cole Porter]
Entire broadcast on **ET:** AFRS One Night Stand 3709

> *sustaining broadcast,* Cafe Rouge, Hotel Statler, New York, N.Y.—December 1954-January 1955

TOMMY DORSEY & HIS ORCH., featuring Jimmy Dorsey
Bill Raymond, Lynn Roberts (vcl)

I'm Gettin' Sentimental Over You [Ned Washington; George Bassman] (theme) / **Stereophonic** [Ernie Wilkins] / **Three Coins In The Fountain** [Sammy Cahn; Jule Styne] / **It Started All Over Again** [Bill Carey; Carl Fisher] / **The Man That Got Away** [Ira Gershwin; Harold Arlen] / **Muskrat Ramble** [Ray Gilbert; Edward "Kid" Ory] *(Dorseyland Jazz Band)* / **Green Eyes** [N. Menendez, E. Rivera, Eddie Woods, A. Utera] vBR&LR (as solo) / **Rain** [Billy Hill; Peter De Rose] (as solo) / **Flagler Drive** [Ernie Wilkins] (as solo)
Entire broadcast on **ET:** AFRS One Night Stand 3712

Flagler Drive, inspiration for the title of Ernie Wilkins' instrumental, was the street where Tommy lived in Greenwich, Connecticut.

sustaining broadcast, Cafe Rouge, Hotel Statler, New York, N.Y.—December 1954-January 1955
TOMMY DORSEY & HIS ORCH., featuring Jimmy Dorsey

I'm Gettin' Sentimental Over You [Ned Washington; George Bassman] (theme) / **Skirts And Sweaters** [Ernie Wilkins] / **It's A Woman's World** [Sammy Cahn] vLR / **I Should Care** [Sammy Cahn, Axel Stordahl, Paul Weston] (as solo) / **Mister Rainbow** vBR (as solo) / **Do It Yourself** [Ernie Wilkins] / **Tangerine** [Johnny Mercer; Victor Schertzinger] vBR&LR (as solo)
Entire broadcast on ET: AFRS One Night Stand 3721

sustaining broadcast, Cafe Rouge, Hotel Statler, New York, N.Y.—December 1954-January 1955
TOMMY DORSEY & HIS ORCH., featuring Jimmy Dorsey

I'm Gettin' Sentimental Over You [Ned Washington; George Bassman] (theme) / **In A Little Spanish Town** [Sam M. Lewis, Joseph Young; Mabel Wayne] (as solo) / **It Happens To Be Me** [Sammy Gallop] (as solo) / **The Night We Called It A Day** [Tom Adair; Matt Dennis] (as solo) / **(Back Home Again In) Indiana** [Ballard MacDonald; James F. Hanley] *(Dorseyland Jazz Band)* (cl solo) / **What Do You Think I Am?** [Hugh Martin, Ralph Blane] / **Stompin' Down Broadway** [Ernie Wilkins] (as solo)
Entire broadcast on ET: AFRS One Night Stand 3726

sustaining broadcast, Cafe Rouge, Hotel Statler, New York, N.Y.—December 1954-January 1955
TOMMY DORSEY & HIS ORCH., featuring Jimmy Dorsey

I'm Gettin' Sentimental Over You [Ned Washington; George Bassman] (theme) / **Lover** [Lorenz Hart; Richard Rodgers] (as solo) / **A Lovely Way To Spend An Evening** [Harold Adamson; Jimmy McHugh] / **Nevada** [Mort Greene; Walter Donaldson] (as solo) / **When The Saints Go Marching In** [traditional] (cl solo) *(Dorseyland Jazz Band)* / **Green Eyes** [N. Menendez, E. Rivera, Eddie Woods, A. Utera] vBR&LR (as solo) / **Rain** [Billy Hill; Peter De Rose] (as solo)
Entire broadcast on ET: AFRS One Night Stand 3731

As 1954 came to a close it became apparent that another venue for the big bands on tour was drying up. According to *Variety* (December 22, 1954, 45), there was increasing interest in jazz on college campuses, with Dave Brubeck and Gerry Mulligan as examples of the jazz combos that were grabbing the campus jobs along with touring concert series like "Jazz At The Philharmonic." Not to be ignored either was the mushrooming rock 'n roll craze that was grabbing the teenagers.

When Jackie Gleason took a two-week midwinter vacation, the Dorseys were called in to substitute for "The Great One."

Stage Show, CBS-TV Studio 50, New York, N.Y.
—8:00-9:00 P.M. Saturday, January 1, 1955
TOMMY DORSEY & HIS ORCH., featuring Jimmy Dorsey
Duke Ellington (p) Johnny Ray, Mindy Carson (vcl)

Stage Show theme / **My Brother Is The Leader Of The Band**
vTD&JD / **Teach Me Tonight** [Sammy Cahn; Gene DePaul] vMC /
I've Got The World On A String [Ted Koehler; Harold Arlen] vMC
/ Duke Ellington Medley: **Don't Get Around Much Anymore; In A
Sentimental Mood; Mood Indigo; I'm Beginning To See The Light**
(as solo); **Sophisticated Lady** (as solo); **Caravan; Solitude** (as solo);
**Do Nothin' Till You Hear From Me; I Let A Song Go Out Of My
Heart; It Don't Mean A Thing If It Ain't Got That Swing**
[Edward K. "Duke" Ellington] / **Alexander's Ragtime Band** [Irv-
ing Berlin] / **If You Believe** [Johnny Ray] vJR / **When The Saints
Go Marching In** [traditional] vJR (cl solo) *(Dorseyland Jazz Band
including Duke Ellington)* / Closing Theme
    Entire show on **CD:** Jazz Band (E) EBCD 2123-2; First six
    selections (including theme) on **TC:** Magic (E) CAWE-37 , **CD:**
    Magic (E) DAWE-37; "Ellington Medley" and "When The Saints
    Go Marching In" on **LP:** Giants Of Jazz GOJ-1008

Stage Show, CBS-TV Studio 50, New York, N.Y.
—8:00-9:00 P.M. Saturday, January 8, 1955
TOMMY DORSEY & HIS ORCH., featuring Jimmy Dorsey
Johnny Ray, Patti Page (vcl)

Stage Show theme / **Opus One** [Sid Garris; Sy Oliver] / **(I Wanna
Go Where You Go, Do What You Do) Then I'll Be Happy** [Sidney
Clare, Lew Brown; Cliff Friend] vPP / **You Too Can Be A Dreamer
(If You Try)** [Mitchell Parish; Jerry Livingston] vPP / *Dorseys
medley*: **There Are Such Things** [Stanley Adams, Abel Baer, George
W. Meyer] (as solo); **Maria Elena** [S. K. (Bob) Russell; Lorenzo
Barcelata] (as solo); **On The Sunny Side Of The Street** [Dorothy
Fields; Jimmy McHugh]; **Holiday For Strings** [David Rose] / **Please
Don't Talk About Me When I'm Gone** [Sidney Clare; Sam H.
Stept] vJR / **Cry** [Churchill Kohlman] vJR / **The Jubilee** vJR / **Quiet
Please** [Sy Oliver]
    Entire show on **CD:** Jazz Band (E) EBCD 2123-2; "Quiet Please"
    on **TC:** Magic (E) CAWE37, **CD:** Magic (E) DAWE37

On Wednesday evening, January 12, the Statler was the scene of a
celebration marking the brothers' two decades as big-band leaders.

sustaining broadcast, Cafe Rouge, Hotel Statler, New
York, N.Y.—CBS, Saturday, January 15, 1955
TOMMY DORSEY & HIS ORCH., featuring Jimmy Dorsey

Skirts And Sweaters [Ernie Wilkins] / **It's A Woman's World**
[Sammy Cahn] vLR / **Rain** [Billy Hill; Peter De Rose] (as solo) /
Mister Rainbow vBR (as solo) / **When The Saints Go Marching In**
[traditional] (cl solo) *(Dorseyland Jazz Band)* / **Teach Me Tonight**

[Sammy Cahn; Gene DePaul] vLR (as solo) / **Peace Pipe** [Ernie Wilkins] (as solo) / **I'm Gettin' Sentimental Over You** [Ned Washington; George Bassman]
"Skirts And Sweaters," "Mister Rainbow" and closing theme on TC: Magic (E) CAWE44, CD: Magic (E) DAWE44

sustaining broadcast, Cafe Rouge, Hotel Statler, New York, N.Y.—CBS, Saturday, January 22, 1955
TOMMY DORSEY & HIS ORCH., featuring Jimmy Dorsey

I'm Gettin' Sentimental Over You [Ned Washington; George Bassman] (theme) / **Peace Pipe** [Ernie Wilkins] (as solo)/ **You Too Can Be A Dreamer** vLR (cl solo) / **Nevada** [Mort Greene; Walter Donaldson] arrHG (as solo) / **Mister Rainbow** vBR (as solo) / **(Back Home Again In) Indiana** [Ballard MacDonald; James F. Hanley] (cl solo) *(Dorseyland Jazz Band)* / **Teach Me Tonight** [Sammy Cahn; Gene DePaul] vLR (as solo) / **Kicking The Blues Around** [Ernie Wilkins] (as solo)

sustaining broadcast, Cafe Rouge, Hotel Statler, New York, N.Y.—CBS, Wednesday, January 26, 1955
TOMMY DORSEY & HIS ORCH., featuring Jimmy Dorsey

Mister Rainbow vBR (as solo) / **When The Saints Go Marching In** [traditional] (cl solo) *(Dorseyland Jazz Band)* / **It Happens To Be Me** [Sammy Gallop] vLR (as solo) / **Flagler Drive** [Ernie Wilkins] (as solo) / **I'm Gettin' Sentimental Over You** [Ned Washington; George Bassman] (theme)

By the end of January, CBS-TV had lined up the Nestlé Company as one of three sponsors for the fall season of *Stage Show,* starring the Dorseys. The network was also trying to sign Gleason's other two sponsors, Schick shavers and Sheaffer pens, but industry sources were saying the two companies were still miffed over Gleason's decision to go to a half-hour filmed *Honeymooners* segment instead of the hour-long live show that had been so successful.

sustaining broadcast, Cafe Rouge, Hotel Statler, New York, N.Y.—CBS Thursday, January 27, 1955
TOMMY DORSEY & HIS ORCH., featuring Jimmy Dorsey

I'm Gettin' Sentimental Over You [Ned Washington; George Bassman] (theme) / **Lover** [Lorenz Hart; Richard Rodgers] (as solo) / **It's A Woman's World** [Sammy Cahn] vLR / **The Night We Called It A Day** [Tom Adair; Matt Dennis] (as solo) / **Mr. Rainbow** vBR (as solo) / **When The Saints Go Marching In** [traditional] (cl solo) *(Dorseyland Jazz Band)* / **Don't Worry 'Bout Me** [Ted Koehler; Rube Bloom] vLR (cl solo) / **Stereophonic** [Ernie Wilkins]
Entire broadcast on ET: AFRS One Night Stand 3737, TC: Imperfect C-119. Last two selections on TC: Magic (E) CAWE37, CD: Magic (E) DAWE37. In addition, ONS 3737 adds "Flagler Drive" from an unknown broadcast as a filler.

Travel itinerary: Tues., Feb. 1—Warner Theater, Erie, Pa., benefit show for Men's Club of Erie.

In February 1955, New York's Manhattan Center was the scene of a joint twentieth anniversary celebration for Tommy Dorsey's Orchestra and the WNEW *Make Believe Ballroom,* hosted by Martin Block.

The Tommy Dorsey Orchestra, featuring Jimmy Dorsey, was on hand along with Tommy's most famous alumnus, Frank Sinatra, who happened to be in town at the famed Copacabana.

> *WNEW Make Believe Ballroom and Tommy Dorsey Orch. 20th Anniversary stage show,* Manhattan Center, New York, N.Y.—Thursday, February 3, 1955

TOMMY DORSEY & HIS ORCH., featuring Jimmy Dorsey
Frank Sinatra (vcl)

(Testimonials: Tommy Dorsey praises Frank Sinatra, Sinatra praises Dorsey) / **I'll Never Smile Again** [Ruth Lowe] vFS / **Oh! Look At Me Now!** [John De Vries; Joe Bushkin] vFS / **This Love Of Mine** [Frank Sinatra; Sol Parker, Henry Senicola] vFS / (Segment closing)
    All on **CD:** Voice (C) V-CD-1103

Beginning Saturday, March 12, the Dorsey band worked the still popular Meadowbrook in New Jersey on weekends. That same night Jackie Gleason took a two-week break and the Dorseys again had a standby band at the Meadowbrook for that part of the Saturday nights in which they filled in for Gleason.

> *Stage Show,* CBS-TV Studio 50, New York, N.Y., 8:00-9:00 P.M. Saturday, March 12, 1955

TOMMY DORSEY & HIS ORCH., featuring Jimmy Dorsey
Count Basie (p) Kate Smith, The DeMarco Sisters (vcl)

Heaven Help Us [Deane Kincaide] / **Two Hearts, Two Kisses** vDMS / **Imitations** vDMS / **I'll Never Smile Again** [Ruth Lowe] / **Yours (Quieremé Mucho)** [Jack Sherr, Augustin Rodriguez; Gonzalo Roig] / **South Rampart Street Parade** [Steve Allen; Ray Bauduc, Bob Haggart] *(Jazz Band)* / **Just One Of Those Things** [Cole Porter] vKS /**When Your Lover Has Gone** [Einar A. Swan] vKS / **I've Got The World On A String** [Ted Koehler; Harold Armstrong] vKS / **One O'Clock Jump** [William "Count" Basie] (p,CB)

One of the March 12 *Stage Show* viewers was Charlie ("Bird") Parker, by then undisputed jazz king of the alto sax and one of the creators of bop. At approximately 8:35, which would place it about the time the Dixieland number was on, Parker reportedly began to laugh, suddenly collapsed and died a few minutes later of a massive heart attack, complicated by lobar pneumonia, ulcers and cirrhosis of the liver.

Scenes from the show on a TV screen were part of the 1988 movie *Bird,* directed by Clint Eastwood. Parker was known to admire Jimmy's techniques, and Jimmy admired his. Parker reportedly was paid $100 to play one night for Jimmy in his hotel room (Bockemuehl 1996, 34). (When Jimmy died *Billboard* called him the Charlie Parker of his day for his work in the twenties.)

Stage Show, CBS-TV Studio 50, New York, N.Y.
—8:00-9:00 P.M. Saturday, March 19, 1955
TOMMY DORSEY & HIS ORCH., featuring **Jimmy Dorsey**
Nat King Cole, The McGuire Sisters (vcl)

Song Of India [Nicholas Rimsky-Korsakoff] / **Comedian's Gallop** [Dimitri Kabalevsky] / **Sincerely** [Harvey Fuqua, Alan Freed] vMgS / **I'd Rather Lead A Band** [Irving Berlin] vMgS / Dorseys Medley: **Street Of Dreams** [Sam M. Lewis; Victor Young] (as solo); **Brazil** (Aquarela do Brasil) [S. K. [Bob] Russell; Ary Baroso] (as solo) ; **Daybreak** [Harold Adamson; Ferde Grofé]; **Oh, What A Beautiful Morning** [Oscar Hammerstein II; Richard Rodgers] / **Pavanne** [Morton Gould] / **Darling, Je Vous Aime Beaucoup** [Anna Sosenko] vNKC/ **It's Crazy, But I'm In Love** vNKC/ **The Sand And The Sea** [Hal Hester, Barry Parker] vNKC / **Stompin' Down Broadway** vNKC [Ernie Wilkins(as solo)]
  Except for "Pavanne" the entire broadcast is on **LP:** Magic AWE-30; "It's Crazy, But I'm In Love" on **TC:** LaserLight 15-750, **CD:** LaserLight 15-750, Delta/Jazzline 20815; "Stomping Down Broadway" on **LP:** Festival (Au) ALB223, Accord 302232, **TC:** LaserLight 15-750, **CD:** LaserLight 15-750, Magic DATOM5, Delta 11086, Delta /Jazzline 20815 (Laserlight 15-750 is also included in the 5-CD Laserlight 915 set).

Look magazine in late April featured the Dorsey Brothers in an article titled "The Dorseys Bring Back the Swing Era." Tommy used it to open up on the "bopsters," calling them "musical communists," adding that they couldn't be danced to, were frustrated and not worth hearing.
  The Dorsey band was on another *Stage Show* May 7, but Jimmy was ill and did not appear. "Toots" Mondello replaced him, Gale Curtis moved from tenor to alto and "Boomie" Richman filled in on tenor.
  Jimmy also missed five cuts made in early May, and later part of either LP set C2L-8: (CO 60071—"Skirts And Sweaters," CO 60073 —"Flagler Drive,") or CL-1240: (CO 60093—"Just Swingin'," CO 60096—"Prelude To A Kiss" and CO 60097—"Ruby") (Seavor 1997).

Columbia, New York, N.Y. Mid to late May, 1955
TOMMY DORSEY & HIS ORCH., featuring **Jimmy Dorsey**
Andy Ferretti for *unknown* (tp) Boomie Richman (ts) replaces Gale Curtis, who moves to (as). Louis Bellson (d) replaces Rich. Lynn Roberts, Gordon Polk (vcl) Dick Jones, Howard Gibeling, Deane Kincaide, Ernie Wilkins, Neal Hefti (arr)

CO60065   **Melancholy Serenade** [Jackie Gleason] (as solo)
      LP: Columbia CL1151 (part of C2L-8), Harmony KH-32014, Music For Pleasure (Au) MFP10001
CO60066   **There Are Such Things** [Stanley Adams, (Contd.)

TOMMY DORSEY & HIS ORCH., feat. Jimmy Dorsey (Contd.)

                    Abel Baer, George W. Meyer] arrDJ (as solo)
        LP: Columbia CL1151 (part of C2L-8), B-2596, Harmony HL-
        7334, KH-32014, Music For Pleasure (Au) MFP10001
CO60067   **Autumn In New York** [Vernon Duke] (cl,as solos)
        LP: Columbia CL1151 (part of C2L-8), Harmony HL-7334, KH-
        32014, Music For Pleasure (Au) MFP10001
CO60068   **Do Do Do** [Ira Gershwin, George Gershwin] arrHG
                    (as solo)
        LP: Columbia CL1151 (part of C2L-8), Harmony KH-32014,
        Music For Pleasure (Au) MFP10001
CO60069   **I Should Care** [Sammy Cahn, Axel Stordahl, Paul
                    Weston] (as solo)
        LP: Columbia CL1151 (part of C2L-8), B-2596, Harmony HL-
        7334, KH-32014, Music For Pleasure (Au) MFP10001
        CD: Sony Special Products 10263
CO60070   **Moonlight In Vermont** [John Blackburn; Karl Suess-
                    dorf] arrNH (as solo)
        LP: Columbia CL1151 (part of C2L-8), Harmony HL-7334, KH-
        32014, Music For Pleasure (Au) MFP10001
CO60072   **Do It Yourself** [Ernie Wilkins] (as solo)
        LP: Columbia CL1151 (part of C2L-8)
CO60076   **Stereophonic** [Ernie Wilkins]
        LP: Columbia CL1151 (part of C2L-8)
CO60077   **I Dream Of You (More Than You Dream I Do)**
                    [Marjorie Goetschius, Edna Osser] (as solo)
        LP: Columbia CL1150 (part of C2L-8), Harmony KH-32014,
        CBS (Brazil) 225024, Music For Pleasure (Au) MFP10001
CO60078   **This Love Of Mine** [Frank Sinatra; Sol Parker, Hen-
                    ry Senicola] arrDJ (cl solo)
        LP: Columbia CL1150 (part of C2L-8), B-2596, Harmony HL-
        7334, KH-32014, Music For Pleasure (Au) MFP10001
CO60079   **Rain** [Billy Hill; Peter De Rose] arrDJ (as solo)
        LP: Columbia CL1150 (part of C2L-8), Harmony KH-32014,
        Music For Pleasure (Au) MFP10001
CO60080   **Nevada** [Mort Greene; Walter Donaldson] arrHG
                    (as solo)
        LP: Columbia CL1150 (part of C2L-8)
CO60081   **Yesterdays** [Otto Harbach; Jerome Kern] arrDJ (as
                    solo)
        LP: Columbia CL1150 (part of C2L-8), Harmony HL-7334
CO60086   **This Is What Gabriel Says** [Deane Kincaide] (as solo)
        LP: Columbia CL1150 (part of C2L-8)
CO60087   **It Started All Over Again** [Bill Carey; Carl Fisher]
                    arrDJ (as solo)
        LP: Columbia CL1150 (part of C2L-8), B-2596, Harmony KH-
        32014, Music For Pleasure (Au) MFP10001
CO60088   **Let's Have A Party** [Friend, Haymes, Baxter] vLR&
                    GP arrHG (cl solo)
CO60089   **Kicking The Blues Around** [Ernie Wilkins] (as solo)

CO60090	**Dixieland Mambo** [Danny Hurd] (cl solo)
CO60091	**Rhumba Montevideo** [Dick Cary, Bud Freeman] (cl solo)
CO60092	**The Time Is Right** [Dick Cary, Bud Freeman] (cl solo)
CO60094	**Stompin' Down Broadway** [Ernie Wilkins] (as solo)
CO60095	**Sweet Sue, Just You** [Will J. Harris; Victor Young] (cl solo)

60088—60095 on **LP:** Columbia CL1240

CO60098	**The Night We Called It A Day** [Tom Adair; Matt Dennis] arrDJ (as solo)
CO60099	**Dipper Mouth Blues** [Joe "King" Oliver, Louis Armstrong] arrHG (cl solo)

60098 and 60099 on **LP:** Columbia CL1240, Harmony HL-7334

In the summer of 1955, Jackie Gleason turned to Paul Whiteman for *America's Greatest Bands* as a summer replacement. The Whiteman hour featured four different big-name bands each week.

This freed Jimmy and Tommy to take the band on the road, mostly for one-nighters in places ranging from Portland, Oregon, to Chicago to Connecticut.

Right after completing their Columbia sessions in May they went to Las Vegas, Nevada, for a week at the Last Frontier Hotel.

Next the brothers struck out for the Northwest. At this time the band's personnel shaped up like this:

TOMMY DORSEY & HIS ORCH., featuring Jimmy Dorsey
Tommy Dorsey (tb,ldr) Charlie Shavers, Lee Castle, Paul Cohen (tp) Vince Forrest, Sam Hyster, Tak Takvorian (tb) **Jimmy Dorsey** (cl,as) Red Press (cl,fl,as) Buzzy Brauner, Bruce Snyder, Gale Curtis (ts) Teddy Lee (bar) Buddy Savarise (p) Billy Cronk (sb) Louis Bellson (d) Shirley Jeanne, Bruce Snyder, Bill Raymond (vcl)

It was while they were touring that Jimmy first noticed increased weakness and complained to Tommy. They were in Winnipeg, Manitoba, Canada, at the time and Tommy had his valet Sonny Tate take his brother to a famous local clinic, where the diagnosis was a growth on his lung. It was another year before the growth was found to be cancerous.

While it was not well documented in the early fifties, later research has shown that Jimmy's was a classic case of the dangers that can come from excessive smoking and drinking in combination, namely, the development of cancer. Jimmy shrugged off his problem at the time and continued the tour.

Of course, the long strings of one-nighters were not the best thing health-wise for either of the brothers, now in their fifties and facing the stresses that came from losing their grip on the top of the heap.

The one-nighter grind was tough enough for musicians in their twenties and thirties, as most musicians who went through that era have confirmed.

In the case of the Oregon and Chicago Dorsey Brothers stints, non-broadcast tape recordings were made, those in Portland by engineer and jazz buff Wally Heider.

private recording, Jantzen Beach Ballroom, Portland, Ore.—Friday, Saturday, June 3, 4, 1955
TOMMY DORSEY & HIS ORCH., featuring **Jimmy Dorsey**
Shirley Jeanne, Bill Raymond, Bruce Snyder (vcl)

Flagler Drive [Ernie Wilkins] (as solo) / **Let's Fall In Love** [Ted Koehler; Harold Arlen] / **Happy Rabbit/ Where Is That Rock?** [Deane Kincaide] / **Tanglefoot** / **Rain** [Billy Hill; Peter De Rose] (as solo) arrDJ / **No Other Love** [Oscar Hammerstein II; Richard Rodgers] vBR / **Moonlight In Vermont** [John Blackburn; Karl Suessdorf] arrNH (as solo)/ **The Man That Got Away** [Ira Gershwin; Harold Arlen] vSJ / **Just Swingin'** [Ernie Wilkins] / (intermission) / **I Should Care** [Sammy Cahn, Axel Stordahl, Paul Weston] (as solo) / **All Of You** [Cole Porter] vBR / **No Bones About It** / **Teach Me Tonight** [Sammy Cahn; Gene DePaul] vSJ (as solo) / **Heaven Help Us /** (intermission / **Melancholy Serenade** [Jackie Gleason] (as solo) / **Love, You Didn't Do Right By Me** [Irving Berlin] vBR / **Sunny Disposish** [Ira Gershwin; Philip Charig] vSJ / **Hot Dawg** vBS / **Puddle Wump** (intermission) **Someone To Watch Over Me** [Ira Gershwin; George Gershwin] *****It Feels So Good** [Sy Oliver] (as solo) / **Green Eyes** [N. Menendez, E. Rivera, Eddie Woods, A. Utera] vBR&SJ (as solo)/ *****On The Sunny Side Of The Street** [Dorothy Fields; Jimmy McHugh] vBS / **Saxophone Mambo** / *****In A Little Spanish Town** [Sam M. Lewis, Joseph Young; Mabel Wayne] (cl,as solos) / (intermission) / *****The Most Beautiful Girl In The World** [Lorenz Hart; Richard Rodgers] / **Ruby** (partial) [Mitchell Parish; Heinz Roemheld] *****Ebb Tide** [Carl Sigman; Robert Maxwell] (as solo with TD tb) / *****Marie** [Irving Berlin] vBR&band (as solo) / (intermission) **I'm Gettin' Sentimental Over You** [Ned Washington; George Bassman] (theme) / **Does Your Mambo** [*sic*] **Come From Ireland?** / Rhumba Parody on Gillette Razor Commercial / **Jingle Bells** / (unknown title) / *****Tangerine** [Johnny Mercer; Victor Schertzinger] vBR,SJ (as solo) / *****Song Of India** [Nicholas Rimsky-Korsakoff] / *****King Size** (as solo) / *****Long Sam** (as solo) / *****Romance** [Edgar Leslie; Walter Donaldson] (cl solo) / *****Danceably Yours** / *****Heart And Soul** [Mike Chapman, Nicky Chinn] (cl solo) / *****Kicking The Blues Around** [Ernie Wilkins] (as solo) / *****Let's Fall In Love** [Ted Koehler; Harold Arlen] (cl,as solos) / **There You Go** / **September Song** [Maxwell Anderson; Kurt Weill] / *****Harlem Express** (as solo) / *****Dipper Mouth Blues** [Joe "King" Oliver, Louis Armstrong] (cl solo) / *****Moonlight In Vermont** [John Blackburn; Karl Suessdorf] arrNH (as solo with TD tb) / **Do It Yourself** / **Cachimba Mambo** / *****Maria Elena** [S. K. (Bob) Russell; Lorenzo Barcelata] vBR (cl solo) / **A Good Man Is Hard To Find** [Eddie Green] vBS / **Oh, What A Beautiful Morning** [Oscar Hammerstein II; Richard Rodgers] / **Don't Worry 'Bout Me** [Ted Koehler; Rube Bloom] vSJ (cl solo) / **Tenderly** [Jack Lawrence; Walter Gross] (as solo) / **Sweet Sue, Just You** [Will J. Harris; Victor Young] (cl solo) / **The Most Beautiful Girl In The World** [Lorenz Hart; Richard Rodgers] / **One O'Clock Jump** [William "Count" Basie] / **I'm Gettin' Sentimental Over You**
Selections marked "*"on **CD**: Jazz Unlimited (Denmark) 2026

Another West Coast appearance by the brothers was at the Los Angeles Home Show at the Pan-Pacific Auditorium for ten days, starting Thursday, June 9 and closing Sunday, June 19. Appearing with them were The Lancers. It was Tommy's second year at the show, and Jimmy's first.

Upon their return to the East Coast they worked another group of one-nighters, including one at West View Park near Pittsburgh, Pennsylvania, Friday, July 1, and another that weekend at Pleasure Beach, a municipally operated amusement park in Bridgeport, Connecticut.

Monitor, Pleasure Beach, Bridgeport, Conn.—NBC, Sunday, July 3, 1955
TOMMY DORSEY & HIS ORCH., featuring Jimmy Dorsey

I'm Gettin' Sentimental Over You [Ned Washington; George Bassman] (theme) / **Just Swingin'** [Ernie Wilkins] (as solo) / **I Think Of You** [Jack Elliot, Don Marcotte] (as solo) / **Let's Fall In Love** [Ted Koehler; Harold Arlen] (cl solo) / **DC-7** (aka **Just For Taking Bows**) (cl solo) / **I Should Care** [Sammy Cahn, Axel Stordahl, Paul Weston] (as solo) / **King Size**
Entire broadcast on **TC:** Cassettes Only 0538

Four weeks later it's known they spent Sunday, July 24, at Ocean Park Ballroom, New London, Connecticut.

That summer Tommy was named chairman of the East Coast Committee of the Dance Orchestra Leaders of America, headed nationally by Les Brown and founded earlier in 1955 to form a united front in the face of declining band business. The action proved to be too late for the big-band era, which had begun to lose its power a decade earlier.

Jimmy went to Hollywood to join Eddie Fisher, Lawrence Welk and Jimmy McHugh as the honored guests at a luncheon of the West Coast Music Men Tuesday, August 1 (*Variety* August 3, 1955, 48).

Travel itinerary: Sun., Aug. 21, to Mon., Aug. 29—Bolero night club, Wildwood, N.J. / Tues., Sept. 27, to Thurs., Sept. 29—Syria Mosque, Pittsburgh, Pa.

private recording, Holiday Ballroom, Chicago, Ill.—Friday, September 30, 1955
TOMMY DORSEY & HIS ORCH., featuring Jimmy Dorsey
Pearl Bailey (vcl guest) Bill Raymond, Bruce Snyder, Shirley Jeanne, Charlie Shavers (vcl)

Just As Though You Were Here [Eddie DeLange; John Benson Brooks] / **Moten Swing** [William "Count" Basie, Eddie Durham] / **I Think Of You** [Jack Elliot, Don Marcotte] / **There Are Such Things** [Stanley Adams, Abel Baer, George W. Meyer] / **Flagler Drive** [Ernie Wilkins] (as solo) / **Something's Gotta Give** [Johnny Mercer] vSJ / **Fooled** [Mann Curtis; Doris Tauber] vBR / **'Deed I Do** [Walter Hirsch; Fred Rose] / **Jazz Mambo** / **All Of You** [Cole Porter] vBR / **Smack Dab In The Middle** [Charles Calhoun] vCS&PB / **Let's Fall In Love** [Ted Koehler; Harold Arlen] / **Ruby** [Mitchell Parish; Heinz Roemheld] vBR / **Just For Taking Bows** /(unknown rumba) (Contd.)

TOMMY DORSEY & HIS ORCH., feat. JIMMY DORSEY (Contd.)

/ **The Man In The Raincoat** [Warwick Webster] vSJ / **Hot Dawg** vBS / (unknown instrumental) / **Miami Beach Rumba** [Irving Fields] / **Maria Elena** [S. K. (Bob) Russell; Lorenzo Barcelata] / **I Should Care** [Sammy Cahn, Axel Stordahl, Paul Weston] (as solo) / **Heart** [Richard Adler, Jerry Ross] vCS,BR&BS / **Dream** [Johnny Mercer] vBR / **In A Little Spanish Town** [Sam M. Lewis, Joseph Young; Mabel Wayne] / **Deep Purple** [Mitchell Parish; Peter De Rose] / **Sweet Sue, Just You** [Will J. Harris; Victor Young] (cl solo) / **Swanee River** [Stephen C. Foster] / **Without A Song** [Billy Rose, Edward Elliscu; Vincent Youmans] vBR / **Girl Of My Dreams** [Sunny Clapp] / **Medley:** I'll Never Smile Again [Ruth Lowe]; I Can't Believe That You're In Love With Me [Clarence Gaskill; Jimmy McHugh]; The Gang That Sang Heart of My Heart [Ben Ryan]; I Can't Give You Anything But Love [Dorothy Fields; Jimmy McHugh]; **Night And Day** [Cole Porter]; **Cecilia** [Herman Ruby; Dave Dreyer]; **Side By Side** [Harry Woods]; **That Old Gang of Mine** [Billy Rose, Mort Dixon; Ray Henderson]; **On The Alamo** [Gus Kahn; Isham Jones]; **My Blue Heaven** [George Whiting; Walter Donaldson]; **April In Paris** [E. Y. Harburg; Vernon Duke] / **Your Daddy's Got The Gleeks** [Charlie Shavers] vCS / **Muskrat Ramble** [Ray Gilbert; Edward "Kid" Ory] / (intermission) / **More Than You Know** [Edward Eliscu, Billy Rose; Vincent Youmans] **I Understand** [Kim Gannon; Mabel Wayne] vBR / **Manhattan** [Lorenz Hart; Richard Rodgers] / **Perfidia** [Milton Leeds; Alberto Dominguez] / **Boogie Woogie** [Clarence "Pinetop" Smith] / **Honeysuckle Rose** vPB [Andy Razaf; Thomas "Fats" Waller] / **Table Money** vPB / **Opus One** [Sid Garris; Sy Oliver] / **Puddle Wump** [Charlie Shavers]

In a controversial move, Jackie Gleason presented *The Honeymooners* for the fall season as a filmed half-hour series and used *Stage Show* as the "warm-up" preceding it. This schedule lasted until February when the order was reversed because of failing ratings.

Stage Show, CBS-TV Studio 50, New York, N.Y.—
8:00-8:30 P.M. Saturday, October 1, 1955
TOMMY DORSEY & HIS ORCH., featuring Jimmy Dorsey
Jane Russell, Dick Haymes (vcl)

(Background music for June Taylor Dancers) / **Something's Gotta Give** [Johnny Mercer] vDH / **Come Rain Or Come Shine** [Johnny Mercer; Harold Arlen] vDH / **South Rampart Street Parade** [Steve Allen; Ray Bauduc, Bob Haggart] *(Dorseyland Jazz Band)* / **Taking A Chance On Love** [John Latouche, Ted Fetter; Vernon Duke] vJR / **Tall Man** vJR

Stage Show, CBS-TV Studio 50, New York, N.Y.—
8:00-8:30 P.M. Saturday, October 8, 1955
TOMMY DORSEY & HIS ORCH., featuring Jimmy Dorsey
Jeanne Crain, Blackburn Twins (vcl)

Dorseys Medley: **There Are Such Things** [Stanley Adams, Abel Baer, George W. Meyer] arrDJ (as solo); **Maria Elena** [S. K. (Bob) Russell; Lorenzo Barcelata] (as solo); **Holiday For Strings** [David Rose] (as solo) / **Darling, Je Vous Aime Beaucoup** [Anna Sosenko] vJC / **Gentlemen Marry Brunettes** vJC&BT
Dorseys Medley on **CD:** Magic (E) DAWE44

Stage Show, CBS-TV Studio 50, New York, N.Y.
—8:00-8:30 P.M. Saturday, October 15, 1955
TOMMY DORSEY & HIS ORCH., featuring Jimmy Dorsey
Dick Haymes, Lillian Briggs (vcl)

I Want You, I Need You, I Love You [Maurice Musels; Ira Kosloff] vLB / **Dark Eyes (Ot Chi Chornya)** [traditional Russian folk song] / Gershwin Medley: **Our Love Is Here To Stay** vDH; **They Can't Take That Away From Me** [Ira Gershwin; George Gershwin] vDH
"Dark Eyes" and Dick Haymes medley on **TC:** Magic (E) CAWE44, **CD:** Magic (E) DAWE44

Sometime early that fall the band put together a quarter-hour program promoting the traditional Christmas Seal fund-raising effort of the American Lung Association.

1955 Christmas Seal Program, unknown studio, New York, N.Y.—Fall 1955
TOMMY DORSEY & HIS ORCH., featuring Jimmy Dorsey

I'm Gettin' Sentimental Over You [Ned Washington; George Bassman] (theme) / **Teach Me Tonight** [Sammy Cahn; Gene DePaul] vLR (as solo) / **This Love Of Mine** [Frank Sinatra; Sol Parker, Henry Senicola] arrDJ / **Just Swingin'** [Ernie Wilkins] / **(Back Home Again In) Indiana** [Ballard MacDonald; James F. Hanley] (as solo) *(Dorseyland Jazz Band)*
All on **ET:** 1955 Christmas Scals Program

Stage Show, CBS-TV Studio 50, New York, N.Y.
—8:00-8:30 P.M. Saturday, October 22, 1955
TOMMY DORSEY & HIS ORCH., featuring Jimmy Dorsey
The Four Aces (vcl)

The Breeze And I [Al Stillman; Ernesto Lecuona] / **Fools Rush In** [Johnny Mercer; Rube Bloom] / **Stompin' Down Broadway** [Ernie Wilkins] (as solo) / **Love Is A Many Splendored Thing** [Paul Francis Webster; Sammy Fain] vFA

On Friday, October 28, 1955, the band played for a union group's private party at the Meadowbrook Ballroom, which by now was welcoming private events, even on Friday nights.
An experimental stereo tape recorder was on hand that evening, two years ahead of the debut of the first hi-fi stereo LPs. The tapes made that

night, portions of which have been released on CD, offer a rare opportunity to hear the Dorseys in true stereo, as well as afford a glimpse of
Tommy, Jimmy and the band in a nonbroadcast atmosphere.

Private party, The Meadowbrook Ballroom, Cedar
Grove, N.J.—Friday, October 28, 1955
TOMMY DORSEY & HIS ORCH., featuring **Jimmy Dorsey**
Bill Raymond, Shirley Jeanne, Lynn Roberts, Charlie Shavers (vcl)

Harold Arlen Salute: **My Shining Hour** [Johnny Mercer; Harold
Arlen] / (unknown title) / **Out Of This World** [Johnny Mercer;
Harold Arlen] / (unknown title) / **Come Rain Or Come Shine**
[Johnny Mercer; Harold Arlen] / **Over The Rainbow** [E. Y. Har-
burg; Harold Arlen] / **Blues In The Night** [Johnny Mercer; Harold
Arlen] / **Right As The Rain** [E. Y. Harburg; Harold Arlen] / **Ac-
Cent-Tchu-Ate The Positive** [Johnny Mercer; Harold Arlen] vSJ /
That Old Black Magic [Johnny Mercer; Harold Arlen] / (unknown
title) / **Between The Devil And The Deep Blue Sea** [Ted Koehler;
Harold Arlen] / Fanfare, introduction and segue to: ***Holiday For
Strings** [David Rose] (as solo) / ***Perfidia** [Milton Leeds; Alberto
Dominguez] (cl solo) / **I Think Of You** [Jack Elliot, Don Marcotte]
(as solo) / ***All Of You** [Cole Porter] vBR (as solo) / ***Let's Fall In
Love** [Ted Koehler; Harold Arlen] (cl solo) / ***Something's Gotta
Give** [Johnny Mercer] vLR / ***Moonlight In Vermont** [John
Blackburn; Karl Suessdorf] arrNH (as solo) / *Medley:* **Brazil**
(Aquarela do Brasil) [S. K. (Bob) Russell; Ary Baroso]; **Once In A
While** [Bud Green; Michael Edwards]; **The Breeze And I** [Al
Stillman; Ernesto Lecuona]; **This Love Of Mine** [Frank Sinatra; Sol
Parker, Henry Senicola]; **All Of Me** [Seymour B. Simons, Gerald
Marks]; **Amapola** [Albert Gamse; Joseph M. Lacalle]; **There Are
Such Things** [Stanley Adams, Abel Baer, George W. Meyer];
Yours (Quieremé Mucho)[Jack Sherr, Augustin Rodriguez; Gonzalo
Roig]; **On The Sunny Side Of The Street** [Dorothy Fields; Jimmy
McHugh]; **Maria Elena** [S. K. (Bob) Russell; Lorenzo Barcelata];
Song Of India [Nicholas Rimsky-Korsakoff]; **Tangerine** [Johnny
Mercer; Victor Schertzinger] (as solo); **I'll Never Smile Again** [Ruth
Lowe]; **Green Eyes** [N. Menendez, E. Rivera, Eddie Woods, A.
Utera] (as solo) / ***Marie** [Irving Berlin] vBR&Band (as solo) / **Star
Dust** [Mitchell Parish; Hoagy Carmichael] vBR / **You Made Me
Love You (I Didn't Want To Do It)** [Joseph McCarthy; James V.
Monaco] vLR / **It's Only A Paper Moon** [E. Y. Harburg, Billy
Rose; Harold Arlen] / ***Baby, Won't You Please Come Home**
[Charles Warfield, Clarence Williams] vCS / ***Smack Dab In The
Middle**[Charles Calhoun] vCS (cl solo) / (intermission) / **I Under-
stand** [Kim Gannon; Mabel Wayne] vBR / (unknown mambo) / **Just
For Kicks** (as solo) / **Tenderly** [Jack Lawrence; Walter Gross] (as
solo) / ***In A Little Spanish Town** [Sam M. Lewis, Joseph Young;
Mabel Wayne] (as solo) / ***Boogie Woogie** [Clarence "Pinetop"
Smith] / ***Without A Song** [Billy Rose, Edward Elliscu; Vincent
Youmans] vBR / ***Swanee River** [Stephen C. Foster] / ***Skirts And
Sweaters** [Ernie Wilkins] / ***Just For Taking Bows** (as solo)
Selections marked "*" on **CD:** Jazz Hour JH1003

Stage Show, CBS-TV Studio 50, New York, N.Y.
—8:00-8:30 P.M. Saturday, October 29, 1955
TOMMY DORSEY & HIS ORCH., featuring **Jimmy Dorsey**
Tommy Dorsey (tb,ldr) John Frosk, Billy Mullens, Charlie Shavers (tp),
Vinny Forrest, Don Rogers, Tak Takvorian (tb) **Jimmy Dorsey** (cl,as)
Gale Curtis (cl,as,ts) Seymour "Red" Press (cl,as,fl,piccolo) Pat Chart-
land (cl,ts) Bruce Snyder (ts,vcl) Bob Carter (p) Bill Cronk (sb) Louis
Bellson (d) Sarah Vaughan (vcl)

> **Don't Give Your Heart** vSV / **C'est La Vie** [Edward R. White;
> Mack Wolfson] vSV / **I'll Never Smile Again** [Ruth Lowe] (as solo)
> / **Yours (Quieremé Mucho)** [Jack Sherr, Augustin Rodriguez; Gon-
> zalo Roig] / **Well, Git It!** [Sy Oliver]

That evening the band also resumed a Friday, Saturday, Sunday
schedule at the Meadowbrook, which lasted to Sunday, January 1, 1956.

Stage Show, CBS-TV Studio 50, New York, N.Y.
—8:00-8:30 P.M. Saturday, November 5, 1955
TOMMY DORSEY & HIS ORCH., featuring **Jimmy Dorsey**
Tony Bennett (vcl) was present, selections unknown

> **Panama** [William N. Tyers] (cl solo) *(Dixieland group)* / **Sweet
> Georgia Brown** [Maceo Pinkard, Kenneth Casey, Ben Bernie]

Stage Show, CBS-TV Studio 50, New York, N.Y.
—8:00-8:30 P.M. Saturday, November 12, 1955
TOMMY DORSEY & HIS ORCH., featuring **Jimmy Dorsey**
Billy Daniels (vcl)

> **Sweet Georgia Brown** [Maceo Pinkard, Kenneth Casey, Ben Bernie]
> / **Three O'Clock In The Morning** [Dorothy Terris; Julian Robleso] /
> **Bye Bye Blackbird** [Mort Dixon; Ray Henderson] vBD / **That Old
> Black Magic** [Johnny Mercer; Harold Arlen] vBD

Stage Show, CBS-TV Studio 50, New York, N.Y.
—8:00-8:30 P.M. Saturday, November 19, 1955
TOMMY DORSEY & HIS ORCH., featuring **Jimmy Dorsey**
Yma Sumac, Shirley Jean, George DeWitt (vcl)

> *Medley*-Native Songs vYS / ***Parade of Dorsey Favorites:*** **Brazil
> (Aquarela do Brasil)** [S. K. (Bob) Russell; Ary Baroso]; **Once In A
> While** [Bud Green; Michael Edwards]; **The Breeze And I** [Al
> Stillman; Ernesto Lecuona]; **This Love Of Mine** [Frank Sinatra; Sol
> Parker, Henry Senicola]; **All Of Me** [Seymour B. Simons, Gerald
> Marks]; **Opus One** [Sid Garris; Sy Oliver]; **Amapola** [Albert Gamse;
> Joseph M. Lacalle]; **There Are Such Things** [Stanley Adams, Abel
> Baer, George W. Meyer]; **Yours (Quieremé Mucho)** [Jack Sherr,
> Augustin Rodriguez; Gonzalo Roig]; **On The Sunny Side Of The
> Street** [Dorothy Fields; Jimmy McHugh]; **Maria Elena** [S. K. (Bob)
> Russell; Lorenzo Barcelata] (as solo); **Song Of India** [Nicholas
> Rimsky-Korsakoff] /*Second Dorsey Medley:* **Tangerine** (Contd.)

Stage Show (Contd.)

[Johnny Mercer; Victor Schertzinger] vGDW&SJ(as solo); **I'll Never Smile Again** [Ruth Lowe]; **Green Eyes** [N.Menendez, E.Rivera, Eddie Woods, A.Utera] vGDW&SJ (as solo); **Marie** [Irving Berlin] vGDW&SJ
   Second Dorseys Medley on **TC:** Magic (E) CAWE-37, **CD:** Magic (E) DAWE-37

Telecast schedule: Sat., Nov. 26, CBS-TV *Stage Show,* 8:30-9:00 P.M. Guests: Eddie Arnold, Gene Sheldon, Gene Nelson.

Stage Show, CBS-TV Studio 50, New York, N.Y.
—8:00-8:30 P.M. Saturday, December 3, 1955
TOMMY DORSEY & HIS ORCH., featuring **Jimmy Dorsey**
Gordon MacRae, Connie Francis (vcl) Kim Novak (actress)

Stage Show theme / **South Rampart Street Parade** [Steve Allen; Ray Bauduc, Bob Haggart] / **My Treasure** vCF / **Well, Git It!** [Sy Oliver] (cl solo) / **If I Loved You** [Oscar Hammerstein II; Richard Rodgers] vGM / medley: **All-American Girl** [Al Lewis]; **You Gotta Be A Football Hero** [Al Lewis, Al Sherman, Buddy Fields] / **I'm Gettin' Sentimental Over You** [Ned Washington; George Bassman]
   Entire show on **VIDEO:** Video Images 258

Monitor, NBC-Radio, Meadowbrook Ballroom, Cedar Grove, N.J.—Early to mid-December 1955
TOMMY DORSEY & HIS ORCH., featuring **Jimmy Dorsey**
Tommy Mercer, Dolly Houston (vcl) Fred Collins (announcer)

The Most Beautiful Girl In The World [Lorenz Hart; Richard Rodgers] / **Amapola** [Albert Gamse; Joseph M. Lacalle] vTM&DH / **King Size** [Ernie Wilkins]
   "King Size" on **CD:** Jazz Hour JH-1003

Telecast schedule: Sat., Dec. 10, CBS-TV *Stage Show,* 8:30-9:00 P.M. Guests: Vaughn Monroe, Jack Carter / Sat., Dec. 17, CBS-TV *Stage Show,* 8:30-9:00 P.M. Guest: Mindy Carson / Sat., Dec. 24, CBS-TV *Stage Show,* 8:30-9:00 P.M. Guests: Tony Bennett, Lionel Hampton, Raymond Massey.

Stage Show, CBS-TV Studio 50, New York, N.Y.
—8:00-8:30 P.M. Saturday, December 31, 1955
TOMMY DORSEY & HIS ORCH., featuring **Jimmy Dorsey**
Tommy Dorsey (tb,ldr) Charlie Shavers, Lee Castle, John Frosk, Dick Perry, Art Tancredi (tp) Tak Takvorian, Vince Forrest, Sonny Russo (tb) **Jimmy Dorsey** (cl,as) Skip Galluccio, Red Press (as) Buzz Brauner, Gale Curtis (ts) Teddy Lee (bar) Doug Talbert (p) Sam Herman (g) Billy Cronk (sb) Louis Bellson (d) Guests: Jack Carter, Morey Amsterdam (comedians) Count Basie (p) Joe Williams, The DeMarco Sisters (vcl)

Every Day I Have The Blues [Peter Chatman] vJW (p,CB) / **What Good Is A Gal Without A Guy?** vDMS / **Moments To Remember**

[Al Stillman; Robert Allen] / **A Hot Time In The Old Town Tonight** [Joe Hayden; Theodore H. Metz]

After the telecast, the band headed for the Meadowbrook for a big New Year's Eve party and two of the traditional end-of-the-year broadcasts. The band was using "Opus One" as their opening theme for much of the fall and winter. When they returned to the more sedate Hotel Statler, things got "Sentimental" once again.

> *sustaining broadcast,* Meadowbrook Ballroom, Cedar Grove, N.J.—NBC, Saturday, December 31, 1955, 11:30-12:00 P.M.

TOMMY DORSEY & HIS ORCH., featuring Jimmy Dorsey
Tommy Mercer, Gordon Polk, Dolly Houston (vcl)

Opus One [Sid Garris; Sy Oliver] (cl solo) / **Kicking The Blues Around** [Ernie Wilkins] (as solo) / **It Started All Over Again** [Bill Carey; Carl Fisher] / **Maria Elena** [S. K. (Bob) Russell; Lorenzo Barcelata] vTM (as solo) / **Brunch** [Ernie Wilkins] (as solo) / **Green Eyes** [N. Menendez, E. Rivera, Eddie Woods, A. Utera] vTM&DH (as solo) / **Let's Call It Swing** [Louis Bellson] (as solo) / **Just For Taking Bows** (as,cl solos) / **Auld Lang Syne** (Robert Burns; traditional Scottish air]

> *sustaining broadcast,* Meadowbrook Ballroom, Cedar Grove, N.J.—CBS, early Sunday, January 1, 1956

TOMMY DORSEY & HIS ORCH., featuring Jimmy Dorsey
Jilla Webb (vcl) replaces Houston, Charlie Shavers (vcl)

Opus One [Sid Garris; Sy Oliver] (cl solo) / **Just Swingin'** [Ernie Wilkins] (as solo) / **This Love Of Mine** [Frank Sinatra; Sol Parker, Henry Senicola] / **Green Eyes** [N. Menendez, E. Rivera, Eddie Woods, A. Utera] vTM&JW (as solo) / **Flagler Drive** [Ernie Wilkins] (as solo) / **Your Daddy's Got The Geeks** [Charlie Shavers] vCS / **Stompin' Down Broadway** [Ernie Wilkins] / **Opus One**
Entire broadcast on **LP:** Fanfare 39-139

> *Stage Show,* CBS-TV Studio 50, New York, N.Y. —8:00-8:30 P.M. Saturday, January 7, 1956

TOMMY DORSEY & HIS ORCH., featuring Jimmy Dorsey
Gary Crosby, The Crew Cuts (vcl)

I Should Care [Sammy Cahn, Axel Stordahl, Paul Weston] (as solo) / **I Just Can't Wait 'Til They Get A Load Of Me** vGC / **Sixteen Tons** [Merle Travis] vGC

After finishing at the Meadowbrook in early January, the Dorseys moved into another old dance spot, Manhattan's Roseland Ballroom, for three Friday-through-Sunday stands, opening Friday, January 13.

Telecast schedule: Sat., Jan. 14, CBS-TV *Stage Show,* 8:30-9:00 P.M. Guests: Jack Carter, Dolores Hawkins, George Raft and Wallis and Carroll.

Down Beat (February 8, 1956, 8) revealed the details of a one-million-dollar contract that Tino Barzie, the Dorseys' manager, had negotiated with the Statler chain, partly on the strength of the Dorseys' TV exposure.   Under it the band would play the New York Statler six months out of every year for the coming five years. The agreement called for the band to open about September 21 of each year and work at the hotel until March.   *Variety* (February 1, 1956, 45) added that the brothers were guaranteed $7,000 a week plus a percentage of the cover charges, which were being increased by fifty cents.

Stage Show, CBS-TV Studio 50, New York, N.Y.
—8:00-8:30 P.M. Saturday, January 21, 1956
TOMMY DORSEY & HIS ORCH., featuring Jimmy Dorsey
The Four Aces (vcl grp)

Nevada [Mort Greene; Walter Donaldson] arrHG

The January 28 *Stage Show* is of special interest since it was the start of a not-often-cited four-week national television introduction of rockabilly star Elvis Presley, often erroneously credited to Ed Sullivan.

Stage Show, CBS-TV Studio 50, New York, N.Y.
—8:00-8:30 P.M. Saturday, January 28, 1956
TOMMY DORSEY & HIS ORCH., featuring Jimmy Dorsey
Elvis Presley, Sarah Vaughn (vcl)

Mister Wonderful [Jerry Bock, Larry Holofcener, George David Weiss] vSV / **Kicking The Blues Around** [Ernie Wilkins] (as solo) / **Heartbreak Hotel** [Mae Axton, Tommy Durden, Elvis Presley] vEP "Heartbreak Hotel" on **LP:** Golden Archives 56-GA-100

Stage Show, CBS-TV Studio 50, New York, N.Y.
—8:00-8:30 P.M. Saturday, February 4, 1956
TOMMY DORSEY & HIS ORCH., featuring Jimmy Dorsey
Elvis Presley (vcl)

Dipper Mouth Blues [Joseph "King" Oliver, Louis Armstrong]

On Friday, February 10, the band moved back to the Statler for another six-month stand. Faced with a drop in ratings opposite the last thirty minutes of Perry Como on NBC-TV, Jackie Gleason switched half-hours with the Dorseys, moving *The Honeymooners* to 8:00 P.M.

Stage Show, CBS-TV Studio 50, New York, N.Y.
8:30-9:00 P.M. Saturday, February 11, 1956
TOMMY DORSEY & HIS ORCH., featuring Jimmy Dorsey
Ella Fitzgerald, Elvis Presley (vcl) Jackie Miles (comedian)

Love Is Sweeping The Country [Ira Gershwin; George Gershwin] / **Same Old Saturday Night** [Sammy Cahn; Frank Reardon] vEF / **Oh! Lady Be Good** [Ira Gershwin; George Gershwin] vEF / **Stompin' Down Broadway** [Ernie Wilkins]

sustaining broadcast, Cafe Rouge, Hotel Statler, New
York, N.Y.—NBC, Wednesday, February 15, 1956
TOMMY DORSEY & HIS ORCH., featuring **Jimmy Dorsey**
Tommy Mercer, Dolly Houston (vcl)

Opus One [Sid Garris; Sy Oliver] (cl solo) / **Once In A While** [Bud
Green; Michael Edwards] (as solo) / **Green Eyes** [N. Menendez, E.
Rivera, Eddie Woods, A. Utera] vTM,DH (as solo) / **Lover** [Lorenz
Hart; Richard Rodgers] (as solo) / **Song Of India** [Nicholas Rimsky-
Korsakoff] / **Tangerine** [Johnny Mercer; Victor Schertzinger]
vTM&DH (as solo)
All but "Green Eyes" on **LP:** Fanfare 39-139 labeled "Dec. 1955")

Stage Show, CBS-TV Studio 50, New York, N.Y.
—8:30-9:00 P.M. Saturday, February 18, 1956
TOMMY DORSEY & HIS ORCH., featuring **Jimmy Dorsey**
Elvis Presley (vcl) Tokayers (acrobats)

Smack Dab In The Middle [Charles Calhoun] vCS&band / **Long
Sam** [Ernie Wilkins] (as solo) / **An Occasional Man** / **Just For
Taking Bows** (as,cl solos) / (Presley sang with his own band)

sustaining broadcast, Cafe Rouge, Hotel Statler, New
York, N.Y.—Saturday, February 18, 1956
TOMMY DORSEY & HIS ORCH., featuring **Jimmy Dorsey**

Smack Dab In The Middle [Charles Calhoun] / **Brunch** [Ernie Wil-
kins] (as solo) / **Tangerine** [Johnny Mercer; Victor Schertzinger] vDH
&TM (as solo) / **Kicking The Blues Around** [Ernie Wilkins] (as solo)

sustaining broadcast, Cafe Rouge, Hotel Statler, New
York, N.Y.—Wednesday, February 22, 1956
TOMMY DORSEY & HIS ORCH., featuring **Jimmy Dorsey**

I'm Gettin' Sentimental Over You [Ned Washington; George
Bassman] (theme) / **Manhattan** [Lorenz Hart; Richard Rodgers] (cl
solo) / **There Are Such Things** [Stanley Adams, Abel Baer, George
W. Meyer] arrDJ (as solo) / **Without A Song** [Billy Rose, Edward
Eliscu; Vincent Youmans] vTM / **Muskrat Ramble** [Ray Gilbert;
"Kid" Ory] (cl solo) *(Dixieland group)* / **I'm Glad There Is You**
[Paul Madeira; Jimmy Dorsey] vDH (as solo) / **Marie** [Irving Berlin]

Stage Show, CBS-TV Studio 50, New York, N.Y.
—8:30-9:00 P.M. Saturday, February 25, 1956
TOMMY DORSEY & HIS ORCH., featuring **Jimmy Dorsey**
Sister Rosetta Tharpe, Dick Haymes, Tommy Mercer (vcl)

I Ain't Gonna Study War No More [traditional] vSRT / **Tenderly**
[Jack Lawrence; Walter Gross] (as solo) / **All At Once You Love
Her** [Oscar Hammerstein II; Richard Rodgers] vTM (as solo) / **Let's
Get Away From It All** [Tom Adair; Matt Dennis] vDH / **The
Carioca** [Gus Kahn, Edward Eliscu; Vincent Youmans] vDH

Monitor, Cafe Rouge, Hotel Statler, New York, N.Y.
—NBC, Sunday, February 26, 1956
TOMMY DORSEY & HIS ORCH., featuring Jimmy Dorsey

Just For Kicks (as solo) / **Kicking The Blues Around** [Ernie Wilkins] (cl solo)

Both Tommy and Jimmy attended services for the veteran operator of the Meadowbrook, Frank Dailey, who died at fifty five on February 27.

sustaining broadcast, Cafe Rouge, Hotel Statler, New York, N.Y.—February 1956
TOMMY DORSEY & HIS ORCH., featuring Jimmy Dorsey

Stereophonic [Ernie Wilkins] / **Moonlight In Vermont** [John Blackburn; Karl Suessdorf] arrNH (as solo) / **Ruby** [Mitchell Parish; Heinz Roemheld] vTM arrHG (as solo) / **In A Little Spanish Town** [Sam M. Lewis, Joseph Young; Mabel Wayne] (cl solo) / **Melancholy Serenade** [Jackie Gleason] (as solo) / **Something's Gotta Give** [Johnny Mercer] vDH
All on **ET: AFRS** One Night Stand 4010

sustaining broadcast, Cafe Rouge, Hotel Statler, New York, N.Y.—February 1956
TOMMY DORSEY & HIS ORCH., featuring Jimmy Dorsey

Brunch [Ernie Wilkins] (as solo) / **I Should Care** [Sammy Cahn, Axel Stordahl, Paul Weston] (as solo) / **The Nearness Of You** [Ned Washington; Hoagy Carmichael] vTM / **Powerglide** / **Flagler Drive** [Ernie Wilkins] (as solo) / **I'm Glad There Is You** [Paul Madeira; Jimmy Dorsey] vDH (as solo)
All on **ET: AFRS** One Night Stand 4015

sustaining broadcast, Cafe Rouge, Hotel Statler, New York, N.Y.—February 1956
TOMMY DORSEY & HIS ORCH., featuring Jimmy Dorsey

Peace Pipe [Ernie Wilkins] (as solo) / **I Dream Of You (More Than You Dream I Do)** [Marjorie Goetschius, Edna Osser] (as solo) / **The Tender Trap** [Sammy Cahn; Jimmy Van Heusen] vTM / **Lover** [Lorenz Hart; Richard Rodgers] (as solo) / **It Started All Over Again** [Bill Carey; Carl Fisher] / **Don't Worry 'Bout Me** [Ted Koehler; Rube Bloom] vDH (cl solo) / **Just Swingin'** [Ernie Wilkins] (as solo)
All on **ET: AFRS** One Night Stand 4016

Stage Show, CBS-TV Studio 50, New York, N.Y.
—8:30-9:00 P.M. Saturday, March 3, 1956
TOMMY DORSEY & HIS ORCH., featuring Jimmy Dorsey
Tommy Dorsey (tb,ldr) Charlie Shavers, Lee Castle, John Frosk, Dick Perry, Art Tancredi (tp) Tak Takvorian, Vinnie Forrest, Sonny Russo (tb) **Jimmy Dorsey** (cl,as) Skip Colluccio, Red Press (as) Buzz Brauner, Gale Curtis (ts) Teddy Lee (bar) Doug Talbert (p) Sam Herman (g) Billy

Cronk (sb) Louis Bellson (d) Helen O'Connell, Bob Eberly (vcl) Wally Brown (comedian) Dancing Clark Brothers

(Unknown title for June Taylor Dancers) / **Time Was** [S. K. (Bob) Russell; Miguel Prado] vHO'C&BE (a parody with Jimmy interjecting comments) / **Tangerine** [Johnny Mercer; Victor Schertzinger] vBE&HO'C (as solo) / **Green Eyes** [N.Menendez, E.Rivera, Eddie Woods, A.Utera] vBE&HO'C (as solo) / (following a commercial delivered by Jimmy the guests sang "Happy Birthday To You" in honor of his "thirteenth" birthday, February 29, 1956) / **Boogie Woogie** [Pinetop Smith] / **I'm Gettin' Sentimental Over You** [Ned Washington; George Bassman] (theme)

Little did the brothers realize the fateful connection with Jimmy's celebrating that thirteenth "leap-year" birthday in 1956.

> *Monitor,* Cafe Rouge, Hotel Statler, New York, N.Y.—NBC, Saturday, March 3, 1956

TOMMY DORSEY & HIS ORCH., featuring Jimmy Dorsey

Harlem Express (as solo) / **Tangerine** [Johnny Mercer; Victor Schertzinger] vTM&DH (as solo) / **Just Swingin'** [Ernie Wilkins] (as solo)

Down Beat (March 7, 1956, 7) reported that *The Fabulous Dorseys* had been released for use on television, that the Dorseys' life story would appear in the March 1956 issue of *Cosmopolitan* magazine and that Edward R. Morrow, CBS's television news star, would soon make a *Person To Person* visit to Tommy's Greenwich, Connecticut, home.

> *sustaining broadcast,* Cafe Rouge, Hotel Statler, New York, N.Y.—NBC, Wednesday, March 7, 1956

TOMMY DORSEY & HIS ORCH., featuring Jimmy Dorsey

I'm Gettin' Sentimental Over You [Ned Washington; George Bassman] (theme) / **Opus One** [Sid Garris; Sy Oliver] (cl solo) / **Maria Elena** [S. K. (Bob) Russell; Lorenzo Barcelata] vTM (as solo) / **In A Little Spanish Town** [Sam M. Lewis, Joseph Young; Mabel Wayne] (cl solo) / **I'm Glad There Is You** vDH [Paul Madeira, Jimmy Dorsey] (as solo) / **Swanee River** [Stephen Foster] / **Who?** [Otto Harbach, Oscar Hammerstein II; Jerome Kern] vTM&band

> *sustaining broadcast,* Cafe Rouge, Hotel Statler, New York, N.Y.—Early March 1956

TOMMY DORSEY & HIS ORCH., featuring Jimmy Dorsey

Just For Kicks (as solo) / **Moonlight In Vermont** [John Blackburn; Karl Suessdorf] (as solo) / **(You Are) Always In My Heart** [Kim Gannon; Ernesto Lecuona] vTM (as solo) / **Powerglide** / **Bouncing With Boots**
All on **ET**: AFRS One Night Stand 4021, 4066

Stage Show, CBS-TV Studio 50, New York, N.Y.
—8:30-9:00 P.M. Saturday, March 10, 1956
TOMMY DORSEY & HIS ORCH., featuring Jimmy Dorsey
The Crew Cuts (vcl)

The Most Beautiful Girl In The World [Lorenz Hart; Richard Rodgers] / **That's Your Mistake** vCC / **Angels In The Sky** [Dick Glasser] vCC

sustaining broadcast, Cafe Rouge, Hotel Statler, New York, N.Y.—NBC, Wednesday, March 14, 1956
TOMMY DORSEY & HIS ORCH., featuring Jimmy Dorsey

I'm Gettin' Sentimental Over You [Ned Washington; George Bassman] (theme) **Lover** [Lorenz Hart; Richard Rodgers] (as solo) / **I Dream Of You (More Than You Dream I Do)** [Marjorie Goetschius, Edna Osser] (as solo) / **(You Are) Always In My Heart** [Kim Gannon; Ernesto Lecuona] vTM (as solo) / **I Should Care** [Sammy Cahn, Axel Stordahl, Paul Weston] (as solo) / **Sweet Sue (Just You)** [Will J. Harris; Victor Young] (cl solo) / **Don't Worry 'Bout Me** [Ted Koehler; Rube Bloom] vDH (cl solo)

The next *Stage Show* featured a St. Patrick's Day theme, and Tess Dorsey, the brothers' mother, was introduced from the audience. On the closing "Irish Reel," the June Taylor Dancers did their bit with solos by Henny Youngman (vn) Jimmy Dorsey (cl) and Tommy Dorsey (tb).

Stage Show, CBS-TV Studio 50, New York, N.Y.
—8:30-9:00 P.M. Saturday, March 17, 1956
TOMMY DORSEY & HIS ORCH., featuring Jimmy Dorsey
Glenn Derringer (organ) Elvis Presley (vcl) Henny Youngman (comedian, vn) June Taylor Dancers

(This Is My) Lucky Day [Buddy De Sylva, Lew Brown] (for June Taylor Dancers) / **Blue Suede Shoes** [Carl Lee Perkins] vEP / **Heartbreak Hotel** [Mae Axton, Tommy Durden, Elvis Presley] vEP / **Boogie Woogie** [Clarence "Pinetop" Smith] (organ,GD) / (Henny Youngman, comedy) / **Irish Reel** [traditional] (cl solo)
Entire show on **VIDEO:** Video Images 751

Monitor, Cafe Rouge, Hotel Statler, New York, N.Y.—NBC, Saturday, March 17, 1956
TOMMY DORSEY & HIS ORCH., featuring Jimmy Dorsey

Just Swingin' [Ernie Wilkins] (as solo) / **Just For Taking Bows** (aka **DC-7**) (as,cl solos)

sustaining broadcast, Cafe Rouge, Hotel Statler, New York, N.Y.—Mid March 1956
TOMMY DORSEY & HIS ORCH., featuring Jimmy Dorsey

Harlem Express (as solo) / **Once In A While** [Bud Green; Michael

Edwards] (as solo) / (You Are) Always In My Heart [Kim Gannon; Ernesto Lecuona] (as solo) vTM / Brunch [Ernie Wilkins] (as solo) / I'm Glad There Is You [Paul Madeira; Jimmy Dorsey] vDH (as solo)
 All on ET: AFRS One Night Stand 4036, 4091

sustaining broadcast, Cafe Rouge, Hotel Statler, New York, N.Y.—Mid-March 1956
TOMMY DORSEY & HIS ORCH., featuring Jimmy Dorsey

Powerglide / Moonlight In Vermont [John Blackburn; Karl Suessdorf] arrNH (as solo) / Ruby [Mitchell Parish; Heinz Roemheld] vTM arrHG (as solo) / Just An Idea [Benny Goodman] / Nevada [Mort Greene; Walter Donaldson] arrHG / An Occasional Man [Hugh Martin, Ralph Blane] vDH
 All on ET: AFRS One Night Stand 4030, 4070

Travel itinerary: Sun., Mar. 18—Pikesville Auditorium, Baltimore, Md., Covenant Guild charity show.

On Tuesday, March 20, Jimmy and Tommy guested on the premiere of a new CBS-TV show, *Guy Lombardo's Diamond Jubilee.* They reportedly performed, but details are unknown.

Stage Show, CBS-TV Studio 50, New York, N.Y. —8:30-9:00 P.M. Saturday, March 24, 1956
TOMMY DORSEY & HIS ORCH., featuring Jimmy Dorsey
Jack E. Leonard (comedian) Glenn Derringer (organ) Elvis Presley (vcl) Condos and Brandow (dancers)

Caravan [Irving Mills; Juan Tizol, Duke Ellington] (GD, organ) / Marie [Irving Berlin] / Money Honey [Jesse Stone] vEP / Heartbreak Hotel [Mae Axton, Tommy Durden, Elvis Presley] vEP

Monitor, Cafe Rouge, Hotel Statler, New York, N.Y.—NBC, Saturday, March 24, 1956
TOMMY DORSEY & HIS ORCH., featuring Jimmy Dorsey

Let's Fall In Love [Ted Koehler; Harold Arlen] (cl solo) / Amapola [Albert Gamse; Joseph M. Lacalle] vTM&DH (as solo)

Telecast schedule: Sat., Mar. 31, CBS-TV *Stage Show,* 8:30-9:00 P.M.

Broadcast schedule (Cafe Rouge): Mon., Mar. 26, NBC, 10:15-10:30 P.M.

NBC Monitor, Cafe Rouge, Hotel Statler, New York, N.Y.—NBC, Saturday, March 31, 1956
TOMMY DORSEY & HIS ORCH., featuring Jimmy Dorsey

Long Sam [Ernie Wilkins] (as solo) / Amapola [Albert Gamse; Joseph M. Lacalle] vTM&DH (as solo) / Just Swingin' [Ernie Wilkins] (as solo)

Stage Show, CBS-TV Studio 50, New York, N.Y.
—8:30-9:00 P.M. Saturday, April 7, 1956
TOMMY DORSEY & HIS ORCH., featuring Jimmy Dorsey
Roberta Sherwood (vcl) Joey Adams (comedian) Lou Wills, Jr. (dancer)

Another Op'nin', Another Show [Cole Porter] (for June Taylor Dancers) / **Opus One** [Sid Garris; Sy Oliver] (cl solo) / unknown background music for Wills / **It's All Over Now** [Sunny Skylar, Don Marcotte] vRS / *Medley:* **If You Knew Susie (Like I Know Susie)** [B. G. De Sylva; Joseph Meyer]; **The Yankee Doodle Boy** [George M. Cohan] (background for Wills and Adams) / unknown title for June Taylor Dancers / **This Train** vRS (with *Dorseyland Jazz Band*)

Monitor, Cafe Rouge, Hotel Statler, New York, N.Y.—NBC, Saturday, April 7, 1956
TOMMY DORSEY & HIS ORCH., featuring Jimmy Dorsey

Harlem Express (as solo) / **Green Eyes** [N. Menendez, E. Rivera, Eddie Woods, A. Utera] vTM&DH (as solo) / **Non Drastic** [Charlie Shavers] (as solo)

Stage Show, CBS-TV Studio 50, New York, N.Y.
—8:30-9:00 P.M. Saturday, April 14, 1956
TOMMY DORSEY & HIS ORCH., featuring Jimmy Dorsey
Bob Eberly, Ella Logan, The Four Aces (vcl)

I Feel A Song Coming On [Dorothy Fields, George Oppenheimer; Jimmy McHugh] vEL / **I May Be Wrong But I Think You're Wonderful** [Harry Ruskin; Henry Sullivan] vEL

sustaining broadcast, Cafe Rouge, Hotel Statler, New York, N.Y.—Mid-April 1956
TOMMY DORSEY & HIS ORCH., featuring Jimmy Dorsey

Lover [Lorenz Hart; Richard Rodgers] (as solo) / **Once In A While** [Bud Green; Michael Edwards] (as solo) / **The Tender Trap** [Sammy Cahn; Jimmy Van Heusen] vTM / **I'm Glad There Is You** [Paul Madeira; Jimmy Dorsey] vDH (as solo) / **Bouncing With Boots**
    All on ET: AFRS One Night Stand 4110, 4046

sustaining broadcast, Cafe Rouge, Hotel Statler, New York, N.Y.—Mid-April 1956
TOMMY DORSEY & HIS ORCH., featuring Jimmy Dorsey

Harlem Express (as solo) / **This Love Of Mine** [Frank Sinatra; Sol Parker, Henry Senicola] arrDJ / **(You Are) Always In My Heart** [Kim Gannon; Ernesto Lecuona] vTM (as solo) / **Brunch** [Ernie Wilkins] (as solo) / **An Occasional Man** [Hugh Martin, Ralph Blane] vDH / **Manhattan** [Lorenz Hart; Richard Rodgers] (cl solo)
    All on ET: AFRS One Night Stand 4051

On Sunday, April 15, the Dorseys began a Sunday afternoon series on

CBS-Radio. Titled *Those Fabulous Dorseys,* the program kicked off a two-hour lineup of music including Guy Lombardo and Percy Faith.

sustaining broadcast, Cafe Rouge, Hotel Statler, New York, N.Y.—Mid-April 1956
TOMMY DORSEY & HIS ORCH., featuring Jimmy Dorsey

Opus One [Sid Garris; Sy Oliver] (cl solo) / **Once In A While** [Bud Green; Michael Edwards] (as solo) / **My First And Last Love** [Remus Harris; Marvin Fisher] vTM / **Harlem Express** (as solo) / **An Occasional Man** [Hugh Martin, Ralph Blane] vDH / **Just As Though You Were Here** [Eddie DeLange; John Benson Brooks]
All on **ET:** AFRS One Night Stand 4042, 4097

Stage Show, CBS TV Studio 50, New York, N.Y. —8:30-9:00 P.M. Saturday, April 21, 1956
TOMMY DORSEY & HIS ORCH., featuring Jimmy Dorsey
Helen O'Connell, Audrey and Jayne Meadows (vcl) 13-year-old Charles Castleman (p) Seven Ashtons (jugglers)

Almost Like Being in Love [Alan Jay Lerner; Frederick Loewe] (for June Taylor Dancers) / **Dungaree Dan And Chino Sue** vA&JM / **Sabre Dance** [Aram Khachaturian] (included in music for Ashtons) / **South Rampart Street Parade** [Steve Allen; Ray Bauduc, Bob Haggart] / *Medley:* **When The Sun Comes Out** [Ted Koehler; Harold Arlen] vHO'C; **It's Love** [Betty Comden, Adolph Green; Leonard Bernstein] vHO'C / **Bumble Boogie** [Jack Fina] CC(p)

Stage Show, CBS-TV Studio 50, New York, N.Y. —8:30-9:00 P.M. Saturday, April 28, 1956
TOMMY DORSEY & HIS ORCH., featuring Jimmy Dorsey
Tony Bennett, DeMarco Sisters (vcl) Roger Ray (comedian) Charles Castleman (p)

Medley: **If You Knew Susie (Like I Know Susie)** [B. G. De Sylva; Joseph Meyer]; **The Yankee Doodle Boy** [George M. Cohan] (background for Ray and Castleman) / *Medley:* **The Poor People Of Paris** [Jack Lawrence; Marguerite Monnot] vDMS; **Once In A While** [Bud Green; Michael Edwards] vDMS / **The Hucklebuck** [Roy Alfred; Andy Gibson]

sustaining broadcast, Cafe Rouge, Hotel Statler, New York, N.Y.—Late-April 1956
TOMMY DORSEY & HIS ORCH., featuring Jimmy Dorsey

Danceably Yours / **I Dream Of You** [Marjorie Goetschius, Edna Osser] arrDJ (as solo) / **All At Once You Love Her** [Oscar Hammerstein II; Richard Rodgers] vTM (as solo) / **Just An Idea** [Benny Goodman] / **Something's Gotta Give** [Johnny Mercer] vDH / **In A Little Spanish Town** [Sam M. Lewis, Joseph Young; Mabel Wayne] arrHG (cl solo) / **Just Swingin'** [Ernie Wilkins] (as solo)
All on **ET:** AFRS One Night Stand 4064

Airchecks of the Dorseys' CBS Sunday afternoon radio series were made between April 15 and June 24, 1956 by a recording service, apparently for checking by Tommy and Jimmy.

It wasn't until after both Dorseys died that their personal manager, Toni Barzee, released the tapes for use on LP, originally by the Top Rank label and later by a myriad others.

The listings that follow are what Top Rank claimed to be complete broadcasts, but in reality many, if not most of them, are edited from several broadcasts.

They are presented here in the sequence created by Top Rank and used in many instances by the successors.

> *The Dorsey Brothers Show, Those Fabulous Dorseys,*
> Cafe Rouge, Hotel Statler, New York, N.Y.—CBS,
> April 15-June 24, 1956

TOMMY DORSEY & HIS ORCH., featuring Jimmy Dorsey

Lover [Lorenz Hart; Richard Rodgers] (as solo) / **The Most Beautiful Girl In The World** [Lorenz Hart; Richard Rodgers] / **Tenderly** [Jack Lawrence; Walter Gross] (as solo) / **It Never Entered My Mind** [Lorenz Hart; Richard Rodgers] vTM / **Skirts And Sweaters** [Ernie Wilkins] / **Dorsey-itis**
  All on **LP:** Top Rank RM328, Jazz Kings 1213, Urania UJ/US41213, **TC:** Drive 41231, **CD:** Drive 41231

> *The Dorsey Brothers Show, Those Fabulous Dorseys,*
> Cafe Rouge, Hotel Statler, New York, N.Y.—CBS,
> April 15-June 24, 1956

TOMMY DORSEY & HIS ORCH., featuring Jimmy Dorsey

Danceably Yours [Ernie Wilkins] / **A Door Will Open** [Don George; John Benson Brooks] (as solo) / **You Taught Me To Love Again** [Charles Carpenter; Tommy Dorsey, Henri Woode] vTM (as solo) / **Manhattan** [Lorenz Hart; Richard Rodgers] (cl solo) / **Panama** [William N. Tyers] (cl solo) *(Dixieland group)*
  All on **LP:** Top Rank RM328, Jazz Kings 1213, Urania UJ/US41213, **TC:** Drive 41231, **CD:** Drive 41231

> *The Dorsey Brothers Show, Those Fabulous Dorseys,*
> Cafe Rouge, Hotel Statler, New York, N.Y.—CBS,
> April 15-June 24, 1956

TOMMY DORSEY & HIS ORCH., featuring Jimmy Dorsey

Song of India [Nicholas Rimsky-Korsakoff] / **On The Sunny Side Of The Street** [Dorothy Fields; Jimmy McHugh] vDH / **Moten Swing** [William "Count" Basie, Eddie Durham] / **I'll Never Smile Again** [Ruth Lowe] (as solo) / **Too Close For Comfort** [Jerry Bock, Larry Holofcener, George David Weiss] vTM / **Serious Business** (cl solo)
  All on: **LP:** Top Rank RM329, Jazz Kings 1214, Urania UJ/US41213; **TC:** Radio Yesteryear 5482; "Song Of India," "Moten Swing," "I'll Never Smile Again" and "Too Close For Comfort" on **TC:** Star Line SLC 61082

The Dorsey Brothers Show, Those Fabulous Dorseys,
Cafe Rouge, Hotel Statler, New York, N.Y.—CBS,
April 15-June 24, 1956
TOMMY DORSEY & HIS ORCH., featuring Jimmy Dorsey

Chasin' The Girls [Neal Hefti] (as solo) / **Without You** [J. D. Miller] vTM (as solo) / **Bula Beige** [Tadd Dameron] (as solo) / **Too Young To Go Steady** [Harold Adamson; Jimmy McHugh] vTM (as solo) / **Let's Fall In Love** [Ted Koehler; Harold Arlen] (cl solo)
All on **LP**: Top Rank RM329, Jazz Kings 1214, Urania UJ/US41213; "Chasin' The Girls," "Without You" and "Bula Beige" on **TC**: Star Line SLC 61082

The Dorsey Brothers Show, Those Fabulous Dorseys,
Cafe Rouge, Hotel Statler, New York, N.Y.—CBS,
April 15-June 24, 1956
TOMMY DORSEY & HIS ORCH., featuring Jimmy Dorsey

Long Sam [Ernie Wilkins] (as solo) / **Street Of Dreams** [Sam M. Lewis; Victor Young] (as solo) / **The Nearness Of You** [Ned Washington; Hoagy Carmichael] vTM (as solo) / **Studio 50** (aka **Dorsey Swing**) [Charlie Shavers] (cl solo) / **Brunch** [Ernie Wilkins] (as solo)
All on **LP**: Top Rank RM330, Jazz Kings 1215; "Street Of Dreams" and "Brunch" on **LP**: Urania UJ/US41214

The Dorsey Brothers Show, Those Fabulous Dorseys,
Cafe Rouge, Hotel Statler, New York, N.Y.—CBS,
April 15-June 24, 1956
TOMMY DORSEY & HIS ORCH., featuring Jimmy Dorsey

Romance [Edgar Leslie; Walter Donaldson] (cl solo) / **Ridin' Around In The Rain** [Gene Austin, Carmen Lombardo] vDH (as solo) / **Let's Call It Swing** [Louis Bellson] (as solo) / **All At Once You Love Her** [Oscar Hammerstein II; Richard Rodgers] vTM (as solo) / **Just For Taking Bows** (as,cl solos)
All on **LP**: Top Rank RM330, Jazz Kings 1215; "Romance" and "Just For Taking Bows" on **LP**: Urania UJ/US41214

The Dorsey Brothers Show, Those Fabulous Dorseys,
Cafe Rouge, Hotel Statler, New York, N.Y.—CBS,
April 15-June 24, 1956
TOMMY DORSEY & HIS ORCH., featuring Jimmy Dorsey

Sweet Cakes [Ernie Wilkins] / **Without A Song** [Billy Rose, Edward Eliscu; Vincent Youmans] vTM / **I'll Always Be In Love With You** [Bud Green, Herman Ruby] vDH (cl solo) / **A Groovy Little Ditty** (as solo) / **I've Grown Accustomed To Her Face** [Alan Jay Lerner; Frederick Loewe] vDH (as solo)
All on **LP**: Top Rank RM331, Jazz Kings 1216; **TC**: Radio Yesteryear 5482; "Sweet Cakes" on **LP**: Urania UJ/US41215, Jazz Kings 1215

The Dorsey Brothers Show, Those Fabulous Dorseys,
Cafe Rouge, Hotel Statler, New York, N.Y.—CBS,
April 15-June 24, 1956
TOMMY DORSEY & HIS ORCH., featuring Jimmy Dorsey

My First And Last Love [Remus Harris; Marvin Fisher] vTM (as
solo) / **In A Little Spanish Town** [Sam M. Lewis, Joseph Young;
Mabel Wayne] (cl solo) / **I Could Have Danced All Night** [Alan Jay
Lerner; Frederick Loewe] vDH (as solo) / **On The Street Where
You Live** [Lerner; Loewe] vTM (as solo) / **Octopus**
    All on **LP:** Top Rank RM331, Jazz Kings 1216; "In A Little
    Spanish Town" and "I Could Have Danced All Night" on **LP:**
    Urania UJ/US41215, Jazz Kings 1215

Tommy and Jimmy were reported in the trade press to have
commissioned Jacques Belasco to compose a concerto for jazz orchestra
with solo trombone and saxophone and symphonic accompaniment. The
idea was to introduce it at a New York concert hall in the early fall.
Belasco was a conductor, composer and orchestrator then working on
The Greatest Story Ever Told radio program (*Down Beat,* May 2, 1956).
    The band also played an unknown location in Montreal, Quebec,
Canada, for two midweek nights in early May 1956, at which time they
spotted Lynn Roberts at the Chez Paree, and invited her to appear on the
May 19 *Stage Show* and rejoin the band in June (Seavor 1997).
    For any appearances out of New York, Tommy hired a replacement
for drummer Louis Bellson, who apparently shunned road trips. For the
Montreal booking, it was Nat Ray.

Stage Show, CBS-TV Studio 50, New York, N.Y.
—8:30-9:00 P.M., Saturday, May 5, 1956
TOMMY DORSEY & HIS ORCH., featuring Jimmy Dorsey
Sarah Vaughan (vcl,p) Morey Amsterdam (comedian)

It's A Big, Wide, Wonderful World [John Rox] (for June Taylor
Dancers) / **Manhattan** [Lorenz Hart; Richard Rodgers] (cl solo) /
Medley: **Hot And Cold Running Tears** vSV; **Over The Rainbow**
[E. Y. Harburg; Harold Arlen] v,pSV) / **Cheese And Crackers** /
Medley: **Aloha Oe (Farewell To Thee)** [Queen Liliuokalani];
Hawaiian War Chant [Johnny Noble, Prince Leleioahaku]

sustaining broadcast, Cafe Rouge, Hotel Statler, New
York, N.Y.—Early May 1956
TOMMY DORSEY & HIS ORCH., featuring Jimmy Dorsey

Studio 50 (aka **Dorsey Swing**) [Charlie Shavers] (as solo) / **Romance**
[Edgar Leslie; Walter Donaldson] (as solo) / **My First And Last
Love** [Remus Harris; Marvin Fisher] vTM / **Powerglide** / **I'll
Always Be In Love With You** [Bud Green, Herman Ruby] vDH (cl
solo) / **I Should Care** [Sammy Cahn, Axel Stordahl, Paul Weston]
arrDJ (as solo) / **Just Swingin'** [Ernie Wilkins] (as solo)
    All on **ET:** AFRS One Night Stand 4071

Stage Show, CBS-TV Studio 50, New York, N.Y.
—8:30-9:00 P.M., Saturday, May 12, 1956
TOMMY DORSEY & HIS ORCH., featuring Jimmy Dorsey
Roberta Sherwood, Dick Haymes (vcl) Colgate Thirteen Choral Group
(vcl grp) Hines Brothers (dancers)

There's No Business Like Show Business [Irving Berlin] (for June
Taylor Dancers) / **Isn't This A Lovely Day?** [Irving Berlin] vDH /
Irving Berlin Tribute Medley: **Blue Skies; Remember; Alexander's
Ragtime Band** / *Medley:* **All Alone** [Irving Berlin] vRS; **Always**
[Irving Berlin] vRS / *Medley:* **Great Day** [Billy Rose, Edward
Eliscu; Vincent Youmans]; **September Song** [Maxwell Anderson;
Kurt Weill] vC13 / **Stompin' Down Broadway** [Ernie Wilkins]
"Alexander's Ragtime Band" on **VIDEO:** MPI 6410

sustaining broadcast, Cafe Rouge, Hotel Statler, New
York, N.Y.—Mid-May 1956
TOMMY DORSEY & HIS ORCH., featuring Jimmy Dorsey

Stereophonic [Ernie Wilkins] / **Do, Do, Do** [Ira Gershwin; George
Gershwin] arrHG (as solo) / **It Never Entered My Mind** [Lorenz
Hart; Richard Rodgers] vTM / **Hanid** / **On The Sunny Side Of The
Street** [Dorothy Fields; Jimmy McHugh] vDH arrSO / **A Door Will
Open** [Don George; John Benson Brooks] vTM (as solo)
All on **ET:** AFRS One Night Stand 4074

Stage Show, CBS-TV Studio 50, New York, N.Y.
8:30-9:00 P.M., Saturday, May 19, 1956
TOMMY DORSEY & HIS ORCH., featuring Jimmy Dorsey
Roberta Sherwood, Kirby Stone Four (vcl grp) Lynn Roberts (vcl) Hines
Brothers, June Taylor Dancers

Kicking The Blues Around [Ernie Wilkins] / **Would You Like To
Take A Walk? (Sumpin' Good Will Come From That)** [Mort
Dixon, Billy Rose; Harry Warren] vLR / **Taking A Chance On Love**
[John Latouche, Ted Fetter; Vernon Duke] vLR / **Waltz In Swing-
time** [Dorothy Fields; Jerome Kern] / *"Fats" Waller Medley:* **Ain't
Misbehavin'** [Andy Razaf; Thomas "Fats" Waller; Harry Brooks];
I've Got A Feeling I'm Falling [Billy Rose; Thomas "Fats" Waller,
Harry Link]; **Honeysuckle Rose** [Andy Razaf; Thomas "Fats"
Waller] (featuring Hines Brothers)
All except medley on **TC:** Ajazz C-1420

In mid-May the brothers faced their first labor union squabble when
the American Federation of Television and Radio Artists (AFTRA)
threatened a strike against *Stage Show* and Jackie Gleason Enterprises
unless the Dorseys joined AFTRA to continue emceeing the shows.

The musicians' union (AFM) opposed the move but AFTRA finally
won out and the brothers agreed to appear only as musicians (*Billboard*
May 19, 1956, 3).

This development must have irked Tommy more than Jimmy, as
Jimmy was always more uncomfortable "up-front."

sustaining broadcast, Cafe Rouge, Hotel Statler, New York, N.Y.—Mid-May 1956
TOMMY DORSEY & HIS ORCH., featuring Jimmy Dorsey

Infinity / **I Dream Of You (More Than You Dream I Do)** [Marjorie Goetschius, Edna Osser] arrDJ (as solo) / **The Tender Trap** [Sammy Cahn; Jimmy Van Heusen] vTM / **Yesterdays** [Otto Harbach; Jerome Kern] arrDJ / **An Occasional Man** [Hugh Martin, Ralph Blane] vDH / **Manhattan** [Lorenz Hart; Richard Rodgers] (cl solo) / **I'll Never Smile Again** [Ruth Lowe] (as solo)
All on **ET:** AFRS One Night Stand 4085

Stage Show, CBS-TV Studio 50, New York, N.Y. —8:30-9:00 P.M., Saturday, May 26, 1956
TOMMY DORSEY & HIS ORCH., featuring Jimmy Dorsey
Eileen Barton (vcl) George Kirby (comedian) Novelles (dog act)

When The Saints Go Marching In (for June Taylor Dancers) / incidental music for George Kirby: **C'Est La Vie** [Edward R. White, Mack Wolfson] (Sarah Vaughan impression); **Oh! Lady Be Good!** [Ira Gershwin; George Gershwin] (Pearl Bailey impression) / **Dorsey-itis** / **Medley: Too Close For Comfort** [Jerry Bock, Larry Holofcener, George David Weiss] vEB; **It's All Right With Me** [Cole Porter] vEB / incidental music for Novelles, including **Dolores** [Frank Loesser; Louis Alter]

sustaining broadcast, Cafe Rouge, Hotel Statler, New York, N.Y.—Late May 1956
TOMMY DORSEY & HIS ORCH., featuring Jimmy Dorsey

Long Sam [Ernie Wilkins] (as solo) / **There Are Such Things** [Stanley Adams, Abel Baer, George W. Meyer] arrDJ (as solo) / **You Taught Me To Love Again** [Charles Carpenter; Tommy Dorsey, Henri Woode] vTM / **Hanid** / **I'll Always Be In Love With You** [Bud Green, Herman Ruby] vDH (cl solo) / **Moonlight In Vermont** [John Blackburn; Karl Suessdorf] arrNH (as solo)
All on **ET:** AFRS One Night Stand 4087

Next is a group of airchecks that are from this period but for which no closer dating, originating station or other information is available.

sustaining broadcast, Cafe Rouge, Hotel Statler, New York, N.Y.—May 1956
TOMMY DORSEY & HIS ORCH., featuring Jimmy Dorsey

Danceably Yours / **There Are Such Things** [Stanley Adams, Abel Baer, George W. Meyer] (as solo) / **The Tender Trap** [Sammy Cahn; Jimmy Van Heusen] vTM / **A Door Will Open** [Don George; John Benson Brooks] vTM (as solo) / **Do It Yourself** [Ernie Wilkins] / **Ridin' Around In The Rain** [Gene Austin, Carmen Lombardo] (as solo) / **Just For Taking Bows** (aka **DC-7**) (as,cl solos)
All on **ET:** AFRS One Night Stand 4108

sustaining broadcast, Cafe Rouge, Hotel Statler, New
York, N.Y.—May 1956
TOMMY DORSEY & HIS ORCH., featuring Jimmy Dorsey

Lover [Lorenz Hart; Richard Rodgers] (as solo) / **This Love Of
Mine** [Frank Sinatra; Sol Parker, Henry Senicola] arrDJ / **The
Tender Trap** vTM [Sammy Cahn; Jimmy Van Heusen] / **Let's Call
It Swing** [Louis Bellson] (as solo) / **I've Grown Accustomed To Her
Face** [Alan Jay Lerner; Frederick Loewe] vDH / **Powerglide**
All on **ET:** AFRS One Night Stand 4111

sustaining broadcast, Cafe Rouge, Hotel Statler, New
York, N.Y.—May 1956
TOMMY DORSEY & HIS ORCH., featuring Jimmy Dorsey

Skirts And Sweaters [Ernie Wilkins] / **I'll Never Smile Again** [Ruth
Lowe] (as solo) / **The Nearness Of You** [Ned Washington; Hoagy
Carmichael] vTM / **Do It Yourself** [Ernie Wilkins] / **I've Grown
Accustomed To Her Face** [Alan Jay Lerner; Frederick Loewe] vDH
/ **Once In A While** [Bud Green; Michael Edwards] (as solo)
All on ET: AFRS One Night Stand 4116

sustaining broadcast, Cafe Rouge, Hotel Statler, New
York, N.Y.—March-May 1956
TOMMY DORSEY & HIS ORCH., featuring Jimmy Dorsey

Let's Fall In Love [Ted Koehler; Harold Arlen] (cl solo) / **Long
Sam** [Ernie Wilkins] (as solo) / **Just Swingin'** [Ernie Wilkins] (as
solo) / (unknown title) / **Opus One** [Sid Garris; Sy Oliver] (cl solo) /
Studio 50 (aka **Dorsey Swing**) [Charlie Shavers] (as solo) / **South
Rampart Street Parade** [Steve Allen; Ray Bauduc, Bob Haggart]
(Dixieland group)

sustaining broadcast, Cafe Rouge, Hotel Statler, New
York, N.Y.—March-May 1956
TOMMY DORSEY & HIS ORCH., featuring Jimmy Dorsey

Just An Idea [Benny Goodman] / **King Size** /**I'll Never Smile** Again
[Ruth Lowe] (as solo) / **Romance** [Edgar Leslie; Walter Donaldson]
(as solo) / **Dorsey-itis** / **Let's Fall In Love** [Ted Koehler; Harold
Arlen] (cl solo) / **Stompin' Down Broadway** [Ernie Wilkins]

sustaining broadcast, Cafe Rouge, Hotel Statler, New
York, N.Y.—March-May 1956
TOMMY DORSEY & HIS ORCH., featuring Jimmy Dorsey

You Make Me Feel So Young [Mack Gordon; Josef Myrow] /
Harlem Express (as solo) / **My Funny Valentine** [Lorenz Hart;
Richard Rodgers] vLR / **Moten Swing** [William "Count" Basie,
Eddie Durham] / **The Tender Trap** [Sammy Cahn; Jimmy Van
Heusen] vTM

sustaining broadcast, Cafe Rouge, Hotel Statler, New York, N.Y.—Early June 1956
TOMMY DORSEY & HIS ORCH., featuring Jimmy Dorsey

Opus One [Sid Garris; Sy Oliver] (cl solo) / **I Dream Of You (More Than You Dream I Do)** [Marjorie Goetschius, Edna Osser] (arr DJ) (as solo) / **It Never Entered My Mind** [Lorenz Hart; Richard Rodgers] vTM / **Bouncing With Boots** / **Too Young To Go Steady** [Harold Adamson; Jimmy McHugh] vDH (as solo) / **Once In A While** [Bud Green; Michael Edwards] (as solo)
All on **ET:** AFRS One Night Stand 4090

Stage Show, CBS-TV Studio 50, New York, N.Y.
—8:30-9:00 P.M. Saturday, June 2, 1956
TOMMY DORSEY & HIS ORCH., featuring Jimmy Dorsey
Sunny Gale (vcl) George Jessell (comedian) Four Step Brothers (dancers)

Unknown selection for June Taylor Dancers / **On The Sunny Side Of The Street** [Dorothy Fields; Jimmy McHugh] vSG / *Medley:* **I Laughed At Love** [Bennie Davis; Abner Silver] vSG; **Smile** [John Turner, Geoffrey Parsons; Charles Chaplin] vSG; **Goodnight, Well It's Time To Go** (aka **Goodnight, Sweetheart, Goodnight**) [Calvin Carter, James Hudson] vSG / **Theme From** *Picnic* [Steve Allen; George Dunning] / **California, Here I Come** [Al Jolson, B. G. De Sylva; Joseph Meyer] (Al Jolson impression) vGJ / **If You Knew Susie (Like I Know Susie)** [B. G. De Sylva; Joseph Meyer] (Eddie Cantor impression) vGJ / incidental music for Four Step Brothers including **Charleston** [Cecil Mack; James P. Johnson]

sustaining broadcast, Cafe Rouge, Hotel Statler, New York, N.Y.—Early June 1956
TOMMY DORSEY & HIS ORCH., featuring Jimmy Dorsey

Opus One [Sid Garris; Sy Oliver] (cl solo) / **This Love Of Mine** [Frank Sinatra; Sol Parker, Henry Senicola] arrDJ / **Without You** [J. D. Miller] vTM (as solo) / **Let's Fall In Love** [Ted Koehler; Harold Arlen] (cl solo) / **Mister Wonderful** [Jerry Bock, Larry Holofcener, George David Weiss] / **I Should Care** [Sammy Cahn, Axel Stordahl, Paul Weston] vDH (as solo)
All on **ET:** AFRS One Night Stand 4104

Stage Show, CBS-TV Studio 50, New York, N.Y.
8:30-9:00 P.M., Saturday, June 9, 1956
TOMMY DORSEY & HIS ORCH., featuring Jimmy Dorsey
Charlie Shavers (vcl) Joe Marsala (cl) Adele Girard (harp) Jack Durante (comedian)

Well, Git It! [Sy Oliver] (for June Taylor Dancers) / **Smack Dab In The Middle** [Charles Calhoun] vCS / music for Durante including **When You're Smiling (The Whole World Smiles At You)** [Mark Fisher, Joe Goodwin, Larry Shay] / **Holiday For Strings** [David Rose] (for June Taylor Dancers) / **Body And Soul** [John Green]

AG,harp / **Schoen Rosmarin** AG,harp & JM,cl / **Boogie Woogie**
[Clarence "Pinetop" Smith] AG,Harp & JM,cl / **I'm Gettin'**
Sentimental Over You [Ned Washington; George Bassman]

The Colts vocal group was scheduled to appear on the last show but
did not. Meanwhile, in mid-June Lynn Roberts rejoined the band, replacing Dolly Houston, a move negotiated earlier that year in Montreal.

Stage Show, CBS-TV Studio 50, New York, N.Y.
—8:30-9:00 P.M., Saturday, June 16, 1956
TOMMY DORSEY & HIS ORCH., featuring Jimmy Dorsey
Connie Francis (vcl) The Edwards Brothers, The Treniers

Whachamajig (as solo) / (music for Edwards Brothers) / **Song Of**
India [Nicholas Rimsky-Korsakoff] / **Puddle Wump** [Charlie
Shavers] / **Medley: When You're Smiling (The Whole World**
Smiles At You) [Mark Fisher, Joe Goodwin, Larry Shay] vCF; **For-**
getting vCF / **On The Sunny Side Of The Street** [Dorothy Fields;
Jimmy McHugh] / **Lover** [Lorenz Hart; Richard Rodgers] (as solo)
  "Whachamajig" on **TC:** Joyce Record Club C-1409

Stage Show, CBS-TV Studio 50, New York, N.Y.
—8:30-9:00 P.M., Saturday, June 23, 1956
TOMMY DORSEY & HIS ORCH., featuring Jimmy Dorsey
Fran Warren (vcl)

Song Of India [Nicholas Rimsky-Korsakoff] / **I Get The Blues**
When It Rains [Marcy Klauber; Harry Stoddard] vFW / **A Sunday**
Kind Of Love [Barbara Belle, Anita Leonard, Stan Rhodes] vFW /
Panama [William N. Tyers] (cl solo) *(Dixieland group)*
  All tunes on **TC:** Joyce Record Club C-1409

Tommy and Jimmy closed at the Cafe Rouge of Hotel Statler on
Friday, June 29. The band did such good business at the hotel, which
was fast becoming their home base, that the management tore down
walls to enlarge the room over the summer. The band was scheduled to
return in late September (*Down Beat,* July 11, 1956, 4).

Stage Show, CBS-TV Studio 50, New York, N.Y.
—8:30-9:00 P.M., Saturday, June 30, 1956
TOMMY DORSEY & HIS ORCH., featuring Jimmy Dorsey
Russ Morgan (tb,p) Helen O'Connell, The Platters (vcl)

Serious Business (cl solo) / **The End Of A Love Affair** [Edward
Redding] vHO'C / **Not So Quiet Please** [Sy Oliver] / *Russ Morgan*
Medley: **Does Your Heart Beat For Me** [Mitchell Parish; Russ
Morgan, Arnold Johnson]; **Somebody Else Is Taking My Place**
[Dick Howard, Russ Morgan, Bob Ellsworth]; **So Tired** [Russ
Morgan, Jack Stuart] (p,vRM) / **I'm Gettin' Sentimental Over You**
[Ned Washington; George Bassman] (trombone duet RM,TD) /
Amapola [Albert Gamse; Joseph M. Lacalle] vHO'C
  All tunes on **TC:** Joyce Record Club C-1409

In mid-week the band went into the Midwest for three days. *Variety* (July 11, 1956, 43) reported that they did a $20,000 gross in two days at the Mesker Amphitheater, Evansville, Indiana, on Tuesday and Wednesday, July 3 and 4. On the way back to New York they grossed $5,000 the next day, Thursday, July 5, at Cedar Point Park, Sandusky, Ohio.

Stage Show, CBS-TV Studio 50, New York, N.Y.
—8:30-9:00 P.M., Saturday, July 7, 1956
TOMMY DORSEY & HIS ORCH., featuring Jimmy Dorsey
Jack Fina (p) Tommy Mercer, Tony Bennett (vcl)

Marie [Irving Berlin] TM&band (as solo) / *Medley:* **Tonight We Love** [Bobby Worth; Freddy Martin, Ray Austin] (p,JF); **Bumble Boogie** [Jack Fina] (p,JF) **Can't You Find It In Your Heart?** vTB / **Tawny** (suite) [Jackie Gleason] (p,JF) / **I'm Gettin' Sentimental Over You** [Ned Washington; George Bassman]
All tunes except theme on **TC:** Joyce Record Club C-1409

Stage Show, CBS-TV Studio 50, New York, N.Y.
—8:30-9:00 P.M., Saturday, July 14, 1956
TOMMY DORSEY & HIS ORCH., featuring Jimmy Dorsey
"Somethin'" Smith & The Red Heads, Tommy Mercer, Lynn Roberts (vcl)

Ol' Man River [Oscar Hammerstein II; Jerome Kern] **Manhattan** [Lorenz Hart; Richard Rodgers] (cl solo) / **All The Things You Are** [Oscar Hammerstein II; Jerome Kern] vTM (also used as background for June Taylor Dancers) / **I've Got The World On A String** [Ted Koehler; Harold Arlen] vLR
"Manhattan," "All The Things You Are" and "I've Got The World On A String" on **TC:** Joyce Record Club C-1420

Telecast schedule: Sat., July 21, CBS-TV *Stage Show,* 8:30-9:00 P.M. Guests: Dick Haymes, Sister Rosetta Tharpe / Sat., July 28, CBS-TV *Stage Show,* 8:30-9:00 P.M. Guests: The Crew Cuts, Eileen Rogers.

After the July 28 telecast the band moved to Hollywood, where on Monday, July 30, NBC-Radio began a two-hour format featuring live big bands Monday through Friday from 10:00 A.M. to noon with a simulcast of the 10:30-11:00 segment on NBC-TV. Called *NBC Bandstand,* the show was insipidly hosted by Bert Parks and co-emceed by a string of music names like Johnny Mercer and Dick Haymes, who bore the title "Mr. (or Miss) Music" for the week. The program showcased what big bands still remained, and the brothers were featured for the first two weeks from Hollywood along with Guy Lombardo from New York, Wayne King from Chicago and Freddy Martin from Hollywood.

The nature of the majority of the bands indicated that NBC was aiming at the housewife. Since the TV and radio sound was separately picked up, NBC promoted a "binaural opportunity" and urged listeners to use the radio and TV sounds side by side to create a "stereo effect."

The television portion lasted only for two months, but the radio program survived for some time.

NBC Bandstand,   Hollywood,   Cal.—NBC   Radio
7:00- 9:00 A.M. PDT, NBC-TV 7:30-8:00 A.M. PDT
Thursday, August 2, 1956
TOMMY DORSEY & HIS ORCH., featuring **Jimmy Dorsey**
Johnny Mercer, Tommy Mercer, Lynn Roberts (vcl)

Rain [Eugene Ford, Carey Morgan, Arthur Swanstrom] (as solo) /
I've Grown Accustomed To Her Face [Alan Jay Lerner; Frederick
Loewe] vLR (as solo) / **In The Cool, Cool, Cool Of The Evening**
[Johnny Mercer; Hoagy Carmichael] vJM / **Too Close For Comfort**
[Jerry Bock, Larry Holofcener, George David Weiss] vTM / **Would
You Like To Take A Walk? (Sumpin' Good Will Come From
That)** [Mort Dixon, Billy Rose; Harry Warren] vLR / **Song Of India**
[Nicholas Rimsky-Korsakoff] / **Surprise Party** vJM / **Too Young To
Go Steady** [Harold Adamson; Jimmy McHugh] vLR (as solo) /
Green Eyes [N. Menendez, E. Rivera, Eddie Woods, A. Utera]
vLR&TM (as solo) / **Swanee River** [Stephen Foster] / **The Tender
Trap** [Sammy Cahn; Jimmy Van Heusen] vTM / **There Are Such
Things** [Stanley Adams, Abel Baer, George W. Meyer] (as solo) /
Yours (Quicremé Mucho) [Jack Sherr, Augustin Rodriguez; Gonzalo
Roig] vLR&TM (as solo) / **Do, Do, Do** [Ira Gershwin; George
Gershwin] (as solo)
 Entire segment on **LP:** Sunbeam SB224, Sandy Hook SH2071,
TC: Sandy Hook CSH-2071; entire segment except "Do, Do, Do"
on **TC:** Radio Days CA 5-1012; "Yours" on **TC:** Imperfect C-19

Stage Show, CBS-TV Studios, Hollywood, Cal.,
—5:30-6:00 P.M. PDT Saturday, August 4, 1956
TOMMY DORSEY & HIS ORCH., featuring **Jimmy Dorsey**
Merv Griffin (vcl,p) Sarah Vaughan (vcl)

Dipper Mouth Blues [Joseph "King" Oliver, Louis Armstrong]

Telecast schedule: Sat., Aug. 11, CBS-TV *Stage Show,* 5:30-6:00 P.M. PDT, Guests:
Gene Baylos, Sunny Howard.

On August 14 the Dorsey Orchestra returned to New York for a
week's engagement at the Paramount Theater with Frank Sinatra, followed by a return to the Hotel Statler. This was the second time in
eighteen months that the Dorseys had worked with Tommy's former
featured vocalist. Sinatra had visited the Manhattan Center WNEW
shindig in New York on February 3, 1955. Neither of these contacts,
however, was other than a pure business arrangement and Frank's bad
feelings about his last days with Tommy were still in evidence.
 The movie at the Paramount was *Johnny Concho* (*Down Beat,* August
8, 1956). There is extant a film of one of the Paramount stage performances (Seavor 1997).

Stage Show, CBS-TV Studio 50, New York, N.Y.,
—8:30-9:00 P.M., Saturday, August 18, 1956
TOMMY DORSEY & HIS ORCH., featuring **Jimmy Dorsey**
Della Reese (vcl)

Stage Show (Contd.)

Well, Git It! [Sy Oliver] / **In The Still Of The Night** [Cole Porter] vDR / **Hesitation** [Hugo Winterhalter] / **Serious Business** (cl solo)
   All tunes on **TC:** Joyce Record Club C-1420

Stage Show, CBS-TV Studio 50, New York, N.Y., —8:30-9:00 P.M. Saturday, August 25, 1956
TOMMY DORSEY & HIS ORCH., featuring Jimmy Dorsey
Dick Haymes (vcl)

September Song [Maxwell Anderson; Kurt Weill] / **Love Is A Great Big Nothin'** vDH
   All tunes on **TC:** Joyce Record Club C-1420

The fiftieth anniversary of Paul Whiteman's first job as a musician was marked in 1956 by an LP.   This was Tommy's last date in a recording studio. Tommy soloed on two of the sides, "My Romance" and "The Night Is Young And You're So Beautiful," while Jimmy did a yeoman's job on his own hit "It's The Dreamer In Me."   Neither appeared on the others' sides.

Grand Award, New York, N.Y. Thursday, August 30, 1956
PAUL WHITEMAN 50TH ANNIVERSARY ORCHESTRA
Charlie Margulis, 3 *unknown* (tp) Bobby Byrne, Charlie Small, Tommy Mitchell (tb) **Jimmy Dorsey** (as) 3 *unknown* (reeds) 5 *unknown* (strings) Buddy Weed (p,celst) George Barnes (g)   Felix Giobbe (sb) Morey Feld (d)

33-901-C-3   **It's The Dreamer In Me** [Jimmy Van Heusen, Jimmy Dorsey] (as solo)
   LP: Grand Award 33-901, London (E) HA-Z2365

Telecast schedule: Sat., Sept. 1, CBS-TV *Stage Show,* 8:30-9:00 P.M. Guests: Morey Amsterdam (comedian), Merv Griffin (p), Martin Brothers (dance team)

Stage Show, CBS-TV Studio 50, New York, N.Y. —8:30-9:00 P.M., Saturday, September 8, 1956
TOMMY DORSEY & HIS ORCH., featuring Jimmy Dorsey

Dipper Mouth Blues ["King" Oliver, Louis Armstrong] / **Obey**
   Both tunes on **TC:** Joyce Record Club C-1420

NBC Monitor, Cafe Rouge, Hotel Statler, New York, N.Y.— NBC Radio, Saturday, September 8, 1956
TOMMY DORSEY & HIS ORCH., featuring Jimmy Dorsey

Skirts And Sweaters [Ernie Wilkins] / **Moten Swing** [William "Count" Basie, Eddie Durham]

Telecast schedule: Sat., Sept. 15, CBS-TV *Stage Show,* 8:30-9:00 P.M. Guests: Eddie Fontaine (comedian), The Crew Cuts (vcl grp) Leo Dalton.

sustaining broadcast, Cafe Rouge, Hotel Statler, New
York, N.Y.—Mid September 1956
TOMMY DORSEY & HIS ORCH., featuring Jimmy Dorsey

Make Believe [Oscar Hammerstein II; Jerome Kern] / **Manhattan**
[Lorenz Hart; Richard Rodgers] (cl solo) / **Ruby** [Mitchell Parish;
Heinz Roemheld] vTM arrHG (as solo) / **Stereophonic** [Ernie Wilkins] / **Let's Zip**
All on **ET**: AFRS One Night Stand 4161B

sustaining broadcast, Cafe Rouge, Hotel Statler, New
York, N.Y.—Mid-September 1956
TOMMY DORSEY & HIS ORCH., featuring Jimmy Dorsey

Skirts And Sweaters [Ernie Wilkins] / **Too Young To Go Steady**
[Harold Adamson; Jimmy McHugh] vDH (as solo) / **Street Of
Dreams** [Sam M. Lewis; Victor Young] (as solo) / **It Never Entered
My Mind** [Lorenz Hart; Richard Rodgers] vTM / **Anything Goes**
[Cole Porter]
All on **ET**: AFRS One Night Stand 4173A

sustaining broadcast, Cafe Rouge, Hotel Statler, New
York, N.Y.—Late September 1956
TOMMY DORSEY & HIS ORCH., featuring Jimmy Dorsey

Bula Beige [Tadd Dameron] (as solo) / **(How Little It Matters) How
Little We Know** [Carolyn Leigh; Philip Springer] / **In A Little
Spanish Town** [Sam M. Lewis, Joseph Young; Mabel Wayne] (cl
solo) / **Harlem Express** (as solo)
All on **ET**: AFRS One Night Stand 4176B

sustaining broadcast, Cafe Rouge, Hotel Statler, New
York, N.Y.—Late September 1956
TOMMY DORSEY & HIS ORCH., featuring Jimmy Dorsey

Lover [Lorenz Hart; Richard Rodgers] (as solo) / **It Never Entered
My Mind** [Lorenz Hart; Richard Rodgers] vTM / **Let's Fall In Love**
[Ted Koehler; Harold Arlen] (cl solo) / **Do It Yourself** [Ernie
Wilkins]
All on **ET**: AFRS One Night Stand 4178

And finally, the closing telecast in the *Stage Show* series.

Stage Show, CBS-TV Studio 50, New York, N.Y.
—8:30-9:00 P.M., Saturday, September 22, 1956
TOMMY DORSEY & HIS ORCH., featuring Jimmy Dorsey
Ella Logan, Gale Storm (vcl) Archie Robbins (comedian)

Unknown titles / "thank yous" from Tommy and Jimmy to production
staff and sponsors (Nestlé Co.) for their support during the series /
I'm Gettin' Sentimental Over You [Ned Washington; George
Bassman] / unknown title

Once the fall television season resumed, CBS reinstated the hour-long *Jackie Gleason Show,* and *Stage Show* was put back in mothballs, as it turned out permanently. The Dorseys returned to the *NBC Bandstand* on Monday, October 8, for two weeks, ending Friday, October 19.

> *sustaining broadcast,* Cafe Rouge, Hotel Statler, New York, N.Y.—Early October 1956

TOMMY DORSEY & HIS ORCH., featuring Jimmy Dorsey

Dancing In The Dark [Howard Dietz; Arthur Schwartz] / **Stormy Weather** [Ted Koehler; Harold Arlen] / **Manhattan** [Lorenz Hart; Richard Rodgers] (cl solo) / **Sunny Disposish** [Ira Gershwin; Philip Charig] / **Ruby** [Mitchell Parish; Heinz Roemheld] vTM (as solo)
All on **ET**: AFRS One Night Stand 4190B

> *sustaining broadcast,* Cafe Rouge, Hotel Statler, New York, N.Y.—Mid-October 1956

TOMMY DORSEY & HIS ORCH., featuring Jimmy Dorsey

Studio 50 (aka **Dorsey Swing**) [Charlie Shavers] (as solo) / **Romance** [Edgar Leslie; Walter Donaldson] (as solo) / **You Taught Me To Love Again** [Charles Carpenter; Tommy Dorsey, Henri Woode] / **Sweet Sue (Just You)** [Will J. Harris; Victor Young] (cl solo) / **The Most Beautiful Girl In The World** [Lorenz Hart; Richard Rodgers]
All on **ET**: AFRS One Night Stand 4192A

> *sustaining broadcast,* Cafe Rouge, Hotel Statler, New York, N.Y.—Mid-October 1956

TOMMY DORSEY & HIS ORCH., featuring Jimmy Dorsey

The Tender Trap [Sammy Cahn; Jimmy Van Heusen] vTM / **There Are Such Things** [Stanley Adams, Abel Baer, George W. Meyer] (as solo) / **On The Sunny Side Of The Street** [Dorothy Fields; Jimmy McHugh] (arrSO) / **Standing Room Only**
All on **ET**: AFRS One Night Stand 4195A

> *NBC Bandstand,* New York, N.Y.—NBC Radio 10:00 A.M-noon, NBC-TV 10:30-11:00 A.M., Wednesday, October 17, 1956

TOMMY DORSEY & HIS ORCH., featuring Jimmy Dorsey
Guy Mitchell, Tommy Mercer, Lynn Roberts (vcl)

I'm Gettin' Sentimental Over You [Ned Washington; George Bassman] (theme) / **Laura** [Johnny Mercer; David Raksin] vTM (as solo) / **All Of You** [Cole Porter] vTM (as solo) / **Park Avenue Patter** (cl solos) / **Belle, Belle (My Liberty Belle)** [Bob Merrill] vGM / **Romance** [Edgar Leslie; Walter Donaldson] (as solo) / **Mister Wonderful** [Jerry Bock, Larry Holofcener, George David Weiss] vLR (cl solo) / **Bouncing With Boots** (as solo) / (theme) / **I've Got The World On A String** [Ted Koehler; Harold Arlen] vLR / **The Most Beautiful Girl In The World** [Lorenz Hart; Richard Rodgers]

/ **The Roving Kind** [Jesse Cavanaugh, Arnold Stanton] vGM / **Stereophonic** [Ernie Wilkins]
　　All selections on **LP:** Sunbeam SB226; "Park Avenue Patter," "Bouncing With Boots" and "The Most Beautiful Girl In The World" on **TC:** Imperfect C-19

NBC Bandstand, New York, N.Y.—NBC Radio, 10:00 A.M-noon, Thursday, October 18, 1956
TOMMY DORSEY & HIS ORCH., featuring **Jimmy Dorsey**
Tommy Dorsey, Jimmy Dorsey (dialogue) Tommy Mercer, Lynn Roberts (vcl)

I'm Gettin' Sentimental Over You [Ned Washington; George Bassman] (theme) / **Wagon Wheels** [Billy Hill, Peter De Rose] / **(You Are) Always In My Heart** [Kim Gannon; Ernesto Lecuona] vTM (as solo) / **Stella By Starlight** [Ned Washington; Victor Young] (as solo) / **The Bells Of St. Mary's** [Douglas Furber; A. Emmett Adams] / **I'm Glad There Is You** [Paul Madeira; Jimmy Dorsey] vLR (as solo) / **Bula Beige** [Tadd Dameron] (as solo) / **My Brother Is The Leader Of The Band** TD&JD dialogue / **Besame Mucho** [Sunny Skyler; Consuello Valazquez] (cl solo) / **Amapola** [Albert Gamse; Joseph M. Lacalle] vTM&LR (cl solo)
　　all except "Bula Beige," "Besame Mucho" and "Amapola" on **TC:** Magic (E) CAWE-37, **CD:** Magic (E) DAWE-37; "Wagon Wheels" on **LP:** Sunbeam SB226; all except "Amapola" on **TC:** Joyce Record Club C-1544 and Ajazz 1544; "Amapola" on **TC:** Joyce Record Club C-1545 and Ajazz 1545

NBC Bandstand, New York, N.Y.—NBC Radio 10:00 A.M.-noon, Friday, October 19, 1956
TOMMY DORSEY & HIS ORCH., featuring **Jimmy Dorsey**

I'm Gettin'Sentimental Over You / **Sandman** [Ralph Freed, Bonnie Lake] (as solo) / **Too Close For Comfort** [Jerry Bock, Larry Holofcener, George David Weiss] vTM / **Deep Purple** [Mitchell Parish; Peter De Rose] (as solos) / **Moonlight In Vermont** [John Blackburn; Karl Suessdorf] (as solo) / **My Funny Valentine** [Lorenz Hart; Richard Rodgers] vLR / **Do It Yourself** [Ernie Wilkins] (as solo) / **Oh, What A Beautiful Mornin'** [Oscar Hammerstein II; Richard Rodgers] (cl solo)
　　Full program on **TC:** Ajazz 1545, Joyce Record Club C-1545

sustaining broadcast, Cafe Rouge, Hotel Statler, New York, N.Y.—Late October 1956
TOMMY DORSEY & HIS ORCH., featuring **Jimmy Dorsey**

Bula Beige [Tadd Dameron] (as solo) / **Too Young To Go Steady** [Harold Adamson; Jimmy McHugh] vLR (as solo) / **You Make Me Feel So Young** [Mack Gordon; Josef Myrow] / **The Night We Called It A Day** [Tom Adair; Matt Dennis]
　　All on **ET:** AFRS One Night Stand 4200B

sustaining broadcast, Cafe Rouge, Hotel Statler, New
York, N.Y.—Early November 1956
TOMMY DORSEY & HIS ORCH., featuring Jimmy Dorsey

Opus One [Sid Garris; Sy Oliver] (cl solo) / **(You Are) Always In
My Heart** [Kim Gannon; Ernesto Lecuona] (as solo) / **Romance**
[Edgar Leslie; Walter Donaldson] (as solo) / **Moten Swing** [William
"Count" Basie, Eddie Durham]
All on **ET**: AFRS One Night Stand 4212A

In addition, AFRS lists other One Night Stand programs from this
period but their details are unknown: 4202A, 4208B, 4214B, 4217A,
4222A, 4225B and 4228A.
A heart attack took the life of the Dorseys' long time associate, fifty-
six-year-old Victor Young, who died Saturday, November 10, in Palm
Springs, California. Passing away that same week at forty-six, was
another friend, jazz pianist Art Tatum.
On Sunday, November 11, Jimmy brought the band (without Tommy
and slightly augmented) into the Capitol studios for four cuts of an LP
and a 45 RPM extended-play record to be released by Fraternity. One
of the tunes in that session, a pseudo-rock version of "So Rare," went on
to set surprising sales records, earning a posthumous gold record for
Jimmy in an era when rock 'n roll was ruling the roost.
First introduced in 1937 by Gus Arnheim on Brunswick, the tune
received little recording activity, and was played, but never recorded, by
several bands including Jimmy's. An aircheck from August, 1937 by the
Benny Goodman Trio, issued on an LP in the late fifties, after Jimmy's
success, and a Decca recording by the Edgar Hayes Quartet are the only
other significant releases of the song.
As was his way throughout his life, Jimmy was reluctant to do the
session, cautioning Fraternity Records producer Harry Carlson he might
"get hurt" by taking a chance "on a has-been" (Wilson 1957).

Capitol, New York, N.Y. Sunday, November 11, 1956
JIMMY DORSEY & HIS ORCHESTRA
Jimmy Dorsey (cl,as,ldr) Lee Castle, John Frosk, Bill Spano, Art
Tancredi (tp) Will Bradley, Vince Forrest, Jack Rains, Billy VerPlanck
(tb) Ralph "Skip" Galluccio, Danny Trimboli (as) Buzzy Brauner, Frank
Maynes (ts) George Perry (bar) Joe Massimino (p,celst) Steve Jordan (g)
Billy Cronk (sb) Tommy Widdicombe (d) Artie Malvin Singers (vcl grp)
Howard Gibeling (arr)

1174   **So Rare** [Jack Sharpe; Jerry Herst] vAMS (as solo)
     45: Dot 16371
     EP: Fraternity F755
     LP: Fraternity FLP1008, Liberty LRP3223, LRP3260, LRP7723,
     Quality (C) V1599, Dot DLP3437, HMV(E) CLP1132, Project3
     PR-2-6036, Pye (E) GGLO289, Trip TLP5815, Gusto GT4-2100
1175   **Sophisticated Swing** [Mitchell Parish; Will
                    Hudson] vAMS (as solo)
     EP: Fraternity F755

LP: Fraternity FLP1008, Quality (C) V1599, Dot DLP3437, HMV(E) CLP1132, Pye (E) GGLO289, Trip TLP5815
CD: Pilz (EC) 2049
1176   **It's The Dreamer In Me** [Jimmy Van Heusen, Jimmy Dorsey] vAMS (as solo)
LP: Fraternity FLP1008, Quality (C) V1599, Dot DLP3437, HMV(E) CLP1132, Pye (E) GGLO289, Trip TLP5815
-0-   **Mambo En Sax** [Perez Prado] vAMS (as solo)
LP: Fraternity FLP1008, Quality (C) V1599, Dot DLP3437, HMV(E) CLP1132, Pye (E) GGLO289, Trip TLP5815

The remaining seven cuts on FLP-1008 and reissues were cut after Jimmy's death. Dick Stabile played Jimmy's parts and the band was led by Lee Castle (see page 589).

Down Beat (December 12, 1956, 7) reported on some recent changes in the band. Tom Widdicombe replaced Louis Bellson (d) and Buzzy Brauner (ts) returned from the armed forces, replacing Pat Chartrand.

Then the magazine added that the band would work the New Frontier Hotel-Casino in Las Vegas, Nevada, for three weeks beginning on January 21, 1957.

The same issue of *Down Beat* reported on a possible West Indies tour, again brought up an exchange of appearances with England, and said that the Dorsey band would return to the Statler on Good Friday, 1957, working until the end of June or possibly to August 15. These events, however, were overshadowed by others occuring before the December 12 issue of the magazine reached the newsstands.

Tommy celebrated his fifty-first birthday on November 19, 1956. He, Jimmy and eighty-two-year-old "Mom" Dorsey, who by now was living on the Upper East Side in New York, celebrated at the Hotel Statler where the combined Dorsey band was playing and Jimmy was in residence.

The following broadcast is claimed by many collectors to be the final recorded broadcast by Tommy Dorsey. As the reader will also see, another is purported to be the last one.

sustaining broadcast, Cafe Rouge, Hotel Statler, New York, N.Y.—CBS Friday, November 23, 1956
TOMMY DORSEY & HIS ORCH., featuring Jimmy Dorsey

Bula Beige [Tadd Dameron] (partial) / **I Dream Of You (More Than You Dream I Do)** [Marjorie Goetschius, Edna Osser] arrDJ (as solo) / **The Tender Trap** [Sammy Cahn; Jimmy Van Heusen] vTM / **The Night We Called It A Day** [Tom Adair; Matt Dennis] / **This Is Romance** [Edward Heyman; Vernon Duke] / **Love Is Here To Stay** [Ira Gershwin; George Gershwin] vTM / **The Left Hand Corner** / **Swingin' For Breakfast** (aka **Just For Takin' Bows**) (as,cl solos)

On the following Sunday evening, the band fed its customary fifteen minute show to CBS. The next is claimed to be that show and thus Tommy's final broadcast; others, just as positively, say it is from an earlier date.

sustaining broadcast, Cafe Rouge, Hotel Statler, New
York, N.Y.—CBS, *Sunday, November 25,* 1956
TOMMY DORSEY & HIS ORCH., featuring Jimmy Dorsey

Harlem Express (as solo) / **Don't Worry 'Bout Me** [Ted Koehler;
Rube Bloom] vLR (cl solo) / **Romance** [Edgar Leslie; Walter
Donaldson] (as solo) / **Something's Gotta Give** [Johnny Mercer]
vLR / **Moten Swing** [Bennie Moten]
   All on **LP**: Joyce LP1086, "Harlem Express" and "Don't Worry
'Bout Me" on **TC**: Joyce Record Club C-1545, Ajazz 1545

After finishing the night's performance at the Statler, Tommy picked
up some Italian food, of which he was especially fond, and brought it
home to Flagler Drive in Greenwich, Connecticut, where he, his
estranged third wife Jane and his mother-in-law shared a late meal.
Then Tommy went to his room alone.
   The next afternoon he was found dead. He had taken Nembutal to
help him sleep, and had suffocated when he regurgitated food particles
which lodged in his throat. The sleeping pills inhibited the cough reflex
that would have cleared his windpipe.
   Jimmy was devastated. With his old friend Cork O'Keefe he rushed
to his mother's apartment on Manhattan's East Side. (Mom Dorsey had
only recently moved to New York from California, where she had lived
since the death of "the father" in 1942.) Lee Castle and other friends of
the family had begun to arrive, but try as he might Jimmy could not find
the courage to tell his mother that "Mac" was dead. The task fell to
personal manager Tino Barzee. After they had left his mother, Jimmy
told O'Keefe: "I don't think I'll last out the year" (Sanford 1972).
   That evening the band played for the diners and dancers at the Cafe
Rouge. In Jimmy's absence Lee Castle led the band, and Tommy's
trombone was placed on a chair in front of the bandstand.
   As word of Tommy's death reached a shocked music world, many
friends rallied to take part in a hastily arranged memorial tribute, hosted
by longtime friend Jackie Gleason and telecast from CBS facilities on
both coasts. Considering the state of television technology in 1956, and
that the show was put together so quickly, it was remarkably well done.
   One of the programs most touching moments was the medley of
Tommy Dorsey hits, introduced by Paul Whiteman and directed by
Jimmy. Vinnie Forrest, the trombonist in the band, whom Tommy had
said played the most like him, played Tommy's solos from behind a
scrim, so only his shadow appeared on the screen.

Tribute To Tommy Dorsey, CBS Television studios,
New York, N.Y., and Hollywood, Cal.—CBS-TV,
8:00-9:00 P.M. Saturday, December 1, 1956
THE FABULOUS DORSEY ORCHESTRA
Lee Castle (ldr) Charlie Shavers, John Frosk, Bill Spano, Art Tancredi
(tp) Tak Takvorian, Vince Forrest, Jack Rains, Billy VerPlanck (tb)
Skip Galluccio, Danny Trimboli (as) Buzzy Brauner, Frank Maynes (ts)
George Perry (bar) Joe Massimino (p) Steve Jordan (g) Billy Cronk (sb)
Tommy Widdicome (d) Dick Haymes (vcl)

Daybreak [Harold Adamson; Ferde Grofé] vDH

TOMMY DORSEY TRIBUTE BAND

Previous personnel augmented or featuring solos by: **Jimmy Dorsey** (ldr) Charlie Shavers, Lee Castle (tp) Vince Forrest (tb) Count Basie (p) Louis Bellson (d) Lynn Roberts, Tommy Mercer, Stuart Foster, Sy Oliver (vcl)

Tommy Dorsey Medley: **Quiet Please** [Sy Oliver] (LB,d); **Once In A While** [Bud Green; Michael Edwards]; **This Love Of Mine** [Frank Sinatra; Sol Parker, Henry Senicola] vTM; **Opus One** [Sid Garris; Sy Oliver] (cl solo); **There Are Such Things** [Stanley Adams, Abel Baer, George W. Meyer] vSF; **On The Sunny Side Of The Street** [Dorothy Fields; Jimmy McHugh] vSO; **Yes, Indeed!** [Sy Oliver] vLR; **Song Of India** [Nicholas Rimsky-Korsakoff]; **I'll Never Smile Again** [Ruth Lowe]; **Boogie Woogie** (CB,p); **Marie** [Irving Berlin] vSF&band (as solo); **I'm Gettin' Sentimental Over You** [Ned Washington; George Bassman] (theme)
LP: Sounds Great SG8014

"Mac" was gone. The younger brother whom he had fought yet just as vigorously defended for two decades, had left "Lad" adrift. Buffeted by the pain and uncertainty of lung cancer and its then rudimentary drug treatments, and increasingly dependent on alcohol, the senior Dorsey brother picked up the reins of the band and his life as best he could—but it would not be an easy task.

A Lost and Lonesome Lad
(1956-1957)

Once the band resumed operations at the Statler, it also assumed a new name: Jimmy Dorsey and the Fabulous Dorsey Orchestra. Patrons at the Statler, however, saw less and less of Jimmy, who often retreated to his hotel room. It increasingly fell to Lee Castle to front the band. Since it was now Jimmy's band, its theme reverted to "Contrasts."

While in recent years Tommy had supervised the bookings himself through TomDor Enterprises, the ailing Jimmy placed the job back in the laps of Music Corporation of America, signing a five-year contract with them. Tommy's offices on Broadway were closed and Tommy's publishing companies were put up for sale by his estate.

It was announced that due to the difficulty in finding a trombonist capable of playing Tommy's parts, many of the arrangements were being shelved and new ones featuring Jimmy introduced.

The real reason for the change in arrangements was that Tommy's estate, which now owned most of them, could make no decisions because Tommy left no will, and an executor had to be named.

The court decided that Tommy's third wife Jane should act in that position. The only other adult parties to the estate under the law, Patsy and Tommy III ("Skipper"), Tommy's children by his first marriage, eventually agreed to this arrangement.

During Christmas and New Year's weeks, Jimmy fronted the band on ten segments of the *NBC Bandstand,* hosted by Bert Parks. Vocalist Tommy Leonetti was the guest on Christmas morning, and while the band now carried Jimmy's name first, by then the show featured an equal number of Tommy's arrangements.

Broadcast schedule: *NBC Bandstand*—NBC, Mon., Dec. 24, 10:00 A.M.-noon.

NBC Bandstand, NBC Radio City Studios, New York, N.Y.—NBC, 10:00 A.M.-noon, Tuesday, December 25, 1956
JIMMY DORSEY AND THE FABULOUS DORSEY ORCHESTRA
Personnel as November 11, 1956 except Will Bradley (tb) out. Tommy Leonetti, Tommy Mercer, Lynn Roberts (vcl)

Contrasts [Jimmy Dorsey] (theme) / **Oh What A Beautiful Mornin'** [Oscar Hammerstein II; Richard Rodgers] (cl solo) / **It Never Entered My Mind** [Lorenz Hart; Richard Rodgers] vTM (cl solo) / **Swanee River** [Stephen Foster] / **I've Grown Accustomed To His Face** [Alan Jay Lerner; Frederick Loewe] vLR / **Go Buy The Ring** vTL / **The Bells Of St. Mary's** [Douglas Furber; A. Emmett Adams]
    Entire contents on **TC**: Ajazz 1537

584

Contrasts (theme) / **There Are Such Things** [Stanley Adams, Abel Baer, George W. Mayer] (as solo) / **You Make Me Feel So Young** [Mack Gordon; Josef Myrow] vTM (as solo) / **The Christmas Song** [Robert Wells; Mel Torme] vTL / **Sweet Sue (Just You)** [Will J. Harris; Victor Young] (cl solos) / **Ridin' Around In The Rain** [Gene Austin, Carmen Lombardo] vLR (as solo) / **Namely You** [Johnny Mercer; Gene DePaul] vTL / **Tenderly** [Jack Lawrence; Walter Gross] (as solo)

"Contrasts" through "Ridin' Around In The Rain" on **TC:** Ajazz 1537; "Namely You" and "Tenderly" on **TC:** Ajazz 1540

Contrasts (theme) / **Stella By Starlight** [Ned Washington; Victor Young] / **Amapola** [Albert Gamse; Joseph M. Lacalle] vTM&LR (cl solo) / **It Started All Over Again** [Bill Carey; Carl Fisher] (as solo) / **(What Can I Say) After I Say I'm Sorry?** [Walter Donaldson; Abe Lyman] vLR (as solo) / **Wagon Wheels** [Billy Hill, Peter De Rose] vTL / **Song Of India** [Nicholas Rimsky-Korsakoff] / **On The Street Where You Live** [Alan Jay Lerner; Frederick Loewe] vTM (as solo) / **Manhattan** [Lorenz Hart; Richard Rodgers] (cl solo) / **Ever Since You Went Away** vTL / **A Foggy Day (In London Town)** [Ira Gershwin; George Gershwin] vLR / **September Song** [Maxwell Anderson; Kurt Weill] (as solo) / **Tangerine** [Johnny Mercer; Victor Schertzinger] vTM&LR (as solo) / **Tears For Souvenirs** vTL [Tom Glaser; Tommy Leonetti] / **Opus One** [Sy Oliver] / **Contrasts** (theme)

"Contrasts" through "A Foggy Day" on **TC:** Ajazz 1540; "September Song" through closing theme on **TC:** Ajazz 1541

Broadcast schedule (all NBC Bandstand—NBC): Wed., Dec. 26, 10:00 A.M.-noon, Guest: Johnny Desmond / Thurs., Dec. 27, 10:00 A.M.-noon / Fri., Dec. 28, 10:00 A.M.-noon

sustaining broadcast, Cafe Rouge, Hotel Statler, New York, N.Y.—CBS-Radio, Saturday, December 29, 1956

JIMMY DORSEY AND THE FABULOUS DORSEY ORCHESTRA

Contrasts [Jimmy Dorsey] (theme) / **Brunch** [Ernie Wilkins] (as solo) / **Tropical Magic** [Mack Gordon, Harry Warren] vTM / **Oh, What A Beautiful Mornin'** [Oscar Hammerstein II; Richard Rodgers] (cl solo) / **It's De-Lovely** [Cole Porter] vLR / **I'll Never Smile Again** [Ruth Lowe] (as solo) / **The Money Tree** [Cliff Ferre; Mark McIntyre] vTM&LR / **Just For Taking Bows** (as solo) / **I'm Gettin' Sentimental Over You** [Ned Washington; George Bassman]

In presenting Tommy's former theme, Jimmy's new arrangement dropped the trombone solo and instead used the second reed chorus.
Two days later, on New Year's Eve, Jimmy was back with the band for another *NBC Bandstand*. Bert Parks again emceed and Vaughn Monroe was on hand as "Mr. Music" on the first half. Only the contents of the second hour are known.

NBC Bandstand, NBC Radio City Studios, New York, N.Y.—NBC, 10:00 A.M.-noon, Monday, December 31, 1956

JIMMY DORSEY AND THE FABULOUS DORSEY ORCHESTRA
Tommy Mercer, Lynn Roberts (vcl)

(Second hour:) ***Contrasts** [Jimmy Dorsey] (theme) / **In A Little Spanish Town** [Sam M. Lewis, Joseph Young; Mabel Wayne] (as solo) / **You Taught Me To Love Again** [Charles Carpenter; Tommy Dorsey, Henri Woode] vTM / **Pet Me Poppa** [Frank Loesser] vLR / **Perfidia** [Milton Leeds; Alberto Dominguez] (cl,as solos) / **The Tender Trap** [Sammy Cahn; Jimmy Van Heusen] vTM / *(unknown instrumental) (as solo) / ***Contrasts** (theme) / **Bula Beige** [Tadd Dameron] (as solo) / **The End Of A Love Affair** [Edward C. Redding] vLR (as solo) / **Love For Sale** [Cole Porter] (as solo) / ***Five Foot Two, Eyes Of Blue** [Sam M. Lewis, Joe Young; Ray Henderson] / **(How Little It Matters) How Little We Know** [Carolyn Leigh; Philip Springer] vTM (as solo) / **Manhattan** [Lorenz Hart; Richard Rodgers] (cl solo) / **Moten Swing** [William "Count" Basie, Eddie Durham] (as solo)

> Except for tunes marked (*) entire show on **TC:** LaserLight (G), (USA) 79 768, **CD:** LaserLight (G), (USA) 15 768; opening through "Love For Sale" on **TC:** Joyce Record Club C-1541, Ajazz 1541; "Five Foot Two" through "Moten Swing" on **TC:** Joyce Record Club C-1544, Ajazz 1544, "In A Little Spanish Town" on **LP:** K-Tel 3744-2

At 11:30 P.M. that evening, the band was back on the air as the midnight hour approached, this time on CBS Radio.

sustaining broadcast, Cafe Rouge, Hotel Statler, New York, N.Y.—CBS-Radio, 11:30-12:00 P.M. Monday, December 31, 1956

JIMMY DORSEY AND THE FABULOUS DORSEY ORCHESTRA

Contrasts (Jimmy Dorsey) (theme) (as solo) / **Just Swingin'** [Ernie Wilkins] (as solo) / **(How Little It Matters) How Little We Know** [Carolyn Leigh; Philip Springer] vTM / **Let's Fall In Love** [Ted Koehler; Harold Arlen] (as solo) / **It's De-Lovely** [Cole Porter] vLR / **Manhattan** [Lorenz Hart; Richard Rodgers] (as solo) / **The Money Tree** [Cliff Ferre; Mark McIntyre] vLR,TM / **Swanee River** [Stephen Foster] / **I'm Gettin' Sentimental Over You** [Ned Washington; George Bassman] / **Auld Lang Syne** [traditional]

AFRS *One Night Stand* 4329-B is said by some to have been made at the Statler January 1-3, 1957, and is announced as "Jimmy Dorsey and His Orchestra under the direction of Lee Castle." However, since the show includes singer Dottie Reed, who replaced Bobbie Baird at a much later date, this is not believed to be correct.

The booking at the Statler ended Thursday, January 3, and the band vacationed until January 21. During the vacation and less than two months after Tommy's death, Jimmy underwent surgery and a lung was removed. Jimmy was not told there was residual cancer. As a "smoke screen" the trade press was advised that Jimmy was vacationing in Palm Springs for three weeks.

More than ever now it fell upon Lee Castle to keep the band going. Despite this Fraternity Records announced (*Billboard,* February 9, 1957, 18) that it had signed a one-year contract with Jimmy and his orchestra, with an option for two more years.

After vacation, the band replaced Lynn Roberts with Bobbi Baird, took on more one-nighters on the road, then played a concert at the Municipal Auditorium in San Antonio, Texas, Wednesday, February 27, and worked three nights at the Jacob Brown Memorial Center, Brownsville, Texas, from Thursday, February 28, to Sunday, March 3.

While the band was still in the Southwest it was announced (*Variety,* March 2, 1957, 60) that Jimmy would play the Blue Note in Chicago for two weeks beginning June 19.

The next two weeks saw more one-nighters in the Midwest including one at the Orpheum Theater in Minneapolis, scene of several triumphal engagements for Jimmy. In a final ignominious action Jimmy stumbled on several of his sax solos because of his weakening condition. He was booed and heckled by the audience and the show was abruptly halted.

Returning east Jimmy and the band began a scheduled stand at New York's Roseland Dance City from Tuesday, March 19, to Sunday, April 14 that was to be followed by a week in the Persian Terrace of Hotel Syracuse. The band did make the dates, but on his doctor's advice Jimmy went south right after returning to New York to stay at the Bel Harbor Hotel in Miami Beach, Florida. When Cork O'Keefe visited him there a week later, he was so shocked by Jimmy's appearance that he had him rushed back immediately to Doctors' Hospital in New York (Sanford 1971).

The Roseland stand is the probable source for AFRS *One Night Stand* 4312-B, which is listed by some as from December 1956. It, like 4329-B, is announced as "under the direction of Lee Castle." After Syracuse, the band returned to the Hotel Statler for a booking through June 29.

There are numerous AFRS *One Night Stands* on which the AFRS announcers introduce the band as "the late Jimmy Dorsey" or "The Jimmy Dorsey Orchestra under the direction of Lee Castle."

They are 4232-A, 4240-B, 4245-A, 4249-B, 4251-B, 4312-B, 4329-B, 4332-A, 4337-A, 4342-B, 4346-B, 4352-A, 4357-A (announced as "Lee Castle leading the Jimmy Dorsey Orchestra"), 4361-A, 4366-A, 4372-A, 4376-A, 4380-A. While some assert that these were made during this period, they were all made after mid-June and are outside the scope of this book.

In one of those ironies of life, as Jimmy's health worsened, his recently released Fraternity recording of "So Rare" began a steady climb up the charts. In *Billboard's* charting, the record rose from ninety-five out of one hundred the week of March 13 to twenty-fifth place April 10 and was at the ninth spot by May 15. The magazine noted that this was the first chart record for either of the brothers in many years.

Billboard (April 20, 1957, 22) also said that the Tommy Dorsey estate was in the process of selling off the two Dorsey publishing firms along with sixty-four unreleased masters recently produced by Tommy on his own. These are the matrices subsequently released on Columbia.

Variety (May 22, 1957, 41) sounded another ominous chord with its story that Jimmy was seriously ill from "internal complications" and that Lee Castle would continue to front the band at Cafe Rouge and subsequent bookings.

Jimmy's daughter, Julie Lou, who by then was divorced from playboy Nicky Hilton and was working as an actress in Hollywood, came to New York while Jimmy was hospitalized. She knew that her father was going to die but kept her knowledge from him by claiming that she was in New York to make a movie. To further the charade, probably one of her most challenging acting assignments, she visited him only two or three times a week, citing busy shooting schedules.

Another close friend who visited Jimmy often over those nearly three months in the hospital, was his former singer, Bob Eberly.

Jimmy died at the age of 53 on Wednesday, June 12, 1957. While Jimmy's father had passed away fifteen years before during World War II, his mother, Tess Dorsey, survived both her sons.

A solemn requiem mass attended by nearly 1,000 was celebrated by Jimmy's boyhood friend Father Thomas Mulhearn at 10:00 A.M. Saturday, June 15, at New York's famed St. Patrick's Cathedral. Two other priests and a monsignor, all Dorsey family friends, were also on hand. In addition to Jimmy's mother, other family members present were daughter Julie Lou and Jimmy's sister, Mrs. Anthony (Mary) Lisella.

The honorary pallbearers included manager Tino Barzie, Lee Castle, Jackie Gleason, Sammy Kaye, Guy and Carmen Lombardo, boxer Rocky Marciano, Jimmy O'Keefe, Tommy Rockwell, nightclub owner Toots Shorr, Dick Stabile, Paul Whiteman and columnist Earl Wilson. Jimmy's body was returned to Shenandoah, Pennsylvania, for burial near his father in Annunciation Church Cemetery.

There was, of course, one final contrast in the brothers' lives—the way their passing was observed. When Tommy died, there was a major one-hour television tribute, and much space was devoted to his passing in the trade press and daily newspapers. Tommy's final resting place is in the somewhat exclusive, non-denominational Kensico Cemetery near White Plains, New York, surrounded by show business and political personages, and his gravestone depicts a trombone and the opening notes of his theme song.

While the trade press notice of Jimmy's death was respectful it was by no means as extensive as his brother's. Though his funeral was large and in New York's most famous cathedral, it was a solemn ceremony followed by a quiet burial in the land from whence he had sprung, the coal-mining country of Pennsylvania.

This is not to say there weren't any tributes to Jimmy. Old pal Jackie Gleason aired a special show over CBS on Friday, June 14, but unlike his tribute to Tommy, this was on radio, not TV, and it was taped and broadcast a day later on WCBS, the New York City CBS outlet, which couldn't clear the time to carry it live. Jimmy's former vocal star Helen O'Connell, who was by then a regular on NBC-TV, devoted much of her show on June 12 to her one-time boss (*Variety*, June 19, 1957, 59).

Five days after Jimmy's death Lee Castle assembled the band in Webster Hall and finished the album for Fraternity that had been started on November 11, 1956. Dick Stabile, who had been named by Jimmy just before he died as his choice "to finish the job," played Jimmy's solos. Recorded that day were long and short versions of "Contrasts" plus "Speak Low," "Jay-Dee's Boogie Woogie," "Maria Elena," "June Night," "Just Swingin'" and "Amapola." A final tune, "No One Ever Lost More," was cut in January 1958.   Jimmy's daughter Julie represented the family at the June session.

Jimmy's former label, Decca, rushed out an album of reissues in July titled *The Great Jimmy Dorsey*.

In late 1957, The American Cancer Society released a quarter-hour transcribed radio program for its 1958 Cancer Crusade, titled *A Tribute To Jimmy Dorsey*, hosted by Jackie Gleason, and featuring Benny Goodman, Gene Krupa, Connie Boswell and Helen O'Connell.

Lee Castle, who had studied under the Dorseys' father in 1938 to correct his embouchure, would continue to actively lead the Jimmy Dorsey band for over thirty years. He died in Florida of heart complications on November 16, 1990.

Further recognition of the significant role played by the Dorseys came September 11, 1996, when the U.S. Postal Service issued a commemorative postage stamp featuring the brothers as part of a four-stamp block honoring bandleaders Count Basie, Benny Goodman and Glenn Miller.

Both brothers have also gained spots in the "Walk Of Fame" in Hollywood, Jimmy in front of 6505 Hollywood Boulevard and Tommy a block or so away at 6675.

The Dorseys weren't the only "brother act" of the big-band era by any means. The Lombardos, the Elgarts, the Teagardens, the Goodmans, even the Eberles come immediately to mind.   But the Dorseys were by far the most colorful, diversified and successful.

Born a year and a half apart, the two brothers came to the end of their time on earth within a half year of each other, and in lifetimes full of contrasts the end was yet another, for one died suddenly and unexpectedly, the other lingeringly and painfully.

For siblings whose roles in developing a major change in America's musical life had been so significant, the end of their lives after only five decades was tragic indeed. In a way, however, it also was a symbolic representation of the end of the big-band era they each had helped mold and were so determined to keep alive to the very end.

Posthumous postal praise. One of four stamps issued by the U.S. Postal Service September 11, 1996 (stamp design © 1996, U.S. Postal Service; reproduced with permission).

Addenda

The first listing below was omitted from the text due to an editing error by the author for which he apologizes, while the remainder became available after the author had submitted his manuscript for the body of this work.

OKeh, New York, N.Y. Friday, July 12, 1929
MIFF MOLE'S MOLERS
Leo McConville, Phil Napoleon (tp) Miff Mole (tb) **Jimmy Dorsey** (cl,as) Arthur Schutt (p) Tommy Felline (g) Stan King (d)

402529-C   **Birmingham Bertha** [Grant Clarke; Harry Akst]
         (as,cl solos)
    78: OKeh 41273, Odeon ONY-41273, (F) 165788, (Arg) 193378, (F) A-189275, A-189307, A-221170, Parlophone (E) R-432, (Au) A-3046
402530-C   **Moanin' Low** [Howard Dietz; Ralph Rainger]
         (cl solos)
    78: OKeh 41273, Odeon ONY-41273, (Arg) 193378, (It) A-2324, (F) A-189275, A-189307, A-221170, (Arg) A-286028, Parlophone (E) R-849, 22525
     Odeon ONY-41273 as EDDIE GORDON'S BAND
Both sides on **LP:** Swaggie (Au) 1297, Parlophone (E) PMC-7126

         sustaining broadcast, Terrace Room, Hotel New Yorker, New York, N.Y.—MBS [WOR], 11:05-11:30 P.M. Saturday, May 14, 1938
JIMMY DORSEY AND HIS ORCHESTRA

    Parade Of The Milk Bottle Caps [Pat McCarthy, Jimmy Dorsey]

         sustaining broadcast, Outdoor Gardens, Meadow-brook Ballroom, Cedar Grove, N.J.—NBC-Blue [WJZ], 5:00-5:30 P.M. Wednesday, June 7, 1939
JIMMY DORSEY AND HIS ORCHESTRA
Helen O'Connell, Don Matteson, Bob Eberle (vcl)

    Contrasts [Jimmy Dorsey] (theme) (as solo) / **Is It Possible?** [Al Dubin; Jimmy McHugh] vHO'C / **All I Remember Is You** [Eddie DeLange; Jimmy Van Heusen] vHO'C / **An Old Fashioned Tune Always Is New** [Irving Berlin] vDM / **Stairway To The Stars** [Mitchell Parish; Matty Malneck, Frank Signorelli] vBE / **Hollywood Pastime** [Toots Camarata] (to station break) / **Shoot The Meatballs To Me, Dominick Boy!** [Toots Camarata, Jimmy Dorsey] vRM (as solo) / **The Lamp Is Low** [Mitchell Parish; Peter De Rose, Bert Schefter]

vBE / **Bugle Call Rag** [Eubie Blake, Carey Morgan] (cl solo) / **Contrasts** (theme)
  Closing theme on **CD**: Reader's Digest CD 056C.   "Bugle Call Rag" reportedly runs nearly seven minutes.

> *sustaining broadcast,* Meadowbrook Ballroom, Cedar Grove, N.J.—NBC-Blue [WJZ], 5:00-5:30 P.M., Tuesday, June 13, 1939

JIMMY DORSEY AND HIS ORCHESTRA
Helen O'Connell, Bob Eberle, Ray McKinley (vcl)

Contrasts [Jimmy Dorsey] (theme) (as solo) / **Show Your Linen, Miss Richardson** [Johnny Mercer] vRM / **Romance** [Otto Harbach, Oscar Hammerstein II; Sigmund Romberg] (cl solo) / **A Home In The Clouds** [Benny Carter, Benny Goodman] vHO'C (as solo) vHO'C / **All Or Nothing At All** [Jack Lawrence; Arthur Altman] vBE (cl solos) / **This Can't Be Love** [Lorenz Hart; Richard Rodgers] (cl solo) / **My Love For You** [Edward Heyman; Harry Jacobson] vBE (cl solo) / **Frasquita Serenade** [Franz Lehar] / **All I Remember Is You** [Eddie DeLange; Jimmy Van Heusen] vHO'C (as solo) / **Honolulu** [Gus Kahn; Harry Warren] (cl solo)
  "My Love For You", "All I Remember Is You" and "Honolulu" on **CD**: Jazz Hour JH-1053

> *sustaining broadcast,* Meadowbrook Ballroom, Cedar Grove, N.J.—October 1939

JIMMY DORSEY AND HIS ORCHESTRA
Helen O'Connell (vcl)

You're A Lucky Guy [Sammy Cahn; Saul Chaplin] vHO'C / **John Silver** [Ray Krise, Jimmy Dorsey] / **One Sweet Letter From You** [Lew Brown, Sidney Clare; Harry Warren] vHO'C / **I Got Rhythm** [Ira Gershwin; George Gershwin]

> *sustaining broadcast,* Meadowbrook Ballroom, Cedar Grove, N.J.—NBC-Red [WEAF], 8:00-8:30 P.M., Saturday, November 4, 1939

JIMMY DORSEY AND HIS ORCHESTRA

Carolina In The Morning [Gus Kahn; Walter Donaldson] (cl solo) / **Major And Minor Stomp** [Joe Lippman, Jimmy Dorsey] (as solo) **Contrasts** (theme)

> *sustaining broadcast,* Panther Room, Hotel Sherman, Chicago, Ill.—NBC-Red, Sunday, January 21, 1940

JIMMY DORSEY AND HIS ORCHESTRA

Major And Minor Stomp [Joe Lippman, Jimmy Dorsey] (as solo)

> *sustaining broadcast,* Panther Room, Hotel Sherman, Chicago, Ill.—NBC-Red, Thursday, January 25, 1940

JIMMY DORSEY AND HIS ORCHESTRA

JIMMY DORSEY AND HIS ORCHESTRA (Contd.)

I Got Rhythm [Ira Gershwin; George Gershwin] / **Contrasts** [Jimmy Dorsey] (theme) (as solo)

> *sustaining broadcast,* Cafe Rouge, Hotel Pennsylvania, New York, N.Y.—NBC-Red [WEAF], 11:30-12:00 P.M., Thursday, May 23, 1940

JIMMY DORSEY AND HIS ORCHESTRA
Bob Eberly (vcl)

Julia [Mallory, Davis, Moran] (cl solo) / **The Breeze And I** [Al Stillman, Ernesto Lecuona] vBE / **Shake Down The Stars** [Eddie DeLange; Jimmy Van Heusen] vBE / **The Nearness Of You** [Ned Washington; Hoagy Carmichael] vBE (cl solo) / **Pagan Love Song** [Arthur Freed; Nacio Herb Brown]

> *sustaining broadcast,* Cafe Rouge, Hotel Pennsylvania, New York, N.Y.—NBC-Red [WEAF], 11:30-12:00 P.M. Thursday, June 20, 1940

JIMMY DORSEY AND HIS ORCHESTRA

The Breeze And I [Al Stillman, Ernesto Lecuona] vBE / **Dolemite** [Buddy Feyne; William Johnson] (as solo)

> *sustaining broadcast,* Cafe Rouge, Hotel Pennsylvania, New York, N.Y.—July 1940

JIMMY DORSEY AND HIS ORCHESTRA

So You're The One [Hy Zaret, Joan Whitney, Alex Kramer] vHO'C / **Shades Of Twilight** vBE

> *sustaining broadcast,* Meadowbrook Ballroom, Cedar Grove, N.J.—MBS [WOR], 8:45-9:00 P.M. Wednesday, November 27, 1940

JIMMY DORSEY AND HIS ORCHESTRA

I Hear A Rhapsody [George Fragos, Jack Baker, Dick Gasparre] vBE / **Blue (And Broken Hearted)** [Grant Clarke, Edgar Leslie; Lou Handman] vBE,HO'C (cl solos)

> *sustaining broadcast,* Meadowbrook Ballroom, Cedar Grove, N.J.—NBC, Monday, December 16, 1940

JIMMY DORSEY AND HIS ORCHESTRA

I Ain't Tellin' (cl solo) / **Contrasts** (theme)

> *sustaining broadcast,* Cafe Rouge, Hotel Pennsylvania, New York, N.Y.—c. March 1941

JIMMY DORSEY AND HIS ORCHESTRA

High On A Windy Hill [Joan Whitney, Alex Kramer] vBE / **I Hear**

A Rhapsody [George Fragos, Jack Baker, Dick Gasparre] vBE / **Au Reet (Au Rote, Au Root)** [Fud Livingston, Arthur Russell, Bob Mosely] vHO'C / **In The Hush Of The Night** [Sammy Lerner; Al Hoffman] vBE&HO'C (as solo) / **Sowing Wild Notes** [Charlie Frazier] (as,cl solos) / **I Give You My Word** [Al Kavelin, Merril Lynn] vBE

Fitch Bandwagon, Radio City, New York, N.Y.— NBC-Red, 7:30-8:00 P.M. Sunday, April 6, 1941
JIMMY DORSEY AND HIS ORCHESTRA

Contrasts [Jimmy Dorsey] (theme) (as solo) / **Turn Right** [Joe Lippman] (as solo) / **It All Comes Back To Me Now** [Hy Zaret, Joan Whitney, Alex Kramer] vBE **Amapola (Pretty Little Poppy)** [Albert Gamse; Joseph M. Lacalle] vBE&HO'C (cl solo) / **Fingerbustin'** [Jimmy Dorsey] (as, cl solos) / **In The Hush Of The Night** / **Sowin' Wild Notes** [Charlie Frazier] (as,cl solos)

During the Fitch show, manager Billy Burton, Jimmy and nine-year-old daughter Julie Lou, who was visiting Jimmy, were all interviewed.

sustaining broadcast, Cafe Rouge, Hotel Pennsylvania, New York, N.Y.—NBC-Blue [WJZ], 7:30-8:00 P.M. Wednesday, April 16, 1941
JIMMY DORSEY AND HIS ORCHESTRA

Mirage / **Yours (Quieremé Mucho)** [Jack Sherr, Augustin Rodriguez; Gonzalo Roig] vBE&HO'C / **Maria Elena** [S. K. (Bob) Russell; Lorenzo Barcelata] vBE (cl solo) / **Man, That's Groovy** vHO'C&band (cl solo) / **Perfidia** [Milton Leeds; Alberto Dominguez] (cl solo) / **The Things I Love** [Lew Harris; Harold Barlow] vBE (as solo) / **Oh Look At Me Now** [John De Vries; Joe Bushkin] vBE&HO'C / **I Ain't Tellin'** (cl solo)

sustaining broadcast, Cafe Rouge, Hotel Pennsylvania, New York, N.Y.—NBC-Blue [WJZ], 7:30-8:00 P.M. Thursday, April 17, 1941
JIMMY DORSEY AND HIS ORCHESTRA

Amapola (Pretty Little Poppy) [Albert Gamse; Joseph M. Lacalle] vBE&HO'C (cl solo) / **Blue Champagne** [Jimmy Eaton, Grady Watts, Frank Ryerson] vBE (as solo) / **My Sister And I** [Hy Zaret, Joan Whitney, Alex Kramer] vBE / **Man, That's Groovy** vHO'C&band (cl solo) / **Sowing Wild Notes** [Charlie Frazier] (as,cl solos)
"Amapola", "Blue Champagne" on **CD:** Reader's Digest CD 056C

sustaining broadcast, Panther Room, Hotel Sherman, Chicago, Ill.—NBC, Saturday, July 5, 1941
JIMMY DORSEY AND HIS ORCHESTRA

Charleston Alley [Robert Bruce] (as solos)

sustaining broadcast, Hollywood Palladium, Hollywood, Cal.—CBS, 9:30-10:00 P.M. PWT, Wednesday, October 21, 1942
JIMMY DORSEY AND HIS ORCHESTRA

Hit The Note [Charlie Frazier] (as,cl solos)

sustaining broadcast, Hollywood Palladium, Holly-
wood, Cal.—CBS, 8:30-9:00 P.M. PWT, Sunday,
November 1, 1942
JIMMY DORSEY AND HIS ORCHESTRA

One O'Clock Jump [William "Count" Basie] (as,cl solos) / Contrasts [Jimmy Dorsey] (as solo)

Command Performance, unknown studio, Los Ange-
les Cal.—Monday, September 6, 1943
JIMMY DORSEY AND HIS ORCHESTRA
Bob Eberly, Kitty Kallen (vcl)

Besame Mucho (Kiss Me Much) [Sunny Skylar; Consuelo Vela-
quez] vBE&KK / King Porter Stomp ["Jelly Roll" Morton]
Both on ET: AFRS Command Performance 83

sustaining broadcast, Pacific Square Ballroom, San
Diego, Cal.—MBS, July 1944
JIMMY DORSEY AND HIS ORCHESTRA
Paul Carley (vcl)

Poinciana [Buddy Bernier; Nat Simon] vPC (as solo) / (I Would Do)
Anything For You [Alex Hill, Bob Williams, Claude Hopkins] (as
solo) / Do Nothin' Till You Hear From Me [Bob Russell; Edward
K. "Duke" Ellington] vGT (as solo) / The Champ

sustaining broadcast, Casino Gardens, Ocean Park,
Cal.—NBC, Saturday, August 25, 1945
JIMMY DORSEY AND HIS ORCHESTRA

J.D.'s Boogie Woogie [Marvin Wright, Jimmy Dorsey] (cl solo)

sustaining broadcast, 400 Restaurant, New York,
N.Y.—NBC [WEAF], 11:30-12:00 P.M. Tuesday,
January 1, 1946
JIMMY DORSEY AND HIS ORCHESTRA
Paul Chapman, Dee Parker (vcl)

Contrasts [Jimmy Dorsey] (theme) (as solo) / Everybody Knew But
Me [Irving Berlin] vPC / Begin The Beguine [Cole Porter] / A Door
Will Open [Don George; John Benson Brooks] vDP / King Porter
Stomp [Ferdinand "Jelly Roll" Morton]

> *sustaining broadcast,* Chase Club, Hotel Chase, St. Louis, Mo.—Friday, October 25, 1946

JIMMY DORSEY AND HIS ORCHESTRA
Bob Carroll, Dee Parker (vcl)

Contrasts [Jimmy Dorsey] (theme) (as solo) / **Lover** [Lorenz Hart; Richard Rodgers] (as solo) / **The Language Of Love** vBC

> *sustaining broadcast,* Meadowbrook Ballroom, Cedar Grove, N.J.—Thursday November 28, 1946

JIMMY DORSEY AND HIS ORCHESTRA

Contrasts [Jimmy Dorsey] (theme) (as solo) / **Apache Serenade** [Jimmy Dorsey, Buddy Kaye, Joe Lippman] vDP (as solo)

> *AFRS Winnie The Wave #22B,* unknown studio, New York, N.Y.—Wednesday, December 18, 1946

JIMMY DORSEY AND HIS ORCHESTRA

Contrasts [Jimmy Dorsey] (theme) (as solo) / **I May Be Wrong But I Think You're Wonderful** [Harry Ruskin; Henry Sullivan] vDP / **Skychief** / **The Language Of Love** vBC

For about six months in early 1949, disk-jockeys Fred Robbins and Bill Williams hosted the television series "Adventures in Jazz" on CBS. Jimmy was a guest on one show, playing with a CBS house band led by old pal Will Bradley.

> *Adventures In Jazz,* CBS-TV Studios, New York, N.Y.—CBS-TV, 8:00-8:30 P.M. Friday, April 15, 1949

WILL BRADLEY ORCHESTRA
Will Bradley (tb,ldr) Warren Covington (tb) **Jimmy Dorsey** (cl,as) Mike Coluccio (p) Al Caiola (g) Gordon "Specs" Powell (d) (others, if any, unknown)

Fingerbustin' [Jimmy Dorsey] (as,cl solos) / **It Had To Be You** [Gus Kahn; Isham Jones] (cl,as solos)

> *sustaining broadcast,* Beach Walk, Edgewater Beach Hotel, Chicago, Ill.—NBC, 11:30-11:55 P.M. Saturday, September 9, 1950

JIMMY DORSEY AND HIS ORCHESTRA
Kenny Martin, Pat O'Connor (vcl)

I Don't Know Why [Roy Turk; Fred E. Ahlert] vKM&PO'C (as solo) / **Count Every Star** [Sammy Gallop; Bruno Coquatrix] vKM / **Jazz Me Blues** [Tom Delaney] (cl solo)

> *sustaining broadcast,* Cafe Rouge, Hotel Statler, New York, N.Y.—Saturday, November 18, 1950

JIMMY DORSEY AND HIS ORCHESTRA

JIMMY DORSEY AND HIS ORCHESTRA (Contd.)
Kenny Martin, Pat O'Connor (vcl) Marvin Wright (arr)

   Nevertheless (I'm In Love With You) [Bert Kalmar, Harry Ruby]
   (as solo) / **Just Say I Love Her** [Martin Kalmanoff, Sam Ward, Jack
   Val, Jimmy Dale] vKM / **I'll Never Be Free** [Bennie Benjamin;
   George David Weiss] vPO'C / **Baby-O, Baby-O** vKM&PO'C (as
   solo) / **Where Do I Go From You** [Walter Bullock; Allie Wrubel]
   vPO'C / **Sirrocco** vKM arrHG / **I've Never Been In Love Before**
   [Frank Loesser] vKM (as solo) / **Alto-Tude** arrMW (as solo)
        ET: AFRS One Night Stand 2357

                    sustaining broadcast, Cafe Rouge, Hotel Statler, New
                    York, N.Y.—Saturday, November 25, 1950
JIMMY DORSEY AND HIS ORCHESTRA
Kenny Martin, Pat O'Connor (vcl)

   Where Do I Go From You [Walter Bullock; Allie Wrubel] vPO'C /
   Sirrocco vKM arrHG / **I'll Never Be Free** [Bennie Benjamin; George
   David Weiss] vPO'C / **Alto-Tude** arrMW (as solo) / **Baby-O, Baby-
   O** vKM&PO'C (as solo) / **It's The Dreamer In Me** [Jimmy Van
   Heusen, Jimmy Dorsey] vKM (cl solo) / **Can Anyone Explain? (No!
   No! No!)** [Bennie Benjamin, George David Weiss] vCH (cl solo) /
   Just Say I Love Her [Martin Kalmanoff, Sam Ward, Jack Val,
   Jimmy Dale] vKM / **In A Little Spanish Town** [Sam M. Lewis,
   Joseph Young; Mabel Wayne] (as,cl solos) / **On The Alamo** [Gus
   Kahn; Isham Jones]
        ET: AFRS One Night Stand 2347

                    sustaining broadcast, Palladium Ballroom, Holly-
                    wood, Cal.—Thursday, May 22, 1952
JIMMY DORSEY AND HIS ORCHESTRA
Blane (tp) out (no replacement); Vince Ferraro (bar) replaces Layton;
White (g) out (no replacement); Sandy Evans, Eleanor Russell (vcl)

   Busy Signal (cl solo) / **Mixed Emotions** [Stuart F. Loucheim] vER /
   I'll Always Be Following You [Bernie Wayne; Lee Morris] vSE /
   Wimoweh ["Paul Campbell" (Pete Seger, Fred Hellerman, Lee Hays,
   Ronnie Gilbert)] / **It's The Dreamer In Me** [Jimmy Van Heusen,
   Jimmy Dorsey] vSE (cl solo) / **Blacksmith Blues** [Jack Holmes] vER
   / **(I Stood And Threw) Confetti** [Michael Carr] vSE / **Warm
   Hearted Woman** vER / **Sweet Georgia Brown** [Maceo Pinkard,
   Kenneth Casey, Ben Bernie] (cl solo) *(Original Dorseyland Jazz
   Band)*
        ET: AFRS One Night Stand 2855

   The following fills in at least partial details on a 1952 television
appearance for Jimmy and the band (page 517).
   While it has been reported that Bob Eberly and Helen O'Connell were
on the show, the following listing provides confirmation of only Helen's
presence.

Saturday Night Dance Party, NBC-TV Studios, New York, N.Y.—9:00-10:00 P.M. Saturday, August 23, 1952

JIMMY DORSEY AND HIS ORCHESTRA
Helen O'Connell, *Bob Eberly* (vcl)

Contrasts [Jimmy Dorsey] (theme) (as solo) / **Wimoweh** ["Paul Campbell" (Pete Seger, Fred Hellerman, Lee Hays, Ronnie Gilbert)] / **Fingerbustin'** [Jimmy Dorsey] (as,cl solos) / **All Of Me** [Seymour B. Simons, Gerald Marks] vHO'C (as solo) / **Long John Silver** [Ray Krise, Jimmy Dorsey] (as,cl solos) / **South Rampart Street Parade** [Steve Allen; Ray Bauduc, Bob Haggart] (cl solo) (other titles, if any, unknown)

Following are recently unearthed details on the last months of air activity by Jimmy, this time at the helm of his late brother's band.

sustaining broadcast, Cafe Rouge, Hotel Statler, New York, N.Y.—CBS-Radio, Saturday, December 8, 1956

JIMMY DORSEY AND THE FABULOUS DORSEY ORCHESTRA

Charlie's Blues / **Just For Takin' Bows**

sustaining broadcast, Cafe Rouge, Hotel Statler, New York, N.Y.—Saturday, December 29, 1956

JIMMY DORSEY AND THE FABULOUS DORSEY ORCHESTRA

Do It Yourself / **Bula Beige**

sustaining broadcast, Cafe Rouge, Hotel Statler, New York, N.Y.—ABC [WABC], Monday, December 31, 1956

JIMMY DORSEY AND THE FABULOUS DORSEY ORCHESTRA
Tommy Mercer, Lynn Roberts (vcl)

Contrasts (Jimmy Dorsey) (theme) (as solo) / **Speak Low** [Ogden Nash; Kurt Weill] vTM / **The Nearness Of You** [Ned Washington; Hoagy Carmichael] vTM / **It Started All Over Again** [Bill Carey; Carl Fisher] (as solo) / **September Song** [Maxwell Anderson; Kurt Weill] (as solo) / **Nevada** [Mort Greene; Walter Donaldson] arrHG / **Standing Room Only** / **I'm Gettin' Sentimental Over You** [Ned Washington; George Bassman]

sustaining broadcast, Cafe Rouge, Hotel Statler, New York, N.Y.—NBC [WNBC], Tuesday, January 1, 1957

JIMMY DORSEY AND THE FABULOUS DORSEY ORCHESTRA

Contrasts (Jimmy Dorsey) (theme) (as solo) / **Just For Takin' Bows** (as solo) / **You Make Me Feel So Young** [Mack Gordon; Joseph My-
(Contd.)

JIMMY DORSEY & THE FABULOUS DORSEY ORCH. (Contd.)

row] vTM (as solo) / **I'll Never Smile Again** [Ruth Lowe] (as solo) / **Pennies From Heaven** [Johnny Burke; Arthur Johnston] vLR (cl solo) / **Perfidia** [Milton Leeds; Alberto Dominguez] (cl,as solos) / **You're Sensational** [Cole Porter] vTM&LR / **I'm Gettin' Sentimental Over You** [Ned Washington; George Bassman]

Bibliography

Allen, Walter C., and Michael Brooks. "The 'TO' Series of the American Record Corp." *Storyville Magazine* 38 (1972): 56-59.

Arnold, Robert. "Jack Miller Biography and Discography." *ARSC Journal* vol. 26, no. 1 (Spring 1995): 23, 33.

Backensto, E. B. "Woody," and Perry Armagnac. "Ed Kirkeby's California Ramblers (Edison)." *Record Research Magazine* 47, 48, 49, 55, 56, 58, 66, 74 (1964, 1965).

————. "Ed Kirkeby's California Ramblers on Columbia-Harmony-OKeh and Associated Labels." Unpublished manuscript (late 1950s).

Beaton, Josephine, and Howard Rye. "More on the ARC 'TO' Series." *Storyville Magazine* 75 (1978): 102-103.

Billings, Josh. *Plunkett's.* New York, N.Y.: Esquire Jazz Book, 1947.

Bockemuehl, Eugene. *On the Road: With the Jimmy Dorsey Aggravation.* San Diego, Calif.: Gray Castle Press, 1996.

Brooks, Michael. Liner notes: *The Boswell Sisters.* New York: Biograph Records BLP-C-3, 1972.

————. Liner notes: *The Boswell Sisters.* New York: CBS Records P316493, 1982.

————. Liner notes: *The Crooners.* New York: Columbia Legacy CT52930, 1993.

Brown, Lawrence. "Acoustic Era to CD: Seger Ellis 1904-1995." *IAJRC Journal* (Winter 1996): 19-21.

Burgess, Paul. Liner notes: *Jazz in a Vertical Groove.* New York: Biograph Records BLP-12057, 1977.

Connor, D. Russell. *Benny Goodman: Listen to His Legacy.* Metuchen, N.J.: Scarecrow Press & The Institute of Jazz Studies / Rutgers—The State University of New Jersey, 1988.

DeLong, Thomas A. *The Mighty Music Box, The Golden Age of Musical Radio.* Los Angeles, Calif.: Amber Crest Books, Inc., 1980.

"Dorsey Brothers' Orchestra, The." *Orchestra World* (Jan. 1935): 7.

Driggs, Frank.   Liner notes: *The Dorsey Brothers' Orchestra: Mood Hollywood*. Scotland: Hep LP1005, 1985.

Evans, Philip R, Stan Hester, Steve Hester and Linda Evans. *The Red Nichols Story: After Intermission, 1942-1965*. Lanham, Maryland: Scarecrow Press & The Institute of Jazz Studies / Rutgers—The State University of New Jersey, 1997.

Firestone, Ross. *Swing, Swing, Swing: The Life & Times of Benny Goodman*. New York, N.Y.: W. W. Norton & Co., 1993.

Frase, Bill, and Steve Abrams. "Corrections and Additions to *The American Dance Band Discography* (Rust)." *Record Research Magazine* 157/158 (1978) through 251/252 (1993).

Garrod, Charles, et al. *Jimmy Dorsey And His Orchestra*. Zephyrhills, Fla.: Joyce Record Club, 1980.

———. *MGM Record Listing 1001 thru 13506*.   Zephyrhills, Fla.: Joyce Record Club, 1989.

———. *Decca New York Master Numbers Vol. 1*.   Zephyrhills, Fla.: Joyce Record Club, 1992.

Garrod, Charles, and Rod Baum. *Associated Transcription Listing, Original Series and A-Series*. Zephyrhills, Fla.: Joyce Record Club, 1991.

Garrod, Charles, Ken Crawford and Dave Kressley.   *World Transcriptions Original Series 1-11268*.   Zephyrhills, Fla.: Joyce Record Club, 1992.

Gleason, Ralph J. *The Men Who Made the Music: The Dorsey Brothers*. New York, N.Y.: Time-Life Records, 1971.

Goodman, Benny, and Irving Kolodin.   *The Kingdom of Swing*. Harrisburg, Pa.: Stackpole Press, 1939.

Hadlock, Richard. *Jazz Masters of the Twenties*.   New York, N.Y.: Macmillan Publishing Co., Inc., 1965.

Healey, Jeff. Liner notes: *The Dorsey Brothers' Orchestra: Volume One 1928*. Toronto, Ontario, Canada: Jazz Oracle Records BDW 8004, 1996.

Hester, Stan. Correspondence with the author. 1992 through 1998.

Hester, Steve. Liner notes: *Red Nichols and His Five Pennies: Volume One 1926-1927*. South Yarra, Victoria, Australia: Swaggie Records 836, 1985.

Hoefer, George. "Eddie Lang." *Jazz Magazine* (Nov. 1966): 14.

Johnson, Richard. *American Dance Band Discography (Rust) Revised.* Aylesbury, Bucks, England, forthcoming.

Kennedy, Rick. *Jelly Roll, Bix and Hoagy.* Bloomington and Indianapolis, Ind.: Indiana University Press, 1994.

Kite, Martin. "American Record Corporation's Theater-Use Records" (unpublished research), 1977.

Kunstadt, Leonard. "Scranton Sirens." *Record Research Magazine* 249/50 (May 1992): 1.

————. "Scranton Sirens Part Two." *Record Research Magazine* 251/52 (April 1993): 1.

Lax, Roger, and Frederick Smith. *The Great Song Thesaurus.* New York, N.Y.: Oxford University Press, 1989.

Lee, Amy. "Tommy Dorsey Fell Asleep on the Job!" *Metronome* (May 1940): 12, 32.

————. "Goldkette Band Greatest of Them All!" *Metronome* (June 1940): 16, 17.

————. "Goldkette Band Rocked Floors in Summer." *Metronome* (July 1940): 20, 21.

————. "The Dorsey Brothers Played for Pennies!" *Metronome* (Sept. 1940): 14, 15.

————. "Jimmy Was Worse than Tommy Dorsey!" *Metronome* (Oct. 1940): 20, 21.

————. "Dorsey Bros. Name Didn't Mean a Thing!" *Metronome* (Nov. 1940): 20, 48, 49.

Lissauer, Robert. *Lissauer's Encyclopedia of Popular Music in America.* New York, N.Y.: Paragon House, 1991.

Lord, Tom. *The Jazz Discography.* Redwood, N.Y.: Cadence Jazz Books, 1993.

McCarthy, Albert. *The Dance Band Era.* London, England: Hamlyn Publishing Group, Ltd., 1974.

McNicholas, John. Liner notes: *The Chronological Bing Crosby, Volume 13, 1932.* England: Jonzo JZ-13, 1990.

McRae, Barry. *The Jazz Handbook.* Boston, Mass.: G. K. Hall and Co., 1989.

Mackenzie, Harry, and Lother Polomski. *One Night Stand Series, 1-1001*. Westport, Conn.: Greenwood Press, 1991.

Meeker, David. *Jazz in the Movies*. New York, N.Y.: Da Capo Press, 1981.

Pugh, Collin. Liner notes: *The Chronological Bing Crosby, Volume 11, 1931*. England: Jonzo JZ-11, 1988.

Raben, Erik, ed. *Jazz Records 1942-80: A Discography*. Copenhagen NV, Denmark: JazzMedia ApS, 1995.

Raichelson, Dick.   Liner notes: *The Cotton Pickers 1929*. Canada: Arcadia Records 2013, 1980.

Riordan, Frank.   Rememberances of the Dorsey Brothers by a family friend. Tape recording, St. Louis, Mo., January, 1998.

Rogers, Alice. "Boyd Senter—Jazz Pilot of the Air." *IAJRC Journal* (Spring 1996): 1.

Rogers, Ginger. *Ginger My Story*. New York, N.Y.: Harper-Collins Publishers, 1991.

Rust, Brian. *The American Dance Band Discography 1917-1942*. 2 vols. New Rochelle, N.Y.: Arlington House, 1975.

―――. *Jazz Records 1897-1942*. 2 vols. New Rochelle, N.Y.: Arlington House, 1978.

―――. *Guide To Discography*. Westport, Conn.: Greenwood Press, 1980.

―――. Liner notes: *The Young Dorsey Brothers 1928 -1930*. England: World Records SHB67, 1980.

Rust, Brian, and Allen G. Debus. *The Complete Entertainment Discography*. New Rochelle, N.Y.: Arlington House, 1973.

Sanford, Herb. *Tommy & Jimmy: The Dorsey Years*.   New Rochelle, N.Y.: Arlington House, 1972.

Schuller, Gunther. *Early Jazz, Its Roots and Musical Development*. New York, N.Y.: Oxford University Press, 1968.

―――. *The Swing Era: The Development of Jazz 1930-1945*.   New York, N.Y.: Oxford University Press, 1989.

Seavor, Ken. "Gettin' Sentimental—The Dorsey Brothers' Orchestra —1928 to 1935." Unpublished manuscript. Wirral, England, 1995-1998.

Shapiro, Nat, and Nat Hentoff. *Hear Me Talkin' to Ya.* New York, N.Y.: Rinehart, 1955.

Shapiro, Nat, and Bruce Pollack. *Popular Music 1920-1979.* 3 vols. Detroit, Mich.: Gale Research Co., 1985.

Shaw, Arnold. *52nd St.: The Street of Jazz.* New York, N.Y.: Da Capo Press, 1977.

———. *The Jazz Age: Popular Music in the 1920s.* New York, N.Y.: Oxford University Press, 1987.

Simon, George T. *The Big Bands.* New York, N.Y.: Macmillan Publishing Co., Inc., 1974.

———. *Simon Says: The Sights and Sounds of the Swing Era.* New York, N.Y.: Gallahad Books, 1971.

Stockdale, Robert L. *Tommy Dorsey: On the Side.* Metuchen, N.J.: Scarecrow Press & The Institute of Jazz Studies / Rutgers—The State University of New Jersey, 1995.

Sudhalter, Richard M., and Philip R. Evans. *Bix, Man & Legend.* New Rochelle, N.Y.: Arlington House, 1974.

Terenzio, Maurice, Scott MacGillivray and Ted Okuda. *The Soundies Distributing Corporation of America.* Jefferson, N.C.: McFarland & Co., Inc., 1991

Thomas, Bob. *The One and Only Bing.* New York, N.Y.: Grosset & Dunlap, 1977.

White, Bozy. *The Eddie Condon "Town Hall Broadcasts" 1944-1945. A Discography.* Oakland, Calif.: Shoestring Records, 1980.

———. *AFRS Basic Music Library, P-1 to P-1200.* Zephyrhills, Fla.: Joyce Record Club, 1988.

———. Continuing research on Bunny Berigan 1929-1941 (unpublished). Oakland, Calif., 1988-1998.

White, Bozy, and Martin L. Kite. Research on Bunny Berigan 1929-1941 (unpublished). Oakland, Calif., and Woodbridge, Va.: 1951-1987.

Whyatt, Bert, et al. "Sam Lanin Discography, 1920-1931" (unpublished). Taunton, Somerset, England, 1967.

Wilson, Earl. Liner notes: *The Fabulous Jimmy Dorsey.* New York: Fraternity Records FLP1008, 1957.

Woods, Bernie. *When the Music Stopped.* New York, N.Y.: Barricade Books, 1994.

General Index

This index includes only those listings found in the narrative text because of their biographical significance. Numerous other cities, performance locations, broadcasts and similar citations in listings throughout the book, such as *Travel Itinerary* and *Broadcast Schedule* are not indexed here.

Performing Artists

This index does not include guests on broadcasts or telecasts for which musical contents are unknown. In the case of recording pseudonyms, the actual performer's name follows in brackets [ ] as do nicknames, which are additionally in quotes.

Luther Trio, Frank (vcl grp) 297
Lyon, Russ (ts) 209
Lyons, Art (ts) 481, 483, 499, 501, 506-508, 510, 511
Lytell, Jimmy (cl,as) 29

McCarthy, Pat (arr) 330, 334
McConville, Leo (tp) 20, 25, 27, 30, 31, 33, 34, 36, 37, 41, 47, 57, 61-66, 69-72, 74-76, 78, 80, 81, 83, 84, 86, 89, 91, 92, 94, 97, 100-107, 109, 110, 112-114, 117-123, 126, 128, 132, 133, 136, 138-140, 142, 143, 149, 151, 154-157, 159, 161, 162, 168, 169, 238, 590
McCormick, John (tp) 521, 522, 534, 536, 540
McCoy, Paul (tp) 414, 415
McDonald, Everett (tp) 481
McDonald, Harold (d,vib) 48, 49, 51, 53-56
McDonough, Dick (g,bj) 25-27, 29, 30, 34, 37-39, 42, 45, 61, 79, 137, 144, 151, 172, 190, 191, 199, 203, 213, 220-223, 226, 228, 229, 232, 234-236, 238, 239, 241-249, 253, 254, 260, 264-285, 289, 293, 295, 297
McGrath, Frank (vcl) 41
McGrath, Fulton (p,celst) 209, 215, 221, 234, 235, 238, 239, 241-243, 245-249, 253, 259, 261, 263, 264, 266, 267, 269, 271, 273, 274, 276-279, 281-284, 285, 287, 289, 292-294, 297-299, 301, 303, 304
McGuire Sisters (vcl grp) 535, 537
McKenzie, Red (vcl) 128, 195, 197, 198, 282, 286
McKinley, Ray (d,vcl) 195, 197, 297-299, 301, 303-305, 313, 316, 317, 320-324, 330, 339, 344, 345, 348, 352, 353, 359, 361,

363, 364, 368, 591
McLean, Hal (cl,as) 46, 48, 51, 53, 55, 56
McPartland, Jimmy (tp) 72, 74, 100, 115
MacRae, Gordon (vcl) 556
Macy, Jerry (vcl) 47
Magee, Erwin [Irving Mills] (vcl) 74
Magnante, Charlie (acc) 60, 127, 146, 162, 251, 261, 270, 271, 292
Malneck, Matty (vn,viola) 46, 48, 49, 51, 54-56, 74, 79, 83, 156, 237, 242, 253, 259, 276, 281
Malvin, Artie, Singers (vcl grp) 580
Mancusi, Fred (tb) 462, 465, 473
Mangano, Mickey (tp) 469
Mann, Belle (vcl) 85
Mann, Dave (p) 428
Manning, Jack [Irving Kaufman] (vcl) 84
Manone, Joseph ["Wingy"] (tp,vcl) 177
Marcus, Harold (cl,as) 76, 79
Margulis, Charlie (tp) 48, 51, 53-56, 164, 167, 173, 187, 191-193, 200-202, 206, 208, 210, 211, 219, 223, 227, 232, 233, 240, 243, 245, 250, 251, 255, 257, 258, 267, 269-271, 273, 279, 281, 283, 285, 289, 294, 295, 297, 576
Markowitz, Marky (tp) 428
Marsala, Joe (cl) 595
Marsh, Andrea [Audrey] (vcl) 225, 257,
Marshall, Billy (tp) 520, 534, 536, 540
Martel, John (tp) 477
Martin, Kenny (vcl) 494-496, 499, 501, 506, 595
Martin, Louis (cl,as) 154, 155, 157, 159, 175, 188
Marvin, Frank (vcl) 172
Marvin, Johnny (uke,vcl) 41, 85, 215, 259
Mason, Paul (ts) 106, 118

Massiminio, Joe (p,celst) 580, 582
Masso, George (tb) 483, 486
Mastren, Carmen (g) 364
Mathieu, Carl [Franklin Baur] (vcl) 23
Matlock, Matty (cl,as) 510
Matteson, Don (tb,vcl) 293, 295, 296, 298, 299, 301, 303-305, 308, 313, 316, 317, 320-324, 330, 333, 344, 346, 348, 352, 353, 355, 358, 360, 362, 364, 368, 376, 382, 386, 387, 397, 401, 462, 465, 473
Matthews, Dave (as,ts,arr) 330, 352, 364
Maxey, Virginia (vcl) 481
Maxon, Chuck (tb) 486, 494
Mayfair, Mitzi (vcl) 430
Mayhew, Bob (tp, cnt) 48-50, 53, 54, 56, 57
Mayhew, Gus (tb) 160
Mayhew, Nye (ts,vcl) 48-50, 51, 54, 64
Maynes, Frank (ts) 486, 490, 492, 494-498, 580, 582
Meadows, Audrey and Jane (vcl grp) 565
Meaken, Gilda (vcl) 476
Mele, Vi (vcl) 358
Mello-Larks (vcl grp) 482
Melton, James (vcl) 251
Men About Town (vcl grp) 187, 295
Mendell, Johnny (tp) 377
Mercer, Johnny (vcl) 284, 510, 575
Mercer, Tommy (vcl) 556, 557, 559, 574, 575, 578, 583, 584, 586, 597
Meresco [Moresco], Joe (p) 190, 207, 223, 225, 228, 235, 237, 238, 250, 251, 254, 255, 257, 258, 260, 267, 270, 272, 275, 279-281, 286-288, 291, 293-294, 296-298, 300
Merman, Ethel (vcl) 254
Mertz, Paul (p,arr) 35, 196
Mettome, Doug (tp) 520,

Recording Groups

This index includes pseudonyms. Vocalists with featured billing on the label are listed under **Performing Artists.** Where the group name includes a person's first and last name, even if a pseudonym, (e.g., Irwin Abrams and His Hotel Manger Orch.), it will be found under the last name (e.g., Abrams). However, Ben Franklin Hotel Dance Orch. will be found under "Ben." Possessives (e.g., Jerry White's Orch.) have been shortened by dropping the " 's" and are listed under the last name.

Titles

For alphabetical indexing purposes "A," "An" and "The" as well as parenthetical phrases are ignored if they are at the beginning of a title. Where known, lyricists and composers are listed in the text at the first occurrence of the title in each session, broadcast, telecast or film.

658

Concerts, Broadcasts and Telecasts

This index lists concerts, broadcasts and telecasts that included Jimmy Dorsey either as a leader, guest or sideman and for which the contents are all or partially known. Except for certain AFRS programs, many sustaining remote broadcasts, listed only by date and time throughout the text, are not indexed here. AFRS series program numbers are shown in boldface and italic (*1234:*) preceding the page number.

About the Author

Robert L. Stockdale has spent a major part of his life working with music and musicians. Now retired, he spent his first career years in radio broadcasting, starting as an announcer, record librarian and production manager at a Syracuse, New York, radio station (WAGE, now WHEN). There he announced almost weekly live remotes both locally and nationally (ABC) featuring bands like Tommy Dorsey, Benny Goodman, Sammy Kaye, Skitch Henderson, Johnny Long, Woody Herman, Eddie Duchin and Lenny Herman, as well as smaller groups like Jan August, the Dardanelle Trio and the Three Suns.

Following a seven-year stint in public relations, he owned and operated the "first country-music stations north of the Mason-Dixon line," WSEN and WSEN-FM in the Syracuse market for fifteen years.

After selling the stations in 1974, he spent seventeen years with the American Cancer Society, including direction of ACS upstate New York computer operations in twenty-two cities.

In high school and college he played piano and drums and for most of his adult life has been an avid record collector, developing a large reference library of single, albums and tapes, including hundreds of hours of big-band airchecks.

He is the author of *Tommy Dorsey: On the Side* (Scarecrow Press 1995), winner of the 1996 Award for Best Research in the Field of Recorded General Popular Music from the Association for Recorded Sound Collections (ARSC), and has been a member of the International Association of Jazz Record Collectors (IAJRC) since 1986. He is also a member of the Jazz Appreciation Society of Syracuse (JASS).